THE GERMAN
RESEARCH COMPANION

Shirley J. Riemer

Roger P. Minert

Jennifer A. Anderson

LORELEI
P•R•E•S•S

ISBN: 0-9656761-6-1

Library of Congress Control Number: 00-091147

Lorelei Press, P.O. Box 221356, Sacramento, CA 95822-8356
E-mail: Lorelei@softcom.net

Introduction

This third edition of *The German Research Companion* is filled with possibilities for researching German family history.

Note the addition of email addresses, recently published books and other aids, website addresses (complete with directions for managing some of them), as well as helpful comments concerning the use of resources.

Perusal of the contents of this third edition should create, the authors hope, some often-welcome optimism for German family historians facing difficult research problems.

The authors, listed below, wish you success in your German genealogical ventures.

Shirley J. Riemer earned her Master of Arts in English degree at Carnegie-Mellon University, then spent 22 years teaching and working in communications. Her first book, *The German Research Companion* appeared in 1997, followed by the second edition in 2000. For the third edition, she was fortunate that two talented German researchers, Dr. Roger P. Minert and Jennifer A. Anderson, agreed to be co-authors. In 2001, she and Dr. Minert co-authored the book *Researching in Germany: A Handbook for Your Visit to the Homeland of Your Ancestors.* She has published *Der Blumenbaum,* quarterly journal of the Sacramento German Genealogy Society since 1992. Every year since 1971, she has visited Germany, collecting a wide variety of cultural and genealogical documents.

Roger P. Minert received his doctoral degree from The Ohio State University in German language history and second language acquisition theory. He taught German language and history for ten years, and then became a professional family history researcher. Accredited by the Family History Library for research in Germany and Austria, he has more than 33,000 hours in research experience. In August 2003 he became an associate professor of family history at Brigham Young University. The author of more than 75 books and articles, he is currently directing the project "German Immigrants in American Church Records" and has completed the first of two volumes of a history of the Church of Jesus Christ of Latter-day Saints in Germany during World War II.

Jennifer A. Anderson earned a B.A. in German and a master's degree in European History from Brigham Young University. After spending three years in Europe, she has become fluent in German. A resident of Provo, Utah, she works as an independent professional researcher in Germanic family history, providing services ranging from simple document searches to extensive family history research. She has amassed thousands of hours researching records from Germany, Switzerland and other German-speaking regions of Europe. She has worked on the "German Immigrants in American Church Records" project with Dr. Roger P. Minert, extracting records of German-born immigrants found in U.S. church records.

Table of Contents

Section 1: German Lands, Past and Present

◆

Chronology of events in German social
and political history
Jurisdictional organization and history
Basic facts about Germany
The three German empires
Geographical and historical considerations

◆

CHRONOLOGY OF EVENTS IN GERMAN HISTORY

1000-100 B.C.: The Germani tribes occupy the lands from the Baltic Sea to the Danube River, and from the Rhine to the Oder River.

9 B.C. - 9 A.D.: The Romans move eastward to the Elbe River. In 9 A.D. they withdraw to the Rhine.

481-511: The king of the Franks, Clovis, establishes the Frankish Empire.

768-814: Charlemagne (*Karl der Große*) rules what is to become the Holy Roman Empire.

800: Charlemagne crowned in Rome as emperor of the Holy Roman Empire of the German Nation.

843: Treaty of Verdun: empire divided among Charlemagne's three grandsons: Charles the Bold — West Franks; Louis the German — East Franks (nucleus of the future German state); Lothar — Middle Kingdom (Alsace-Lorraine)

919-1024: German tribes unified

925: Lorraine becomes a German duchy.

936-973: Otto I rules.

962: Otto I crowned (Holy Roman) Emperor in Rome, founding Holy Roman Empire of the German Nation, lasting until 1806.

1000-1500: Jewish expulsions: from German areas (1000-1350), from Hungary (1300s), and from Austria (1400s)

1096: Beginning of first Crusade

1123-24: Plague sweeps France and Germany.

1141-81: "Saxons" (mostly Franks) invited to settle in Transylvania to defend Hungary's eastern border.

1152-90: Reign of Frederick I (Barbarossa), of the Hohenstaufen dynasty, who converts the Slavs to Christianity. Age of chivalry.

1190: Teutonic Order founded

1200: Early Gothic period begins (Rheims, Cologne, constructed).

1241: Hanseatic League formed

1273-1806: Hapsburg dynasty begins; ends with abolition of Holy Roman Empire by Napoleon in 1806.

1348-65: More than 25 million Europeans die in the Bubonic plague.

1356: The Golden Bull, an ecclesiastic document, laid down rules for election of the king, to be elected in Frankfurt and crowned in Aachen.

1417: Frederick of Nürnberg of Hohenzollern family appointed Elector of Brandenburg

c. 1440: In Mainz, Johann Gutenberg invents the art of printing with movable type.

1500: Surnames are in common use throughout German territories of Europe by 1500.

1517: Protestant Reformation begins; Luther said to have fastened 95 theses on Wittenberg church door. First significant non-Catholic religions among Germanic people.

1518-23: Ulrich Zwingli begins Reformation in Switzerland, leading to formation of Reformed (Calvinist) Church

c. 1520: Anabaptist movement develops in Switzerland and Germany.

1521: Luther's arrest by Charles V, for Diet of Worms. Luther translates New Testament into German, devising new written form of German.

1524-26: Peasants Revolt. Peasants influenced by Luther's teachings rise up against their feudal overlords and 5,000 peasants are massacred.

1524: Protestant church records begin in Nürnberg.

1530: Augsburg Confession (creed) adopted by Lutherans

1534: A standardized German language is established with the publication of the Old Testament in Luther's translation of the Bible from Hebrew and Greek into vernacular German.

1536: Menno Simons leaves the Church and begins "Mennonite" preaching.

1541: Reformation introduced in Switzerland by John Calvin.

1545: Catholic Counter-Reformation begins.

1555: Peace of Augsburg: Doctrine of *cuius regio, eius religion* adopted,

mean-ing that the religion of the prince deter-mined the religion (Catholic or Lutheran) of his subjects.

1556: Palatinate becomes Lutheran.

1562: Wars of Religion in France between Catholics and French Calvinists (Huguenots, of French "Reformed" faith)

1563: The rulings of the Catholic Council of Trent require priests to include more detail (principally the names of sponsors and witnesses) in the baptism and marriage records they are already keeping.

1568: Protestants in the Spanish Netherlands, including Belgium, are persecuted by the Duke of Alva. Walloon Calvinists flee, especially to the Palatinate, Hessen, and Brandenburg; Dutch-Flemish-Frisian Mennonites flee to Danzig area.

1583: Gregorian calendar is adopted by most Catholic countries of Europe — by Prussia in 1612, by most Protestant countries in 1700, by Great Britain in 1752, and by Russia in 1917.

1598: In France, Edict of Nantes gives Huguenots political and some religious rights in some places.

1618-48: Thirty Years War devastates Holy Roman Empire. France emerges as Europe's leading power. Some records are burned. Population drops from 20 million to 13 million.

1622: Pfalz suffers great destruction in the war. January 1 declared as beginning of the year (previously began March 25)

1633: Outbreak of plague in Bavaria

1639-60: Grain crisis in Europe

1648: Peace of Westphalia ends Thirty Years War. Holy Roman Empire dis-solved. France gets Alsace-Lorraine. By this time, there are 350 different German states. Switzerland officially recognized as independent from the Holy Roman Empire. Reformed Church members granted same rights as those Lutherans had been granted almost 100 years earlier.

1650: Essentially all Catholic and

Protestant churches are keeping vital records in the German-language territories of Europe.

1652: Famine in Lorraine and surrounding lands

1653: Germans from Heidelberg introduce vineyards and winemaking to America.

1654: Spain occupies Palatinate.

1671-77: William Penn first visits Germany to propagate Quaker faith.

1681: William Penn founds Pennsylvania

1683: First permanent German settlement in the United States is founded at Germantown, Pennsylvania. Encouraged by American Quaker William Penn, Franz Daniel Pastorius organizes the immigration of 13 Mennonite families from Krefeld, beginning German group immigration to North America.

1685: King Louis XIV of France revokes the Edict of Nantes (see 1598). Persecution and forcible conversion of Huguenots (French Protestants) causes flight to Switzerland, Germany, the Netherlands, Great Britain and North America. Friedrich Wilhelm, the Great Elector, helps many immigrate to Brandenburg.

1687-97: Invasion of France into the Palatinate

1689-97: War of the League of Augsburg results in French burning down many towns in the Palatinate and mass flight of the population.

1694: Johann Kelpius leads a group of German mystics to America and forms a brotherhood on Wissahickon Creek near Philadelphia.

1700: The last German Protestant areas finally switch to the Gregorian calendar.

1701: Frederick III, elector of Brandenburg, renames his duchy the Kingdom of Prussia, and he becomes King Frederick I.

1701-14: War of Spanish Succession; Palatines leave for England.

1708: Joshua Kocherthal brings 61 Protestant emigrants from the Rhenish Palatinate to America.

1709: Thousands more of the Palatine Germans, fleeing destruction caused by the invading French, emigrate to the Hudson River Valley and Pennsylvania. Large numbers of emigrants, called Palatines (*Pfälzer*), leave the Pfalz region of Germany for England and America.

1710: A group of German and Swiss immigrants settle New Bern, North Carolina.

1710-11: First relatively large-scale immigration of Swiss and Palatines to American colonies.

1711: An estimated 500,000 die of plague in Austria and German areas.

1714: Christopher von Graffenried brings miners from Siegen, Westphalia to Virginia to work Governor Spotswood's iron mines.

1719: Peter Becker brings the first German Baptist "Dunkers" to Germantown. The sect's founder, Alexander Mack, comes to America with another group ten years later.

1727: The German population of Pennsylvania numbers around 20,000.

1727: Beginning of Philadelphia port records

1722: Austro-Hungarian monarchs begin inviting Germans to settle parts of their empire.

1730: Beginning of community at Ephrata (Pennsylvania)

1731-38: Expulsion of Salzburg Protestants, some of whom come to America, most going to East Prussia and other European areas.

1732: Benjamin Franklin publishes the first German language newspaper in America, the *Philadelphische Zeitung.*

1732: Conrad Beissel, a Seventh Day Dunker from the Palatinate, founds the Ephrata Cloisters near Lancaster, Pennsylvania.

1733: Members of the Schwenkfelder sect from Silesia settle in Montgomery County, Pennsylvania.

1734: Refugees from Salzburg arrive in Savannah, Georgia.

1736: The Herrnhuters, or Moravians, found their first settlement, in Georgia, under the leadership of August Gottlieb Spangenberg.

1740-86: Under Frederick II of Prussia (Frederick the Great), Prussia becomes a great power.

1740-48: War of Austrian Succession between Prussia and Austria; Prussia wins new territories, thus becoming a major European power.

1742: Silesia becomes part of Prussia in the war with Austria.

1742: Nikolaus Ludwig, Count of Zinzendorf and Pottendorf, founds the Moravian settlement of Bethlehem, Pennsylvania.

1743: Christopher Saur of Philadelphia prints a German-language Bible: the first complete Bible published in America.

1748: George Washington first encounters German immigrants in the Shenandoah Valley.

1749: Settlement of New Germantown (Braintree), Massachusetts.

1749-53: Peak of Germanic immigration to colonial America, mostly from near the Rhine valley about 1750.

1750: Beginning of Pennsylvania-German emigration to North Carolina. Also, the first Germans arrive in Nova Scotia.

1753: Europeans found the town of Lunenburg, to become the most important ship-building center of Nova Scotia. Moravians begin settlement on the Wachovia tract, North Carolina.

1754: The Schwenkfelder sect of Pennsylvania establishes the first Sunday School in America.

1755: Beginning of French and Indian War

1756-63: Germans play a significant role in fighting the French in the French and Indian War.

1756-63: Seven Years War. An Anglo-Prussian alliance faces off against a coalition of Austria, Saxony, France, and Russia. Prussia wins more territory and goes on to become a great power.

1759: Michael Hillegas opens America's first music store in Philadelphia.

1763: Catherine the Great begins inviting Germans to settle in Russia, granting them free land, freedom from military service, and many other special privileges

1764-67: Heavy immigration of Germans to Volga River region in Russia

1766: France acquires Lorraine.

1771: Patronymic naming system is to be abolished in Schleswig-Holstein.

1772-95: Partition of Poland by Russia, Prussia and Austria in three stages: 1772, 1793, and 1795. Poland disappears as an independent country until 1918.

1775-83: American Revolution, with independence declared in 1776; 30,000 Hessian and other German mercenaries fight for Great Britain. Thousands remain in United States and Canada.

1776: Henry Miller's *Staatsbote* is first American newspaper to print news of the Declaration of Independence.

1778: General Friedrich Wilhelm von Steuben takes over the training of the Continental Army.

1781: Palatine emigration (since 1709) to U.S. continues.

1781: Freedom of religion guaranteed in Austria, opening the way for immigration of Protestants.

1781-1864: Feudalism is phased out in northern Europe. Key dates: Austria (1781, again in 1848 after being reinstituted); France (1789); Prussia (1807); all German territory (by 1848); Hungary (1853-54); Russia (1861); Russian Poland and Romania (1864).

1782-87: Heavy German immigration to Danube region of southern Hungary, Galicia and Bukovina, all recently acquired by Austria under Emperor Joseph II.

1783: German is decreed as the language of all church records in Austria (replacing

Latin in many cases).

1783: German Loyalists settle in Upper Canada, where the town of Berlin (whose name was changed to Kitchener during World War I) would become the center of a predominantly German area.

1785-1844: Jews required to adopt family names in all Austrian-ruled lands except Hungary (1785-87), in France and Germany (1802-12), and in Russia and Poland (1844)

1786: German Mennonites from Pennsylvania begin to emigrate to Ontario, more heavily after 1807.

1789: Paris mob storms Bastille; *Declaration of Rights of Man and of Citizen* is published. French Revolution begins.

1789: Frederick Augustus Mühlenberg becomes first Speaker of United States House of Representatives.

1789-1824: Heaviest German immigration to Black Sea region of Russia (now Ukraine)

1789-1917: Jews emancipated, being granted equality by law in France (1789), Prussia (1850); Austro-Hungarian Empire (1867); Germany (1871); Switzerland (1874) and Russia (1917)

1792: France starts civil registration in German territories west of the Rhein.

1792: French Republican Calendar begins, used 8-13 years in some areas.

1792-1815: Napoleonic wars against revolutionary France by Prussia, Austria and other countries. Napoleon forces end Holy Roman Empire in 1806; Hapsburg family continues to rule Austria, but no longer influential in German lands. Rhenish Confederation founded in 1806.

1794: Changing of surnames is forbidden in Prussia.

1795: Franco-Prussian War. Prussia defeated.

1798: Switzerland declares neutrality.

c. 1800: Industrial Revolution underway

1803: Disruption of trade following resumption of war between England and France makes emigration from conti-nental Europe practically impossible.

1803-15: Napoleonic Wars. Napoleon annexes Rhine, abolishes 112 states and free cities, which are absorbed by larger kingdoms, and secularizes monasteries, giving their lands as rewards to friends for their loyalty.

1804: Napoleon creates French Empire and proclaims himself emperor. *Code Napoleon* is issued as a comprehensive compilation of French civil laws.

1804: George Rapp, founder of a communal religious sect, establishes the settlement of Harmony in Pennsylvania.

1805-07: Napoleon compels emperor Francis I of Austria to renounce his title and position, bringing the Holy Roman Empire of the German Nation to an end.

1806: Holy Roman Empire dissolved, ending tradition of German kings being elected Holy Roman Emperors since 800.

1806-13: German states bordering France unite under Napoleon's protection in the Confederation of the Rhine. Bavaria, Westphalia and Württemberg are raised to status of kingdoms; new states and grand duchies are created. Areas ruled by 16 German princes become allied with France.

1806-67: Austrian Empire

1807: Prussians again defeated by Napoleon

1808: First locomotive built

1810-11: Trading regulations and business taxes destroy the guilds' monopoly over certain trades, establishing the principle of freedom of trade (*Gewerbefreiheit*).

1811: Decree to end the use of patronymic surnames in Ostfriesland

1812: War of 1812 brings immigration to America to a complete halt.

1813-15: Prussia rallies German states to rise and drive the French from German soil. War of Liberation. Napoleon defeated at Battle of Leipzig, exiled to Elba in 1814. Spirit of national unity sweeps through German states.

1814: Treaty of Ghent ends War of 1812.

First great wave of U.S. immigration: 5 million German immigrants, 1815-1860.

1814: Napoleon weakens. German states begin to reorganize under the leadership of Prussia.

1815: Napoleon defeated at Waterloo.

1815: German Confederation formed: Congress of Vienna restores Prussian territories, reduces number of independent states to 39 by increasing new territories of Prussia and Austria. (German Confederation is dissolved 1866)

1816: "The year without a summer" (attributed to the 1815 eruption of a volcano on an island of Indonesia)

1816: Crop failures and famine spark first significant emigration from Germany and Luxembourg to the United States.

1817: Lutheran and Reformed Churches are ordered to merge into Evangelical Church in Prussia, and merge elsewhere about the same time.

1818: 597 German immigrants land at New Orleans.

1818: Black Ball Line of sailing packets begins regular Liverpool-to-New York service; Liverpool becomes main port of departure for Irish and British along with considerable numbers of Germans and Norwegians.

1819: U.S. Congress passes the Passenger Act, ending redemptioner trade.

1819: The first steamship crosses the ocean, from Savannah to Liverpool, in 29 days, ushering in a new era of transatlantic travel.

1826-37: Cholera ravages Europe, with 900,000 victims in 1831 alone.

1828: Patronymic naming is outlawed in Schleswig-Holstein (then part of Denmark).

1830: Gradually increasing German emigration to United States and Canada, coinciding with beginning of Industrial Revolution in the German states.

1830s: German-Americans introduce decorated Christmas trees in America.

1830-48: Local and regional patriotism begins to give way to a new spirit of national patriotism previously unknown by Germans. It is Napoleon who more than any other person spreads pan-German thought.

1834: Zollverein (customs union of the Germanic Confederation) is created.

1835: First German railway between Nürnberg and Fürth

1835: "Männerchor von Philadelphia" is the first German-American "Gesangsverein" (choral society).

1837: Laws in Pennsylvania and Ohio permit public schools to be conducted in German.

1838-54: Main wave of emigration of "Old Lutherans," who rejected the Evangelical merger – to New York, Wisconsin, Missouri, Michigan and Texas. About one third go to Australia and Canada.

1840: Cunard Line founded, beginning era of steamship lines especially designed for passenger transportation between Europe and the United States.

1840-50: German immigration in Gulf Coast region

1840-75: Worldwide cholera, millions of deaths

1841: Heinrich Hoffmann von Fallersleben writes text to *Deutschland über Alles* hymn as the rallying cry of liberals urging national rather than Bavarian, Saxon, or Rhenish patriotism.

1843-59: First large wave of Germans to the United States (1846-1857), especially from Palatinate and Rhineland. Emigration peaks in 1854 and is largely stopped by the Panic of 1857. Most German emigration to Texas occurs in this period.

1844: Prince Carl von Solms-Braunfels brings first German settlers to Texas; in 1845 he founds town of New Braunfels.

1845: First propeller-driven steamship crosses Atlantic

1846: Crop failures in Germany and the Netherlands, followed by foreclosures, encourage Germans to emigrate to America.

1847: Missouri Synod of the Lutheran

Church organizes in protest against Americanization and liberalization of the Lutheran Church in America.

1848: German Revolution. A self-appointed group of liberals meets in the Paulskirche in Frankfurt/Main to draft a constitution for a new German nation to include all Germans states except Austria. Emigration to U.S. increases.

1848: German Revolution. Forty-Eighter Friedrich Hecker is greeted by a crowd of 20,000 German-Americans upon his arrival in New York.

1848: National civil registration adopted in Switzerland after brief civil war.

1848: Revolution in Germany fails, resulting in emigration of political refugees to America.

1849: Mass emigration of the Forty-Eighter political refugees to the U.S.

1849: Gold discovered in California

1850: First *Turnverein* in the U.S. opens in Cincinnati; bloody clashes between anti-foreign nativists ("Know-Nothings") and German Americans begin and continue throughout decade.

1850: Hamburg passenger lists begin to document the origins or places of residence of Europeans leaving for the Americas, Africa, and Australia.

1853: Immigrant Heinrich Steinweg founds the piano-manufacturing firm Steinway & Sons in New York.

1854-55: Anti-foreign movement active in New York City; immigrants beaten by mobs; depression of 1854; two-year cholera outbreak reaches peak in late 1854 aboard ships and at port.

1855-90: Castle Garden serves as a processing center for immigrants.

1855: Know-Nothings – anti-Catholic, anti-alien – at height of their influence

1856: A kindergarten is organized by Margaretha Meyer Schurz, wife of Carl

1857: Depression in U.S. (Panic of 1857)

1861-65: American Civil War; 23 percent of the 2,213,363 soldiers in the Union army are German-Americans; 500 officers in the Union army born in Germany.

1862: Homestead (Morrill Act) makes free land available in the United States.

1862: Otto von Bismarck begins long career as a powerful leader in Prussia (later Germany)

1863-75: Cholera causes deaths of millions (300,000 alone in 1866 in Eastern Europe).

1864: War with Denmark. Prussia conquers Schleswig-Holstein.

1865-74: Second large wave of emigrants to the U.S., peaking in 1873

1866-67: South German states join Prussia and North German states to form the North-German Confederation.

1866: Seven Weeks War. Bismarck leads Prussia in the defeat of Austria, forcing Austria to share power with Hungary as Austro-Hungarian Empire is established in 1867. Prussia annexes Hannover, Nassau, Hessen-Kassel, Schleswig-Holstein, and Frankfurt am Main.

1867: Karl Marx publishes Volume I of *Das Kapital.*

1867-1918: Austro-Hungarian Empire

1869: Carl Schurz becomes first German-born citizen elected to the U.S. Senate.

1870-71: German-Americans hail the defeat of France in the Franco-Prussian War and the unification of Germany on January 18, 1871. Prussia's victory over France leads to creation of the Second German Empire, taking Alsace and part of Lorraine from France. Second German Reich begins; Otto von Bismarck becomes chancellor.

1871: Special privileges of Germans are revoked in Russia, sparking emigration to North and South America.

1871-1907: Anti-Jewish pogroms in Russia. Many Jews emigrate to U.S.

1871-1918: Second German Empire

1873-79: Depression in the U.S. (Panic of 1873)

1874: Prussia introduces civil registration.

1874: Migration of German-speaking Mennonites from Russia to the prairies of Manitoba begins.

1876: Civil Registration is instituted throughout Germany where not already in practice.

1877: Carl Schurz becomes Secretary of Interior, holding this office until 1881.

1880s: Industrialization of Germany. Colonizing increases, especially in Africa.

1880-90: Largest number of Luxembourg emigrants come to the U.S.

1880-93: Third wave of German emigrants to the U.S, peaking in 1882

1881-88: Large numbers of Swiss emigrants come to the U.S.

1888-1918: Reign of Kaiser Wilhelm II, also known as the "Wilhelmine Age."

1889-90: Influenza epidemic, affecting 40% of world, causes deaths of millions

1892-1954: Ellis Island serves as U.S. Immigration Center, through which about 20 million immigrants pass.

1893-94: Renewed worldwide outbreak of cholera

1910-20: Largest number of Swiss emigrants come to the U.S.

1914: Assassination of Archduke Franz Ferdinand triggers World War I.

1914-18: World War I. German economy in ruins. Alsace-Lorraine returned to France. Parts of eastern Germany ceded to Lithuania and Poland. Bolshevik Revolution of 1917 and civil war cause emigration from Russia.

1917 (6 April): United States declares war against Central Powers; German-Americans suffer wave of severe discrimination as America enters World War I.

1917-19: Influenza epidemic, with deaths estimated as high as 50 million

1918: Kaiser abdicates. End of the second German Reich.

1919 (8 June): Versailles Peace Treaty signed. West Prussia with Posen and Upper Silesia come under Polish rule. New state of Thüringen created from seven small principalities. Germany cedes Alsace-Lorraine to France; Upper Silesia, most of Posen, and West Prussia

to Poland; North Schleswig to Denmark; Eupen and Malmédy to Belgium, part of Jutland to Denmark; Danzig becomes a free city; Memel is ceded to Lithuania; Saarland is to be administered by the League of Nations for 15 years.

1919-33: Weimar Republic, ill-fated German effort at parliamentary democracy

1920s: Following calming of anti-German sentiment, many German skilled workers and technicians migrate to Canada to work in industrial centers of Ontario.

1921: Treaty of Riga establishes boundaries of new Poland.

1921: Hitler joins the Nazi Party (NSDAP, or *National sozialistische deutsche Arbeiterpartei*).

1921-23: Extreme inflation in Germany ($1 = 4.3 trillion marks).

1921-24: Immigration severely curtailed by new American laws.

1923: Hitler's Munich beer-hall Putsch

1929-34: The Great Depression: Mass unemployment in Germany during worldwide financial crisis. One-third of the potential work force is unemployed.

1933: Start of the emigration of German artists and intellectuals to the U.S.

1933: Third Reich begins with Hitler's appointment as chancellor. Nazi rule begins. Hitler's anti-Semitic campaign drives many German Jews to seek refuge in the U.S, but quotas imposed in 1929 limit numbers allowed.

1938 (9-10 November): *Reichskristallnacht* pogrom carried out throughout Germany, opening way for the Nazis' attempt to exterminate European Jewry.

1938: Hitler annexes Austria. Munich Pact provides legal framework for Nazi occupation of largely German-speaking Sudeten areas of Czechoslovakia.

1939-45: Germany occupies the rest of Czechoslovakia and invades Poland, thus starting World War II. Many German records destroyed in war.

1939-45: World War II. East Prussia divided between Poland and Russia.

Most of Pomerania, West Prussia, Brandenburg, and Silesia come under Polish administration.

1941 (11 December): Hitler declares war on the U.S.

1941-45: One-third of the 11 million soldiers in the U.S. armed forces in World War II are of German descent.

1944-48: Mass flight from Eastern Europe before the advancing Soviet armies. Population of West Germany increases 25% as 9 million ethnic Germans arrive.

1945 (8 May): Unconditional surrender of Germany to the Allies. Germany is divided into four occupation zones: American, British, French, and Soviet sectors; Berlin, Austria and Vienna are all divided on the same basis. The end of the war period is referred to in German as *Stunde Null,* the "zero hour."

1945: Hitler suicide. End of Third Reich

1948 (June): Beginning of the Berlin Blockade and the western allies' Berlin Airlift, which lasts 10 months

1948: The Displaced Persons Act allows additional ethnic Germans, expelled from Eastern Europe, to emigrate to America.

1949: The Federal Republic of West Germany and the German Democratic Republic of East Germany are created.

1950s: About 250,000 Germans, many of them skilled workers, migrate to Canada.

1955: Federal Republic of West Germany becomes member of NATO. The German Democratic Republic of East Germany becomes member of the Warsaw Pact.

1957: The European Economic Community is established, of which West Germany is a part.

1961 (13 August): Construction of Berlin wall begins.

1969-70: West Germany signs a nonaggression treaty with the U.S.S.R. and recognizes the Oder-Neisse line as Poland's western frontier.

1973: Both East and West Germany are admitted to the United Nations.

1987: *Glasnost* leads to emigration of many ethnic Germans and Jews from the Soviet Union and East Central Europe.

1989 (9 November): Fall of the Berlin Wall, the period in history commonly referred to by Germans as the *Wende,* or the "turning point."

1990 (3 October): German reunification completed with the annexation of the German Democratic Republic by the Federal Republic of Germany

1991 (June): Bundestag decides to move government and parliament to Berlin.

1993 (1 January): Czechoslovakia split into Czech Republic and Slovakia.

SUMMARY OF GERMAN POLITICAL ORGANIZATION

◆370-568 AD: The Great Migrations (*Die Völkerwanderung*)

◆768-814: Charlemagne and Frankish expansion

◆962-1806 Holy Roman Empire of the German Nation *(Heiliges Römisches Reich deutscher Nation,* or *Das Alte Reich*)

◆1806-1815: Confederation of the Rhine (*Der Rheinbund*)

◆1815-1866: German Confederation (*Der Deutsche Bund*)

◆1866-1871; North German Confederation (*Der Norddeutsche Bund*)

◆1871-1918: Second German Empire (*Das Deutsche Reich*)

◆1918-1933: The Weimar Republic (*Die Weimarer Republik*)

◆1933-1945: Third German Empire (*Das Dritte Reich*)

◆1949-1990: German Democratic Republic (*Deutsche Demokratische Republik*)

◆1949- : Federal Republic of Germany (*Bundesrepublik Deutschland*)

LEGAL AND COURT TERMINOLOGY

Abhilfe .... remedy or cure

Aburteilung .... trial
Advocat .... lawyer
Amtmann .... district judge
Amtsrichter .... county judge
Amtsvogt .... district judge
Anwalt .... lawyer
Appellationsgericht .... court of appeal
Behörde .. authority, board, department
Berufungsgericht .... appeals court
Beweismittel .... evidence
Bundesgericht .... federal court
                                          or tribunal
Bundesverfassungs- .... federal
gericht   constitutional court
Entscheidung .... legal decision
Erbgericht .... inheritance court
Erlaß .... decree, edict
Gau(Go-) .... regional district
Gericht   provincial court
gelehrte Richter .... learned judge
Gemeindegericht .... municipal court
Gerichts Buch .... court record
Gerichts Protokolle .... court record
Gerichts Schöffen .. court of lay judges
                          or of jury courts
Gerichtsakten .... court records
Gerichtsbezirk .... circuit court,
                          judicial district court
Gerichtshof . court of justice, law court
Gerichtsurteil .. judgment of the court
Handelsgericht .... court dealing
                          with commerce
Hofgericht .... appellate court
Kammergericht .... supreme court
Kirchengericht ..... ecclesiastical court
Kreisgericht .... court of an
                          administrative district
Kreisrichter .. county or district judge
Landesgericht .... law of the land/
                          municipal law
Landmarschallschengericht . appellate
                                          court
öffentlich .... public
Patrimonialgericht .... court on a
                          noble estate
Polizeibehörden .... police authorities
Prozeß .... lawsuit, trial, litigation
Recht .... right, law, justice,
                          due process of law

Rechtsanwalt .... lawyer
Rechtsordnung .... legal system
Reichsgesetz .... federal law
Reichsverfassung .... constitution of
                          the German Empire
Richter .... judge
Scharfrichter .... executioner, hangman
Schöffe .... lay judge
Schöffengericht .... court with trial
                          by jury
Schultheißegericht .... local or
                          communal court
Staatsrecht constitutional or public law
Stadtgericht .... city court
Stadtrecht .... city law, municipal law
Strafgericht .... criminal court
Strafmittel .... disciplinary matters
Untergericht .... lower court
Urteil .... judgment, decision,
                          sentence, verdict
Verbrechen .... crime, felony
Vorschriften .... rule, regulation
Zivilprozeß .... civil action

COURTS OF THE GERMAN EMPIRE

German courts of the German Empire,
from 1877, from lowest to highest:
+ **Amtsgericht** (county court): jurisdiction in petty criminal and civil cases; the
Amtsrichter was the judge. The Amtsgericht was presided over by a single
judge, whose jurisdiction covered petty
criminal and civil cases, up to 300 marks.
Petty criminal cases were heard by the
Amtsrichter sitting with two Schöffen
(assessors) selected by lot from the jury
lists. Prisoners were tried for offenses
punishable with a fine not exceeding 600
marks or confinement, or with imprisonment of not more than three months.
+ **Landesgericht:** (regional court): revised the decisions of the Amtsgerichte,
had original jurisdiction in criminal and
civil cases and in divorce proceedings.
+ **Oberlandesgericht** (higher regional
court): had original jurisdiction in grave

offenses; it was composed of seven judges. There were 28 such courts in the empire in 1910. Only Bavaria had an *Oberstes Landesgericht* (highest regional court) which could revise the action of the *Oberlandesgericht*.

Reichsgericht (supreme court): composed of 92 judges, called *Reichsgerichtsräte*, appointed by the emperor. The supreme court seat was at Leipzig.

The *Rechtsanwalt*, or advocate, was required to study law at a university for four years and to pass two state examinations in order to be admitted to practice by the *Amtsgericht* or *Landesgericht*.

Source: *Encyclopedia Britannica*: *Dictionary of Arts, Sciences, Literature and General Information.* University Press, New York, 11th ed., 1910.

FACTS ABOUT THE FEDERAL REPUBLIC OF GERMANY (Bundesrepublik Deutschland)

Geographic location
Central Europe, common borders with Denmark (68 km), the Netherlands (577 km), Belgium (167 km), France (451 km), Switzerland (334 km), Austria (784 km), Luxembourg (138 km), the Czech Republic (646 km), and Poland (456 km).

Total area
356,910 sq km; land area 349,520 sq km

Comparative area
Slightly smaller than Montana

Capital
Berlin (The shift from Bonn to Berlin took place largely in 1999, but continued for several years with Bonn retaining some administrative functions.)

Ports, seaboard and interior
Berlin, Bonn, Brake, Bremen, Bremerhaven, Cologne, Dresden, Duisburg, Emden, Hamburg, Karlsruhe, Kiel, Lübeck, Magdeburg, Mannheim, Rostock, Stuttgart

Jurisdictional history

◆ **January 18, 1871:** German Empire unification

● **1945:** Divided into four zones of occupation (United Kingdom, United States, Union of Soviet Socialist Republics, and later France) following World War II

◆ **May 23, 1949:** Federal Republic of Germany (or West Germany) proclaimed, which consisted of the former zones of the United Kingdom, United States, and France

◆ **October 7, 1949:** German Democratic Republic (or East Germany) proclaimed and included the former USSR zone

◆ **October 3, 1990:** Unification of West Germany and East Germany; on this date the states of Mecklenburg-Vorpommern, Brandenburg, Sachsen-Anhalt, Thüringen, and Sachsen were established and became part of the Federal Republic of Germany; the eleven districts of East Berlin merged with the state of Berlin.

◆ **March 15, 1991:** rights of all four occupation powers relinquished; returned to full sovereignty

Constitution
The Basic Law of May 23, 1949 for West Germany became (with some modifications) the constitution for reunited Germany on October 3, 1990.

Suffrage
18 years of age; universal

Executive branch
Head of state: Federal President; elected for five years by the Federal Assembly *(Bundestag* plus the same number of delegates from the states*)*

Head of government
Elected by the Federal Parliament (*Bundestag*) for its duration (maximum of four years); Chancellor Angela Merkel since Nov 22, 2005.

Cabinet
Appointed by the president upon the proposal of the chancellor

Major political parties
◆ Christian Democratic Union (CDU), in all Germany except Bavaria

◆Christian Social Union (CSU), only in Bavaria
◆Free Democratic Party (FDP)
◆Social Democratic Party (SPD)
◆Green Party (*Die Grünen*)
◆Party of Democratic Socialism (PDS)
◆Republikaner
◆National Democratic Party (NPD)
◆Communist Party (DKP)

Legislative branch

Bicameral chamber (no official name for the two chambers as a whole)

Federal Parliament (*Bundestag*)

Elected by direct popular vote under a system combining direct and proportional representation; a party must win 5 percent of the national vote or three direct mandates to gain representation; for reunited Germany, first elected on December 2, 1990; term of office is four years

Federal Council (*Bundesrat*)

State governments are directly represented; each has three to six votes (depending on size), which must be voted as a block.

Judicial branch

Federal Constitutional Court *(Bundesverfassungsgericht)*; criminal courts (*Strafgerichte*); civil courts (*Zivilgerichte)*; administrative courts (*Verwaltungsgerichte*); tax courts (*Finanzgerichte*); labor dispute courts *(Arbeitsgerichte)*; social affairs courts (*Sozialgerichte*)

Population

82.3 million; including foreigners)

Ethnic divisions

German 91.2%, Turkish 2.1%, Italians 0.5%, Greeks 0.4%, Poles 0.4%

Religions

Protestant 34%, Roman Catholic 31%, Muslim 0.4%, unaffiliated or other 34%

States (*Länder*)

Baden-Württemberg, Bayern, Berlin, Brandenburg, Bremen, Hamburg, Hessen, Mecklenburg-Vorpommern, Niedersachsen, Nordrhein-Westfalen, Rheinland-Pfalz, Saarland, Sachsen, Sachsen-Anhalt, Schleswig-Holstein, Thüringen

Diplomatic representation in the United States

Chancery at 4645 Reservoir Road NW, Washington, DC 20007; tel. (202) 298-8140

Consulate(s) general

Atlanta, Boston, Chicago, Houston, Los Angeles, Miami, New York, San Francisco, Washington D.C.

U.S. Embassy in Berlin

Pariser Platz, Berlin

Consulate(s) general

Frankfurt, Hamburg, Leipzig, Munich, and Stuttgart

Flag

Three equal horizontal bands of black (top), red, and gold

THE THREE GERMAN EMPIRES

Historically, there have been two periods when Germany was a realm (*Reich*) ruled by an emperor (*Kaiser*).

First empire

The first German Reich was called the "Holy Roman Empire of the German Nation."

It began in the tenth century and lasted 850 years until its dissolution in 1806 by Napoleon's conquest of Europe. This Reich was ruled by the dual power of the Kaiser and of the feudal nobles who elected him.

From the fifteenth century on, the Austrian House of Hapsburg supplied the heirs to the throne.

Second empire

The second German Reich was founded by the German federated states, leaving out Austria, after the Franco-Prussian War of 1870-71. Otto von Bismarck, who was then Prime Minister of Prussia, played the decisive role in forging the second Reich, which lasted until Kaiser Wilhelm II abdicated in 1918 as a result of the first World War.

Third empire

Adolf Hitler became chancellor in 1933. National Socialist (Nazi) Germany became known as the "Third Reich." The Third Reich ended when Germany capitulated on May 8, 1945, thus ending the Second World War.

Source: Federal Republic of Germany: Questions and Answers, ed. Susan Steiner. German Information Center, New York, 1996

SIGNIFICANCE OF 'REICH' AND 'EMPIRE'

The term "empire" is from *imperium,* Latin for "command and the power to issue it," as well as "the area subjected to this power."

The German term is *Reich,* related to Latin *regnum*: "rule, government over country and people," which in the Middle Ages meant "kingly rule." From early medieval times, *imperium* and *Reich* were taken as practically synonymous. They were also universalized to signify "worldwide rule," though the extent and limits of the "world" to which this claim related varied considerably from moment to moment. The constant theme was the reference to imperial Rome, where, from the days of Augustus, *imperium* had signified "empire."

The *Reich* was the *Kaiserreich* (*Kaiser* from Caesar, the paradigmatic Roman ruler); the *imperium* was the *imperium romanum* which, according to the historical theory prevailing throughout the Christian Middle Ages, was expected to last to the end of time.

The medieval (German) empire was, therefore, the successor to, and continuation of, the ancient Roman Empire, the authority and sway of which were guaranteed by Scriptural prophecy to endure until the return of Christ (Dan. 2:31-45).

Source: *Dictionary of the Middle Ages*, Vol. 5, ed. Joseph R. Strayer. Charles Scribner's Sons, New York, 1985

HOLY ROMAN EMPIRE OF THE GERMAN NATION

The Holy Roman Empire of the German Nation

(Heiliges Römisches Reich Deutscher Nation)

Since Konrad II, the East Frankonian Empire was known as the *Romanum Imperium* (*Römisches Reich*, or the Roman Empire).

It was called the *Sacrum Imperium* (*Heiliges Reich*, or Holy Empire) since 1157, and since the mid-thirteenth century the name *Sacrum Romanum Imperium* (Holy Roman Empire) gradually came into use.

The addition, *Nationis Germaniae* (*Deutscher Nation,* or German Nation) was added only in the fifteenth century.

The German (or Roman) king was selected by a College of Electors since 1356 (the Golden Bull). However, starting with Otto I, the German Kaiser was crowned by the pope, a tradition that ended with Karl V in 1530.

Since the fifteenth and sixteenth centuries, the Holy Roman Empire was dominated by power struggles between the Kaiser and the *Reichsständen* (the Imperial Diet) until after the Peace of Westphalia when German history took place almost solely on the level of the many territorial states.

In 1806, the Holy Roman Empire of the German Nation was dissolved.

PRUSSIAN AND GERMAN EMPIRE RULERS

The Hohenzollerns

(In 1417, the Hohenzollerns were granted the Electorate of Brandenburg.) **Electors of Brandenburg (Kurfürsten von Brandenburg):**

◆Friedrich I (1417-1440)
◆Friedrich II (1440-1470)
◆Albrecht Achilles (1480-1486)
◆Johann Cicero (1486-1499)
◆Joachim I (1499-1535)
◆Joachim II (1535-1571)
◆Johann Georg (1571-1598)
◆Joachim Friedrich (1598-1608)
◆Johann Sigismund (1608-1619)
◆Georg Wilhelm (1619-1640)
◆Friedrich Wilhelm, der Große Kurfürst (1640-1688)
◆Friedrich III. (1688-1701)

Kings of Prussia
(Könige von Preußen)
◆Friedrich III, König in Preußen under the name of Friedrich I (1701-1713)
◆Friedrich Wilhelm I (1713-1740)
◆Friedrich II, der Große (1740-1786)
◆Friedrich Wilhelm II (1786-1797)
◆Friedrich Wilhelm III (1797-1840)
◆Friedrich Wilhelm IV (1840-1861)
◆Wilhelm I (1861-1871)

The German Empire
(Das Deutsche Reich)
In 1871, King Wilhelm I of Prussia was proclaimed as the German Kaiser and thus the basis for the empire was reestablished.
Emperors *(Kaiser):*
◆Wilhelm I (1871-1888)
◆Friedrich III (9 Mar.-15 June 1888)
◆Wilhelm II (1888-1918)
Chancellors *(Kanzler):*
◆Otto von Bismarck (1871-1890)
◆Georg Leo von Caprivi (1890-1894)
◆ Chlodwig Fürst zu Hohenlohe-Schillingsfürst (1894-1900)
◆Bernhard von Bülow (1900-1909)
◆ Theobald von Bethmann-Hollweg (1909-1917)
◆Georg Michaelis (1917)
◆Georg von Gertling (1917-1918)
◆Max von Baden (1918)

The Weimar Republic
(Die Weimarer Republik)

Presidents of the Republic:
◆Friedrich Ebert (1919-1925)
◆Paul von Hindenburg (1925-1934)
Chancellors:
◆Philipp Scheidemann (1919)
◆Gustav Bauer (1919-1920)
◆Hermann Müller (1920)
◆Konstantin Fehrenbach (1920-1921)
◆Joseph Wirth (1921-1922)
◆Wilhelm Cuno (1922-1923)
◆Gustav Stresemann (1923)
◆Wilhelm Marx (1923-1925)
◆Hans Luther (1925-1926)
◆Wilhelm Marx (1926-1928)
◆Hermann Müller (1928-1930)
◆Heinrich Brüning (1930-1932)
◆Franz von Papen (1932)
◆Kurt von Schleicher (1932-1933)
◆Adolf Hitler (1933)

The Third Empire
(Das Dritte Reich)
◆Adolf Hitler, Führer und Reichskanzler (1933-1945)
◆Karl Dönitz (1945)

The two Germanys
(Die Beiden deutschen Staaten)
After the fall of the German Empire on May 8, 1945, the four powers, the USA, USSR, Great Britain, and France, took over the government.
Germany was divided into four occupied zones, by the Potsdam Agreement of August 2, 1945.
In the western zones was established the Federal Republic of Germany; in the Soviet occupied zone, the German Democratic Republic.

Federal Republic of Germany
(Bundesrepublik Deutschland)
Presidents *(Bundespräsidenten):*
◆Theodor Heuss (1949-1959)
◆Heinrich Lübke (1959-1969)
◆Gustav Heinemann (1969-1974)
◆Walter Scheel (1974-1979)
◆Karl Carstens (1979-1984)
◆Richard von Weizsäcker (1984-1994)

◆Roman Herzog (1994-1999)
◆Johannes Rau since 1999
◆Horst Köhler since Jul 1, 2004
Chancellors *(Bundeskanzler):*
◆Konrad Adenauer, CDU (1949-1963)
◆Ludwig Erhard, CDU (1963-1966)
◆Kurt Georg Kiesinger, CDU (1966-1969)
◆Willy Brandt, SPD (1969-1974)
◆Helmut Schmidt, SPD (1974-1982)
◆Helmut Kohl , CDU (1982-1990; 1990-1998, chancellor of united Germany)
◆Gerhard Schröder, SPD, 1998-2005
◆Angela Merkel, CDU, 2005 -

German Democratic Republic
(Deutsche Demokratische Republik)
Heads of state *(Staatschefs):*
◆Wilhelm Pieck (1949-1960)
◆Walter Ulbricht (1960-1973)
◆Willi Stoph (1973-1976)
◆Erich Honecker (1976-1989)
◆Manfred Gerlach (1989-1990)

First Secretary of the ZK
of the SED
(Erste Sekretäre des ZK der SED):
◆Walter Ulbricht (1950-1971)
◆Erich Honecker (1971-1989)
◆Egon Krenz (Oct. - Dec. 1989)
◆After the downfall of communist East Germany: L. de Maizière, Ministerpräsident, 12 April - 2 October 1990
Source: *Meyers Memo: Das Wissen der Welt nach Sachgebieten.* Meyers Lexikonverlag. Mannheim, 1991

THE SECOND GERMAN EMPIRE (1871-1918)

Information shown in italics indicates where each political subdivision of the Second German Empire (1871-1918) is located today. Dates indicate when the political body was acquired or allied with states making up the Empire.

Four kingdoms
(Königreiche)

◆ **Bayern** (Bavaria) 1871: *Germany (former West Germany).*
◆ **Königreich Sachsen** (Kingdom of Saxony), 1871: *Germany (former East Germany).*
◆**Württemberg,** 1871: *Germany (former West Germany).*
◆ **Königreich Preußen**, Kingdom of Prussia, including provinces of
–**Brandenburg,** 1415: *Germany (former East Germany) and Poland*
–**Hannover,** 1866: *Germany (former West Germany)*
–**Hessen-Nassau,** 1867: *Germany (former East Germany and West Germany)*
–**Hohenzollern,** 1415: *Germany (former West Germany)*
–**Ostpreußen** (East Prussia), 1813: *Poland and former USSR*
–**Pommern** (Pomerania), 1648, 1720 (Swedish Pomerania 1815): *Germany (former East Germany) and Poland*
–**Posen,** 1793: *Poland*
–**Rheinland/Rheinprovinz** (Rhineland), 1814/1824: *Germany (former West Germany) and Belgium*
–**Provinz Sachsen** (Province of Saxony), 1816: *Germany (former East Germany)*
–**Schlesien** (Silesia), 1742: *Germany (former East Germany), Poland and Czech Republic*
–**Schleswig-Holstein,** 1864: *Germany (former West Germany) and Denmark*
–**Westfalen** (Westphalia), 1815: *Germany (former West Germany)*
–**Westpreußen** (West Prussia). 1772, 1793: *Poland*

Grandduchies
(Großherzogtümer)
◆**Baden,** 1852: *Germany (former West Germany).*
◆ **Hessen (Hessen-Darmstadt),** 1871: *Germany (former West Germany).*
◆**Mecklenburg-Schwerin,** 1866: *Germany (former East Germany)*
◆**Mecklenburg-Strelitz,** 1866: *Germany*

(former East Germany)
◆**Oldenburg**, 1866: *Germany (former West Germany)*
◆**Sachsen-Weimar-Eisenach** (in Thüringen*), 1871: *Germany (former East Germany)*

Duchies
(Herzogtümer)
◆**Anhalt**, 1871: *Germany (former East Germany)*
◆ **Braunschweig** (Brunswick), 1866: *Germany (former East Germany and West Germany)*
◆**Sachsen-Meiningen** (in Thüringen*), 1871: *Germany (former East Germany)*
◆**Sachsen-Altenburg** (in Thüringen*), 1871: *Germany (former East Germany)*
◆**Sachsen-Coburg-Gotha** (in Thüringen*), 1871: *Germany (former East Germany)*

Principalities
(Fürstentümer)
◆**Schwarzburg-Rudolstadt** (in Thüringen*): *Germany (former East Germany)*
◆ **Schwarzburg-Sondershausen** (in Thüringen*): *Germany (former East Germany)*
◆**Waldeck**, 1868: *Germany (former West Germany)*
◆ **Reuß-ältere Linie** (in Thüringen*): *Germany (former East Germany)*
◆**Reuß-jüngere Linie** (in Thüringen*): *Germany (former East Germany)*
◆**Schaumburg-Lippe**, 1866: *Germany (former West Germany)*
◆**Lippe (Lippe-Detmold)**, 1867: *Germany (former West Germany)*

Free Hanseatic cities
(Freie Städte)
◆**Bremen**, 1866: *Germany (former West Germany)*
◆**Hamburg**, 1871: *Germany (former West Germany)*
◆**Lübeck**, 1866: *Germany (former West Germany)*

Imperial province
(Reichsland)
◆**Elsaß-Lothringen** (Alsace-Lorraine), 1871: *France*
*Thüringen described a geographical region; it had no political boundaries during the time of the Second German Empire. See below.

THÜRINGEN (THURINGIA)

Smaller Saxon states in the area between the Thuringian Forest on the south, the Harz Mountains on the north, the Werra River on the west, and the Saale River on the east were sometimes grouped together and called Thüringen.

Thüringen also included parts of the Kingdom of Saxony, the Kingdom of Bavaria, and the Saxony Province of the Kingdom of Prussia.

The eight independent states of Thüringen were,

Grand duchy
◆ Sachsen-Weimar-Eisenach (Saxe-Weimar-Eisenach)

Duchies
◆ Sachsen-Altenburg (Saxe-Altenburg)
◆ Sachsen-Coburg-Gotha (Saxe-Coburg-Gotha)
◆ Sachsen-Meiningen (Saxe-Meiningen)

Principalities
◆ Reuß-ältere Linie (Reuss-elder line), also known as Reuß-Greitz (Reuss-Greitz)
◆ Reuß-jüngere Linie (Reuss-younger line), also known as Reuß-Schleitz-Gera (Reuss-Schleitz-Gera)
◆ Schwarzburg-Rudolstadt
◆ Schwarzburg-Sondershausen

Following World War I, Thüringen became a political state.

Source: William J. Toeppe, "Dewey and His System (Part 3A), *German Genealogical Society Newsletter* , Vol. IV, No. 6, July 1995

STATES OF THE GERMAN EMPIRE, 1871-1918, IN ENGLISH AND GERMAN

English	German
Alsace-Lorraine (State)	Elsaß-Lothringen (Reichsland)
Anhalt (Duchy)	Anhalt (Herzogtum)
Baden (Grandduchy)	Baden (Großherzogtum)
Bavaria (Kingdom)	Bayern (Königreich)
Berlin (City)	Berlin (Stadt)
Brandenburg (Province)	Brandenburg (Provinz)
Bremen (Free City-State)	Bremen (Freistadt)
Brunswick (Duchy)	Braunschweig (Herzogtum)
East Prussia (Province)	Ostpreußen (Provinz)
Hamburg (Free City-State)	Hamburg (Freistadt)
Hanover (Province)	Hannover (Provinz)
Hesse (Grandduchy)	Hessen (Großherzogtum)
Hesse-Nassau (Province)	Hessen-Nassau (Provinz)
Hohenzollern (State)	Hohenzollern (Reichland)
Lippe (Principality)	Lippe (Fürstentum)
Lübeck (Free City-State)	Lübeck (Freistadt)
Mecklenburg-Schwerin (Grandduchy)	Mecklenburg-Schwerin (Großherzogtum)
Mecklenburg-Strelitz (Grandduchy)	Mecklenburg-Strelitz (Großherzogtum)
Oldenburg (Grandduchy)	Oldenburg (Großherzogtum)
Pomerania (Province)	Pommern (Provinz)
Posen (Province)	Posen (Provinz)
Prussia (Kingdom)	Preußen (Königreich)
Reuß-Greiz (Principality)	Reuß ältere Linie (Fürstentum)
Reuß-Schleiz-Gera (Principality)	Reuß jüngere Linie (Fürstentum)
Rhineland (Province)	Rheinland (Provinz)
Saxe-Altenburg (Duchy)	Sachsen-Altenburg (Herzogtum)
Saxe-Coburg-Gotha (Duchy)	Sachsen-Coburg-Gotha (Herzogtum)
Saxe-Meiningen (Duchy)	Sachsen-Meiningen (Herzogtum)
Saxe-Weimar-Eisenach (Grandduchy)	Sachsen-Weimar-Eisenach (Großherzogtum)
Saxony (Kingdom)	Sachsen (Königreich)
Saxony (Province)	Sachsen (Provinz)
Schaumburg-Lippe (Principality)	Schaumburg-Lippe (Fürstentum)
Schleswig-Holstein (Province)	Schleswig-Holstein (Provinz)
Schwarzburg-Rudolstadt (Principality)	Schwarzburg-Rudolstadt (Fürstentum)
Schwarzburg-Sondershausen (Principality)	Schwarzburg-Sondershausen (Fürstentum)
Silesia (Province)	Schlesien (Provinz)
Waldeck (Principality)	Waldeck (Fürstentum)
West Prussia (Province)	Westpreußen (Provinz)
Westphalia (Province)	Westfalen (Provinz)
Württemberg (Kingdom)	Württemberg (Königreich)

Germany (Empire)	Deutschland (Reich)

Source: Steven W. Blodgett, *Germany Genealogical Research Guide.*The Genealogical Department of the Church of Jesus Christ of Latter-day Saints, 1989. Reprinted by permission.

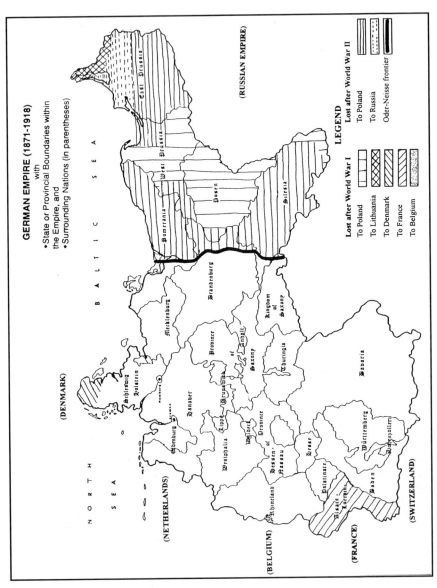

Map courtesy of Paul F. C. Mueller

'DEUTSCH,' 'DEUTSCHLAND'

The German nation grew out of a number of tribes, known as Germanic tribes. There were Franks and Saxons, Bavarians and Swabians, Alemani and Frisians, and many others. During the 8th century, the word *deutsch* (German) began to be used to designate the people who did not speak a Roman dialect and who lived in the eastern part of the Frankish realm.

Soon the region they lived in became known as "Deutschland" (Germany). The English words "German" and "Germany" are derivatives of the Latin "Germanus," a word used by the Romans in reference to the non-Roman tribes living in the central part of Europe.

Source: German Information Center

THE TEUTONIC KNIGHTS

The Teutonic Knights are also known as the Teutonic Order (*Deutscher Orden*). Formally, they were called the House of the Hospitalers of Saint Mary of the Teutons in Jerusalem, or the *Deutscher Orden,* as the *Deutscher Ritterorden*, or as *Haus der Ritter des Hospitals Sankt Marien der Deutschen zu Jerusalem.*

The order was known in Latin as *Domus Sanctae Mariae Theutonicorum in Jerusalem.*

This religious order played a major role in eastern Europe in the late Middle Ages and underwent various changes in organization and residence from its founding in 1189/90 to the present.

Its major residences, marking its major states of development, were 1) Acre, Palestine (modern Akko, Israel), its original home beginning with the Third Cru-

sade (1189-90 - c. 1291); 2) Marienburg, Prussia (modern Malbork, Poland), the center of its role as a military principality (1309-1525); 3) Mergentheim, Württemberg, to which it moved after its loss of Prussia (1525-1809); and 4) Vienna, where the order gathered the remains of its revenues and survives as a purely hospital order (from 1834).

The German Order, whose symbol is the black cross (modified today in the form of the Iron Cross), still exists as a religious order which owns hospitals throughout Germany and Austria.

Partial source: "Teutonic Order," *Encyclopaedia Britannica Online,* accessed 19 January 2000

ENCLAVES AND EXCLAVES

Many states of the Second German Empire were composed of parts of different areas of the Empire.

A state might completely surround a part of another state whose main part was distant. This completely surrounded state was an enclave as far as the surrounding state was concerned. These situations arose when a ruling noble family would obtain land outside the main areas ruled by them.

To the state which owned the surrounded part, the surrounded part was an exclave.

In other situations, one part of a state might be separated from another part but not completely surrounded by a single state. If the separated part was a small part of the total area of the state, the separated part might also have been called an exclave.

With the elimination of the ruling of these areas by the noble families following World War I, the need to recognize these enclaves and exclaves was eliminated.

Source: William J. Toeppe, ed. *Newsletter,* German Genealogical Society of America,

Vol. IV, No. 6, 1995. Reprinted by permission.

LEAD-UPS TO WORLD WAR II

Jan. 30, 1933: German President Hindenburg appoints Hitler as Reich Chancellor
Aug. 2, 1934: Hindenburg dies. Hitler becomes chancellor and president
Mar. 13, 1938: Germany annexes Austria (*Anschluss*)
Sep. 29, 1938: German occupies Sudetenland
Nov. 9, 1938: Reichskristallnacht: Jewish pogroms throughout Germany
Mar. 15, 1939: Germany occupies Czechoslovakia
Aug. 23, 1939: Non-aggression pact between Germany and Russia
Sep. 1, 1939: Germany invades Poland

THE TREATY OF VERSAILLES

On June 28, 1919, Germany signed the Treaty of Versailles in the Hall of Mirrors in the palace of Versailles, where Bismarck had proclaimed the German Empire in 1871.
As the results of the Treaty of Versailles,
♦Alsace-Lorraine was ceded to France.
♦The Polish Corridor, created to give Poland an outlet to the Baltic, went to Poland, thus dividing East Prussia from the rest of Germany. (The Polish Corridor was created from land which had previously been Posen and West Prussia; what was left of these two areas which remained part of Germany was combined in the Prussian province of *Grenzmark*, meaning "border area.")
♦Eupen, Malmédy, and Moresnet went to Belgium after a plebescite.
♦After a plebescite, the League of Nations divided German Upper Silesia between Germany and Poland.

♦Memel went to Lithuania.
♦Schleswig was returned to Denmark
♦The Rhineland was occupied by the Allies.
♦The industrial region of the Saar was placed under international control, but came effectively under French influence
♦All German colonies were transferred to the Allies as mandates.
♦The German army was limited to 100,000 men
♦The navy was strongly reduced, and the air force eliminated.
♦German munitions were restricted, and poison gas prohibited.
♦Germany was held responsible for the damages of the war (in the "war-guilt" clause). Reparations payments to the victor nations will cripple the German economy for several years.

GERMAN TERRITORIAL LOSSES AFTER WWII (1945)

Germany lost East Prussia and the territory east of the Oder and Neisse Rivers, i.e., parts of the states of Brandenburg and Pomerania and most of Silesia. The northern half of East Prussia is now part of Russia. Ther remaining territories were added to Poland, which had lost land to the Soviet Union in the east. Germany lost about 44,310 sq. miles with a population of 9,621,000. The population either fled from advancing Soviet forces or was expelled after the end of the war. Ethnic Germansa were also expelled from Czechoslovakia and other countries in eastern or southeastern Europe.

THE BASIC LAW, OR CONSTITUTION (Grundgesetz)

The German constitution is called the *Grundgesetz* (Basic Law) and was put into effect in May 1949 for West Germany.

The name *Grundgesetz* was chosen to emphasize the provisional character of this constitution.

As its preamble declared, a definite constitution was to be formulated by the Parliament of a reunited Germany. However, the *Grundgesetz* proved to be so successful that it was retained under the same name by reunited Germany with only minor changes.

In contrast to other constitutions, in which civil liberties are placed in the preamble or in amendments, the Basic Law places civil liberty protection in the constitution itself.

The first paragraph of Article I states that the dignity of the individual must not be threatened.

The third paragraph lists basic rights that all executive and judicial authorities are bound to defend. These include freedom in writing and painting; outlawing of sterilization or medical experiments (even with volunteers); equal rights for men and women; include nondiscrimination regarding sex, descent, race, language, and religious or political views.

Article IV guarantees freedom of religion and conscience, the free profession of religious or philosophical views, and the right to refuse to serve in the military for reasons of conscience.

Article V protects freedom of opinion, research, and teaching. Article VI protects marriage and the family. The right of assembly and the right to join and found organizations is also guaranteed.

The Basic Law draws heavily from the Bill of Rights and American civil liberties, with additional anti-Nazi-inspired guarantees.

The Basic Law adopts the principle of the American Constitution in that powers of the federal government are expressed and enumerated, while those of the *Länder* (states) are residual.

But it also borrows from the Swiss in building its definition of federalism with the heavy intermingling of federal and state governments in their direct effect on the people.

Sources:

♦Judith M. Gansberg, Stalag: USA. *The Remarkable Storyof German POWs in America.* Thomas Y. Crowell Company, New York, 1977

♦Rainer Thumshirn, Heimstetten, Germany

THE GERMAN FLAG

1813-18: During the War of Liberation against Napoleon, university students wore the black-red-gold colors as a symbol of the struggle for German unity. These colors are said to have originated in the black coats with red epaulettes and gold buttons worn by members of the irregular force which von Lutzöw raised in 1813 to fight Napoleon. Because the force was recruited largely from democratically-minded German university students, the colors became a symbol of freedom.

1817: The tricolors were flown by students from the University of Jena and other universities at the rally at the Wartburg Castle in Erfurt.

1832: The flag was again displayed at the castle of Hambach when some 30,000 Germans demonstrated for the cause of unity, justice, and freedom. Many German princes took this action as a sign of subversion and banned the flag.

1848: The colors became the symbol of the German Confederation.

1852: After the failure of the revolution in this year, the tri-colors were outlawed, in the interest of "law and order."

1867: North German Confederation originated, adopting the first German national flag, a horizontal tricolor of black at the top, white in the center, and red at the bottom. The red and white represented the old Hanseatic League,

The German Research Companion

GERMAN CITIES WITH POPULATIONS OVER 100,000 IN 1905

Locality	State	Population
Berlin	Preußen	2,040,148
Hamburg	Hamburg	802,793
München	Bayern	538,393
Dresden	Sachsen	516,996
Leipzig	Sachsen	502,570
Breslau	Preußen	470,751
Köln	Preußen	428,503
Frankfurt/Main	Preußen	334,951
Nürnberg	Bayern	294,344
Düsseldorf	Preußen	253,099
Hannover	Preußen	250,032
Stuttgart	Württemberg	249,443
Chemnitz	Sachsen	244,405
Magdeburg	Preußen	240,661
Charlottenburg	Preußen	239,512
Essen	Preußen	231,396
Stettin	Preußen	224,078
Königsberg	Preußen	219,862
Bremen	Bremen	214,953
Duisberg	Preußen	192,227
Dortmund	Preußen	175,575
Halle	Preußen	169,899
Altona	Preußen	168,301
Straßburg	Elsaß-Lothringen	167,342
Kiel	Preußen	163,710
Elberfeld	Preußen	162,682
Mannheim	Baden	162,607
Danzig	Preußen	159,685
Barmen	Preußen	156,148
Rixdorf	Preußen	153,650
Gelsenkirchen	Preußen	147,037
Aix-la-Chapelle	Preußen	143,906
Schöneberg	Preußen	140,992
Braunschweig	Braunschweig	136,423
Posen	Preußen	137,067
Kassel	Preußen	120,446
Bochum	Preußen	118,455
Karlsruhe	Baden	111,200
Krefeld	Preußen	110,347
Plauen	Sachsen	105,182
Wiesbaden	Preußen	100,953

Source: *Encyclopedia Britannica*, University Press, New York, 1910, 11th ed.

and the black and white came from Prussia.

1871: Following Bismarck's leadership in the unification of Germany, he chose a flag of black-white-red, the colors of Prussia and other northern German states combined.

1918: With the creation of the Weimar Republic, the tricolor of black-red-gold (the "Weimar Colors – Schwarz-Rot-Gold") became the national flag of Germany. Reactionary forces were vehemently opposed to the flag they identified with liberalism and democracy. (One of their cries was, "Down with the black-red-mustard Republic.")

1933: With the Nazis' rise to power, the black-red-gold tricolor was replaced with the pre-World War I black-red-white, which was in turn replaced with the swastika *(Hakenkreuz)* on September 15, 1935.

1933-35: Display of the black-red-gold became a criminal offense. In 1933, it was decreed that two national flags were to be hoisted together: the black, white, and red (black at the top and red at the bottom), and the *Hakenkreuz* flag. The *Hakenkreuz* flag was red, charged with a white circle bearing the emblem of the Nazi Party, a "swastika" in black.

1949: Since this date, the constitutionally adopted "schwarz-rot-gold" has served as the national colors of the Federal Republic of Germany.

Sources: "Banner of Unity, Flag of Hope," by Gerhard Weiss. *German Life*, August/ September 1995; and *Flags of the World*, by E.M.C. Barraclough, Frederick Warne & Co., New York, 1971

NATIONAL ANTHEM

The national anthem of the Federal Republic of Germany is the third stanza of the *Lied der Deutschen.*

The lyrics of *Lied der Deutschen* were written in 1841 by August Heinrich

Hoffmann von Fallersleben (1798-1874), as an appeal for unity to his country, at the time split into some 30 states, loosely united in the *Deutscher Bund* (German Federation) since 1815. It represented what seemed to be a naive hope that the German lands could be unified into one.

Hoffmann wrote his appeal for unity while in Heligoland, an island in the North Sea which had belonged to Denmark, Schleswig-Holstein and Great Britain. It was on this remote island that the anthem was played officially for the first time in 1890, when Great Britain left Heligoland.

The melody, composed by Joseph Haydn (1732-1809), is that of the old Austrian *Kaiserhymn* (Imperial Anthem), first played in 1797.

In 1922, the first President of the Weimar Republic, Friedrich Ebert, introduced the *Deutschlandlied* as the official national anthem. It had been an unofficial national anthem in the second half of the 19th century.

After 1933, Hitler allowed only the aggressive first verse *("Deutschland, Deutschlan d über alles")* to be sung officially.

The anthem was banned after World War II until 1952, when Theodor Heuss, President of the Federal Republic of Germany *(Bundesrepublik Deutschland)*, proclaimed the third stanza of the *Deutsch-landlied* as the official anthem of the Federal Republic of Germany:

Einigkeit und Recht und Freiheit
Für das deutsche Vaterland
Danach laßt uns alle streben,
Brüderlich mit Herz und Hand,
Einigkeit und Recht und Freiheit
Sind des Glückes Unterpfand
Blüh' im Glanze dieses Glückes,
Blühe, deutsches Vaterland

Unity, justice, and freedom
For the German Fatherland,
This is what we all must strive for,

Brotherly with heart and hand.
Unity, justice, and freedom
Are the foundation of happiness.
Bloom in the radiance of this
happiness,
Bloom, oh German Fatherland.
        (Translation by Eberhard
        Reichmann)
Sources: *Deutschland,* June/July 1999;
German Information Center; Eberhard
Reichmann, *Indiana German Heritage
Society Newsletter,* Fall 1997

THE NAZI PARTY

The term "Nazi" is the abbreviation
for the National Socialist German Workers Party (*Nationalsozialistische
Deutsche Arbeiterpartei,* or NSDAP),
which came onto the political scene after World War I as just one of many nationalist splinter groups.

Under the leadership of Adolf Hitler,
a frustrated artist gradually gained the
support of right-wing industrialists and
military leaders, and eventually rose in
prominence.

In 1923, Hitler attempted an uprising
against the Weimar Republic in Munich,
but failed. He was imprisoned for 13
months, during which time he wrote
Mein Kampf (My Struggle), a book that
explicitly laid out the Nazi Party doctrine.
The book is overwhelmingly anti-
Semitic; it propagates Aryan racial su-
periority and leadership, to be achieved
by eliminating Jews from Germany, and
eventually from the entire world. National strength and destiny were to be
achieved through strict discipline in following an authoritarian leader (*Führer*).

In addition, the NSDAP advocated
anti-parliamentarianism, and anti-Marx-
ism. The Nazis blamed Germany's defeat in World War I on the Jews and Com-
munists, and they rejected the Treaty
of Versailles. Their appeal was highly
emotional.

Under Hitler's leadership, the Nazi
Party was organized on a semi-military
basis, with a uniformed militia known as
the S.A. (*Sturmabteilung,* or Storm
Troops.) They held mass rallies and
made use of elaborate pageantry.

Although "workers" was included in
its name, the Nazi movement had little
worker support. Most of its members
came from the lower middle class.
Source: German Information Center

THE SWASTIKA (HAKENKREUZ)

The swastika was understood to represent a sun wheel. In 1933, a decree was
issued in Germany that the national flags
were to be the black, white and red tricolor (from top: black, white, red) and
the *Hakenkreuz.* The two flags were to
be hoisted together.

The *Hakenkreuz* (literally, "hooked
cross") flag had a red background, a
white disk in the middle, on which was
superimposed the swastika, the emblem
of the Nazi Party. On September 15, 1935
it became the national flag.

After World War II, the occupying
powers ordered that no flags or emblems
of the Nazi regime were to be flown.
Sources:
◆*Flags of the World,* ed. E.M.C. Barraclough.
Frederick Warne & Co., New York, 1971
◆ Wilfried Fest, *Dictionary of German
History 1806-1945.* St. Martin's Press, New
York, 1978

NOVEMBER 9: FOUR MARKERS IN A CENTURY

1918 (9 November): Abdication of Kaiser Wilhelm II, ending the Second German Empire
1923 (9 November): Arrest of Adolf Hitler
following his Beer Hall Putsch
1938 (9 November): Date of the *Reichs-
kristallnacht* ("The Night of Broken

Glass"), portent of the Final Solution (see "Crystal Night," on the next page).

1989 (9 November): The opening of the Berlin Wall

Note: Reunification of Germany is celebrated not on November 9, the day the wall was opened in 1989, but on October 3, the day in 1990 when the two Germanys were formally united. The reason, as one Berliner stated: "We'd like to celebrate the good November 9's, but we are always concerned that those who want to remember the bad ones will be celebrating too."

Source: "Nov. 9, a Day of Horror and Glory," by Amity Shlaes, *Wall Street Journal*, Novem-ber 9, 1999

THE BERLIN WALL

The Berlin Wall, a reaction by the German Democratic Republic to the constant flow of East Germans across the open border to West Germany and the western parts of Berlin, appeared suddenly on August 13, 1961, as a barbed-wire barrier, and was supplemented over time.

The effect was to create two Berlins – East Berlin, the capital of the German Democratic Republic, and West Berlin, a virtual island 110 miles inside East Germany.

Residents of West Berlin had West German citizenship.

The government in Berlin sent non-voting representatives to the Bundestag in Bonn.

On November 9, 1989, the East German regime announced that East Germans were free to travel without restrictions.

By November 11, the no-man's-land at Potsdamer Platz was opened. Ten years later, in many places, no trace remained, although a few short stretches were designated for preservation, the longest being what is known as the East

Side Gallery because of the colorful murals painted on it in the early 1990s.

Since 1961, when the wall went up, 191 people had been shot to death trying to escape the East German "death strip."

Sources: *Federal Republic of Germany: Questions and Answers*, Susan Steiner, ed., German Information Center, NY, 1996; and *Wall Street Journal*, September 21, 1999

'CRYSTAL NIGHT,' 1938

On November 9-10, 1938, Nazi officials led attacks on Jews, synagogues and businesses owned by Jews throughout Germany in a pogrom now known as "Crystal Night" (*Reichs-kristallnacht*).

Nearly 100 people were killed, 267 synagogues were set ablaze, and some 30,000 Jews were arrested for deportation to concentration camps.

Source: *The Week in Germany*, German Information Center, New York, November 15, 1996.

THE BRANDENBURG GATE: A CHRONOLOGY

1788: Frederick Wilhelm II ordered the city gate at the end of the avenue Unter den Linden to be replaced. (The design, by Carl Gothard Langhan, was based on the Propylaeum in Athens. It was the first bulding in the classical style in Gemany.) This city gate was also a triumphal arch at the end of the avenue which leads to the royal palace.

1791: The Gate was officially opened.

1793: Johann Gottfried Schadow's huge statue of Victory in a chariot was placed on the roof.

1806 (27 October): Napoleon was welcomed by crowds along Unter den Linden as he made his triumphal entry through the Gate. Napoleon, after stating his admiration for the Gate, dragged the chariot off to Paris. But as time went on, public opinion turned against the French, the chariot became a national symbol, and the empty Brandenburg Gate became a reminder of a shameful defeat.

1814 (7 August): Friedrich Wilhelm III and Field Marshal Blücher led the triumphal march through the Gate as the chariot was returned to Prussia on six enormous wagons surrounded by enthusiastic crowds. The square in front of the Brandenburg Gate was renamed Pariser Platz in memory of the defeat of France.

1864, 1866: In both these years, victorious Prussian troops marched through the Brandenburg Gate, which was no longer a memorial to the victory in the wars of liberation, but rather had become a symbol of Prussian military strength.

1871 (16 June): A parade of 42,000 soldiers marched through the Gate, led by the 87-year-old General von Wrangel, who had crushed the Berlin revolution of 1848, followed by Bismarck, Moltke, and Roon, and then by the Kaiser. By this time, the Brandenburg Gate had become the triumphal arch of the new Reich.

1919: President Ebert welcomed the defeated army at the Brandenburg Gate, now a sad reminder of past glories.

1933 (30 January): The SA (*Sturmabteilung*, or storm troops) led a torchlight procession through the Gate to celebrate Hitler's appointment as chancellor.

1939: A huge parade was held at the Gate for Hitler's fiftieth birthday.

1940: Victory over France was celebrated with great pomp and ceremony

1945: The victorious Allies paraded through the badly damaged Brandenburg Gate. By then, the Gate, now in the Soviet sector, was seen by some as a symbol of imperialist aggression. It was restored and proclaimed to be the "gate of peace" in the East.

In the West, it was seen as a symbol of a divided nation.

1989 (9 November): The Brandenburg Gate was opened and has since signified national unity.

Source: *The Cambridge Illustrated History of Germany,* by Martin Kitchen, Cambridge University Press, 1996

REUNIFICATION OF GERMANY

On October 3, 1990, less than one year after the opening of the Berlin Wall, the German Democratic Republic acceded to the Federal Republic and adopted its laws. The accession took place in three steps:

1. On May 18,1990, the Federal Republic of Germany and the German Democratic Republic signed a treaty establishing monetary, economic and social union between the two states.

This took effect on July 1, when the West German D-Mark was introduced into East Germany together with West Germany's laws, rules, and regulations governing such matters as commerce, taxation, and social security .

2. On August 31, 1990, a second treaty was signed under which the five East German states – Mecklenburg-Vorpommern, Brandenburg, Saxony-Anhalt, Thuringia, and Saxony – acceded to the Federal Republic of Germany under Article 23 of the Basic Law.

This, the formal unification treaty, took effect on October 3, 1990.

3. On September 12, 1990, the Federal Republic of Germany, the German Democratic Republic, France, the Soviet Union, Britain and the United States concluded a "Treaty of the Final Settlement with Respect to Germany."

With this treaty, the four Powers agreed to the establishment of a "united Germany" consisting of the territories of the Federal Republic of Germany, the German Democratic Republic and all of

Berlin. In doing so, they also agreed to relinquish their rights and responsibilities relating to Berlin and Germany as a whole.

They also permitted united Germany to be a member of alliances. The Soviet Union thus agreed to united Germany's continuing membership in NATO. The Soviet Union agreed to withdraw its forces from the territory of the GDR by the end of 1994.

Source: German Information Center, *Federal Republic of Germany: Questions and Answers,* ed. Susan Steiner. New York, 1996.

CAPITALS OF GERMANY

Berlin was the capital of Germany between 1871 and 1945. Prior to that there was no German capital because Germany did not exist as a single state.

During the years when two German states existed (1949-1990), Bonn was the seat of government google.cof West Germany and Berlin (East) was the capital of East Germany. A law dated February 2, 1957 designated Berlin as the capital of the Federal Republic of Germany.

When East Germany merged with West Germany, Berlin became united Germany's capital.

Source: German Information Center, *Federal Republic of Germany: Questions and Answers,* ed. Susan Steiner. New York, 1996

POLITICAL STRUCTURE, MODERN GERMANY

Modern Germany has a six-level political hierarchy:
1. *Bundesrepublik Deutschland* (Federal Republic of Germany)
2. *Land* (State)
3. *Bezirk* or *Regierungsbezirk** (District)
4. *Kreis*** (a county-like entity – literally,

a "circle")
5. *Gemeinde* (Official Community)
6. *Habitation*
*Not applicable to the city states or Saarland **Not applicable to city states
Source: William J. Toeppe, "Dewey and His System (Part 3A), *German Genealogical Society Newsletter* , Vol. IV, No. 6, July 1995

PLACE-NAME PREFIXES

The following place-name prefixes are shown with their meanings (in parentheses) and examples of their use:
Alt (old): .... Alt Meiershof
Am (at the): .... Am Sonnenberg
Bad (bath, spa): .... Bad Kissingen
Groß (large): .... Groß Buckow, Großgartach
Hinter (back): .... Hinter Bollhagen, Hinterweiler
Hohe (high): .... Hohe Mühle, Hohenkirchen
Im (in the): .... Im Holze
Klein (small): .... Klein Eschefeld
Neu (new): .... Neu Grambow, Neuhardenberg, Neuendorf
Nieder (lower): .... Niederzimmern
Ober (upper): .... Oberbachheim
St. (*Sankt*) .... St. Martin (meaning saint)
Schloß (castle, palace): .... Schloß Neuhaus
Unter (lower): .... Untergrombach
Vorder (front): .... Vor Wangern

POPULATION OF GERMAN EMPIRE STATES, 1871

Kingdoms

Prussia	24,691,433
Bavaria	4,863,450
Saxony	2,556,244
Württemberg	1,818,539

Grand Duchies

Baden	1,461,562
Hesse	852,894
Mecklenburg-Strelitz	96,982
Oldenburg	314,459

Duchies

Brunswick	311,764
Saxe-Meiningen	187,957
Saxe-Altenburg	142,122
Saxe-Coburg-Gotha	174,339
Anhalt	203,437

Principalities

Schwarzburg-Sondershausen	76,523
Schwarzburg-Rudolstadt	67,191
Waldeck	56,224
Reuss-Greiz	45,094
Schaumburg-Lippe	32,059
Lippe	111,135

Free Hanseatic Cities

Lübeck	52,158
Bremen	122,402
Hamburg	338,974

Imperial Province

Alsace-Lorraine	1,549,738

German Empire	41,058,792

Source: *Encyclopedia Britannica*: *Dictionary of Arts, Sciences, Literature, and General Information,* 11th edition, University Press, New York, 1910.

FOUNDING DATES OF GERMAN STATES (Bundesländer)

Baden-Württemberg	1952
Bayern	1946
Berlin	1946
Brandenburg	1990
Freie Hansestadt Bremen	1947
Freie Hansestadt Hamburg	1949
Hessen	1945
Mecklenburg-Vorpommern	1990
Niedersachsen	1946
Nordrhein-Westfalen	1946
Rheinland-Pfalz	1946
Saarland	1957
Sachsen	1990
Sachsen-Anhalt	1990
Schleswig-Holstein	1946

Thüringen	1990

COMMON ELEMENTS IN GERMAN PLACE NAMES

Au	low area
Bach	brook
Bad	spa, resort
Berg	mountain
Bostel	living place
Brücke	bridge
Brunnen (Brunn, Bronn)	spring, well
Burg	fortress
Büttel	building
Dorf	village
Ecke	corner
Eiche	oak
Feld	field
Fels	rock
Frieden	peace
Furt	ford
Gau	district
Groß	large
Hafen (Haven)	harbor, port
Hain (Hagen)	grove
Haus	house
heilig	holy
Heiligen	saints
Heim	home
Hof	courtyard, farm
Hohen	high
Kirche	church
klein	small
lang	long
Lar	open pastureland
Leben	ancient settlement
Loh	forest
Mar	border, swamp
mittel	middle
Münster	monastery, cathedral
Mühle	mill
nieder	lower
neu	new
Nord	north
ober	upper
Ost	east
roden (and variations – often "t" instead of "d")	to clear land

THE GERMAN STATES (LÄNDER)

Map courtesy of the German Information Center, Washington DC

See .... lake
Siedlung .... settlement
Stadt .... city
Stein .... stone
Süd .... south
Tal, Thal .... valley
über .... over, above
unter .... lower
Wald .... forest
Weiler .... hamlet
West .... west
Wiese .... meadow
Zelle (Celle) .... monk's chamber,
                          prayer chamber

PLACE-NAME ENDINGS TYPICAL IN VARIOUS GERMAN AREAS

-a: Posen, Sachsen, Schlesien
-ach: Baden, Bayern, Elsaß-Lothringen
-ath: Rheinland
-au: Hessen-Nassau, Ostpreußen, Westpreußen, Posen, Sachsen (prov.), Sachsen, Schlesien
-bach: Baden, Bayern, Elsaß-Lothringen, Hessen-Nassau, Hessen, Rheinland, Württemberg
-beck: Hannover, Westfalen
-bek: Schleswig-Holstein
-berg: Baden, Bayern,Pfalz, Brandenburg, Braunschweig,Elsaß-Lothringen, Hannover, Hessen-Nassau, Hessen, Mecklenburg, Oldenburg, Ostpreußen, Westpreußen, Pommern, Rheinland, Sachsen (prov.), Sachsen, Schlesien, Westfalen, Württemberg
-brok: Oldenburg
-bruck: Hannover
-brucken: Pfalz
-bull: Schleswig-Holstein
-burg: Baden, Bayern, Pfalz, Brandenburg, Braunschweig, Elsaß-Lothringen, Hannover, Hessen-Nassau, Hessen, Mecklenburg, Oldenburg, Ostpreußen, Westpreußen, Pommern, Rheinland, Sachsen (prov.), Sachsen, Schlesien, Westfalen, Württemberg

-by: Schleswig-Holstein
-chen: Elsaß-Lothringen
-dorf: Brandenburg, Braunschweig, Elsaß-Lothringen, Hannover, Hessen-Nassau, Mecklenburg, Oldenburg, Ostpreußen, Rheinland, Sachsen (prov.), Schlesien, Schleswig-Holstein
-e: Sachsen (prov.)
-en: Ostpreußen, Rheinland, Sachsen (province), Sachsen, Schlesien, Westfalen, Württemberg
-erk: Rheinland
-feld: Sachsen, Württemberg
-felde: Braunschweig, Westpreußen
-gard: Pommern
-gen: Baden, Elsaß-Lothringen, Westfalen, Württemberg
-hagen: Baden, Mecklenburg, Pommern
-hain: Hessen-Nassau
-hausen: Bayern, Brandenburg, Braunschweig, Hannover, Hessen-Nassau, Sachsen (prov.), Westfalen
-haven: Hannover
-helm: Bayern, Pfalz, Elsaß-Lothringen, Hessen, Württemberg
-hofen: Elsaß-Lothringen
-horn: Oldenburg
-ich: Rheinland
-ig: Sachsen
-in: Brandenburg, Mecklenburg, Pommern, Posen
-ing: Bayern, Schleswig-Holstein
-ingen: Braunschweig
-itz: Mecklenburg, Westpreußen, Pommern, Posen, Sachsen (prov.), Sachsen, Schlesien
-kehmen: Ostpreußen
-ken: Ostpreußen
-kirchen: Hessen-Nassau, Oldenburg, Rheinland
-lau: Brandenburg
-lin: Brandenburg
-litz: Brandenburg
-low: Brandenburg
-lund: Schleswig-Holstein
-mar: Hessen-Nassau
-mark: Brandenburg
-nau: Baden
-nitz: Brandenburg

-**now:** Brandenburg
-**o:** Posen
-**ow:** Mecklenburg, Pommern
-**pitz:** Brandenburg
-**reuth:** Bayern
-**rode:** Branschweig, Hannover
-**rum:** Braunschweig
-**rup:** Schleswig-Holstein
-**scheid:** Rheinland
-**schin:** Posen
-**see:** Westpreußen, Pommern
-**stadt:** Bayern, Pfalz, Hessen, Sachsen (prov.), Württemberg
-**stede:** Oldenburg
-**stedt:** Braunschweig, Hannover, Sachsen (prov.), Schleswig-Holstein
-**stein:** Bayern, Hessen-Nassau, Hessen, Westfalen
-**stett:** Baden
-**sum:** Hannover
-**thal:** Brandenburg
-**walde:** Brandenburg, Westpreußen
-**weiler:** Elsaß-Lothringen
-**witz:** Brandenburg, Schlesien
-**wo:** Posen
-**zig:** Brandenburg, Westpreußen, Posen
Source: Larry O. Jensen, *A Genealogical Handbook of German Research.* Rev. ed. Pleasant Grove, Utah, 1995

THE 16 STATES (LÄNDER): POPULATION, CAPITALS AND OTHER CITIES

Note: Other cities named below are those with populations of more than 100,000.
* **Baden-Württemberg** (10.3 million). Capital: Stuttgart. Other cities, Freiburg, Heidelberg, Heilbronn, Karlsruhe, Mannheim, Pforzheim, Ulm
* **Bayern** (12 million). Capital München. Other cities, Augsburg, Erlangen, Fürth, Ingolstadt, Nürnberg, Regensburg, Würzburg
* **Berlin** (3.46 million). Capital: Berlin.
* **Brandenburg** (2.6 million). Capital Potsdam. Other city, Cottbus

* **Bremen** (0.68 million). Capital: Bremen
* **Hamburg** (1.7 million). Capital: Hamburg
* **Hessen** (6.0 million). Capital: Wiesbaden. Other cities, Darmstadt, Frankfurt a. M., Kassel, Offenbach
* **Mecklenburg-Vorpommern** (1.8 million). Capital: Schwerin. Other city, Rostock
* **Niedersachsen** (7.8 million). Capital: Hannover. Other cities, Braunschweig, Göttingen, Hildesheim, Salzgitter, Wolfsburg
* **Nordrhein-Westfalen** (18 million). Capital Düsseldorf. Other cities, Aachen, Bielefeld, Bonn, Dortmund, Duisberg, Essen, Hamm, Köln, Leverkusen, Münster, Paderborn, Recklinghausen, Siegen
* **Rheinland-Pfalz** (4 million). Capital: Mainz. Other cities, Koblenz, Ludwigshaven
* **Saarland** (1.1 million). Capital: Saarbrücken.
* **Sachsen** (4.5 million). Capital: Dresden. Other cities, Chemnitz, Leipzig, Zwickau
* **Sachsen-Anhalt** (2.7 million). Capital: Magdeburg. Other cities, Dessau, Halle
* **Schleswig-Holstein** (2.7 million). Capital: Kiel. Other city, Lübeck
* **Thüringen** (2.5 million). Capital: Erfurt. Other cities, Gera, Jena

AREA IN SQUARE MILES OF STATES OF THE GERMAN EMPIRE (1900 STATISTICS)

Kingdoms

Preußen	134,463
Bayern	29,282
Württemberg	7,528
Sachsen	55,787

Imperial Province

Elsaß-Lothringen	5,668

Grand Duchies

Baden	5,821
Hessen	2,965
Mecklenburg-Schwerin	5,135

Mecklenburg-Strelitz 1,131
Oldenburg 2;,479
Sachsen-Weimar 1,388
Duchies
Braunschweig 1,424
Sachsen-Meiningen 953
Sachsen-Coburg-Gotha 755
Sachsen-Altenburg 511
Anhalt 998
Principalities
Waldeck 433
Lippe 469
Schwarzburg-Rudolstadt 363
Schwarzburg-Sondershausen 333
Schaumburg-Lippe 131
Reuß-Greitz 122
Reuß-Schleitz-Gera 31
Free Hanseatic Cities
Bremen 99
Hamburg 158
Lübeck 115
Total: 208,830
Source: Max Kade Institute, Madison,
Wisconsin

GERMAN COLONIES

The age of European colonialism began around 1500, when Spanish, Portu-
guese, French, Dutch and English sailors discovered new overseas territories
and took them over for their countries.

Settlement and economic exploitation
of these lands were a major factor in the
rise of the respective home countries to
major powers.

Germany, inward-looking, divided into
a multitude of small states, and lacking a
sizable fleet, could not try to join this
dividing-up of the world except for two
short-lived ventures: one into Venezuela 1528-1555 by the merchants Ehingen
and Welser, and another by Prussia into
Africa's Gold Coast 1683-1718.

Although tens of thousands of German emigrants helped to settle and develop many of the new colonies, they
usually severed ties to their former

homelands which did not gain any ad-
vantages from their former subjects'
colonization efforts.

This changed only in the 1880s, when
German explorers and merchants urged
the newly established *Deutsches Reich*
to acquire colonies of its own, before
none would be left. Chancellor Bismarck
realized that the remaining available areas for colonization were of little economic value and acquired some of them
for the *Deutsches Reich* without enthu-
siasm. They were officially called *Schutz-
gebiete* (protectorates), and Bismarck is
said to have avoided the term colony.

These areas were,
◆Togo, Kamerun [Cameroon], Deutsch-
Ostafrika [Tanzania] and Deutsch-
Südwestafrika [Namibia] in Africa
◆Kiautschau and Tsingtau in China
◆The South Sea Islands of Palau, the
Marianas, Caroline Islands, Solomon
Islands, and parts of New Guinea. (The
Melanesian Islands off the northeast
coast of New Guinea are still called
Bismarck Archipelago today.)

The acquisitions were short-lived
however, as they were lost after World
War I when they were taken over by
other countries or put under the jurisdiction of the League of Nations.
Source: Rainer Thumshirn, Heimstetten,
Germany

GEOGRAPHIC NAMES, GERMAN-TO-ENGLISH

Adria .... Adriatic (Sea)
Ägäis .... Aegean (Sea)
Ägypten .... Egypt
Albanien .... Albania
Alpen .... Alps
Alpenvorland .... foothills of the Alps
Amerika .... America
Ardennen .... the Ardennes
Atlantik .... the Atlantic (Ocean)
Australien .... Australia
Balkanhalbinsel .... Balkan Peninsula

Balkanstaaten .... Balkan States,
                                  the Balkans
Baltikum .... the Baltic (States),
                                  the Baltics
Basel .... Basle
Bayerischen Alpen .... Bavarian Alps
Bayerische Wald .... Bavarian Forest
Bayern .... Bavaria
Belgien .... Belgium
Benelux Länder .... Benelux Countries
Beringmeer .... Bering Sea
Beringstraße .... Bering Strait
Berner Alpen .... Bernese Alps
Bessarabien .... Bessarabia
Bodensee .... Lake Constance
Böhmen .... Bohemia
Böhmen und Mähren .... Bohemia-
                                  Moravia
Böhmerwald .... Bohemian Forest
Bosnien .... Bosnia
Brandenburger Tor . Brandenburg Gate
Brasilien .... Brazil
Breslau .... Wroclaw/Breslau
Bretagne .... Brittany
Brügge .... Bruges
Brüssel .... Brussels
Bundesrepublik .... Federal Republic
Deutschland   of Germany
Chiemsee .... Lake Chiem/Chiemsee
Dänemark .... Denmark
Danzig .... Gdansk/Danzig
Danziger Bucht Bay of Gdansk/Danzig
Den Haag .... The Hague
Deutsche Demokratische .... German
Republik   Democratic Republic
Deutschland .... Germany
Dnjepr .... Dnieper
Dnjestr .... Dniester
Donau .... Danube
Eismeer, ... See *Nordpolarmeer*
Nördliches Eismeer,
Südliches .... See *Südpolarmeer*
Elsaß .... Alsace
Elsaß-Lothringen .... Alsace-Lorraine
Erzgebirge .... Erzgebirge, Ore
                                  Mountains
Estland .... Estonia
Europa .... Europe
Finnischer Meerbusen . Gulf of Finland

Finnland .... Finland
Franken .... Franconia
Frankfurt .... Frankfurt (on the Main
am Main   [River]
Frankfurt an der Oder Frankfurt (on the
                                  Oder [River])
Frankreich .... France
Friesische Inseln .... Frisian Islands
Galicien .... Galicia
Genf .... Geneva
Genfer See .... Lake Geneva
Gent .... Ghent
Germanien .... Germania
Glarner Alpen .... Glarus Alps
Griechenland .... Greece
Grönland .... Greenland
Großbritannien ..... Great Britain, Britain
Helvetien .... Helvetia,
                                  Switzerland
Hannover .... Hanover
Hessen .... Hesse
Innerasien .... Central Asia
Ionisches Meer .... Ionian Sea
Irische See .... Irish Sea
Island .... Iceland
Italien .... Italy
Jugoslawien .... Yugoslavia
Kanada .... Canada
Karibik .... Caribbean
Karpaten .... Carpathians,
                                  Carpathian
                                  Mountains
Kaspisches Meer .... Caspian Sea
Kaukasus .... Caucasus
Kiew .... Kiev
Kleinasien .... Asia Minor
Köln .... Cologne
Königsberg .... Kaliningrad,
                                  Königsberg
Konstanz .... Constance
Kroatien .... Croatia
Lateinamerika .... Latin America
Lettland .... Latvia
Litauen .... Lithuania
Lothringen .... Lorraine
Lüneburger Heide ...... Lüneburg Heath
Mähren .... Moravia
Mark Brandenburg .... Brandenburg
                                  Marches

Mecklenburg- .... Mecklenburg-
Vorpommern   Western Pomerania
Mittelamerika .... Central America
Mittelasien .... Central Asia
Mitteldeutschland ..... Central Germany
Mitteleuropa .... Central Europe
Mittelmeer .... Mediterranean (Sea)
Mittlerer Osten .... Middle East
Moldau .... Moldavia
Mosel .... Moselle
Moskau .... Moscow
Mülhausen .... Mulhouse
München .... Munich
Naher Osten .... Near East
Neufundland .... Newfoundland
Neuseeland .... New Zealand
Niederbayern .... Lower Bavaria
Niederlande .... Netherlands, Holland
Niederösterreich .... Lower Austria
Niederrhein .... Lower Rhine
Niedersachsen .... Lower Saxony
Niederschlesien .... Lower Silesia
Nordamerika .... North America
Norddeutsche Tiefebene .... North(ern)
                              German Plain
Norddeutschland . North(ern) Germany
Nordeuropa .... North(ern) Europe
Nordfriesischen Inseln .. North Frisians
Nord-Ostsee-Kanal .... Kiel Canal
Nordpol .... North Pole
Nordpolarmeer .... Arctic Ocean
Nordrhein-Westfalen   North Rhine-
                              Westphalia
Nordsee .... North Sea
Norwegen .... Norway
Nürnberg .... Nuremberg
Oberbayern .... Upper Bavaria
Oberfranken .... Upper Franconia
Oberitalien .... Northern Italy
Oberösterreich .... Upper Austria
Oberpfalz .... Upper Palatinate
Oberrhein .... Upper Rhine
Oberrheinische Tiefebene Upper Rhine
                              Valley
Oberschlesien .... Upper Silesia
Ostasien .... East Asia
Ostdeutschland .... Eastern Germany;
                     German Democratic
               Republic, East Germany

Österreich .... Austria
Österreich-Ungarn .... Austria-Hungary
Osteuropa .... Eastern Europe
Ostfriesische Inseln .... East Frisians
Ostpreußen .... East Prussia
Ostsee .... Baltic (Sea)
Pazifik .... Pacific (Ocean)
Peloponnes .... Peloponnese,
                              Peloponnesus
Persischer Golf .... Persian Gulf
Pfalz .... Palatinate
Polarkreis .... Arctic Circle
Polen .... Poland
Posen .... Poznán
Prag .... Prague
Preßburg .... Bratislava, Pressburg
Preußen .... Prussia
Pyrenäen .... Pyrenees
Rhein .... Rhine
Rheinhessen .... Rhinehessen
Rheinland .... Rhineland
Rheinland-Pfalz ... Rhineland-Palatinate
Rom .... Rome
Rotes Meer .... Red Sea
Rumänien .... Romania
Rußland .... Russia
Saargebiet .... Saar(land)
Sachsen .... Saxony
Sachsen-Anhalt .... Saxony-Anhalt
Sächsische Schweiz .... Saxon
                              Switzerland
Schlesien .... Silesia
Schottland .... Scotland
Schwaben .... Swabia
Schwäbische Alb .... Swabian Jura
Schwarzes Meer .... Black Sea
Schwarzwald .... Black Forest
Schweden .... Sweden
Schweiz .... Switzerland
Schweizer Mittelland .. Swiss Midlands
Serbien .... Serbia
Siebenbürgen .... Transylvania
Skandinavien .... Scandinavia
Slowakei .... Slovakia
Slowenien .... Slovenia
Sowjetunion .... Soviet Union
Spanien .... Spain
Stettin .... Szczecin, Stettin
Straßburg .... Strasbourg

Südamerika .... South America
Süddeutschland ... South(ern) Germany
Sudetenland .... Sudetenland,
                                       the Sudeten
Südeuropa .... South(ern) Europe
Südpolarmeer .... Antarctic Ocean
Südsee .... South Pacific,
                                       South Seas
Südtirol .... South Tyrol
Suezkanal .... Suez Canal
Teutoburger Wald ... Teutoburg Forest
Themse .... Thames
Thüringen .... Thuringia
Thüringer Wald .... Thuringian Forest
Tirol .... Tyrol
Totes Meer .... Dead Sea
Trient .... Trento
Tschechoslowakei .... Czechoslovakia
Türkei .... Turkey
Ungarn .... Hungary
Union der Sozia- .... Union of Soviet
listischen Sowjet-   Socialist
republiken   Republics
Unterfranken .... Lower Franconia
Ural .... Urals
Venedig .... Venice
Vereinigtes Königreich von Großbritan-
nien und Nordirland .... Kingdom (of
     Great Britain and Northern Ireland)
Vereinigte Staaten .... United States
(von Amerika)   (of America)
Vierwaldstätter See .... Lake Lucerne
Vogesen .... Vosges (Mountains)
Vorderasien .... Middle (or Near) East
Vorpommern .... Western Pomerania
Weichsel .... Vistula
Weißrußland .... B(y)elorussia,
                                       White Russia
Westdeutschland ... Western Germany,
                          Federal Republic
                             of Germany
Westeuropa .... West(ern) Europe
Westfalen .... Westphalia
Westfriesische Inseln ..... West Frisians
Westpreußen .... West Prussia
Wien .... Vienna
Wolga .... Volga
Zürich .... Zurich

Major source: *Langenscheidts Großes
Schulwörterbuch Deutsch-Englisch,*
Langenscheidt, Berlin, 1996

PLACE NAMES,
GEOGRAPHIC AREAS

✦**Allgäu:** Region in southern Germany
along the Austrian border from Lake
Constance (*Bodensee*) to Füssen in
Bavaria, Germany.
✦**Alsace:** Region of eastern France along
the southwestern border of Germany.
Called *Elsaß* in German
✦**(Das) Alte Land:** Marshy region of
northwestern Germany between the
North Sea and Hamburg.
✦**Altmark:** Region around Magdeburg,
Saxony-Anhalt, in the eastern part of
Germany.
✦**Banat:** Area around the Tisza River in
Romania.
✦**Batschka:** Part of Croatia and Hungary.
✦**Bergisches Land:** Region of Germany
east of the Rhine River in the Ruhr district
northeast of Cologne (*Köln*).
✦**Bessarabia:** Region of northeastern
Romania along the southwestern border
of the Ukraine.
✦**Black Forest:** See *Schwarzwald.*
✦**Bohemia:** Western portion of the
Czech Republic bounded by Germany
(to the west and north), Poland (to the
east), and Austria (to the south). Called
Böhmen in German.
✦**Brandenburg:** Region west and east
of the Oder River in the western part of
Poland along the German state of
Brandenburg.
✦**Breisgau:** (1) Region of northern
Baden-Württemberg, Germany, south of
Heidelberg and lying between the Rhine
River and the Neckar River; (2) region
between the Rhine River and and the
Black Forest.
✦**Bukovina:** Region of northern Romania
along the borders of the Ukraine and
Moldava.

◆**Burgenland:** Region of southeastern Austria bordering and extending into western Hungary.

◆**Byelorussia:** Region in Eastern Europe between Lithuania, Poland, Russia and the Ukraine. Also known as White Ruthenia.

◆**Carinthia:** Region of southern Austria along the northern borders of Italy and Slovenia.

◆**Carniola:** Region of Slovenia just south of Croatia.

◆**Courland:** Region of western Latvia along the Baltic coast. Known in German as Kourland.

◆**Dobrogea:** See *Dobrudscha.*

◆**Dobrudscha:** Portion of eastern Romania between the Black Sea and the Danube River.

◆**Egerland:** Part of northwest Bohemia, along the Eger River.

◆**Eifel:** Mountainous southwestern part of Northrhine-Westphalia and northwestern part of Rhineland-Palatinate, between the northern Bonn-Aachen line and the southern Trier-Koblenz line.

◆**Elsaß:** See **Alsace.**

◆**Emsland:** Region of northern Germany, south of the North Sea, west of Bremen, and along the eastern border of the Netherlands.

◆**Ermland:** Region of Poland southeast of Danzig.

◆**Erzgebirge:** Mountainous region along southeastern Saxony, Germany, and northwestern Bohemia, Czech Republic.

◆**Franconia:** Region of northern Bavaria, Germany. Divided into Unterfranken (the northernmost part), Mittelfranken or Mainfranken (the middle part), and Oberfranken (the southern part). Called *Franken* in German.

◆**Franken:** See *Franconia.*

◆**Galicia:** Region around the upper part of the Dniester River. The western part of Galicia is in Poland and the eastern part in the Ukraine.

◆**Gorizia:** Western portion of Slovenia along the Adriatic Sea north of Trieste, Italy.

◆**Gottschee:** Ethnic German area of northern Slovenia between Italy (on the west), Austria (on the north), Hungary (on the northeast), and Croatia (on the south).

◆**Great Poland:** The heartland of Poland.

◆**Grenzmark:** Region of eastern Pomerania, just north of Posen and now part of Poland.

◆**Gross Polen:** See *Great Poland.*

◆**Haardt:** Region of Rhineland-Pfalz, Germany, between the Rhine River at Worms, Germany, and extending west into Alsace, France.

◆**Halich Ruthenia:** Prairie-like region along the Dniester River, Ukraine. Also known as Little Russia and better known as Galicia. Ukrainians lived in eastern Galicia and Poles in the western part known as Little Poland.

◆**Harz:** Mountainous region of north-central Germany east of the Weserbergland.

◆**Harzgebirge:** Mountainous region of the southern part of Niedersachsen and the southeastern part of Sachsen-Anhalt. Thüringen occupies a small strip northwest of the "südliches Harzvorland."

◆**Hauerland:** Region of south central Slovakia along the northern border of Hungary.

◆**Hegau:** Region of southwestern Germany between Lake Constance (Bodensee), the Black Forest, and the Danube and Rhine rivers.

◆**Hunsrück:** Mountainous region of the Rhineland-Palatinate state, Germany, west of the Rhine River, and north of the Saarland.

◆**Ingermanland:** Region of Russia, east of Estonia and Latvia, west of St. Petersburg, Russia.

◆**Ingria:** See *Ingermanland.*

◆**Karinthia:** Region of Austria south of Salzburg. Known in German as *Kärnten.*

◆**Kärnten:** See *Karinthia.*

◆**Kashubia:** Region of Poland south and west of Danzig.

◆**Kourland:** See *Courland.*

◆**Kraichgau:** Region east of the Rhine River between the Black Forest and the Odenwald in northern Baden-Württemberg, Germany.

◆**Krain:** See *Carniola.*

◆**Kujawien:** Region of Poland along the Vistula River around Thorn. Also known as *Kuyavia.*

◆ **Kulmerland:** Region of northern Poland, named after the town Kulm on the Weichsel (Vistula) River in the northeastern part of the former West Prussia, bordering the formerly southwestern part of East Prussia.

◆**Kurpie:** Region in Russia around the Narew River, northeast of Warsaw.

◆**Lauenburg:** 1) Lauenburg (Lebork) in Pomerania, Poland; and 2) Lauenburg, county and town on the Elbe, east and northeast of Hamburg, north of the Elbe River (Elbe region at the town of Lauenburg).

◆**Lausitz:** Region of eastern Germany between Meissen and Berlin and the Elbe and Bobr rivers.

◆ **Lithuania:** An independent nation along the eastern Baltic coast between Poland, Russia and Latvia.

◆**Little Poland:** Region along the upper Vistula River near Crakow, Poland. (See *Halich Ruthenia.*)

◆ **Little Russia:** See *Halich Ruthenia.*

◆**Livland:** Region of eastern Latvia and southern Estonia.

◆**Livonia:** Region along the Baltic coast, now known as Latvia.

◆ **Lorraine:** Region of eastern France northwest of Alsace, south of Luxembourg, and west of Germany. Known in German as *Lothringen.*

◆**Lothringen:** See *Lorraine.*

◆**Lusatia:** See *Lausitz.*

◆**Mähren:** See *Moravia*

◆**Markgräflerland:** Region southwest of the Black Forest in Germany and south of the Breisgau, east of the Rhine River.

◆ **Masuria:** Region of northeastern Poland near Lithuania.

◆ **Mazovia:** Region of central Poland between the Warthe and Vistula rivers.

◆**Memel:** Coastal region of Lithuania along the Baltic Sea.

◆**Mittelmark:** Region of Brandenburg, Germany, west of the Oder River.

◆**Moldavia:** Region lying between the Ukraine and Romania, now the independent state of Moldava.

◆**Moravia:** Region of the Czech Republic between Poland (to the north and east), the Slovak Republic (to the east and south), and Austria (to the south). Known in German as *Mähren.*

◆**Münsterland:** Region of Germany east of the Rhine River, north of the Ruhr district, and bordering the Netherlands.

◆ **Neumark:** Region east of the Oder River in Brandenburg and now part of Poland.

◆**Oberland:** See Oberschwaben.

◆**Oberland:** Lake region south of Königsberg, Poland, along the Polish/Russian border.

◆**Oberpfalz:** Region of eastern Bavaria, Germany, along the Czech border.

◆ **Oberschlesien (Upper Silesia):** A former Prussian province, the southern part of Silesia with the chief city being Kattowitz. Area now belongs to Poland.

◆ **Oberschwaben:** Region of southern Germany between the Danube River, the Black Forest, Lake Constance, and the Allgäu.

◆**Ostpreussen (East Prussia):** A former Prussian province, composed of districts (and cities) of Königsberg, Bumbinnen, Allenstein, and (until 1939) the province of West Prussia, but after 1922, without the Memel region. Now the territory is divided, with Poland having the southern part and Russia the northern part.

◆**Palatinate:** See *Pfalz.*

◆ **Pfalz:** (1) Region west of the Rhine River, today the southern part of the state of Rhineland-Palatinate, Germany. For most of the 19th century, it was part of

Bavaria, Germany; (2) Region in eastern Bavaria, Germany, known as the *Oberpfalz* (Upper Palatinate).

♦ **Podhale:** Region of southern Poland just north of the Carpathian Mountains.

♦ **Podlachia:** Region around Bretst-Litovsk, divided between eastern Poland and eastern Belarus. Known in German as *Podlachien.*

♦ **Podlachien:** See *Podlachia.*

♦ **Podlasie:** Region around the Bug and Narew rivers, with the western part in central Poland the eastern part in Byelorussia.

♦ **Podolia:** Region between the Dniester and Boh Rivers, with the western part in central Poland and the eastern part in Byelorussia.

♦ **Polesie:** Swampy region around the Pripet Marshes in southern Byelorussia.

♦ **Pomerania:** See *Pommern.*

♦ **Pomerelia:** See *Pommerellen.*

♦ **Pommerellen:** Region in Poland south of Danzig.

♦ **Pommern:** Region in northwestern Poland along the Baltic Sea. Often called Pomerania.

♦ **Posen:** Region of northwestern-central Poland, just south of Pomerania.

♦ **Red Ruthenia:** See *Ruthenia.*

♦ **Rheingau:** Region of Hessen east of the Rhine River to the western slopes of the Taunus Mountains between Weisbaden and Bingen

♦ **Rheinpfalz:** See *Pfalz.*

♦ **Ruthenia:** Region of the Ukraine, also known as Red Ruthenia.

♦ **Salzkammergut:** Region of Austria east of Salzburg.

♦ **Samgallen:** Region in Latvia along the borders of Lithuania and Belarus.

♦ **Samland:** Area of East Prussia, north of Ermland and south of Memel, around Königsburg.

♦ **Samogita:** Region of northwestern Lithuania.

♦ **Sauerland:** Region of Germany east of the Rhine River, between the Ruhr and Sieg Rivers. Not to be confused with Hauerland.

♦ **Schlesien:** See *Silesia.*

♦ **Schleswig:** Southern part of the combined state of Schleswig-Holstein, between the North Sea and the Baltic Sea.

♦ **Schwaben (Swabia):** Region stretching from the Black Forest in the west to the Lech River in the east, and from the middle Neckar River in the north to Lake Constance in the south. Covers parts of Baden-Württemberg and Bavaria.

♦ **Schwalm:** Region on both sides of the upper reaches of the Schwalm River, south of Kassel in northern Hessen.

♦ **Schwarzwald:** Mountainous region of southwestern Germany, east of the Rhine River. Better known in America as the Black Forest.

♦ **Semegalia:** A region of Latvia

♦ **Siebenburgen:** See *Transylvania.*

♦ **Silesia:** Southern border region of Poland, along the border of the Czech Republic. Known in German as *Schlesien.*

♦ **Slovakia:** An independent nation, the Slovak Republic, east of the Czech Republic, south of Poland, west of the Ukraine, and north of Hungary.

♦ **Slovonia:** Eastern region of Croatia, south of Hungary, west of Vojvodina, and north of Bosnia.

♦ **Srem:** See *Syrmien.*

♦ **Steiermark:** See *Styria.*

♦ **Styria:** Region of southeastern Austria along the northern border of Slovenia. Known in German as the *Steiermark.*

♦ **Sudetenland:** Region of northern, western, and southern Czech Republic, bordered by Germany, Austria and Poland.

♦ **Syrmien:** Region south of the Danube River northwest of Belgrade. Known in German as *Srem.*

♦ **Taunus:** Hilly region of Germany in southeastern Hessen, north of the Main River.

♦ **Taurida:** See *Taurien.*

♦ **Taurien:** Region of the Crimea, Ukraine, along the Black Sea.

◆**Terek:** Region of Russia along the Terek River near the Caspian Sea.
◆**Thüringen (Thuringia):** State in the east central part of Germany composed of the former imperial German states of Sachsen-Altenburg, Sachsen-Coburg-Gotha, Sachsen-Meiningen, Sachsen-Weimar-Eisenach, and the former principalities of Schwarzburg-Rudolstadt, Schwarzburg-Sonderhausen, Reuss (elder line) and Reuss (younger line).
◆**Tirol:** Region of western Austria south of Germany and north of Italy.
◆**Transnistria:** See *Transnistrien.*
◆**Transnistrien:** German name for the region of southwestern Ukraine between the Bug and Dniester Rivers.
◆ **Transylvania:** Region of central Romania. Known in German as Siebenburgen.
◆**Uckermark:** Region of northeastern Brandenburg, Germany, and eastern Mecklenburg, Vorpommern, Poland.
◆**Unterfranken:** See Franconia.
◆ **Vogtland:** Region of southwestern Saxony, Germany.
◆ **Volhynia:** Region of northwestern Ukraine, south of Belarus and east of Poland.
◆ **Voralberg:** Westernmost part of Austria, south of Germany, and north of Italy and Switzerland.
◆**Vorpommern ("Near Pomerania"):** Former Prussian province lying west of the Oder River around Rostock and Neubrand-enburg in Mecklenburg-Vorpommern.
◆ **Walachia:** Region of southern Romania.
◆**Warmia:** See *Samland.*
◆**Warthegau:** Region along the Warthe River, between Posen and Warsaw in west-central Poland.
◆**Wasgau:** Region of Germany, west of the Rhine River, along the eastern French border between the Vosges Mountains and the Haardt area of Germany.
◆ **Weizacker:** Region of southwestern

Pomerania along the Brandenburg, Germany, border, now partly in Poland, and mostly in Germany.
◆**Weserbergland:** Mountainous region of northern Germany along the Weser River, west of the Harz Mountains and east of the Teutoberger Forest.
◆**Westerwald:** Region of Germany east of the Rhine River and covering parts of Hessen and Rhineland-Palatinate.
◆**Westpreussen (West Prussia):** Former Prussian province between the Baltic Sea, Pomerania, Brandenburg, Posen, Russian and East Prussia. Now part of Poland.
◆**Westrich:** Region of Germany east of the Rhine River and covering parts of Hessen and Rhineland-Palatinate.
◆ **Wetterau:** Region of Germany in Hessen, north of the Main River above Frankfurt/Main.
◆**White Ruthenia:** See *Byelorussia.*

HISTORICAL REGIONS OF GERMANY

Historical name	Present state/ country location
Allgäu	Bayern, Baden-Württemberg
Altes Land	Niedersachsen
Altmark	Sachsen-Anhalt
Ammerland	Niedersachsen
Angeln	Schleswig-Holstein
Anhalt	Sachsen-Anhalt
Baar	Baden-Württemberg
Baden	Baden-Württemberg
Baiern	Bavaria
Bergisches Land	Nordrhein-Westfalen
Böhmen	Czech Republic
Börde	Sachsen-Anhalt
Brandenburg	Brandenburg
Breisgau	Baden-Württemberg
Chiemgau	Bayern
Dithmarschen	Schleswig-Holstein
Donau-Moos	Bayern
Donau-Ried	Bayern
Egerland	Czech Republic

Eichsfeld	Thüringen	Rodgau	Hessen
Eiderstedt	Thüringen	Ruppertigau	Bayern
Emsland	Niedersachsen	Saarland	Saarland
Gäuboden	Bayern	Schlesien	Poland
Goldene Aue	Sachsen	Schleswig	Schleswig-Holstein
Grabfeld	Bayern	Schönbuch	Baden-Württemberg
Grenzmark	Poland	Schwaben	Bayern
Hadeln	Niedersachsen	Stormarn	Schleswig-Holstein,

Eichsfeld .... Thüringen
Eiderstedt .... Thüringen
Emsland .... Niedersachsen
Gäuboden .... Bayern
Goldene Aue .... Sachsen
Grabfeld .... Bayern
Grenzmark .... Poland
Hadeln .... Niedersachsen
Havelland .... Brandenburg
Hessen .... Hessen
Hohenloher Land Baden-Württemberg
Holledau (Hallertau) .... Bayern
Holstein .... Schleswig-Holstein
Isarwinkel .... Bayern
Jeverland .... Niedersachsen
Kehdingen .... Nidersachsen
Kraichgau .... Baden-Württemberg
Kulmerland .... Poland
Lüneburger Heide .... Niedersachsen
Margräfler Land .. Baden-Württemberg
Masuren .... Poland
Mecklenburg .... Mechlenburg-
Vorpommern
Memelland .... Lithuania
Mittelfranken .... Bayern
Mittelmark .... Lithuania
Münsterland ...... Nordrhein-Westfalen
Natangen .... Russia
Neumark .... Poland
Nieder-Lausitz .... Brandenburg
Nordfriesland .... Schleswig-Holstein
Oberes Gäu .... Baden-Württemberg
Oberbayern .... Bayern
Oberfranken .... Bayern
Ober-Lausitz .... Sachsen, Poland
Oberpfalz .... Bayern
Oberschlesien .... Poland
Ostfriesland .... Niedersachsen
Ostpreußem .... Poland, Russia
Pfalz .... Rheinland-Pfalz
Pomesanien .... Poland
Pommern .... Mecklenburg-
Vorpommern, Poland
Posen .... Poland
Prignitz ...... Mecklenburg-Vorpommern
Rangau .... Bayern
Rheinhessen .... Rheinland-Pfalz
Ried .... Hessen
Ries .... Bayern

Rodgau .... Hessen
Ruppertigau .... Bayern
Saarland .... Saarland
Schlesien .... Poland
Schleswig .... Schleswig-Holstein
Schönbuch .... Baden-Württemberg
Schwaben .... Bayern
Stormarn .... Schleswig-Holstein,
Hamburg
Stroh-Gäu .... Baden-Württemberg
Sudetenland .... Czech Republic
Thüringen .... Thüringen
Tucheler Heide .... Poland
Uckermark .... Brandenburg
Unterfranken .... Bayern
Vogtland .... Thüringen
Vorpommern Mecklenburg-Vorpommern
Wagrien .... Schleswig-Holstein
Werdenfelser Land .... Bayern
Westfalen .... Nordrhein-Westfalen
Westpreußen .... Poland
Wetterau .... Hessen
Württemberg ...... Baden-Württemberg

Source: Rainer Thumshirn, Heimstetten, Germany

GERMANY'S TOPOGRAPHY

With an area of 356,959 square kilometers, Germany extends 853 kilometers from its northern border with Denmark to the Alps in the south. It is the sixth largest country in Europe. At its widest, Germany measures approximately 650 kilometers from the Belgian-German border in the west to the Polish frontier in the east.

With its irregular, elongated shape, Germany provides an excellent example of a recurring sequence of land forms found the world over. A plain dotted with lakes, moors, marshes and heaths retreats from the sea and reaches inland, where it becomes a landscape of hills crisscrossed by streams, rivers, and valleys. These hills lead upward, gradually forming high plateaus and woodlands and eventually climaxing in spectacular

RIVERS OF EUROPE

Name of river	Length (km)	Mouth
Volga *(Wolga)*	3,531	Caspian Sea *(Kaspisches Meer)*
Danube *(Donau)*	2,850	Black Sea *(Schwarzes Meer)*
Dnieper *(Dnjepr)*	2,200	Black Sea *(Schwarzes Meer)*
Don	1,870	Sea of Azov (Asowsches Meer)
Rhine *(Rhein)*	1,320	North Sea *(Nordsee)*
Elbe	1,165	North Sea *(Nordsee)*
Vistula *(Weichsel)*	1,047	Baltic Sea *(Ostsee)*
Loire	1,020	Atlantic Ocean *(Atlantischer Ozean)*
Tagus *(Tajo, Tejo)*	1,007	Atlantic Ocean *(Atlantischer Ozean)*
Meuse *(Maas)*	925	North Sea *(Nordsee)*
Ebro	910	Mediterranean *(Mittelmeer)*
Oder	854	Baltic Sea *(Ostsee)*
Rhone *(Rhône)*	812	Mediterranean *(Mittelmeer)*
Seine	776	English Channel *(Ärmelkanal)*
Weser (with *Werra*)	732	North Sea *(Nordsee)*
Po	652	Adriatic Sea *(Adriatisches Meer)*
Garonne	650	Bay of Biscay *(Golf von Biskaya)*
Tiber	405	Tyrrhenian Sea *(Tyrrhenisches Meer)*
Thames *(Themse)*	346	North Sea *(Nordsee)*

Source: *Brockhaus Enzyklopädie*, Sechster Band. F.A. Brockhaus, Mannheim, 1988.

mountain ranges.

As of the mid-1990s, about 37 percent of the country's area was arable; 17 percent consisted of meadows and pastures; 30 percent was forests and woodlands; and 16 percent was devoted to other uses. Geographers often divide Germany into the following four distinct topographic regions:

North German Lowland

The North German Lowland is a part of the Great European Plain that sweeps across Europe from the Pyrenees in France to the Ural Mountains in Russia. All of the *Länder* of Schleswig-Holstein, Hamburg, Bremen, Mecklenburg-Western Pomerania, Brandenburg, Berlin, most of Lower Saxony and Saxony-Anhalt, and parts of Saxony and Northrhine-Westphalia are located in this region.

Hills in the lowland only rarely reach 200 meters in height, and most of the region is well under 100 meters above sea level. The lowlands slope almost imperceptibly toward the sea.

The North Sea portion of the coastline is devoid of cliffs and has wide expanses of sand, marsh, and mud flats *(Watten)*. The mud flats between the Elbe estuary and the Netherlands border are believed to have been above sea level during Roman history and to have been inundated when the shoreline sank during the 13th century.

In the western area, the former line of inshore sand dunes became the East Frisian Islands. The mud flats between the islands and the shore are exposed at very low tides and are crossed by innumerable channels varying in size from those cut by small creeks to those serving as the estuaries of the Elbe and Weser rivers. The mud and sand are constantly shifting, and all harbor and shipping channels require continuing maintenance.

The offshore islands have maximum

elevations of fewer than 35 meters and have been subject to eroding forces that have washed away whole sections during severe storms. Shorelines most subject to eroding tides were stabilized during the late 19th and early 20th centuries.

Although the East Frisian Islands are strung along the coast in a nearly straight line, the North Frisian Islands are irregularly shaped and are haphazardly positioned. They were also once a part of the mainland, and a large portion of the mud flats between the islands and the coast is exposed during low tides.

The Baltic Sea coast of Schleswig-Holstein differs markedly from its North Sea coast. It is indented by a number of small deep fjords with steep banks, which were carved by rivers when the land was covered with glacial ice. Farther to the east, the Baltic shore is flat and sandy. Rügen, Germany's largest island, lies just offshore of Stralsund.

Wherever the region's terrain is rolling and drainage is satisfactory, the land is highly productive. This is especially true of the areas that contain a very fertile siltlike loess soil, better than most German soils. Such areas, called *Börden*, are located along the southern edge of the North German Lowland beginning west of the Rhine near the Ruhr Valley and extending eastward and into the Leipzig Basin. The Magdeburg *Börde* is the best known of these areas. Other *Börden* are located near Frankfurt am Main, northern Baden-Württemberg, and in an area to the north of Ulm and Munich. Because the areas with loess soil also have a moderate continental climate with a long growing season, they are considered Germany's breadbasket.

Central German Uplands

The Central German Uplands are Germany's portion of the Central European Uplands; they extend from the Massif Central in France to Poland and the Czech Republic. Germany's uplands are generally moderate in height and seldom reach elevations above 1,000 meters.

The region encompasses all of the Saarland, Hesse, and Thuringia; the north of Rhineland-Palatinate; substantial southern portions of Northrhine-Westphalia, Lower Saxony, and Saxony-Anhalt; and western parts of Saxony.

In the west, the Central German Uplands begin with the Rheinish Uplands, a massive rectangular block of slate and shale with a gently rolling plateau of about 400 meters in elevation and peaks of about 800 to 900 meters.

The Rheinish Uplands are divided by two deep and dramatic river valleys – the Mosel and the Rhine. The high hilly area to the south of the Mosel is the Hunsrück; the one to its north is the Eifel.

The Rhine separates these areas from their extensions to the east, the Taunus, and, to the north, the Westerwald. To the north and east of the Westerwald are further distinct areas of the Rheinish Uplands, most notably the small range of hills known as the Siebengebirge, across the Rhine from Bonn, and the larger hilly regions – the Siegerland, Bergisches Land, Sauerland, and the Rothaargebirge. The higher elevations of the Rheinish Uplands are heavily forested; lower-lying areas are well suited for the growing of grain, fruit, and early potatoes.

Because of the low elevations of its valleys (200 to 350 meters), the Uplands of Hesse provide an easily traveled passageway through the Central German Uplands. Although not as dramatic as the Rhine Valley, for hundreds of years this passageway – the so-called Hessian Corridor – has been an important route between the south and the north, with Frankfurt am Main at one end and Hanover at the other, and Kassel on the Weser River in its center.

The headwaters of the Weser have created a number of narrow but fertile valleys. The highlands of the Uplands of Hesse are volcanic in origin. The most notable of these volcanic highlands are the Rhön (950 meters) and the Vogelsburg (774 meters).

To the north of the Uplands of Hesse lie two low ranges, the Teutoburger Wald and the Wiehengebirge, which are the northernmost fringes of the Central German Uplands. It is at the Porta Westfalica near Minden that the Weser River breaks through the latter range to reach the North German Lowland.

One of the highest points in the Central German Uplands is at Brocken (1,142 meters) in the Harz Mountains. This range is situated about 40 kilometers to the northeast of Göttingen and forms the northwestern boundary of the Leipzig Basin, an extension of the North German Lowland.

The Harz are still largely forested at lower levels; barren moors cover higher elevations. An important center for tourism in the 1990s, the range was once an important source for many minerals.

The Thüringer Wald, located in southwest Thuringia, is a narrow range about 100 kilometers long, with its highest point just under 1,000 meters. Running in a northwesterly direction, it links the Central German Uplands with the Bohemian Massif of the Czech Republic and forms the southwestern boundary of the Leipzig Basin.

The basin's southeastern boundary is formed by the Erzgebirge range, which extends to the northeast at a right angle to the Thüringer Wald. Part of the Bohemian Massif, the Erzgebirge range reaches 1,214 meters at its highest point.

The southeasternmost portion of the Central German Uplands consists of the Bohemian Forest and the much smaller Bavarian Forest. Both ranges belong to the Bohemian Massif. The Bohemian Forest, with heights up to 1,450 meters, forms a natural boundary between Germany and the Czech Republic.

Southern Germany

Between the Central German Uplands and the Alpine Foreland and the Alps lies the geographical region of Southern Germany, which includes most of Baden-Württemberg, much of northern Bavaria, and portions of Hesse and Rhineland-Palatinate.

The Main River runs through the northern portion of this region. The Upper Rhine River Valley, nearly 300 kilometers long and about 50 kilometers wide, serves as its western boundary.

The Rhine's wide river valley here is in sharp contrast to its high narrow valley in the Rheinish Uplands. The southern boundaries of the region of Southern Germany are formed by extensions of the Jura Mountains of France and Switzerland. These ranges are separate from those of the Central German Uplands. One of these Jura ranges forms the Black Forest, whose highest peak is the Feldberg at 1,493 meters, and, continuing north, the less elevated Odenwald and Spessart hills.

Another Jura range forms the Swabian Alb and its continuation, the Franconian Alb. Up to 1,000 meters in height and approximately 40 kilometers wide, the two albs form a long arc – 400 kilometers long – from the southern end of the Black Forests to near Bayreuth and the hills of the Frankenwald region, which is part of the Central German Uplands.

The Hardt Mountains in Rhineland-Palatinate, located to the west of the Rhine, are also an offshoot of the Jura Mountains.

The landscape of the Southern Germany region is often that of scarp and vale, with the eroded sandstone and limestone scarps facing to the northwest. The lowland terraces of the Rhine, Main, and Neckar river valleys, with their dry and warm climate, are suitable for agriculture and are highly productive. The loess and loam soils of the Rhine-Main Plain are cultivated extensively, and orchards and vineyards flourish. The

Rhine-Main Plain is densely populated, and Frankfurt am Main, at its center, serves both as Germany's financial capital and as a major European transportation hub.

Alpine Foreland and the Alps

The Alpine Foreland makes up most of Bavaria and a good part of Baden-Württemberg. The foreland is roughly triangular in shape, about 400 kilometers long from west to east with a maximum width of about 150 kilometers north to south, and is bounded by Lake Constance and the Alps to the south, the Swabian and Franconian albs to the north, and the Bavarian Forest to the east. Elevation within the foreland rises gently from about 400 meters near the Danube, which flows along its north, to about 750 meters at the beginning of the Alpine foothills.

With the exception of Munich and the small cities of Augsburg, Ingolstadt, and Ulm, the foreland is primarily rural. Soils are generally poor, with the exception of some areas with loess soil, and much of the region is pasture or is sown to hardy crops.

Germany's portion of the Alps accounts for a very small part of the country's area and consists only of a narrow fringe of mountains that runs along the country's border with Switzerland and Austria from Lake Constance in the west to Salzburg, Austria, in the east. The western section of the German Alps are the Algäuer Alps, located between Lake Constance and the Lech River.

The Bavarian Alps, the central section, lie between the Lech and Inn rivers and contain Germany's highest peak, the Zugspitze (2,963 meters). The Salzburg Alps, which begin at the Inn River and encircle Berchtesgaden, make up the easternmost section of Germany's Alps.

Source: Germany: A Country Study, Eric Solsten, ed. Federal Research Division, Library of Congress, 1996

GERMANY'S SCENIC ROUTES (Ferienstraße)

♦ *Grüne Küstenstraße*, "Green Coastal Route" (coastal marsh and meadowlands): Pinneberg, North Sea coast, Tønder in Denmark

♦ *Störtebekerstraße*, "Störtebecker Route" (famous pirate, a kind of Robin Hood of the seas): Leer, East Frisian coast, Cuxhaven, Stade

♦ *Alte Salzstraße,* "Old Salt Route" (salt transport): Lüneburg, Nature Park of Lauenburg Lakes, Lübeck

♦ *Deutsche Märchenstraße*, "German Fairy Tale Route" (locations mentioned in fairy tales by the Grimm brothers): Hanau, Kassel, Weser valley, Bremen

♦ *Hamalandroute*, "Hamaland Route" (region of Hamaland): Western Münsterland, Raesfeld, Wulfen

♦ *Osning-Route*, "Osnig Route" (Osnig Mountain, part of the Teutoburg Forest): Bad Laer, Osnabrück, Teutoburg Forest, Detmold

♦ *Ahr-Rotweinstraße/Grüne Straße Eifel-Ardennen/Deutsche Wildstraße*, "Red Wine Route" along River Ahr/ Green Route from Eifel Mountains to Ardennes/German Game Route: Sinzig, Ahr Valley, Daun, the Eifel, meeting point of Germany, Belgium, and Luxemburg

♦ *Mosel-Wein-Straße*, "Mosel Wine Route": French border, Trier, Mosel valley, Koblenz

♦ *Kannebäcker-/Bäderstraße*, "Pottery Route/Spa Route": Montabauer, the Taunus mountans, Wiesbaden

♦ *Rheingau-Riesling-Route/Rhein-goldstraße*, "Rhineland Route/Rhine-gold Route" (Nibelungen saga): Wiesbaden, the Rheingau, castles of the Middle Rhine, Koblenz

♦ *Deutsche Edelsteinstraße*, "German Gem Route" (gem cutting and polishing industries): Idar-Oberstein, Idar Forest

♦ *Deutsche Weinstraße*, "German Wine Route": Bockenheim, Rheinhessen and

Pfalz wine areas, Schweigen
* *Nibelungenstraße/Siegfriedstraße*, "Nibelungen Route/Siegfried Route": Worms, the Odenwald, Miltenberg
* *Burgenstraße*, "Route of Castles," Mannheim, the Odenwald, Rothenburg o.d.T., Nürnberg
* *Bergstraße*, "Mountain Route" (western slopes of the Odenwald mountains, Rhine): Darmstadt, Heidelberg, Karlsruhe
* *Straße der Staufer*, "Staufer Route" (Staufen dynasty of German kings and emperors, c. 1050-1268, Friedrich I, Barbarossa): Lorch, Schwäbisch Gmünd, Göppingen
* *Schwäbische Albstraße*, "Swabian Mountain Route": Aalen, Tuttlingen
* *Schwarzwaldbäderstraße*, "Black Forest Spas Route": Northern Black Forest, Pforzheim, Hirsau, Nagold, and Freudenstadt, Wildbad, Bad Herrenalb
* *Schwarzwaldhochstraße*, "Black Forest Mountains Ridge Route": Black Forest, Baden-Baden, the Mummelsee, Kniebis, Gutachtal, Titisee, Waldshut-Tiengen
* *Oberschwäbische Barockstraße*, "Upper Swabian Baroque Route": Ochsenhausen, Birnau, Steinhausen, Zwiefalten
* *Badische Weinstraße*, "Wine Route of Baden,": Baden-Baden, wine area of the upper Rhine valley, Freiburg, Kaiserstuhl
* *Romantische Straße*, "Romantic Route": Würzburg, Dinkelsbühl, Nördlingen, Augsburg, Füssen, Neuschwanstein
* *Straße der Residenzen*, "Route of Palaces": Aschaffenburg, Coburg, Bamberg, Nürnberg, Regensburg, Landshut, Salzburg
* *Fichtelgebirgsstraße/Bayerische Ostmarkstraße*, "Fichtelgebirge Route/ Bavaria's Eastern Region Route": Bad Berneck, Luisenburg, Oberpfälzer Forest, National Park of the Bavarian Forest, Passau
* *Deutsche Alpenstraße*, "German Alpine Route,": Allgäu Alps, Wetter-

stein and Karwendelgebirges, Watzmann Mountain at Königsee
* *Artlandroute*, "Artland Route" (region of Artland): Dinklage, Ankum, Berge
* *Bier- und Burgenstraße*, "Beer and Castles Route": Kulmbach, Kronach, Lauenstein
* *Bramgauroute*, "Region of Bramgau": Neuenkirch, Hagenbeck, Neuenkirchen
* *Deutsche Ferienstraße Alpen*, "German Vacation Route from the Alps to the Baltic Sea": Puttgarden, Celle, Michelstadt, Kehlheim, Traunstein, Berchtesgaden
* *Deutsche-französische Touristikroute*, "German-French Tourist Route": Schweigen, Neustadt/Weinstraße, Bitche, Schweigen
* *Deutsche Hopfenstraße*, "German Hops Route" (hops growing area): Zolling, Au, Abensberg
* *Deutsche Schuhstraße*, "German Shoes Route" (shoe manufacturing industries): Waldfischbach, Leimen, Pirmasens, Dahn
* *Deutsche Weinstraße*, "German Wine Route": Rheinhessen and Pfalz area
* *Eichenlaubstraße*, "Oak Leaf Route" (oak forests): Oberlenken, Nonnweiler, Oberkirchen
* *Elbufer-Straße*, "Banks of the River Elbe Route": Schnackenburg, Gorleben, Niedermarschacht
* *Elmhochstraße*, "Elm Mountains Ridge Route": Helmstedt, Worlenbüttel
* *Feldbergstraße*, "Feldberg Route (mountain in the Black Forest): Freiburg, Titisee, Neustadt, Feldberg
* *Ferienstraße Südeifel*, "Southern Eifel Mountains Route": Baustert, Nattenheim, Baustert
* *Frankenwaldhochstraße*, "Frankenwald Mountains Ridge Route": Steinwiesen, Nordhalben, Reichenbach, Rothenkirchen
* *Frankenwaldstraße*, "Frankenwald Mountains Route": Mitwitz, Kronach, Hof
* *Freundschaftsstraße*, "Friendship

Route" (in commemoration of Franco-German friendship): Stuttgart, Straßburg, Metz

✦ *Glasstraße*, "Glass Route," (glassmaking industries): Fichtelberg, Warmensteinach, Bayreuth

✦ *Grüne Straße/Route Verte*, "Green Route" (dense forests): Epinal, Colmar, Freiburg, Donaueschingen, Lindau or Konstanz

✦ *Harz-Heide-Straße*, "Harz Mountains - Heathlands Route": Lüneburg, Braunschweig, Göttingen

✦ *Harz-Hochstraße*, "Harz Mountains Ridge Route": Seesen, Braunlage

✦ *Hochrhönring*, "Upper Rhön Mountains Circular Route": Kleinsassen, Oberhausen

✦ *Hochrhönstraße*, "Upper Rhön Mountains Route,": Bischofsheim, Leubach, Fladungen

✦ *Hochtaunusstraße*, "Upper Taunus Mountains Route": Bad Homburg, Oberursel, Camberg

✦ *Hunsrück-Höhenstraße*, "Hunsrück Mountains Ridge Route": Koblenz, Moorbach, Saarburg

✦ *Hunsrück Schieferstraße*, "Hunsrück Mountains Slate Route" (slate quarries): Kirn, Bundenbach, Simmern

✦ *Idyllische Straße*, "Idyllic Route": Welzheim, Spiegelberg, Eschach, Welzheim

✦ *Kehlsteinstraße*, "Kehlstein Mountain Route" (to Adolf Hitler's mountain retreat): Obersalzberg, Kehlstein

✦ *Kesselbergstraße*, "Kesselberg Mountain Route": Kochel am See, Kesselberg, Walchensee

✦ *Liebfrauenstraße*, "Route of Our Lady": Worms, Mainz

✦ *Loreley-Burgenstraße*, "Loreley and Castles Route": Kamp, St. Goarshausen, Kaub

✦ *Nahe-Weinstraße*, "River Nahe Wine Route": Bad Kreuznach, Sobernheim, Schweppenhausen, Bad Kreuznach

✦ *Nordstraße*, "Northern Route": Flensburg, Gundelsby, Kappeln

✦ *Obstmarschenweg*, "Marshlands-Orchards Route": Itzwörden, Stade, Neuenfelde

✦ *Ostsee-Bäderstraße*, "Baltic Sea Spas Route": Travemünde, Burg auf Fehmarn, Eckernförde, Glücksburg

✦ *Panoramastraße*, "Panoramic Route": Bischofsgrün, Ochsenkopf, Fichtelberg

✦ *Panoramastraße*, "Panoramic Route": Heppenschwant, Attlisberg, Höchenschwand

✦ *Porzellanstraße*, "China Route" (china manufacturing industries): Selb, Marktredwitz

✦ *Roßfeld-Ringstraße*, "Rossfeld Mountain Circular Route": Berchtesgaden, Roßfeld

✦ *Schauinslandstraße*, "Schauinsland Mountain Route": Freiburg, Todtnau

✦ *Schwäbische Bäderstraße*, "Swabian Spas Route": Bad Buchau, Bad Wurzach, Bad Wörishofen

✦ *Schwäbische Dichterstraße*, "Swabian Poets' Route": Bad Mergentheim, Marbach, Tübingen, Meersburg

✦ *Schwäbische Weinstraße*, "Swabian Wine Route": Gundelsheim, Heilbronn, Esslingen

✦ *Schwarzwald-Tälerstraße*, "Valleys of the Black Forest Route": Karlsruhe, Freudenstadt, Schenkenzell

✦ *Spessart-Höhenstraße*, "Spessart Mountains Ridge Route": Steinau, Wiesen, Hösbach

✦ *Spielzeugstraße*, "Toys Route": Nürnberg, Arnstadt, Coburg, Neusstadt, Rödental, Sonneberg, Waltershausen

✦ *Spitzingstraße*, "Spitzing Mountain Area Route": Schliersee, Spitzingsee

✦ *Steigerwald-Höhenstraße*, "Steigerwald Mountains Ridge Route": Ebersbach, Neustadt/Aisch, Uffenheim

✦ *Wesertalstraße*, "River Weser Valley Route": Münden, Höxter, Hameln, Minden

Partial Source: "Die schönsten Ferienstraßen in Deutschland," Grieben Reiseführer, Grieben Verlag, 1987.

Section 2: The Tools, Contacts and Resources

◆

The Family History Library and its resources
Researchers, organizations, opportunities
Finding the German immigrant's place of origin
Communicating with Germany
Useful addresses for German
family history-related communications

◆

FAMILY HISTORY LIBRARY: HOURS, TELEPHONE NUMBERS

The Family History Library in Salt Lake City is located at 35 North West Temple Street, Salt Lake City, Utah, 84150-3440.

Hours of opening
Monday: 8:00 am - 5:00 pm
Tuesday-Saturday: 8:00 am - 9:00 pm
Sunday: closed

Holidays
Closed: New Year's Day, Fourth of July, Thanksgiving Day, and Christmas Day

Shortened hours
◆ Pioneer Day (24 July, a Utah state holiday): 11:00 am - 5:00 pm
◆ Day before Thanksgiving: 8:00 am - 5:00 pm
◆ Christmas Eve: 8:00 am - 3 pm
◆ New Year's Eve: 8:00 am - 5 pm

Telephone numbers
International .... (801) 240-3433
Brief research consultation
by telephone: .... (801) 240-2584

.... or (866) 406-1830
To arrange group visits: (801) 240-4673
or fax: (801) 240-3718

FAMILY HISTORY LIBRARY: THE FLOORS

The researcher in Germanic ancestry will be interested in materials on these floors of the Family History Library (book call numbers):

European (943-949) .... Basement 1
U.S. Family History .... Main Floor
  Books (929.273)
U.S./Canada Reference .... Third Floor
  (929.27305)
U.S. Microforms .... Second Floor
U.S. Books .... Third Floor
Scandinavia (948) .... Basement 1
British Isles (941-942) .... Basement 2
Canada Books (971) .... Third Floor
Canada Family History .... Main Floor
  Books (929.271)

DEWEY DECIMAL NUMBERS
FOR MAJOR AREAS OF GERMANIC RESEARCH

	Geography	Genealogy	History
Europe, general	914	929.34	940
Germany	914.3	929.343	943
Austria	914.36	929.3436	943.6
Czech Republic	914.37	929.3437	943.7
Poland	914.38	929.3438	943.8
France	914.4	929.344	944
Russia	914.7	929.347	947
Scandanavia	914.8	929.348	948
Norway	914.81	929.3481	948.1
Sweden	914.85	929.3485	948.5
Denmark	914.89	929.3489	948.9
Other European	914.9	929.349	949
Switzerland	914.94	929.3494	949.4

DEWEY DECIMAL NUMBERS WITHIN THE 929 CATEGORY

929.0 .... Genealogy, names, insignia
.... (general)
929.1 .... Genealogy
929.2 .... Family histories
929.3 .... Genealogical sources
929.4 .... Personal names
929.5 .... Cemetery records
929.6 .... Heraldry
929.7 .... Royal houses, peerage, gentry, knighthood
929.8 Awards, orders, decorations, etc.
929.9 .... Forms of insignia and identifications

Source: Frank Fuqua, in Mission Oaks Genealogy Club *Newsletter,* Winter 1997.

DEWEY DECIMAL NUMBERS BY STATE

The beginning numbers of the Dewey Decimal Classification Scheme for the states of the United States:

Alabama	976.1
Alaska	979.8
Arizona	979.1
Arkansas	976.7
California	979.4
Colorado	978.8
Connecticut	974.6
Delaware	975.1
District of Columbia	975.3
Florida	975.9
Georgia	975.8
Hawaii	996.9
Idaho	979.6
Illinois	977.3
Indiana	977.2
Iowa	977.7
Kansas	978.1
Kentucky	976.9
Louisiana	976.3
Maine	974.1
Maryland	975.2
Massachusetts	974.4
Michigan	977.4
Minnesota	977.6
Mississippi	976.2
Missouri	977.8
Montana	978.6
Nebraska	978.2
Nevada	979.3
New Hampshire	974.2
New Jersey	974.9

New Mexico	978.9
New York	974.7
North Carolina	975.6
North Dakota	978.4
Ohio	977.1
Oklahoma	976.6
Oregon	979.5
Pennsylvania	974.8
Rhode Island	974.5
South Carolina	975.7
South Dakota	978.3
Tennessee	976.8
Texas	976.4
Utah	979.2
Vermont	974.3
Virginia	975.5
Washington	979.7
West Virginia	975.4
Wisconsin	977.5
Wyoming	978.7

FAMILY HISTORY LIBRARY TOOLS (FamilySearch)

FamilySearch is a computerized system of genealogical information, developed by the Family History Department of The Church of Jesus Christ of Latter-day Saints (LDS Church). It is available at the Family History Library in Salt Lake City, in nearly 5,000 Family History Centers worlwide and via the internet at www.familysearch.org.

Family History Library Catalog
The Family History Library Catalog, or FHLC, describes the records (books, microfilms, maps, and other materials) in the Family History Library. The FHLC provides an explanation of each of these records. The catalog is updated constantly.

FHLC GERMAN LOCALITY SECTIONS

When searching for information about a particular area of German lands

in the Family History Library Catalog (FHLC), go first to the "Locality Section" of the Catalog, and select a geographic area from those listed below to determine the pertinent locality resources which may be available.
- Baden
- Bayern
- Bayern/Pfalz
- Braunschweig
- Elsass-Lothringen
- Hamburg
- Hessen
- Lippe
- Mecklenburg-Schwerin
- Mecklenburg-Strelitz
- Niedersachsen
- Oldenburg
- Preussen/Brandenburg
- Preussen/Hannover
- Preussen/Hessen-Nassau
- Preussen/Ostpreussen
- Preussen/Pommern
- Preussen/Posen
- Preussen/Rheinland
- Preussen/Sachsen
- Preussen/Schlesien
- Preussen/Schleswig-Holstein
- Preussen/Westfalen
- Preussen/Westpreussen
- Sachsen
- Sachsen-Altenburg
- Sachsen-Coburg-Gotha
- Sachsen-Meiningen
- Sachsen-Weimar-Eisenach
- Schaumburg-Lippe
- Schwarzburg-Rudolstadt
- Schwarzburg-Sondershausen
- Sudetenland
- Thüringen
- Waldeck
- Württemberg

FHLC TOPICS FOR 'GERMANY'

Every resource entry provided in the "Germany" portion of the Family History Library Catalog has been classified within one or more of the following topics. A study of these categories of topics can lead to a better understanding of how the Germany portion of the Catalog is arranged.

Almanacs
Archives and libraries
Archives and libraries - Bibliography
Archives and libraries - Dictionaries
Archives and libraries - Directories
Archives and libraries - Handbooks, manuals, etc.
Archives and libraries - History
Archives and libraries - Indexes
Archives and libraries - Inventories, registers, catalogs
Archives and libraries - Periodicals
Bibliography
Bibliography - Periodicals
Biography
Biography - Bibliography
Biography - Indexes
Biography - Portraits
Business records and commerce
Business records and commerce - Directories
Business records and commerce - History
Business records and commerce - Periodicals
Cemeteries
Cemeteries - Maps
Census
Census - Indexes
Centennial celebrations, etc.
Chronology
Chronology - Handbooks, manuals, etc.
Church directories
Church history
Church history - Archives and libraries
Church history - Bibliography
Church history - Inventories, registers, catalogs
Church history - Maps
Church history - Periodicals
Church history - Societies
Church history - Sources
Church history - Yearbooks
Church records
Church records - Bibliography
Church records - Dictionaries
Church records - Directories

Church records - Handbooks, manuals, etc.
Church records - History
Church records - Indexes
Church records - Inventories, registers, catalogs
Church records, Sources
Civil registration
Civil registration - Handbooks, manuals, etc.
Civil registration - History
Civil registration - Indexes
Church records - Inventories, registers, catalogs
Church records - Sources
Civil registration
Civil registration - Handbooks, manuals, etc.
Civil registration - History
Civil registration - Indexes
Civil registration - Inventories, registers, catalogs
Civil registration - Sources
Colonization
Court records
Court records - Indexes
Description and travel
Description and travel - Guide-books
Directories
Dwellings
Dwellings - Bibliography
Emigration and immigration
Emigration and immigration - Bibliography
Emigration and immigration - Handbooks, manuals, etc.
Emigration and immigration - Indexes
Emigration and immigration - Inventories, registers, catalogs
Emigration and immigration - Law and legislation
Emigration and immigration - Maps
Emigration and immigration - Periodicals
Emigration and immigration - Sources
Encyclopedias and dictionaries
Ethnology
Ethnology - Bibliography
Ethnology - Periodicals
Folklore
Folklore - Dictionaries
Folklore - Periodicals
Gazetteers
Gazetteers - Bibliography
Genealogy
Genealogy - Almanacs

Genealogy - Bibliography
Genealogy - Bibliography - Periodicals
Genealogy - Collected works
Genealogy - Collected works - Indexes
Genealogy - Dictionaries
Genealogy - Directories
Genealogy - Handbooks, manuals, etc.
Genealogy - History
Genealogy - History - Collected works
Genealogy - Indexes
Genealogy - Indexes - Periodicals
Genealogy - Inventories, registers, catalogs
Genealogy - Names, Personal - Collected
  works
Genealogy - Periodicals
Genealogy - Periodicals - Bibliography
Genealogy - Periodicals - Indexes
Genealogy - Societies
Genealogy - Societies - Directories
Genealogy - Societies - Periodicals
Genealogy - Source
Genealogy - Yearbooks
Handwriting
Handwriting - Handbooks, manuals, etc.
Heraldry
Heraldry - Bibliography
Heraldry - Collected Works
Heraldry - Dictionaries
Heraldry - Directories
Heraldry - Encyclopedias and dictionaries
Heraldry - Handbooks, manuals, etc.
Heraldry - Indexes
Heraldry - Inventories, registers, catalogs
Heraldry - Periodicals
Heraldry - Periodicals - Indexes
Heraldry - Societies
Heraldry - Societies - Periodicals
Historical geography
Historical geography - Bibliography
Historical geography - Dictionaries
Historical geography - Maps
History
History - Almanacs
History - Bibliographies
History - Dictionaries
History - Encyclopedias and dictionaries
History - Handbooks, manuals, etc.
History - Indexes
History - Maps
History - Newspapers
History - Newspapers - Indexes
History - Periodicals

History - Societies
History - Societies - Directories
History - Sources
History - Sources - 843-1273
History - Sources - Inventories, registers,
  catalogs
History - Yearbooks
Jewish history
Jewish history - Bibliography
Jewish history - Sources
Jewish records
Jewish records - Indexes
Jewish records - Inventories, registers, cata-
  logs
Land and property
Land and property - History
Land and property - Periodicals
Language and languages
Language and languages - Dictionaries
Language and languages - Handbooks,
  manuals, etc.
Language and languages - History
Language and languages - Periodicals
Law and legislation
Law and legislation - History
Manors
Maps
Maps - Bibliography
Maps - Collected works
Maps - Indexes
Medical records
Migration, Internal
Military history
Military history - Bibliography
Military records
Military records - World War I, 1914-1918
Military records - Indexes
Military records - Periodicals
Military records - Sources
Minorities
Minorities - Biography
Minorities - Business records and commerce
Minorities - Directories
Minorities - Emigration and immigration
Minorities - Genealogy
Minorities - Genealogy - Sources
Minorities - History
Minorities - History - Sources
Minorities - Law and legislation
Minorities - Occupations
Minorities - Periodicals
Minorities - Periodicals - Indexes

Minorities - Population
Minorities - Religion and religious life
Minorities - Societies - Bibliography
Minorities - Statistics
Names, Geographical
Names, Geographical - Dictionaries
Names, Geographical - Periodicals
Names, Personal
Names, Personal - Dictionaries
Names, Personal - Encyclopedias and dictionaries
Names, Personal - Indexes
Names, Personal - Periodicals
Native races
Naturalization and citizenship
Newspapers
Newspapers - Bibliography
Nobility
Nobility - Bibliography
Nobility - Biography
Nobility - Collected works
Nobility - Dictionaries
Nobility - Encyclopedias and dictionaries
Nobility - Genealogy
Nobility - Genealogy - Collected works
Nobility - Genealogy - Indexes
Nobility - Genealogy - Periodicals
Nobility - Genealogy - Sources
Nobility - Heraldry
Nobility - History
Nobility - Indexes
Nobility - Periodicals
Nobility - Portraits
Nobility - Societies - Yearbooks
Nobility - Yearbooks
Obituaries
Obituaries - Indexes
Obituaries - Indexes - Periodicals
Occupations
Occupations - Dictionaries
Occupations - Indexes
Officials and employees
Officials and employees - Genealogy -
  Sources
Pensions
Periodicals
Periodicals - Bibliography
Politics and government
Politics and government - Bibliography
Population
Population - History
Postal and shipping guides

Probate records
Public records
Public records - Handbooks, manuals, etc.
Religion and religious life
Religion and religious life - Bibliography
Religion and religious life - Periodicals - Inventories, registers, catalogs
Schools
Schools - Bibliography
Schools - Directories
Schools - Heraldry
Slavery and bondage
Slavery and bondage - History
Social life and customs
Social life and customs - Periodicals
Societies
Societies - Handbooks, manuals, etc.
Societies - History
Societies - Periodicals - Indexes
Societies - Yearbooks
Taxation

Record Search Pilot

This is a collection of original documents as digitized images, principally church, civil and census records. Some of these records are not available in microform. This collection is constantly growing and can be accessed through familysearch.org, under the tab "Search Records."

FAMILY SEARCH GENEALOGICAL DATABASES

The major genealogical collections within the www.familysearch.org website are as follows:

Ancestral File

The Ancestral File provides a collection of genealogies that link individuals into families and pedigrees. People throughout the world have been invited to send their genealogies to Ancestral File, the information from which is made available for research. The information includes names, with dates and places of birth, marriage, and death. The file also contains names and addresses of the individuals who have contributed the information.

Names are organized into family groups and pedigrees.

Information from the Ancestral File should be carefully researched and used merely as a clue to further research. Many of the dates given in the file are estimates. Errors occur with some frequency due to individuals' reports of incorrect information.

No data will be added to the Ancestral File.

Pedigree Resource File (PRF)

This database, which grows by millions of names each month, is the successor to Ancestral File. Genealogists worldwide are invited to submit their personal data collections to this database. Access to the PRF is through the website www.familysearch.org. Only the index, however, can be seen. The full collection is included in 140 CDs, any of which may be purchased at www.ldscatalog.com. Researchers in the Family History Library will find the PRF as part of the library's computer network, where CDs are not used.

The IGI

The International Genealogical Index, or the IGI, is a worldwide index of several hundred million name entries of deceased persons, based on government, church, and personal records. The bulk of the names come from vital records from the early 1500s to 1875. A very large number of names from German-speaking countries are contained in the IGI.

The IGI, prepared by the Church of Jesus Christ of Latter-day Saints, is an index of surnames available on microfiche, on compact disk through Family History Centers, and through the online FamilySearch.

A search in the area called Germany may be filtered to one of these nine German states: Alsace-Lorraine (France); Baden; Bayern; "German, Misc."; Hesse-Darmstadt; Prussia; Sachsen;

Thüringen; and Württemberg. Filtering to "Germany, Misc." provides only the small states and free cities of Anhalt, Braunschweig, Bremen, Hamburg, Lippe, Lübeck, Mecklenburg, Oldenburg, Schaumburg-Lippe, and Waldeck.

The IGI is particularly useful for searching records of births or christenings and marriages.

The source for an IGI listing is either a film number, or a batch number plus a film number.

The extraction entries are the most valuable, taken from records of births, christenings, or marriages, and these can be traced directly to the source cited. There is no submitter for extraction records.

Many names in the index come from vital records from the early 1500s to 1885.

To find the source of an entry in the IGI, read the directions in the Family History Library's publicaton, *Resource Guide: Finding an IGI Source,* usually available at Family History Centers as well as at the Family History Library.

Note: It is worth checking the "Country Unknown" section of the IGI, which contains about 738,000 entries on 54 microfiche, in which the computer did not recognize the place names involved. About 26 percent of the entries are from Germany.

Social Security Death Index

The U.S. Social Security Death Index lists several million deceased people who had social security numbers and whose deaths were reported to the Social Security Administration. (See the index to locate Social Security Administration dates and other information.) Primarily, it covers deaths since 1962, but some go back to 1937. Many names are added every year.

The computer file is available on compact disc.

This index includes only those persons who had a social security number, are deceased and whose death was re-

ported to the Social Security Administration.

New Family Search

Thewebsite www.new.familysearch.
org was designed specifically as a tool
to help members of the Church of Jesus
Christ of Latter Day Saints determine
which of their ancestors have already
been identified.

Access to this data base is currently
available to most LDS members worldwide. Administrators of the program will
open the site to everyone as soon as it
is determined that the support mechanism can handle what is anticipated to be
a very large number of users. In general,
www.new. familysearch.com is a
combination of the data bases Ancestral
File, Pedigree Resource File, and
International Genealogical Index
(described above.)

ESSENTIAL FHL AIDS
FOR GERMAN RESEARCH

The following publications of the
Family History Library, Church of Jesus
Christ of Latter-day Saints, are extremely
useful in pursuing family history research. These (and many others) can be
viewed at www.familysearch.org (Research Helps).

* *Germany: Research Outline* covers
numerous research strategies and
suggested resources for conducting
German research. This excellent guide is
the biggest bargain among all research
aids available for German research.

* *Tracing Immigrant Origins: Research
Guide* provides information on search
strategies, country-of-arrival records,
and country-of-origin records

* *United States: Research Outline* re-
views the many facets of United States
research, necessary before conducting
German research.

* *German Letter-Writing Guide:
Research Outline* contains sample

letters and phrases for non-German
speakers' use in correspondence.

FAMILY HISTORY CENTERS IN
EUROPE

There are more than 100 European
Family History Centers (branches of the
Family History Library).

These centers are used by local residents, but are not designed to assist
patrons from North America.

Patrons of European centers are usually there only to use microfilms of
records from locations many miles away.

Family History Centers are located in
LDS meeting houses; some have telephones but none can receive mail. Family History Centers are located in a number of German cities, but U.S. visitors
should not expect to find them useful. Addresses of Family History Centers in Germany and other countries can be found
at: www.familysearch.org/eng/library/
fhc/frameset_fhc.asp

Addresses for Austria, Germany and
Switzerland, can be found at www.
familysearch.org. Click on "Library,"
"Family History Centers" and "Country."

ABBREVIATIONS:
GENEALOGICAL
ACCREDITATIONS,
ORGANIZATIONS, RESOURCES

AAGRA: Australasian Association of
Genealogists and Record Agents
AAHGS: African American Historical
and Genealogical Society
AG: Accredited Genealogist
AGoFF: Arbeitsgemeinschaft ost-
deutscher Familienforscher e.V. (Interest
Group of Eastern German Genealogists)
AGRA: Association of Genealogists and
Record Agents (England)
AHSGR: American Historical Society of
Germans from Russia

AIS: Accelerated Indexing Systems

AJGS: Association of Jewish Genealogical Societies

ALA: American Library Association

AP: Association of Professional Genealogists

APG: Association of Professional Genealogists

APGQ: *Association of Professional Genealogists Quarterly*

ASG: American Society of Genealogists

BCG: Board for Certification of Genealogists
The following titles relate to the BCG's areas of specialty:

–**CAILS:** Certified American Indian Lineage Specialist, as of 1999 folded into the CLS category.

–**CALS:** Certified American Lineage Specialist, as of 1999 folded into the CLS category.

–**CG:** Certified Genealogist

–**CGI:** Certified Genealogical Instructor, a secondary teaching certification of BCG.

–**CGL:** Certified Genealogical Lecturer, a secondary teaching certification of BCG.

–**CGRS:** Certified Genealogical Record Specialist

–**CLS:** Certified Lineage Specialist, a certification category of the BCG, developed in 1999. CLS is one of its three major categories (the other two are CGRS and CG).

BIFHS-US: British Isles Family History Society-USA

BLM: Bureau of Land Management

BYU: Brigham Young University

CCGS: Colorado Council of Genealogical Societies

CDA: Colonial Dames of America

CGC: Council of Genealogy Columnists

CIG: Computer Interest Group, a group within a society with a special interest in using computers in genealogy.

CPJG: Committee of Professional Jewish Genealogists

CSG: Connecticut Society of Genealogists

CWSS: Civil War Soldiers System

DAC: Daughters of American Colonists

DAGV: *Deutsche Arbeitsgemeinschaft genealogischer Verbände* (German Federation of Genealogical Societies)

DAR: Daughters of the American Revolution

DCH: Dames of the Court of Honor

DCW: Daughters of Colonial Wars

DFPA: Daughters of Founders and Patriots of America

DLP: Descendants of Loyalists and Patriots

DRT: Daughters of the Republic of Texas

EZA: *Evangelisches Zentralarchiv* (Evangelical [Protestant] Central Archives)

FASG: Fellow American Society of Genealogists

FGS: Federation of Genealogical Societies

FGSP: Fellow, Genealogical Society of Pennsylvania

FHC: Family History Center (one of many branches of the Family History Library)

FHL: Family History Library of the Church of Jesus Christ of Latter-day Saints (in Salt Lake City)

FHLC: Family History Library Catalog

FNGS: Fellow, National Genealogical Society

FSAG: Fellow of the Society of Australian Genealogists

FSG: Fellow, Society of Genealogists (England)

FUGA: Fellow, Utah Genealogical Association

GIMA: Genealogical Institute of Mid-America

GLO: General Land Office

GRHS: Germans from Russia Heritage Society (focus on Germans from western Black Sea area)

GRINZ: Genealogical Research Institute of New Zealand

GSG: Genealogical Speakers Guild

GSMD: General Society of Mayflower Descendants

GStA: *Geheimes Staatsarchiv preussischer Kulturbesitz* (Prussian State Privy Archives, in Berlin)

HETRINA: *Hessische Truppen im [in dem] amerikanischen Unabhängigskeitskrieg* (Hessian Troops in the American War of Independence)

HOFFM: The Hereditary Order of the First Families of Massachusetts

IAJGS: International Association of Jewish Genealogy Societies

IGHR: Institute of Genealogy and Historical Research (Samford University)

IGI: International Genealogical Index

IGS: Institute of Genealogical Studies, Dallas, Texas; Immigrant Genealogical Society, Burbank California; Indiana Genealogical Society

IRC: International Reply Coupon

ISBGFH: International Society for British Genealogy and Family History

JGS: Jewish Genealogical Society

LC: Library of Congress

LDS: Church of Jesus Christ of Latter-day Saints

LSG: Librarians Serving Genealogists

MGS: Minnesota Genealogical Society

MLS: Master of Library and Information Science

NARA: National Archives Records Administration

NDC: National Society of the Daughters of the American Colonists

NEHGR: *The New England Historical and Genealogical Register*

NEHGS: New England Historic Genealogical Society

NGS: National Genealogical Society

NGSQ: National Genealogical Society Quarterly

NHS: National Huguenot Society

NIGR: National Institute on Genealogical Research (National Archives)

NSCD-17: National Society of the Colonial Dames of the XVII Century

NSCDA: National Society Colonial Dames of America

NYGB: New York Genealogical and Biographical Society

NYGBR: *The New York Genealogical and Biographical Record*

OFPA: Order of Founders and Patriots of America

OGS: Ohio Genealogical Society

PAF: Personal Ancestral File (software program)

SAC: Sons of American Colonists

SAR: Sons of the American Revolution

SASE: Self-addressed stamped envelope

SC: The Society of the Cincinnati

SCV: Sons of Confederate Veterans

SDP: Sons and Daughters of the Pilgrims

SIG: Special Interest Group

SIW: Sons of the Indian Wars

SOG: Society of Genealogists

SR: General Society Sons of the Revolution

SRT: Sons of the Republic of Texas

TAG: *The American Genealogist*

TG: *The Genealogist*

TSGS: Texas State Genealogical Society

UDC: United Daughters of the Confederacy

UGA: Utah Genealogical Association

USD 1812: National Society United States Daughters of 1812

WPGS: Western Pennsylvania Genealogical Society

LOCATING CREDENTIALED RESEARCHERS

Lists of accredited or certified genealogists may be available from these organizations:

The Association of Professional Genealogists
P.O. Box 350998
Westminster, CO 80035-0998
www.apgen.org
admin@apgen.org
Tel. (303) 465-6980

The Association of Professional Genealogists supplies lists of researchers and persons supplying related services who agree to a code of professionalism.

◆**The Board for Certification of Genealogists**
P.O. Box 14291
Washington, DC 20044
www.bcgcertification.org
The Board provides tests and certified researchers in the U.S., Canada, and abroad. BCG-certified persons must abide by a code of ethics and renew their certification every five years.
International Commission for the Accreditation of Professional Genealogists (ICAPGen)
P.O. Box 970204
Orem, UT 84097-0204
www.icapgen.org
information@icapgen.org
ICAP tests candidates for the title Accredited Genealogist (AG^{SM}) in specialized areas. Members promise to abide by a code of ethics and must renew their certification every five years.

GERMAN GENEALOGY AND HERITAGE ORGANIZATIONS

◆**FEEFHS: Federation of East European Family History Societies,** P.O. Box 510898, Salt Lake City, UT 84151-0898. feefhs@feefhs.org; http://feefhs.org
◆**Genealogical Society of Pennsylvania,** 1300 Locust Street, 2nd Floor, Philadelphia, PA 19107-5699. Tel. (215) 545-0391; Fax: (215) 545-0936; ExecDir@GenPa.org; www.genpa.org
◆**German-American Heritage Center,** 712 W. Second Street, Davenport, IA 52802-1410. Tel. (563)322-8844; Director@gahc.org; www. gahc.org
◆**German American Heritage Society of Greater Washington, DC,** c/o Gary Grassl, 4207 Oxford Drive, Silver Hill, MD 20746-3030. GaryGrassl@aol.com
◆**German Genealogical Group**, P.O. Box 1004, Kings Park, NY 11754-1004. hans521@optonline.net; www. German GenealogyGroup.com; *Der Ahnen-*

forscher
◆**German Interest Group-Wisconsin,** GIG-WI, P.O. Box 2185, Janesville, WI 53547-2185. www.rootsweb. com/~wigig/index.html. *Newsletter*
◆**German Interest Group** (of the Seattle Genealogical Society, P.O. Box 15329, Seattle, WA 98115-0329. www.rootsweb. ancestry.com/~waseags
◆**German Interest Group,** 628 East Grand Avenue, Des Moines, Iowa 50309-1924. Tel. (515) 276-0287; Fax: (515) 727-1824; www. iowa genealogy. org/sigs/german.html
◆**German Research Association, Inc.,** P.O. Box 11293, San Diego, CA 92111. http://gragen.org. *The German Connection*
◆**German Society of Pennsylvania,** 611 Spring Garden Street, Philadelphia, PA 19123. Tel. (215) 627-2332; Fax: (215) 627-5297; www.german society.org. (Home of the Joseph Horner Memorial Library, with one of the largest holdings of German books in the United States)
◆**Germanic Genealogy Society,** P.O. Box 16312, St. Paul, MN 55116-0312. www.rootsweb.ancestry.com/~mnggs/ GGS.html. *Germanic Genealogy Journal*
◆**German Immigrant Genealogical Society,** P.O. Box 7369, Burbank, CA 91510-7369. Tel. (818) 848-3122.http://feefhs. org/igs/frg-igs.html Home of the Immigrant Library. *German American Genealogy; German Genealogy Journal*; *Die Pommerschen Leute*
◆**IUPUI Max Kade German-American Center, in conjunction with the Society for German American Studies.** mkgac@iupui.edu;http://www. ulib.iupui.edu/collections/kade/. *SGAS Newsletter*
◆**Mid-Atlantic Germanic Society,** P.O. Box 2642, Kensington, MD 20891-2642. President@magsgen.com. *Der Kurier*
◆**Palatines to America,** 611 E. Weber Rd., Columbus, OH 43211-1097. Tel. (614) 267-4700. www.PalAm.org. *The Palatine Im-*

migrant
- **Pennsylvania German Society,** P.O. Box 244, Kutztown, PA 19530-0244. Tel. (484) 646-4227; pgs@kutztown.edu; www.pgs.org
- **Sacramento German Genealogy Society,** P.O. Box 660061, Sacramento, CA 95866-0061. SGGS@Forevermail.com; www.SacGerGenSoc.org. *Der Blumenbaum*
- **Southern California Genealogical Society and Family Research Library,** 417 Irving Drive, Burbank, CA 91504. Tel. (818) 843-7247; Fax (818) 843-7262; scgs@earthlink.net;www.scgs genealogy.com
- **Society for German-American Studies,**c/o William D.Keel, University of Kansas, Lawrence, Kansas 66045; Tel. (785) 864-4657; WKeel@ku.edu; www.lib.iupui.edu/kade/sgas/sgasin. html.

SPECIALIZED SOCIETIES

(Addresses change. Check the Internet for current web and email addresses.)

- **American Historical Society of Germans from Russia,** 631 D Street, Lincoln, NE 68502-1199. Tel. (402) 474-3363. Fax (402) 474-7229; ahsgr @ahsgr.org; www.ahsgr.org. *American Historical Society of Germans from Russia Newsletter*
- **American/Schleswig-Holstein Heritage Society,** P.O. Box 506, Walcott, IA 52773-0506. Tel. (563) 284-4184; ASHHS@ASHHS.org; www.ashhs.org
- **Anglo-German Family History Society,** located in Great Britain. www.agfhs.org.uk
- **Balch Institute of Ethnic Studies:** See Historial Society of Pennsylvania.
- **Bukovina Society of the Americas,** P.O. Box 81, Ellis, KS 67637-0081. info@bukovinasociety.org; www.bukovina society.org.

- **Center for Pennsylvania German Studies,** C. Richard Beam, Director, 406 Spring Drive, Millersville, PA 17551. www. millersville.edu
- **Eastern Europe Genealogical Society,** P.O. Box 2536, Winnipeg, MB Canada R3C 4A7. Tel. (204) 989-3292; info@eegsociety.org;www. eegsociety.org
- **Fraktur: Russell D. Earnest Associates,** P.O. Box 1132, Clayton, DE 19938. RDEarnest@aol.com
- **Frankenmuth Historical Museum,** 613 South Main Street, Frankenmuth, MI 48734. Tel.: (989) 652-9701; www. frankenmuthmuseum.org
- **Galizien German Descendants,** Betty Wray, 2035 Dorsch Road, Walnut Creek, CA 94598-1126. Tel. (925) 944-9875; ggd@galiziengermandescendants.org; www.galiziengermandescendants.org
- **Georgia Salzburger Society,** 2980 Ebenezer Road, Rincon, GA 31326. Tel. (912) 754-7001; www.georgiasalzburgers. com
- **German Bohemian Heritage Society,** P.O. Box 822, New Ulm, MN 56073-0822. Rpaulgbhs@comcast.net
- **German-Texan Heritage Society,** 507 East 10th Street, P.O. Box 684171, Austin, TX 78768-4171. Tel. (866) 482-4847; info@GermanTexans.org; www.gths.net
- **Germanna: Memorial Foundation of theGermanna Colonies in Virginia, Inc.,** P.O. Box 279, Locust Grove, VA 22508-0279. Tel. (540) 423-1700; www.germanna.org
- **Germans from Russia Heritage Society,**1125 West Turnpike Avenue, Bismarck, ND 58501. Tel. (701) 223-6167. grhs@grhs.org; www. grhs.org
- **Germantown Historical Society,** 5501 Germantown Ave., Philadelphia, PA 19144. www.germantown history.org.
- **Glückstal Colonies Research Association,** 611 Esplanade, Redondo Beach, CA 90277. Tel. (310) 540-1872; gcra31 @aol.com; www. glueckstal.org
- **Gottscheer Heritage and Genealogy**

Association, P.O. Box 725, Louisville, CO 80027-0725. www.gottschee. org. (*The Gottschee Tree*)
♦Old Economy Village, 270 Sixteenth Street, Ambridge, PA 15003-2298. Tel. (724)266-4500; www.oldeconomy village.org
♦Historical Society of Pennsylvania, 1300 Locust Street, Philadelphia, PA 19107 Tel. (215) 732 6200; www.hsp.org (Balch Institute of Ethnic Studies merged with the Historical Society of Pennsylvania in 2002).
♦ Huguenot Historical Society, 18 Broadhead Ave., New Paltz, NY 12561-0339. Tel. (845) 255-1660; hhsoffice@ h h s - n e w p a l t z . o r g ; w w w . h h s - newpaltz.org
♦Huguenot Society of Wisconsin, 8920 No. Lake Drive, Bayside, WI 53217-1940. Tel. (414) 351-0644; CChew@exec pc.com; www.execpc.com/~drg/wihs. html
♦Indiana German Heritage Society, 401 East Michigan Street, Indianapolis, IN 46204. Tel. (317) 464-9004; mkgac @iupui.edu; www. ighs.org
♦Johannes Schwalm Historical Association, (Hessian troops research), P.O. Box 127, Scotland, PA 17254-0127.
♦Krefeld Immigrants and Their Descendants, stuebing@worldnet.att. net
♦Lancaster Mennonite Historical Society, 2215 Millstream Road, Lancaster, PA 17602-1499. Tel. (717) 393-9745; www.lmhs.org
♦ Mennonite Historians of Eastern Pennsylvania, Mennonite Heritage Center, 565 Yoder Road, P.O. Box 82, Harleyville, PA 19438. Tel. (215) 256-3020; info@mhep.org; http://mhep.org
♦Mennonite Historical and Genealogical Society of Oregon, 5326 Briar Know Loop, Scotts Mills, OR 97375. Tel. (503) 873-6406
♦Mennonite Historical and Genealogical Society, Illinois. 675 State Route 116, Metamora, IL 61548-7732. Tel. (309) 367-2551; info@imhgs.org; http://imhgs. org

♦Mifflin County Mennonite Historical Society, 3922 W. Main Sreet, P.O. Box 5603, Belleville, PA 17004. Tel. (717) 935-5574; http://mifflincomhs. mennonite.net
♦Moravian Heritage Society, 214 E. Center Street, Nazareth, PA 18064. Tel. (610) 759-5070; info@moravian historicalsociety.org; www. moravian historical society.org
♦ Moravian Archives, 41 W. Locust Street, Bethlehem, PA 18018. Tel. (610) 866-3255; info@moravianchurch archives.org; www.moravianchurch archives.org
♦ National Huguenot Society, 9033 Lyndale Ave. S. #108, Bloomington, MN 55420-3535. Tel. (952) 885-9776; http://huguenot.netnation.com
♦Orangeburg German-Swiss Genealogical Society, P.O. Box 974, Orangeburg, SC 29116-0974. www. ogsgs.org
♦ Ostfriesland Genealogy Society of America, 1670 S. Robert Street, Ste. #333, West St. Paul, MN 55118. www.ogsa.us. *Newsletter*
♦OHS Ostfriesland Heritage Society, 18419 205th Street, Grundy Center, IA 50638
♦Palatines to America, P.O. Box 141260, Columbus, OH 43214. www.palam.org
♦ Die Pommerschen Leute (German Pomeranian newsletter). See "German Immigrant Genealogy Society."
♦ Pommerscher Verein Freistadt Rundschreiben (Pomeranian Society of Freistadt), P.O. Box 204, Germantown, WI 53022. http://pommerscher vereinfreistadt.org
♦Schwenkfelder Library and Heritage Center, 105 Seminary Street., Pennsburg, PA 18073. Tel. (215) 679-3103; i n f o @ S c h w e n k f e l d e r . c o m ; www.schwenkfelder.com
♦Slovak Genealogical Research Center, 6862 Palmer Court, Chino, CA 91710-7343. Tel. (909) 627-2897; rplutko@ aol.com; http://feefhs.org/slovak/frg-sgrac.html
♦Slovenian Genealogy Society, 52 Old

Farm Road, Camp Hill, PA 17011.
www.sloveniangenealogy.org
◆**Steuben Society of America**, 6705 Fresh
Pond Road, Ridgewood, NY 11385. Tel.
(718) 381-0900; http://steuben
society.org
◆ **Texas Wendish Heritage Museum**,
1011 County Road 212, Giddings TX
78942. Tel. (979) 366-2441; wendish@
bluebon.net; http://wendish. concordia.
edu
◆ **Wandering Volhynians Genealogy
Society**, 3492 West 39th Avenue,
Vancouver, BC, Canada V6N 3A2. Tel.
(604)263-3458; jfrank@cadvision.com

NATIONAL AND UMBRELLA
GENEALOGY SOCIETIES

◆**Federation of Genealogy Societies**
P.O. Box 200940
Austin, TX 78720-0940
Tel. (888) 347-1500
Fax (888) 380-0500
http://www.fgs.org
fgs-office@fgs.org
Covers member societies throughout the
United States, as well as Canada, Ger-
many, Ireland, and the United Kingdom.
Quarterly magazine: *Forum*
◆**Federation of East European Family
History Societies** (FEEFHS)
P.O. Box 510898
Salt Lake City, UT 84151-0898
info@feefhs.org
http://feefhs.org
FEEFHS is a multi-ethnic umbrella
organization which disseminates infor-
mation about Eastern and Central Eu-
rope and serves as a clearinghouse for
member societies.
◆**International Association of Jewish
Genealogical Societies**
The International Association of Jewish
Genealogical Societies (IAJGS) is an in-
dependent non-profit umbrella organization coordinating the activities and
annual conference of more than 75 na-

tional and local Jewish genealogical societies around the world.
http://iajgs.org
◆**National Genealogical Society**
3108 Columbia Pike, Suite 300
Arlington, VA 22204-4370
Tel. (800) 473-0060
Fax: (703) 525-0052
www.ngsgenealogy.org
ngs@ngsgenealogy.org
The Society provides members with
educational offerings, publications and
materials, research and research guid-
ance, and opportunities to interact with
others.

BALCH INSTITUTE
FOR ETHNIC STUDIES

The Balch Institute for Ethnic Studies
merged with the Historical Society of
Pennsylvania in 2002.
The collection focuses on American
ethnic, racial and immigration experiences
from an historical and contemporary perspective.
Records relating to Germans are reflected through newspapers, diaries,
church histories, German organizations,
and original documents, to name a few.
The registers and inventories described
in the "Guide to Manuscript and Microfilm Collections of the Research Library
of the Balch Institute for Ethnic Studies" are available through interlibrary
loan.

AERIAL PHOTOS
OF GERMAN VILLAGES

The Cartographic and Architectural
Branch of the National Archives is able
to provide aerial photographs of German villages taken in 1945.
To initiate a request, send a map on
which the location of the village is
marked, or provide exact geographic co-

ordinates (latitude and longitude) of the village, along with any variant spellings that the village name may have. Give also the Kreis or Provinz name, and perhaps the name of the nearest city.

The Cartographic and architectural Branch will reply with an order form and the negative numbers it has for the village, as well as a cost list and list of vendors who can do the photographic reproduction. (A 10" x 10" negative will give better detail than a 5" x 5".)

Address the request to the Cartographic and Architectural Branch (NNSC), National Archives and Records Administration, 8601 Adelphi Road, College Park, MD 20740-6001.

PHOTOGRAPHY AND TOURS OF ANCESTRAL VILLAGES IN EUROPE

European Focus Inc.
508 S. Pineapple Avenue
Sarasota, FL 34236
Tel. (800) 401-7802
Fax (941) 330-0878
www.eurofocus.com
info@europeanfocus.com>

James A. Derheim's services provide professional photography of family history searchers' European ancestral towns in more than 15 countries in Europe; private ancestral and other tours for groups from 2 to 10. Also available are German locality photographs for general purchase.

GENEALOGICAL INSTITUTES, CONFERENCES, LEARNING PROGRAMS

(Check the Internet for newer web and email addresses.)

◆**National Institute of Genealogical Research (NIGR)**

P.O. Box 118
Greenbelt, MD 20768-0118
www.rootsweb.ances try.com~natgenin
NatInsGen@juno.com
◆**Samford University's Institute of Genealogy and Historical Research (IGHR)**
Samford University Library
800 Lakeshore Drive
Birmingham, AL 35229
Tel. (205) 726-4447
www.samford.edu/schools/ighr/
ighr@samford.edu
◆**Institute of Genealogical Studies (IGS)**
Dallas Genealogical Society
P.O. Box 12446
Dallas, TX 75225-0446
Tel. (866) 968-2347 (voice mail)
www.dallasgenealogy. org
info@dallasgenealogy. org
◆**Salt Lake Institute of Genealogy**
Utah Genealogical Association
P.O. Box 1144
Salt Lake City, UT 84110
www.infouga.org
info@infouga.org
◆**Virginia Institute of Genealogical Research (VIGR)**
Virginia Genealogical Society
1900 Byrd Avenue, Suite 104
Richmond, VA 23230-3033
Tel. (804) 285-8954
mail@vgs.org
National conferences
◆**NGS Conference in the States**
3108 Columbia Pike, Ste. 300
Arlington, VA 22204-4370
Tel. (703) 525-0050 or (800) 473-0060
conference@ngsgenealogy. org
◆**FGS Conferences**
Federation of Genealogical Societies
P.O. Box 200940
Austin, TX 78720-0940
Tel. (888) 347-1500
Fax (888) 515-2303
www.fgs.org
office@fgs.org
◆**Brigham Young University, Genea-**

logy and Family History Conference
BYU Conferences and Workshops
136 Harman Building
Provo, UT 84602
http://ce.byu.edu/cw/cwgen
◆**GENTECH, Inc.**[computers and genealogy conference]
P.O. Box 140277
Irving, TX 75014-0277
Fax (888) 522-7313 (toll free in the 48 contiguous states)
Home study courses
◆**The National Genealogical Society's Home Study Course**
3108 Columbia Pike, Ste. 300
Arlington, VA 22204-4370
Tel. (800) 473-0060
Fax: (703) 525-0052
www.ngsgenealogy.org
ngs@ngsgenealogy.org
◆**The Brigham Young University Independent Study Course**
BYU offers a Certificate Program in Family History as an independent study course. College credit is granted for each course successfully completed within the certificate program, but the certificate is not a college degree.
Brigham Young University
Department of Independent Studies
P.O. Box 21514
Provo, UT 84602-1514
(801) 422-5078 or (800) 914-8931
http://ce.byu.edu/is/
◆**University of Washington: Certificate Program in Genealogy and Family History**
On-campus instruction in genealogy, with a nine-month Certificate Program in Genealogy and Family History
Tel. (206) 685-8936
◆**Bellevue Community College**, Bellevue, Washington, online instruction
Tel. (425) 564-2263
www.conted.bcc.ctc. edu
◆**Heritage Genealogical College**
1449 E. 3300 South
Salt Lake City, UT 84106
Phone: 801-944-0254

Fax 801-484-2875
www.genealogy.edu
heritagegenealogycollege @yahoo.com
◆**Global Genealogy.com Inc.**
158 Laurier Avenue
Milton, ON, Canada L9T 4S2
1-800-361-5168
sales@globalgenealogy.com
www.globalgenealogy.com

HOME AND COMMUNITY SOURCES FOR SEARCHING GERMAN FAMILY HISTORY

Clues useful to family history projects may surface through examination of any of the following sources — from one's own family members, as well as from the community.

From family members
◆**Family Bible:** For family birth-marriage-death records, also for scraps of papers, programs, letters, and other miscellanea tucked haphazardly among the pages
◆**Old letters:** Some letters may be from Germany. If they are still inside their envelopes, they may reveal a location and a date. Old letters mailed from within the United States may be equally valuable.
◆**Newspaper clippings**
◆**Old photographs and albums:** The pictures may themselves provide clues; also, names and dates may be written on their reverse sides.
◆**Family scrapbooks,** journals, diaries, histories, autograph books, personal address books, receipt books
◆**Needlework** containing a family name or date
◆ **Newspaper clippings** or notes on births, marriages, deaths, retirements, awards, and other events
◆**Certificates of any kind**
◆**Birth announcements**
◆**Baptismal certificates**
◆**Wedding announcements, invitations**

◆ **Memorial cards or funeral cards/ folders**
◆ **Passports** (often contain names of parents and grandparents)
◆ **Citizenship papers:** Particularly the "Declaration of Intent" papers, or naturalization papers, or citizenship certificates
◆ **Land records:** Deeds, mortgage papers, other official papers regarding purchase or sale of land
◆ **Military records:** Pension files, applications, correspondence, discharge papers — all papers regarding military service
◆ **School report cards, diplomas**
◆ **School notebooks or essays** containing biographical information
◆ **School yearbooks**
◆ **Family traditions and treasures:** Stories collected through interviews of family members
◆ **Old family artifacts**, which may be imprinted or otherwise marked with the name of a place of origin or of manufacture

　　　　From community sources
◆ **Cemetery office records**
◆ **Tombstone inscriptions**
◆ **Mortuary records**
◆ **Vital records** (birth, marriage, death)
◆ **Paraphernalia and records** from professional organizations, lodges, fraternal societies
◆ **City directories**
◆ **German-American newspapers**, other newspapers
◆ **Trade journals**
◆ **County atlases**, county plat books, insurance maps
◆ **County histories**
◆ **Family genealogies, family histories**
◆ **Local histories**
◆ **Genealogical magazines, newsletters**
◆ **Wills, probate records**, other papers related to a death
◆ **Other court records**
◆ **Passenger arrival lists, ship arrival lists**

◆ **Federal census records**
◆ **State census records**
◆ **Alien registrations**

SELECTED HISTORICAL EVENTS AFFECTING GERMAN GENEALOGICAL RESEARCH

1517: Martin Luther proclaims his "95 Theses" in Wittenberg, thus beginning the religious Reformation.
1521: Martin Luther translates the New Testament into his middle German dialect.
1524: Start of Lutheran and Reformed records in Germany, written in German
1555: Peace of Augsburg: Henceforth princes would determine religion in their respective territories ("cuius regio, eius religio" – whose region, whose religion)
1582: Pope Gregory XIII authorizes a calendar correction, adopted in Catholic areas 1583-85, but in Protestant areas much later
1583: Start of church records in Catholic areas (usually written in Latin)
1618-48: Thirty Years War – massive destruction of records, razing of villages, and population decimation, heaviest in ??? the Pfalz
1648: Peace of Westfalia, allowing only three religions – Catholic, Lutheran, and Reformed. Treaty declares *"cujus regio, ejus religio"* – people's religion to be determined by that of the ruler.
1683: First permanent settlement of Germans in America
1763: Catherine the Great begins inviting Germans to settle in Russia
1771, 1820, 1822: Laws outlawing patronymic surnames in Schleswig-Holstein (1811 in Ostfriesland)
1775-83: American Revolution: German states, led by Hessen, provide troops for British
1789: French Revolution. German lands invaded by French.
1792: Civil marriage ceremonies required

in German areas under French control
1792-1815: Civil registration introduced in western German lands
1799: Hamburg begins civil registration
1803-15: Napoleon annexes the Rhine, abolishes 112 states and free cities
1804: Napoleon crowns himself Emperor. Code Napoleon: compilation of French civil laws
1806: End of Holy Roman Empire of the German Nation
1817: Lutheran and Reformed churches merge into the Evangelical Church ("Church of the Prussian Union")
1830: Beginnings of industrialization in German lands
1839: First major railroad begins operation, between Leipzig and Dresden
1840s: Police records (*Melderegister*) begin, mostly in Hamburg, Sachsen, and Thüringen
1840-46: Worldwide cholera
1841: Laws making marriages difficult; illegitimacies rise
1845: First propeller-driven steamship crosses the Atlantic
1846-47: Serious crop failures, setting off an upward spiraling in the cost of grains
1848: Failed German "revolution" causes emigration to America (especially intellectuals)
1849: Gold discovered in California
1850-1934: Passengers from Hamburg listed on records still available
1855-90: Castle Garden serves as a processing center for immigrants
1857: Economic panic/depression in the United States
1863: First U.S. national draft of males (born between 1818 and 1843) residing in Union States
1866: Austro-Prussian War; Austria is separated from Germany
1867: Prussia absorbs armies of all other states except Bayern, Sachsen, and Württemberg
1867: Railway system in Germany completed

1870-71: Prussia wins Franco-Prussian War. Unification of Germany; beginning of the Second Reich
1873-79: Depression in the United States
1874: Prussia introduces civil registration.
1875: Bremen passenger lists destroyed by German government to save storage space
1876: Civil registration introduced in all of the German Empire. (see 1792)
1880s: Period of industrialization in Germany
1892: Ellis Island opens (closes in 1954)
1905: Census taken of Prussian lands (*Gemeindelexikon für das Königreich Preußen*)
1910: U.S. port authorities require noting immigrants' hometowns on ship captains' passenger lists
1912: Publication of *Meyers Orts- und Verkehrslexikon*
1917-18: U.S. requires draft registration of male aliens and citizens born between 1873 and 1900
1918: Treaty of Versailles, end of the Second Reich; Poland recreated, taking in parts of Prussia
1920: Eight duchies and principalities of Sachsen became state of Thüringen
1922: *Sütterlinschrift* is adopted by Prussian schools, then spreads to other parts of Germany
1941 (September 15): The Reich education ministry (*Reicherziehungsministerium*) decrees that the old German Script is to be replaced by the Latin handwriting alphabet and the Fraktur type set with the antiqua type. The process of transition will take several years.
1943: Prussian military records destroyed by bombing
1944: Bremen passenger lists destroyed by bombing (see 1875)
1983: *Datenschutz* – landmark ruling by the German Supreme Court on privacy of personal data

2009 (January 1): The revised law of the civil registry (*Personenstands- gesetz*) allows public access to birth records after 110 years, marriage records after 90 years and death records after 30 years. Civil registrars are required to offer older records to government archives
Source: "Selected Historical Events Affecting German Genealogical Research," by Shirley J. Riemer, *Der Blumenbaum,* Vol. 17, No. 2, 1999.

SOME PRINTED RESOURCES FREQUENTLY USED IN GERMAN GENEALOGY

♦ Anderson, Chris and Ernest Thode, *A Genealogist's Guide to Discovering Your Germanic Ancestors*, Betterway Books, Cincinnati, OH 2000.

♦ Arndt, Karl J.R. and May E. Olson, comp. *German-American Newspapers and Periodicals, 1732-1955.* 2nd rev. ed., Johnson Reprint Corporation, New York, 1965.

♦ _____, *The German Language Press of the Americas, 1732-1968.* Verlag Doku-mentation, Pullach, 1973.

♦ Bahlow, Hans, *Deutsches Namen-lexikon* [Encyclopedia of German (family and first) names]. Keysersche Verlagsbuch-handlung, Munich, 1967.

♦ _____, *Dictionary of German Names.* Translated by Edda Gentry. Ed. Henry Geitz and Charlotte L. Brancaforte. Max Kade Institute for German-American Studies Translation Series, Henry Geitz, ed., University of Wisconsin-Madison, 1993.

♦ Baxter, Angus, *In Search of Your German Roots: A Complete Guide to Tracing Your Ancestors in the Germanic Areas of Europe.* Genealogical Publishing Co., Inc., Baltimore, 3rd ed., 1994.

♦ Bentley, Elizabeth Petty, *County Courthouse Book.* Genealogical Publishing Co., Inc., Baltimore, 1995.

♦ _____, *Directory of Family Associations.* Genealogical Publishing Co., Inc., Baltimore, 1993.

♦ _____, *The Genealogists's Address Book.* Genealogical Publishing Co., Inc., 3rd ed., Baltimore, 1995.

♦ Bentz, Edna M., *If I Can You Can Decipher Germanic Records.* Edna M. Bentz, 1982.

♦ Blodgett, Steven W., *Germany: Genealogical Research Guide.* Genealogical Society of Utah, Salt Lake City, 1989.

♦ Brandt, Edward R., Ph.D., Mary Bellingham, Kent Cutkomp, Kermit Frye, and Patricia Lowe, *Germanic Genealogy: A Guide to Worldwide Sources and Migration Patterns.* Germanic Genealogy Society, St. Paul, 2007.

♦ *Cassell's German-English, English-German Dictionary,* rev. by Harold T. Betteridge. MacMillan Publishing Co., New York, 1978.

♦ Colletta, John Philip, *They Came in Ships: A Guide to Finding Your Immigrant Ancestor's Arrival Record,* 3rd ed., Ancestry, Salt Lake City, 2002.

♦ Dearden, Fay and Douglas Dearden, *The German Researcher: How to Get the Most Out of Our Family History Center.* 4th ed., revised and expanded, Family Tree Press, Minneapolis, 1983. 1990.

♦ Eakle, Arlene and Johni Cerny, eds., *The Source: A Guidebook of American Genea-logy.* Ancestry, Salt Lake City, 1984.

♦ Edlund, Thomas Kent, comp., *An Introduction and Register to Die Ahnenstammkartei des deutschen Volkes of the Deutsche Zentralstelle für Genealogie Leipzig 1922-1991.* Family History Library, Salt Lake City, 1993.

♦ Eichholz, Alice, ed., *Ancestry's Red Book: American State, County, and Town Sources.* Ancestry Publishing, Salt Lake City, 1989, 1992.

♦ Everton, George B., Sr., ed. *The Handy Book for Genealogists,* 9th ed., Everton

Publishers, Inc., Logan, Utah, 1999.
◆Ferguson, Laraine, "Locating Church and Civil Registration Records," *German Genealogical Digest,* Vol. 1, No. 3, pp. 202-203, 1985.
◆Filby, P. William, and Mary K. Meyer, *Passenger and Immigration Lists Index: A Guide to Published Arrival Records of about 500,000 Passengers Who Came to the United States and Canada in the Seventeenth, Eighteenth, and Nineteenth Centuries.* 1st ed., 3 vol. plus annual sup-plements, Gale Research Co., c 1981.
◆Filby, P. William, ed., *Passenger and Immigration Lists Bibliography, 1538-1900: Being a Guide to Published Lists of Arrivals in the United States and Canada.* 1st ed., Gale Research Co., De-troit, c1981.
◆Glazier, Ira A. and P. William Filby, ed., *Germans to America: Lists of Passengers Arriving at U.S. Ports.* Scholarly Resources, Wilmington, Del., c1988- [Series begins with 1850 arrivals and is intended to continue through 1893.]
◆Greenwood, Val D., *The Researcher's Guide to American Genealogy.* Genea-logical Publishing Co., Baltimore, 1990.
◆Gregory, Winifred, ed. *American News-papers, 1821-1936, and Canada.* W.H. Wilson, New York, 1937.
◆Hall, Charles M., *The Atlantic Bridge to Germany,* 10 vols. The Everton Pub-lishers, Inc., Logan, Utah.
◆Haller, Charles R., *Across the Atlantic and Beyond: The Migration of German and Swiss Immigrants to America.* Heritage Books, 1993.
◆Jensen, Larry O., "Basic Principles in Resolving Naming Practice Problems," *German Genealogical Digest,* Vol. 4, No. 1, 1988, pp. 17-19.
◆ Jensen, Larry O., *A Genealogical Handbook of German Research.* Pleasant Grove, UT, Everton Publishers, Logan, Utah, 2 vols., 1980-1983.
◆Johnson, Dr. Arta F., ed. *Bibliography and Source Materials for German-*

American Research. Vol. 1, Arta F. John-son, 1982. Updated 1984.
◆Jones, George F., *German-American Names.* Genealogy Unlimited, Inc., 2nd. ed., Orem, Utah, 1995.
◆Kemp, Thomas Jay, *International Vital Records Handbook.* 3rd ed., Genealogical Publishing Co., Baltimore, 1995.
◆Kirkham, E. Kay. *A Survey of American Church Records: Major Denominations before 1880,* vol. 1. Everton Publishers, Logan, Utah, 1971.
◆_____, *A Survey of American Church Records: Minor Denominations,* vol. 2. Everton Publishers, Logan, Utah, 1969.
◆Law, Hugh T., *How to Trace Your An-cestors to Europe.* Cottonwood Books, Salt Lake City, 1989.
◆Minert, Roger P., *Deciphering Hand-writing in German Documents.* GRT Pub-lications, 2001.
◆_____, *German Immigrants in American Church Records.* Picton Press, Rockland, ME, 2006-. (Vol. 1 Indiana Protestant; Vol. 2 Wisconsin Northwest Protestant; Vol. 3 Wisconsin Northeast Protestant; Vol. 4 Wisconsin Southwest Protestant; Vol. 5 Wisconsin Southeast Protestant; Vol. 6 Nebraska Protestant; Vol. 7 Iowa West Protestant; Vol. 8 Iowa Northeast Protestant; Vol. 9 Iowa Southeast Protestant. www.pictonpress.com
◆_____, *Place Name Indexes (Alsace-Lorraine; Baden; Bavaria; Branden-burg; Braunschweig/Oldenburg/ Thuringia; East Prussia; Hanover; Hesse; Hesse-Nassau; Mecklenburg; Palatinate; Pomerania; Posen; Rhine-land; Schleswig-Holstein, Westphalia (including Hohenzollern, Lippe, Schamburg-Lippe, and Waldeck); West Prussia; Württemberg; and Switzerland* (CD only). GRT Publications.
◆_____, and Shirley J. Riemer, *Researching in Germany.* Sacramento, CA, Lorelei Press, 2000. www.lorelei-press.com.

* _____, *Spelling Variations in German Names: Solving Family History Problems Through Applications of German and English Phonetics*, GRT Publications, Woods Cross, UT, 2000.
* Müller, Friedrich, *Müllers großes deutsches Ortsbuch* (Müller's large German gazetteer). Post- und Ortsbuchverlag Postmeister a.d. Friedrich Müller, Wuppertal-Barmen, Germany, 1958.
* Neagles, James C. and Lila Lee Neagles, *Locating Your Immigrant Ancestor: A Guide to Naturalization Records.* Everton Publishing Co., Logan, Utah, 1975.
* Newman, John J., *American Naturalization Processes and Procedures, 1790-1985.* Family History Section, Indiana Historical Society, Indianapolis, 1985.
* Parker, J. Carlyle, *Going to Salt Lake City to Do Family History Research.* Marietta Publishing Company, 3rd ed., Turlock, Cal., 1996.
* Ribbe, Wolfgang, and Eckhard Henning, *Taschenbuch für Familiengeschichteforschung.* Verlag Degener, Neustadt/Aisch, 1995.
* Schaefer, Christina K., *Guide to Naturalization Records of the United States.* Genealogical Publishing Co., Baltimore, 1997.
* Schenk, Trudy and Ruth Froelke, *Württemberg Emigration Index.* Ancestry, Inc., Salt Lake City, 1986 ff.
* Schweitzer, George K., *German Genealogical Research.* George K. Schweitzer, 407 Ascot Court, Knoxville, TN 37923, 1995.
* Smith, Clifford Neal and Anna Piszczan-Czaja Smith, *Encyclopedia of German-American Genealogical Research,* R.R. Bowker Co., New York, 1976.
* Smith, Kenneth L., *German Church Books: Beyond the Basics.* Picton Press, Camden, Maine, 1989.
* Smith, Juliana Szucs Smith, *The Ancestry Family Historian's Address Book: A Comprehensive List of Local, State, and Federal Agencies and Institutions, and Ethnic and Genealogical Organizations,* Ancestry, Inc., 1997.
* Stumpp, Dr. Karl, *The Emigration from Germany to Russia in the Years 1763-1862.* Translation by Prof. Joseph S. Height and others. American Historical Society of Germans from Russia, Lincoln, Neb., 1978.
* Suess, Jared H., *Central European Genealogical Terminology.* Everton Publishers, Logan, Utah, 1978.
* Thode, Ernest J., Jr., Thode, *Address Book for Germanic Genealogy.* Genealogical Publishing Co., Baltimore, 5th ed. 1994.
* _____, *Atlas for Germanic Genealogy*, Heritage House, Marietta, Ohio, 1982, 1988.
* _____, *German-English Genealogical Dictionary.* Genealogical Publishing Co., Inc., Baltimore, 1992.
* "Tracking Immigrant Origins," in *The Source: A Guidebook of American Genealogy*, Arlene Eakle and Johni Cerny, ed., Ancestry Publishing, Salt Lake City, 1984.
* Üncapher, Wendy K., *Lands of the German Empire and Before*, Origins, Janesville, Wisconsin, 2000 (see Maia's Books).
* Ütrecht, Dr. E., ed. *Meyers Orts- und Verkehrs-Lexikon des deutschen Reichs.* (Meyer's Directory of Places and Commerce in the German Empire). Bibliographisches Institut, Leipzig, Germany. 1912, 2 vols.
* *Where to Write for Vital Records: Births, Deaths, Marriages and Divorces.* U.S. Department of Health and Human Services.
* Wittke, Carl, *The German-Language Press in America.* University of Kentucky Press, Lexington, 1957.
* Wright, Raymond S. III, *Ancestors in German Archives: A Guide to Family History Sources.* Genealogical Publishing Co., Inc., Baltimore, 2004.
* Zimmerman, Gary J. and Marion Wolf-

ert, *German Immigrants: Lists of Passengers Bound from Bremen to New York 1847-1854 with Places of Origin.* Genealogical Publishing Co., Baltimore, 1993.

SELECTED SOURCES FOR 'PLACE OF ORIGIN' CLUES

The following sources are recommended as means for finding clues that may lead to locating an immigrant ancestor's German place of origin. The groupings (A, B, C, etc.) are arranged in descending order of their potential for reasonably quick success.

This list is not intended to represent all the possible approaches aimed at locating a German place of origin.

A.   Potential clues close to the researcher's home or in the researcher's family

__A1. Family bible, hymn books, prayer books

__A2. Programs, certificates of every kind

__A3. Old letters (with envelopes), postcards

__A4. Birth announcements

__A5. Church certificates (christening/ confirmation/marriage)

__A6. School records, diplomas

__A7. Death certificates

__A8. Marriage certificate (note witnesses, clergyman, church)

__A9. Family heirlooms, artifacts, photographs

__A10. Interviews with older relatives, distant "cousins"

__A11. Review of notes from long-ago family history searches

B. Searches in area of immigrant's U.S. settlement town and county

__B1. Naturalization papers (declaration of intent, certificate); after Sept. 27, 1906 papers filed with INS (See *Guide to Naturalization Records of the United States,*

by Christina K. Schaefer, GPC, 1997) FHL 973 P4s

__B2. U.S. church records from place of settlement – christenings, marriages, deaths, memorials, burials. (Be sure to check FHLC for church records in settlement area church.)

__B3. Surname and obituary card-indexes in public library of immigrant's U.S. settlement area

__B4. Newspaper obituary in area where immigrant died or resided for a long time

__B5. Newspapers: marriage notices, anniversary memorials (especially 50th wedding anniversary reports) deaths, births

__B6. City/town histories

__B7. City directories, to find fellow passengers on emigration ship who settled in the same U.S. town, also other neighbors

__B8. Biographical sketches (also "vanity books") mentioning fellow townspeople (but not necessarily the immigrant ancestor)

__B9. Tombstone inscriptions

__B10. Cemetery office records

__B11. Funeral home, mortuary office

__B12. Hospital/caretaker/home/school/ university records

__B13. The most active, enthusiastic, consumed genealogist/historian now living in the U.S. town of settlement

__B14. German organizations, German interest groups (genealogy) people in town

__B15. Trade/industry publications (based on occupation of immigrant and siblings)

__B16. Fraternal organization records

__B17. Fellow immigrants' records (the same records as those checked for the immigrant, like those on this list)

__B18. Records of immigrants' neighbors

__B19. Records of immigrants' siblings

__B20. Local telephone directories

__B21. County biographies (but not just

for the immigrant)

__B22. Wills, probate records

__B23. County marriage records

__B24. County death records

__B25. County family histories

__B26. County tax lists

__B27. State Adjutant General annual reports

__B28. Histories of early settlers in the area

__B29. Witnesses to marriages or births

__B30. Birth certificate of immigrant's child

__B31. Records of immigrant's spouse (if they were married or knew each other before they emigrated)

__B32. Local Turn Verein records; see *Research Guide to the Turner Movement in the United States,* by Eric L. Pumroy and Katja Rampelmann, comps., Greenwood Press, 1996

__B33. Published history of church in settlement locality

__B34. Veteran organization records

C. Records in immigrant's settlement state

__C1. State censuses (after 1855 they give birth places); see State Censuses, annotated bibliography. FHL 973.X23s

__C2. State genealogy society

__C3. State library, for variety of statewide indexes

__C4. German-American, English-language newspapers in state libraries

D. Other sources in the United States

__D1. Passports; passport applications (mandatory starting in 1916, but many citizens nevertheless applied for them). Incomplete indexes for 1791-1925 available through National Archives

__D2. U.S. Census, to find area of origin, year of immigration, parents' birthplace

__D3. Passenger arrival lists (for year of arrival, see 1880, 1900, 1910, 1920 U.S. ; censuses; see also *They Came in Ships: A Guide to Finding Your Immigrant*

Ancestor's Arrival Record, by John Colletta, Ancestry, 1993. FHL book 973 W27c

__D4. Military records: pension and service records, applications, correspondence, discharge papers (National Archives has military service, pension, and bounty land records and indexes for pre-World War I soldiers)

__D5. Land and property records: deeds, Homestead files

__D6. Newspapers in Microform, United States, Library of Congress, 1973 -

__D7. *A Survey of American Church Records,* E.K. Kirkham, Everton, 1978. FHL 973 K2k)

__D8. *Preliminary Guide to Church Records Repositories,* A.R. Suelflow, 1969. FHL film 908,962 item 1

__D9. Draft registrations, World War I

__D10. Social Security applications (since 1936) through Social Security Death Index

__D11. Bounty and warrant applications

__D12. Ancestral File in *FamilySearch* program

__D13. Civil War draft records

__D14. International Genealogical Index (IGI) in *FamilySearch*

__D15. Surname section of Family History Library Catalog

__D16. *Directory of Family Associations*

__D17. *Everton's Genealogical Helper,* March-April issues for family associations

__D18. Homestead Act records (may contain naturalization papers and/or military records)

__D19. Alien registrations (scarce)

__D20. PERiodical Source Index (on CD-ROM)

__D21. Government employment records

__D22. *Family History Library Resource Guide: The Hamburg Passenger Lists, 1850-1934*

__D23. *The Research Outline: Germany,* published by the Family History Library

__D24. *Research Outline: Tracing Im-*

migrant Origins, by the Family History Library).

__D25. *German-American Newspapers and Periodicals, 1732-1955: History and Bibliography,* 1961 (microfilm: 824091 item 1); and *The German Language Language Press of the Americas 1732-1968: History and Bibliography. Die deutsch-sprachige Press der Amerikas,* by Karl J.R. Arndt and May E. Olson,, comps., 2 vols., München, 1973-1976, FHL 973 B33a 1976 and 973 B33a 1976 v. 2

__D26. *Germans to America: Lists of Passengers Arriving at U.S. Ports, 1850-* by Ira A. Glazier and P. William Filby, ed. (973 W2ger)

__D27. "Military Service Records in the National Archives of the United States," General Information Leaflet No. 7, rev. 1985, National Archives and Records Administration

__D28. *Locating Your Immigrant Ancestor: a Guide to Naturalization Records,* by James C. Neagles and Lila Lee Neagles, Everton Publishing, c 1975. FHL film 6117121)

__D29. *Passenger and Immigration Lists Bibliography, 1538-1900: Being Published Lists of Arrivals in the United States and Canada,* P. William Filby , ed., Gale Research, Detroit, 1988. FHL 973 W33p 1988

__D30. *Passenger and Immigration Lists Index,* P. William Filby, Gale Research, Detroit, 1981

__D31. Library of Congress bibliographies: *A Complement to Genealogies in the Library of Congress: A Bibliography,* Kaminkow, Marion J., ed. FHL book 016.9291 K128c

__D32. *German-American Newspapers and Periodicals, 1732-1955,* NY: Johnson Reprint, 1985. FHL film 824091

__D33.*The Württemberg Emigration Index,* Trudy Schenk and Ruth Froelke, Salt Lake City, 1986. FHL 943.47 W22st

__D34. Published lists of emigrant applications, such as: Braunschweig, 1846-

1871; Hessen-Kassel, 1840-1850; Hessen-Nassau, 1806-1866; Lippe, to 1877; Minden, Westfalia, 1816-1900; Münster, Westfalia, 1803-1850; Rheinland Palatine and Saarland, 1700s; Waldeck, 1829-1872. (For emigration lists, search in Family History Library Catalog by Country - State- Emigration and Immigration)

__D35. *How to Trace Your Ancestors to Europe,* Hugh T. Law, Cottonwood Books, 1987. FHL 940 D23L

__D36. *German Immigrants: Lists of Passengers Bound from Bremen to New York,* Gary J. Zimmerman and Marion Wolfert, Baltimore, 1993. FHL 974.71 W3g

__D37 *American Passenger Arrival Records: A Guide to the Records of Immigrants Arriving at American Ports by Sail and Steam,* by Michael H. Tepper, Genealogical Publishing Co., 1988. FHL 973 W27 am 1993

__D38. *Pennsylvania German Pioneers: A Publication of the Original Lists of Arrivals in the Port of Philadelphia from 1727 to 1808,* Ralph Beaver Strassburger, comp., and William John Hinke, ed., Pennsylvania German Society, 1934. FHL 974.811 W3s 1992

__D39. *Passenger and Immigration Lists Index: A Guide to Published Arrival Records of about 500,000 Passengers Who Came to the United States and Canada in the 17th, 18th, and 19th Centuries,* P. William Filby and Mary K. Meyer, eds., Supplemental volumes

__D40. Search of back entries in FaNa (*Familienkundliche Nachrichten*), through the Immigrant Genealogical Society (Burbank, California)

__D41. Locality search for Germany-born mother or wife's maiden name

__D42. Widow's request for Civil War pension

__D43. National Union Catalog of Manuscript Collections, NUCMC Washington, DC, Library of Congress, 1959 - (surnames may be checked in the index)

E. Searches in Germany and in German records

__E1. German telephone directory (www.dastelefonbuch.de and www.tele auskunft.de)

__E2. Geogen, view surname distribution in modern Germany (http://christoph. stoepel.net)

__E3 HETRINA, *Hessische Truppen im Amerikanischen Unabhängigkeits-krieg,* for unusual names only. FHL 943 M2h; film 1,320,516, items 6-7 (A-L), and 1,320,542, items 5-6 (M-Z)

__E4 *Deutsches Namenlexikon,* by Hans Bahlow FHL 943 D46ba; or its English translation, *Dictionary of German Names,* by Hans Bahlow, FHL D46ba 1993) translated by Edda Gentry, Friends of the Max Kade Institute for German-American Studies, Madison, Wisc., 1993

__E5. *Der Schlüssel* (German periodical index, 9 volumes), using the Name Index. FHL book 943 D25sc (not on film)

__E6. *Familiengeschichtliche Quellen* (German periodical index, 17 volumes; each volume must be searched separately. FHL book 943 B2fq; microfiche 6000817

__E7. *Deutsches Geschlechterbuch* (German lineage books, more than 200 volumes; available at Family History Library, not filmed for Family History Centers)

__E8. *Bibliographie gedruckter Familien-geschichten,* 1946-1960 (bibliography of printed family histories), Heinzmann, Düsseldorf, 1990. FHL 943 D23he

__E9. *Deutsches biographisches Archiv* (DBA) (the German Biographical Archive. FHL fiche 6002159. Contains about 225,000 biographical sketches; use to search for a clue to a location where a surname may have come from.

__E10. *Die Quellenschau für Familien-forscher* (Sources for Family Research, a three-volume index, including a surname index (*Personen Register*) FHL 943 A3kp; film 0924491 items 4-6

__E11. "Germanic Emigrants Register." FHL microfiche 6312192. FHLC Computer Number 445448

__E12. *Die Ahnenstammkartei des deutschen Volkes an introduction and register* (of the *Zentralstelle für Genealogie* Leipzig, 1922-1991, by Thomas Kent Edlund. FHL 943 A33e 1995

__E13. Card index to emigrants to and from the United States listed in German periodicals (primarily from *Deutsches Familienarchiv,* FHL film 1125001)

__E14. *Die Ahnenlisten-Kartei* (Ancestor List Catalog, (14 volumes), an index to ancestors, as submitted by German genealogists

__E15. German genealogy society in general area of Germany, if the area is known

F. Creative search techniques

__F1. Inquire at settlement town's public library for the unofficial "town historian" (usually a hobbyist)

__F2. Submit queries for publication by ethnic organizations

__F3. Submit queries in German periodicals (FaNa, PraFo)

__F4. Letters to clergy (for possible posting, accompanied by a church contribution) in German village(s) where the surname of interest is prominent

__F5. Letters to same-name people in U.S., from U.S. telephone directory (include SASEs)

__F6. Queries in U.S. genealogical publications in immigrant's settlement area

__F7. Stab-in-the-dark letters to same-surname people in Germany (from German telephone directory)

__F8. Internet queries, surname lists

__F9. Paid newspaper ads in area of Germany where the name is prevalent. See latest edition of *Europa World Year Book* for addresses of current newspapers in Germany. (Addresses for such newspapers in Germany in 1999 are included in this edition of *The German Research*

Companion, beginning on page 601.)
__F10. Correspondence with persons researching the same surname
Source: © Shirley J. Riemer, 2000.

OTHER CLUES FOR FINDING PLACE OF ORIGIN

German immigrants to America not only tended to travel together, but also to live in the same neighborhoods with one another. It is almost impossible to count the number of American "German quarters" that were once known by such names as "Kleindeutschland," or "Dutch Land," or "Little Germany." Such all-German neighborhoods could be found in New York, Philadelphia, Baltimore, Charleston, New Orleans, Charleston, New Orleans, Cincinnati, Chicago, Milwaukee, St. Louis and in so many other American cities.

And then there were the settlements that were not German "quarters," but rather whole communities, each set up as a sort of "New Germany," like Hermann, Missouri; New Fredericksburg and New Braunfels, Texas; Frankenmuth, Michigan; New Ulm, Minnesota; and Ebenezer, Georgia.

Researchers should be especially aware that German immigrants in their predominantly German neighborhoods in America formed churches of their respective faiths– where christenings, marriages, and deaths were recorded in precisely the same manner as the churches of their homeland had recorded them. German immigrants' church records in America can therefore be of great value, for these German-American records reveal not only the names of a newborn child's parents, but also the immigrant parents' place of German origin.

With such large German emigrations occurring in the 18th and 19th centuries (in 1880, for instance, German immigrants in New York and their American-born children made up almost a third of the New York population), we now find many accounts and histories that have been collected by local historians and genealogical societies, most of these materials now residing in public libraries and with historical societies in the respective areas.

These accounts may not mention a specific ancestor being searched, but they may nevertheless offer clues based on the origins of German immigrants who settled in all-German neighborhoods and communities. Therefore, one of the best research "tools" for German family history researchers is their ancestors' penchant for "togetherness."

RECORDINGS OF GENEALOGY CONFERENCES

Jamb Tapes, Inc.
P.O. Box 2885
St. Louis, MO 63111
Tel. (800)-809-9284
Jamb Tapes Inc. provides CDs of sessions of conferences of the National Genealogical Society (NGS), the Federation of Genealogical Societies (FGS), and conferences of some other organizations, beginning in 2007.

When searching the website, click on the category "Genealogy."

Repeat Performance
2911 Crabapple Lane
Hobart, IN 46324
Tel. (219) 465-1234
Fax (219) 477-5492
www.audiotapes.com
info@audiotapes.com
Repeat Performance has audio-recordings of past national genealogical conferences up to and including 2004 and makes the cassettes available for purchase.

See the Repeat Performance website cited above for the catalog listing of available cassettes. (Click on "Geneal-ogy" to begin).

WRITING QUERIES

Preparing to write the query for a United States publication

♦In a first draft, as a means of ensuring that the problem is presented in a focused and clear fashion, write down the question to be posed — as simply, as directly, and as briefly as possible.

♦List the facts available concerning the question, organizing them in appropriate order

♦Cut long sentences into two or three sentences. Cross out unnecessary words.

♦ Emphasize facts and other vital statistics; eliminate extraneous personal or anecdotal material.

♦Adjust the order of items; compose the second draft.

Composing the query

♦ Use a word-processor to write the query. Do not write it in longhand.

♦Use all capital letters for surnames.

♦Use standard-size paper (8°" x 11")

♦If possible, limit the length of the query to a half page, double-spaced.

♦Consider breaking a long query into two – one for each of two related ances-tors.

Small courtesies

♦Pose a reasonable request.

♦ Offer to pay respondents for photo copies of relevant information.

Be sure to include:

♦The name of the German village and *Kreis* (county) if known

♦Any alternate spellings of the surname that may have appeared in the research

♦Umlauts, when known

♦If available, the date of immigration and points of United States settlement through the ancestor's lifetime

♦ Locations as well as dates of births, marriages, and deaths (use date estimates if necessary, but be sure to state them as estimates)

♦The emigrant's religion, if known

♦ Your name and address; optionally, your telephone number, e-mail address, or fax number in addition to the address

♦A stamped, self-addressed envelope if a copy of the published query is requested of the publications' editor

ABBREVIATIONS USED IN QUERIES

abt	about
ae	age
aft	after
anc	ancestor(s)
ans	answer
arr	arrived
b	born
bap/bapt	baptized
bdt	birthdate(s)
bef	before
bel	believed
bet	between
bp/bpl	birthplace
bro	brother
bur	buried
ca	circa, about
cem	cemetery
cen	census
cert	certificate
ch	child(ren)
CivW	Civil War
Co	County
corr/corres	correspond
csn	cousin
d	died, death
dau	daughter
desc	descendant(s)
desr	desire
div	divorced
dp/dpl	death place
dt	date(s)
em/emigr	emigrated/emigrant
Eng.	England
enl	enlisted
est	estate

f	female
fa	father
fam	family/families
1st	first
1/hus	first husband
1/w	first wife
fol	following
fr	from
g	grand-
gg	great grand-
gen	genealogy
Ger	Germany
hus	husband
id	identity
immig	immigrant/immigrated
info	information
int	interested
kn	known
/law	in-law (e.g. mo/in-law)
liv	living
loc	location
M	male
m	married
m/1	married first
m/2	married second
M.D.	doctor
mo	mother
mov	moved
Ms	manuscript
ndt	no date
npl	no place
nr	near
obit	obituary
orig	original
par	parents
per	perhaps
pl	place
pos/poss	possibly
PR	Prussia
pro	probate
prob	probably
re	regarding
rec	record
ref	reference
rel	related/relative(s)
rem	remained
req	requested
res	resided, residence
rsch	research

Rev.	Reverend
RevW	Revolutionary War
s	son(s)
SASE	self-addressed stamped envelope
2nd	second
set	settled
sib	sibling(s)
sis	sister
sol	soldier
terr	territory
tn	town
trad	tradition
twp/Tp	township
unk	unknown
unm	unmarried
V.S.	vital statistics
ver	verify
vic	vicinity
w	wife
wid	widow
widr	widower
wt	want(ed)
xch	exchange
yng	young
yr	year

WRITING TO GERMANY

The sample German-language letter shown on these pages, can be adapted for mailing to -
A) a town archive (*Stadtarchiv*), or B) a local civil registration office (*Standesamt*), or C) a church office (*Pfarramt*).

The address
A) *for a village/town archive:*
    Stadtarchiv [*locality name*]
    [*zip code*] [*locality name*]
  Germany
B) *for a local civil registry office:*
    Standesamt [locality name]
    [zip code] [*locality name*]
  Germany
C) *for a Catholic church office:*
    Katholisches Pfarramt
    [*zip code*] [*locality name*]

EXAMPLE OF A LETTER TO GERMANY
(USING THE FORM LETTER ON THE PREVIOUS PAGE)

Ernest Schneider   15. März 2010
120 Beach Street
Mytown, IA 55555
U.S.A.

Evangelisches Pfarramt
36115 Ehrenberg
Germany

Sehr geehrter Herr Pfarrer,

Vorfahren meiner Familie haben in Ehrenberg gelebt. Um meine Familienchronik

vervollständigen zu können, bitte ich um Kopien vorhandener Dokumente über

HARTMANN Heinrich Georg geb. 22 Januar 1832 in Ehrenberg sowie

gegebenenfalls auch über seine Vorfahren (Eltern, Großeltern).

Ich versichere ausdrücklich, daß die erbetenen Unterlagen meine eigene Familie

betreffen und nur der privaten Familienforschung dienen.

Natürlich bin ich gern bereit, Ihnen die üblichen Gebühren zu entrichten.

Für Ihre Unterstützung bedanke ich mich bereits jetzt.

Mit freundlichem Gruß

(signature)

Ernest Schneider

Germany
or, *for a Lutheran church office:*
Evangelisches Pfarramt
[*zip code*] [*locality name*]
Germany
Salutation
A & B: Sehr geehrte Damen und Herren,
C: Sehr geehrter Herr Pfarrer,
Body of the letter:
Vorfahren meiner Familie haben in [*locality*] gelebt. Um meine Familienchronik vervollständigen zu können, bitte ich um Kopien vorhandener Dokumente über [*last name, in all capital letters*] [*first name*] geb. [*birthdate*] in [*place of birth*] sowie gegebenenfalls auch über [seine/ihre*] Vorfahren (Eltern, Großeltern).

Ich versichere ausdrücklich, daß die erbetenen Unterlagen meine eigene Familie betreffen und nur der privaten Familienforschung dienen.

Zum Ausgleich entstehender Unkosten füge ich einen Verrechnungsscheck über ⌐ [*amount*] bei und bitte um Nachricht, falls dies nicht ausreicht.

Für Ihre Unterstützung bedanke ich mich bereits jetzt.

Mit freundlichem Gruß
[*writer's signature and name*]
(*Use *seine* for a male immigrant, or *ihre* for a female immigrant.)
English translation
Dear Sir or Madam,

Ancestors of my family lived in [*locality name*]. To complete my family history, I request copies of any available documents concerning [*last name, in all capital letters*] [*first name*] born [*date of birth*] in [*place of birth*] as well as his/her ancestors (parents, grandparents).

I do expressly declare that these documents concern my own family and serve for private genealogical research only.

I will be pleased to pay the customary fee for your services.

Thank you for your assistance.

Sincerely yours,
[signature of sender]
[name of sender]
Example of a finished letter
Note how the date is written on the letter on the previous page. Months of the year in German are as follows:
January .... Januar
February .... Februar
March .... März
April.. April
May .... Mai
June .... Juni
July .... Juli
August .... August
September .... September
October .... Oktober
November .... November
December .... Dezember
Examples of the envelope address
◆Katholisches Pfarramt
36115 Ehrenberg
Germany
◆Standesamt Ehrenberg
36115 Ehrenberg
Germany
◆Stadtarchiv Ehrenberg
36115 Ehrenberg
Germany

ADDRESSING GERMANS: USING DU AND SIE

Unlike English, German has two ways to address another person – either using *Du* (*jemanden duzen* – to *Du* someone), or using *Sie* (*jemanden siezen* – to *Sie* someone). There is a world of difference between the two.

Changes in Du and Sie usage through history.

In the original Germanic dialects – which were only spoken, not written – people regardless of age or social status addressed each other in the second person singular: *Du*. Since about the fourth century AD, the Roman tradition of addressing people of higher social status in the third person singular – *Er* – was adopted to flatter them. In the late fifteenth century, a Byzantine tradition to address high-ranking individuals with a respectful noun was introduced: *Eure Hoheit* (your highness) or *Euer Ehren* (your honor). Emperor Karl V (1500-1558) was the first to be called *Eure Majestät* (your majesty). By the seventeenth century, the conventional manner of address in educated and higher circles had switched to the third person plural – *Sie*. Now there were four ways to address a person – to ask him/her, for example, "Where are you?"

Wo bist Du?
Wo seid Ihr?
Wo ist Er/Sie?
Wo sind Sie?

Anybody of equal or higher social status was to be addressed using *Sie*. This included children. For example, when young Goethe or Mozart talked to their parents, it was *"Herr Vater/Frau Mutter, darf ich Sie etwas fragen?"* (Mr. Father/Mrs. Mother, may I ask you something?")

In letters during the eighteenth and nineteenth centuries, flattering nouns were substituted for the name, graduated according to social status and aristocratic rank:

Euer Wohlgeboren
Euer Hochgeboren
Euer Hoch- und Wohlgeboren
Euer Hochwohlgeboren

Used respectively for the Roman Catholic clergy were:

Euer Ehrwürden
Euer Hochwürden
Euer Hochehrwürden

By the end of the eighteenth century, in general usage only *Du* and *Sie* were left and used – as they basically still are today – with *Du* being used between relatives, close friends, and toward children – and *Sie* for everybody else.

Siezen and *Duzen* in modern times

While the basic rule mentioned above seems simple enough, there still are many variations that may cause confusion. In German, the invitation to continue a relationship on a first-name basis, *"Sagen Sie doch einfach Du zu mir!"* (Just call me by my first name and *Du*!) is usually the major step when it crosses the threshold from formal to close and cordial. Usually – but this is just a rule of thumb – it is up to the more senior or higher ranking person to take the initiative: father to daughter's boyfriend or fianceé; or boss to employee. If the situation permits, this may turn into quite a ceremony called *Duz-Bruderschaft trinken* (to drink a toast to the brotherhood of *Du*), sometimes in a complicated maneuver of intertwined arms (see below). Afterwards you stand on a *Duzfuß* (*Du*-footing) with the other person, and you are his or her *Duz-Bruder* (*Du*-brother).

Examples of traditional conventions

♦ Members of trade unions and leftist political parties (including the Social Democratic Party, SPD) address each other using *Du*, formerly accompanied by *Genosse* (comrade), and either the last or the first name.

♦ Members of conservative or centrist political parties tend to use *Sie*.

♦ Blue collar workers, construction workers, farm laborers, etc. usually use first names and *Du* among one another.

♦ When hiking or climbing in the Alps, not only does tradition demand that you greet everybody you meet (*Grüß Gott* – not northern German *Guten Tag!*), but a mountaineer's rule also states: *Über tausend Meter wird geduzt* (The first-name zone starts 3,300 feet above sea level).

♦ In rural areas in Bavaria, even local dignitaries like the local priest or the mayor are addressed with a *Du*. In contrast to the chummy *Du* that farmers use among one another, this is a different, respectful *Du* used in connection with the appropriate title: *Du, Herr Pfarrer* or *Du, Bürgermeister.*

♦In a beer hall, a rustic tavern, or at a *Volksfest*, people may join you at your table (even if others are still empty) and strike up a conversation, addressing you as *Herr Nachbar/Frau Nachbarin* (Mr./Mrs. Neighbor) either with a *Du* or a *Sie.*

♦ When animals and things are addressed (as in songs: *Oh Du schöner Deutscher Wald. . . * Oh you beautiful German forest), *Du* is always used. It is quite common to hear Germans inquire of dogs, *"Ja, wer bist denn Du?"* (Who might you be?) – without expecting *Sie* in an answer, of course.

♦To top it all off: If you want to show your contempt for someone or want to insult him or her, use *Du* in combination with some derogatory remark or invective. This, however, is not advisable, for the other person may bring you to court under §185 of Germany's Penal Code.

Even more dangerous is the use of *Du* when speaking to an official, as *Beamten-beleidigung* (insulting an official) is a crime punishable under §193 (3) of the Penal Code.

Du-Sie adjustments in recent years

The boundary between *Sie* and *Du* has become increasingly blurred in recent years. It has become fashionable with younger people to use *Du* and first names without preliminary ceremonies as a way to show that they are doing away with antiquated formalities.

While in private life these adjustments evolve without causing much stir, in professional life they can cause situations that range from awkward to funny. In more traditional-minded companies and administrative authorities, where hierarchies are still intact, it is strictly *Sie*. People who for 20 years sit in the same office, facing each other across

adjoining desks, may still address each other as *Herr K.* and *Herr F.*

However, modern management methods emphasize teamwork instead of hierarchies, and the use of *Du* and first names is considered symbolic. This is especially true with American companies operating in Germany, where this new theory coincides with an established use of first names.

In a library I recently found a handbook on how to address correctly, orally and in writing, more than 1,500 different categories of people (Helga Pfeil-Braun, *Das große Anredenbuch,* Verlag Moderne Industrie, München, 1973). It started with *Abgeordneter* (congressman) and *Abt* (abbot) and ended with *Zollwachtmeister* (customs official) and *Zugführer* (train conductor). Although the book was already in its third edition, dated 1973, it showed little signs of use – proving the point that formalities like these have gradually diminished in importance.

Some practical advice

What is a non-German to do, when there are so many subtle nuances in how Germans address one another? It's fairly easy – most of them don't apply to non-Germans.

Which form of address you use probably depends mostly on whose home turf you meet.

If you are hosting Germans in the United States, do as you would with anyone else you know. However, keep in mind that Germans who have had little or no previous experience with easygoing American manners may consider *Du* and first names as an invitation to intimacy and close friendship to an extent you may not have intended.

When in Germany, remember that –

♦The German language offers two ways to address a person: "You" translates as either *"Du"* or *"Sie."*

♦*Du* usually is reserved for addressing

relatives, close friends and children (up to about 16 years) together with the first name.

♦ *Sie* should be used in all other cases, together with appropriate titles like *Herr* (Mr.), *Frau* (Mrs.) or *Fräulein* (Miss) and also together with the last name.

♦ When in doubt, always use *Sie* and wait for the other person to use *Du*.

♦ Avoid calling a person (adult) by his or her first name unless invited to do so.

♦ Also avoid offering to be called by your own first name ("Hi, I'm Bob") – at least right away and unless you really want to start a closer relationship.

Letter writing

♦ In letter writing, the letter should start with *Sehr geehrte Damen und Herren* (if you know no name) or *Sehr geehrte(r) Frau (Herr) Maier*; (the literal translation of Dear Mr. Maier would be *Lieber Herr Maier*, which would be appropriate only if you knew Herr Maier very well)

♦ If the person addressed (either verbally or in writing) holds a doctorate in any field, it should be used:

– *Frau Doktor (Dr.)* Maier
– *Herr Doktor (Dr.)* Maier

Wait for him or her to invite you to drop the "Doctor" – then call him (her) *Herr (Frau) Maier*. Almost all other titles (academic or otherwise) may be omitted without serious "breach of etiquette" – even if you should know them.

♦ When writing, be aware that – contrary to English usage – the addressee merits capital letters as a sign of respect in *Du* and *Sie* (instead of you), whereas modesty requires that *ich* starts with a small letter (instead of with a capital I).

Source: Rainer Thumshirn, "Du or Sie: A little Knigge on how Germans address one another," *Der Blumenbaum,* Vol. 15, No. 1, 1997.

THE GERMAN HANDSHAKE PACKET

Travelers to German-speaking countries who do not speak German may be interested in ordering a set of personalized introductory materials to ease the way. The German Handshake Packet is prepared by the Sacramento German Genealogy Society specifically for non-German speaking members in search of information about their German ancestors.

The Packet consists of several items designed to be helpful in communicating with German-speaking officials encountered in libraries, archives, and municipal offices, as well as to help in communicating with community members who may have information to offer. The Packet includes the following items:

Letter 1

This letter is written in German on the society's official letterhead (embossed with its official seal) and signed by the Society's president.

It introduces the traveler by name as a valued member of the Sacramento German Genealogy Society and states that, although the bearer of the letter does not speak German, he or she is researching his or her German ancestry during the trip abroad. It also states that the Society will appreciate any consideration the reader of the letter shows on behalf of the traveler.

The traveler carries one copy of this letter to each of the archives or libraries visited..

Letter 2

This letter, also written in German, is headed with the traveler's own address and carries the traveler's signature.

It explains that the bearer of the letter does not speak German but that the traveler's purpose in making the journey is to conduct research concerning one or more German ancestors.

It states that attachments to this letter provide whatever vital records the traveler has learned concerning the immigrant. The letter asks for the reader's suggestions for further research of the named ancestor and thanks the reader for any help given. Both letters (this one and the letter described above) are written in formal, polite German by a native German speaker.

The traveler carries about ten copies of this letter, to be used as needed.

Attached items

A set of attachments to Letter 2 consists of the major data thus far known about the ancestor(s) being researched. Written entirely in German, this information gives name, birth date, birth place, residence, year of emigration, and place of residence in the United States (insofar as such information is known) for the immigrant and for the immigrant's father and mother (as applicable). Attachments for more than one immigrant (each including the immigrant's parents) may be prepared at additional cost.

Translations

English translations of all three documents named above are included in the Packet.

Ordering

The German Handshake Packet must be ordered at least one month before the traveler's departure date. All applications must be submitted on the application form supplied by the Society. It is necessary to complete a separate application form for each additional immigrant. To obtain an application form, write to Sacramento German Genealogy Society, P.O. Box 660061, Sacramento, CA 95866-0061

Cost

The Packet is individually prepared for Society members for $5 for one immigrant ancestor (and parents). Preparation of data concerning additional immigrant ancestors (with parents) cost $5 each.

Applicants who are not members of the Sacramento German Genealogy Society pay an additional amount to cover annual dues in the Society ($30 or $35), as the letters introduce travelers as *members of the Society.*

PAYING IN EURO

There are times when researchers in other lands need to pay fees to persons or agencies in European countries where the Euro is used. Personal checks are not acceptable in Germany, foreign paper money is subject to lower exchange rates, and sending Euro currency incurs greater fees and is not totally reliable. A company known as the International Currency Express (ICE) can do this for you. Call (888) 278-6628 and ask them to prepare a "draft" (not a "check") to a person or agency you identify and for the Euro amount you wish to pay. ICE will collect that amount from you as a credit card transaction or a personal check (the cheaper option by about 3%) that you then mail to Europe. You may also pay by electronic transfer, but this requires additional account numbers from your bank. ICE then mails the draft to you in three to seven working days, after which it is your responsibility to send the draft to Europe.

A draft in Euro can also be ordered from ICE over the Internet. Follow these steps: 1) Go to www.foreignmoney.com . In the gray box click on "Buy foreign draft," and then click on "Order now." 2) Read "Please note the following," and then from "Select currency," select "Euro draft." Enter the amount of "foreign currency" you want, such as 20.00 for 20 Euro. Click on "Quote me," and then on "Next." 3) Review the quotation and click "Enter payee." Type in the payee's name. In the "Purpose" block, enter "gift" or "genealogy" or any other appropriate term (an entry is required). You may leave the "Reference" block blank. Click "Submit." 4) Review your order and edit it if necessary. Note that a fee of $10 has been added. 5) Click "Secure checkout" and provide the required information and your shipping address. Complete checkout. 6) In three to seven working days, you will receive your draft in the mail. You are responsible for mailing it to the payee in Europe.

AN ALTERNATE PAYMENT PLAN

Calling Germany

At times it may be necessary to pay small charges or make minimal donations to agencies or people in Europe. Rather than sending a check that will incur fees almost as great as the amount to be paid, it is still possible to send small bills (€ 5. € 10, € 20) through the mail to Germany and Austria. If one chooses to do so, it is a good idea to hide the bill(s) between two or three sheets of paper (that can still be sent from the United States at the lowest air mail rate). The same is true of U.S. currency, because some Europeans specifically request payments of $10 or $20.

THE GERMAN CARD

The German Card, laminated and the size of a credit card when folded, and containing eight panels that fold up, accordion-style, is designed to be carried in the German researcher's wallet at all times.

A creation of the Sacramento German Genealogy Society, *The German Card* provides the following information:
♦The complete German alphabet in the old Gothic script, both printed and handwritten, in both upper and lower case characters
♦A brief list of immigration information

as it applies to the various United States Federal Census records from 1850 through 1920
♦The key for interpreting the German genealogy symbols (birth, death, burial, christening, etc.) commonly used in German vital statistic records
♦The rules and the code for the Soundex system, necessary for finding census records
♦A list of some basic German genealogy resources, with Family History Library call numbers
♦Dates of civil registration in the German Empire

To purchase *The German Card*, send to the Sacramento German Genealogy Society, P.O. Box 660061, Sacramento, CA 95866-0061 the following:
♦A check for $5, payable to "SGGS," a
♦A long (business-size) envelope, self-addressed, and containing first class postage (the standard lowest rate)

TELEPHONING
TO AND FROM GERMANY

Calling Germany
from the United States

♦Dial 011, the code for reaching Europe; but a different code may be required for some long distance carriers and calling cards.
♦ Next, dial 49, the country code for Germany.
♦Next, dial the remaining digits of the telephone number, which consist of the area code* and the recipient's individual telephone number.
*The area code (*Vorwahl*), as usually printed on a business card, a letterhead, or an advertisement, begins with a zero. Note that German area codes may have 3, 4, or 5 digits, including the 0. The telephone number itself (the digits following the area code) consists of from 3 to 8 digits.

When calling from the United States,

do not dial the zero which precedes the area code. It is needed only if the call is placed within Germany from a location outside the calling area of the recipient. In other words, the zero serves the same purpose in Germany that the "1" serves in the United States.

Example: Calling 0 64 32 4501, dial 011 49 64 32 4501

Calling the United States from Germany

• Dial 001* (the country code for the United States and Canada).

• Next, dial the area code and the individual's telephone number.

Example: Calling (415) 232-5555, dial 001 415 232 5555.

*Some calling cards may be used to call the United States.

Long-distance telephone rates in Germany have dropped to historic lows. Germans can call the United States for as little as ⸜ 0.12 (U.S. $0.02), i.e., about one dollar per hour. Therefore it is not only no longer impolite to ask to use the host's phone for this purpose, but it is usually expected. Of course, you should continue to offer to pay for the privilege.

SELECTED TELEPHONE COUNTRY CODES

The following country codes are needed to call the respective countries *from the United States.*

To call these countries from Germany, add 00 before each code (Austria, 0043, etc.)

Note that the German words for the countries listed below are shown in parentheses (unless the German word is the same as that given):

• Austria (*Österreich*): 43
• Czech Republic (*Tschechische Republik*): 42
• Denmark (*Dänemark*): 45

• Finland (*Finnland*): 358
• France (*Frankreich*): 33
• Germany (*Deutschland*): 49
• Great Britain and North Ireland (*Großbritannien und Nordirland*): 44
• Hungary (*Ungarn*): 36
• Ireland (*Irland*): 353
• Italy (*Italien*): 39
• Japan: 0081
• Latvia (*Lettland*): 371
• Liechtenstein: 41
• Lithuania (*Litauen*): 370
• Luxemburg: 352
• Netherlands (*Niederlande*): 31
• Northern Ireland (*Nordirland*): 0044
• Poland (*Polen*): 48
• Russia (*Russische Föderation*): 7
• Spain (*Spanien*): 34
• Sweden (*Schweden*): 46
• Switzerland (*Schweiz*): 41
• Norway (*Norwegen*): 47

TELEPHONE CONVERSATION ALPHABET KEY

The following set of spelling aids is commonly used in the German language, especially in telephone conversations when it may be difficult to distinguish the difference, for example, between the sounds d and t, s and f, p and b, and so on.

A	Anton
Ä	Ärger
B	Berta
C	Cäsar
CH	Charlotte
D	Dora
E	Emil
F	Friedrich
G	Gustav
H	Heinrich
I	Ida
J	Julius
K	Kaufmann
L	Ludwig
M	Martha
N	Nordpol

O	Otto
Ö	Ökonom
P	Paula
Q	Quelle
R	Richard
S	Samuel
Sch	Schule
T	Theodor
U	Ulrich
Ü	Übermut
V	Viktor
W	Wilhelm
X	Xanthippe
Y	Ypsilon
Z	Zacharias

TIME ALERT!

When telephoning Germany or other western European countries, remember that –
◆Germany is on Central European Time, which is 6 hours ahead of Eastern Standard Time, and 9 hours ahead of Pacific Standard Time.
◆ Western Europe changes to daylight time on the last Sunday in March, and changes back again on the last Sunday in October.

GOETHE-INSTITUT
IN THE UNITED STATES

(Check the Internet for newer web and email addresses.)

◆ **Atlanta:** Goethe-Institut, German Cultural Center, Colony Square, Plaza Level, 1197 Peachtree Street, NE, Atlanta, GA 30361-2401. Tel. (404) 892-2388; Fax (404) 892-3832; info@atlanta.goethe.org
◆ **Boston:** Goethe-Institut, German Cultural Center for New England, 170 Beacon Street, Boston, MA 02116. Tel. (617) 262-6050; Fax (617) 262-2615; info@boston.goethe.org
◆ **Chicago:** Goethe-Institut, German Cultural Center, Suite 200, 150 North Michigan Avenue, Chicago, IL 60601. Tel. (312) 263-0472; Fax (312) 263-0476; info@chicago.goethe.org
◆**Cincinnati:** (closed June 1997)
◆ **Houston:** Goethe-Institut, German Cultural Center, 3120 Southwest Freeway, Suite 100, Houston, TX 77098. Tel. (713) 528-2787; Fax (713) 528-4023; program@goethe-houston.org
◆ **Los Angeles:** Goethe-Institut, 5750 Wilshire Boulevard 110, Los Angeles, CA 90036. Tel. (323) 525-3388; Fax (323) 934-3597; gila@artnet.net
◆**New York:** Goethe House New York, German Cultural Center, 1014 Fifth Avenue, New York, NY 10028. Tel. (212) 439-8700; Fax (212) 439-8705; library@goethe-newyork.org
◆ **San Francisco:** Goethe-Institut, 530 Bush Street, San Francisco, CA 94108. Tel. (415) 263-8765; Fax (415) 391-8715; gisfprog@aol.com
◆ **Seattle** Goethe-Institut, Mutual Life Building, 605 First Avenue, Suite 401, Seattle, WA 98104. Tel. (206) 622-9694; Fax (206) 623-7930; goethe@eskimo.com
◆**Washington, DC:** Goethe-Institut, 810 Seventh Street NW Washington, D.C. 20001-3718. Tel. (202) 289-1200; Fax (202) 289-3535; info@goethe-de.org

GOETHE-INSTITUT IN GERMANY

◆**Berlin:** Goethe Institut berlin@goethe.de
◆**Bonn:** Goethe Institut bonn @goethe.de
◆**Bremen:** Goethe Institut bremen@goethe.de
◆**Dresden:** Goethe Institut dresden@goethe.de
◆**Düsseldorf:** Goethe Institut duesseldorf@goethe.de
◆**Frankfurt am Main:** Goethe-Institut frankfurt@goethe.de
◆**Freiburg:** Goethe Institut

freiburg@goethe.de
◆**Göttingen:** Goethe Institut
goettingen@goethe.de
◆**Mannheim-Heidelberg**
mannheim@goethe.de
◆**München:**
muenchen@ goethe.de
◆**Schwäbisch Hall:**
schwaebisch-hall@goethe.de
◆**Weimar:**
weimar@goethe.de

MAX KADE INSTITUTES

◆**Max Kade Institute for German-
American Studies at the University of
Wisconsin-Madison,** 901 University
Bay Drive, Madison, WI 53705. Tel.
(608) 262-7546; Fax (608) 265-4640;
maxkade@macc.wisc.edu
◆**Max Kade German-American
Research Institute,** 304 Burrowes
Building, Pennsylvania State
University, University Park, PA 16802-
6203. Tel. (814) 863-9537; Fax (814) 865-
5482; gari@psu.edu
◆**Max Kade German-American
CenterIndiana University-Purdue
University at Indianapolis,** 401 East
Michigan Street, Indianapolis, IN
46204. Tel. (317) 464-9004; Fax (317)
630-0035
◆**Max Kade German-American
Document and Research Center,**
Department of Germanic Languages
and Literatures, University of Kansas,
Lawrence, KS 66045.

THE GERMAN
INFORMATION CENTER

**German Information Center
Embassy of the Federal Republic of
Germany
4645 Reservoir Road, NW
Washington, DC 20007
Tel. (202) 298-4000**

**gic1@ix.netcom.com
www.germany-info.org**

Hours
Monday-Thursday, 8 am to 4:30 pm
Friday 8 am to 3 pm.
Programs
The German Information Center in
New York welcomes media profession-
als, students, and researchers to use its
resources for information about many
aspects of German life.
The German Information Center
should not, however, be considered a
genealogical resource.
Fact-checkers from major publications regularly use German Information
Center services to ensure accuracy in
writing stories pertaining to individual
Germans and topics concerning Germany.
Library
The library's 3,500-volume library is
open to the public. Most of its books
are written in German, although quite a
few English-language books are included as well. Political, historical and
economic texts make up the bulk of the
collection.
Access to the German Information
Center's archive is available upon request. Since 1961, it has collected newspaper clippings, press releases, and government publications on a broad range
of topics.
Areas of particular concentration are
German domestic politics, German-
American relations, German social policy,
and environmental protection.
The German Information Center is a
major source of information on Germany,
but it does *not* cover such topics as family history, tourism, culture, and business.
Publications
The Week in Germany, an Internet
newsletter in English, is available upon
request and continues to provide readers with the latest information on poli-

tics, the economy, sports and the arts in Germany.

Deutschland Nachrichten is a weekly newsletter in German that covers politics, economics, cultural, and supports news from Germany and includes a review of German newspaper editorials.

Subscriptions to both these publications are free upon request.

GERMAN EMBASSIES AND CONSULATES

United States

♦ Embassy of the Federal Republic of Germany, 4645 Reservoir Road N.W., Washington, DC 20007-1998. Tel. (202) 298-4000

♦ **Atlanta:** Consulate General of the Federal Republic of Germany, Marquis Two Tower, Ste. 901, 285 Peachtree Center Avenue, NE, Atlanta, GA 30303-1221. Tel. (404) 659-4760; Fax (404) 659-1280. Jurisdiction: Alabama, Georgia, Mississippi, North Carolina, South Carolina, Tennessee

♦ **Boston:** Consulate General of the Federal Republic of Germany, 3 Copley Place, Suite 500, Boston, MA 02116. Tel. (617) 369-4900 or (617) 369-4934 (operator); Fax (617) 369-4940. Jurisdiction: Connecticut (except Fairfield County), Maine, Massachusetts, New Hampshire, Rhode Island, Vermont

♦ **Chicago:** Consulate General of the Federal Republic of Germany, 676 North Michigan Avenue, Ste. 3200, Chicago, IL 60611. Tel. (312) 202-0480; Fax (312) 202-0466. Jurisdiction: Illinois, Iowa, Kansas, Minnesota, Missouri, Nebraska, North Dakota, South Dakota, Wisconsin

♦ **Houston:** Consulate General of the Federal Republic of Germany, 1330 Post Oak Blvd., Ste. 1850, Houston, TX 77056-3818. Tel. (713) 627-7770. Jurisdiction Arkansas, Louisiana, New Mexico, Oklahoma, Texas

♦ **Los Angeles:** Consulate General of the Federal Republic of Germany, 6222 Wilshire Boulevard, Ste. 500, Los Angeles, CA 90048. Tel. (323) 930-2703; Fax (323) 930-2805. Jurisdiction: Imperial, Kern, Los Angeles, Orange, Riverside, San Bernardino, SanDiego, SanLuis Obispo, Santa Barbara, and Ventura of the state of California; Arizona

♦ **Miami:** Consulate General of the Federal Republic of Germany, 100 N. Biscayne Bouevard, Ste. 2200, Miami, FL 33132. Tel. (305) 358-0290; Fax (305) 358-0307. Jurisdiction: Florida, Puerto Rico, Ameri-can Virgin Islands

♦ **New York:** German Consulate General 871 United Nations Plaza, New York, NY 10017. Tel. (212) 610-9700; Fax (212) 610-9702. Jurisdiction: New York; New Jersey; Pennsylvania; Fairfield County; Connec-ticut; Bermuda

♦ **San Francisco:** Consulate General of the Federal Republic of Germany, 1960 Jackson Street, San Francisco, CA 94109. Tel. (415) 775-1061; Fax (415) 775-0187. Jurisdiction: California (except Imperial, Kern, Los Angeles, Orange, Riverside, San Bernardino, San Diego, San Luis Obispo, Santa Barbara, and Ventura Counties); Colorado, Hawaii, Nevada, Utah, Wyoming, and the U.S. territories (Baker, Howland, Jarvis, Johnston, Midway, and Palmyra Islands)

GERMAN CHAMBERS OF COMMERCE IN THE UNITED STATES

♦ **Atlanta:** German American Chamber of Commerce, 3475 Lenox Road N.E., Ste. 620, Atlanta, GA 30326. Tel. (404) 239-9494; Fax (404) 264-1761. Jurisdiction: Alabama, Florida, Georgia, North Carolina, South Carolina, Tennessee

♦ **Chicago:** German American Chamber of Commerce, 401 North Michigan Avenue, Ste. 2525, Chicago, IL 60611-4212,

Tel. (312) 644-2662; Fax (312) 644-0738. Jurisdiction: Illinois, Indiana, Iowa, Kansas, Kentucky, Michigan, Minnesota, Missouri, Nebraska, North Dakota, Ohio, South Dakota, Wisconsin
◆**Houston:** German American Chamber of Commerce, 5599 San Felipe, Ste. 510, Houston, TX 77056. Tel. (713) 877-1114; Fax (713) 877-1602. Jurisdiction: Arkansas, Louisiana, Mississippi, Oklahoma, Texas
◆**Los Angeles:** German American Chamber of Commerce,5220 Pacific Concourse Drive, Los Angeles, CA 90045. Tel. (310) 297-7979; Fax (310) 297-7966. Jurisdiction: Arizona, California (south of Fresno), Colorado, Nevada (southern part – Las Vegas), New Mexico, Utah
◆**New York:** German American Chamber of Commerce, 40 West 57th Street, 31st Floor, New York, NY 10019-4092. Tel (212) 974-8830; Fax (212) 974-8867. Jurisdiction: Connecticut, Delaware, Maine, Massachusetts, New Hampshire, New Jersey, New York, Rhode Island, Vermont, Puerto Rico
◆**Philadelphia:** German American Chamber of Commerce, Philadelphia Chapter, 1515 Market Street, Ste. 505, Philadelphia, PA 19102. Tel. (215) 665- 1585; Fax (215) 665-0375. Jurisdiction: Delaware, southern New Jersey (includ-ing Princeton), eastern Pennsylania (including Harrisburg)
◆ **San Francisco:** German American Chamber of Commerce, 465 California Street, Ste. 910, San Francisco, CA 94104. Tel (415) 392-2262; Fax (415) 392-1314. Jurisdiction: Alaska, Bahamas, California (north of Fresno), Hawaii, Idaho, Montana, northern Nevada (Reno), Oregon, Washington, Wyoming

---

GERMAN TOURISM HEAD-QUARTERS IN THE UNITED STATES

◆**German National Tourist Office**
122 East 42nd Street, 20th Floor, Ste.

2000; New York, NY 10168-0072. Tel. (212) 661-7200; Fax (212) 661-7174; GermanyInfo@d-z-t.com; www.cometo germany.com

---

GERMAN-RELATED ORGANIZATIONS IN THE UNITED STATES

◆**German Wine Information Bureau**
245 Fifth Avenue, Suite 2204, New York, NY 10016. Tel. (212) 896-3336; Fax (212) 896-3342; info@german-wineusa.org; www.germanwineusa.org
◆**German Village Meeting Haus,** 588 Third Street, Columbus, OH 43215. Tel. (614) 221-8888
◆**German-American Joint Action Committee (GAJAC),** P.O. Box 5488, Washington, DC 20016-5488. (Umbrella organization of the first three German-American organizations listed immediately below, which work together to prepare German American Day)
◆**German-American National Congress (DANK):** Deutsch-Amerikanischer Nationalkongress Executive Offices, 4740 N. Western Avenue, Ste. 206, Chicago, IL 60625-2013. Tel. (773) 275-1100; Fax (773) 275-4010; office@dank.org
◆**Steuben Society of America,** National Council, 6705 Fresh Pond Road, Ridgewood, NY 11385. Tel. (718) 381-0900; Fax (718) 628-4874
◆**United German-American Committee of the USA (UGAC-USA),** Vereinigtes Deutsch-Amerikanische Komitee: (headquarters) 9130 Academy Road, Philadelphia, PA 19114; (business office) UGAC-USA, 583 Broadway, Westwood, NJ 07675. Tel. (201) 664-2400; Fax (201) 664-9478; ugac@bellatlantic.net; www.ugac.org
◆**American Association of Teachers of German, Inc. (AATG),**112 Haddontowne Court No. 104,Cherry Hill, NJ 08034-3668. Tel. (856) 795-5553; Fax

(856)795-9398; aatg@ bell atlantic. net
♦**German Studies Association,** Arizona State University, Box 87 32 04, Tempe, AZ 85287-3204. Tel. (602) 965-4839; Fax (602) 965-8989
♦**German Language Society,** P.O. Box 4811, Washington, DC 20008. Tel. (202) 333-6281
♦**Society for German American Studies,** Blegen Library, University of Cincinnati, P.O. Box 210 113, Cincinnati, OH 45221-0113. Tel. (513) 556-1959; Fax: (513) 556-2113
♦**Center for German & European Studies,** Edmund A. Walsh School of Foreign Service, Georgetown University, Washington, DC 20057. Tel. (202) 687-5602; Fax (202) 687-8359
♦**Center for German & European Studies,** University of California, 254 Moses Hall, Berkeley, CA 94720-2316. Tel. (510) 643-5777; Fax (510) 643-5996; cges@berkeley.edu
♦**Center for German and European Studies,** 214 Social Science Building, 267 19th Avenue South, Minneapolis, MN 55455.; www.cges.umn. edu
♦**American Council on Germany,** 14 East 60th Street, Ste. 1000, New York, NY 10022. Tel.: (212) 826-3636. Fax: (212) 758-3445.E-Mail info@acgusa.org
♦**American Institute for Contemporary German Studies,** The Johns Hopkins University, 1400 16th Street, N.W., Suite 420, Washington, D.C. 20036-2217. Tel. (202) 332-9312; Fax (202) 265-9531 aicgsdoc@jhunix.hcf.jhu.edu
♦**Deutsches Historisches Institut,**1607 New Hampshire Avenue, NW, Washington, DC 20009. Tel. (202) 387-3355; Fax (202) 387-6437
♦**Center for Immigration Research Temple University - Balch Institute for Ethnic Studies,** 18 South 7th Street, Philadelphia, PA 19106. Tel.: (215) 922-3454; Fax: (215) 922-3201
♦**The German Marshall Fund of the United States,** 11 Dupont Circle, NW, Ste. 750, Washington, DC 20036. Tel.

(202) 745-3950; Fax (202) 265-1662
♦**Germanic-American Institute,** (formerly the Volksfest Association of Minnesota), 301 Summit Avenue, St. Paul, MN 55102. Tel. (651) 222-7027; Fax (651) 222-6295.
♦**Institute for German-American Relations,** 9380 McKnight Road, Ste. 102, Pittsburgh, PA 15237. Tel (412) 364-0812; Fax (412) 364-1539
♦**Ellis Island Immigration Museum,** Statue of Liberty National Monument, Ellis Island/Liberty Island, New York, NY 10044. Tel. (212) 363-3200; Fax (212) 363-8347

GERMAN SCHOOLS IN THE UNITED STATES

♦**Deutsche Schule Washington, DC,** 8617 Chateau Drive, Potomac, MD 20854. Tel. (301) 365-4400; Fax: (301) 365-3905
♦**Deutsche Schule New York,** 50 Partridge Road, White Plains, NY 10605. Tel. (914) 948-6514; Fax: (914) 948-6529
♦**Deutsch-Amerikanische Schule San Francisco,** 275 Elliott Drive, Menlo Park, CA 94025. Tel. (415) 324-8617; Fax: (415) 324-9548
♦**German Language School Conference (GLSC),** 154 Middle River Road, Danbury, CT 06810. Tel. (203) 792-2795. (An association of private German language schools in the United States (for the most part Saturday schools.)
♦**German School, Sacramento Turn Verein German-American Cultural Center,** 3349 J Street, Sacramento, CA 95816. Tel. (916) 488-7922; Fax: (916) 488-0688; ai_sch@ pacbell.net

INTERNATIONAL BOOK FINDING SERVICE (IBIS)

The International Book Import Service (IBIS) offers years of import experience and comes highly recommended.

The service provices bookstores, libraries, school, and individuals with any title
published in Germany (and in other
countries as well) either from the IBIS
inventory or by special order.

Individuals may prepay by credit
card, check, or money order. The email
address (the best way to order or send
an inquiry) is: ibis@IBIService.com. Telephone: (800)-277-4247 (8:00 a.m. to 4:00
p.m. CST, Monday-Friday). Mailing address: International Book Import Service,
Inc., 161 Main Street, P. O. Box 8288,
Lynchburg, TN 37352-8188.

HIRING A PROFESSIONAL FAMILY HISTORY RESEARCHER

There comes a time when the
researcher cannot (or prefers not to)
do the work for her- or himself and
decides to engage a professional
researcher to assist or to take on the
project independently. A look in one's
favorite Internet search engine for
"professional genealogists German"
(or similar wording) will yield several
websites announcing such persons. A
specific inquiry should be addressed
to each candidate with questions such
as these:

1) Are you qualified to do the work
I need to have done?

2) When can you begin or complete
the project?

3) What do you charge per hour?

4) Do you require a retainer and if
so, how much?

5) How or when is the payment to
be made?

6) In what form do you report your
research results?

7) Can you provide references?

Hiring a qualified professional can
be a very rewarding experience and
can allow a family tree to grow,
whereas the research otherwise might
be stymied. The following article
offers more suggestions regarding the
relationship between the client and
the professional researcher:

Roger P. Minert, "Professional Family
History Researchers and Their Clients:
Working Together for the Common
Good." *Palatine Immigrant*, 30:1
(2005), n.p.

Section 3: Emigration and Immigration

•

The emigration/immigration experience
The records: Ship departures and arrivals
Transportation to the ports in German lands
Immigration processing and naturalization
Germans' neighbors in and outside the
former German Empire

•

TIMELINE OF EMIGRATION LAWS AND POLICIES IN EUROPE

1724: A Palatinate ordinance threatened confiscation of property in response to the heavy emigration to Pennsylvania. Further Palatine ordinances followed in 1752, 1753, 1764, 1766, 1767, 1769, 1770, and 1779 "to counteract with the necessary vigour the evil whose injuriousness grows the longer it persists." (Between 1709 and 1815, Württemberg issued 18 similar ordinances.)

1768: Emperor Joseph II's edict prohibited "all migration by German imperial subjects to foreign countries having no connection with the empire." The edict contained severe punishments to be imposed on those who disobeyed, called for the immediate arrest of those involved in secret emigration, and even imposed a ban on assemblies. A contemporary document from Upper Hesse reads, "The alleged reasons, namely a great burden of debt and insufficient food supplies, are not enough to justify the supplicants fleeing in such arbitrary manner from their hereditary sovereign and from the country in which they were born, brought up and hitherto nourished; on the contrary, it is their bounden duty to remain in the country and . . . to hope for the return of better and more blessed times."

1815 and following: With the establishment of the German Confederation in 1815 came a liberalization of emigration policy. Also, several individual states wrote the principle of freedom of emigration into their constitutions or granted that freedom through ordinances or laws. As early as 1803, Baden took such measures, followed by Württemberg in 1815, Prussia in 1818, and Hesse in 1821. In almost all states of the Confederation, conditions were laid down before permission to emigrate was granted: Men had to have completed their military service, men with families required the consent of their wives, and all debts had to be paid.

1832: In an early example of beginnings of government protection of emigrants, the city state of Bremen passed an ordinance protecting emigrants from bad treatment, at the same time cultivating the city's traf-fic in emigration as it sought to compete with the ports of Rotterdam, Antwerp and Le Havre.

The ordinance of 1832 set out guidelines by which shipowners were required to keep passenger lists, to have food supplies for 90 days on board, and to provide proof of the seaworthiness of their ships.

1837 onwards: Similar ordinances were adopted in Hamburg.

1846-47: Following the great wave of emigration in these years, the Frankfurt National Assembly tried but failed to adopt a uniform emigration policy. In 1878, a similar bill was presented to the Reichstag, but it too failed.

1897: Finally, a uniform, imperial ruling, the Imperial Act on Emigration, was achieved, which contained detailed regu-lations for agents and entre-preneurs involved in the transport of emigrants. Its goal was to steer emigrants into territories where colonies would serve the interests of the empire.

1975: The Federal Republic of Germany enacted a law superseding that of 1897 by which freedom of migration was estab-lished, with the government serving in an advisory capacity only.

Source: Ingrid Schöberl, "Emigration Policy in Germany and Immigration Policy in the United States," *Germans to America: 300 Years of Immigration, 1683-1983,* ed. Günter Moltman, Institute for Foreign Relations, Stuttgart, in cooperation with Inter Nationes, Bonn, Bad Godesberg, 1982.

THE REDEMPTIONERS

Redemption was a system of payment for ship passage through labor given by emigrant passengers.

La Vern Rippley, in his book *The German Americans*[1] (which should be required reading for German family history searchers) offers the following explanation of "redemptioning":

"Shipping companies often transported European emigrants to America without directly charging the passengers.

"Occasionally, a local ruler in a German principality also resorted to selling his 'sons' to a shipper or a foreign government for what little they would bring on the auction block. 'Redemptioning' was, therefore, the process by which agents loaded ships with able-bodied men and proceeded to anchor in an American port where the newcomers were sold to the highest bidder.

"Since the shipping company had born the costs of transportation without charging the passenger, potential employers in America reimbursed the shipper when paying the going price for an emigrant who in turn worked for as many years as were necessary to redeem the cost of passage.

"In a land where the sale of black slaves was taken for granted, we should not be surprised to learn that the redemption of Germans was scarcely frowned upon by anyone.

"American laws binding the contracts of redemption continued in effect until 1819 when the United States Congress passed a law, not abolishing redemption, but limiting the weight of passengers permitted on ships docking at United States ports . . . .

"This action effectively outlawed shipment in steerage, which brought with it an end to the system of redemption because the law ruled out the possibility of huge profits."

Further information

German Immigration Servant Contracts: Registered at the Port of Philadelphia, 1817-1831. Farley Grubb. Baltimore, MD, Genealogical Publishing Co.,

1994.

[1]La Vern J. Rippley, *The German Americans.* University Press of America, New York, 1984.

HOW THE 'REDEMPTIONING' SYSTEM WORKED

Gottlieb Mittelberger, an emigrant to Pennsylvania from Württemberg in 1750, wrote this account of his first-hand experiences with the redemptioner system:

"When the ships have landed at Philadelphia after their long voyage, no one is permitted to leave them except those who pay for their passage or can give good security; the others who cannot pay must remain on board the ships till they are purchased, and are released from the ships by their purchasers.

"The sick always fare the worst, for the healthy are naturally preferred and purchased first; and so the sick and wretched must often remain on board in front of the city for two or three weeks, and frequently die, whereas many a one if he could pay his debt and was permitted to leave the ship immediately might recover. . . .

"The sale of human beings in the market on board the ship is carried on thus: Every day, Englishmen, Dutchmen, and High German people come from the city of Philadelphia and other places, some from a great distance, say 60, 90, and 120 miles away, and go on board the newly arrived ship that has brought and offers for sale passengers from Europe, and select among the healthy persons such as they deem suitable for their business, and bargain with them how long they will serve for their passage money, for which most of them are still in debt. When they have come to an agreement, it happens that adult persons bind themselves in writing to serve three, four, five, or six years for the amount due by them, according to their strength and age. But

very young people, from 10 to 15 years, must serve until they are 21 years old.

"Many persons must sell and trade away their children like so many head of cattle; for if their children take the debt upon themselves, the parents can leave the ship free and unrestrained; but as the parents often do not know where and to what people their children are going, it often happens that such parents and children, after leaving the ship, do not see each other again for years, perhaps no more in all their lives.

"When people arrive who cannot make themselves free, but have children under five years of age, they cannot free themselves by them; for such children must be given to somebody without compensation to be brought up, and they must serve for their bringing up till they are 21 years old. Children from five to ten years, who pay half price for their passage, must likewise serve for it until they are 21 years old; they cannot, therefore, redeem their parents by taking the debt of the latter upon themselves. but children above 10 years can take part of their parents' debts upon themselves.

"A woman must stand for her husband if he arrives sick, and in like manner a man for his sick wife, and take the debt upon herself or himself, and thus serve five or six years not alone for his or her own debt, but also for that of the sick husband or wife.

"But if both are sick, such persons are sent from the ship to the hospital, but not until it appears probable that they will find no purchasers. As soon as they are well again they must serve for their passage, or pay if they have means.

"It often happens that whole families, husband, wife and children, are separated by being sold to different purchasers, especially when they have not paid any part of their passage money.

"When a husband or wife has died at sea, after the ship has completed more than half her trip, the survivor must pay or serve not only for himself or herself, but also for the deceased.

"When both parents died after the voyage was more than half completed, their children, especially when they are young and have nothing to pawn or pay, must stand for their own and their parents' passage, and serve till they are 21 years old.

"When one has served his or her term, he or she is entitled to a new suit of clothes at parting, and, if it has been so stipulated, a man gets, in addition, a horse; and a woman a cow.

"When a servant has an opportunity to marry in this country, he or she must pay for each year he or she would still have to serve £5 or £6. But many a one who has thus purchased and paid for his bride, has subsequently repented of his bargain, so that he would gladly have returned his dear ware and lost his money in addition.

"If a servant in this country runs away from his master who has treated him harshly, he cannot get far. Good provision has been made for such cases so that a runaway is soon recovered. He who detains or returns a deserter receives a good reward.

"If such a runaway has been away from his master a single day, he must serve an entire week for it; if absent a week, then a month, and for a month, half a year. But if the master does not care to keep the runaway when he gets him back, he may sell him for as many years as he has still to serve."[1]

[1]*The Pennsylvania-German Society Proceedings and Addresses at Ephrata, Oct. 20, 1899*. Vol. X, 1900; Chapter III.

FOOD ON BOARD EMIGRANT SHIPS

The food served on German immigrant ships in the 1850s seems to have been fairly standardized. This is an example of a week's menu:

Sunday: salt meat, meal pudding, and prunes
Monday: salt bacon, pea soup, and potatoes
Tuesday: salt meat, rice, and prunes
Wednesday: smoked bacon, sauerkraut, and potatoes
Thursday: salt meat, potatoes, and bean soup
Friday: herring, meal, and prunes
Saturday: salt bacon, pea soup, and potatoes
Source: Richard O'Connor, *The German-Americans: An Informal History*. Little, Brown and Co., Boston, 1968.

Another recorded menu for steerage passengers traveling in 1846 from Bremen to New York, Baltimore, Philadelphia, New Orleans and Galveston offered the following fare:

Sunday: Meat or salt pork and pudding with potatoes
Monday: Meat or salt pork and beans or peas with potatoes
Tuesday: Meat or salt pork and beans or peas with potatoes
Wednesday: Salt pork and sauerkraut with potatoes
Thursday: Meat or salt pork and peas or beans with potatoes
Friday: Meat and rice soup or oatmeal soup with potatoes
Saturday: Rice or barley with prunes and syrup.

The portions for each passenger per week are listed as follows: 3 pounds of black bread, 2 pounds of white bread, 3/8 pound of butter, 2° pounds meat, and 1 pound of salt pork or ∫ pound smoked pork In addition, "Each morning coffee and every afternoon tea or coffee. [Also] sufficient vegetables and drinking water."

PACKING FOOD
FOR THE OCEAN VOYAGE

In 1822, not long after his arrival in America, the nineteen-year-old German immigrant Louis Jüngerich wrote a long letter to his mother, brother, and sister in Hessen, from the farm where he was living in Lancaster County, Pennsylvania.

In his letter, he gave specific instructions for any family members who were anticipating a trip to America, including advice on what food to pack for the trip.

He advised his relatives back home to sign onto a ship for the the ocean voyage only (to "cut the cost of provisioning by thirty Gulden"), and then to obtain food supplies on their own, to last 90 days. (The voyage could be expected to last that long.)

His list of recommended provisions to pack *for each person* for the voyage reads as follows:

* 55 pounds of ship's zwieback or hardtack
* "6, 8, 9, or 10, or even 12 pounds of butter, depending on circumstances"
* 2 bushels of potatoes or more
* salt
* 15 pounds of flour
* 8 pounds of rice
* 4 pounds of barley
* "any amount of peas, beans, and some meat stock for a fresh soup"
* vinegar to drink   ("absolutely necessary"; described by Jüngerich as "ship's water"; vinegar was considered helpful for   digestion and as an antidote to scurvy)
* tea, sugar, chocolate, and brandy ("as you wish")
* 20 pounds of well salted beef
* 6 pounds of bacon for fat
* lemons
* dried plums ("and other small items")
* pepper

Cooking utensils recommended for the ship passage included,
* "2 tin kettles to cook meals, and one for liquids"
* spoons, knives, forks and cups

The young immigrant reported to his family his favorite meal aboard ship:

"Our best meals were as follows: I took the ship's zwieback or hardtack that was handed out to us and butter, soaked the zwieback so that it became spongy, and cooked it in water, adding the butter. This was our best dish and could not compare with what was given out on the ship only at the noon hour."

(A translation note on this item of the letter explains that the zwieback referred to was not "the familiar twice-toasted rusks, but rather a biscuit-like bread product baked especially to travel well and remain palatable in the process.")

Source: Levine, Neil Ann Stuckey, Ursula Roy, and David J. Rempel Smucker, "Trans-Atlantic Advice: An 1822 Letter by Louis C. Jüngerich (1803-1882)," *Pennsylvania Mennonite Heritage,* Vol. XIX, No. 3, July 1996.

OVERVIEW OF GERMAN
EMIGRATION TO AMERICA

* **Colonial period:** 65,000 to 100,000 Germans (about 8% or 9% of total population of the colonies)
* **1816-1914:** 5.5 million Germans
* World War I to present: About 1.5 million more Germans
* **Altogether:** More than 7 million Germans (this number does not take into account return migration)
* **Peak years of German immigration:** 1854 (215,000); and 1882 (250,000)
* **Second half of nineteenth century:** Americans born in Germany as a rule made up more than 30 percent of all Americans born abroad and more than 4 percent of the total population
* **Total immigration to the United States since 1920:** More than 46 million, of which Germans made up the largest

GERMAN IMMIGRATION BY DECADE

Decade	Total Immigration	German Immigration	German as Percentage of Total Immigration
1820-29	128,502.	5,753	4.5
1830-39	538,381	124,726	23.2
1840-49	1,427,337	385,434	27.0
1850-59	2,814,554	976,072	34.7
1860-69	2,081,261	723,734	34.8
1870-79	2,742,137	751,769	27.4
1880-89	5,248,568	1,445,181	27.5
1890-99	3,694,294	579,072	15.7
1900-09	8,202,388	328,722	4.0
1910-19	6,347,380	174,227	2.7
1920-29	4,295,510	386,634	9.0
1930-39	699,375	119,107	17.0
1940-49	856,608	117,506	14.0
1950-59	2,499,268	576,905	23.1
1960-69	3,213,749	209,616	6.5
1970	373,326	10,632	2.8
Total	45,162,638	6,917,090	15.3

U.S. Bureau of Census

share, about 15 percent. The table on the next page indicates patterns of German immi-gration in a 150-year period, as well as the relative concentration of Germans among all immigrants.

Source: Günter Moltmann, "Three Hundred Years of German Emigration to North Ameri-ca," translated by William D. Graf. Günter Moltmann, ed., *Germans to America: 300 Years of Immigration 1683-1983,* Institute for Foreign Cultural Relations, Stuttgart, with Inter Nationen, Bonn-Godesberg, 1982.

THE FIRST GERMANS IN AMERICA

In 1997, an historic marker was placed at Jamestown by the German Heritage Society of Greater Washington, DC to commemorate the arrival of the first Germans in America in Jamestown in 1608.

The text of the marker, headed, "First Germans at Jamestown," reads,

"The first Germans to land in Jamestown, the first permanent English settlement in Virginia, arrived aboard the Mary and Margaret about October 1, 1608.

"These Germans were glass makers and carpenters. In 1620, German mineral specialists and saw millwrights followed to work and settle in the Virginia colony.

"These pioneers and skilled craftsmen were the forerunners of the many millions of Germans who settled in America and became the single largest national group to populate the United States."

This marker at Jamestown, confirming the history of the arrival of the first Germans in America, is an important step toward celebration of the German-American quadricentennial in the year 2008.

The project was sponsored by the German American Heritage Society of Greater Washington DC, 4207 Oxford Dr., Suitland, MD 2074. Tel. (301) 423-3937. **Source:** *Society for German American Studies Newsletter,* Vol. 17, No. 4, Dec. 1996.

HAMBURG PASSENGER LISTS

The Hamburg passenger lists may be accessed either through the microfilms of the Family History Library or online as part of the Ancestry.com Immigration Collection.

Go to www.ancestry.com, press the drop down arrow next to the "Search" tab and select "Card Catalog." In the "Title" window, type "Hamburg lists" and press "Search."

Images in this collection are available to browse, but have not yet been indexed for a keyword search.

Using the microfilms

To find the microfilm numbers for the Hamburg Passenger Lists, go to the Family History Library Catalong. Select "Place," enter "Hamburg" and select "Germany, Hamburg, Hamburg." Then select "Emigration and Immigration" and find the entry beginning with the words "Auswanderer Listen 1850-1934."

On the compact disc version of the Family History Library Catalog, select the computer number search and enter 11064.

Direct and Indirect lists

♦Direct Lists (with index): for passengers traveling directly, non-stop, from Hamburg to a foreign destination
♦Indirect (with index): for passengers who traveled from Hamburg to a foreign destination, but who made a stop between the two points

Indexes

Most of the Hamburg passenger lists have been indexed. The lists for 1850-1854 do not require indexing because they are arranged alphabetically.

The two sets of indexes are,
1. The 15-year index to the Direct Hamburg Passenger Lists, 1856-1871
2. The regular indexes

Steps in using the indexes

♦If the departure was between 1850 and 1854, search the alphabetical passenger *lists* for those years.
♦If the departure was between 1856 and 1871, search the 15-year index first (but this is not a complete list).
♦If the person is not found in the 15-year index, search the regular index. (Both the direct and the indirect passenger lists have regular indexes, divided into segments for a year or part of a year. The direct indexes begin in 1854 and end in 1934. The indirect indexes begin in 1854 and end in 1910.)

Index contents

The index entry shows:
♦Name of ship
♦Departure date
♦Name of passenger
♦Name of ship's captain
♦Name of destination port
♦Page number on which information is found on the actual passenger lists

Availability

The microfilmed lists and indexes may be borrowed from the Family History Library in Salt Lake City, through its local Family History Centers. For more information see:
♦ *The Hamburg Passenger Lists* (Salt Lake City, Utah; Genealogical Society of UT, 1984; FHL fiche 6000034).
♦ *Register and Guide to the Hamburg Passenger Lists, 1850-1934.* Research Paper Series C, No. 30. Salt lake City: The Genealogical Department of The Church of Jesus Christ of Latter-day Saints.

COORDINATING THE HAMBURG PASSENGER LISTS WITH U.S PASSENGER LISTS

Once it has been determined that a ship arrived in the United States on a specific date from Hamburg, the book listed below will show the researcher the date of departure and the FHL microfilm that includes the Hamburg passenger list for that ship and voyage. This book also identifies the location (volume number and page number) of the transcibed U.S. passenger list in the series *Germans to America*. The book thus allows the researcher to forego a search of the indexes of the Hamburg passenger lists.

Minert, Roger P., Kathryn Boeckel and Caren Winters, *Germans to America and the Hamburg Passenger Lists: Coordinated Schedules* [Heritage Books, Westminster, MD 2005].

HAMBURG POLICE RECORDS

Because Hamburg was a major port city, thousands of Germans (and those of other ethnic groups) took up temporary residence there before departing the country. In accordance with the regulations in force in the German lands, it was necessary for travelers to register at the resident registration office, whose records have been preserved. Usually it was the police department that was in charge of such registrations.

The information in these records is often better than that of the passenger lists, and they begin several years earlier than the Hamburg passenger lists that are available.

The resident registers give the former residence of the traveler as well as the actual place of birth. The passenger lists, however, give only the last place of residence.

The types of records available

through the Family History Library are,
* Passport Applications (*Reisepaß Proto-kolle*), 1852-1929
* Register of Non-citizen Resident Servants (*Allgemeine Fremden Melde-protokolle*) 1843-1890
* Register of Male and Female Non-citizen Laborers and Domestics (*Fremde Männ-liche und Weibliche Dienst-boten*) 1834-1899
* Register of Guilded Journeymen (*Fremde zünftige Gesellen*) 1850-1867

Search the Family History Library Catalog for microfilm and microfiche numbers, listed under Germany - Hamburg - "Emigration and Immigration," "Occupations," and "Population."

PASSENGER LIST INDEXES IN THE NATIONAL ARCHIVES

The years of passenger list indexes created by the WPA during the Depression, available through the National Archives and Records Administration include, from these ports:
* Baltimore: 1820-1897 and 1897-1952
* Boston: 1848-1891, 1902-1906, and 1906-1920
* New Orleans: 1853-1899 and 1900-1952
* New York: 1820-1846, 1897-1902, 1902-1943, and 1944-1948
* Philadelphia: 1800-1906 and 1883-1948

Other indexes to passenger arrivals and other resources are available to substitute for the missing periods above.

Passenger list indexes allow researchers to identify specific passengers, then locate them on passenger ship arrival lists.

STEAMSHIP ARRIVALS (MORTON ALLAN DIRECTORY)

The Morton Allan Directory of European Passenger Steamship Arrivals lists ships arriving in United States ports

– at New York for the years 1890 to 1930; and at New York, Philadelphia, Boston, and Baltimore in the years 1904-1926.

This source lists by years the names of the shipping lines, their ports of departure and stops, the names of the ships, and their specific dates of arrival in the United States ports named above.

The directory lists ports from a wide range of countries in the western hemisphere, including several in Great Britain (mostly Liverpool).

The shipping lines whose European points of departure may have relevance for researchers of German emigrants, are listed below.

The European ports listed below are not necessarily ports of origin. All American cities shown here are ports of debarkation.

American Merchant Line: Hamburg (1930 only); New York

American Line: Hamburg; Antwerp (1924 only); New York

Anchor Line: Havre (1926 only); New York

Baltic S.S. Corp. of America: Havre; Danzig; New York

Baltic-America Line: Hamburg; Danzig; New York

Cunard Line: Havre; Hamburg; New York

French Line: Havre; Bordeaux; Danzig (1920 only); New York

Hamburg American Line: Hamburg; New York; Philadelphia; Baltimore; Boston

Holland American Line: Rotterdam, Amsterdam, Boulogne; New York; Boston

North German Lloyd: Bremen; New York; Baltimore; Philadelphia

North-West Transportation Line: Rotterdam; Hamburg; New York

Polish-American Navigation Corporation: Danzig (1921 only); New York

Red Star Line: Antwerp; Danzig (1920 and after); Hamburg (1924 only); New York; Philadelphia; Boston

Royal Mail Steam Packet Company: Hamburg (1921 and after); New York

Royal Holland Lloyd: Amsterdam; New York

Russian-American Line: Rotterdam; New York

U.S. Mail Steamship Company: Hamburg; Danzig; New York

United States Line (1921 and after): Bremen; Danzig; New York

United American Lines, Inc. (1922 and after): Hamburg; New York

Uranium Steamship Company: Rotterdam; New York

White Star Line: Antwerp (1927 and after); Bremen (1922 only); Hamburg (1923 and after); New York

Source: *Morton Allan Directory of European Passenger Steamship Arrivals: For the Years 1890 to 1930 at the Port of New York and for the Years 1904 to 1926 at the Ports of New York, Philadelphia, Boston and Baltimore,* Genealogical Publishing Company, Inc., Baltimore, 1993.

A SELECT BIBLIOGRAPHY FOR RESEARCHING PASSENGER LISTS

◆ Burgert, Annette K., *Eighteenth Century Emigrants from German-Speaking Lands to North America.* Vols. 16 and 19. Pennsylvania German Society, Breinigsville, Pa., 1983 and 1985.

◆Colletta, John P., *They Came in Ships.* 3rd ed. Ancestry Publishing, Salt Lake City, 2002.

◆Ferguson, Laraine K., "Hamburg, Germany, Gateway to the Ancestral Home." *German Genealogical Digest*, Vol. 2, no. 1, 1985.

◆Filby, P. William, *Passenger and Immigration Lists Bibliography, 1538-1900: Being a Guide to Published Lists of Arrivals in the United States and Canada.* Gale Research Co., Detroit, 1988.

◆Filby, P. William, with Mary K. Meyer, eds. *Passenger and Immigration Lists*

Index: A Guide to Published Arrival Records of about 500,000 Passengers Who Came to the United States in the New World Between the Sixteenth and the Early Twentieth Centuries. 3 vols. Gale Research Company, 1981 - present. Supplemental volumes.

◆Glazier, Ira A., and P. William Filby, eds. *Germans to America: Lists of Passengers Arriving at U.S. Ports*, 1850-1855. Scholarly Resources, Wilmington, Del., 1988-present (ongoing).

◆ Minert, Roger P. et al., *Germans to America and the Hamburg Passenger Lists: Coordinated Schedules.* Westminster, MD: Heritage, 2005.

◆National Archives Trust Fund Board, *Immigrant and Passenger Arrivals: A Select Catalog of National Archives Microfilm Publications.* National Archives Trust Fund Board, Washington, D.C., 1983.

◆ Schenk, Trudy, and Ruth Froelke, comps. *The Württemberg Emigration Index.* Ancestry, Salt Lake City, 1986-88.

◆Strassburger, Ralph Beaver, comp., and William John Hinke, ed. *Pennsylvania German Pioneers: A Publication of the Original Lists of Arrivals in the Port of Philadelphia from 1727 to 1808.* Vols. 42, 43, 44. Pennsylvania German Society, Norristown, Pa., 1934.

◆ Tepper, Michael H., *American Passenger Arrival Records: A Guide to the Records of Immigrants Arriving at American Ports by Sail and Steam.* Genealogical Publishing Co., 1988.

◆Yoder, Don, ed. *Pennsylvania German Immigrants, 1709-1786: Lists Consolidated from Yearbooks of The Pennsylvania German Folklore Society.* Genealogical Publishing Co., Baltimore, 1980.

◆Zimmerman, Gary J., and Marion Wolfert, comps. *German Immigrants: Lists of Passengers Bound from Bremen to New York, 1847-1854.* Genealogical Publishing Co., Baltimore, 1985.

TRAVEL IN STEERAGE, 19TH CENTURY

Up to the second half of the nineteenth century, the transport of emigrants was only a subsidiary branch of cargo transport, and emigrants consequently traveled in cargo ships temporarily adapted for the conveyance of passengers. A deck was built between the upper deck and the hold, thus providing he necessary space for passengers. (In German, this was known as the *Zwischendeck.*) The accommodation in the steerage was primitive, as can be imagined. The berths, which were removed again at the end of the passage, since the space was needed on the return journey for cargo, were knocked together out of mere planks, narrow and mostly too short. Mattresses and bedding had to be provided by the passengers themselves. There were few latrines, and ventilation was provided for the most part only through ten hatches. The steerage was at once a bedroom, dining-room and living-room. There were no separate quarters for women or the sick.

All the passengers were crowded into the poorly-lighted deck by day and night. Only if the weather was good was it possible for them to emerge onto the upper deck. Medical care was not available; in an emergency, the sufferer was dependent on the captain's medical knowledge. Feeding was the passengers' own concern; they had to provide their own food and crockery, and the only amenity provided for them was a ration of water. For the preparation of food there were usually only one or two fireplaces, often leading to quarrels between passengers about their use. Many went for days without a hot meal.

By about the end of the 1870s, the steamship had replaced the sailing ship for emigrants. This development improved conditions almost at once. The passage was reduced to seventeen days — nine in the fast steamers introduced in the 1890s. Since the ships were fitted expressly for passenger transport, they were better ventilated. The employment of physicians and the segregation of the sexes had been introduced before the end of emigration by sail. Food became more plentiful, especially since it had become possible to keep provisions fresh until the end of the passage.

Gradually, the passengers were also offered a degree of service. After the steerage had been equipped, toward the end of the 1880s, with chairs and benches, eating in the bunks or even standing up, which had hitherto been the practice, became a thing of the past. The provision of mattresses, bedding and crockery was taken over by the forwarding agents. Shortly before the First World War, some ships were fitted out with special dining rooms for steerage passengers, in which they were served by stewards. At the beginning of the 1920s, a third class, consisting of four-berth cabins, was introduced on all emigrant ships, and the steerage disappeared completely.

Source: *Germans to America: 300 Years of Immigration 1683-1983.* ed. Günther Moltmann. Institute for Foreign Cultural Relations, Stuttgart.

RIVER TRAVEL

After 1807, when Fulton built the first commercially successful steamboat, steam-powered boats became increasingly popular on Germany's waterways.

Germany has a large number of rivers, but they converge into relatively few seaports.

The important ones for transatlantic travelers were the Rhine, Weser, Elbe, and the Oder. The Rhine and its tributaries, (the Lippe, Ruhr, Mosel, Lahn, Nahe, Main, Neckar, Regnitz, Saar, Sieg, Tauber,

etc.) end in Rotterdam.

The Weser that passes Bremen on its way to Bremerhaven on the North Sea includes the Aller, Fulda, Hunte, and Werra.

The Elbe brings the waters of the Elbe, Havel, Mulde, Saxon Saale, Schwarze Elster and Weisse Elster to the North Sea at Hamburg.

The Neisse and Warta join the Oder before it gets to Stettin.

The Danube and its tributaries, (the Enns, Inn, Naab, Regen, Traub, and others), however, empty into the Black Sea. Germany also has many canals.

Many immigrants also left from Le Havre, the French seaport at the mouth of the Seine, which flows through Paris on its way to the English Channel. Undoubtedly, in France and western Germany, "all roads led to Paris." For those who chose this route, it was probably easier, safer, and/or more economical than a North Sea or Baltic port.

Source: Excerpted from "How Our Ancestors Got to the Sea," by Bruce Walthers and Rolf Wasser. *The German Connection*, Vol. 18, No. 2 (1994).

GERMAN HARBORS AND INLAND WATERWAYS

The total volume at Germany's North Sea and Baltic ports was 161.4 million metric tons in 1991. The most important seaports with numbers of respective metric tons are,

Hamburg	60.33
Wilhelmshaven	17.76
Bremen	14.12
Bremerhaven	13.98
Lübeck	11.32
Rostock	7.44

The most important waterway is the Rhine River, accounting for two-thirds of the inland waterway goods transportation.

A network of canals links the major

rivers to the European waterways system. The *Rhein-Main-Donau Kanal* (Rhine-Main-Danube Canal) was finished in 1993 and connects the North Sea with the Black Sea via the Rhine, Main and Danube rivers. The Nord-Ostsee Kanal connects the North and Baltic seas.

The major inland ports are Duisburg, Mannheim, Hamburg, Cologne, Ludwigshafen, Wesseling, Gelsenkirchen, and Karlsruhe. Inland ships make use of a network of rivers, canals and lakes totaling some 4,400 kilometers (2,700 miles).

Source: German Information Center, *Federal Republic of Germany: Questions and Answers*, ed. Susan Steiner , New York, 1996.

EARLY 19TH CENTURY SHIPS

Fulton was not the first to build a steam-powered ship, but his (1807) paddle-wheel design was the first commercially successful model. Germany undoubtedly had steam-powered boats within a few years. The design was also used in ocean service, even though paddle-wheels on a rolling ship were often lifted completely out of the water and the exposed mechanism was easily damaged.

1819: *The American Savannah*, using steam as auxiliary power, was the first steam-powered ship to cross the Atlantic. It used its engines for 105 hours of the 29-day voyage and was out of fuel when it arrived. The first all-steam-powered crossing was made by a British-built ship (the *Curaçao*) in 1827.

1838: The British sidewheeler *Sirius* became the first ship to offer regularly scheduled service under steam power. The transatlantic crossing took 18° days.

1843: The *Great Britain*, launched in 1843 became the first passenger ship

with a screw propeller to cross the Atlantic. (The screw propeller had been invented in Bohemia in 1827.)

Sail and steam existed together well into the twentieth century, however. The largest sailing ship ever built, the *Preußen*, was launched in 1902.

Source: Excerpts from "How Our Ancestors Got to the Sea," by Bruce Walthers von Alten and Rolf Wasser. *The German Connection*, Vol. 18, No. 2 , 1994.

MARITIME MUSEUMS, LIBRARIES

◆**Steamship Historical Society of America,** 1029 Waterman Avenue, East Providence, RI 02914. Tel. (401) 274-0805; Fax; (401) 274-0836; www.ss hsa.org

The Steamship Historical Society *of* America (SSHSA) is dedicated to recording, preserving, and distributing information about all types of engine-powered vessels. Its services are threefold. One, it offers images of vessels, crews and passengers both electronically and in hard copy (over 400,000 images are stored in its archives and approximately 40,000 images are viewable online.) Two, it provides historical research on ships and their voyages. Three, it sponsors a journal about ships and shipping-lines. Since its founding in 1935, the SSHSA has published some forty volumes.

Currently, the SSHSA does not allow public access to its resources. It-house staff research is possible. Members and non-members, alike, are encouraged to send photo requests to photobank@sshsa.org and research requests to assistant@sshsa.org.

◆**Maine Maritime Museum**
243 Washington Street, Bath, ME 04530. Tel. (207) 442-0961; Fax (207) 443-1665; www.mainemaritimemuseum .org

◆**Mariner's Museum Library**
100 Museum Drive, Newport News, VA

23606-3759. Tel. (757) 596-7334; Fax (757) 591-7320; www.mariner.org; marketing@ marinersmuseum.org.

The museum's Research Library and Archives is open Monday-Saturday, 10 am to 5 pm; call in advance to confirm hours.

◆ Mystic Seaport, G.W. Blunt White Library
95 Greenmanville Ave., Mystic, CT 06355. Tel. (860) 572-5367; Fax (860) 572-5394; library@mysticsearport.org; www. collections@mysticseaport.org.

The G.W. Blunt White Library specializes in American maritime history and has ships register finding aids. Open Thursday-Friday 10:00 am - 5 pm.

◆ National Maritime Museum, J. Porter Shaw Library
Bldg. E, Fort Mason Center, San Francisco, CA 94102. Tel. (415) 561-7080.

Focuses on sail and steam on the West Coast; also has some general ship registers. Call about opening hours.

◆ Phillips Library, Peabody Essex Museum
East India Square, Salem, MA 01970. Tel. (508) 745-1876; Fax (508) 744-0036.

Phillips Library has 400,000 rare books and more than 1 million photographs. It is open Tuesdays, Wednesdays, and Fridays from 10 am to 5 pm, and Thursdays from 1 pm to 8 pm. In June, July and August, the library is open on Mondays, 10 am to 5 pm as well.

◆ San Diego Maritime Museum
1492 North Harbor Drive, San Diego, CA 92101. Tel. (619) 234-9153.

Museum has a Master Ship Index database. Library, open by appointment to non-members, has a collection of 11,000 photos and can supply reproductions.

◆ San Francisco Maritime Museum
860 Beach Street, San Francisco, CA 94109-1110. Tel. (415) 556-9870.

The 14,000-volume library focuses on commercial maritime history, with holdings on sail and steam on the West Coast and in the Pacific Basin from 1520 to the

present. It provides reference service. Limited open hours.

◆ Texas Seaport Museum
Pier 21 - #8, Galveston, TX 77550-1631. Tel. (409) 763-1877; Fax (409) 763-3037; tsm@phoenix.net.

This museum has the nation's only computerized listing of immigrants to Galves-ton. More than 130,000 passengers from the period 1846 to 1948 have been entered. The database lists only those who first disembarked in Texas. There are very few entries between 1871 and 1894.

◆ National Maritime Historical Society
5 John Walsh Boulevard, P.O. Box 68, Peekskill, NY 10566. Tel. (914)-737-7878; Fax (914) 737-7816; www.seahistory.org; nmhs@seahistory.org.

Prints, photographs, and artists' paintings of ships.

◆ Deutsches Schiffahrtsmuseum
Hans-Scharoun-Platz 1, 27568 Bremerhaven, Germany. Tel. 49 471 48 207 0; Fax 49 471 48 207 55; www.dsm.museum. edsm.htm; info@dsm.museum.

Photocopies as well as black and white and color prints or slides available from the museum's archives and library.

◆ National Maritime Museum, Manuscripts Section
Greenwich, London, SE10 9NF, Great Britain.

The website www.nmm.ac.uk has pictures, charts, maps, and more.

◆ Glasgow University Archives and Business Records Centre
FAO Duty Archivist, Archives and Business Records Centre, University of Glasgow, 13 Thurso Street, Glasgow G11 6PE, Scotland, United Kingdom; Tel. 44 141 330 5515; Fax 44 141 330 4158; enquiries@archives.gla.ac.uk; www.gla.ac.uk.

Collections concentrate on business records, including ship-building records, ship photographs, and technical drawings of ships.

SHIP REFERENCES

◆Michael J. Anuta, *Ships of Our Ancestors*, Ships of Our Ancestors, Inc., Menominee, Mich., 1983. Contains many ship illustrations. FHL 973 U3an; fiche 6104022; reprint: FHL 973 u3an 1993.
◆Lawrence B. Bargerter, *The Compass: A Concise and Factual Compilation of All Vessels and Sources Listed, with Reference Made of All of their Voyages and Some Dates of Registration*, 2 vols.,: (1983-1990); volume 1 lists ships arriving at Baltimore between 1820-1891; and volume 2 lists ships arriving at Boston 1820-1860.
◆Carl Cutler, *Queens of the Western Ocean: The Story of America's Mail and Passenger Lines*, United States Naval Institute, Annapolis, Md., 1961. FHL 973 U3c
◆C.R. Vernon Gibbs, *Passenger Liners of the Western Ocean: A Record of the North Atlantic Steam and Motor Passenger Vessels from 1838 to the Present Day*, Staples Press, London, 1952. FHL 387.243 G353p
◆Arnold Kludas, *Die Geschichte der deutschen passagierschiffahrt, Band I: Die Pionierjahre von 1850 bis 1890*, Ernst Kabel Verlag, Hamburg, 1986.(Note: Vol. 2 covers 1890-1900; vol. 3, 1900-1914; vol. 4, 1914-1930; and vol. 5 1930-1990.) FHL 943 U3k
◆Arnold Kludas, Charles Hodges, trans., *Great Passenger Ships of the World*, Patrick Stephens Ltd., Wellingborough, England, 1975, 6 vols. Covers 1858-1975. Vol. 1: 1858-1912; Vol. 2: 1913-1923; Vol. 3: 1924-1935; Vol. 4: 1936-1950; Vol. 5: 1951-1976; Vol. 6: 1977-1986. FHL 973 U3k (vols. 1-6)
◆*Morton Allan Directory of European Passenger Steamship Arrivals for the Years 1890 to 1930 at the Port of New York and for the Years 1904 to 1926 at the Port of New York, Philadelphia, Boston, and Baltimore*, New York Immigration Bureau, 1931. Reprinted by Genealogical Publishing Co., Baltimore, 1993 (also in 1979, 1980, and 1987). FHL 973 U3m 1993
◆Claus Rothe, *Deutsche Ozean-Passagierschiffe 1896 bis 1918*, Steiger Verlag, 1986
◆Eugene W. Smith, *Passenger Ships of the World: Past and Present*, George H. Dean, Boston, 1978. FHL 387.243 Sm55p
◆Bradley Steuart, *Passenger Ships Arriving in New York Harbor, 1820-1850*, 1991. FHL 974.71 W3s

SHIP-NAME ENTRIES IN ANUTA'S SHIPS OF OUR ANCESTORS

Information about the ships listed below is included in Michael J. Anuta's Ships of Our Ancestors, FHL 973 U3an; fiche 6104022.
Note that the asterisks (*) indicate ship names that are included at the end of the book's index, out of alphabetical order. These ship names have been inserted alphabetically in this listing:
Key
*= Indicates ship names listed at the end of the index (after Z), and unalphabetized.
Aachen 1895; Abangarez 1909; Abyssinia 1870; Acadia; Acropolis 1890; Adristic 1871; Alaska 1882; Aleppo 1865; Alesia 1906; Alfonso XII 1890; Alfonso XIII 1888; Algeria 1875; Allemania 1865; Aller 1886; America*; America 1857, 1881,1884, 1904, 1905, 1908, 1940, 1872; Amsterdam 1897; Anchoria 1875; Andrea Doria 1953; Andre Lebon 1912, 1913; Anglia 1864; Aquitania 1914; Arabic 1903; Aragon 1905; Arandora Star 1927; Arcadia 1896; Arcadian 1899; Arctic 1849; Argentina 1905; Arizona*; Arizona 1879; Armadale Castle 1903; Armenia 1896; Arundel Castle 1921; Asama Maru 1929; Ascania 1911; Assyria 1908; Astoria 1885; Athlone Castle 1936; At-

lantic 1871, 1927; Atlas 1860; Augusta Victoria 1888; Augusta 1927; Augusta 1952; Aurania 1883; Aurania 1924; Austral 1881; Australia, 1870, 1881; Avoca 1891; Avon 1907; Baltic 1904; Baltimore 1868; Barbarossa 1896; Batavia 1870, 1899; Bavarian 1900; Belgenland I 1878; Belgenland 1917, 1878; Belgravia 1899; Berengaria 1912; Bergensfjord 1950; Berlin 1875, 1908; Bermudian 1904; Berrima 1913; Birma 1894 Bluecher 1901; Bohemian 1900; Bonn 1895; Borussia 1855; Bothnia 1874; Braemar Castle 1898; Brandenburg 1901; Brasil 1958; Brasilia 1897; Brasilian 1890 Brazil 1928 Bremen 1858, 1897, 1929, 1939; Breslau 1901; Britannia 1840; Britannic*; Britannic 1874, 1914, 1930; British Prince 1882; British Princess 1899; Brooklyn 1869; Buenos Aires 1887; Buenos Ayrean*; Buenos Ayrean; Buffalo 1885; Bulgaria 1898; Bulow 1906; Burgunida 1882; Cairnrona 1900; Calabria 1857, 1901; Caledonia 1904, 1925; California 1907, 1923; Californian 1891; Cambria 1869; Cambroman 1892; Campania 1893; Canada 1848, 1865, 1896, 1911; Canadian 1872, 1900; Canopic 1900; Cap Arcona 1927; Cap Lay 1922; Capetown Castle 1938; Carinthia 1895; Carnarvon Castle 1926; Caronia 1905, 1948; Carpathia 1903; Carthaginian 1884; Caspian 1870; Cassel 1901; Castilian 1898, 1890; Catalonia 1881; Cataluna 1883; Cedric 1903; Celtic I 1872; Celtic 1901; Centennial State 1921; Cephalonia I 1882; Cestrian 1896; Champlain 1932; Chateau La Fitte 1881; Chester 1873; Chimborazo 1871, China 1862; Christian Huygens 1928; Cimbria 1867; Circassia I 1878; Circassia 1902; Circassian 1873; Citta Di Milano 1897; Citta Di Napoli 1871; Citta Di Torino 1898; City of Antwerp 1876; City of Baltimore 1854; City of Berlin 1875; City of Brooklyn 1869; City of Brussels 1869; City of Chester 1873; City of Chicago 1883; City of Cork 1863; City of London 1863; City of Manchester 1851; City of Montreal 1872; City of New York II 1865; City of New

York 1930; City of Paris 1888; City of Richmond 1873; City of Rome*; City of Rome 1881; City of Washington 1853; Ciudad De Cadiz 1878; Cleveland 1908; Clyde 1890; Colima 1873; Colorado 1865; Columbia I 1866; Columbia 1889, 1889, 1902; Columbus 1914; Constantinople 1896; Constitution 1951; Conte Biancamano 1925; Conte Grande 1927; Conte Rosso 1922; Conte Verde 1923; Corcovado 1907; Corean 1881; Corinthian 1900; Corsican 1907; Crefeld 1895; Cretic 1902; Cristoforo Colombo 1953; Cuba 1864; Cufic 1888; Cunard, Etruria Umbria*; Cuzco 1871; Cymric 1898; Czar 1912; Camascus 1856; Dania 1889; Dante Alleghieri 1915; Darmstadt 1890; Demerara 1872; Denmark 1865; Derfflinger 1907; Deseado 1912; Deutschland 1866, 1900; Devonia 1877; Devonian 1900; Devonian II 1902; Dominion 1894; Don 1872; Donau 1868; Douro 1865; Dresden 1888, 1914; Drottningholm 1905; Dubbeldam 1891; Duca D'Aosta 1909; Duca Degli Abruzzi 1907; Duca Di Genova 1907; Ducadi Galliera 1883; Duchess Di Genoa 1883; Duilio 1923; Dunnottar Castle 1890; Dunvegan Castle 1896; Edinburgh 1854; Edinburgh Castle 1872, 1910; Edison 1896; Egypt*; Egypt 1871; Eider 1884; Eisenach 1908; Elbe 1881; Elysia I 1872; Empress of Australia 1914; Empress of Britain 1906; Empress of Britain 1955; Empress of Canada 1955; Empress of France 1913; Empress of India 1908 Empress of Ireland 1906; Empress of Japan 1891; Empress of Scotland 1905; Ems 1884; England 1863; Entella 1883; Erin 1864; Erra 1932; Espagne 1909; Esperanza 1901; Ethiopia 1873; Etna 1855; Etruria 1884; Etruria Umbria, Cunard*; Eugenia 1906; Europa 1848, 1867, 1907, 1930; Excalibur 1944; Ferdinand De Lesseps 1875; Finland 1902; Flandre 1914, 1952; Florida 1905; Floride 1905, 1862, 1907; Fort Victoria 1913; France 1865, 1912; Francesca 1905; Franconia 1873; Franconia 1910; Frankfurt 1899;

Frederick VIII 1913; Friedrich Der Grosse 1896; Friesland 1889; Frisia 1872, 1909; Fulda*; Fulda 1882, 1924; Furnessia 1880; Furst Bismark 1890; Gallia 1878, 1883, 1914; Garibaldi 1906; Gellert 1874; General Von Steuben 1922; General Werder 1874; George Washington 1908; Georgia 1908; Georgic 1895; Gera 1890; Germania 1870, 1902, 1874; Germanic*; Gerolstein 1904; Gerty 1903; Giulio Cesare 1951; Gneisenau 1903; Goeben 1906; Goethe 1872; Gothic 1848; Gothland 1894; Gottardo 1883; Graf Waldersee 1898; Grampian 1907; Great Britain 1843; Greece 1863; Grosser Kurfurst 1899; Guadeloupe 1908; Guglielmo Marconi 1963; Guilia 1904; Guiseppi Verdi 1915; Habana 1872; Haiti 1913; Hamburg 1899; Hammonia 1854; Hammnia 1866; Hammonia III 1882; Hannover 1899; Hanoverian 1882; Hanoverian 1882, 1902; Hansa 1860 Hansa 1899; Havel 1890; Haverford 1901; Hecla 1860; Hekla 1884; Hellig Olav 1902; Helvetia 1864; Herder 1872; Hermann 1847, 1865; Hesperian 1908; Hibernian 1861; Himalaya 1949; Hohenstauffen 1874; Hohenzollern 1872, 1889; Holland 1858; Holsatia 1868; Homeland 1905; Homeric 1913; Hudson 1858; Hungarian 1859; Iberia 1881; Iberia 1954; Ile De France 1926; Illinois 1873; Ilsenstein 1904; Imperator 1912; Imperatrice Eugenie 1866; Independence 1950; India 1869 Indiana 1873, 1905; Infanta Isabel 1912; Infanta Isabel De Borbon 1913; Inman Steamship Company*; Iowa I 1879; Iowa 1902; Irishman 1898; Isla De Panay 1882; Island 1882; Israel 1955; Italia 1872, 1904, 1928; Italy 1868; Ivernia 1900; Jacques Cartier 1908; Jan Pieterszoon Coen 1915; Java 1865; Jerusalem 1913, 1957; John Bell 1854; Justicia 1915; Kaiser Friedrich 1898; Kaiser Wilhelm II*; Kaiser Wilhelm II 1889, 1903; Kaiser Wilhelm Der Grosse 1897, 1902; Kaiserin Auguste Victoria 1905; Kaiserin Maria Theresia 1890; Kangaroo 1853; Kansas 1882; Karlsruhe 1900; Kedar 1860;

Kensington 1894; Kiautschou 1900; King Alexander 1908; Kleist 1906; Klopstock 1872; Kohln 1899; Konig Albert 1899; Konig Friedrich August 1906; Konig Wilhelm II 1907; Konigen Luise 1896; Konigstein 1907; Koningen Emma 1913; Koscuiszko 1915; Kristianafjord 1913; Kronprinz Wilhelm 1901; Kronprinzessin Cedilie 1906; Kroonland 1902; Kungsholm 1902, 1928; Kursk 1910; La Bourdonnais 1904; La Bourgoyne 1886; Labrador 1865, 1891; La Bretagne 1886; La Champagne 1886; Laconia 1912, 1922; Lady Hawkins 1928; Lafayette 1864; La Gascogne 1886; La Guardia 1944; Lahn 1837; Lake Champlain 1874, 1900; Lake Erie 1900; Lake Huron 1881; Lake Manitoba 1880, 1901; Lake Megantic 1884; Lake Nepigon 1875; Lake Ontario 1887; Lake Simcoe 1884; Lake Superior 1885; La Navarre 1893; Lancastria 1922; La Normandie 1882; Lapland 1908; La Provence 1905; L'Aquatine 1890; La Savoie 1901; La Touraine 1890; Laura 1907; Laurentian 1872; Laurentic 1908; Layfayette 1915; Lazio 1899; Leconte Delisle 1922; Leerdam 1882, 1921; Legazpi 1904; Leipzig 1869; Leon XIII 1888; Leonardo Da Vinci 1925, 1960; Lessing 1874; Letitia 1912; L'Europe 1865; Leviathan 1914; Leberte 1928; Liguria 1901; Livonian 1881; Lombardia 1901; Lone Star State 1921; Lorraine 1900; Louisiane 1862; Lucania 1893; Ludgate Hill 1881; Luetzow 1908; Lurline 1932; Lurline 1932; Lusitania 1871, 1907; Lydian Monarch 1881; Maas 1872; Maasdam 1871, 1952; Macedonia 1912; Macoris 1902; Madonna 1905; Main 1868, 1899; Majestic 1890, 1920; Malawa 1908; Manchuria 1904; Manhattan 1866, 1932; Manilla 1873; Manitoba 18892; Manitou 1898; Manuel Calvo 1892; Marathon 1860; Marco Minghetti 1876; Marco Polo 1942; Marglen 1898; Mariposa 1883, 1931; Marloch 1904; Marnix Van Sint Aldegonde 1930) Marques De Comillas 1928; Marquette 1898; Martello 1884;

Martha Washington 1908; martinique 1883; Marvale 1907; Massachusetts 1892; Massilia 1902; Mauretania 1907, 1939; Mayflower 1902; Media 1947; Medway 1877; Megantic 1909; Meknes 1913; Melita 1918; Mendonza 1904; Menominee 1897; Merion 1902; Mesaba 1898; Metagama 1915; Mexico 1884; Mexique 1915; Michigan 1887, 1890; Milwaukee 1897, 1929; Minneapolis 1900; Minnedosa 1918; Minnehaha 1900; Minnekahda 1917; Minnesota 1866, 1901; Minnetonka 1902; Minnewaska 1894, 1909; Missanable 1914; Mississippi 1871, 1903; Mobile 1893; Mohawk 1892; Moltke 1901; Mongolia 1905; Mongolia 1905, 1891; Montacalm 1921; Montana 1872; Montcalm 1897; Monteagle 1899; Monterey 1897; Monte Rosa 1930; Monte Videan 1887; Monte Video 1889; Montequma 1899; Montfort 1899; Montnairn 1908; Montreal 1896, 1900, 1906; Montrose 1897, 1922; Montroyal 1906; Montserrat 1889; Mooltan 1923; Moravia 1883; Moreas 1902; Morivian 1864; Morro Castle 1930; Mosel 1872; Mount Clay 1904; Mount Clinton 1921; Mount Temple 1901; Munchen 1922; Neckar 1874, 1910; Nederland 1873; Neptunia 1920; Nestorian 1866; Neustria 1883; Nevada 1869; New England 1898; New York 1858, 1864, 1888, 1922, 1927; Niagara 1848, 1908; Nieuw Amsterdam 1906; Noordam 1901; Noordland 1884; Nord America 1882; Normandie 1935; Normannia 1890; Norseman 1882, 1897; North America 1862; Northern Star; Norwegian 1861; Nova Scotia 1926; Nova Scotian 1858; Numidian 1891; Nurnberg 1873; Oaxaca 1883; Obdam 1880; Ocean Queen 1857; Oceana 1891; Oceania 1907; Oceanic 1871, 1870, 1899; Oder 1873; Ohio 1869, 1873, 1923; Oldenburg 1890; Olinde Rodriguez 1873; Olympia 1871, 1953; Olympic*; Olympic 1911; Olympus & Hecla 1860; Ontario 1867; Oranje 1903; Orbita 1915; Orca 1918; Orduna 1914; Oregon 1883; Oriana 1960; Orient 1879;

Orion 1935; Orient 1879; Orion 1935; Orione 1883; Ormuz 1886; Oronsay 1951; Orontes 1902; Oropesa 1920; Orotava 1889; Orsova 1954; Oscar II 1902; Oslofjord 1938, 1947; Osterley 1909; Otranto 1909; Ottawa 1875; P. Calend 1874; P. De Satrustegui 1890; Pacific 1849; Palatia 1895; Palermo 1907; Palmyra 1866; Panama 1865, 1875; Pannonia 1904; Paris 1889, 1921; Parisian 1881; Parthia 1870, 1943; Pasteur 1938; Pastores 1912; Patria 1894, 1913; Patricia 1902; Patris 1909; Pavonia 1882; Pendennis Castle 1959; Pennland 1870; Pennsylvania 1863, 1873, 1896, 1929; Pereire 1866; Perou 1906; Perseo 1883; Persia 1856; Perugia 1901; Peruvian 1863; Pesaro 1901; Philadelphia 1889; Phoenicia 1894; Pilsudski 1935; Pisa 1896; Pittsburg 1922; Pocahontas 1900; Poland 1898; Polonia 1910; Polynesian 1872; Pomeranian 1882; Pomerania 1871; President Arthur 1900; President Fillmore 1899; President Grant 1900; President Lincoln 1907; President Monroe 1920; President Polk 1921; President Roosevelt 1922; President Taft 1921; President Van Buren 1920; President Wilson 1948, 1912; Pretoria 1897; Pretorian 1901; Preussen 1886; Prince George 1898, 1910; Princepessa Yolanda 1907; Princess Helene 1930; Princess Marguerite 1949; Princess Matoika 19000; Principe De Piemonte 1907; Principe De Udine 1908; Principe Umberto 1909; Principello 1907; Prinz Adalbert 1902; Prinz Eitel Friedrich 1904; Prinz Friedrich Wilhelm 1907; Prinz Oskar 1902; Prinz Sigismund 1903; Prinzess Alice 1900; Prinzess Irene 1900: Prinzessin Victoria Luise 1900; Provence 1906; Providence 1915; Prussia; Puerto Rico 1913; Pulaski 1912; Quaker City 1867; Quebec 1896; Queen Elizabeth 1940; Queen Mary 1935; Re D'Italia 1907; Regina Elena 1907; Regina Margherita 1884; Reina Del Mar 1956; Reina Maria Christina 1888; Reliance 1920; Republic 1871, 1907; Republic II 1903; Resolute 1920; Re Vittorio 1907; Rex 1932; Rhaetia 1883; Rhaetia II 1905;

Rhein 1899; Rhynland I 1878; Rijndam 1901; Rijndam 1901; Rochambeau 1911; Roma 1901, 1926; Romanic 1898; Roon 1903; Rosarian 1887; Roslin Castle 1883; Rotterdam 1872, 1908, 1959; Rotterdam II 1878; Rotterdam III 1897; Roussillon 1906; Royal Edward 1908; Royal George 1907; Rugia 1882; Rugia II 1905; Runic 1899; Russia 1867, 1889; Ryndam 1951; Saale 1886; Sachem 1893; Sachsen 1886; Sagamore 1892; Saint Germain 1874; St. Laurent 1866; St. Louis 1895, 1929; St. Paul 1895; Saint Simon 1874; Salier 1875; Samaria 1868; Samland 1903; San Giorgio 1886, 1907; San Guglielmo 1911; Sannio 1899; Santa Anna 1910; Santa Inez 1929; Santa Maria 1928; Santa Rita 1929; Santa Rosa 1932; Saragossa 1874; Sardegna 1902; Sardinian 1875; Samatian 1871; Sarnia 1882; Saturnia 1910, 1927; Savannah 1819; Savoia 1897; Saxonia 1857, 1900, 1900 Souvenir Plate, 1954; Scandia 1889; Scandinavian 1870, 1898; Scanmail 1919; Scharnhorst 1904; Schiller 1873; Schleswig 1903; Scotia 1862, 1890; Scotian 1898; Scotsman 1899; Scythia I 1875; Scychia 1920; Servia*; Servia 1881; Seven Seas 1940; Seydlitz 1902; Siberia 1867; Sicilian 1899; Sicilian Prince 1889; Sierra, 1900, 1928; Sierra Ventana 1923; Silesia I (1869

Slavoina 1903; Smolensk 1901; Sobieski 1939; Southwark 1893; Spaarddam 1922; Spain 1871; Spree 1890; Stampalia 1909; State Line*; State of California 1891; State of Indiana 1874; State of Nebraska 1880; State of Nevada*; State of Nevada 1874; State of Pennsylvania 1873; State Steamship Company*; Statendam 1898, 1929; Stirlingcastle 1936; Stockholm 1900, 1940, 1947; Strassburg 1872; Stuttgart 1889; Suevia 1874; Suffren 1901; Susquehanna 1899; Switzerland 1874; Taormina 1908; Tarsus 1931; Tennyson 1900; Teresa 1900; Teutonia 1856; Teutonic 1889; Thames 1890; The Queen 1864; Thingvalla 1874; Thuringia 1922; Tigre 1862; Tintagel Castle 1896; Tirpitz I 1914; Titanic*s; Ti-

tanic 1911; Toloa 1917; Tomaso Di Savoia 1907; Toronto 1880; Tortona 1909; Transvaal Castle 1961; Transylvania 1914; Trave 1866; Trent 1900; Trinacria 1871; Tripoli 1863; Tunisian 1900; Tuscania 1914; Ultonia 1826; Umbria 1884; United States 1903, 1952; Utopia 1874; Vaderland 1873; Vancouver 1884; Vandalia 1870; Vanderbilt 1855; Vasco Nunez De Balboa 1891; Vasconia 1899; Vaterland 1914; Vanderland 1940; Vedic 1918; Veendam 1871; Venezia 1907; Venezuela 1906; Ventura 1900; Verona 1908; Vicksburg 1872; Victoria I 1872; Victoria 1931; Victoria Luise 1899; Victorian 1895, 1904; Ville De Bordeaux 1870; Ville De Brest 1870; Ville De Marseille 1874; Ville De Paris 1866; Ville De St. Nazaire 1870; Ville Du Havre 1866; Virginian 1905; Vladimir 1895; Volendam 1922; Vulcania 1928; Waesland 1867; Waldensian 1861; Washington 1864, 1880, 1933; Weimar 1891; Werkendam 1882; Werra 1882; Westernland*; Westernland 1884, 1918; Westphalia 1868, 1923; Wieland 1874; Wilhelmina 1909; Willehad 1894; Willem Ruys 1947; Winchester Castle 1930; Winifredian 1899; Winnipeg 1918; Wisconsin 1870; Wittekind; Wyoming 1870; Yorck 1906; Yorkshire 1889; Ypiranga 1908; Zaandam 1882, 1939; Zeeland 1901; Zeppelin 1914; Zieten 1902; Zion 1956; Zuiderkruis 1944

SHIP-NAME ENTRIES IN KLUDAS' DIE GESCHICHTE DER DEUTSCHEN PASSAGIER-SCHIFFAHRT DER WELT

Information about the following ships is included in Arnold Kludas' book, *Die Geschichte der deutschen Passagierschiffahrt* [history of German passenger ships], volume 1, *Die Pionierjahre von 1850-1890* [the pioneer years from 1850 to 1890], FHL 943 U3k:

Abydos 1888; Abyssinia; Acadia;

Ada; Aden; Adler; Admiral; Admiral 1890; Adolphe Woermann 1886, 1888; Adrien David; Ägir; Aeroligh; Africshore; Aglaia; Alaska; Albano; Albatross 1872; Albingia 1888; Alecto; Alfeld; Alfonso XII; Alice; Aline; Aline Woermann 1879, 1890, 1891; Allemannia 1865, 1881; Aller; Alsatia 1872, 1873; Amalfi 1881; Amazonas 1890; Amazone; Amboto; America 1862, 1881; Amicizia; Ammiraglio Viale; Andros; Anna Strowig; Anna Villa; Anna Woermann 1884; Apenrade; Apollonia; Aracaty; Argentina 1872, 1894; Argonaut; Arizona; Armistice; Arno; Ascan Woermann 1893; Ascania; Assam; Assyria; Atlantica; Augusta Victoria 1888; Auguste Victoria 1888; Aurora; Australia 1881; Austria 1857; Austsria; Aval; Aviles; Babelsberg; Bahia 1871, 1886; Bahrenfeld; Baltimore; Bamberg; Bankoku Maru; Barcelona; Barmen; Batavia; Baumwall 1881, 1890; Bavaria 1856; Bayern 1886; Baysarnia; Belgique; Belgrano 1888; Bellagio; Bellona 1887, 1895; Bengore Head; Berezan; Berlin 1867; Bermudez; Blokshif; Boba; Bohemia 1881; Bolivia 1889; Borussia 1855; Bosporus; Branksome Tgower; Brasilien 1869; Braunschweig 1872; Brazilian 1869; Brava; Bremen 1858, 1896; British Queen; Buenos Aires 1872, 1893; Bulgarie; Bundesrath 1890; California 1882; Camilia; Campania; Campidano; Campinas 1886; Canadia 1889; Canadian; Carl Woermann 1881; Carlton; Cassius; Catania 1881; Catarina; Ceara 1882; Celikkale; Ceres 1896; Cetvrti; Charles Morse; Chemnitz 1889; Chios; Christiania 1890; Chubut 1889; Cimbria 1867; Cintra 1889; Citta di Napoli; Citta di Savona; City of Amsterdam; Citsy of Mecca; City of New York; City of Paris; City of Sydney; Ciudad Condal; Clan MacLeod; Clermont; Colonia 1887; Columbia 1889; Commodore Bateman; Comodoro Rivadavia 1890; Cork; Cornigliano; Cornwallis; Corona; Corrientes 1881, 1894; Crathie; Cremon 1871; Criterion; Croatia

1888; Curityba 1887; Cuxhaven; Daghestan; Dagmar; Dago; Dahome; Dalecarlia 1882; Dalmatia 1871; Dan; Dania 1889; Danzig 1886; David; Delaware; Della 1897; Denderah 1872, 1883; Denise; Desertas; Desterro 1885; Deutschland 1866; Devonshire; Diamant; Dnestr; Don; Don Matias; Donau; Douglas; Doumlou Pounar; Dresden 1888; Dumlupinar; Dunkeld; Dupleix; Eduard Bohlen 1889, 1890; Edward & Charlotte; Egeo; Elbe 1881; Elberfeld 1889; Ella; Ella Woermann 1883; Ems; Ems 1884; Enrique Lihn; Erato 1894; Erda; Erich Woermann 1893; Eritrea; Erlangen 1889; Erna Woermann 1884; Ernest Renan; Ernst Moritz Arndt 1872; Erzherzog Johann; Essen 1889; Ethel Wolf; Etruria; Euripos; Europa 1865; Feldmarschall Moltke 1873; Fides; Fido; Flandre; Flandria 1888; Francia 1886; Franconia 1873; Frankfurt 1869; Franklin 1871; Frascati; Fred B. Taylor; Frieda Woermann 1888; Frisia 1872; Fürst Bismarck 1890; Fulda 1882; Fulton; Gäa; Gaisen Maru; Galata; Gellert 1874; General 1890; General H. F. Hodges; General Werder 1874; Georgia 1880; Georgie; Gerda 1892; Germania 1840, 1863, 1879; Gertrud Woermann 1885; Gin Yun; Glengarry; Goethe 1873; Golden Fleece; Gothia 1884; Graecia; Graf Bismarck 1870; Grand liban; Grasbrook 1882; Great Western; Gresford; Grimm 1890; Guaratuba; Guinee; Gyptis; Habana; Habsburg 1875; Hachiro Maru; Haelen; Haian Maru; Hamburg 1878; Hammonia 1855, 1866, 1882; Hansa 1847, 1861; Hannover 1869; Harpon; Hathor 1895; Havel 1890; Hedjin; Heidelberg; Hejaz; Helena Sloman 1850; Helene Woermann 1888; Helios; Hellas; Helvetia; Hercynia 1889; Herder 1873; Hereford; Hermann; Hermann 1865; Herodot 1890; Hertha 1894; Herzogin Sophia Charlotte; Hispania 1890; Hochfeld; Hohenzollern 1873, 1889; Hohenstaufen 1873; Holland; Holsatia 1868; Hourriet; Housatonic; Hudson 1858; Huemul; Humboldt 1871;

Hungaria 1884; Huntsgulf; Ibis 1873; Ida; India 1881; Indian Empire; Indra; Ingeborg; Irene 1893; Irish Beech; Isis 1889; Italia 1889; Itaparica 1889; J. L. Luckenbach; Jacatra Jason; Jeanette Kayser; Jenfeld; Jugoslaven Prvi; Kätie 1880; Kaijo Maru; Kaiser Friedrich 1897; Kaiser Wilhelm der Grosse 1897; Kaiser Wilhelm II 1889; Kaiserin Maria Theresia 1890; Kambyses 1884; Karnak 1872, 1887; Katinitsa; Kayseri; Kehrewieder; Kehrwieder 1872; Kentish Knock; Khalif; Kinko Maru; Klopstock 1874; Köln 1870; König Wilhelm I 1879; Königsberg; Komagata Maru; Kong Magnus; Koning Willem III; Koshun Maru; Kreta; Kriemhild 1889; Kronprinz Friedrich Wilhelm 1870; Kuban; Kum Chow; Kurt Woermann 1883; L'Aquitaine; La Bourgogne; La Champagne; La Touraine; Lachta; Lady Mitchell; Lady of the Lake; Lahn 1887; Lake Huron;Lake Simcoe; Lamentin; Lauenburg; Lawang; Le Levant; Leipzig 1869; Lemnos; Leros; Lessing 1874; Libano; Liberia; Licata; Ligure; Lipsos; Lisa; Lissabon 1883; Liverpool; Lome; London City; Loong Yue; Lothar Bohlen 1888; Lotharingia 1873; Louise; Louisiana; Lourdes; Lucania; Ludwig; Lübeck 1886; Luisa; Luise M. Fuller; Lulu Bohlen 1886; Lusitania; Luxor 1873, 1894; M. Bruzzo; Maasdam; Macapa; Macassar; Madison; Main 1868, 1900; Maine; Majestic; Malvinas; Maracaibo 1873; Margaret Fraenkel; Marga Hemsoth; Marie Woermann 1887; Marsale 1882; Marseille; Martha 1884; Mascotta; Maurice; Melbourne; Melita Bohlen 1883; Metshta; Memphis 1872, 1894; Mendes Barata; Mendoza 1894; Menes 1881; Mentana; Messina; Meteoro; Midnight Sun; Mikado Maru; Milano; Milos; Minister Roon 1873; Missouri; Misurata; Mobile; Moel Eilian; Montevideo; Montevideo 1873, 1888; Montserrat; Moravia 1883; Mosel 1872; Moskva; München 1889; Murat Murvet; Myrtoon; Naguyla; Nanto Maru; Naxos;

Neapel; Neckar 1873; Nedjat; Neko 1882, 1891; Nepaul; Nerthe; New York 1858; New York; Nijni Novgorod; Niobe; Nisshin Maru; Nordsee; Normannia 1888, 1890; Nubian; Nürnberg; Nürnberg 1873; Oceana 1889; Oceanic; Oder 1873; Odessa; Ohio 1868; Olinda 1887; Olinde Rodrigues; Orazio; Oregon; Orrik; Osiris 1889; Oxenholme; Pacifica; Padang; Paranagua 1878; Paraguassu 1890; Parma; Paros; Patagonia 1890; Patria; Patriota; Pauline Constance Eleonore; Pavia; Pentaur 1889; Pera; Pergamon; Pernambuco   1883;   Petersburg; Petropolis 1856, 1882; Phoenicia 1894; Pickhuben 1890; Piemontese; Polaria 1882; Pollockshields; Polonia 45; Polynesia 1881; Pommerania 1873; Pompei; Pompeji; Port de Cette; Porto Alegre 1888; Presidente Mitre 1894; Preussen 1886; Princess; Princess of Wales; Prinzessin von Joinville 1857; Priok 1891; Procida 1871; Professor Woermann 1882; Provincia di Sao Paulo; Puglia; Quatre Amis; Ramses 1876, 1893; Rapido; Rattler; Real; Regina; Reichstag 1889; Reinfeld; Reval; Rhaetia 1882; Rhein; Rhein 1868; Rhenania 1874, 1880; Rhone; Rio 1870, 1892; Rio Gallegos 1890; Rio Santa Cruz; Roma; Rosalind; Rosario 1881, 1893; Rossiya; Rostsov; Roumelia; Rudolf; Rugia 1882; Runhild; Russ; Russia 1889; Ryoyu Maru; S. Primo; Saale 1886; Sabah; Sachsen 1886; Saint Germain; Saint Simon; Sakarya; Sakkarah 1872; Salatiga 1890; Salier 1874; San Giusto; San Nicolas 1888; Santa Ana; Santa Barbara; Santos 1869, 1877; Sarnia 1892; Savannah; Savoia 1889; Saxonia 1857; Scandia 1889; Scandinavia 1889; Schiller 1873; Schwinge; Scotia; Scotia 1890; Senegambia; Senta 1895; Serapis 1890; Serbia 1894; Seriphos; Setos 1883; Siam; Sibiria 1894; Sicilia 1890; Sidi Mabrouck; Siegfried; Silesia 1869, 1887, 1896; Simson; Sizily; Skutari 1890; Slavonia 1883; Smidt 1867; Solingen 1889; Somali 1889; Sommerfeld 1889; Somali 1889;

Sommerfeld 1889; Sorrento 1881; Sovetskaya Rossija; Sparta; Sperber; Sperrbrecher; Spezia; Spree 1890; Stw. Pauli; St. Petersburg; Staincliff; Stambul; Stassfurt 1891; Steinhöft 1889; Stettin 1886; Stolberg; Stork; Strassburg 1872; Strathclyde; Stubbenhuk 1890; Suchan; Sud America; Suevia 1874, 1896; Sultan; Sultan 1891; Sumatra; Sumatra 1889; Sumner; Sunk; Taiholku Maru; Tanis 1891; Taormin 118; Taormina 1884; Tarapaca; Tebea; Temerario; Tenedos; Terek; Teutonia 1856; Teutonic; Thasos; Theben 1872, 1879; Thekla 1895; Theodor Körner; Theta; Thorwaldsen 1872; Thuringia 1870; Tiber; Tijuca 1886; Tinos; Titanic; Tsogo; Tom G. Corpi; Tosari 1890; Totmes 1884; Toto Maru; Trave 1886; Turkiye; U 22; U 32; U 34; U 39; U 48; U 53; U 61; UB 63; Ub 125; UC 16; UC 73; Uarda 1880; Umbria; Union; Union 1866; United States; Ural; Uralker; Urayasu Maru; Uruguay 1883; Valdivia; Valdivia 1886; Valencia 1886; Valparaiso 1873; Vandalia 1871; Varazze; Vatan; Venetia 1890, 1891; Venezia; Venus; Versailles; Ville de Damas; Ville de Nancy; Ville de Nantes; Virginia 1891; Vojslav; Vorsetzen 1881; Wachusett; Wally 1896; Wandrahm 1881, 1890; Warren; Washington; Washington 1873; Werra 1882; Weser 1858, 1867; Westphalia 1868, 1887; Wieland 1874; Wild Flower; Wildflower; Willie; Winland; Wittenberg; Yorihime Maru; Zaandijk

SHIP-NAME ENTRIES IN KLUDAS' DIE GROSSEN PASSAGIERSCHIFFE DER WELT

Information about the following ships is included in Arnold Kludas' *Die grossen Passagierschiffe der Welt* [great passenger ships of the world], Vol. 1, titled *1858-1912*:

Adriatic; Aeneas; Aeolus; Afric; Agamemnon; Albant; Alberta; Alcala;

Alcantara; Aliya; Almanazora; Amazon; America; American; American Shipper; Amerika; Anchises; Andes; André Lebon; Antillan; Arabic; Aragon; Araguaya; Arcadian; Arctic Queen; Argentina (pan.)

Argentina (span.); Argyllshire; Arlanza; Armadale Castle; Ascanius; Asturias; Asuncion; Atlantis; Athenic; Audacious; Auriga; Avoca; Avon; Ballarat; Balmoral Castle; Baltic; Barbarossa; Batavia; Bavaria; Bavarian; Belgia; Belgic; Belgravia; Beltana; Benalla; Bergensfjord; Berlin 1907; Berlin 1909; Berlin 1925; Berrima; Blücher; Borda; Borussia; Boston; Bothnia; Brasil; Brasilia; Bremen 1897, 1900, 1929; Britannic; Briton; Buenos Ayres; Bulgaria; Budigala; Burma; Cairo; Californian, Cameronia; Campania; Canada; Canopic; Cap Finisterre; Cap Trafalgar; Carmania; Caronia; Carpathia; Catlin; Cedric; Celt; Celtic; Ceramic; Chicago; Chiyo Maru; Cincinnati; City of Honolulu; City of Los Angeles 1896, 1900; City of New York; City of Paris; Clan Urquhart; Cleveland; Columbus; Commonwealth; Comus; Constantinople; Corinthic; Corsican; Covington; Cretic; Cymric; Czar; Daisy; Dakota Darre; Demerara; Demosthenes; Deseado; Desna; Devonian 1900, 1902; Deutschland; Drina Drottningholm; Edinburgh Castle; Edison; Edmund B. Alexander; Elbe; Eleonore Woermann; Embleton; Empire Evenlode; Empire Pakeha; Empire Waimana; Empress of Asia; Empress of Britain; Empress of China; Empress of India; Empress of Ireland; Empress of Russia; Empress of Scotland; Eolo; Espagne; Europa; Ferdinando Palasciano; Finland; Florida; Foxhound. France; France IV; Franconia; Frankfurt; Friedrich der Große; Galician; Gange; Garonne; Generale Diaz; George Washington 120; Gertrud; Gladiator; Graf Waldersee; Grampian; Great Eastern; Greif; Grenadier; Großer Kurfürst; Guadeloupe; Hamburg; Hanoverian;

Hansa; Harrisburg; Harvard; Harvard Queen; Haverford; Hawke; Hawkes Bay; Hektoria; Heleopolis; Hellig Olav; Helvetia; Hercules; Hermes; Herminius; Heroic; Hesperian; Highflyer; Homeland; Hudson; Huron; Indrapura; Infanta Isabel de Borbon; Instructor; Ionic; Irishman; Italia; Ivernia; Ixion; Jacob van Heemskerk; Jerusalem; Kaiser Franz Joseph I; Kaiser Friedrich; Kaiser Wilhelm der Große; Kaiser Wilhelm II; Kaiserin Auguste Victoria; Kapiti; Karlsruhe 1900; Karlsruhe SMS; Kashmir; Kenilworth Castle; Kiautschou; Kincora King Alexander 1897, 1909; Knoxville; König Albert; Königin Luise; Koordistan; Korea; Korea Maru; Kraljica Marija; Kristianiafjord; Kronprinz Wilhelm; Kronprinzessin Cecile; Kroonland; Kungsholm; La Lorraine; La Picardie; La Proavence; La Savoie; La Touraine; Laconia; Lapland; Laristan; Laurentic; Leopoldina; Leviathan; Lorraine II; Loughborough; Louisville; Lucania; Lucigen; Lusitania; Macedonia; Madura; Main; Majestic; Makarini; Maloja; Malwa; Mamari; Mamilius; Manchuria; Mantua; Mar Bianco; Marburn; Marco Polo; Marglen; Marguerite Ryan; Marije; Marloch; Marmora; Martand; Martano; Marvale; Mauretania; Mayflower; Medic; Medina; Megantic; Mercury; Merion; Mesaba; Michigan; Minneapolis; Minnehaha; Minnekahda; Minnelora; Minnetonka; Minnesota; Minnewaska; Minnewaska; Mississippi; Mobile; Moltke; Mongolia; Monteith; Monticello; Montlaurier; Montnairn; Montreal; Montroyal; Morca Mount Temple; Mount Vernon; Mounsey; Munamar; Munster; Myriam; Nansemond; Nantucket Lightship; Narragansett; Nestor; New England; New Rochelle; New Sevilla; New York; Niagara; Nieuw Amsterdam; Nipponia; Noordam; Norseman; Northern Light; Northland; Oceana; Oceanic; Olympic; Omar; Orama; Orcoma; Orinoco; Orion; Orsova; Orvieto; Oscar II; Osterley; Otranto; Otway; Pakeha Panamanian; Paris; Patricia; Paul Lecat; Pavia; Peel; Pelagos; Pennsylvania; Pericles; Persic; Pesaro; Philadelphia; Philippines; Pinguin; Pisagua; Pishchevaya Industriya; Plattsburg; Pocahon-tas; Polonia; Port Adelaide; Port Napier; Port Nicholson; Potsdam; Powhatan; President Arthur; President Buchanan; President Fillmore 1900, 1904; President Grant; President Johnson; President Lincoln; President Wilson; Pretoria; Princess Matoika; Prinz Friedrich Wilhelm; Prinzess Alice; Prinzess Irene; Provence II; Rangatira; Red Cross; Reina Eugenia Victoria; Remuera; Reno; Republic 1903, 1907; Resolution; Revenge; Rhein; Riga; Rijndam; Rochambeau; Romanic; Rotorua; rotterdam; Royal Edward; Royal George; Ruahine; Ronic; Saale; St. Louis; St. Paul; Samland; San Giovannino; Santa Cruz; Savoie; Saxon; Saxonia; Scandinavian; Scotian 1898, 1903; Scourge; Servian; Seydlitz; Shinyo Maru; Shropshire; Siberia; Siberia Maru; Skytteren; Slavonia; Solglimt; Sonderburg; Southland; Spadefish; Statendam; Stockholm; Storstad; Suevic; Suffren; Susquehanna; Taiseiyo Maru; Taiyo Maru; Talthybius; Taruyasu Maru; Tenyo Maru; Teutonia; Teutonic; Themistocles; Thomas; Tiger; Titanic; Transbalt; Troy; Tung Shing; Tunisian; U 20; U 24; U 33; U 35; U 39; U 48; U 50; U 52; U 53; U 55; U 62; U 64; U 70; U 73; U 80; U 81; U 86; U 90; U 94; U 96; U 103; U 138; U 160; U 515; U 608; UB 8; UB 47; UB 64; UC 1; UC 17; UC 49; UC 65; UC 66; Ultonia; Ulysses; United States 1901, 1903; Uruguay; Vaderland; Vandyck; Vasari; Vauban; Vestris; Victoria Luise; Victorian; Virginian; Vittoria; Volturno; Von Steuben; Waimana; Walmer Castle; Wanganella; Wechawken; White Palace; Wiltshire; Winifredian; Wyoming; Yale; Yamuna; Zealandic; Zeeland; Zero; Zwarte Zee

GERMANS TO AMERICA (PASSENGER LISTS)

Germans to America: Lists of Passengers Arriving at U.S. Ports, **edited by Ira A Glazier and P. William Filby.**

This is a set of volumes offering an index of immigrants with German surnames taken from original passenger lists filed by ships entering U.S. ports between 1850 and 1893.

This six volume set includes ships that departed from German ports or carried passengers who declared themselves to be of German origin. Information includes first and last names, age, sex, occupation, date of arrival, and province and village of origin (when available) provided for each emigrant.

The entries for 1850 through 1855 cover only ships on which at least 80 percent of passengers had German names; the entries since 1856 reportedly include all passengers with German names.

Many recording errors have been found in this work; researchers are advised to check the passengers lists themselves to confirm the accuracy of extracted data.

A complete index of names is included at the end of every volume.

Publisher: Scholarly Resources, 104 Greenhill Avenue, Wilmington, DE 19805-2897. Tel. (800) 772-8937; Fax (302) 654-3871.

Dates covered by volume

vol. 1 .... Jan 1850 - May 1851
vol. 2 .... May 1851 - Jun 1852
vol. 3 .... Jun 1852 - Sep 1852
vol. 4 .... Sep 1852 - May 1853
vol. 5 .... May 1853 - Oct 1853
vol. 6 .... Oct 1853 - May 1854
vol. 7 .... May 1854 - Aug 1854
vol. 8 .... Aug 1854 - Dec 1854
vol. 9 .... Dec 1854 - Dec 1855
vol. 10 .... Jan 1856 - Apr 1857
vol. 11 .... Apr 1857 - Nov 1857

vol. 12 .... Nov 1857 - Jul 1859
vol. 13 .... Aug 1859 - Dec 1860
vol. 14 .... Jan 1861 - May 1863
vol. 15 .... Jun 1863 - Oct 1864
vol. 16 .... Nov 1864 - Nov 1865
vol. 17 .... Nov 1865 - Jun 1866
vol. 18 .... Jun 1866 - Dec 1866
vol. 19 .... Jan 1867 - Aug 1867
vol. 20 .... Aug 1867 - May 1868
vol. 21 .... May 1868 - Sep 1868
vol. 22 .... Oct 1868 - May 1869
vol. 23 .... Jun 1869 - Dec 1869
vol. 24 .... Jan 1870 - Dec 1870
vol. 25 .... Jan 1871 - Sep 1871
vol. 26 .... Oct 1871 - Apr 1872
vol. 27 .... May 1872 - Jul 1872
vol. 28 .... Aug 1872 - Dec 1872
vol. 29 .... Jan 1873 - May 1873
vol. 30 .... Jun 1873 - Nov 1873
vol. 31 .... Dec 1873 - Dec 1874
vol. 32 .... Jan 1875 - Sep 1876
vol. 33 .... Oct 1876 - Sep 1878
vol. 34 .... Oct 1878 - Dec 1879
vol. 35 .... Jan 1880 - Jun 1880
vol. 36 .... Jul 1880 - Nov 1880
vol. 37 .... Dec 1880 - Apr 1881
vol. 38 .... Apr 1881 - May 1881
vol. 39 .... Jun 1881 - Aug 1881
vol. 40 .... Aug 1881 - Oct 1881
vol. 41 .... Nov 1881 - Mar 1882
vol. 42 .... Mar 1882 - May 1882
vol. 43 .... May 1882 - Aug 1882
vol. 44 .... Aug 1882 - Nov 1882
vol. 45 .... Nov 1882 - Apr 1883
vol. 46 .... Apr 1883 - Jun 1883
vol. 47 .... Jul 1883 - Oct 1883
vol. 48 .... Nov 1883 - Apr 1884
vol. 49 .... Apr 1884 - Jun 1884
vol. 50 .... Jul 1884 - Nov 1884
vol. 51 .... Dec 1884 - Jun 1885
vol. 52 .... Jul 1885 - Apr 1886
vol. 53 .... May 1886 - Jan 1887
vol. 54 .... Jan 1887 - Jun 1887
vol. 55 .... July 1887 - April 1888
vol. 56 .... May 1888 - Nov 1888
vol. 57 .... Dec 1888 - Jun 1889
vol. 58 .... Jul 1889 - Apr 1890
vol. 59 .... May 1890 - Nov 1890
vol. 60 .... Dec 1890 - May 1891

Vol. 61	Jun 1891 – Oct 1891
Vol. 62	Nov 1891 – May 1892
Vol. 63	Jun 1892 – Dec 1892
Vol. 64	Jan 1893 – Jul 1893
Vol. 65	Aug 1893 – Jun 1894
Vol. 66	Jul 1894 – Oct 1895
Vol. 67	Nov 1895 – Jun 1897

Series II: from 1840 to 1849 inclusive

Vol. 1	Jan 1840 – Jun 1843
Vol. 2	Jul 1843 – Dec 1845
Vol. 3	Jan 1846 – Oct 1846
Vol. 4	Nov 1846 – Jul 1847
Vol. 5	Jul 1847 – Mar 1848
Vol. 6	Apr 1848 – Dec 1849
Vol. 7	Oct 1848 – Dec 1849

Digital sources of Germans to America are available online. Volumes 1-56 are found at www.genealogy.com, listed under the International and Passenger Records collection. CDs may be purchased at www.ancestry.com (CD 355 1850-1874 and CD 356 1875-1888).

GERMANS TO AMERICA AND THE HAMBURG PASSENGER LISTS: COORDINATED SCHEDULES

Minert, Roger P. et al. (Westminster, MD: Heritage, 2005)

This book allows the researcher to match directly a passenger arrival list shown in *Germans to America* with the corresponding list of passengers leaving the port of Hamburg. Follow these steps in using this book: 1) Identify the ship on which the person arrived or reportedly arrived. To do so, search the indexes of the volumes of *Germans to America*. 2) Once the immigrant is found, determine where the ship began its voyage— specifically whether the ship departed Hamburg. 3) If the immigrant left the port of Hamburg, search for the ship

name by arrival date in *Coordinated Schedules*. On the same line you will find the date on which the ship left Hamburg and the page numbers of the passenger lists compiled by the Hamburg port authority. 4) Procure the microfilm listed on the same line and search the film for the lowest page number of the Hamburg passenger list. A title page with that number should show the name of the ship, the name of its captain, the nationality of its owner, the date of departure and the port to which it was sailing. Note: the page numbers were often written large in grease pencil and may be challenging to read. Scanning pages before and after will allow you to identify the number.

GERMAN PASSENGERS MISSING FROM GERMANS TO AMERICA

A great number of German immigrants' names were omitted from the *Germans to America* volumes. In Volumes 1 to 9 the compilers disregarded passenger lists showing (apparently) fewer than 80 percent Germans on board. Beginning with Volume 10 (1885), passengers of German origin from all ships were extracted.

The German Research Association (GRA) in San Diego is involved in the ambitious project of extracting the names that were omitted in the first nine volumes of *Germans to America*.

Several issues of GRA's quarterly publication, *The German Connection*, offer lengthy lists of passengers' names extracted from passenger lists by GRA researchers.

GRA's addresses:
German Research Association
P.O. Box 711600
San Diego, CA 92171-1600
www.gragens.org

Source: Antonius Holtmann, "Germans to America: 50 Volumes that Are Not to be Trusted," *The Palatine Immigrants*, Vol XXII, no. 2 (March 1997), 80-87.

PORTS OF DEBARKATION

During the 18th century, emigrants usually used transportation on boats or rafts downstream to ports of overseas embarkation (mainly Rotterdam). As a result of the Navigation Act of the 17th century, European goods (and immigrants bound for the English colonies) had to be transported via England as of 1664.

Therefore, all such ships had to touch an English port (usually London or Cowes) before leaving for America.

The completion of the German railroad system in the 1860s enabled the emigrants to choose among several competing ports of embarkation. All such choices may have depended upon the passage rates and the conditions offered by the travel agent, knowledge of experiences of other emigrants who had traveled from specific ports, and whether the emigrant was leaving his country illegally (and thus, trying to go abroad as quickly as possible, chose a foreign port).

The following are some ports of embarkation from which emigrants traveled, with related comments on the passenger lists and supporting records discovered so far:

Libau (Russia)
Served as a port of embarkation for emigrants from Russia, including Russia-Germans. No information available.

Stettin
(today Szczecin, Poland)
This port had very limited importance from 1869 onward. Passenger lists for the years 1869 to 1898 have been preserved at the Greifswald state archives (*Vorpommersches Landesarchiv Greifswald*) [being prepared by the author for publication].

Hamburg
No emigration lists preserved for the period before 1850. The Staatsarchiv Hamburg (SAHbg) has the following lists for the period after 1850:

1850-1855: Passenger lists contain name, often also the first name and occupation, place of birth or former residence, name of ship, port of destination, date of departure.

1855 - : Passenger lists contain first and last name, age, former place of residence, country or province, occupation, numbers or names of family members, destination, name of ship and captain, date of departure.

Direct emigration
(from Hamburg to an overseas destination port)
1850-1914: 280 volumes, 140 index volumes (*SAHbg Auswanderungsamt* VIII.A.Nr 1f.).

The lists for 1850-1855 are arranged according to the first letter of the surname; later lists are arranged by ships with a separate index.

There is a gap between January and 25 September 1853 (in the lists of direct emigration only).

1871-1887: 2 volumes. Persons who traveled overseas, but not in emigrants' ships (*ibid.* Nr 3).

1850-1914: Lists of emigrants' ships leaving Hamburg (*ibid.* Nr 4).

Indirect emigration
(from Hamburg to an English port and then overseas)
1854-1910: 122 volumes, 25 index volumes. (*SAHbg Auswanderungsamt* VIII.C.Nr 1).

Marriages of emigrants
1850-1853, 1857-1865: Certificates of marriages performed before the U.S. consul at Hamburg, usually among emigrants who could not get a marriage license at home. (For details, see Clifford Neal Smith, *Encyclopedia of German-*

American Genealogical Research, New York: R.R. Bowker 1976, p. 197).

Indexes to these lists

◆The regular indexes beginning in 1855 are organized only by the first letter of the surname, and they are difficult to use.

◆An incomplete card index to the years 1856-1871 was compiled by a group of Church of Jesus Christ of Latter-day Saints volunteers in 1969. It is unknown how complete this index is.

◆The card index to the direct lists 1850-1870 and the indirect lists 1850-1867 was compiled during the last few decades by the Hamburg genealogist Karl Werner Klüber. This index is kept at the Staatsarchiv Hamburg.

◆The indexes to the *Germans to America* book series includes passenger arrivals of ships from Hamburg.

The original passenger lists and the original indexes are no longer available for public use, although they have been microfilmed. There are several ways to obtain access to these films:

◆ The films may be searched in the Family History Centers of the Family History Library of the Church of Jesus Christ of Latter-day Saints.

◆ A professional genealogist in or near Hamburg may be retained.

References

◆ Erika Suchan-Galow, *"Hamburger Quellen zur Auswandererforschung."* *Deutsches Archiv für Landes- und Volksforschung* 7 (1943) 90-98 (Hamburg as a port of embarkation, survey of available sources).

◆Karl-Werner Klüber, "Die Hamburger Schiffslisten." *Archiv für Sippenforschung* (1964) 386-390 (and other articles by the same author with a description of the Hamburg passenger lists and name lists of passengers).

◆ Karl-Egbert Schultze, *"Zur Bearbeitung der Hamburger Auswandererlisten, insbesondere: kann man sie drucken?" Zeitschrift für nieder-*

sächsische Familienkunde 41(1966) 7-9.

◆Karl-Werner Klüber, *"Die Hamburger Auswanderlisten (Schiffslisten)". Mitteilungen der westdeutschen Gesellschaft für Familienkunde* 56 (1968) 278-282 (response by K.W. Klüber to Schultze's considerations).

◆The Genealogical Department of The Church of Jesus Christ of Latter-day Saints (ed.), *The Hamburg Passenger Lists.* Salt Lake City 1976 (Hamburg as a port of emigration, description of the lists and their indexes, case studies).

◆Birgit Gelberg, *Auswanderung nach Übersee. Soziale Probleme der Auswandererbeförderung in Hamburg und Bremen von der Mitte des 19. Jahrhunderts bis zum ersten Weltkrieg.* (Beiträge zur Geschichte Hamburgs 10). Hamburg: Christiansen 1973 (social problems connected with the transportation of emigrants).

◆The Hamburg Passenger Lists," *The Genealogical Helper* 44 (1990) 28.

◆Martin A. Diestler, "Some suggestions on tracing emigrants through Hamburg police records," *The Palatine Immigrant,* vol. 14, no. 1 (March 1989) pp. 16-18.

Partial publications of the Hamburg passenger lists

Note: PILB = William F. Filby (ed.), *Passenger and Immigration Lists Bibliography, 1538-1900. Being a Guide to Published Lists of Arrivals in the United States and Canada.* Detroit (MI): Gale 1981.

This list contains also some passenger lists taken from American arrival lists.
1845 to New Orleans: see PILB 6127.
1849 ship *Deutschland*: see PILB 3967.
1849-1851 Karl Werner Klüber, "Deutsche Auswanderung nach Australien 1849-1851." Genealogie 15 (1966) 186-194 (emigrants to Australia, partially from the Hamburg passenger lists).
1849-1855: see PILB 3879 (entries in the Hamburg passenger lists compared with

emigration announcements in the gazettes of the Bavarian districts of Oberpfalz and Oberfranken).

1850: see PILB 3948 (emigrants from Thuringia).

1850: Karl Welrner Klüber, "Badische Auswanderer nach Übersee." Badische Familienkunde 8 (1965) 131-138 (emigrants from Baden).

1850-1851: see PILB 3941 (emigrants from Bavaria).

1850-1851: see PILB 3935 (emigrants from the Prussian Rhine Province).

1850-1852: see PILB 3886 (emigrants from Anhalt and the Prussian districts of Magdeburg and Merseburg).

1850-1855: see PILB 3960 (emigrants from the city of Leipzig).

HARBURG

Harburg was in the Kingdom of Hannover, across the Elbe River from Hamburg. Transportation of emigrants started 10 April 1851 (see the *Karlsruher Zeitung* 16 April 1851) but never gained much importance.

Reference

♦ Hans-Georg Mercker, *Alphabetisches Register der von und über Harburg ausgewanderten Personen von 1841 bis 1884.* Typescript 1964, one copy located at the Genealogische Gesellschaft, Sitz Hamburg e.V. in Hamburg (list of emigrants from and through the port of Harburg, 1841-54, and returning emigrants).

EMDEN

This port was in the Kingdom of Hannover, Ostfriesland. Transportation of emigrants never gained importance. Some passenger lists were published for 1855-1857. See PILB 9670.

BREMEN

Due to limited storage space and to the authorities' assumption that the emigrants were lost to their native country, the Bremen passenger lists were destroyed annually beginning in 1875, except for the two preceding years. This

procedure continued until about 1907. The emigration lists from 1905 to May 1914 were preserved.

They contained surname and first name of the emigrants, age, number of persons, last residence including country or province, name of ship and country or port of destination. Non-German emigrants were also listed. Passenger lists of ships to England were missing. Those of ships to East Asia, Australia, North and South America were incomplete. These surviving lists were taken to the *Statistisches Landesamt* (Bureau of Statistics) in Bremen in 1931.

In addition, there were police registers from 1898 to 30 July 1914 with the names of German emigrants who traveled in steerage and by third class. These lists were preserved in the *Nachweisungsbüro für Auswanderer* in Bremen.

In 1941, three students extracted records on 8,500 emigrants from Westphalia for the years 1898 to 1914. A small part of this material is preserved in Nordrhein-Westfälisches Staatsarchiv Münster, section Verein für das Deutschtum im Ausland (VDA), cartons 55, 56, and 128.

As this work progressed, duplicates of the lists for 1905 to 1914 were discovered in a shed on the Lloyd platform of the Bremen main railroad station. An evaluation was begun by the Deutsches Auslands-Institut (DAI), Stuttgart, in 1941.

Twenty students were ordered to the Marburg State Archives where they could feel safe from air raids, and the lists (600 kilograms) were trucked there from Bremen. The students limited the task to extractions of Germans or people of German descent. About 80 percent of the lists' emigrants were Slavs, Hungarians, and Jews.

At the end of four weeks, only a fifth of the entries had been extracted, mainly for the years 1907-1908 and 1913-1914.

The lists and the extracts were taken to the DAI and stored there. The extracts for German emigrants were sorted into the Central Emigration File (now in the Bundesarchiv Koblenz, R 57 Kartei 1).

The others, mainly Eastern European extracts, were sorted according to the country of origin and year (now in the Bundesarchiv Koblenz, R 57 Kartei 12). The address of these archives: Am Wöllershof 12, 56068 Koblenz, Germany. These card files were microfilmed by the LDS church.

The lists in Bremen were totally destroyed in an air raid on October 6, 1944. The duplicates in Stuttgart were probably destroyed when the DAI building was hit by bombs on September 12 and 19/20, 1944. Possibly they were stored for safe keeping somewhere in the Württemberg countryside at the end of the war. They have not been recovered.

In 1989, the archives of the Bremen chamber of commerce (*Handelskammer*) had only a very few passenger lists from 1834, 1854, and 1866. The lists for 1920-1923 and 1925-1939 were returned to East Germany in 1988.

Bibliography

♦ Bodo Heyne, *"Über bremische Quellen zur Auswanderungsforschung."* Bremisches Jahrbuch 41 (1944) 358-369 (survey of available passenger lists from 1834 on). Quoted as "Heyne"

♦ Gustav Wehner, *"Das Schicksal der Bremer Auswanderer-Listen"* Norddeutsche Familienkunde 1 (1952) 74-78, 96-98, 113-118. Quoted as "Wehner"

♦ Rolf Engelsing, *Bremen als Auswandererhafen 1683/1880. Ein Beitrag zur bremischen Wirtschafts-geschichte des 19. Jahrhunderts.* (Veröffentlichungen aus dem Staatsarchiv der Freien Hansestadt Bremen 29). Bremen: Schünemann 1961. (Detailed account of the city of Bremen as a port of emigration).

♦ Peter Marschalck (comp.), *Inventar der Quellen zur Geschichte der Wander-*

ungen, besonders der Auswanderung, in Bremer Archiven. (Veröffentlichungen aus dem Staatsarchiv der Freien Hansestadt Bremen 53). Bremen: Staatsarchiv Brem-en 1986.

♦ Gunnar Nebelung, *"Auswanderung über Bremerhaven,"* Genealogie 41 (1992) 250.

Bremen lists

Following are publications of Bremen passenger lists and of passenger arrival lists for ships arriving from Bremen:

1826-1828: Lists of emigrants to Brazil: Staatsarchiv Bremen 2-C.12.e. Published by Peter Marschalck, *"Brasilienauswanderer aus dem Saar-Hunsrück-Raum in Bremen 1826-1828."* Zeitschrift für die Geschichte der Saargegend 34 (1986).

1832-1849: Friedrich Spengemann, *Die Reisen der Segelfregatten "Isabella" "Pauline" "Meta" und "Uhland" nach Nordamerika.* Bremen: Vahland & Co. 1937. (Passenger lists taken from a logbook, indexed in Wehner 75ff.).

1834: 67 passenger lists of the shipping companies F. D. Lüdering and Westhoff & Meier still existed in 1944 (Heyne p. 363) Two of these lists have been published.

1834: Ship Ferdinand, see Heyne p. 368 (76 persons to Baltimore)

1834: Ship Wallace, see Heyne p. 369 (76 persons to New York)

All of these lists were stored at a safe place at the end of the war but have not been recovered.

1842: Ship Friedrich Lucas, see PILB 5270.

1845: To New Orleans, see PILB 6127.

1845: To Texas, see PILB 2474-2476.

1847-1854: Gary J. Zimmerman, Marion Wolfert (eds.), *German Immigrants. Lists of Passengers Bound from Bremen to New York, 1847-1854.* Baltimore: Genealogical Publishing Company, 1985 (includes only those passengers whose German place of origin is given in the New York passenger arrival lists).

1848-1869 (mainly 1850-1855):
Numerous passenger lists have been
published in print in the contemporary
paper *Allgemeine Auswanderungs-
Zeitung* and are currently being
published by the author (30,060).
1848: Ship Burgundy (shipwrecked),
see PILB 5153.
1850: Ships Itzstein and Welcker, see
PILB 3967.
1851: Ship Reform (and Magnet) to Galveston, see PILB 2514
1854: Ship Johann Georg, see Alfred
Rubarth, *"Auswanderer" Zeitschrift für
niederdeutsche Familienkunde 51*
(1976) 92-93 (26 names).
1855-1862: Gary J. Zimmerman, Marion
Wolfert (eds), *German Immigrants. Lists
of Passengers Bound from Bremen to
New York, 1855-1862.* Baltimore:
Genealogi-cal Publishing company, 1986
(continuation of the book listed above
for 1847-1854).
1863-1867: Gary J. Zimmerman, Marion
Wolfert (eds.), *German Immigrants. Lists
of Passengers Bound from Bremen to
New York, 1863-1867.* Baltimore:
Genealogical Publishing company, 1988
(continuation of the book listed above
for 1855-1862).
1864: Karen P. Neuforth (ed.),
"Passenger List: The Bark Atalanta
Bremen to New York, 1864," *Omnibus 11*
(1990) 692ff.
1875-1876: see PILB 2966.
1875: Ship Ohio, see PILB 2969.
1876: Ship Mosel, see PILB 2971.
1882: Ship Salier, see PILB 6206.
1886: Hans Arnold Plöhn, *"Im Februar
1886 nach New York ausgereiste
Personen,"* Zeitschrift für niederdeutsche Familienkunde 54* (1979) 73-
74 (emigrants on the steamer Ems to New
York, 20 February 1886, from American
sources).

Although the actual passenger lists
are lost, the Bremen state archives has
records about the births, marriages and
death on board Bremen ships from 1834

until 1939. Questions about a particular
ship and the passage can usually be
answered, often when only a picture of
the ship is available.(Staatsarchiv
Bremen, Am Staatsarchiv 1, 28203
Bremen, Germany).

LIVERPOOL
Apparently many German emigrants
took the train from Hull to Liverpool and
embarked there to continue their journey at the cheap British fares.

No passenger lists have been preserved for Liverpool before 1890, probably none for England before that year
at all.

To have a search done in the Passenger Lists Outwards, it is necessary to
know the name of the ship, the year and
month of departure, and the port from
which the ship sailed.

Presumably a search in the Passenger Lists Inwards requires similar data.
These records are open to public search
at the Public Record Office (Ruskin Avenue, Kew, Richmond, Surrey TW9 4DU).

References
♦"From the Old World to the New. The
Half-Way House to the West." *The
Liverpool Review*, 5 and 12 May 1888
(observations on emigrants' housing
and transportation in Liverpool).
♦Public Record Office, Lists and Indexes
Supplementary Series No. IX, Board of
Trade Records to 1913, London: 1964.

GLASGOW
Known to have been a port of embarkation for Russia-Germans in 1879, 1905,
and 1911. No additional information
available.

AMSTERDAM
According to a letter from Gemeente-
archief Amsterdam, 18 January 1987,
there are passenger lists in the Archives
of the Waterschout (Port Administration). No passenger lists at all have been
found, but it is doubtful whether any

were kept.

ROTTERDAM

Rotterdam is at the mouth of the Rhine River and was thus the main port of embarkation during the 18th century. Only the passenger arrival lists for the port of Philadelphia have been preserved for the years 1727 to 1808. These were edited by Strassburger and Hinke.

The available passenger lists of the mass emigration of 1709 have been published:

◆Walter Allen Knittle, *Early Eighteenth Century Palatine Emigration*. Philadelphia 1927, Reprints Baltimore: Genealogical Publishing Company 1965, 1970 (pp. 243-282 include the Rotterdam sailing lists of 1709, the London Census of the Palatines of 1709, not in the original order and with some errors).

◆ Lou D. MacWeathy, *The Book of Names* (etc.), St. Johnsville (NY) 1933, Reprint Baltimore: Genealogical Publishing Company 1969 (pp. 75-111 the London Census of the Palatines of 1709, with some errors).

◆Henry Z. Jones, John P. Dern, "Palatine Emigrants Returning in 1710."

◆Karl Scherer (ed.), *Pfälzer-Palatines.* Kaiserslautern: Heimatstelle Pfalz 1981, 52-77 (lists of passengers who returned from London to Rotterdam in 1710).

◆ Henry Z. Jones, Jr., *The Palatine Families of New York. A Study of hte German Immigrants Who Arrived in Colonial New York in 1710*. 2 vols. Universal City (CA): privately published by the author, 1985 (this is not a publication of the passenger lists, but an extensive investigation on those emigrants who later settled in colonial New York and New Jersey).

◆John P. Dern, *London Churchbooks and the German Emigration of 1709. Die deutsche Auswanderung von 1709 in den Londoner Kirchenbüchern. (Schriften zur Wanderungsgeschichte der Pfälzer* 26). Kaiserslautern:

Heimatstelle Pfalz 1968 (listed here as it pertains to the 1709 emigration).

Note: According to a letter from *Gemeente Rotterdam*, Archiefdienst (Robert Fruinstraat 52, 3021 XE Rotterdam, Netherlands), 18 January 1987, the Archives of the Waterschout were destroyed in the Second World War, including the passenger lists.

The archives of the Holland-Amerika Line shipping company contain "passagestaten" and "passagiers-registers" from 1900 on. These passenger lists contain many Germans.

ANTWERP

General information: G. Kurgan, E. Spelkens, *Two Studies on Emigration through Antwerp to the New World.* Brussels: Center for American Studies 1976 (con-tains an essay by G. Kurgan-van Hen-tentryk on Belgian emigration to the United States and other overseas countries at the beginning of the 20th century, and a statistical investigation by E. Spelkels on Antwerp as a port of emigration 1843-1913).

Only the embarkation lists of 1855 have survived and been published: Charles M. Hall (ed.), *The Antwerp Emigration Index.* Salt Lake City: Heritage International (NY) – name, age, place of origin, name of ship and place where passport was issued, for about 5,100 emigrants, many of them from Germany.

Registers for other years were destroyed by German troops in 1914.

The Ludwigsburg State Archives preserves a list of Württemberg emigrants on the ship *Vaterlands-Liebe,* leaving Antwerp for Philadelphia in May 1817 (Staatsarchiv Ludwigsburg D 41, Büschel 4408, reproduced in Günter Moltmann (ed.) *Aufbruch nach Amerika.* Tübingen: Wunderlich 1979, 263-268).

Additional records in the City Archives of Antwerp have been checked for names of German emigrants: hotel registers 1801-1821 and 1858-1887

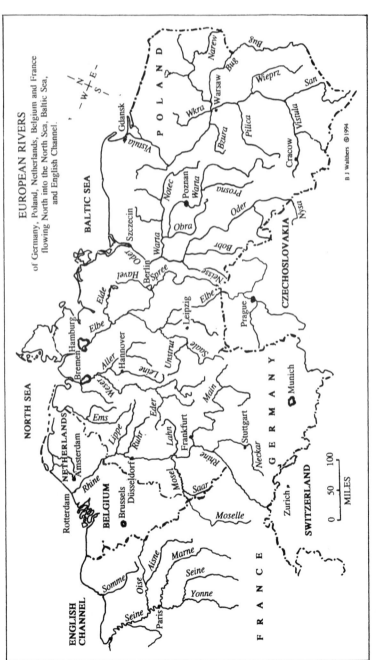

EUROPEAN RIVERS

of Germany, Poland, Netherlands, Belgium and France flowing North into the North Sea, Baltic Sea, and English Channel.

(MA2641, MA2645, MA2669, MA2672), lists of emigres 1793-1815 (MA447/1, MA450/1) sojourn registers 1840-1871 (MA2670/1-12, MA2671/1), general records on German emigrants 1850-1856 (MA674/1), passport and visa registers 1798-1857 (MA2643, MA2644) passenger arrivals from Rotterdam and London 1843-1844 (MA2636). Most of these lists are incomplete. None contains German emigrants in transit.

LE HAVRE

The port of LeHavre was mainly used by emigrants from southern Germany during the period from about 1830 to 1870.

General information: Jean Braunstein, *"L'emigration allemande par le port du Havre au XIXe siecle."* Annales de Normandie 34 *(*1984) 95-104 (statistical evaluation of the available data).

The passenger lists are kept at the Archives Departementales de la Seine Maritime, Cours Clemenceau, 76036 Rouen Cedex, France (6 P 6 no. 1-600 for 1750-1898, also for later years).

They give name, description and destination of the ship (mostly to French colonies), name, sometimes age and occupation of the passengers, their place of birth or residence (or the place where their passport was issued), and the names or numbers of family members.

These lists were delivered by the captains when they returned to LeHavre, which may have been one or two years after their departure.

They are filed by the date of delivery and therefore they are hard to locate. Only passenger lists for French ships were delivered, and therefore these lists cover only a small part of the emigrants through this part.

A card index to about 40,000 passenger entries was discovered in the 1980s and thus saved from destruction. This information was supplied by M. Jean-Paul Portellette of LeHavre, who is in charge of the preparation of a letter-by-letter series of publications containing the data from this index.

For details, one may write to Cercle Genealogique et Heraldique de Normandie, 17 rue Louis Malliot, 76000 Rouen, France (without any guarantee of receiving an answer).

Supporting information

The civil registration (*Etat civil*) registers do not contain entries on German emigrants who were married or had a child born in LeHavre. Entries of this kind might be found in the registers of the churches (mainly of the Saint Francois Church). The marriages from 1867 to 1870 have been published:

Jean-Paul and Elisabeth Portelette (eds.), *"La Chapelle des Allemands du Havre."* Revue genealogique normande no. 17 (1986) 11-14 (list of 148 marriages, not giving the places of origin, which are also not given in the original records, Archives Departementales de la Seine Maritime, I J 368).

The names of 3,987 passengers from 1848 to 1855, mainly 1850 to 1854 were published by Friedrich R. Wollmershäuser under the title *Vielen Dank, Herr Bielefeld.*

Sources replacing the passenger lists of various ports

♦ Lists of emigrants signing a letter of thanks to the travel agent for his goods and services. These lists were then published by the agent for advertising purposes. Lists of this type are found in many German newspapers of the 1850s and sometimes 1860s.

♦ Ship passenger lists published in the *Allgemeine Auswanderungs-Zeitung* (printed in Rudolstadt 1846-1871). Two lists of this type (for the ships *Itzstein & Welcker* leaving Bremen for New Orleans, and *Helena Sloman*, Hamburg to New York, both in 1850) were published by Karl Werner Klüber (see

PILB 3967 and 3921).

Final notes

◆*Clues* (a magazine of the American Historical Society of Germans from Russia) regularly publishes lists of Russia-German passengers to American and Canadian ports.

◆ The remaining passenger arrival lists of the US-American ports from 1850 onward are being published in the following book series:
Ira A. Glazier, P. William Filby (eds), *Germans to America. Lists of Passengers Arriving at U.S. Ports* [1850-1855], vol. 1ff, Wilmington DE: Scholarly Resources 1988ff. and continued.

◆ Michael Palmer, "Published Passenger Lists: A Review of German Immigrants and Germans to America." *German Genealogical Society of America Bulletin* vol. 4 (1990) pp. 69, 71-90, and not continued (a very detailed account on the available United States arrival lists and the com-pleteness and quality of their publication).

Source: Friedrich R. Wollmershäuser, M.A. The author, an Accredited Genealogist, lives at Herrengasse 8-10 , 89610 Oberdischingen, Germany ©Friedrich R. Wollmershäuser, 1997.

LIST OF GERMAN EMIGRANTS

◆ **Baden Emigration Indexes**
http://wwancestry.com/search/rectype/inddbs/4610a.htm
This index contains the names of over 28,000 persons who legally emigrated from Baden between 1866 and 1911. Entries include such information as the immigrant's name, residence, birthplace and departure year.

Brandenburg Emigration Indexes
http://www.ancestry.com/search/db.aspx?dbid=4121\
This source is a partial index to names of emigrants leaving the government

district of Potsdam, Brandenburg, Prussia after 1810. Of the original source, which consists of emigration applications for 44 Brandenburg counties, this database contains a partial index of more than 61,000 persons. A complete index may be viewed at the Salt Lake Family History Library under the title Auswanderungskartei (Fiche 6109219 and 6109220).

◆ **Bremen to New York: Lists of Passengers Bound from Bremen to New York, with Places of Origin**
http://www.ancestry.com/search/db.aspx?dbid=7486
This database of immigrants is part of Ancestry's Passenger and Immigration Lists Index, 1500s-1900s. It contains a partial reconstruction of Bremen passenger lists between 1847 and 1871. Not all Bremen passengers are included; only those for whom a specific place of origin is known.

Places of origin, are not included in Ancestry's results. If you find your ancestor in this database, look up the original source from which Ancestry took its data. This will lead you to the actual place name.

The original volumes, compiled by Gary J. Zimmerman and Marion Wolfert, remain on hand at the Salt Lake City, LDS Family History Library (974.71 W3g Vols. 1-4).

◆ **Bremen Passenger Lists 1920-1939**
http://www.passengierlisten.de/
In 1851 the Bremen Chamber of Commerce established the *Nachweisungsbureau für Auswanderer* (the Information Office for Emigrants), to which ship captains had to deliver complete lists of their passengers. Unfortunately, from 1875 to 1908, the staff of the *Nachweisungsbureau*, lacking office space, destroyed all lists older than 3 years. Only 2,953 passenger lists (totaling about 637,880 passengers)

survived for the years 1920 to 1939. The surviving lists of passengers are fund in this database.

♦Deutsche Auswanderer-Datenbank
http://www.deutsche-auswanderer-datenbank.de/
This project is dedicated to gathering and indexing passenger lists and all other emigration to North America via German ports. The site has no online database. You may request a search by filling out an online form.
They presently have data on 4.4 million emigrants, spanning the following years: 1820-1833, 1840-1891, 1904, and 1907.

♦Mecklenburg Emigration Index
http://www.imar-my.com/ind_eng.htm
About 250,000 people from Mecklenburg left their homeland between 1850 and 1900, most of them going to the United States.
The Institute for Migration and Ancestral Research (IMAR) has at its disposal an extensive database that contains the particulars of some 25,000 emigrants from Mecklenburg. This database is continuously updated. Although the database is *not* online, institute members are ready to research inquiries from descendants or Mecklenburg emigrants, via written request.

♦Schleswig-Holstein Emigration index
http://www.rootdigger.de/Emi.htm
This database contains an alphabetical list of 59,000 emigrants, found mainly in parish records, but also found in printed media, personal gedcom files and Ancestry charts available in libraries and genealogical societies. A few names come from passenger lists (Hamburg) and applications to emigrate.

♦Westphalia Emigration Index

http://www.genealogy.net/vereine/wggf/PDF/Mueller%20I%20Aus wanderer.pdf
This database contains the names and places of origin for 6,453 individuals or families who legally and secretly emigrated from Westphalen (Westphalia) between 1803 and 1850.

♦Württemberg Emigration Indexes

Württemberg and Baden Indexes of Glatzle & Müller
http://www.auswanderer-bw.de/sixcms/detail.php?template=a_articel&id=6591&sprache=en&PHPSESSID=
This database contains approximately 250,000 entries with names and hometown information of immigrants who left Württemberg and Baden in the 19th century. The information contained herein was extracted from Oberamt files now stored in the state archive of Stuttgart.

Ancestry's Württemberg Index
http://www.ancestry.com/search/db.aspx?dbid=3141
This source contains about 60,000 persons who made application to emigrate from Württemberg between 1808 and 1890.
The information, compiled by Trudy Schenk and Ruth Froelke, appeared first in book form.

♦ Palatine Project: Reconstructed Passenger Lists, 1683-1819
http://hera.progenealogists.com/palproject/index.html
"The Palatine Project is an ongoing effort, using sources from German-speaking countries as well as early colonial American sources, to annotate and/or reconstruct the passenger lists of Germans who came to America in the first large wave of emigration in the 18th century.

German railway system, 1845.

These annotated lists ware to provide a 'bridging the gap' tool for identifying the original emigrants to America while identifying sources that indicate where they came from in their ancestral country. This is an ambitious project and will require many years. Its success will depend on contributions of information, finances, and other assistance from the public and genealogical communities."

EARLY RAIL TRAVEL

On September 27, 1825, the Englishman George Stephenson's steam powered railway carried 450 people at 15 miles per hour over the 25-mile route from Stockton to Darlington, thus opening

German railway system, 1850.

the way for practical use of the new technology. His success won him a contract to build a line from Liverpool to Manchester.

Several people had previously built self-propelled steam engines, but efforts to build a steam-powered railway had failed due to the cost of construction and the relative inefficiencies of the engine. Thousands of miles of railroad were built during the middle of the 19th century.

Within a few years of Stephenson's 1825 triumph, railroads had been built in Belgium, Italy, Austria and the Netherlands. France built its first in 1832, the Russians in 1837. The first German railroad opened on December 7, 1835, powered by der Adler (the eagle), a Stephenson-built locomotive, and provided transportation between Nürnberg and Fürth. By 1850, 3,000 miles of railroads were in operation in Germany. It was possible to travel from Munich to Hamburg,

German railway system, 1880.

Stettin, the Rhineland, or Silesia by rail. Anyone going to America after 1850 most certainly could have traveled at least part of the way across the continent by rail.

Source: Excerpted from "How Our Ancestors Got to the Sea," by Bruce Walthers and Rolf Wasser. *The German Connection*, Vol. 18, No. 2 , 1994.

DEVELOPMENT OF THE GERMAN RAILWAY SYSTEM: 1835-1866

Following are completion dates, first-stretch completion dates, and dates of a few other significant events in the development of the German railway, connecting German cities as well as a few cities in Switzerland, Belgium, Holland, and Austria:

1827-1832: Horsedrawn railway from Linz to Budweis
1835 (7 Dec): first stretch of railway between Nürnberg and Fürth opened.
1837 (24 Apr.): Leipzig-Dresden (first stretch), completed 7 Apr. 1839 (including the first German railway tunnel). This was the first long-distance railroad line and the first line of major consequence in German lands.
1838 (29 Oct.): Berlin - Potsdam
1938 (1 Dec.): Braunschweig-Wolfenbüttel
1838 (20 Dec.): Düsseldorf - Erkrath
1838: Mannheim - Basel
1838: Wien - Wagram
1839: Wien - Brünn
1839 (29 Jun.): Magdeburg - Halle - Leipzig (first stretch), completed 18 Aug. 1840
1839 (2 Aug.): Köln - Aachen (first stretch), completed 1 Sep. 1841; in 1843 extended to Antwerp
1839 (1 Sep): München - Augsburg (first stretch), completed 4 Oct. 1840
1839 (26 Sep): Taunusbahn Frankfurt - Wiesbaden (first stretch), completed 19 May 1840
1839: Dresden - Leipzig (extended to Magdeburg the next year)
1839: Amsterdam - Haarlem
1840 (12 Sep): Mannheim - Heidelberg
1841: Berlin - Anhalt
1842: Berlin - Stettin
1842: Berlin - Frankfurt on der Oder
1843: The Köln - Aachen line crossed over the border into Belgium
1843: Elberfeld - Dortmund
1844: Nürnberg-Erlangen-Bamberg
1846: Berlin - Hamburg
1847: Köln - Minden (to connect with Hannover - Berlin); by 1848 it was possible to travel by rail between Köln and Berlin.
1847: Hamburg and Bremen were both connected to Hannover
1847: By this year, the Rhine and Weser rivers were connected by rail, providing wider access to major ports.

1847: Frankfurt - Basel
1847: Baden - Zürich
1851: First *Schnellzug* (speed train) between Berlin and Köln (17 hours)
1858: Rosenheim - Kiefersfelden (first railway connection between Germany and Austria)
1859: München - Wien
1859: The first railroad bridge over the Rhine built at Köln.
1863: Rhine railway ferry operated between Mannheim and Ludwigshafen
1866: By this year, the German railway system was completed, followed by a knitting together of lines occurring over the next 20 to 25 years.

Rail webs by 1848

By 1848, German railways radiated from a number of regional centers. Some of these include,
♦**Berlin:** Linked to the north by lines to Stettin and Hamburg, to the east by a line to Breslau, and to the west by a line running through Braunschweig and Hannover, and then turning south into Westfalen and on to Köln
♦**Port cities:** Both Hamburg and Bremen connected to Hannover, in turn connecting to a number of routes to the east, west, and south
♦ **Köln:** Joined upper Rhine cities in southwestern localities to major port cities in the north.
♦ **München:** From München north to Plauen, rails linked cities such as Augsburg, Nürnberg, Bamberg, and Hof
♦**Frankfurt am Main:** The city central to a north-south railway line connecting southern cities such as Freiburg, Stuttgart, Karlsruhe, Heidelberg and Mannheim, to northern cities like Kassel, Hannover, and Bremen.

Sources:
♦Asmus, Carl, *Die Ludwigs-Eisenbahn: Die erste Eisenbahnlinie in Deutschland,* Orell Füssli Verlag, Zürich, 1984.
♦Hans-Peter Friedrich and Ulrich Schefold, *Die Eisenbahn von A-Z: Das Lexikon für*

Väter und Söhne, Südwest Verlag, München, 1983.

♦Hajo Holborn, *A History of Modern Germany 1840-1945*, Princeton University Press, 1969.

♦Martin Kitchen, *The Cambridge Illustrated History of Germany*, Cambridge University Press, 1996.

♦Thomas Nipperdey, Daniel Nolan, trans., *Germany from Napoleon to Bismarck 1800-1866*, Princeton University Press, 1996.

♦Werner Walz, *Deutschlands Eisenbahn 1835-1985*, Motorbuch Verlag, Stuttgart, 1985.

♦*Zug der Zeit - Zeit der Züge Deutsche Eisenbahn 1835-1985*, Bd. 1, Wolf Jobst Siedler Verlag, Berlin, 1985.

BEHIND THE GERMAN MIGRATIONS

A book in circulation during the mid-nineteenth century, *Hand- und Reisebuch für Auswanderer* [Handbook and Travel Guide for Emigrants], by Traugott Bromme, offers these reasons for German emigration:

"The innate human urge to forge ahead, to improve one's position, as well as distress, dependent situations, pressures from all sides, often among the best of the most highly placed persons, are reasons why thousands are leaving their fatherland, seeking a new homeland, thousands more are preparing to follow them, and hundreds of thousands are dejectedly and longingly watching the emigrants whom they, for lack of funds, are unable to follow, even though they desire a change, an improvement in their situation just as ardently as the fortunate ones."[1]

A twentieth century writer, Peter Marschalck, has written,

"There is a natural outflow from areas containing too many people in a space toward those with too few people in a space.

"Space is the (not only material) possibility of existence (e.g. political oppression is too small a space for the possibility of political existence; overpopulation is too small a space for the possibility of economic existence) . . . .

"The relationship between people and space, whenever it is not in equilibrium, strives for equilibrium in the long term by adaptation and in the short term by migrations."[2]

An 1851 emigrant song went like this:
Mein Vetter schrieb noch kürzlich mir aus diesem schönen Land
Und Ich bleib' wahrlich nicht mehr hier, will hin zum schönen Land
Rosinen, Mandeln ißt man da, wie hierzuland das Brot
Denn in dem Land Amerika hat man gar keine Not[3]

Translation
My cousin wrote me just a while ago from this beautiful land
And I really won't stay here much longer, I want to go to the beautiful land
Raisins, almonds are eaten there as in this country one eats bread,
For in the land of America there is no want.

[1]Traugott Bromme, Hand- und Reisebuch für Auswanderer nach den Vereinigten Staaten von Nord-Amerika

[2]Peter Martschalck, *Deutsche Überseewanderung im 19. Jahrhundert* [German Migration Overseas in the 19th Century], Stuttgart 1973

[3]Text of the poem in Karl Andree, "Umwandlungen im Weltverkehr der Neuzeit" [Changes in World Traffic in Modern Times], *Deutsche Vierteljahrsschrift*, 18 (1855).

Source for all of the above: Günter Moltmann, *Germans to America: 300 Years of Immigration, 1683 to 1983.* Institute for Foreign Cultural Relations in cooperation with Inter Nationes, Bonn-Bad Godesburg, 1982.

SOME EARLY RAILROAD LINES
IN ENGLAND AND CONTINENTAL EUROPE

1825 ...... Stockton to Darlington, England (20 miles)
1827 ...... Kerschmarm to Budweiss, Austria(started in 1827)
1827 ...... St. Etienne to Andrezieux, France (used horsepower until 1832)
1830 ...... Mancester to Liverpool, England
1831 ...... Rotterdam to Amsterdam, Netherlands (North Sea port)
1832 ...... Linz to Budweiss, Austria-Hungary (used horsepower until 1837)
1832 ...... St. Etienne To Lyon, France (38 miles, begun in 1828)
1835 ...... Brussels to Malines, Belgium
1835 ...... Nürnberg to Fürth, Bavaria (using a Stephenson-built locomotive)
1836 ...... Linz to Gmunden, Austria (opened in 1836)
1837 ...... Linz to Budweiss, Austria (originally horse-drawn)
1837 ...... Paris to St. Germain, France (13 miles, originally horsedrawn)
1837 ...... Vienna to Brno, Austria
1838 ...... Berlin to Posdam, Prussia
1838 ...... Brunswick to Wolfenbüttel, Brunswick
1839 ...... Haarlem to Amsterdam, Netherlands(Rhine, North Sea port; opened in 1839)
1839 ...... Cologne to Müngersdorf, Prussia
1839 ...... Frankfurt to Hattersheim, Hesse
1839 ...... Leipzig to Dresden, Saxony (carried 412,000 passengers the first year)
1839 ...... Magdeburg, Prussia to Calbe (Saale), Saxony/Anhalt
1839 ...... Munich to Maisach, Bavaria
1839 ...... Naples to Portici, Italy
1839/40 ..Paris to Versailles, France (two competing lines)
1840 ...... Berlin to Wittenberg, Prussia (first section finished)
1840 ...... Frankfurt to Wiesbaden, Hessen
1840 ...... Magdeburg, Prussia, to Leipzig, Saxony
1840 ...... Mannheim to Heidelberg, Baden
1841 ...... Berlin, Prussia, to Köthen, Saxony/Anhalt
1841 ...... Berlin to Stettin, Prussia (Oder, Baltic port)
1841 ...... Düsseldorf to Elberfeld, Prussia
1841 ...... Strasbourg to Basel, Switzerland (the first international line)
1842 ...... Bergedorf to Hamburg, Hamburg (Elbe, North Sea port)
1842 ...... Minden to Cologne, Prussia
1843 ...... Angermünde to Stettin, Prussia (Oder, Baltic port)
1843 ...... Cologne, Prussia to Brussels-Antwerp, Belgium
1844 ...... Hamburg, Hamburg to Altona, Schleswig-Holstein
1846 ...... Stargard to Stettin, Prussia (Oder, Baltic port)
1847 ...... Celle, Hannover to Harburg-Wilhelmsburg-Hamburg, Hamburg
.... (Elbe, North Sea port)
1847 ...... Copenhagen to Roskilde, Denmark (first in Scandanavia)
1847 ...... Wunstorf, Hannover, to Bremen, Bremen (Weser, North Sea port)
1847 ...... Zürich, Switzerland, to Baden
1848 ...... Barcelona to Mataro, Spain
1848 ...... Mürzzuschlag to Gloggnitz, Austria (started in 1848, finished about 1854)
1848 ...... Schwerin to Wismar, Mecklenburg (Baltic port)

1850 ...... Bad Kleinen to Rostock, Mecklenburg (Baltic port)
1851 ...... Moscow to St. Petersburg, Russia (Baltic port)
1856 ...... Cologne, Prussia, to Amsterdam/Rotterdam, Netherlands (Rhine, North Sea
.... port)
1856 ...... Münster/Westphalia, Prussia to Emden, Hannover (Ems, North Sea port)
1862 ...... Bremen to Bremerhaven, Bremen (Weser, North Sea port)
1867 ...... Oldenburg, Oldenburg, to Bremen, Bremen (Weser, North Sea port)

©Copyright 1997 Bruce Walthers von Alten and Rolf Wasser, originally published in *The German Connection*, Vol. 18, No. 2. Reprinted with permission.

TIMELINE OF IMMIGRATION LAWS IN THE UNITED STATES

1819: Under An Act Regulating Passenger Ships and Vessels, ship captains had to submit to customs officials a list of passengers, describing name, age, sex, vocation, country of origin, and country of destination of each passenger. Passengers ill with contagious diseases had to be quarantined. States carried out provisions of this law.

1847 and 1848: Congress passed laws on accommodation of passengers on ships.

1855: An act of Congress superseded the laws of 1819, 1847, and 1848, whereby it stated the amount of space to which immigrants were entitled aboard ship and required issue of at least one hot meal per day for steerage passengers. The law was not very effective in correcting the problems of abuse to immigrants.

1864: An Act to Encourage Immigration provided for the naming of a Commissioner of Immigration, in order to encourage contract labor, to increase the numbers of farm workers, and to build American industry.

Immigrants were granted exemption from military service for as long as they remained citizens of a foreign country and did not voluntarily apply for American citizenship. The act was repealed four years later, but competition among the states to attract new citizens grew.

1875: The Immigration Act of 1875 provided for inspection of vessels by state officials. The law barred the admission of ex-convicts as well as Chinese and Japanese who were brought to the United States against their will.

1882: An act was passed by which every immigrant was charged a poll tax of 50 cents.

Subsequent increases had the effect of reducing immigration. In the 1880s authority over immigration, including enforcement of the Federal statutes, remained at the state level.

1885: A law was passed prohibiting contract labor. It was designed to end the practice of signing up foreign laborers to work in America for low wages. No immigrant could have a job or a promise of a job before landing.

1891: The Immigration Act of 1891 provided for the federal government to take over entirely the job of processing immigrants. Federal inspectors examined immi-grants on arrival. All immigrants had to pass a medical exam and answer questions about their background and intentions in America. Shipping lines were forbidden to solicit immigrants in foreign countries. The law also barred from admission persons suffering from "loathesome or dangerous diseases," those convicted of crimes involving "moral turpitude," polygamists, and those whose passage was paid for by others. Those rejected for immigration were deported at the expense of the shipping companies which had transported them to the United States.

As a result of this law, all duties previously deferred to the States were transferred by the June 30, 1891 to United States inspection officers. The Bureau of Immigration began operations in the Treasury Department as the first Federal immigration agency. Besides its headquarters in Washington, DC, the Bureau opened 24 inspection stations (including Ellis Island in January 1892) at ports of entry along both borders and in major seaports.

1903: The Bureau of Immigration was moved to the newly established Department of Commerce and Labor and given broader responsibilities.

1903, 1907: Further laws were passed to impose stricter standards of admission, the object being to exclude untrained workers and anarchists.

1917: A law was enacted prescribing a literacy test for immigrants, affecting primarily eastern and southeastern Europeans.

1921: From this date, all immigration was controlled by a quota system. Starting in this year, quotas allowed only three per-cent of the share of a nationality in the total American population, as determined by the 1910 census.

1924: The quota was reduced to two per-cent, with the calculation based on the 1890 census. (In that census year, immigration from eastern and southeastern countries had not been so high.)

1929: American consuls in the countries of emigration were given the decision as to the granting of visas, thus influencing immigration. (In 1921, the maximum immigration for Germany was set at 68,051, which dropped to 51,227 following the act of 1924, and was reduced to 25,967 in 1929. In 1923, Germany exhausted its quota within six months. After 1930, German immigration to the United States almost came to a stop.)

1965: New regulations gave every country a limit of 20,000 immigrants, but not more than 290,000 persons could be admitted annually (170,000 from the eastern and 120,000 from the western hemisphere).

Sources:
♦"Emigration Policy in Germany and Immigration Policy in the United States," by Ingrid Schöberl.
♦*Germans to America: 300 Years of Immigration 1683-1983,* ed. Günter Moltmann, Institute for Foreign Relations, Stuttgart, in cooperation with Inter Nationes, Bonn. Bad Godesberg, 1982. Also, U.S. Immigration and Naturalization Service.

NATURALIZATION TIMELINE

1607-1740: Naturalization was granted through the British Crown or Parliament, but colonial governors also granted natur-alization for the colony (but not for British citizenship).

1740: Naturalization by colonies required seven years' residency in the colony, an oath of allegiance to the Crown, profession of Christian belief in a colonial court, and evidence of taking of the sacrament in a Protestant and Reformed Congregation (exemptions allowed for Jews and Quakers).

Revolutionary War period: Most of the newly formed states required an oath of allegiance, demonstration of good character, a specified period of residency, and a disavowal of allegiance to a foreign power.

1790: Under the Constitution, the control of the several states was replaced with federal naturalization, requiring one year's state residence, two years' residence in the United States, and a loyalty oath taken in a court.

1795: Requirements for naturalization were residency in the United States for five years, one year's residency in the state where naturalized, a declaration of intent three years before the oath, an oath of allegiance, good moral character, renunciation of any title of nobility, and the foreswearing of allegiance to the reigning foreign sovereign.

1798: The requirement changed to 14 years' residency, with the declaration of intent to be filed five years before the loyalty oath.

1802: Provisions as required in 1795 (above) were restored. Any court which kept records (U.S., state, county, city) could carry out the declaration and oath. The alien was to register with the court, which was "to ascertain the name, birthplace, age, nation and allegiance of each alien, together with the country whence he or she migrated. . .." Automatic citizenship was provided for wives and children of naturalized males and for men who received an honorable discharge for U.S. military service.

1828: The registry requirements of the 1802 law were repealed, but by the late 1820s, the registry and declaration were frequently united as one document. Procedures of the naturalization process: 1) Report and Registry of Aliens, 1798-1828, either separate from or combined with 2) the Declaration of Intention, 3) the Petition for Naturalization, 4) the order of the court granting citizenship, based upon the petition and oath of allegiance, and 5) Certificate of Naturalization. (Note: the first two steps did not always occur at the same time or in the same court.)

1868: With enactment of the Fourteenth Amendment, national citizenship was guaranteed and extended to all persons born or naturalized in the United States and subject to its jurisdiction.

1906: The Bureau of Immigration and Naturalization was created and given authority to make rules, one of which was that the courts had to use only officially produced blank forms and records. (Before 1906, the courts were totally responsible for the naturalization process.)

1913: The Division of Naturalization became the Bureau of Naturalization, which it remained until 1933 when the name was changed to the Immigration and Naturalization Service, in the Department of Labor. This agency was transferred to the Department of Justice in 1940.

1929: An act provided a major refinement of the 1906 law, among other matters clarifying the requirements for registry of aliens and providing for certificates of derivative naturalization. American consuls in countries of emigration were given the responsibility for deciding who could and could not emigrate.

1930: Due to strict implementation of American immigration restrictions, German migration to the United States almost completely stopped after this year.

NATURALIZATION RECORDS: AN OVERVIEW

Naturalization papers are records of a court procedure granting U.S. citizenship to noncitizens. They usually include three documents — a Declaration of Intent to become a citizen, Petition, and Naturalization Certificate. Prior to 1906, the court record was the only record of a naturalization. After implementation of the Basic Naturalization Act of 1906, a second copy of the records was sent to the then new Bureau of Naturalization in Washington, DC, now part of the U.S. Immigration and Naturalization Service.

Note

Naturalization records exist only for those immigrants who sought citizenship. No such records were drawn for persons who gained citizenship by being born in the United States, by being the wife or child of a naturalized male, or by other derivative citizenship processes.

The main attraction for naturalization

was that it provided the right to vote; it was never required for residency. For many German immigrants, naturalization may not have been particularly appealing. In 1901, for example, 65.4 percent of eligible German aliens were naturalized.

Evidence of time and place of naturalization may be found in federal and state censuses, passenger manifests, homestead applications, passport applications, and voter registrations. Filby's *Passenger and Immigration Lists Index* may also provide clues.

DOCUMENTS INCLUDED IN THE NATURALIZATION PROCESS

◆ Declarations of Intent (commonly known as "First Papers")
Through the Declaration of Intent, the applicant renounced allegiance to a foreign government and stated an intention to become a United States citizen.

It usually appeared two years before other documents. (Between 1798 and 1828, an immigrant, upon arrival, may have filed at a local court of record for a "certificate of report and registry.")

The Declaration of Intent was sometimes not required if the applicant served in the military with an honorable discharge, or entered the country as a minor.

If an alien filed a Declaration of Intent but never followed through with the final papers, the document should nevertheless have remained on file.

◆ Naturalization petitions (or "Second," or "Final Papers")
Naturalization petitions were used to make formal applications for citizenship by those who had met residency requirements and who had declared their intention to become citizens.

Usually the residency requirement was five years in the United States, and one year in the state in which applica-

tion was being filed.

◆ Naturalization depositions
These depositions are formal statements by other persons supporting the applicant's petition for naturalization.

◆ Records of Naturalization/Oaths of Allegiance
These records document the granting of U.S. citizenship to petitioners.

Such records, later filed in the form of certificates, may typically appear in the court of naturalization in chronological arrangement, often in bound volumes which include surname indexes. Sometimes the records of a petitioner are bound in the form of a "petition and record."

◆ Final Certificate
The certificate of citizenship was given to the immigrant.

INFORMATION FOUND IN NATURALIZATION RECORDS

Before September 27, 1906, there was no uniform method of creating naturalization records. As a result, pre-1906 records may contain little information, or may contain a wealth of data. Records before 1906 do not give birth date or town of birth.

After September 26, 1906, naturalization records take a standard format and contain prescribed information. They include the place and date of birth of the immigrant and other family members, port of arrival, vessel name, and date of arrival.

Usual content of records
◆ Declarations of Intent prior to 1906:
Name, country of birth or allegiance, date of application, and signature. Some provide the date and port of arrival in the United States.

◆ Declarations of Intent after 1906:
Applicant's name, age, occupation, and personal description; date and place of birth; citizenship; present address and

last foreign address; vessel and port of em-barkation for the United States; date of application and signature

◆**Naturalization petitions**: Name, residence, occupation, date and place of birth, citizenship, personal description; date of emigration; port of embarkation and arrival; marital status; names, dates, places of birth, and residence of applicant's children; date at which U.S. residence commenced; time of residence in state; name changes; and signature.

Frequently interfiled with these petitions are copies of declarations of intention, certificates of arrival, and certificates of completion of citizenship classes. Petitions after 1930 often include photographs of the applicants.

◆**Naturalization depositions:** Period of applicant's residence in a certain locale and other information, including witnesses' appraisals of the applicant's character.

◆**Certificate of Naturalization/Oaths of Allegiance:** The petition for naturalization, affidavits of the petitioner and witnesses, the oath of allegiance, and the order of the court admitting the petitioner to citizenship

◆ **Petition and Record:** Documents gathered together into a "Petition and Record," providing the petition for naturalization, affidavits of the petitioner and witnesses, the oath of allegiance, and the order of the court admitting the petitioner to citizenship

THE SEARCH FOR NATURALIZATION RECORDS

◆ For naturalizations occurring before September 27, 1906, there are court records only, which may be found in court houses, state and federal archives, historical societies, and libraries. See *Guide to Naturalization Records of the United States*, by Christina K. Schaefer, for locations of records by state and

county. FHL 973 P4s

◆Beginning September 27, 1906, there were two copies of naturalization records filed — one with the court and one with the Bureau of Immigration and Naturalization, now part of the Immigration and Naturalization Service. Also, copies of the records are usually kept with the records of court which handled them or at a state archives.

Court copies

◆Most (but not all) Federal court records are now in the custody of the National Archives.

wMany state and local court records are stored by other institutions, such as a State Archive.

◆County records are listed in the Family History Library Catalog under the state, then the county, then "Naturalization and Citizenship."

◆ For any court naturalization record, write the Clerk of Court in the county (or coun-ties) where it is likely the immigrant may have applied.

National Archives

The regional archives of the National Archives and Records Administration hold original records of naturalizations filed in most of the federal courts (and, in some cases, non-federal courts) located in their respective regions. The available records span the period from 1790 to 1950, but coverage varies from region to region. Due to the variability in records and finding aids available in each region, researchers should contact the appropriate regional archives for specific information.

Immigration and Naturalization Service (INS)

The INS kept records of naturalizations from September 26, 1906 to March 2003, but those records are available only through Freedom of Information Act (FOIA)/Privacy Act (PA) request.

However, copies of most records made by the INS may also be available at public institutions without FOIA/PA restrictions.

Locating the records

♦Homestead and passport applications, normally stored in the National Archives, include the name of the court where a naturalization was certified.The naturalization records are often found with these respective applications.

♦In the Family History Library Catalog, search under one of the following: [State] - Naturalization and Citizenship; [State], [County], - Naturalization and Citizen-ship; and [State], [County], [City] - Naturalization and Citizenship.

♦The National Archives' 11 regional archives hold original records of naturalizations filed in most of the federal courts (and, in some cases, nonfederal courts) located in their regions.

The available records span the periods from 1790 to 1950, but coverage varies from region to region.

Due to the variability in records and finding aids which are available in each region, researchers should contact the appropriate regional archives for specific information.

♦ When the 1870 census shows an immigrant to have become a citizen, it is apparent that naturalization papers exist.

♦Check censuses, homestead records, passports, voting registers, and military papers for indications that an immigrant met citizenship requirements.

♦An excellent guide detailing this topic is found in the *Research Outline: United States*, published by the Family History Library and available for printing out on www.FamilySearch.org.

DERIVATIVE CITIZENSHIP

Derivative citizenship is that which is based on the citizenship of another person or on service performed by an applicant. Included below are provisions of derivative citizenship, not including

group citizenship (which includes blocks of people such as Native Americans or Chinese).

1790: Children of naturalized citizens automatically became citizens.

1790-1922: During this timespan, the wife became naturalized when her husband gained citizenship.)

1804: Widows and minor children of a deceased applicant who had filed his declaration of intention but who died before the naturalization proceeding, could be declared citizens upon taking the oath required by law.

1824: Minor aliens who had lived in the United States three years before age 21 and for two years thereafter could apply for naturalization. (Repealed in 1906).

1922: An 1855 law granting citizenship to a woman by marriage to a citizen was repealed. Under this law, a married woman now had to be naturalized on her own.

CITIZENSHIP: MILITARY SERVICE AND LAND PURCHASE

1862: An alien of age 21 or more with an honorary discharge from the regular or volunteer armies could petition to become a citizen without any previous declaration of intention and with proof of one year's residence. This legislation applied to any war, including the Mexican, Indian, and the Spanish-American wars.

1894: The same privilege of naturalization was given without filing a declaration of intent to a man who had been honorably discharged after five consecutive years in the Navy or one enlistment in the Marine Corps.

1918: The various laws regarding naturalization of soldiers, sailors and veterans were consolidated, and rules for aliens serving in World War I were lib-eralized.

Land Purchase

1862: The Homestead Act required that

before a settler could purchase land under the Act, he either had to be a U.S. citizen or had to have filed a declaration of intention. The National Archives has Homestead records before May 1, 1908; the Bureau of Land Management has them for the period after that date. The most valuable of the Homestead records are the applications.

CHRONOLOGY OF IMMIGRANT PROCESSING IN AMERICA

Castle Garden

Castle Garden, at the Battery on the tip of Manhattan, was originally built as a fort, called Castle Clinton (named for DeWitt Clinton, governor of New York), one of five forts built to defend New York harbor.

1807-1811: Circular gun battery emplacement is built

1824: The fort, now named Castle Garden, serves as a fashionable amphitheater. Later, in 1845, it is renovated as a concert hall where public figures including Lafayette, Kossuth, and President Jackson were received, and where artists such as Jenny Lind were presented.

1850: Increasing immigration through New York harbor demands a centralized receiving station. Disembarking from 1,912 ships, 212,796 newcomers arrive.

1855 (1 August): Castle Garden, on the Battery at the tip of Manhattan, officially opens as the first United States receiving station for immigrants arriving through the nation's principal port of entry at New York City. More than 7 million newcomers come to the United States between 1855 and 1890.

1864: Castle Garden becomes a recruiting quarters for the Union Army; many German and Irish immigrants sign up for service as soon as they arrive in New York.

1876: Fire destroys most of the structure, but service to immigrants continues.

1881: Some 455,600 immigrants pass through Castle Garden, more than doubling the past average annual rate, and increasing to 476,000 the following year.

1882: First federal immigration law enacted; bars lunatics, convicts and those likely to become public charges.

1882: Outbreak of anti-semitism in Russia spurs sharp rise in Jewish immigration.

1885: Foran Act prohibits importing contract labor, does not prohibit individuals from assisting immigration of relatives and friends.

1886 (28 October): Statue of Liberty dedicated, as resistance to immigration becomes stronger.

1887: Castle Garden's facilities are found hopelessly inadequate for flow of immigration.

1890: Last group passes through Castle Garden. Federal government assumes full control of immigration for previous state-contracted management of New York Port.

1891: New legislation places all national immigration under full federal control, creating the Bureau of Immigration under the Department of the Treasury; legislation adds health requirements to immigration restrictions. Russian pogroms spur large volume of Jewish immigration. Immigration through the Barge Office represents 80 percent of the national total.

1896-1941: Castle Garden serves as the New York City Aquarium.

1950: Castle Garden is declared a national monument.

ELLIS ISLAND

In its 62 years as an immigration station, detention center, and deportation center (1892-1954), Ellis Island served as the gateway to America for an estimated

22 million immigrants. Passenger Lists are searchable at www.ellisisland.org.

1892 (1 January): Ellis Island Immigration Center formally opens as an immigration station; first and second cabin passengers processed on board and directly disembark in Manhattan.

1892: Immigration through the New York port totals 445,987, showing a shift from northern and western Europeans to southern and eastern Europeans.

1893: Shipowners are required to prepare manifests containing detailed information on individual immigrant passengers.

1893: Cholera epidemic and national economic depression result in immigration decrease, to continue for several years.

1894: Immigration Restriction League organized, favoring the "old" (northern and western European) over the "new" (southern and eastern European) immigrants.

1897: Literacy test for immigrants, aimed at restricting Italian influx, vetoed by President Cleveland

1897 (13 June): Fire destroys Ellis Island's wooden buildings, along with immigration records dating from 1855-1890 housed in old Navy magazine. Processing temporarily transferred back to Barge Office (14 June) – until 17 December 1900.

1898: U.S. immigration reaches low point of 229,299, with New York port's share only 178,748, following years of national economic depression.

1900 (17 December): New Ellis Island Immigration Station reopens as an immigration station, on a larger scale, with a total of 2,251 immigrants received for inspection on this day. The new complex, unlike the former station, is situated to retain some green space and show to best advantage to approaching ships.

1902: Procedures to ensure efficient, honest and sanitary treatment of immigrants are instituted.

1903: Immigration control transferred to the newly established Department of Commerce and Labor.

1903: New legislation denies entry to anarchists and prostitutes, imposes fines on steamship companies bringing in immigrants with loathsome or contagious diseases.

1903: On one day, 12,600 immigrants arrive at New York Port, with nearly half required to remain in steerage for several days due to inadequate facilities to process all in a day or provide overnight quarters at Ellis Island. This is to become a common occurrence over the next several years.

1904: New 160-foot "Ellis Island" ferry completed, with capacity for 600. Steerage immigrants transported to Ellis from docks at the Battery by barges and tugs provided by steamship companies; when cleared for admission, new ferry runs them hourly to their "new land" at New York.

1905: There are 821,169 immigrants processed at Ellis Island, with many logistical problems regarding numerous detainees frequently required to remain for several days.

1907: Climax of immigration, with 1,004,756 received at Ellis Island.

1909: Following a sharp falloff in 1908, immigration again rising.

1911: Greatest number of exclusions to date; 13,000 immigrants of the 650,000 arrivals at Ellis Island are deported.

1914-18: World War I ends period of mass migration to the United States. 1914: 1,218,480 total U.S. immigration, 878,052 through New York Port. 1915: 326,700 admitted, 178,416 through New York Port (a 75% increase). 1918: Only 28,867 immigrants enter New York Port.

1917: Literacy test for immigrants adopted, having been defeated in seven previous proposals from 1896-1915.

1917: United States enters war. German merchant ship crews held in New York Harbor at Ellis Island; suspected enemy aliens are taken to Ellis Island under custody.

1918-19: U.S. Army Medical Department and U.S. Navy take over main facilities of Ellis Island; inspection of arriving aliens conducted on board ship or at docks.

1919: Thousands of suspected alien radicals interned at Ellis Island; hundreds deported under new legislation based on principal of guilt by association with any organization advocating revolt.

1920: Ellis Island Station reopened for immigration inspection, while continuing to function as a deportation center.

1920: Immigration takes a noticeable upturn, with 225,206 aliens admitted through New York.

1921: Immigration rises to nearly pre-war proportions; 560,971 immigrants pass through the New York Port — of a national total of 805,228.

1921: Emergency immigration restriction law introduces the quota system, weighted in favor of natives of northern and western Europe; the number of any given European nation's immigrants to the United States annually can not exceed 3 percent of foreign-born persons from that nation living in the United States in 1910. An annual total of admissible immigrants is set at 358,000, with not more than 20 per-cent of the quota to be received in any given month. Steamship companies rush to land each month's quota of immigrants in keen competition, overloading the pro-cessing capacities of Ellis Island.

1921-23: Steamship companies find steer-age no longer profitable; new liners are designed instead with comfortable third-class cabins, marking the passing of the steerage era.

1924: National Origins Act (or, the Second Quota Law) further restricts immigration, changing the quota basis from the census of 1910 to that of 1890, and reducing annual quota immigration to 164,000. The Act further requires

selection and qualification of immigrants at countries of origin, with inspections conducted by staff of U.S. consuls in Europe.

1924: Mass immigration ends; Ellis Island no longer used for primary inspection of immigrants, who are now inspected in countries of origin.

1929: National Origins Act amended, with new quotas based on 1920 census, and the maximum number of admissions annually lowered to 150,000. Act increases bias against southern and eastern Europeans.

1930: Principal function of Ellis Island changed to detention station. Immigration sharply reduced during economic depression following stock market crash.

1931: Many aliens voluntarily seek depor-tation to escape economic depression.

1933: In contrast to only 4,488 incoming aliens through Ellis Island, there are 7,037 outgoing aliens.

1933: Hitler initiates anti-Semitic campaign; Jewish refugees come to United States, but quota system barriers not lifted to admit large numbers in jeopardy in Ger-many.

1933: Immigration and Naturalization Bureaus are merged.

1940: Alien Registration Act requires registration of all aliens, adds to the list of deportable classes, and calls for finger-printing arriving aliens.

1941: United States enters World War II. Ellis Island again used for detention of suspected alien immigrants.

1946: War Brides Act provides for admis-sion of foreign-born wives of American servicemen.

1950: Internal Security Act excludes arriving aliens who were ever members of Communist and Fascist organizations.

1952: Immigration and Naturalization Act makes the quota system even more repressive.

1953-56: Refugee Relief Act granted

visas to some 5,000 Hungarians after 1956 revo-lution; President Eisenhower invites 30,000 more on parole.

1954: Ellis Island Station is vacated, declared excess federal property, and closed.

1965: Ellis Island is added by Presidential Proclamation to the Statue of Liberty National Monument.

1976: The site is opened to the public for limited seasonal visitation.

1984: Ellis Island closed for $160 million restoration.

1990 (10 September): Ellis Island re-opened with extensive museum exhibits and facilities.

Partially based on: *The Ellis Island Source Book,* by August C. Bolino, Kensington Historical Press, Washington, DC, 1985 (chapter IX, Appendix A1; author took information from Tedd McCann, et al. *Ellis Island Study*, Washington: National Park Service, May 1978, pp. C-1 to C-18; D 1-2; E1 to E3).

U.S. IMMIGRANT RECEIVING CENTERS CHRONOLOGY

Official reception of immigrants entering the United States took place as follows:

◆August 1, 1855 - April 18, 1890: Castle Garden

◆ April 19, 1890 - December 31, 1891: Barge Office

◆January 1, 1892 - June 13, 1897: Ellis Island

◆ June 14, 1897 - December 16, 1900: Barge Office

◆ December 17, 1900 - 1924: Ellis Island

Source: John P. Colletta, *They Came in Ships,* Ancestry, Salt Lake City, 1993.

STATUE OF LIBERTY

Original name of statue: "Liberty Enlightening the World"

Designer: Alsatian sculptor and architect Frédéric Auguste Bartholdi, with engineering assistance from Alexandre Gustave Eiffel, later to become famous for the Eiffel Tower in Paris

Location: Liberty Island, a small island southwest of Manhattan in Upper New York Bay, Liberty Island (called Bedloe's Island before 1956)

Size, weight: 151 feet, 1 inch high, weighing 225 tons, on a 142-foot high pedestal. Right arm, 42 feet long and 12 feet in diameter at its thickest point, extends 300 feet above sea level. Head is 10 feet wide. Each eye is 2.5 feet wide.

Construction: Hand-hammered copper plates over an iron skeleton; 142 steps in- side the statue

Presentation from France to the United States: July 4, 1884

Dedication of statue, "Liberty Enlightening the World,": October 28, 1886, as a memorial to the alliance between France and the American colonists who fought for independence in the Revolutionary War in America.

The statue's later influence: During World War I, the statue took on greater symbolism. Its image was used to boost sales of what came to be known as "Liberty Bonds" to help support the war effort. Thus the statue's title, "Liberty Enlightening the World" became more commonly known as the "Statue of Liberty."

National Monument: In 1924, the Statue of Liberty was declared a national monument. In 1933, the National Park Service first took on the responsibility for maintaining the statue.

Note: The Statue of Liberty, located in New York Harbor, is open daily except Christmas from about 9:30 am to 5:00 pm. Access is by Circle Line Statue of Liberty Ferry which leaves from the Battery in Lower Manhattan and from Liberty State Park in New Jersey. For boat schedules and prices call (212) 269-5755.

'THE NEW COLOSSUS'

"The New Colossus" was written in 1883 by American poet Emma Lazarus.

The sonnet is engraved on the pedestal of the Statue of Liberty.

Not like the brazen giant of Greek fame,
With conquering limbs astride from
   land to land;
Here at our sea-washed, sunset gates
   shall stand
A mighty woman with a torch, whose
   flame
Is the imprisoned lightning, and her name
Mother of Exiles. From her beacon-hand
Glows world-wide welcome; her wild
   eyes command
The air-bridged harbor that twin
   cities frame.
"Keep, ancient lands, your storied
   pomp!" cries she
With silent lips. "Give me your tired,
   your poor,
Your huddled masses yearning to
   breathe free,
The wretched refuse of your teeming
   shore.
Send these, the homeless, tempest-tost
   to me.
I lift my lamp beside the golden door!"

THE AMERICAN IMMIGRANT WALL OF HONOR

The American Immigrant Wall of Honor at the Ellis Island Immigration Museum on Ellis Island in New York contains more than 500,000 names of immigrants to America. For a $100 donation (tax deductible), the name of either an individual or a family may be permanently engraved on the Wall, which overlooks New York Harbor. Two-individual entries may be entered for a $200 donation.

Country of origin does not appear on the Wall, but is listed in the computer data bank and is shown on the Certificate of Registration.

Names on this memorial, the largest wall of names in the world, is arranged in alphabetical listings: Those names registered before 1993 are listed on panels 7 through 484; those registered between 1993 and 1995 are listed on panels 485 through 578. Other sections are being added.

To determine on which panel a name is inscribed, check the Wall of Honor computer, which displays all registered immigrant names with the corresponding panel number on which each name may be found. In addition to the immigrant's name and the position on the wall, the computerized information includes the country of origin and the donor's name.

(It is important to note that all data inscribed on the Wall has been submitted by individuals. The information on the wall is not taken from official documents or records.)

Whether an ancestor first set foot on American soil at Ellis Island or entered through another gateway, the name may be included on the Wall.

Donations to The American Immigrant Wall of Honor fund the creation of The American Family Immigration History Center.

Each Wall of Honor donor receives a certificate personalized with the name and country of the individual being honored. Contributions of $1,000, $5,000 and $10,000 receive special places of honor. Contributions are tax-deductible.

For information on how to participate, write to: The Statue of Liberty-Ellis Island Foundation, Inc., P.O. Box Ellis, New York, NY 10163. Tel. (212) 883-1986; www.wallofhonor.com.

THE ELLIS ISLAND
ORAL HISTORY PROJECT

At the Oral History Studio on the second floor of the Ellis Island Immigration Museum, the visitor may listen to interviews made by about 1,200 immigrants and former immigration employees, who have shared their Ellis Island memories. About 300 additional interviews are in the process of transcription. The Oral History Library is a project of the Statue of Liberty-Ellis Island Foundation.

Individual interviews are listed in the library's computers by name, country of origin, immigration date, ship, and a few by topic. In order to review interviews given by German-Americans, it is possible to display on the library computers a list of all Germans in the database, alphabetically arranged by surnames. Women are listed by both maiden and married names. Each interview runs from about 10 minutes to two hours.

The Oral History Library is equipped with 20 listening stations and 50 sets of headphones. Up to four people at one time can listen to the same interview.

Taped interviews may be purchased on standard cassettes at a cost of $10.00 per hour of interview.

Project leaders continue to seek potential interviewees who entered the United States through Ellis Island or who worked at the station during its years of operation.

To hear to one or more of these oral-history interviews, make an appointment with a librarian by calling (212) 363-5807. The fax number is (212) 363-6302.

AMERICAN FAMILY
IMMIGRATION HISTORY CENTER

The American Family Immigration History Center, located in the Ellis Island Immigration Museum on Ellis Island in New York Harbor, is preparing the ambitious project of gathering information on 17 million people who immigrated through the port of New York from 1892 to 1924, the peak years of Ellis Island processing.

The data are being taken directly from the ships' passenger manifests, which are currently on microfilm at the National Archives and Records Administration. The documents are, for the first time, being digitized and entered into an electronic database. The information will cover 11 fields of information, including the immigrant's given name, the immigrant's surname, the ship name, the port of origin, the arrival date, the line number on the manifest, the immigrant's gender, and his/her age, marital status, nationality, and last residence (town and country).

For a nominal fee, visitors to the Center will have the opportunity to order a printout of an immigrant's family data, a scanned reproduction of the original ship's manifest on which the ancestor's entry appears, and a picture of the ship on which the immigrant arrived.

The extraction of records from microfilm and digitizing the information for the Center's database is being undertaken by The Church of Jesus Christ of Latter-day Saints.

The Center is scheduled to open in 2000, when it is to make available a prototype of the user-friendly database. The first phase of the Center is planned to be completed in 2001. Future plans call for making the immigrant arrival records accessible through the Internet, and expanding the database to include additional years and ports of entry.

Information about The American Family Immigration Center may be requested from: The Statue of Liberty-Ellis Island Foundation, Inc., P.O. Box ELLIS, New York, NY 10163. Tel. (212) 883-1986; pr@ellisisland.org

THE STATUE OF LIBERTY NATIONAL MONUMENT AND ELLIS ISLAND IMMIGRATION MUSEUM

Ellis Island and the Statue of Liberty are located in New York Harbor.

The Ellis Island Immigration Museum, on Ellis Island in New York Harbor, is located in the Main Building of the former immigration station complex and tells the story of 400 years of American immigration.

Highlights of the museum

♦ The historic Great Hall, or Registry Room, where new arrivals were processed, now restored to its 1918-1924 appearance

♦ "Through America's Gate," a step-by-step view of the Ellis Island immigrant process

♦ "Ellis Island Galleries," illustrates the history of the Island and its restoration and containing displays of actual immigrant artifacts brought from the Old World and donated to the museum by descendants of the immigrants.

♦ "Peak Immigration Years, 1880-1924," which covers the immigrants' journey to America and the many aspects of their settlement throughout the United States

♦ The Oral History Archives, where visitors may hear taped reminiscences of Ellis Island immigrants and former Ellis Island employees

♦ "The Peopling of America," a graphic, colorful look at the history of immigration to America

w Two theaters, featuring the film, "Island of Hope, Island of Tears"

♦ More than 30 galleries of artifacts, historical photos, posters, maps etc.

w A Learning Center and student orientation center (reservations required)

♦ The American Immigrant Wall of Honor

Hours

Both the Statue of Liberty and the Ellis Island Immigration Museum are open daily except Christmas Day. Winter hours: 9:30 am - 5 pm. Summer hours: 9:30 am - 5:30 pm

Transportation

Boats leave daily from the Battery in Lower Manhattan and Liberty State Park in New Jersey about every half hour from 9:30 am to 3:30 pm. The schedule is subject to change. For specific departure times, call Circle Line - Statue of Liberty Ferry Company at (212) 269-5755. The ferry runs between the Statue of Liberty and Ellis Island.

IMMIGRATION/EMIGRATION VOCABULARY

Abfahrt, Abreise: departure
Abschied: leave-taking
Ankunft: arrival
auf dem Wege: on the way
Ausländer: foreigner(s)
*Auswanderer:*emigrant(s)
Auswandererbahnhof: emigrant train station
Auswandererhafen: emigrant port
auswandern: to emigrate
Auswanderung: emigration
Auswanderungskartei: emigration register
Auswanderungsverzeichnis: emigrant list
Binnenwanderung: internal migration
Dampfschiff, Dampfer: steamship
das gelobte Land: the promised land
Einschiffung: the embarking, the going on board
Einwanderer: immigrant(s)
einwandern: to immigrate
Einwanderung: immigration
Einwanderungsbeschränkung: immigration restrictions
Eisenbahn: railroad
Flüchtlinge: refugee

Hafen: port, harbor
Heimweh: homesickness
Jahrhundert: century
Kai, Kaje: pier
Motive: cause
Passagiere: passengers
Reisepass: passport
Rückwanderer: return emigrant
Rückwanderung: return emigration
Segelschiff, Segler: sailing ship
Überfahrt: ocean crossing
Übersee: overseas
Ufer: shore, bank
Vereinigte Staaten von Amerika: United States of America
Verzeichnis: register, index
Wartehalle, Warteraum: waiting room
Zuwanderer: immigrant(s)
Zuwanderung: immigration
Zwischendeck: steerage

OVERVIEW OF GERMAN IMMIGRATION

♦ More persons immigrated to the United States from Germany than from any other country in the world.
♦ Between 1820 and 1996 the largest ethnic groups were, in order, Germany (7 million), Mexico (5.5 million), Italy (5.3 million); Great Britain (5.1 million), and Ireland (5.1 million).
♦ Little immigration occurred between 1776 and 1819 (because of the War of Independence, 1775-1783; and The War of 1812-14).
♦ About 5,000 Hessian prisoners of war stayed in America after the War of Independence.
♦ Many German speakers emigrated from Austria-Hungary and Russia but were not counted as Germans.
♦ German immigrants, choosing the best farmland, settled mainly in Maryland, Pennsylvania, Ohio, Indiana, Michigan, Wisconsin, Illinois, Minnesota, Iowa, Missouri, North Dakota, South Dakota, Nebraska, and Kansas.
♦ In 1900, about 40 % of the farmlands of the U.S.A. were owned by German Americans.
♦ Many U.S. cities had a high percentage of Germans. In 1900, American cities had the following percentage of German immigrants and their children compared to total populations: Milwaukee (70%), Davenport (62%), Hoboken (58%), Cincinnati (54%), St. Louis (45%), Buffalo (43%) and Detroit (41%).
♦ Baltimore, the terminal of immigration ships from Bremerhaven in 1900 counted 28% of its population as first and second generation Germans. Among whites that year, 42% first- and second-generation Germans inhabited Baltimore.
♦ Other large American cities with a high percentage of first- and second-generation Germans in 1900 were New York (32%), Chicago (35%), and Cleveland (38%).

Source: Edward A. Fleckenstein, "The Distinguished German Ethnic Population of America – (XVI)" in *Der Volksfreund/ People's Friend* (Buffalo) May/June 1998; as reported in "Germans: The largest immigrant group in the United States," by Gary Carl Grassl, *The German-American Heritage Society of Greater Washington, D.C. Newsletter,* Vol. XVII, No. 4, July 2000.

FAMILY HISTORY LIBRARY EMIGRANT LISTS FOR SOME GERMAN PROVINCES

Lists of emigrants such as these are usually cataloged in the Family History Library Catalog (www.FamilySearch.org) under "Gemany, [Province or Region name] - Emigration and Immigration."
♦ **Baden:** Emigration Index 17th-20th Century (*Auswanderer, 17. bis 20.*

Jahrhundert). FHL films beginning with 1180096

♦**Brandenburg:** *Auswanderungskartei* (emigrants for Potsdam district, FHL fiche 6109220); *Auswanderungskartei* (emigrants for Frankfurt/Oder district, FHL fiche 6109219)

♦**Grand Duchy of Hessen-Darmstadt:** Emigration Index 1800-1900, incomplete (FHL 1124278, 1124279, 1124280, 1124319, 1124320); Gieg, Ella *Auswanderungen aus dem Odenwaldkreis* (FHL 943.41 W2gi), five volumes; Schmahl, Helmut, *Die Auswanderung aus Rheinhessen im 18. und 19. Jahrhundert* (FHL 943.41 W2sh)

♦**Hessen-Nassau:** Struck, Wolf-Heino, *Die Auswanderungen aus dem Herzogtum Nassau* (FHL 943.42 W2s); Auerbach, Inge, *Hessische Auswanderer – Auswanderer aus Hessen -Kassel 1840-1850* (FHL 943.41 W29a); Auerbach, Inge, *Auswanderung aus Kurhessen* (FHL 943.41 W2ai)

♦ **Waldeck:** Thomas, Karl, *Die Waldecksche Auswanderung zwischen 1829 und 1872* (FHL 943.41 W2tk)

♦**Lippe-Detmold:** Verdenhaven, Fritz, *Die Auswanderer aus dem Fürstentum Lippe* (FHL 943.55 W2v)

♦ **Schaumburg-Lippe:** Rieckenberg, Heinrich, *Schaumburger Auswanderer* (FHL 943.59 H2ss v. 48)

♦**Rhineland:** Mergen, Joseph, *Auswanderungen aus dem Saarland* (FHL 943.42 W29m)

♦ **Westfalen:** Müller Friedrich, *Westfälische Auswanderer im 19. Jahrhundert* (*Auswanderung aus dem Regierungsbezirk Müster, 1. Teil 1803-1850*) (FHL 943.42 56 D25b v. 22-24); Müller, Friedrich, *Westfälische Auswanderer im 19. Jahr- hundert* (*Auswanderung aus dem Regierungsbezirk Münster, 2. Teil*) (FHL 943.56 D25b v. 38-39); Müller, Friedrich, *Westfälische Auswanderer im 19. Jahrhundert* (*Auswanderung aus dem Regierungsbezirk Minden – heimliche*

Auswanderung, 1814-1900) (FHL 943.56 D25b v. 47-48); *Wittekindsland – Beiträge zur Geschichte, Kultur und Natur des Kreises Herford* (FHL 943.56 H2w)

♦**Württemberg:** Schenk, Trudy, and Froelke, Ruth, *The Württemberg Emigration Index* (943.47 W22st), 8 vols.

Source: Baerbel K. Johnson and Marion Wolfert, "German Emigration and Immigration Sources," Family History Library, 2002

OATHS OF ALLEGIANCE

By the Oath of Allegiance mandate adopted on June 29, 1906 (Chapter 3592, Public Law 338), applicants became new U.S. citizens.

The law stated –

"He shall, before he is admitted to citizenship, declare an oath in open court that he will support the Constitution of the United States, and that he absolutely and entirely renounces and abjures all allegiance and fidelity to any foreign prince, potentate, state, or sovereignty and particularly by name to the prince, potentate, state, or sovereignty of which he was before a citizen or subject; that he will support and defend the Constitution and laws of the United States against all enemies, foreign and domestic, and bear true faith and allegiance to the same."

On December 6, 1957, an Oath of Allegiance was established that contained elements similar to those established earlier. (Code of Federal Regulations, Title 8, Sec. 337.1).

UNITED STATES PASSPORT APPLICATIONS

United States passport applications are rich in primary information concerning immigrants.

Passport requirements

The National Archives reports that except for a short time during the Civil War, passports were not required of U.S. citizens traveling abroad before World War I. They were frequently obtained when not required, however, because of the added protection they might afford. The National Archives has passport applications received by the Department of State, with related records, 1791-1925.

Contents of passport applications

A passport application varies in content, the information being ordinarily less detailed before the Civil War than afterward. It usually contains the name, signature, place of residence, age, and personal description of the applicant; names or number of persons in the family intending to travel; the date; and, where appropriate, the date and court of naturalization. It sometimes contains the exact date and place of birth of the applicant and of spouse and minor children, if any, accompanying the applicant, and, if the applicant was a naturalized citizen, the date and port of arrival in the United States, name of vessel on which the applicant arrived, and date and court of naturalization.

For the period 1906-1925, each application includes name of applicant, date and place of birth, name and date and place of birth of spouse or children (when applicable), residence and occupation at time of application, immediate travel plans, physical description, and photograph. Often accompanying applications are transmittal letters and letters from employers, relatives, and other attesting to the appli-cant's purpose for travel abroad.

Record locations
(passports issued before 1925)

Records of all United States passports issued between 1795 and March 1925

are maintained by the National Archives and may be requested for a fee. Passport applications for these years are are also available (with a paid membership) online at www.ancestry.com.

To search for your ancestor in Ancestry's online database of U.S. passport applications, 1795-1925, do the following: Go to www.ancestry.com, press the drop down arrow next to the "Search" tab and select "Card Catalog." Under "Keywords" type "us passport applications" and press the "Search" button.

U.S. Passport applications held at the National Archives can be ordered three ways: by regular mail, by email or by online request.

When making your request, please include the name of your ancestor along with all known dates and places pertaining to his/her life. Do not forget to include your own mailing address and email address. The initial search is free. If the archival staff locates your ancestor's passport application, it will send you a price quote by regular mail or email. This will include a minimum charge of $15.00, which covers five pages. If the application is longer, there may be added fees of about $2.90 for each additional page.

To order by regular mail, send a letter to: National Archives and Records Administration, Attn: Archives I Research Support Branch (NWCC1), 700 Pennsylvania Avenue, NW, Washington, DC 20408-0001. Tel. 202-357-5400.

To order by email, send a letter to enquire@nara.gov.

To order online, go to www. archives.gov/genealogy/passport/ #where. Scroll down to the heading "Part 4: Where to Find these Records" and follow the steps outlined under the subheading, "To obtain passport applications through an online request."

Records of all United States passports issued between 1795 and Mar 1925 are maintained by the National Archives and may be requested for a fee. Passport applications for these years are also available (with a paid membership) online at www.ancestry.com.

Record location
(passports issued since 1925)

Records of passports issued since 1925 are maintained by the Department of State, Passport Services Directorate. Genealogical researchers wishing to gain access to its records should submit a typed or clearly printed request bearing signature and including full name, date and place of birth of the file subject, and the dates that the file subject may have applied for a United States passport. Also included should be a fee of $60 for *each* subject. Checks or money orders should be made payable to the Department of State.

In addition, if the file subject was born after 1900, the Department of State requires either *notarized* consent for the file subject authorizing release of the information for his/her passport record to the requestor, or convincing evidence of death in the form of a newspaper obituary or a death certificate.

You may submit your request to: The Department of State, Office of Information Resources Management, Programs and Services, 515 22nd St. NW, Washington, DC 20522-6001.

Additional information can be found at the Department of State's website: http://travel.state.gov/passport/services/copies/copies_872.html.

Important note

Unless a person who travelled abroad or intended to travel abroad had obtained United States citizenship, it is useless to initiate a search of the passport files.

GERMAN IMMIGRANT AID SOCIETIES

Although it was recognized by Germans during the early years of emigration to America that many of their country-men's lives were being made miserable by swindlers at the docks, robbers, and dishonest agents, little attention was paid to the emigrants' plight.

The government's interest was in trying to prevent emigration, or at least making it more difficult. Therefore, its only steps were aimed at regulating the activities of the emigration agents, beginning in the late 1930s. With government unconcerned, private groups sprang up to try to alleviate the emigration problem.

The two types of organizations that appeared were the settlement societies and the aid societies. Settlement societies were business ventures through which money was invested in land and potential settlers were offered cheap passage tickets and help in starting their new lives.

Two of the well known settlement societies were the Texas Society (*Texas-Verein*, founded in 1842, and famous for its incompetent planning and organization) and the Hamburg Colonization Society (*Hamburger Kolonisationsverein*, founded in 1849 for the purpose of establishing a colony in Brazil).

The aid societies, on the other hand, were formed to help emigrants as they journeyed to the new land. These societies first formed at points of crossing on the emigration routes, like Frankfurt am Main, Cologne, and Darmstadt, and, most importantly, in the harbor cities of Bremen and Hamburg where emigrant conditions were at their worst. Nevertheless, emigrants had to be wary. For example, one emigration agent in Koblenz, well known as a swindler, named his business the "Office for the Protection of Emigrants to America and Australia."

Many of the aid societies distributed information about travel routes and prices, and descriptions of the climate and economic conditions in various destination points. They also helped migrants who had been cheated in legal fights for compensation and brought to the public's attention to cases of fraud.

The National Society for German Emigration and Settlement (*Nationaler Verein für deutsche Auswanderung und Ansiedlung*, founded in 1848) had local sections in most southern German states, where emigration was heavy during this period.

The Berlin Society for the Centralization of German Emigration and Colonization (*Berliner Verein zur Centralisation deutscher Auswanderung und Kolonisation,* founded in 1849) opened a branch in Hamburg in 1850, operating Hamburg's version of the Bremen information office for emigrants beginning in 1851. Most of these societies were short-lived and local in scope.

Although the churches would seem to have been logical agents for aid to emigrants, it was not until the 1870s that Lutheran and Catholic churches took on the task. Their earlier arguments were that only rootless people with no true faith in God would leave their homes, that God-fearing Christians should stay at home. As more and more requests came in from abroad for German-speaking pastors, the churches' positions changed.

The Protestant Langenberg Society (or Evangelical Society for Germans of Protestant Faith in North America) was established in 1837 to train pastors for service in America. Before about 1860, Catholic Germans had no choice but to join already established parishes in the United States, and these were dominated mainly by Irish immigrants, with whom ethnic conflicts frequently flared.

Active Christian groups became involved in the embarkation process at the ports and began distributing Bibles and pamphlets to the steerage passengers.

In the Bremerhaven *Auswanderer-*haus, Protestant services were held twice a week and Catholic masses every two weeks.

Church reaction to the needs of emigrants came late. A Lutheran pastor for emigrants in Hamburg and Bremen was appointed in 1870, and a Catholic chaplain was appointed in 1871.

A society of Catholic laymen was active in Le Havre beginning in 1854, but it was 15 years before these active Catholics could convince the church hierarchy that there was a need to help the emigrants.

In 1871, Peter Paul Cahensly, a Le Havre merchant, obtained authorization to establish the Raphael Society to aid emigrants. By 1877, society officials were working in Bremen, Hamburg, Le Havre, Liverpool, London, and Rotterdam.

By the end of the 19th century, both Protestants and Catholics were operating immigrant housing facilities in New York. The Lutheran immigrant house opposite Castle Garden opened in 1873, offering low-cost shelter for about 400 people.

The Leo House, which Catholics opened in 1885, offered similar facilities. Protestant groups such as Baptists and Methodists set up operations for immigrants of other ethnic groups as well.

In the 1880s, German and American Jews joined together to establish a massive aid program for Jews fleeing from pogroms. (See files for the Hebrew Immigrant Aid Society in www. FamilySearch.org.)

The first organization in America to dedicate itself to the welfare of German immigrants was the German Society of Philadelphia, founded in 1764, which responded to the miserable conditions faced by the German redemptioners.

The functions filled by these societies included locating housing and employment, finding relatives, and the changing and transferring of money. The societies saw themselves as guardians of national honor, a goal which unfortunately often provoked hostile reactions among other Americans.

The German Society of New York was the most active of the societies aiding German immigrants because it was New York where most of them entered the country. This society worked closely with the Commissioners of Emigration and, after 1892, with officials at Ellis Island.

Source: Agnes Bretting, "From the Old World to the New: Immigrant Aid Societies," *Fame, Fortune and Sweet Liberty: The Great European Emigration*, Dirk Hoerder and Diethelm Knauf, ed.,(Bremen: Edition Temmen, 1992).

FOUNDING DATES OF GERMAN IMMIGRANT AID SOCIETIES

These aid societies are listed in chrono-logical order by founding dates:

◆ **Deutsche Gesellschaft von Pennsylvanien** [German Society of Pennsylvania], Philadelphia, Pa. Founded December 26, 1764

◆**German Friendly Society**, Charleston, South Carolina. Founded 1766 [No longer in existence by 1892]

◆**Deutsche Gesellschaft von New York** [German Society of New York], New York, N.Y. Founded August 20, 1784

◆**Deutsche Gesellschaft von Maryland** [German Society of Maryland], Baltimore, Maryland. Founded February 6, 1817

◆ **Deutscher Hilfsverein von Boston** [German Relief Society of Boston], Boston, Massachusetts. Founded February 6, 1847

◆**Deutsche Gesellschaft von New Orleans, Louisiana** [German Society of New Orleans, Louisiana], New Orleans, Louisiana. Founded May 24, 1847

◆**Deutsche Gesellschaft von St. Louis** [German Society of St. Louis], St. Louis, Missouri. Founded 1847

◆ **Allgemeine Deutsche Unterstützungs- Gesellschaft** [German Public Assistance Society], San Francisco, California. Founded January 7, 1854

◆**Deutsche Gesellschaft von Chicago** [German Society of Chicago], Chicago, Illinois. Founded August 1, 1854

◆ **Deutscher Einwanderungs- und Unterstützungs Verein** [German Immigration and Assistance Society], Cincinnati, Ohio. Founded 1854

◆**Allgemeine Deutsche Unterstützungs-Gesellschaft** [German Public Assistance Society], Portland, Oregon. Founded February 7, 1871

◆ **Deutsche Gesellschaft von Lehigh County** [German Society of Lehigh County], Allentown, Pennsylvania. Founded November 9, 1871

◆**Einwanderer Hilfsverein** [Immigrants Relief Society], Pittsburg, Pennsylvania. Founded April 15, 1880

◆**Deutsche Gesellschaft von Milwaukee** [German Society of Milwaukee], Milwaukee, Wisconsin. Founded May 28, 1880

◆**Deutsche Gesellschaft von Kansas City** [German Society of Kansas City], Kansas City, Missouri. Founded July 14, 1882

◆**Deutsch-Amerikanische Gesellschaft** [German-American Society], Rochester, New York. Founded October 8, 1883

◆ **Allgemeine Deutsche Unterstützungs-Gesellschaft** [German Public Assistance Society], Seattle, Washington. Founded February 22, 1884

◆**Deutsche Gesellschaft von Dorchester** [German Society of Dorchester], Dorchester, Wisconsin. Founded May 5, 1885

◆ **Deutsche Gesellschaft** [German Society], St. Paul, Minnesota. Founded October 10, 1889

◆**Deutsche Gesellschaft von New Haven** [German Society of New Haven], New Haven, Connecticut. Founded March 2, 1890

◆ **Deutsche Gesellschaft** [German Society], Petersburg, Virginia. Founded

April 29, 1890
♦**Deutsch-Amerikanische Gesellschaft von Virginien** [German-American Society of Virginia], Richmond, Virginia. Founded September 8, 1890
Source: Reprinted from the program of the *German Day Celebration of the German Society of Pennsylvania*, 1892.

IMMIGRANT AID BY THE LUTHERAN CHURCH IN NEW YORK CITY

Care given to German immigrants at the German Lutheran and Emigrant House[1], 1871 and 1889

	Type and Amount of Care Given	
	In 1871	**In 1889**
Letters exchanged	3,125	xxx
Meals Given	915	1,850
Persons Lodged	410	12,439
Persons Employed	404	xxx
Calls at Office	5,604	xxx
Lodging	xxx	12,058

[1]This house was opposite Castle Garden (the immigration station) in New York.
Source: James Sigurd Lapham, "The German-American of New York City 1860-1890," Ph.D. dissertation, St. John's University, New York, 1977.

THE 'ENGLISH LANGUAGE VOTE NEVER TAKEN'

"The Mühlenberg myth" says that in the United States in the 1770s, a vote was taken to decide whether German or English should be the national language and that English won by one vote.

The tie-breaker was a German, one Frederick Augustus Mühlenberg, the first Speaker of the House — or so the story goes.

In the late 1700s, the German language was prevalent, especially in Virginia, Maryland, and Pennsylvania. The German language was especially concentrated in Pennsylvania, where Germans made up 33 percent of the state population in the 1790s.

When Pennsylvania's State Librarian Thomas L. Montgomery searched in 1927 through Pennsylvania state archives for documentation of the vote, he found no mention of it.

In May 1990, The U.S. State historian wrote that he was "unable to document that a vote in the U.S. Congress ever took place with regard to making German the national language. . . ."

Despite the strong use of the German language in Pennsylvania, the United States census figures for 1790 show that a mere 6 percent of the population spoke German.

Mühlenberg, as Speaker of the House, did cast a tie-breaking vote during his congressional career, on April 26, 1796.

This vote contained no reference to Germans or the German language.
Source: "A Ballot for Americans: A Famous Vote That Was Never Taken," by Michelle Buswinka, *Munich Found*, April 1992.

GERMAN IMMIGRANT CASUALTIES ABOARD SHIP

Number of German immigrants arriving in New York City 1865-1867 and number of deaths due to transatlantic travel (number of deaths shown in parentheses)

1865:	11,264 (128)
1866:	14,335 (387)
1867:	8,788 (199)

Source: James Sigurd Lapham, "The German-Americans of New York City 1860-1890," Ph. D. dissertation, St. John's University, New York, 1977.

GERMAN-AMERICANS IN THE 1990 CENSUS

The first group of German settlers arrived in the American colonies in 1683, where they established what later became known as Germantown.

By 1800, about 9 percent of the total population of the United States had ties to Germany.

Mass immigration started after 1815 and reached a high during the 1880s when more than 1.5 million Germans arrived.

The peak year was 1882, when a record 250,000 Germans immigrated. At the turn of the century, German immigration began to slow.

Since the 1970s, only about 150,000 Germans have come to the United States. Over three centuries, about 8 million Germans have come to what is now the United States.[1]

German descendants in the 1990 census

Dr. Don Heinrich Tolzman, president of the Society for German-American Studies, provides the following analysis of the 1990 U.S. Census as it relates to the German-American element:[2]

Final results of the 1990 United States Census indicate that the total United States population in that year was 248,709,873.

The five major groups and their percentages of the total population are as follows:

1. German	57,985,595	(23.3%)
2. Irish	38,739,548	(15.6%)
3. English	32,655,779	(13.1%)
4. Italian	14,714,939	(5.9%)
5. Polish	9,366,106	(3.8%)

The German category does not include Germans from other German-speaking states and regions of Europe and the Americas.

Hence, to the German statistic, the following can be added:[3]

1. Alsatian	16,465
2. Austrian	870,531
3. Luxemburger	49,061
4. Swiss-German (estimated)	700,000
5. German-Russian	10,153
6. Pennsylvania German	305,841

These six additional German ethnic groups total 1,952,051. The total of all seven German ethnic categories is 59,937,646.

Without question, there are thousands more German-Americans who were not counted because they failed to note their ethnic roots on the census reports.

Nevertheless, the census results clearly indicate that German-Americans constitute a full one-fourth of the population. German-Americans can take pride in the fact that they are without question the major ethnic group in America.

Source: "German Americans," German Embassy, March 1996; eds. Ekkehard Brose, Betsy Wittleder, Ina-Marie Blomeyer, Andrea Metz.
[2]*UGAC-USA Newsletter*, 3 September 1992.

[3]These numbers represent only the people who claimed respective origins for the census reports. Many more descendants of immigrants from these areas were not counted.

GERMAN-AMERICAN UNIONS OF NEW YORK CITY, 1860-1890

Numbers of members are shown in parentheses

1860s: German Joiners Association (1,000)
1860s: Cabinetmakers (550)
1860s: United Piano Forte Union (250)
1870: Cigarmakers (9,292) (U.S.)
1870: Shoemakers (19,631) (U.S.)

1871: German Social Democratic Work-
ingmen's Union (293)
1881: .... Brewery Workmen's Union of
New York City and Vicinity, Local 1, AFL
(121)
1890: Brewery Worker's Local 69, #3
Knights of Labor (1,000)
1890: New York Typographia [German]
Local #6 (1,400)
Source: James Sigurd Lapham, "The
German-American, New York City 1860-
1890," Ph. D. dissertation, St. John's
University, New York, 1977.

SUICIDES
IN NEW YORK CITY, 1870

**The Nationality of Suicides in New York
City, October to December 1870**

Nationality and number of suicides:
German 50
American 25
Irish 20
English 4
"Uncanny" Scot 1

The German suicide rate remained at
a high level into the 1870s. In 1875, the
percentage of German suicides among
the foreign element (one third of the foreign population was German) of the city
was 37 percent.
Source: James Sigurd Lapham, "The
German-Americans of New York City
1860-1890." Ph. D. dissertation, St.
John's University, New York, 1977.

THE PENNSYLVANIA GERMANS
('PENNSYLVANIA DUTCH')

"Pennsylvania Dutch" describes the
Germans who came to Pennsylvania in
the late 1600s and in the 1700s, mostly
from the Rhineland, Württemberg,
Baden, and Alsace. Also among these
emigrants, but in smaller numbers were

French Huguenots and the Swiss.
   The word "Dutch" came from
English speakers' misunderstanding
of the word the Germans used to
describe themselves – the *Deutsche*
(Germans). In past centuries,
"*Deutsch*" referred to anyone from
a wide range of German regions,
which we now know as Netherlands,
Belgium, Germany, Austria, and
Switzerland.
   Between 1702 and 1704, two books
praising the new lands of William Penn
circulated widely in Germany. One of
them, *Curieuse Nachright von Pensyl-
vania in Norden-America* (A Novel Report from Pennsylvania in North
America) by a German, Daniel Falckner,
was written upon his return home from a
1699 visit to Pennsylvania. In it he wrote
glowing accounts of the New World and
gave specific advice on how to emigrate
to Penn's colony.
   A book published by Gabriel Thomas
in 1698 supplied similar information
about Penn's settlements.
   Many Pennsylvania Germans, besides representing the Lutheran and
German Reformed churches, belonged
to several sects — like the Amish,
Brethern, Mennonites, French Huguenots, Moravians, and Schwenkfelders —
growing out of the religious movement
in Europe called pietism, which rejected
formal religious practices.
   These separatist sects generally opposed formal religious practices. Even
today, many Pennsylvania Germans,
most of whom settled in southeastern
Pennsylvania, are referred to as the
"plain people."
   These German emigrants tended to
stay together, traveling in groups across
the ocean and then colonizing the new
lands. They governed themselves and
maintained their language and customs
to such an extent that Benjamin Franklin
urged the English Parliament to restrict the
high immigration of "Palatine Boors" for

fear that the English colonists "be not able to preserve our language, and even our government will become precarious."

In 1790, the Pennsylvania Germans made up a third of the state's population. Their dialect has only recently been dying out.

Although it is impossible to draw a strict boundary line around the Pennsylvania German communities, one writer, Fredric Klees, in his book, *The Pennsylvania Dutch* (1952), includes a map of Pennsylvania Dutch settlements that covers the area from the New Jersey line on the east, through Huntington County, Pennsylvania, on the west, and Luzerne County, Pennsylvania in the north, to Baltimore, Maryland, in the south.

There still remain pockets, especially in rural areas, where "Dutch" is spoken in the home.

Society
Pennsylvania Dutch Folk Culture Society, Bauer Memorial Library, Folklife Museum, Main and Willow streets, Lenhartsville, PA 19534. Tel. (215) 562-4893

PENNSYLVANIANS' GERMAN ANCESTRY

The number of Pennsylvanians claiming German as a single ancestry rose by 9.7 percent during the 1980s, according to the Pennsylvania State Data Center at Penn State Harrisburg. Almost 1.9 million of all Pennsylvanians who reported a single ancestry in the 1990 Census claimed German ancestry. That works out to 28.4 percent of the total in that category.
Source: *Focus Magazine*, 1 Sep.1992.

RESOURCES FOR PENNSYLVANIA RESEARCH

♦ Beam, C. Richard, *Pennsylvania Ger-*

man Dictionary: English to Pennsylvania Dutch, revised 1991, Brookshire Publications, Lancaster, Pa. 1994.
♦ Burgert, Annette Kunselman, "Are Your Pennsylvania Dutch Ancestors Really Swiss?" *The German Connection,* First quarter 1995.
♦Burgert, Annette Kunselman, Locating Your Colonial German families in Pennsylvania, AKB Publications, Worthington, Ohio, c. 1983, pamphlet. FHL 974.8 A1 No. 375
♦ _____, *Locating Your Pennsylvania German Ancestor in Europe,* AKB Publications, Worthington, Ohio, c. 1983, pamphlet. FHL 974.8 A1 no. 377
♦ _____, *Using Pennsylvania German Church Records,* AKB Publications, Worthington, Ohio, c. 1983, pamphlet. FHL 974.8 A1 no. 376
♦ _____, *Eighteenth Century Emigrants from German-speaking Lands to North America,* Pennsylvania German Society, 1983-1985. 2 vols. of Pennsylvania German Society. FHL 974.8 B4pgp v. 16, 19
♦ _____, *Notes on Research Sources for Emigration Studies from Archives and Societies in Southern Germany,* AKB Publications, Worthington, Ohio, pamphlet. FHL 974.8 A1 no. 379
♦ Burgert, Annette Kunselman and Henry Z. Jones, *Westerwald to America: Some 18th Century German Immigrants,* Picton Press, Camden, Me., c. 1989. FHL 943.42 W2b
♦ Center for Pennsylania German Studies, 406 Spring Drive, Millersville, PA 17551-2021.
♦ Clint, Florence, *Pennsylvania Area Key: A Guide to the Genealogical Records of the State of Pennsylvania; Including Maps, Histories, Charts, and Other Helpful Materials.* 2nd ed. Area Keys, Denver, 1976. (An area key is also available for each county.)
♦ Daly, John C., *Descriptive Inventory of the Archives of the City of Philadelphia,* 1970; supplement, 1980. FHL

974.811 A3d; film 1036003 item 4
◆Druktor, Robert M., *The Guide to Genealogical Sources of the Pennsylvania State Archives,* 2nd ed., Pennsylvania Historical and Museum Commission, Harrisburg, Pa., 1998. (For information, telephone (800) 747-7790 or (717) 783-2618).
◆John W. Heisey, *Handbook for Genealogical Research in Pennsylvania.* Heritage House, Indianapolis, Ind., 1985.
◆ Hocker, Edward W., *Genealogical Data Relating to the German Settlers of Pennsylvania and Adjacent Territory from Advertisements in German Newspapers Published in Philadelphia and Germantown, 1743-1800.* Genealogical Publishing Co., Baltimore, 1980.
◆Hoenstine, Floyd G., *Guide to Genealogical and Historical Research in Pennsylvania.* 3rd ed., F. Hoenstine, Hollidaysburg, Pa., 1978.
◆ Humphrey, John T., *Pennsylvania Births* (series, for these counties: Berks, Bucks, Chester, Delaware, Lancaster, Lebanon, Lehigh, Montgomery, Northampton, and Philadelphia), John T. Humphrey, P.O. Box 15190, Washington, DC 20003.
◆ Klees, Fredric . *The Pennsylvania Dutch.* The Macmillan Co. New York, 1952. (out of print).
◆ *Pennsylvania German Church Records: Births, Baptisms, Marriages, Burials, Etc.* with an introduction by Don Yoder,. 3 vols., Genealogical Publishing Co., Baltimore, 1983.
◆*Pennsylvania Line: A Research Guide to Pennsylvania Genealogy and Local History.* 3rd ed. Southwest Pennsylvania Genealogical Services, Laughlintown, Pa., 1983.
◆Philadelphia Archives, 401 N. Broad Street, Philadelphia, PA 19108. Tel. (215) 686-1580.
◆*Research Outline: Pennsylvania,* Family History Library, Church of Jesus Christ of Latter-day Saints. Available in most Family History Centers.
◆ Schweitzer, George K., *Pennsylvania Genealogical Research.* G. Schweitzer, Knoxville, Tenn., 1986.
◆ Strassburger, Ralph Beaver, William John Hinke, ed., *Pennsylvania German Pioneers: A Publication of the Original Lists of Arrivals in the Port of Philadelphia from 1727 to 1808,* Pennsylvania German Society, reprint, 1934. FHL 974.811 W3s 1992
◆Yoder, Don, ed., *Rhineland Emigrants: Lists of German Settlers in Colonial America.* Genealogical Publishing Co., Baltimore, 1981. Reprinted 1985.

SELECTED COLLECTIONS OF PENNSYLVANIA CHURCH RECORDS

◆Evangelical & Reformed Historical Society, James and College Street, Lancaster, PA 17603
◆Genealogical Society of Pennsylvania, 1300 Locust Street, Philadelphia, PA 19107
◆State Library of Pennsylvania, P.O. Box 1601, Harrisburg, PA 17126
◆ Lutheran Theological Seminary, 61 West Confederate Avenue, Gettysburg, PA 17325
◆Lutheran Theological Seminary, 7310 Germantown Avenue, Mt. Airy, Philadelphia, PA 19119
◆Moravian Archives, 41 West Locust Street, Bethlehem, PA 18018
◆Family History Library, Salt Lake City, Utah
Source: Annette K. Burgert, *Locating Your Ancestor in the Keystone State: Genealogical Research in Pennsylvania,* NGS Conference in the States, 1995.

PENNSYLVANIA GERMAN BIRTHS

John T. Humphrey has extracted names from baptismal records of German

Lutheran parishes in Pennsylvania and published the compilations in eighteen books. Details are available at www.librarything.com/author/humphreyjohnt

PENNSYLVANIA SOCIETIES

♦**Genealogical Society of Pennsylvania** : 1305 Locust Street, 3rd Floor, Philadelphia, PA 19107. Tel. (215) 545-0391; Fax (215) 545-0936; gsppa@aol.com; www.libertynet.org/~gspa
♦**Historical Society of Pennsylvania,** 1300 Locust Street, Philadelphia, PA 19107-5699. Tel. (215) 732-6200; Fax (215) 732-2680; hsppr@aol. com; www.libertynet. org/pahist
♦**German Society of Pennsylvania,** 611 Spring Garden Street, Philadelphia, PA 19123. Tel. (215) 627-2332 [home of the Joseph Horner Memorial Library, with one of the largest holdings of German books in the United States]
♦**Germantown Historical Society,** 5501 Germantown Avenue, Philadelphia, PA. Tel. (215) 844-0514
♦**Historical Society of Pennsylvania,** 1300 Locust Street, Philadelphia, PA 19107-5699. Tel. (215) 732-6200; Fax (215) 732-2680; hsppr@aol. com
♦**Lancaster Mennonite Historical Society,** 2215 Millstream Road, Lancaster, PA 17602-1499. Tel. (717) 393-9745
♦**Pennsylvania German Society,** P.O. Box 244, Kutztown, PA 19530-0244. Tel. (610) 894-9551; Fax: (610) 894-9808; www.pgs.org
♦**Western Pennsylvania Genealogical Society**, 4400 Forbes Avenue, Pittsburgh, PA 15213-4080. Tel. (412) 687-6811

PENNSYLVANIA STATE ARCHIVES

Records of the Pennsylvania State Archives in Harrisburg date from 1664 to the present and cover a wide range of topics relating to almost every aspect of Pennsylvania history.

Records of specific genealogical interest include passenger lists, primarily of German and Swiss arrival at the port of Philadelphia, 1727-1808; official naturalization lists, 1740-1773; oaths of allegiance, 1777-1790; septennial census returns, 1779-1863; naturalization records of the Pennsylvania Supreme Court, Eastern District, 1794-1868; Western District 1812-1867; and Southern District, 1815-1829; and records relating to military service.

Available on microfilm are certain records of 58 counties, including wills, deeds, slave registers, and tax lists.

Federal population schedules

Microfilm holdings include copies of the federal population schedules for Pennsylvania, 1800-1920 (1790 being published and indexed), the 1880-1920 Soundexes and the 1870 and 1880 censuses on industry and manufacturers.

Military service records

Official records relating to service with Pennsylvania military units covering the period 1775-1945 are found among the records of the Departments of Military Affairs, Treasury, Auditor General, and State; and also of the Office of the Comptroller General, and Pennsylvania's Revolutionary Governments. They consist primarily of muster rolls, military returns, clemency petitions, bonus files, pension records, commissions, and military accounts.

Land records

The State Archives holds the records

of Pennsylvania's Land Office, which document the original purchases of land from the Penn family or the Commonwealth, consisting of applications, warrants, surveys, patents, and other related records. Papers relating to Donation and Depreciation Lands are available for finding grants of land to soldiers of the Pennsylvania Line in the Revolution. Also on file are warrant tract maps for about 48 percent of the counties, showing the locations of original surveys within current township boundaries. A list of the maps of counties and townships completed may be obtained upon request.

Published State Archives

Of the nine series of the *Pennsylvania Archives,* consisting altogether of 135 volumes, those that are of most use to genealogists are the Second, Third, Fifth, Sixth, and Seventh. See the *Guide to the Published Archives of Pennsylvania*, by Henry Howard Eddy. FHL 974.8 A5pe; film 1036386 item 11

Ethnic studies

Individual collections of personal papers, organizational records, runs of foreign-language newspapers, and church anniversary histories are part of a general ethnic studies collection.

Maps

The map collection consists of more than 900 maps and panoramic views. Dating from 1681 to the present, these maps are mainly state road and turnpike, political subdivision and boundary, and military maps.

Address

The Pennsylvania State Archives is located at the corner of Third and Forster streets in Harrisburg. Mailing address: Pennsylvania State Archives, P.O. Box 1026, Harrisburg, PA 17108-1026. Tel. (717) 783-3281.

Hours

The library is open Tuesday through Friday, and Saturday (for microfilm only) except state and legal holidays. Check for the hourly schedule.

THE STATE LIBRARY OF PENNSYLVANIA

The State Library of Pennsylvania in Harrisburg is not the holder of offical or unofficial records but rather it holds compilations made from other sources, as well as an extensive collection of Pennsylvania newspapers.

A microfiche group titled Genealogy/ Local History, is a collection of local histories, genealogies and primary source materials indexed by author, title, geographical area, and name. The collection also contains unpublished compilations of church and cemetery records and a file of miscellaneous family materials.

Surname/Place Name indexes

The Surname/Place Name Indexes contain almost 2 million cards, with information gathered from the indexes of titles which were in the collection proior to 1968 and from seveeral special collections. Since 1968, no new cards have been added to either of these indexes.

Pennsylvania newspapers

The State Library's collection of retrospective Pennsylvania newspapers, the largest known to exist, is a primary source for identifying birth and death dates.

More than 61,000 microfilm reels are maintained by the library. Staff at libraries with access to OCLC can search for specific newspaper holdings by means of the "Pennsylvania Union List of Newspapers," a database maintained on the OCLC computer.

Reels of newspaper microfilm are available for interlibrary loan for use in any library in North America

Online catalog

Dial access to LUIS, the library's online catalog, is available to libraries and individuals with the capability to access it. For complete instructions, write to the State Library (address below) to request its publication, "Dial Access to LUIS."

Librarians at local public libraries may borrow a copy of the Reel Index to the Microfilm Collection of Pennsylvania County and Regional Histories. The librarian should specify the titles being requested, as well as the reel numbers, on the interlibrary loan form.

Address

The library is located in the Forum building on Commonwealth Avenue at Walnut Street, Harrisburg.

Write to Pennsylvania Department of Education, State Library of Pennsylvania, Library Services Division, Box 1601, Harrisburg, PA 17105-1601. Tel. (717) 787-4440 (Reference, information); fax: (717) 783-2070 (Interlibrary Loan)

PENNSYLVANIA LIBRARIES: LISTINGS WITH GENEALOGICAL INFORMATION

The book noted below is a county-by-county compilation of Pennsylvania libraries where it is known that genealogical and/or local history information is found in collections. The book includes library addresses, telephone numbers, and comments, including special genealogical/local history holdings, restrictions on use, and user fees, if known.

John W. Heisey, *Pennsylvania Genealogical Library Guide*. Masthof Press, Route 1, Box 20, Mill Road, Morgantown, PA 19543-9701 (formerly Old Springfield Press).

SOUTHEASTERN AND OTHER PENNSYLVANIA GERMAN COUNTIES, WITH THEIR PARENT COUNTIES

Listed below are some southeastern and nearby counties in Pennsylvania, the dates they formed, and their respective parent counties (in the right column). Germans who immigrated into Pennsylvania in the early years settled in these (and some other) counties.

Adams (1800) .... York
Berks (1752) .... Chester, Lancaster, Philadelphia
Bucks (1662) .... Original County
Chester (1682) .... Original County
Cumberland (1750) .... Lancaster
Dauphin (1785) .... Lancaster
Delaware (1789) .... Chester
Juniata (1831) .... Mifflin
Lancaster (1729) .... Chester
Lebanon (1813) ..... Dauphin, Lancaster
Lehigh (1812) .... Northampton
Northampton (1752) .... Bucks
Northumberland (1772) .... Bedford, Berks, Lancaster
Perry (1820) .... Cumberland
Philadelphia (1682) ..... Original County
Schuylkill (1811)... Berks, Northampton
York (1749) .... Lancaster

Source: John W. Heisey, *Pennsylvania Genealogical Library Guide*, Masthoff Press, Route 1, Box 20, Mill Road, Morgantown, PA 19543-6860.

GERMAN IMMIGRANTS IN AMERICAN CHURCH RECORDS

The series of books under the above title consists of genealogical data for German immigrants compiled from German-language church records. The first nine volumes of the series feature more than 72,000 immigrants from Indiana, Wisconsin, Nebraska and Iowa. Additional volumes are in preparatio (see www.germanimmigrants.org). Each volume has an every-name index.

Roger P. Minert, ed., *German Immigrants in American Church Records*, Rockland, ME: Picton Press (www.pictonpress.com).

GERMANS FROM RUSSIA: CHRONOLOGY OF EVENTS

1763: Catherine the Great of Russia invites Germans to settle in Russia.

1764-1786: About 23,000 Germans establish 104 colonies along the Volga River.

1789: Mennonites begin settling in the Black Sea region.

1804: Czar Alexander I's Manifesto, with the promise of free land and political privileges, brings many Germans from southern Germany and West Prussia to colonize the Black Sea area in South Russia.

1848: Russia invokes universal military service.

1854-1859: Mennonites colonize the Volga region.

1860: About 300 colonies established in Russia — 104 on the Volga, 13 in areas around St. Petersburg and Moscow, and 181 in the Black Sea region.

1862: The Homestead Act is enacted, and the lure of free land in America begins acting as a magnet.

1871: Provisions of the manifestos are abrogated by the Russian government. Canada offers the immigrant a homestead of 160 acres for ten dollars, to become his property after three years.

1873: Ethnic Germans from the Black Sea and Volga regions in Russia move into North and South America. This emigration continues until the beginning of World War II.

1874: Military Reform Decree enacted, extending military service to the colonists, inducing many of them to emigrate. Mass migrations of Germans

from Russia to the United States begin.

1903: *The Dakota Freie Presse* is purchased by Friedrich W. Sallet, who makes the newspaper the organ of the Black Sea Germans; the newspaper ceases publication in 1954.

1909: Sallet announces success of his campaign to establish a system whereby eye examinations are given to potential emigrants before boarding ships in Europe. (Trachoma plagues the Germans from Russia during this period.)

1912: The *Welt-Post* newspaper, devoted to Volga German interests, begins publication; continuing (in Omaha and Lincoln) until 1954.

1917: Russian and Bolshevik revolutions. Conditions temporarily improve for Ger-mans in Russia.

1920: *The Dakota Freie Presse* moves to New Ulm, Minnesota.

1921-22: Crop failure and famine

1928-29: Stalin begins ruthless collectivization. Churches close.

1932-33: Crop failure and famine

1936-38: Peak of the period of banishment and liquidation of pastors, teachers, doctors, and officials

1941: Russia begins resettlement of Germans in the Crimea and South Caucasus and banishment of the Volga Germans to Siberia and Central Asia

1955: Civil rights restored to ethnic Germans, but confiscated property is not returned. Germans are denied right to return to their original homes.

1964: Soviets lift deportation order of 1941.

1992: Autonomous Volga Republic established.

PROVISIONS OF MANIFESTOS OF CATHERINE II AND ALEXANDER I

Catherine II's Manifesto, 1763
♦Free practice of religion
♦Tax exemption for ten years

♦Freedom from military service
♦Cash grant, to be repaid in 20 years
♦ Treatment equal to that of native Russians
♦Each family may bring into the country 500 rubles in cash or property duty-free.
♦ Professionals and laborers permitted to join guilds and unions
♦After 10 years, an annual tax to be paid on land received
♦ Freedom to depart, but only after paying debts to crown and five years' real estate taxes

Alexander I's Manifesto, 1804

The decree of 1804 was similar to that of Catherine II, but its intent was to restrict immigration into Russia to colonists who were well-to-do, experienced farmers who could serve as models for agricultural occupations and handicrafts.

GERMANS IN RUSSIA, BY SETTLEMENT AREAS

♦Black Sea Germans
♦Baltic Germans
♦Lithuanian Germans
♦Polish and Volhynian Germans
♦Petersburg Germans
♦Volga Germans
♦Germans in Transcaucasia
♦Germans in other parts of European and Asiatic Russia

GERMANS FROM RUSSIA, SETTLEMENTS IN THE UNITED STATES

Black Sea emigrants

Settled primarily in the Dakotas and were mostly Protestant. These were the first to arrive in America, in 1873.

Volga River emigrants

Settled shortly after the Black Sea emigrants in the central Great Plains states and were, as a rule, Catholic. The center of their settlements was Ellis and Rush Counties, Kansas, south and east of the town of Hays. Protestant Volga Germans tended to settle in Lincoln or Sutton, Nebraska, and later worked in the sugar beet fields of Colorado
.

Emigrants from other areas

Small numbers from Bessarabia, Volhynia, Caucasus and elsewhere. They were Catholic, Protestant (Reformed or Lutheran), and Mennonite.

Source: La Vern J. Rippley, The German-Americans, University Press of America, Inc., Lanham Md, 1984.

PHASES OF GERMANS-TO-RUSSIA MIGRATIONS

The "Germans from Russia," seeing freedom from oppressive rulers and an opportunity of self-determination, accepted the inducements that included numerous privileges to become colonists in czarist Russia.

The German homelands included principally Hesse, the Rhinelands, Baden, Württemberg, and Bavaria — in fact, most of southwest Germany, the German-speaking French Alsace, and the northern portion of Switzerland along with the Danzig region adjacent to the Vistula River in Polish Prussia.

Notwithstanding the fact that Germans had been living in the Baltic Regions since the return of the Teutonic Knights from the Crusades in the 1300s, the settlements in Russia were developed in several distinct phases:

1763-1768: The Volga German colonies extending from Saratov to Kamyschin on both sides of the lower Volga under Czarina Catherine II to develop the virgin lands and to act as a buffer against the mar-auding Khirgiz and Kalmuck tribes. Also in this period, some 2,000 people who did not make it to the Volga settled in the St. Petersburg area where they engaged in small truck farming.

1764-1768: The Chernigov and Voronezh separated colonies by immigrants who were probably destined for but did not reach the Volga Region

1789-1820: The Mennonite colonies along the Kneper River by a pietistic religious sect that obtained special autonomy under Catherine II and Paul I

1790-1850: The Volhynian Germans in the Zhitomir region of Russia from Polish areas that became their homelands after the Partitions of Poland (1772-1795)

1804-1840: The Black Sea German colonies established in the Odessa region of South Russia under Alexander I for the purpose of developing those lands agri-culturally which they also succeeded in making into the breadbasket of Europe

1814-1830: The Bessarabian German colonies between the Dniester and Prut Rivers following Russian acquisition of that area of the Treaty of Bucharest in 1812

1818-1820: The Trans-Caucasus German settlements in the Tiflis (Tbilisi) region of the Caucasus under Alexander I by a separatist religious group

1850-1900: The Don River, North Caucusus along the Kuban River and East of the Urals settlements developed by new immigrants along with settlers from earlier established and later overpopulated com-munities.

With the development of the Plains Regions, the western United States and Canada in the latter half of the nineteenth century, these eastern European Germans joined the mass immigration to the western hemisphere where they again became pioneers.

They brought along the Red Turkey wheat that had made Ukraine so prosperous and, with that as a basis, succeeded in creating the "bread basket of the world" in the states of North Dakota and Kansas, and in the Province of Saskatchewan.

The millions who remained in the eastern European regions fell prey to the Russian Revolution and communism and suffered their personal holocaust. Millions perished during the contrived famines. Those who survived that holocaust but were unwilling to accept forced collectivization were systematically disappro-priated, driven out of their homes and dispersed into forced (slave) labor camps throughout Asiatic Russia and Siberia — a process that again caused the untimely deaths of thousands.

Source: Arthur E. Flegel, C.G "Phases of the German Migrations," *Der Blumenbaum,* Vol. 12, No. 3, 1995.

SOME GERMAN SETTLEMENTS IN SOUTHEASTERN EUROPE.

Germans settled in what had previously been parts of the Austro-Hungarian Empire. These peoples include:

♦ The Polish Galician, Bohemian and Moravian Germans from the northern areas of the Hapsburg Empire

♦ The Germans who settled in Slovenia, the Batschka (Bazca) and Banat along the Danube River basin (1740-1800)

♦ The Siebenbürgen (Transylvanian) Germans in Central Romania whose ancestors had been in that region as early as the 1200s

♦ The Bukowina Germans, who settled from 1770-1790 in northern Moldavia where Romania borders the Ukraine

♦ The Romanian Germans of the Dobrudscha (Dobruja, Dobrogea) region, who settled along the Black coast of Eastern Romania from 1850-1900 when it was part of the Ottoman Turkish Empire

Source: Contributed by Arthur E. Flegel, C.G.

MAJOR RESOURCES FOR GERMANS-FROM-RUSSIA RESEARCH

*American Historical Society of Germans from Russia**, 631 D Street, Lincoln, NE 68502-1199. www.ahsgr.org.
Collection emphasis: Bessarabian, Black Sea, Crimean, Volga, and Volhynian Germans
*Germans from Russia Heritage Society**, 1125 West Turnpike Avenue, Bismarck, ND 58501. www.ghrs.org
Collection emphasis: Bessarbian, Black Sea, and Crimean Germans
*Germans from Russia Heritage Collection**, North Dakota State University Libraries, P.O. Box 6050, Fargo, ND 58108-6050.
   Collection emphasis: Bessarabian and Black Sea Germans. Annotated bibliography to the collection: *Researching the Germans from Russia: Annotated Bibliography of the Germans from Russia Heritage Collection*
*Heimatmuseum der Deutschen aus Bessarabien e.V.**, Florianstraße 17, 70188 Stuttgart, Germany.
Collection emphasis: Bessarabian Germans
*Landsmannschaft der Deutschen aus Russland**, Raitelsbergerstraße 49, 70188 Stuttgart, Germany.
Collection emphasis: Black Sea, Crimean, Mennonite, Volga, and Volhynian Germans
Source: Contribution of collections emphases by Professor Michael M. Miller, Germans from Russia bibliographer, Germans from Russia Heritage Collection, North Dakota Institute for Regional Studies, North Dakota State University.

MICROFILMED CARDFILE: GERMANS FROM RUSSIA

   The FHL microfilms titled *Bestandskartei der Russlanddeutschen, 1750-1943* (Card file of Russian Germans, 1750-1943) are described in the Family History Library Catalog as follows:
   "Index cards of ethnic Germans in Russia, arranged alphabetically by surname.
   "While not all the cards contain the same amount of information, many of them supply the given name, present address, birth place and date, place and date of death, earlier and present citizenship; place of origin, year of emigration, and names of ancestors who first emigrated from Germany; places of residence in Russia; year of emigration from Russia; earlier occupation and later activities; religion, whether pedigrees exist; name, places and dates of birth, marriage, and death, occupation for spouse; names, birthplaces and dates for children; and documentary sources."

Aab-Anton	1335722
Antoni-Bastian, Alexander	1335723
Bastian, Alexander-Bekker (Becker)	1335724
Belajeff-Bleeck, Alfred	1335725
Bleeck, Alfred-Braun, Ida	1335726
Braun, Ida-Busse, Arthur	1335727
Busse, Arthur-Dietrich	1457135
Dietsch-Eckhard	1457136
Eckhard-Esch	1528980
Esch-Fischer, Josef	1528981
Fischer, Josef-Fritz, Elisabeth	1528982
Fritz, Elisabeth-Geissler	1528983
Geist-Goltz	1528984
Goltz-von Bynz-Rekowski	1528985
Haab-Hartman	1528986
Hartman-Helke	1528987
Hell-Hilzendeger	1529015
Hilzendeger-Hornbacher	1529016
Hornbacher-Janzen	1529017
Janzen-Kalkowski	1529018
Kalkowski-Kircher	1529019
Kircher-Knecht	1457323
Knechtel-Kox	1457324
Kraas-Krscheminski	1457325
Krüber-Lang, Daniel	1457326
Lang, Daniel-Lindt	1457327
Lindt-Mahn	1538533

Mahn-Mayer	1538534
Mayer-Mössner	1538535
Mössner-Neufeld	1538536
Neufeld-Ozenberger	1538537
Pabst-Prieb	1538538
Prieb-Reinbold	1538539
Reinbold-Roduner	1538540
Röchert-Sattler	1538541
Sattler-Scheydemanns	1538542
Schibat-Schmied	1538613
Schmied-Schuhmacher, Karl	1538614
Schuhmacher, Karl-Sell	1538615
Sell-Starke	1538616
Starke-Subarewa	1538617
Subarewa-Trost	1538714
Trost-Vüst	1538715
Waade-Webert	1538716
Wechinger-Wieb	1538717
Wieb-Wößner	1538718
Wogaraki-Zimmerman, C.	1538830
Zimmerman, C.-Zyres	1538831

RESOURCES FOR GERMANS-FROM-RUSSIA RESEARCH

♦ Ruben Goertz Collection: Germans-from-Russia materials at Augustana College, Collections of the Center for Western States, 2113 South Summit, Sioux Falls, SD 57105
♦ Mennonite Library and Archives, Information and Research Center, North Newton, KS 67117
wMennonite Historical Library, Goshen College, Goshen, IN 46526

Suggested reading
♦ Adam Giesinger, *From Catherine to Khruschev*, Marian Press, Battleford, Saskatchewan, Canada, 1974. FHL 947 F2ga (see index, next entry)
♦ Freeman, Robert, *Index to Place Names Found in From Catherine to Khruschev by Adam Giesinger,* R&M Freeman, Santa Monica, 1986. FHL 947 F2ga index; film 1666773 item 6
♦ Joseph S. Height, *Homesteaders on the Steppe*, Gulde-Druck, Tübingen, Ger-

many; Bismarck, ND, 1975.
♦ Joseph S. Height, *Paradise on the Steppe*, Gulde-Druck, Tübingen, Germany; Bismarck, ND, 1972.
♦ P.Conrad Keller, *The German Colonies in South Russia: 1804-1904*, vols I and II, translated by A. Becker, Mercury Printers, Ltd., Saskatoon, Saskatchewan, Canada, 1973.
♦ Timothy J. and Rosalinda Kloberdanz, *Thunder on the Steppe*, American Historical Society of Germans from Russia, 1993.
♦ Richard Sallet, *Russian-German Settlements in the United States*, translated by LaVern Rippley and Armond Bauer, Institute for Regional Studies, Fargo, North Dakota, 1974.
♦ Karl Stumpp, *The Emigration from Germany to Russia in the Years 1763-1862.* Translation by Prof. Joseph S. Height and others. American Historical Society of Germans from Russia, Lincoln, NE, 1978.
♦ Karl Stumpp, *The German-Russians: Two Centuries of Pioneering*, Atlantic Forum, 1971.

ALSACE-LORRAINE

CHRONOLOGY OF ALSACE AND LORRAINE JURISDICTIONS

Before 1648: Alsace is part of the Holy Roman Empire
1648: Most of Alsace becomes part of France.
1766: Lorraine becomes part of France.
1871: Alsace and part of Lorraine ("German Lorraine") are annexed by Germany under the name Elsaß-Lothringen. Bismarck takes from Napoleon III the French départements of Bas-Rhin, Haut-Rhin, and Moselle. The western part of Haut-Rhin becomes the territory of Belfort.
1919: Alsace becomes part of France, following World War I. (The old Alsatian

départments of Bas-Rhin and Haut-Rhin are restored. The Lothringen section becomes the départment of Moselle.) **1940-1945:** Alsace becomes part of Germany during World War II. **1946 to present:** Alsace is part of France. (Alsace takes in the departments of Bas-Rhin, Haut-Rhin and, since 1871 the Territory of Belfort; Lorraine corresponds to the departments of Moselle, Meurthe-et-Moselle, and parts of the départments of Meuse and of Vosges.)

RESOURCES FOR ALSACE-LORRAINE RESEARCH

♦"Alsace Family History Research," by Adeline Vigelis. *The German Connection* (The German Research Association), Vol. 18, No. 3, 1994.
♦ Annette Kunselman Burgert, *Eighteenth Century Emigrants from the Northern Alsace to America.* Picton Press, Camden, Maine, 1992.
♦Hugh T. Law, "Locating the Ancestral Home in Elsaß-Lothringen (Alsace Lorraine)," *German Genealogical Digest*, Vol. VI, No. 3, 1990.
♦ Cornelia Schrader-Muggenthaler, *Alsace Emigration Book*, 3 vols. Apollo, PA: Closson Press. 1989-1991.
♦Friedrich Müller. *Ortsbuch für Eupen-Malmedy, Elsass-Lothringen und Luxemburg* [Gazetteer for Eupen-Malmedy (Belgium), Alsace-Lorraine, and Luxembourg]. 1942.

ARCHIVES FOR ALSACE-LORRAINE RESEARCH

Alsace
(Elsaß)
♦ Archives Departementales du Bas-Rhin, 5-9 rue Fischart, 67000 Strasbourg, France
♦ Archives Departementales du Haut-Rhin, Cité administrative, 68026 Colmar Cedex, France
♦Archives Departementales du Territoire de Belfort, 2 rue de l'Ancien Théâtre, 90020 Belfort Cedex, France

Lorraine
(Lothringen)
♦Archives Departementales de Meurthe et Moselle, 1, rue de la Monnaie, 54052 Nancy Cedex, France
♦ Archives Departementales de la Meuse, 20, rue Mgr. Aimond, 55012 Bar-le-Duc, France
♦ Archives Departementales de la Moselle, 1, allée du Château, 57070 St.-Julien-lès-Metz, France
♦Archives Departementales des Vosges, Allée des Hêtres, Z.I. La Voivre, 88000 Épinal, France

ALSACE EMIGRATION INDEX

FHL microfilm numbers for the Alsace Emigration Index for surnames beginning with the specified letters of the alphabet are listed below:

A-C	1,125,002
D-G	1,125,003
H-K	1,125,004
L-P	1,125,005
Q-S	1,125,006
T-Z	1,125,007

Birthplaces, ages and dates of emigration found on these films can become the basis for searches in French civil or parish records.

After 1792, civil records for Alsace and the department of Moselle are mostly in German.

Parish records of Lutherans are usually in German. Parish records of Catholics are in Latin, or sometimes in French.

'OPTIONS' OF ALSATIANS AND LORRAINERS

After Germany annexed much of Alsace and Lorraine after the Franco-Prussian War in 1871, about 160,000 residents of the area, as well as many others, recorded their options to leave.

A list of 523,000 persons who registered their options are recorded on FHL microfilm. Included are names, birth dates, and places of birth.

Some places of destinations are also given.

These lists were originally published in supplements to the *Bulletin des Lois* (Bulletin of the Laws).

Microfilm numbers for these "Options of Alsatians and Lorrainers" are FHL 787154 (beginning in the middle) to 787166. Film numbers 787165 and 787166 contain information about persons whose destinations were given as New York, New Orleans, Louisville, St. Louis, San Francisco, Baltimore, Boston, Chicago, Cincinnati, Washington, Quebec, etc.

Source: Hugh T. Law, M.A., A.G., "Locatiing the Ancestral Home in Elsass-Lothringen," *German Genealogical Digest*, Vol. VI, No. 3 (1990), p. 83.

AUSTRIA

CHRONOLOGY OF AUSTRIA AND THE AUSTRO-HUNGARIAN EMPIRE

Late 13th century: The Habsburg Dynasty comes into power, rules until 1918.
15th, 16th centuries: Austrian rulers are Holy Roman Emperors; thus Austria is part of the First Reich.
c. 1650: Austrian lands include present-day Austria, in addition to Lorraine, Burgundy, Alsace, Breisgau, Belgium, the Netherlands, Bohemia, Moravia, Silesia

and other territories.
1731: 23,500 Salzburg Protestants are expelled, settling for the most part in East Prussia and Brandenburg.
1740-48: War of the Austrian Succession. Prussia gains Silesia from Austria.
1781: The Patent of Tolerance provides new freedoms to non-Catholics, opening the way for Protestants to settle in Austria. (Therefore, all immigrants before this date would have been Catholics.) German peasants are invited to settle in Galicia.
1783: Under Emperor Joseph I, ministers must keep separate registers of christenings, marriages, and deaths. in German. The German language is to replace Latin and any other languages in the church books.
1804-13: Napoleonic Wars
1805-1807: The end of the Holy Roman Empire and the creation of the Austrian Empire is brought about through the Napoleonic Wars.
1848: Insurrections occur throughout the Austrian Empire.
1866: Seven Weeks War. Prussia defeats Austria, forcing Austria to share power with Hungary as Austrian-Hungarian Empire is established in 1867.
1867: The dual monarchy of Austria-Hungary is formed, lasting until World War I.
1914-18: World War I. End of the Austrian-Hungarian Empire (1919), with its division into Austria, Czechoslovakia, Hungary, Italy, Poland, Romania, Russia and Yugoslavia. (In 1914, the Austrian-ruled half consisted of Austria proper, Bohemia, Bosnia and Herzegovina, Bukovina, Carinthia, Carniola, Dalmatia, Galicia, Istria, Moravia, Salzburg, the Austrian part of Silesia, Styria, Trent, Tyrol, and Vorarlberg. Hungary ruled Croatia, Slavonia, and Transylvania, in addition to Hungary proper, then much larger than today. After World War I, Austria and Hungary each became a separate small country. A part of the

ethnically mixed Burgenland region, which hitherto had belonged to Hungary, became part of Austria pursuant to a plebiscite.[1])

1938: Hitler annexes Austria and the Sudetenland region of Czechoslovakia. Civil registration begins in Austria.

1939-1945: World War II. Following the war, Austria's previous boundaries are restored.

1955: Allied occupation forces leave Austria on condition that Austria maintain neutrality, not confederate with West or East Germany, and not restore the Habsburgs.

[1]Brandt, Edward R., et al, *Germanic Genealogy: A Guide to Worldwide Sources and Migration Patterns*. Germanic Genealogy Society, St. Paul. 1995.

AUSTRO-HUNGARIAN EMPIRE (ENDING IN 1919)

Austrian Crownlands
* Niederösterreich/Lower Austria
* Oberösterreich/Upper Austria
* Salzburg/Salzburg
* Kärnten/Carinthia
* Steiermark/Styria
* Krain/Carniola
* Goerz and Gradiska/Goritz
* Triest and surrounding area/Triest
* Istrien/Istria
* Dalmatien/Dalmatia
* Tirol/Tyrol
* Vorarlberg/Vorarlberg
* Böhmen/Bohemia
* Mähren/Moravia
* Schlesien/Silesia
* Galizien/Galicia
* Bukowina/Bukovina

Hungarian Crownlands
* Ungarn with Siebenbürgen/Hungary with Siebenbürgen
* Kroatien-Slovonien/Croatien-Slovenia
* Fiume and surrounding area/Fiume and surrounding area

Occupied Areas
* Bosnien/Bosnia
* Herzegowina/Hercegovina

GEOGRAPHIC AREAS OF AUSTRO-HUNGARY

Alpenländer: Erzherzogthum (Archduchy) Oesterreich, Steiermark, Tirol, Kärnten, Krain, Lombardie
Sudetenländer: Böhmen, Mähren with Schlesien
Seeküstenländer: Venedig, Illirisches Littorale, Kroatien, Dalmatien
Karpathenländer: Galizien, Ungarn, Siebenbürgen

RESEARCH SUGGESTIONS FROM THE AUSTRIAN NATIONAL TOURIST OFFICE

The Austrian National Tourist Office provides the following advice and caution:

For any birthdates prior to November 1918, make certain the town listed as the birthplace is within present-day Austria. Generally, Austria is given as a country of birth prior to 1918 for any birth in the provinces of the Austrian Empire and, later on, the Austro-Hungarian Monarchy. At the end of World War I, this entity disintegrated into a number of different countries, and a birthplace listed as being in Austria may actually be in any of these modern-day countries. In the past, the following organizations in some of these successor countries to the Austro-Hungarian Monarchy and the Austrian Empire have been genealogically helpful:

* **Czech Republic:** Archivni Sprava, Trida Obrancy Miru 133 Prague 6
* **Hungary:** Magyar Leveltar Orszagos, Becsi Kapu ter 4, Budapest
* **Poland:** Naczelna Dyrekcja Archiwow Panstwowych, ul. Wicza 9a, Warsaw 10

Nobility

Contact this organization (which keeps complete lists of families and coats of arms) about any degree of nobility discovered:

Heraldisch-Genealogische Gesellschaft Adler, Landstrasser Hauptstrasse 140 A-1030 Wien Austria

Military records

Files on military personnel (*Militärmatrikeln*) may be accessed at the address below. Note, however, that the person being searched would have to be positively identified as having served in the Imperial Army or the Imperial Navy, and basic data on the time and location of military postings or assignments or a date of discharge would have to be known as well.

Bundesministerium für Inneres Abteilung 9/M Karl-Schweighofer-Gasse 3 A-1070 Wien Austria

Church records

In general, under the administrative system introduced by Empress Maria Theresia, personal documents such as certificates of birth, marriage or death were issued and the corresponding records kept by the religious communities in the respective localities. Therefore, it is necessary to establish, through documents, letters, and the correct affiliation (Roman Catholic, Lutheran, Calvinist, Jewish), and then contact the respective religious community in that town, such as a parish (*Pfarramt*) or a synagogue.

In some cases, files have been transferred to regional archives (such as those of a diocese) of the various religious denominations, and it may be helpful to contact those.

After 1870, the administrative districts and self-administering cities started registers (*Meldeamt*) for persons without religious affiliation

See the Austrian church archive addresses below.

CHURCH ARCHIVES IN AUSTRIA (KIRCHENARCHIVE)

Catholic diocesan archives (Diözesanarchive)

♦Diözese Eisenstadt: Diözenanarchiv, St. Rochus-Str. 21, A-7001 Eisenstadt

♦ Diözese Feldkirch: Archiv der Diözese, Bahnhofstr. 13, A-6800 Feldkirch

♦ Diözese Graz-Seckau: Diözesanarchiv, Bischofsplatz 4, A-8010 Graz

♦ Diözese Gurk in Klagenfurt, Archiv der Diöze, Mariannengasse 6, A-9020 Klagenfurt

♦Diözese Innsbruck: Diözesanarchiv, Riedgasse 9, A-6021 Innsbruck

♦ Diözese Linz: Diözesanarchiv, Harrachstr. 7, A-4020 Linz

♦Diözese St. Pölten: Diözesanarchiv, Domplatz 1, A-3100 St. Pölten

♦ **Archdiocese:** Erzdiözese Salzburg, Konsistorialarchiv, Kapitelplatz 2, A-5010 Salzburg

♦ **Archdiocese:** Erzdiözese Wien,: Diözesanarchiv, Wollzeile 2, A-1010 Wien Protestant church archives

Protestant church archives

♦ Archiv des Evangelischen Oberkirchen-rates A.u.H.B., Severin Schreiber-Gasse 3, A-1180 Wien

♦ Archiv des Evangelischen Oberkirchen-rates H.B., Archiv der Evangelischen Pfarrgemeinde H.B. Wien-Innere Stadt, Dorotheergasse 16, A-1010 Wien

Jewish archive

♦Israelitische Kulturgemeinde, Schottenring 25, A-1010 Wien

Sources: *Archive in der Bundesrepublik Deutschland, Österreich und der Schweiz,* Ardey-Verlag, Münster, 1995;

and Austrian National Tourist Office.

AUSTRIAN CITY/TOWN ARCHIVES (STADTARCHIVE)

Amstetten: Stadtarchiv, Rathausstr. 1, A-3300 Amstetten
Baden bei Wien: Standtarchiv, Weikersdorfer-platz 1, A-2500 Baden bei Wien
Bludenz: Stadtarchiv, Rathaus, Postfach 120, A-6700 Bludenz
Braunau am Inn: Stadtarchiv, Palmplatz 8, A-5280 Braunau am Inn
Bregenz: Stadtarciv, Rathausstr. 4, A-6900 Bregenz
Bruck an der Leitha: Stadtarchiv, Rathaus, Hauptplatz 16, A-2460 Bruck an der Leitha
Dornbirn: Stadtarchiv, Rathaus, A-6850 Dornbirn
Drosendorf: Stadarchiv, Rathaus, Hauptplatz 1, A-2098 Drosendorf
Durnstein: Stadtarchiv, Rathaus, A-3601 Dürnstein
Eferding (Oberösterreich): Stadtarchiv, Stadtplatz 31, A-4070 Eferding (Oberösterreich)
Eisenstadt: Stadtarchiv Eisenstadt (stored in *Burgenländischen Landesarchiv Eisenstadt*)
Enns: Stadtarchiv, Hauptplatz 16, A-4470 Enns
Feldkirch: Stadtarchiv, Palais Liechtenstein, A-6800 Feldkirch (Vorarlberg)
Gleisdorf (Steiermark): Stadtarchiv, Rathaus, A-8200 Gleisdorf (Steiermark)
Gmunden (Oberösterreich): Stadtarchiv (stored in Oberösterreichischen Landesarchiv Linz)
Graz: Stadtarchiv, Hans-Sachs-Gasse 1, A-8010 Graz
Grein Oberösterreich: Stadarchiv (stored in Oberösterreichischen Landsarchiv Linz)
Groß-Siegharts: Stadtarchiv, Rathaus, Schloßplatz 1, A-3812 Groß-Siegharts
Haag (Niederösterreich): Stadtarchiv, Rathaus, A-3350 Haag (Niederösterreich)

Hainburg an der Donau: Stadtarchiv Bauhof der Stadtgemeinde, Dorrekstr. 2, A-2410 Hainburg an der Donau
Hall in Tirol: Stadtarchiv, Oberer Stadtplatz 1, A-6060 Hall in Tirol
Hallein (Salzburg): Stadtarchiv, Keltenmuseum, A-5400 Hallein (Salzburg)
Horn: Stadtarchiv, Rathausplatz 4, A-3580 Horn
Innsbruck: Stadtarchiv, Badgasse 2, A-6020 Innsbruck
Kitzbühel (Tirol): Stadtarchiv, Kirchgasse 2, A-6370 Kitzbühel (Tirol) (Stadtgemeinde, Kulturreferat, Rathaus, A-6370 Kitzbühel)
Klosterneuburg: Stadtarchiv, Rathausplatz 1, A-3400 Klosterneuburg
Korneuburg: Stadtarchiv, Hauptplatz 39, A-2100 Korneuburg
Krems an der Donau: Stadtarchiv, Körnermarkt 13, A-3500 Krems an der Donau
Laa an der Thaya: Stadtarchiv, Rathaus, A-2126 Laa an der Thaya
Langenlois (Niederösterreich): Stadtarchiv, Rathausstr. 2, A-3550 Langenlois (Niederösterreich)
Leoben: Stadtarchiv, Kirchgasse 6, A-8700 Leoben
Lienz: Stadtarchiv, Museum Schloß Bruck, A-9900 Lienz
Linz: Stadtarchiv, Hauptstr. 1-5, Postfach 1000, A-4041 Linz
Mödling: Stadtarchiv, Rathausgasse 8, A-2340 Mödling
Neunkirchen: Stadtarchiv, Heimatmuseum, Dr. Stockhammergasse 13, A-2620 Neunkirchen
Pinkafeld (Burgenland): Stadtarchiv, Hauptplatz 1, A-7423 Pinkafeld (Burgenland) (handled through the *Burgenländische Landesarchiv Eisenstadt*)
Pöchlarn (Niederösterreich): Stadtarchiv, Regensburger Str. 11, A-3380 Pöchlarn (Niederösterreich)
Retz: Stadtarchiv, Stadtamt, Hauptplatz 30, A2070 Retz
Ried im Innkreis: Stadtarchiv, Kirchenplatz 13, A-4910 Ried im Innkreis
Rust (Burgenland): Stadtarchiv, Con-

radplatz 1, A-7071 Rust (Burgenland)
Salzburg: 1) Stadtarachiv mit Archiv des Salzburger Museums Carolino-Augusteum, Museumsplatz 6, A-5020 Salzburg 2) Archiv der Stadt Salzburg, Magistrats-Abt.ZV/o4, Fürbergstr. 47, Postfach 63, A-5024 Salzburg
St. Pölten: Stadtarchiv, Prandtauerstr. 2, A-3100 St. Pölten
Schwechat: Stadtarchiv, Stadtamt, A-2320 Schwechat
Steyr (Oberösterreich): Stadtarchiv, Stadtplatz 27, A-4400 Steyr (Oberösterreich)
Stockerau: Stadtarchiv, Belvederschlößl, Belvederegasse 5, A-2000 Stockerau
Traiskirchen (Niederösterreich): Stadt-archiv, Hauptplatz 13, A-2514 Trais-kirchen (Niederösterreich)
Tulln (Niederösterreich): Stadtarchiv, Nußalle 4, A-3430 Tulln (Niederösterreich)
Villach: Stadtarchiv, Widmanngasse 38, A-9500 Villach
Vöcklabruck (Oberösterreich): Stadt-archiv Vöcklabruck (Oberösterreich) (stored in Oberösterreichischen Landesarchiv Linz)
Bad Vöslau: Stadtarchiv, Altes Rathaus, A-2540 Bad Vöslau
Waidhofen an der Thaya: Stadtarchiv, Rathaus, Hauptplatz 1, A-3830 Waidhofen an der Thaya
Waidhofen an der Ybbs: Stadtarchiv, Ybsitzerstr. 18, A-3340 Waidhofen an der Ybbs
Weitra (Niederösterreich): Stadtarchiv, Rathausplatz 1, A-3970 Weitra (Niederösterreich)
Wels: Stadtarchiv, Rathaus, A-4601 Wels
Wiener Neustadt: Stadtarchiv, Wienerstr. 63, A-2700 Wiener Neustadt
Ybbs an der Donau: Stadtarchiv, Hauptplatz 1, A-3370 Ybbs an der Donau
Zwettl (Niederösterreich): Stadtarchiv, Stadtamt, Gartenstr. 3, A-3910 Zwettl (Niederösterreich)

Source: *Archive in der Bundesrepublik Deutschland, Österreich und der Schweiz,* Ardey-Verlag, Münster, 1995.

GAZETTEERS FOR AUSTRIA

•**Raffelsperger, Franz,** *Allgemeines geographisch-statistisches Lexikon aller österreichischen Staaten* [gazetteer of the Austrian Empire comprising areas later located in Austria, Czechoslovakia, Poland, Ukraine, Hungary, Romania, Yugoslavia, and Italy]. FHL 943.6 E5r; also,
A-Balig: film 1187928 item 4
Balin-G: film 1187929
H-Megyes: film 1187930
Megyes-Sanct Lor: film 1187931
Sanct Lor-Warm: film 1187932
Warm-Z; Karten: film 1187933 items 1-2
♦ *Allgemeines Verzeichnis der Ortsgemeinden und Ortschaften Österreichs: Nach den Ergebnissender Volkszählung vom 31. Dezember 1910* [gazetteer of the Austrian Empire, based on the 1910 census]. FHL film 1186712 item 2. These volumes can now be viewed at www.lib.byu.edu/fhc/. In the "Browse" window, press the down arrow, select "Gazetteers" and press "Go." The document is free to browse and print, but has not been indexed for a keyword search.
♦ Mayerhofer, Hans, *Österreich-ungarisches Orts-Lexikon enthaltend die Pfarrorte, Culbisgemeinden und Filialen aller Confessionen: Österreich-Ungarns, Bosniens, und der Herzegowina* [gazetteer of the Austro-Hungarian Empire showing all parishes and church jurisdictions]. FHL film 1256324 item 4
♦ Skwor, Johann, *Orts-Lexicon der im Reichsrathe vertretenen Königreiche und Länder von Oesterreich* [gazetteers of the Austrian crown lands]. FHL film 1188663 item 3
♦**www.ihff.at** This is the website of the

prime research resource for modern and historic Austria. The director is Felix Gundacker and his agency has published several gazetteers and churchbook inventories for the Austrian Crownlands.

OTHER HELPFUL RESOURCES FOR AUSTRIAN RESEARCH

♦ *Genealogical Guide to German Ancestors from East Germany and Eastern Europe* [English translation of *Wegweiser für Forschungen nach Vorfahren*, by Arbeits-gemeinschaft ostdeutscher Familien-forscher]. FHL 943 D27gg
♦ Mikoletzky, Hans Leo, *Genealogical Research in Austrian Archives*. FHL 929.1 W893 D7; film 897214 item 30; fiche 6039327
♦ Schuster, Gustav, *Die Matrikenbestande der rom.-kath. Pfarren Niederöstereichs und Wiens* [parish register inventory and parish jurisdictions for Niederösterreich und Wien]. FHL 943.612 K23s; film 1183572 item 2
♦ Senekovic, Dagmar, *Handy Guide to Austrian Genealogical Records*. FHL 943.6 D27s

RIVERS OF AUSTRIA

The Danube River begins in Germany and flows through Linz and Vienna. It is the principal river of Austria.

Its tributaries include the Inn, which forms part of Austria's border with Germany; the Traun; the Enns; and Ybbs rivers.

The Mur and Mürz rivers are in the south.

AUSTRIAN WAR ARCHIVES (KRIEGSARCHIV)

Kriegsarchiv

Nottendorfergasse 2-4
1030 Wien
Austria

The War Archives (*Kriegsarchiv*) in Vienna contains holdings of the central military offices, the territorial authorities, and the field chancelleries of the Imperial Army and the Royal Army.

Records older than 30 years are opened to the public if they do not fall under the provisions of the Information Protection Act and the Personal Information Act.

A *partial* list of holdings follows:

Personnel records
♦ Roll call records (personnel lists) 1740-1820
♦ Basic service sheets 1820-1918
♦ Enlistment registers and enrollment lists 1862-1918
♦ Retirement and pension books 1749-1920
♦ Pay registers for persons on staff 1753-1819
♦ Records of soldiers' children 1770-1870
♦ Death notices and press clippings 1918-1996

Parish registers and war casualties
♦ Military parish registers
♦ Military units and institutions 17th century-1920
♦ World War I 1914-1918
♦ Military hospitals (death registers) 1779-1922
♦ Card index to military parish registers 1914-1918*
♦ Lists of war casualties 1914-1918
♦ Prisoners of war (lists and card indexes) 1914-1918*
♦ Military hospitals (patients' sheets) 1914-1918
♦ Burial records 1914-1918
♦ Soldiers' returns 1918-1920*
* = restricted access

Reference
For further information about the War Archive in Vienna, see:

◆Blodgett, Steven W., "Great Grandfather was in the Imperial Cavalry: Using Austrian Military Records as an aid to writing family history," *World Conference on Records*, Corporation of the President, Salt Lake City, 1980.
◆Egger, Rainer, *The Kriegsarchiv* [the Vienna War Archives collection of military records for the former Austrian Empire]. FHL 943.613/W1 J5e; fiche 6001424

AUSTRIAN TOURIST OFFICES

New York
Austrian National Tourist Office
P.O. Box 1142
New York, NY 10108-1142
Tel. (212) 730-8400
Fax (212) 730-4568
ANTONYC@ibm.net

Austrian Cultural Institute
11 E. 52nd Street
New York, NY 10022
Tel. (212) 319-5300
Fax (212) 644-8660
desk@acfny.org

Los Angeles
Austrian National Tourist Office
6520 Platt Avenue #651
West Hills, CA 91307-3218
Tel. (818) 999-4030
antolax@ix.netcom.com

OTHER ADDRESSES

Austrian Chamber of Commerce
165 West 46th Street, Suite 1112
New York, NY 10036-2501
Tel. (212) 819-0117
Fax (212) 819-0345

Austrian Embassy
3524 International Court, NW
Washington, DC 20008-3027

Consular Section
Tel. (202) 895-6700
Fax (202) 895-6750

BOHEMIA/BOEHMEN
SUDETENLAND

GERMAN BOHEMIANS

The *Böhmisch* (Bohemians) descend from Germanic peoples who lived outside of what was until recently Czechoslovakia (for example: Bavaria, Silesia, and Austria), though they forged a distinct identity after living as long as 900 years in Bohemia.

German-Bohemians were settlers from as long ago as the seventh century in the mountainous area that extend around Bohemia and Moravia, which much later, in 1918, became Czechoslovakia.

Around 1900, these areas came to be known as the Sudetenland and the people as Sudeten-Germans. By this time, ethnic Germans constituted 35 percent of Bohemia's population and almost 28 percent of the population of Moravia; these populations were overwhelmingly Roman Catholic.

In 1938, these territories were taken over by Germany until the end of World War II, when Czechoslovakia's pre-war borders were restored. Most ethnic Germans were expelled from the country. In 1948, most of the border villages were bulldozed to the ground.

Many of the *Böhmisch* emigrants settled near New Ulm, Minnesota in Brown and Nicollet counties, starting in 1856 and continuing until 1914. Early emigrants settled near Dubuque, Iowa, but then moved on toward New Ulm to find better land.

Church registers
Church registers in Bohemia and Moravia were taken into state possession in 1952. No civil registration existed

until the twentieth century.

Resources
♦La Vern Rippley and Robert Paulson, *The German-Bohemians: The Quiet Immigrants.* St. Olaf College Press, Northfield Minnesota. 1995.
♦Ken Meter and Robert Paulson, *Border People: The Bohemisch* [German-Bohemians] *in America.* Crossroads Resource Center and the German-Bohemian Heritage Society. 1993.
♦ Gundacker, Felix, *Genealogical Gazetteer of Bohemia*, IHFF, Vienna, Austria (undated) Genealogy societies.

Bohemian Societies
♦**German-Bohemian Heritage Society,** P.O. Box 822, New Ulm, MN 56073-0822. contactgbhs@gmail.com; www.roots web.ancestry.com/~gbhs/index.html – [GBHS founder] Robert Paulson, 800 W. Idaho Avenue, St. Paul, MN 55117. rpaulgb@comcast.net
This is the primary society in the United States for German-Bohemian research, with a German-Bohemian Family Data Base available on the Internet. They publish the German-Bohemian Heritage Society Newsletter (quarterly; free queries)
♦ **Vereinigung Sudetendeutscher Familienforscher (VSFF),** Erikaweg 58, 93053 Regensburg
♦**Czechoslovak Genealogical Society International,** P.O. Box 16225, St. Paul, MN 55116-0255
♦ **Minnesota Genealogical Society Library,** 1650 Carroll Avenue, St. Paul, MN 55104
♦ **Minnesota Historical Society,** 345 Kellog Blvd. West, St. Paul, MN 55102-1906
♦**Brown County Historical Society**, 2 North Broadway, New Ulm, MN 56073

BOHEMIA RESOURCES

The best English-language guide to ethnic German genealogical research in the former Czechoslovakia is –
♦ Arbeitsgemeinschaft ostdeutscher Familienforscher e.V., Herne, **Genealogical Guide to German Ancestors from East Germany and Eastern Europe** (AGoFF-Wegweiser - English Edition), translated by Joachim O.R. Nuthack and Adalbert Goertz. Verlag Degener, Neustadt/Aisch, 1984.
♦ *Bestandsverzeichnis der Deutschen Zentralstelle für Genealogie Leipzig Teil II Die archivalischen und Kirchenbüchunterlagen deutscher Siedlungsgebiete im Ausland Bessarabien, Bukowina, Estland, Lettland und Litauen, Siebenbürgen, Sudetenland, Slowenien und Südtirol.* [inventory of holdings of the German Central Office for Genealogy in Leipzig for former German settlements in . . . .] Shows microfilm holdings for towns in each area. Indexed]. FHL 943.21/L2 K23w pt. 2
♦ Leo Baca, ed., *Czech Immigration Passenger Lists.* 9 volumes Old Homestead Publishing Co., Hallettsville, Tex., 1983-1998.

Archive
Sudetendeutsches Archiv, Hochstraße 8/11, 81669 München. Tel. (089) 48 00 03-30
The Sudeten German Archive collects historic primary sources, documents, newspapers, magazines, pictures and recordings of the political, economic and cultural development of the Sudeten Germans before and after their expulsion. Its focus is local historical and geographical history and the Sudeten German and Czechoslovakian press.

District archives
Archives in the Czech Republic are divided into these eight districts:

1. West Bohemian district: State district archives Pilsen (Pilzen)
2. North Bohemian district: State district archives Leitmeritz (Litomerice)
3. Middle Bohemian district: State district archives Prague (Praha)
4. South Bohemian district: State district archives Wittingau (Trebon)
5. East Bohemian district: State district archives Zamrsk
6. North Moravian district: State district archives Troppau (Opava)
7. South Moravian district: State district archives Brünn (Brno)
8. Prague: Archive of the capital of Prague (Praha)

BUKOVINA

BUKOVINA GERMANS

Formerly a province of Romania, Bukovina lies in the foothills of the eastern Carpathian Mountains. Until 1769, it was ruled by the Ottoman Turks and occupied by Russia. In 1775, having been taken over by Austria, Bukovina became part of Galicia until 1849, when it was made a separate crownland or province. In the late 1700s and early 1800s, the ruling Hapsburg family recruited German-speaking people to settle its virgin forests.

The German colonists consisted of three groups: 1) Swabians and Palatines from what is now Baden-Württemberg and Rheinland-Pfalz, in southwest Germany; 2) German Bohemians, from the Bohemian forest (*Böhmerwald*), now in the Czech Republic; and 3) Zipsers, from the Zips mountains, now Spis county, Slovakia. The Bukovina Germans never exceeded 10 percent of the population of the province. Although a minority, they lived in ethnic German villages and communities, preserving their language and customs.

After one to two generations in Buko-

vina, land became scarce and the New World looked promising. Agents for the railroads passed out flyers throughout Europe to recruit the hard-working Germans to settle along their lines. Newspapers brimmed with ads announcing free homestead land, and, in the case of South America, free passage. Some 70 famiilies chose Ellis, Kansas as their destination during a span of 15 years beginning in 1886. Later arrivals located in Rooks, Trego, Ness and other western Kansas counties. Two other colonies were started, one in Yuma County, Colorado, and one in Lewis County, Washington. After 1900, some Bukovina Germans located in New York and Chicago. Stepping off the train in western Kansas in the middle of a vast prairie was a stark contrast to their forested ancestral lands, but the hardy pioineers carved out successful lives as the largest concentration of Bukovina Germans in the United States.

At the end of World War I, when the Austro-Hungarian Empire was dissolved, Bukovina became independent and joined Romania as a province. During World War II (in 1940), Bukovina and Bessarabia were ceded to the Soviet Union but were occupied by German and Romanian forces from 1941-1944. Through an armistice in 1944, northern Bukovina and Bessarabia became part of the Soviet Union, and southern Bukovina remained in Romania. The ancestral villages of the Ellis Buko-vina Germans today are in Romania.

Societies
◆**Bukovina Society of the Americas**, P.O. Box 81, Ellis, KS 67637-0081
w**Landsmannschaft der Buchenland-deutschen e.V.**, Bukowina Institut, Alter Postweg 97a, 86159 Augsburg, Germany. (This organization was formed in 1949 by refugees who had resettled from Bukovina to Germany and Austria during and after World War II.)

◆ **Raimund Friedrich Kaindl-Gesell-schaft e.V.**, Waldburgstr. 251, 70655 Stuttgart, Germany (a genealogical society)

Resources
◆ Irma Bornemann, *The Bukovina Germans*; published in Germany as *Die Buchenlanddeutschen*, vol. 13 of *Kulturelle Arbeitschelfte*, ed. Barbara Konitz (Bonn: Bund der Vertriebenen, 1986). English translation by Sophie A. Welisch, © 1990 by the Bukovina Society of the Americans, Ellis, Kansas.
◆ Sopie A Welisch, *Bukovina Villages/Towns/Cities and Their Germans.* Published 1990 by the Bukovina Society of the Americas, Ellis, Kansas.
◆ Oneita Jean Bollig, *Extracted Parish Records from Ellis, Kansas.* Each book includes the Register of Baptisms, Register of Confirmations, Register of Marriages, and Register of Funerals for the cited years.
◆ Irmgard Hein Ellingson, *The Bukovina Germans in Kansas: A 200 Year History of the Lutheran Swabians.* No. 6 of Ethnic Heritage Studies, published by Fort Hays State University, 1987. (Irmgard Ellingson, P.O. Box 97, Ossian, IA 52161-0097).
◆ Oren Windholz, *Bohemian Germans in Kansas: A Catholic Community from Bukovina.* Published by the author, 1993 (Oren Windholz, P.O.Box 1083, Hays, KS 67601. owindholz@ruraltel.net).
◆ Almar Associates, *Bukovina Families: 200 Years.* Almar Associates, Ellis, Kansas, 1993. Primary emphasis on families from Pojana Mikuli. (Almar Associates, 300 N. Washington Street, Ellis, KS 67637).

Records
After World War II, many of the Roman Catholic and Lutheran parish records were brought out of Romania when the Bukovina Germans left there in the *Umsiedlung* (resettlement) of 1940.

Most of them were collected in *Die Deutsche Zentralstelle für Genealogie* in Leipzig. All these records have been microfilmed and are available through Family History Centers. See: *Bestandsverzeichnis der Deutschen Zentralstelle für Genealogie Leipzig Teil II Die archivalischen und Kirchenbüchunterlagen deutscher Siedlungsgebiete im Ausland Bessara-bien, Bukowina, Estland, Lettland und Litauen, Siebenbürgen, Sudetenland, Slowenien und Südtirol.* [inventory of holdings of the German Central Office for Genealogy in Leipzig for former German settlements in . . . .] Shows microfilm holdings for towns in each area. Indexed] FHL 943.21/L2 K23w pt. 2

CANADA

GERMAN-CANADIANS

German-speaking and German-descended populations are found in the greatest numbers in the rural areas of Manitoba, Saskatchewan, and Alberta. They are found in Ontario in and near the cities of Kitchener (formerly Berlin) and Waterloo, the town of New Hamburg and the Niagra area, and in the Royal York area of metropolitan Toronto.

ARCHIVES
The National Archives of Canada
395 Wellington Street
Ottawa, Ontario, Canada K1A 0N3

Regional archives
◆ Montreal Federal Records Centre
665A Montee de Liesse
Ville St. Laurent, Quebec, Canada H4T 1P5
◆ Quebec City Federal Records Centre
75 de Hambourg
◆ St. Augustan, Quebec, Canada G3A 1S6
◆ Ottawa Federal Records Centre

Bldg. #15 Tunneys Pasture, Goldenrod Street
Ottawa, Ontario, Canada K1A 0N3
◆Toronto Federal Land Record Centre
190 Carrier Drive
Rexdale, Ontario, Canada M9W 5R1
◆Winnipeg Federal Records Center
201 Weston Street
Winnipeg, Manitoba, Canada R3E 3H4
◆ Edmonton Federal Records Centre
8707 51st Avenue
Edmonton, Alberta, Canada T6E 5H1
◆Vancouver Federal Records Centre
2751 Production Way
Lake City Industrial Park
Buraby, British Columbia, Canada V5A 3G7
◆Halifax Federal Records Centre
131 Thornhill Drive
Halifax, Nova Scotia, Canada B3B 1S2

St. Albans passenger arrival records

The St. Albans Passenger Arrival Records record those people who crossed the border from Canada to the United States, including passengers arriving by train through substations, ports, or along the borders from Washington State to Maine.

The Immigration and Naturalization Service at St. Albans, Vermont, maintained these records, which are part of Group 85 records of the Immigration and Naturalization Service. It has been estimated that as many as 40 percent of the passengers arriving in Canada were actually bound for the United States. They were traveling through Canada because of the low railway and steamship fares.

Records Group 85 indexes

The four indexes for this INS Records Group 85 are,
◆ **M1461** (400 rolls of microfilm), "Soundex Index to Canadian Border Entries through the St. Albans, Vermont, District, 1895-1924"
◆**M1462** (6 rolls of microfilm), "Alphabetical Index to Canadian Border Entries through Small Ports in Vermont, 1895-1924"
◆**M1463** (98 rolls of microfilm), "Soundex Index to Entries into the St. Albans, Vermont, District through Canadian Pacific and Atlantic Ports, 1924-1958."
◆**M1478** (117 rolls of microfilm), "Card Manifests (Alphabetical) of Individuals Entering through the Port of Detroit, Michigan, 1906-1954"

Immigrants who came to the United States through any Canadian port were reported to the St. Albans Immigration office, the records for which are found in the #M1463 index.

For more information, see "St. Albans Passenger Arrival Records," by Constance Potter, *Prologue*, National Archives, Washington, Spring 1990, pp 90-93.

Canadian passenger ship manifests

Manifests are available to researchers for the ports of Montreal/Quebec City, 1865-1919; Halifax, 1880-1919; North Sydney, 1906-1919; Saint John, 1900-1918; Vancouver, 1905-1919; Victoria and small coastal ports, 1905-1919.

Microfilms of these manifests are available at Family History Centers of the Family History Library of the Church of Jesus Christ of Latter-day Saints in Salt Lake City, as well as at locations in Canada. Almost none of the manifests are indexed. The information is arranged chronologically by year and date. For further information, see "Canadian Passenger Ship Manifests," by Glen Eker. *Ancestry*, March/April 1996.

Resources

◆ Baxter, Angus, *In Search of Your Canadian Roots.* Genealogical Publishing Co., Inc., Baltimore. 2nd ed. 1994.
◆Lehman, Heinz, *The German Canadians, 1750-1937,* trans. Prof. Gerhard P. Bassler. Jesperson Press, St. John's,

The German Research Companion

173

Newfoundland, 1986 .
(This is a very detailed history of German
settlements in Canada, including places
of origin for many settlers)
◆**German-Canadian Studies at the University of Winnipeg**, 516 Portage Avenue, Winnipeg, Manitoba R3B 2E9
Canada. Tel. (204) 786-9007; Fax (204)
772-0472; www. uwinnipeg.ca/
~germcan/index.html

Consulate General
Canadian Consulate General
550 South Hope Street, 9th floor
Los Angeles, CA 90071
Tel. (213) 346-2700
Fax (213) 346-2767
lngls@international.gc.ca
Sources:
◆"Road less travelled used by some
'back door' immigrant ancestors," by
John W. Heisey, *AntiqueWeek*, August
28, 1995.
◆"A History of German Canadians," by
William A. Hynes. *German Life*,
February/March 1996.
◆ "Canadian Passenger Ship Mani-
fests," by Glen Eker. *Ancestry*, March/
April 1996.

CZECHOSLOVAKIA

**CZECHOSLOVAKIA
(CZECH REPUBLIC, SLOVAKIA)**

1918: Czechoslovakia is born from
the disbanded Austro-Hungarian Empire
after World War I. (The regions of
Bohemia, Moravia, and Silesia – now
known as the Czech Republic – had fallen
under the rule of the Austrian crown.
Before 1918, Czechs were known as Austrians. The Slovaks were occupied by
the Hungarian monarchy, and later the
dual Austro-Hungarian Empire.) The 1918
creation of Czecho-Slovakia soon becomes referred to simply as Czechoslovakia.

1938: Bohemia and Moravia become a
Protectorate of the Third Reich following
the Nazi invasion. Slovakia becomes an
"independent" puppet state of the Nazi
government.
1945: At the end of World War II, the
nation once more becomes Czechoslovakia.
1946: With the Communist takeover, the
country becomes the Czechoslovak
Socialist Republic.
1989: Through the "Velvet Revolution,"
the Czechoslovak Federal Republic is
born, soon followed by the Czech and
Slovak Federal Republic.
1993: The country divided into the
Czech Republic and the Slovak Republic,
more commonly known as Slovakia.

Archives
The Czech Republic archives are divided into regional branches, with five
Bohemian archives and two Moravian
archives. All parish registers, beginning
in the 1890s, remain in the city or village
repositories.
Books completed during the last decade of the nineteenth century and those
prior to them were sent to regional archives for preservation and cataloging.
They may be accessed, but with some
rather stringent restrictions.
Slovak records for the three major regional archives in Slovakia are available
through the Family History Library.
Source: Dr. Paul S. Valasek, "Multiple
border, national boundary changes
test skills of the Czech, Slovak
researchers." *AntiqueWeek,* February
10, 1997. (Dr. Valasek is a founding
member of the Czech & Slovak
American Genealogy Society of Illinois
and serves as the editor to its journal,
Koreny ("roots"). He is also a member
of the Slovak Heritage & Folklore
Society International and serves as the
Illinois Represntative for the Moravian
Heritage Society (see addresses
below). He welcomes letters and

comments and may be reached at 2643 W. 51st Street, Chicago, IL 60632-1559.)

Societies
◆**Czech and Slovak American Genealogy Society of Illinois,** P.O. Box 313, Sugar Grove, IL 60554
◆**Slovak Heritage & Folklore Society International,** 151 Colebrook Drive, Rochester, NY 14617-2215
◆ **Moravian Heritage Society,** 28485 Tomball Parkway #381, Tomball, TX 77375

CZECH, SLOVAK RESOURCES

◆Gardiner, Duncan B., *German towns in Slovakia and Upper Hungary: A Genealogical Gazetteer* [Gazetteer of German towns in the former kingdom of Hungary, now in Slovakia, Hungary, and Ukraine. Includes section on doing genealogical research on Germans in Eastern Europe and on Czech and Slovak research] FHL 943.73 E5g 1991; film 1183659, item 18
◆ *Genealogical Guide to German Ancestors from East Germany and Eastern Europe* [English translation of *Wegweiser für Forschungen nach Vorfahren*]. FHL 943 D27gg
◆ Miller, Olga K., *Czechoslovankian Roots,* 1980. FHL 929.1 W893 1980 v. 7 pt. 11; films 1760721-1760740; fiche 6085777
◆Miller, Olga K., *Genealogical Research for Czech and Slovak Americans.* FHL 943.7 D27 m
◆ Schlyter, Daniel M., *A Handbook of Czechoslovak Genealogical Research.* FHL 943.7 D27s
◆ Wellauer, Maralyn A., *Tracing Your Czech and Slovak Roots.* FHL 943.7 D27wm

'DANUBE SWABIANS'

A large-scale migration of Germans into eastern and southeastern Europe during the eighteenth century resulted in many settling in the Austrian Empire, who became known as Hungarian Germans because the area was part of Greater Hungary of that day. Since 1919, these settlers have been referred to as the "Danube Swabians" because a majority of these settlements were now in Romania or Yugoslavia.

As to the reason these settlers became known as "Swabians," genealogist and author Edward R. Brandt, explains that it was because they embarked at Ulm in Swabia and sailed down the Danube to their destination near Belgrade. In fact, there stands in Ulm today a statue dedicated to these Danube Swabians who departed from that city.

A major resource
Anton Scherer, *Donauschwäbische Bibliographie, 1935-1955: das Schrifttum über die Donauschwaben in Ungarn, Rumänien, Jugoslawien und Bulgarien sowie – nach 1945 – in Deutschland, Österreich, Frankreich, USA, Canada, Argentinien und Brasilien.* [Bibliography of the Danube Swabians in Hungary, Romania, Yugoslavia, Bulgaria, and after 1945 in Germany, Austria, France, USA, Canada, Argentina, and Brazil]. FHL 943 A3sa; film 928004 item 1
Societies
◆**Society of Danube Swabians,** 4219 N. Lincoln Avenue, Chicago, IL 60618
◆**Donauschwaben Society in Chicago,** 625 E. Seegers Road, Des Plains, IL 60016. (847) 296-6172
◆**Danube Swabian Association,** 1277 Southampton Road, Philadelphia, PA 19116. www.danubeswabian.com

FRANCE

THE ANDRIVEAU COLLECTION

The Andriveau family in Paris has made available indexes of civil and church records of many French cities. These have been filmed and are available through the Family History Library.

To obtain the FHL numbers for these 1,068 rolls of microfilm, see the Family History Library Catalog, "Author" section, under "Andriveau, B."

The collection's manuscript card index of parish registers includes, **Paris** 1700-1860; **Bruxelles**, 1800-1880; **Anvers**, 1760-1880; **Le Mans**, 1700-1888; **Le Merlerault**, 1700-1830; **Argentan**, 1700-1830; **Bordeaux**, 1700-1820; **Ancenis**, 1700-1820; **Niort**, 1700-1882; **Poitiers**, 1700-1882; **Tours**, 1700-1882; **Montpellier**, 1700-1875; **Mortain**, 1759-1863; **Le Havre**, 1700-1883; **Amiens**, 1700-1885; **Louviers**, 1700-1883; **Arras**, 1700-1885; **Valenciennes**, 1759-1909; **Dijon**, 1700-1869; **Epernay**, 1700-1862; **Chalon-sur-Marne**,1700-1862; **Laon**, 1700-1890; **Lure**, 1700-1890; **Vitry-le-Francois**, 1700-1890; **Strasbourg**, 1700-1870; **Metz**, 1700-1870; **Nancy**, 1700-1870; **Reims**, 1750-1891.

The contents of the films are listed in the index as follows:
Paris: baptisms, marriages, 1800-1860; deaths, 1795-1850; marriages 1700-1850. **Bruxelles**: marriages, 1800-1880. **Anvers**: marriages, 1760-1880. **Le Mans**: marriages, 1700-1888. **Le Merlerault**: marriages 1700-1830. **Argentan**: marriages 1700-1830. **Bordeaux**: marriages 1700-1820. **Ancenis**: marriages 1700-1820. **Niort**: marriages, 1700-1882. **Poitiers**: marriages, 1700-1882. **Tours**: marriages, 1700-1882. **Montpellier**: marriages, 1700-1875. **Mortain**: marriages, 1759-1863. **Le Havre**: marriages, 1700-1883. **Louviers**: marriages, 1700-1883. **Amiens**: marriages,

1700-1885. **Arras**: marriages, 1700-1885. **Valenciennes**: marriages, 1759-1909. **Dijon**: marriages, 1700-1869. **Epernay**: marriages, 1700-1862. **Chalons-sur-Marne**: marriages, 1700-1862. **Laon**: marriages, 1700-1890. **Lure**: marriages, 1700-1890. **Vitry-le-Francois**: marriages, 1700-1890. **Strasbourg**: marriages, 1700-1870. **Metz**: marriages, 1770-1870. **Nancy**: marriages, 1750-1869. **Reims**: marriages, 1750-1891.

FHL microfilm numbers range (with breaks) from 1147628 through 1296860.

See the microfiche noted above (Family History Library Catalog, Author section, microfiche #0032) for the listing of microfilm numbers arranged alphabetically by surname.

GALICIA/GALIZIEN

GALICIA (GALIZIEN) TIMELINE

Galicia, now part of southeastern Poland and western Ukraine, was formerly an Austrian crown land. The background:

11th, 12th centuries: An important Slavic principality, later belonged to Poland

1772: Galicia becomes part of the Austrian Empire (as a result of the first partition of Poland) and remains an Austrian Crownland until 1918, when it was claimed by the new Polish Republic.

1919: West Galicia is assigned to Poland by the Treaty of Versailles following World War I. East Galicia is later given the right of self-determination

1919: East Galicia is given autonomy under a Polish protectorate that lasted 20 years. Galicia comprises the Polish provinces of Kraków, Lwów, Stanislawów and Tarnopol.

1939: The provinces of Kraków, Tarnopol, and part of Lwów, after the invasion of Poland by Germany and the Union of Soviet Socialist Republics, are included in the Soviet Zone of Occupation.

1945: Galicia is assigned to the USSR and incorporated into the Ukrainian SSR under a Polish-Soviet agreement.

1991: Ukraine becomes independent.

Resources

◆**Ukrainian Genealogical & Historical Society,** Box O, Blaine Lake, SK, Canada, SOJ0J0. Tel./Fax (306) 497-2770; UkranianGenealogist@sasktel.net

◆Lenius, Brian J., comp. *Genealogical Gazetteer of Galicia,* Anola, Manitoba, 1994.

LIECHTENSTEIN

ARCHIVES IN LIECHTENSTEIN

◆**Liechtensteinisches Landesarchiv,** FL-9490 Vaduz, Liechtenstein. This archive features a family registry for the entire principality.

◆**Hausarchiv der regierenden Fürsten von Liechtenstein,** Schloß, FL-9490, Vaduz, Liechtenstein

◆ **Civil registry office:** Kanzlei der Regierung des Fürstentums Liechtenstein, FL-9490 Vaduz, Liechtenstein

RESOURCES FOR LIECHTENSTEIN RESEARCH

◆ Suess, Jared H., and Daniel M. Schlyter, *Liechtenstein: Sources for Genealogical Research and Gazetteer.* FHL 943.64 D2s; fiche 6001768

◆ Jansen, Norbert, *Nach Amerika: Geschichte der liechtensteinischen Auswanderung nach den Vereinigten Staaten von Amerika.* FHL 943.64 W2j. For an inventory of family history records in the Liechenstein National Archive, see www.eye.ch/swissgen/kibu/flkb_a-z.htm.

LITHUANIA

LITHUANIAN RESEARCH

Lithuanian Global Genealogy Society 38 Saint John Street Schuylkill Haven,PA 17972. www.lithuaniangenealogy.org **Balzekas Museum of Lithuanian Culture, IHG/LAGS 6500 S. Pulaski Road Chicago, IL 60629-5136 info@balzekasmuseum.org**

The Lithuanian American Genealogy Society (LAGS), part of the Balzekas Museum of Lithuanian Culture, maintains the largest collection of Lithuanian library and research materials outside Lithuania and is the only American genealogy organization that holds an institutional relationship with the Lithuanian Archives, whose records date back to the year 1359.

Research services are offered by LAGS and the Immigration History & Genealogy Department (IHG) of the Balzekas Museum.

LITHUANIA RESOURCES

◆*Gazetteer of Lithuania: Names Approved by the United States Board on Geographic Names.* FHL 947.E5g; film 1573242 item 1

◆*Gemeindelexikon für das Königreich Preußen: auf Grund der Materialen der Volkszählung vom 1. Dezember 1905 un anderer amtlicher Quellen* [gazetteer of the Kingdom of Prussia, based on the 1905 census]. FHL film [for Ostpreußen] 1187921 item 2

◆*Genealogical Guide to German Ancestors from East Germany and Eastern Europe* [English translation of

Wegweiser für Forschungen nach Vorfahren]. FHL 943 D27gg

NATIONAL ARCHIVES, LITHUANIA

Lietuvos Valstybinis Istorijos Archyvas, Gerosios Vilties 10, 2015 Vilnium, Lithuania

MORAVIA/MAEREN
(See also BOHEMIA)

GERMAN MORAVIANS

The Moravian territory is roughly the eastern one-third of the modern Czech Republic. This area is the home of the "Moravians," a significant group of separatists who are represented among early German immigrants in the North American colonies. Additional details are found under the topic "Bohemia" above.
Source: Gundacker, Felix, *Genealogical Gazetteer of Moravia*, IHFF, Vienna, Austria (undated).

NETHERLANDS

NETHERLANDS RESEARCH BASICS

◆ Civil registration was introduced in some southern parts of Netherlands in 1796; it was in general use in 1811. Records are available through 1912, with indexes, on microfilm through the Family History Library in Salt Lake City.
◆ Population registers (by families), show birth and death dates and places, and frequently show arrival and departure dates. Passport applications are found in these records.
◆ Church records were kept by the Dutch Reformed Church during the time of the

Republic of the United Netherlands (1586-1795); within these records are often found records of Catholics, Mennonites, Jews, and others. Most registers were handed over to civil authorities during the French occupation (1796-1813), and they are now in custody of the archives.
◆ Notarial records (wills, divisions of estates, marriage contracts, deeds and other items) date from 1531.
◆ Copies of almost all original church registers are available through the Family History Library.
Source: "Dutch Research," by Gene Weston Cheney. Presentation at 1995 NGS Conference in the States.

NETHERLANDS-RELATED ADDRESSES

◆ Consulate General of the Netherlands
One Rockefeller Plaza, #1100
New York, NY 10020-2094
www.cgny.org
(The central state archive)
◆ Central Bureau for Genealogy
Postbus 11755
2502 at The Hague
Netherlands
Tel. 011-31-70/3814651

Genealogy/heritage societies
Nederlandse Genealogische Vereniging,
Postbus 26
1380 AA Weesp
The Netherlands
www.ngv.nl
◆ **Herrick District Library**
300 South River Avenue
Holland, MI 49423-3290
Tel. (616) 355-3100
www.herrickdl.org
(The Genealogy Department holds records of Dutch emigrants to America, primarily 1820-1880.)

ARCHIVES IN THE NETHERLANDS

◆Algemeen Rijksarchief, Prins Willem-Alexanderhof 26, Postbus 90520, NL-2509 LM's Gravenhage
◆ Rijksarchief in Drenthe, Brink 4, Postbus 595, NL-9400 AN Assen
◆Rijksarchief in Flevoland, Visarenddreef, Postbus 55, NL-8200 AB Leleystad
◆Rijksarchief in Friesland, Boterhoek 3, Postbus 97, NL-8900 AB Leeuwarden
◆Rijksarchief in Gelderland, Markt 1, Postbus 1130, NL-6811 BC Arnhem
◆ Rijksarchief in Groningen, St.-Jansstraat 2, NL-9712 JN Groningen
◆Rijksarchief in Limburg, Achter de Oude Minderbroeders 3, Postbus 845, NL-6200 AV Maastricht
◆Rijksarchief in Noord-Brabant, Zuid-Willemsvaart 2, Postbus 1169, NL-5211 NW's Hertogenbosch
◆Rijksarchief in Noord-Holland, Kleine Houtweg 18, NL-2012 CH Haarlem
◆Rijksarchief in Overijssel, Eikenstraat 20, Postbus 1227, NL-8001 BE Zwolle
◆ Rijksarchief in Utrecht, Alexander Numankade 201, NL-3572 KW Utrecht
◆ Rijksarchief in Zeeland, At.-Pieterstraat 38, NL-4331 EW Middelburg
◆ Rijksarchif in Zuid-Holland (See Alge-meen, above)
◆International Institute of Social History (IISH), Cruquiusweg 31, NL-1019 AT Amsterdam
◆ Zentraal Bureau voor Genealogie, Prins Willem Alexanderhof 22, NL-2595 BE 's Gravengage

GENEALOGICAL ORGANIZATIONS IN THE NETHERLANDS

◆Zentraal Bureau voor Genealogie
Postbus 2502 AT
The Hague
the Netherlands

Tel. +31-70 3150500
Fax +31-70-3478394
[Central office for genealogy; street address given at end of preceding section]
◆ Nederlandse Genealogische Vereniging
Netherlands genealogy society (See "Netherlands-Related Addresses," above)

FAMILY HISTORY RESOURCES FOR NETHERLANDS RESEARCH

◆Franklin, Charles M., *Dutch Genealogical Research,* C.M. Franklin, c 1982. FHL 949.2 D27cf
◆ Hart, Simon, *Bridging the Atlantic: Finding the Place of Origin of Your Germanic Ancestor: the Netherlands.* FHL 929.1 W893 D1; film 897214 item 21; fiche 6039324
◆Jensen, Larry O., **"Were Your Ancestors Dutch or Deutsch?"** *German Genealogical Digest,* Vol. 9, no. 3, 1993.
◆Köster Henke, W.L.H., *Alphabetische lijst van dorpen, gehuchten, buurten, enz. in Nederland . . . .* [alphabetical list of communities and the jurisdictions of the civil registration offices in the Netherlands]. FHL 949.2 E5k; fiche 6001586
◆*Major Genealogical Record Sources in the Netherlands.* FHL 929.1 G286gs ser. C, no. 3 1972; fiche 6000039
◆ Nederhand, Erica H., *Ancestral Research in the Netherlands: Textbook for an Advanced Study in Dutch Records and Methods of Genealogical Research,* Salt Lake City, 1966. FHL 949.2 D27ne; film 845093 items 1-2
◆Swierenga, Robert P., comp. *Dutch Immigrants in U.S. Ship Passenger Manifests, 1820-1880: An Alphabetical Listing by Household Heads and Independent Persons.* 2 vols., Scholarly Research, Wilmington, Del. FHL 973 W3sr
◆**Dutch word list:** English translations of key genealogical terms found in Dutch records FHL 6068526; also available in

Family History SourceGuide.

DUTCH-ENGLISH GENEALOGICAL TERMS

Gezinsblad .... family group sheet
Acternaam .... family name
Voornamen .... given names
Geb. plaats .... birth place
Geb. datum .... birth date
Ged. plaats .... place of baptism
Ged. datum .... date of baptism
Ovl datum .... place of death
Beg. plaats .... place of burial
Geloof .... religion
Beroep .... profession
Ouders (man) .... parents (father)
Getrouwd .... marriage
Tr. plaats .... wedding place
Tr. plaats (K) .. wedding place (church)
Kinderen .... children
Ambtenaar .... registrar
Rijksarchief .... state archive
Burgerlijke Stand .... civil registration
Primary source: *German-American Genealogy,* Immigrant Genealogical Society, Spring 1996.

POLAND

POLAND SINCE THE 16TH CENTURY: Partitions, boundary changes

1569: The two realms of Poland are united with Lithuania. Protestantism is no longer a significant religion after 1600.
1572: Polish nobility takes complete control of the country.
1772, 1793,1795: Three partitions result in treaties whereby the Russian Empire, Prussia, and Austria divide the territory under their respective controls, causing the Polish state to disappear from the map of Europe for almost 125 years. (In the third partition, in 1795, nearly all of western and central Poland, beyond the Vistula River, comes under Prussian rule.)
1808: Napoleon establishes civil registration in the Russian part of Poland (with records written in Polish — one copy remaining in the parish, the other going to the appropriate civil court).
1815: Congress of Vienna creates the kingdom of Poland ruled by the Russian emperor, establishes Kraków as a city republic, and gives the rest of the country to Russia, Austria, and Prussia.
1831: Russians squelch a powerful movement for Polish independence and severe Russianization activities ensue.
1848, 1861, 1863: Polish insurrections result in intensification of Russian repressions. Russian language is introduced in Polish schools in an attempt to replace Polish. Those parts of Poland ruled by Russians become mere provinces of the Russian Empire. Those under Prussian rule are made to endure a Germanization policy; but Austrian Poles are treated more liberally.
1917: A Polish government, following the downfall of the Russian Empire, is estab-lished, controlled by Germans.
1918-1919: The Republic of Poland is recreated as an independent state, with its boundary with Germany running east of the Oder River. Treaty of Versailles grants Poland territory along Vistula River (the "Polish corridor") and large sections of Posen and West Prussia. The former Austrian province of Galicia becomes part of the republic.
1920-1921: Following war with Soviet Russia, Poland annexes parts of Belarussia and Ukraine.
1921-1922: Poland acquires parts of Upper Silesia.
1939: German invasion of Poland results in its partition by Germany and USSR.
1944-1945: Many Germans in central Poland flee before advancing Soviet armies or are expelled.
1945: Following World War II, Poland, as an independent state, is given adminis-trative rights over Upper and

Lower Silesia, Danzig, and parts of Brandenburg, Pomerania, and East Prussia. Poland's eastern boundary of 1939 is restored, and the western border moves to the Oder-Neisse line. Most Germans living east of the Oder-Neisse line who had not already fled are expelled. The German Democratic Republic (East Germany) recognizes the line as the German-Polish border, but the German Federal Republic (West Germany) does not. USSR acquires considerable formerly Polish territory.
1947-1989: Poland is dominated by a Communist-ruled government.
1990: Reunited Germany approves treaty recognizing the Oder-Neisse line as the German-Polish border, and the following year a treaty of friendship and cooperation is ratified.
Sources:
• "Poland," Microsoft (R) Encarta; Microsoft Corporation and Funk & Wagnalls Corporation. 1994.
• "Family Origins in Eastern Europe: Using the Records of the Genealogical Society of Utah, Modern Poland," by Zdenka Kucera. Church of Jesus Christ of Latter-day Saints, 1980.
• "Chronology of German-Polish Relations," *German Life*, December 1996/January 1997.

RESOURCES
FOR POLISH RESEARCH

Many of the Polish records held by the Family History Library in Salt Lake City come from the Polish state archive system, including:
♦ Civil registration records (beginning 1808 or later) from the area of Napoleon's Duchy of Warsaw and later under Imperial Russian rule.
These include many Jewish communities.
♦ Civil/church registration records from the former province of Galicia, some

going back to 1784.
♦ Catholic and Protestant parish registers from as early as 1529, most starting in the mid to late 1700s (most from parishes in former German and Russian-ruled areas).
For records later than 1865 or 1870, one must write to the headquarters of the Polish State Archives in Warsaw.

Publications
♦ Chorzempa, Rosemary A. *Korzenie Polskie: Polish Roots*, Genealogical Publishing Co., Baltimore, 1993. FHL 943.8 D27c
♦ *Genealogical Guide to German Ancestors from East Germany and Eastern Europe* [English translation of *Wegweiser für Forschungen nach Vorfahren*]. FHL 943 D27gg
♦ Müllerowa, Lidia, **Roman Catholic Parishes in the Polish People's Republic in 1984.** Genealogy Unlimited, Orem, Ut. FHL 943.8 K24m
♦ Lewanski, Richard Casimir, comp., *Guide to Polish Libraries and Archives.* East European Monographs, No. VI. Boulder, Colorado, 1974. FHL film 1045441 item 3
♦ Schlyter, Daniel M., *Essentials in Polish Genealogical Research*. FHL 943.8 D27sd 1993
♦ Schlyter, Daniel M., *A Gazetteer of Polish Adjectival Place Names,* 1980. FHL 943.8 E5sd; film 1181581 item 4; fiche 6000843
♦ "Poland: Maps, Gazetteers, Aids," by Dolores Semon. *The German Connection,* Vol. 17, No. 1, January 1993.
♦ "Acquiring Polish Records" by Dolores Semon. *The German Connection,* Vol. 17, No. 1, January 1993.
♦ Wellauer, Maralyn A., *Tracing Your Polish Roots.* Private printing, Milwaukee, WI, 1991.
♦ Palmer, Michael P., *Genealogical Resources in Eastern Germany (Poland).* Privately published, Claremont, CA 1993.

♦FHL word list for translation of Polish genealogical words into English. FHL fiche 6068529; also on FHL's *Family History SourceGuide.*

Societies
♦ **Polish Genealogical Society of America,** 984 N. Milwaukee Avenue, Chicago, IL 60622-4199
♦ **Polish Genealogical Society of the Northeast,** 8 Lyle Road, New Britain,CT 06053-2104
♦ **Polish Genealogical Society of Michigan,** c/o Burton Historical Collection, Detroit Public Library, 5201 Woodward Avenue, Detroit, MI 48202-4007
♦**Polish Genealogical Society of Texas,** 15917 Juneau Drive, Houston, TX 77040-2155
♦ **Polish Genealogical Society of California,** P.O. Box 713, Midway City, CA 92655-0713
♦**Polish Genealogical Society of Greater Cleveland**, 906 College Avenue, Cleveland, OH 44113
♦ **Polish Genealogical Society of Massachusetts,** P. O. Box 381, Northhampton, MA 01061-0381
♦ **Polish Genealogical Society of Minnesota,** P.O. Box 16069, St. Paul, MN 55116-0069
♦**Polish Genealogical Society of New Zealand**, 16 Nugent Street, Plymouth, New Zealand
♦ **Polish Genealogical Society of Western New York,** 299 Barnard Street, Buffalo, NY 14206-3212
♦ **Polish Genealogical Society of Wisconsin,** 3731 Turnwood Drive, Richfield, WI 53076
Sources:
♦"Poland: Maps, Gazetteers, Aids," by Dolores Semon. *The German Connection,* Vol. 17, No. 1, January 1993.
● "Acquiring Polish Records," by Dolores Semon. *The German Connection*, Vol. 17, No. 1, January 1993.

SILESIA

SILESIA (Schlesien)

Silesia (in German, *Schlesien*) falls mostly in what is now southwestern Poland. It also included parts of North Moravia,, the Czech Republic, and the states of Brandenburg and Saxony in eastern Germany.

In the eleventh century, it was part of the kingdom of Poland. In the fourteenth century, it was acquired by Bohemia.

In 1742, it was annexed by Prussia, after having been ruled for more than 200 years by the Austrian Habsburgs.

The German population was expelled after World War II when almost all of Prussian Silesia reverted to Poland.

Society
Silesian Genealogical Society,
ul. Dubois3/1
PL-50-208 Wroclaw
Poland
http://eurogento.org

RESOURCES FOR SILESIA

♦*Gemeindelexikon für das Königreich Preußen: auf Grund der Materialen der Volkszählung vom 1. Dezember 1905 und anderer amtlicher Quellen* [Gazetteer of the Kingdom of Prussia, based on the 1905 census. Shows jurisdictions of Protestant and Catholic parishes and civil registration districts. Includes statistical data and indexes]. FHL film 1183537 item 5
♦ Kowallis, Otto K., *A Genealogical Guide and Atlas of Silesia.* FHL 943.85 E5k
wWermes, Martina, *Bestandsverzeichnis der Deutschen Zentralstelle für Genealogie Leipzig Teil I: Die Kirchenbuchunterlagen der östlichen Provinzen, Posen Ost- und Westpreußen, Pommern*

und Schlesien. [Inventory of parish registers in the Zentralstelle für Genealogie for areas formerly in Germany. Arranged by parish within each province, etc.]. FHL 943.21/L2 K23w pt. 1 1994

SUDETENLAND
(See BOHEMIA AND MORAVIA)

SWITZERLAND

SWISS CITIZENSHIP

In Switzerland, each family name is connected to its original place of origin or citizenship, or its *Bürgerort.*

A Swiss person is first and foremost a citizen of a community and, as such, a citizen of the canton and automatically a Swiss citizen. (A child born outside Switzerland is born a Swiss citizen if his or her father is Swiss.)

Vital records are registered at the place where the person lives but also at the "home community," which is in charge of the family registry.

A Swiss citizen may never see his or her home community.

The place of origin is necessary for the proper identification of the family, as there are often several unrelated families with the same surname.

Places of birth, baptism, marriage and death are also important, but the place of civil registration is always the place of birth.

Family history researchers need to remember that although the children in one family may be citizens of the same town, they may have been born in different places.

Every locality in Switzerland is responsible to one specific record center for all its citizens, regardless of their place of current residence.

CIVIL REGISTRATION IN SWITZERLAND (Zivilstands-Register)

Civil registration was required in all cantons beginning January 1, 1876. Some of the areas in which it was started earlier include:

Basel-Land	1827
Fribourg	1849
Genève	1798
Glarus	1849
Neuchâtel	1825
Schaffhausen	1849
Solothurn	1836
St. Gallen	1867
Ticino	1855
Valais	1853
Vaud	1821

SWISS PARISH REGISTERS (PFARRBÜCHER)

Protestant areas

Parish registers began in the 1520s (especially the Zürich and Bern areas); they were kept in village churches in the second half of the 16th and the early 17th centuries.

Catholic areas

Most began in the first part of the 17th century (usually in Latin).

Parish registers include: baptism records *(Taufbücher)*, marriage records *(Ehebücher)*, and burial records *(Beerdigungen).*

Parish register inventories

These inventories, listing years for which parish registers are accessible, are available for Cantons Solothurn, Basel, Aargau, Zürich, Schaffhausen, St. Gallen (FHL film 908,641, item 4), Glarus (FHL film 908,641, item 5), and Luzern. (The inventories are available at the Family History Library in print form for all these

Cantons, as well as on microfilm for the two Cantons noted above.)

SWISS CIVIL REGISTERS

Civil registration began officially on January 1, 1876. It began earlier in some areas.

Civil registers are of two types:

A-Registers: Recorded all births, marriages, and deaths occurring *within* a political community

B-Registers: Recorded vital events of citizens of a political community occurring *outside* the jurisdiction of that community. In 1928, these records were discontinued and the information was continued in the Family Registers (*Familienregister*), which consist of a page of vital records for each married couple and their children. Before Family Registers were in use, Citizens' Books (*Bürgerbücher*) were kept.

Church censuses began in 1634 and were continued until the early 1700s.

Bürgerbücher (citizens' books), similar to family registers, began around 1820.

SWISS POSTAL ABBREVIATIONS

The postal abbreviations below represent Switzerland's 23 cantons , three of which are divided into half-cantons.

Asterisks signify half-cantons, which were formed for administrative convenience.

Postal
Abbreviation   **Canton**
AG .... Aargau
AI .... *Appenzell (Inner Rhoden)
AR .... *Appenzell (Ausser Rhoden)
BE .... Bern
BL .... *Basel-Land
BS .... *Basel-Stadt
FR .... Freibourg
GE .... Geneva (Genève)

GL .... Glarus
GR .... Graubünden (Grisons)
JU .... Jura
LU .... Lucerne (Luzern)
NE .... Neuchâtel
NW .... *Nidwalden
OW .... *Obwalden
SG .... Sankt Gallen
SO .... Solothurn (Soleure)
SH .... Schaffhausen
SZ .... Schwyz
TG .... Thurgau
TI .... Ticino
UR .... Uri
VD .... Vaud
VS .... Valais
ZG .... Zug
ZH .... Zürich

SWITZERLAND CHRONOLOGY

58 BC: The Helvetii, earliest inhabitants of Switzerland, are conquered by the Romans. (The Romansh language, still spoken in the cantons of Graubunden and Ticino, derives from this period.)

1518: Huldreich Zwingli sparks the Protestant Reformation in Switzerland; city of Zürich, supported by its merchants, revolts against church dogma and with other towns such as Basel and Bern, supports independence from the Roman Catholic Church and the Holy Roman Empire.

1536: Geneva, newly adopted home of the French theologian John Calvin who organizes his new church here, revolts against the duchy of Savoy and refuses recognition of the Roman Catholic bishop.

1541-1564: Geneva is the stronghold of Calvinism.

1648: Through the Peace of Westphalia following the Thirty Years War, Switzerland is recognized as a completely independent state.

1798: Swiss revolutionaries of the French Revolution occupy all Swiss territory. Napoleon unifies the country under the name Helvetic Republic, instituting a constitution strongly resented by the Swiss.

1803: Napoleon withdraws his occupation forces; by the Act of Mediation, a new constitution is established, with Swiss approval

1815: The Congress of Vienna guarantees the perpetual neutrality of Switzerland.

1847: The Roman Catholic cantons form the *Sonderbund*, a league denounced by the federal government as a violation of the constitution, and civil war results. The federal government defeats the *Sonderbund*.

1848: The resulting constitution greatly increases federal power.

1874: Another constitution is enacted, basically still in force today, turning a group of cantons into a federal state, which in turn relegates power to the cantons and their individual communes. A law is enacted to require all cantons to begin civil registration as of January 1, 1876

1876: Civil registration begins

Source: *Microsoft Encarta,* Microsoft Corporation, Funk & Wagnall's Corporation, 1994.

STATE ARCHIVES, SWITZERLAND (Staatliche Archive)

◆Schweizerisches Bundesarchiv, Archivstr. 24, CH-3003 Bern

◆ Staatsarchiv des Kantons Aargau, Obere Vorstadt 6, CH-5001 Aargau

◆ Staatsarchiv des Kantons Appenzell Ausserrhoden, Regierungsgebäude, CH-9100 Herisau

◆Landesarchiv Appenzell Innerrhoden, Landeskanzlei, CH-9050 Appenzell

◆ Staatsarchiv des Kantons Basel-Landschaft, Wiedenhubstr. 35, CH-4410 Liestal

◆Staatsarchiv des Kantons Basel-Stadt, Martinsgasse 2, CH-4001 Basel

◆ Staatsarchiv des Kantons Bern, Falkenplatz 4, CH-3012 Bern

◆ Archives de l'Etat de Fribourg, 4 chemin des Archives, CH-1700 Fribourg

◆Archives d'Etat de Genève, 1 rue de l'Hotel de Ville, Case postale 164, CH-1211 Genève 3

◆ Landesarchiv des Kantons Glarus, Postgasse 29, CH-8750 Glarus

◆Staatsarchiv des Kantons Graubünden, Karlihofplatz, CH-7001 Chur

◆Archives historiques de la Règpublique et Canton du Jura, Office du patrimoine historique, Hotel des Halles, CH-2900 Porrentruy 2

◆ Staatsarchiv des Kantons Luzern, Schützenstr. 9, Postfach, CH-6000 Luzern 7

◆ Archives de l'Etat de Neuchâtel, Chateau de Neuchâtel, CH-2000 Neuchatel

◆Staatsarchiv des Kantons Nidwalden, Mürgstr. 12, CH-6370 Stans

◆Staatsarchiv des Kantons Obwalden, Rathaus, CH-6060 Sarnen

◆Staatsarchiv des Kantons St. Gallen, Regierungsgebäude, CH-9001 St. Gallen

◆Staatsarchiv Schaffhausen, Rathausbogen 4, CH-8200 Schaffhausen

◆ Staatsarchiv des Kantons Schwyz, Bahnhofstr. 20. Postfach 357, CH-6430 Schwyz

◆Staatsarchiv des Kantons Solothurn, Bielstr. 41, CH-4500 Solothurn

◆ Staatsarchiv des Kantons Thurgau, Regierungsgebäude, CH-8500

◆Archivio cantonale, Via Carlo Salvioni 14, CH-6501 Bellinzona

◆Staatsarchiv des Kantons Uri, Bahnhofstrasse 13, CH-6460 Altdorf

◆ Archives cantonales vaudoises, Rue de la mouline 32, CH-1022 Chavanne-près-Renens

◆Staatsarchiv des Kantons Wallis, 7 rue des Vergers, CH-1951 Sion

◆ Staatsarchiv des Kantons Zug, Verwaltungszentrum an der Aa,

Aabachstr. 5, CP 897, CH-6301 Zug
• Staatsarchiv des Kantons Zürich, Winterthurerstr. 170, CH-8057 Zürich

TOWN ARCHIVES, SWITZERLAND (Stadtarchive)

◆Stadtarchiv, Rathaus, Rathausgasse 1, CH-5000 Aarau
◆Stadtarchiv, Rathaus, CH-4663 Aarburg
Talarchiv Ursern, Rathaus, CH-6490 Andermatt
• Archives communales d'Avenches, Municipalité, CH-1580 Avenches
◆Stadtarchiv c/o Historisches Museum Baden, Landvogteischloß, CH-5400 Baden
• Stadtarchivund Dokumentationsdienst, Erlacherhof, Junkerngasse 47, CH-3011 Bern
◆Stadtarchiv, E.-Schülerstr. 23, CH-2502 Biel
◆Stadtarchiv, Rathaus, CH-5620 Bremgarten
◆Stadtarchiv, Stadthaus, CH-5200 Brugg
Burgerarchiv (= altes Stadtarchiv [old town archive]), Bernstr. 5, CH-3400 Burgdorf
• Stadtarchiv (= neues Stadtarchiv ab 1832 [new town archive since 1832]), Rathaus, Kirchbühl 19, CH-3400 Burgdorf
◆Stadtarchiv, Rathaus, CH-7002 Chur
Bürgerarchiv (= altes Stadtarchiv [old town archive]), Bürgergemeinde, CH-8500 Frauenfeld
• Stadtarchiv (= neues Archiv [new archive]), Rathaus, CH-8500 Frauenfeld
Archives de la Ville, Maison de Ville, CH-1700 Fribourg
◆Archives de la Ville, Palais Eynard, rue de la Croix-Rouge 4, CH-1211 Genève 3
• Stadtarchiv, Schulhaus I, CH-2540 Grenchen
◆Stadtarchiv, Rathaus, CH-8434 Kaiserstuhl
◆Stadtarchiv, Propsteigebäude, CH-5313

Klingnau
• Archives communales, c/o Musée d'Histoire et Médaillier, rue des Musées 31, CH-2300 La Chaux-de-Fonds
• Stadtarchiv, Rathaus, CH-4335 Laufenburg
◆Archives de la Ville, rue du Maupas 47, Case postale CH-1000 Lausanne 9
◆Stadtarchiv, Rathaus, CH-5600 Lenzburg
• Archivio della città di Locarno, Via Rusca 1, CH-6600 Locarno
• Archivio della città di Lugano, strada di Gandria 4, CH-6976 Castagnola
◆Stadtarchiv, Industriestr. 6, CH-6005 Luzern
• Stadtarchiv, Rathaus, CH-5507 Mellingen
◆Archives de la Commune de Montreux, p.a. Greffe municipal, Grand-Rue 73, CH-1820 Montreux
◆Archives communales, Place de l'Hôtel de Ville 1, CH-1110 Morges
◆Stadtarchiv, Rathaus, CH-3280 Murten
• Archives de la Ville, Départment Historique du Musée d'Art et d'Histoire, Quai Léopold-Robert, case postale 876, CH-2001 Neuchâtel
◆Stadtarchiv, Stadthaus, Dornacherstr. 1, CH-4600 Olten
◆Stadtarchiv der Ortsgemeinde, Rathaus, CH-8640 Rapperswil
• Stadtarchiv, Rathaus, CH-4310 Rheinfelden
• Stadtarchiv (Vadiana), Notherstr. 22, CH-9000 St. Gallen
◆Stadtarchiv, Fronwagplatz 24, CH-8200 Schaffhausen
◆Archives communales, Hôtel de Ville, Grand-Pont 12, CH-1950 Sion
• Bürgerarchiv, Bürgergemeindehaus, Unterer Winkel 1, CH-4500 Solothurn
◆Stadtarchiv, Rathaus, CH-8260 Stein am Rhein
◆Stadtarchiv, Rathaus, CH-6210 Sursee
◆Stadtarchiv, Hofstettenstr. 14, CH-3600 Thun
◆Burgerarchiv, Rathausplatz 1, CH-3600 Thun

◆Archives communales de Vevey, Hôtel de Ville, rue du Lac 2, CH-1800 Vevey
◆Bürgerarchiv (= altes Stadtarchiv [old town archive]), Ortsbürgergemeinde, Präsidium, Toggenburgerstr. 86, CH-9500 Wil
◆Stadtarchiv, Stadthaus, CH-8400 Winterhur
◆Stadtarchiv, Hintere Hauptstr. 20, CH-4800 Zofingen
◆Bürgerarchiv (= altes Stadtarchiv [old town archive]), Rathaus, CH-6300 Zug
◆ Stadtarchiv, St.-Oswalds-Gasse 21, Postfach 362, CH-6301 Zug
◆ Stadtarchiv, Neumarkt 4, CH-8001 Zürich
Source: *Archive in der Bundesrepublik Deutschland, Österreich und der Schweiz,* Ardey-Verlag Münster, 15th ed., 1995.

SWISS CHURCH ARCHIVES (Kirchliche Archive)

Diocesan archives
(Diözesanarchive)
Diocese and Prince-Bishopric, Basel [before 1815]: Fondation des Archives de l'ancien Evêché de Bâle, Hôtel de Glér-esse, 10 rue des Annonciades, CH-2900 Porrentruy
Bishopric of Basel (since 1828): Bischôf-liches Archiv, Baselstr. 58, CH-4501 Solo-thurn
Bishopric of Lausanne, Genève and Fribourg: Archives épiscopales, 86 rue de Lausanne, case postale 271, CH-1701 Fribourg
Bishopric of Lugano: Bischöfliches Archiv, Curia Vescovile, via Borghetto 6, DH-6900 Lugano
Bishopric of St. Gallen: Bischöfliches Archiv, Klosterhof 6 B, CH-9000 St. Gallen
Bishopric of Sitten/Sion: Archives épiscopales, Avenue de la Tour 12, CH-1950 Sion

Protestant archive
(Evangelische Kirchenarchiv)
Archiv der Basler Mission, Missions-str. 11, CH-4003 Basel
Source: *Archive in der Bundesrepublik Deutschland, Österreich und der Schweiz.* Ardey-Verlag Münster. 15th ed., 1995.

SWITZERLAND GAZETTEERS

◆ Jacot, Arthur, *Schweizerisches Orts-lexikon* [Swiss postal guide and gazetteer]. FHL fiche 6053515
◆**United States Board on Geographic Names.** *Preliminary Gazetteer:* Switzerland, Washington, DC, 1950.
◆ Knapp, Charles, **Geographisches Lexikon der Schweiz** [gazetteer of Switzerland]. FHL films 599323-599326
–As-Kraialpass: 599323
–Krailigen-Schweiz: 599324
–Schweiz-Tavetsch: 599326
–Tavetsch-Zybachsplatt, and supplement: 599325
◆**Ortsbuch der Schweiz** [gazetteer of Switzerland]; includes all towns, even very small ones. FHL 949.4 E5s; film 1181544 item 2

MICROFILMED RECORDS

Records from Switzerland have been microfilmed and are available through the Family History Library in these cantons:
◆Basel-Land
◆Basel-Stadt
◆Zürich
◆Bern
◆Sankt Gallen
◆ Thurgau
◆Ticino
◆Vaud
◆Geneva
◆Lucerne
◆ Appenzell-Ausser-Rhoden
◆ Appenzell-Inner-Rhoden
◆Neuchâtel

◆Graubünden
◆Solothurn
◆Jura
◆Uri
   The city of Küssnacht, canton of Schwyz, has been filmed.

SELECTED RESOURCES FOR SWISS RESEARCH

General reference works
   (Note: The most valuable by far of the works listed below will likely be *Familiennamenbuch der Schweiz.*)

◆Attinger, Victor *Historisch-Biographisches Lexikon der Schweiz.* [historical biographical encyclopedia of Switzerland] 7 vols. plus supplement.
   A very useful set of biographical and genealogical pieces on Swiss families and places, submitted by experts in the field, accompanied by good bibliographies for further consultation. FHL 949.4 D36hb; film 1181541 (A-Gue), 1181542 (Gue-Sant D), 1181543 (Saint G-Z and supplement; fiche 6000814

◆Bartholdi, Albert, ed. *Prominent Americans of Swiss Origin.* James T. White & Co., New York, 1932

◆Billeter, Julius C., *Verzeichnis der genealogischen Arbeiten von Julius Billeter* [bibliography of genealogies compiled by Julius Billeter].
   This Swiss genealogist spent more than 50 years tracing Swiss lines. Many entries in his books date from about 1550 to 1900. The research has been filmed. Film numbers can be found by checking the Family History Library Catalog surname section.
   See also this bibliograpahy and p. 57 ff. of *Handy Guide to Swiss Genealogical Records,* by Jared H.Suess, listed under "Research Guides" at the end of this section.

◆Burgert, Annette Kunselman, *Notes on Research Sources for 18th Century Emigration from the Swiss Cantons Basel-Land, Basel-Stadt, Bern, and Zürich.* FHL 974.8 A1 no. 378

◆*Deutsches Geschlechterbuch: Genealogisches Handbuch Bürgerlicher Familien* [German families lineage book] Verlag von C.A. Starke, Limburg an der Lahn, Görlitz, 1889. See volumes 42, 48, 56, 65, and 77. FHL 943 D2dg; FHLC computer number 278503; films 491876-491981

◆*Familiennamenbuch der Schweiz,* [Register of Swiss Surnames], 3rd edition. Polygraphischer Verlag, Zürich. 3 vols. FHL 949.4D4f; film 441670; fiche 6053507
   Official inventory of names of families which in 1962 possessed citizenship in a Swiss community.
   Surnames are followed by cantons, arranged in alphabetical order, according to the official names of the place of citizenship; the year in which citizenship was granted (acquired before 1800, acquired in the nineteenth century, 1801-1900; or citizenship acquired 1901-1962).

◆Faust, Albert B. and Galus M. Brumbaugh. *Lists of Swiss Emigrants in the Eighteenth Century to the American Colonies.* National Genealogical Society, Washington, DC, 1925. Reprinted with Dr. Leo Schelbert's *Notes on Swiss Emigrants,* Genealogical Publishing Co., Inc., Baltimore, Md., 1976.
   Contains descriptive lists of early emigrants from Zürich, 1734-1744; Bern, 1706-1795; and Basel, 1734-1794, compiled from records found at the state archives in Switzerland. Indexed. FHL 973 W2fa 1968; fiche 6048998.

◆Grueningen, John Paul von, ed., *The Swiss in the United States.* Swiss

American Historical Society, Madison, WI, 1940. Contains information derived from census data explaining the distribution of the Swiss throughout the United States. FHL 973 F2gj; fiche 6125340.

♦Haller, Charles R., *Across the Atlantic and Beyond: The Migration of German and Swiss Immigrants to America*. FHL 973 W2aa.

♦Macco, Herman Friedrich, *Swiss Emigrants to the Palatinate in Germany and to America, 1650-1800, and Huguenots in the Palatinate and Germany*. 6 vols. and index. FHL films 823861 (A-L), and 823862 (M-Z and index).

♦ Minert, Roger P. and Jennifer A. Anderson, *Switzerland Place Name Indexes* (CD), GRT Publications, Provo, UT, 2008.
   This CD allows a quick search for places names in Switzerland on the national and the cantonal level.
   The researcher can also search for place names using the reverse alphabetical method. Each place is also associated with a political community.

♦ Moos, Mario von, *Bibliography of Swiss Genealogies*. Picton Press, Rockland, ME, 1993.
   Lists published genealogies of non-noble Swiss families, with a place index and a surname index. FHL 949.4 D23a no. 6, v.1.

♦ Schrader-Muggenthaler,C.C.F. Lendorff, Basel, Verlag Genealogisches Institut Zwicky, Zürich, 1904-65. 12 vols. FHL 973 W2smc.
♦Strassburger, Ralph B. and William J. Hinke, eds., *Pennsylvania German Pioneers*. 3 vols. Pennsylvania German Society, Norristown, PA, 1934. [Transcriptions of the original lists of arrivals at the port of Philadelphia.] FHL 974.811 W3s 1992.

♦ Tobler-Meyer, Wilhelm, *Deutsche Familiennamen nach ihrer Entstehung und Bedeutung, mit besonderer Rücksichtnahme auf Zürich und die Ostschweiz* [German-Swiss surnames with origins and meanings, with emphasis on Zürich and Eastern Switzerland]. FHL 949.4 D4t; film 908216 item 2.

Research Guides
♦Nielson, Paul A., *Swiss Genealogical Research: An Introductory Guide.* Donning Co. Publishers, Virginia Beach, VA, 1979. FHL 949.4 D27n.
♦Suess, Jared H., *Handy Guide to Swiss Genealogical Records.* Everton Publishers, Inc., Logan, UT, 1979. FHL 949.4 D27s.
♦Wellauer, Maralyn A., *Tracing Your Swiss Roots.* Wellauer, Milwaukee, WI, 1979. (1988, 1991). FHL 949.4 D27wm.
Note: Maralyn A. Wellauer, editor of *The Swiss Connection,* contributed to this list.

Swiss websites
   A list of Swiss websites for Swiss genealogical research is available at www. TheSwissCenter.com. Click on "Swiss Roots."

SWISS EMBASSY AND CONSULATES GENERAL IN THE UNITED STATES AND CANADA

UNITED STATES
Washington, DC
Embassy of Switzerland
2900 Cathedral Ave. NW
Washington, DC 20008
Tel. (202) 745-7900
Fax (202) 387-2564

Atlanta
Consulate General of Switzerland
1275 Peachtree Street NW, Suite 425
Atlanta, GA 30309-3555
Tel. (404) 870-2000
Fax (404) 870-2911

Chicago
Consulate General of Switzerland
Olympia Center, Suite 2301
737 N. Michigan Avenue
Chicago, IL 60611
Tel. (312) 915-0061
Fax (312) 915-0388

Houston
Consulate General of Switzerland
Wells Fargo Plaza, Ste 5670
1000 Louisiana
Houston, TX 77002
Tel. (713) 650-0000
Fax:(714) 650-1321

Los Angeles
Consulate General of Switzerland
11766 Wilshire Blvd., Suite 1400
Los Angeles, CA 90025
Tel. (310) 575-1145
Fax (310) 575-1982

New York
Consulate General of Switzerland
633 Third Avenue, 30th Floor
New York, NY 10017-6706
Tel. (212) 599-5700
Fax (212) 599-4266

San Francisco
Consulate General of Switzerland
456 Montgomery Street, Suite 1500
San Francisco, CA 94104-1233
Tel. (415) 788-2272
Fax (415) 788-1402

SWISS TOURISM CONTACTS, UNITED STATES AND CANADA

UNITED STATES
New York
Swiss Center
608 Fifth Avenue
New York, NY 10020-2303
Tel. (212) 757-5944
Fax (212) 262-6116

Chicago
Swiss National Tourist Office
150 North Michigan Avenue
Chicago, IL 60601-7553
Tel. (312) 630-5840
Fax (312) 630-5848

Los Angeles, California
Swiss National Tourist Office
222 North Sepulveda Boulevard
Suite 1570
El Segundo, CA 90245-4300
Tel. (310) 335-5980
Fax (310) 335-5982

San Francisco, California
Swiss National Tourist Office
260 Stockton Street
San Francisco, CA 94108
(415) 362-2260

CANADA
Swiss National Tourist Office
154 University Avenue
Toronto, ON M5H 3Y9
Canada
Tel. (416) 971-9734-2090

CONTACTS FOR SWISS GENEALOGICAL RESEARCH

Societies
♦**Swiss-American Historical Society**
www.swissamericanhistory.org
♦**Zentralstelle für genealogische Auskünfte** [Central Office for Genealogical

Information]
Schweizerische Gesellschaft für
Familienforschung
Postfach 54
3608 Thun
Switzerland
♦ **Schweizerische Vereinigung für
jüdische Genealogie** [Jewish Genealogical Society of Switzerland]
c/o Rene Loeb
P.O. Box 876
CH-8021 Zürich
Switzerland

Library

Craven County Library
400 Johnson Street
New Bern, NC 28560-4098
Tel. (252) 638-7800
Fax: (252) 638-7817

WENDS/SORBS

WENDS (WENDISCH)

Wends was the name that Germans in medieval times gave to the Slavic tribes from an area west of the Oder River. Some 500 of these Wends (who called themselves Sorbs) sailed from their homes in Lusatia (Lausitz), the area now divided between Upper Lusatia in Saxony and Lower Lusatia in Brandenburg.

Led by their spiritual leader, The Rev. Jan Killian, they arrived at the harbor at Galveston, Texas in 1854, seeking religious liberty and the right to speak their Wendish tongue.

Their settlement was established on 4254 purchased acres in what is now Lee County. They named their new town Serbin, near Giddings. In Serbin, they established what became the first Missouri Synod Lutheran church in Texas, with the only Wendish school in America.

The colonists moved on into other parts of Texas in the late 1800s, and they founded sub-colonies in places like Austin, Houston, Warda, Fedor, Swiss Alp, Giddings, Port Arthur, Manheim, Copperas Cove, Vernon, Walburg, The Grove, Bishop, and the Rio Grande Valley – in each place building a new church affiliated with the Missouri Synod, thus helping to spread its congregations throughout Texas.

Many more Wends immigrated in the second half of the nineteenth century.

Resources
♦ Texas Wendish Heritage Museum, 1011 County Road, Giddings, TX 78942 (archives, library, museum). Tel. (409) 366-2441
♦ Sophienburg Museum, 401 W. Coll, New Braunfels, TX 78130. Tel. (830) 629-1572
♦ Sophienburg Archives, 200 N. Seguin Avenue, New Braunfels, TX 78130. Tel. (830) 629-1572
♦ Gillespie County Historical Society, 312 West San Antonio, P.O. Box 765, Fredericksburg, TX 78624 (archives, historical society). Tel. (830) 997-2835.
♦ Winedale Historical Center, University of Texas, Farm Road 2714-Winedale, P.O. Box 11, Round Top, TX 78954 (historical center). Tel. (409) 278-3530; Fax (409) 278-3531
♦ University of Texas Institute of Texan Cultures, Library (library, museum, research institution).Mail: 801 S. Bowie Street, San Antonio, TX 78205-3296. Tel. (210) 226-7651; Fax (210) 222-8564
♦ Barker Texas Historical Center, University of Texas at Austin, SRH 2.101, Austin, TX 78712. Tel. (512) 495-4515; Fax (512) 495-4542

Sorb museum
♦ Sorbisches Museum, Ortenburg 3, 02065 Bautzen, Germany. Tel. (03591) 42403; Fax (03591) 42425

Section 4:
United States Resources

•

National Archives and Records Administration
Censuses – federal and state
Land in America
American military matters
Libraries and other resources
Fraternal organizations

•

UNITED STATES BOARD ON GEOGRAPHIC NAMES

The U.S.Board on Geographic Names (BGN) is the single authority in the United States to which all problems and inquiries concerning geographic names throughout the world may be addressed.

The Geographic Names Information System (GNIS) is the nation's official data base for domestic geographic names information.

GNIS is maintained by the U.S. Geological Survey and can often provide information on name changes. This data base contains 2 million entries, including the names of places that no longer exist as well as other or secondary names for existing places.

The automated system also contains the names of every type of feature except roads and highways. It is especially useful for genealogical research because it contains entries for very small and scattered communities as well as churches and cemeteries, including entries for those that no longer exist.

Selected place-name sources

The U.S. Geological Survey's GNIS will respond to written and phone inquiries about present past, and secondary names and locations of any of more than two million place and geographic feature names, large and small, in the United States. The service is free.

U.S. names information

To contact the U.S. Board on Geographic Names (BGN), write to: USGS National Center, 12201 Sunrise Valley Drive, Reston, VA 20192. Tel. (703) 648-4000; http://geonames.usgs.gov.

Foreign names information

For information about geographic names in foreign countries, contact: USGS Executive Secretary for Foreign Names, Defense Mapping Agency A-20, 8613 Lee Highway, Fairfax, VA 22031-2137. Tel. (703) 285-9518.

Geographic names database

The Geographic Names Information System is an online gazetteer of the United States that consists of three databases: 1) The National Geographic

Data Base (with almost 2 million entries, 2) the Toponymic Map Names Data Base (an inventory of all USGS published topographic maps), and 3) the Reference Data Base (a collection of annotated bibliographies of all sources used in compiling information for the National Geographic Names Data Base). It covers 154,243 populated places, streams, rivers, creeks, lakes, swamps, mountains, etc. and other named places such as churches and cemeteries, including 57,782 places that no longer exist.

To view this gazetteer, go to http://geonames.usgs.gov/domestic. From there, you can search for a single domestic place name or download geographical data for entire states. Contact information: Tel. (703) 648-5953; gnis_manager@usgs.gov.

CEMETERIES, UNITED STATES

The following are some sources available for locating and researching cemeteries in the United States:

◆**www.findagrave.com:** More than 35 million cemetery records since 1700.

◆**www.internment.net:** Online library of burial records from thousands of cemeteries across the world.

◆ *United States Cemetery Address Book,* by Elizabeth Gorrell Kot and James Douglas Kot. Indices Publishing, 228 Sandy Neck Way, Vallejo, CA 94591-7850. Tel. (707) 554-4814. Lists 28,000 U.S. cemeteries and locations. [FHL 973 V34k].

◆*The Cemetery Record Compendium: Comprising a Directory of Cemetery Records and Where They May Be Located,* John D. Stemmons, ed., Everton Publishers, Logan, UT, 1979. [FHL 973 V34s; FHL fiche 6126201].

◆**The Association for Gravestone Studies,** Greenfield Corporate Center, 101 Munson Street, Suite 108, Greenfield, MA 01301. Tel. (413) 772-0836;

info@gravestonestudies.org; www.gravestonestudies.org.

Resources for locating cemeteries
◆Obituaries, wills, death certificates and church records
◆CD-ROMs of telephone listings
◆County courthouses
◆Queries to pertinent genealogical and historical societies
◆Online cemetery listings

VETERANS BURIAL LOCATION ASSISTANCE

The National Cemetery System, Department of Veterans Affairs, provides burial location assistance to the next-of-kin, relatives, or close friends of decedents thought to be interred in a Department of Veterans Affairs national cemetery.

The NCS has a "Nationwide Gravesite Locator" on its website (http://gravelocator.cem.va.gov), allowing researchers to search for veterans buried in VA national cemeteries since the Civil War.

The database now exceeds five million names, including veterans and their family members. Records generally include the veteran's rank, branch of service, the war in which he/she served, birth and death date, name and location of the cemetery, and (in most cases) a map of the cemetery plot.

If the veterean cannot be found in the online database, researchers can request a secondary search from NCS personnel by writing to: U.S. Department of Veterans Affairs, National Cemetery Administration (41C1), 810 Vermont Avenue, N.W., Washington, DC 20420.

One should provide the following information when submitting a request: veteran's full name, date and place of birth, date and place of death, state from which the veteran entered active duty, and branch of the military (Army, Navy,

Air Force, Marine Corps, Coast Guard).

No form is required and no fee is charged for this service. Most requests take approximately four weeks for a reply. Be sure to include your return mailing address, phone number or e-mail address.

Source: National Cemetery System, Public and Consumer Affairs Division, Washington, DC 20420.

FUNERAL DIRECTORS

The directory noted below lists 22,000 funeral homes with addresses and telephone numbers classified by country, state, city, and county. It also includes some international locations:

The Yellow Book of Funeral Directors, Nomis Publications, Inc., 1987. Contact: Nomis Publications, Inc., P.O. Box 5159, Youngstown, OH 44514. Tel. (800) 321-7479; Fax (800) 321-9040; info@nomispublications.com; www.yelobk.com.

This full size edition lists addresses for daily newspapers in the United States and Canada. It also includes a national hospital directory as well as information about cemeteries and Veterans Administration.

A more recent source (2002) *American Blue Book of Funeral Directors,* was put out by the National Funeral Directors' Association. This may be found in larger libraries.

PROBATE RECORDS VOCABULARY (UNITED STATES)

Administration: The process of setting in motion the legal machinery required to settle the estate of a deceased person.
Administrator(trix): A person appointed by the court to settle the estate of a deceased person (usually when there is no will).

Affinity: A relationship by marriage rather than by blood.
Bequeath: To give personal property by will as opposed to devise which relates to real property.
Chattel: Personal property which is more than simple goods as it can include living property. In earlier times, it may act as a synonym for slaves.
Child of tender years: A child under 14
Codicil: A supplement or addition to a will.
Conjoint Will: A will two or more people make together; popular with the Dutch in New York.
Consanguinity: A blood relationship
Corporeal property: Property which can be seen and handled. For instance, a house is corporeal; but rent is incorporeal.
Decedent: Deceased person
Devise: A gift of real property by will
Dower: The land and tenements to which a widow has claim (in life estate) after the death of her husband, for the support of herself and her children.
Endowment: Assigning or setting off the widow's dower.
Escheat: The revision of property to the state when there are no heirs.
Estate: The sum total of a person's property.
Et uxor: Often written "et ux.," Latin for "and wife," often used in indexing.
Executor(trix): The person named in the will by the testator to see that the provisions of the will are carried out after the testator's death.
Friendly suit: A suit brought by a creditor against an executor or administrator (being actually a suit by the executor or adminis-trator against himself in the name of the creditor) to compel the creditors of an estate to take an equal distribution of assets.
Guardian: A person who is invested with the right, and so charged, to manage the rights and property of another person. A *testamentary guardian* is

named in a deed or last will of a child's father. Otherwise, the guardian is chosen by the election of the child, if over 14, or by appointment if under 14.

Heir: A person who inherits or succeeds through legal means, after the death of another.

Heirs and Assigns: Under common law, these words were necessary to convey any fee simple title. They are no longer necessary, but they are often used.

Holographic Will: A will written, dated, and signed in the testator's own handwriting.

Infant: Any person not of full legal age; a minor.

Intestate: A person who dies without making a valid will.

Issue: All lineal descendants of a common ancestor; not children only.

Legacy: Same as bequest

Life Estate: An estate that lasts only during the life of a person, or for the duration of someone else's life. Often, in a will a life estate is devised to a widow.

Moiety: Half of anything

Natural Affection: Affection which exists naturally between near relatives.

Nuncupative Will: An oral will valid in last sickness, sudden illness or combat; it must be witnessed and be clear that it is the intent of the decedent.

Probate: An inclusive term which refers to all matters over which the probate court has jurisdiction including the settling of an estate (whether testate or intestate) and guardianship matters.

Real Property or **realty:** Relating to land

Relict: The surviving spouse when one has died.

Testate: A person who dies leaving a valid will.

Testament: Document outlining the disposition of personal property after death.

Will: Document outlining the disposition of real and personal property after death.

Source: M. Bell, "Definitions taken from or adapted from *Black's Law Dictionary* and from Val D. Greenwood," in *The Researcher's Guide to American Genealogy,* (Baltimore: Genealogical Publishing Co., 1990.)

NATIONAL ARCHIVES (NARA) REGIONAL CENTERS

The National Archives and Records Administration maintains updated information for all its primary and regional locations at www.archives.gov/locations/.

National Archives

The primary sites of the NARA are in Washington, DC (Archives I,) College Park, MD (Archives II) and Suitland, MD:

♦District of Columbia: Washington
National Archives and Records Administration, 700 Pennsylvania Avenue, NW Washington, DC 20408-0001. Tel. (202) 357-5400; Fax (202) 501-7170.

♦Maryland: College Park
Office of Regional Records Services, National Archives and Records Administration, 8601 Adelphi Road, College Park, MD 20740-6001. Tel. (301) 837-2000; Fax (301) 837-0483; inquire@nara.gov.

♦Maryland: Suitland
Washington National Records Center, 4205 Suitland Road, Suitland, MD 20746-8001. Tel. (301) 778-1600; Fax (301) 778-1621; suitland.transfer@nara.gov. Records center holdings for Federal agency headquarters offices in the District of Columbia, Maryland, and Virginia; Federal agency field offices in Maryland, Virginia, and West Virginia; Federal courts in the District of Columbia; and U.S. Armed Forces worldwide.

Regional Archives

The following are NARA's regional records services facilities:

♦Alaska: Anchorage

NARA, Pacific Alaska Region, 654 W. Third Avenue., Anchorage, AK 99501. Tel. (907) 261-7820; Fax (907) 261-7813; alaska.archives@nara.gov.

◆**California: Riverside**
Riverside Federal Records Center, NARA, Pacific Region, 23123 Cajalco Rd., Perris, CA 92570. Tel. (951) 956-2000; Fax (951) 956-2029; riverside.refer ence@nara.gov.

◆**California: San Bruno** (San Francisco) NARA, Pacific Region, 1000 Commodore Drive, San Bruno, CA 94066-2350. Tel. (650) 238-3501; Fax (650) 238-3510; sanbruno.archives@nara.gov.

◆**Colorado: Denver**
NARA, Rocky Mountain Region, Denver Federal Center, Building 48, P.O. Box 25307, Denver, CO 80225. General Information: Tel. (303) 407-5740; Genealogy: (303) 407-5751; Fax (303) 407-5709; denver.archives@nara.gov.

◆**Georgia: Morrow**
NARA, Southeast Region, 5780 Jonesboro Road, Morrow, GA 30260. Tel. (770) 968-2100; Fax (770) 968-2547; morrow.resources@nara.gov.

◆**Illinois: Chicago**
NARA, Great Lakes Region, 7358 South Pulaski Road, Chicago, IL 60629-5898. Tel. 773-948-9000; Fax (773) 948-9050; chicago.archives@nara.gov. Archival holdings from Federal agencies and courts in Illinois, Indiana, Michigan, Minnesota, Ohio, and Wisconsin. Records center holdings from Federal agencies in Illinois, Minnesota, and Wisconsin, and from Federal courts in Illinois, Indiana, Michigan, Minnesota, Ohio, and Wisconsin. Microfilm holdings.

◆**Massachusetts: Boston (Waltham)**
NARA, Northeast Region, Frederick C. Murphy Federal Center, 380 Trapelo Road, Waltham, MA 02452-6399. Tel. (781) 663-0130; Fax (781) 663-0154; waltham.archives@nara.gov.

◆**Massachusetts: Pittsfield**
NARA, Northeast Region, Silvio O. Conte National Records Center, 10 Conte Drive, Pittsfield, MA 01201-8230. Tel. (413) 236-3600; Fax (413) 236-3609; pittsfield.archives@nara.gov.

◆**Missouri: Kansas City**
NARA, Central Plains Region, 400 West Pershing Road, Kansas City, MO 64108. Tel. (816) 268-8000; Fax (816) 268-8038; kansascity.archives@nara.gov. Archival holdings from Federal agencies and courts in Iowa, Kansas, Missouri, and Nebraska. Records center holdings from the same states. Microfilm holdings.

◆**Missouri: Lee's Summit**
NARA, Central Plains Region, 200 Space Center Drive, Lee's Summit, MO 64064-1182. Tel. (816) 268-8100; Fax (816) 268-8159; leessummit.reference@nara.gov. Records center holdings from Federal agencies and courts in New Jersey, New York, Puerto Rico, and the U.S. Virgin Islands, and from most Department of Veterans Affairs and Immigration and Naturalization Service offices nationwide.

◆**Missouri: St. Louis**
– NARA, National Personnel Records Center, Civilian Personnel Records, 111 Winnebago Street, St. Louis, MO 63118-4126. Tel. (314) 801-9250; Fax (314) 801-9269; cpr.center@nara.gov. Civilian personnel records from Federal agencies nationwide; selected military dependent medical records
– NARA, National Personnel Records Center, Military Personnel Records, 9700 Page Avenue, St. Louis, MO 63132-5100. Tel. (314) 801-0800; Fax (314) 801-9195; mpr.center@nara.gov. Military personnel records, and military and retired military medical records from all services; selected dependent medical records, morning reports, rosters, and Philippine army and guerilla records

◆**New York: New York City**
NARA, Northeast Region, 201 Varick Street, 12th Floor, New York, NY 10014. Tel. (212) 401-1620; Fax (212) 401-1638; newyork.archives@nara.gov. Archival

holdings from Federal agencies and courts in New Jersey, New York, Puerto Rico, and the U.S. Virgin Islands. Microfilm holdings.

◆**Ohio: Dayton**
NARA, Great Lakes Region, 3150 Springboro Road, Dayton, OH 45439-1883. Tel. (937) 425-0600; Fax (937) 425-0640; dayton.reference@nara.gov. Records center holdings from Federal agencies in Indiana, Michigan, and Ohio; Federal bankruptcy court records from Ohio; Defense Finance Accounting System records nationwide and from Germany and Korea; and Internal Revenue Service records from selected sites nationwide.

◆**Pennsylvania: Philadelphia**
– NARA, Mid Atlantic Region (Center City Philadelphia), 900 Market Street, Philadelphia, PA 19107-4292. Tel. (215) 606-0100; Fax (215) 606-0116; philadelphia.archives@nara.gov.
– NARA, Mid Atlantic Region (Northeast Philadelphia), 14700 Townsend Road, Philadelphia, PA 19154-1096. Tel. (215) 305-2000; Fax (215) 305-2038; philadelphia.reference@nara.gov.

◆**Texas: Fort Worth**
NARA, Southwest Region, 501 West Felix Street, Building 1, Fort Worth, TX 76115-3405. Tel. (817) 831-5620; Fax (817) 334-5621; ftworth.archives@nara.gov.

◆**Washington (state): Seattle**
NARA, Pacific Alaska Region, 6125 Sand Point Way NE, Seattle, WA 98115-7999. Tel. (206) 336-5115; Fax (206) 336-5112; seattle.archives@nara.gov. Archival holdings from Federal agencies and courts in Idaho, Oregon, and Washington (state). Records center holdings for Federal agencies and courts in the same states and Alaska. Microfilm holdings.

NATIONAL ARCHIVES AT COLLEGE PARK (ARCHIVES II)

The following information may be helpful to those conducting research at the National Archives at College Park (Archives II).

◆The National Archives at College Park is located at 8601 Adelphi Road, College Park, Maryland, 20740-6001.

◆Unless one already has a research card, it is necessary to apply for one in the reception area.

◆ Research room hours (except legal holidays) are 9 am to 5 pm, Monday, Tuesday and Saturday; and 9 am to 9 pm, Wednesday, Thursday, and Friday. Subject matter specialists are not on duty after 5:15 pm. The research rooms, open on Satur-day from 8:45 am to 4:45 pm, with reduced staff, are closed on Sunday.

◆ Requests for records must be made before 3:30 pm Monday through Friday; no requests can be made on Saturday. The telephone number for the Archives II Reference Branch is (301) 837-2000.

Source: National Archives at College Park, Textual Reference Branch, 1996.

SOCIAL SECURITY ACT TIMELINE

1935: Enactment of Social Security Act.
1936 (December 1): First social security card issued.
1937 (January 1): United States workers begin accumulating credits toward benefits.
1951: Domestic workers, farm and agricultural laborers, Americans working abroad for United States companies, temporary employees of the federal government, and the self-employed covered under Social Security.
1955: Self-employed farmers are covered.
1957: Beginning of coverage of persons serving in the Armed Forces.
1961: Internal Revenue Service begins using Social Security numbers as taxpayer identification numbers.
1963 (July 1): Persons registered with

the Railroad Retirement board are no longer issued special Social Security numbers.

1965: Medicare program enacted.

1967 (July 4): Freedom of Information Act provides public access to federal gov-ernment files, including the Social Security Death Master File.

1973: Starting this year, the first three digits of a person's Social Security number are determined by the zip code of the mailing address shown on the application for a social security number.

1984 (January 1): All federal employees hired after this date earn retirement benefits under Social Security. Employees of nonprofit organizations receive mandatory coverage.

1990s: Information from the Social Security Death Master File become generally available to genealogists.

Source: Jacob Gehring, "Social Security Death Master File: A Much Misunderstood Index," *Genealogical Journal* Utah Genealogical Association, Vol. 24, No. 2 (1996).

HELPFUL FACTS ABOUT THE SOCIAL SECURITY DEATH MASTER FILE

♦Only those who were involved with the Social Security program are included in the Social Security Death Master File.

♦ A person's death is recorded only if the Social Security Administration was informed of the death, usually through a family member's application for a lump sum benefit at death.

♦ The file lists the state where an individual resided or the state where the Social Security card was received, which may not have been the place of the person's birth.

♦ A married woman is generally listed under her married name.

♦ The zip code indicated for the last residence may or may not represent the area where the death occurred.

♦ Most of the deaths recorded in the index occurred after 1962, when the Social Security Administration began maintain-ing the file electronically.

♦The Social Security Death Master File index is available online at www.family search.org and also at http://ssdi. rootsweb.ancestry.com/.

Source: "Social Security Death Master File: A Much Misunderstood Index," by Jacob Gehr-ring. *Genealogical Journal*, Utah Genealogical Association, Vol. 24, No. 2 (1996).

SOCIAL SECURITY NUMBER DESIGNATIONS BY LOCALITY

The first three digits of the social security number indicate the state in which the holder applied for the card:

001-003	NH
004-007	ME
008-009	VT
010-034	MA
035-039	RI
040-049	CT
050-134	NY
135-158	NJ
159-211	PA
212-220	MD
221-222	DE
223-231	VA
232	WV and NC
233-236	WV
237-246	NC
247-251	SC
252-260	GA
261-267	FL
268-302	OH
303-317	IN
318-361	IL
362-386	MI
387-399	WI
400-407	KY
408-415	TN
416-424	AL
425-428	MS

429-432	AR
433-439	LA
440-448	OK
449-467	TX
468-477	MN
478-485	IA
586-500	MO
501-502	ND
503-504	SD
505-508	NE
509-515	KS
516-517	MT
518-519	ID
520	WY
521-524	CO
525	NM
526-527	AZ
528-529	UT
530	NV
531-539	WA
540-544	OR
545-573	CA
574	AK
575-576	HI
577-579	DC
580	VI, PR
581-584	PR
585	NM
586	Guam, Philippine Islands, American Samoa
587	MS
700-728	Railroad Retirement Board (all states)

SOCIAL SECURITY APPLICATIONS

It is possible to send for a copy of the SS-5 record, which is the form that social security card holders filled out when they applied for coverage.

Ordering an SS-5

SS-5 copies can be obtained for oneself, for deceased individuals, and for persons who would be over 100 years old if they were still living.

When the social security number is known, researchers can generate a letter of request upon locating an ancestor in the SSDI at Rootsweb (www.ssdi.rootsweb.ancestry.com). Researchers are asked to send $27.00 (if the social security number is known) with this letter or $29.00 (if the number is unknown or incorrect) to this address: Social Security Administration, OEO FOIA Workgroup, 300 N. Green Street, P.O. Box 33022, Baltimore, MD 21290-3022.

When writing to this office, request a full copy of the individual's SS-5 and his/her social security number, if known.

The Social Security Death Master File provides the deceased person's social security number. If the social security number is not known, provide identifying information. Provide proof of death (such as a copy of an obituary, a death certificate, or even the printout from the Social Security Death Master File).

To request a copy of a living person's SS-5, that person's signature is required. Make the check payable to "Social Security Administration."

Information provided on the SS-5

The SS-5 record provides spaces for the following information which was to be supplied by the applicant:
◆Full name of the applicant
◆Place of residence at the time of application
◆Name and address of the employer
◆Date and place of birth
◆Father's full name
◆Mother's full maiden name
◆Date of application
◆The applicant's signature

The SS-5 may be especially helpful to genealogists by providing
◆ A clue to the applicant's early occupation
◆ A residence address that is probably more recent than that shown on the latest available U.S. federal census
◆ The maiden name of the applicant's

mother
- The full name a German-American may have been given at christening.

Where to search for the social security number

- Social Security Death Master File
- Death certificate
- Insurance policies, bank statements, income tax returns
- Military and military discharge records
- Pension applications
- Employment records
- Funeral home records
- Voter registration rolls
- Drivers license offices
- Fraternal, business, trade organizations
- Schools, colleges, alumni associations
- Hospital records

U.S. RAILROAD RETIREMENT BOARD

The U.S. Railroad Retirement Board began keeping records of covered rail service in 1937, and therefore the Board's service records are limited to individuals who worked in the rail industry after 1936.

If a person was not actually working for a railroad after 1936, the person would not be listed in these records, nor would the Board generally have any pertinent records of persons whose rail service was performed on a casual basis and/or was of short duration. Its records apply only to persons covered under the Railroad Retirement Act. Street, interurban, or suburban electric railway employees are not covered under this Act.

The Board will provide information from its records for deceased persons, but if the person of interest is still living, a written consent is required.

The records are organized by the railroad employee's social security number, which often appears on the death certificate. If the social security number is not known, it is necessary to provide the complete name, including middle name or initial, and complete dates of birth and death. This information may not be sufficient, however, if the surname is relatively common. In most cases it is not possible to make a positive identification without the employee's social security number.

The fee for searching the records is $27 for each railroad employee and must be paid before the search is attempted. Allow 30-60 days for responses to genealogical inquiries. Fees are non-refundable, even if the information requested cannot be located. Checks or money orders should be made payable to the Railroad Retirement Board and sent to:

U.S. Railroad Retirement Board
Congressional Inquiry Section
844 North Rush Street
Chicago, IL 60611-2092

For updated information, visit the Railroad Retirement Board online, www.rrb.gov/mep/genealogy.asp.
Source: Railroad Retirement Board

BEGINNINGS OF STATEWIDE VITAL RECORDS LAWS

The beginning of registration of vital records (births, marriages, deaths) in the United States varies widely among the states. The dates shown below, indicating the year in which states began to require vital records registration, or the year in which statewide records actually began, can be misleading for these reasons:

- Certain counties in some states often collected vital records before the state required them
- After a statewide requirement was put in force, several years elapsed before the state came into full compliance.
- Gaps in the years of registration activity often occurred.
- Registration of vital records in some large cities was accomplished separately from that conducted in the state's regis-

tration offices.
◆ Some states began registering births at a different time from the year death records were collected.
◆ Many states began to register marriages later than births and deaths.
For these reasons, the dates for vital records registration shown here should be considered as guidelines only. For more complete information about vital records registration history in a specific state, see the reference noted as the source at the end of this list.

AL	1908
AK	1913
AZ	1909[1]
AR	1914[2]
CA	1905[3]
CO	1907
CT	1897
DE	1881[4]
DC	1874
FL	1899
GA	1919
HI	1896[5]
ID	1911
IL	1916
IN	1907[6]
IA	1880
KS	1911[7]
KY	1911
LA	1914
ME	1892[8]
MD	1898
MA	1841
MI	1867
MN	1900
MO	1863
MT	1907
NE	1905[9]
NV	1867
NH	1901
NJ	1878
NM	1880
NY	1880
NC	1913[10]
ND	1899[11]
OH	1867
OK	1908

OR	1903
PA	1906
RI	1853
SC	1915[12]
SD	1905[13]
TN	1914
TX	1903
UT	1905[14]
VT	1955[15]
VA	1912
WA	1907
WV	1917
WI	1907
WY	1909[16]

[1]Marriages: 1891
[2]Marriages: 1917
[3]Includes marriages
[4]Also 1861-63
[5]Actually began earlier, but few records in existence before this date
[6]Births: 1907; deaths: 1900
[7]Marriages: 1913
[8]Includes marriage registration
[9]Marriages: 1864
[10]Deaths: 1930. Marriages: 1962
[11]Also 1893-95
[12]Marriages: 1950
[13]Includes marriages
[14]Marriages: 1887
[15]Includes marriages. Vital records were kept in the towns from 1760
[16]Marriages: 1941

Source: George B. Everton, Sr., *The Handy Book for Genealogists,* Eighth Ed., Everton Publishers, Inc., Logan, UT, 1991.

US CITIES AND STATES REQUIRING GOVERNMENT REGISTRATION BY 1880

Cities

New Orleans	1790
Boston	1848
Philadelphia	1860
Pittsburgh	1870
Baltimore	1875

States

Delaware	1860

Florida	1865
Hawaii	1850
Iowa	1880
Massachusetts	1841
Michigan	1867
New Hampshire	1840
New Jersey	1878
New York	1880
Rhode Island	1853
Vermont	1770
Virginia	1853
Wisconsin	1876
Washington, D.C.	1871

Source: Arlene Eakle and Johni Cerny, *The Source, A Guidebook of American Genealogy.* Ancestry Publishing Co., Salt Lake City, 1984.

ACCESSING U.S. VITAL RECORDS

The following sources are helpful in tracking down vital records in the United States:

♦**www.labs.familysearch.org:** Go to the Internet site, click "Record Search," and select "Browse our record collections." Click on the map of the United States and scroll through periodically updated U.S. record collections.

♦**www.progenealogists.com/genealogy sleuthb.htm:** Access regularly updated links to U.S. vital records online.

♦ *Where to Write for Vital Records: Births, Deaths, Marriages, and Divorces,* U.S. Department of Health and Human Services.

Information provided (state by state) in this publication includes the costs of certified copies, the address of the office having custody of the records, and remarks concerning the types of records available and the period of time they cover.

This publication is now available online in both pdf and html formats. In addition to the features outlined in the previous paragraph, the online versions

specify when a state's vital records (e.g. birth, marriage or death) have been placed on the Internet and, if so, provides a direct link to the digitized collection:

– www.cdc.gov/nchs/data/misc/09-16-08.w2w.pdf
– www.cdc.gov/nchs/w2w.htm

To access updated informaion about these and other genealogical sources offered by the U.S. Government Printing Office, visit http://catalog.gpo.gov and search for terms such as "vital records" or "genealogy."

♦ *International Vital Records Handbook,* by Thomas J. Kemp, 3rd Ed., Genealogi-cal Publishing Co., Baltimore, 1995.

This book not only offers most of the information listed in the DHHS publication described above, but it also provides a sample copy of the necessary application forms for each office, which may be photocopied for mailing to state offices. Procedures for ordering birth, marriage, and death certificates from each state, province, territory, and country are given. The book includes addresses of key archives and libraries in 200 countries and territories. [FHL 973 V24k].

♦ *The Handy Book for Genealogists,* by George B. Everton, Sr., 9th ed., The Everton Publishers, Inc., Logan, UT, 1999; provides county mailing addresses. [FHL 973 D27]

♦ *Ancestry's Red Book: American State, County, and Town Sources,* Alice Eichholz, ed., Ancestry Publishing, Salt Lake City, UT, 1989, 1992. County addresses as well as New England town addresses may be found in this book. [FHL 973 D27rb].

♦ *County Courthouse Book.,* by Elizabeth Petty Bentley, Genealogical Publishing Co., Inc., Baltimore, 1995.

The book, arranged by state, provides a summary of each state's court system with current addresses and telephone numbers for 3,351 county courthouses. It includes location and dates of coverage for land records, naturalization records, probate records, and vital records and often gives alternative places to locate records.[FHL 973 D24bena]

♦ *Research Outlines* for the states of the United States, published by the Family History Library of the Church of Jesus Christ of Latter-day Saints, Salt Lake City, Utah.

These outlines, which give specific vital records information for each state, can be extremely useful. They may be viewed at www.familysearch.org. Go to "Research Helps" and search alphabetically by state.

Source: "375 Years of Vital Records in the United States: Where and How to Access Them in 1995," lecture by William C. Kleese, Family History Land, Tucson, AZ, at the National Genealogy Society Conference of the States, 1995.

WORKS PROGRESS ADMINISTRATION (WPA) RECORDS

The Work Projects Administration, established in 1935, was responsible for the relief program associated with the "New Deal." (The name was changed to Works Progress Adminstration in 1939.) One WPA project was the Historical Records Survey Program, which was responsible for the Soundex index to the U.S. population censuses of 1880, 1900, 1910, and 1920, as well as naturalization indexes — both areas microfilmed by the National Archives.

The goal of the Historical Records Survey Program was to locate and describe records at the county level across the United States.

Few of the projects were completed, and many records that were compiled were destroyed or lost. The agency was discontinued in 1942.

The Historical Records Survey produced bibliographies, inventories, indexes, and other historical materials. Because the projects were conducted during the lifetimes of an extraordinary number of German immigrants in America, it could be profitable to investigate specific areas of German settlements to determine whether pertinent records from the Historical Records Survey exist.

Surviving records of the Historical Records Survey are found in the National Archives' "Records of the Work Projects Administration," Record Group 69. The National Archives does not have the microfilm publications or the unpublished project material of the Historical Records Survey. These sources are listed in the Work Projects Administration *Bibliography of Research Projects Reports, Check List of Historical Records Survey Publications,* Technical Series, Research and Records Bibliography 7 (Washington: Work Projects Administration, 1943). The bibliography has been reprinted by the Genealogical Publishing Co., Baltimore, 1969. Names and addresses of the state depositories for the unpublished project material appear in an appendix to this bibliography.

Other references

♦ *The WPA Historical Records Survey: A Guide to the Unpublished Inventories, Indexes, and Transcripts,* compiled by Loretta Hefner (Chicago: Society of American Archivists, 1980), contains lists of the specific holdings of Historical Records Survey materials in each repository where they have been located.

♦ Major pertinent publications of the National Archives and Records Administration (NARA): 1) *Index to Reference Cards for Work Project Administration Project Files, 1935-1937* [NARA film T936, 79 rolls]; 2) *Index to Reference Cards for Work Project Administration Project Files, 1938* [NARA film T937, 15 rolls]; and 3) *Index to Reference Cards*

for Work Project Administration Project Files, 1939-1942 [19 rolls]
♦ *Territorial Papers of the United States:* a multi-volume documentary historical publication of the National Archives and Records Administration, published for territories northwest of the Ohio River, territories south of the Ohio River, Mississippi, Indiana, New Orleans, Michigan, Louisiana, Missouri, Illinois, Alabama, Arkansas, and Florida. [NARA microfilm M721, 15 rolls].
Also:
–*The Territorial Papers of the United States: The Territory of Wisconsin, 1836-48* [NARA film M236, 122 rolls]
–*The Territorial Papers of the United States: The Territory of Iowa, 1838-46,* [NARA film M325, 102 rolls]
–*The Territorial Papers of the United States: The Territory of Minnesota, 1849-1858.* Incomplete. (NARA film M1050, 11 rolls]
–*The Territorial Papers of the United States: The Territory of Oregon, 1848-1859* Incomplete. [NARA film M1049, 12 rolls]

SANBORN MAPS

In 1867, Daniel A. Sanborn founded the National Insurance Diagram Bureau. Still in operation today, the company's archives contain over 1.2 million Sanborn maps for approximately 12,000 cities and towns in the United States.

The maps were produced for fire insurance companies which were easily wiped out following major fires. They served the purpose of documenting property owned and destroyed. They maps show building outlines, street names, street adress numbers, number of stories of the structures, general building use, and construction details.

As the mapping business developed, there were added to the maps fire protection devices and the location of potential fire hazards. Insurers used this information to evaluate risks and to set premiums.

These fire insurance maps can locate an ancestor's home and place of business, showing all details such as sheds, garages, wells, and the number of rooms.
Availability
The Library of Congress has a huge collection of fire insurance maps. The entire digitized collection may be viewed by visitors to the LOC. Patrons visiting the LOC are permitted to view the entire digitized collection. Due to copyright laws, however, patrons requesting copies by mail can only request copies of maps published before 1923.

of Sanborn maps. in person, have access to all Sanborn maps. Those requesting copies When requesting a copy of Reproductions of the Sanborn maps are available from the Library of Congress, Photoduplication Services, 101 Independence Avenue SE, Washington, DC 20540-4570. Tel. (202) 707-5640; Fax (202) 707-1771; photoduplication@loc.gov; www.loc.gov/preserv/pds/.

Maps published more than 75 years ago are in the public domain and can be reproduced without restriction. The Library of Congress is permitted to reproduce 50 or fewer paper copies or color slides from Sanborn maps for noncommercial customers.

Many public libraries have duplicate sets of Sanborn maps.

To order Sanborn Maps from the LOC, When ordering, be sure to specify the exact community, house number or building, or boundary of area by streets. The LOC will send you a scanned, black and white image of the map (at least 300 dpi).

The Sanborn Map Company is located at 629 Fifth Avenue, Pelham, NY 10803. Tel. (800) 930-3298; Fax (917) 738-1680; http://www.sanbornmap. com/
Sources:

◆ "Sanborn City Maps," by Jo White Linn, , *Heritage Quest*, #32.

◆"Fire insurance maps are 'hot' with collectors," by Diane L. Oswald, *AntiqueWeek*, August 5, 1996.

◆ "Fire insurance documents may offer valuable information about ancestors," by John W. Heisey, *AntiqueWeek*, September 9, 1996.

U.S. CENSUS INFORMATION RELATING TO IMMIGRATION

Census information relating to immigration or providing clues relating to immigration is categorized below according to the census years in which the various relevant questions were recorded:

◆**Place of birth of person:** 1860, 1870, 1880, 1900, 1910, 1920, 1930, 1940, 1950
◆**Place of birth of parents:** 1880, 1900, 1910, 1920, 1930
◆**Whether person or parents foreign-born:** 1870, 1880, 1900, 1910, 1920, 1930, 1940, 1950. (The 1820 and 1830 censuses ask for the number of non-naturalized foreigners in the household)
◆**Whether naturalized:** 1900, 1910, 1920, 1930, 1940,1950
◆**Year of immigration:** 1900, 1910, 1920, 1930
◆**Year of naturalization:** 1920
◆**Number of years in the United States:** 1900
◆**Number of years married**: 1900, 1910
◆**Ability to speak English:** 1900, 1910, 1920, 1930
◆**Mother tongue of person and parents:** 1910
◆**Mother tongue of foreign born:** 1920, 1930

THE SOUNDEX SYSTEM

"Soundex" is a surname index to the census schedules. The index was prepared by the Works Progress Adminis-tration between 1938 and 1940. The system was developed in order that a surname may be found even though it may have been recorded under various spellings.

Soundex Code

The Soundex index enables the researcher to search for specific surnames in the 1880, 1900, 1910, and 1920 federal census records and in some passenger list records. (The index for 1910 is called Miracode.)

The surname code (see below) is used to search in the microfilmed Soundex card index, which is organized by state, then by Soundex code, and then alphabetically by first name or initial.

The Soundex code may be determined by using a special feature of *Personal Ancestral File* (PAF) software program.

How to use the Soundex code

Every Soundex code consists of the first letter of the surname plus a three-digit number.

Steps for finding the Soundex code for a surname are,

1. The first letter of the surname is the first element of the Soundex code for the surname. Every surname code begins with this first letter of the name.

2. Write down the surname. After the first letter of the name, cross out every a, e, i, o, u, w, y, and h.

3. To each of the remaining letters assign a number, according to the following guide:

1	b,p,f,v
2	c,s,k,g,j,q,x,z (also the German tz)
3	d,t
4	l
5	m,n
6	r

Exceptions

◆ If there are any side-by-side letters having the same number equivalents, these letters should be treated as one letter. For example, in the surname Stadtler, the *d* should be crossed out because *d* and *t* both have 3 as their code number.

♦If the surname has any doubled letters, they are treated as a single letter. For example, in the surname Lloyd, the second *l* is crossed out; in Hess, the second *s* is crossed out.

♦ If the result is three digits, the task is finished; the three digits become the numbers of the code. For example, Rasmus = R252.

♦If fewer than three digits resulted, add enough zeros so that there are three digits. For example, Kern = K650; Hull = H400.

♦If the result is more than three digits, ignore the digits following the three needed ones. For example, Knierenschild = K565.

Special cases

♦If the surname has a prefix – *Van, Von, De, Di,* or *Le,* for example – code it with the prefix and again without the prefix because the surname may be given either code.

♦ *Mc* and *Mac* are not considered prefixes.

♦If the first letter of the surname could differ due to misspelling, code it in different ways. For example, Cole (C400) could be spelled Kohl (K400).

♦ The surnames of Catholic nuns are usually coded as "Sister."

♦Be careful of a surname like Tutt, which is indexed as T300 rather than T000 because the last two Ts are doubled but are not next to the first one.

♦Watch for misspellings in the records. For example, Glover may be found misspelled as Clover; Buesch as Ruesch.

♦To account for possible mistakes in the coding of surnames, try different codes for a surname.

Online Soundex Converters

Several genealogy websites now provide online soundex conversion programs that quickly generate soundex

codes.
♦ http://resources.rootsweb.ancestry. com/cgi-bin/soundexconverter
♦ www.progenealogists.com/soundex. htm
♦ www.bradandkathy.com/genealogy/ yasc.html (converts entire lists of surnames all at once)

FEDERAL CENSUS INDEXES

Census indexes and original census images may be viewed at www.ances try.com and www.labs.familysearch.org.

Federal Indexes exist for the 1790-1850 censuses and most of the 1860 and 1870 censuses, usually in print form, with some on microfilm or microfiche.

The Accelerated Indexing Systems International (AIS) indexes all the 1790 to 1850 censuses and a few later censuses, on microfiche.

The 1880, 1900, and 1920 censuses have been indexed through the Soundex system.

The 1880 census

All households with children aged ten years and under are indexed on Soundex, on microfilm. Book indexes are available at the Family History Library for Arizona, Colorado, Idaho, Minnesota, Montana, North and South Dakota, Nevada, Ohio. Oregon, Texas, Utah, Washington, West Virginia, and Wyoming.

1890 census

Although most of this census was destroyed, the few records remaining are indexed on FHL film 1,421,673 and on FHL film 543,341-42.

1900 census

Every household is Soundexed, for all states, on microfilm.

1910 census

Soundex and "Miracode" indexes to the 1910 census are available for 21 states: Alabama, Arkansas, California, Florida, Georgia, Illinois, Kansas, Kentucky, Louisiana, Michigan, Mississippi, Missouri, North Carolina, Ohio, Oklahoma, Pennsylvania, South Carolina, Tennessee, Texas, Virginia, and West Virginia, on microfilm.

Some cities and counties are indexed separately from the state in the 1910 indexes of Alabama, Georgia, Louisiana, Pennsylvania, and Tennessee.

Published indexes are available for Hawaii, Nevada, and Wyoming.

The following resource is very helpful for searching states whose 1910 censuses are not Soundexed:

G. Eileen Buckway, compiler, *U.S. 1910 Federal Census: Unindexed States: A Guide to Finding Census Enumeration Districts for Unindexed Cities, Towns, and Villages,* compiled by C. Eileen Buckway; assisted by Marva Blalock, Elizabeth Caruso, Ray Matthews, and Kenneth Nelson (Salt Lake City: Family History Library, 1992, FHL US/CAN REF AREA 973 X2bu 1910 and microfiche 6101540, 8 microfiches).[1]

Tip

The 1910 Miracode index system can be confusing: On some of the indexed entries, a row of numbers near the upper right corner appears without any indication of what they represent. The following example illustrates how this number (always in three parts) is used:

095 0222 0162

The first number (95), the volume number, is not always necessary for a search and can often be ignored. The second number (222) is the "Enumeration District" number. The third number (0162) is the family number, found on the census to the left of the family name, indicating the order in which the family residence was visited.

Non-Soundexed states, 1910 census

There are no statewide indexes for Alaska, Arizona, Colorado, Connecticut, Delaware, District of Columbia, Indiana, Iowa, Maine, Maryland, Massachusetts, Minnesota, Montana, Nebraska, New

Hampshire, New Jersey, New Mexico, New York, North Dakota, Oregon, Puerto Rico, Rhode Island, South Dakota, Utah, Vermont, Washington, and Wisconsin.

The 1920 census

This census is completely Soundexed, for all states.

The 1940 and later censuses

The 1940 census remains closed until the year 2012, according to the agreement reached in 1952 that population schedules will "remain closed for seventy-two years after the enumeration date for each census" for privacy reasons.

[1]J. Carlyle Parker, *Going to Salt Lake City to Do Family History Research.* Rev. ed. Turlock, California: Marietta Publishing Company, 1996.

Sources:

•*Research Outline: United States,* Family History Library, Church of Jesus Christ of Latter-day Saints, Salt Lake City, Utah.

•National Archives and Records Administration, Washington, DC.

NON-POPULATION CENSUS SCHEDULES

The "nonpopulation" census schedules — agriculture, manufacturing, mortality, and social statistics may be found in the National Archives or in state archives.

Agriculture, mortality, and social statistics schedules are available for the census years of 1850, 1860, 1870, and 1880.

Manufacturing schedules are available for 1820, 1850, 1860, 1870, and 1880. They are arranged by state, then by county, and then by political subdivision.

Agricultural schedules of 1850, 1860, and 1880

These schedules show for each farm listed the owner or manager's name, number of acres, the farm's cash value, farming machinery, livestock and many other details. In 1850, small farms that produced less than $100 worth of products were not included. By 1870 the minimum farm size was three acres; the minimum production, $500.

Manufacturing schedules in 1820, 1850, and 1860

These schedules provide the name of the manufacturer, the type of business, capital invested, value of materials used in the business, cost of labor, and many other details.

Mortality schedules

Recording deaths in the year preceding the taking of the census, these schedules include name, age, sex, marital status, state or country of birth, month of death, occupation, cause of death, and length of final illness.

Social statistics schedules for 1850 through 1870

This source indicates for each political subdivision the value of real estate, annual taxes, number of schools, teachers, and pupils, as well as specific information concerning libraries, newspapers, churches, paupers, criminals, wages of laborers, and more. They do not provide information about specific individuals, but rather statistical data.

The 1880 schedules provide information about deaf, dumb, blind, and criminal persons who are listed by name.

Other special censuses

For information about other special censuses (1840 List of Pensioners; Federal Territorial Censuses; and Colonial, State, and Local Censuses), see *Research Outline: United States*, Family History Library, Church of Jesus Christ of Latter-day Saints, Salt Lake City, Utah, page 13.

Source: "The Nonpopulation Census Schedules," by Claire Prechtel-Kluskens, *The Record: News from the National Archives and Records Administration*, Vol. 2, No. 1, September 1995.

'CENSUS DAY'

The "census day" is, by law, the day for which census statistics were to be taken. This list shows dates for "census days" for each U.S. Federal Census year:

1790	August 2
1800	August 4
1810	August 6
1820	August 7
1830 through 1900	June 1
1910	April 15
1920	January 1
1930	April 1
1940	April 1

YEARS OF STATE CENSUSES (INCLUDING ONLY STATES IN WHICH THE CENSUSES COVERED THE MAJORITY OF THE RESPECTIVE STATES)

AL	1816, 1855, 1907 Conf. Vet
AZ	1864, 1866
AR	1829
CA	1852
CO	1885
DAKOTA	1885
FL	1814, 1885
HI	1878, 1890
IL	1855, 1865
IN	1807
IA	1836, 1856, 1885, 1895, 1905, 1915, 1925
KS	1855, 1865, 1875, 1885, 1895
MD	1776
MA	1855, 1865
MI	1884, 1894
MN	1836, 1849, 1857, 1865, 1875, 1885, 1895, 1905
MS	1810, 1816, 1841, 1845, 1853
NE	1855, 1885
NV	1875
NH	1732, 1776
NJ	1855, 1885, 1895, 1905, 1915
NY	1825, 1835, 1855, 1865, 1875, 1892, 1905, 1915, 1925

NYC	1890, 1905, 1915, 1925
NC	1784, 1787
ND	1915, 1925
OK	1890
RI	1774, 1782, 1865, 1875, 1885, 1915, 1925, 1936
SD	1905, 1915, 1925, 1935, 1945
TX	1840
UT	1856
VT	1771
WI	1836, 1842, 1846, 1847, 1855, 1875, 1895, 1905

References

◆Anne S. Lainhart, *State Census Records,* Genealogical Publishing Company, Inc., Baltimore, 1992. This book identifies each state census taken for 40 of the 50 states; indicates repositories holding the origi-nals; whether microfilmed; the years extant; which counties survive for each census taken; whether an index to the state census exists, and the address of any repository holding state census records. FHL 973 X2Lai

◆The Family History Library Catalog (part of *FamilySearch)* can be searched for each state, under "Census," to locate which of these records are available.

U.S. CENSUS ABBREVIATIONS

Citizenship Status

A	Alien
NA	Naturalized
PA	First papers filed

Other abbreviations

A	aunt
Ad	adopted
AdCl	adopted child
AdD	adopted daughter
AdGcl	adopted grandchild
AdM	adopted mother
AdS	adopted son
Al	aunt-in-law
Ap	apprentice
Asst	assistant
At	attendant
B	brother

B Boy	bound boy
B Girl	bound girl
Bar	bartender
Bl	brother-in-law
Bo	boarder
Boy	boy
Bu	butler
C	cousin
Cap	captain
Cha	chambermaid
Cil	cousin-in-law
Cl	child
Coa	coachman
Com	companion
Cook	cook
D	daughter
Dl	daughter-in-law
Dla	day laborer
Dom	domestic
Dw	dishwasher
Emp	employee
En	engineer
F	father
FaH	farm hand
FaL	farm laborer
FaW	farm worker
Fi	fireman
First C	first cousin
Fl	father-in-law
FoB	foster brother
FoSi	foster sister
FoS	foster son
Gcl	grandchild
Gd	granddaughter
Gf	grandfather
GGF	greatgrandfather
GGGF	great great grandfather
GGGM	great great grandmother
GGM	great grandmother
GM	grandmother
Gml	grandmother-in-law
Gn	great or grand nephew
Gni	great or grand niece
Go	governess
God Cl	God child
Gs	grandson
Gsl	grandson-in-law
Gua	guardian
Guest	guest

H Maid .... housemaid
Hb .... half brother
Hbl .... half brother-in-law
He .... herder
Help .... help
HGi .... hired girl
HH .... hired hand
Hk .... housekeeper
Hlg .... hireling
HSi .... half sister
HSil .... half sister-in-law
Husband .... husband
Hw .... house worker
Inmate .... inmate
L .... lodger
La .... laborer
Lau .... laundry
M .... mother
Maid .... maid
Man .... manager
Mat .... matron
Ml .... mother-in-law
N .... nephew
Ni .... niece
Nil .... niece-in-law
Nl .... nephew-in-law
NU .... nurse
O .... officer
P .... patient
Pa .... partner
Ph .... physician
Por .... porter
Pr .... prisoner
Pri .... principal
Prv .... private
Pu .... pupil
R .... roomer
S .... son
Sa .... sailor
Sal .... saleslady
Sbl .... stepbrother-in-law
Scl .... stepchild
Sd .... stepdaughter
Sdl .... stepdaughter-in-law
Se .... servant
SeCl .... servant's child
Sf .... stepfather
Sfl .... stepfather-in-law
Sgd .... stepgranddaughter

Sgs .... stepgrandson
Si .... sister
Sl .... son-in-law
Sm .... stepmother
Ss .... stepson
Ssl .... stepson-in-law
SSsil .... stepsister-in-law
Su .... superintendent
Ten .... tenant
U .... uncle
Ul .... uncle-in-law
Vi .... visitor
W .... wife
Wa .... warden
Wai .... waitress
Ward .... ward
Wkm .... workman
W t .... waiter

WARD MAPS

◆Ward maps of 35 major cities, showing
census districts and political divisions
of large cities, and 232 maps representing
35 cities are available on FHL film
1,377,700; microfiche 6016554-782.
◆To find which maps to use with each
U.S. census, see Michael H. Shelley,
*Ward Maps of United States Cities: A
Selective Checklist of Pre-1900 Maps
in the Library of Congress*, FHL film
928,210, item 16.
◆To find U.S. county boundary maps
for census decades, see William
Thorndale and William Dollarhide, *Map
Guide to the U.S. Federal Censuses,
1790-1920*, FHL 973 X2th. This book
shows 400 U.S. county boundary maps
for the census decades from 1790 to 1920
superimposed on modern county
boundaries.

GLOSSARY OF LAND AND PROPERTY TERMS

Abstract of title: A history of the chain
of title to a piece of property

Base line: A principal east/west line used for surveying and from which townships are numbered north and south

Bounds: Description of property boundaries by physical attributes

Bounty land: Land awarded to veterans in payment for military service

Cadaster: A public record of the extent, ownership, and value of land for taxation purposes; *adj.* cadastral

Chancery court: An equity court which decides the "reasonable justice" or the "common good," where following the letter of the law would be unjust

Chattel: Movable, personal property

Crown colony: A colony established by the king

Deed: A written document by which ownership of property is conveyed

Defendant: The party against whom a suit is brought

Fee: An estate in land, or the land so held

Fee simple: A fee without limit or restriction on transfer; highest form of ownership

Field notes: A written record of a survey

Freehold estate: The privileges of ownership extended to a tenant under a lease; e.g., voting rights

Grantee: One who receives a grant; buyer

Grantor: One who makes a grant; a seller

Hereditament: Any property that can be inherited

Homestead: n. A tract of land acquired from U.S. public lands by filing a record, living on, and improving the tract; v. to acquire or settle on land under a homestead law

Improvements: Additions to real property, such as buildings

Intestate: Having no valid will

Jurisdiction: The territorial range of authority; a political subdivision

Land warrant: A negotiable government certificate that entitles the holder to possess a designated amount of public land

Lease: A title transfer less than fee, subject to payment of rent for a certain time

Metes: Description of property boundaries by measurement; length and direction; literally, "measures"

Patent: An instrument in writing granting land ownership

Principal meridian: A principal east/west line used for surveying and from which ranges are numbered north and south

Public domain: The realm of property rights belonging to the community at large

Quitrent: An annual tax, or token payment by the tenant of a freehold estate

Range: A north-south row of townships, six miles wide, numbered east and west from the principal meridian

Survey: A delineation of a tract of land

Source: J. Loren Kemper , researcher and lecturer, Yorba Linda, California.

LAND TRANSACTIONS IN AMERICA

1606-1732: British Crown made grants (charters) to colonies and individuals

1607-1776: Colonies transferred land to individual colonists

1780-1876: States and foreign powers transferred land to individuals

1785-1934: Federal government transferred land to individuals

1607-present: Individuals transferred land to other individuals

Source: Janice G. Cloud, "Give Deeds Their Due: Lessons from the Land," 1996.

LAND RECORDS CONTENTS

Land records may reveal one or more of the following:

♦ Name of wife, possibly her maiden name
♦ Occupation

◆Age and marital status
◆Names of children, including son-in-law
◆Names of heirs
◆Location of previous and next home
◆Description and location of property, plus number of acres
◆Names of previous owners
◆Length of time at one location
◆Religious and educational practices (as many settlers donated land for churches and schools)
◆ Economic circumstances (owned a great deal of land, or land was sold to pay debts, for example)
◆ Names of neighbors and witnesses who may be relatives
◆ Perhaps transactions of personal property
Source: *Newsletter*, St. Louis Genealogy Society, September 1994.

AMERICAN LAND MEASUREMENT TERMS

◆**Acre:** 160 square rods (43,560 square feet)
◆ **Arpent:** Similar to an acre, used in French sections of the United States. The side of an arpent equals 191.994 feet; one square arpent = 0.84625 acre. In Missouri, an arpent = .8507 acres, or 192.5 square feet.
◆**Chain:** Invented by Edmund Gunter in 1620, a chain is 66 feet long with 100 links. One mile is 80 chains.
◆**Degree:** 1/360th of the distance around a circle.
◆**Furlong:** 660 feet
◆**Link:** 1/100th of a chain, 7.92 inches long; 25 links = 1 rod.
◆**Metes & Bounds:** A type of survey based on measurements (chains, rods, poles, perches, etc.) and country markers (trees, stakes, streams, etc.)
◆**Mile:** 5,280 feet (80 chains, 32 rods, 8 furlongs)
◆**Minute:** 1/60th of a degree

◆**Perch:** Same as a rod
◆**Rectangular Survey:** Adopted in the United States in 1785 and used in public land states (most states west of the Appalachian Mountains). Based on certain longitude and latitude lines (meridians and base lines), land is described in terms of range, township, sections, and quarter-sections, etc.
◆**Rod:** 16.5 feet. Measured as ˉ of a chain or 25 links. Also called pole or perch.
◆**Section:** 1 square mile (640 acres)
◆**Township:** 36 square miles
◆**Vara:** Unit of measure used in parts of the United States settled by Spain. Varying lengths, with the Texas vara being 33.3333 inches (36 varas = 100 feet), the Florida vara being larger, and the southwestern vara being smaller.
Source: Most from "Terminology Found on Plat Maps," *Antique Week*, July 15, 1996.

PUBLIC LAND STATES

Alabama, Alaska, Arizona, Arkansas, California, Colorado, Florida, Idaho, Illinois, Indiana, Iowa, Kansas, Louisiana, Michigan, Minnisota, Mississippi, Missouri, Montana, Nebraska, Nevada, New Mexico, North Dakota, Ohio, Oklahoma, Oregon, South Dakota, Utah, Washington, Wisconsin, Wyoming.

FEDERAL LAND SALES

In the 19th century, the U.S. government sold land at exceedingly low prices to settlers. Records are available for many of the transactions. Some of these sales are:
◆**Military Wagon Roads**: Income from sales from land lying on both sides of a proposed military road, given in order to facilitate access of troops to certain sensitive frontier areas, were used to pay for road construction. Projects were instituted in Ohio (1823, 1827), in Indiana

(1827), Michigan (1863), Wisconsin (1863), and Oregon (1856-1869).

◆**Canals:** Land sales to finance canals occurred in Indiana (1827), Ohio (1848), Illinois (1827), Wisconsin (1838, 1846, 1866), and Michigan (1852,1865,1866).

◆ **River Improvements:** Land was granted to states to sell in order to make river improvements in Alabama (1828), Wisconsin (1846), Iowa (1846), and Louisiana (1824).

◆**Railroads:** To develop the railroads, the government gave land to the states — starting in Illinois (1833). During the Civil War until 1871, Congress made huge land grants to railroad companies for construction of rail lines.

◆**"Settlement Lands":** Settlers in 1842 and 1843 were encouraged to take and develop land in Florida, Oregon/Washington, and New Mexico/Arizona.

◆ **Miscellaneous grants:** The Legislature handed out land in the unoccupied land gained by the Louisana Purchase (1803); to British Army deserters in 1776; to Hessians with the British Army in Amer-ica during the Revolution (if they deserted); in Ohio, to Canadian refugees of the Revolution; and numerous others, including federal bounty and other special land grants made to American veterans of various wars and for other purposes.

Source: John W. Heisey, "Territorial expansion enhanced by federal land 'giveaway' programs," *Antique Week,* Knightstown, IN   46148.

HOMESTEAD ACT OF 1862

The Homestead Act of 1862 offered 160 acres to buyers (only 80 acres in railroad grant areas) if the settler (after January 1, 1863) improved the holding and lived there for five years. Most homestead papers were filed between 1863 and 1917.

The person had to be at least 21 years old and a United States citizen, or had to have filed a declaration of intent to become a citizen. The only cost was a small fee for filing a claim.

Homesteading land was located in Alabama, Florida, Illinois, Indiana, Louisiana, Michigan, Mississippi, Wisconsin, and all states west of the Mississippi River except Texas.

The homesteading entry had to be made by a citizen or by an immigrant who had filed papers to become a citizen.

Other Acts of Congress making land available in the West included the Desert Reclamation Act of 1894, the Kincaid Act of 1904 (which gave out 640-acre tracts in western Nebraska), the Enlarged Homestead Act of 1909 (covering land in seven mountain states of the West), and the Stockraising Homestead Act of 1916.

United States Government records covering more than 6.5 million patents to individuals who got public land, filed in 11,550 volumes; more than 4,000 books containing 25 million entries for tracts in public domain land; and some 8 million case records – are available through the Bureau of Land Management in the United States Department of the Interior.

Information likely to be found in these records include:

◆A Homestead final certificate file, which should include an application form and the certificate of publication that the individual intends to complete his/her claim.

◆Final proof of homesteading (testimony from the claimant and witnesses)

◆ Certificate of naturalization, if necessary

◆Claimant's name

◆Claimant's age

◆Post office address

◆Descriptions of the house and land

◆Date of residence established

◆ Number and relationship of family members

◆Citizenship

♦Acres under cultivation

Homestead records may be found in the National Archives and Records Administration. They have not been microfilmed.

Reference

William Thorndale, "Land and Tax Records," Chapter 7 of *The Source: A Guidebook of American Genealogy*, Arlene Eakle and Johni Cerny, eds., Ancestry Publishing Co., Salt Lake City, 1984.

COUNTY LAND RECORDS: WHAT TO LOOK FOR

Names: All names are important, as any of them may be relatives' names. Follow up with research on people associated with the ancestor.

Dates: Analysis of land records can place a family in chronological perspective by these means:

♦Estimating arrival and removal dates of a family in a county, based on the earliest land purchase and final sale of land in the county.

♦ Estimating minimum ages of male children by the date when they first owned land (generally after they reached their majority, age 21). Or probable birth order of brothers may be deduced, based on the order in which they begin to appear in the land records.

When a death date is not available, note the last date on which a person appears in the records and indicate on the family group sheet that he/she died after that date. Or indicate that a person died before a particular date if he/she is named in the deed as being deceased.

Places: Deeds and patents always give the place of residence (county and state) of the grantor and the grantee (or patentee).

Relationships: Relationships may be stated or implied in deeds between family members.

♦Look for clues in the wording of a deed, such as "for and in consideration of $1 and the natural love and affection which I bear. . . ." This indicates a gift deed, usually between parent and child.

♦Deeds resulting from probate proceedings often list names of heirs and state family relationships. This is an excellent source of information when a person dies without leaving a will.

Time frame: Deeds and patents do not have to be recorded to be legally binding. Some are never recorded at all. Previously unrecorded deeds or patents are sometimes recorded when the land is subsequently sold or going through probate. Land documents may be recorded as many as 100 years after they are written.

Source: "Yes, In*deed*! American County Land Records" lecture materials, by Barbara E. Leak, Loomis, California, lecturer on topics of land and military genealogy.

BUREAU OF LAND MANAGEMENT

The Bureau of Land Management's Eastern States organization is the steward of the public lands and resources under the jurisdiction of BLM in the 31 states east of and bordering on the Mississippi River.

BLM's land records include some 7.5 million ownership titles covering 1.5 billion acres of present or former Public Domain land. More than 5 million of these title documents are stored and maintained at BLM's Eastern States office in Virginia.

The records

As the Public Domain was surveyed, the government began transferring title of land parcels to private citizens, companies and local governments. Most titles were transferred through patents (deeds) from the federal government. Records of these patents and other conveyances of title - such as railroad grants, swamp grants, school grants, Indian allotments, and private land claims - are contained in huge tract books.

First developed around 1800 and maintained in local land offices, tract books have long served as the essential reference source for all transactions involving public lands. They tell who obtained what land from the federal government and when.

BLM's Eastern States office maintains 10,000 tract books containing the land records for the 13 public land states under its jurisdictions:
Alabama, Arkansas, Florida, Illinois, Indiana, Iowa, Louisiana, Michigan, Minnesota, Missouri, Mississippi, Ohio and Wisconsin.

The Eastern States office maintains almost 5 million federal land conveyance documents which precede and follow the ratification of the constitution; they include homesteads, cash sales, miscellaneous warrants, private land claims, swamp lists, State selections, and railroad lists.

General Land Office Project

The Bureau of Land Management (BLM) and the General Land Office (GLO) provide access to Federal land conveyance records for the Public Land States. They also provide image access to more than three million Federal land title records for Eastern and Western Public Land States, issued between 1820 and 1908. Currently, they are adding images of Military Land Warrants. These land patents were issued to individuals as a reward for their military service. Images related to survey plats and field notes, dating back to 1810, are added to the site state-by-state as each state's documents are completed. Due to organization of documents in the GLO collection, this site does not yet contain every Federal title record issued for the Public Land States.

The three search types available at www.glorecords.blm.gov include Federal Survey Plats and Field Notices, Federal Land Status Reports and Federal Land patents. Federal Land Patents are the most useful of these collections and may be viewed at www.glorecords.blm.gov/PatentSearch/. The Land Patent search site offers researchers a source of information on the initial transfer of land titles from the Federal government to individuals. In addition to verifying title transfer, this information will allow the researcher to associate an individual (Patentee, Assignee, Warrantee, Widow, or Heir) with a specific location (Legal Land Description) and time (Issue Date). The database may be searched using the Last name and state associated with your ancestor. Although users can view the original land patent online, they may also request certified copies of land patents electronically or through the mail.

For information, contact the GLO Records Access Staff, Bureau of Land Management, Eastern States, 7450 Boston Boulevard, Springfield, VA 22153. Tel. (703) 440-1600; Fax (730) 440-1609; records@es.blm.gov; www.blm.gov.

Compact disks (CDs) available

Contact BLM concerning compact disks containing the data base only (not the images) for patents prior to 1908 by the General Land Office, available from the Government Printing Office. These are available for the nine states mentioned above (Alabama, Arkansas, Florida, Louisiana, Michigan, Minnesota, Mississippi, Ohio, and Wisconsin).

Other states

Because the 13 original colonies and their territories were not part of the federal lands acquired during national expansion, BLM does not maintain land records of 18 eastern non-public land states or the District of Columbia. They are,

Connecticut, Delaware, Georgia, Kentucky, Maine, Maryland, Massachusetts, New Hampshire, New Jersey, New York, North Carolina, Pennsylvania,

Rhode Island, South Carolina, Tennessee, Vermont, Virginia, and West Virginia.

Inquiries concerning land records for these states should be directed to the individual state archives, land records offices, or the National Archives and Records Administration in Washington, DC.

BUREAU OF LAND MANAGEMENT STATE OFFICES

◆**Alaska State Office**
Bureau of Land Management
222 W. 7th Avenue #13
Anchorage, AK 99513
(907) 271-5960; Fax (907) 271-3684

◆**Arizona State Office**
Bureau of Land Management
One North Central Avenue Ste. 800
Phoenix, AZ 85004-4427
(602) 417-9200

◆**California State Office**
Bureau of Land Management
2800 Cottage Way Ste. W-1623
Sacramento, CA 95825
(916) 978-4400; Fax (916) 978-4416

◆**Colorado State Office**
Bureau of Land Management
2850 Youngfield Street
Lakewood, CO 80215-7093
(303) 239-3700

◆**Eastern States Office**
Bureau of Land Management
7450 Boston Boulevard
Springfield, VA 22153-3121
(703) 440-1600; Fax (703) 440-1701

◆**Idaho State Office**
Bureau of Land Management
1387 South Vinnell Way
Boise, ID 83709
(208) 373-4000; Fax (208) 373-3899

◆**Montana State Office**
[North Dakota, South Dakota]
Bureau of Land Management
5001 Southgate Drive
Billings, MT 59101

P.O. Box 36800
Billings, MT 59107
(406) 896-5013; Fax (406) 896-5281

◆**Nevada State Office**
Bureau of Land Management
1340 Financial Boulevard
Reno, NV 89502
P.O. Box 12000
Reno, NV 89502
(775) 861-6400; Fax (775) 861-6601

◆**New Mexico State Office**
[Oklahoma, Texas)
Bureau of Land Management
1474 Rodeo Road
Santa Fe, NM 87505
P.O. Box 27115
Santa Fe, NM 87502-0115
(505) 438-7400; Fax (505) 438-7435

◆**Oregon State Office**
[Washington]
Bureau of Land Mangement
333 S.W. 1st Street
Portland, OR 97204
(503) 808-6001; Fax (503) 808-6308

◆**Utah State Office**
Bureau of Land Management
440 West 200 South, Ste. 500
Salt Lake City, UT 84145-0155
(801) 539-4001; Fax (801) 539-4013

◆**Wyoming State Office**
Bureau of Land Management
5353 Yellowstone Road
Cheyenne, WY 82009
P.O. Box 1828
Cheyenne, WY 82003-1828
(307) 775-6256; Fax (307) 775-6129

SELECTED LARGE AMERICAN LIBRARIES WITH GERMAN GENEALOGICAL HOLDINGS

◆**Allen County Public Library**
900 Library Plaza
Fort Wayne, IN 46802
Tel. (260) 421-1252
Fax (260) 421-1386
ask@acpl.info
www.acpl.lib.in.us

[Among a huge collection are *Deutsches Geschlecterbuch* and Siebmacher's *Grosses Allgemeines Wappenbuch*. This library is headquarters for the Periodical Source Index (PERSI).]

◆Balch Institute for Et hnic Studies
Center for Immigrant Research
The mission and collections of the Balch Institute (concerning the country's ethnic and immigrant experience) have been integrated into the Historical Society of Pennsylvania.
History Society of Pennsylvania
1300 Locust Street
Philadelphia, PA 19107
Tel. (215) 732-6200
Fax (215) 732-2680
library@hsp.org
www.hsp.org

◆ Public Library of Cincinnati and Hamilton County
800 Vine Street
Cincinnati, OH 45202-2009
Tel. (513) 369-6900
www.cincinnatilibrary.org

◆Cleveland Public Library
325 Superior Avenue NE
Cleveland, OH 44114
Tel. (216) 623-2800
Fax (216) 623-7015
info@library.cpl.org
www.cpl.org

◆Dallas Public Library
1515 Young Street
Dallas, TX 75201-5415
Tel. (214) 670-1433 (Genealogy Dept.)
genealogy@dallaslibrary.org
www.dallaslibrary.org

◆Denver Public Library
Western History/Genealogy
10 West 14th Avenue Parkway
Denver, CO 80204-2731
Tel. (720)-865-1821

Fax (720) 865-1800
www.history.denverlibrary.org
◆Detroit Public Library
5201 Woodward Avenue
Detroit, MI 48202
Tel. (313) 833-1000
Fax (313) 832-0877
uonyema@detroitpubliclibrary.org
www.detroit.lib.mi.us/Special_Collec tions/special_collections.htm
[The library's Burton Historical Collection holds all the sources used in Filby's Passenger and Immigration Lists Index. A library form is sent upon request for searching sources, requiring in advance a moderate fee.]

◆Family History Library
35 North West Temple
Salt Lake City, UT 84150
Tel. (801) 240-2331
www.familysearch.org

◆Houston Public Library: Clayton Library
Center for Genealogical Research
500 McKinley Street
Houston, TX 77002

◆Immigration History Research Center, University of Minnesota
Elmer L. Andersen Library, Suite 311
222 - 21st Avenue S
Minneapolis, MN 55455
Tel. (612) 625-4800
Fax (612) 626-0018
ihrc@umn.edu
www.ihrc.umn.edu
[Archival and published resources documenting immigration and ethnicity on a national scope. Emphasis on groups originating in eastern, central, and southern Europe and the Near East.]

◆Leo Baeck Institute
German-Jewish Families
15 West 16th Street
New York, NY 10011
Tel. (212) 744-6400

Fax (212) 988-1305
lbaeck@lbi.cjh.org
www.lbi.org

◆Library of Congress
101 Independence Avenue SE
Washington, DC 20540

◆Los Angeles Library System
History and Genealogy Department
630 W. Fifth Street LL4
Los Angeles, CA 90071-2097
Tel. (213) 228-7400
Fax (213) 228-7409
history@lapl.org
www.lapl.org/central/history.html
[Holds all 203 volumes of the *Deutsches Geschlechterbuch;* about 10,000 family history titles, of which about 20 percent of which are not in the Library of Congress; 102 volumes of J. Siebmacher's *Grosses und Allgemeines Wappenbuch;* passenger arrival lists of ships docking in San Francisco, Boston, and Philadelphia, and records for New York ships between 1820 and 1846; many local histories; an excellent map and newspaper collection.]

◆Library of Michigan
Michigan Library and Historical Center
702 W. Kalamazoo Street
Lansing, MI 48916

◆National Society, Daughters of the American Revolution Library
1776 D Street, N.W.
Washington, DC 20006-5303

◆New York Public Library
U.S. History, Local History, and Genealogy Division
Fifth Avenue at 42nd Street
New York, NY 10018-2788
Tel. (212) 930-0849 & (212) 930-0829
Fax (212) 921-2546
histref@nypl.org
www.nypl.org/research/chss/lhg/genea.html

[One of the largest genealogical and local history collections open to the public in the country.]

◆Newberry Library
60 W. Walton Street
Chicago, IL 60610
Tel. (312) 943-9090
Reference: (312) 255-3506
Genealogy: (312) 255-3512
genealogy@newberry.org
www.newberry.org
[A very inclusive library. See *Guide to Local and Family History at the Newberry Library,* by Peggy Sinko, 1989].

◆Orlando Public Library
Genealogy Department
101 East Central Boulevard
Orlando, FL 32801-2471

◆St. Louis Public Library
1301 Olive Street
St. Louis, MO 63103
Tel. (314) 241-2288
Fax (314) 539-0393
webmaster@slpl.org
www.slpl.org

◆Seattle Public Library
Humanities Department
1000 4th Avenue
Seattle, WA 98104-1109
Tel. (206) 386-4636
www.spl.org

◆Sutro Library
[branch of the California State Library, Sacramento]
480 Winston Drive
San Francisco, CA 94132
Tel. (415) 731-4477
Fax: (415) 557-9325
sutro@library.ca.gov
www.onelibrary.com/Library/calslsut.htm
[This branch of the California State Library, holds the largest collection of

genealogical materials west of Salt Lake City, including more than 10,000 family histories. Special collections: Royal and noble genealogy; heraldry and vexillology; Crusades, knighthood, chivalry; historical maps; insignia, medials and decorations; medieval Europe; the Celts; archaeology and anthropology.]

◆**Wisconsin, State Historical Society of, Library**
816 State Street
Madison, WI 53706
Tel. (608) 264-6534
Fax (608) 264-6520
www.shsw.wisc.edu
[This library has probably the largest collection of German newspapers and the largest general newspaper collection except for the National Archives. It also holds all Wisconsin newspapers and many ethnic newspapers.]

◆**Western Reserve Historical Society Case Western Reserve University History Library**
10825 East Boulevard
Cleveland, OH 44106
Tel. (216) 721-5722
www.wrhs.org/sites/library.htm
[Major emphasis on northeastern Ohio and area of the United States east of the Mississippi]

LIBRARY OF CONGRESS

The Library of Congress
101 Independence Avenue SE
Washington, DC 20540
Tel. (202) 707-5000
Fax (202) 707-5844
Recorded information telephone numbers: Visitors' information: (202) 707-8000; Reading room hours: (202) 707-6400; Researchers: (202) 707) 6500
www.loc.gov
The buildings
Thomas Jefferson Building: 1st Street,

SE between East Capitol Street and Independence Avenue
James Madison Memorial Building: Independence Avenue between 1st and 2nd Streets, SE
John Adams Building: 2nd Street SE, between East Capitol Street and Independence Avenue
Local History and Genealogy Reading Room
Location: Thomas Jefferson Building ("LJ"), ground floor
Card catalogs for this reading room:
◆Family Name Index
◆Analyzed Surname Index
◆U.S. Biographical Index
◆Coats-of-arms Index
◆Subject Catalog
◆Local History Shelf List
◆Computer catalog (for books added to the collection since 1980)

For a comprehensive guide to the Library of Congress, for use by genealogists, see *The Center: A Guide to Genealogical Research in the National Capital Area*, by Christina K. Schaefer. Genealogical Publishing Company, Inc., Baltimore, 1996; this guide (FHL 975.3 A3sc) is the source of the information above.

U.S. LIBRARIES WITH GERMAN-AMERICAN HOLDINGS

Below are listed a few of the many United States libraries with collections offering information related to German family history research.

In brackets after most listings is a brief description of the collection or holding that gives the library its special interest to German family historians. Each holdings category shown in brackets below may be only one of several other special-interest topics for which the library is known.
◆**Weld Library District Lincoln Park Branch, Special Collections,** 919 7th

Street, Greeley, CO 80631. Tel. (970) 350-9215; www.mylibrary.us *[Germans from Russia: history, genealogy, personal reminiscences]*

• **University of Illinois, Illinois Historical Survey,** 346 Library, 1408 W. Gregory Drive, Urbana, IL 61801. Tel. (217) 333-1777; Fax (217) 333-2214; www.library.uiuc.edu/ihx *[German immigration]*

•**St. Louis Public Library, Rare Book & Special Collections Department,** Central Library, 1301 Olive Street, St. Louis, MO 63103-2389. Tel. (314) 241-2288; Fax (314) 539-0393; webmaster@slpl.org; www.slpl.lib.mo.us *[German-American Heritage Archives]*

•**Wagner College, Horrmann Library,** 631 Howard Avenue, Staten Island, NY 10301. Tel. (718) 390-3401; Fax (718) 390-3107; www.wagner.edu *[German-American Newspapers – 118 reels of microfilm]*

• **University of Cincinnati, German-Americana Collection,** Blegen Library, P.O. Box 210033, Cincinnati, OH 45221-0133. Tel. (513) 556-1515; Fax: (513) 556-6325; http://archives.uc.edu/german *[German-American literature, history, and culture]*

•**Ursinus College, Myrin Library,** Special Collections, Collegeville, PA 19426-1000. Tel. (610) 489-4111; Fax: (610) 489-0634; http://myrin.ursinus.edu *[Pennsylvania German culture, German Reformed Church]*

PUBLISHERS AND BOOKSELLERS

•**Adam Apple Press,**1249 Edge Hill Road, Box E, Bedminster, PA 18910. Tel. (215) 795-2149; Fax (215) 795-2694

• **AKB Publications,** 691 Weavertown Road, Myerstown, PA 17067-2642. Tel. (717) 866-2300

• **Ancestry, Inc.,** P.O. Box 476, Salt Lake City, UT 84110-0476. Tel. (800) 262-3787; info@ancestry.com; www.ancestry.com (also www.myfamily.com)

•**Tamara J. Bentz,** 9150-187 Gramercy Drive, San Diego, CA 92123-4001. Tel. (858) 278-2377

•**R.R. Bowker & Co.,**121 Chanlon Road New Providence, NJ 07974 .Tel. Sales: (800) 521-8110; Fax: (908) 464-3553; info@reedref.com

•**Edward R. Brandt,** 13 - 27th Avenue S.E., Minneapolis, MN 55414-3101. Tel. (612) 338-2001

•**Clearfield Company, Inc.,** 200 E. Eager Street, Baltimore, MD 21202-3761. Tel. (410) 625-9004

•**Deseret Book Direct,** 40 East South Temple, Salt Lake City 84111. Tel. (800) 453-4532; Fax (801) 517-3392; http://deseretbook.com

•**The Everton Publishers, Inc.,** 3223 S. Main Street, P.O. Box 368, Logan, UT 84323-0368. Tel. (800) 443-6325 or (801) 752-6022; Fax (801) 752-0425

•**Facts On File, Inc.,**11 Penn Plaza,New York, NY 10001. Tel. (800) 322-8755; (212) 967-8800

•**Family Line Publications,**Rear 63 E. Main Street, Westminster, MD 21157. Tel. (800) 876-6103

•**Family Tree Press,** 2912 Orchard Avenue N., Minneapolis, MN 55422. Tel. (612) 588-5824

• **Frontier Press,** 15 Quintana Drive, Suite 2, Galveston, TX 77554-9350. Tel. (800) 772-7559 (to order); Fax (409) 740-0138;kgfrontier@aol.com; www.doit.com/frontier

•**Gale Research Inc.,** The Gale Group, P.O. Box 9187, Farmington Hills, MI 48333-9187. Tel. (800) 877-4253 or (800) 877-GALE (customer service); Fax (800) 414-5043; galeord@gale.com; www.gale.com

•**Genealogical Publishing Co. Inc.,** 1001 N. Calvert Street, Baltimore, MD 21202-3897. Tel. (800) 296-6687; (410) 837-8271; Fax (410) 752-8492; orders@genealogical.com

•**Genealogical Sources Unlimited,** 407

Ascot Court, Knoxville, TN 37923-5807. Tel. (423) 690-7831

✦**Germanic Genealogy Society,** P.O. Box 16312, St. Paul, MN 55116-0312. Tel. (612) 777-6463

✦**Greenwood Publishing Group,** 88 Post Road West, P. O. Box 5007, Westport, CT 06881. Tel. (800) 225-5800; (203) 226-3571; Fax (203) 222-1502; bookinfo@greenwood.com

✦ **GRT Publications,** P.O. Box 1845, Provo, UT 84603-1845. Tel. (801) 374-2587; grtpublications@juno.com

✦**Hearthside Press,** 8405 Richmond Highway, Suite H, Alexandria, VA 22309-2425. Tel. (703) 360-6900

✦**Heritage Books, Inc.,** 1540-E Pointer Ridge Place, Bowie, MD 20716-1800. Tel. (800) 398-7709 or (301) 390-7708; fax (800) 276-1760;heritage books@usa.pipeline.com

✦**Heritage House,** P.O. Box 39128, Indianapolis, IN 46239. Tel. (317) 862-3330; (800) 419-0200; Fax (317) 862-2599

✦ **Heritage Quest Genealogical Services,** P.O. Box 329, Bountiful, UT 84011-0329. Tel. (800) 760-2455; Fax (801) 298-5468; sales@heritagequest.com; www.heritagequest.com

✦**John Kallmann, Publishers,** 701 West North Street, Carlisle, PA 17013. Tel. (717) 258-0919; Fax (717) 258-4161; Tel. (888) 411-3810 (orders)

✦**Links Genealogy Publications,** Iris Carter Jones, 7677 Abaline Way, Sacramento, CA 95823-4224. Tel. (916) 428-2245; ralphj@ix.netcom.com

✦**Lorelei Press,** P.O. Box 221356,Sacramento, CA 95822-8356. Fax (916) 421-8032; lorelei@softcom.net; www.softcom.net/users/lorelei/index.html

✦**Maia's Books & Misc.,** 5480 North Meadows Blvd., Columbus, OH 43229. Tel. (614) 838-1280; Martha@MaiasBooks.com; www.MaiasBooks.com

✦**Marietta Publishing Company,** 2115 North Denair Avenue, Turlock, CA 95382. Tel. (209) 634-9473

✦**Masthof Press***[formerly Olde Spring-field Shoppe],* Route 1, Box 20, Morgan-town, PA 19543-9701. Tel. (610) 286-0258; Fax (610) 286-6860; masthof@ptdprolog.net

✦**National Archives and Records Administration,** 601 Pennsylvania Ave. NW, Rm. G9 Washington, DC 20408. Tel. (202) 501-5212; (800) 234-8861 (orders); Fax (202) 501-7170; www.nara.gov

✦**Park Genealogical Books,** P.O. Box 130968, Roseville, MN 55113-0968. Tel. (612) 488-4416; Fax (612) 488-2653

✦**Picton Press,** P.O. Box 1111, Camden, ME 04843-1111. Tel. (203) 236-6565

✦**Roots International**, 3239 N. 58th Street, Milwaukee, WI 53216-3123. Tel. (414) 871-7421

✦**K.G. Saur,** Subsidiary of R.R. Bowker Co., 121 Chanlon Road, New Providence, NJ 07974-1541. Tel. (908) 665-3576; (800) 521-8110 (orders only); Fax (908) 771-7792

✦ **Scholarly Resources, Inc.,** 104 Greenhill Avenue, Wilmington, DE 19805-1897. Tel. (800) 772-8937 or (302) 654-7713; Fax (302) 654-3871

✦**Dr. George K. Schweitzer**: See Genealogical Sources Unlimited

✦**Jonathan Sheppard Books,** Box 2020, Plaza Station, Albany, NY 12220

✦ **Kenneth L. Smith,**523 S. Weyant Avenue,Columbus, OH 43213-2275

✦**Suhrkamp Publishers New York, In,** 175 Fifth Avenue, New York, NY 10010-7703. Tel. (212) 460-1653

✦**Ernest Thode (Thode Translations),** RR 7, Box 306 Kern Road , Marietta, OH 45750-9437. Tel. (614) 373-3728

✦**University of Utah Press,** University of Utah, 101 University Service Building, Salt Lake City, UT 84112. Tel. (800) 773-6672; (801) 581-6771; Fax (801) 581-3365; mkeele@media.utah.edu

✦**University Press of America, Inc.,** 4720 Boston Way. Lanham, MD 20706. Tel. (301) 459-3366; (800) 462-6420; Fax (301) 459-2118

◆Ye Olde Genealogie Shoppe, P.O. Box 39128, Indianapolis, IN 46239. Tel. (800) 419-0200; Fax (317) 862-2599; yogs@iquest.net

AMERICAN INVOLVEMENT IN WARS

Wars related to American colonization

1701-13: Queen Anne's War — between England and French/Indians. Britain gains control of French Acadia (modern Nova Scotia), Newfoundland, and the region around Hudson Bay.

1744-48: King George's War — between England and France, fought for control of North American colonial territories, but ending without significant territorial changes.

1754-63: French and Indian War — between England and France over colonial territories in North America, resulting in Great Britain's conquest of French Canada.

American national wars and engagements

1775-83: American Revolution — American forces against Great Britain allied with France and Spain (April 19, 1775 - April 11, 1783)

1791-94: Whiskey Rebellion — in Pennsylvania, near Uniontown; farmers protest whiskey tax

1812-14: ..... War of 1812 — between United States and Great Britain (June 1812 to December 1814)

1832: Black Hawk War — Indian tribes push west across the Mississippi (began April 26, ended September 21).

1835: Toledo War — Ohio-Michigan boundary dispute

1846-48: Mexican-American War — between United States and Mexico, resulting in United States' annexation of Mexican territory, comprising present United States southwest and California

1861-65: American Civil War — War

Between the States (began April 12, 1861, ended April 9, 1865)

1898: Spanish-American War — United States defeats Spanish colonial forces in Philippines and Cuba (began April 25, ended July 17).

1899-1901: Philippine-American War (United States involvement) — outgrowth of the Philippine War of Independ-ence (began February 4, 1899, ended March 23,1901)

1917-18: World War I (United States involvement) — United States enters the war April 6, 1917

1941-45: World War II (United States involvement) — United States enters the war December 8, 1941

1950-53: Korean War — United States intervention following North Korea's attack on South Korea (began June 30, 1950, ended July 27, 1953)

1964-73: Vietnam War (United States involvement) — American participation following the 1964 attack in the Gulf of Tonkin (began February 1965, ended January 1973)

Sources

◆Bruce Wetterau, *The New York Public Library Book of Chronologies*. Prentice Hall, NY 1990.

◆*The World Almanac and Book of Facts*. World Almanac, New York, 1993.

◆David Brownstone and Irene Franck, *Timelines of War: A Chronology of Warfare from 100,000 BC to the Present*. Little, Brown and Company, Boston 1994.

AMERICAN MILITARY RECORDS

Among the German immigrants who arrived in the mid- and later-nineteenth century waves of immigration were many who served in United States military units during those years and on into the early twentieth century. For this reason, it is worth searching military records, especially for the vital records and notations of places of origin that may reside there. The following information is excerpted from a publication of the National Archives and Records Administration concerning its military service records:

United States military service

Records relating to service in the United States Regular Army by officers, 1789-1917, and enlisted men, 1789-1912, during peace and war are in the National Archives Building.

Records relating to service of Regular Army enlisted men include registers of enlistments, muster rolls of regular units, and medical and other records. Registers of enlistments show for each man his name, age, place of birth, date and place of enlistment, occupation at enlistment, regiment and company, physical description, and date and reasons for discharge.

Pension files

Records of pensions granted or applied for under laws providing for military pensions are in the National Archives Building. The pension files relate to claims based on service in the Army, Navy, or Marine Corps between 1775 and 1916.

Documents submitted in support of some pension claims include affidavits attesting to service, pages from family bibles, and copies of records of birth, marriage, and death.

For service in the Civil War and later, a pension file may also include Bureau of Pensions questionnaires sent out in 1898 and 1915, which contain genealogical information.

Information in the Records

Pension application files usually show name, rank, and military unit of the veteran and period of his service. If a veteran applied, the file usually shows his age or date of birth and place of residence at the time he applied, and sometimes his place of death. If his widow applied, the file shows her age and place of residence, her maiden name, the date and place of their marriage, and the date and place of his birth. When application was made on behalf of minor children or by heirs of the veteran, their names and sometimes their ages or dates of birth are shown.

Bounty Land Warrant Application Files

Bounty land warrant application files relate to claims based on wartime service between 1775 and March 3, 1855. These as well as pension files are recorded at the National Archives.

Bounty land warrant application files usually show name, rank, and military unit of the veteran and period of his service.

If a veteran applied, the file usually shows his age or date of birth and place of residence at the time he applied, and sometimes his place of death. If his widow applied, the file shows her age and place of residence, her maiden name, the date and place of their marriage, and the date and place of his birth.

When application was made on behalf of minor children or by heirs of the veteran, their names and sometimes their ages or dates of birth are shown.

Availability of unrestricted records

Photocopies of unrestricted original documents are available for a fee. The National Archives and Records Administration will conduct a search for the documents if, in addition to the full name of the serviceman, the war in which he served, and the State from which he entered service, an inquirer can supply other identifying information.

Ordering unrestricted records from the National Archives

Requests for copies of veterans records housed in the National Archives Building should be submitted on National Archives Trust Fund (NATF) Forms 85 (pension and bounty land warrant applications) and 86 (service records for Army veterans discharged before 1912). To download these forms or to submit your document request online, visit http://archives.gov/contact/inquire-form.html.

The forms should be filled out according to the instructions and with as much information as possible. Forms submitted by mail should be addressed to the National Archives and Records Administration, 8th and Pennsylvania Avenue, NW, Washington, DC 20408.
Source: "Military Service Records in the National Archives of the United States," General Information Leaflet, No. 7, rev. 1985 (with an address correction supplied by NARA, July 1996), National Archives and Records Administration, Washington, DC 20408.

Internet Sources
www.footnote.com
www.ancestry.com

HESSIAN SOLDIERS IN THE AMERICAN REVOLUTION

Background: The number of German mercenary troops who remained in America after serving Great Britain in the American Revolution (1775-1783) is estimated at between 7,000 and 12,000 of the approximate 30,000 who were sent to North America. These Hessians comprised about 30 percent of the British forces.

"Hessian" troops in America: All German mercenaries who fought in the revolutionary war came to be referred to as "Hessians," probably because the largest contingent of troops — 15 infantry regiments, four grenadier battalions, one courier corps, one artillery corps, totaling about 15,000 men — was from Hessen-Kassel. Others came from such small kingdoms as Braun-schweig, Ansbach-Bayreuth, Hesse-Hanau, Anhalt-Zerbst, and Waldeck.

The majority of the German troops arrived in August 1776. Hessians were involved in battles between 1776 and 1783. Many of the surviving troops were returned to their homelands in 1783.

Availability of records: The microfilm titled *Hessische Truppen im amerikanischen Unabhängigkeitskrieg* (Hessian Troops in the American War for Independence) lists valuable information about individual German mercenaries. See FHL films 1,320,516 items 6-7 (A-L), and 1,320,542 items 5-6 (M-Z). (The acronym HETRINA is taken from the German name of the collection: *Hessische Truppen im [in dem] amerikanischen Unabhängig-keitskrieg*. Note: In German, *im = in dem*.)

Content of HETRINA microfilm: The following key is supplied with the HETRINA records, the information from which is arranged in 11 columns (the key for reading the data is shown below verbatim) —

Column 1: No. of unit in computer list
Column 2: Family name
Column 3: First name
Column 4: Yr. of birth (o/o=no statement of age)
Column 5: Place of origin (historical place names after slash; names in parentheses are aids to location)
Column 6: Code no. of towns with abbr. for the *Land* (+ = town in Hessen-Kassel)
Column 7: Rank (see list of abbreviations)
Column 8: Unit (regiment or battalion and company)
Column 9: Categories of presentation (see list)
Column 10: Date of entry in unit books (mo. and yr. in numbers)
Column 11: Archive code of the source

The researcher with a German ancestor born between 1735 and 1762 (approximately) may want to look into the possibility of descent from a Hessian soldier. The researcher working on an unusual German surname (not necessarily known to belong to a German mercenary), may want to look for that name in HETRINA. Because "place of origin" (see column 5 above) may have been the soldier's place of birth, it could be useful to search church records in the home village of a same-name Hessian soldier to see if the surname is prevalent there. Once in a while, a long-shot like this can pay off.

References

◆Eckhart G. Franz, compiler. *Hessische Truppen im amerikanischen Unabhängig-keitskrieg (HETRINA)*. [Hessian Troops in the American Revolution] Marburg, Germany: Archivschule. 1971-1976, 1987. 3 vols. FHL 943 M2mg; see film numbers above).
◆ Don Heinrich Tolzmann. *German-Americans in the American Revolution: Henry Melchior Muhlenberg Richards' History*. 1908. Reprinted by Heritage Books, Bowie, MD, 1992.
◆Clifford Neal Smith, *Cumulative Surname Index and Soundex to Monographs 1 through 12 of the German-American Genealogical Research Series*. McNeal, Ariz.: Westland Publishing, 1983. FHL 973 W2smn no. 13
◆ "Die Hessische Soldaten – The Hessian Soldiers," by William S. Cramer, *German American Genealogy*, Spring 1991, p. 23.

JOHANNES SCHWALM HISTORICAL ASSOCIATION

The Johannes Schwalm Historical Association researches, collects and disseminates data relating to German auxiliaries to the British Crown who fought in the Revolutionary War and their descendants.

All books and material owned by the Association are available for research and examination by the public at the Gratz Historical Society, Gratz, Pennsylvania, which is the official depository of the Association's records. JSHA issues a color certificate to authenticate a person's ties to Hessian forebearers.

Mailing address: Johannes Schwalm Historical Association, P.O. Box 127, Scotland, PA 17254-0127. halschwalm@prodigy.net; www.jsha.org.

AMERICAN MILITARY INDEX

The Military Index of the *FamilySearch* program of the Family History Library is available through *FamilySearch* at local Family History Centers and at the Family History Library in Salt Lake City. It contains death records of those who died in the Korean (1950-1957) and Vietnam (1957-1975) conflicts. Other military records are added to the program as they become available. See the publication, *FamilySearch: Military Index*, a one-page summary available through the Family History Library (Series FS, No. 2, 1991).

UNITED STATES DRAFT REGISTRATIONS (WORLD WAR I)

If a male ancestor (whether native born or alien) was born between 1873 and 1900, and lived in the United States in 1917 and 1918, his draft registration card may well be one of the 24 million collected by the Selective Service System during World War I. These draft registrations include German males who immigrated into the United States in the massive immigration of the 1880s.

These draft records identify about 44 percent of the entire U.S. male population in 1918 and contain information important to researchers of German immigrants and their descendants.

The records do not reveal whether the registrants actually served in the military (many were not called into service), but the records do provide important information relative to the man's birthplace, his citizen status, and much more.

Registration dates

There were three World War I registrations in 1917 and 1918:

First registration: June 5, 1917, for all men between the ages of 21 and 31.

Second registration: June 5, 1918, for those who turned 21 after 5 June 1917; a supplemental registration was held on August 24, 1918 for those turning age 21 after June 5, 1918.

Third registration: September 12, 1918, for men age 18 through 45.

Record content

The contents of the three registration questionnaires are summarized below. The numbers following each item identify which of the three registration forms (from the first, second, and third registrations, listed above) asked for a response to the item.

Name: 1,2,3
Address of home: 1,2,3
Age in years: 3
Birth date: 1,2,3
Birthplace (town, state, country): 1,2,3
Father's birthplace: 2
Exemption claimed: 1
Married or Single: 1
Military Service (rank, branch, years, nation): 1
Naturalized: 1,3
Native born: 1,2,3
Citizen by father's naturalization: 3
Alien: 1
Alien with declared intent: 1,3
Alien without declared intent: 3
Alien nationality: 1,2,3
Occupation: 1,3
Employer's name: 1,2,3
Place of business or employment: 1,2,3
Physical description: 1,2,3
Race: 1,2
Race (white, black, oriental, Indian citizen or non-white): 3
Relatives solely dependent (wife, sister, etc.): 1

Nearest relative's name: 2,3
Address of nearest relative: 2,3

National Archive records

Draft registration cards are part of Record Group 163 of the National Archives. Searches are made for a small fee as long as the full name and city and county of residence are known. For certain large cities, a home address is needed (city directories may be helpful here).

A complete home address is needed for these cities: Los Angeles, San Francisco, Washington (DC), Atlanta, Chicago, Indianapolis, Louisville (KY), New Orleans, Baltimore, Boston, Minneapolis, St. Paul, Kansas City, St. Louis, Jersey City, Newark, Albany, Buffalo, New York City, Syracuse, Cincinnati, Cleveland, Luzerne County (PA), Philadelphia, Pittsburgh, Providence, Seattle, and Milwaukee. To obtain a search form, write to: National Archives, Southeast Region, 5780 Jonesboro Road, Morrow, GA 30260. Tel. (770) 968-2100; Fax (770) 968-2547; atlanta.archives@nara.gov.

Family History Library records

The Family History Library Catalog (1995 editions) lists 3,680 microfilms for draft cards, arranged by states, from Alabama through Tennessee, and including Wisconsin. (Look for this list of states to expand.) Microfilm readers with a 65X lens are recommended for viewing these microfilms.

The film numbers may be found in the microfiche Locality catalog under United States — Military Records — World War I, 1914-1918. In the Author-Title microfiche catalog, the records are listed as United States, Selective Service System, World War I Selective Service System draft registration cards, 1917-1918.

The records are arranged alphabetically first by state; then alphabetically by county or city; then for each draft board by an alphabetical list of the names of registrants. An individual might not have registered where he resided, but instead where it was most convenient for him on the particular day of the draft registration.

Available on microfilm is *Lists of World War I Draft Board Maps* (FHL film 1498803) providing maps of certain U.S. cities: Albany, Allegheny (PA), Atlanta, Baltimore, Birmingham, Boston, Bridgeport (CT), Bronx, Brooklyn, Buffalo, Chicago, Cincinnati, Cleveland, Dallas, Denver, Hartford, Indianapolis, Jersey City, Kansas City, Los Angeles, Louisville (KY) Luzerne Co. (PA), Manhattan, Milwaukee, Minneapolis, New Haven, New Orleans, Philadelphia, Pittsburgh, Queens, Reading (PA), Richmond (NY), Rochester, St. Paul, San Diego, Schenectady, Seattle, Syracuse, Toledo, Washington (DC), and Westmoreland Co. (PA).

The Family History Library keeps a notebook with selective service addresses for major cities (not on microfilm or fiche). It lists the draft boards and their number and addresses for Allegheny (PA), Baltimore, Boston area, Buffalo, Chicago area, Cincinnati, Cleveland, Denver, Detroit, Indianapolis, Jersey City, Kansas City, Los Angeles, Luzerne Co. (PA), Milwaukee, Minneapolis, New Orleans, New York City, Newark, Philadelphia, Pittsburgh, Portland, Providence, St. Louis, St. Paul, San Francisco, and Seattle.

Ancestry.com

World War I Draft Registration cards have been digitized and are availbale at www.ancestry.com.

Source: "U.S. Selective Service System: Draft Registration Records, 1917-1918," by Jayare Roberts, A.G., *Genealogical Journal.* Utah Genealogical Association. Vol.24, No. 2. 1996.

GERMAN UNITS IN THE AMERICAN CIVIL WAR

German Units: Companies and regiments in the Union Army, American Civil War.

NEW YORK
- 5th New York Militia
- 7th New York Regiment, Steuben Rifles
- 8th New York Infantry, First German Rifles
- 20th New York Infantry, United Turner Regiment
- 29th New York Regiment, Astor Rifles
- 41st New York Regiment, DeKalb Regiment
- 45th New York Regiment, German Rifles No. 5 or Platt Deutsch Regiment
- 46th New York Regiment, Frémont Regiment
- 52nd New York Regiment, Sigel Rifles
- 54th New York Regiment, Schwarze Jäger
- 58th New York Regiment, First Morgan Rifles (part German)
- 68th New York Volunteers, Cameron Rifles (part German)
- 103rd New York Regiment, German Rifles No. 3 (one elite company composed entirely of former German officers)
- 119th New York Regiment (one-third German)
- 149th New York Regiment (part German)
- 190th New York Regiment (part German)

Artillery:
- Brickel's artillery, 1st New York Independent Battalion Light Artillery
- Battery Sigel in the 46th New York Regiment (composed of experienced Germans)
- 15th New York Heavy Artillery
- Schirmer's battery, 2nd Independent New York Battery
- Von Sturmfel's battery, Light Artillery Company A, later 13th Independent Battery
- Wiedrich's battery, 1st Regiment Light Artillery, Battery I

Cavalry:
- Dickel's mounted rifles, 4th Regiment Cavalry (largely German)
- 1st Regiment New York Cavalry (four companies German)

NEW ENGLAND

Infantry:
- 1st Regiment Connecticut Volunteer Infantry, Company B
- 6th Regiment Connecticut Volunteer Infantry, Company H (from Bridgeport, Meriden, and New York. There was also Company B from New Haven, Norwich, and Waterbury under Captain Klein.)
- 11th Connecticut Regiment, company under Captain Mögling
- 17th Massachusetts Regiment, one company recruited in Boston (one-third German)
- 29th Massachusetts Regiment, one company (one-third German)

PENNSYLVANIA
Infantry:
- 27th Pennsylvania Regiment
- 73rd Regiment, Pennsylvania Troops
- 74th Pennsylvania Regiment
- 75th Pennsylvania Regiment
- 98th Pennsylvania Regiment, originally the 21st Männerchor Rifle Guards (Home guards)

NEW JERSEY
Cavalry:
- 3rd New Jersey Cavalry, from Hoboken

Artillery:
- Battery A, 1st New Jersey Artillery
- Batteries B and C, 1st New Jersey Artillery (largely German)

OHIO
Infantry:
- 9th Ohio Regiment, Ohio Turners, 1st German regiment, from Cincinnati
- 28th Ohio Regiment, 2nd German regiment, from Cincinnati
- 37th Ohio Regiment, 3rd German regiment, from northern Ohio
- 47th Ohio Regiment (over one-half German)
- 58th Ohio Regiment (over one-half German)
- 74th Ohio Regiment (over one-half German)
- 106th and 6th Ohio Regiment, 4th German regiment
- 107th Ohio Regiment, 5th German regiment

- 108th Ohio Regiment, 6th German regiment
- 165th and 65th Ohio Regiment (over one-half German)

Cavalry:
- 3rd Ohio Cavalry (partly German)

Artillery:
- Dilger's battery, Battery I, 1st Light Artillery, originally Von Dammert's battery from Cincinnati
- Hofman's battery, 4th Ohio Battery, from Cincinnati
- Markgraf's battery, 8th Independent Battery, from Cincinnati (half German)
- 20th Ohio Independent Battery, from Cleveland (about half German)

INDIANA
Infantry:
- 14th Indiana Regiment (half German; Company E, wholly German)
- 24th Indiana Regiment (half German)
- 32nd Indiana Regiment
- 136th Indiana Regiment, from Evansville (half German)

Artillery:
- Behr's battery, 6th Independent Indiana Battery, from Indianapolis
- Klaus's battery, 1st Independent Indiana Battery, from Evansville

ILLINOIS
Infantry:
- 9th Illinois Regiment, a three months regiment (half German)
- 24th Illinois Regiment, Hecker's Jäger (largely but not wholly German)
- 27th Illinois Regiment (half German)
- 36th Illinois Regiment (half German)
- 43rd Illinois Regiment (second-generation Germans from Belleville)
- 44th Illinois Regiment (half German)
- 45th Illinois Regiment (half German)
- 45th Illinois Regiment (half German)
- 57th Illinois Regiment (half German)
- 58th Illinois Regiment (half German)
- 82nd Illinois Regiment, second Hecker regiment

Artillery:
- Battery E, 2nd Illinois Light Artillery (almost wholly German)

Cavalry:
•12th Illinois Cavalry, Company B
•13th Illinois Cavalry (half German)
Thielemann's battalion of dragoons,
Company A, 16th Illinois Cavalry
•Schambeck's independent cavalry
company, or Washington Light Cavalry;
later, Company B, 1st Regiment Dra-
goons; then Company C, 16th Illinois
Cavalry (half German)
Artillery:
•Gumbert's battery of artillery, Battery E,
•2nd Light Artillery (half German)
•D'Osband's battery of artillery (half
German)
•Stollemann's battery of artillery (half
German)
MISSOURI
Infantry:
•1st Missouri Volunteers including three
Turner companies of St. Louis and one
Irish company, after the three months
service, an artillery regiment (half
German)
•2nd Missouri Regiment (Germans and
German-Americans)
•3rd Missouri Regiment, Sigel's regiment
•4th Missouri Regiment, Black Jägers
(including a few native Americans and a
number of Bohemians)
•5th Missouri Regiment, from southern
portion of St. Louis and adjacent
counties
•7th Missouri Regiment, Company I
•12th Missouri Regiment, Osterhaus'
regiment until he became brigadier
general
•17th Missouri Regiment, Western
Turner Rifles, composed of Turners
drawn from a wide area
•18th Missouri Regiment, Company K
•39th Missouri Regiment (half German)
•40th Missouri Regiment (half German)
•41st Missouri Regiment (half German)
•Home guards, five regiments
Artillery:
•Backhoff's independent battalion light
artillery, Batteries B and C, 1st Missouri
Light Artillery

•Essig's   Landgräber's,   Mann's,
•Neustadter's, and Wölfe's batteries
•Essig's, Battery A, Franz Backhoff's
independent battalion light artillery, three
months service
•Neustädter's   Battery   C,   Franz
Backhoff's independent battalion light
artillery
•Mann's, Battery B, Franz Backhoff's
independent battalion light artillery, later
Battery C, First Missouri Regiment Light
Artillery
•Landgräber's,   Battery   F,   1st
Independent •Battery Flying Artillery,
later 2nd Regiment Missouri Light
Artillery
Pioneer Company, created by Sigel
Cavalry:
•1st Missouri Cavalry, Company A
•4th Missouri Cavalry, Frémont Hussars
(almost wholly German)
WISCONSIN
•5th Wisconsin Militia (overwhelmingly
German)
•6th Wisconsin Regiment, Company F
(more than half German)
•9th Wisconsin Regiment, called Salomon
Guards, in honor of the governor
•18th Wisconsin Regiment (more than
half German)
•20th Wisconsin Regiment (more than
half German)
•23rd Wisconsin Regiment (more than
half German)
•26th Wisconsin Regiment
•27th Wisconsin Regiment (more than
half German)
•34th Wisconsin Regiment (more than
half German)
•35th Wisconsin Regiment (more than
half German)
•45th Wisconsin Regiment (one-half
German)
Artillery:
•2nd Wisconsin Independent Battery
Light Artillery
•12th Wisconsin Battery, Platt Deutsch
Battery, from Sheboygan
IOWA

•16th Iowa Infantry, Companies B,G,K (half German)
•5th Iowa Cavalry, Company F (two-thirds German), from Dubuque and Burlington
(The 1st Iowa Regiment contained many Germans, but it was not, strictly speaking, a German unit.)

MARYLAND
•Color Company, Public Guard Regiment,
•5th Maryland Infantry
•Several companies organized just before Gettysburg

NEBRASKA
•1st Veteran Nebraska Cavalry (half German)

MINNESOTA
Infantry:
•1st Minnesota Regiment (more than one-third German; Company A almost one-half German)
•2nd, 4th, and 6th Minnesota Regiments (one-third German)
Artillery:
•Münch's battery of Pfänder's battery, 1st Independent Battery (a Turner unit)
Cavalry:
•Brackett's cavalry, 3rd Independent Battalion Cavalry

KANSAS
•1st Kansas Regiment (Company A about one-half German)
•2nd Kansas Regiment (about one-half German)

WEST VIRGINIA
•Dilger's Mountain Howitzer Battery, Company E, 1st Battalion Light Artillery

KENTUCKY
Infantry:
•5th Kentucky Regiment, from Louisville (half German)
•6th Kentucky Regiment, from Louisville, considered the best regiment of the state (half German)
Cavalry:
•Second Kentucky Cavalry (many Germans)
Artillery:
•Stone's Battery, Battery A, 1st Regiment

Light Artillery, independent (contained many Germans, though it was not, strictly speaking, a German unit.)

TEXAS
•1st United States Regiment (almost all of the 600 men were German)

Source: Ella Lonn, *Foreigners in the Union Army and Navy.* Greenwood Press, New York, 1951.

RESEARCHING CIVIL WAR DOCUMENTS

The Family History Library of the Church of Jesus Christ of Latter-day Saints in Salt Lake City issues a guide providing specific suggestions for researching Civil War documents:

Service Records

Civil War military service records may provide rank, dates of service, place of residence prior to enlistment, age, physical description, and date and place of discharge or death.

Union records: In order use the service records, the state of enlistment must be known, as there is no master index to the soldiers in the Union Army. See *Register of United States Federal Military Records: Civil War* (vols. 2 and 4). Available at the Family History Library are indexes for all states and the service records of Union Army regiments enlisted from southern states, but they show only the name, rank, and unit. To obtain copies of the service records, request NATF form 86 (service records for Army veterans discharged before 1912).

To download this form or to submit your document request online, visit http://archives.gov/contact/inquire-form.html. You may also request form 86 by writing to the National Archives & Records Administration, General Reference Branch (NNRG), 7th and Pennsylvania Avenue NW, Washington, DC 20408.

Confederate records: A general index to

the names of Confederate soldiers as well as indexes of soldiers in each state is available at the Family History Library. For additional information and library microfilm numbers, consult Register of United States Federal Military Records: Civil War (vol. 2, pp. 145-6 and vol. 4 supplemental).

Pension Records

Union records: Soldiers who met the proper criteria received pensions from the federal government.

Pension records may include information on a soldier's military service, family members, places of residence, and other genealogical information.

The Family History Library has three indexes to Union pensions, which have not been microfilmed. One of these indexes, *Organization Index to Pension Files of Veterans Who Served Between 1861 and 1900* (T289), may be accessed through the Family History Library Catalog under United States - Military Records - Pensions - Indexes. Use NATF Form 85 to obtain copies of a pension file.

Confederate records: Soldiers who fought in the Confederate Army did not receive pensions from the federal government.

Most of the southern states, however, paid pensions from state funds in order to compensate disabled veterans and widows. Pension files may include information on a soldier's military service, family members, places of residence, or other genealogical data. It is necessary to know the *state of residence* of a veteran after the war in order to locate his pension record.

The microfilm numbers and additional information on the records from most states are listed in *Register of United States Federal Military Records: Civil War* (vol. 2 and vol. 4 supplemental).

Union and Confederate published records

Many rosters of soldiers, lists of vet-

eran burials, and compilations of biographical data have been published. See the Family History Library research outline for the state from which the soldier served to determine what records may be searched.

Also worth checking is the Family History Library Catalog under [State]-Military Records - Civil War, 1861-1865.

For Confederate records, see *Confederate Veteran* magazine and its index. FHL 973 B2cv

OFFICIAL RECORDS ('OR'), AND OTHER RESOURCES FOR CIVIL WAR RESEARCH

A useful place to research an ancestor's regiment is this work:

A Compendium of the War of the Rebellion, by Frederick H. Dyer; 3 vols; reprint of original published in Des Moines, 1908. Vol. 1: FHL 973 M2df 1959; Vol 2: 973 M2df 1959; Vol. 3: FHL 973 M2df 1959

Volume 1 records the number and organization of the armies of the United States; volume 2 contains a chronological record of the campaigns, battles, engagements, actions, combats, sieges, skirmishes, etc. in the United States, 1861-1865; and volume 3 offers brief regimental histories – arranged by state, then type of unit (cavalry, artillery, infantry), then in numerical order by unit designation. Note: This *Compendium* refers only to Union organization.

Confederate regiments

For Confederate regiments, see

Compendium of the Confederate Armies, by Steward Sifakis, 10 vols. FHL 975 M2ss

Similarly arranged, it is composed of ten volumes (generally, a volume devoted to each state). The entries are arranged by state, type of unit (artillary, cavalry, infantry), then in numerical order by unit designation.

The 'OR'

Considered one of the best places for civil war research is,

The War of the Rebellion: A Compilation of the Official Records of the Union and Confederate Armies, by Frederick H. Dyer.

Over time, this work has been given the shortened title of "Official Records," or "OR."

Delving into this work can be an intimidating experience for the novice, as it consists of a general index, four series consisting of 70 volumes divided into 128 "Parts" (volumes), each "Part" containing its own specific index. Also, there is an atlas containing 1,006 maps and sketches to accompany the records. The OR's oversize atlas is considered the premier atlas of the Civil War.

Source, and for further information: "Official Records (OR) and Related Resources Researching Civil War Regiments," by Glenn V. Longacre, Archivist, NARA-Great Lakes Region, FGS Forum, Vol. 10, Number 4 (Winter 1998).

CONTRIBUTIONS OF GERMAN-AMERICANS BY STATES TO THE UNION ARMED FORCES IN THE CIVIL WAR 1861-1865

State	Number	Percent
New York	256,252	21%
Ohio	168,210	14%
Pennsylvania	138,244	11%
Illinois	130,804	11%
Wisconsin	123,879	10%
Missouri	88,487	7%
Indiana	66,705	5%
Maryland	43,884	4%
Michigan	38,787	3%
Iowa	38,555	3%
New Jersey	33,772	3%
Kentucky	27,227	2%
California	21,646	2%
Minnesota	18,400	1%
Massachusetts	9,961	**
Connecticut	8,525	**
Kansas	4,318	**
Territories	4,093	**
District of Columbia	3,254	**
Delaware	1,263	**
Oregon	1,078	**
Rhode Island	815	**
New Hampshire	412	**
Maine	384	**
Vermont	219	**
Total German-Americans	1,229,174	100%

**Less than 1% from a State (District, or Territory). Aggregate total of these 11 "States" is only 5%.

Source: Ella Lonn, *Foreigners in the Union Army and Navy.* Greenwood Press, NY, 1951.

CIVIL WAR SOLDIERS AND SAILORS SYSTEM

The Civil War Soldiers and Sailors System (CWSS), is a joint project of the National Park Service, the Civil War Trust, the Federation of Genealogical Societies, the Genealogical Society of Utah, and the National Archives.

The system includes a computerized database containing very basic facts about 6.3 million soldiers who served on both sides during the Civil War; a list of regiments in both the Union and Confederate Armies; identifications and descriptions of some of the major battles of the war; references that identify the sources of the information in the database; and suggestions for where to find additional information.

The facts about the soldiers come from millions of documents about Union and Confederate Civil War soldiers maintained by the National Archives and Records Administration. Additional information comes from historical works about soldiers, sailors, regiments, battles, as well as prisoner-of-war records and cemetery records.

In the words of Curt B. Witcher, a System coordinator representing the Federation of Genealogical Societies, "...the names of well over three million individuals who participated in the Civil War formed the nucleus of the largest, most integrated, and most widely accessible historical database ever created."

The project identifies 7,000 regiments and units formed during the war and provides the location of some of the soldiers buried in Civil War cemeteries managed by the Park Service.

The Names Index is limited to fewer than 10 pieces of information on each of the 6.3 million General Index Cards. The most important pieces of information are the name of the individual, rank in and out, and the name of the organizational unit (such as regiment and sometimes the company).

The home page of the Civil War Soldiers and Sailors system is found at www.itd.nps.gov/cwss/. To search for the records, one needs to know only the name of a soldier. The system identifies and allows access to information about the regiment to which the selected soldier served and battles in which that regiment fought.

If there is additional information available in the database, the researcher is told how to view it. The system also tells researchers how to request copies of the actual National Archives records for their selected soldier names.

Select records also include photographs of individual soldiers, and even original photos of battlefields.

HEADSTONES OF UNION CIVIL WAR VETERANS

The graves of 166,000 Union soldiers are recorded on National Archives and Records Administration (NARA) film

M1845, "Card Records of Headstones Provided for Deceased Union Civil War Veterans, ca. 1879-ca. 1903" (22 rolls).

An Act of Congress of February 3, 1879 required that the government should provide gravestones to soldiers buried in private cemeteries. Therefore, a card record of all headstones provided for Union Civil War soldiers was established.

These records consist of 3- by 4-inch cards arranged alphabetically by surname, then by first name. The cards include some or all of the following information about each soldier: rank, company, and regiment; place of burial, including the cemetery's name, and the community, county, and state in which it is located; grave number, if any; date of death; name of contractor who supplied the headstone; and the date of the contract under which the stone was provided.

Most of the burials occurred in private cemeteries, probably in the county of the soldier's last residence.

The soldiers for whom these gravestones were provided were Union Civil War soldiers who died between about 1861 and about 1903; however a few War of 1812 veterans and at least one Revolutionary War soldier are also included.

The gravestones were provided by the Federal Government between about 1879 and about 1903.

NARA film M1845 is available for public viewing at the National Archives Building, Washington, DC and at the 13 NARA regional records services facilities.

Roll breaks for the 22 rolls of M1845 film are as follows:

1. Aab-Barwis; 2. Baschensky-Brand; 3. Brandan-Carlisle; 4. Carlie-Coop; 5. Cooper-Dery; 6. DeSantos-Erxleben; 7. Esbin-Gardipe; 8. Gardner-Haisley; 9. Hake-Higgins; 10. Higgs-Jaynes; 11. Jeamrings-Knittle; 12. Knobbe-Lowyles; 13. Loy-McFurlow; 14. McGaffee-

Morford; 15. Morgan-Osom; 16. Ossinger-Pugh; 17. Pugsley-Rohrscheib; roll 18. Roice-Sheldon; 19. Sheley-Starkes; 20. Starkey-Truax; roll 21. Trubee-Wertz; 22. Westrooks-Zylerwiez.

NARA microfilms are available for sale as well. To order, call (800) 234-8861.

Source: "Headstones of Union Civil War Veterans," by Claire Prechtel-Kluskens, *The Record,* National Archives and Records Administration, Vol. 4, No. 4, March 1998.

GRAND ARMY OF THE REPUBLIC (GAR)

The major veterans' organizations [from the American Civil War] were the Grand Army of the Republic (for the Union) and the United Confederate Veterans. The records of these organizations survive only in collections in individual state archives and other manuscript repositories. No nationwide inventory of what has survived exists. For the GAR, no complete collection of even the printed annual proceedings of its state departments, a rich source of genealogically valuable death notices, are known to survive, although the GAR did not officially disband until 1955 (the Daughters of Union Veterans of the Civil War still exists). For the United Confederate Veterans, copies of their magazine, *Confederate Veteran,* survive and have been reprinted with an index.

Source: "From the Ashes of War: Some Little Known Black and White Civil War Organizations," by Robert S. Davis, Jr., Heritage Quest, #57, Man/June 1995.

ADDRESSES FOR CIVIL WAR VETERAN ORGANIZATIONS

✦**Grand Army of the Republic Museum and Library,** 4278 Griscom Street, Philadelphia, PA 19124-3954.

Tel. (215)-289-6484; garmuslib@verizon.net; www.garmuslib.org.
✦**Daughters of Union Veterans of the Civil War, 1861-65** (library and museum): 503 S. Walnut Street, Springfield, IL 62704-1932. Tel. (217) 544-0616; duvcw@sbcglobal.net; www.duvcw.org.
✦**Sons of Union Veterans of the Civil War** (has a grave registration committee that marks graves of Civil War veterans); P.O. Box 1865, Harrisburg, PA 17105; Tel. (717) 232-7000; www.suvcw.org; SUVCW may also be contacted at the Grand Army of the Republic Civil War Museum and Library (see above).
✦**Sons of Confederate Veterans,** International Headquarters, P.O. Box 59, Columbia, TN 38402. Tel. (800) 380-1896; Fax (931) 381-6712; www.scv.org.
✦**Ladies of the Grand Army of the Republic,** Tel. (330) 279-4393; JMCLGAR@aol.com; www.suvcw.org/LGAR/.

CIVIL WAR RECORDS

Institute of Civil War Research
7913 67th Drive
Middle Village, NY 11379
Tel./Fax (718) 894-3164
ICWRJOHN@aol.com
This organization researches the history of small units during the American Civil War, available on 7860 units, including the following:
✦Capsule histories of units
✦Official histories of Union and Confederate Army units
✦Naval histories, relating to Union and Confederate war ships
✦Union soldiers' records, including as available enlistment and discharge papers, brief physical description, times at which the soldier was present with a unit or detachment, hospital and casualty reports.

◆Union soldiers' pension files (sometimes containing marriage, birth and death certificates, photographs, and personal correspondence)

◆Confederate soldiers' records; although many were lost or destroyed, records exist for more than 2 million individuals.

◆Confederate state-pension records, as available

Contact the Institute for a fee schedule.

CIVIL WAR DRAFT RECORDS

Civil War draft records may hold a key to determining where an immigrant ancestor was born. Even if a direct ancestor is not found in these records, a brother or other relative may have registered for the draft and may appear in records giving his birthplace.

The first national draft in United States history was established by the Enrollment Act signed by President Abraham Lincoln on March 3, 1863. It was passed to supply men to fight for the Union after the number of volunteers continued to dwindle.

Under the draft act, all eligible males between the ages of 20 and 45, white citizens and aliens who had declared their intent to naturalize, were eligible for the draft. Males 20 to 35 were to be drafted first. Males ages 17 to 20 could serve with the consent of a parent or guardian.

The records of the draft include men born between 1818 and 1843 who served in the Army during the Civil War and those who did not. The draft applied only to men residing in states of the United States under Union control. The records are in the National Archives I in Washington, DC and National Archives II in College Park, Maryland. Some are available by mail and some by research on-site only.

There are five record groups housed

at the National Archives that can be used to find more details on ancestors living during this period of American history:
1. Consolidated Lists
2. Descriptive Rolls
3. Case Files on Drafted Aliens
4. Medical Record of Examinations
5. Statement of Substitutes

Note to German place-of-origin searchers

The Record Groups above numbered 1, 2, 4, and 5 record "Place of Birth" information. All five ask for place of residence and age. The Drafted Aliens files (number 3 above) ask for country of citizenship.

A guide to Civil War draft records

A book that describes fully and clearly how to access these records is,

Civil War Draft Records: An Index to the 38th Congressional Districts of 1863, by Nancy Justus Morebeck, 1997.

The book's index shows in what Congressional District each county in each state was located during the time of the 38th Congress. The index is necessary if one is to search in the National Archives for four of the five record types listed above.

Contained in this book are many examples reproduced from the original lists, form letters to use to request information from the files in the National Archives, and examples of replies from the National Archives.

As of the publication date of this book, there was no charge by the National Archives for mail requests for information from any of the record groups that are available by mail (some are not). The records are held in tightly bound volumes and have not yet been microfilmed. The Archives will provide a transcription of the record for free or a microfilmed copy for a minimum fee of $10.00. A mail request should include as much identifying information as possible, such as name, county of residence, age, marital status, and Congressional District.

Source: *Der Blumenbaum,* Sacramento German Genealogy Society, Vol. 16, No. 2 (1998).

MAJOR ETHNIC GROUPS IN THE UNION ARMED FORCES DURING THE CIVIL WAR, 1861-1865

Irish 1,526,541
German 1,229,174
English 414,582
British American 246,940
Scots... 101,409
Source: Ella Lonn, *Foreigners in the Union Army and Navy.* Greenwood Press, NY, 1951.

CIVIL WAR HISTORICAL RESEARCH, IMAGES

The United States Army Military History Institute maintains a collection of 1.2 million Civil War images. To search the collection's online index, go to www.usahec.org and select "Search AHEC Collections."

The institute also maintains a library, which includes unit histories and many materials relating to the Grand Army of the Republic (GAR). Indexes to these holdings are likewise accessible via the website.

Send inquiries relating to photographs or artifacts to: U.S. Army Military History Institute, 950 Soldiers Drive, Carlisle, PA 17013-5021. Tel. (717) 245-3949; carl_usamhi@conus.army.mil.

OTHER RESOURCES FOR CIVIL WAR RESEARCH

♦*Research Outline, U.S. Military Records,* published by the Family History Library, Salt Lake City, Utah, 2000, is an excellent guide to family history research relating to the Civil War (and other wars). This guide provides many reference sources, directions for locating service records and draft records, as well as information about census records, cemetery records, and veteran and lineage organization records — for Union and Confederate soldiers.

The outline is available at the Family History Library and at many Family History Centers. Copies are also hosted online. Go to www.familysearch.org, click on the "Research Helps" tab, select the letter "U" and scroll down to "U.S. Military Records Research Outline."

♦**National Archives in Washington, DC** The National Archives headquarters in Washington, DC holds all the original service records of Civil War soldiers. Requests for copies of service records should be submitted on National Archives Trust Fund (NATF) Form 86. To download this form or to submit a request online, visit http://archives.gov/contact/inquire-form.html.

Forms submitted by mail should be addressed to the National Archives and Records Administration, 8th and Pennsylvania Avenue, NW, Washington, DC 20408.

♦ **Published state adjutant generals' reports**
♦**Regimental histories**
♦**Confederate Descendants Society,** P.O. Box 233, Athens, AL 35611

Other sources

♦Henry Putney Beers. *A Guide to the Archives of the Government of the Confederate States of America,* Washing-ton, D.C.: National Archives and Records Service, 1968.

♦Nancy J. Carroll. "Unusual References to Confederate Military Service." *Ancestry Newsletter,* 8 (July-August 1990): 1-3.

♦Charles E. Dornsbusch. comp. *Military Bibliography of the Civil War.* New York: New York Public Library, 1961,

1967, 1972.

◆Bertram Hawthorne Groene, *Tracing Your Civil War Ancestor.* Winston-Salem, NC, John F. Blair, 1973.

◆ Manrial Phillips Joslyn. "Was Your Civil War Ancestor a Prisoner of War." *Ancestry Newsletter*, 11 (July-Aug 1993): 1-5.

◆Wilhelm Kaufmann, *The Germans in the American Civil* (with a Biographical Directory), Steven Rowan trans., Don Heinrich Tolzmann, ed., John Kallmann, Publishers, Carlisle, Pa., 1999.

◆Kenneth W. Munden and Henry Putney Beers. *A Guide to Federal Archives Relating to the Civil War,* Washington DC, National Archives and Records Service, 1962.

◆Michael P. Musick. "The Little Regiment. Civil War Units and Commands." *Prologue* 27 (Summer 1995): 151-171.

◆ James C. Neagles. *Confederate Research Sources: A Guide to Archive Collections*. Salt Lake City, UT: Ancestry, 1986.

◆ James C. Neagles. *U.S. Military Records: A Guide to Federal and State Sources*. Salt Lake City, UT: Ancestry, 1994.

◆Ken Nelson. "Civil War Sources for Genealogical Research." *Genealogical Journal* 15 (Winter 1986): 187-199; 17 (1988)/1989)89-9.

◆ *Official Records of the Union and Confederate Armies in the War of the Rebellion*, published from 1880 to 1900 by the U.S. War Department in 128 volumes.

◆George K. Schweitzer, *Civil War Genealogy,* Knoxville, Tenn., 1988.

THE TURNVEREIN IN GERMANY

In Germany today, the Turnverein serves its members as a framework for sports activities, both competitive and "just for fun." It also serves, however, as a social club. The "Vereinsheim" is virtually a guesthouse where members of all ages meet.

Organized competitive sports events are practically nil at German high schools, colleges, and universities – this is what the *Turn-* und *Sportvereine* do.

But the Turnverein has evolved through the years from a concept that began quite differently.

The 'Verein'

The word *"Verein"* is derived from *"sich vereinigen,"* (to unite). Today, a *Verein* is an association of people pursuing a common non-profit interest. Under German law, a *Verein* may become incorporated by registering with a court. This is shown by the abbreviated appendix of "e.V.," for *"eingetragener Verein"* (registered Verein), as in "Turnverein 1848 Schwabach e.V.," for example.

The right for Germans to found a *Verein* is guaranteed by the *Grundgesetz* (the constitution) in Article 9. The way a *Verein* may operate is regulated by 58 paragraphs (out of 2,385) in Germany's Civil Code (*Bürgerliches Gesetzbuch*).

After registration, a *Verein* becomes a legal entity which can perform legal business and transactions in its own name independently from the individual members.

Laws regulating the *Verein* system began appearing around 1867.

Historical background

The idea of the Verein developed around the turn of the eighteenth to nineteenth century as a way for people to emancipate themselves from their status as "subjects" of autocratic aristocratic (or sometimes clerical) rule.

Democratic ideas just started appearing in Germany at that time, when they were already well established in the United States.

To get listened to, individuals had to unite. That of course was not allowed because rulers realized that the emergence of political groups would mean the emergence of political power other than their own and would therefore become a threat to absolutism. Political parties were unknown then, since there was nothing to vote on.

Although people didn't have any political rights other than those the ruler chose to grant them, most rulers were far from being tyrants. This is shown by their being called *"Landesvater"* or *"Landesmutter."* The rulers referred to their subjects as *"meine Landeskinder"* for whom they had to care. And mostly they did, or at least they tried to. This, of course, was helped by the fact that a "Germany" didn't exist, but rather consisted of a Milky Way of more or less sovereign states, few of which exceeded county-size. Even for a stagecoach, it was easy to cross several borders (including customs) on a single day in some areas.

So, while this kind of patriarchal rule had a mostly benevolent intent, it also created a stifling atmosphere for social and political life. There was no room to express new ideas or individualistic notions. Every aspect of life was ruled by decrees, religion or convention.

Friedrich Jahn, along with several others, rediscovered some sports activities with a long history – like running, discus-throwing, and javelin-throwing – and added new ones to them, like the parallel bars and the horizontal bar. He also invented the word *"Turnen"* for these activities which he formed into a comprehensive system of physical exercises both for education in school and for the population in general.

'Frisch, Fromm, Fröhlich, Frei'

Jahn's theory was that a lively mind depended upon a physically fit body *(Frischer Körper – frischer Geist)*. The kind of person he wanted to help create was described in the motto, *Frisch, Fromm, Fröhlich, Frei* ("Lively, Pious, Merry, Free").

Jahn opened his first "Turnplatz" (ath-letic grounds) outside Berlin at Hasenheide ("rabbit's heath") in 1811 and published an important book, *Deutsche Turnkunst* (the German Art of Gymnastics) in 1816. For all this he became known as "Turnvater Jahn."

The second important idea the followers of the *Turnen* movement pursued was that of national unity, which was meant to break up the feudal mini-states and to bring more freedom to the population. The idea was natural and even overdue at that time, considering what was going on in England, France, Spain and Austria.

On the other hand, this basically sound idea was exaggerated and even perverted, especially by Friedrich Jahn and his *Turnen* movement. Jahn is accused by historians of laying the groundwork for an ugly nationalism whose outward aggressiveness did not stay purely rhetorical later on.

Soon, the Turner movement worked closely together with student fraternities *(Burschenschaften)* which shared the goals of liberalization and national unity. Both groups, therefore, were fiercely opposed by the reactionary rulers.

Thus it was quite logical that members of both groups also supported the 1813-1815 *Befreiungskriege* ("wars of liberation") of European states and peoples against Napoleon, which ended with his defeat at Waterloo. Many students and Turners died in this war.

Crisis for the Turner movement

After a student who happened to be a member of a *Turnverein* murdered August von Kotzebue, the publisher of a reactionary political magazine, all *Turnverein* activities were banned from 1820 until 1842. However, such activities were continued underground in many places. Jahn was arrested and held in custody for five years.

In 1842, this ban was lifted and the *Turnverein* movement started on a large scale both in schools and in the *Verein*.

In 1848, most of the *Turnvereinie* supported the *Nationalversammlung (National Assembly)* in Frankfurt, which tried to find a way to German political unity and to write a constitution. When the assembly failed, many *Turnvereine* joined in the subsequent unrest and uprisings.

However, soon after that, by the middle of the nineteenth century, the *Turnverein* movement itself had become discredited in liberal circles by its nationalistic behavior.

By this time, modern competitive athletics and sports as we know them today had developed in England and spread to the Continent and throughout the world. They held much greater appeal for young people than the original *Turnen*.

On the other hand, this modern sports movement, by its international character and outlook and by allowing colorful dress and even shorts, was regarded with horror by the traditionalists. This was when the more modern "*Sportverein*" movement separated from the more conservative *Turnverein* movement. The *Sportverein* idea thrived, while the old *Turnverein* idea remained more or less stagnant.

To study the history of the *Turnverein* in America is to realize that the particular Germans who founded them emigrated because they had better chances there to realize the positive ideas which the German *Turnvereine* stood for. And certainly it was the negative aspects that were among the reasons these Germans left Germany.

Germany today

In Germany today, practically all organized sports activities take place within a *Sportverein*. Even professional soccer teams are run as departments within a *Sportverein*.

The sheer numbers of *Sportverein* members in Germany show the important role the *Sportverein* plays in Germany's social life. Even activities like playing chess, white-water canoeing, bowling, driving horse-drawn buggies on a slalom course, or show-dancing are conducted mostly within a *Sportverein*. Cardplayers have their *Vereine* too, but much to their regret, their attempts to join the *Sportsvereine* system have not been successful.

These numbers also prove the saying that whenever more than two Germans meet, they immediately form some kind of *Verein*. This tendency is described by the word *Vereinsmeierei* (clubbiness).

While the *Turnvereine* may be a little more tradition-minded and generally cater to more conservative interests than other *Sportvereine*, they are no longer fundamentally different. Like any other *Sportverein*, they are both service-organizations for activities of their members and centers of social life.

The best evidence of this is that, while in the nineteenth century a *Turnverein* would have loudly protested at having their activities called *Sport* (a word of English! origin), today Sport is accepted as the general term, with *Turnen* as one of its branches, no longer separated by idealogical beliefs.

Source: Excerpted from "Frisch, Fromm, Fröhlich, Frei," by Rainer Thumshirn, *Der Blumenbaum,* Vol. 11, No. 2, 1993.

TURNERS IN AMERICA

By the time of the failure of their 1848 revolution, Germans, including many Turners, were entering the United States in droves. It was natural, then, for them to want to start up their own *Turnvereine* in this country.

The earliest American Turnvereine included those founded in Cincinnati in 1848, in San Francisco in 1852, in Milwaukee in 1853, and in Sacramento in

1854. At the peak of the movement in America, there were about 300 Turnvereine.

Many fresh immigrants joined these clubs. The *Turnverein* was for them "a home away from home," where German was spoken. The rich social life offered opportunities for camaraderie and freedom from loneliness in a new land. The athletic program was challenging.

During the American Civil War, Turner organizations raised military units and were among the first to volunteer for military service. They earned recognition for their discipline and courage. Many became war casualties.

Turnvereine were founded in many cities and communities with heavy German immigrant populations.

The membership records and other extant documents produced by the these Turnvereine in America were inventoried and published in 1996. (See below)

RECORDS OF TURNVEREINE IN AMERICA

The Turner organizations listed below are those for which records have been located and identified. Following the name of each organization is its founding date.

Addresses of current Turner organizations begin on page 243.

ALABAMA
Birmingham: Deutscher Turnverein, 1887
Mobile: Mobile Turnverein, 1851

CALIFORNIA
Los Angeles: Los Angeles Turners, 1870-71 as Los Angeles Turnverein
Oakland: Oakland Turnverein, 1867
Sacramento: Sacramento Turn Verein, 1854
San Diego: San Diego Turners, 1884 as *Eintracht Turnverein*

San Francisco: San Francisco Gymnastic Club, 1852 as San Francisco Turnverein
San Jose: San Jose Turnverein, 1868

COLORADO
Boulder: Boulder Turnverein [date of organization unknown]
Denver: Denver Turnverein, Inc., 1865 as East Denver Turnverein

CONNECTICUT
Hartford: Hartford Turnerbund, 1878
Meriden: Meriden Turner Society, Inc., 1866 as Meriden Turnverein
New Britain: Socialer Turnverein, 1853 as *Sozialer Turn Verein*
New Haven: New Haven Turnverein, 1852
Rockville: Rockville Turnverein, 1857
Waterbury: *Turnverein Vorwärts*, 1893

DELAWARE
Wilmington: Wilmington Turners, 1859 as *Social Demokratischer Turnverein*

ILLINOIS
Alton: Alton Turnverein, 1864
Aurora: Aurora Turnverein, 1857; *Turnverein Frisch Auf*, 1907
Belleville: Belleville Turners, 1855 as Belleville *Turngemeinde*
Bloomington: Bloomington Turnverein, 1858
Chicago: [See *The Research Guide to the Turner Movement in the United States'* summary of the movement in Chicago]
Chicago: American Turners Northwest Chicago, 1956 (consolidation of the Social Turners, Forward (*Vorwärts*) Turners, and Swiss Turners
Chicago: Aurora Turnverein, 1864
Chicago: Chicago Turners, 1852 as Chicago Turn Verein
Chicago: Turn Verein Lincoln, Inc., 1885 as Lincoln Turn-Verein
Chicago: Turn Verein Eiche, 1890 — merger of Pullman-Kensington *Turngemeinde* (1887), *Turnverein*

Eintracht (1885), and Pullman *Männerchor* (1884)
Chicago: Swiss Turners of Chicago, 1882
Chicago: Social Turners, 1886 as *Sozialer Turnverein*
Chicago: Turnverein *Vorwärts*, 1867
Columbia: Columbia Gymnastic Association, 1866 as Columbia Turnverein
Elgin: Elgin Turners, 1883 as Elgin Turnverein
Highland: Highland Gymnastic Association, 1853 as Turnverein Highland
Moline: Moline Turners, 1866 as Moline Turnverein
Mt. Olive: Mt. Olive Gymnastic Society, 1897 as Mt. Olive Turnverein
Peoria: Peoria Turnverein, 1851
Smithton: Smithton Turnverein, 1867 as Georgetown Turnverein

INDIANA
Evansville: Central Turners, 1869 as *Turnverein Vorwärts*
Fort Wayne: Fort Wayne Turners, 1897 as *Turnverein Vorwärts*
Indianapolis: Athenaeum Turners, 1851 as Indianapolis *Turngemeinde*
Indianapolis: South Side Turners, 1893 as *Südseite Turnverein*
South Bend: American Turners South Bend, 1861 as South Bend Turnverein
Tell City: Tell City *Socialer Turnverein*, 1859

IOWA
Clinton: Clinton Turners, Inc., 1883 as *Turnverein Vorwärts*
Davenport: Central Turners, 1852 as *Socialistischer Turnverein*
Davenport: Northwest Davenport Turner Society, 1871
Davenport: East Davenport Turners, 1891 as *Ost Davenport Turnverein*
Garnaville: Garnaville *Sozialer Turnverein*, 1869
Holstein: Holstein Turnverein, 1884
Keystone: Keystone Turners, Inc., 1892

as Keystone Turnverein
Muscatine: Muscatine *Turnverein Vorwärts*, 1907
Postville: Postville Turnverein, 1873
KANSAS
Atchison: Atchison Turnverein, 1859
Leavenworth: Leavenworth Turnverein, 1857
Seneca: Seneca Turnverein, 1897
Topeka: Topeka Turnverein, 1867

KENTUCKY
Covington: Covington Turner Society, 1855 as Covington *Turngemeinde*
Louisville: American Turners Louisville, 1848-1850, as Louisville *Turngemeinde*
Newport: Newport Gymnastic Association, 1852 as Newport Turnverein

LOUISIANA
New Orleans: New Orleans Turnverein, 1851

MARYLAND
Baltimore: American Turners Baltimore, Inc., 1849 as *Social Democratischer Turnverein*
Baltimore: Baltimore *Turnverein Vorwärts*, 1867

MASSACHUSETTS
Adams: Adams Turners, Inc., 1889 as Adams Turn Club [in same year changed name to Adams *Turn Verein Vorwärts*]
Boston: Boston Turnverein, 1849
Clinton: Clinton Turn Verein, 1867 as *Turnverein Frohsinn*
Fitchburg: Fitchburg Turners, Inc., 1886 as Fitchburg Turnverein
Holyoke: Holyoke Turn Verein, 1871
Holyoke: Springdale Turners, Inc., 1886 as Springdale *Vorwärts Turn Verein*
Lawrence: Lawrence Turn Verein, 1866
Malden: Malden Turn Verein, 1889
Springfield: Springfield Turnverein, Inc., 1855
Westfield: Westfield Turnverein, 1897
Worcester: Worcester *Socialer Turnverein*, 1859

MICHIGAN

Detroit: American Turners Detroit, 1852 as Detroit *Socialer Turnverein*
Saginaw: Germania Turnverein, 1856 as Saginaw Turnverein

MINNESOTA

Minneapolis: St. Anthony Turnverein, 1857
Minneapolis: West-Minneapolis Turnverein, 1866
New Ulm: *Ansiedlungsverein des Socialistischen Turnerbundes*, 1856
New Ulm: New Ulm Turnverein, 1856
St. Paul: St. Paul Turners, Inc., 1858 as St. Paul Turnverein
St. Paul: West Side Turnverein, 1888

MISSOURI

Boonville: Boonville *Turn und Gesang Verein*, about 1852 as Boonville Turnverein
Brunswick: Brunswick Turn Verein, 1866 or 1867
Kansas City: Kansas City Turners, 1858 as Kansas City *Sozialer Turnverein*
Lexington: Lexington Turner Society, 1859 as Lexington Turnverein
St. Louis: [See the summary of the Turner movement in St. Louis which introduces the section on St. Louis in *Research Guide to the Turner Movement in the United States*.]
St. Louis: St. Louis Turnverein, 1850 [other societies formed after the Civil War]
St. Louis: Carondelet *Germania Turnverein*, 1875 as Carondelet Turnverein [closed 1887, reopened 1890 as Carondelet Germania Turnverein]
St. Louis: Concordia Gymnastic Society, 1874 or 1875 as St. Louis Concordia Turnverein
St. Louis: North St. Louis Gymnastic Society, 1868 as North St. Louis *Turnschule* and *Kindergarten*
St. Louis: Schiller Turners, Inc., 1906

St. Louis: St. Louis Turnverein, 1850
St. Louis: South St. Louis Turnverein, 1864 as *Süd St. Louis Turnverein*
St. Louis: South West Gymnastic Society, 1893 as *Süd-West St. Louis Turnverein*
St. Louis: Tower Grove Gymnastic Society, 1906
St. Louis: West St. Louis Turnverein, 1879 [which was founded earlier as the Schiller Club]
Washington: Washington Turnverein, 1859 [disbanded during Civil War, reorganized 1865]

NEBRASKA

Omaha: South Side Turners, 1892 as *Süd Seite Turnverein*

NEW HAMPSHIRE

Manchester: Manchester Turnverein, 1870

NEW JERSEY

Carlstadt: Carlstadt Turnverein, 1857 as *Sozialer Turnverein von Carlstadt*
Elizabeth: Elizabeth *Turnverein Vorwärts,* 1872 [as successor to Turner society active prior to the Civil War]
Hoboken: Hoboken Turnverein, 1857 as Hoboken *Turngemeinde*
Jersey City: Hudson City Turnverein, 1863
New Brunswick: New Brunswick Turnverein, 1867
Newark: Newark Turnverein, 1878
North Bergen: Union Hill Turners, 1872 as Union Hill Turn Verein
Passaic: Passaic Turners, Inc., 1892
Paterson: Riverside Athletic and Singing Club, 1867 as *Socialer Turnverein*
Plainfield: Plainfield *Gesang und Turnverein*, Inc., 1886
Riverside: Riverside Turners (Turnverein Progress), 1860 as Turnverein Progress
Riverside: Riverside Turners Inc., 1897 as Riverside *Turngemeinde*
Trenton: Trenton *Turnerbund,* 1924

NEW YORK

Buffalo: Buffalo Turn Verein, Inc., 1853 as Buffalo Turn Verein

Newburgh: Newburgh Turnverein, 1863

New York City: [Turner activities began in the city in the early 1840s; in 1848 the New York *Turngemeinde* was formed. See *The Research Guide to the Turner Movement in the United States'* summary of the Turner movement in New York City, which introduces the New York City section.]

New York (Bronx): American Turners, Bronx, Inc., 1881 as *Deutsch-Amerikanischer Turnverein*

New York (Brooklyn): American Turners of Brooklyn, Inc., 1883 as *Turnverein Vorwärts*

New York: American Turners New York, Inc., 1850 as *Sozialistischer Turnverein*

New York (Bloomingdale): Bloomingdale Turnverein, 1850s

New York (Brooklyn): Brooklyn Eastern District Turnverein, 1853 as Williamsburgh Turnverein

New York: Central Turnverein of the City of New York, 1886

New York (Long Island): Long Island Turners, Inc., 1875 as Long Island City Turnverein

New York: Mt. Vernon Turners, Inc., 1891 as Mt. Vernon Turnverein

Rochester: Rochester Turners, Inc., 1852 as *Socialer Turnverein*

Schenectady: Schenectady Turners, Inc., 1891

Syracuse: Syracuse Turners, Inc., 1854 as *Socialer Turn Verein*

Troy: Troy Turnverein, 1852

Utica: Utica Turnverein, 1854

OHIO

Akron: Akron Turner Club, 1885 as Akron Turnverein

Cincinnati: Cincinnati Central Turners Inc., 1848 as Cincinnati *Turngemeinde*

Cincinnati: North Cincinnati Gymnasium, 1881 as *Nord Cincinnati Turnverein*

Cleveland: Cleveland East Side Turners, 1849 as Cleveland Turnverein

Cleveland: Germania Turnverein [covered in history of the Cleveland East Side Turners]

Cleveland: Swiss Gymnastic Society of Cleveland, 1891 as *Schweizer Turnverein*

Cleveland: American Turners S.T.V. Cleveland, 1867 as *Socialer Turnverein*

Cleveland: *Turnverein Vorwärts* [covered in the history of the Cleveland East Side Turners]

Dayton: Dayton Liederkranz Turners, 1853 as Dayton *Turngemeinde*

Toledo: American Turners Toledo, 1926 [in 1930s known as the *Toledo Turn und Sport Verein* and the German-American Athletic Club]

Toledo: Toledo Turnverein, active in late 1850s, reorganized 1866

Toledo: Toledo *Turnverein Vorwärts*, 1880s

OREGON

Portland: Portland *Socialer Turnverein*, 1858 as Portland Turnverein

PENNSYLVANIA

Ambridge: *Harmonie Männerchor, Gesang und Turn Verein*, 1904

Beaver Falls: Beaver Falls Turners, 1871 as Beaver Falls Turnverein

Charleroi: Charleroi Turn Verein, 1905

Erie: East Erie Turners, 1874 as Erie Turn Verein

Homestead: Eintracht Music and Turn Hall Association, 1886 as *Turn und Gesang-Verein Eintracht von Homestead*

Johnstown: Johnstown Turners, 1866 as Johnstown Turnverein

McKeesport: McKeesport Turners, 1880 [merged with Harmony Singing Society to form the *McKeesport Turn und Gesang Verein*]

Monaca: Monaca Turn Verein, 1883

Monessen: Monessen Turn Verein, 1905

Monongahela: Monongahela Turners, 1889 as *Eintracht Gesangverein*

Philadelphia: [See *The Research Guide to the Turner Movement in the United States'* summary of the Turner movement in Philadelphia, which introduces the Philadelphia section.]

Philadelphia: Philadelphia Turners, 1849 as Philadelphia *Turngemeinde*

Philadelphia: Roxborough Turners, 1873 as *Unabhängige Turner von Roxborough* [offshoot of *Turnverein von Manayunk*, founded 1854]

Philadelphia: West Philadelphia *Turn-und Schul-Verein*, 1904

Rochester: Central Turn Verein Rochester, 1851 as *Socialer Turnverein*

RHODE ISLAND

Providence: Providence Turnverein, 1852 as Providence Turnverein

Providence: Providence Turners, 1896 as *Turnverein Vorwärts*

TENNESSEE

Chattanooga: American Turners of Chattanooga, 1866 as Chattanooga Turnverein

TEXAS

[See *The Research Guide to the Turner Movement in the United States'* summary of the Turner movement in Texas, which introduces the Texas section.]

Belleville: Piney Concordia Turnverein, about 1870

Fredericksburg: *Fredericksburg Sozialer Turnverein*, 1871

New Braunsfeld: New Braunsfeld Turnverein, 1853

WEST VIRGINIA

Morgantown: Turnverein Concordia, 1897

WISCONSIN

Farmington: Farmington Turner Society, 1862 as Farmington Turn Verein

Fond Du Lac: Fond Du Lac Turnverein, 1855 as *Sozialer Turnverein von Fond du Lac*

La Crosse: La Crosse Turnverein, 1865 as La Crosse Turnverein

Madison: Madison Turners, 1855 as Madison Turnverein

Milwaukee [See *The Research Guide to the Turner Movement in the United States'* summary of the Turner movement in Milwaukee, which introduces the Milwau-kee section.]

Milwaukee: *Turnverein Bahn Frei*, 1890 as off-shoot of the North Side Turnverein

Milwaukee: Milwaukee Turner Foundation, 1853 as *Socialer Turn Verein*

Milwaukee: *Turnverein der Nordseite*, 1869 as West Hill Turning Society, changed name to *Turnverein der Nordseite* by 1870

Sheboygan: Sheboygan Turners, Inc., 1854 as *Socialer Turnverein*

Note: The entry for each organization listed in Chapter 3 of this book includes a brief historical sketch, listings of its archival collections and publications, and the location of its records. The book lists repository codes for use in locating historical records available for each society. In addition, an appendix attempts to identify all past and present Turner societies which have been active in the United States. The compilers do not, however, claim the list, which includes more than 700 Turner organizations, to be definitive.

Source: Eric L. Pumroy and Katja Rampelmann [comp.], *Research Guide to the Turner Movement in the United States,* [comp]. Greenwood Press, Westport, Conn., 1996.

TURNER ADDRESSES

National organization

National Council of the American Turners, 1127 E. Kentucky Street, P.O. Box 4216, Louisville, KY 40204. Tel. (502) 636-2395

Repository for the American

Turners' archives

Ruth Lilly Special Collections and Archives, IUPUI University Library, 755 W. Michigan Street, Indianapolis, IN 46202. Tel. (317) 274-0464

LOCAL TURNER ORGANIZATIONS
* = independent society
(not belonging to the National Council of the American Turners)

California
•Los Angeles Turners, 8946 Sepulveda Eastway, Los Angeles, CA 90045-4812. www.laturners.com
•*Sacramento Turn Verein, 3349 J Street, Sacramento, CA 95816. www.sacramentoturnverein.com

Colorado
•Denver Turnverein, Inc., 1570 Clarkson Street, Denver, CO 80030

Connecticut
•*Meriden Turner Society, Inc., 800 Old Colony Road, Meriden, CT 06450

Delaware
•Wilmington Turners, 701 S. Claymont Street, Wilmington, DE 19805. (302) 658-9011

Illinois
•Aurora Turner Club, 1335 Mitchell Road, Aurora, IL 60505. (630) 859-2267
•American Turners Northwest Chicago, 3825 Willow Street, Schiller Park, IL 60176-2353. (847) 671-1300
•Turn Verein Lincoln, Inc. 1019 W. Diversey Parkway, Chicago, IL 60614
•*Columbia Gymnastic Association, 211 E. Cherry Street, Columbia, IL 62236. (618) 281-5393
•Elgin Turners, 112 Villa Street, Elgin, IL 60120. (847) 697-4431
•Central Turners of Rockford: Contact American Turners National Office for current address.
•*Smithton Turner Hall, 15 North Julia Street, Smithton, IL 62285-1621. (618) 277-9690
•Turn Verein Eiche, 16767 S. 80th Avenue, Tinley Park, IL 60477-2361

Indiana

•Fort Wayne Turners, 3636 Parnell Avenue, Fort Wayne, IN 46895. (260) 471-8876
•South Side Turners, 3702, Raymond Street, Indianapolis, IN 46203
•Athenaeum Turners, 401 E. Michigan Street, Indianapolis, IN 46204. (317) 630-4569
•American Turners South Bend, 53666 N. Ironwood Road, South Bend, IN 46635-1532

Iowa
•Northwest Davenport Turner Society, 1602 Washington Street, Davenport, IA 52804-3614
•Keystone, Turners, 91 2nd Avenue, Keystone, IA 52249

Kentucky
•Covington Turner Society, 447 Pike Street, Covington, KY 41011
•River City Turners, 8009 Terry Road, Louisville, KY 40258
•American Turners Louisville, 3125 Upper River Road, Louisville, KY 40207

Maryland
•American Turners Baltimore, 9124 Lennings Lane, Baltimore, MD 21237-4367

Massachusetts
•Adams Turners, Inc., 6 Turners Avenue, Adams, MA 01220
•Clinton Turnverein, 60 Branch Street, Clinton, MA 01510-2732
•Springfield Turnverein, 176 Garden Street, Feeding Hills, MA 01030
•Holyoke Turn Verein, 624 S. Bridge Street, Holyoke, MA 01040-5538

Michigan
•American Turners Detroit, 26214 Virginia, Warren, MI 48091

Minnesota
•St. Paul Turners, Inc., 2500 Lexington Avenue South, Mendota Heights, MN 55120
•New Ulm Turnverein, 102 South State Street, New Ulm, MN 56073

Missouri
•Concordia Gymnastic Society, 6432 Gravois Road, St. Louis, MO 63116-1124

•North St. Louis Turners, 1928 Salisbury Street, St. Louis, MO 63107
•Schiller Turners, 200 Weiss Avenue, St. Louis, MO 63125
New Jersey
•Carlstadt Turnverein, Inc., 500 Broad Street, Carlstadt, NJ 07072-1102
•Riverside Turners Inc., 300 Rancocas Avenue, Riverside, NJ 08075
New York
•American Turners New York, 748 Clarence Avenue, Bronx, NY 10465
•Buffalo Turn Verein, 3200 Elmwood Avenue, Buffalo, NY 14217
•Long Island Turners Inc.: Contact American Turners National Office for current address.
•Schenectady Turn Verein, P.O. Box 3157, Schenectady, NY 12303
•Syracuse Turners, Inc., 619 N. Salina Street, Syracuse, NY 13208-2508
Ohio
•Akron Turner Club, 547 Munroe Falls Road, Tallmadge, OH 44278-3305
•Cincinnati Central Turners, 2200 Pinney Lane, Cincinnati, OH 45231
•American Turners Toledo, 26280
•Glenwood Road, Perrysburg, OH 43551-4850
•Cleveland East Side Turners, 1622 East 55 Street, Cleveland, OH 44103
•Cleveland Turners STV, 7412 Lawn Avenue, Cleveland, OH 44103
•*Dayton Liederkranz Turners, 1400 E. Fifth Street, Dayton, OH 45402-2224
Pennsylvania
•Beaver Falls Turners, 615 8th Street, Beaver Falls, PA 15010-4544
•*East Erie Turners Hall, 829 Parade Street, Erie, PA 16503
•*South Erie Turners, 2663 Peach Street, Erie, PA 16508
•Johnstown Turnverein, 632 Railroad Street, Johnstown, PA 15901-2232
•McKeesport Turners & Gesang Verein, 2701 Walnut Street, McKeesport, PA 15132-7066
•Monaca Turn Verein, 1700 Old Broadhead Road, Monaca, PA 15061

•Monongahela Turners, 127 E. Main Street, Monongahela, PA 15063
•Roxborough Turners, 418 Leverington Avenue, Philadelphia, PA 19138
•Central Turn Verein Rochester, 338 Pennsylvania Avenue, Rochester, PA 15074
Rhode Island
•Providence Turners, 118 Glenbridge Avenue, Providence, RI 02909-2093
Texas
•*Boerne Turn Verein, 221 East Theissen Street, Boerne, TX 78006-2349
•*Houston Turn Verein, 5202 Almeda Road, Houston, TX 77004-5909
•San Antonio Turner Club, 120 Ninth Street, San Antonio, TX 782151548
Wisconsin
•Madison Turners, Inc., 3001 S. Stoughton Road, Madison, WI 53716-3347
•Milwaukee Turners Foundation, Inc., 1034 N. 4th Street, Milwaukee, WI 53203
•Sheboygan Turners, Inc., 3714 Lakeshore Road, Sheboygan, WI 53083
•*Watertown Turners, W. 1604 Silver Creek Road, Watertown, WI 53098

OTHER FRATERNAL ORGANIZATIONS

The fraternal organizations which immigrants joined in the second half of the nineteenth century and the early twentieth century played a strong role in the social integration of the American newcomers.

The influence of these organizations is aptly described by Alvin J. Schmidt in his book, *Fraternal Organizations* (see "Source" at the end of this text):

"As the members [of fraternal organizations] participated in their lodge sessions, they slowly learned some of the democratic processes of their newly adopted country by seeing them practiced in their fraternal society's meetings. They soon learned and appreciated the value of free speech and the expression of opinions without fear of reprisal. They also learned how to conduct meetings and the importance of voting. Having learned and internalized these American values, the immigrant became a better-integrated citizen, and much credit belonged to the fraternal societies."

The following information concerning some of the organizations to which German and East European immigrants belonged is culled from the above-mentioned book, *Fraternal Organizations*. Current addresses, provided as available, come from other sources.

Aid Association for Lutherans

AAL began its work in 1899 in Appleton, Wisconsin (as the Aid Association for Lutherans in Wisconsin and Other States) with the purpose of establishing a fund for family protection. It received its charter from the state of Wisconsin in 1902. (AAL avoided use of the word "life insurance," or the German word *Lebens-versicherung,* because the purchaser of life insurance was considered to be lacking in trust in God, or to be engaged in usury, which Luther had condemned.) In 2002, AAL merged with Lutheran Brotherhood to form Thrivent Financial for Lutherans.

See the AAL's former quarterly, *Correspondent*; a brief article, "Our Pioneers Are Gone, But What a Legacy They Left" appears in the summer 1969 issue of this periodical.

Address: Thrivent Financial for Lutherans, 4321 N. Ballard Road, Appleton, WI 54919-0001. Tel. (800) 847-4836; Fax (800) 225-2264; www.thrivent.com.

The Alliance of Poles

The Alliance of Poles was formed in 1895 in Ohio, beginning as a fraternal benefit organization. In 1914, the name was changed to its present form, The Alliance of Poles of America. Prospective members have been required to be between 15 and 65 years old. The society's newspaper is *The Alliancer* (or, in Polish, *Zwiazkowiec*).

Address: The Alliance of Poles in America, 6966 Broadway, Cleveland, OH 44105. Tel. (216) 883-3131; Fax (216) 883-3172.

Alliance of Transylvania Saxons (ATS)

A number of Saxons founded this ethnic organization in 1902 in Cleveland, Ohio, as the *Siebenbürger Bund*. At the group's first convention the same year, the name was changed to *Central Verband der Siebenbürger Sachsen.* In 1965, the name was changed to The Alliance of Transyl-vania Saxons.

The society is a fraternal benefit insurance organization seeking to keep alive its 800 years of Saxon heritage. To join the society, prospective members must be "of Transylvanian Saxon birth or a descendant thereof, or married to a Saxon or descendant thereof, or of German birth or a descendant thereof." The age requirement is 16 to 60 years of age.

See the *Saxon Year Book, 1902-1977*, published in 1977 upon the society's 75th anniversary. The organization also publishes a weekly, *Saxon News (Volksblatt)*.

Address: Alliance of Transylvanian Saxons, 5393 Pearl Road, Cleveland, OH. Tel. (440) 842-8442; office@atsaxons.com; www.atsaxons.com.

Bavarian National Association of North America.

This organization was founded in 1884 by Bavarian immigrants as a fraternal benefit group seeking to protect families. In 1934, the society merged with Unity Life and Accident Insurance Association. See Alfred Preuss, *A Dictionary of Secret and Other Societies* (1924).

Concordia Mutual Life Association

This group was formed in 1908 to provide life insurance for Lutherans. They merged with National Mutual

Benefit in 2001.

Address: National Mutual Benefit, P.O. Box 1527, Madison, WI 53701-1527. Tel. (608) 833-1936; fraternal@nmbfrat.org; www.nmblife.org.

German Order of Harugari

This organization, also known as *Deutscher Orden der Harugari*, was formed in 1847 in New York to provide German immigrants with the opportunity to socialize and to practice speaking their mother tongue. ("*Harugari*" was selected as a name to honor the old Teutons who were called *Harugaris* because they met in the forests; *Haruc* meant grove or forest). See the society's publication, *Der Harugari*; also Albert C. Stevens, *Cyclopedia of Fraternities* (1907).

Address: German Order of Harugari, c/o Max Math, 7625 Hooker Street, Westminster, CO 80030.

Knights of Luther

This was a secret society organized in 1912 in Des Moines, Iowa "for the purpose of fighting the Romanist Church with weapons like those with which it fights." It apparently no longer exists. See Arthur Preuss, *A Dictionary of Secret and Other Societies* (1924).

**Improved Order
of Knights of Pythias**

Following the refusal of the Supreme Lodge of the Knights of Pythias to allow its lodges to print the ritual of the order in any language but English, some German members seceded to form the Improved Order of Knights of Pythias in 1895 in Indianapolis. The organization dissolved around the time of World War I. See Albert C. Stevens, *Cyclopedia of Fraternities* (1907).

**Lutheran Life Insurance
Society of Canada**

This organization came into existence with the merger of the Aid Association of Lutherans and the Lutheran Brotherhood in 1972. Members must belong to the Lutheran church. The society offers life insurance to its members, offers mortgage funds at reduced rates to Lutheran churches, and provides scholarships to Canadian Lutheran educational institutions and individuals. In 2009, the name of this society was changed to Faith Life Financial, 470 Weber Street North, Waterloo, ON N2L 6J2, Canada. Tel. (519) 886-4610; Fax (519) 886-0350; www.faithlifefinancial.ca. Some early records from LLIS are now kept at Thrivent Financial for Lutherans, www.thrivent.com.

Order of Sons of Hermann

A group of German Americans in New York City in 1840 formed The Order of Sons of Hermann to protect their German culture and heritage. (Hermann, called Arminius by the Romans, is a German folk hero who led the destruction of three Roman legions in the Battle of Teutoberg Forest in 9 AD.) The organization spread from New York to many other states.

In 1937, English rather than German began to be used in conducting meetings, and membership was opened to those of northern European lineage who did not have German ancestry.

The Order of the Sons of Hermann in the State of Texas, founded in 1861, publishes the Hermann Sons News, and has 155 local lodges in 140 communities in Texas. Headquarters is located at 515 South St. Mary's Street, San Antonio, TX 78205. Tel. (210) 226-9261; lee@texashermannsons.org; www.texashermannsons.org. Mail inquiries to P.O. Box 1941, San Antonio, TX 78297.

The Order of Hermann Sons and Sisters of the State of California, incorporated in 1923, publishes monthly *Der Hermann-Sohn* (in German and English). The organization is made up of 13 lodges: Harmonie Lodge No. 4 (San Jose), Sacramento Lodge No. 11, Fresno Lodge No. 18, Teutonia Lodge No. 19 (Napa), Berkeley Lodge No. 21, Santa Rosa Lodge No. 25, Petaluma Lodge No. 26, Stockton Lodge No. 26, Vallejo Lodge No. 30, Armin Bakersfield Lodge No. 35, Sutter Lodge No. 36 (Yuba City), Stanislaus Lodge No. 50 (Modesto), and Elmhurst Lodge, No. 53 (Hayward).

The newspaper is based in San Lorenzo, California

United Lutheran Society

This society is the product of a merger of two organizations: 1) the Slovak Evangelical Union, founded in 1893 in Freeland, Pennsylvania (providing fraternal insurance for men who were Slo-vak Lutherans), and 2) the Evangelical Slovak Women's Union, organized in 1906. The two groups merged in 1962 to form the United Lutheran Society. In 2007, United Lutheran merged with and into Great Beneficial Union of Pittsburgh.

Address: Greater Beneficial Union, 4254 Clairton Boulevard, Pittsburgh, PA 15227-3394. Tel. (412) 884-5100; Fax (412) 884-9815; info@gbu.org; www.gbu.org.

Source: Alvin J. Schmidt, *Fraternal Organizations* [part of *The Greenwood Encyclopedia of American Institutions* series] Greenwood Press, Westport, Conn., 1980.

Section 5: Language and vocabularies

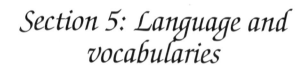

♦

Abbreviations
German, Latin, and French vocabularies
Old medical terms, illnesses, causes of death
Family relationships, terminologies
Gothic characters, alphabets, dialects

♦

GERMANIC LANGUAGES

Germanic languages are spoken by more that 480 million people in northern and western Europe, North America, South Africa, and Australia.

About 7 million people in Austria, about 300,000 in Luxembourg, 3,400,000 in northern Switzerland, and about 1,500,000 in Alsace-Lorraine speak German – in addition to about 330,000 people in Canada, 550,000 in Brazil, and 250,000 in Argentina.

The largest number of people outside Europe using German as their mother tongue live in the United States. The Pennsylvania Germans, who immigrated from the Palatinate during the late 17th and the 18th centuries and who settled in southeastern Pennsylvania, speak the Rhine-Franconian dialect mixed with some English.

In seven countries of the world, German is an official language. In Germany, Austria, and Liechtenstein, it is the only official language. In Switzerland, it is a co-official language, together with French and Italian. In Luxembourg, it is also a co-official language, together with French and Letzeburgisch. It is a regional official language in Italy, in Bolzano-South Tyrol (together with Italian) and in Belgium (in the German-speaking, eastern part of the country).

Sources:
•"The German Language: Lingua Franca Overshadowed by English?" by Ulrich Ammon. *Deutschland,* No. 1, 2/1994
•"German Language," *Microsoft Encarta,* Funk & Wagnalls Corp., 1994

CHRONOLOGY AND OVERVIEW OF THE GERMAN LANGUAGE

•**Until middle of 14th century:** Latin was the official written language of the Holy Roman Empire of the German Nation (comprising most of the German-speaking regions of present-day Europe)
•**Reign of Louis IV, Holy Roman Empire, 1314-47):** German was adopted as the language of official court docu-ments
•**Between 1480 and 1500:** German was

introduced for official use in many municipalities and courts of Saxony and Meiss-en and was adopted by the universities of Leipzig and Wittenberg
•**By 1500:** German generally was accepted as the official language of all parts of Sax-ony and Thuringia and was the written lan-guage of the educated classes. Publication of books in German increased in Wittenberg, Erfurt, and Leipzig as well as in Mainz, Straßbourg, Basel, Nürnberg, and Augsburg, resulting in a reduction of regional differences and the standardi-zation of the literary language.
•**First quarter of 16th century:** Standard written German emerged in areas such as Erfurt, Meissen, Dresden, and Leipzig, where the dialect spoken was based on Middle and Upper German dialects of High German. The High German standard, due largely to Luther's translations and writings, spread throughout the rest of Germany.
•**By 1600:** The literary language was well established, even though it did not become recognizable in its present form until about the middle of the 18th century.
•**Until the 20th century:** Different standards of spelling were adhered to in various parts of Germany and in other parts of Europe.
♦ In 1898, a commission of university professors and representatives of the Ger-man theater formed the basis of codified rules of pronunciation in *Deutsche Buhnenaussprache* (German Stage Pronunciation), published first in 1898 and later in 1957 as *Deutsche Hochsprache* (Standard German).

Following the spread of High German, that term came to have two meanings: It referred to all German dialects except those included in the Low German branch of the language, as well as to the official language of Germany.
Source: "German Language," *Microsoft Encarta.* Funk & Wagnalls Corp., 1994

OVERVIEW OF GERMAN LANGUAGE REFORM

Before Germany became a nation in 1871, no binding rules governing spelling existed for the entire German-speaking area of Europe.
♦ In 1901, representatives of northern and southern Germany, Austria, and Switzerland participated in a conference through which they devised a uniform system of orthography which was later accepted.

This system is outlined in *Rechtschreibung der deutschen Sprache* (Orthography of the German language) by the famous German philologist Konrad Du-den. This work became the official Ger-man spelling guide and went through many editions.
♦ Since the 1970s, experts from Germany, Austria and Switzerland worked on simplifying and systematizing German spelling.
♦ In July 1996 in Vienna, the three countries signed a joint reform of the rules.Long before this, the 20th edition of *Duden – Die deutsche Rechtschreibung* already contained the major innovations and recommendations in a special index.
♦ Also in 1996, a group of 100 writers, literary scholars, teachers and publishers from around the German-speaking nations put their names to a strongly critical declaration presented to the public during the Frankfurt Book Fair.

The "Frankfurt Declaration" called on public officials in Austria, Germany and Switzerland to reconsider their plans to introduce modifications in German spelling rules. The declaration contended that the changes would "waste millions of working hours, create decades of confusion, harm the standing of the German language at home and abroad, and cost more than a billion marks." Among the best known of the Germans to put their names to the declaration were the novelists Günter Grass, Siegried Lenz, and Martini Walser.

♦On August 2, 1999, German newspapers and magazines accepted and began using the new rules. At that time, the reforms were planned to be incrementally adopted by the year 2005. Until July 31, 2005, violation of the new rules were not to be corrected in red color as "mistakes" by teachers, but only marked in green as "outdated" or "traditional."

It is claimed that only one half of one percent of all German words were changed by the spelling reform.

Overview of the changes

♦ **The "eszett," was reduced in frequency.** Written as "ß" and pronounced like a double "s," the eszett became used only after long vowels, as in "Maß," or after dypthongs, as in "heiß." A double "s" is used after short vowels, as in "dass."

♦**Words are spelled according to the root words from which they originate,** as with "platzieren" instead of the former "plazieren." The word originates from the word "Platz." Even if such a change leads to three consonants appearing together in a word, so be it. "Schifffahrt" (the new spelling), for example, was formerly spelled "Schiffahrt." The word comes from "Schiff" plus "Fahrt."

♦**Foreign words may be Germanized,** but need not be – for example, "Delfin" instead of "Delphin" (dolphin in English).

♦**Capitalization is more consistently applied,** in general, as in "der Einzige" or "Rad fahren" – which were previously spelled entirely in lowercase letters.

♦**Compound words were, in general, to be separated**, as in "kennen lernen," instead of the former "kennenlernen."

♦**Comma rules were greatly simplified.** In many cases, the use of commas is left to the discretion of the writer.

♦**Syllabification was simplified.** The old rule drummed into the heads of elementary pupils, "*Trenne nie st / Denn es tut*

ihm weh!" (Never separate *st* / because it would be hurt!"). Under the old spelling rules, the word "lustig" separated as "*lu-stig*," but under the new rules, *lustig* is the proper division.

Examples of spelling changes

Former	New
Kuß (kiss)	Kuss
bißchen (little bit)	bisschen
Eislaufen (ice skate)	Eis laufen
Panther (Panther)	Panter
Mayonnaise	Majonäse
Open-Air Festival	Openairfestival
Bettuch (bedsheet)	Betttuch
Spaghetti	Spagetti
Mißstand (nuisance)	Missstand
selbständig (self-reliant)	selbstständig
angst machen (frighten)	Angst machen

Sources:

•"German Language," *Microsoft Encarta*. Funk & Wagnalls Corp., 1994

•"'Frankfurt Declaration Attacks Much Debated Language Reform," *The Week in Germany*, Ger-man Information Center, October 11, 1996, p. 6

•*Munich Found*, August/September 1996, p. 6

•"German Spelling in the 21st Century," by Gerhard Weiss. *German Life*, October/November 1995, p. 64

♦Janet Schayan, "Neue Regeln für die deutsche Rechtschreibung," *Deutschland*, February/March 1999., p. 56

♦Rainer Thumshirn, "The new spelling reform: Now it's official – maybe," *Der Blumenbaum*, Vol. 16, No. 2, 1998

BASIC GERMAN ALPHABET CHARACTERISTICS

•**Umlauted vowels:** The German alphabet has three vowels that are in addition to the English-language alphabet – letters containing umlauts *(Umlaute)*. They are ä. ö, and ü (Ä. Ö, and Ü). In certain lists and dictionaries created by Germans, the lists put an umlauted vowel before the same vowel that is unumlauted. Sometimes the umlaut is omitted, and the letter *e* is added. (For example, *Schröder* becomes *Schroeder*.)

•**The *Eszett:*** This letter (ß) is the equivalent of *ss* and is alphabetized as if it were *ss*. (But note the changes affecting the *eszett* in German spelling rules.) In a headline or other printed form using all capital letters, the ß is printed as *SS*. The ß is used only with lower-case forms of printed words.Thus the word *Haß* retains the *Eszett* when the word is written in lower case; but when it is composed in all capital letters, it is shown as *HASS*.

Handwritten letters

Although the old German Gothic handwritten script is another topic altogether, it may be useful to list here two other special features of German spelling.

•**The *U-Bogen* or (U-loop):** This is a curved figure that was writtenover the letter *u* to help the reader distinguish it from the *n*..

•**The *Verdoppelungsstrich* (doubling dash) or *Faulheitsstrich* (lazy dash):** This little "dash," or straight line placed over the handwritten *m* or *n* was used as an indication that the respective letter was to be doubled. For example, the surname *Hammer* might be written as *Hamer*, with a little dash placed over the *m* to indicate that the *m* should be doubled. Thus writers using the "lazy dash" saved themselves the bother of writing two letters, writing instead just one with a simple little straight-line dash on top of it.

ALPHABETIZATION OF UMLAUTS AND THE ESZETT

The German alphabet has three vowels not known to English: ä, ö, ü. In modern indexes, these are ordered alphabetically as if spelled *ae*, *oe*, and *ue*.For example, in *Das Postleitzahlenbuch* (the German postal code directory), the fol-

lowing villages appear in this alphabetical order: Lübz – Lüssow – Lützen – Luftschiff – Luppa.

Note, however, that German lists and indexes constructed by non-German researchers will likely be alphabetized with umlauted and unumlauted vowels intermingled. It is a good idea to search for a surname in an index by checking for both the umlauted and unumlauted vowels.

Words containing the *ß* (*Eszett*) are usually alphabetized as if it were *ss*.

THE GERMAN DIALECTS

Dialects in the German-speaking areas of Europe show an almost incomprehensible linguistic diversity. These dialects are linked to the historic tribal sub-structure of the German-speaking people(s) who settled in Central Europe and in England (Anglo-Saxons) during the *Völkerwander-ung* (migration of nations) around 500 AD.

The major tribes, from north to south, were the Frisians (*Friesen*), the Saxons (*Sachsen*), the Franks (*Franken*), the Thuringians (*Thüringer*), the Alemanni (*Allemannen*), and the Bavarians (*Bayern*). Each of these tribes developed its own dialect and subdialects.

In the course of history, dynastic territorial actions – war, marriage, or inheritance – altered the political borders of the original tribes, but seldom did these acquisitions/losses affect the ethno-linguistic delineations of the tribes. In the southern part of the German-speaking area, for example, the Alemanni had settled in what today is Alsace, Baden, Württemberg, western Bavaria, western Austria, Liecht-enstein and two-thirds of Switzerland. They formed the duchy (*Herzogtum*) of Schwaben.

Even after 1500 years, the overarching Alemannic dialect base still makes it possible for people in these areas to communicate in their respective subdialects.

The visitor in Augsburg, 30 miles from München, may be surprised to hear *schwäbisch* rather than *bayerisch*, and in Nürnberg and Würzburg it is *fränkisch* rather than *bayerisch* that one hears, yet Bavaria is Germany's largest *Bundesland.*

The Alemanni in Alsace speak *elsässisch*, an Alemannic subdialect, and French.

The Austrian dialect is given the linguistic designation of *südbayerisch* (south Bavarian), but it must be recalled that most of Austria was settled by Bavarians well over 1,000 years ago, hence the legitimacy of the designation.

These examples demonstrate that political and ethno-linguistic borders may not necessarily coincide. In the course of history, the latter have shown more permanence than the former.

The map shown here illustrates these incongruities. It provides an overview of the three large dialect bands spanning German-speaking Central Europe, with each, in turn, showing subgroups.

From north to south:

NIEDERDEUTSCH
[PLATTDEUTSCH, LOW GERMAN]
- Friesisch [Frisian]
- Niederfränkisch [Low Franconian]
- Niedersächsisch [Low Saxon]

MITTELDEUTSCH
[MIDDLE GERMAN]
- Fränkisch [Franconian]
  - Mittelfränkisch [Middle Franconian], Ripuarisch [Ripuarian], Moselfränkisch [Moselle-Franconian]
  - Rheinfränkisch [Rhine Franconian]
- Thüringisch [Thüringian]
- Obersächsisch [Upper Saxon]
- Schlesisch [Silesian]

OBERDEUTSCH
[UPPER GERMAN],
(SOMETIMES CONFUSED WITH HIGH GERMAN)

German Dialects Around 1930

Map based on one by Theo van Dorp in Adolf Bach's *Geschichte der deutschen Sprache,* 9th ed. (Wiesbaden: VMA-Verlag, n.d.), p. 102

◆Ober-Fränkisch [Upper Franconian]
  –Süd-Fränkisch [South Franconian]
  –Ostfränkisch [East Franconian]
◆Alemannisch [Alemannic]
  –Schwäbisch [Swabian]
  –Niederalemannisch [Low Aleman-
  nic]
◆Oberalemannisch [Upper Alemannic]
◆Bayerisch [Bavarian]
  –Nord-Bayerisch [North Bavarian]
  –Mittel-Bayerisch [Middle Bavarian]
  –Süd-Bayerisch [South Bavarian]

A phenomenon called the "Second or Old High German Soundshift" (*Zweite oder Althochdeutsche Lautverschiebung*) between the fifth and ninth centuries created the three big dialect bands. It affected especially the consonants p, t, and k.

In the Upper German area, they were shifted, depending on position within a given word, as follows:

p to pf, ff
t to s, ss, z, tz
k to ch

Middle German participated to a somewhat lesser degree: a Frankfurter likes his "Äbbelwoi" (apple wine), not "Apfel-wein." The line separating Upper and Middle German is also referred to as the "Appel/Apfel" line.

Low German (including Anglo-Saxon) was not affected by the soundshift at all. The line between Low and Middle German is called the *maken/machen* line. The Low German band of the map shows less differentiation than the Middle and Upper bands, but Mecklenburg, West- and East Pomerania, Brandenburg and East Prussia certainly also have dialects variants of their own. Along the Ruhr River one hears *Westfälisch*, 50 km east of there it is *Ostfälisch*, then *Elb-Ostfälisch*.

Source: Dr. Eberhard Reichmann, Professor of Germanic Studies (Emeritus), from a paper presented to the Palatines to America National Convention, 1997

HIGH, MIDDLE, LOW GERMAN

The names "high German," "middle German," and "low German" take their names from the geographical altitude of the areas where they are spoken.

High German is a blend of *Oberdeutsch* (upper, or mountain) German and *Mitteldeutsch* (midway German or middle upland) German.

Remnants of Low German (north of an imaginary boundary called the Benrath line), which is no longer spoken officially, are found as *Plattdeutsch* in rural areas north of the Benrath line. *Platt* is much like English. The Low Franconian dialect farther south merges with the Rhenish Franconian dialects.

It was a coincidence that led to High German rather than Low German becoming the accepted dialect. As a result of the attempt by the duke of Saxony in the early 1500s to standardize the dialects in his duchy, a language for state affairs called *Kanzleisprache* was adopted. This occurred just at the time Martin Luther translated the Bible from Latin, using the very same German dialect.

Luther explained his task in these words: *"Ich habe keine gewisse, sonderlich, eigene Sprache im Deutschen, sondern brauche die gemeine deutsche Sprache, daß mich beide, Ober- und Niederländer verstehen können."* (I have no special, definitive language in German, but I am using the common German tongue so that both High German and Low German will be able to understand me.) Martin Luther was compromising between the extremes of upper and lower German. The real coincidence was that he came from the Saxon area and wrote many manuscripts, including the Bible, in the *Kanzleisprache*.

This blending of dialects grew into what is called New High German, with a grammar taught in the schools to all Germans. It is sometimes called *Bühnen-*

sprache (stage language) or *Schrift-deutsch* (written German).

Although everyone writes High German, almost no one speaks it all the time. At home and among friends, Germans speak in their own local dialects. This tradition reflects the reverence and devotion of the German to his local region, hometown, and territorial district.

The common parent of English and German is Saxon. Both also share a single grandfather, Gothic.

Long before the Romans moved into German territory, many Germanic tribes roamed Europe, one of which was the Goths. After the Christian era began, the Goths migrated to southern Russia. There, in about 350 AD, Bishop Wulfilas translated the Bible into Gothic. It is from this document that linguists have been able to compare the Gothic language with later Saxon documents — and to determine that Saxon evolved from the root language of Gothic.

Thus the parent language of modern English was Anglo-Saxon, and that of modern German was Saxon.

Source: *Of German Ways,* by LaVern Rippley. Dillon Press, Minneapolis, 1970

NUMBERS VOCABULARY

0	null
1	eins
2	zwei
3	drei
4	vier
5	fünf
6	sechs
7	sieben
8	acht
9	neun
10	zehn
11	elf
12	zwölf
13	dreizehn
14	vierzehn
15	fünfzehn
20	zwanzig
21	einundzwanzig
30	dreißig
31	einunddreißig
40	vierzig
41	einundvierzig
50	fünzig
51	einundfünzig
60	sechzig
61	einundsechzig
70	siebzig
71	einundsiebzig
80	achtzig
81	einundachtzig
90	neunzig
91	einundneunzig
100	hundert
101	hundert(und)eins
200	zweihundert
1000	tausend
2000	zweitausend
1,000,000	eine Million
1,000,000,000	eine Milliarde
1,000,000,000,000	eine Billion

Ordinal numbers

1	erste
2	zweite
3	dritte
4	vierte
5	fünfte
6	sechste
7	sieb(en)te
8	achte
9	neunte
10	zehnte
11	elfte
20	zwanzigste
21	einundzwanzigste
30	dreißigste
40	vierzigste
50	fünfzigste
60	sechzigste
70	siebzigste
80	achtzigste
90	neunzigste
100	hundertste
101	hundert(und)erste
1000	tausendste
1,000,000	millionste
2,000,000	zweimillionste

The Old German Alphabet

𝔄	a	𝔑 R	r
𝔅	b	𝔖 S	ſs
ℭ	c	𝔗	t
𝔇	d	𝔘 U	u
𝔈	e	𝔙 V	v
𝔉	f	𝔚 W	w
𝔊	g	𝔵 X	x
ℌ	h	𝔜 Y	y
ℑ	i	𝔷 Z	z
ℨ	j	ch
𝔎	k	ck
𝔏	l	ng
𝔐	m	pf
𝔑	n	ph
𝔒	o	ſch
𝔓	p	ſſ
𝔔	q	tz

IDENTIFYING GERMAN SCRIPT

O	A	U	Y*
G	Q	P	H*
I	T	F*	J
J	Y*	H*	Z
B	L	C	Ch
E	F*	D	
K	R	X*	X*
S	St	N	M
V	W		

c*	c*	i	d	sch
e	n	nn	u	m
o	a	acht	nach
r	v	w	vier
b	k	l	d	s (final)	t*	t*
g	q	j	p	x	y	z
f	h	s	ss	sz	st
ein	er	en
ie	und	zwei

(c) 1996 Bruce Walthers

* alternate forms

Gothic—Roman Alphabet Comparison

Gothic	Roman		Gothic	Roman
𝔄	A	𝔘	U	
𝔅	B	𝔙	V	ℌ P
ℭ	C	𝔈	E	𝔊 G 𝔖 S
𝔇	D	𝔒	O	𝔔 Q
ℑ	I	𝔍	J	𝔉 F
𝔎	K	𝔑	N	ℜ R
𝔐	M	𝔚	W	
ℍ	H	𝔏	L	𝔗 T
𝔛	X	𝔜	Y	ℨ Z

Gothic	Roman		
a	a	o	o
b	b	d	d	v v
c	c	e	e	r r x
g	g	p	p	q q
f	f	ſ	s	
i	i	j	j	k k	l l	t t
n	n	u	u	h h	y y
m	m	w	w	
s	s	z	z	ß ss

The Sütterlin Alphabet

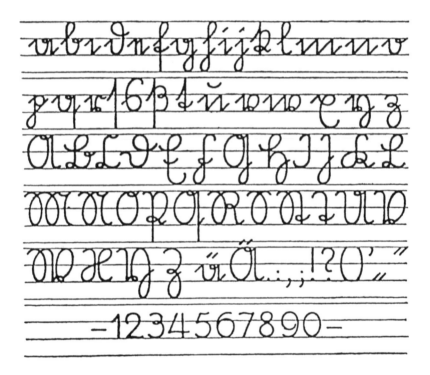

The Sütterlin alphabet (*Sütterlinschrift*) was named after an art teacher from Berlin, Ludwig Sütterlin, who first published his proposal for this simplification of the standard script in 1917.

It was adopted by Prussian schools in 1922 and soon spread to the other parts of Germany.

The teaching of the Sütterlin alphabet was phased out beginning in 1941.

There is some confusion in Germany when people use the term Sütterlin to describe the handwriting of old church records.

This alphabet was never used in church or civil records.

ABBREVIATIONS
GERMAN AND LATIN

a. .... *am, an/aus*: at/from
Abb. .... *Abbildung:* illustration,
   figure (fig.)
a. St. .... *alten Stils*: old style (of
   calendar)
a.a.O. .... am angeführten Orte [= loc.
cit]:   the place cited
abb. .... *Abbildung*; illustration
abds. .... *abends*; in the evening
Abf. .... *Abfahrt:* departure
Abk. .... *Abkürzung*: abbreviation
Abs. .... *Absender*: sender
Abt. .... *Abteilung,* department
a.c. .... *anno currente, Lat.*: of the
   current year
A.C. .... *anno Christi, Lat.*: in the
   year
   of the Lord
A.C. .... Augsburg Confession
   (Lutheran Creed)
a.D. .... *außer Dienst:* retired
A.D. .... *anno Domini, Lat.*: in the
   .... year of our Lord
ADAC .... Allgemeiner Deutscher
Automobil-Club: General German
   Automobile
   Association
Adr. .... *Adresse*: address
a.e. .... *anno edicto, Lat.*: in the
   year
   mentioned
AG .... *Aktiengesellschaft:*a
   cor-poration whose shares
   can be traded on the
   German stock exchanges
AG. .... *Amtsgericht*: district court
   AGoFF
   Arbeitsgemeinschaft ost-

   deutscher Familienfor-
   scher: society for east
   German family history
   research
A.H. .... *alter Herr*: old gentleman
allg. .... *allgemein;* general

Ank. .... *Ankunft*; arrival
Anm. .... *Anmerkung*: note;
   Anmeldung: registration
ao. .... *anno, Lat.*: in the year
a.pr.   anno prioris, Lat.: in the
   previous year
ARD .... *Arbeitsgemeinschaft der*
   R u n d f u n k a n s t a l t e n
   Deutsch-lands: Germany's
   first pub-lic TV network
Ausg. .... *Ausgabe*: edition
b. .... *bei(m)* (with persons) [=c/
   o]:
   in care of
B.-Rhin ...... *Bas-Rhin*: Lower Rhine
b.w.   *bitte wenden:* please turn
   over (page)
BA. .... *Bezirksamt*: district office
BAFöG ...... Federal Education
   .... Promotion Act; provides
   scholarship money for
   German university students
BCE .... Before Common Era (Jewish
   term for B.C.)
Bd. .... *Band:* volume (book)
Bde. .... *Bände:* volumes (books)
begr. .... *Begräbnis:* burial; buried
beil. .... *beiliegend:* enclosed
Bem. .... *Bemerkung:* remark
bes. .... *besonders:* especially
betr. .... *betreffend*: concerning,
   about
bez.,bz. .... *bezahlt*: paid
Bez. .... *Bezirk:* district
Bhf. .... *Bahnhof:* train station
bisw. .... *bisweilen*: sometimes,
   occasionally
Br. .... *Bruder; Breite*: brother;
   latitude
BRD .... *Bundesrepublik Deutsch-*
   land; FRG, Federal Repub-
   lic of Germany, West
   Germany
Bz. .... *Bezirk:* district
bzgl. .... *bezüglich:* with reference to
bzw. .... *beziehungsweise:*
   respectively; or
C .... *Tschechoslowakei*:
   Czechoslovakia

c. .... *copuliert,* Lat.: married
c. .... *currentis/circa,* Lat.; of the current year\about
c.a., ca. .... *currentis anni,* Lat.: of the current year
CDU .... *Christlich Demokratische Union*: the Christian Democratic Union (a political party)
CE .... Common Era, Jewish term for A.D.
c.f.l. .... *conjugium filius legitimus/ filia legitima,* Lat.: legitimate child
CH .... *Confoederatio Helvetica:* Lat. for "Swiss Confederation"
c.l. .... *citato loco,* Lat.: in the place cited
C.N. .... *Code Napoléon*: Code Napoleon
ca. .... *circa, Lat.*: approximately
Chr. .... *Christus,* Lat.: Christ
conj .... *conjux,* Lat.: wife
Cop. .... *copulatio,* Lat.: marriage
cr. .... *currentis,* Lat.: of the current year
CSU .... *Christlich-Soziale Union:* Christian Social Union, Bavarian sister party of the CDU
CVJM .... *Christlicher Verein Junger Männer*: YMCA
d. .... Lat.: *dicta/us,* named (Ger.: *genannt)*
d. .... *den; des*: on the (date); of the
D. .... *Deutschland*: Germany
d.a. .... *dicti anni,* Lat.: of the year mentioned
d.Ä. .... *der Ältere*: the elder; senior
DAX .... *Deutscher Aktien-Index:* index of stocks in Ger-many (similar to the Dow-Jones index)
DB .... *Deutsche Bahn AG:* German Rail
d.Bl. .... *dieses Blattes*: of this page
d.d. .... *de dato,* Lat.: on this date

DDR. .... Deutsche Demokratische *Republik:* (former) East Germany
D.dw .... *Euer dienstwilliger:* your obedient servant
dgl. .... *dergleichen:* the like
d.Gr. .... *der Große;* the Great
d.h. .... *das heißt:* that is [i.e.]
d.i. .... *das ist:* that is
Di. .... *Dienstag:* Tuesday
DIN .... *Deutsche Industrie-Norm:* German Industry Standards
Dipl. .... *Diplom* (holding a)
d.J. .... *der Jüngere/des Jahres*: the younger; junior/of the year
d.l. .... *dicto loco,* Lat.: in the place mentioned
d.l.J. .... *des laufenden Jahres:* of the current year
d.M. .... *dieses Monats:* this month [=inst.]
DM .... *Deutsche Mark:* German mark(s)
d.M. .... *dieses Monats*: this month; instant
D.N. .... *Dominus Noster* Lat.: Our Lord
d.O. .... *der Obige:* the above
Do. .... *Donnerstag:* Thursday
dom. .... *dominica* Lat.: Sunday
dch. .... *durch*: through
dgl. .... *dergleichen/desgleichen*: (of) the same
Di. .... *Dienstag:* Tuesday
do./dto. ...... *ditto:* ditto
Do. .... *Donnerstag:* Thursday
dom. .... *dominica,* Lat.: Sunday
dpa .... *Deutsche Presse-Agentur:* German Press Agency
Dr. .... [See "university degrees"]
ds.J(s) .... *dieses Jahres:* of this year
ds.M(ts) ..... *dieses Monats*: of this month
d.s.p. .... *decessit sine prole,* Lat.: he/ she died without issue
d.s.p.l. .... *decessit sine prole legitima,* Lat.: he/she died without legitimate issue

d.s.p.m. ...... *decessit sine prole mascula,* Lat.: he/she/died without male issue

d.s.p.s. .... *decessit sine prole supersite,* Lat.: he/she/died without surviving issue

dt. .... *deutsch:* German

d.Verf. .... *der Verfasser:* the author

dz. .... *derzeit:* then, at that time

DZG .... Deutsche Zentralstelle *für Genealogie* (in Leipzig)

e.a. .... *ejusdem anni,* Lat.: of the same year

ead. .... *eadem,* Lat.: likewise

ebd. .... *ebenda(selbst):* in the same place; ibidem

eccl. .... *ecclesia,* Lat.: church

Ecu .... European Currency Unit

e.g. .... *exempli gratia:* for example

EG .... *Europäische Gemeinschaft:* European Community (EC), now known as the European Union (EU)

Ehefr. .... *Ehefrau:* wife, married woman

ehel. .... *ehelich:* legitimate (child)

Ehl. .... *Eheleute:* a married couple

eigtl. .... *eigentlich:* actually; proper(ly)

ejusd. .... *Ejusdem:* of the same

E.K. .... *Eisernes Kreuz:* Iron Cross (military medal)

E.K.D. .... Evangelische Kirche in *Deutschland:* Protestant Church in Germany (usually Lutheran)

e.m. .... *ejusdem mensis,* Lat.: in the same month

e.o. .... *ex officio,* Lat.: by virtue of one's office

eod. .... *eodem:* the same

eod.q.s. .... *eodem quo supra,* Lat.: on the same day as above

Ep. .... *Epiphania:* Epiphany

e.p. .... *en personne,* Fr.: in person

EU .... *Europäische Union:* European Union

e.V. .... *eingeschriebener Verein:* a registered association, usually a nonprofit organization

E.v. .... *Eltern von:* parents of

ev.luth. .... *evangelish-lutherisch:* Evangelical Lutheran

ev.ref. .... *evangelisch-reformiert:* Evangelical Reformed

evtl. .... *eventuell:* possibly

EWG .... Europäische Wirtschaftsgemeinschaft: European Common Market

Expl. .... *Exemplar:* sample, copy

f. .... *für/folgende/folium:* for/following (page)/page

f. .... *filius/filia,* Lat.: son/daughter

F. .... *Frankreich:* France

Fa. .... *Firma:* firm, company

F.-Geb. .... *Fehlgeburt:* stillbirth; abortion

f.c. .... *filius/filia civis,* Lat.: son/daughter of a citizen

f.d.A. .... *für die Ausfertigung:* attesting to this document

FDJ .... *Freie Deutsche Jugend:* Free German Youth, youth wing of SED (in former East Germany)

FDP .... *Freie Demokratische Partei:* Free Democratic Party

ff. .... *folgende (Seiten):* following (pages)

ff. .... *filii,* Lat.: sons

fr. .... *frater,* Lat.: brother

f.l. .... *filia legitima, filius legitimus,* Lat.: legitimate child

Fr. .... *Frau:* wife, Mrs

Fr. .... *Freitag:* Friday.

Frdh. .... *Friedhof:* cemetery

Frl. .... *Fräulein:* Miss; unmarried young woman

frz .... *französisch:* French

geb. .... *geboren/geborene:* born, birthname

gefl. .... *gefälligst:* if you please

gegr. .... *gegründet:* founded

gem. .... *gemelli/gemellae (Lat.):* male/female twins; *gemäß:* according to

gen. .... *genannt:* named, mentioned

gesch. .... *geschieden:* divorced; *geschätzt: estimated*

geschr. .... *geschrieben:* written

gest. .... *gestorben:* died

Gestapo ..... *Geheimesstaatspolizei:* Secret State Police (Nazi)

get. .... *getauft:* baptized, christened

getr. .... *getraut:* married

Gev. .... *Gevatter(n):* sponsor(s)

gez. .... *gezeichnet:* signed

g.f. .... *generis femini,* Lat.: of female sex

g.g.F. .... *gegebenen Falls:* in that case

G.G. .... *Grundgesetz:* Basic Law (federal Constitution)

G.K. .... *Gregoranischer Kalender,* Lat.: Gregorian calendar

g.m. .... *generis masculini,* Lat: of male sex

GmbH .... *Gesellschaft mit beschränk-ter haftung:* a closed corporation or limited liability company (Ltd.)

g.z. .... *gehört zu:* belongs to

h .... *hora,* Lat.: hour; o'clock

H .... *Helvetica:* Switzerland; *Herr*: Mr.

h. .... *hora,* Lat.: hour

H. .... *Hafen:* port

h.a. .... *hoc anno/hujus anni,* Lat.: in this year/of this year

ha .... *Hektar:* hectare (about 2.47 acres)

Hapag .... *Hamburg-Amerikanische Paketfahrt-Aktien-Gesell-schaft:* German merchant shipping company

Hausfr. .... *Hausfrau:* wife, housewife

Hbf. .... *Hauptbahnhof:* main train station

HC .... Helvetic Confession (for the Reformed creed)

h.e. .... *hoc est,* Lat.: that is

Hg.,Hrsg. ... *Herausgeber:* editor

hins. .... *hinsichtlich:* with regard to

hl. .... *heilig:* holy

h.l. .... *hoc loco,* Lat.: at this place

Hpt. .... *Haupt-:* chief, main

Hr. .... *Herr:* Mr.

H.R.I.P. .... *Hic Requiescat In Pace,* Lat.: here rests in peace

H.R.R. .... *Heiliges Römisches Reich:* Holy Roman Empire

h.t. .... *hoc tempore,* Lat.: at this time

I .... *Italien:* Italy

i.D.. .... *im Durchschnitt:* on the average

i. .... *in; im:* (in place names) in

I. .... *Iesus,* Lat.: Jesus

i.allg. .... *im allgemeinen:* in general

ib(d). .... *ibidem,* Lat.: in the same place

IC .... *InterCity* (German long-distance train)

ICE .... *InterCity Express* (German high speed train)

i.d. .... *in der, in dem:* in the

i.e. .... *id est,* Lat.: that is

i.f. .... *ipso facto,* Lat.: by its very nature

i.f. .... *in fine,* Lat.: in conclusion

i.f., i.folg. ... *im folgenden:* in the following

i.J. .... *im Jahre:* in the year

inkl. .... *Inklusive:* including

i.R .... *im Ruhestand:* retired

J .... *Johann/Jahr(e):* Johann/ years

j. .... *jährlich*: annually

Jg. .... *Jahrgang:* year (of issue of a publication)

Jgfr. .... *Jungfrau:* unmarried young woman

Jh./Jhdt. .... *Jahrhundert:* century

jhrl. .... *jährlich:* yearly, annually

Jngfr. .... *Jungfrau:* unmarried young woman

Joes .... *Johannes*

Joh. .... *Johann:* Johann
jr. .... *junior:* younger of two people of same name
jun. .... *junior:* younger of two people of same name
juv. .... *juvenis,* Lat.: young, youth
-k. .... *-keit/-kunde/-kunst:* -ness/ knowledge/-skill
Kap. .... *Kapitel:* chapter
kath. .... *katholisch:* Catholic
K.B. .... *Kirchenbuch:* church record book
KG .... *Kommanditgesellschaft:* a limited partnership
KGaA .... *Kommanditgesellschaft auf Aktien:* a partnership, with the partners holding stock
k.J .... *kommenden/künftigen Jahres:* of the coming year
Kl. .... *Klasse:* class
k.M. .... *kommenden/künftigen Monats:* of the coming month
Kr(s). .... *Kreis:* district
Kripo .... *Kriminalpolizei:* criminal investigation department (C.I.D.)
Kt. .... *Kanton:* canton
k.u.k. .... *kaiserlich und königlich:* imperial and royal
k.W. .... *kommende Woche:* next week
L .... *Luxemburg:* Luxembourg
l. .... *legitimata,* Lat.: legitimate
l. .... *lies!/links:* read!/left
l.b. .... *liegen bei:* (documents) are enclosed
LB .... *Landesbezirk:* administrative district
l.c. .... *loco citato,* Lat.: the place cited
led. .... *ledig:* unmarried
lfd. .... *laufend:* current
L.G. .... *Landgericht:* district court
l.J. .... *laufenden Jahres/letzten Jahrs:* of the current year/ of last year
Lkw .... *Lastkraftwagen:* truck, semi
l.l. .... *loco laudato,* Lat.: in the place cited

L.-Nr. .... *Listennummer:* list number
l.o. .... *links oben:* top left
l.p.m.s. .... *legitimatus per matrimonium subsequens,* Lat.: legitimized by subsequent marriage
l.p.r.p. .... *legitimatus per rescriptum principis,* Lat.: legitimate by order of the ruler
l.p.s.m. .... *legitimatus persubsequens matrimonium,* Lat.: legitimitzed by subsequent marriage
lt. .... *laut:* according to
l.u. .... *links unten:* bottom left
luth. .... *lutherisch:* Lutheran
m. .... *mit:* with
M. .... *Magister, Meister:* master
MA. .... *Mittelalter/Meldeamt:* Middle Ages/registration office
m.a. .... *mit anderen:* with other things
männl. .... *männlich:* masculine
m.a.W. .... *mit anderen Worten:* in other words
m.E. .... *meines Erachtens:* in my opinion
MEZ .... *Mitteleuropäische Zeit:* Central European Time (CET)
Mgl. .... *Mitglied:* member
Mi. .... *Mittwoch:* Wednesday
mlat. .... *mittellatein:* Middle Latin
m.m.p. .... *manu mea propria,* Lat.: with my own hand
m.n. .... *more novo,* Lat.: according to the new custom
Mo. .... *Montag/Monat:* Monday month
m.p. .... *manu propria,* Lat.: with one's own hand
Mskr. .... *Manuskript:* manuscript
Mstr. .... *Meister:* master
m.v. .... *more vetere,* Lat.: old style of calendar
m.Vn. .... *männerlicher Vorname:* male given name

m.W. .... *meines Wissens*: as far as I know

MW .... *Mittelwelle:* medium wave, AM radio

Mwst. .... *Mehrwertsteuer:* value-added tax, VAT

N .... *Nord(en)/Niederlande:* north/Netherlands

n. .... *nördlich*: north

n. .... *nata/natus*, Lat.: born

nachm. .... *nachmittags:* in the afternoon; P.M.

nat. .... *nata/natus*, Lat.: born

N.B. .... *nota bene!* Lat.: note well

n. Chr. .... *nach Christus:* after Christ, A.D.

n. Chr.G. ..... *nach Christus Geburt:* after the birth of Christ, A.D.

nep. .... *nepos, neptis*, Lat.:nephew/grandson

n.J. .... *nächsten Jahres:* next year

NL .... *Niederlande*: Netherlands

n.M. .... *nächsten Monat(s)*: next month

N.N./n.n. .... *nomen nescio*, Lat.: name unknown

Nr(n). .... *Nummer(n):* Number(s)

N.S. .... *Nachschrift*: postscript (P.S.)

NSDAP ...... *National sozialistische Deutsche Arbeiterpartei*: National Socialist German Workers' Party, or Nazis

NVA .... *National Volksarmee:* National People's Army, GDR army

o. .... *obiit*, Lat.: died

O. .... *Ost(en)*: east

o.ä. .... *oder ähnliche(s):* or similar

ÖBB .... Österreichische Bundesbahnen: Austrian Federal Railways

od. .... *oder:* or

o.g. .... *oben genannt:* mentioned above

oHG .... *offene Handelsgesellschaft:* general partnership

o.J. .... *ohne Jahr:* without a year; no\ date

o.O. .... *ohne Ort*: without place

o.O.u.J. ...... *ohne Ort und Jahr:* without place and year

P. .... *Pater*, Lat.: father, pastor

p.a. .... *per annum*, Lat.: per year

p.A(dr) ...... *per Adresse*: in care of (c/o)

par .... *parentes,* Lat.: parents

pat. .... *pater,* Lat.: father

patr. .... *patrini;* Lat.: godparents

p.Chr. .... *post Christi*, Lat.: after Christ; A.D.

p.d. .... *post datum*, Lat.: after the date

pd. .... *pridie*, Lat.: the day before

PDS .... *Partei Deutscher Sozialisten:* Party of German Socialists, Communist successor to SED after 1990

Pf. .... *Pfennig*: penny

Pfd. .... *Pfund:* German pound(s)

Pfl. .... *Pflege*: ward; care

Pkw .... *Personenkraftwagen:* auto- mobile

P.L. .... *Pastor Loci*, Lat.: pastor of this parish

p.m. .... *post mortem,* Lat.: after death

p.n.Chr. ..... *post nativitatem Christi, Lat.*: after the birth of Christ; A.D.

Pr. .... *Preußen*: Prussia

prot. .... *protestantisch:* Protestant

Prov. .... *Province*: province

p.s.m.l. .... *per subsequens matrimonium legitimatus*, Lat.: legitimized by subsequent marriage

p.t. .... *pro tempore*, Lat, : for the time

pzt. .... *prozentig*: percent

q.e. .... *quod est*, Lat.: which is

Q.I.P. .... *quiescat in pace*, Lat.: may he/she rest in peace

qkm .... *Quadratkilometer*: square kilometer

qm .... *Quadratmeter:* square meter

Q.M.O. .... *qui mortem obiit*, Lat.: the one who died

qu. .... *quasi*, Lat.: questioned, questionable

q.v. .... *quod vide*, Lat.: which see

q.v._annos: Lat., who lived ___years

R.-Bez .... *R e g i e r u n g s b e z i r k* : government district

rd. .... *rund*: approximately

rel. .... *relictus, relicta*, Lat.: widower, widow

ren./renat. . *renata, renatus*, Lat.: baptized

resp. .... *respektive*: respectively

Rh. .... *Rhein*: Rhine (River)

R.I.P. .... *Requiescat in pace*, Lat.: rest   in peace

röm .... römisch: Roman

Rr. .... *Richter*: judge

ß .... *Schilling*: coin

s. .... *siehe*: see, refer to

S. .... *Süd(en)*: south

S. .... *Seite*: page

S., sel. .... *selig*: late, deceased

s.a. .... *sine anno*, Lat.: without the year

s.a. .... *(S)siehe auch (Seite)*: see also (page)

SA .... *Sturmabteilung:* storm troops of the NSDAP, founded 1921

Sa. .... *Samstag*: Saturday

SAE .... *saeculum*, Lat.: century

s.a.e.l. .... *sine anno et loco*, Lat.: without year and place

Sa. .... *Samstag:* Saturday

SAE .... *saeculum* Lat.: century

SBB .... *Schweizerische Bundes- bahnen:* Swiss Federal Railways

SCL .... *saeculo*, Lat.: in the century

s.d. .... *siehe dies!*: see this!

S.d. .... *Sohn der/desson*: son of (the)

SD .... *Sicherheitsdienst:* Nazi Security Service

SED .... *Sozialistische Einheits- partei Deutschlands:* Socialist Unity Party of Germany, East German Communist party

sen. .... *senior,* Lat.: older; elder (of the two)

sep. .... *sepulta, sepultus,* Lat.: buried

seq. .... *sequens,* Lat.:   (the) following

s.o. .... *siehe oben!*: see above!

So. .... *Sonntag:* Sunday

SPD .... *S o z i a l d e m o k r a t i s c h e Partei Deutschlands:* Social Demo- cratic Party of Germany

s.p.l. .... *sine prole legitima,* Lat.: without legitimate issue

spons. .... *sponsus, sponsa,* Lat.: bridegroom, bride

s.p.m. .... *sine prole mascula, Lat.:* without male issue

spur. .... *spurius, spuria,* Lat. illegitimate child

sq. .... *sequens,* Lat.: following

s.R. .... *siehe Rückseite:* see reverse (side)

sr. .... *senior:* the older of two people of the same name

SS .... *Schutzstaffel:* special formation of the NSDAP; founded as the bodyguard for National Socialist leaders

Stasi .... *Staatssicherheitsdienst:* former East Germany's state security agency

StB .... *Staatsbibliothek:* state library

Std./Stdn ... *Stunde(n)*: hour(s)

StdA. .... *Standesamt:* civil registra- tion office

Str. .... *Straße*: Street, Road

stud. .... *studiosus,* Lat.: student

susc. .... *susceptor, susceptores, susceptrix,* Lat.: godparents

s.u. .... *siehe unten:* see below

S.v. .... *Sohn von:* son of

SW .... *Schweiz:* Switzerland

s.Z. .... *seinerzeit:* in those times, formerly

T. .... *Tag(e):* day(s)

T.d. .... *Tochter des/der:* daughter

of

testes	*testes* Lat.: godparents
To.	*Tochter:* daughter
Tr.	*Trinitatis:* Trinity
Tsd.	*Tausend:* thousand
TT...............	*testamentum* Lat.: will
TÜV	*Technische Überwachungsverein:* German auto safety testing agency
T.v.	*Tochter von:* daughter of
T.V.	*Turnverein:* gymnastic society
Tz.	*Taufzeuge:* male baptismal sponsor
Tzi.	*Taufzeugin:* female baptismal sponsor
u.	*und:* and
u.Ä	*und Ähnliches:* and similar
u.a.	*und ander(s)* or *unter ander- em/anderen:* and others, among other things
u.a.m.	*und andere mehr:* among others
U-Bahn	*Untergrundbahn:* subway
u.d.	*und der/und des:* and of (the) *u. desgl. und desgleichen (mehr):* and the like
Ufa	*Universum Film-Aktiengesellschaft:* German film studio founded in the 1920s
u.ff.	*und folgende (Seiten):* and the following (pages)
u.i.	*ut infra:* as below
UKW	*Ultrakurzwellen:* FM radio
ult.	*ultimo,* Lat.: last day of month or year
Umgeb.	*Umgebung:* vicinity
unehel.	*unehelich:* illegitimate (child)
u.s.	*ut supra,* Lat.: as above
usf.	*und so forth:* and so forth
usw.	*und so weiter:* etc.
u.U.	*unter Umständen:* in (certain) circumstances, possibly
u.v.a.	*und viel anderes:* and much more
u.W.	*unseres Wissens:* as far as we know
ux.	*uxor:* wife, spouse
u.zw.	*und zwar:* that is; namely; in fact
v.	*von, vom:* from (the)
v. Chr.	*vor Christus:* before Christ, B.C.
v.Chr.G.	*vor Christi Geburt:* before Christ's birth; B.C.
v.d.	*vor dem/der:* before the
vdt.	*vidit,* Lat.: has seen
Verf.	*Verfasser:* author
verh.	*verheiratet:* married
verl.	*verlobt:* engaged (to marry)
verm.	*vermählt:* married
verw.	*verwitwetet/verwundet:* widowed/wounded
Verw.-Bez...	*Verwaltungsbezirk:* administrative district
Verz.	*Verzeichnis:* list
vgl.	*vergleiche!:* compare!; see!
v.H.	*vom Hundert:* percent
vid.	*vide,* Lat.: see
vid.	*viduus, vidua* Lat.: widower, widow
VID	*vidua, viduus* Lat.: widow, widower
vix.	*vixit,* Lat.: he/she lived
v.J.	*vorigen Jahres:* of last year
v.M.	*vorigen Monats:* of last month
v.s.p	*vide subsequente pagina* Lat.: see the following page
v.v.	*vice versa:* the other way around
vw.	*verwitwet:* widowed
W.	*West(en):* west
WC	*water closet:* rest room, toilet
weibl.	*weiblich:* feminine
weil.	*weiland:* late, deceased
weyl.	weyland: deceased
Wlr.	*Weiler:* hamlet
Wo.	*Woche:* week
w.o.	*wie oben:* as above
w.u.	*wie unten:* as below
w.v.	*wie vorher:* as previously
Wwe.	*Witwe:* widow
X; Xs.	*Christus:* Christ

Xstnacht .... *Christnacht:* Christmas
Z. .... *Zeile/Zahl/Zeuge*: line (on
          a page)/number/witness
z.B. .... *zum Beispiel*: for example
ZDF .... *ZweitesDeutsches Fern-
          sehen:* Germany's second
          public TV network/channel
Zi. .... *Zimmer:* room (number)
z.J. .... *zum Jahr*: in the year
z.T .... *zum Teil*: partly, to some
          extent
Ztg. .... *Zeitung:* newspaper
z.Zt. .... *zur Zeit:* at this time
Other short forms:
September:
7br. 7ber. 7bris. VIIber.:
October:
8br. 8ber. 8bris. VIIIber.
November:
9br. 9ber. 9bris. IXber.
December:
Xbr. Xber. Xbris. 10ber. 10bris
Christ:
Xus or *Xg:* Christus
Christianus, Christian: *Xian. Xiang:*

GERMAN GENEALOGY VOCABULARY

Note: In German, all nouns are capitalized.

Abend/abends: evening/in the evening
Abendmahl: communion
Abgang: departure
Abkürzung(en): abbreviation(s)
abmelden: to report in on departure
Abriß: synopsis, summary
Abschrift: copy, extract
Abstammungsurkunde: birth certificate
absterben: to die
Abtei: abbey
Abteilung: department, section
Ackermann: farmer (old term)
Adel: nobility
adoptieren/adoptiert: to adopt/adopted
Adreßbuch/(-bücher) address book(s),
          city directory(ies)
Ahne(n): ancestor(s)

Ahnenforschung: family research
Ahnenliste: ancestral line chart
Ahnentafel: pedigree chart
Akte(n): document(s), deed; records
          (plural)
allgemein: (adj.) general(ly), common(ly)
allhier: in this place
Almosen: welfare
alt: (adj.) old
Alter: age
älter: (adj.) elder, senior
Altertum: antiquity
Ältester: elder [noun]
Amt: office, jurisdiction
Amtsbücher: official books
Amtsgericht (AG.): district court
Amtssprache: official language
Angehöriger: relative, family member
angenommenes Kind: adopted child
angezeigt durch: registered by
Anhang: appendix of a book
anmelden: to report in on arrival
Anmerkung: note, comment
Anschrift(en): address(es)
Anzeige: notice
Arbeitsgemeinschaft: society
Arbeitsmann: workman
Archiv(e): archive(s)
archivisch: (adj.) archival
arm: (adj.) poor
Armenregister: poor record
aufbieten: to publish marriage banns
Aufenthaltsort: place of residence
Aufgebote(n): proclamation(s), bann(s)
Aufstellung: list
Augenfarbe: color of eyes
Ausblick: outlook, prospect, view
ausgestorben: (adj.) (line) died out
Aushebungsliste: military muster rolls
Ausland: foreign country
Außenstelle: branch office
Auswanderer: emigrant
auswandern: to emigrate
Auswanderung: emigration
Auswanderungsliste: emigration record
Ausweis: identification papers
Auszug: extract (of a record)
Bahnhof: railway station
Baiern: Bavaria

Band/Bände: volume/volumes
Baptisten: Baptists
Bauer: peasant, farmer
Bauernhof: farm
Bauernkrieg: Peasant War (1525)
Bayern: Bavaria
Beamter: official
beerdigt: (adj.) buried
Beerdigung: funeral, burial
Beerdigungsregister: burial register
begraben: to bury
Begräbnis, Beerdigung: burial
Begriffe: idea(s), notion(s)
Bekenntnis: religious faith (Catholic, ...
   Lutheran, etc.)
Bemerkungen: remarks
Benutzungshinweis(e):useful
   comment(s)
Bereich: area, region
Berg: mountain, hill
Beruf: occupation, calling
Berufsakten: occupation records
Berufsbezeichnung(en): name(s) of
   occupation(s)
Beschäftigung: occupation
Bescheinigung: certificate
besonders: particular, special
Bestand/Bestände: holdings (in archive)
Beständer: leaseholder (Austria)
Bestandskataloge: catalog of holdings
Bestandsübersichten: summary of
   holdings
Bestätigung: certificate
bestatten: to bury
Bestattung: burial, funeral
Bestimmungsort: distination
Bevölkerungsliste: population list,
census
Bevölkerungsgruppe(n): population
   group(s)
Bevölkerungsverzeichnis: population
list,census
Bezeichnunge(n):indication(s),
   representation(s)
Bezifferung: numbering
Bezirk: district
Bezirksamt: district office
Bezirkskommando (Bkdo.): district ....
   military command

Bezugsquelle(n): source(s)
Bibliographie(n): bibliography(ies)
Bibliothek: library
Biographieforschung: biographical
   research
Bischof: bishop
bischöflich: ecclesiastical
bisheriger Wohnort: former residence
Bistum: diocese
Blätter: newspaper/periodical
Blutverwandtschaft: blood relationship
Böhmen: Bohemia
Braunschweig: Brunswick
Braut: bride
Bräutigam: bridegroom
Brautkind: premarital child
Brief: letter
Brinksitzer: farmer (old term)
Bruder: brother, monk, member of a
   fraternity
Brüdergemein(d)e: Moravians
Brüdergemeine: fraternity; Moravian
   Brethern
Bruderschaft: brotherhood, fraternity
Buch/Bücher: book/books
Bundes: federal
Burg: fortress, castle
Bürger: person with full rights of
   citizenship
Bürgerbuch/(-bücher): citizenship
   record(s)
Bürgereid: citizen's oath
Bürgerrecht: citizenship
Bürgerregister: citizenship record
Burggut: castle estate
Burghof: castle court (=inside)
Christnacht: Christmas Eve
Chronik(en): chronicle(s)
Dachverband: holding, umbrella
   association; parent organization
Dampfschiff: steamship
Datenschutz: (personal) data
protection
Datum: date
Datum d. Abgang: date of departure
deutsche: (adj.) German
deutscher Sprachraum: German-
   speaking area
Deutsches Reich: German Empire

Diakon: deacon
Diener: servant
Diener Gottes: minister
Dienstherr: employer
Dienstjunge/Dienstmagd: farmhand
  (child)
Dienstmagd: maidservant
Dienststelle: government office, place .
  of employment, service office
Diözese: diocese
Dom: cathedral
Domäne: estate
Dorf/Dörfer: village/villages
ebenda: at the same place
Ehe: marriage
Ehebrecher: adulterer
Ehebücher: marriage registers
Ehefrau: (legitimate) wife
Ehegatte: spouse, husband
Ehegattin: spouse, wife
Eheleute: married couple
ehelich: (adj.) legitimate
ehemalig: former
Ehemann: husband
Ehepaar: married couple
Ehescheidung: divorce
Eheschließung: marriage ceremony
Ehesohn: legitimate son
Ehestiftung: marriage contract
Ehetochter: legitimate daughter
Ehevertrag: marriage contract
Eid: oath
einbürgern: to naturalize
einführend: (adj.) introductory
Einführung: introduction
Eingekäufter: peasants who had
  bought into the land
Einnahmsregister: receipt book
einpfarren: to assign to a parish
Einrichtung(en): regulation(s)
Eintrag, Eintragung: entry
Einwanderung: immigration
Einwilligung: permission
Einwohner: inhabitant, resident
Einwohnerliste: list of inhabitants
einzeln: (adj.) single, individual
Eisenbahn: railroad
ejusdem: (adj.) the same
Elsaß: Alsace

Eltern: parents
Erbe: heir
erben: to inherit
Erbrecht: right of succession
Erbschaft: inheritance, legacy
erfolgte am: occurred on (date)
Erforschung: research
Erlaubnis: permission
Erschließung: development
Erstkommunionen: confirmation
  records (Catholic)
Erwachsen(e): adult(s)
Erzbistum: archbishopric
evangelisch: (adj.) Protestant
Familie: family
Familienarchiv: family archive
Familienbuch: family book/register
Familienforschung: family research
Familiengeschichte: family history
Familiengeschichtsforschung: family
  history research
Familienkunde: genealogy
Familienname: surname
Familienregister: family register
Familienstand: marital status
Familienverband: family organization
Feld: field
Filiale: branch church, branch office
Findling: foundling
firmen: to confirm (Catholic)
Firmung: confirmation (Catholic)
Firmungsbücher: confirmation books
  (Catholic)
Flecken: hamlet
Flitterwochen: honeymoon
Fluß/Flüsse: river/rivers
Forscher: researcher
Forschung: research
Frankreich: France
französisch: (adj.) French
Frau: wife
Fräulein: unmarried female
Freiherr: baron
Freie Reichsstadt: free city-state
Friedhof, Friedhöfe: cemetery/
  cemeteries
frühe Neuzeit: early modern times
Fürst(in): prince(cess), aristocrat
Fürstbischof: prince bishop

Fürstentum: principality
Garnison: military garrison
Gärtner: gardener
Gäste: attendees
Gatte/Gattin: husband/wife
Gebiet(e): territory, region
geboren: to be born
geboren am: born on (birthdate)
geboren in: born at (birthplace)
geborene, geb.: maiden name
Gebühr(en): charge(s), fee(s)
Geburt: birth
Geburtsdatum: birth date
Geburtsname: maiden name
Geburtsort: place of birth
Geburtsurkunde: birth certificate
geheiratet: (adj.) married
gehören zu: to belong to
Geistlicher: clergyman
Geld: money
Gemeinde: community/parish
Gemeindelexikon: gazetteer
Gemeindeverwaltung: municipal
  administration
Gemeindsmann: person with rights of
  citizenship
genannt: (adj.) alias, known as, called
Genealogie: genealogy
genealogische Forschungsstelle:
  genealogical research institution
Generallandesarchiv: national archives
Gericht: court
Gerichtsbuch: court record
Gerichtsprotokoll: court register
Geschichte(n): history (histories)
Geschichtsverein: historical society
geschieden: (adj.) divorced
Geschlecht: gender; family lineage
Geschlechterbuch: lineage book
Geschlechtsname: family name
Geschwister: siblings
Geselle(n): journeyman(men)
Gesellschaft: society, community, asso- .
  ciation
Gesetz: law
gestern: yesterday
gestorben am: died on (date)
getauft: (adj.) baptized
getraut: (adj.) married

getrennt: (adj.) separated
Gevatter: godfather, cousin, good friend
Gewerbe: trade/occupation/profession
gewesen: (adj.) former
Gilde: guild
Glaubensgemeinschaft: religious society
Glockenbuch: bell toll register
Graf/Gräfin: count/countess
Grafschaft: county
Größe: size; height
Großeltern: grandparents
Großherzogtum: grandduchy
Großmutter: grandmother
Großvater: grandfather
Grund: land
Grundbuch: land register
Gut: possessions; estate
Gutsherr: estate owner
Gutsverwalter: estate manager
Hafen: harbor, port
Handbuch: handbook, manual
Handel: trade
Handlung: act/action, store
Handschrift: handwriting
Hannover: Hanover
HAPAG: Hamburg-Amerikanische
Packetfahrt-Aktiengesellschaft
(shipping line)
Haupt-: head, main
Häuserbuch: book of houses
Häusler: cottage industries
Häusling: owns house (no farm)
Hebamme: midwife
Heft: number (of periodical)
Heimat: homeland
Heimatkunde: local history
Heimatortskartei(en): home town card-
  file(s)
Heirat/heiraten: marriage/to marry
Heiratsdatum: date of marriage
Heiratsliste: list of marriages
Heiratsurkunde: marriage certificate
Heraldik: heraldry
Herkunft: origin
Herkunftsname: a surname representing
a place of origin
Herkunftsort: place of origin
Heroldsamt: heraldic office
Herrengut: noble estate

Herzog/(-tum)/-in: duke/duchy/duchess
Hessen: Hesse
hiesiger Ort: of this place
Hinterbliebene: surviving relatives
hinterlassen: to leave (behind)
Hinweis(e): comment(s), remark(s)
historisch: (adj.) historical
Hochschulmatrikel(n): roll(s)/register(s)
  of school of higher education
Hochstift: independent bishopric,
  subject only to the Reich (similar to
Freie Reichsstadt)
Hochzeit: wedding
Hof: farm, estate
Hofgut: estate
Hofland: land strictly the property of
  the lord
Hofverwalter: estate manager
Hugenotten: Huguenots
Hurenkind: illegitimate child
Hutmacher: hat maker
Hypothekenbuch: mortgage book
Impfliste: vaccination list
Inhalt, Inhaltsverzeichnis: table of
  contents
Innungsregister: guild register
Institut: institution, establishment
Jahr/im Jahre: year/in the year (date)
Jahrbuch: annual register/chronicle
Jahrgang: age group (wine: vintage)
Jahrhundert: century
Judisch: Jewish
Junge: boy
jünger: (adj.) younger, junior
Jungfer: unmarried woman
Jungfrau: virgin/single woman
Junggeselle: bachelor
Jüngling: young man, bachelor
Kalender: calendar, almanac
Kapitel: chapter (of a book)
Kartei: card file
Katholik: Catholic
katholisch: (adj.) Catholic
Kaufmann: merchant
Kind(er): child(ren)
kinderlos: (adj.) childless
Kirche: church
Kirchenbuch/-bücher: church (vital
  records) book(s)

Kirchenbuchduplikat: parish register
  duplicates
Kirchenbücherverzeichnis(se):church
  book list(s), register(s), index(es)
Kirchengemeinde: congregation
Kirchensprengel: diocese, parish
Kirchenvorsteher: church warden
Kirchenzehnt: tithe
Kirchenzweitschrift: parish transcript
Kirchgemeinde : parish
Kirchhof: church cemetery
kirchlich getraut: married in church
Kirchspiel: parish
Kirchsprengel: parish
Kirchweih: church dedication
Kleinstadt: small town
Kloster: cloister
Knabe: boy
Knecht: farmhand (male)
Kommunikanten: communicants
  (Catholic)
Konfession: religion
Konfirmation: confirmation
(Protestant)
konfirmiert: (adj.) confirmed
  (Protestant)
König/-reich: king/kingdom
Kopfzahl: census, number of persons
Kopulation: marriage
Kötner: farmer (old term)
Krankheit: disease/illness
Krankheitbezeichnung(en): illness
  terminology(ies)
Kreis: district/county
Krieg: war
Kunde: science, knowledge,
information
Kunst: arts, crafts
Kurfürst: elector
Kurfürstentum: electorate
Kusin/Kusine: cousin (male/female)
Küster: sexton
Lagerbücher: military levy books
Land/Länder: state(s)/province(s)
Landesarchiv: state archive
Landesherr: territorial ruler
Landgericht: district court
Landgraf: Landgrave (aristocrat)
Landgrafschaft: Landgraviate

Landkarte: map
Landkreis: rural administrative area
  (county
Landschaft: province, district
Landwehr: militia
Landwirt: farmer (new term)
lateinisch: (adj.)Latin
lebendig: (adj.) living, alive
Lebensdokumente: vital records
ledig: (adj.) single (unmarried)
legitimieren: to legitimize
Lehrling: apprentice
Lehrlingsbuch: apprentice record
Leibeigenschaft: personal servitude
Leibzüchter: retired farmer entitled to
  receive a livelihood for life
Leichen: funeral
Leichenpredigt(en): funeral sermon(s)
letzter Wille: last will
Lexikon: dictionary, encyclopedia
Literatur: bibliography
Lothringen: Lorraine
lutheranisch: Lutheran
Mädchen: girl
Mädchenname: maiden name
Magd: farmhand (female)
Magyarország: Hungary
Mähren: Moravia
männlich: (adj.) male
Mannzahl: census, number of males
Mark: boundary/border
Markgraf: margrave
Markgrafschaft: margravate
Marktflecken: market town
Matrikel: register; enrollment; roll
Maurermeister: master mason
Maurer: mason
Meier: leaseholder; dairy farmer
Meister: master
Meldebehörden: registration
authorities
melden: to register
Mennonit/(-isch): Mennonite [noun/
adj.]
Mennoniten: Mennonites
Mieter: tenant
Militär: the military
Militärverhältnis: military standing
minderjährig: underage

Mitglied(er): member(s)
Mittag: midday/noon
Mitteilung: message/news
Möbel: furniture
Monat: : month
Morgen/morgen: morning/tomorrow
morgens: in the morning
Musterungslisten: military lists
Mutter: mother
Nachfahr: descendant
Nachfahrentafel: descendancy chart
nachgelassene(r): (adj.) surviving
Nachkomme(n): descendant(s)
Nachkommenforschung: descendant ..
  research
Nachlaß: legacy, estate
Nachlaßgericht: probate court
Nachlässe: personal effects of estate
nachmittags: in the afternoon
Nachricht: news
Nachschlagewerk: reference book
Nacht: night
Nachtrag: supplement (of a book)
Name(n): name(s)
Namenlexikon: name encyclopedia
Namenregister: name index
Namensverzeichnis: name index
Nationalität: nationality
Nebenfrau: mistress, concubine
Neffe: nephew
Nichte: niece
noch lebende: still living
Nottaufe: emergency baptism
Nummer: number
Oberamt: principal government office
Oberslandesgericht: high court
Oheim: uncle
Onkel: uncle
Ort(e): location(s), place(s)
Ort der Geburt: place of birth
Ortsbuch: gazetteer
Ortschaft: village
Ortschaftsverzeichnis: gazetteer
Ortsfamilienbücher: lineage books
Ortslexikon: gazetteer
Ortsliste(n): place list(s)
Ortsnamenverzeichnis: gazetteer
Ortsregister: locality index/list
Ortssippenbuch: locality family book

Ortsteil: suburb/district
Österreich: Austria
Österreich-Ungarn: Austria-Hungary
Ostpreußen: East Prussia
Pächter: farmer, tenant
Parochie: parish
Paten: witnesses, godparents
Personenregister: surname index
Personenstandsregister: civil
   registration records
Pfalz: Palatinate
Pfalzgraf: Count Palatine
Pfalzgrafschaft: Palatine county
Pfarramt: church office/parish
Pfarrbezirk: parish
Pfarrbuch: parish register
Pfarrei: parish
Pfarrer: pastor/priest
Pfarrerverzeichnis(se): index(es) of
   clergymen
Pfarrkirche: parish church
Pfarrsprengel: parish district
Pflege: care, maintenance
Pflegesohn: foster son
Platz: place
Polen: Poland
Polizeiregister: police register
polnish (adj.): Polish
Polska: Poland
Polterabend: party held on eve of
   wedding ceremony
Pommern: Pomerania
Porzellan: porcelain/china
Postfach: post office box
Predigt: sermon
Preußen: Prussia
Priester: priest
Proklamation: banns, proclamation
protestantisch: (adj.) Protestent
Protokolle: official records
Provinz: province
preußisch (adj.): Prussian
Quelle(n): source(s)
Quellenverzeichnis(se): list of sources
Rangliste: list of military officers
Rathaus: town hall
Realteilungsrecht: division of the
   family farm among many
descendants

Rechtsanwalt: lawyer
reformiert: (adj.) Reformed (church);
   Calvinistic
Regierungsbezirk (RB.) provincial
   district
Register: register(s)
Reich: empire
Reichs-: national
Reichsland: Area subject to the Reich
   itself
Reichsfreiherr: baron (prince of the
Holy Roman Empire)
Reiseziel: destination
Religion: religion
Rentkammer: board of revenue
Rentner: retired person
Rheinland: Rhineland
Ritter: knight
Rittergut: knight's estate
Rufname: the given name one goes by
Saargebiet: Saarland, Saar
Sache: thing
Sachregister: subject index
Sachsen: Saxony
Sachsen-Altenburg: Saxe-Altenburg
Sachsen-Coburg-Gotha: Saxe-Coburg-
   Gotha
Sachsen-Meiningen: Saxe-Meiningen
Sachsen-Weimar-Eisenach: Saxe-
   Weimar-Eisenach
Sammelwerk: compilation
Sammlung: collection
Scheidung: divorce
Schein: certificate
Schiffsliste: ship list
Schlesien: Silesia
Schloß: palace
Schloßgut: palace estate
Schmied: blacksmith
Schuhmacher: shoemaker
Schule: school
Schullehrer: teacher
Schultheiß: village mayor
Schweiz: Switzerland
Seelenregister: membership register
Seite: page
selbe: (adj.) same
Selbsmord: suicide
selbständig: (adj.) self-sufficient, self-

employed
Selbstzeugnis(se): documentation(s) of one's own life
Siegelkunde: information about seals
siehe (abbrev.: *s.*): see (refer to something)
Sippe: group of related persons, kin
Sippenforschung: ancestral research
Sippennamen: lineage names
Sippenverband: lineage
Sohn/Söhne: son/sons
Sohn von: son of
Söhnchen: son (diminutive)
Sonderdruck: special edition
sonstig: (adj) other, remaining; former
Staat: state, nation
Staatsangehörigkeit: citizenship/ nationality
Staatsarchiv: state archive; public records office
Stadt: city, town
Stadtarchiv: city archives
Stadtbuch: town or city record
Stadtchronik: town history
Stamm: family line
Stammbaum: family tree, pedigree
Stammbuch: book in which family records are kept
Stammliste: pedigree list
Stammrolle: military muster rolls
Stammtafel: pedigree
Stammvater: originating ancestor
Stand: status/position/occupation
Standesamt/(-ämter): civil registry office(s)
standesamtlich getraut: married in a civil ceremony
Standesbeamter: civil clerk at civil registry office
Standesregister: civil registry record
Standort: site, location
starb: died
Stelle: place, office
Stellung im Berufe: position in profession
Sterbefall: death
sterben: to die
Sterbeurkunde: death certificate
Sterbeursache: cause of death

Steuer(n): tax(es)
Steuerbuch: tax record
Steuerrolle: tax rolls
Stiefkind: stepchild
Stift: religious institution, convent
Stiftung: foundation
Straße: street
Stunde: hour
Tag der Taufe: day of baptism
Tag : day
Tagelöhner: day laborer(s)
Tal: valley
Taufdatum: date of christening
Taufe: christening, baptism
taufen: to baptize
Taufpaten: godparents
Taufrodel: baptismal record (Swiss)
Tauftag: christening date
Taufzeuge: godfather
Taufzeugin: godmother
Teil: part (as in *part of*, or *Part I*)
Testament: will/testament
Thüringen: Thuringia
Tirol: Tyrol
Tochter/Töchter: daughter/daughters
Tochter von: daughter of
Töchterchen: daughter (diminutive)
Tochtergemeinde: church branch, filial church
Tod: death
Todesanzeige: obituary
Todesursache: cause of death
tot: (adj.) dead
Totenbücher: death books
Totengeläutbücher: death bell tolling books
totgeborenes Kind: stillborn child
Trauung: wedding, marriage ceremony
Übersetzung: translation
Übersicht: overview, list
um: at about, around
unbekannt: (adj.) unknown
unehelich: illegitimate
Ungarn: Hungary
ungefähr: about, approximately
Universität: university
Universitätsmatrikel(n): university roll(s)/registry(ies)
Unterschrift: signature

unverheiratet: (adj.) unmarried
Urgroßvater/-mutter: great
  grandfather/-mother
Urkunde: old (original) document,
  certificate, deed; *zu Urkund*
  dessen=in witness whereof
Ursache: cause
Vater: father
Verband/Verbände: society/societies
verehelicht: (adj.) married
Verein: society, union
Vereinigte Staaten: United States
Vereinigung: association
Verfasser(in): author/writer
verheiratet: (adj.) married
Verlag: publisher
Verlobte: engaged couple
Verlobung: engagement
Verlobungsanzeige: banns
vermählt: (adj.) married
Veröffentlichung(en): publication(s)
verstorben: (adj.) deceased, defunct
verstorben am: died on
Verstorbene(r): the deceased
verwandt: (adj.) related
verwandte Publikationen: related
  publications
Verwandtschaft: relatives
verwitwet: (adj.) widowed
Verzeichnis(se): list(s)/index(es)
Vetter: male cousin
Viertel: town quarter
Volk: people/nation
Volkszählung: census
volljährig: (adj.) of legal age
von: of/from
Vorfahr(en): ancestor(s)
Vormund: guardian
Vormundschaft: guardianship
Vorname(n): given name(s)
Vorwerk: residence; farm outside the
            castle walls
Waise: orphan
Wappen: coat-of-arms
Wappenkunde: heraldry
Wäsche: laundry/underclothes
Weib: wife/woman
weiblich: female
weiland: deceased, former

Weiler: hamlet
Westfalen: Westphalia
Westpreußen: West Prussia
wichtig: (adj.) important
Wiedertäufer: Anabaptist
Wissenschaften: science
Witwe/(-r): widow/widower
wohin: where to? (destination)
wohnen: to live (reside)
Wohnhaft: place of residence
Wohnort/Wohnplatz: place of
residence
Wohnsitz: residence
Wörterbuch: dictionary
wurde geboren: was born
wurde getauft: was baptized
Zehntregister: tithe register
Zeichen: symbol
Zeit: time
Zeitschrift(en): periodical(s), journal(s)
Zeitung(en): newspaper(s)
Zentral: central
Zentralstelle: center, central repository
Zeuge(n): witness(es)
Zeugnis: testimony, certificate
Ziel der Auswanderung: emigrant's
  destination
Zivilstand: marital status
Zivilstandsamt: civil registry
Zivilstandsregister: civil registry (vital
  records)
Zollverein: Customs Union
Zuname: surname
Zunft: guild
Zunftbuch: guild record
Zweitschriften: transcripts
Zwilling: twin

DESIGNATIONS FOR GERMAN OCCUPATIONS, TRADES, AND TITLES (BERUFSBEZEICH-NUNGEN)

Abbauer .... farmer on newer farm
Abdecker ...... dealer in animal cadavers
Abentürer .... jewelry maker
Abortfeger .... toilet cleaner
Abstreifer .... dealer in animal cadavers

Ackerer, Acker(s)mann .... farmer
Ackerknecht .... farm laborer,
ploughman
Adeliger .... nobleman
Aderlasser .... blood-letter, surgeon
Advocat .... attorney
Akademiker .... academician
Altbuzer .... cobbler, shoe repairman
Altmacher ...... cobbler, shoe repairman
Altreifer .... cobbler, shoe repairman
Altreuser .... cobbler, shoe repairman
Amtmann .. magistrate, warden, district
judge
Amtsdiener .... court usher
Amtsknecht .... servant, messenger
Amtsverwalter .... administrator
Amtsverweser .... deputy
Anbauer .... peasant
Angestellter .... employee
Ankerschmied .... anchor maker
Anstreicher .... painter
Anwalt .... lawyer, guardian, notary
Anweiser .... attorney
Anwohner .... nearby resident
Apotheker .... pharmacist
Arbeiter .... worker, laborer
Architekt .... architect
Armbruster .... bow-maker
Arzt(in) .... (male/female) physician
Ätzer .... etcher
Aufseher .... guard, supervisor
Auktionator .... auctioneer
Ausgeber .... distributor
Ausländer .... foreigner
Auslaufer .... errand boy
Ausrufer .... town crier
Auswanderer .... emigrant
Auszahler .... paymaster
Bader .... barber, surgeon
Bauer .... farmer
Bäcker .... baker
Badeknecht/-magdbaths servant (male/
female)
Bader .... bathhouse operator, barber
Bahnarbeiter .... railroad employee
Ballierer .... polisher
Bamutter .... midwife
Bandfabrikant .... ribbon maker
Bankangestellte .. bank employee/teller

Barbier .... barber
Barrettmacher .... bonnetmaker
Bartscherer .... barber
Bauarbeiter .... construction worker
Bauer .... farmer/builider
Bauernknecht/-magd .... farm servant
Bauernbursche .... country lad, yokel
Bauernfrau/Bauerin .... farmer's wife
Bauhandwerker .... assigner of building
contracts
Bauingenieur .... architect
Baumeister ..... architect, master builder
Baumgärtner .... orchard gardener
Bauzeichner .... structural draftsman
Beamte, Beamter .. official, civil servant
Beauftragter ..... deputy, representative
Becherer .... turner
Bechermacher ...... mugs or cups maker
Becker, Beck .... baker
Behelfer .... tutor
Beinhauer .... butcher
Beisass .... cottager, resident
without citizenship
Beischer .... whipmaker
Beisitzer .... assessor
Bekenmacher .... cooper
Bender .... cooper
Berater .... counselor, advisor
Bergarbeiter .... miner
Bergknappe .... miner
Bergleute .... miners
Bergmann .... miner
Berittener .... mounted horseman
Bernsteinschleifer ..... amber gem cutter
Beschlägemacher .... tinsmith
Beschleißer .... custodian, caretaker
Beschneider .... animal castrator
Besenbinder .... broom maker
Besitzer .... owner, proprietor
Bettler .... beggar
Bettziechenweber ...... bed cover maker
Beutler .... (leather) bagmaker
Bewaffneter .... arms bearer
Beysass .... lay assessor
Bienenpfleger .... bee-keeper
Bienenzüchter .... bee cultivator
Bierbrauer .... beer brewer
Biereigen .... home brewer
Bierfahrer .... beer delivery man

Bierschenk(er) .... tavern keeper
Bierschröter .... beer hauler
Biersieder .... beer brewer
Bildgießer .... educator
Bildhauer .... sculptor
Bildschnitzer .... woodcarver
Bildweber .... wood-cutter
Binder .... binder, cooper, barrel maker
Bischof .... bishop
Blaufärber .... dyer of blue cloth
Blecharbeiter .... sheet metal worker,
                                                    plumber
Blechschmied .... sheet metal/tin smith
Bleicher .... bleacher
Bleigießer .... lead smelter
Bletzer .... cobbler, shoe repairman
Boddeker .... cooper
Bogenmacher .... bowmaker
Bogenschütze .... archer
Bogner, Bogener .... bowmaker
Bohrerschmied .... drill smith
Börsenmakler .... stock broker
Bortenwirker .... lace worker
Bote .... messenger
Böttcher .... cooper, barrelmaker
Brandweinbrenner .... distiller
Brauer .... brewer
Brauknecht .... brewery worker
Brettschneider .... sawyer
Briefbote, -träger .... mailman
Brillenmacher .... maker of eyeglasses,
                                                   optician
Brinksitzer .... farmer
Bruchschneider .... physician, surgeon
Brückenzöllner .... bridge toll-taker
Brummifahrer .... truck driver
Brunnengraber .... well digger
Brunnenmeister   supervisor of well
                                            construction
Brücker .... bridge worker
Buchbinder .... bookbinder
Buchdrucker .... printer
Buchführer .... bookkeeper
Buchhalter .... bookkeeper
Buchhändler .... book dealer
Buchschließenmacher .... maker
                   of miniature locks for books
Büchsenmacher ..... gunsmith, armorer
Büchsenschäfter .... gunstock maker

Büchsenschmied .... gunsmith
Büdner .... stallkeeper, cottager
Bürge .... guarantor, sponsor
Bürger .... citizen
Bürgermeister .... mayor
Burggraf .... baron
Burgmann .... castle steward
Bürstenmacher .... brush maker
Bürstenbinder .... brush maker
Büttel .... overseer, bailiff, jailor
Büttner .... cooper
Chemiker .... chemist
Chirurg .... surgeon
Civilbeamt .... civil officer
Colon(us) .... farmer, settler
Conditor .... see Konditor
Corber .... basketweaver
Dachdecker .... thatcher, roof tiler
Dechanat .... dean
Dekan .... dean (of university)
Dengler .... blademaker (scythes)
Dichter .... author, poet
Dieb .... thief
Diener/-in .... servant (male/female),
                                                    waiter
Dienstbote .... domestic servant
Dienstknecht .... servant boy
Dienstmädchen .... servant woman
Dirne . female servant, maid, farm hand
Doktor .... learned person
Domherr .... canon
Dosenfasser .... tinsmith
Dosenmacher .... can maker
Dosenmaler .... jar painter
Dragoner .... dragoon
Drahtzieher .... wire drawer/maker
Drechsler .... thresher, (wood) turner
Dreher .... turner
Drogist .... druggist, chemist
Drucker .... printer, print maker
Durchreisender .... stranger, transient
Edelknecht .... squire
Edelmann .... nobleman
Edelsteinhändler ..... dealer in precious
                                                      stones
Eichbeamter ...... weights and measures
                                         representative
Eierhändler .... egg dealer
Eigengärtner .... independent gardener

Eigenkätner ...... independent cottager
Eigentümer .... property owner
Einlieger .... lodger, tenant farmer,
day laborer
Einnehmer .... collector (of money)
Einwohner .... inhabitant
Eisengießer .... iron founder
Einsiedler .... hermit, recluse
Eisengießer .... iron founder
Eisenhändler .... iron monger
Eisenhauer .... miner, iron-hewer
Eisenmeister .... iron master
Eisenschmied .... blacksmith
Erntearbeiter .... harvester
Erzbildner .... bronze sculptor
Erzbischof .... archbishop
Erzgießer .... caster, brass founder
Erzgräber .... ore miner
Erzherzog/(-in) archduke/archduchess
Erzieher .... educator
Eseltreiber .... donkey driver
Essenkehrer .... chimneysweep
Estrichmacher .... stone floor maker
Fabrikant manufacturer, factory owner
Fabrikarbeiter .... factory worker
Fächermacher .... fan maker
Fachmann .... expert, specialist
Fackelträger .... torch carrier
Fadenmacher .... threadmaker
Fahn(en)träger, -rich .... flagbearer
Fährmann .... ferryman
Faktor .... manager, supervisor
Falder .... baker
Falkner .... falconer
Färber .... dyer
Färbergeselle .... dyer journeyman
Faßbinder .... cooper, barrel-maker
Faßler .... cooper
Federschmücker .... feather maker,
plumassier
Federviehhändler ...... poultry merchant
Feilenhauer .... file maker
Feldarzt .... military medical officer
Feldherr .... commander-in chief,
general
Feldmesser .... (land) surveyor
Feldprediger .... chaplain (military)
Feldscherer ...... military medical officer
Feldsher .... army surgeon

Feldschütz .... sergeant
Feldwebel .... sergeant
Feldzeugmeister .... quartermaster
Ferkelbeschneider .... pig castrator
Fernfahrer .... truck driver
Fertigmacher .... finisher, foreman,
adjuster
Feuerschlossmacher ..... flintlock maker
Feuerwehrleute .... fire brigade workers
Feuerwerker .... explosives expert
Fiedler .... fiddler
Figurist .... sculptor
Finanzbeamte .... finance official
Finanzer .... tax-collector
Finanzmann .... financier
Fischer .... fisherman
Flachshändler .... flax merchant
Flachshausierer .... flax peddler
Flaggermacher .... flag maker
Flaschenmacher .... bottlemaker
Flaschner .... plumber
Flecksieder ...... cleaner/boiler of animal
entrails for further use
Fleischer .... butcher
Fleischhauer .... butcher
Flicker .... mender
Flickschneider .... tailor who mends
Flickschuster .. cobbler, shoe repairman
Flieger .... aviator
Fliesenmacher .... tiler
Flößer .... raftsman
Flötenbläser .... flute player
Fluchtling ... refugee, fugitive, deserter
Flugkapitän .... airplane pilot
Flurhüter .... keeper, ranger
Fohlenbeschneider .... foal castrator
Folterknecht .... torturer, executioner
Förster .... forest ranger
Fotograf .... photographer
Fourier .... quartermaster
Frachmakler .... shipping agent
Franziskaner .... Franciscan monk
Freibauer .... independent peasant,
Freiherr/(-in) .... baron/baroness
freeholder
Friseur .... barber, hairdresser (male)
Führer .... director, manager, driver,
conductor
Fuhrknecht .... grooms attendant

Fuhrleute .... freight haulers
Fuhrmann . coachman, wagoner, driver
Fürsprech .... advocate
Fürst/(-in) .... prince/princess
Füselier .... light infantryman
Fußsoldat .... foot soldier
Fußvolk .... footmen
Futterhändler .. animal feed tradesman
Futteralmacher .... case maker
Galanteriearbeiter .... worker with fancy
                            goods and jewelry
Garkoch .... cook
Garmmeister .... fisherman
Gartenkünster .... landscape artist
Gärtner .... gardener
Gastwirt(h) .... innkeeper
Gaukler .... juggler, vagabond, minstrel
Geächteter .... outlaw
Gebißmacher .... bridle bit maker
Gefäßformer .... ceramic mold maker
Geflügelhändler .... poulterer
Geheimschreiber confidential secretary
Gehilfe .... assistant, helper
Geiger .... violinist
Geißhirte .... goat herder
Geistlicher .... priest, pastor, clergyman
Gelbgiesser .... brazier
Geldeinnehmer .... money collector
Geldleiher .... money lender
Geldwechsler .... money changer
Gelehrter .... scholar
Geistlicher .... clergyman
Gemeindearbeiter ...... municipal worker
Gemeindediener .... beadle,
                       community messenger
Gemeindemann .... officer
Gemeindeschreiber .... town
                             or parish clerk
Gemüsegärtner .... market gardener
Gemüsehändler .... vegetable seller,
                              green grocer
Gerber .... tanner
Gerichtsdiener ...... servant in the court
Gerichtsmann des Gerichts magistrate
                                of the court
Gerichtsschöffe .... juryman,
                       lay member of the court
Gerichtsschreiber ...... clerk of the court
Gerichtsverwandter: ..... lay member of

the court; juryman
Geschäft .... trade, business
Geschäftsführer .... manager
Geschäftsmann .... businessman
Geschmeidemacher .... jewelry maker
Geschützgiesser .... cannon founder
Geselle .... journeyman, apprentice
Getreidehändler .... grain dealer
Gewandschneider .... garment cutter
Gewehrschmied .... gun smith
Gewerbe .... trade, occupation
Gewürtz -krämer/-händler .... grocer,
                                 spice dealer
Gießer .... founder, caster, molder
Gilde .... guild
Gipser .... plasterer
Glasgeselle .... glazier
Glaser .... glassmaker, glazier
Glasmacher .... glassmaker
Glasmaler .... glass painter
Glasschleifer .... glass grinder
Gläubiger .... creditor, mortgagee
Glockengießer .... bell founder
Glöckner .... sexton, bellringer
Goldarbeiter .... gold worker
Goldschlager .... maker of gold leaf
Goldschmied .... goldsmith
Goldsticker .... gold embroiderer
Goldzieher .... gold wire drawer
Graf .... count
Grapengiesser .... iron pot caster
Graphiker .... graphic artist
Graveur .... engraver
Greis .... old man
Grenadier .... grenadier, infantryman
Grobschmied .... blacksmith
Großhändler .... wholesaler
Großherzog/(-in) ...... grand duke/grand
                                      duchess
Großuhrmacher ...... maker of big clocks
                       (for churches, etc.)
Grützer .... grain miller
Gurtelmacher .... beltmaker
Gürtler .... beltmaker, brass worker
Gutsbesitzer .... estate owner
Gutspächter .... brass founder
Häcker .... vine grower
Hafner .... potter
Halbbauer .... half-share farmer

Hammerschmied .... blacksmith
Handarbeiter .... manual laborer
Handelsmann .... merchant
trader
Händler .... dealer, trader, retailer
Handschuhmacher .... glove maker
Handwerker .... artisan, craftsman
Handwerksmann .... craftsman
Harfner .... harpist
Harnischmacher .. armor/harness maker
Häscher .... bailiff
Hauer .... miner
Hauptmann .... captain, chief
Hausdiener .... house servant
Hausgenosse .... household member
Hausierer .... door-to-door salesman,
peddler
Häusler .... cottager, landless laborer
Hausmeister .... caretaker
Hebamme .... midwife
Heftelmacher .... hook-and-eye maker
Heger .... keeper, forester, game warden
Heizer .... stoker, fireman
Hellebardenmacher .... halberd maker
Helmmacher .... helmet maker
Helmschmied .... helmet smith
Hemd(en)macher .... shirtmaker
Henker .... hangman, executioner
Herr .... master, lord, Lord, mister
Herstellen .... manufacturer
Herzog/(-in) .... duke/duchess
Heuerling .... day laborer, hired man
Hilfsgeistlicher ..... assistant clergyman
Hirte .... shepherd, cowherd
Hochseefischer ...... deep sea fisherman
Hof: .... farm estate; court
Hofleute .... bondsmen, courtiers
Hofmann .... courtier, bailiff, steward
Hofmarschall ...... master of ceremonies
Holzarbeiter .... woodworker
Holzbitschenmacher .... cooper
Holzbildhauer .... wood sculptor
Holzdrechsler .... turner (wood)
Holzflösser .... raftsman
Holzgraveur .... wood engraver
Holzhändler .... lumber dealer
Holzhauer .... woodcutter
Holzschläger .... woodcutter
Holzschneider .... wood cutter

Holzschuhhändler .... trader in
wooden shoes
Holzschuhmacher .... wooden shoe
maker
Holztroghauer .... maker of wooden
troughs
Homusikus .... crowns musician
Hopfenbauer .... hops grower
Hornrichter .... comb maker
Hospitaler .... nursing home resident
Hucker .... peddler
Hüfener .... farmer with full size farm
Hufschmied .... farrier, blacksmith
Hüter .... guardian, warden, herdsman
Hutmacher .... hatmaker, milliner
Hüttenarbeiter .... foundryman
Imker .... beekeeper
Ingenieur .... engineer
Jagdgenosse .... hunter's assistant
Jäger .... huntsman
Journalist .... journalist
Jurist .... lawyer
Juwelier .... jeweler
Kacheler .... tiler
Kachelmacher .... tiled stove maker
Kachelmaler .... tile painter
Kalkbrenner .... chalk burner
Kalkmacher .... chalkmaker
Kameenschneider .... cameo engraver
Kaminkehrer .... chimneysweep
Kammerdiener .... butler
Kämmerer (city) treasurer, chamberlain
Kammmacher .... comb maker
Kämmerer .... chamberlain
Kampferer .... warrior
Kandelgießer .... pewter caster
Kannengießer .... pewter caster
Karrenmann .... coachman
Karrenzieher .... cart puller
Kantor .... choirmaster, organist, singer
Kanzleibeamter .... chancery clerk
Kaplan .... chaplain
Kärcher .... coachman
Kärrner, Karrer .... coachman
Kartenstecher ...... map/chart engraver
Kartenzeichner .... cartographer
Käsehändler .... cheese dealer
Käser .... cheesemaker
Käsmacher .... cheesemaker

Kastellan .... steward
Kastenmacher .... boxmaker
Kastrierer .... castrator
Kartendrucker .... calico print maker
Kattunweber .... cotton weaver
Kaufbudeninhaber .... shop/stall owner
Kaufleute ...... merchants, businessmen
Kaufmann .... shopkeeper, merchant,
                                            businessman
Kehrrichtlader .... rubbish collector
Kelchmaker .... cup maker
Kellereiverwalter .... keeper of
                                            the wine cellar
Kellermeister ..... cellarmaster/cellarman
Kellner(in) .... (male/female) waiter
Kerkermeister .... jailer, master jailer
Kerzengießer .... candlemaker
Kerzenmacher .... candlemaker
Kerzenzieher .... candlemaker
Kesselflicker .... tinker
Kesselschmied .... boilermaker
Kessler .... boilermaker, tinker,
                                            coppersmith
Kettenschmied .... chainsmith
Kieffer .... cooper
Kielfedernschneider .... quill feather
                                            cutter
Kindermagd .... nanny
Kirchenpfleger .... church caretaker
Kirchenschöffe .... church assessor
Kirschner .... cherry brandy maker
Kisten-Truhenmacher .... cabinetmaker
Kistenmacher cratemaker, woodworker
Kistler .... box/crate maker
Klausner .... hermit, recluse
Kleiber .... daub and wattle worker
Kleidermacher .... clothesmaker
Kleinbauer .... peasant, farmer
Kleinbüttscher .... cooper
Kleinplastiker .... miniature sculptor
Kleinschmied .... edge-toolmaker
Kleinverschlüssen .... maker of
                                            fasteners and locks
Klempner .... plumber, tinsmith
Klingenschmied .... sword smith
Klopffechter fencing artist (circus, etc.)
                                   or fencing teacher
Klosterschaffner .... financial adviser
                                            of an abbey

Knappe .... page, squire
Knecht .... (male) servant, farmhand
Knochenhauer .... butcher
Knopfmacher .... buttonmaker
Koch/Köchin .... cook (male/female)
Kohlenbrenner .... coal-maker/sorter
Köhler .... charcoalmaker
Kolonist .... settler, pioneer
Komödiant .... play-actor, clown
Konditor .... pastry-cook
Kopist .... copyist
Korber   basket weaver
Korbflechter .... basket weaver
Korbmacher .... basket weaver
Korbwagenmacher ...... basket-carriage
                                            maker
Kornfruchthändler .... cereals dealer
Kornhändler .... grain merchant
Kornhausverwalter .... granary
                                            administrator
Konmesser .... corn measurer
Kornmüller .... grain miller
Korsettmacher .... corsetmaker
Kostgänger .... boarder
Kötner .... farmer
Krämer .... shopkeeper, tradesman,
                                            peddler
Krankenpfleger . caregiver for the sick
Krankenschwester .... nurse
Krankenwärter ...... male nurse, orderly
Krausenbäcker .... jar potter
Kräutermann .... herbalist
Krautkrämer .... druggist
Kriegsknecht .... mercenary
Krüger .... innkeeper, publican
Krugführer .... innkeeper
Küchenbäcker .... confectioner
Küchenmeister .... head cook
Küchenmädchen .... kitchen maid
Küchlebäcker/Küchler .... pastry baker
Küfer .... cellarman; (dial.) cooper
Küher .... cowherd
Kuhhirt .... cowherd
Kuhhirtin .... cowherd (female)
K.U.K. Oberleutnant .... regimental
                                            sergeant major
Kunstdilettant .... amateur artist
Kunsthändler .... art dealer
Kunsthandwerker .... artisan

Künstler .... artist
Kunstschlosser .... art metal worker
Kunsttischler .... cabinetmaker
Kupferdrucker .... copperplate printer
Kupfergiesser .... copper founder
Kupferschmied .... coppersmith
Kupferstecher .. copperplate engraver,
.... etcher
Kuppler .... matchmaker
Kürschner .... furrier
Küster ..... church caretaker, custodian
Kutschenbauer .... coach maker
Kutscher .... coachman
Küster .... sexton
Kutscher .... coachman
Kuttler .... offal seller
Lackierer .... varnisher, lacquerer
Ladenangestellter .... shop keeper
Laie .... layman
Landarbeiter .... farm laborer, farmhand
Landarzt .... country doctor
Landgärtner .... landscape gardener
Landmann .... farmer
Landmesser .... surveyor
Landsknecht: .... German mercenary
Landstreicher .... tramp
Landwirt(h) .... farmer
Landwirt(h) .... farmer
Lastträger .... porter
Laternenmacher .... lanternmaker
Laufbursche .... errand boy,
printer's devil
Läufer .... messenger
Laufschmied .... gun barrel maker
Lebkücher .... gingerbread baker
Lederbereiter .... leather dresser
Lederbeutelmacher .. leather bag maker
Lederer .... leather maker
Lederhändler .... leather dealer
Lederkünstler .... leather artist
Lehmarbiter .... potter or brickmaker
Lehnsherr .... liege lord
Lehnsmann .... vassal
Lehrmeister .... master of a trade
Lehmfahrer .... clay pit
.... (transportation worker in)
Lehmverstreicher .... grouter
Lehnsmann .... vassal (slave)
Lehrer/(-in) .... teacher (male/female)

Lehrling .... apprentice
Leibarzt .... personal physician
Leibzüchter .... retired farmer
Leichenbestatter .... undertaker
Leichenbitter .... inviter to funerals
Leichenlader .... undertaker or inviter to
funerals
Leierkastenmann .... organ grinder
Leinwanddrucker .... cloth printer
Lein(en)weber .... linen weaver
Leitender Arzt .... head physician
Leiter .... director
Leutnant .... lieutenant
Leutpriester .... lay priest
Lichtenmacher .... candlemaker
Lichtzieher .... candlemaker
Litterati .... writer
Lkw-Fahrer .... truck driver
Lodenfärber .... wool or cloth dyer
Lodenmacher/-weber ... maker of coarse
woolen cloth
Loder .... maker of Loden cloth
Lohgerber .... tanner
Lohnarbeiter .... hired worker
Lohnkutscher .... hired coachman
Lumpensammler .... ragpicker
Magd .. female domestic servant, maid
Magister .... schoolmaster
Mahler .... painter, artist
Mahlmüller .... miller
Maier .... overseer
Major .... major
Makler .... broker, jobber
Maler .... painter, artist
Mälzer .... beer distiller, malt miller
Malzmüller .... malt miller
Mantelmacher .... coatmaker
Marktaufseher .... market supervisor
Marktschreier .... charlatan
Marmorkünstler .... marble artist
Marmorsteinmetz .... marble mason
Matratzenmacher .... mattressmaker
Matrose .... sailor
Mattenmacher .... mat maker
Maurer .... bricklayer, mason
Mauerpolier .... foreman bricklayer,
head-mason
Mechaniker .... fitter, mechanic
Medaillenstecher .... medal engraver

Mehlhändler .... flour merchant
Meier .... farm administrator, dairy
    farmer, tenant, castle overseer
Meister .... master
Melder .... dispatch rider, messenger
Melker .... milker (male)
Messerschmied .... cutler, knifemaker
Messergriffmacher knife-handle maker
Messerschneidenmacher .. knife-blade
                                   maker
Messingschmied .. brassworker, cutler
Messner .... sexton
Metalplastiker .... metal sculptor
Metzger .... butcher
Mietling .... male renter, tenant,
                               mercenary
Mietsgärtner .... tenant gardener
Mietsmann .... male tenant
Milchträger .... milkman
Milchviehzüchter ...... dairy farm leaser
Milizer .... militiaman
Möbelhändler .... furniture merchant
Möbelschnitzer .... furniture carver
Möbeltischler .... cabinetmaker
Modist .... milliner
Mönch .... monk, friar
Müller .... miller
Mundschenk .... butler, cupbearer
Münster: .... monastery; later a
    Klosterkirche, or cloister church
Münzer .... (coin) minter
Münzmeister .... (coin) minter
Münzscheider .... assayer
Musiker, Musikant .... musician
Nachahmer .... copyist
Nachtwächter .... night watchman
Nadelfertiger .... needle finisher
Nadelhändler .... needle merchant
Nadelmacher .... needlemaker
Nadelmaler .... needlepointer
Nadler .... needlemaker, haberdasher
Nagelschmied, Nagler .... nailsmith
Näherin .... dressmaker
Nähler .... sewer
Nestler .... shoelace maker
Neuling .... novice
Niederrichter .... lower judge
Notar .... notary, civil lawyer
Oberkoch .... master chef

Oberleutnant .... first lieutenant
Oberpfarrer .... rector
Oberst .... colonel
Obsthändler .... fruit seller
Ochsenknecht .... cowherder
Ofensetzer .... stove fitter
Ölmacher .... oilman, chandler
Ölmüller .... oil-miller
Ölschlager .... oil press operator
                         (oil from seeds)
Örgelbauer .... organ builder
Orgelmacher .... organ builder
Ortsfremder .... stranger
Pächter .... lessee, tenant
Packer .... packer
Paneelenmacher .... panelmaker
Pantoffelmacher .... slipper maker
Panzermacher ..... maker of body armor
Papierarbeiter .... paper worker
Papierhändlerstationer, paper merchant
Papiermacher .... papermaker
Parfümmacher .... perfume maker
Parillenmacher .... eye-glass maker
Pastetenverkäufer .... pie seller
Pauker .... kettle drummer, duellist
Pelzhändler .... fur dealer
Pergamentmacher .... parchment maker
Perlmuttergraveur ...... mother-of-pearl
                                engraver
Perück(en)macher .... wigmaker
Pfalzgraf .... Earl, count palatine
Pfandgeber .... pawnbroker
Pfandnehmer .... pawnbroker
Pfannenschmied .... pan smithy
Pfarrer .... clergyman, pastor, priest
Pfarrkind .... parishioner
Pefferhändler .... pepper trader
Pfeifenfabrikant .... pipe maker
Pfeifenmacher .... pipe maker
Pfeifer .... fife player
Pfeilmacher .... arrowmaker
Pferdehändler .... horse merchant
Pferdeknecht .... stable worker
Pferdeschlächter .... horse butcher
Pferdeverleiher .... livery stable worker
Pflasterer .... street paver, plasterer
Pfleger .... nurse (male)
Pflüger .... plowman
Pflugschmied .... plowsmith

Pförtner .... doorman, porter
Philosoph .... philosopher
Physicus ------------------------- doctor
Pilger .... pilgrim
Piscator .... fisherman
Plattner .... (flattening) smith,
body armor maker
Polierer .... burnisher, polisher
Polizei .... police
Polsterer .... upholsterer
Porträtmaler .... portrait painter
Posamentierer   braidmaker, lacemaker,
haberdasher
Postbeamte .... postal worker
Posthalter .... post-horse keeper
Postillion .... coachman
Postreiter .... courier
Pottaschbrenner .... potash burner
Prediger .... preacher
Priester .... priest
Prinz/(essin) .... prince/princess
Probst .... dean
Prüfer .... examiner
Puppenmacher .... dollmaker
Putzfrau .... cleaning woman
Putzmacherin .... milliner (female)
Quacksalber .. quack doctor, charlatan
Rademacher .... wheelwright
Rahmenmacher .... frame maker
Ranglisten: .... officers' rolls
Rat .... council
Rathsverwandter: .... member of the
(town) council
Ratsdiener .... council employee
Ratsherr .... town councilman
Ratsmitglied .... member of council
Ratsverwandter town council assistant
Rauchfangkehrer .... chimneysweep
Rauchfleischmetzger ..... smoked meat
dealer
Rebmann .... wine farmer
Rechenmeister .... accountant
Rechtsanwalt .... attorney
Rechenmeister .... accountant
Reepschläger .... rope maker
Regenschirmmacher ... umbrella maker
Reisender .... traveler
Reiter .... rider
Rekrut .... recruit

Rektor .... dean
Rentner .... retired person (male)
Reseler .... cobbler, shoe repairman
Restaurator .... restorer
Revenirer .... confectioner
Richter .... judge, justice
Riemenschneider .... harness maker
Riemer .... saddler, strapmaker
Rinderhirt .... cowherd
Ritter .... knight, cavalryman
Rittergut: .... noble, landed estate
Rittmeister .... captain (of cavalry)
Rosenkranzmacher .... maker of
rose garlands
Roßtäuscher .... horse merchant
Rotgerber .... red tanner
Rotgießer .... coppersmelter
Rutenbinder .... broommaker
Sachmacher .... sack maker
Sachwalter .... attorney
Säckler .... pursemaker, sackmaker
Sägenmacher .... sawmaker
Säger .... sawyer
Salbenhändler ...... dealer in ointments
Salpetergräber .... saltpeter digger
Salzhändler .... salt merchant
Salzpetersieder .... saltpeter boiler
Salzsieder .... salt works laborer
Salzverlader, Salzhändler .... salt trader
Sämann .... sower
Samtweber .... velvet weaver
Sänger .... singer
Sattelmacher .... saddle maker
Sattler ...... saddlemaker, harnessmaker
Sauhirt .... swineherd
Sauter .... shoemaker
Schachtelmacher .... boxmaker
Schäfer .... sheepherder
Schaffer .... tub maker
Schäf(f)ler .... cooper
Schaffner .... conductor
Schafhirt .... sheepherder
Schaftstiefelmacher . sheepskin maker
Schalknarr .... clown
Schankwirt .... publican
Scharfrichter .... executioner
Schätzer .... (expert) valuer, adjuster
Schatzmeister .... treasurer
Schauspieler/-in .... actor/actress

Schenkwirt .... innkeeper
Scheibler .... salt carrier
Schellenmacher .... bell maker
Scherenschleifer .. scissors sharpener
Scherenschnitkünstler ....
                               silhouette cutter
Schiedsrichter .... arbiter, judge
Schieferdecker .... roofer
Schiffbauer .... ship builder
Schiffer .... sailor (inland waters)
Schiffsführer .... ship captain
Schiffstaumacher ..... ship cable maker
Schindelhändler ...... shingle merchant
Schindelhauer, -macher . shinglemaker
Schindelmacher .... shinglemaker
Schinder .... renderer, skinner
Schirmer .... umbrella maker
Schirmmacher .... umbrella maker
Schlachtenmaler .... battle painter
Schlächter .... butcher
Schlagzeuger .... timpanist
Schleierverkäufer .... veil dealer
Schleifer . grinder, polisher, gem-cutter
Schlichter .... mediator, dresser
Schließer .... door-keeper, porter, jailer
Schlosser .... locksmith, mechanic
Schlossherr(in) .... lord (lady)
                               of the manor
Schlosswache .... palace guard
Schlüsselträger .... key carrier
Schmelzer .... caster, founder, molder
Schmid, Schmied .... blacksmith
Schmuckgestalter .. jewellery designer
Schnallengiesser/macher buckle maker
Schneider .... tailor
Schnitter .... harvester, reaper
Schnittwarenhändler .... dry goods
                                        merchant
Schnitzer .... carver
Schnurmacher .... lace maker
Schöffe .... lay assessor
Schöffer .... juror
Schornsteinfeger .... chimneysweep
Schrader .... tailor, cutter
Schrammermeister .... scratcher for
                               washer boards
Schreiber .... writer, scribe, clerk
Schreiner .... joiner, cabinetmaker
Schriftgießer .... type founder

Schriftsetzer .... compositor, typesetter
Schriftsteller .... author
Schröder .... tailor, carter, cooper
Schuhflicker .... shoemaker
Schuhknecht .... book-jack
Schuhmacher .... shoemaker
Schuldiener .... school caretaker
Schülerstudent (below university level)
Schulhalter .... teacher
Schullehrer .... teacher
Schulmeister .... schoolmaster
Schultheiß .... village mayor
Schulte, Schulze .... village mayor
Shuhplätzer ... cobbler, shoe repairman
Schuster .... cobbler
Schutzverwandte .... foreigner
                or stranger enjoying the rights
                               of a citizen
Schwarzbrotbäcker .... baker of
                               black bread
Schwarzkünstler .... sorcerer
Schwarzschmied .... blacksmith
Schweinebeschneider swine castrator
Schweinehändler .... swine dealer
Schweinehirt .... swineherd
Schweinmetzger .... swine butcher
Schwertfeger .... armorer, bladesmith
Schwerdtschleifer .... sword sharpener
Schwörer .... public servant/
                official sworn by oath
                to perform his duties correctly
                (surveyor, inspector of
                seawalls, weights, etc.)
Seeleute .... seamen
Segelmacher .... sail maker
Seifensieder .... soapmaker
Seidenkrämer .... silk merchant
Seidenmacher .... silk maker
Seidensticker .... silk embroiderer
Seidenwirker .... silk worker
Seifensieder .... soapmaker
Seigner .... fisherman
Seiler .... rope maker, rope merchant
Seilmacher .... ropemaker
Seiltänzer .... tightrope walker
Semmler ...... baker (white bread, cake)
Sensenschmied .... scythe smith
Siebmacher .... sieve maker
Siedler .... settler, colonist

Siegelbewahrer .... keeper of the seal
Silberschmied .... silversmith
Silbertreiber .... silver embosser
Silhouetteur .... silhouette cutter
Soldat .... soldier
Söldner .... mercenary
Sonnenschirmmacher ..... parasolmaker
Spangenmacher .... brass worker
Spediteur .... (freight) forwarder
Spengler .... tinsmith
Spenhauer .... carpenter
Spezereihändler .... grocer
    Sieber   sieve maker
Spiegelmacher .... mirror maker
Spiegler .... mirror maker
Spielmann .... minstrel
Spielzeugmacher .... toymaker
Spinnerin .... spinster, female spinner
Spinnermann .... spinner
Spinrockenmacher ... maker of spinning
                                              distaffs
Spion .... s p y
Spitalpfleger .... male nurse
Spitzenhändler .... lace merchant
Spitzenklöppler .... lace maker
Sporenmacher, Sporer .... spur maker
Sporenschmied .... spursmith
Sporer .... spursmith
Sprechmeister .... musician
Stablstecher .... steel engrver
Stadtbote .... civil official
Stadtknecht .... town worker
Stadtschreiber .... town clerk
Stallknecht .... stable servant
Stallmeister .... riding master
Stärkefabrikant .... starchmaker
Stärkemehlmacher .... starch flour maker
    Statzauner   phamacist
Stecher .... engraver
Steinhauer .... stone cutter
Steinmetz .... stone mason
Stecknadelmacher .... pinmaker
Steinbrecher . stone mason, quarryman
Steinbrenner .... maker of lime
Steinbrücker .... bridgepaver
Steindecker .... stone paver
Steindrechsler .... stone turner
Steinhauer .. stone cutter, stone mason
Steingutwarenhändler .... stoneware

                                              merchant
Steinmetz .... stone mason
Steinschneider ...... gem cutter, lapidary
Steinsetzer .... paver
Stellmacher .... wheelwright
Stellvertreter .... deputy, substitute
Stempeischneider .... stamp cutter
Steuereinnehmer .... tax collector
Steuereintreiber .... tax collector
Steurrat .... tax board
Sticker .... embroiderer
Stockmeister .... jailer
Stoffmaler .... textile painter
Straßenfeger .... road sweeper
Strumpffabrikant .... stocking producer
Strumpfstricker .... stocking knitter
Stückgiesser .... cannon founder
Stückweber .... piece weaver
Student .... student
Studienrat .... teacher
Stuhlmacher .... chairmaker
Stuhltischler .... chairmaker
Sulzer .... saltmaker
Tabaksteuereinnehmer .... tobacco
                                         tax collector
Tafelmacher .... carpenter (for tables)
Tag(e)löhner .... day laborer
Tagwerker .... day laborer
Tambour .... drummer
Tapezierer .... paperhanger, decorator,
                                         upholsterer
Tapissier .... tapestry craftsman
Taschenmaker .... bag/purse maker
Taschner .... bag/purse maker
Taucher .... diver
Teppichsticker .... tapestry embroiderer
Teppichweber .... carpet weaver
Teppichwirker .... carpet worker
Theologe .... theologian
Tierarzt .... veterinarian
Tierbildhauer .... animal sculptor
Tiermaler .... animal sculptor
Tischler .... carpenter, cabitnetmaker
Tonbildhauer .... clay sculptor
Töpfer .... potter
Topfhändler/-krämer ...... pots merchant
Torwächter .... gatekeeper
Torwart .... gatekeeper
Totengräber .... gravedigger

Träger .... porter
Treideler .... tower of ships
     in canal or river
Trödler secondhand, old clothes dealer
Trommler .... drummer
Trompeter .... trumpeter
Troßbube .... baggage servant
Trossknecht .... camp follower
Truchsess .... lord high steward
Tuch .... cloth, fabric, material
Tücher .... whitewasher
Tucher .... clothmaker
Tüchermacher .... cloth maker
Tuchhändler .... cloth dealer, draper
Tuchmacher .... fabric maker
Tuchscherer .... cloth cutter
Tuchschneider .... tailor
Tüncherer .... whitewasher
Türhüter .... doorkeeper, porter
Turner .... gymnast
Tütenmacher .... paper bag maker
Uhrmacher .... watch- or clock-maker
Unterhändler .... agent, negotiator
Unteroffizier .... corporal
Unvermögende .... pauper
Vergolder .... gilder
Verkäufer .... salesman
Vermögensverwalter .... estate
     administrator
Vertreter .... agent, representative
Verwalter .... administrator, manager
Verwaltungsbeamter ...... administrative
     official
Verweser .... administrator
Viehbeschneider .... cattle castrator
Viehhändler .... cattle dealer/trader
Viehhirt .... cattle herder
Vogeler .... bird-catcher, fowler
Vogelmaler .... bird painter
Vogt .... overseer, warden, steward
Vormund .... legal guardian
Vorsänger .... choir leader,
     officiating minister
Vorsteher .... director, manager, chief
Waagemeister .. master of weights and
     measures
Wachszieher ...... candle maker or seller
Wächter .... watchman, guard
Wachtmeister .... sergeant major,
     policeman
Waffenschmied .... weapon maker,
     gunsmith
Wagenbauer coach builder, cartwright
Wagenmachercoach builder, cartwright
Wagenmeister .... wagonmaster
Wagner .... coach builder, wheel maker
Wahrsager .... fortune-teller
Waise .... orphan
Waisenpfleger .... orphan nurse
Waldhüter .... forest ranger
Walker .... fuller
Wappenkünstler .... heraldic artist
Wappenmaler .... blazoner
Wappenschneider .. carver of coats-of-
     arms
Wäscher/-in .... laundry man/
     washerwoman
Wasenmeister .... skinner, renderer
Wassermüller .... watermill operator
Weber .... weaver
Webergeselle .... weaver
Wechsler .... money changer
Weg(e)macher .... road mender
Wehmutter .... midwife
Weinbauer .... wine farmer
Weinbrenner .... brandy maker
Weingärtner .... vine-dresser
Weinhändler .... wine merchant
Weinprüfer .... wine tester
Weinschenker .... waiter
Weinwirt .... keeper of a wine tavern
Weißbinder .... cooper, whitewasher
Weißbrotbäcker .... white bread baker
Weißfrau .... midwife
Weißgerber ...... tanner (of fine leather)
Werbeberater .... publicity agent
Werghändler .... hemp tradesman
Werkmeister .... master mason
Wiedertäufer .... Anabaptist
Wildbrethändler . game, venison trader
Wildhändler .... game dealer
Wildzaunwärter .... game keeper
Winzer .... vintner, wine farmer
Wirker .... knitter
Wirt(h) .... innkeeper, landlord, hotel/
     restaurant proprietor
Wissenschaftler .... scientist
Witwe/Witwer .... widow/widower

Wollkämmerer .... wool comber
Wollspinner .... wool spinner
Woll(en)weber .... wool weaver
Wucherer .... money lender
Wundarzt .... surgeon
Würdenträger .... high official
Würfelmacher ..... wood turner for dice
Würfelspieler .... dice player
Wurstmacher .... sausage maker
Würth .... innkeeper
Zahlmeister .... paymaster
Zahnbrecher .... dentist
Zangenschmied .... blacksmith
Zauberer .... magician
Zaumschmied .... bridle maker
Zaumstricher .... bridle maker
Zeichner .... graphic artist, draftsman
Zeidler .... beekeeper
Zeiner .... basketmaker
Zentgraf.................................... captain
Zerrenner .... blacksmith, iron smelter
Zeuge .... witness
Zeugkrämer .... cloth merchant
Zeugmacher .... clothmaker
Zeugschmied .... toolsmith
Ziegelbrenner, Ziegler .... brickmaker
Ziegelbrenner .... brick/tile maker
Ziegler .... brick/tile maker
Zigeuner .... gypsy
Zimmermädchen .... (chamber)maid
Zimmermann .... carpenter, joiner
Zinkenbläser .... bugler
Zinkenist .... bugler
Zinngießer .... tin founder, pewterer
Zinsbauer .... farmer who pays tithes
Zinsnehmer ... collector of taxes or rent
Zirkelschmied .... compass maker
Zofe .... chambermaid
Zögling .... trainee, pupil
Zöller .... customs official
Zöllner .... toll collector
Zuchtmeister .... taskmaster
Zuckerbäcker .... confectioner
Zuhälter .... pimp
Zunftmeister .... master of a guild
Zwirnmacher ..... thread or twine maker
Zwischenhändler . (commission) agent, intermediary

GERMAN TERMINOLOGY ADOPTED BY AMERICANS

Angst: fear, anxiety
Blitzkrieg: "lightning war"
Doppelgänger: phantom double
Drang nach Osten: drive toward the east
ersatz: fake, imitation
Gastarbeiter: guest workers
Gesellschaft: society, association
Gleichschaltung: assimilation, coordination
Heimat: homeland, area that is the source of one's local identity
Historikerstreit: historians' controversy
Kleinstaaterei: profusion of small states
Kulturkampf: struggle between Catholic Church and German government in Bismarck's Reich from 1872 to 1887
Lebensraum: living room, elbow room
Mitbestimmung: working together of management and labor
Realpolitik: politics of realism, pragma-tism
Rechtsstaat: state based on the rule of law
Schadenfreude: pleasure at someone else's misfortune
Stasi: Staatssicherheitsdienst (secret police of East Germany)
Stunde Null: Zero Hour, 1945, when Germany had to build itself from scratch
Sturm und Drang: storm and stress
verboten: forbidden
Vergangenheitsbewältung: coming to terms with the past
Vertriebene: exiles
Volksgeist: national spirit
Wanderlust: "call of the open road"
Weltanschauung: philosophy, outlook, idealogy
Weltschmerz: world weariness
Weltstadt: international metropolis

Wirtschaftswunder: (Germany's post-war) economic miracle
Wunderkind: child prodigy
Zeitgeist: spirit of the times
Source: Based in part on *The Germans: Who Are They Now?* by Alan Watson. editionq., inc., Chicago, 1993

LATIN DESIGNATIONS FOR OCCUPATIONS, TRADES AND TITLES

abatissa .... abbess
abbas .... abbot
abiectarius .... cabinetmaker
actionarius .... shopkeeper (Krämer)
acupictor .... embroiderer
adumbrator .... draftsman
advocatus .... lawyer
aedilis .... chief, head
aedituus .... sexton
aerarius veteramentarius .... tinker
aerarius faber .... coppersmith
agaso .... stable boy
agittarius .... crossbow maker
agricola .... farmer
albator .... bleacher
altarista inhaber .... chaplain
alumnus .... boarding student
amiger .... page, squire
ampularius .... bottle maker
anachoreta .... hermit
ancilla .... female servant
annonarius .... dealer in grain
annutarius faber .... armor maker, chainsmith
antistes .... clergyman
apiarius .... bee-keeper
apothecarius .... pharmacist
apparitor .... overseer, bailiff
arator .... farmer
arcarius faber .... box/cabinet maker
archiater, archigenes .... physician
architriclinus ...... conductor, master of ceremonies
arcularius .... carpenter, cabinetmaker
argentarius ..... banker, money changer
armbruster .... bow maker

aromatopola   herb/spice dealer/peddler
arrendator .... lessee
artifex calcarium .... spur maker
artifex loricarius .... harnessmaker
artopoeus .... baker
assator .... cook
aucellator .... falconer
aulaeorum opifex .... carpet weaver
aurifaber .... gold and silver smith
auriga .... wagoner, carter
baccalaureus .... scholar, lowest degree academedician
baiulus .... messenger, porter
balistarius .... bowmaker, archer
bapirifex .... paper maker
barbarius .... barber
becharius .... (wood) turner
bedellus .... bailiff
bergarius .... sheepherder
biadarius .... grain dealer
bibliopegus .... bookbinder
birmenter .... parchment maker
bombardarius .... tinsmith
bombicinator .... silk maker
bractearius .... gold beater
brasiator .... maltser
breiser .... haberdasher
bubulcus .... cowherd
burgravius .... baron
bursarius .... bag maker
cacubarius .... tiled stove maker
caduceator .... agent, bridge and   road mender
caelator .... engraver
caementarius .... stonemason
caicariator .... spur maker
calciator .... shoemaker
califex .... pewterer
calopedarius .... wooden shoe maker
calvarius .... nail smith
cambiator .... money changer
campanarius .... sexton
campsor .... money changer
candidarius .... bleacher
caniparius .... waiter
cantafusor .... pewterer
capellanus .... curate
capillamentarius .... wig maker
capsarius .... box maker

carator .... nurse (male)
carbonarius .... charcoal maker
carnarius.................................... butcher
carnifex ..... hangman, knacker, butcher
carpentarius .... cartwright
carrucarius .... driver
casier .... cheese maker
castellanus .... steward
castrator .... cattle castrator
catopticus .... mirror maker
cauno .... publican
caupo .... innkeeper
cellarius .... cellarmaster
cementarius .... mason
cerdo .... tanner, workman, artisan
cereficiarius .... wax chandler
cerevisiarius .... brewer
cermenarius .... day laborer
cervillarius .... helmet smith
chaicographus ... copper plate engrver
chelista .... violinist
chelius .... violinist
chirothecarius .... glove maker
chirurgus .... surgeon
chymiater .... alchemist
cingularius .... belt maker
circulator .... tramp, vagrant, peddler
cistarius .... box/chest maker
claustrarius .... doorkeeper, janitor
clausurmacher .... lockmaker
claviorum artifex .... art metal worker
clericus .... clergyman
clibanarius .... oven caster
clusor .... smith
coctor .... brewer
cocus .... cook
collector .... tax collector
colonus .... settler, peasant farmer
colorator .... painter
comes .... Count Palatine
commissarius .... deputy, agent
commutator .... money changer
concionator .... clergyman
conducticius .... day worker
conflator .... foundryman
consilianus, consul . councilman,mayor
conterfetter .... portrit painter
coqua .... cook (female)
coquus .... cook (male)l

corbo .... basket maker
cordarius .... rope maker
coreator, coriarius .... tanner, leather
worker
corrigiarius .... strap maker
credenzer .... waiter
crumenarius........ bottle and bag maker
crustularius .... confectioner
culcitarius .... coat maker
cuparius.................................. cooper
cupendinarius .... confectioner
cuprifaber .... coppersmith
custodius .... watchman
custos .... custodian, guard, clerk
dantler .... peddler
dapifer .... lord high steward
deaurator .... gilder
decanus .... dean, prior, provost
deglubitor .... knacker, flayer
dignitarius .... high official
disceptator .... arbiter, judge
discipulus .... student
dispensator .... conductor
doliarius .... cooper
domicellus .... nobleman
dulciarius .... confectioner
ebursator .... paymaster
edentarius .... dentist
ennoyeus .... goat herder
ephipparius .... saddler
ephorus .... director, manager
episcopus .... bishop
eques .... cavalryman, knight
equester................ mounted horseman
equicida .... horse butcher
equicius .... horse dealer
eremita .... hermit, recluse
ergastularius .... taskmaster, jailer
eruginator .... sword sharpener
exactor .... tax collector
exclamator .... town crier
faber, Fabricius .... smithy
faber ferrarius .... farrier (horseshoe
maker)
faber lignarius .... woodworker
falcarius .... scythe sharpener
falconarius .... falconer
famula/famulus . servant (female/male)
farcher .... swine dealer

fartor	sausage maker
feniseca	harvester, reaper
fibulator	plumber
fidicen	fiddler, minstrel
figulus	potter, tiler
filicarius	paver, stone mason
fistulator	fife/flute player
flator	caster, foundryman
flebotomarius	blood-letter
foeniseca	reaper, harvester
forestarius	forester
fornacarius	stove fitter
fossarius	grave digger
fossor	gravedigger, ditch digger
fragner	tradesman
frenarius	strapmaker
frumentarius	grain salesman
fuderer	feed tradesman
fullo	fuller, draper
funarius	rope maker
funicularius	belt/strap/thongs maker
funifex	rope maker
furnarius	oven fitter
gailer	tramp, begger
gantier	glove maker
garcifer	cook
gemmarius	jeweler
geraria	nanny
gerulus	messenger, porter
girator	tramp, vagrant
gladiarius	swordsmith
grammaticus	schoolmaster
guardianus	guard
haragius	magician, fortune teller
harpator	harpist
hauderer	cabman
herbarius	dealer in herbs
hortulanus	gardener
hospes	innkeeper
hospinianus	innkeeper
impressor	printer
inbursator	money collector
incisor	tailor
indusiarius	shirt maker
infector	painter
institor	peddler, shopkeeper
ioculator	juggler
iudex	judge
judex	judge
kaviller	knacker
laaber	cheesemaker
laborator	worker, day worker
laborius	worker, laborer
lacticinator	milker
laganator	plumber
laminarius	sheet metal smith
laniator	butcher
lanifex	clothmaker
lanio	butcher
lanitextor	clothmaker
lapidarius	quarryman
lapper	jobbing cobbler
lapsator	gem polisher
lasiterer	saltpeter digger
laterator	brickmaker
lavandarius	laundryman
leno	matchmaker
lepper	cobbler
liber rusticus	free peasant
librarius	book dealer
libripens	inspector of weights and measures
lictor	bailiff, jailer
ligator	cooper
lignarius	joiner, cabinetmaker
lignicidus	woodcutter
ligularius	thong/shoelace maker
limbolarius	braid maker, haberdasher
linarius	hemp and flax dealer
linifex	linen weaver
lintearius	hemp and flax dealer
liticen	minstrel
lodex	weaver, coatmaker
lorarius	strap maker
ludimagister	schoolmaster, teacher
ludimoderator	teacher of lower classes
ludirector	school director
lutorissa	washer woman
lychnopoeus	candlemaker
macellator	butcher
mactator	butcher
magirus	cook
magister	master, teacher
magister civium	mayor
magus	magician
malleator	blacksmith
mamburnus	administrator
mansuarius	farmer

marcellarius .... butcher
marinarius .... sailor
marpahis .... riding master
marsuparius .... purse/satchel maker
massarius .... dairy farmer
materialista .... merchant
matiarius .... sausage maker
medicus .... physician
medicus equarius .... veterinarian
medicus dentium .... dentist
mellicida .... bee farmer
membranarius .... parchment maker
mendicus .... beggar
mensator .... cabinetmaker
mercator .... merchant, businessman
mercenarius .... daylaborer
meretrix .... prostitute
messor .... examiner (check)
miles .... soldier, knight
miles enautoratus .... retired soldier
mindrita .... shepherd, monk
minutor .... bloodletter, surgeon
molendarius .... miller
molineus .... miller
molitor .... miller
murarius .... mason
mylius .... miller
nauta .... sailor
navector .... ferryman
negotiant .... businessman, merchant
netor .... tailor
netrix .... seamstress
nigromanticus .... sorcerer, magician
notarius .... clerk, notary
nummularius .... minter
nuntius .... messenger
nutrix .... wet-nurse
obsequa ...... domestic servant (female)
obstetrix .... midwife
oenopola .... tavern keeper
official, officialis .... agent
olearius .... oil presser (from seeds)
operarius .... laborer
operator .... laborer
opifex .... craftsman
opilio .... sheepherder
ornitander .... fowler
ostiarius .... caretaker, guard
palaeopater .... patriarch

panifex .... baker
pannarius .... clothmaker
pannicida .... cloth-, drapery cutter
pannifex .... clothmaker
pantopola .... wholesaler
papyrifex .... paper worker
paramentier .... lace maker
parochus .... clergyman
pastellator .... pan smithy
pastor .... shepherd, pastor
paternosterer ... maker of rose garlands
paur .... farmer
pectinator .... wool comber
pellifex .... furrier
pellificator .... furrier
pellio .... furrier
pelviarius .... boilermaker
pelvifex .... boilermaker
pelzer .... furrier
penesticus .... second-hand dealer
pensator weights and measures official
perator .... leather bag maker
pharmacopola ..... pharmacist, scented
                                          oil merchant
phlebotomarius ... bloodletter, surgeon
picarius .... cooper
picator .... cooper
pictaciarius .... mender
pictor .... painter
pilearius .... drayman
pileo .... drayman
piscator .... fisherman
pistor .... baker
plastes .... sculptor
plebanus .... clergyman
plumbarius .... tin founder, pewterer
poeta .... poet
polentarius ..... maltzer, brewery worker
polio .... flattening smith
pollinctor .... undertaker
pomarius .... fruit dealer
pontifex .... bishop
popinarius .... cook
practious .... lawyer
praeceptor .... schoolmaster
praeco .... town crier
praefectus .... adminstrator, overseer
praefectus .... magistrate
praenobilis .... of ancient nobility

praepositus .... dean
praestes .... director, manager
praetor .... manager, mayor
praetorius .... mayor, judge
praxator .... brewer
presser .... printer
procarius .... swineherd
procurator .... deputy, advocate
proirnus .... head cook
promocondus ..... cellarmaster, steward
proreta .... ship captain
proxeneta .... (commission-) agent
puer exercitus .... baggage boy
quaestor .... tax collector, treasurer
receptor .... tax assessor
rector ecclesia .... minister
reddituarius .... lessee, tenant
redemptor .... dealer, merchant
regius, Rex .... king
repositor .... treasurer
restiarius .... ship cable/rope maker
restio .... ship cable/rope maker
rhedarius .... wagoner
ribaldus .... tramp, vagrant
rurensis .... brewer
rusticus .... peasant, farmer
saccellarius .... treasurer
sacellanus .... chaplain
sacerdos .... priest
sagittarius .... bow and arrow maker,
                                                     marksman
sakristan .... sexton
salarius .... salt works laborer
salifex .... salt dealer
salinator .... salt dealer
sallarius .... salt works laborer
salpista .... trumpeter
salsuciarius .... prepares entrails for
     further use (sausage,   strings, etc.)
samiator .... grinder, gem polisher
sapicida .... stone mason
sartor .... tailor
satellites .... servant, farmhand
sator .... sower
scabinus .... juror
scandularius .... shinglemaker
schacherer .... peddler
sclopetarius .... handler of guns
scoparius .... road sweeper

scorifex .... tanner
scriba .... scribe, writer, clerk
scriniarius .... confidental secretary,
                           archivist, cabinetmaker
scrutarius .... second-hand dealer
scultetus .... village mayor
segristanus .... sexton
sellarius .... saddler
sensal .... broker, jobber
serator .... locksmith
sericarius .... silk worker
serrarius .... saw maker
servus .... male servant, knight
similarius .... bread baker
simulator .... copyist
smigator .... soapmaker
socius .... apprentice, comrade
speciarius .... herb peddler
speculator .... guard, spy
sportularius .... basketmaker
stabularis .... stable servant
stannarius .... pewterer
staterarius .... wagonmaker
stationarius .... shopkeeper
stipus .... beggar
stratarius .... saddler
studiosus .... student
stupenator .... baths owner
subulcus .... swineherd
sufferator .... blacksmith
superattendens .... superintendent
sutor, sutoris .... cobbler, shoemaker
tabellarius .... messenger
talemetarius .... baker
tector .... roofer
tegularius .... brickmaker
teleonarius .... tax collector
textor, textoris .... weaver
tinctor .... dyer
tiro .... novice, student
tomeator .... thresher
tomio .... thresher
tonsor .... gem cutter
tritor .... thresher
tunnarius .... cooper
tutor .... guardian
tyropola .... cheese dealer
unguentarius .... perfume and
                                   scented oil maker

urinator .... diver
usurarius .... money lender
vadius .... guarantor
valvarius .... custodian, caretaker
vassus .... servant, vassal
vector .... coachman
venator .... hunter
venditor .... merchant, businessman
verganter .... auctioneer
vespillo .... gravedigger
vestiarius .... tailor
veteramentarius ... second-hand dealer
viego .... cooper
vietor .... cooper
vigilarius .... guard
vilicus .... foreman, manager
villicus ..... lower court judge, overseer
vinctor .... cooper
vinitor .... vintner
virgulator .... broom maker
vitriarius .... glassmaker
xylocopus .... carpenter
zonarius .... belt maker
zythopepta .... brewer
zytopoeus .... brewer

MEDICAL TERMS, ILLNESSES, CAUSES OF DEATH (GERMAN AND LATIN)

Abtreibung .... abortion
Abszeß .... abscess
Abweichen .... diarrhea
Abzehrung .. consumption, emaciation
Agonia .... throes of death
Altengeschwürn .... varicose veins
Alter .... age, old age
Altermarasmus .... weakness of old age
Altersschwäche .. weakness of old age
Anfall .... seizure
Angst .... fear, anguish
Ansteckung .... contagion
Apoplexie .... apoplexy, stroke
außerer Schaden .... external damage
Aussatz .... leprosy
Auszehrung .... consumption
Bandwurm .... tapeworm
Bauchschuß . gunshot wound in belly

bettlägerig .... bed-ridden
Beule .... swelling, bruise, boil
Beulenpest .... plague
Blasenentzündung .... cystitis
Blasengeschwulst .... bladder tumor
Blattern .... smallpox of chicken pox
Blätterrose .... shingles, erysipelas with
        bullae or pustules
Blinddarm .... appendicitis
Blinddarmentzündung .... typhlitis
        (inflammation of cecum
        of intestine), appendicitis
Blödigkeit der Augen .... myopia
Blödigkeit .... weakness of mind,
        imbecility; weakness of sight
Blutfluß .... hemorrhage, dysentery,
        haematorrhoea
Blutgang.... flow of blood, hemorrhage
Blutsturz .... violent hemorrhage
Blutsucht .... hemophilia
Blutvergiftung .... blood poisoning,
        toxemia
Böse Flecken .... bubo
Brand am Fuß .... gangrene of foot
Brand .... gangrene, necrosis
Bräune ...... quinsy, angina, sore throat
Brechdurchfall .... bloody diarrhea
Brechruhr .... cholera
Bruckschaden .... hernia
Brustentzündung, Brustfieber ....
        pleurisy, bronchitis,
        inflammation of the chest
Brustkrampf .... cramps, spasms,
        convulsions
Brustkrankheit: .... lung disease,
        tuberculosis
Brustwassersucht: .... hydrothorax,
        dropsy of the chest
Cholera .... cholera
Diptherie .... diphtheria
Drüsenkrankheit .... disease of lymph
        glands
Durchfall .... diarrhea
Eiterbeule .... abscess, boil, pustule
Eiterbläschen .... pustule
Engbrüstigkeit .... tightness of chest,
        asthma
Englischen Krankheit .... rickets
Entkräftung .... weakening,

exhaustion, debilitation
Entkräftung .... weakness of old age
Epilepsie .... epilepsy
Erdbeerpocken .... yaws (contagious
disease common in Tropics)
Erstickung .... suffocation
Ertränkung .... drowning (homicidal
or suicidal)
fallende Sucht .... epilepsy
Fallsucht .... epilepsy
Fallübel .... epilepsy
Fäule .... decay, or cancer
Faulfieber ..... putrid fever; also typhus
febril .... feverish
Febris putrida .... putrid fever
Fehlgeburt .... miscarriage
Fettsucht .... obesity
Fieber: .... fever
Flecken, rote .... rubella
Fleckfieber .... typhus
Flecktenkrankheit .... dry scalp
Flecktyphus .... typhoid fever
Fleisch, faules .... wound, cancer
Fluß .... flow, flux, catarrh, stroke
Flußfieber ... rheumatic fever; influenza
Folgen chirurgieschen .... condition
resulting from a surgical operation
Französischekrankheit .... syphilis
Frühgeburt .... premature birth
Furunkel .... boil
Gallenfieber .... bilious fever, typhus
Gallensucht .... old term for many
diseases attended by symptoms
connected with the bile apparatus
Gedärmbrand, Gedärmfrasz .... intesti-
nal gangrene (ulcerative colitis)
Gehirnhauptkrankheit .... meningitis
Gehirnschlag .... cerebral apoplexy
Gelbes Fieber .... yellow fever
Gelbsucht .... jaundice
Gelenkrheumatismus .... articular
rheumatism
Geschwulst .... swelling or tumor
or goiter
Geschwür im Hals: .... ulcer in throat
Geschwür .... ulcer, abscess
Gesichtsrose ...... erysipelas of the face
Gicht .... arthritis, gout
Gichter .... (infantile) convulsions,

spasms
Gift .... poison, venom, contagion
Glaukom .... glaucoma
Gliederstopfung .... apoplexy
Goitre .... goiter
Goldene Ader .... hemorrhoids
Gravidität .... pregnancy
Gürtelrose .... herpes, shingles
Haemorrhoia .... hemorrhaging
Hals abgeschniten .... throat cut
Halsbräune .... quinsy, suppurative
tonsillitis, perhaps strep throat
Halsenzüendung .... tonsillitis
Halsgicht .... gout in throat or neck,
diphtheria
Halskrankeit disease of throat or neck,
diphtheria
Halsentzündung .... throat infection
Halsschwindsucht .... laryngeal or
tracheal phthisis
Harnruhr .... diabetes insipidus
Hauptkrankheit .... typhus, primary
disease
Herzkrankheit .... heart disease
Herzschlag .... heart attack; paralysis
of heart
Hictericus .... jaundice
Hinfälligkeit .... infirmity, decrepitude
Hirnentzündung .... brain infection,
meningitis
Hitziges Fieber .... high fever, quick
fever
Hitzschlag .... heat apoplexy
höhes Fieber .... high fever (typhoid)
Hüftweh .... sciatica, pain in the hip
Husten .... coughing
Husten, blauer .... whooping cough
Icterus (Hictericus) .... jaundice
ikterisch .... jaundiced
Icterus .... jaundice
Influenze .... influenza
innerliche Krankheit ... internal disease
Inokulierung ..... (smallpox) vaccination
Ischias .... sciatica
Jammer .... epilepsy, cramps
or convulsions
Jucken .... itching of the skin
Kälte .... chills
Kaltenbrande .... frostbite

Family relationships
in German and English

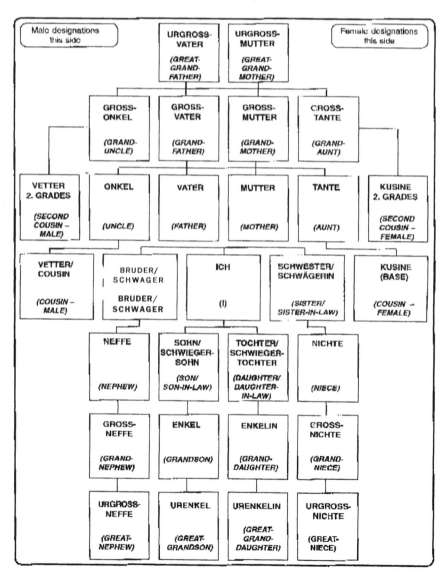

Kaltenerkältung .... influenza
Kelch .... goiter
Keuchhusten .... whooping cough
Kindbettfieber .... puerperal fever
Kinderbett gestorben, im .... died while
                                              giving birth
Kindbettfieber .... childbed fever,
                                            puerperal fever
Kinderblattern (-flecken) .... smallpox
Kinderflecken .... measles
Kinderlähmung .... infantile paralysis
Kinderpocken .... chicken pox
Knochenbrüchen .... broken bones
Knochenfäule .... osteomylelitis
Knochenfraß .... caries
Knochenkrebs .... bone cancer
Knollsucht ...... lepra, nodosa (leprosy)
Knoten .... nodosa
Kolik .... colic
kontagios .... contagious
Kontraktur .... cramp
Kopfwassersucht .... hydrocephalus
Krämpfen .... cramps, convulsions,
                                                    spasms
Krampfadern .... varicose veins
krank .... sick, ill
Krankheit, hitzige .... typhus
Krankheit .... illness
Krankheit, englische .... rickets
Krankheit, fallende .... epilepsy
Krankheiten und Urin .... illness of
                            urine-producing organs
Krätze .... scabies
Krebs .... cancer
Krebsgeschwür .... carcinoma, cancer
Krips .... grippe, influenza
Kropf .... goiter
Krupp .... diphtheria, convulsions,
                                                        croup
Kurzatmigkeit .... asthma
Langwierige Krankheit .... prolonged
                                                       illness
Lebensschwäche .... fraility of life
Leibverstopfung .... constipation
Lethargie .... somnolence, lethargy
Lues .... syphilis
Luftröhrenentzündung .... bronchitis
Lungenentzündung .... pneumonia
Lungenkatarrh .... pulmonary catarrh

Lungenlämung .... disability of lungs
Lungenpest .... plague
Lungenschwindsucht ... consumption,
                                             tuberculosis
Lungentuberkulose .... pulmonary
                                             tuberculosis
Lustseuche .... syphilis
Magenkatarrh .... gastritis
Magenkrebes .... stomach cancer
Magenschwäche .... dyspepsia
                                              (indigestion)
Magerkeit .... thinness, emaciation
Mandelbräune .... tonsillitis, angina
Mandelentzündung .... tonsillitis
Manie .... mania
Marasmus (senilis) ..... senility, old age
Mase .... scar from wound or disease,
                                                    smallpox
Masern .... measles
Melancholie .... depression
Melancholie und Wahnsin ....
                          depression and madness
Milzbrand .... anthrax
Milzverhärtung ...... anthrax, induration
                                            of the spleen
Nekrose .... necrosis, gangrene
Nerven fieber ... nervous fever, typhus
Nervenentzündung .... neuritis
Nesselwurm .... tape worm
Nichtbestimmte Krankheit .... unknown
                                                       illness
Nierengeschwür .... kidney tumor
Nierenkrebs .... kidney cancer
Nierensteine .... kidney stones
Nierentzündung .... kidney infection
Organ. Herzfehler .... organic heart
                                                       failure
paralytisch .... lame, paralytic
Pedechien .... typhoid fever
Pest .... plague
Pestbeule .... bubo
Phrenesia ...... mania from inflammation
                                            of the brain
Pocken .... pox, smallpox
Podagra, podager .... (foot) gout/
                                            arthritis, lame
Potatschen .... spotted fever, spotted
                                                      typhoid
Quartanfieber .... intermittent fever,

malaria
Rachenbräune .... angina, pharyngitis
Räude (böse Räudigkeit) .... mange
Rheuma .... arthritis; also head cold
Röteln .... German measles, rubella
Rotlauf .... erysipelas
Ruhr .... diarrhea, dysentery
ruhrartig .... dysentery
ruhrkrank ...... suffering from dysentery
Samenfluß .... gonorrhea
Scharbock .... scurvy
Scharlach .... scarlet fever
Scharlachfieber .... scarlet fever
Schlarachriesel .... scarlet fever
Schlafkrankheit .... coma, lethargy;
sleeping sickness,
epidemic encephalitis
Schlag(anfall) .... apoplectic attack,
stroke
Schlagfluß .... apoplexy, stroke
Schleichendem Fieber .. consujmption,
tuberculosis
Schleimfieber ... mucous, typhoid fever
Schnupfen .... head cold
Schnupfenfieber .... influenza
Schwäche .... weakness
Schwachsinn .... feeblemindedness
Schwamm(e) .... (cancer) tumor, spongy
growth, fungus
Schwartzgalligkeit .... depression
Schwarzer Tod .... plague
Schweißsucht .... consumption
Schweiß .... heavy fever, sweating
sickness
Schwemmen .... external growth
(spongy growth)
Schwindsucht .... acute tuperculosis
Schwulst .... swelling, cancer
Selbstmord .... suicide
Spanischekrankhei .... syphilis
Spasmus .... cramp, convulsion
Steinbeschwerde .... kidney stones
Stickfluß .... bronchitis, asthma,
suffocating catarrh, angina pectoris
Stickhusten .... whooping cough
Strangurie .... strangury, dysuria
(both: difficult urination)
Sucht .... epidemic, chronic disease
Sucht, fallende .... epilepsy

Sumpffieber .... malarial fever,
swamp fever
Synkopa .... fainting, unconsciousness
Tabes (Tabitudo) .... neurosyphilis
Tabis dorsalis .... spinal tuberculosis
Tobsucht .... raving madness
Tod schwarzer .... plague
Tripper .... gonorrhea
Trunksucht .... chronic alcoholism
Tuberkulose .... tuberculosis
Tuberkulsucht .... tuberculosis
Typhus .... typhoid fever
unbekannt .... unknown (disease)
unbestimmte Krankheit .... undefined
disease
Unfall .... accident; epilepsy
Unglück .... accident
Unterleibsentzündung .... peritonitis
due to intestinal bacteria
released in the abdominal cavity
Unterleibstyphus .... typhoid
Varicosus .... varicose veins
Variola .... pockmarks
Veitstanz .... chorea, St. Vitus' dance
Venäsektion .... blood-letting
venerische Erkrankung .... venereal
disease
Vergiftung .... poisoning
Vergrößerung der Vorsteherdrüse ....
enlargement of prostate gland
Verunstaltende Gelenkentzündung .....
arthritis deformans
Wasserkopf .... hydrocephalus
Wassersucht .... dropsy
Weichselzopf .... hair infested by lice
or disease
weiße Ruhr .... diarrhea, dysentery
Windgeschwulst .... chicken pox
Windpocken .... chicken pox
Wochenbettfieber .... childbed fever
Wolf .... lupus
Würmer .... worms
Wurmfieber .... intestinal cold,
typhus, "worm fever"
(in young children
Zahnfieber .... gingivitis
Zahnfleischentzündung .... gingivitis
Zahnung .... teething
Zellgewebsentzündung .... cellulitis

Ziegenpeter .... mumps
Zuckerkrankheit .... diabetes
Zuckung .... cramps, convulsions,
palpitations
Zwang .... tenesmus, compulsion
diarrhea
Zysten .... cysts

FAMILY RELATIONSHIPS VOCABULARY: GERMAN, LATIN, OTHER

Ahn(e) .... ancestor
Ahnfrau .... female ancestor
Ahnherr .... male ancestor
angenommenes Kind ...... adopted child
Artschwager/(in) .... brother/
(sister)-in-law
Awwe .... grandmother
Base .... female cousin
Bessmoder, Bessmoer ..... grandmother
Blutsfreund .... blood relative
Bruder .... brother
conius/conjus, ... spouse
Cousin .... male cousin
Cousine .... female cousin
dogter, *Dutch* .... daughter
Ehefrau .... wife
Ehegatte .... husband
Ehegattin .... wife
Ehem .... mother's brother: uncle
Ehemann .... husband
Ehni .... grandfather
Eltern .... parents
Elternpaar .... parents
En(c)kel/-in .... grandson/-daughter
En(c)kelkind .... grandchild
En(c)kelsohn .... grandson
En(c)keltochter .... granddaughter
et exor, *Lat.* .... and wife
Findling .... foundling
frater *Lat.* .... brother: cousin;
brother-in-law; kinsman
frater consanguineus, *Lat.* half-brother
frater germanus, *Lat.* .. son of a brother
frater uterinus, *Lat.* .... half-brother
(with same mother)
Frau .... woman; wife; Mrs./Ms.

Fräulein .... unmarried woman, miss
Gatte .... husband
Gattin .... wife
Gebärerin .... mother
Gemahl .... (male) spouse;
(esteemed) husband
Gemahlin .... (female) spouse;
(esteemed) wife
genetor, *Lat.* .... father; begetter
genitores, *Lat.* .... parents
genetrix, *Lat.* .... mother
germanus, *Lat.* .... (full) brother
germen,*Lat.* .... descendant; son; junior
Geschäger .... brother-in-law
Geschwei/Geschwey .... mother-in-law;
sister-in-law
Geschwister .... siblings
Geswige .... sister-in-law
Geswiger .... brother-in-law
Gevatter .... godfather
Gevatterin .... godmother:
Grememm .... grandmother
grootmoeder, *Dutch* .... grandmother
grootvader, *Dutch* .... grandfather
Großeltern .... grandparents
Großen(c)kel/-in .... grandson,
granddaughter
Großkind .... grandchild
Großmama/Großmutter .... grandma,
grandmother
Großpapa/Großvater .... grandpa,
grandfather
Großsohn .... grandson
Großtochter .... granddaughter
Halbbruder .... half-brother
Halbgeschwister .... half-siblings
Halbschwester .... half-sister
Halfbole .... half-brother
Hausehre .... wife; housewife
Hausvater ... (father and) head of family
Hussfrow, Hußfraw .... wife
Kusine .... female cousin
liberi, *Lat.* .... children; grandchildren
Majoratserbe .... first son;
heir by primogeniture
mater meretrix, *Lat.* ...... mother of child
born out of wedlock
matrinia, *Lat.* .... stepmother
Mauser .... son born out of wedlock

Mutter .... mother
Nachfahr(e)/Nachkomme .. descendant
Neffe ....nephew
Nichte .... niece
noverca, *Lat.* .... stepmother
novercus, *Lat.* .... stepfather
Omi/Oma .... grandma
Onkel ....uncle
Opi/Opa .... grandpa
Pate/Pathe .... godparents
Patenkind/Pathenkind .... godchild
Patensohn/Pathensohn............ godson
Patin, Pathin .... godmother,
             sometimes goddaughter
pater, *Lat.* .... father
pater familias, *Lat.* .... father of a family
pater ignoratus, *Lat.* ... father unknown
pater patris, *Lat.* .... father's father
pater sponsae, *Lat.* .. father of the bride
patrui, *Lat.* .... father's brother
Pflegekind .... ward; foster child
Pflegemutter .... foster mother
Pflegesohn/tochterfoster son/daughter
Pflegevater .... foster father
prefigna/prefignus, *Lat.* .... step-
             daughter/stepson
progenita, *Lat.* ....daughter
progenitor *Lat.* (male) .... progenitor;
             ancestor
progenitrix *Lat.* ....female ancestor
progenitus *Lat.* .... son
protavus *Lat.* .... great-grandfather
rechte Geschwister .... full siblings
Schnorr .... mother-in-law
Schnur(r) .... daughter-in-law
Schwager .... brother-in-law
Schwägerin .... sister-in-law
Schwägerschaft .... relationship
             (through the spouse)
Schwäher .... father-in-law;
             brother-in-law
Schweher, Schwehr .... father-in-law
Schwester ....sister
Schwesterkind .... sister's child
Schwestermann........ sister's husband;
             brother-in-law
Schwestersohn ... sister's son; nephew
Schwestertochter ..... sister's daughter;
             niece

Schwieger .... mother-in-law
Schwieger- .... -in-law
Schwiegermutter .... mother-in-law
Schwiegereltern .... parents-in-law
Schwiegerkind .... child relative
             through marriage
Schwiegersohn .... son-in-law
Schwiegervater .... father-in-law
Schwieger/Schwiegermutter .... mother-
             in-law
Schwippschwager/wägerin ..... brother/
          sister of one's brother-
          in-law or sister-in-law
Schwöster .... sister
Seitenverwandte ..... collateral relatives
Sibbe ....relatives
sobrina, *Lat.* .... (female)
             (maternal first) cousin
socer, *Lat.* .... father-in-law
soceri, *Lat.* .... parents-in-law
socrinus, *Lat.* .... brother-in-law
socrus, *Lat.* .... mother-in-law
Sohn .... son
Söhnin/Sohnsfrau ...... daughter-in-law
soror germana, *Lat.*............... half-sister
soror patruelis, *Lat.* ... nephew or niece
sororis filia, *Lat.* ....niece;
             sister's daughter
sororis filius, *Lat.* nephew; sister's son
sororius, *Lat.* .... brother-in-law;
             husband of sister
Stammverwandte(r)........................... kin
Stiefbruder ... stepbrother; half-brother
Stiefkind .... stepchild
Stiefmutter .... stepmother
Stiefschwester ... stepsister; half-sister
Stiefsohn .... stepson
Stieftochter .... stepdaughter
Stiefvater ....stepfather
struprator, *Lat.* ....father of child born
             out of wedlock
Suhnerin ....daugher-in-law
Süster ....sister
Tante .... aunt
Taufpaten .... godfather
Taufpatin .... godmother
Taufzeuge .... godfather
Taufzeugin .... godmother
Tochter ....daughter

Tochtermann .... son-in-law
Ullersmann .... father of the bride
Uren(c)kel .... great-grandson
Uren(c)kelin .... great-granddaughter
Uren(c)kelkind .... great-grandchild
Urgroßeltern .... great-grandparents
Urgroßkind .... great-grandchild
Urgroßmutter/vater .... great-
         grandmother/great-grandfather
Urur- .... great-great-
uterini, *Lat.* .... half-siblings by
                            the same mother
uxor, *Lat.* .... wife, spouse
vader, *Dutch* .... father
Vater .... father
Vatersschwester .... father's sister
Vedeke .... cousin, aunt
vedova/vedovus, *Lat.* widow/widower
Verhältnis .... family relationship
Verwandtschaft .... relationship
Vetter .... cousin (male), relative
Vetternschaft .... cousins; relatives
vitrica, *Lat.* .... stepmother
vitricus, *Lat.* .... stepfather
Vorkinder .... stepchildren from
                            a former marriage
Vorsohn/Vortochter .. stepson/daughter
                       from a previous marriage
Vorvater .... forefather
vrouw, *Dutch* .... wife
Wäschen .... cousin; aunt
Weib(e); Wyb, Wyp .... wife
Witwe .... widow
Witwer .... widower
zuster, *Dutch* .... sister
Zwillingsbruder/schwester .... twin
                               brother/sister
Zwillingskind .... twin child
Source: Primarily, *German-English
Genealogical Dictionary*, by Ernest Thode.
Genealogical Publishing Co., Inc., Baltimore,
1992

BIRTHS, CHRISTENINGS, GUARDIANSHIPS VOCABULARY

angenommenes Kind ...... adopted child
Brautkind .... premarital child

ehelich .... born legitimate(ly),
                              in marriage
ehelos .... unmarried
geboren .... born
Geborene .... born
gebornene .... née (with maiden/birth
                                     name)
Geburt .... birth
gebürtig: .... native, by birth
Geburtsakt .... birth record
Geburtsanzeige .... printed birth
                            announcement
Geburtsbrief: .... birth letter
Geburtsdatum .... birth date
Geburtsfest .... celebration of a birth
Geburtshelfer(in) . obstetrician, midwife
Geburtsjahr .... year of birth
Geburtsort .... place of birth
Geburtsregister .... birth register
Geburtsschein .... birth certificate
Geburtszeugnis
Geburtsstätte ... house or place of birth
Geburtsurkunde .... birth documents
Geburtsverzeichnis .... birth index
getauft .... baptized
Getaufte .... the person baptized
Hebamme .... midwife
Herkunftszeugnis .... proof of origin
Hurenkind .... illegitimate child
infans adulterinus ...... child born out of
(or spurius), *Lat.*   wedlock
infantulus, *Lat.* .... little child, infant
Jungfernkind .... child born out of
                            wedlock; first-born
Jüngste .... youngest one   (female)
Jüngster.............. youngest one (male)
Kinderheim .... children's home,
                                  foster home
kinderlos .... childless
Kindermädchen .... nanny
Kindervater .... father of a child
Kinderverding, . contract for placement
Kinderzug   of a child
Kinderzahl .... number of children
Kindesabtreibung .... abortion
Kindesmutter .... (unmarried) mother;
Kindestaufe .... baptism of a child
Kindesvater .... father (of an out-of-
                              wedlock child)

Mutter .... mother
mutterlos .... motherless
Nottaufe .... emergency baptism
Pate .... godfather
Paten .... godparents
Pateneltern .... godparents
Patenkind .... godchild
Patin .... godmother
Söhnchen .... little son(s)
Stiefkind .... stepchild
Taufbücher .... christening records
Taufe .... christening, baptism
Taufeltern .... godparents
Taufkind .... child being christened
Taufpate .... godfather
Taufpaten .... godparents
Taufpatin .... godmother
Taufprotokolle ..... christening records
Taufregister .... christeninig register
Taufurkunde .... christening record
Taufzeuge .... godfather
Taufzeugin .... godmother
Totgeburt .... stillbirth
unehelich .... illegitimate
Vater .... father
Vorkind(er) .... stepchild(ren)
Vormund .... guardian
Waise .... orphan
Zeugen .... witnesses

MARRIAGE VOCABULARY

Ablobung .... (arranged) marriage
ac quaestus coniugalis .... community
                                              property
acte de mariage, *Fr.* .... marriage
                                              certificate
Äe, Aee .... marriage
affinitas, Lat. ...... relationship through
                                              marriage
alliance, *Fr.* .... marriage
amensa et toro, *Lat.* .... divorced
angeheiratet ...... married into (a family)
ante nuptius, *Lat.* .... before the
                                    marriage; prenuptial
Anulehe .... secret marriage
Anulfrau .... secretly married woman
anverwandt .... related by marriage

aufbieten .... proclaim (marriage banns)
Aufgebotsverzeichnis ..... list of procla-
                          mations (of marriage banns)
bans, *Fr.* .... (marriage) banns
bestatten (sich) .... marry;
                                  (lit."bury oneself")
bigami, *Lat.* .... remarried widower
binuba/binubus, Lat. .... woman/man
                              married for second time
Braut .... bride
Brautausstattung,- .. trousseau; dowry
aussteuer
Brautbitter .... marriage arranger
Brauteltern .... parents of the bride
Bräutigam .... bridegroom
Brautkind .... child born to
                                    an engaged couple
Brautleute/ .... engaged couple;
Brautpaar   bride and bridegroom
Brautmacher .... bridegroom
Brautmesse ..... (Catholic) nuptial mass
Brautschatz .... dowry
Brautstand .... time of engagement;
                                              betrothal
Brautsuche .... search for a wife
Brautmutter/-vater .... bride's
                                    mother/father
Brautwein .... tax payable by newly
                                    married couples
Brautwerber .... marriage arranger
Bruthavent .... dowry
Brutlacht .... wedding
Brutmaker/ .... bridegroom
Brutmann .... bridegroom;
                                    witness at wedding
Brutschat(t) .... dowry
Civilehe .... civil marriage
collateralis, *Lat.* .... wife
conjus, conjux, *Lat.* .... spouse
conjugatis, *Lat.* .... married
Connubium .... marriage
connubius, *Lat.* .... marriage
copulatio, *Lat.* .... marriage
discidium, *Lat.* ..... separation; divorce
dos inter nuptias, *Lat.* .... dowry
dos adventitia, *Lat.* woman's property
                                    brought to marriage
dos profectitia, *Lat.* ...... man's property
                                    brought to marriage

Eheberedung: .... marriage contract
Ehebücher .... marriage registers
Ehebündis .... wedlock
Ehefrau .... wife, married woman
Ehegatte .... husband
Eheherr(in) .... husband/wife
eheherrlich .... of husband's rights in a
                                                    marriage
Ehejahr .... year of marriage
Ehekonsens............ (parental) consent
                                          to a marriage
Eheleute.......................... married couple
ehelichen .... marry; wed
ehelos .... unmarried
Ehemakler .... matchmaker
Ehemangel .... reason for nullity
                                        of a marriage
Ehemann .... husband; married man
Ehemittler(in) .... matchmaker
ehemündig .... of legal age to marry
Ehepaar .... married couple
Ehepaktenbuch .... marriage
                                          contract book
Ehepartner(in) .... spouse
Eheregister .... marriage register
Ehesakrament ... sacrament of marriage
Ehescheidung .... divorce
Ehescheidungsklage .... petition for
                                                    divorce
Ehescheidungsurteil .... divorce decree
Eheschließung .... marriage
Ehestand .... matrimony
Ehestifter/(in) .... matchmaker \(male/
                                                    female)
eheunmündig not of legal age to marry
Eheverbot............. prohibition to marry
Eheverkündigung .... marriage
                                          announcement
Ehevertrag .... marriage contract
eingeheiratet .... married into
enviandé/(e), Fr. .... married
                                          (male/female)
épouse, Fr. .... bride; wife
épouser, Fr. .... marry
Fastenehe .... secret marriage
geheurat(h)et .... married
geschieden .... divorced
Heirat .... marriage
heiraten .... to marry

Heirat(h)sbüro .... marriage bureau
Heirat(h)sgesuch . petition for marriage
                                                    permit
Heiratsakt .... marriage record
Heiratserlaubnis.............. arriage permit
Heiratsgesuch ..... petition for marriage
                                                    permit
Heiratsgut .... dowry
Heiratsregister .... register of marriages
Heiratsrottel .... marriage contract
Heiratsstifter .... matchmaker
Heiratsurkunde .... marriage record
Heiratsvermittler .... matchmaker
Heiratsversprechen .... engagement
                                                    (to marry)
Heiratsvertrag .... marriage contract
Heurat(h) .... marriage
heymelike Ehe .... secret marriage
Hillcheit .... marriage
Hochzeitsbrauch............ marriage rites
Hochzeitszeremoniell............. wedding
                                                    ceremony
Hürat(h)en .... to marry
innuba, innupta, Lat. .... unmarried
                                                    (female)
innubus, innupta, Lat. .... unmarried
                                                    (male)
iugere, Lat. ....join; marry
Josephsehe .... quasi-marriage
Keuschheitsehe .... unconsummated
                                                    marriage
kirchenrufen ....proclaim
                                          (marriage) banns
Konkubinat .... common-law marriage
Konleute....................... married couple
Kopulation .... marriage
Kriegstrauung .... wartime wedding
ledig arried; single
Ledige/r .... unmarried woman/man
liber matrimoniorum, Lat. ....marriage
                                                    register
Liebesheirat.............. marriage for love;
                                          love match
marier, Fr. .... get married
mariés, Fr. .... married couple
matrimonia, Lat. .... marriage
matrimonium ....secret marriage
clandestinum, Lat.
matrimoniumconscientiae, Lat. ... secret

matrimonium .... unconsummated marriage
   claudicans, *Lat.*
matrimonium .... unequal (in status) marriage
   morganaticum, *Lat.* .... marriage
matrimonium putativum, *Lat.* .... invalid marriage
matrimonium virgineum, *Lat.*, .. uncom-summated marriage
neosponsa/neosponsus, *Lat.* ..... bride/bridegroom
Notzivilehe .. emergency civil marriage
nouveaux-mariés, *Fr.* .... newlyweds
nuptiae, *Lat.* .... marriage
Nupturienten .... bride and groom
ongehuwd, (*Dutch*), ... unmarried
pacta , Lat.), ... marriage contract
pactum connubiatis, *Lat.* .... marriage contract
Proclamation(en) .... proclamation of the marriage banns
Quasimatrimonium, *Lat.* .... quasi-marriage; unconsummated marriage
reconciliatio, Lat. .... (second) marriage, this time before clergy with jurisdiction
Reinigungseid ... oath of marital fidelity
relicta/relictus *Lat.* ...... widow/widower
Ringehe .... secret marriage (esp. of priests in Middle Ages)
sacro ledo copulati, *Lat.* ... married after a mass
schecken .... get engaged without parental permission
Scheidung .... divorce
secunda vota, *Lat.* ..... second marriage
sedes vidualis, *Lat.* .... widowhood
Trauzeuge, erster .... best man at a wedding
Trauzeuge, zweiter .... groomsman (at a wedding)
Trauzeugnis .... marriage certificate
Truwe .... loyalty; marriage
Truwe, heymelike .... secret marriage
Ullersmann .... father of the bride
unverheiratet .... unmarried
vacara/vacarus, Lat. .... unmarried (female/male)
verehelichungsbücher ....marriage registers

verheiratet .... married
uxor (abbrev. ux., *Lat.* ..... wife; spouse
uxor militaris, *Lat.* .... soldier's wife
uxorata/-is, *Lat.* .... female/male
uxoratis, *Lat.* .... married
vacara/-us, *Lat.* .... unmarried (female/male)
verehelichen .... marry
verehelicht .... married
Verehelichung .... marriage; wedding
Verkündigen ....proclaim (marriage banns)
Verkündigung .... proclamation (of marriage banns)
verlobt .... engaged
Vermühlen (sich) .... (formally) marry
vermählt .... (formally married)
Vermählung .... (formal) marriage
Vermählungsanzeige .... marriage announcement
Verwandtenehe .... marriage between (blood) relatives
vierge, *Fr.* ..... virgin; unmarried woman
wiederverheiratet, ... remarried
wiedergeheiratet
Wiederheirat, ... remarriage
Wiederverehelichung
wiederverehelicht .... remarried
Witfrau, Witib, ... widow
Wittib, Wittwe
Witmann, Wittiber, ...widower
Wittler, Wittling, Wittmann
Wittwenschaft .... widowhood
Würt .... husband
Why, Wyp .... wife; woman
Zeugen .... witnesses

DEATH VOCABULARY

acte de décès, *Fr.* .... death certificate
annales funesti, *Lat.* ...... death register
beerdigen .... to bury, inter
Beerdigung .... burial
Begräbnis .... burial
Bestattung .... burial, funeral
   Beulenpest   bubonic plague
   Blatterrose   shingles

Blindarm   appendicitis
Blutfluss, Blutlauf, Blutgang
hemmorrhage
Braune
Erbschaft .... inheritance
Erbsteuer .... death or estate duties
Ertrunken .... drowned
Friedhofsparzelle .... cemetery lot
Friedhof .... cemetery
Friedhofsprotokoll ...... cemetery record
gesetzlicher Erbe .... legal heir
gestorben .... dead, died
Grab .... grave, tomb, sepulchre
Grabgeleit .... funeral procession
Grabgewölbe .... tomb, vault
Grablegung ... burial, interment, funeral
Grabrede .... funeral oration, eulogy
Grabschrift .... epitaph, inscription
Grabstätte ...... burial place, grave, tomb
Grabstein .... grave stone
Graburne .... funeral urn
Hinterlassenschaft .. (testator's) estate
Leiche .... corpse, remains
Leichenacker .... cemetery,
                                          burying ground
Leichenausgrabung .... exhumation
Leichenbegängnis .... funeral, burial
Leichenbegleiter .... mourner
Leichenbegleitung .. funeral procession
Leichenbeschau .... inspection of body;
                                                     inquest
Leichenbeschauer ..... coroner; medical
                                                    examiner
Leichenbesichtigung .... inspection
                                          of body; inquest
Leichenbesorger .... undertaker
Leichenbestatter .... undertaker
Leichenbestattung .... funeral, burial
Leichenbitter .... person who invites
                                     persons to a funeral
Leichenbuch ..... book of the deceased
Leicheneröffnung .... autopsy
Leichenfeier .... funeral service
Leichengeburt ..... birth of child after its
                                           mother's death
Leichengefolge ...... funeral procession
Leichengewölbe .... burial vault
Leichengruft .... burial vault
Leichenhalle, Leichenhaus ..... mortuary

Leichenkapelle .... mortuary chapel
Leichenpredigt .... funeral sermon
Leichenrede .... funeral sermon
Leichenschauhaus .... morgue
Leichenschmaus .... funeral meal
Leichenstein .... tombstone
Leichenträger .... pallbearer
Leichenverbrennung .... cremation
Leichenwache .... death vigil, wake
Leichenwagen .... hearse
Leichenzug .... funeral procession
Leichnam .... corpse
Leichsstein ..... burial stone in a church
Leicht .... burial
Leich(t)mann .... undertaker, funeral
                                                     director
Leich(t)versorger .... undertaker, funeral
                                                     director
letzter Wille .... last will
letztwillig .... in the will
Mord .... murder
obiit, Lat. .... (he; she; it) died
obire, Lat. .... die; go away
obita, Lat. .... dead (female)
obitus, Lat. .... dead (male)
Parta .... obituary notice
Sterbe .... death
Sterbedatum .... date of death
Sterbeeintrag .... death record
Sterbegeld .... death benefit
                                  (of mutual aid society)
Sterbekasse .. (funeral) benefit fund (of
                                      mutual aid society)
Sterbelager .... deathbed
sterben .... to die
sterbenskrank .... deathly sick
Sterberegister .... register of deaths
Sterbesakrament .... last rites
Sterblichkeit .... mortality (statistic)
Testament .... last will and testament
Tod .... death
Todesanzeige .... death notice
Todesdatum .... date of death
Todeseintrag .... death entry
Todeserklärung (official) declaration of
                              death of a missing person
Todesfall .... a death (or casualty,
                                               as in war)
Todeskampf .... death struggle;

death throes
Todesmesse .... funeral mass
Todesnachweis .... proof of death
Todestag ...... anniversary of a death
Todesursache .... cause of death
Todfallsgeld .... money paid by a
burial fund
todkrank .... deathly ill
Todtgeboren .... stillbirth
tot .... dead
To(d)tenbuch .... book of deaths
To(d)tenhof .... cemetery
To(d)tenregister .... death register
to(d)tgeboren .... stillborn
Totenacker .... cemetery
Totenamt .... burial service
Totenausleger .... undertaker
Totenbahre .... bier
Totenbeschauer ... physician attending
death; medical examiner; coroner
Totenbett .... deathbed
Totenbuch .... book of the dead
Totenfeier .... funeral rites
Totenfest .... festival in
commemoration
of the dead
Totenfrau .... female undertaker
Totengebet .... prayer for the dead
Totengedächtnis .... memorial service
for the dead
Totengeläutbuch ..... death knell record
Totengeleit .... funeral cortege
Totengesang .... funeral dirge
Totenglocke .... death knell
Totengottesdienst .... funeral service;
memorial service
Totengräber ... grave digger, undertaker
Totengruft .... vault, sepulchre
Totenhalle, Totenhaus .... mortuary;
funeral home
Totenhof .... cemetery
Totenkirche .... memorial chapel
Totenklage .... dirge, wake
Totenlade .... coffin
Totenlied .... funeral dirge
Totenliste .... list of deaths
Totenmann .... undertaker
Totenmesse .... mass for the dead
Totenname .... name of the deceased

Totenregister .... register of deaths
Totenschein .... death certificate
Totenschau .... coroner's inquest;
post-mortem examination
Totenverbrennung .... cremation
Totenwache .... death vigil; wake
Totenwagen .... hearse
Totenzeugnis .... death certificate
toter Leib .... dead body
totgeboren .... stillborn
Totgeburt .... stillbirth
totgesagt .... reported dead
totsagen .... declare dead
Trauergottesdienst .... funeral service
Tumulus, *Lat.* .... grave
Unschlingung der Nabelschnur um den
Hals-Erstichung ....
stillbirth due to strangulation
by umbilical cord
Verstorbene .... deceased (person)
Verunglückt .... accidental death
Waise .... orphan
wijlen, *Dutch* .... deceased
Wurmfrass .... being eaten by worms

LATIN GENEALOGICAL VOCABULARY

a, ab .... from, out
acotholica/us .... not Catholic
aedituus .... church guardian, church
warden
aegra ill
aetas suae .... aged
aetatis .... age
aetatis suae .... his age
affinis .... related through marriage
agricola .... peasant
ambo ex .... both from
amita .... father's sister
amita magna .... grandfather's sister
ancilla .... maid, maiden
anima(e) .... person(s)
anno .... in the year of
annorum .... years
annus .... year
arx .... castle, fortress
Ascensio Domini .... Ascension Day

avia .... grandmother
avuncula .... mother's sister
avunculus .... mother's brother
avus .... grandfather
balneator .... bather, surgeon, barber
baptisma .... the baptism
baptizatus .... baptized
baptizatus est .... was baptized
beatae memoriae .... of blessed memory
calendae ianuariis .... first of January
cantor .... singer
capellanus .... chaplain
carnifex .... executioner
chirurg, chirurgus .... surgeon
Circumcisio Domini .... January 1
coelebs .... single, unmarried
cognatus .... related; uncle
commorantes in .... residing in
concionator .... preacher
condictus .... named
conditio .... condition, situation
coniugalis .... legitimate
coniugata .... married
coniugatus .... married
coniuges .... spouses
coniugo .... married
coniiugium .... marriage
coniugum .... husband
coniugum ex .... husband from
coniunctus .... married
coniunx .... husband
coniux .... spouse
conjunx, conjux .... wife
consobrinus .... child of siblings
consobrini .... children of siblings
copulati ..... the ones who were married
copulatio, copulation .... marriage
coriarius .... the tanner
cum .... with
decem .... ten
defuncta .... deceased (female)
defunctus .... deceased (male)
diaconus ..... deacon, assistant minister
dierum .... days
die, dies .... day
dies Jovis .... Thursday
dies Lunaw .... Monday
dies Martis .... Tuesday
dies Mercurii .... Wednesday

dies Sabbathi .... Saturday
dies Solis .... Sunday
dies Veneris .... Friday
domi .... at home
Dum medium ... Sunday after Christmas
ecclesia .... church
ecclesia parrochiali .... parish church
ejusdem .... same day, as above
emeritus .... retired, emeritus
eodem .... same day
eodem dienatus .... was born
et baptizatus .... and baptized
on the same day
Epiphanie .... 6th of January
eques .... rider, knight, servant
et .... and
ex .... from, out(of), of
Exaudi .... 6th Sunday after Easter
exinde .... of the same place
extra .... beyond
extra matrimonium .... illigitimate
faber .... smith
faber lignarius .... woodworker
familia .... family, household
famula .... servant (female)
famulus .... servant (male)
feria quarta .... Wednesday
feria quinta .... Thursday
feria secunda .... Monday
feria sexta .... Friday
feria tertia .... Tuesday
filia .... daughter
filia insipiens .... mentally disabled
filia legitima .... legitimate daughter
filia putativa .... daughter who had
a child before marriage
or had cohabited
filiola .... little daughter
filiolus .... little son
filius .... son
filius adoptivus ..... adopted or stepson
filius legittimus .... legitimate son
figulus .... potter
frater .... brother
frater germanus .... half-brother
fratria .... brother's wife
gemelli .... twins
gener .... son-in-law
gens .... clan

glos .... husband's sister
heri .... yesterday
hic jacet .... here lies
ibidem .... in the same place
incola .... resident
inferior .... the lower
in periculo mortis .... in danger of death
in praesente .... in the presence of
inquilinus   house resident, renter,
                                              inhabitant
institor .... merchant
judex .... judge
junior .... the younger
juvenis .... young man/young woman
levantes .... witness, godparent
liber .... book
liber baptizatorum .... baptismal book
liber matrimoniorum .... marriage book
liber mortuorum .... death book
ludimoderafor .... schoolmaster
ludirector .... school director
maritus .... husband, spouse
mater .... mother
mater mariti ...... mother of the husband
mater uxoris .... mother of the wife
maternitas .... motherhood
materta .... sister of the mother
materta magna .... great aunt
matrimonialis   legitimate, pertaining
                                         to marriage
matrimonium .... marriage
matrina .... godmother
mensis .... month
mensium .... months
miles .... soldier
molitor .... miller
mortuus .... died
nata .... born (female)
natale .... birthday
natales .... origin, birth
natalis dies .... birthday
nativitas Domini .... Christmas (25 Dec.)
natus .... born (male)
natus est .... was born
nepos .... nephew; grandson
neptis .... niece; grandaughter
nescitur quo loco .. residence unknown
N.N. ... nomen nescio (unknown name)
nobilis .... noble, nobility

novem .... nine
noverca .... stepmother
nurus .... daughter-in-law
nutrix .... nurse
obiit. .... deceased
obstetrix .... midwife
octo .... eight
opilio .... shepherd
pannifex .... clothmaker
parentes .... parents
parochia .... parish
parochus .... minister
partus .... birth
Pascha .... Easter
pastor .... pastor, minister
pater .... father
pater mariti .... father of the husband
pater uxoris .... father of the wife
patrini .... godparents, witnesses
patrinus .... godfather
patruus .... father's brother
patruus magnus .... great uncle
pauper .... poor
persona libera .... free person
pharmacopola .... pharmacist
physicus .... doctor
piscator .... fisherman
pistor .... baker
postero die .... on the following day
post pascha .... Monday after Easter
postridie baptizatus   baptized on the
                                         following day
practious .... lawyer
praeceptor .... house teacher
praefectus .... administrator, director
preces .... blessing
pridie idus septembris   on the 12th of
                                            September
pridie natur .... born the day before
primogenita .... first born (female)
primogenitus .... first born (male)
prius .... previous
privigna .... step-daughter
privignus .... step-son
proamita .... great grandfather's sister
proavia .... great grandmother
proavus .... great grandfather
proclamatio .... banns, the ones
                                         who planned

on getting married
proles .... child, offspring
promaterta .... great great aunt
pronepos .... great grandson
proneptis .... great granddaughter
propatruus .... great granduncle
puella .... girls
puer .... boy
quasi modo geniti .... first Sunday
after Easter
quaestor .... tax collector
quam primum natus fuit right after birth
rector .... rector, minister
rector ecclesia .... minister
relicta .... left behind,
surviving (female)
relictus ..... left behind, surviving (male)
renata .... baptized (female)
renatus .... baptized (male)
sabbato .... Saturday
sartor .... tailor
schola .... school
scriba .... scribe, write
senator .... councilman, counselor
senatus .... city council
septum .... seven
sepultatio .... the burial
sepultus .... buried
sequenti die .... on the following day
servus .... servant, knight
socer .... stepfather
socrus .... stepmother
soror .... sister
soror germana .... half sister
sororius .... sister's husband
sponsa .... the engaged (female)
sponsalia .... engagement
sponsus .... the engaged (male)
spuria .... illegitimate (female)
spurius .... illegitimate (male)
superattendens .... superinitendent
superior .... the above
susceperunt .... they lifted (out of
baptism)
suscipientes ..... godparents, witnesses
sutor .... shoemaker
testes .... witnesses, godparents
testis .... witness, godparent
textor .... linenweaver

trigemini .... triplets
tutor .... guardian
unica .... the only one (female)
unicus .... the only one (male)
uxor .... wife
vacat .... empty
vagus .... not a resident
vicarius .... vicar
vidua .... widow
viduus .... widower
virgo .... virgin, unmarried
vitricus .... step-father
vivus .... living
xenodochium .... hospital,
pilgrim's house

Abbreviated date indicators

7bris .... in September
VIIber .... in September
8bris .... in October
VIIIber .... in October
9bris .... in November
IXber .... in November
10bris .... in December
Xber .... in December
Note: See *septem, octo, novem, decem
above.*

ROMAN NUMERALS

I 1
II 2
III 3
IV 4
V 5
VI 6
VII 7
VIII 8
IX 9
X 10
XI 11
XII 12
XIII 13
XIV 14
XV 15
XX 20
XXIV 24
XXIX 29
XXXI 31

XL	40
L	50
LX	60
LXX	70
LXXX	80
XC	90
C	100
CI	101
CV	105
CXI	111
CXLI	141
CL	150
CC	200
CCC	300
CCCC	400
CD	400
D	500
DC	600
DCLV	655
DCC	700
DCCC	800
DCCCC	900
CM	900
M	1000
MDCCVI	1706
MDCCCLXV	1865
MDCCCXC	1890
MCMIX	1909
MCMXLVIII	1948
MCMXCVIII	1998

GENEALOGICAL AIDS IN INTERPRETING LATIN

♦ C. Russell Jensen, Ph.D., *Parish Register Latin: an Introduction*. Vita Nova Books, Salt Lake City, 1988. Out of print (FHL 475 J453p)
♦ Minert, Roger P., Ph.D. *Deciphering German Handwriting in German Documents*. GRT Publications, Woods Cross, Utah, 2001 *[This book features chapters on Latin and French.]*
♦ Kenneth L. Smith, *German Church Books; Beyond the Basics*. Picton Press, Camden, Maine, 1989
♦ Ernest Thode, *German-English Genealogical Dictionary*. Genealogical

Publishing Company, Baltimore, 1992. *[Note: Besides German, this dictionary contains many Latin words and phrases.]*
♦ Wolfgang Ribbe and Eckart Henning, *Taschenbuch für Familiengeschichtsforschung*. Verlag Degener & Co., Neustadt/Aisch, 1995

TOMBSTONE LATIN

A.D. – Anno Domini: In the Year of Our Lord . . .
Ad perpetuam rei memoriam: For a perpetual record of the matter
Adsum: Here I am
Ars longa, vita brevis: Art is long, life is short
Beatae memoriae: Of blessed memory
Carpe diem: Enjoy the present day
Dei gratia: By the grace of God
Deo volente (D.V.): God willing
Dominus vobiscum: The Lord be with you
Durante vita: During life
Elapso tempore: The time having passed
Errare humanum est: To err is human
Et sequentes (sequentia): And those who follow
Ex voto: According to one's wishes
Faber suae fortunae: A self-made man
Fecit.: Made it. Executed it
Fidei defensor: Defender of the faith
Filius terrae: A son of the soil.
Gloria patri: Glory be to the Father
Hic jacet: Here lies
Hoc nomine: In his name.
In articulo mortis: At the point of death
In facie ecclesiae: Before the church
In futuro: Henceforth
In memoriam: In memory of . . . .
In nomine Domini: In the name of the Lord . . . .
In perpetuum: For ever
In secula seculorum: For ever and ever
Jubilate Deo: Rejoice in God
Laus Deo: Praise to God
Monumentum aere perennius: A monu-

ment more lasting than brass
Mors omnibus communis: Death is common to all
Natus est: Was born
Obit: Died
Pace tua: By your leave
R.I.P. – Requiescat in pace: May he (she) rest in peace
Scripta litera manet: The written word remains.
Sic transit gloria mundi: Thus passes away the glory of the world.
Taedium vitae: Weariness of life
Tempus fugit: Time flies.
Ubi supra: Where above mentioned
Ut infra: As below
Ut supra: As above
Source: Raymond Lamont Brown, A Book of
Epitaphs. Taplinger Publishing Co., New York, 1969

DAYS, MONTHS IN LATIN

Sunday: dominica, dies dominica (dominicus), dies Solis, feria prima
Monday: feria secunda, dies Lunae
Tuesday: feria tertia, dies Martis
Wednesday: feria quarta, dies mercurii
Thursday: feria quinta, dies Jovis
Friday: feria sexta, dies Veneris
Saturday: feria septima, sabbatum, die sabbatinus, dies Saturni

Months (nominative form)

January: Januarius
February: Februarius
March: Martius
April: Aprilis
May: Maius
June: Junius
July: Julius
August: Augustus
September: September
October: October
November: November
December: December

OLD LATIN NAMES FOR CITIES

Agrippina Colonia: Köln
Albiorum: Wittenberg
Albis: Elbe (river)
Alisum: Heilbronn
Altena: Altona
Aquae Aureliae, Badena, Thermae inferiores: Baden-Baden
Aquae Mattiacae: Wiesbaden
Aquisgranum: Aachen
Astnidensis civ.: Essen
Augusta Vindelicorum: Augsburg
Augusta Trevirorum, Treveris: Trier
Aula Cotelini: Quedlinburg
Auriacum: Aurich
Balticum mare: Ostsee, Baltic Sea
Baruthum: Bayreuth
Batavia: Passau
Bermensis civ.: Barmen
Berolinum: Berlin
Bilveldia: Bielefeld
Bingium, Vincum: Bingen
Bonna: Bonn, Rheinprovinz
Bostanium: Potsdam
Brandeburgum novum: Neubrandenburg
Brema: Bremen
Brunsvicum: Braunschweig
Bruchsella, Bruxella: Brussel
Brunsvigia: Braunschweig
Budissa: Bautzen
Caesarealutra, Lutria, Lutra imperialis: Kaiserslautern
Caroli hesychium: Karlsruhe
Cassala: Kassel
Cella: Celle
Chemnitium: Chemnitz (Karl Marx Stadt)
Chilonium: Kiel
Colmaria: Colmar
Colonia Agrippinensis, Ubiopolis: Köln
Confluens: Münster im Münstertal
Confluentes: Koblenz
Cotbusium: Cottbus
Cuxhavia: Cuxhaven
Dachhovia, Tachovia: Dachau
Danubius: Donau (river), Danube
Darmstadium: Darmstadt

Dispargum: Duisberg, Rheinprovinz
Dresda: Dresden
Dusseldorpium, Dusselodorvum: : Düsseldorf
Dvorce: Hof
Elberfeldia: Elberfeld
Emda: Emden
Erfordia: Erfurt
Erlanga: Erlangen
Facibusd: Füssen
Fauces: Füssen
Flenopolis: Flensburg
Frankfordia super Oderam: Frankfurt an der Oder
Francofurtum ad Moenum: Frankfurt am Main
Friburgum, Freyburga, Friburgium Brisigavorum:: Freiburg i. Breisgau
Fuldense coenobium: Fulda
Furtha, Furtum: Fürth
Gedanum: Danzig
Genava: Genf (Genéve)
GissaHassorum: Gießen
Gorlicium: Gorlitz
Gotaha: Gotha
Gotinga: Göttingen
Hailprunna: Heilbronn
Halla: Halle
Halla Suevorum, Hallis Swewie: Schwäbisch Hall
Hamala: Hameln
Hammonia: Hamburg
Hannovera: Hannover
Hassia: Hessen
Haylprunna, Halbrunna, Hellprunna: Heilbronn
Heidelberga: Heidelberg
Herbipolis: Würzburg
Hildesia: Hildesheim
Hydropolis: Feuchtwang(en)
Ilmena: Ilmenau
Ingolstadium, Ingolsavia: Ingolstadt
Islebia: Eisleben
Jhena, Athenae ad Salam: Jena
Lipsia: Leipzig
Lubica Vetus, Lubeca: Lübeck
Luneburgum: Lüneburg
Lutetia Parisiorum: Paris
Magnopolis: Mecklenburg

Maguncia, Moguntiacum, Castrum
Moguntiacum: Mainz
Manhemium: Mannheim
Marbugum, Mappurga: Marburg
Mariae Verda: Marienwerder
Marianopolis: Marienburg
Mimida, Munda ad Visurgium: Minden (in Westfalen)
Misna, Mixna: Meißen
Moenus: Main (river)
Moguntiacum: Mainz
Monacum: München
Monasterium, Mimigardefordum: Münster
Mosel: Mosel (river)
Nemetis: Speyer
Noremberga, Nurenberga: Nürnberg
Oeni pons: Innsbruck
Oldenburgum: Oldenburg, in Oldenburg
Osnabruga, Asnoburgensixs: Osnabrück
Parthenopolis: Magdeburg
Pingwia, Pigwia: Bingen
Plavia: Plauen
Poznan, Posna, Posnania: Posen
Praha, Boiobinum: Prague
Quedlinburgum: Quedlinburg
Rafelspurga, Ravispurga: Ravensburg
Ratisbona, Regina Castra: Regensburg
Regiomontanum, Regiomontum: Königs-   berg
Rhein: Rhein (river), Rhine
Rhodopolis: Rostock
Rotenburgum: Rothenburg ob der Tauber
Rugia: Rügen
Sarae pons, Saraepontum: Saarbrücken
Schaffnaburgum: Aschaffenburg
Sedinum: Stettin
Sigedunum: Siegen
Spira, Augusta Nemetum, Noviomagus: Speyer
Spreha: Spree (river)
Spuirsina: Schwerin
Stadium: Stade
Stargardia: Stargard
Stetina, Sedinum: Stetstin
Stralsunda: Stralsund
Strasbourg: Straßburg
Strelicia: Strelitz

Stutgardia: Stuttgart
Swicia: Switzerland
Tabernarum Castsellum: Bernkastel
Tachovia: Dachau
Teutoburginum: Detmold
Teutonicorum terra: Deutschland
Thiotmelli: Detmold
Thorunium: Thorn
Trajectum ad Oderam: Frankfurt an der
    Oder
Tremonia: Dortmund
Tricollis, Zeapolis: Dinkelsbühl
Ulma Suevorum: Ulm
Verdingen: Krefeld
Vienna, Wienna, Wyenna, Vindobona,
    Flaviana casstra: Wien (Vienna)
Vimania: Wangen
Visbada: Wiesbaden
Visurgia: Weser (river)
Warmacia, Wormacia, Wurmacia,
    Borbetomagus: Worms
Wimaria: Weimar
Wratislavia, Brateslavia, Bratislavia:
    Breslau
Wurtemberga: Württemberg
Ysenacum: Eisenach
Zeapolis: Dinkelsbühl
Zwickau: Zwickau

Sources:

◆*Orbus Latinus*, Klinkhardt and Biermann,
Braunschweig, 1971

◆Ernst Wilhelm Weidler and Paul A.Grun,
Latein II für den Sippenforscher. C.A. Starke
Verlag, Limburg/Lahn, 1969

FRENCH GENEALOGY
VOCABULARY

accoucher .... to give birth
actes de naissance .... birth records
actes de notaire............ notary records
alliance ....marriage
l'an, l'année.................................. year
aujourd'hui .... today
avec .... with
le baptême .... baptism
bans .... banns
le célibataire .... bachelor

le citoyen .... citizen
la commune .... community
conjoindre .... marriage
les conjoints............................. couple
le cordonnier .... shoemaker
le curé .... priest, minister
de, de la, de l', du .... of (the)
le décès .... death
décédé .... deceased
le défunt .... the deceased
demain .... tomorrow
le demeurant.......................... residing in
le domicile .... residence
l'église .... church
Église Catholique .... Roman
Romaine   Catholic Church
l'emploi .... occupation
enfant ....child
enseveli .... burial
enterré .... burial
l'enterrement .... burial
épouser .... to marry; marriage
époux .... husband
et .... and
expiré .... death
la famille.....................................family
la fille .... girl, daughter
la fille légitime .... legitimate daughter
le fils .... son
le fils naturel .... illigitimate son
le frére .... brother
funébre .... burial
le garçon... boy
le grand-pére .... grandfather
la grand-mere .... grandmother
hébreu .... Jewish
l'heure ....hour, time of day
hier .... yesterday
l'homme .... man
hôtel de ville .... town hall
inanimé .... death
inhumé .... burial
israélite .... Jewish
le jour.. day
juif... Jewish
juive .... Jewish
le lieu ....place
mairie .... town hall
maison de ville .... town hall

le mari .... husband
marié .... husband
le mariage .... marriage
le même mois .... the same month
mensuel .... month
la mére .... mother
le mois .... month
la mort .... death
mort-né .... stillborn
la naissance .... birth
naguit .... born
né, née .... born
nom .... surname
nom de baptême .... given name
nom de famille .... surname
parents .... parents
la paroisse, paroissiaux, ... parish
paroissiales
le parrain, la marraine   godfather,
                                godmother
le pére .... father
pére et mére .... parents
pour .... for
le prénom .... given name
le prêtre .... priest
publications .... banns
registres paroissiaux .... parish registers
registres de l'État Civil ... civil registers
répertoire .... index
la sépulture .... burial
la soeur .... sister
le soir .... evening
tables .... index
la tante .... aunt
le témoin .... witness
le temps .... time
le testament .... will
le tome .... volume
unir .... marriage
veuve, veuf .... widow, widower
(de cette) ville .... (from this) city

NUMBER WORDS IN FRENCH

1 .... un
2 .... deux
3 .... trois

4 .... quatre
5 .... cinq
6 .... six
7 .... sept
8 .... huit
9 .... neuf
10 .... dix
11 .... onze
12 .... douze
13 .... treize
14 .... quatorze
15 .... quinze
16 .... seize
17 .... dix-sept
18 .... dix-huit
19 .... dix-neuf
20 .... vingt
21 .... vingt-et-un
30 .... treinte
40 .... quarante
50 .... cinquante
60 .... soixante
70 .... soixante-dex, septante
80 .... quatre-vingts, huitante
90 .... quatre-vingt-dix
100 .... cent
1,000 .... mil, mille
1,000,000 .... million

DAYS, MONTHS IN FRENCH

Days

lundi .... Monday
mardi .... Tuesday
mercredi .... Wednesday
jeudi .... Thursday
vendredi .... Friday
samedi .... Saturday
dimanche .... Sunday

Months

janvier .... January
février .... February
mars .... March
avril .... April
mai .... May
juin .... June
juillet .... July

août	August
septembre (7bre)	September
octobre (8bre)	October
novembre (9bre)	November
décembre (10bre)	December

ABBREVIATIONS OF FRENCH GIVEN NAMES

A.	Albert
Ch.	Charles
Fr^s	François
Fr^{se}	Françoise
G	Ghislain
G^e	Ghislaine
H.	Henri
H^e	Henriette
J.	Joseph
J^e	Josèphe
J^{ne}	Joséphine
L.	Louis
L$^{e.}$	Louise
M.	Marie
P.	Pierre
Th.	Thérèse

YIDDISH

Yiddish, the language of Eastern and Central European Jews, is written with Hebrew letters but is mainly Germanic, with some words from Hebrew and Slavic languages.

Before the Holocaust, during which half the 12 million Yiddish speakers died, the cities of central and eastern Europe supported a rich and varied Yiddish culture. The language was abandoned by many Jews who emigrated to America, Canada, Argentina, and Western Europe.

Still spoken by about 700,000 people worldwide, in large part by ultra-Orthodox Hasidim, who tend to have very large families, Yiddish is predicted by some to grow in absolute terms, even as elderly Jewish immigrants die out.

In Germany are established two pro-fessorial chairs in Yiddish studies, one in Düsseldorf, the other in Trier. In the United States, Harvard has endowed a chair in the study of Yiddish, and other colleges have created Yiddish faculty positions: Ohio State, UCLA, UC Berkeley, and the Universities of Michigan and Texas.

Sources:
- Tina Rosenberg, "Living an American Life – in Yiddish," *New York Times*, Sept. 3, 1999.
- "Scholars See Modest Yiddish Renaissance," *The Week in Germany*, German Information Center, Oct. 30, 1998
- David Klinghoffer, "Schumer's Yiddish Lesson," *Wall Street Journal*, Nov. 6, 1998

FRAKTUR

The decorated manuscripts made primarily by the Pennsylvania Germans are called Fraktur. Most of them are birth and baptism certificates (*Geburts- und Taufschein*) produced from about 1760 to the early years of the twentieth century, almost always in German. By around 1900, Fraktur are frequently found written in English.

From about 1760 to 1818, freehand Fraktur were created by schoolmasters. Later Fraktur, from about 1810 to 1900, were preprinted and filled out by persons highly skilled in producing decorative handwriting.

Areas in which Fraktur were common are the present states of Pennsylvania, Virginia, West Virginia, Ohio, Maryland, New Jersey, New York, Indiana, the Carolinas, and Ontario, Canada. Their heaviest concentration was in southeast Pennsylvania. They were most popular among Lutheran and Reformed families because the majority of them were baptism certificates, representing an important sacrament among followers of these faiths.

"Fraktur" (pronounced FROCK-TUR), short for *Frakturschriften* (broken writing) derives from a Latin word meaning "fractured," or "broken," for as the letters are formed, instead of writing cursively, without lifting the pen, the writer lifts the pen, which is thus "broken" from the page.

Usually the Fraktur birth and baptism certificates include the father's name, the mother's name including her maiden name, the date of birth of the child, the place of birth, the name of the child, the date of baptism, and the name of the pastor who baptized the child. Names of witnesses or sponsors at the baptism, who were usually related to the child, are also listed.

Fraktur are highly prized for their beauty and historical value. The data they preserve have been found to be highly reliable

Collections of fraktur may be found at the Free Library of Philadelphia; the Abby Aldrich Rockefeller Folk Art Center in Williamsburg, Virginia; and The Henry Francis du Pont Winterhur Museum in Winterhur, Delaware. They are also held at the National Archives, the Library of Congress, and in some public libraries.

A great many Fraktur have been published and indexed by Russell and Corinne Earnest in East Berlin, Pennsylvania. Among the books they have published on Fraktur are *Papers for Birth Dayes: Guide to the Fraktur Artists and Scriveners; The Genealogist's Guide to Fraktur: For Genealogists Researching German-American Families*; *German-American Family Records in the Fraktur Tradition*, and *Fraktur: Folk Art & Family.*

To submit photocopies of Fraktur to the Earnests for sharing with others, or for information about publications, write to Russell D. Earnest Associates, P.O. Box 1007, East Berlin, PA 17316. Enclose a long, self addressed stamped envelope. Tel. (717) 259-0299.

Sources: Corinne P. Earnest, *Antique Week*; and Kenneth L. Marple, Palatines to America National Conference, June 1994

FRAKTUR GLOSSARY

Bücherzeichen: Bookplate. Bookplates show ownership. In American Fraktur, they sometimes also give genealogy data, such as date of birth.

Familientafel: Family register, a type of Fraktur

Fraktur, Fractur: Term applied to the typeset word used in Germany prior to 1941. Americans often use the term erroneously in regard to old German handwriting. In America, this term is used to describe a body of manuscript art. It is an umbrella term, under which there are many types, the most popular of which was the *Taufschein.*

Frakturschriften: Fraktur writing

Geburts- und Taufschein: Birth and baptism certificate

Infill: Genealogy data recorded on prefabricated freehand or printed birth and baptism certificates. Some scriveners who infilled genealogy data on Fraktur called themselves *Ausgefüller,* or "filler-outers."

Schein: Certificate

Script: Cursive writing. Unlike Fraktur lettering which is printed by hand, cursive writing is faster. In Fraktur lettering the pen is lifted from the page between letters of the alphabet, as in hand printing. In cursive writing or script, letters are strung together with ligatures to form words. Most written languages have both hand-printing and script.

Scrivener: A penman who filled out printed Fraktur. These penmen were often itinerant, moving from farm to farm to fill in Bible records and *Taufscheine* in their extraordinarily beautiful hands. Most knew German and English, and sometimes other languages as well. They worked from about 1810 into the twentieth century.

Taufe: Baptism

Taufpatenbrief: Baptism letter given by sponsors to the child

Taufschein: Baptism certificate. The *Taufschein* (or *Geburts- und Taufschein,* birth and baptism certificate) was the most popular type of American Fraktur. The German plural for *Taufschein* is *Taufscheine.*

Taufzedel, Taufzettel: A type of Swiss *Taufpatenbrief* given by sponsors to children at baptism.

Vorschrift: A type of Fraktur; a writing exercise, often made by schoolmasters as a teaching tool, so that students might copy the Fraktur lettering and German script.

Source: "Fraktur: A Special Kind of Genealogical Record," by Corinne and Russell Ernest. *Der Blumenbaum,* Vol. 15, No. 3, January/February/March 1999

MINORITY LANGUAGE PROTECTION IN GERMANY

On January 1, 1999, a treaty growing out of the Council of Europe's convention on the protection of minority languages went into effect, obliging the German government to protect and promote the use of Sorbic, Danish, Frisian, Low German, and Romany within Germany's borders.

It was estimated that this program would affect at least 150,000 German citizens.

Some 50,000 people ·in the states of Sachsen and Brandenburg speak Sorbic, a Slavic language that has been used in the region for centuries.

Northern Germany boasts about 20,000 Danish speakers, while thousands of Germans in the northern states of Niedersachsen and Schleswig-Holstein speak Frisian, a Germanic language closely related to English. The area is also home to several hundred thousand speakers of *Plattdeutsch,* or Low German.

Programs supporting Sorbic and Danish had been in place for decades, but Frisian and Low German benefited for the first time from this convention.

Romany, the Indo-Iranian language of the Sinti and Roma, also enjoyed its first official boost from German authorities. The language is spoken by an estimated 70,000 citizens, primarily in the industrial areas along the Rhine, the Ruhr and the Main rivers.

Some officials were surprised to learn that Frisian and Low German could be added to the list, as many had considered *Platt* to be dialect rather than a separate language, one that developed independent of High German. In the Hanseatic period of the 14th century, *Platt* was the language of trade on the North Sea and Baltic coasts.

The convention on the protection of minority languages calls for specific changes in cultural policy, public administration, education, and business practices.

Source: "With New Year, New Protections for Germany's Minority Languages," *The Week in Germany,* German Information Center, January 8, 1999

THE LORD'S PRAYER: HOCHDEUTSCH, POMERANIAN PLATT, AND PENNSYLVANIA GERMAN

Hochdeutsch
Das Gebet des Herrn
Vater unser, der du bist im Himmel.
  Geheiliget werde dein Name.
Dein Reich komme.
Dein Wille geschehe, wie im Himmel, also
  auf Erden.
Unser Täglich Brot gib uns heute.
Und vergib uns unsere Schuld, als wir
  vergeben unsern Schuldigern.
Und führe uns nicht in Versuchung,
  sondern erlöse uns von Übel.
Denn dein ist das Reich, und die Kraft

und die Herrlichkeit in Ewigkeit.
Amen

Pomeranian Platt

Unse Vader de du buest in'n Himmel:
Laat hilligt warrn dienen Willen, so as
in'n Himmel, so ok op de Eerd.
Uns' daaglich Brood gigg uns vundag.
Un vergiff uns unse Schuld,
as we de vergeben doot,
de an uns schuellig suend.
Un laat uns nich versoecht warrn.
Maak du uns loos un frie vun dat Boese.
Denn dien is dat Riek un de Kraft un de
Herrlichkeit in Ewigkeit.

Pennsylvania German

Em Herr Sei Gebaed

Unser Vadder, os ist im Himmel.
 Geheilicht is Dei Naame.
Dei Kaenichreich soll kumme.
 Dei wille soll geduh warre uff die Erd
 graat wie im Himmel.
Geb unns heit unser daeglich Brod.
 Vergeb unns unser schulde, wie mier
 anner ehre schulde vergewwe.
Fiehr unns net in versuchung awwer
 erlase unns vunn iwwel.
Ver Dei is es Keenichreich, unn die grofft,
 unn die Harlichkeit, in Aewichkeit.
 Amen

Source of Pomeranian Platt prayer: *Der Maibaum,* Deutschheim Association Journal, Vol. VI, No. 1, Spring 1998. (Submitted by Harolyn Schulz, of Hermann, Mo.)

OLD BIBLE TRANSLATIONS: THE LORD'S PRAYER

Hochdeutsch 1518

Der herr regieret mich und mir geprist
nichts, und an der stat der weide, da setzt
er mich. Er hat mich gefüret auf dem
wasser der widerspringung, er bekeret
mein sel. Er fürt mich auss auf die steig
der gerechtigkeit, vmb seinen namen.
Wann ob ich gen in mitte des schatten
des todes, ich fürcht nit die üblen ding,
wann du bist bei mir: Dein ruot und dein
stab, die selben haben mich getröstet.

Niederdeutscher Druck 1522:

De here regeret mi und mi schal nicht
gebreken, in de stede der weide, dar he
mi satte. He ledde mi up dat water der
weddermakinge, he bekerte mine sele. He
ledde mi ut up den wech der rechtfer-
dichkeit, dorch sinen namen. Wente efte
ick ga in dem middel des schemen des
dodes, ick schal nein quat forchten,
wente du bist mit mi: din rode und din
staf, de hebben mi getrost.

Luthers Wortlaut 1534:

Der Herr is mein Hirte, mir wird nichts
mangeln. Er weidet mich auff einer
grünen Awen und füret mich zum frischen
Wasser. Er erquicket meine Seele. Er füret
mich auf rechter Straße, vmb seines
namens willen. Und ob ich schon
wandert im finstern tal, fürchte ich kein
Unglück, denn Du bist bey mir, Dein
stecken und stab trösten mich.

Source: Hans Ebeling, *Deutsche Geschichte,* Georg Westermann Verlag, Braunschweig, 1960

COMPUTER TRANSLATION

Several websites offer free translations among a number of languages. For example, the user can enter a short message in English (the "source" language) and have it translated into German (the "target" language).

Most websites offer a free translation of text up to 150 words, and then quote fees for longer texts. This method can produce a basic translation into the target language, but experts have found that the translation should be checked by a person well-versed in that language. Small misunderstandings could lead to huge difficulties.

To find a free translation service, use your favorite search engine and enter the term "translation English to German free." Several websites will appear to offer the same service.

In translating older German texts from church or civil vital records into English, users should be aware of many possible problems that will lead to mistranslations. The following article investigates these problems in depth: "Computer Translation of Old Church Book Entries: What Quality Can We Expect?" *Everton's Genealogical Helper,* 62:4 (July/August 2008), 56-60.

HISTORIC GERMAN ALPHABET FONTS FOR THE COMPUTUER

For those researchers who would like to create the old look of German with computer fonts of old alphabets, this German website will be of interest: www.delbanco-frakturschriften.de.

The site can be read only in German. At the top left of the home page, there are the following seven groups of fonts: *Gotisch* (older type-set), *Kursiv* (older type-set), *Deutsche Schreibschrift* (20th century handwritten), *Schwabacher* (newer type-set), *Fraktur* (older type-set), *Sonstige Schriften* (type-set for other languages), *Verschiedenes* (literature for various fonts). All purchases are made in Euro on a Mastercard or Visa credit card. Each order must reach a minimum of 15 Euro, and discounts are given beginning at 50 Euro. The user must be adept at reading German to make the purchase.

Section 6:
German Resources

♦

Church and civil registration records
Abbreviations
Finding and using gazetteers
Maps and atlases
German indexes, other German resources
Postal codes
Lineages

♦

GERMAN CHURCH RECORDS

Church records are about the only primary sources of genealogical data before 1875 for emigrants from German areas (except west of the Rhine, Baden, Württemberg, Hessen, and Frankfurt).

Church registers began between 1524 and 1650. The primary motive for creating them was the church's interest in recording the religious events associated with baptisms, marriages, and burials of persons living in its respective parishes.

The aristocrats ruling most Protestant communities were responsible for early church registers, beginning in Hesse, Saxony, and parts of Thuringia and the old duchy of Württemberg) in the mid 16th century, and about a century later in other parts of Germany.

Keeping of church records varied, depending on religious practices in various lands. Sometimes part of a population was Lutheran, another Reformed (Calvinist), each keeping separate church records. In Prussia within its borders of 1817, in Nassau and in the Rhenish part of the grand-dukedom of Hessen, the Lutherans and Calvinists were united in 1818. Since then, only combined "Protestant" (*evangelisch*) church registers exist rather than separate registers for each denomination.

Catholic church registers were written in Latin until the early 19th century, by mandate of the Council of Trent (*Trient*) of 1563.

Small denominations like the Mennonites and the Moravian Brethren (called "Herrnhuter" in Germany) often had their own church registers. The registers of the oldest Moravian settlement in Germany, Herrnhut in Saxony, began in 1739.

Most church registers in Germany are kept in the parish offices. Some, in the formerly French communities west of the Rhine, can still be found in the local mayor's office, in compliance with a French decree of May 1798. Some are kept in certain special archives, as in Brühl near Cologne, or in Detmold.

To determine what records should be available for a specified parish and where to write for information on these records, consult church record inventories (see index). These are listed in the "Locality" section of the Family History Library Catalog under "Church Records." For more information, see *Research Outline: Germany*, available online through www.familysearch.org.

GERMAN CHURCH BOOKS (KIRCHENBÜCHER)

Church books, or parish registers, contain records made by priests and pastors concerning births, baptisms, marriages, deaths, and burials. In general, the detail increases over time. Church books sometimes include account books (recording fees for tolling bells, fees for masses for the dead, and so forth), lists of confirmations, lists of members, and family registers.

Types of church records
♦ *Kirchenbücher Duplikate*
Parish register transcripts, or duplicates. These date from 1807 in Bavaria; from 1740 in Mecklenburg; from 1899 in Prussia; and from 1808-1875 in Württemberg.

♦ *Taufregister*: **christening/baptism registers**
These records usually provide the child's name and sex; baptism date, and some-times birthdate; place of baptism; name of mother; name and occupation of father; legitimacy of birth; names and residence of witnesses or godparents' (unless the child is illegitimate, in which case the father's name is not always mentioned)

♦ *Geburtsregister*: **birth registers**
These usually provide the child's name, date of birth, legitimacy, parents and godparents' names

♦ *Konfirmationsregister*: **Confirmation registers**
Confirmation usually occurred at age 14 for Protestants, and at about age 12 for Catholics. Usually the records provided (at the discretion of the recording minister) name of participant; age; date/place of event; and sometimes name and occupation of father, and name of mother. Some registers give only the names and dates of confirmation.

♦ *Trauregister*: **marriage registers**
These registers usually provided the name and age of the bride; marriage date and place; residence/occupation of bride-groom; names of bridegroom's parents, their residence and fathers' occupations; name of bride, her age, and names of her parents; occupation of her father; names of witnesses, their residences and occupations; and name of previous spouse if the bride or bridegroom was widowed.

♦ *Sterberegister*: **death registers (or)** *Begräbnisse*: **burial registers**
Usually provided are the name of the deceased, profession, age at death (some-times cause of death), occupation, date/place of death, date/place of burial.

♦ *Familienbücher, Familienregister*: **family registers**
This record type is often found in southern Germany, especially in Baden and Württemberg, dating from the early nineteenth century.

Provided are names, birth dates/places, marriage dates, sometimes death dates of husband/wife, their parents' names, birth dates/places, children's names in order of birth, birthdates, and birthplaces.

"The Evolution of Content in German Church Records: A Case Study, "by Roger P. Minert and Erin Clark Collins, *Pal-Am Immigrant*, 33: 1 (2007), 2-13.

SYMBOLS FOUND IN GERMAN CHURCH RECORDS

The following symbols were commonly written into many church record books:

* = geboren (born)

∞ = verheiratet (married)

† = gestorben (died)

(*) = außereheliche Geburt (illegitimate-ly born)

〜〜 = getauft (christened)

° = verlobt (engaged)

▢ = begraben (buried)

†* = Totgeburt (stillborn)

O|O = geschieden (divorced)

✕ = gefallen (killed in action)

o-o = uneheliche Verbindung (common-law marriage, illegitimate union)

The following symbols can be found in older records:

Ƴ = getauft (christened)

Ψ = geboren (born)

✕ = verheiratet (married)

⋏ = gestorben (died)

⋔ = begraben (buried)

DEVELOPMENT OF GERMAN CHURCH, CIVIL RECORDS

Late 1400s: Church record beginnings. Catholic: 1480-1540. Protestant: 1524-1560

1618-48: Thirty Years War leaves many records destroyed.

End of 1700s: Civil registration begins west of the Rhine, in 1792/1798. Some church records stop, but restart by 1813.

Early 1800s: During the French occupation (1794-1815), the system of civil registration west of the Rhine is introduced. (Often these records are found written in French.)

1808-76: Parish register transcripts are produced for areas not covered by civil registration. (These registers are not necessarily stored according to parish jurisdictions.)

1874/76: Official beginning dates of civil registration – October 1, 1874 in Prussia and January 1, 1876 in all of the German Empire. The procedure continues to the present day.

CIVIL REGISTRATION (Reichspersonenstandsgesetz)

The recording of vital data (births/baptisms, marriages, and deaths/burials) was first done by the churches beginning in the late 15th century. When France occupied German-language territories along the Rhine River beginning in the 1790s, administrative officials introduced in those regions the same system of civil registration that had been used in France since the French Revolution.

The justification for the recording of vital data by the government was that only the civil authority (*Standesamt*) could guarantee that church authorities could not forbid marriages between persons of different faiths (so-called *Mischehe*). Civil records (*Standesregister*) were established and maintained in several large cities not in the Rhineland as well, such as Hanover and Bremen, but many closed down as soon as the French forces had been driven from German territories. Researchers therefore see in the Family History Library Catalog terms such as 1798-1813 for civil records. The French system also required that church officials cease the recording of vital events, but the fact that some clerics continued the practice in secret is of great importance to family history researchers. The Family History Library has sporadic groups of civil records in other regions of Germany beginning in about 1810 and those records can be found categorized as "civil registration."

In the new German Empire (1871-1918), Prime Minister Otto von Bismarck pushed for the adoption of the French civil registry system and was successful in seeing it introduced in the Prussian provinces on October 1, 1874 and in the entire Empire as of January 1, 1876. The system is still in use. In addition to recording all births, marriages and deaths within his/her jurisdiction, the official in charge (*der Standesbeamte, die Standesbeamtin*) conducts marriages (after which the parties may also have a church ceremony if they choose, but no marriage in Germany is valid under law until performed by the civil registrar).

Originally, only the principal in the record or his relatives and assigns had access to the civil records. Thanks however to the revised law (*Personenstandsgesetz*) of January 1, 2009, access to older civil records is now more easily obtained. Birth records more than 110 years old, marriages more than 90 and deaths more than 30 must now be offered by the civil registrar to the local government archive and anybody may study them. Records not yet that old are retained in the *Standesamt* and are subject to the original restrictions.

Because older civil registry documents are now being moved from their origins to local archives, researchers should use the Internet to contact the *Standesamt* to learn the disposition of the records. Inquiries may be sent via email in most cases, but the fees are established by the archives and may be as much as $50 per record found and copied. A sample search might follow this route: www.heidelberg.de, *Politik und Verwaltung, Rathaus, Standesamt.* Other terms of import are *Verwaltung, Behörden, Ämter, Bürgerservice, Urkunden* and *Suchdienst.* Inquiries should be written in or translated into

German. Payment for copies will usually be required before the documents are sent.

Meyers Orts- und Verkehrsverzeichnis des Deutschen Reichs identifies with the symbol *StdA* the location of the *Standesamt* for each community. Large cities usually have more than one *Standesamt*.

Source: "Privacy Law and the German Civil Registry: The Case of Col. Gen. Alfred Jodl," by Roger P. Minert. *German Genealogical Digest,* 21:2 (Fall 2005), n.p.

SOME OTHER GOVERNMENT RECORDS

◆ *Passagierlisten*: **passenger lists**
Hamburg passenger list information includes date of embarkation, husband's name, place of last residence, occupation, and age; given names and ages of wife and children; sometimes port of destination.

◆ *Steuerlisten, Steuerbücher*: **tax lists, books**
Providing names and addresses, these date from the beginning of the 15th century.

◆ *Leichenpredigten*: **funeral sermons**
Following the Reformation, funeral sermons replaced the elaborate funeral mass of the Catholic church, taking the form of a graveside eulogy (*Leichenpredigt,*) which often recounted the life of the deceased in considerable detail. These sermons were printed and circulated to friends and family of the deceased. Funeral sermons are found from about 1500 to 1800.

◆ *Auswandererlisten, Auswandererakten*: **emigration lists/records**
Usually these provide the name of the emigrant, date and place of emigration (sometimes destination), date and place of birth, place of residence, occupation, given names and ages of wife and

children. Not all emigrants were listed. These lists date from the early 19th century.

◆ *Testamente, Testamentsakten*: **wills**
Usually these documents contained names of heirs and their relationship to the deceased, probate records, name and sometimes age of testator, residence, relationships, description of property, date of will and probate, and witnesses. These records, dating from the 13th century, are found in the *Amtsgerichte* (local courthouses).

◆ *Volkszählungslisten, Bauernverzeichnisse, Einwohnerlisten*: **census records**
Originally called Tax and Tithing Records (*Steuer- und Zehntregister*), these exist only for specific places and times.

Usually provided are name, age, place of origin, occupation, and residence. Census records occur in Mecklenburg: 1677-1689, with intervals, and in 1819; in Schleswig-Holstein, 1803-1860; and in some other areas. They date from the 16th to 18th centuries.

◆ *Bürgerbücher/-listen*: **Citizenship registrations.**
New immigrants applying for citizenship in a town had to produce a birth or baptism certificate with names of the parents. Some citizenship records contain the burgher's genealogy. Found in *Stadtarchive,* (state archives), they date from the 13th to the mid-19th century.

◆ *Polizeiregister/Einwohnermeldelisten*: **police registers, resident registration lists.**
Usually provided are the name and address of every resident. Kept at the *Einwohnermeldeamt* (town registration office) and dating from about 1830.

◆ *Grundbücher*: **land books**
These land books contain descriptions of specific parcels of land, the owners' names, and records of mortgages on property. Kept by the *Amtsgericht* (lower court), they date from the 11th century and sometimes earlier.

◆ *Adressbücher*: **city directories**

Provided are names and addresses of residents of a given locality. Dating from the early 1800s, these directories are found in local archives. See Ribbe and Henning's *Taschenbuch für Familiengeschichts-forschung* for lists of years in which *Adressbücher* exist for many localities in Germany.

◆ *Gildenbücher, Zunftbücher, Innungsbücher*: **apprentice and guild books**
Usually provided are names, parents' names, occupation, and residence of employer. Dating from the 16th to 19th centuries, the availability of these books is sporadic.

◆ *Kriegslisten, Militärakten*: **military records**
These records are found in local and state archives near areas where soldiers were stationed.

◆ *Dorfsippenbücher, Ortssippenbücher*: **local histories**
These are lineage books showing the genealogy of all residents of a particular village, usually ending before 1900.

◆ *Hausbücher*: **house books**
Dating from the 16th to the 19th century, these histories of houses generally include house owners' names, occupations, and social and economic status.

See below for a more extensive list of government records.

VOCABULARY OF GERMAN RECORD TYPES AND RELATED TERMS

Abendmahlsgästelisten: communion attendance lists
Abmeldescheine: permits to move away from a place
Achtbücher: proscription books (names of persons tried in absentia)
Adels Geschlechterbücher: genealogies of nobility
Adreßbücher: address books (similar to city directories)

Allgemeine Akten: general documents
Almosenliste: welfare lists
Amtsbücher: civil records
Anniversarien: records of donations given for saying prayers on anniversaries of deaths
Arbeitsbücher: employment books
Arbeitssachen: business accounts
Archivinventare: archive inventories
Armen- und Wohltätigkeitssachen: welfare matters
Armenregister: registers of the poor, welfare lists
Atlanten: atlases
Aufgebote: marriage banns/marriage registers
Aufgelöste Ehen: divorces
Aushebungsrollen: conscription lists (muster rolls)
Aushebungsverzeichnisse: conscription lists (muster rolls)
Auswandererverzeichnisse: emigrant lists
Auswanderungsakten: emigration records
Auswanderungsgesuche: emigration applications
Auswanderungslisten: emigration records
Bauernlisten: census records
Beerdigungsregister: burial registers
Begräbnisregister: burial registers
Begräbnisse, Ordnungen bei: orders of precedence for funerals
Beiakten: supplementary records
Berufsakten: occupational records
Berufsangehörigenverzeichnisse: lists of members of a profession
Bestandsverzeichnis: register of holdings
Bestattungsbücher: burial books
Bevölkerungslisten: population lists
Bevölkerungsverzeichnisse: population lists
Bibliothekskataloge: library catalogs
Bibliotheksverzeichnisse: library catalogs
Bruderschaftsurkunde: brotherhood (fraternity) records

Bürgerbücher: citizen rolls
Bürgerlisten: citizen rolls
Dezennaltabellen: decennial index of vital records (west-Rhine)
Dienerbücher: servants' books
Dorfsippenbücher: village lineage books
Ehebücher: marriage records
Ehelichkeitserklärung: declaration of legitimacy
Eheregister: marriage registers
Ehescheidung: divorce, dissolved marriage
Ehestiftunen: matchmakings, donations on the occasion of a marriage by the couple (not *to* the couple)
Eheverkündigungen: marriage proclamations (banns)
Eheverträge: marriage contracts
Einbürgerungen: naturalizations
Einnahmeregister: receipt registers
Einwanderungen: immigrations
Einwohnerlisten: lists of inhabitants
Einwohnermelderegister: inhabitant registration registers/police registration
Einwohnerverzeichnisse: census records
Erbebücher: inheritance books
evangelisch- : Protestant-
Familienbücher: family books
Familiengeschichten: family histories
Familienregister: family registers
Firmungen: confirmations
Flurbücher: field or parcel records
Garnisonskirchenbücher: Military (garrison) church records
Geburtsbriefe: birth letters/certificates
Geburtsregister: birth registers
Geburtsscheine: birth certificates
Geburtsurkunden: birth certificates
Geburtszeugnisse: birth certificates
Gefangener: See *Kriegsgefangener*
Gemeindelexikon: gazetteer
Gerichts und Polizeisachen: court and police matters
Gerichtsakten: court documents
Gerichtsbücher: court books

Gerichtsprotokolle: court minutes
Geschlechterbücher: family lineage books
Geschlechterkunde: inventories
Gesellenbücher: journeymen books
Gilderbücher: guild books
Glockenbücher: bell-tolling books
Grabregister: grave registers
Grundbücher: land records
Güterbücher: chattel records
Handbücher: handbooks, manuals
Hausbücher: books recording owners of houses
Häuserbücher: See *Hausbücher*
Hauslisten: house directories
Heimatsscheine: place of origin certificates
Heiratsbeilage: marriage documents (supplements)
Heiratsprotokolle: marriage records
Heiratsregister: marriage registers
Heiratsurkunden: marriage records
Heiratsverzeichnis: marriage indexes
Herkunftszeugnisse: certificates of origin
Hochschulmatrikeln: student registers
Hypothekenbücher: mortgage books
Impflisten: vaccination records
Innungsbücher: guild books
Inventare: inventories
Jahrbücher: yearbooks
Jüdische Akten: Jewish documents
Kartei: card file
katholisch- : Catholic-
Kaufbücher: property records
Kaufverträge: contracts of sales
Kirchenbuchämter: parish record offices/archives
Kirchenbuchduplikate: inventory of church book duplicates
Kirchenbücher: church books
Kirchenbüchverzeichnisse: parish register inventories
Kirchenchroniken: church chronicles
Kirchengeschichte: church histories
Kirchenlagerbücher: church account books
Kirchenvisitationen: church

visitations
Kirchenzweitschriften: church duplicates
kirchliche Adressbücher: church directories
Klosterverzeichnisse: monastery records
Kommunikanten: communicants
Konfirmandenverzeichnisse: confirma-tion books
Konfirmationsregister: confirmation registers
Kopfzahlregister: census registers
Kopulationsregister: marriage registers
Kriegsgefangener: prisoner of war
Kriegslisten: military records
Lagerbücher: property/warehouse records, military levy books
Landkarten: maps
Lebensabrisse: biographical sketches
Lebensbilder: biogaphical sketches
Lebensläufe: biographical histories
Legitimationen: legitimations
Lehnbriefe: fief certificates
Lehnbücher: fief records
Lehrlingsbücher: apprentice books
Leibgedingsbriefe: documents providing support of a wife upon husband's death
Leichenpredigten: funeral sermons
Libri de statu animarum: family registers
Mannzahlregister: census registers
Matrikelamt: register office
Matrikeln: see *Universitätsmatrikeln*
Meisterbuch: book of masters
Melderegister: registers of residents
Militärakten: military records
Militärkirchenbücher: military church-book records
Militärurkunden: military records
Mitgliederlisten: membership lists
Musterrollen: military lists
Musterungslisten: military lists
Nachlässe: estates
Nachlaßprotokolle: estate records
Namenregister: indexes
Necrologien: records of recent deaths

Offizier-Stammlisten: lists of officers and their assignments
Ortschaftverzeichnis: gazetteer
Ortslexika: gazetteers
Ortssippenbücher: village lineage books
Passagierlisten: passenger lists
Personenstandsregister: registry of vital statistics
Pfarranstellungsakten: ministers' contracts
Pfarrbücher: parish records
Pfarrerverzeichnisse, Pfarrbücherverzeichnisse: indexes of parish records
Politische Akten: public records
Polizeiregister: police registers *(Meldebücher)*
Proklamationsbücher: banns register
Prozessakten: court records
Quelle: sources
Ranglisten: military lists
Rassenkunde: ethnology
Ratsrechnungen: municipal accounting records
Reichspersonenstandsgesetz: civil registration law
Reiseführer: travel guide books
Reversen: lists of properties reverted to the owners
Scheidungsprozesse: divorce records
Schiffslisten: passenger lists
Schöffenbücher: records of the jurors of the court of first instance
Schulakten: school records
Schulberichte: school records
Schuldbücher: records of indebtedness
Schülerverzeichnisse: alumni lists
Seelenregister/Seelenlisten: person registers (census records)
Staatsdienstakten: civil service records
Stadtbücher: city records
Stadtchroniken: city chronicles
Stadtrechnungen: municipal account books
Stammrollen: military rosters
Standesamtregister: vital record office registers
Standesbücher: registry books
Sterberegister: death registers
Sterbeurkunde: death record

Steuerbücher: tax books
Steuerlisten: tax lists
Steuerregister: tax lists
Synodalbücher: synod records
Tagebücher: diaries, journals
Taschenbuch: handbook, guide
Taufregister: christening registers
Teilungsverträge: contracts of division and inheritance agreements
Telefonbücher: telephone books
Testamente: wills
Testamentsakten: probate records
Todesanzeigen: obituaries
Todesregister: death registers
Toten-Annalen: annals of the dead
Totengeläutbücher: death bell tolling books
Trauregister: marriage registers
Überschreibungen: property transfer records
Übersicht über - : inventory of -
Universitätsmatrikeln: university enroll-ments, registrations
Untertanenurkunden: serf records
Urkunden: certificates/documents
Vaterschaftsanerkennung: acknowledgements of fatherhood
Verehelichungen: marriages
Verkaufsbriefe: contracts of sales
Verkündbücher: announcment books
Verlobungen: engagements (to marry); promises of donations to a church
Verlustlisten: casualties lists
Verschiedene Akten: various documents
Verwaltungsakten: administration documents
Verzeichnis: index, register
Visitationen: (church) inspections
Völkerkunde: ethnology
Volkszählungslisten: census records
Volljährigkeitserklärung: declaration of majority (age)
Vormünderbücher: guardian books
Vormundschaften: guardian records
Wahlfähigkeitslisten: election lists
Wanderbücher: documents carried by journeymen (*Geselle*) on their journeys
Wanderzettel: guild attestation to

member's competence
Wörterbücher: dictionaries
Zehntregister: tithe registers
Zeitungen: newspapers
Zivilstandsamturkunde: civil registry records
Zivilstandsregister: vital records registers
Zunftbücher: guild records
Zuzugsgenehmigungen: permits to move into other areas
Zweitschriften: transcripts, duplicates

PARISH REGISTERS

What are parish registers?

Parish registers are books maintained by parish offices to record ecclesiastical events. These records include:
◆Baptisms (recorded initially without the date of birth
◆Confirmations (around the age of 14)
◆Marriages, or banns before marriages, or permissions to marry in another parish
◆Burials (initially without the date of death)
◆Lists of parish members
◆Lists of persons taking the communion or sacrament
◆Family registers (*Seelenregister, Familienregister*) as compilations of family groups on one page
◆Lists and biographies of clergymen
◆Historical and miscellaneous notes

The following records are not parish registers:
◆Books maintained by parish offices to record financial, construction, and other matters
◆ Vital registers maintained by state authorities
◆Private records of sacristans, cemetery administrations, etc.
◆ Accounts of baptismal, marriage and burial fees
◆Proceedings of moral courts (*Kirchenconventsprotokolle, Kirchenzensurprotokolle).*

The following types of records may replace missing parish registers:
◆Duplicates of parish registers (from about 1780 to 1876 only)
◆Printed parish registers (in the newspapers of towns)
◆Abstracts which were made at a time when the parish registers were still there
◆State vital registers, the earliest starting in 1798

Birth registers
◆ Birth certificates (*Geburtsschein, Mannrecht*)
◆Entries of penalties for illegitimate births
◆Entries in registers of bonded serfmen

Marriage registers
◆marriage contracts
◆Marriage licenses
◆Entries concerning the payment of a marriage fee (*Brautlauf, Salzscheibe*)

Death registers
◆Death notices in newspapers
◆Death dates in probate records, which often include detailed notifications about the death of the deceased (*Sterbefall-anzeigen*)
◆Tombstones after 1870
◆Funeral sermons
◆ Entries on the death tax of bonded serfmen (*Hauptrecht*)
◆ Petitions of widows, entries on a second marriage
◆Orphans records

Time period
The time in which these parish registers existed varies considerably. In the Protestant territories, the oldest ones usually start when the Reformation was introduced in the pertinent domain (from the 1520s onward); in Catholic lands in the late 1400s. Some of these old books were destroyed during the Thirty Years War (1618-1648), by the French invasions around 1690, and during the Second World War (1939-1945).

Most parish records have separate event catagories and even event books. In some parishes, the records are kept separately, i.e. arranged according to communities within the parish.

The scope of the entries may vary from church to church and from parish to parish. When church and state officials published guidelines for the recording of vital events within their jurisdictions, some uniformity in content and form ensued.

Where can parish registers by found?

Originally, parish registers were kept at the local parish offices, but some may have been forwarded to other places, such as,

♦To another parish office if the original parish no longer exists

♦To a central parish register office in a city

♦To a central ecclesiastical archive

♦To a state archive

♦To a municipal archive

Beginning in the 18th century, many states and church offices required that exact duplicates of church records be submitted to county offices or church archives at the end of each calendar year. This practice generally ended by 1876 when the civil registry system was established throughout the German Empire.

The Church of Jesus Christ of Latter-day Saints has copied many original parish registers and duplicates on microfilm or as digital images. Therefore, parish registers may be searched in a local family history center as well as in the repositories of original records in Europe.

Hints and cautions in the use of parish registers

♦Make sure the initial entry is correct. When starting with a known birth date, verify it before searching the marriage and death entries of the parents.

♦Become aware of the organization of the books and the methods of recording the entries.

♦Look for biological inconsistencies. A woman giving birth at age 50 is just as suspicious as a first child being born five years after the marriage of the parents.

♦ Don't trust indexes. If an index does not prove helpful, search through the original register page by page. The entry may be recorded and indexed by a slightly different name (Clais, instead of Klais, for example), or by a quite different name (an illegitimate child was recorded with the mother's surname, and may have later have been assigned the surname of the father).

♦When the date of a death entry of a man shows his widow to be still fairly young, look for her second marriage before searching for the record of her death. She may have remarried and be registered in the death register under the surname of her second husband.

♦Places of origin are sometimes listed in unexpected places in the registers, such as,

–In an entry on a relative

–In an entry of the sponsors of the children

– In an entry on the confirmation of a child

–At the death of the person

–In the death entry of a person's father, father-in-law or other relative

–In the records of a group of people who moved to the same place at the same time from the same area of origin

–In the record of a person's mother who moved to a new location when she married

♦ Abstract all information given in an entry. Every detail could be important for further research – like the word *weiland* in a marriage entry (indicating that a person was deceased), or the mention of someone's ruler, or the person's nickname, or the occupation.

♦Be careful not to mix up two bearers of the same name.

♦If it is not certain that the birth entry belongs to the person being searched, check the death, confirmation, and marriage registers to find out if the child survived childhood.

♦Interpret obsolete dates, such as the

Tuesday after the Sunday Rogate of 1769. Observe the historical calendar reforms.

* Become aware of local customs, especially as they concern name-giving and the selection of sponsors.

◆Friedrich R. Wollmershäuser, M.A., Accredited Genealogist, Herrengasse 8-10, 89610 Oberdischingen, Germany. © Friedrich R. Wollmershäuser, 1997.

◆Roger P. Minert, *Deciphering Handwriting in German Documents: Analyzing German, Latin, and French in Vital Records in Germany,* Provo, Utah: GRT Publications, 2001.

BEGINNINGS OF CIVIL REGISTRATION

Civil (government) registration records (*Zivilstands-register* or *Personenstandsregister)* include birth, marriage and death events. This system began for the entire German Empire on 1 January 1876. In the Prussian provinces it began on 1 October 1874. In some areas records began even earlier, as shown in the following list:

◆**National civil registration:** 1 January 1876
◆**Prussia:** 1 October 1874
◆**Baden:** 1 January 1870 - (marriages only)
◆**Bavaria (Pfalz – west of the Rhine):** 1 May 1798-
◆**Bremen:** 1811 -
◆**Alsace-Lorraine:** 1792 -
◆**Hamburg:** 1811-1815; 1866- (births, deaths; 1596- (marriages)
◆**Hessen (parts west of the Rhine):** 1 May 1798-
◆**Duchy of Nassau:** 1 November 1817 -
◆**Frankfurt (Grand Duchy):** 1 January 1810 - 1 February 1814
◆**Frankfurt (free city):** 1 May 1851-
◆**Lübeck:** 1811 -
◆**Oldenburg (Birkenfeld County):** 1 May 1798 -
◆**Rheinland (parts west of the Rhine):** 1 May 1798 -
◆**Rheinland (Berg - Grand Duchy):** 1 January 1810-1815
◆**Westfalen:** 1 January 1808-1814
◆**Württemberg:** 15 November 1807 (family books)

Civil records became another prime source for genealogical research after the date of their introduction because of the high amount of detail and accessibility, and the availability of indexes. The reliability of civil registers is excellent.

Sources: *Germany: Genealogical Research Guide,* by Steven W. Blodgett. The Genealogical Department of the Church of Jesus Christ of Latter-day Saints, Salt Lake City, Utah, rev. 1989. Reprinted by permission of the author.

"Privacy Law and the German Civil Registry: The Case of Col. Gen. Alfred Jodl," by Roger P. Minert. *German Genealogical Digest,* 21:2 (Fall 2005), n.p.

CHURCH RECORD INVENTORIES, DIRECTORIES

Church book inventories

In order to search church records, the researcher must first determine to which parish a particular village or town belonged. To access church inventories for specific German states, check the Family History Library Catalog as follows: Search under "Place Search" for "Germany" and the heading "Germany – Church Records – Inventories, Registers, Catalogs."

The following resources are generally useful in church record searches:

◆ *Archive und Archivare in der Bundesrepublik Deutschland, Österreich und der Schweiz,* 15th ed., Munich, 1995. (FHL 943 J54a)
◆Steven W. Blodgett, *Germany: Genealogical Research Guide.* FHL 943 D27bs; film 1,573,115 item 2; fiche 6001630
◆ Wolfgang Eger, *Verzeichnis der*

Militärkirchenbücher in der Bundes-republik Deutschland. (FHL 943 K23va Vol. 18)

◆Laraine K. Ferguson, "German Church Records," *German Genealogical Digest*, Vol. 11, No. 1, Spring 1995.

◆ C. Russell Jensen, *Parish Register Latin: An Introduction,* Vita Nova Books, Salt Lake City, 1988. (FHL 475 J453p)

◆C. Russell Jensen, *Parish Register German: An Introduction*, Vita Nova Books, Salt Lake City, 1994. FHL 943 G2j; film 1573234 item 6

◆*Meyers Orts- und Verkehrslexikon des deutschen Reichs,* Leipzig, 1912, to determine if a particular locality had a parish. (FHL 943 E5mo; film 496640 (A-K) and 496641 (L-Z); fiche 6000001-29)

◆ *Minerva-Handbücher, Archive im deutschsprachigen Raum*, Walter de Gruyter, New York, 1974.

◆Ernest Thode, *Address Book for Germanic Genealogy,* 5th edition, Genealogical Publishing Company, Baltimore, 1994.

Church directories

Parishes in a church region generally provide lists of parishes in a diocese and the villages belonging to specific parishes. Addresses of parish churches and of diocese headquarters are also often included.

◆To search Roman Catholic dioceses for a particular parish, see the *General-Schematismus der katholischen Geistlichkeit Deutschlands* (Directory of the Catholic clergy of Germany. FHL film 1,340,500 – also:

– *Handbuch über die katholischen Kirchenbücher in der Ostdeutschen Kirchenprovinz östlich der Oder und Neiße und dem Bistum Danzig* (Inventory of Catholic parish registers for the former German areas east of the Oder-Neiße, including Ostpreußen, Pommern, Branden-burg, Westpreußen, and Schlesien; now located in Poland, Lithuania, and Russia). FHL 943.8 K23k;

film 0908101 item 2; fiche 6001308

◆To search Protestant jurisdictions, see *Deutsches kirchliches Adreßbuch* (German church directory). FHL 943 K24d 1934; film (1929 edition) 476,672 – also:

–*Deutsches kirchliches Adreßbuch: ein kirchlicher Führer durch die evangelischen Landeskirchen Deutschlands* (Directory of Protestant churches in Germany, including German Protestant churches throughout the world). FHL 943 K24d; film 0584897

GERMAN CENSUSES

Census records are found under terminologies such as *Volkszählungen* (censuses), *Bevölkerungsliste* (population lists), *Bürgerlisten* (citizen lists), *Einwohnerlisten* (resident lists), *Hausbesitzerverzeichnis* (list of house owners), *Mannzählregister* (population count), *Seelenlisten* (church memberships), and *Untertannenlisten* (list of serfs).

Those records identified as *Volkszählungen* are found in the Family History Library Catalog under "Census." Records identified by other names (see the list above) are usually listed under the subject heading "Population."

In Germany, no national census was taken until the late 1800s, but local censuses began as early as the 1500s, most of them appearing in the late 1700s and early 1800s. Most were taken on a city or district level, but some were taken on a kingdom, province, or duchy level.

Censuses provided information on required military service, income taxes, the local populace for the indirect taxes, and custom assessment of the populace.

Census records may be found mixed in with other record groups.

Experienced researchers consult an archive's website to determine if the catalog can be searched. Archivists will be pleased to answer email inquiries, as well.

It is wise to write to an archive to obtain a copy of its printed inventory in order to determine whether censuses are included.

For an excellent overview of German census records, see *German Genealogical Digest,* Vol. VI, No. 1, 1990.

In addition to searching the Family History Library Catalog, it may be necessary to write to the appropriate *Landesarchiv/Stadtarchiv* (state archive) or the *Kreisarchiv* (county archive) to learn whether census records are available.

Source: "Insights to Research: German Census and Other Population Records," *German Genealogical Digest,* Vol. VI, No.1.

CHURCH VOCABULARY

Abt .... abbot
Äbtissin .... abbess
Bischof .... bishop
Bistum .... diocese
Dechant, Dekan .... dean
Erzbischof .... archbishop
Erzbistum .... archdiocese
Erzherzogtum .... archduchy
Fürstbischof................... prince bishop
geistlicher Beamter .... ecclesiastical official
Geistlicher .... clergyman, minister
Gemeinde .... congregation
Gemeindeschreiber .... parish clerk
Glöckner .... sexton, bell ringer
Hilfsgeistlicher .... curate, assistant
Hochstift .... independent bishopric, subject only to the Reich (similar to *Freie Reichstadt*)
Kantor .... cantor, choir director, organist
Kaplan .... chaplain
Kirchenbuch/-bücher . parish register/s
Kirchendiener .... (church) sexton
Kirchner....................... (church) sexton
Kirchenpfleger .... church curator
Kirchenrat .... Protestant church official

Kirchenschöffe .... church assessor
Küster .... church caretaker, sexton
Meßner .... sexton
Oberpfarrer .... rector, head minister
Pfarrer .... minister, pastor
Prediger .... preacher
Priester .... priest
Propst .... dean, provost
Rektor .... dean
Vikar .... vicar
Vorsänger .... choir leader

BÜRGERBÜCHER (Citizen books)

Bürgerbücher, Bürgerrechtslisten, or citizens books, a very old resource concerning city dwellers (but not those in rural areas and villages), record persons who attained the privilege of new citizenship.

Those persons who were successful after applying for citizenship received rights including 1) acquisition of real property; 2) use of the *Allmende,* the common lands, such as meadows and woodlands; 3) pursuit of a trade or enterprise; and 4) access to candidacy for public municipal office, unless such offices were the exclusive prerogative of the patrician families.

To achieve the goal of citizenship, the applicant must have been of legitimate birth as proved by presentation of the *Geburtsbrief,* the birth certificate from his native residence, as well as evidence of descent from blameless parents and a believer of the Christian faith. At one time, ownership of real property within the city was a requirement of citizenship, but this regulation was often exempted.

If the requirements of citizenship were met, the applicant had to swear the *Bürgereid* (*Eid* = oath) and to pay his *Bürgergeld,* a fee for admission to citizenship

Information found in the citizenship rolls can include date of admission, amount of fee, name, trade and native origin of the applicant, and name of his father. Sometimes the name of both parents, as well as those of witnesses and sponsors are listed.

Bürgerbücher may be found in city archives or may have been transferred to the pertinent state archives. These records ceased to exist in the mid-19th century.

Source: "The Role of Citizen Books or Lists in German Genealogy," by Horst A. Reschke. *The German Connection*, German Research Association, Vol. 21, No. 3, 1997.

BÜRGERBUCH REFERENCES

Below is a list of German towns that have *Bürgerbücher*:

Wolfgang Ribbe and Eckart Henning, *Taschenbuch für Familiengeschichtsforschung*, Verlag Degener & Co., 11th ed., Neustadt an der Aisch, 1995, pp. 192-233. (FHL 943 D27r)

The cities and towns for which such references are provided in this book are as follows:

Aachen, Abensberg, Ahaus, Ahlen, Alfeld, Allenburg, Alsfeld, Altona, Alt-Zlabings, Amberg, Andreasberg, Angerburg, Angermünde, Anklam, Ansbach, Appenzell-Ausserrhoden, Appenzell-Innerrhoden, Arensburg, Arneburg, Arns-berg, Arnstadt, Augsburg

Babenhausen, Bad Bevensen, Bad Driburg, Bad Freienwalde, Bad Hersfeld, Bad Kreuznach, Bad Lippspringe, Bad Münder, Bad Oldesloe, Bad Schönfliess, Bad Segeberg, Baden, Bahn, Balga, Barnstorf, Barten, Bartenstein, Basel-Land, Basel-Stadt, Bauske, Bautzen, Beelitz, Bensheim, Bentheim, Bergedorf, Bergen, Berleburg, Berlin, Bern (Land), Bern (Stadt), Bernau, Bernburg, Beromünster, Betschwanden, Beuthen/O.S., Bevensen, Bevergern, Biberach an der Riss, Biedenkopf, Bingen, Birnbaum, Bischopswerder, Blaubeuren,

Blieskastel, Blomberg, Bocholt, Bochum, Bockenem, Bömisch-Leipa, Bopfingen, Bottingen, Bozen, Brakel, Brandenburg, Brand-enburg i. Pr., Braunsberg, Braunschweig, Bremen, Breslau, Bretten, Bromberg, Bruchsal, Brünn, Brüx, Brugg, Buer, Büren, Bütow, Bunzlau, Burg, Burg/Fehmarn, Burgbern-heim, Burghausen, Burgsteinfurt, Buxte-hude

Celle, Charlottenburg, Chemnitz, Chur, Coburg, Cölln, Coesfeld, Colmar, Corbach

Dachau, Danneberg, Danzig, Darkehmen, Dessau, Detmold, Deutsch-Kralupp, Diepholz, Dietzenbach, Dillenburg, Ding-olfing, Dinklage, Dinslaken, Dir-schau, Doberlug/Niederlausitz, Domnau/Ost-preußen, Dornburg, Dorpat, Dortmund, Dramburg, Drengfurt, Dresden, Driburg, Düren, Duisburg, Durlach

Eberswalde, Eckernförde, Eisenstadt, Eisleben, Elbing, Eldagsen, Elze, Emden, Emmendingen, Emmerich, Engi, Erfurt, Erlangen, Erlinghausen, Essen, Eversberg

Faldern, Fellin, Fischhausen, Flensburg, Frankfurt/Main, Frankfurt/Oder, Frauenburg, Fraustadt, Freiberg, Freienwalde, Freiburg/Uechtland (Stadt und Kanton), Freising, Freudenheim, Freystadt, Friedberg, Friedeberg, Friedland, Friedrichstadt, Friesack, Fürstenau, Füssen, Fulda

Gaflenz, Garnsee, Geithain (Sachsen), Gemünden, Genf, Gera, Gerbstedt, Gilgenburg, Glarus, Glückstadt, Görlitz, Göttingen, Goldap, Goldingen, Goslar, Gossmannsdorf, Gotha, Graudenz, Graz, Grebenstein, Greiffenberg/Schlesien, Greiz, Grobin, Grossalsleben, Gumbinnen, Gunzenhausen

Hachenburg, Hadamar, Hadersdorf am Kamp, Hadersleben, Haldensleben, Hall, Hamburg, Hanau, Hannover, Hartberg, Havelberg, Haynau, Heide, Heidelberg, Heidersbach, Heiligen-AA, Heiligenbeil, Heiligenhafen, Heimiswil, Heinsberg, Helmstedt, Hemau, Herborn,

Heringen, Hersbruck, Hersfeld, Hessisch Oldendorf, Hildburghausen, Hirschberg/Schlesien, Hofgeismar, Hohenstein, Holten, Hornburg, Hoyerswerda, Husum

Iglau, Innsbruck, Insterburg, Iserlohn, Isny

Jastrow, Johannisburg

Kaaden, Kahla, Kaiserslautern, Kalkar, Kamen, Kamenz, Kammin, Karlsruhe, Kassel, Kaemnath, Kempen, Kempten, Kiel, Kirchberg, Kirchhain, Kitzingen, Köln, Königsberg/Neumark, Königsberg/Preußen, Köpenick, Köthen, Kolmar, Konitz, Kosten, Krakau, Krefeld, Kremmen, Krempe, Kreuzburg/Ober-schlesien, Kreuznach, Kromau, Kühls-heim, Küstrin, Kulm, Kulmbach, Kurland

Labiau, Lambsheim, Lamspringe, Landau, Landsburg/Ostspreußen, Lands-berg/Warthe, Landshut, Langenzenn, Langewiesen, Laubach, Lauban, Lauenburg/Elbe, Lauenburg/Pommern, Laufen, Lautenthal, Leba, Leibnitz, Leipzig, Lemgo, Lengfeld, Leutenberg, Libau, Lichtenberg, Liebemühl, Liebstadt, Liegnitz, Liestal, Limburg, Lingen, Linz/Donau, Linz/Rhein, Lippspringe, Lipp-stadt, Lissa, Lobloch, Löbau, Lötzen, Lohr, Luckenwalde, Lübbecke, Lübeck, Lüdenscheid, Lüdge, Lüneburg, Luzern, Lyck

Maastricht, Magdeburg, Mainz, Marbach/Neckar, Marburg/Lahn, Marienburg/Ostpreußen, Marienwerder, Margra-bowa, Markgröningen, Markneukirchen, Markt Bergel, Marktredwitz, Marsberg, Mayen, Meersburg, Meldorf, Melsungen, Meme, Memmingen, Mengede, Merse-burg, Meseritz, Meteln, Meyenburg/Prignitz, Minden, Mitau, Mömpelgard (Montbéliard), Mohrungen, Mollis, Mühlhausen/Ostpreußen, Mühlhausen/Thüringia, Mülhausen/Elsaß, Münder, Münster, Murten

Näfels, Narva, Nauen, Naumburg/Bober, Naumburg/Saale, Neidenburg, Neresheim, Neuchatel, Neuern, Neu-haldensleben, Neuhausen, Neumarkt, Neuruppin, Neuss, Neustadt/Holstein, Neustadt am Rübenberge, Neustädt-chen, Neuteich, Neu-Titscherin, Nidwalden, Niedermarsberg, Nijmegen, Nordhausen, Nordhorn, Northeim, Nürnberg

Oberglogau, Obermarsberg, Obersitz-ko, Oderberg, Oederan, Oelde, Ofen, Ohrdruf, Oldenburg i Holstein, -i. Oldenburg, Oldesloe, Olmütz, Oppenheim, Orsoy, Ortelsburg, Oschersleben, Osterode/Harz, Osterode/Ostpreußen, Ottenstein, Otterberg, Otterndorf, Ottweiler

Paderborn, Passenheim, Peisern, Pernau, Pfullendorf, Pillkallen, Plauen, Plettenberg, Posen, Potsdam, Prag, Prenzlau, Preussisch Eylau, Preussisch-Holland, Preussisch-Mark, Pritzwalk

Quakenbrück

Ragnit, Rastenburg, Ratingen, Ratze-burg, Rauschenberg, Ravensburg, Rawitsch, Recklinghausen, Rehau, Reich-enberg, Rein, Rethem, Reval, Rheda, Rheine, Rhodt, Ried, Riesenburg, Rietberg, Riga, Rinteln, Rockenhausen, Ronneburg, Rosenheim, Rosenthal, Rostock, Rüdesheim, Rügenwalde, Russheim

Saalburg, Saalfeld, Saarbrücken, Saaz, Salfeld, Sankt Andreasberg, Sankt Gallen, Schaffhausen, Schaken, Schippenbeil, Schirwindt, Schleiz, Schleswig, Schlicht-ingsheim, Schloppe, Schlotheim, Schmal-lenberg, Schmölln, Schöneck, Schönfliess, Schöningen, Schöppenstedt, Schon-gau, Schwabach, Schwäbisch Hall, Schwanberg, Schweinfurt, Schwelm, Sdhwerin, Schwyz, Segeberg, Sehesten, Selb, Senftenberg, Sensburg, Siegburg, Siegen, Simmern, Sion, Sissach, Sömmerda, Soest, Soldau, Sonderburg, Sorau, Spandau, Spangenberg, Sprottau, Stade, Stadthagen, Stallupönen, Stamm-bach, Stargard, Stassfurt, Steele, Steinau, Stendal, Stettin, Stolp, Stralsund, Strasburg, Strassburg, Stuttgart, Sulzfeld,

Swinemünde, Szegediin

Tanna, Taus, Telgte, Teltow, Thamsbrück, Thorn, Thun, Thurgau, Tilsit, Tirschtiegel, Tönning, Tondern, Torgau, Treffurt, Treptow, Treuburg, Treuenbrietzen, Tribsees, Triebes, Trier, Trogen

Uelzen, Uerdingen, Unna, Unterwalden, Urach, Usedom, Uttrichshausen

Vacha, Visselhövede

Waadt, Wallis, Warendorf, Wehlau, Weilburg, Weimar, Weinheim, Weissenburg, Weissenfels, Weissensee, Weissen-stadt, Wenden, Werl, Werne, Werni-gerode, Wertheim, Wesel, Wetter, Wetzlar, Wiedenbrück, Wien, Wiesbaden, Wildemann, Wilsdruff, Wimpfen, Windau/Kurland, Winterthur, Wismar, Wittingen, Wittmund, Witzenhausen, Wöhrd, Woldenberg, Wolfhagen, Wol-gast, Wriezen, Würzburg, Wunsiedel, Wuppertal

Ybbsitz

Zehden, Zellerfeld, Zerbst, Zierenberg, Zinten/Ostpreußen, Zofingen, Zollikon, Zossen, Zweibrücken, Zürich, Zug

DATENSCHUTZ (Privacy laws)

Since a landmark ruling in 1983 by the *Bundesverfassungsgericht* (Supreme Court), privacy of personal data is taken very seriously in Germany. Strict laws now regulate what kind of personal data may be collected by authorities and private organizations, how they may be processed and used, and to whom they may be released.

The framework is contained in the *Bundesdatenschutzgesetz* (Federal Privacy Law) with corresponding State Privacy Laws. *Datenschutzbeauftragte* (Data Protection Commissioners) supervise observance of these laws and follow up on complaints by individuals.

They also issue annual reports on their findings to the respective legislatures who appoint them.

Obviously, this affects genealogists who wish to study restricted records in these two important sources: the *Einwohnermeldedatei* (residents' registration files) and the *Stadt- und Kreisarchive* (City and County Archives).

All residents in Germany are required by the *Meldegesetz* (Registration Law) of their respective States to register with the local *Einwohnermeldeamt* (residents' registration office). Personal data like name, maiden name, former and present address, citizenship, birthday, marital status, religion, legal guardian, criminal record, and date of death are filed there for official use. If a person moves, all these data are transferred to the *Einwohnermeldeamt* of the new residence.

This system has basically been in effect in most of Germany for approximately 200 years - in large cities first.

When these files are no longer current (there is no strict nationwide time limit for this), they are transferred to the *Stadtarchiv* (City Archive) or *Kreisarchiv* (County Archive) – if a small town or village does not have an archive of its own).

Access to these data is restricted by Privacy Laws referred to above.

For purposes like genealogical research, according to provisions in the *Meldegesetz* (registration law), the *Einwohnermeldeamt* (resident's registration office) will usually provide a *Melderegisterauskunft* (information on registry files) consisting of the name and current address of a person – of the last address if deceased. In most cases, a written request is required and a fee is charged.

The *Stadt- und Kreisarchive* can be more generous, as they do not deal with current data. Also, they are not regulated by specific laws but use the *Bundesarchivgesetz* (Federal Archives Law) more or less literally as a guideline.

Under the new law (January 1, 2009),all civil registry records are available to the public as of the following dates:
- 110 years for birth records
- 80 years for marriage records
- 30 years for death records

Any records of more recent date are available only to the person in question, his or her immediate relatives, and other persons who can demonstrate what the law refers to as a "justified interest." This would allow a civil registrar to release a document for genealogical research purposes, but it is left to his judgment (Paragraph 62 of the *Personenstandtsgesetz*).

MELDEREGISTER (City registers)

As stated in the previous section, Germany's residential registration law (*Meldegesetz*) required that residents be registered by the municipal office, specifically the *Einwohnermeldeamt*, upon entering and leaving the city (as well as when they moved to different locations within the city). The resulting *Melderegister* (resident registers) therefore provide valuable information about some urban populations in the 19th and 20th centuries. They are especially valuable in indicating when a particular resident entered or left the city.

Column headings of a typical *Melderegister* might call for the following information: the person's first and last name; occupation; age; birthplace; religious faith; whether single, married or widowed; military status; whether the newcomer is self-supporting or requires public welfare; and when and from whence the newcomer came. The *Melderegister* also typically records when a resident leaves the city as well as his destination.

If the Family History Library holds a filmed *Melderegister* for a particular locality, it will be recorded in the Locality section, in most cases catalogued under "Population." Occasionally, however, these records are catalogued under "Civil Registration" or "Migration, Internal."

GERMAN CEMETERIES

For centuries, cemeteries usually surrounded the church, which in turn was located in the center of the town or village . Therefore, space in cemeteries was limited, and graves were used repeatedly in some parishes. Bones dug up when a new corpse was entered were often removed to a *Beinhaus* or *Karner* (house for bones) where they were sorted and stored.

Although this practice was discontinued in the 19th century and most of the *Beinhäuser* have been dismantled, some of them can still be seen in remote alpine areas. In Vienna and Paris, huge underground vaults full of bones are accessible as macabre museums.

The increase of the population in the 19th century also made necessary more and more new cemeteries, which were then often located on the outskirts of towns and operated by the municipality. Being non-denominational, they could serve for the entire population.

Cemeteries operated by a parish usually are called *Kirchenfriedhof* and are the older ones.

Cemeteries operated by a municipality are called *städtischer Friedhof* or *Gemeindefriedhof* and are the newer ones.

There are also jointly operated cemeteries where these terms then apply to the different sectors.

Gravesites usually contain more than one burial spot. Depending on the chemistry of the soil and local laws, these may be reused after about 20 to 30 years.

The gravesites themselves are usually leased for 20 to 50 years, and the lease may be extended for as long as someone pays for it.

When the lease for a gravesite expires, it may be leveled and made available for another burial.

Some older cemeteries in urban areas have been given up entirely with only old maps to show where they were located. Others have been turned into parks with restrictions for use by the public.

Even in cemeteries that have existed for centuries and continue to be used, wooden markers rotted, iron ones rusted, and even rocks eroded or were removed to make room for new ones. So, unless the person buried was considered enough of a celebrity to preserve his or her tombstone for historical reasons, the only traces of most graves used in the 20th century may be found today in a *Grabbuch* (burial record).

As these were much less important than birth or marriage records, less care was taken to preserve them.

If records still exist, those for a *Kirchenfriedhof* may be found in the church archive and those for a *städtischer Friedhof* or *Gemeindefriedhof* in the municipal archive of the office of the *Friedhofsverwaltung* (cemetery administration).

Unfortunately, there rarely (if ever) is a central register if there is more than one cemetery. They would have to be checked one by one.

In a city such as Munich, for example, which has 28 municipal cemeteries, 29 church cemeteries, and about a dozen abandoned cemeteries, it would be difficult to locate the gravesite used in the 19th century for a specific family or even a person. There would rarely be more than a slim chance of success without a lead from other sources on where to start a search.

Source: "How Long Is Eternal?" by Rainer Thumshirn, *Der Blumenbaum*, Sacramento

German Genealogy Society, Vol. 15, No. 4, June 1998.

MEYERS ORTS- UND VERKEHRSLEXIKON

One of the most valuable resources for German research is the gazetteer commonly known as "Meyers." *Meyers Orts- und Verkehrs-Lexikon des Deutschen Reichs* (Meyer's locality and commerce directory of the German Empire), was compiled by Erich Ütrecht in 1912. Printed in Fraktur type, *Meyers* lists over 210,000 German place names as they existed in the German Empire between 1871 and 1918.

Important Uses

Note these two major uses of this gazetteer:

1. *Meyers* specifies the local civil registry office. Look for the "*StdA*" (StdA) abbreviation (short for *Standesamt* , or the civil registration office). The *StdA*, followed by a comma or a semicolon, indicates that the locality had its own civil registration office. If the *StdA* is not followed by a comma or semicolon, the civil registration office was located in the place named immediately following *StdA*.

2. *Meyers* indicates the existence of churches in the locality. Look for the abbreviations *ev.Pfk* (Lutheran church), *reform Pfk* (Reformed church), *kath.Pfk* (Catholic church), or *Syn* (synagogue). If none of these ecclesiastical terms is present, there is no church in that. In such cased it is necessary to look in other gazetteers to determine parish affiliation (international floor, B1).

Where to Find *Meyers*

Visitors to the Family History Library can find these two volumes (bound in red) on the international floor in the bookshelf just to the right of the Germany consultation desk (FHL Book 943 E5mo).

Researchers may also order microfilmed copies of this gazetteer through local family history centers (Film 496,640 localities A-K & Film 496,641 localities L-Z). To find the nearest family history center, visit www.familysearch.org/eng/library/FHC/frameset_fhc.asp.

The *Meyers* gazetteer is now available online:

♦ **Harold B. Lee Library's digitized Family History collection:** Go to www.lib.byu.edu/fhc. In the "Title" window, type "meyers orts" and press "Go." The pages are free to browse, but have not been indexed for keyword searches.

♦ **Ancestry's German collection:** Go to www.ancestry.com, press the drop down arrow next to the "Search" tab and select "Card Catalog." In the "Title" win-

dow type "meyers gazetteer" and press "Search." Access to this document is free, but requires a brief registration process that includes entering your name and email address. Images can be browsed, but have not been indexed for keyword searches.

Reading and abbreviations

Listed below are some of the most commonly-used abbreviations in the *Meyers* gazetteer. The first column shows gazetteer abbreviations as they appear in the old Fraktur type. The second column shows the same abbreviations, but in Roman type. The third column spells out the full words or phrases in German, followed by their English translations.

ABBREVIATIONS: MEYERS ORTS- UND VERKEHRSLEXIKON

A	A	*Amt (Amtsbezirk):* district, county
Ab.(e)	Ab.(e)	*Abbau(e) oder Ausbau(e):* surface mine(s)
Abt.	Abt.	*Abteilung:* division, section, department
a / d	a/d	*an der, auf der:* at the, on the
Ag., -ag.	Ag., -ag.	*Agentur, -agentur:* agent/agency, -agency
AG	AG	*Amtsgericht:* lower/district court
AH	AH	*Amtshauptmannschaft:* main county administrative office
AK	AK	*Armeekorps:* army corps
AktGes	AktGes	*Aktiengesellschaft:* joint-stock company
a.L.	a.L.	*ältere Linie:* of the old lineage
AllGut.	AllGut.	*Allodialgut:* small proprietary lands; allodial estate
Anh.	Anh.	*Anhalt:* Anhalt (former duchy)
Ansdl.	Ansdl.	*Ansiedlung:* colony, settlement
Anst., -anst.	Anst., -anst.	*Anstalt, -anstalt:* institution, -institution
Arb.	Arb.	*Arbeiter:* worker
Art.	Art.	*Artillerie:* artillery
Ausg.	Ausg.	*Ausgaben:* expenditures
B.	B.	*Bezirk:* district
BA	BA	*Bezirkamt:* district office
Bat.	Bat.	*Bataillon:* battalion
Batt.	Batt.	*Batterie:* battery
Bay.	Bay.	*Bayern:* Bavaria
Bgb., -bgb.	Bgb., -bgb.	*Bergbau, -bergbau*: mining, -mining
Bgrem.	Bgrem.	*Bezirksgremium:* district board
Bgw.	Bgw.	*Bergwerk:* mine
Bhf.	Bhf.	*Bahnhof:* train station

𝕭𝕶ꝺₒ	BKdo	*Bezirkskommando:* district military command
𝕭ₙ, -ᵇⁿ.	Bn, -bn	*Bahn, -bahn:* railroad, -railway
𝕭ᵣₐₙꝺᵇᵍ.	Brandbg.	*Brandenburg:* Brandenburg
𝕭ᵣₐᵤₙₛ𝔠ₕ𝔴.	Braunschw.	*Braunschweig:* Braunschweig
-ᵇ ᵣ ₑ	-bre	*-brüche:* -swamp, moor, quarry, pit
𝕭ᵣᵍₘ.	Brgm.	*Bürgermeister (ei):* mayor; mayor's office
𝕭ᵣ ᵢ ᵍ.	Brig.	*Brigade:* brigade
𝕭ₛ 𝔠 ₕ.	Bsch.	*Bauernschaft:* farmers' association
ᵇ ᶻ	bz.	*beziehungsweise:* respectively; or
D		*Dampfer- oder Motorbootverbindung:* steam or motorboat connection
SD		*ditto, in der Saison, -Sommer:* same as above (but ..... boat available in summer season only)
ꝺ ₐ ₛ.	das.	*daselbst:* there, at that place
𝕯., 𝕯ᵣ.	D., Dr.	*Dorf, Dörfer:* village, villages
𝕯ᵢᵣ., -ꝺᵢᵣ.	Dir., -dir.	*Direktion, -direktion:* management, head office
𝕯ᵣ ₗ.	Drl.	*Darlehen:* loan
𝕯ₒₘ.	Dom.	*Domäne, Dominium:* domain, state-owned estate
𝕯ₒₘA.	DomA.	*Domäneamt:* estate office
ꝺ ₛ ᵍ ₗ.	dsgl.	*(desgleichen) bezieht sich auf unmittelbar Vorher-gehendes:* (the same) refer directly to the preceding
- ꝺ ₜ.	-dt.	*-distrikt:* -district
E		*Eisenbahnstation, Haltestelle:* train station, stop .... *mit Personen-und Güterverkehr:* - with passengers and goods
ꞇE		*-mit Bahntelegraph:* -with telegraph
EGt		*-nur mit Güterbeförderung:* -with transportation of goods only
EPs		*-nur mit Personenverkehr:* -with passengers only
E†		*-mit Eisenbahnauskunftsstelle:* -with railroad information desk
𝕰		*Einwohner:* population
𝕰ᵢₙ.	Ein.	*Einöde:* wilderness, outlying (farm)house
𝕰ᵢₙₙ., -ₑᵢₙₙ	Einn., -einn	*Einnahme, -einnahme:* income, revenue, tax office
𝕰ᵢ ₛ.	Eis.	*Eisenbahn:* railroad
𝕰ₗ ₖ ₜ ᵣ.	Elktr.	*Der Ort hat elektr. Licht & (od.) Kraftqu.:* The place has electric light and/or a source of power
𝕰ₗ ₖ ₜ ᵣ 𝔴.	Elktrw	*Elektrizitätswerk:* power plant
𝕰ₗ ₛ.	Els.	*Elsaß:* Alsace
𝕰ₛ ₖ.	Esk.	*Eskadro:* cavalry troop (squadron)
𝕰ₜ ₐ ᵦ ₗ	E t a b l	*Etablissement:* establishment
ₑ𝔳., 𝕰𝔳.	Ev., Ev.	*Evangelisch, Evangelische:* Protestant, (Lutheran)
F		*Fernsprecher:* telephone
ꞇF		*Fernsprecher und Telegraph:* telephone and

telegraph

𝔉br., -fbr.	Fbr., -fbr.	*Fabrik, Fabrikation:* factory, works, mill
𝔉il.	Fil.	*Filiale:* branch of an institution
𝔉l.	Fl.	*Flecken:* borough (village with some rights of a township)
𝔉örst.	Först: *Försterei*, forester ranger's house
fr.	fr.	*früher:* former, formerly
𝔉rht.	Frht.	*Freiheit:* a *Flecken* or market town (borough in Rhineland and Westphalia)
𝔉ürstt.	Fürstt.	*Fürstentum:* principality
𝔊.	G	*Gericht:* court
𝔊arn.	Garn.	*Garnison:* garrison
𝔊𝔅.	GB.	*Gerichtsbezirk:* court district
𝔊ef.	Gef.	*Gefängnis:* prison, jail
geh.	geh.	*gehörig:* belonging to
𝔊em.	Gem.	*Gemeinde:* community, congregation
𝔊en.	Gen.	*General:* general, commander
𝔊enoss.	Genoss.	*Genossenschaft:* company, cooperative
𝔊es.	Ges.	*Gesellschaft:* society, association
𝔊ew., gew.	Gew., gew.	*Gewerbe; gewerblich:* trade, business; industrial
glchn.	glchn.	*gleichnamig:* of the same name
𝔊r.,	Gr.	*Groß:* Great- (part of place name)
𝔊sth.	Gsth.	*Gast-, Wirtshaus, Krug:* guesthouse, inn, lodging
𝔊𝔗g.	GTg.	*Gerichtstag:* jurisdictional area of a court
𝔊ymn.	Gymn.	*Gymnasium:* academically oriented high school
ℌ. (ℌr.)	H. (Hr.)	*Haus, (Häuser):* house (houses)
-ℎ	-h	*-haus, -heim:* -house, -home
ℌann.	Hann.	*Hannover:* Hanover (former Prussian province)
ℌdl.	Hdl.	*Handel(s):* commerce, or business establishment
ℌersch.	Hersch.	*Herrschaft:* manor, estate
ℌessen-N.	Hessen-N	*Hessen-Nassau:* Hessen-Nassau (former Prussian province)
ℌf	Hf.	*Hafen:* port, harbor
ℌosp.	Hosp.	*Hospital:* hospital
ℌpt-	Hpt-	*Haupt:* main
ℌr	Hr.	*Häuser:* houses
ℌrgr.(n)	Hrgr.(n)	*Häusergruppe(n):* group of houses
hzl.	hzl.	*herzoglich:* ducal
ℌzt. (-hzt.)	Hzt. (-hzt.)	*Herzogtum (-herzogtum):* duchy, dukedom
ℑnd.	Ind.	*Industrie:* industry
ℑnf.	Inf.	*Infanterie:* infantry
ℑnsp.	Insp.	*Inspektionz:* inspection
ℑnst.	Inst.	*Institut:* institute
ℑnt., -int.	Int., -int.	*Intendantur:* superintendent, quartermaster general's department
ℑ.	J	*Juden, Israeliten, israelitisch:* Jews; Israelites; Israeli (adj.)
j.𝔏.	j.L.	*jüngere Linie:* of the younger lineage

𝕶. .... K .... *Kirche:* church
- 𝕶 .... -k .... *-kasse oder -kirche:* -collecting agency; -church
𝕶 a m. .... Kam. .... *Kamme*; treasury: departments of a court (civil, criminal, trade); houses of parliament; chamber (like Chamber of Commerce)
𝕶 a p . ... Kap. .... *Kapelle*: chapel
𝕶 a t . ... Kat. .... *Kataster*: land-register
k a t ḥ . , 𝕶 a t ḥ .... kath., Kath. ...... *katholisch, Katholiken:* Roman Catholic (adj.), Catholics
𝕶 a v . ... Kav. .... *Kavallerie:* cavalry
𝕶 d o .... Kdo .... *Kommando*:   command post
k g l . ... kgl. .... *königlich:* royal
- k ḥ l b g b . ... -khlbgb. .... *-kohlenbergbau:* coal-mine
𝕶 l - .... Kl- .... *Klein-:* Little- (part of place names)
𝕶 l b n . ... Klbn. .... *Kleinbahn:* narrow-guage railroad
k m .... km .... *Kilometer:* 1000 meters, 0.6 miles
𝕶 o l . ... Kol. .... *Kolonat, Kolonie:* .... hereditary leasehold to a farm belonging to an estate
𝕶 o m . ... Kom. .... *Kommandantur:* commandant's office, garrison headquarters
𝕶 o m m. .... Komm. .... *Kommission*: commission
𝕶 r . ... Kr. .... *Kreis:* county, district
𝕶 r e d 𝖁 o r . ... Kred.Vor .... *Kredit- & od. Vorschussverein:* loan association
𝕶 r . 𝕳 . ... Kr.H. .... *Kreishauptmannschaft:* county office
𝕶 r 𝕾 t . ... KrSt. .... *Kreisstadt:* capital of a Kreis
𝕶 s p . ... Ksp. .... *Kirchspiel:* parish
𝕶 t .... Kt. .... *Kanton:* county (state) in France and Switzerland
l . ... l. .... *links*: to the left
𝕷 . ... L. .... *Land(es)*: land, region
𝕷 d e p l . ... Ldepl. .... *Ladeplatz:* wharf, loading point
𝕷 𝕲 .... LG .... *Landgericht:* county court
𝕷 𝕲 e m . ... LGem. .... *Landgemeinde:* citizens of a county
𝕷 ḥ e r r - (e n) s c ḥ .... Lherr-(en) sch. *Landherr(en)schaft:* sovereign possession, rulers (collectively)
𝕷 𝕶 r . ... Lkr. .... *Landkreis*: county
𝕷 t ḥ r . ,   𝕷 o t ḥ . .. Lthr-, Loth. ...... *Lothringen:* Lorraine (as in Alsace-Lorraine)
𝕷 r 𝔄 . ... LrA. .... *Landratsamt:* office of county commission
𝕷 w . ,   l w . ... Lw., lw. .... *Landwirtschaft:* farm, agriculture
m .... *Meter überm Meer*: meters above sea level
𝔐 a g . ... Mag. .... *Magazin:* warehouse, depot, armory
𝔐 a s c ḥ . ... Masch. .... *Maschine(n):* machine(s)
𝔐 d g . ... Mdg. .... *Mündung:* mouth of a river, estuary
𝔐 e c k l . - 𝕾 c ḥ w ... Meckl.-Schw. .... *Mecklenburg-Schwerin:*   Mecklenburg-Schwerin
𝔐 e c k l . - 𝕾 t r . .... Meckl.-Str. .... *Mecklenburg-Strelitz:*Mecklenburg-Strelitz
𝔐 i l . ... Mil. .... *Militär:* the military
𝔐 k t f l . ... Mktfl. .... *Marktflecken:* market or small county town; a Flecken (borough) chartered to hold markets
𝔐 k t 𝕲 k . ... MktGk. .... *Martflecken-Gerechtigkeit:*   m a r k e t

jurisdiction

Ml., -ml.	Ml., -ml.	*Mühle, -mühle:* mill, -mill	
N., (n.)	N., (n.)	*Norden (nördlich), neben*: north, northerly; next to	
- n	-n.	*-nebenstelle:* -branch office	
Nd.-	Nd.-	*Nieder-:* Lower- (part of place names)	
Neum.	Neum	*Neumark*: eastern part of province of Brandenburg	
NO. (nö.)	NO. (nö)	*Nordosten, nordöstlich:* northeast, northeasterly	
NW., nw.	NW., nw.	*Nordwesten, nordwestlich:* northwest, northwesterly	
NZA.	NZA.	*Nebenzollamt:* branch custom office	
O.	O. Ober-	*Upper-:* (part of place names)	
O. (ä.)	O. (ö)	*Osten (östlich):* east (easterly)	
OA.	OA.	*Oberamt:* county (in Württemberg)	
OForst.	Oforst.	*Oberförsterei:* head forester's office	
Oldenb.	Oldenb.	*Oldenburg:* Oldenburg	
OLG.	OLG.	*Oberlandesgericht:* provincial supreme court	
OPDir.	OPDir.	*Oberpostdirektion:* top postal service administration	
Ortsch.	Ortsch.	*Ortschaft:*(inhabited) place, village	
Ostpr.	Ostpr.	*Ostpreußen*: East Prussia	
P		*Postanstalt:* post office	
P		*Post und Fernsprecher:* post office with telephone	
P		*Post und Telegraph:* post office with telegraph	
P		*Post, Fernsprecher und Telegraph:* post office with telephone and telegraph	
PDir.	PDir.	*Postdirektion:* post authorities	
Pf.-	Pf.-	*Pfarr.-:* parish-	
Pfk.	Pfk.	*Pfarrkirche:* parish church	
Pomm.	Pomm.	*Pommern:* Pomerania	
Pr., (pr.)	Pr., (pr.)	*Preußen, (preußisch)*: Prussia, Prussian	
Präs.	Präs.	*Präsidium:*presidency, chairmanship, head office	
Prov.	Prov.	*Provinz(ial):*province (provincial)	
Pw.		*Personenpostwagen oder Autoverkehr*: statecoach or automobile traffic	
Pz. (Dt.)	Pz. (Dt.)	*Polizei (-distrikt):* police (police district)	
r.	r.	*rechts:* to the right	
R.	R.	*Regierung(s):* government, administration	
Raiffbk.	Raiffbk.	*Raiffeisenbank:* a rural loan institution	
RB.	RB.	*Regierungsbezirk*: provincial district	
Rbkh.	Rbkh.	*Reichsbankhauptstelle:* main office of national bank	
Rbkn.	Rbkn.	*Reichsbankhauptstelle:* national bank's main office	
Rbkst.	Rbkst	*Reichsbankstelle:* German National Bank office	
Ref.	Ref.	*Reformierte:* Calvinist, member of the Reformed	

Church
𝕽 e g . ... *Reg.* .... *Regiment: government, authority, regiment (mili-tary)*

𝕽 g . ... *Rg.* .... *Rittergut:* nobleman's landed estate

𝕽 h e i n l . ... *Rheinl.* .... *Rheinland, -provinz:* Rhineland, Rhine Province

𝕽 i t t . ... *Ritt.* .... *Ritterschaft(s):* knights, knighthood

𝕽 i t t A . ... *RittA.* .... *Ritteramt:* estate office

𝕾 . ... *S.* .... *Sankt, in Verbindung mit Ortsnamen, Kirchen, Stiften:* Saint, in connection with place names, churches, or monasteries

s .   (a.) .... *s. (a.)* .... *siehe (auch):* see (also)

𝕾 .   (s.) .... *S. (s.)* .... *Süden (südlich):* south (southerly)

𝕾 a . ... *Sa.* .... *Sachsen (Staat od. Prov.):* Saxony, state or .... province

𝕾 a . - A .... *Sa.-A* .... *Sachsen-Altenburg:* Saxony-Altenburg (former .... duchy)

𝕾 a - ℭ . - ⑥ . ... *Sa-C-G.* .... *Sachsen-Coburg-Gotha:* Saxony-Coburg-Gotha (former duchy)

𝕾 a . - 𝕸 . ... *Sa.-M.* .... Sachsen-Meiningen: .... Saxony-Meiningen (former duchy)

𝕾 a . - 𝕸 . - 𝕰 . ... *Sa.-W.-E.* .... *Sachsen-Weimar-Eisenach:* Saxony-Weimar-Eisenach (former duchy)

𝕾 a n a t . ... *Sanat.* .... *Sanatorium:* sanatarium

𝕾 ch . ,   - sch . .... *Sch., sch.* .... *Schule, -schule:* school, -school

𝕾 ch a u m b - 𝕷 . ... *Schaumb-L.* ..... *Schaumburg-Lippe:* Schaumburg-Lippe

𝕾 ch i f f . ... *Schiff.* .... *Schiffahrt(s):* naval, maritime

𝕾 ch l . ... *Schl.* .... *Schleuse:* sluice (lock)

𝕾 ch l e s . ... *Schles.* .... *Schlesien:* Silesia

𝕾 ch l e s w - 𝕳 o l s t . ... Schlesw-Holst.   *S c h l e s w i g - Holstein:* Schleswig-Holstein

Schwarzb.-Rud. ...... Schwarzb.-Rud. *Schwarzburg-Rudolstadt:*   Schwarzburg-Rudolstadt

𝕾 ch w a r z b - 𝕾 o n d . ... Schwarzb.Sond.*Schwarzburg-Sondershausen:* Schwarzburg Sondershausen

𝕾 ch w ⑥ .... SchwG .... *Schwurgericht:*court with a jury

𝕾𝕯 .... see *D (Dampfer . . . .)*

𝕾 e m . ... Sem. .... *Seminar:*   seminary; training college (for teachers)

𝕾 l g . ... Slg. .... *Sammlung:* collection, compilation

𝕾𝕯 .   (sö.) .... SD. (sö) .... *Südosten   (südöstlich):*   southeast (southeasterly)

𝕾 o z . ... Soz. .... *Sozietät:*   society,   partnership, company

𝕾 p 𝕯 r l . ... SpDrl. .... *Spar- & Darlehnskassenverein:* savings and loan union

𝕾 p k . ... Spk. .... *Sparkasse:* savings bank

𝕾 t .... St. .... *Stadt (städtisch):* city (municipal)

𝕾 t a t . ... Stat. .... *Station:* station, stop

𝕾 t d A . ... StdA. .... *Standesamt:* civil registry office

StKr.	StKr.	*Stadtkreis:* urban district
Strbn. (-verz.)	Strbn. (-verz.)	*Straßenbahn (-verzeichnis):* streetcar (-register)
Sv.	Sv.	*Servisklasse (Wohnungsgeldzuschluß):* lodging allowance for civil servants
svw.	svw.	*sovielwie:* so far as, according to
SW. (sw.)	SW. (sw.)	*Südwesten(südwestlich):* s o u t h w e s t (southwester-ly)
Syn.	Syn.	*Synogoge:* synagogue
T		*Posttelegraph:* telegraph office
T		*Eisenbahntelegraph auf der Station:* railway telegraph at the station
T		*Fernsprecher und Telegraph:* telephone and telegraph
T		*Post, Fernsprecher, und Telegraph:* post office telephone, and telegraph
T		*Post und telegraph:* Post office and telegraph
Thür.	Thür.	*Thüringen:* Thuringia
u.	u.	*und:* and
U.	U.	*Unter-:* Lower- (part of place names)
USt.	USt.	*Unmittelbare Stadt:* independent township
v.	v.	*von:* of, from
Ver.(e)	Ver.(e)	*Verein(e):* club(s), union(s)
Vers.	Vers.	*Versicherung:* insurance, insurance company
Verw.	Verw.	*Verwaltung:* administration, government
VerwA.	VerwA.	*Verwaltungsamt:* administration office
Vw.	Vw.	*Vorwerk:* outlying farm belonging to a main estate; first line of defense at a fortified place
-w.	-w.	*-waren (in Verbindung mit Fbr.):* -goods (as related to a factory or plant)
-W. (we.)	-W. (we.)	*-werk, (-werke):* -works
W.,(w)	W.,(w)	*Westen, westlich:* west, westerly
Westf.	Westf.	*Westfalen:* Westphalia
Westpr.	Westpr.	*Westpreußen:* West Prussia
Wlr.	Wlr.	*Weiler:* very small village
Wp.	Wp.	*Wohnplatz:* place of residence
Wst., -wst.	Wst., -wst.	*Werkstätte (-werkstätte):* workshop (-workshop)
Württ.	Württ.	*Württemberg:* Württemberg (former kingdom)
Z.	Z.	*Zoll:* custom, duty
ZA.	ZA.	*Zollamt:* customs office
Zgl.	Zgl.	*Ziegelei:* brickworks, tile works
Zh.	Zh.	*Zollhaus:* custom house
Zk.	Zk.	*Zinken:* small village (Weiler) in Baden
zw.	zw.	*zwischen:* between, among
[.....] transpor-etc.)		*Verkehrsanstalt nur zu gewisser Zeit:* tation available station (railway, bus, operating at certain times
*		*siehe dieses:* see this

MÜLLERS GROSSES DEUTSCHES ORTSBUCH (MÜLLER'S LARGE GERMAN GAZETTEER)

Friedrich Müller. *Müllers grosses deutsches Ortsbuch.* Wuppertal-Barmen, Germany: Post- und Ortsbuchverlag Postmeister a.d. Friedrich Müller. 1958. 18th edition 1974

Müllers großes deutsches Ortsbuch [Müller's large German gazetteer] lists more than 107,000 places in present-day Germany, including very small communities, as they existed before the 1990 reunification of Germany. It is cross-referenced to the Shell Atlas.

The book is printed in modern type and indicates the states to which specific communities belonged before World War II (1945).

The entries are listed alphabetically, with the name of the respective state and county given at the end of each entry.

The book also contains a section listing localities under Polish or Russian jurisdictions in Germany after World War I. FHL 943 E5m 1958; film 1,045,448; fiche 6000340-6000354). *Müllers* is also available on CD at several online bookstores.

Clues for use of the gazetteer
◆The abbreviation for the German state where an entity was located appears at the end of each entry.
◆Places having the same name are listed separately.
◆The Kreis (district, abbreviated as *Kr.*) appears in boldface type.
◆Suburbs of large cities are listed directly after the city and are preceded with a hyphen (-).
◆Many of the indicators included in an entry are abbreviated. See the key to abbreviations below.

ABBREVIATIONS USED IN MÜLLERS GROSSES DEUTSCHES ORTSBUCH

A: *Abtei* [abbey]
a: *an* [at, on]
Aa: *Arbeitsamt* [employment office]
Ab: *Abbau/Ausbau* [outskirts, suburb/ renovation]
A Fr: Amt *Frankenberg* [Frankenberg District
Ag: *Amtsgericht* [local court]
Ans: *Ansiedlung* [settlement]
Arbg: *Arbeitsgericht* [labor court]
AT: *Aussichtsturm* [observation tower]
Außenst: *Außenstelle* [branch office]
b: *bei* [at, near, by]; *beschränkt* [restricted by railroad regulations]
Bad Württ: Baden Württemberg
Bay: *Bayern* [Bavaria]
Bd: *Bad* [spa, health resort]
Bf/Bhf: *Bahnhof* [train station]
Bf   Ex: *Bahnhof   mit Expreßgutabfertigung* [train station with express freight]
Bf Gü: *Bahnhof mit Güterabfertigung* [train station with freight]
Bf P: *Bahnhof mit Personenverkehr* [train station with passengers]
Bg: *Bauerngut, Bauernhöfe* [farm settlement]
Bgw: *Bergwerk* [mine]
Bh: *Baurnhof, Bauernhöfe* [farm(s)]
Brandb: *Brandenburg* [Brandenburg]
Brem: *Bremen* [city of Bremen]
Bsch: *Bauernschaft* [farmers collectively]
Bz/Bez: *Bezirk* [district]
bzw: *beziehungsweise* [or else; respectively]
Chh: *Chausseehaus* [toll house]
Ctb: *Cottbus* [city of Cottbus]
D: *Dorf* [village]
DB: *Deutsche Bundesbahn* [Federal Railway]
DDR: *Deutsche Demokratische Republik* [German Democratic Republic\— former East Germany]

Dm: *Domäne* [state-owned estate]
Dsdn: *Dresden* [city of Dresden]
E: *Eisenbahnpersonenhaltestelle bzw. Eisenbahnhof mit beschränkten Abfertig-ungsbefugnissen* [passenger train station with a limited schedule]
Eg: *Eisenbahngüterbahnhof* [railroad freight yard]
Eg Klb: *Eisenbahngüterbahnhof einer nicht bundeseigenen Eisenbahn (Kleinbahn bzw. Privatbahn)* [railroad freight yard not federally owned, with small or private trains]
ehem: *ehemalig (nicht mehr bestehender Ort)* [former (no longer existing locality)]
Ep: *Eisenbahnpersonenbahnhof* [passenger train station]
Ei: *Einöde* [wilderness]
Ep Klb: *Eisenbahnpersonenbahnhof einer nicht bundeseigenen Eisenbahn* [passenger train station, not federally owned, for small or private trains]
Epg: *Eisenbahnbahnhof für Personen-, Gepäck-, Expreßgut und Güterverkehr* [train station for passengers, luggage, express freight and regular freight]
Epg (Gü b): *wie bei Epg, jedoch mit beschränkter Expreßgutabfertigung* [same as above, but with limited freight traffic]
Epg (o Gü): *Eisenbahnbahnhof für Personen-, Gepäck-, und Expreßgut-verkehr (ohne Güterabfertigung)* [train station for passengers, luggage, and express freight (without regular freight)]
Epg (o Ex): *Eisenbahnbahnhof für Personen-, Gepäck-, und Güterverkehr (ohne Expressgutabfertigung)* [train station for passengers, luggage, and freight (without express freight)]
Epg (o P): *Eisenbahnbahnhof für Gepäck-, Expreßgut und Güterverkehr (ohne Personenabfertigung)* [train station for luggage, express freight and regular freight (without passengers)]
Epg Klb: *Eisenbahnbahnhof für Personen-, Gepäck-, Expreßgut und Güterverkehr einer nicht*

bundeseigenen Eisenbhn (Kleinbahn bzw. Privatbahn) [small or private train station for passengers, luggage, express freight and regular freight, not federally owned]
Eft: *Erfurt* [city of Erfurt]
Ew: *Einwohner (Einwohnerzahl vorange-stellt)* [residents (employed population)]
Ex: *Expreßgut (Abfertigungsbefugnis)* [express freight (authorized shipments)]
EXA: *Expreßgutabfertigung* [authorized express freight]
FA: *Finanzamt* [finance office]
FamG: *Familiengericht* [family court]
Fb: *Fabrik* [factory]
Fbz: *Forstbezirk* [forest area]
Ffo: *Frankfurt (Oder)* [city of Frankfurt/ Oder]
Fg: *Finanzgericht* [finance court]
Fgbz: *Forstgutsbezirk* [forest district]
Fi: *Finanzamt* [financial office]
Fl: *Flecken* [small town]
Fö, Fo: *Försterei, Forsthaus* [forest area, forester's house]
G: *Gut, Güter* [farmstead, estate]
Ga: *Gesundheitsamt* [board of health]
Gbf: *Güterbahnhof* [railroad freight station]
Gbz/Gtsbz: *Gutsbezirk* [estate district]
Geb: *Gebirge* [mountain range]
GewA: *Gewerbeaufsichtsamt* [industrial inspection board]
Gh: *Gasthaus, Gehöft* [inn]
GK: *Generalkarte, Deutsche* [reference to set of maps used with Müllers gazetteer]
Gm: *Gemeinde* [community]
gmfr Gebiet: *gemeindefreies Gebiet* [area independent of jurisdiction of a town or village]
Gmk: *Gemarkung* [(village, town, township) limits]
Gr: *Grube* [mine, quarry]
Grafsch/Grfsch: *Grafschaft* [county; earldom]
Grenzm: *Grenzmark* [border territory; esp. between Posen and West Prussia]
Gr Krst: *Große Kreisstadt* [county seat]

Gtb: *Gemeindetarifbereich* [local tariff area]

Gü: *Abfertigungsbefugnis für Güterverkehr* [clearance permits to ship goods]

Güb: *beschränkte Abfertigungsbefugnis für Güterverkehr* [limited authorizations to ship goods]

H: *Haus, Häuser, Hofstelle, Höfe, Hof* [house(s), manor, farm, estates]

Hal: *Halle* [city of Halle]

Hamb: *Hamburg* [city of Hamburg]

Hbf: *Hauptbahnhof* [main train station]

Hfe: *Höfe* [country estates]

Hess: *Hessen* [Hesse]

Hgbf: *Hauptguterbahnhof* [central freight train station]

Hgr: *Häusergruppe* [group of houses]

h.j.: *heißt jetzt* [now known as]

Hofg: *Hofgut* [domain]

Hptzo: *Hauptzollamtsbezirk* [main customs district]

Hw: *Hammerwerk, Hüttenwerk* [foundry, ironworks]

IHK: *Industrie- und Handelskammer* [chamber of commerce]

Jgh: *Jagdhaus* [hunting lodge]

K: *Kotten* [cottage]

Kirchsp: *Kirchspiel* [parish]

Kirchspeilgm, Ksplgm: *Kirchspielgemeinde* [parish congregation]

Kl: *Kloster* [monastery, convent]

Klbf: *Kleinbahnhof* [small train station]

Klg: *Klostergut* [cloister lands]

km: *Kilometer* [kilometer]

KMSt: *Karl-Marx-Stadt* [Chemnitz, formerly called Karl-Marx-Stadt]

Kol: *Kolonie* [colony]

Kr: *Kreis (Landkreis)* [district, rural district]

Krarbg: *Kreisarbeitsgericht* [county labor court]

kreisfr St: *kreisfreie Stadt* [city with no obligation to a kreis]

Krfi: *Kreisabgabeamt* [county revenue office]

Krg: Kreisgericht [county court]

Krkhs: *Krankenhaus* [hospital)

Krst: *Kreisstadt* [county seat]

Ksplgm: *Kirchspielslandgemeinde* [regional parish]

LarG: *Landesarbeitsgericht* [state or regional labor court]

Lchtt: *Leuchtturm* [lighthouse]

Lg: *Landgericht* [rural court]

LsG: *Landessozialgericht* [state or regional social court]

l U: *linkes Ufer* [left bank of a river]

Lzg: *Leipzig* [city of Leipzig]

m: *mit* [with]

M: *Mühle* [mill]

Mei: *Meierei* [dairy farm]

Mfl/Marktfl: *Marktflecken* [market town]

M Fr: *Mittelfranken* [an area of Bavaria]

Mgb: *Magdeburg* [city of Magdeburg]

Mkt: *Marktgemeinde* [market community]

Nebenst: Nebenstelle [branch office]

Neubdb: *Neubrandenburg* [city of Neubrandenburg]

NL: *Niederlausitz* [Lower Lusatia]

Niedersachs: *Niedersachsen* [Lower Saxony]

Nm: *Neumark* [region northeast of Berlin]

Nordrh Westf: *Nordrhein-Westfalen* [North Rhine-Westphalia]

Obus: *Kraftomnibus* [bus]

Oelm: *Ölmühle* [oil mill]

OFD: *Oberfinanzdirektion* [upper finance administration]

Ofö: *Oberförsterei* [chief forester's office]

O Fr: *Oberfranken* [Upper Franconia]

Okl: *Ortsklasse* [class of a locality according to size]

OL: *Oberlausitz* [Upper Lusatia]

Olg: *Oberlandesgericht* [provincial supreme court]

O Pf: *Oberpfalz* [Upper Palatinate]

Ortstl: *Ortsteil* [part of a town]

OS: *Oberschlesien* [Upper Silesia]

Osch: *Ortschaft* [locality, community, settlement]

OstPr: *Ostpreußen* [East Prussia]

Ovg: *Oberverwaltungsgericht* [administrative appeals court]

P: *Zustellpostanstalt* [delivery post of-

fice]
P (nach Bf) [referring to a train station): *Personenbahnhof* [passenger train station]
Pbf: *Personenbahnhof* [passenger train station]
Pdm: *Potsdam* [city of Potsdam]
Pom: *Pommern* [Pomerania]
Prov: *Provinz* [province]
pV: *polnische Verwaltung* [under Polish administration]
RB: *Regierungsbezirk* [governing district]
Rbz: *Regierungsbezirk* [governing district]
Rg: *Rittergut* [knightly landed estate]
Rheinl: *Rheinland* [Rhineland]
Ro: *Rotte* [squad]
Rst: *Rostock* [city of Rostock]
rU: *rechtes Ufer* [right bank of a river]
s: *siehe* [see, refer to]
Saarl: *Saarland* [Saarland]
Sch: *Schule* [school]
Schl: *Schlesien* [Silesia]
Schl: *Schloß* [castle, fortress, manor house]
Schl   Hol: *Schleswig-Holstein* [Schleswig-Holstein]
Schw: *Schwerin* [city of Schwerin]
Si: *Siedlung* [settlement]
Sg: *Sozialgericht* [social court]
Sgb: *Stückgutbahnhof* [parcel train station]
Sgo: *Stückgutort* [freight train station]
spr: *sprich* [say! (pronounce)]
St: *Stadt* [city]
Sta: *Standesamt* [registrar's office]
Stadtbz: *Stadtbezirk* [city district]
Stadtg: *Stadtgut* [municipal property]
Stadtkr: *Stadtkreis* [(combined) city/county]
Stdttl: *Stadtteil* [section of town; ward; borough; (former) village (now) incorporated into a town]
Stgm: *Stadtgemeinde* [city community]
sV: *sowjetische Verwaltung* [under Soviet administration]
Sw: *Sägewerk* [sawmill]
Te: *Ortsnetzkennziffer*   *für*

Telefonvorwahl [local code number for telephone exchange]
Tl: *Teil* [portion, share]
TW: *Teutoburger Wald* [Teutoburg Forest]
u: *und* [and]
U: *Unterkunfthaus* [lodging; house of refuge]
Unterfr/U Fr: *Unterfranken* [Lower Fran-conia]
Va: *Verkehrsamt* [tourist office]
VB: *Verwaltungsbezirk* [administrative district]
Vg: *Verwaltungsgericht* [administrative court]
vorl: *vorläufig* [temporary]
Vw: *Vorwerk* [residence; farm (outside castle walls)]
W: *Weiler* [hamlet; small village; farm; (hist.) Lordship]
Weinstr: *Weinstraße* [on the wine road]
Wh: *Wirtshaus, Wirtschaft* [inn, farm]
Wm: *Wassermühle* [watermill]
Wohnpl: *Wohnplatz* [residence, populated place]
Württ: *Württemberg* [Württemberg]
Ww: *Westerwald*
Zg: *Ziegelei* [brickyard]
Zk/Zi: *Zinken* [outlying farm]
Zo: *Zollamtsbezirk* [customs district]
Zweigst: *Zweigstelle* [branch office]

PRUSSIAN GAZETTEER (GERMAN EMPIRE), BASED ON THE 1905 CENSUS

♦*Gemeindelexikon für das Königreich Preußen* (Gazetteer of the Kingdom of Prussia) is a reliable source to have when searching for the Catholic or Lutheran parish linked with your ancestor's Prussian hometown. It is based on information gathered in the 1905 Census and from other official sources.

1908 filming
Each of the Prussian provinces listed below has its own index: The first number

given after each place name in the index signifies the *Kreis* (county) to which the place belonged, and the second number given represents the town number, shown in the first column of the gazetteer page. Usually the most useful columns are columns 25 and 26, which name, respectively, the Lutheran and Catholic parish jurisdictions.

–**Brandenburg:** Film 806635 item 1
–**Hannover:** Film 806634 item 2
–**Hessen-Nassau:** Film 1187921 item 4
–**Hohenzollern:** Film 1187921 item 5
–**Ostpreußen (East Prussia):** Film 1186701 item 3; also 11879211 item 2
–**Pommern (Pomerania):** Film 806634 item 4
–**Posen:** Film 806635 item 3
–**Rheinprovinz:** Film 1186702 item 2
–**Sachsen (Province of Saxony):** Film 806634 item 2
–**Schlesien (Silesia):** Film 806633 item 4
–**Schleswig-Holstein:** Film 806635 item 3
–**Westfalen (Westphalia), with Waldeck and Pyrmont:** Film 491042
–**Westpreußen (West Prussia):** Film 1186701 item 4; also Film 1187921 item 3

1930s filming

This film set includes the provinces listed below. The indexes for these volumes are organized in the same manner as those for the 1908 filming, but note that the columns showing Lutheran and Catholic parishe affiliations are numbers 14 and 15 respectively.

–**Brandenburg, Berlin:** Film 806636 item 2
–**Grenzmark, Posen, and Westpreußen:** Film 806636 item 4
–**Hannover:** Film 806637 item 4
–**Hessen-Nassau:** Film 806637 item 6
–**Hohenzollern:** Film 475862 item 1
–**Niederschlesien:** Film 806636 item 5
–**Oberschlesien:** Film 806637 item 1
–**Pommern:** Film 806636 item 3
–**Rheinland:** Film 457862 item 2

–**Sachsen:** Film 806637 item 2
–**Schleswig-Holstein:** Film 806637 item 3
–**Westfalen:** Film 806637 item 5

Where to Find
Gemeindelexikon Preußen

♦Visitors to the Family History Library can find these twelve volumes (bound in blue) on the international floor in the bookshelf just to the right of the Germany consultation desk (FHL Book Ref 943 E5kp).

♦ Researchers can order microfilmed copies of this gazetteer through their local family history centers. To find an office nearest to you, visit www.familysearch.org/eng/library/FHC/frameset_fhc.asp

♦The *Gemeindelexikon Preußen* is now available online (with paid membership). Go to www.ancestry.com, click on the drop down arrow next to the "Search" tab and select "Card Catalog." In the "Title" window, type "gemeindelexikon preussen" and press "Search." Patrons may browse the digitized pages of the gazetteer, but keyword searching is not yet available.

INVENTORIES OF PARISH REGISTERS (AND A FEW OTHER GUIDES)

Note: The resources listed here should be considered in addition to the sections of the *Gemeindelexikon für das Königreich Preußen* (Gazetteer of the Kingdom of Prussia), described in the previous section, as they are also useful in locating a parish church.

Anhalt

♦Starke, *Statistisches Handbuch der Landwirtschaft und geographisches Ortslexikon vom Herzogthum Anhalt* [gazetteer and statistical handbook, Duchy of Anhalt]. FHL 943.19 E5; film 496846 item 4

◆Specht, Reinhold, *Das Land Anhalt* [Anhalt handbook]. FHL 943 B4fw no. 7-9

◆Krieg, R. *Bestand und Alter Kirchenbücher in der Provinz Sachsen, dem Herzogtum Anhalt und einingen thüringischen Staaten* [inventory of parish registers in the province of Sachsen, the duchy of Anhalt, and the Thuringian states of Sachsen-Weimar-Eisenach, Sachsen-Coburg-Gotha, Schwarzburg-Sondershausen, Reuß ältere Linie, Schwarzburg-Rudolstadt, and Sachsen-Altenburg]. FHL 943.18 K23k; film 1183571 item 34

◆Schlyter, Daniel, *Duchy of Anhalt Gazetteer,* 1983. FHL 943.19 E5s

Baden

◆Franz, Hermann, *Die Kirchenbücher in Baden.* [inventory of parish registers] 1957. FHL fiche 6000833 (4 fiche)

Bayern/Pfalz

◆Eger, Wolfgang, *Die protestantischen Kirchenbücher der Pfalz.* [inventory of Protestant parish registers of the Pfalz]. FHL 943.43 Bvp v. 8; film 845166 item 2; fiche 6000835

◆ Eger, Wolfgang, *Verzeichnis der protes-tantischen Kirchenbücher der Pfalz.* [Protestant parish registers]. FHL 943.43 B4vr v. 26.

◆ *Index evangelischer Kirchenbücher im Landeskirchenarchiv Speyer.* [index of Protestant parish registers]. FHL film 476268 item 5

◆*Kirchenbücher Verzeichnis* [inventory of parish registers in Protestant archives in Karlsruhe]. FHL film 1336627 item 4

◆Müller, Anton *Die Kirchenbücher der bayerischen Pfalz.* [inventory of parish registers of the Bavarian Palatinate]. FHL 943 B5az supp. no.1; film 415618

◆*Ortschaften-Verzeichnis für den Frei-staat Bayern* [gazetteer for Bavaria in 1928]. FHL 943.3 B4fr no. 109; film 924721

Berlin

◆Themel, Karl, *Die evangelischen Kirchenbücher von Berlin* [inventory

of Protestant parish registers, Berlin]. FHL 943.155/B1 K23t

Brandenburg

◆Schwartz, Paul, *Die Kirchenbücher der Mark Brandenburg* [inventory of Brandenburg parish registers]. FHL 943.15 K23s; film 1181819 item 1

◆Themel, Karl, *Übersicht über die Bestände der Pfarr und Kirchenarchive in den Sprengeln Cottbus, Eberswalde und Potsdam der Evangelischen Kirche in Berlin Brandenburg* [Inventory of Protestant churchbooks]. FHL 943.155B

◆*Übersicht über den Bestand der Kirchenbücher und kirchlichen Archivalien der Provinz Brandenburg, Preußen* [inventory of parish registers and other church records, Brandenburg]. FHL fiche 957868 item 1

◆Vorberg, Georg, *Die Kirchenbücher der Mark Brandenburg* [inventory of Brandenburg parish registers; includes Berlin, Lebus, and Frankfurt an der Oder]. FHL 943.15 K23s pt. 2; film 1181819 item 2

Braunschweig

◆ Kleinau, Hermann, *Geschichtliches Ortsverzeichnis des Landes Braun-schweig,* 1968. FHL 943.59 E6kh

◆ Meyer, K., *Die Kirchenbücher der Kirchengemeinden und Zivil-standregister im Besitz des Braun-schweigischen Staatsarchivs zu Wolfenbüttel und des Stadtarchivs zu Braunschweig* [inventory of parish registers]. FHL film 1181597 item 2

Bremen

◆ *Kirchenbuch-Inventar der Freien Hansestadt Bremen.* [inventory of parish registers]. FHL film 953001 item 1

Elsaß-Lothringen (Alsace-Lorraine)

◆Koch, Herbert, *Die Kirchenbücher von Elsaß-Lothringen,*1911. [inventory of parish registers]. Lists parishes, not all localities. Volume 9 lists Lutheran par-ishes, and Volume 10 lists Reformed and Catholic parishes. FHL films (Vol. 9)

492890 and (Vol. 10) 492892
* Thode, Ernest, *Genealogical Gazetteer of Alsace-Lorraine.* FHL 944.38 E5t

Hamburg
* Loose, Hans-Dieter, *Bestände des Staats-archivs des Freien und Hansestadt Ham-burg* [inventory of Hamburg state archives, with description of parish registers] FHL film 1181595 item 1

Hannover
* Garbe, Fritz, *Die Kirchenbücher in der ev.-luth. Landeskirche Hannovers,* Hannover, 1960. [Protestant parish register inventory]. FHL 943.59 K23g and film 1181595 item 5
* Krieg, R., *Das Alter und der Bestand der Kirchenücher in der Provinz Hannover* [inventory of parish records]. FHL 943.59 K23k

Hessen
* Elsenberg, Erich, *Kirchenbuchver-zeichnis der evangelischen Kirche von Kurhessen-Waldeck,* 1973 [inventory of Protestant parish registers of Kurhessen-Waldeck]. FHL 943.41 K23e
* Praetorius, Otfried, *Kirchenbücher und Standesregister für alle Wohnplätze im Land Hessen.* [inventory of parish registers and civil records for the Grandduchy of Hessen]. FHL 943.41 K23p; film 492895; fiche 6053529 (3 fiche)

Hohenzollern
* Koch, Herbert, *Inventare der katholischen Kirchenarchive in Fürstentume Hohenzollern* [inventory of Catholic parish registers]. FHL 943.49 K23k; film 1181595 item 10

Lübeck
* Jensen, Wilhelm, *Die Kirchenbücher Schleswig-Holsteins, des Landesteil Lübeck und der Hansastädte* [inventory of parish registers of Schleswig-Holstein, Oldenburg, and the Hanseatic cities]. FHL film 1183522 item 5

Mecklenburg-Schwerin,

Mecklenburg-Strelitz
* Endler, Carl August and Edm. Albrecht, *Mecklenburgs familiengeschichtliche Quellen.* 1936. [inventory of parish registers]. FHL 943.2 A5e; film 496473 item 8; fiche 6000834 (2 fiche)
* Schubert, Franz, *Kopulationsregister aus Mecklenburgischen Kirchen-büchern von 1751 bis 1800* [marriage registers with index]. FHL 943.17 B4s, ser. 6

Oldenburg
* *Kirchenbuch-Verzeichnis der Ev.-Luth. Kirche in Oldenburg* [church records before 1800 in Duchy of Oldenburg]. FHL 943.59 K23e
* Koch, Ludwig, *Die kirchlichen familien-kundlichen Quellen des Herzogtums Oldenburg,* Leipzig, 1929. [church sources in the duchy of Oldenburg (part of the grandduchy of Oldenburg)]. FHL 943.59 K23kL; film 1045463 item 16
* *Ortschaftsverzeichnis des Großherzog-tums Oldenburg,* 1911 [gazetteer of the grandduchy of Oldenburg]. FHL 943.1 E5L; film 806633 item 1; fiche 6053541 (4 fiche)

Ostpreußen
* Grigoleit, Eduard, *Neues Verzeichnis ostpreußischer Kirchenbücher* [inventory of parish and civil registers before 1874 of East Prussia]. FHL 943.83 K2g; film 1045344 item 2

Pfalz: See Bayern/Pfalz

Pommern
* Schubert, Franz, *Trauregister aus den ältesten Kirchenbüchern* [early church marriage records for western Pomerania]. FHL 943.81 B4s Ser. 2
* Wehrmann, M., *Die Kirchenbücher in Pommern* [inventory of parish registers]. FHL 943.81 K23w; film 1945971 item 3; fiche 6053534

Rheinprovinz
* Krudewig, Anton, *Neues Verzeichnis der Kirchenbücher der ehemaligen Rhein- provinz* [inventory of parish reg-isters]. FHL 943.42 K34k; film 889342 item

4; fiche 6053535

♦ *Neues Verzeichnis der Kirchenbücher der ehemaligen Rheinprovinz* [inventory of parish registers]. FHL 943.42 K23k; film 1183547 item 3; fiche 6053535

Sachsen (Kingdom of Saxony)

♦ Blaschke, Karlheinz, *Historisches Ortsverzeichnis von Sachsen*. 1957. [gazetteer of the kingdom of Sachson, including church jurisdictions]. FHL 943.21 E5bk; fiche 6000830 (7 fiche).

♦ Köhler, Hermann, *Verzeichnis der Kirchenbücher und der übrigen für die Sippenforschung wichtigen Amtsbücher.* [index of towns in kingdom of Sachsen, showing Protestant parish jurisdictions]. FHL 943.21 K23k; film 1183522 item 13; fiche 6053524

♦ Kolbe, Arthur, *Handbuch der Kirchen-Statistik für das Königreich Sachsen.* [directory of Protestant clergy and churches in the kingdom of Sachsen]. FHL film 823778 item 2

♦ Schumann, August, *Vollständiges Staats, Post, und Zeitungs Lexikon von Sachsen* [gazetteer of kingdom of Sachsen, based on years 1815-1823; includes Thüringen]. FHL fiche 6000822; films 824319-824325

Schaumburg-Lippe

♦ *Adreßbuch über die Provinz Westfalen und die Fürstentümer Lippe, Lippe-Schaumburg* [index of towns in the kingdom of Sachsen showing Protestant parish jurisdictions]. FHL 943.56 E5b; film 873823 item 2

Sachsen (province)

♦ Machholz, Ernst, *Die Kirchenbücher der evangelischen Kirchen in der Provinz Sachsen,* 1925. [gazetteer, including church jurisdictions]. FHL 943 B4m v. 30; film 1183522 item 12; fiche 6053532

♦ *See Anhalt (Krieg)*

Schlesien

♦ *A Genealogical Guide and Atlas of Silesia,* Everton Publishers, Logan, Utah, 1976. FHL 943.85 E5k

♦ *Die Kirchenbücher Schlesiens*

beider Confessionen [inventory of both Protestant and Catholic parish registers]. FHL 943.85 K23k; film 1183571

♦ Randt, Erich, *Die älteren Personenstandsregister Schlesiens.* [inventory of parish and civil registers]. FHL 943.85 K2r; film 862039; fiche 6053530

Schleswig-Holstein

♦ Jensen, Wilhelm, *Die Kirchenbücher Schleswig-Holsteins der Landeskirche Eutin und der Hansestädte.*[Parish inventory for Schleswig-Holstein, Oldenburg, and the Hanseatic cities]. FHL 943.512 D2q vol. 2

♦ Schubert, Franz, *Trauregister aus den ältesten Kirchenbüchern Schleswig-Holstein von den Anfängen bis zum Jahre 1704.* [marriage records to 1704]. FHL 943.512 K29s. vols. 1-14

Thüringen

♦ Karl Guldenapfel, *Die evangelischen Kirchenbücher Thüringens.* [description of Protestant church records, including Reuss-jüngere-Linie, Sachsen-Altenburg, Sachsen-Coburg-Gotha, Sachsen-Meiningen, Sachsen-Weimar-Eisenach, Schwarzburg-Rudolstadt, and Schwarzburg-Sondershausen]. FHL film 1858093-1858097

♦ *See Anhalt (Krieg)*

Westfalen: Lippe, Schaumburg-Lippe, Waldeck-Pyrmont

♦ Bertelsmann, W., *Adreßbuch über die Provinz Westfalen und die Fürstentümer Lippe, Lippe-Schaumburg und Waldeck-Pyrmont.* [gazetteer of Westphalia, etc.]. FHL 943.56 E5b; film 873823 Item 2

♦ *Die evangelischen Kirchenbücher in Waldeck-Pyrmont* [inventory of Protestant parish registers of Waldeck-Pyrmont]. FHL 943.41 K2e

Westpreußen

♦ Bär, Max, *Die Kirchenbücher der Provinz Westpreußen* [inventory of parish records of West Prussia]. FHL 943.82 B4a V. 13; film 1045433 item 5;

fiche 6000826
Württemberg
♦ Dunker, M. *Verzeichnis der württembergischen Kirchenbücher* [inventory of parish registers]. FHL 943.47 K23d; fiche 6053528; film 492889 item 1
♦*Ortschaftsverzeichnis des Königreichs Württemberg* [gazetteer of Württemberg, from the census of 1910]. FHL film 806633 item 3

COLLECTION ANALYSIS REPORTS

The Family History Library in Salt Lake City has recently printed compilations of church record inventories by province. Each book shows the age and availability of baptism, marriage and burial data for all churches in the province. The books are available only at the reference desk on the international floor (B1) of the library. The compiler is Steven W. Blodgett and the set comprises the following provinces: Anhalt, Baden, Brandenburg, Brauschweig, Hessen-Nassau, Hohenzollern, Lippe, Pfalz, Pommern, Posen, Rheinprovinz, Sachsen (province), Schaumburg-Lippe, Schlesien, Thüringen, Waldeck, Westfalen, Westpreußen, Württemberg,

Inventories of parish registers for larger or combined areas
♦**Protestant church inventories of Germany:** Eger, Wolfgang and Karlheinrich Dumrath, *Die zentralen Archive in der evangelischen Kirche* [Archive inventories of Protestant churches in Germany, with index]. FHL 943 K23va no. 3; film 1045349 item 2

♦**Lippe, Birkenfeld, Lübeck, Waldeck, Schaumburg:** Krieg, R., *Alter und Bestand der Kirchenbücher in den Fürstentümern Lippe, Birkenfeld, Lübeck, Waldeck, und*

Schaumburg [inventory of parish registers for these localities]. FHL film 1181595 item 8

♦**Protestant churches in Germany:** *Deutsches kirchliches Adreßbuch: Ein kirchlicher Führer durch die evangelischen Landeskirchen Deutschlands und die Kirchen und Kirchengemeinschaften des deutschen Auslandes* [directory of Protestant churches in Germany and throughout the world]. FHL 943 K24d 1934

♦**Catholic parish registers, east of Oder-Neiße:** Kaps, Johannes, *Handbuch über katholischen Kirchenbücher in der Ostdeutschen Kirchenprovinz östlich der Oder und Neiße und dem Bistum Danzig.* [inventory of Catholic parish registers east of the Oder-Neiße]. FHL 943.8 K23k

SELECTED BASIC GAZETTEERS FOR GERMAN RESEARCH

♦ *Genealogical Guide to German Ancestors from East Germany and Eastern Europe*, Joachim O.R. Nuthack and Adalbert Goertz, trans., Neustadt a.d. Aisch, Verlag Degener & Co., 1984. This is the third edition of the above work, in English translation. FHL 943 D27gg

♦*Müllers Verzeichnis der jenseits der Oder-Neiße gelegenen, unter fremder Verwaltung stehenden Ortschaften* [Müller's gazetteer of localities lying east of the Oder-Neisse (line which are) under foreign administration]. Kaemmerer, Wuppertal-Barmen, Post und Ortsbuchverlag, n.d., a supplement to *Müllers großes deutsches Ortsbuch*). Identifies localities in terms of their pre-and post-World War II names. The two parts of this gazetteer (the first two editions of which are out of print) are 1) an alphabetical list of all communities, using the German names, and 2) a list arranged according to post-1945 locality names.

The title of the third edition, prepared by a different publisher, changed to *Ortsnamenverzeichnis der Ortschaften jenseits von Oder und Neiße* [Gazetteer for localities east of the Oder and Neisse (rivers)], M. Kaemmerer, ed., Leer, Verlag Gerhard Rautenberg, 1988. This edition, including about 7,600 localities, lists German and Polish names of localities lost by Germany to Poland after World War II. It contains a set of maps of the former German areas which have been part of Poland since 1945. This gazetteer does not cover former German areas included in the Polish Republic created between 1919 and 1921 (Posen, West Prussia, Hultschiner District, East Upper Silesia, Soldauer Zipfel, Memel District, and parts of the districts Groß Wartenberg and Guhrau). It does include the western portions of Posen and West Prussia (Grenzmark Posen-Westprussia) that remained German until 1945.

FHL 943 E5m 1958; Supp.; film 1,045,448; fiche 6000343-6000354. See also fiche 6000340-6000342

♦*Amtliches Gemeindeverzeichnis der deutschen Ostgebiete unter fremder Verwaltung* [Official Gazetteer for the Localities in the (former) German East under Foreign Administration], 3d ed., 3 vols, Bundesanstalt für Landeskunde, Remagen, 1955. Contains German and the foreign language names of most localities that were part of Germany on September 1, 1939, but which became part of Poland or the Soviet Union after 1945. German localities that belonged to Poland before 1939 are not included.
– **Volume 1: Alphabetisches Ortsnamenverzeichnis der deutschen Ostgebiete unter fremder Verwaltung nach dem Gebietsstand am 1.9. 1939** [Alphabetical Gazetteer of German Eastern Areas under Foreign Administration on September 1,

1939]. Divided into four parts: Part 1) Prussian jurisdictions that were transferred to Poland and the Soviet Union in 1945, including communities that belonged to each *Kreis* (county), arranged both alphabetically and by *Verwaltungsbezirk* (administrative district); Parts 2 and 3) the *Kreise* (counties) and communities that were dissected by the drawing of Poland's 1945 boundaries; and Part 4) communities that underwent name changes, with the new name for each locality (regarding place name changes that occurred in East Prussia and Silesia between 1933 and 1939, before they became Polish).
– **Volume 2:** *Alphabetisches Ortsnamenverzeichnis (Wohnplatzverzeichnis) der deutschen Ostgebiete unter fremder Verwaltung nach dem Gebietsstand am 1.9. 1939: deutsch-fremdsprachig* [Alphabetical gazetteer (populated area gazetteer) of eastern German areas under foreign administration on September 1, 1939: German-to-foreign language]. Divided into Parts A, B, and C.

Part A consists of an alphabetical listing of about 35,000 localities (*sämtlicher bewohnter Plätze*, or "all inhabited places") in German jurisdictions now in Poland or the Soviet Union. Each entry provides the German place names for the Polish place names, and the standard sheet number for the map series (1:25,000), *Topographische Karte, Amtlicher Anstalt für Kartographie und Kartendruck*, Berlin, 1937; as well as the German *Gemeinde* (township/community) and *Kreis* (county) in which the locality was found, together with the previous German name and its present Polish name and county. Localities in the Soviet-governed Kaliningrad often appear only under the German place name.

Part B is a register of places found in the 1905 gazetteer of Prussia (*Gemeindelexikon für das Königreich Preußen auf Grund der Volkszählung vom 1. 12. 1905*, Verlag des Königlichen

Statistischen Landesamts, Berlin, 1907-1909) and elsewhere that had been re-named by 1955.

This part provides an alphabetical list of (Polish) communities in former German areas for which an official Polish name exists, but no official German name as of September 1, 1939. In other words, these dwelling places receiving a new name after September 1, 1939 were not included in the official gazetteer of 1939, nor were communities that developed after 1939.

Part C lists the applicable Polish names for communities listed in Part B.

– **Volume 3:** Same title as Volume 2, with the words *fremdsprachig-deutsch* (foreign language to German) replacing *deutsch-fremdsprachig* (German to foreign language) in Volume 2's title. This volume is divided into Part A and part B:

Those localities showing an asterisk can be found under their German equivalent name in volume two, part B, where more information is given about the name changes that occurred.

FHL 943.8 E5b; film (Volumes 1 and 2) 824243 item 2, and film (Volume 3) 1045449 item 5; fiche 6053256 [11 fiche]. Polish-to-German name changes: film 1045449 item 5

♦ *Deutsch-fremdsprachiges (fremd-sprachig-deutsches) Ortsnamenver-zeichnis* [Gazetteer of places with German and foreign-language names] (Otto Kredel and Franz Thierfelder eds., Deutsche Verlagsgesellschaft, Berlin, 1931). This gazetteer is organized geographically, covering German localities that became parts of other nations as a result of Germany and Austria's defeat in World War I – including France, Belgium, Denmark, Poland, Lithuania, Russia, Czechoslovakia, Hungary, Yugoslavia, Italy, Switzerland, Latvia, Estonia, Luxemburg, and Romania.

Under the section entitled *"Die abgetretenen Gebiete Ostpreußens, West-preußens, Posens und Obers-chlesiens und das übrige Polen"* (The Ceded Territories of East Prussia, West Prussia, Posen and Upper Silesia and the Rest of Poland), one finds German-to-foreign-language and foreign-language-to-German gazetteers for localities that became part of Poland before 1931. Each entry in the German-to-foreign-language part provides the foreign language equivalent to the German name, the German *Kreis* (county) name, and an abbre-viation for the former German province. In the foreign-language-to-German sec-tion, the foreign language name of the locality is followed by the German name, the German *Kreis* (county) and the ab-breviation for the former German prov-ince. Place names that did not change names are missing from this gazetteer, as are place names with predictable changes in spelling (e.g., sch=sz).

FHL Ref Q 940 E5kt; film 583457, and duplicate film 590387

♦ *Henius großes Orts- und Verkehrs-Lexikon für das Deutsche Reich* [Henius geographical and commercial lexicon of the German Empire] (H. Höpker, Neufeld & Henius, Berlin 1934). In the section titled, *"Alphabetisches Verzeichnis sämt-licher vom Deutschen Reich abgetretenen Städte, Landgemeinden und Guts-bezirke,"* pages 925-992, are listed alphabetically all cities, towns, and estates taken from Germany following World War I, together with their foreign equivalents. Volume 1: A-L; Volume 2: M-Z. FHL 943 E5ho; film 973171 items 1-2

♦ *Gemeindeverzeichnis für Mittel- und Ostdeutschland und die früheren deutschen Siedlungsgebieten im Ausland* [Gazetteer for Middle and East Germany and the earlier German settlements in foreign lands] (Verlag für Standesamts-wesen, Frankfurt am Main, 1970): Locates places removed from

Germany after both world wars. Modern place names are also shown, but no cross reference system is in place to connect the changed names in this register. FHL 940 E5g

♦ *Namensänderungen ehemals preuß-ischer Gemeinden von 1850 bis 1942 (mit Nachträgen bis 1950)* [Name changes of former Prussian communities from 1850 to 1942, with additions to 1950] (Fritz Verdenhalven, Verlag Degener & Co., Neustadt an der Aisch, 1971): A key to name changes, incorporations, and mergers of city and state communities over a period of one century in Prussia.
– **English translation of abbreviations key:**
51-99: covers years 1851-1899
00-50: covers years 1900-1950
-29: name of community until 1929
29x: name of community starting in 1929
26/29: the change took place between these years
E: Incorporated into . . . (town/city)
Z: Merged with . . . (town/city)
N: Reorganized with . . . (town/city)
NZ: New name and merged with other communities
(080): code number indicating rural district locality belonged to at time of name change
(St): city
K: parish
j: now
t: in part
p: current Polish name
r: current Russian name
=: indicates endings of other town names that start with the same first letters
FHL 943 E5vf; fiche 6001700

♦ *The U.S. Board on Geographic Names* has published gazetteers for various countries or areas, providing names of geographic features such as streams, lakes, cliffs, rivers, valleys, farms, tow-ers, woods, hills, passes, waterfalls, channels, passes, islands, bays, and many others. These gazetteers have been published under the name of the political jurisdiction at the time of publication, but they include names of localities belonging formerly to other countries. Therefore, for the German Empire, one would refer to one of these gazetteers of the U.S. Board on Geographic Names:
– **Federal Republic of West Germany and West Berlin:** Volume 1 (A-K) film 874458; Volume 2 (L-Z) film 874459
–**Germany: Soviet Zone and East Berlin:** film 1182601 item 1
–**Poland:** Volume 1 (A-M) film 1184075; Volume 2 (N-Z) film 1184076 item 1-2
– **USSR:** Volume 1, film 928609; Volumes 2 and 3, film 928610; Volumes 4 and 5, film 874455; Volumes 6 and 7, film 874456. fiche (Volumes 1-7) 6053504

♦ *Vollständiges geographischtopo-graphischstatistisches Orts-Lexikon von Deutschland sowie der unter Österreichs und Preußens Botmäßigkeit: stehenden nicht deutschen Länder* [The complete geographical, topographical and statistical gazetteer of Germany, as well as non-German lands governed by Austria and Prussia] by H. Rudolph. Most localities are named in German, but otherwise they are listed in the local language. Entries typically include the name of the locality, the type of place (estate, village, etc.), administrative jurisdiction, location in reference to some other place, and population. Often the name of the nearest post office or administrative office is included. FHL film (A-R) 1256334 item 2-3; (S-Z) 1256335 item 1
Source: In part, "Finding Former German Localities Now in Poland," by Dr. Raymond S. Wright III, *FEEFHS Quarterly,* Volume VI, Numbers 1-4 (1999).

MAP GUIDE TO GERMAN PARISH REGISTERS

This new series is designed to help the researcher identify on the map the parish in Germany in which an ancestor lived. Each map indicates the locations of Catholic and Protestant parishes. For towns without churches, parish affiliations are given. The compiler of the series is Kevan Hansen. For a current list of volumes in this series, consult the publisher:

Family Roots Publishing Co.
P.O. Box 830
Bountiful, Utah 84011
Tel. (801) 992-3705
Fax: (815) 642-0103
www.familyrootspublishing.com

REVERSE ALPHABETICAL PLACE-NAME INDEXES

One of the most troublesome problems of German research is the deciphering of handwritten German place names. When available, the "reverse alphabetical index" can come to the rescue. Such an index lists each locality alphabetically by the spelling from the *ends* of names rather than their beginnings. It can be one of the most valuable tools for re-starting a dead-end search.

For example, in a reverse alphabetical index, these towns would be listed in this order:

Kohlgrube
Taschengrube
Silbergrube
Kaisergrube
Breitenhaide
Heide

Here are some situations in which the reverse alphabetical index is useful:
+ **The beginning of a place name is missing or illegible.**

The researcher comes across a place name for which the first character, or the first few characters, are missing or illegible, even though the final characters of the name can be read without great difficulty. For example, the best interpretation of a handwritten place name might, after serious study, be " - - - - -rgrube". Obviously, without knowing the first character or the first few characters of the word, it is almost impossible to check the name in a gazetteer.

With a "reverse alphabetical index," however, one may search alphabetically from the end of the word rather than from its beginning. Therefore, the researcher would check the appropriate reverse-alphabetical index for " -rgrube." Using the sample from the index segment displayed above, it is clear that "Silbergrube and Kaisergrube" should be strong candidates for identifying the "mystery" town.

+ **The town "doesn't exist"**

The researcher is working with the name of a locality known to be situated in a particular German state or province – a town name that has been read, for example, as *Sangwaden*. Yet no *Sangwaden* appears in any gazetteer or on any map of the German area being searched. The researcher, after checking a reverse alphabetical index and finding no such name, discovers a listing for *Langwaden*. It then becomes obvious that the handwritten capital L of Langwaden, as found in the old record, was being mistakenly read as a capital S.

+ **Archaic spelling prevents searching for the locality under its modern name.**

A researcher is working with three spellings of an old town name: *Bärfelden, Berfelden,* and *Behrfelden.* No such name turns up in gazetters or on maps of the area. All three share the same ending: *-rfelden.* A search of a reverse alphabetical index reveals that these three archaic names are now spelled as *Beerfelden,* the modern name for the town, as listed in modern gazetteers.

Availability of reverse alphabetical place-name indexes

Place Name Indexes with reverse alphabetical listings are available for the following entities of the German Empire: Alsace-Lorraine, Anhalt, Baden, Bavaria, Brandenburg, Braunschweig, Bremen, East Prussia, Hamburg, Hannover, Hesse, Hesse-Nassau, Lippe, Lübeck, Mecklenburg-Schwerin, Mecklenburg-Strelitz, Oldenburg, Palatinate, Pomerania, Posen, Rheinprovinz, Saxony (kingdom), Saxony (province), Schaumburg-Lippe, Schleswig-Holstein, Silesia, Thuringia,Waldeck, Westphalia, West Prussia, Wuerttemberg. A CD is also available for Switzerland.

Minert, Roger P., GRT Publications, P.O. Box 1845, Provo, UT 84603-1845 Tel. (801) 374-2587. grtpublications@juno.com; www.grtpublications.com.

MAJOR GAZETTEERS FOR EASTERN EUROPE

Austria: *Gemeindelexikon der in Reichsrate vertretenen Königreiche und Länder* [Gazetteer of the crownlands and territories represented in the imperial council]. Vienna. K.K. Statistisches Zentralkommission, 1903-1908.

This fourteen volume gazetteer is comprised of data from the 1900 Census in Austria's crownlands. Each volume is accessible online as part of the Harold B. Lee Library's (Brigham Young University) Family History Collection.

Go to www.lib.byu.edu/fhc, press the drop down arrow next to the "Browse" window and select "Gazetteers." Images from the gazetteers are free to browse, but have not been indexed for keyword searches.

The gazetteer is also available at the Family History Library (FHL 943.6 E5g; film (see below); 13 fiche 6001723).

Film numbers for states of the Austrian Empire, volumes 1 through 14, are as follows:

- Volumes 1, Niederöstrreich; 2, Oberösterreich; and 3, Salzburg: film 1187925 item 2-4.
- Volumes 4, Steiermark; 5, Kärnten, 6, Krain; 7, Küstenland; and 8, Tirol and Vorarlberg: film 1187926
- Volumes 9, Böhmen; and 11, Schlesien: film 1187927
- Volume 10, Mähren: film 924736 item 1
- Volumes 12, Galizien; 13, Bukowina; 14, Dalmatien: film 1187928 item 1-3

Austro-Hungarian Empire: *Allgemeines geographisches statistisches Lexikon aller österreichischen Staaten* [General gazetteer of all Austro-Hungary]. Vienna. Franz Raffelsperger, 1845-1853. FHL 943.6 E5r; film 1187928-1187933

Hungary: *Magyarország Helységnévtára* [Gazetteer of Hungary], János Dvorzák, comp. Budapest: "Havi Füzetek," 1877. FHL 943.9 E5; films 599564 item 3 (index), and 973041 (localities)

German Empire: Ütrecht, E., comp. *Meyers Orts- und Verkehrslexikon des Deutschen Reichs* [Meyer's gazetteer and directory of the German Empire]. Leipzig: Bibliographisches Institut, 1912. **Prussia:** *Gemeindelexikon für das Königreich Preußen* [Gazetteer for the Kingdom of Prussia]. Berlin: Verlag des Königlichen statistischen Landesamts, 1907-1909.

Russian Empire: Sulimierski, Filip, ed. *Slownik Geograficzny Królestwa Polskiego i Innych Krajów Slowiañskich* [Geographical dictionary of the Kingdom of Poland and other Slavic countries prior to World War I]. 15 Vol. Warsaw: Sulimierski i Walewski, 1880-1902. FHL 943.8 E5c; film 920957-920972; fiche 6068506 (173 fiche)

Czechoslovakia: *Administratives Gemeindelexikon der Cechoslovakischen Republik* [Administrative gazetteer of the Czechoslovak Republic]. Prague.

Statis-tischen Staatsamte, 1927-1928.
FHL 943.7 E5a; films 496719 and 496720
item 1

**Areas of Hungary later in Czechoslo-
vakia:** *Majtán, Milan. Názvy Obci na
Slovensku za OstatnΩch Dvesto Rokov*
[Place names in Slovakia during the last
200 years]. Bratislava. Slovenská Akadé
mie Vied, 1972. FHL 943.73 E2m; film
1181569 item 1

Poland: *Spis Miejscowosci Polskiej
Rzeczypospolitej Ludowej* [Gazetteer of
Polish People's Republic localities].
Warsaw: Wydawnictwakomunikacj i
lacznosci, 1968. FHL 9433.8 E5s; films
2037058 item 2, and 844922; fiche
6000369-6000383

Also *Skorowidz Miejscowosci
rzeczypos-politej Polskiej* [Gazetteer of
the early Polish Republic (based on 1921
census)]. FHL film 804242 item 3-6

Romania: *Indicatorul Localitatilor din
Romania* [Index of localities of
Romania]. Bucuresti: Editura Academiiei
Republicii Socialiste Romania, 1974. FHL
949.8 E5i; film 1181561 item 1

Yugoslavia: *Imenik mesta u Jugoslaviji*
[Place names in Yugoslavia]. Beograd:
Novinski Ustanova Sluzbeni List SFRJ,
1972. FHL 949.7 E5im; fiche 6053513

REGIONAL GAZETTEERS

The multi-volume set of gazetteers,
The Atlantic Bridge to Germany, by
Charles M. Hall (Everton Publishers,
Inc., Logan, Utah) provides maps, lists
of community names, and archive infor-
mation about the various entities of the
German Empire (including Alsace-
Lorraine) and Switzerland, with each vol-
ume concentrating on a given area.

These volumes are helpful in locating ancestral towns. A typical volume
offers an index to the *Gemeinde* (communities) of an area, the list of *Kreise*
(counties), many regional maps, biblio-

graphic listings of resources pertinent
to the area, and types of records available at specific archives.

The series covers the following localities:

Volume 1: Baden-Württemberg
Volume 2: Hessen, Rheinland-Pfalz
Volume 3: Bayern (Bavaria)
Volume 4: Saarland, Elsaß-Lothringen
(Alsace-Lorraine), Switzerland
Volume 5: Schleswig-Holstein, Bremen,
Hamburg
Volume 6: Mecklenburg
Volume 7: Nordrhein-Westfalen
Volume 8: Preußen (Prussia): Branden-
burg, Ostpreußen (East Prussia), West-
preußen (West Prussia), Pommern (Pom-
erania)
Volume 9: Sachsen (Kingdom and
Province) / Thuringia/nine duchies
Volume 10: Hannover: Niedersachsen,
Braunschweig,   Oldenburg,
Schaumburg-Lippe (Volume 10 is co-
authored by Alice Woods Schiesswohl).
Additional volumes are in preparation
by a new publisher:
Source: Martha Mercer
Maia's Books & Misc.
www.MaiasBooks.com

MAPS AND ATLASES FOR
PRACTICAL USE

Maps for
United States research

♦State maps: AAA American Automobile
Association maps have good indexes
and details
♦ County maps: *The Handy Book for
Genealogists* (Everton Publishers)
shows changes in county borders. FHL
973 D27
♦Township maps: *Township Atlas of the
United States,* by J. L. Andriot, is
available through the National Archives,
university libraries, and genealogy
departments of libraries. FHL 973 E7an;
film 1597808 item 2

Maps for driving in Germany

Road maps are produced in scales too small to read easily while underway. Recommended is this atlas:

◆*Der große Autoatlas Bundesrepublik Deutschland 2000/2001,* by Falk Verlag, is revised biennially. In convenient 7°" x 11" size, this book fits comfortably on the lap when opened. Each of the five maps, proceeding from north to south, has foldout sections as needed. With a map scale of of 1:500,000, this atlas has an easy-to-read index with current zip codes given. Names of towns are easily visible in strong type, and *Tankstelle* (gas station) and *Rastplatz* (rest stop) locations are indicated.

Maps for German research

Small scale maps: Maps drawn to a smaller scale, which show large areas with less detail, varying from about 1:500,000 to 1:200,000, are used to ascertain the location of one state or country as it relates to another, or to locate a large region within a state – for example, the Black Forest in Württemberg, the Vogtland in Sachsen, and the borders of a former duchy or principality.

Large-scale maps: Larger-scaled maps, showing small villages, their main streets, and building locations, vary from about 1:25,000 to 1:150,000. These two scales are the most commonly used.

◆*Maps of the German Empire of 1871,* by Jensen Publications, Pleasant Grove, Utah, contains 21 unindexed maps of 1871 kingdoms, duchies, and provinces in varying small scales. Territory borders are clearly marked. With each map is a very useful and concise one-page history of the region.

◆*Karte des Deutschen Reiches* (Map of the German Empire) also of 1871, with a scale of 1:100,000, has the most detail. Originally produced for military use, it consists of 674 maps, including all cities, towns, villages, hamlets, manorial estates, and groups of houses. It is suit-

able for conducting an area search to gather more information on ancestors in neighboring settlements.

This map is of special significance because it is coordinated with listings in the gazetteer, *Meyers Orts- und Verkehrs- lexikon. Karte des Deutschen Reiches* is found on FHL film 068814 and fiche 6000063-6000197.

◆The *Atlas of the German Empire, 1892* (published by Thomsen's Genealogical Center, Bountiful, Utah) covers the period of greatest emigration. It contains 24 indexed maps of the German regions and those now in Poland, with scales varying between 1:850,000 and 1: 1,700,000.

Best "workhorse" map scales for research are 1:200,000 and 1:100,000

◆*Shell: Die Generalkarte.* Of very fine quality, in a scale of 1:200,00, are the 36 individual Shell maps produced by Mairs Geographischer Verlag and available at German Shell gas stations and German bookstores.

These show many geographical features and all but the tiniest hamlets.

◆ *Falk Autoatlas Deutschland 2008/ 2009* (formerly by RV Verlag), has a scale of 1:200,000. It is spiral-bound in 8" x 11" size, has 237 maps showing 90,000 towns, a town-name index, and zip codes. There are 75 city maps (1:20,000).

The new atlases are now being produced in larger sizes and in the larger scale of 1:150,000.

This scale may yield a few more of the tiny villages than the 1:200,000 scale, but both sizes will show town layout and church location, forests, individual mountain tops, castles, working estates, quaintly named farms – even goat huts –any of which may provide clues to the place of origin.

The following atlases in the 1:150,000 scale are rewarding to use.

◆ *Falk Super Auto Atlas Deutschland* has 228 maps of 11" x 15" size, 90,000 entries, place name index with zip codes, legends, and keys in German and English.

◆ *ADAC* (German Auto Club) *Maxi Atlas Deutschland* has 208 maps, in the same size and numbers of entries, index and zip codes as in the Falk map described above, including legends, and keys in five languages.

For German areas now in Poland
◆ *Poland Road Atlas,* by GeoCenter, is an excellent Polish atlas in a scale of 1:200,000, with 236 area maps. The legend is in English, with town names and index in Polish. It also contains 65 city maps in Polish, in a large scale of 1:20,000.

Topographical maps
Each state of Germany has a *Landesvermessungsamt* (topographical survey office) which produces a series of maps of its state in scales of 1:25,000, 1:50,000, 1:100,000, and 1:500,000. (See "German Topographical Maps.") For genealogists, the 1:25,000 scale map is probably of most interest.

City maps
Falk and ADAC *Stadtplan* maps for large and small cities vary in scale from about 1:10,000 to 1:30,000, depending on the city's size. Clear and colorful, they include street indexes and zip codes.

German postal codes
The *Postleitzahlen* (postal codes) for German localities can be found on the website of the German postal system at www.deutschepost.de. Look for "Online Services" and click on "Postleitzahl Suchen." Click on the "English" link at upper right and enter what you know. You may enter a town name only.

Meyers gazetteer
There are clues in *Meyers Orts- und Verkehrslexikon* to help find a town on a map. Immediately following a town's name is its location – country, state; then nearby services, like courts and administrative offices, post office and telegraph – and also the train station if it is not within the town itself. FHL film 496640 (A-K), and 496641 (L-Z); fiche 6000001-29.

The town can then be searched on one's own map, or on *Karte des Deutschen Reiches*, as previously noted. FHL film 068,814; fiche 600063-6000197.

(Insert description of Meyers at FHL and Ancestry. Copy from chapter 3.)

Older maps
Older maps, which can be useful because of boundary or governmental changes, may be found in university and city public libraries. These may not, however, have the advantage of modern topographical methods developed by the end of the eighteenth century. Copies of old maps can be purchased in large libraries such as the state libraries in Berlin and Munich, and in the Library of Congress.
Source: Betty Heinz Matyas, of Sacramento, California.

MAP SCALES

A map scale (in German, *Maßstab*) is expressed as a ratio between map distance and ground distance.

For example, a map scale designated as *1:100,000* indicates (using the metric system for this example) that 1 centimeter on the map represents 100,000 centimeters on the ground. One needs to know that 100,000 centimeters equals one kilometer. Therefore, in this case, one centimeter on the map represents one kilometer on the ground.

The larger the number given as the

ratio of the "1," the less the detail that is found on the map. For example, a scale of 1:25,000 shows a smaller area in greater detail than does one in the scale of 1:250,000.

Emily Gann, "Understanding European Map Scales," *Der Blumenbaum*, vol. 21-2 (October 2003) 84-86.

TWO WELL-STOCKED MAP SHOPS IN GERMANY

♦**Landkarten Schwarz**
Kornmarkt 12
60311 Frankfurt am Main
Tel. 069 55 3869
Hours: Monday through Friday, 10 am - 7 pm; Saturday, 10 am - 6 pm

♦**Geobuch** [usually referred to as "Geo"]
Rosenthal 6
80331 München
Tel. 089 265030 or 089 263713
Hours: Monday through Saturday, 10 am - 7pm
(Geobuch is near the *Viktualienmarkt*)

GERMAN TOPOGRAPHICAL MAPS

Topographical maps are available through the topographical survey office *(Landesvermessungsamt)* of a given German state. A scale of 1:25,000 is recommended.

Baden-Württemberg
Landesvermessungsamt Baden-Württemberg
Büchsenstr. 54
70174 Stuttgart
Tel +49-711-1232831
Fax +49-711-1232979

Bayern
Bayerisches Landesvermessungsamt
Alexandrastr. 4

80538 München
Tel. +49-89-21621735
Fax +49-89-21621770

Berlin
Senatsverwaltung für Bau- und Wohnungswesen
Abt. V - Vermessungswesen
Mansfelder Str. 16
10713 Berlin
Tel. +49-30-8675628
Fax +49-30-8673117

Brandenburg
Landesvermessungsamt Brandenburg
Aussenstelle Potsdam
Heinrich-Mann-Allee 103
14467 Potsdam
Tel. +49-331-87491
Fax +49-331-872387

Bremen
Kataster- und Vermessungsverwaltung Bremen
Wilhelm-Kaisen-Brücke 4
28195 Bremen
Tel. +49-421-3611
Fax +49-421-3614947

Hamburg
Vermessungsamt der Freien und Hansestadt Hamburg
Wexstr. 7
20355 Hamburg
Tel. +49-40-349132169
Fax +49-40-349133196

Hessen
Hessisches Landesvermessungsamt
Schaperstr. 16
65195 Wiesbaden
Tel. 49-611-535236
Fax: 49-611-535309

Mecklenburg-Vorpommern
Landesvermessungsamt Mecklenburg-Vorpommern
Lübecker Str. 289
19059 Schwerin

Tel. +49-385-48216
Fax +49-385-48398

Niedersachsen
Niedersächsisches Landesverwaltungs-
amt
Landesvermessung
Warmbüchenkamp 2
30159 Hannover
Tel. +49-511-3673288
Fax +49-511-3673540

Nordrhein-Westfalen
Landesvermessungsamt Nordrhein-
West-falen
Muffendorfer Str. 19-21
53177 Bonn
Tel. +49-228-846535 or +49-228-846536
Fax +49-228-846502

Rheinland-Pfalz
Landesvermessungsamt Rheinland-
Pfalz
Ferdinand-Sauerbruch-Str. 15
56073 Koblenz
Tel. +49-261-492232
Fax +49-261-492492

Saarland
Landesvermessungsamt des Saarlandes
Von der Heydt 22
66115 Saarbrücken
Tel. +49-681-9712241
Fax +49-681-9712200

Sachsen
Landesvermessungsamt Sachsen
Olbrichtplatz 3
01099 Dresden
Tel. +49-351-5983608
Fax +49-351-5983202

Sachsen-Anhalt
Landesamt für Landesvermessung und
Datenverarbeitung Sachsen-Anhalt
Barbarastr. 2
06110 Halle/Saale
Tel. +49-345-4772440
Fax +49-345-4772002

Schleswig-Holstein
Landesvermessungsamt Schleswig-
Holstein
Mercatorstr. 1
24106 Kiel
Tel. +49-431-3832015
Fax +49-431-3832099

Thüringen
Thüringer Landesverwaltungsamt
Landesvermessungsamt
Schmidtstedter Ufer 7
99084 Erfurt
Tel. +49-361-51301
Fax:+49-361-26910

For maps of the German Empire, borders of 1935
Institut für Angewandte Geodäsie
Stauffenbergstr. 13
10785 Berlin
Tel. +49-30-2611156 or +49-30-2611157
Fax +40-30-2629499

ABBREVIATIONS USED ON GERMAN MAPS

A. .... Alps (*Alpen*)
Arch. .... archipelago (*Archipel*)
B. .... creek (*Bach*)
B. ... mountain, mountains (*Berg, Berge*)
B. .... bay (*Bucht*)
b., bch. .... creek (*-bach*)
bg., bgn. ...... mountain (*-berg, -bergen*)
bg. .... castle (*-burg*)
Bhf. .... train station (*Bahnhof*)
Br. .... well (*Brunnen*)
D. .... German (*Deutsch*)
df. .... village (*-dorf*)
Fj. .... fjord (*Fjord*)
Fl. .... river(*Fluß*)
Ft. .... fort (*Fort*)
G .... Gulf(*Golf*)
Geb. .... mountain range (*Gebirge*)
Gl. .... glacier (*Gletscher*)
Gr. .... Great- (Groß)
H. .... behind, in back of (*hinter*)

H.	hill, high (*Höhe, Hügel, Hoch, Hohen*)
hfn.	harbor (*-hafen*)
H.I.	peninsula (*Halbinsel*)
hm.	-home (*-heim*)
hsn.	place, town (*-hausen*)
I., Iⁿ	island (*Insel, Inseln*)
K.	cape (*Kap*)
K., Kan.	channel (*Kanal*)
Kl.	small (*Klein-*)
Kr.	county (*Kreis*)
lbn.	-live (*-leben*)
Ld.	land (*Land*)
lgn.	(*-lingen*)
M., Mitt.	middle (*Mittel*)
Nd., Ndr.	Low-, Lower- (*Nieder-*)
Ob.	Upper- (*Ober-*)
P.	pass (*Paß*)
Q.	spring, source (*Quelle*)
R.	reef (*Riff*)
rde.	-rode (*-rode*)
S.	lake (*See*)
Schl.	palace (*Schloß*)
Schn.	rapids (*Schnellen*)
Sd.	sound (*Sund*)
Sp.	peak (*Spitze*)
St.	stone (*Stein*)
St.	Saint (*Sankt*)
Str.	stream (*Strom*)
Str.	street, strait (*Straße*)
T., Th., t., th.	valley (*Tal, Thal, -tal, -thal*)
U.	Lower- (*Unter-*)
V.	volcano (*Vulkan*)
W.	west (*West*)
wd.	-wood (*-wald*)
wlr.	-hamlet (*-weiler*)

Source: *Minerva Atlas*, Leipzig, 1927

MOUNTAIN RANGES IN AND AROUND GERMANY

Locations of mountain ranges listed in the left column are indicated in the right column by a nearby major town or city.

KEY:

s = south of
w = west of
n = north of
e = east of
sw = southwest of
se = southeast of
nw = northwest of
sw = southwest of

Adlergebirge	sw Breslau
Allgäuer Alpen	s Oberstdorf
Alpen, Allgäuer-	s Oberstdorf
Alpen, Bayerische-	s München
Alpen, Salzburger-	s Salzburg
Altvater Gebirge	s Breslau
Ardennen	nw Luxemburg
Bayerische Alpen	s München
Bayerischer Wald	se Regensburg
Beskiden	s Krakau
Böhmerwald	e Regensburg
Deister	sw Hannover
Donnersberg	ne Kaiserslautern
Eggegebirge	e Paderborn
Eifel	sw Bonn
Elbinger Höhe	e Danzig
Elbsandsteingebirge	s Dresden
Erzgebirge	s Chemnitz
Eulengebirge	sw Breslau
Fichtelgebirge	e Bayreuth
Fläming	sw Berlin
Fränkische Alb (Fränkischer Jura)	se Nürnberg
Fränkische Schweiz	sw Bayreuth
Frankenhöhe	e Rothenburg a. d. T.
Frankenwald	e Coburg
Gesenke	s Breslau
Glatzer Schneegebirge	s Breslau
Haar	e Dortmund
Haßberge	nw Bamberg
Harz	ne Göttingen
Hessisches Bergland	s Kassel

Heuscheuer .... sw Breslau
Hohe Tatra .... s Krakau
Hohes Kenn .... w Bonn
Hunsrück .... s Koblenz
Isergebirge .... se Dresden
Kaiserstuhl .... nw Freiburg
Kaiserwald .... e Eger
Katzengebirge .... n Breslau
Kernsdorfer Höhe .... sw Allenstein
Lausitzer Gebirge .... se Dresden
Oberpfälzer Wald .... ne Regensburg
Odenwald .... ne Heidelberg
Pfälzer Wald .... s Kaiserslautern
Rheinisches Schiefergebirge ..... e Köln
Rhön .... e Fulda
Reichensteiner Gebirge .... s Breslau
Riesengebirge .... sw Breslau
Rothaargebirge .... e Bonn
Sächsisches Bergland .... s Zwickau
Salzburger Alpen .... s Salzburg
Schwarzwald.................... sw Stuttgart
Schwabische Alb .... s Stuttgart
  (Schwäbischer Jura)
Solling .... nw Göttingen
Spessart .... se Frankfurt
Steigerwald .... w Bamberg
Süntel .... sw Hannover
Tarnowitzer Höhen .... n Gleiwitz
Taunus .... nw Frankfurt
Teutoburger Wald .... w Bielefeld
Thüringer Wald .... sw Erfurt
Turmbert .... sw Danzig
Vogelsberg .... ne Frankfurt
Vogesen (Fr. Vosges) .... w Straßburg
Wesergebirge (Weser- ... sw Hannover
  bergland)
Westerwald .... ne Koblenz
Zobten .... sw Breslau

Source: Rainer Thumshirn, Heimstetten, Germany.

READING GERMAN PLACE NAMES

Spelling Variations in German Names:
Solving Family History Problems Through Applications of German and English Phonetics[1]
by Roger P. Minert, Ph.D., A.G.

This book, new to German family history, fills a crucial gap in the self-help literature.

One of the most common and challenging problems for researchers in German family history is the occurrence of variant spellings. Whether for surnames or place names, one constantly confronts versions of a name in which consonants or vowels or combinations of both have been changed.

A surname or town name can be spelled one way in the hometown German church record and quite another way in the New World. The great majority of such spelling variations are based on natural, logical, and predictable phonetic rules.

This book describes the basic principles of German and English phonetics and illustrates how such rules are reflected in variant German name-spellings on both sides of the Atlantic.

Spelling Variations in German Names is designed for use by researchers at all levels of experience. Novices will not be intimidated nor experts disappointed. No knowledge of the German language is presumed. The book emphasizes the fact that most spelling variations described are natural, logical, and predictable. The phonetic principles discussed are illustrated in examples.

Some already know that the consonants p, t, k alternate respectively with b, d, g, in German, and the vowels i and e with ü and ö respectively, but few know why. Knowing why, when and how such changes take place can enable the researcher to more efficiently guess where to look in indexes, how to recognize variants of the same name, and what parts of Europe might be more likely origins for the mystery ancestor.

This book features hundreds of sample names, many illustrations from genuine vital records, and an every-name index. A trouble-shooting chart with more than 200 names invites the reader to postpone a close reading of the phonetic descriptions in favor of a quick look at specific surname changes or vowel/consonant alteration patterns.
Source: GRT Publications, P.O Box 1845, Provo, UT 84602-1845. Tel. (801) 374-2587; grtpublications@juno.com; www.grt publications.com.

ATLAS FOR GERMANIC GENEALOGY

Ernest Thode, *Atlas for Germanic Genealogy.* **Heritage House, Marietta, Ohio, 1982. 3rd edition 1988.**

This atlas, instead of showing geographic details, provides such information as the geographic areas for particular religions, the geographic reasons that an ancestor may have emigrated from a particular port, the given names and surnames that are peculiar to specific areas, and the geographic regions that may have jurisdiction over records for a given region.

DICTIONARY OF GERMAN NATIONAL BIOGRAPHY

The *Dictionary of German National Biography* is a 10-volume work, edited by Walther Killy and Rudolf Vierhaus, avail-

able in larger libraries.

DER SCHLÜSSEL
(German periodical index)

Der Schlüssel: Gesamtinhaltsverzeichnisse für genealogische, heraldische und historische Zeitschriftenreihen mit Orts-Sach-, und Namenregistern [The Key: comprehensive index of genealogical, heraldic, and historical serials with place, subject, and name indexes], Heinz Reise-Verlag, Göttingen, Deutschland, 9 volumes, 1950ff.

This periodical index is valuable because it is an immense source of information offered through German genealogy and local history publications. Many German genealogists, in order to have their research results published, submit them to these periodicals.

Description
Der Schlüssel is a nine-volume index to more than 90 German, Austrian, and Swiss genealogical and heraldic periodicals from 1870 to 1975 (some date as early as 1860 and as late as 1981).

Indexes include titles (*Titelnachweis*), place names (*Ortsquellenverzeichnis*), subjects (*Sachverzeichnis*), and surnames (*Namenverzeichnis*).

The first three volumes are indexed within each volume; The others are indexed together. The work is written in German.

Format
The Title Index, or *Titelnachweis,* (the main body of each volume) lists authors alphabetically with the titles of their articles. The numbers assigned to each author-title are referred to in the place, subject, and surname indexes.

The Place Name Index, or *Ortsquellenverzeichnis,* lists places, areas, and countries found in the Title Index. The number following each place name is the number of the article in the Title Index.

The List of Subjects, or *Sachverzeichnis,* lists specific topics, such as emigration, census, tax, or occupation records.

The Name Index, or *Namenverzeichnis,* lists surnames found in titles of articles as they appear in the Title Index, but not surnames within particular articles. The number following each name is the article number.

Locating the periodicals

If a periodical being sought is in the collection of the Family History Library and is not under copyright protection, copies of articles may be obtained by using the Library's "Request for Photocopies" form. Write to:

Photoduplication Service
Family History Library
35 North West Temple Street
Salt Lake City, UT 84150

Copies of periodicals may also be requested through interlibrary loan from university and public libraries.

Further information

A thorough set of instructions, from which the above information is taken, is included in "Locating a Surname, Locality or Topic in German Genealogical Periodicals: Der Schlüssel - The Key," by Laraine K. Ferguson, *German Genealogical Digest,* Vol. 9, No. 2, 1993.

Availability

Der Schlüssel is found in the Family History Library and other well stocked genealogical libraries; it is not available on microfilm or fiche. It may be found at the Family History Library as FHL 943 D25sc.

GLENZDORF'S DIRECTORY

GlenzdorfsInternationales Genealogen-Lexikon (Glenzdorf's International Directory of Genealogists) vol. I and II. Wilhelm Rost Verlag, Bad Münder am Deister, (Vol. I) 1977; (Vol. II) 1979; (Vol. III) 1984).

The three volumes of the Glenzdorf directory list alphabetically the German genealogists who submitted their genealogical information to this project.

The submissions include biographical data and an index of surnames which were being researched by these German genealogists, including the submitters' names. There is also an index of the localities from which the surnames came.

Genealogists' names from all three volumes are listed alphabetically in Volume III. FHL 943 D27gi

QUERIES IN THE GERMAN PUBLICATION: FANA

A publication in Germany accepts queries submitted in English, which its staff translates into German. The cost of submitting queries varies according to the length of the query. A $20-$30 fee is common.

Query publisher

Familienkundliche Nachrichten (Genealogical News), commonly referred to as "FaNa," is a query periodical which is enclosed with virtually all regular publications of German genealogical societies. (For details, see below.)

To submit a query to FaNa

The following instructions are reproduced almost verbatim from the informational brochure circulated by FaNa:

Familienkundliche Nachrichten (Family Information News) is published six times a year. Its pages are devoted entirely to queries for missing ancestors. It has a circulation of more than 13,000 and is a very popular way to publicize genealogical questions.

Familienkundliche Nachrichten is

added to almost every important German genealogical paper; it has also reached a wide distribution in the Netherlands and the United States within the past few years. The *Familienkundliche Nachrichten* is sent to more than 100 genealogical societies abroad where they are held at any reader's disposal.

The typical query costs about US $20.00.

The *Familienkundliche Nachrichten* (FaNa) is delivered on the first days of January, March, May, July, September, and November.

The publisher must receive the information at least six weeks prior to the date of publication. The address of the publisher is,

Familienkundliche Nachrichten
Verlag Degener & Co.
P.O. Box 1340
91413 Neustadt /Aisch
Germany

Send a written narrative (in English or German) detailing all that is known about the German background of the ancestor in question, as well as the approximate date when the ancestor departed for America. Verlag Degener will take that information and formulate a precise query in German.

Verlag Degener & Co. will provide the submitter with a free copy of the issue of *Familienkundliche Nachrichten* in which the query appears.

Since this publication is widely distributed and extensively read, the submitter is almost assured of receiving responses. The submitter, upon receiving a response, is asked to send the person a note of thanks along with reimbursement for the postage.

Some organizations bind single issues of *Familienkundliche Nachrichten*, there-by providing these queries with a long-lasting effect.

Here is an example of a query for which $20.00 would be charged:

Behrmann, Emily Dorothe, *Königreich Hannover, 24.3.1850; engewandert in die usa 1856. Eltern: Augustus B. und Wilhelmina Hock. Andere Kinder: Anna, William, Augusta, Ida.*
1441 Lone Oak Rd., Eagan, Minnesota 55121, USA. Gary Maag

English translation: Behrmann, Emily D. Born in the kingdom of Hanover, 24 March 1850. Came to U.S. in 1856. Parents: Aug. B. & Wilhelmina Hock. Other children: Anna, William, August, Ida. Send information to: [name and address of the writer of the query]

To review queries

The Immigrant Genealogy Society (IGS) keeps indexes to all issues of FaNa published since 1964. It prints in the IGS publication *German American Genealogy* the surnames contained in FaNa submissions in six-month segments.

One may request from IGS a copy of a query containing a specific surname. Send $7.00 for each surname requested to Immigrant Genealogy Society, P.O. Box 7369, Burbank, CA 91510-7369. IGS will copy the query, translate it into English, and supply a German-English form letter to use to correspond with the submitter.

For updated fees and contact information (or to print out a ready-made form letter addressed to the Immigrant Genealogy Society), visit their website at www.immigrantgensoc.org.

FAMILIENGESCHICHTLICHE QUELLEN (German periodical index)

Oswald Spohr, *Familiengeschichtliche Quellen: Zeitschrift familiengeschichtlicher Quellennachweise* [Family history sources: periodical of family history source references] 17 vols. Degener Verlag, Neustadt/Aisch, 1926-

Each volume of this index and biblio-

graphical guide to many German genealogical publications begins with a numbered bibliography of genealogy periodicals and books. Following is the index of surnames, each citing a number
listed in the bibliography. Each volume
must be searched separately for the surname being sought. The researcher follows up on a named source by locating
it in order to find the information cited.
Written in German, but not difficult to
use.

The publication was suspended from
1960 to 1983.

Scope
The index contains 2.5 million surname citations from more than 2,300
sources on 6,400 pages. This work indexes the first 92 volumes of *Deutsches
Geschlechterbuch.*

Availability
FHL 943 B2fq. Fiche 6000817; film: vol.
1, 547171 item 3; vols. 2-8, 496680;
vols. 9-11, 496681; vol. 9, 823778 item
3; vols. 12-13, 496682.

DEUTSCHES GESCHLECHTER-
BUCH (German lineage books)

Deutsches Geschlechterbuch **[German
lineage book]. C.A. Starke, Limburg/
Lahn, 1889-2001 (www.starkeverlag.de/
shopfactory/enter.html). Written
entirely in German.**
This series of German lineage books
includes 216 volumes and an index of
445,000 names. The index can be
searched on CD no. 6224 at the Family
History Library. The CDs can be purchased from the publisher at
www.starkeverlag.de.

All volumes are in the German language and the first 119, known as *die
alte Reihe* (the old series), were printed
in Fraktur type. Volumes printed after
1943 were in modern type.

These books provide genealogies of
many royal, noble or other high-class
German families (less than three percent
of the German population). For each family a brief history is given with a discussion of the origin of the name, a coat of
arms if appropriate, places where the family lived, and a complete genealogy.

The work includes lineages from all
parts of Germany, including the former
German territories lost after World War
II. Many of the volumes are dedicated
to specific German states (see the list
below) and others deal with families from
various areas.

For each family is given a brief family history, information about the origin
of the surname, a coat of arms if appropriate, places where the family has lived,
and a complete genealogy.

Indexes
♦Each volume contains a surname index.
In 1969 a cumulative index was published
for the first 150 volumes in *Stammfolgen-
Verzeichnisse für das genealogische
Handbuch des Adels und das deutsche
Geschlechterbuch* [Index of the
genealogical handbook of nobility and
the German lineage books], Limburg/
Lahn: C.A. Starke, 1969; FHL 943 D2dg
index 1969; or fiche 6053506; or film
1183565 item 5. In 1994 an updated index
appeared covering 199 volumes of
Deutsches Geschlechterbuch.
♦The 1963 index covering volumes 1-
134 has been filmed. FHL 943 D2dg index
1963; film 1,183,565 item 5; fiche 6053506.
♦ Volumes 1 through 92 have been
indexed in the *Familiengeschichtliche
Quellen,* by Oswald Spohr.

Availability
There are at least 190 volumes of
Deutsches Geschlechterbuch at the
Family History Library. See FHL 943
D2dg; FHLC computer number 278503.
The first 125 volumes have been micro-
filmed (FHL film 491876-491981), but the

films of volumes published in the last 56 years may not be circulated to Family History Centers because of copyright restrictions. They are available at the Family History Library only.

The volumes

The numbers shown below pertain to specific volumes of *Deutsches Geschlechterbuch* as each relates to the respective area indicated:

Baden: 81,101,120,161,189
Baltic: 79
Berg (Bergische): 24,35,83,168,183
Brandenburg: 111,150,160
Darmstadt: 69,96
German-Swiss: 42,48,56,65,77
Eifel: 99,123
Hamburg: 18,19,21,23,27,44,51,63,127-128,142,171, 200 (due in 1997)
Harz: 106
Hessen: 32, 47, 52, 54, 64, 66, 69, 84, 96, 98, 107, 119, 121, 124, 138, 144, 157, 159, 175, 176
Kurpfalz (Pfalz): 58, 86, 149, 197
Lippe: 72
Magdeburg: 39
Mecklenburg: 57, 74, 88, 105
Nassau: 49
Neumark: 93
Niedersachsen: 46, 76, 89, 102, 113, 122, 129, 131, 141, 143, 151, 158, 166, 167, 180, 187
Obersachsen: 33
Ostfriesland: 26, 31, 59, 103, 134, 190
Ostpreußen: 61, 68, 117
Pommern: 40, 67, 90, 115, 136, 137, 145, 155, 174, 191
Posen: 62, 78, 116, 140
Ravensberg: 82, 194
Reutlingen: 34, 41
Sauerland: 38, 53, 97
Schlesien: 73, 112, 153, 178
Schleswig-Holstein: 91, 162, 186
Schwaben: 34, 41, 42, 55, 71, 75, 110, 146, 170
Siegerland: 95, 139, 163, 164, 198, 199
Swiss (German): 42,48,56,65, 77
Thüringen: 87, 114,

Westfalen: 108, 152, 156, 172, 182, 184, 187, 193
Westpreußen: 126, 132, 133
General: 1-17, 20, 22, 25, 28-30, 36, 37, 45, 50, 60, 70, 80, 85, 92, 100, 104, 109, 118, 125, 130, 135, 147, 148, 154, 165, 169, 172, 177, 185, 188, 192, 195, 196, 201, 203

The first 35 volumes were titled *Genealogisches Handbuch Bürgerlicher Familien* [Genealogical Handbook of Patrician (non-noble, upper-class) Families]. The volumes that followed were titled *Deutsches Geschlechterbuch.*

The indexes to the above volumes

For further information

See "The German Lineage Book," by Horst A. Reschke, *German Genealogical Digest*, Vol. 12, No. 2, Summer, 1996.

THE INDEX TO DEUTSCHES GESCHLECHTERBUCH (Stammfolgen- Verzeichnesse 1994)

Stammfolgen-Verzeichnisse 1994, **C.A. Starke Verlag, Limburg, Germany.**

Before this index of 1994 was published, the index to the *Deutsches Geschlechterbuch* [German lineage books] series, published in 1969, covered the first 150 volumes. This index covers 199 volumes. As of 1997, this index covered all volumes except numbers – 200, 201, and 203.

See the previous item for information about the *Deutsches Geschlechterbuch* series.

FAMILIENGESCHICHTLICHE BIBLIOGRAPHIE: An index to German periodicals

Familiengeschichtliche Bibliographie, by Friedrich Wecken, eds. Johannes Hohlfeld, and Heinz Friedrich Fried-

erichs, Verlag Degener & Co., Neustadt (Aisch), 1920-1945
This work is a bibliography of German family history since 1897. The first seven volumes cover German genealogical literature published between 1897 and 1945. See the explanation of this index available at the European Reference Desk at the Family History Library in Salt Lake City, entitled *Bibliography of Family History.*

See FHL 943 A3fb. Films: vols. 1-2 (1900-1926): 492936; vols 3-4 (1927-1934: 492937; vols 5-6 (1935, 1897-1899, 1936-1937, Index to vol. 1-6: 492938. Fiche 6000820 (vols. 1-7)

DIE AHNENLISTEN-KARTEI (Ancestor List Catalog)

Die Ahnenlistenkartei [Ancestor List Catalog], Verlag Degener, Neustadt/ Aisch, Germany, 1975-, 14 Lieferungen [volumes]
Die Ahnenstammkartei des deutschen Volkes (aka ASTAKA) is a large index of genealogies representing all parts of present-day Germany and former German lands, including an emphasis on eastern areas. Started in 1922, this collection of genealogies housed at the *Deutsche Zentralstelle für Genealogie* in Leipzig remained open to submissions until 1993. It is now estimated to contain nearly 5 million individual names in well over 11,300 pedigree files. Why is this collection important? For those who have tried every other avenue to find the birthplace of their German ancestor, these pedigrees may provide a list of Germanic hometowns associated with your name. The Federation of East European Family History Societies has placed the index to these pedigree collections online.
www.feefhs.org/links/Germany/ ahnstamm.html

If you find your surname in the index, write down the microfilm number to the right. A copy of the original pedigree(s) can be found on this microfilm at the Salt Lake City, LDS Family History Library. When conducting research at the Family History library, patrons can access this same information (FHL 943 A33e 1995; and fiche 6001616 (2 fiche)).

These volumes serve as an index used to access the ancestor lists submitted by many German family history researchers to what is known as the *Ahnenlistenumlauf* (ancestor list exchange).

The *Ahnenlistenkartei* volumes index information submitted by a group of German researchers, such information consisting of the surnames, the locations from which these surnames originate, and the time periods in which the surnames appear. Once one finds a nearly identical match of these factors with those of his or her own ancestors, the microfilms showing these pedigrees may be ordered, to be examined for details. The microfilm numbers are listed in the next section.

The *Ahnenlistenkartei* volumes are generally found in libraries specializing in German genealogical research.

Publication dates of volumes
The *Ahnenlistenkartei* volumes were published in the following years: Vol. 1, 1975; Vol. 2, 1976; Vol. 3, 1977; Vol. 4, 1978; Vol. 5, 1978; Vol. 6, 1979; Vol. 7, 1980; Vol. 8, 1981; Vol. 9, 1981; Vol. 10, 1982; Vol. 11, 1983; Vol. 12, 1985; Vol. 13, 1986; Vol. 14, 1988; Vol. 15, 1996; Vol. 16, 1996; Vol. 17, 1996

For further information
♦ Helen Boyden, "Die Ahnenlisten-Kartei." *The German Connection* (newsletter of the German Research Association), January 1988, p. 8ff.
♦ Laraine K. Ferguson, "Ahnenlisten-umlauf: Circulating German Ancestor

Lists a Rich Source for the Genealogist." *German Genealogical Digest*, Fall 1995.
* Betty Heinz Matyas, "Using the Ahnenlisten-Kartei." *Der Blumenbaum* (journal of the Sacramento German Genealogy Society), Vol. 11, No. 1 (Summer 1993).

THE AHNENLISTENUMLAUF ON MICROFILM

The numbers in the left column below represent the various submitters to the *Ahnenlistenumlauf* (ancestor list exchange) collection, each of whom is assigned a specific "AL" number.

In the right column are the corresponding Family History Library microfilm numbers where the pedigree and surname information donated by the respective submitters may be found. Films should be ordered by the title *Ahnenlistenumlauf.* These films are used in research that results from perusing the *Ahnenlistenkartei.*

AL 1001-1032	FHL 1861935
AL 1032a-1075	FHL 1864551
AL 1076-1128	FHL 1864552
AL 1129-1188	FHL 1864592
AL 1181-1239	FHL 1864593
AL 1240-1284	FHL 1864594
AL 1285-1329	FHL 1864701
AL 1330-1384	FHL 1864702
AL 1385-1440	FHL 1864703
AL 1441-1504	FHL 1864870
AL 1505-1555	FHL 1864871
AL 1556-1726	FHL 1864904
AL 1727-2011	FHL 1864905
AL 2012-2079	FHL 1873641
AL 2080-2157	FHL 1873642
AL 2158-2204	FHL 1873643
AL 2205-2221	FHL 2374314
AL 3001-3043	FHL 2374315
AL 3044-3086	FHL 2374316
AL 3097-3114	FHL 2374317
AL 3115-3124	FHL 2374318

DIE AHNENSTAMMKARTEI DES DEUTSCHEN VOLKES (ASTAKA)

ASTAKA (acronym for *Die Ahnenstammkartei des deutschen Volkes*, or pedigree index of Germans) is an index of the ALU *(Ahnenlistenaustausch,* or ancestor list exchange) with later ancestor lists that were added to it. These data consist of nearly 5 million names from all parts of present-day Germany and the former German lands, with emphasis on eastern areas.

ASTAKA is housed in *Die Deutsche Zentralstelle für Genealogie* (The German Center for Genealogy) in Leipzig.

Those who use the microfilmed ASTAKA would do well to become familiar with the register for these films, which is titled,

An Introduction and Register to Die Ahnenstammkartei des deutschen Volkes of the Deutsche Zentralstelle für Genealogie Leipzig 1922-1991, compiled by Thomas Kent Edlund, The Family History Library, Salt Lake City, 1993. This register is divided into these sections:

* "Part I, Surname Index," which is the pedigree index. The material represented by this index is recorded on 638 rolls of Family History Library microfilm. In this section of the register, microfilm numbers are listed by alphabetical order of surnames. Before a surname is searched in this index, however, its spelling must be converted according to a specific set of rules listed on pages 1 and 2 of the register.

* *"Ahnenlisten"* (ancestor lists): This section of the register indexes more than 12,000 pedigrees, or ancestor lists, by AL (Ancestor List) numbers. Starting on page 66, the section is headed *"Ahnentafeln* (AL) Manuscript Numbers, Part II."

* *Ahnenlisten Nummernkartei* (ancestor-list index): This index (page 64

of the register) gives the name of the submitter by AL numbers. Use this index to find the submitter's name, then go to the *Einsend-erkartei* (see below) to find the submitter's address.

◆*Einsenderkartei* (submitter index): This index indicates on which films the addresses of the submitters may be found (page 64 of the register).

◆ *Nummernkartei* (index of sources): This is an index (page 65 of the register) of the sources of the "literature" notations recorded on the *Ahnenstammkartei* cards in the pedigree index. (The term "literature" in this sense refers to materials other than the submitted pedigree information, such as books, manuscripts, and journal articles pertaining to specific surnames).

◆Three other indexes, all on one roll of microfilm:

– *Berühmtenkartei*, for genealogical material about well known people

– *Ortskarte*i, an index of places, listed alphabetically (these locality listings were made before 1945)

– *Sachkartei*, an index of miscellaneous materials

Die Ahnenstammkartei des deutschen Volkes may be found in FHL 943 A33e 1995; and fiche 6001616 (2 fiche).

VOCABULARY HELP WITH THE AHNENLISTENUMLAUF

These German words, phrases, abbreviations and symbols may be useful for interpreting notations in the *Ahnenlisten-Kartei* and other resources contained in the *Ahnenlistenumlauf:*

Ahnenlisten: list of ancestors

Ahnenlistenkartei: ancestor list catalog

Ahnentafel: pedigree chart

AL-Nr.: number assigned to the submitter of the surname information

ALA: short for *Ahnenlistenaustausch,* or ancestor list exchange (established in 1921)

ALU: *Ahnenlistenumlauf* (ancestor list exchange), the collection of submitted pedigrees available on microfilm at the Family History Library and its centers

Anschriftenänderungen der AL Einsender: address changes of submitters

ASTAKA: acronym for *Ahnenstammkartei des deutschen Volkes*, the indexed 5-million-name collection stored at the Zentralstelle für Genealogie in Leipzig

Einsender: submitter(s)

Land: state or country

Länderschlüssel: state/country key

Name: surname

Orte: (literally, "places") The postal code for the place in which a surname is found

Ortsliste: list of places

Postleitschlüssel: zip code key

Proband: the principal or main person with which the pedigree begins, which is sometimes listed as "*Haupt,*" or "main"

Quellenverzeichnis or *Quellenangaben:* list of sources, like church books, published sources, home sources, refer-ences to other pedigrees.

Siehe Teilliste: See the continuation of the name under the wife's surname

Zeit: the century in which a surname is found (for example, "16" or "18")

MINERVA HANDBÜCHER

Minerva-Handbücher: Archive im deutschsprachingen Raum [Minerva Handbooks: Archives in German-speaking Regions]. Berlin: Walter de Gruyter. 2nd edition 1974. 2 vols.

The *Minerva Handbook* (written in German) serves as a guide to the collections of archives and libraries in Germany (including East and West Germany, at the time it was written), and Austria, Switzerland, Luxembourg, Lichtenstein, Poland, and Czechoslovakia. It identifies every archive of any kind existing when the work was compiled.

(continued)

**Overview of the postal code areas of Germany,
effective July 1, 1993**

Most valuable for family history researchers are the listings in the *Bestände* (holdings) section for each archive entry. Records listed there are not limited to genealogical holdings; for example, listings might be given for glassworkers' archives, university archives, or other specialty areas that could tie into an ancestor's occupation. Also useful are listings for holdings in a given location that record events in an entirely different area. The work is not useful for the archive addresses listed, as many of these have changed.

The volumes are available at the Family History Library and at larger libraries. FHL 943 A5m 1974 Vol.1-2.

BIBLIOGRAPHY OF PRINTED FAMILY HISTORIES

Bibliographie gedruckter Familiengeschichten, 1946-1960 **[Bibliography of printed family histories, 1946-1960], by Franz Heinzmann and Christoph Len-hartz, (Heinzman, Düsseldorf, 1990)**

This bibliography of printed German family histories lists 6,486 family history titles by the main family discussed in each history, and also contains indexes providing access to collateral lines, authors, and localities.

It is found as FHL 943 D23he.

DEUTSCHES BIOGRAPHISCHES ARCHIV (DBA)

Deutsches biographisches Archiv **[The German Biographical Archive.], K.G. Saur, München, 1980-.**

Known as the "DBA," the German Biographical Archive consists of about 225,000 biographical sketches compiled from 264 biographical dictionaries, encyclopedias, almanacs, handbooks and other such collections which were published from the early 18th century through the early 20th century. Many of the subjects represented (writers, theologians, artists, philosophers and others of sufficient reputation to have earned their place in biographical publications) lived much earlier, however.

Format

Biographies are alphabetized by surname and published on 1,431 microfiche. A four-volume index (*Deutscher Biographischer Index*) of the DBA is available but is not necessary in order to access the DBA. The *Quellenverzeichnis* ("List of Sources") is included in each index volume.

The DBA may be used to search for an ancestor who was prominent in his time and place; to determine from what kingdom, principality, duchy or other political locality of the old German Empire persons of a specific surname came; or to find information about a specific profession or occupation by searching for it in the *Quellenverzeichnis.*

Availability

FHL fiche 6002159 (The surname being searched must accompany the request for the fiche, as the fiche copies are filed alphabetically by surname.) The *Quellen-verzeichnis* is found on FHL fiche 6002158 (16 microfiche)

THE GERMAN POSTAL CODE DIRECTORY (in alphabetical order)

Das Postleitzahlenbuch: Alphabetisch geordnet **[The postal code book, in alphabetical order]. (₵ 6,95 at www.deutschepost.de).**

The *Postleitzahlenbuch* is the directory for the postal code system that was revamped (following the 1990 reunification of Germany) in 1993. On July 1 of that year all postal codes in Germany changed from four- to five-digit numbers.

Using the directory

The *Postleitzahlenbuch: Alphabetisch geordnet* is divided into three parts:

Part 1: Index of locations *(Teil 1: Orteverzeichnis)*

Part I provides an every-locality index, listing alphabetically every village, town, and city in Germany, whether it has its own post office code or is combined with the code of a nearby location. Beside each location name is the appropriate postal code — except in cases where the town or city is large enough to be assigned more than one postal code. In such case, the listing directs the user to Part 2 with this phrase: *"s. Teil 2, Straßenverz.,"* "(see Part 2, Street Index)."

Part 2: Street index *(Teil 2: Straßenverzeichnis)*

Part 2 provides sets of street indexes, arranged alphabetically, for all locations in Germany that have more than one postal code number. With each of these multi-code listings is a map showing the geographic borders of each of its postal code numbers. Below each map begins an A-to-Z listing of every street name in the locality, with the postal code given for each street or portion of a street.

Part 3: Index to suburbs *(Teil 3: Ortsteileverzeichnis)*

Part 3 lists in alphabetical order the new postal codes for multi-code localities, showing the suburbs or other subdivisions of each. For example:

51143 Köln
Langel, Porz•, Zündorf

The solid black circle (•), or *Punkt,* shown after the name *Porz* indicates that in this district or subdivision certain streets fall in postal code 51143, but other streets in Porz fall in another postal code

area. In such a case, one must turn to Part 2, the Street Index, to search in the street-name index of Köln for the specific street name in order to learn the proper postal code.

No *Punkt* is shown with the district names of *Langel* and *Zündorf,* above, indicating that all the streets in these districts fall in the 51143 postal code area.

Note: The postal zone borders do not coincide with the borders of the German states *(Länder).* It is possible, however, instantly to determine to which state *(Land)* a particular village, town, or city belongs without consulting a map. See the postal code key to the 16 German states in the section following this one.

Availability

The German postal code book may be found in most libraries with genealogy collections. (FHL 943 E8p 1993; fiche 9,000,033-34). It may be purchased at German post offices; or through Postamt Marburg, Dienststelle 113-21, Postfach 1100, 35035 Marburg, Germany; and through some genealogical publisher outlets in the United States.

POSTAL CODES KEYED TO GERMAN STATES (Länder)

The geographic borders of German postal codes do *not* coincide with borders of German states *(Länder).*

To determine quickly, without consulting a map, in which state *(Land)* a given locality currently lies, simply find that locality's postal code number in the list below.

For information about how to find the postal code for a specific locality, see the previous article.

Postal codes by German state

01001-01936	Sachsen
01941-01998	Brandenburg
02601-02999	Sachsen

03001-03253 .... Brandenburg	26001-27478 .... Niedersachsen
04001-04579 .... Sachsen	27483-27498 .... Schleswig-Holstein
04581-04639 .... Thüringen	27499 .... Hamburg
04641-04889 .... Sachsen	27501-27580 .... Bremen
04891-04907 .... Brandenburg	27607-27809 .... Niedersachsen
04910 .... Sachsen-Anhalt	28001-28779 .... Bremen
04911-04938 .... Brandenburg	28784-29399 .... Niedersachsen
06001-06548 .... Sachsen-Anhalt	29401-29416 .... Sachsen-Anhalt
06551-06578 .... Thüringen	29431-31868 .... Niedersachsen
06601-06928 .... Sachsen-Anhalt	32001-33829 .... Nordrhein-Westfalen
07301-07907 .... Thüringen	34001-34329 .... Hessen
07917 .... Sachsen	34331-34355 .... Niedersachsen
07919-07950 .... Thüringen	34356-34399 .... Hessen
07951 .... Sachsen	34401-34439 .... Nordrhein-Westfalen
07952-07980 .... Thüringen	34441-36399 .... Hessen
07982 .... Sachsen	36401-36469 .... Thüringen
07985-07989 .... Thüringen	37001-37194 .... Niedersachsen
08001-09669 .... Sachsen	37195 .... Hessen
10001-12527 .... Berlin	37197-37199 .... Niedersachsen
12529 .... Brandenburg	37201-37299 .... Hessen
12531-12623 .... Berlin	37301-37359 .... Thüringen
12625 .... Brandenburg	37401-37649 .... Niedersachsen
12627-14199 .... Berlin	37651-37688 .... Nordrhein-Westfalen
14401-16949 .... Brandenburg	37689-37691 .... Niedersachsen
17001-17259 .... Mecklenburg-Vorp.	37692-37696 .... Nordrhein-Westfalen
17261-17290 .... Brandenburg	37697-38479 .... Niedersachsen
17301-17322 .... Mecklenburg-Vorp.	38481-38489 .... Sachsen-Anhalt
17323-17326 .... Brandenburg	38501-38729 .... Niedersachsen
17327-17331 .... Mecklenburg-Vorp.	38801-39649 .... Sachsen-Anhalt
17335-17337 .... Brandenburg	40001-48432 .... Nordrhein-Westfalen
17345-19306 .... Mecklenburg-Vorp.	48442-48465 .... Niedersachsen
19307-19357 .... Brandenburg	48466-48477 .... Nordrhein-Westfalen
19361-19417 .... Mecklenburg-Vorp.	48478-48480 .... Niedersachsen
20001-21037 .... Hamburg	48481-48485 .... Nordrhein-Westfalen
21039 .... Schleswig-Holstein	48486-48488 .... Niedersachsen
21041-21149 .... Hamburg	48489-48496 .... Nordrhein-Westfalen
21202-21218 .... Niedersachsen	48497-48531 .... Niedersachsen
21220 .... Hamburg	48541-48739 .... Nordrhein-Westfalen
21221-21449 .... Niedersachsen	49001-49459 .... Niedersachsen
21451-21521 .... Schleswig-Holstein	49461-49549 .... Nordrhein-Westfalen
21522 .... Niedersachsen	49551-49849 .... Niedersachsen
21524-21529 .... Schleswig-Holstein	50101-51597 .... Nordrhein-Westfalen
21601-21789 .... Niedersachsen	51598 .... Rheinland-Pfalz
22001-22143 .... Hamburg	51601-53359 .... Nordrhein-Westfalen
22145 .... Schleswig-Holstein	53401-53579 .... Rheinland-Pfalz
22147-22769 .... Hamburg	53581-53604 .... Nordrhein-Westfalen
22801-23919 .... Schleswig-Holstein	53614-53619 .... Rheinland-Pfalz
23921-23999 .... Mecklenburg-Vorp.	53621-53949 .... Nordrhein-Westfalen
24001-25999 .... Schleswig-Holstein	54201-55239 .... Rheinland-Pfalz

55240-55252 .... Hessen	88181-89198 .... Baden-Württemberg
55253-56869 .... Rheinland-Pfalz	89201-89449 .... Bayern
57001-57489 .... Nordrhein-Westfalen	89501-89619 .... Baden-Württemberg
57501-57648 .... Rheinland-Pfalz	90001-96489 .... Bayern
58001-59966 .... Nordrhein-Westfalen	96501-96529 .... Thüringen
59969-63699 .... Hessen	97001-97859 .... Bayern
63701-63774 .... Bayern	97861-97877 .... Baden-Württemberg
63776 .... Hessen	97888-97892 .... Bayern
63777-63939 .... Bayern	97893-97900 .... Baden-Württemberg
64201-64753 .... Hessen	97901-97909 .... Bayern
64754 .... Baden-Württemberg	97911-97999 .... Baden-Württemberg
64756-65556 .... Hessen	98501-99998 .... Thüringen
65558-65582 .... Rheinland-Pfalz	
65583-65620 .... Hessen	
65621-65626 .... Rheinland-Pfalz	
65627 .... Hessen	
65629 .... Rheinland-Pfalz	
65701-65936 .... Hessen	
66001-66459 .... Saarland	
66461-66509 .... Rheinland-Pfalz	
66511-66839 .... Saarland	
66841-67829 .... Rheinland-Pfalz	
68001-68309 .... Baden-Württemberg	
68501-68519 .... Hessen	
68520-68549 .... Baden-Württemberg	
68601-68649 .... Hessen	
68701-69234 .... Baden-Württemberg	
69235-69239 .... Hessen	
69240-69429 .... Baden-Württemberg	
69430-69431 .... Hessen	
69434-69469 .... Baden-Württemberg	
69479-69488 .... Hessen	
69489-69502 .... Baden-Württemberg	
69503-69509 .... Hessen	
69510-69514 .... Baden-Württemberg	
69515-69518 .... Hessen	
70001-74592 .... Baden-Württemberg	
74594 .... Bayern	
74595-76709 .... Baden-Württemberg	
76711-76891 .... Rheinland-Pfalz	
77601-79879 .... Baden-Württemberg	
80001-87491 .... Bayern	
87493-87561 .... Bayern	
87567-87569 .... Bayern	
87571-87789 .... Bayern	
88001-88099 .... Baden-Württemberg	
88101-88146 .... Bayern	
88147 .... Baden-Württemberg	
88149-88179 .... Bayern	

THE GERMAN POSTAL CODE DIRECTORY (in numerical order)

Das Postleitzahlenbuch: Numerisch geordnet [postal code book, in numerical order] (a partner publication of *Das Postleitzahlenbuch: Alphabetisch geordnet (postal code book in alphabetical order).*

The German postal code directory *"numerisch geordnet"* (in numerical order) lists all postal codes in Germany in numerical order with the localities each refers to.

(The *alphabetisch geordnet* directory, on the other hand, lists localities alphabetically, with their respective matching postal codes).

Both directories are on sale at German post offices and through Postamt Marburg, Dienststelle 113-21, Postfach 1100, 35035 Marburg, Germany.

Organization

The *numerisch geordnet* directory is divided into four parts:

PART 1:
Comparison of postal codes — new to old
(Teil 1: Gegenüberstellung der Postleitzahlen Neu/Alt)

This major section of the directory (240 pages) lists in numerical order all the "new" (post-1993) postal codes in Germany and their respective localities, starting with 01001 (part of Dresden), and ending with 99998 (Körner). These new codes are matched with the old (pre-1993) codes for the same respective localities. ♦Many of the new codes are marked in the second column with the abbreviation "Pf," for *Postfach*, meaning "post office box."

Under the new postal code system, the business which uses a post office box address has a postal code different from that of the private residence may be situated just next door. Therefore, in almost all cases, a postal code designated with a "Pf" should be ignored (unless one is searching for the postal code of a business). The word "Zustellung" indicates a postal code area where mail is delivered directly to the street address.

♦ Part I is organized in sections 1 to 9, in order of the first digit of each new code. The order goes like this: Leitzone 0 (postal code zone 0, in which all new codes begin with 0), Leitzone 1, Leitzone 2, Leitzone 3, etc. The zones are structured like this: :

Leitzone 0: all in former East Germany
Leitzone 1: all in former East Germany except for former West Berlin codes
Leitzone 2: all in former West Germany
Leitzone 3: codes in both the former East and West Germany
Leitzone 4, 5, 6, 7, 8: all in former West Germany
Leitzone 9: codes in both the former East and West Germany:

♦ This first section of the book is especially helpful for determining the names of localities geographically situated very close to a particular locality.

To look for localities in the vicinity of a town of interest, first note the postal code of the given locality in *Das Postleitzahlen-buch: Alphabetisch geordnet*.

Then find that some code number in the first section of *Das Postleitzahl-enbuch: Numerisch geordnet* to find the names of surrounding localities (that is, localities with code numbers only slightly higher or slightly lower than that of the locality of interest).

PART 2:
Comparison of postal codes — old to new
(Teil 2: Gegenüberstellung der Postleitzahlen Alt/Neu)

This section of the directory (163 pages) lists in numerical order the old postal codes in Germany and their respective localities, matching them with the new codes for the same localities.
♦The beginning pages of Part 2 list in numerical order all the old postal codes of the former *East Germany* (in order of old postal codes with first digits from 0 to 9), giving their respective new codes.
♦The succeeding pages of Part 2 list in numerical order all the old postal codes of the former *West Germany* (in order of old postal codes with first digits from 0 to 9), giving their respective new codes.

PART 3:
Index to districts
(Teil 3: Ortsteileverzeichnis)

This section of the directory lists in numerical order the new postal codes for cities, showing subdivisions or outlying areas of each city.

For example, here is shown one of the postal codes for the city of Leipzig:
04349 Leipzig
Portitz,
Schönefeld-Ost ●,
Thekla

The solid black circle (●), *or Punkt*, shown after the district name Schönefeld-Ost indicates that some of the streets in this district of Leipzig fall in postal code 04349, but other streets of that district fall in other postal code areas.

To determine the postal code for a

particular street in the Schönefel-Ost district of Leipzig, it is necessary to go to the main postal code directory *(Das Postleit-zahlenbuch: Alphabetisch geordnet)* to search in the Leipzig street-name index.

Obviously, because no *Punkt* is shown after Portitz and Thekla, all streets in these districts carry the 04349 postal code.

PART 4:
Index of place-names in bi-lingual areas of Sachsen and Brandenburg
(Teil 4: Verzeichnis der Orte im Zweisprachigen Gebiet von Brandenburg und Sachsen)

This section lists locations, in numerical order by postal codes, which are known by both their Sorbish and their German names. The first column lists the postal code, the second the German name for the locality; the third the matching Sorbish name for the locality. For example:

01920	Johannisbad	Janska kupjel
01920	Lehndorf b Kamenz	Lejno p Kamjenc

Note: The designation *b Kamenz* (short for "bei Kamenz"), above, indicates that Lehndorf is an outlying locality of Kamenz.

ABBREVIATIONS USED IN THE POSTAL CODE DIRECTORIES

In the front of each of the two postal code directories *(Postleitzahlenbücher)* is a page providing a key to abbreviations *(Abkürzungen)*. Some of the most commonly used are,

a d = *an dem/an den/an der/auf der* (on the)
b = *bei/beim* (at, near)
d = *der/dem* (of the)
GE = *Postleitzahlen für Großempfänger* (special codes for recipients of great quantities of mail, such as businesses handling catalog sales)
GrGE = *Postleitzahlen für Gruppen von Großempfängern* (postal code shared by several recipients of large quantities of mail)
i = *im/in* (in)
i d = *in dem/in den/in der* (in the)
Kr = *Kreis* (county)
Pf = *Postfachbezogene Postleitzahlen* (postal code for post office box)
PLZ = *Postleitzahl* (postal code)
str = *-straße* (street)

THE GERMAN RESEARCH OUTLINE

The *Research Outline: Germany,* published by the Family History Library (FHL) of the Church of Jesus Christ of Latter-day Saints in Salt Lake City, Utah, is the best brief guide (60 pages) to German genealogy available in the United States.

This publication provides an overview of the many resources available to the researcher of German family history, complete with book call numbers and microfilm and microfiche numbers.

The publication is particularly valuable to beginning researchers of German family history.

This publication can be printed from the website www.familysearch.org. Go to "Research Helps," select the letter "G." and look for "Germany Research Outline." Click on pdf to view and/or print the desired pages.

THE ANCESTOR PASSPORT (Ahnenpaß)

During the Nazi era, Adolf Hitler's Nationalist Socialist Party required certain citizens, especially members of the Nazi party and government employees, to complete an *Ahnenpaß* (ancestor passport) as a means of proving their "racial purity" (lack of Jewish ancestry).

Applicants for German citizenship also had to show proof that they were not of Jewish descent. The *Ahnenpaß* documented what Hitler called *Der Begriff der arischen Abstammung* (the concept of Aryan descent). It was used to prove "Aryan" origins by means of a multi-generation search into the holder's ancestry.

Those people who were obliged to produce an *Ahnenpaß* conducted thorough investigations of civil and church records for past generations in order to prove their forebears' "purity."

The *Ahnenpaß* consisted of up to 48 pages which included a discussion of Hitler's concept of the "Aryan race," followed by an *Ahnentafel* (ancestor table) which summarized the holder's family for five generations, back to the third-great-grandparents.

Government and military personnel were required to research six generations.

On the typical *Ahnenpaß,* the holder's name is entered in the box at the bottom of the page. Moving upward from that line, one notes the names of the holder's four grandparents (*Großeltern*), then the 8 great-grandparents (*Urgroßeltern*), the 16 great-great grandparents (*Ur-Urgroß-eltern*), and finally the 32 great-great-great grandparents (*Ur-Ur-Urgroßeltern*).

On the other pages, space was provided for writing in the required information about each ancestor, including 1) surname, 2) given name, 3) birth date, 4) birth place, 5) names of parents, 6) religion, 7) death date, 8) death place, 9) occupation, 10) indication of the source of the information, 11) certification of the correctness of the information acquired from civil and church authorities. Each of the direct ancestors was assigned a number, in a manner similar to that of today's pedigree charts.

To the extent they exist at all, these records are held by family members al-most entirely, rather than by archives.
Source: Roger P. Minert, "The Ahnenpaß: An Approach to Family History under National Socialism," *German genealogical Digest,* 13:4 (Winter 1997), 102-113.

VOCABULARY ASSISTANCE FOR THE AHNENPASS

These words and phrases appear frequently in an *Ahnenpaß* document:

Bekenntnis .... religious faith
Beruf .... occupation
Eheschließung .... marriage
erfolgte am .... occurred on (date)
Familienname .... surname
gestorben am .... died on (date)
Mutter/Vater von .... mother/father of
Ort .... place (of residence, birth, death, etc.)
Pfarramt .... parish
Vornamen .... given (first) name

DIE QUELLENSCHAU FÜR FAMILIENFORSCHER (Index to genealogical periodicals and various records)

[A Display of Sources for Family Research]. Köln/a/Rhein: Paul Kuschbert, 1938. vols. 1-3.

Die Quellenschau für Familien-forscher is a three-volume index to periodicals and various records, consisting of two sets, each having two parts. Both sets index localities (*Orts Register*), areas (*Gebiets Register*), subjects *(Sach Register)*, and surnames *(Personen Register)*. Written in German, in Roman type, the work contains thousands of surnames and localities.

Vol. 1: Part 1 of the first set: Contains *Orts* (locality), *Gebiets* (area), *Sach* (subject), and *Personen* (surname) indexes

Vol. 2: Part 2 of the first set: Contains 1,000 indexed sources

Vol. 3: Four indexes plus a different

1,000 sources
   More than half of both sets are indexes to German periodicals.
   Because the indexes tie surnames to localities, the work is useful in identifying places where immigrant ancestors may have lived.

Further information

See *German Genealogical Digest,* 1989 Vol V., No. 4, for detailed instructions on the use of this resource.

Availability

FHL 943 A3kp; film 0924491 items 4-6

VILLAGE LINEAGE BOOKS (Dorfsippenbücher, Ortssippenbücher)

A *Sippenbuch is* a family book or local lineage book, which usually gives considerable information about most of a particular town's residents. These books usually recount the town records from the sixteenth century, forward to the twentieth century. They often contain local history – including such lists as war casualties, mayors, members of specific occupations (e.g., bakers, weavers), and pastors.
   A table of contents appears in the front of these books.
   Compilers of *Ortssippenbücher* and *Ortsfamilienbücher* (family books of a given locality) typically base their information on local church records, tax lists and other pertinent local records. They begin in the 1500s or 1600s.
   Information obtained from *Ortssippen-bücher* needs to be verified.
   Note the listings in the following two sections as well as the reference to Franz Heinzmann's bibliography of German lineage books listed among the references shown there.

THE DORFSIPPENBUCH PROJECT OF 1937

In 1937, the *Arbeitsgemeinschaft für Sippenforschung und Sippenflege* was organized, with plans to index every parish in Germany in order to provide vital information for each individual in the parish and to link each family member and each generation. There were an estimated 52,000 parishes in Germany. By 1938, 30 volumes of *Dorfsippenbücher* (village "clan" books, recording all families) were compiled, but World War II prevented the completion of the task.
   The name *Dorfsippenbücher* was changed in 1950 to *Ortssippenbücher* (village family books), when *Sippenbücher* were compiled for cities as well as villages and communities.
Contents: Each book took a similar form — a table of contents, a brief history and a map, and a surname and locality index. Dates and places of births, marriages, and deaths are listed in the entries, as well as information about citizenship and occupations.
Scope: There are 122 volumes in Series A *Ortssippenbucher* and 33 volumes in Series B, which included *Sippenbücher* from localities that had belonged to the Austrian-Hungarian Empire and that were later in areas that became Czechoslovakia and Yugoslavia. (The difference between Series A and Series B is primarily the size of the book, not in the format or contents.)
Availability: The Family History Center in Salt Lake City has many of the *Ortssippenbücher* volumes resulting from this project. Many are available on micro-film. To find the microfilm number for a location, search the Locality section of the Family History Library Catalog, under the town name, then under "Genealogy."
   Growing numbers of *Ortssippen-bücher* are available at the *Deutsche*

Zentralstelle für Genealogie (German Center for Genealogy) in Leipzig.

Towns and villages represented by the work of the project described above are combined to include all *Dorf-sippenbücher* and the A and B series of *Ortssippen-bücher.*

Key

In the list below, *Sippenbücher* available at the Family History Library in Salt Lake City are marked with an asterisk (*). Those which the Library has filmed, at least in part, are shown in italics.

ANHALT: *Grosswangen, Petersmark*

BADEN: *Altdorf (Ortenaukreis)**, Altenheim**,* Assamstadt, Bauschlott, *Binzen & Ruemmingen, Britzingen, Broggingen, Büsingen, Dundenheim,* Efringen-Kirchen*, Egringen, *Eimeldingen, Eppingen,* Friesenheim*, *Fischingen, Freiamt, Gochsheim, Göbrichen, Grafenhausen, Grenzach,* Haltingen, Heidelbert-Handschuhsheim*, Heidelberg-Wieblingen,   Herbolzheim, *Hüfingen, Huttingen & Istein, Ichenheim, Istein & Huttingen, Kippenheim,* Kippenheim-weiler, *Kleinkems, Ladenburg, Lauf, Löffingen (Bachheim, Neuenburg), Mahlberg-Orschweier, Meissenheim, Mietersheim, Muellen, Münchweier, Nonnenweier, Oberacker,* Obergrom-bach*, *Oberweier, Oetlingen, Otto-schwanden, Philippsburg, Poppenhausen, Rheinhausen,* Ringsheim*, *Rümmingen & Binzen, Rust,* Sandhausen*, *Schmieheim,* Schuttertal, *Schutterzell, Schweigern, Sexau, Tannenkirch,* Tutschfelden*,   *Weingarten,* Wittenweier, *Wittlingen, Wollbach, Zaisenhausen*

BAYERN: Anhausen*, *Aschach,* Ebermergen*, Gabelbach*, Kreuth

BAYERN-PFALZ: Imsweiler, *Maudach, Mehlbach,   Mittel-Hengstbach,* Munden-heim, Oppau-Edigheim*, *Pirmasens, Sambach*

BRANDENBURG: *Freyenstein, Stor-beck*

BRAUNSCHWEIG: Kirchbrake*, *Wedtlenstedt*

HANNOVER: Adensen-Nordstemmen, *Dehmerbrok, Dehrenberg,* Fürstenhagen*, Gustedt*, Gladebeck*, *Hambühr-en,* Hannover-Grarnison*, Hohenbostel*, Krautsand*, Lenthe*, Misselwarden*, *Mulsum, Vechelade, Woquard*

HANNOVER OSTFRIESLAND: Amdorf*, *Aurich-Oldendorf, Backenmoor, Bagstede, Breinermoor, Dehrenbert, Fürstenhagen, Gustedt, Gladebeck, Hannover-Garnison, Hesel,* Holtrop*, Insel Spieckeroog*, *Insel Baltrum, Kirchborgum,   Leerort,   Loga, Logabirum,   Middels,* Neuburg*, *Nortmoor,   Ochtelbur,   Reepsholt, Timmel,* Uphusen*,   *Werdum,* Westerbur*, *Westerende*

HESSEN: Bickenbach*, Grüningen, *Heppenheim, Ingelheim, Vasbeck,* Volkhardingshausen

HESSEN-NASSAU: Ahausen, *Alpenrod, Altweilnau,* Ehringen, *Kassel, Schlotzau, Sontra*

MECKLENBURG: *Boitin,* Grossupahl

OLDENBURG: Neunkirchen/Nahe, Wolfersweiler

RHEINLAND: Freisen, *Fürth, Hangard,* Heide/Unterberggemeinden, Leitersweiler*, Mettlach-Keuchingen*, *Oberkirchen,* Remmesweiler*, St. Sebastian, Stein-Wingert*,   Wenau/Sankt Katharina*, Welschbillig

RIESENGEBIRGE: Rochlitz a.d. Iser*

SACHSEN: *Leutewitz*

SACHSEN (PREUSSEN): *Neuhof*

SCHAUMBURG-LIPPE: Bückeburg*

SCHLESIEN: Klitten*, Königsbruck, Winsdorf*

SCHLESWIG-HOLSTEIN: Reinbeck

THÜRINGEN: *Altenroda, Hausen, Nermsdorf,* Tottleben*, Wiegleben*

WALDECK: Affoldern*, *Berich, Berndorf,* Bringhausen-Edertal*, Bühle*, Buhlen-Edertal*,   Eppe*, *Frebershausen,   Gembeck*,*

Goddelsheim, *Goldhausen*, Helmscheid, Helsen*, *Hillersbausen*, Immighausen*, *Landau*, Lelbach*, Len-gefeld*, *Lütersheim*, Mandern*, *Mehlen*, Meineringhausen*, Mühlhausen*, *Nieder-Ense*, Niederschleidern, *Nordenbeck, Ober-Ense*, Rattlar, *Rhena*, Schmillings-hausen-Arolsen, Schwalefeld, Strothe*, Twiste*, Vasbeck, Wellering-hausen, Wethen*, Wetterburg*
WESTFALEN: Bergkirchen, Hartum
WÜRTTEMBERG: Altensteig*, *Altensteigdorf, Baiersbronn, Berneck, Beuren-Balzholz, Bondorf, Gaildorf, Kloster-reichenbach, Mötzingen, Müster/Unterrot*, Nagold, *Nebringen*, Ober-jettingen*, *Öschelbronn, Tailfingen*, Unterjettingen*, *Walddorf*
CZECHOSLOVAKIA MORAVIA: Briesen*, Pohorsch*
HUNGARY BANAT: Apatin, *Brestowatz,* Filipowa, Gajdobra-Neugajdobra*, Hodschag*, Jahrmarkt, Miletitsch*, *Palanka*, St. Hubert-Schmidt, Stanischitsch, Ischatali, Weprowatz
Source: "Dorfsippenbücher and Ortssippenbücher," by Larry O Jensen, *German Genealogical Digest*, Vol. VII, No. 2, 1991

SOME PUBLISHED ORTSSIPPENBÜCHER

From: **Wolfgang Ribbe and Eckart Henning,** *Familiengeschichtsforschung.* **Verlag Degener & Co., Neustadt an der Aisch, 1995.**
In the book cited above can be found publication data concerning the *Ortssippenbücher* for the villages and towns listed as follows:
Abentheuer, Abthausen, Abtweiler, Achtelsbach, Adensen (Nordstemmen/Niedersachsen), Affoldern (Waldeck), Ahausen, Allertshofen, Alpenrod, Alsenborn, Altdorf, Altenheim, Altenroda, Altensteig, Altensteigdorf,

Altweilnau, Amdorf, Andernach, Anhausen, Anraff, Apatin/Batschka, Amsfeld (Bad Wild-ungen/Waldeck), Arnsfeld, Arolsen, Asbach, Aschach, Assamstadt, Asterode, Atschau-Vértesacsa, Aurich-Oldendorf, Außen (Schmelz)
Bachheim, Backemoor, Bärendorf, Bagband (Große Fehn/Ostfriesland), Bahnbrücken (Kraichtal), Baiersbronn, Baltrum, Balzholz, Bangstede, Bantorf, Barstede/Ostfreisland, Bartschdorf/Schlesien, Bassenheim, Batschsentiwan, Bauschlott (Pforzheim/Baden), Bedekaspel (Südbrookmer/Ostfriesland), Beihingen (Nagold), Bergkirchen, Berglangenbach, Barglas, Berglicht, Berich, Berndorf/Waldeck, Berneck, Berschweiler, Bettingen (Schmelz), Beuren/Balzholz, Beutha, Bickenbach/Bergstraße, Bierbach, Bietzen, Billings, Binzen, Birkenfeld, Bischofsdhron, Bleider-dingen, Blies, Bliesen, Bliesmengen, Blosenberg, Bobenneukirchen, Bösdorf/Elster, Bösingen, Boitin, Bondorf, Bonerath, Borr, Bosen, Brandau (Modautal), Braunsen, Braunshausen, Bredenbeck/Deister, Breinermoor, Breitenkamp, Bremm, Brensbach, Brestowatz/Batschka, Briesen (Schönhengst), Bringhausen, Britzingen, Bröckingen Broggingen, Broich, Brücken, Brünnsee, Bubenheim, Buchhagen, Bückeburg, Bühle, Bürig, Bürstadt (Hessen), Büsingen, Buhlen (Edertal/Waldeck), Buisdorf, Burgholzhausen, Burkersdorf (Kirchberg), Burkhardtsgrün, Burscheid, Buweiler
Caßdorf, Contwig, Contwig, Cunersdorf (Zwickau)
Dambach, Damflos, Dattingen, Dechengrün, Dehmkerbrock, Dehrenbert, Derlin, Diedelsheim (Bretten/Baden), Dillingen, Dilshofen, Dobeneck, Dörnholzhausen/Waldeck, Dorthain, Dudweiler, Düppenweiler, Dürrbach, Dunden-heim
Ebermergen, Ebersberg, Eckersweiler,

Edigheim, Efringen-Kirchen, Egringen, Ehlingen, Ehringen, Eichstock:, Eicks, Eimeldingen, Einig, Eiweiler, Eisen, Eisenach, Ellweiler, Elm, Elmern, Emmersweile, Engelhardtsgrün, Enkenbach-Alsenbom/Pfalz, Ensdorf, Eppe, Eppingen, Erbach, Erfweiler, Ernsthofen, Eschweiler, Eslarn, Ettenheim, Eulenstein, Euren, Evestorf, Eyersheim

Faha, Filipowa/Batschka, Filsch, Finsterntal, Fischingen, Flögeln, Fohren-Linden, Folperviller, Frebershausen, Freiamt, Freisen, Frei-Weinheim, Freyenstein, Friedel, Friedrichsdorf (Hugenotten),Friedrichsdorf (Dillingen), Friesenheim, Friesheim/Pfalz, Fürstenberg (Lichtenfels/Waldeck), Fürstenhagen, Fürth/Bayern, Fürth/Odenwald

Gabelbach, Gäufelden, Gaildorf, Gajdobra/Batschka, Gappenach, Geisfeld, Geislautern, Gembeck, Gemünden/Hunsrück, Gensbach, Georgenhausen, Gering, Gersweiler, Geyer, Gierschnach, Gießen, Gilzum, Gimbweiler, Gladebeck, Gochs-heim, Goddelsheim/Waldeck, Göbrichen, Göswein, Goldbach (Schmelz), Goldhausen, Grabatz/Baden, Grafenhausen, Grafenhausen, Grenzach, Gresaubach, Griesborn, Gronig, Groß-Bieberau, Großrosseln, Groß-Upahl, Großurleben, Großwangen, Großzöbern, Grüningen, Grumbach, Güdesheim, Güttigheim, Gundernhausen, Gustedt, Gusterath, Gutenbrunnen, Guthmannshausen, Gutweiler

Hägerfelde, Hahnweiler, Haiterbach, Gallerburg, Haltingen, Hambühren, Hameln, Hamm, Handschuhsheim, Hangard, Hannover-Schloßkirche, Harlingen, Harrachsdorf, Hartenau, Hartmannsdorf (Kirchberg), Hartum, Haslach (Herrenberg), Hausen, Hausen/Odenwald, Hausen (Günzburg-Krumbach), Haustadt, Heidelberg-Handschuhsheim, Heimbach (Neuwied), Heinersgrün, Heinrichshagen, Held, Helenenberg, Helmscheid, Helsen, Hengstbach, Hentern, Heppenheim,

Herb-itzheim, Herbolzheim, Herchenrode, Hermühlheim, Hesel, Heyda, Hilberts-hausen, Hillershausen, Hinzenburg, Hinzert, Herschfeld, Hitdorf, Hochmark, Hodschag/Batschka, Höringhausen, Hohen-bostel/Deister, Hohendorf, Holtensen (Weetzen), Holtland/Ostfriesland, Hol-trop, Holzerath, Honnef, Honzrath, Hoppstädten, Horbach, Hornbach, Horsten, Hoxhol, Hüfingen, Huttingen

Ichenheim, Igelsbach, Ihrhove, Immighausen/Waldeck, Imsweiler, Imweiler, Ingelheim, Irsch,, Itzbach

Jägersfreude, Jahmen, Jahrmarkt/Banat

Kaan, Kärlich, Kaisen, Kaiserslautern, Kalt, Kappel/Rhein, Karcheez, Karden, Karlsbrunn, Kaschel, Kassel (französische Gemeinde), Kastel, Keldung, Kerben, Kesselheim, Kettig, Keuchingen, Kieselberg, Kimmlingen, Kippenheim, Kippenheimweiler, Kirchberg/Hunsrück, Kirchberg/Sachsen, Rirchborgum, Kirchbrak, Kirdorf, Kirschhausen, Klarenthal-Krughütte, Klein-Bieberau, Kleinkems, Kleinurleben,Klitten, Klosterreichenbach, Klosterreichenbach, Klotten, Knausholz, Kobeln, Koblenz, Köllertal, Kölln, Königsbruch/Schlesien, Köppern, Kolbitzschwalde, Kolling, Kordel, Koslar (Stadt Jülich), Kostenbach, Kozma, Krautsand, Kreuth, Kreuzweiler, Kringelsdorf, Krughütte, Kürrenberg, Küttig

Ladenburg, Lambsheim, Lampaden, Landau/Waldeck, Landsweiler-Reden, Langenbach, Lasserg, Lauf, Lauschbrünn, Lauterbach/Saar, Lebach, Leerort, Leich-lingen, Leitersweiler, Leitzweiler, Lel-bach, Lengefeld, Lenthe, Leutewitz, Lichtenberg, Liebling/Banat, Liederbach/Taunus, Lilienthal, Limberg, Linden, Lippa/Banat, Lisdorf, Loga, Logabirum, Lohne, Longkamp, Losheim, Lovas-bereny, Ludweiler-Warndt, Lübzin, Lütersheim, Lützelbach, Lützelwig, Lut-tringhausen

Machern/Lothringen, Magwitz, Mahlberg-Orschweier, Mandern/ Waldeck, Marbach, Marburg, Marcusgrün, Markersbach, Massenhausen, Maßweiler, Maudach, Maxdorf, Mayen, Meckenbach, Medelsheim, Mehlbach, Mehlen, Meindorf, Meineringhausen, Meißenheim, Menden, Menningen, Menzingen (Kraichtal), Merscheid, Mertloch, Merzenich, Merzkirchen, Messbach, Metternich, Metternich, Mett-lach-Keuchingen, Mettnich, Mettweiler, Middels, Mietersheim, Miletitsch/Batschka, Mimbach, Minheim, Minkelfeld, Mis-selwarden, Mittelbach-Hengstbach, Mittershausen, Mittweida, Modau, Möhn, Mötzingen, Monzelfeld, Morscheid, Mühlfeld, Mühlhausen/Waldeck, Mül-heim/ Kärlich, Mülldorf, Müllen, Münch-weier, Münster (Gaildorf), Münster-maifeld, Münzesheim, Muggardt, Mul-sum (Wesermünde), Mulsum (Stade), Mundenheim

Nagold (Württemberg), Nalbach, Namborn, Naunheim, Nebringen, Nermsdorf, Neuburg, Neudorf (Lippa/Banat), Neuenburg, Neugajdobra/Batschka, Neuhof, Neuhütten, Neukirchen (Boben), Neunkirchen, Neunkirchen (Nahe), Neunkirchen (Modautal), Neuried, Neutsch, Newel, Niederense, Niedergailbach, Niederhofen, Niederhofheim, Nieder-Ingelheim, Niederkainsbach, Niederliederbach, Niederlinxweiler, Nieder-Modau, Niederpleis, Nieder-Schleidern, Nitz, Nonnenweier, Nonnweiler, Nonrod, Nordenbeck, Nortmoor, Nothberg, Nüttermoor/Ostfriesland

Oberacker, Oberense, Obergrombach, Oberjettingen, Oberkirchen/Saar,Ober-Hambach, Ober-Ingelheim, Oberleuken, Oberliederbach, Oberlimberg, Ober-Modau, Oberschar, Oberschmiedeberg, Oberschwandorf/Württemberg, Obersötern, Oberthal, Oberweier (Kreis Lahr, Schwarzwald), Ochtelbur, Ochtendung, Ölsa, Öschelbronn, Öschelbronn, Öt-

lingen, Oftersheim, Oggersheim (Ludwigshafen), Olk, Ollmuth, Opladen, Oppau, Ormsheim, Orschweier, Osenbach, Ottengrün, Ottenhausen, Ottoschwanden

Palanka/Batschka, Pellingen, Peppenkum, Pessingshausen, Petersmark, Pferds-dorf-Spichra, Philippsburg, Pillig, Pirmas-ens, Plaidt, Planschwitz, Pluwig, Po-horsch, Polch, Poppenhausen, Posteholz, Potshausen-Ostrhauderfehn, Prausitz, Primstal

Ramstein, Rath, Rathen, Rattlar/ Waldeck, Reden, Reepsholt, Rehlingen, Reinbek, Reippersberg, Remmesweiler, Reusrath, Rheindorf, Rheingönheim, Rheinhausen, Rhena, Ringsheim, Rinschheim, Riveris, Rochlitz/Iser, Rodau, Rodenbeck, Rodenkirchen (Köln), Rodenstein, Rodheim, Rohrbach, Rosenthal, Rübenach, Rüber, Rückweiler, Rümmingen, Ruitsch, Ruppertsgrün, Rust

Saarbrücken, Saar/Schildgebirge, Sambach, Sandhausen, Sarreguemines, Saupersdorf, Sausenthal, Scheuerberg, Schilliingen, Schlebuschrath, Schlotzau, Schmidt (Nideggen), Schmiedebert, Schmieheim, Schmillinghausen/ Waldeck, Schönberg (Adorf/Vogtland), Schönberg, Schöndorf, Schuttertal (Lahr/Baden), Schutterzell, Schwalbach, Schwalefeld/Waldeck, Schwarzbach, Schwarzenbach/Saar, Schwarzenberg, Schweigern, Seckmauern, Sekitsch/ Lavcenac, Seligenstadt, Sexau, Seyweiler, Simmern, Sindlingen, Sötern, Sonderbach, Sontra/Hessen, Spichra, Spiekeroog, Sprengen, Staffel, Stangengrün, Stanischitsch/Batschka, Stein, Steinau, Stein-Wingert, St. Nikolaus, Storbeck, Straßberg, Strothe, St. Sebastian, Syrau, Szar

Tailfingen, Taltitz, Tannenkirch, Thalexweiler, Thalfang, Thalwinkel, Thierfeld, Thomaswalde, Timmel, Tottleben, Traunen, Treisberg, Trupe-Lilienthal, Tschatali/Batschka, Tschatalmer-Csataljer, Tutschfelden, Twiste/Waldeck

Uchtelfangen, Überberg, Überlingen, Ückesdorf, Unterhambach, Unterjettingen, Unterliederbach, Unterrot (Gaildorf), Unterscheibe, Uphusen, Urleben, Urmitz, Utweil

Vasbeck, Vechelade, Veldenz, Vértesacsa/Otschau, Verteskozma, Vielbrunn, Völklingen, Voitersreuth, Volkhardinghausen, Vorland, Vrsenda

Wadern, Walddorf, Wald-Erlenbach, Waldfischbach, Waldstetten, Walkenried, Wallesweilerhof, Wangen, Webenheim, Webern, Wedtlenstedt, Weiersbach, Weingarten, Weisenheim, Weissenthurm, Weiten, Welferding, Welleringhausen/Waldeck, Welschbillig, Wenau, Weprowatz/Batschka, Werdum, Werschend, Westerbrak, Westerbur, Westerende, Wethen, Wetterburg, Wiblishausen, Wichtringhausen, Wieblingen/Baden, Wiedersberg, Wiegleben, Wierschen, Wiesdorf, Wildbach, Wilhelmsbruch, Wilkau, Winninghausen, Winsdorf/Oberschlesien, Winterbach, Wirschem, Wittenweier, Wittlingen, Wördeholz, Wolfersweiler, Wollbach, Woltersgrün, Woquard, Wolfskaute, Wustweiler

Zaisenhausen, Zeilhard, Zerf, Zittau, Zöbern (Groß-), Zschocken, Züsch, Zweifall

VILLAGE LINEAGE BOOKS AVAILABLE IN LEIPZIG

The following book contains the names of approximately 5000 towns for which village lineage books (*Ortsfamilienbücher*) exist in Leipzig in the German Library (*Deutsche Bücherei,* or "DB") and the German Central Office for Genealogy (*Deutsche Zentralstselle für Genealogie,* or "DZfG"):

Volkmar Weiss und Katja Münch-ow, *Bestandsverzeichnis der Abt. Deutsche Zentralstelle für Genealogie im Sächsischen Staatsarchiv Leipzig: Teil IV, Ortsfamilienbücher mit Standort*

Leipzig in Deutscher Bücherei und Deutscher Zentralstelle für Genealogie," 2nd ed., Verlag Degener & Co., 91403 Neustadt/Aisch, 1998. FHL 943.21/L2 K23w pt. 4 1998. See pages 216-542.

The list includes localities in the German Empire as well as German-language communities in Poland, the Czech Republic, Hungary, the former Yugoslavia, Romania, Italy, Alsace-Lorraine, the Netherlands, and Luxembourg. The key to the regions appears on page 213.

INTERNET INDEXES OF VILLIAGE LINEAGE BOOKS (ORTSIPPENBÜCHER

♦ Village lineage books in the Leipzig collection are indexed online at www.v-weiss.de/publ5.html. Scroll down to "Ortsfamilienbücher in Mitteleuropa."
♦ The *Verein für Computergenealogie* hosts an online index of *Ortsfamilienbücher* in print or on CD: http://wiki-de.genealogy.net/Kategorie: Ortsfamilienbuch.

PURCHASING VILLAGE LINEAGE BOOKS

Family lineage books are traditionally self-published and printed in very small quantities. In many cases, the books are sold out in a matter of months and are generally not reprinted. Fortunately, remaining originals and used books can often be found through the Internet.

An inquiry to the town hall (Stadtverwaltung) will usually find its way into the hands of a staff member who knows whether such a book exists for that town.

An Internet search for these books may be done using the following terms: *Ortfamilienbuch, Ortsippenbuch,*

Dorfsippenbuch.

State and church archives in Germany are popular repositories for family lineage books. Inquiries should be sent to the archives via their websites.

REFERENCES HELPFUL IN THE USE OF ORTSSIPPENBÜCHER

♦ Larry O. Jensen, "Dorfsippenbücher and Ortssippenbücher," *German Genealogical Digest,* Vol. VII, No. 2, 1991.

♦ Heinzmann, Franz. *Bibliographie der Ortssippenbücher in Deutschland* [Biblio-graphy of village lineage books in Germany]. Heinzmann, Düsseldorf:, 1991. Lists 668 village lineage books in alphabetical order by town name. FHL 943 D23h 1991

♦ Ribbe, Wolfgang and Henning, Eckart, *Taschenbuch für Familiengeschichtsforschung*, 13th ed., Verlag Degener & Co., Neustadt an der Aisch. 2006. Almost 1,000 *Ortsfamilienbücher* are listed with the respective locations and time periods, and publication dates.FHL 943 D25

♦ *Die deutsche Zentralstelle für Genealogie* in Leipzig holds about a great number of *Ortssippenbücher*, with more being added every year. See "Family Lineage Books" in the preceding section.

Note: Most *Ortssippenbücher* and *Ortsfamilienbücher* references appear under the topic "Genealogy" in the Family History Library Catalog.

ADRESSBÜCHER (City directories)

Since the 18th century, German directories (*Adreßbücher*) have been published listing adult residents or tradesmen in a locality. Many have been published annually. In large cities, the directory can be useful in determining the ancestor's parish by locating his place of residence in the city.

Some *Adreßbücher* may include, besides residents' names and addresses, occupations, town maps, civil registration offices, and cemeteries.

To learn whether a directory for a particular locality is available through the Family History Library, check the Locality section of the Family History Library Catalog through the name of the German state or the German town.

About 1600 localities in Germany, with the years in which directories have been published for each, are listed on pages 301-328 of this book:

Ribbe, Wolfgang and Eckart Henning, *Taschenbuch für Familiengeschichtsforschung,* 13th ed., Verlag Degener & Co., Neustadt an der Aisch, 2006.

PASSPORTS

In many cases a resident of a German locality had to apply for a passport to emigrate, although laws varied from place to place.

Passport records and indexes, when they exist and have been filmed, are catalogued in the Family History Library Catalog under the topic "Emigration and Immigration" in its Locality section.

THE GERMANIC EMIGRANTS REGISTER

The Germanic Emigrants Register is an ambitious project of six genealogists in Germany by which information has been extracted concerning emigrants who were listed in German newspapers as persons ("deserters") who left their homeland without official permission and before completing their military service. The database consists of more than a half million entries.

The time period of the newspapers covered in the project, when it is complete, will range from 1820 to 1918.

That range of dates can be confusing, however: The *Reichsanzeiger*, a newspaper published by the *Reichsregierung* (Government of the Deutsches Reich) between 1871 and 1918 contained all official government announcements. (The organ fulfilling a similar purpose today is the *Bundesanzeiger*).

The database of the Germanic Emigrants Register is compiled from newspaper notices dated at the time the government discovered a specific person was missing.

This date of the published notice, therefore, could be 40 to 60 years after the emigrant's actual departure.

The Family History Library has the 1991 edition of the Register index on microfiche, containing about 118,000 names. The index shows name, event year, birth date, emigration date, destination, and last known residence. It does not give place of origin, but one may pay a fee to obtain that information. The 1992 edition indexes about 177,000 emigrants' names in the *Deutscher Reichsanzeiger* from 1820 to 1914. Contact: Germanic Emigrants Register, Postfach 1720, 49347 Diepholz, Germany.

Availability

German Emigrants Register (1991), ten microfiche: FHL microfiche 6312192 (10 microfiche, no circulation to family history centers; FHLC Computer Number 445448.

GERMAN TELEPHONE NUMBERS ON THE INTERNET

To find a current German telephone number, go to www.teleauskunft.de. Click on the pink link "Das Telefonbuch" and enter the person's surname and given name in the window "Wer/Was" as well as the town name in the window "Wo."

Click on the pink "Finden" to the right. For information:
Website: <http://www.detemedien-software.de>
E-mail: <bestellung_cd@detemedien.de>
Tel. 01805/99 99 66
Fax 01805/99 99 55
Note: Information about telephone numbers in Germany may also be accessed through TeleAusKunft Online's website, <http://www.teleauskunft.de> or through <http://www.teldir.com>.

GERMAN LOCAL TELEPHONE DIRECTORIES

With use of a German telephone directory listing current telephone users in your ancestral locality, you can search names and street addresses as well as names and addresses of churches, for possible use in correspondence. Surnames appearing in smaller towns and villages surrounding the locality of interest may also be searched. Still another use for the telephone directory is to check for surnames of your ancestor's fellow German immigrant neighbors in the United States, as well as for those of witnesses at special events.

Print copies of German local telephone directories may be ordered from Deutsche Telekom Medien GmbH. For information contact DeTeMedian at:
Website: <http://www.detemedien.de>
E-mail <telefonbuchversand@t-online.de> Fax 0931 / 33 33 19

MEYERS KONVERSATION LEXIKON

The 16-volume encyclopedia, *Meyers Konversation Lexikon: eine Encyklopädia des allgemeinen Wissens* (encyclopedia of general knowledge) can be helpful even to those who don't read German, especially for the purpose of understanding a particular area of the German Empire from which an ancestor emigrated. It has important information about major towns and cities.

The work is on both FHL film and fiche. The fiche copy consists of 251 fiche, starting with FHL 6000815.

Volume 17 is a supplemental volume and index to volumes 1-17. Volumes 18 and 19 are supplements for 1880 and 1892.

CASTLES AND PALACES

Deutsche Burgenvereinigung e.V.
Marksburg
56338 Braubach/Rhein, Germany
The full name of the *Deutsche Burgen-vereinigung e.V. zur Erhaltung der historischen Wehr- und Wohnbauten* (address above), translates as "German castle association for the preservation of the historic defense and residential structures."

With a library of some 20,000 volumes of castle-related titles, *Deutsche Burgenvereinigung* researches the history of castles and palaces. It also advises owners of these structures on how to preserve, utilize and restore their historic sites.

The library staff responds to inquiries, with fees ranging from 50 Pfennige for one page to 25 deutschemarks for extensive projects.

The librarian reports, "As a rule the society does not research genealogical questions."

The society's headquarters is the Marksburg Castle, eight miles south of Koblenz.

The society's membership is open. It publishes a semi-annual journal, *Burgen und Schlösser* (castles and palaces) and other publications.

Source: Horst A. Reschke, "Preserving Castles & Fortresses." *German Genealogical Digest*, Vol. 12, No. 2, Summer, 1996

GERMAN PICTURE DICTIONARIES

It is not unusual for supplemental volumes of multi-volume German encyclopedias to be titled "*Bildwörterbuch*," or "picture dictionary." Sometimes a *Bildwörterbuch* is not part of an encyclopedia at all, but rather a self-contained work.

A *Bildwörterbuch* consists of hundreds of line-drawings portraying the instruments and other accouterments of many trades, occupations, industries, and businesses, with the many details of each picture numbered and keyed to the names of the respective objects.

The key generally provides the name of each object in German, English, and French. Thus, this picture-word book can be instructive to the researcher who finds evidence of an ancestor's occupation, with references to the objects pertaining to that occupation. It is likely that many of the specialized words found in such references will not be found in a regular German-English dictionary.

When the occupation of the ancestor is not known, it can sometimes be determined through a search of references to the tools or other objects mentioned in the ancestor's letters or documents.

For example, the researcher may come across the word *Abschneider* in relation to the ancestor. An *Abschneider* is a cutting tool, but no indication of the occupation with which it might be associated is evident. The German-language section of the *Bildwörterbuch* index reveals that it is an instrument used in a brickworks (*Ziegelei*) and that it is also the name of an instrument used by a watchmaker (*Uhrmacher*), thus providing new clues.

Ancestors who lived in German areas occupied by the French in the early nineteenth century may have left documents written in French. A *Bildwörterbuch* may be helpful in such case as well, as its thousands of references are given in French, as well as in German and English. A separate index is provided for each of the three languages.

The index of the German-language section can be useful for searching for a technical word whose spelling is difficult to determine because of poor handwriting or deteriorating paper. In fact, it may at times be helpful to search only the huge indexes of a *Bildwörterbüch* in order to investigate poorly interpreted spellings of German words found in cer-

tain kinds of documents. All words listed in all three indexes of the *Bildwörterbuch* are nouns.

An example of a useful *Bildwörterbuch* is a supplemental volume to *Meyers Enzyklopädisches Lexikon*. The title of the volume is *Bildwörterbuch: Deutsch-Englisch-Französisch* (Bibliographisches Institut, Lexikon Verlag, Mannheim, 1981).

Source: "A German Dictionary You Can Read: And the Pictures are the Best Part," *Der Blumenbaum,* Vol. 16, No. 2, October, November, December 1998

Section 7: Archives

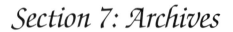

•

Archives in German lands and in the
United States
German archive terminologies
German archives: federal, state, local
Church and university archives
German genealogical societies, historical
societies

•

GERMAN TERMS RELATING TO ARCHIVE CATEGORIES

Bundesland: .... land of the Federal
Republic of Germany
Regierungsbezirk: .... primary
administrative division
of the country; a district
Landkreis: .... administrative division
of a Regierungsbezirk;
similar to a county
kreisfreie Stadt: .... town with the
administrative rank
of a Landkreis
**Hauptstaatsarchiv, Landeshaupt-
archiv**: .... archives corresponding
to the area of a Bundesland
Staatsarchiv, Landesarchiv: ... archives
corresponding to the
area of a Regierungsbezirk
Kreisarchiv: ..... archives corresponding
to the area of a Landkreis
Stadtarchiv: .... town archive
Universitätsarchiv: university archives
Bistum: .... diocese, bishopric
Diözese: .... diocese

Diözesanarchiv: .. archives of a diocese

TERMINOLOGY USED IN GERMAN ARCHIVAL RECORDS

Abbildung: .... image, reproduction
Abkürzung: .... abbreviation
Abschrift: .... transcript
Abteilung: .... subdivision of
an archive group
Abzug: .... print (picture)
Akt: .... act
Akten: .... files
Aktenband: .... file (organized unit of
documents)
Aktenheft: .... file (organized unit of
documents)
Aktenzeichen: .... reference number
amtliches Schriftstück: .. official record
Amtsbuch: .... register
Anlage: .... records/archives kept
in separate place
Annexe: .... records not kept with
principle ones
Arbeitsunterlagen: ..... working papers
Archiv-Karton: .... box

Archivaris: .... archivist
Archivbestand: .... archive group
Archwische Zuständigkeit: .... archival
                                 jurisdiction
Aufzeichnung: .... minutes
Auslaufserie: .... chronological file
Aussenstelle: .... records/archives
                          kept in separate place
Austellung: .... exhibition
Auszug: .... extract
Band: .... volume (of a book)
Beglaubigung: .... certification
Benutzer: .... user (person)
Beständegruppe: .... collective record
                                         group
Beständeübersicht: .... guide to all or
                              part of holdings
Bestandsaufnahme: .... survey
Betreffakte: .... subject file
Bild: .... image, reproduction
Binden: .... binding
Blatt: .... leaf, sheet of paper
Briefwechsel: .... correspondence
Datei: .... file
Dia(positiv): .... slide
Druck: .... print (picture)
Durchschlag: .... carbon copy
Durchschlagserie: ..... chronological file
Eintrag: .... entry
Erwerbung: .... acquisition
Etikett: .... label
Exemplum: .... record copy
gemeinschaftliches Archiv: .... joint
                                       archives
Gesamtbestand: .... holdings
Geschäftsbuch: .... register
Geschlossene Akte: .... closed file
geschlossener Bestand: .... closed record
                                         group
Gruppe: .... class (subdivision of an
                                archive group)
Handschrift: .... manuscript
Hanschriftensammlung: .... manuscript
                                   collection
Heraldik: .... heraldry
Inventar: .... inventory
Kartei: .... card index
Kassette: .... cartridge
Kasten: .... box

Katalog: .... catalogue
Kataster: .... survey, land-register
Kircharchiv(e): .... church archive(s)
Kirchenbücher: .... parish registers
Kirchliches Archivgut: .. church archives
Kohlecopie: .... carbon copy
Kommunalarchive: .... local archives
Lagerkonkordanz: .... location index,
                                         register
Lagerungsübersicht: .... shelf list
Lagerungsübersicht: .... location index,
                                         register
laufende Akten: .... current records
(Land) Karte: .... map
lebende Registratur: ... current records
Luftaufnahme: .... aerial photography
Magazin(e): .... stacks (in storage area)
Mischbestand: .... collection
mündliche Überlieferung: .. oral history
Münzkunde: .... numismatics
Mutterkopie: .... master copy
Namenkunde: .... onomastics
Numismatik: .... numismatics
Öffnungszeiten: .... opening hours
                                Mo, Di, Mi, Do, Fr:
                  Monday, Tuesday, Wednesday,
                            Thursday, Friday
Protokoll: .... minutes, proceedings
Rechnung: .... account
Regal: .... shelf
Registratur: .... registry
Registraturgut: .... records
Reihe: .... row (of shelving)
Reinkonzept: .... minutes
Repertorium: .... inventory
Rückvermerk: ...... endorsement, matter
                  written on back of a document
Sachakte: .... subject file
Sammelbestand: .... collective record,
                                     collection
Sammlung: .... collection
Samtarchiv: .... joint archives
Schenker: .... donor
Schriftgut: .... records
Schriftstück: .... document
Schriftwechsel: .... correspondence
Siegelstempel: .... seal
siehe auch: .... see also
Signatur: .... reference number

Sitzungsbericht: proceedings, minutes
Spule: .... reel
Stammkopie: .... master copy
Standesregister: .... civil registration
stehende Aufbewahrung: .... vertical
filing
Stich: .... print (picture)
Stichwort: .... key word
Stifter: .... donor
Tagebuch: ...... daybook, diary, journal
Teilabschrift: .... extract
Tresor(raum): .... vault
Umschlag: .... envelope
Urheberrecht: .... copyright
Urschrift: .... original document
Verhandlungsbericht: ...... proceedings,
minutes, minute-book
Veröffentlichungen: .... publications
Verordung: ..... ordinance (government
regulation)
Verschlußakte(n): .... closed file(s)
Verschlußsachen: .... closed file
Vertragsurkunde: .... deed
Vertraulichkeit: .... confidentiality
Verwahrung: .... custody
Volkszählungsliste: ...... census return/
schedule
Wappenkunde: .... heraldry
Wirtschaftarchiv(e): business archives
Wirtschaftsarchiv(gut): .... business
archives
Wortgetreue: .... transcript
Zeichen: ..... character (letter, digit, etc.)
Zeitrechnungslehre: .... chronology
Zentralarchiv(e): ...... central archive(s)
Zivilstandsregister: ... civil registration
Zugang: .... acquisition
zurück zu: .... back to
Zusammengefaßter Bestand: collective
record group
Zweigarchiv: .... branch repository

Source: Primarily, *Dictionary of Archival Terminology*, ed. Peter Walne, K.G. Saur, München 1984.

STATE ARCHIVES IN GERMANY (Staatsarchive or landesarchive)

State archives are prime collection points for emigration records, censuses, military, property and duplicate church records.

Names of states in the list of state archives *(Staatsarchive)* below are shown first with their German names, followed by their anglicised names in parentheses.

The word *Außenstelle* indicates a branch archive. The *Hauptstaatsarchiv* is the main archive for the state.

Once the website has been located, researchers will find these terms to be helpful: *Familiengeschichte* (family history), *Familienforschung* (family history research), *Ahnenforschung* (family history research), *Frau Archivarin* (female archivist), *Herr Archivar* (male archivist) and *Bestände* (collection).

Baden-Württemberg
(Baden Wuerttemberg)

Website links (and updated contact information) for the following regional archives in Baden-Württemberg are provided on the state archive's main webpage:

www.landesarchiv-bw.de

Select the city name under the heading "Archivabteilungen" on the menu at the lefthand side of the page.

• Baden-Württembergisches Hauptstaatsarchiv Stuttgart, Konrad-Adenauer-Str. 4, 70173 Stuttgart. hstastuttgart@la-bw.de; www.landesarchiv-bw.de/web/49689

• Staatsarchiv Ludwigsburg, Arsenalplatz 3, 71634 Ludwigsburg. staludwigsburg@la-bw.de; www.-landesarchiv-bw.de/web/47251

—Außenstelle Hohenlohe-Zentralarchiv Neuenstein: Schloß, 74632 Neuenstein (Württemberg). hzaneuenstein @la-bw.de; www.

landesarchiv-bw.de/web/47260
* Generallandesarchiv Karlsruhe, Nördliche Hildapromenade 2, 76133 Karlsruhe. glakarlsruhe@la-bw.de; www.landesarchiv-bw.de/web/47245
* Staatsarchiv Freiburg, Colombistr. 4, 79098 Freiburg i Br., Postfach 323, 79003 Freiburg i. Br.
* Staatsarchiv Sigmaringen, Karlstr. 1+3, 72488 Sigmaringen, Postfach 526, 72482 Sigmaringen
* Staatsarchiv Wertheim, Bronnbach Nr. 19, 97877 Wertheim

Bayern (Bavaria)
Website links (and updated contact information) for the following regional archives in Bayern are provided on the state archive's main webpage:
www.gda.bayern.de/archive/
* Bayerisches Hauptstaatsarchiv, Schönfeldstr. 5, 80539 München
* Staatsarchiv Amberg, Archivstr. 3, 92224 Amberg
* Staatsarchiv Augsburg, Salomon-Idler-Str. 2, 86159 Augsburg
* Staatsarchiv Bamberg, Hainstr. 39, 96047 Bamberg, Postfach 2668, 96017 Bamberg
* Staatsarchiv Coburg, Herrngasse 11, 96450 Coburg
* Staatsarchiv Landshut, Burg Trausnitz, 84036 Landshut
* Staatsarchiv München, Schönfeldstr. 3, 80539 München, Postfach 22 11 52, 80501 München
* Staatsarchiv Nürnberg, Archivstr. 17, 90110 Nürnberg
* Staatsarchiv Würzburg, Residenz-Nordflügel, 97070 Würzburg

Berlin
Updated contact information for the following archives in Berlin is provided on the city's webpage:
www.landesarchiv-berlin.de
* Landesarchiv Berlin, Kalckreuthstr. 1-2, 10777 Berlin (Schöneberg)
— *Außenstelle Breite Straße:* Breite Str. 30-31, 10178 Berlin

Brandenburg

Website links (and updated contact information) for the following regional archives in Brandenburg are provided on the state archive's main webpage:
www.landeshauptarchiv-brandenburg.de
Select "Service" from among the icons on the top of the homepage and choose "Archivportal" from the drop down menu.
* Brandenburgisches Landeshauptarchiv, An der Orangerie 3, 14469 Potsdam, Postfach 60 04 49, 14404 Potsdam
— *Außenstelle Bornim:* Am Windmühlenberg, 14469 Potsdam
— *Außenstelle Cottbus:* Gulbener Str. 24, 03046 Cottbus
— *Außenstelle Frankfurt/Oder:* Große Scharrnstr. 59, 15230 Frankfurt/Oder
— Außenstelle Lübben: Gerichtsstr. 4, 15907 Lübben

Bremen
* Staatsarchiv Bremen, Am Staatsarchiv 1, 28203 Bremen; www.ica.org/en/member/staatsarchiv_bremen

Hamburg
* Staatsarchiv der Freien und Hansestadt Hamburg, ABC-Str. 19 A, 20354 Hamburg; http://134.76.163.162/

Hessen
(Hesse)
Updated contact information for the following archives in Hessen is provided on the city's webpage:
www.hauptstaatsarchiv.hessen.de
* Hessisches Hauptstaatsarchiv, Mosbacher Str. 55, 65187 Wiesbaden
* Hessiches Staatsarchiv Darmstadt, Karolinenplatz 3, 64289 Darmstadt
* Hessisches Staatsarchiv Marburg, Friedrichsplatz 15, Postfach 540, 35037 Marburg

Mecklenburg-Vorpommern
(Mecklenburg-Western Pomerania)
Website links (and updated contact information) for the following regional archives in Mecklenburg-Vorpommern are provided on the state archive's main

webpage:
www.kulturwerte-mv.de
Select "Links" from the menu on the left side of the homepage.
◆ Mecklenburgisches Landeshauptarchiv Schwerin, Graf-Schack-Allee 2, 19053 Schwerin
◆Vorpommersches Landesarchiv Greifswald, Martin-Andersen-Nexö-Platz 1, 17489 Greifswald, Postfach 323, 17463 Greifswald

Niedersachsen
(Lower Saxony)
Updated contact information for the following regional archives in Niedersachsen is provided on the state archive's main webpage:
www.nla.niedersachsen.de
Select "Abteilungen" from the menu along the top of the homepage and choose from the list of regional archives.
◆ Niedersächsisches Hauptstaatsarchiv Hannover, Am Archiv 1, 30169 Hannover
◆ Niedersächsisches Staatsarchiv in Aurich, Oldersumer Str. 50, 26603 Aurich
◆ Niedersächsisches Staatsarchiv in Bückeburg, Schloß, 31675 Bückeburg, Postfach 1350, 31665 Bückeburg
◆ Niedersächsisches Staatsarchiv in Oldenburg, Damm 43, 26135 Oldenburg
◆ Niedersächsisches Staatsarchiv in Osnabrück, Schloßstr. 29, 49074 Osnabrück
◆ Niedersächsisches Staatsarchiv in Stade, Am Sande 4 C, 21682 Stade
◆ Niedersächsisches Staatsarchiv in Wolfenbüttel, Forstweg 2, 38302 Wolfenbüttel

Nordrhein-Westfalen
(North Rhine Westphalia)
Updated contact information for the following regional archives in Nordrhein-Westfalen is provided on the state archive's main webpage:
www.archive.nrw.de/
LandesarchivNRW/
Select "Kontakt" from the menu on the left side of the homepage.
◆ Nordrhein-Westfälisches Haupt-staatsarchiv, Mauerstr. 55, 40476 Düsseldorf
◆Nordrhein-Westsfälisches Staatsarchiv Münster, Bohlweg 2, 48147 Münster
◆Nordrhein-Westfälisches Staatsarchiv Detmold und Nordrhein-Westfälisches Personenstandsarchiv Westfalen-Lippe, Willi-Hofmann-Str. 2, 32756 Detmold
◆ Nordrhein-Westfälisches Personenstandsarchiv Rheinland, Schloß Augustusburg (Eingang Schloßstr. 12), 50321 Brühl

Rheinland-Pfalz
(Rhineland-Palatinate)
Updated contact information for the following regional archives in Rheinland Pfalz is provided on the state archive's main webpage:
www.lha-rlp.de
Select "Kontakt" from the menu on the left side of the homepage.
◆ Landeshauptarchiv Koblenz, Karmeliterstr. 1/3, 56068 Koblenz, Postfach 1340, 56013 Koblenz
◆Landesarchiv Speyer, Otto-Mayer-Str. 9, 67346 Speyer, Postfach 1608, 67326 Speyer

Saarland
◆Landesarchiv Saarbrücken, Scheidter Str. 114, 66123 Saarbrücken, Postfach 102431, 66024 Saarbrücken; www.saarland.de/landesarchiv.htm

Sachsen
(Saxony)
Updated contact information for the following regional archives in Sachsen is provided on the state archive's main webpage:
www.archiv.sachsen.de/4360.htm
◆ Sächsisches Hauptstaatsarchiv, Archiv-str. 14, 10097 Dresden, Postfach 100450, 01074 Dresden
— *Außenstelle Bautzen:* Seidauer Str. 2, 02625 Bautzen
— *Außenstelle Chemnitz*, Schulstsr. 38, 09125 Chemnitz, Postfach 525, 09005 Chemnitz
— *Außenstelle Freiberg:* Kirchgasse 11, 09599 Freiberg

— *Depot Kamenz:* Macherstr. 41, 01917 Kamenz

• Sächsisches Staatsarchiv Leipzig, Reichsgerichtsgebäude, Beethovenstr. 4, 04107 Leipzig, Postfach 100947, 04009 Leipzig

•Deutsche Zentralstelle für Genealogie, Schongauerstr. 1, 04329 Leipzig

Sachsen-Anhalt
(Saxony-Anhalt)

Updated contact information for the following regional archives in Sachsen-Anhalt is provided on the state archive's main webpage:

www.sachsen-anhalt.de/LPSA/
index.php?id=33242

• Landesarchiv Magdeburg-Landeshaupts-archiv, Hegelstr. 25, 39104 Magdeburg, Postfach 4023, 39015 Magdeburg

— *Außenstelle Wernigerode:* Lindenallee 21 (Orangerie), 38855 Wernigerode, Postfach 61, 38842 Wernigerode

— *Außenstelle Möckern:* Schloß, 04159 Möckern

• Landesarchiv Merseburg, König-Heinrich-Str. 83, 06217 Merseburg

•Landesarchiv Oranienbaum, Schloß, 06782 Oranienbaum

Schleswig-Holstein

• Landesarchiv Schleswig-Holstein, Prinzenpalais, 24837; Schleswig; www.schleswig-holstein.de/LA/

Thüringen (Thuringia)

Updated contact information for the following regional archives in Sachsen-Anhalt is provided on the state archive's main webpage:

www.thueringen.de/de/
staatsarchive/

Select the city name from the menu on the lefthand side of the homepage and choose "Kontact" from the drop down menu that appears.

• Thüringisches Hauptstaatsarchiv Weimar, Marstallstr. 2, 99423 Weimar, Postfach 726 99408 Weimar

•Thüringisches Staatsarchiv Altenburg,

Schloß 7. 04600 Altenburg, Postfach 149, 04581 Altenburg

• Thüringisches Staatsarchiv Gotha, Schloß Friedenstein, 99867 Gotha, Postfach 296, 99854 Gotha

• Thüringisches Staatsarchiv Greiz, Oberes Schloß 7, 07973 Greiz

• Thüringisches Staatsarchiv Meiningen, Schloß Bibrabau, 98617 Meiningen, Postfach 272, 98606 Meiningen

• Thüringisches Staatsarchiv Rudolstadt, Schloß Heidecksburg, 07407 Rudolstadt

Sources: Raymond S. Wright III et al, *Ancestors in German Archives: A Guide to Family History Sources,* Baltimore: Genealogical Publishing Co., 2004.
Archive in der Bundesrepublik Deutschland, Österreich und der Schweiz. 15. Ausgabe, Ardey-Verlag Münster, 1995.

COUNTY ARCHIVES (Kreisarchive) IN GERMANY

The German terms *Kreisarchiv* and *Landkreis* both refer to an administrative division of a *"Regierungsbezirk"* - something like a county:

County archives are most often helpful when looking for land and probate records. In Germany, however, there is no consistent guideline as to which records are kept in which type of repository. For example, in one area the property records may be kept in the state archives and in a neighboring area property records may be in the city archives. For researchers who want to know the full extent of record holdings available for a specific German county, it is important to contact that county's archive.

To give the public greater access, many county archives have websites and some even host inventories of their holdings online. Researchers searching the Internet for the address of a county archive will find the ensuing list of archive names and terms helpful:

Kreis Aachen: Kreisarchiv, Kreisverwalt-ung, Bachstr. 39, 52066 Aachen, Postfach 910, 52010 Aachen

Landkreis Ahrweiler: Kreisarchiv, Kreisverwaltung, Wilhelmstr. 24/30, 53474 Bad Neuenahr-Ahrweiler; Postfach 1369, 53458 Bad Neuenahr-Ahrweiler

Alb-Donau-Kreis: Landratsamt Alb-Donau-Kreis, Haupt- und Personalamt, Registratur- und Archivwesen, Schillerstr. 30, 89077 Ulm/Donau

Landkreis Altenburg: Landratsamt [Altenburg], Kreisarchiv, Lindenaustr. 9, 04600 Altenburg (Außenstelle Schmölln, Kreisarchiv, Postfach 141, 04621 Schmölln, Amtsplatz 8, 04626 Schmölln, Dienstsitz: Karl-Marx-Str. 1 b-c, 04621 Schmölln)

Landkreis Altenkirchen: Kreisarchiv, Kreisverwaltung, Parkstr. 1, 57610 Altenkirchen

Landkreis Anklam: See Landkreis Ostvorpommern

Landkreis Annaberg: Kreisarchiv, Paulus-Jenisius-Str. 24, 09456 Annaberg-Buchholz

Landkreis Angermünde: Kreisarchiv. Schwedter Str. 20, 16278 Angermünde

Landkreis Anhalt-Zerbst: Kreisarchiv [Zerbst], Fritz-Brandt-Str. 16, 39261 Zerbst

Landkreis Apolda: See Landkreis Weimar-Land

Landkreis Arnstadt: See Ilm-Kreis

Landkreis Artern: See Kyffhäuser-Kreis

Aschersleben-Straßfurter-Landkreis: Kreisarchiv [Aschersleven], Briete Str. 22, 06449 Aschersleben
−*Außenstelle Staßfurt*, Kreisarchiv, Bernburger Str. 12, 39418 Staßfurt

Landkreis Aue: Landratsamt Aue, Dezernat I, Kreisarchiv/Heimatpflege, Wettiner Str. 64, 08280 Aue; Postfach 10319, 08273 Aue

Landkreis Auerbach: Kreisarchiv [Auerbach], Friedrich-Engels-Str. 22,
08223 Falkenstein

Landkreis Bad Doberan: Kreisarchiv, August-Bebel-Str. 3, 18209 Bad Doberan

Landkreis Bad Freienwalde: Kreisarchiv, Schulstr. 1, 16259 Bad Freienwalde

Landkreis Bad Langensalza: See Unstrut-Hainich-Kreis

Landkreis Bad Salzungen: See Wartburgkreis

Landkreis Barnim: Kries- und Stadtarchiv [Eberswalde], Heegermühler Str. 75, 16225 Eberswalde, Postfach 100448, 16204 Eberswalde
−*Außenstelle Bernau*, Kreisarchiv, Breitscheidstr. 59, 16321 Bernau

Landkreis Bautzen: Kreisarchiv, Bahnhofstr. 9, 02625 Bautzen

Landkreis Beeskow: See Landkreis Oder-Spree

Landkreis Belzig: Kreisarchiv, Niemöller-Str. 1-2, 14806 Belzig

Landkreis Bernau: See Landkreis Barnim

Landkreis Bernburg: Stadt- und Kreisarchiv, Karlsplatz 37, 06406 Bernburg

Landkreis Berkastel-Wittlich: Kriesarchiv, Schloßstr. 10, 54516 Wittlich

Landkreis Biberach an der Riß: Kreiskultur- und Archivamt, Rollinstr. 9, 88400 Biberach an der Riß; Postfach 1662, 88396 Biberach an der Riß

Landkreis Birkenfeld: Kreisarchiv, Kreisverwaltung, Schloßallee 11, 55765 Birkenfeld; Postfach 301240, 55760 Birkenfeld

Landkreis Bischofswerda: Kriesarchiv, Kirchstr. 25, 01877 Bischofswerda

Landkreis Bitterfeld, Kreisarchiv, Glück-Auf-Str. 2, 06749 Bitterfeld

Bodenseekreis: Kreisarchiv, Pestalozzistr. 5, 88677 Markdorf

Landkreis Böblingen, Kriesarchiv, Landratsamt, Parkstr. 16, 71034 Böblingen; Postfach 1640, 71006 Böblingen

Landkreis Bördekreis: Kriesarchiv [Oschersleben], Bahnhofstr. 5, 39387 Oschersleben
− *Außenstelle Wanzleben*, Kreisarchiv,

Ritterstr. 17-19, 39164 Wanzleben
Kreis Borken: Kriesarchiv, Kreisverwalt-ung, Burloer Str. 93, 46325 Borken, Postfach, 46322 Borken
Landkreis Borna: Kreisarchiv, Leipziger Str. 75, 04552 Borna
Landkreis Brand-Erbisdorf, Kreisarchiv, Dr.-W.-Külz-Str. 15, 09618 Brand-Erbisdorf
Landkreis Brandenburg-Land: Kriesarchiv, Bäckerstr. 29, 14770 Brandenburg
Landkreis Breisgau-Hochschwarzwald: Kreisarchiv, Landratsamt, Stadtstr. 2, 79104 Freiburg im Breisgau
Landkreis Bützow: Kreisarchiv, Kreisverwaltung, Schloßplatz 6, 18246 Bützow
Landkreis Burg: See Landkreis Jerichower Land
Burgenlandkreis: Kreisarchiv [Naumburg], Georgenberg 6, 06618 Naumburg (Außenstelle Nebra, Kreisarchiv, 06642 Nebra)
–Außenstelle Zeitz, Zentrales Stadt- und Kreisarchiv, Schloßstr. 6, 39249 Zeitz
Landkreis Calau: Kreisarchiv, J.-Gottschalkstr. 36, 03205 Calau
Landkreis Calw: Kreisarchiv, Vogteistr. 44, 75365 Calw
Landkreis Celle: Kreisarchiv, Kreisverwaltung, Trift 26,Gebäude 6, 29221 Celle
Landkreis Chemnitz: Kreisarchiv, Rußdorfer Str. 1, 09212 Limbach-Oberfrohna
Kreis Coesfeld: Kreisarchiv, Postfach 1543, 48651 Coesfeld
Landkreis Cottbus-Land: Kreisarchiv, Karl-Liebknecht-Str. 30, 03046 Cottbus
Landkreis Cuxhaven: Archiv des Landkreises Cuxhaven, Markstr. 2, 21762 Otterndorf (Niederelbe)
Landkreis Delitzsch: Stadt- und Kreisarchiv, Landratsamt, Markt 10/11, 04509 Delitzsch
Landkreis Demmin: Kreisarchiv, A.-Pompe-Str. 12-15, 17109 Demmin
Landkreis Diepholz: Kreisarchiv, Kreisverwaltung, Postfach, 49356 Diepholz

Landkreis Dippoldiswalde: Kreisarchiv, Dr.-Külz-Str. 1, 01744 Dippoldiswalde
Döbeln: Kreisarchiv, Landratsamt, Dez. III, Straße des Friedens 20, 04720 Döbeln
Landkreis Dresden: Kreisarchiv, Landratsamt, Riesaer Str. 7, 01129 Dresden; Postfach 230100, 01111 Dresden
Kreis Düren: Stadt- und Kreisarchiv, Rathaus, Kaiserplatz, 52349 Düren; Postfach, 52348 Düren
Landkreis Eberswalde: See Landkreis Barnim
Landkreis Eichsfeld: Kreisarchiv [Heiligenstadt], Petristr. 34, 37308 Heilbad Heiligenstadt
–Außenstelle Worbis, Kreisarchiv, Friedensplatz 1, 37339 Worbis
Landkreis Eilenburg: Kreisarchiv, Kranoldstr. 15, 04838 Eilenburg
Landkreis Eisenach: See Wartburgkreis
Landkreis Eisenberg: See Holzlandkreis
Landkreis Eisenhüttenstadt: Kreisarchiv, Glashüttenstr. 6, 15890 Eisenhüttenstadt
Landkreis Eisleben: See Landkreis Mansfelder Land
Landkreis Emmendingen: Kreisarchiv, Bahnhofstr. 2/4, 79312 Emmendingen
Landkreis Emsland: Kreisarchiv, Postfach 1562, 49705 Meppen
Kreis Ennepetal: (placed in Staatsarchiv Münster)
Enzkreis: Kreisarchiv, Landratsamt, Zähringeralle 3, 75177 Pforzheim; Postfach 1080, 75110 Pforzheim
Erftkreis: Kreisarchiv, Willy-Brandt-Platz 1, 50126 Bergheim
Landkreis Erfurt: See Landkreis Sömmerda
Landkreis Esslingen: Kreisarchiv, Landratsamt, Pulverwiesen 11, Postfach 145, 73726 Esslingen am Neckar
Kreis Euskirchen: Kreisarchiv, Kreisverwaltung, Jülicher Ring 32, 53879 Euskirchen; Postfach 1146, 53861 Euskirchen
Landkreis Finsterwalde: Kriesarchiv, Sonnewalder Str. 2-4, 03238 Finsterwalde

Landkreis Flöha (Sachsen): Kreis- und Verwaltungsarchiv, Landratsamt, August-usburger Str. 88, 09557 Flöha

Landkreis Forst: Kreisarchiv, Promenade 26, 03149 Forst

Landkreis Freiberg: Kreisarchiv, Hauptstr. 87, 09633 Krummenhennendorf

Landkreis Freital: Kreisarchiv, Uhlandstr. 13, 01705 Freital

Landkreis Freudenstadt: Kreisarchiv, Landratsamt, Landhausstr. 4, 72250 Freudenstadt; Postfach 620, 72236 Freud-enstadt

Landkreis Fürstenwalde: See Landkreis Oder-Spree

Landkreis Fürth: Landratsamt, Stresemannplatz 11, 90763 Fürth

Landkreis Gadebusch: See Landkreis Nordwestmecklenburg

Landkreis Gardelegen: See Landkreis Westliche Altmark

Landkreis Geithain: Kreisarchiv, Bahnhofstr. 6, 04643 Geithain

Landkreis Genthin: See Landkreis Jerichower Land

Landkreis Gera: See Landkreis Greiz

Landkreis Gießen: Kreisarchiv, Postfach 110760, 35352 Gießen

Landkreis Gifhorn: Kreisarchiv, Schloßstr. 1, 38518 Gifhorn

Landkreis Glauchau: Kreisarchiv, Heinrich-Heine-Str. 7, 08371 Glauchau

Landkreis Göppingen: Kreisarchiv, Schloß Filseck, 73066 Uhingen; Postanschrift: Landratsamt, Postfach 809, 73008 Göppingen

Landkreis Görlitz: Kreisarchiv, Postplatz 18, 02826 Görlitz

Landkreis Göttingen: Kreisarchiv, Reinhäuser Landstr. 4, 37083 Göttingen

Landkreis Gotha: Landratsamt Gotha, Kreisarchiv, Postfach 47, 99867 Gotha, 18.-März-Str. 50, 99867 Gotha (Dienstsitz: Bürgeraue 2, 99867 Gotha)

Landkreis Gräfenhainichen: See Landkreis Wittenberg

Landkreis Greifswald: See Landkreis Ostvorpommern

Landkreis Greiz: Landratsamt [Greiz], Kreisarchiv, Postfach 166, 07962 Greiz; Dienstsitz: Dr.-Rathenau-Platz 11, 07962 Greiz

–Außenstelle Gera; Kreisarchiv, Postfach 68, 07501 Gera; Dienstsitz: Puschkinplatz 3, 07545 Gera.

–Außenstelle Zeulenroda, Verwaltungsarchiv, Postfach 7 und 11, 07931 Zeulenroda; Dienstsitz: Goethestr. 17, 07937 Zeulenroda

Landkreis Grimma: Kreisarchiv, Leipziger Platz 6, 04668 Grimma

Landkreis Grimmen: See Landkreis Nordvorpommern

Landkreis Grevesmühlen: See Landkreis Nordwestmecklenburg

Lankreis Großenhain: Kreisarchiv, Meißner Str. 41a, 01558 Großenhain

Landkreis Guben: Kreisarchiv, Uferstr. 22, 03161 Guben

Landkreis Güstrow: Kreisarchiv [Güstrow], 18273 Güstrow

Kreis Gütersloh: Kreisarchiv, Wasserstr. 14, 33378 Rheda-Wiedenbrück

Kreis Gummersbach: See Oberbergischer Kreis

Landkreis Hagenow: Kreisarchiv, Landratsamt, Hagenstr. 23, 19230 Hagenow

Landkreis Hainichen: Kulturamt, Kreisarchiv Hainichen, Am Landratsamt 3, 09648 Mittweida (The Hainichen district is expected to join with the Rochlitz district)

Landkreis Halberstadt: Kreisarchiv, Friedrich-Ebert-Str. 42, 38820 Halberstadt

Landkreis Haldensleben: See Ohre-Kreis

Landkreis Hameln-Pyrmont: Kreisarchiv, Am Stockhof 2, 31785 Hameln

Landkreis Hannover: Kreisarchiv, Schloßstr. 1, 31535 Neustadt am Rübenberge

Landkreis Harburg: Kreisarchiv, Rote-Kreuz-Str. 6, 21423 Winsen/Luhe

Landkreis Havelberg: See Landkreis Östliche Altmark

Landkreis Heidenheim: Kreisarchiv,

Landratsamt, Felsenstr. 36, 89518 Heidenheim an der Brenz, Postfach 1580, 89505 Heidenheim an der Brenz
Landkreis Heilbronn: Kreisarchiv, Landratsamt, Lerchenstr. 40, 74072 Heilbronn
Landkreis Heiligenstadt: See Landkreis Eichsfeld
Kreis Heinsberg: Kreisarchiv, Valkenburger Str. 45, 52525 Heinsberg
Kreis Herford: Kommunalarchiv, Archiv des Kreises und der Stadt: See Stadtarchiv Herford
Landkreis Herzberg: Kreisarchiv, Ludwig-Jahn-Str. 2, 16835 Herzberg
Landkreis Hettstedt: See Landkreis Mansfelder Land
Landkreis Hildburghausen: Kreisarchiv [Hildburghausen], Friedrich-Rückert-Str. 22, 98646 Hildburghausen
–Außenstelle Suhl, Kreisarchiv, Köhlersgehäu 12, 98544 Zella-Mehlis
Landkreis Hildesheim: Kreisarchiv, Bischof-Janssen-Str. 31, 31134 Hildesheim
Hochsauerlandkreis: Kreisarchiv, Kreisverwaltung, Steinstr. 27, 59870 Meschede
Hochtaunuskreis: Kreisarchiv, Schulstr. 27, 61440 Oberursel
Kreis Höxter: Kreisarchiv, Kreisverwaltung, 37671 Höxter
Hohenlohekreis: Kreisarchiv, Hohenlohe-Zentralarchiv, Schloß, 74632 Neuen-stein
Landkreis Hohenmölsen: See Landkreis Weißenfels
Landkreis Hohenstein-Ernstthal: Kreisarchiv, Am Bach 1, 09353 Oberlungwitz
Holzlandkreis: Landratsamt [Eisenberg], Kreisarchiv, Schloß 1-6, 07607 Eisenberg *–Außenstelle Jena,* Kreisarchiv, Postfach 100337 Jena; Dienstsitz: Ammerbach 108, 07745 Jena; *–Außenstelle Stadtroda,* Kreisarchiv, Schloßstr. 2, 07646 Stadtroda
Landkreis Hoyerswerda: Kreisarchiv, Landratsamt, S.-G.-Frentzel-Str. 1, 02977 Hoyerswerda
Ilm-Kreis: Stadt- und Kreisarchiv [Arnstdt], Ritterstr. 14, 99310 Arnstadt
–Außenstelle Ilmenau, Kreisarchiv, Krankenhausstr. 12, 98693 Ilmenau
Landkreis Ilmenau: See Ilm-Kreis
Landkreis Jena: See Holzlandkreis
Landkreis Jerichower Land: Kreisarchiv [Burg], Magdeburger Str. 44, 39288 Burg
–Außenstelle Genthin
Landkreis Jessen: See Landkreis Witten-berg
Landkreis Jüterbog: Kommunalarchiv Jüterbog, Am Dammtor 16, 14913 Jüterbog
Landkreis Kamenz: Kreisarchiv, Rosa-Luxemburg-Str. 1, 01911 Kamenz
Landkreis Karlsruhe: Kreisarchiv im Generallandesarchiv Karlsruhe, Nördliche Hildapromenade 2, 76133 Karlsruhe
Kreis Kleve: Kreisarchiv, Kapuzinerstr. 34, 47608 Geldern
Landkreis Klingenthal: See Landkreis Auerbach
Landkreis Klötze: See Landkreis Westliche Auerbach
Landkreis Königs Wusterhausen: Kreisarchiv, Thälmannplatz 4, 15771 Königs Wusterhausen
Landkreis Köthen: Kreisarchiv, Springstr. 28, 06366 Köthen
Landkreis Konstanz: Landratsamt Konstanz, Benediktinerplatz 1, 78467 Konstanz, Postfach 101238, 78412 Konstanz; Kreisarchiv. Rathaus, Löwengasse 12, 78315 Radolfzell am Bodensee, Postfach 1480, 78304 Radolfzell am Bodensee
Kyffhäuser-Kreis: Landratsamt [Sondershausen], Kriesarchiv, Postfach 15, 99701 Sondershausen, Markt 8, 99706 Sondershausen, Dienstsitz: Dickkopf *–Außenstelle Artern,* Kreisarchiv, Bergstr. 4, 06556 Artern)
Landkreis Kyritz: Kreisarchiv, Perleberger Str. 2, 16866 Kyritz
Kreis Herzogtum Lauenburg: Archiv

des Kreises, Am Markt 10, 23909 Ratzeburg; Postfach 1140, 23901 Ratzeburg

Landkreis Leipzig: Kreisarchiv, Landratsamt Leipzig, Tröndlinring 3, 04105 Leipzig (The districts of Borna, Geithain and Leipzig-Land are expected to join together.)

Landkreis Lobenstein: See Saale-Orla-Kreis

Landkreis Löbau: Kreisarchiv, Georgewitzerstr. 25, 02708 Löbau

Landkreis Luckau: Kreisarchiv, Karl-Marx-Str. 21, 15926 Luckau

Landkreis Luckenwalde: Kreis-und Verwaltungsarchiv, Grabenstr. 23, 14943 Luckenwalde

Landkreis Ludwigsburg: Kreisarchiv, Landratsamt, Hindenburgstr. 40, 71638 Ludwigsburg; Postfach 760, 71607 Ludwigsburg

Landkreis Ludwigslust: Kreisarchiv, Alexandrienstr. 5/6, 19288 Ludwigslust

Landkreis Lübben: Kreisarchiv, Lohmühlengasse 12, 15907 Lübben

Lankreis Lübz: See Landkreis Parchim

Landkreis Lüchow-Dannenberg: Kreisarchiv, Königsberger Str. 10, 29439 Lüchow

Landkreis Lüneburg: Kreisarchiv, Auf dem Michaeliskloster 4, 21335 Lüneburg

Märkischer Kreis: Kreisarchiv und Landeskundliche Bibliothek des Märkischen Kreises, Bismarckstr. 15, 58762 Altena

Landkreis Märkisch-Oderland: Kreisarchiv, Klosterstr. 14, 15331 Strausberg

Main-Kinzig-Kreis: Kreisarchiv, Barbarossastr. 16-18, 63571 Gelnhausen; Postfach 1465, 63569 Gelnhausen

Main-Tauber-Kreis: See Staatsarchiv Wertheim (Archivverbund Main-Tauber)

Main-Taunus-Kreis: Kreisarchiv, Am Kreishaus 1-5, 65719 Hofheim am Taunus; Postfach 1480, 65704 Hofheim am Taunus

Landkreis Mansfelder Land: Kreisarchiv [Eisleben], Bahnhofstr. 29, 06295 Eisleben (The holdings of Kreis Hettstedt may also be found here.)

Landkreis Marienberg: See Mittlerer Erzgebirgkreis

Landkreis Mecklenburg-Strelitz: Kreisarchiv [Neubrandenburg], Bienenweg 1, 17033 Neubrandenburg
–Außenstelle Neustrelitz, Kreisarchiv, Woldegker Chaussee 35, Haus 4, 17235 Neustrelitz; Postfach 1145, 17221 Neustrelitz)

Landkreis Meiningen: See Schmalkalden-Meiningen

Landkreis Meißen: Kreisarchiv, Loosestr. 17/19, 01662 Meißen

Landkreis Merseburg-Querfurt: Zentralregistratur (Archiv) [Merseburg], Domplatz 9, 06217 Merseburg
–Außenstelle Querfurt, Kreisarchiv, Burgring 31, 06268 Querfurt

Kreis Mettmann: Kreisarchiv, Schloß Linnep, Linneper Weg 17, 40885 Ratingen-Breitscheid; Postfach 105147, 40858 Ratingen

Kreis Minden-Lübbecke, Kommunalarchiv Minden [archive of the city of Minden and Kreis Minden-Lübbecke], Tonhallenstr. 7, 32423 Minden; Postfach 3080, 32387 Minden

Mittlerer Erzgebirgskreis: Kreisarchiv [Marienberg], Bergstr. 07, 09496 Marienberg

Landkreis Mühlhausen: See Unstrut-Hainich-Kreis

Landkreis Müritz: Kreisarchiv, Kietzstr. 10/11, 17192 Waren

Landkreis Nauen: Kreis- und Verwaltungsarchiv, Goethestr. 59/60, 14632 Nauen

Landkreis Naumburg: See Burgenlandkreis

Landkreis Nebra: See Burgenlandkreis

Landkreis Neubrandenburg: See Landkreis Mecklenburg-Strelitz

Landkreis Neuhaus am Rennweg: See Landkreis Sonneberg

Landkreis Neuruppin: Kreisarchiv, Virchowstr. 14/15, 16816 Neuruppin

Kreis Neuss: Kreisarchiv, Burg Friedestrom, Schloßstr. 1, 41541 Dormagen-Zons

Landkreis Neustrelitz: See Landkreis Mecklenburg-Strelitz

Landkreis Nienburg/Weser: Kreisarchiv, Kreishaus am Schloßplatz, 31582 Nienburg/Weser; Postfach 1000, 31580 Nienburg/Weser

Landkreis Niesky: Kreisarchiv, Robert-Koch-Str. 1, 02906 Niesky

Kreis Nordfriesland: Kreisarchiv, Schloß vor Husum, 25813 Husum

Landkreis Nordhausen: Kreisarchiv, Grimmelallee 20, 99734 Nordhausen

Landkreis Nordvorpommern: Kreisarchiv Stralsund, Tribseer Damm 1a, Postfach 1165, 18401 Stralsund

−Außenstelle Grimmen, Kreisarchiv, Bahnhofstr. 12/13, 18507 Grimmen;

−Außenstelle Ribnitz-Damgarten, Kreisarchiv, Damgartner Chaussee 40, 18311 Ribnitz-Damgarten

Landkreis Nordwestmecklenburg: Kreisarchiv Grevesmühlen, Börzower Weg 1, 23936 Grevesmühlen

−Außenstelle Gadebusch, Kreisarchiv, Postfach 1263, 19202 Gadebusch;

−Außenstelle Wismar, Kreisarchiv, Rostocker Str. 76, 23970 Wismar)

Oberbergisher Kreis: Kreisarchiv Moltkestr. 42, 51643 Gummersbach; Postfach 1549, 51605 Gummersbach

Odenwaldkreis: Kreisarchiv, Landratsamt, Michelstädter Str. 12, 64711 Erbach

Landkreis Oder-Spree: Kreisarchiv [Fürstenwalde], Hegelstr. 22, 15517 Fürstenwalde

−Außenstelle Beeskow, Kreisarchiv, Rudolf-Breitscheid-Str. 7, 15841 Beeskow

Landkreis Oelsnitz/Vogtland: Kreisarchiv, Schloßstr 32, 08606 Oelsnitz/Vogtland; Postanschrift: Landratsamt Oelsnitz, SG 11 - Archiv, Stephanstr. 9, 08606 Oelsnitz

Landkreis Östliche Altmark: Kreisarchiv [Stendal], Schönbeckstr. 23, 39576 Stendal

−Außenstelle Havelberg, Kreisarchiv,

Genthiner Str. 17, 39539 Havelberg;

−Außenstelle Osterburg, Kreisarchiv, Ernst-Thälmann-Str. 1, 39606 Osterburg (Altmark)

Ohre-Kreis: Kreis- und Stadtarchiv [Haldensleben], Bülstringer Str. 30, 39340 Haldensleben (Außenstelle Wolmirstedt)

Kreis Olpe: Kreisarchiv, Kurfürst-Heinrich-Str. 34, 57462 Olpe (Biggesee); Postfach 1560, 57445 Olpe (Biggesee)

Landkreis Oranienburg: Kreisarchiv, Poststr. 1, 16515 Oranienburg

Ortenaukreis: Kreisarchiv, Landratsamt, Badstr. 20, 77652 Offenburg; Postfach 1960, 77609 Offenburg

Landkreis Oschatz: Kreisarchiv Oschatz, Friedrich-Naumann-Promenade 9, 04758 Oschatz

Landkreis Oschersleben: See Bördekreis

Ostalbkreis: Kreisarchiv, Landratsamt, Stuttgarter Str. 41, 73430 Aalen; Postfach 1440, 73404 Aalen

Osnabrück: Arbeitskreis für Familienforschung, Kiwittstr. 1 a, 4980 Osnabrück

Landkreis Osterburg: See Landkreis Östliche Altmark

Landkreis Osterholz: Kreisarchiv, Amt 41, Postfach 1262, 27702 Osterholz-Scharmbeck

Landkreis Osterode am Harz: Kreisarchiv, Herzberger Str. 5, 37520 Osterode am Harz

Landkreis Ostvorpommern (Usedom-Peene-Kreis): Kreisarchiv [Anklam], Demminer Str. 71-74, 17389 Anklam

−Außenstelle Wolgast, Kreisarchiv, Burgstr. 7, 17438 Wolgast;

−Außenstelle Greifswald-Land, Kreisarchiv, Martin-Andersen-Nexö-Platz 1, 17489 Greifswald

Kreis Paderborn: Kreisarchiv, Lindenstr. 12, 33142 Büren

Landkreis Parchim: Kreisarchiv, Moltkeplatz 2, 19370 Parchim; Postfach 53 und 54, 19361 Parchim

Landreis Pasewalk: See Landkreis

Uecker-Randow
Landkreis Peine: Kreismuseum und -archiv, Stederdorfer Str. 17, 31224 Peine; Postfach 1360, 31221 Peine
Landkreis Perleberg: Kreisarchiv, Berliner Str. 49, 19348 Perleberg
Kreis Pinneberg: Kreisarchiv, Moltkestr. 10, 25421 Pinneberg; Postfach 1751, 25407 Pinneberg
Landkreis Pirna: Kreisarchiv, Zehistaer Str. 9, 01796 Pirna
Landkreis Plauen: Kreisarchiv, Kreisverwaltung, Neundorfer Str. 96, 08523 Plauen
Kreis Plön: Kreisarchiv, Hamburger Str. 17/18, 24306 Plön
Landkreis Pößneck: See Saale-Orla-Kreis
Landkreis Potsdam: Kreis- und Verwaltungsarchiv Potsdam, Friedrich-Ebert-Str. 79/81, 14469 Potsdam
Landkreis Prenzlau: Kreisarchiv, Leninstr. 21, 17291 Prenzlau
Landkreis Pritzwalk: Kreisarchiv, Meyenburger Tor, 16928 Pritzwalk
Landkreis Quedlinburg: Kreisarchiv, Heilige Geist Str. 7, 06484 Quedlinburg
Landkreis Querfurt: See Landkreis Merseburg-Querfurt
Landkreis Rastatt: Landratsamt Rastatt, Kreisarchiv, Herrenstr. 13, 76437 Rastatt; Postfach 1863, 76408 Rastatt
Landkreis Rathenow: Kreisarchiv, Platz der Freihiet 1, 14712 Rathenow
Landkreis Ravensburg: Landratsamt Ravensburg, Kreisarchiv, Postfach 1940, 88189 Ravensburg; Dienstgebäude: Friedensstr. 6 (= Hauptgebäude)
Kreis Recklinghausen: Kreisarchiv, Kreisverwaltung, Kurt-Schumacher-Allee 1, 45657 Recklinghausen; Postfach 100864 und 100865, 45608 Recklinghausen
Landkreis Reichenbach (Vogtland): Kreisarchiv, Dr.-Külz-Str. 6, 08468 Reichenbach (Vogtland
Rems-Murr-Kreis: Kreisarchiv, Alter Postplatz 10, 71332 Waiblingen
Landkreis Reutlingen: Kreisarchiv,

Bismarckstr. 16, 72764 Reutlingen; Postfach 2143, 72711 Reutlingen
Rheinisch-Bergischer-Kreis: Kreisarchiv, Am Rübezahlwald 7, 51469 Bergisch Gladbach
Rhein-Neckar-Kreis: Kreisarchiv, Trajanstr. 66, 68526 Ladenburg; Postfach 1206, 68521 Ladenburg
Rhein-Sieg-Kreis: Kreisarchiv, Kaiser-Wilhelm-Platz 1, 53721 Siegburg, Postfach 1551, 53705 Siegburg
Landkreis Ribnitz-Damgarten: See Landkreis Nordvorpommern
Landkreis Riesa: Kreisarchiv, Kirchstr. 46, 01591 Riesa-Gröba
Landkreis Rochlitz: Kreisarchiv, Waldstr. 2, 09306 Wechselburg; Post: Landratsamt Rochlitz/Hainichen, DI-Kulturamt, Archivwesen, Am Landratsamt 3, 09648 Mittweida
Landkreis Röbel: Kreisarchiv, Bahnhofstr. 13, 17207 Röbel
Landkreis Roßlau: See Landkreis Anhalt-Zerbst
Landkreis Rostock: Kreisarchiv, Friedrich-Engels-Str. 6-8, 18055 Rostock
Landkreis Rotenburg/Wümme: Kreisarchiv, Bremer Str. 38, 27432 Bremervörde; Postf. 1363, 27423 Bremervörde
Landkreis Rottweil: Kreisarchiv, Landratsamt, Archiv- und Kulturamt, Königstr. 36, 78628 Rottweil
Landkreis Rudolstadt: See Schwarza-Kreis
Landkreis Rügen: Kreisarchiv, Billrothstr. 5, 18528 Bergen
Saale-Orla-Kreis: Kreisarchiv [Schleiz], Oschitzer Str. 4, Postfach, 07907 Schleiz
–Außenstelle Lobenstein, Kreisarchiv, Heinrich-Behr-Str., 07356 Lobenstein;
–Außenstelle Pößneck, Kreisarchiv, Wohlfarthstr. 3-5 07381 Pößneck
Landkreis Saalfeld: See Schwarza-Kreis
Landkreis Saalkreis: Kreisarchiv, Wilhelm-Külz-Str. 10, 06108 Halle/Saale
Stadtverband Saarbrücken: Archiv, Amt 10 (Hauptamt), Schloßplatz 6/7, 66119 Saarbrücken
Landkreis Saarlouis: Kreisarchiv,

Landratsamt, Kaiser-Wilhelm-Str. 6, 66740 Saarlouis; Postfach 1840, 66718 Saarlouis

Landkreis Salzwedel: See Landkreis Westliche Altmark

Landkreis Sangerhausen: Kreisarchiv, Rudolf-Breitscheid-Str. 20-22, 06526 Sangerhausen

Landkreis Schleiz: See Saale-Orla-Kreis

Kreis Schleswig-Flensburg: Kreisarchiv, Suadicanistr. 1, 24837 Schleswig

Landkreis Schmalkalden-Meiningen: Kreisarchiv [Meiningen], Schloß Bibrabau, Schloßplatz 1, 98617 Meiningen

–Außenstelle Schmalkalden, Kreis- und Stadtarchiv, Schloßküchenweg 15, 98574 Schmalkalden

Landkreis Schmölln: See Landkreis Altenburg

Landkreis Schönebeck/Elbe: Kreisarchiv Schönebeck, Cokturhof, 39218 Schönebeck/Elbe

Landkreis Schwäbisch Hall: Kreisarchiv, Landratsamt, Münzstr. 1, 74523 Schwäbisch Hall; Postfach 100440, 74504 Schwäbisch Hall

Schwarza-Kreis: Kreisarchiv [Saalfeld], Schloßstr. 24, 07318 Saalfeld; Postfach 2244, 07308 Saalfeld

–Außenstelle Rudolstadt, Kreisarchiv, Schwarzburger Chaussee 12, 07407 Rudolstdt, Postfach 85, 07392 Rudolstadt

Landkreis Schwarzenberg: Kreisarchiv, August-Bebel-Str. 11, 08340 Beierfeld, Kreisverwaltung, Hofgarten 1, 08340 Schwarzenberg

Schwarzwald-Baar-Kreis: Kreisarchiv, Am Hoptbühl 2, 78048 Villingen-Schwenningen

Landkreis Schwerin: Kreisarchiv, Wismarsche Str. 132, 19053 Schwerin

Landkreis Sebnitz: Kreisarchiv, Promenade 32, 01855 Sebnitz

Landkreis Seelow: Kreisarchiv, Puschkinplatz 12, 15306 Seelow

Landkreis Senftenberg: Kreisarchiv, Dubinaweg 1, 01968 Senftenberg

Landkreis Sigmaringen: Kreisarchiv, Landratsamt, Leopoldstr. 4, 72488 Sigmaringen; Postfach 440, 72482 Sigmaringen

Landkreis Sömmerda: Kreisarchiv [Sömmerda], Kreisverwaltung, Bahnhofstr. 9, 99610 Sömmerda (Außenstelle Erfurt-Land, Kreisarchiv, Postfach 206, 99005 Erfurt; Dienstsitz: Juri-Gagarin-Ring 110, 99084 Erfurt)

Kreis Soest: Kreisarchiv, Villa Plange, Sigefridwall 8, 59494 Soest; Postfach 1752, 59491 Soest

Landkreis Soltau-Fallingbostel: Kreisarchiv, Vogteistr. 19, 29683 Fallingbostel

Landkreis Sondershausen: See Kyffhäuser-Kreis

Landkreis Sonneberg: Kreisarchiv [Sonneberg], Postfach 158, Bahnhofstr. 66, 96515 Sonneberg

–Außenstelle Neuhaus am Rennweg, Kreisarchiv, Sonneberger Str. 1, 98724 Neuhaus am Rennweg

Landkreis Spremberg: Kriesarchiv, Schloßbezirk 3, 03130 Spremberg

Landkreis Stadtroda: See Holzlandkreis

Landkreis Staßfurt: See Aschersleben-Staßfurter-Landkreis

Kreis Steinburg: Gemeinsames Archiv des Kreises Steinburg und der Stadt Itzehoe, Markt 1, 25524 Itzehoe

Kreis Steinfurt: Kreisarchiv, Tecklenburger Str. 8, 48565 Steinfurt; Postfach 1420, 48544 Steinfurt

Landkreis Stendal: See Landkreis Östliche Altmark

Landkreis Sternberg: See Landkreis Parchim

Landkreis Stollberg: Kreisarchiv, Hohndorfer Str., 09366 Oelsnitz/Erzgebirge

Kreis Stormarn: Kreisarchiv, Stormarnhaus, Mommenstr. 11, 23843 Bad Oldesloe

Landkreis Stralsund: See Landkreis Nordvorpommern

Landkreis Strasburg: See Landkreis Uecker-Randow

Landkreis Strausberg: See Landkreis

Märkisch-Oderland
Landkreis Suhl: See Landkreis Hildburg-hausen
Landkreis Templin: Kreisarchiv, Prenzlauer Allee 7, 17268 Templin
Landkreis Teterow: See Landkreis Güstrow
Landkreis Torgau: Kreisarchiv, Schloßstr. 27, 04860 Torgau
Landkreis Traunstein: Kreisarchiv, Landratsamt, Ludwig-Thoma-Str. 2, 83278 Traunstein; Postfach 1509, 83265 Traunstein
Landkreis Tübingen: Kreisarchiv, Doblerstr. 13-21, 72074 Tübingen; Postfach 1929, 72009 Tübingen
Landkreis Tuttlingen: Kreisarchiv, Landratsamt, Bahnhofstr. 100, 78532 Tuttlingen; Postfach 4453, 78509 Tuttlingen
Landkreis Ueckermünde: See Landkreis Uecker-Randow
Landkreis Uecker-Randow: Kreisarchiv [Pasewalk], Am Markt 1, 17309 Pasewalk, Postfach 1242, 17302 Pasewalk
–Außenstelle Strasburg, Kreisarchiv, Markt 22, 17335 Strasburg; Außenstelle Ueckermünde, Kreisarchiv, Ueckerstr. 47, 17373 Ueckermünde
Landkreis Uelzen: Kreisarchiv, Veerßer Str. 53, 29525 Uelzen; Postfach 1761, 29507 Uelzen
Kreis Unna: Kreisarchiv, Kreisverwaltung, Friedrich-Ebert-Str. 17, 59425 Unna, Postfach 2112, 59411 Unna
Unstrut-Hainich-Kreis: Kreisarchiv [Mühlhausen], Bonatstr. 50, 99974 Mühlhausen (Thüringen).
–Außenstelle Bad Langensalza, Kreisarchiv, An der Alten Post 3, 99947 Bad Langensalza; Dienstsitz: Thamsbrücker Str. 20, 99947 Bad Langensalza
Usedom-Peene-Kreis: See Landkreis Ostvorpommern
Landkreis Verden: Kreisarchiv, Bremer Str. 4, 27283 Verden (Aller), Postfach 1509, 27281 Verden
Kreis Viersen: Kreisarchiv, Thomasstr. 20, 47906 Kempen

Landkreis Waldshut: Archiv des Landkreises, Dr.-Rudolf-Eberle-Str. 34, 79774 Albbruck
Landkreis Wanzleben: See Bördekreis
Landkreis Waren: See Landkreis Müritz
Kreis Warendorf: Kreiszentralarchiv, Kreisverwaltung, Waldenburger Str. 2, 48231 Warendorf
Wartburgkreis: Dienstelle Bad Salzungen, Kreisarchiv, Andreasstr. 11, 36433 Bad Salzungen; Dienstsitz: August-Bebel-Str. 2, 36433 Bad Salzungen; Dienstelle Eisenach, Kreisarchiv, Markt 22, 99817 Eisenach
Landkreis Weimar-Land: Kreisarchiv [Apolda], Bahnhofstr. 44, 99510 Apolda; Postfach 134, 99503 Apolda, Dienstsitz: Dorngasse 4, 99510 Apolda.
–Außenstelle Weimar, Kreisarchiv, Schwanseestr. 17, 99423 Weimar
Landkreis Weißenfels: Kreisarchiv [Weißenfels], Am Stadtpark 6, 06667 Weißenfels
–Außenstelle Hohenmölsen, Kreisarchiv, Ernst-Thälmann-Str. 58, 06679 Hohen-mölsen
Landkreis Weißwasser (Oberlausitz): Kreisarchiv, Jahnstr. 53, 02943 Weißwasser (Oberlausitz); Postfach 6, 02931 Weißwasser (Oberlausitz))
Landkreis Werdau: See Landkreis Zwickau
Landkreis Wernigerode: Kreisarchiv, Rudolf-Breitscheid-Str. 10, 38855 Wernigerode
Kreis Wesel: Kreisarchiv, Kreisverwaltung, Reeser Landstr. 31, 46483 Wesel
Landkreis Westliche Altmark: Kreisarchiv [Salzwedel], Karl-Marx-Str. 32, 29410 Salzwedel
–Außenstelle Gardelegen, Kreisarchiv, Philipp-Müller-Str. 13, 39638 Gardelegen; Außenstelle Klötze, Kreisarchiv, Poppauer Str. 42, 38486 Klötze
Landkreis Wismar: See Landkreis Nord-westmecklenburg
Landkreis Wittenberg: Kreisarchiv [Wittenberg], Landratsamt,

Möllensdorfer Str. 13a, 06886 Wittenberg *–Außenstelle Gräfenhainichen,* Kreisarchiv, Karl-Liebknecht-Str. 12, 06773 Gräfenhainichen; Außenstelle Jessen, Robert-Koch-Str. 18, 16917 Jessen
Landkreis Wittstock: Kreisarchiv, Walter-Schulz-Platz, 16909 Wittstock/Dosse
Landkreis Wolgast: See Landkreis Ostvorpommern
Landkreis Wolmirstedt: See Ohre-Kreis
Landkreis Worbis: See Landkreis Eichsfeld
Landkreis Wurzen: Kreisarchiv, Friedrich-Ebert-Str. 2, 04808 Wurzen
Landkreis Zeitz: See Burgenlandkreis
Landkreis Zerbst: See Landkreis Anhalt-Zerbst
Landkreis Zeulenroda: See Landkreis Greiz
Landkreis Zittau: Landratsamt, Kreisarchiv, Hochwaldstr., 02763 Zitta
Zollernalbkreis: Kreisarchiv, Hirschberg-str. 29, 72336 Balingen
Landkreis Zossen: Kreis- und Verwaltungsarchiv Zossen, Jasminweg 18/19, 15834 Rangsdorf
Landkreis Zschopau: Kreisarchiv, August-Bebel-Str. 17, 09405 Zschopau
Landkreis Zwickau: Landratsamt Zwickauer Land, Kreisarchiv, Schulstr. 7, 08412 Werdau, Postfach 4, 08401 Werdau *–Außenstelle,* Reichenbacher Str. 158, 08056 Zwickau
Source: *Archive in der Bundesrepublik Deutschland, Österreich und der Schweiz.* Ardey-Verlag, Münster, 1995.

TOWN/CITY ARCHIVES (STADTARCHIVE) IN GERMANY

The term *Stadtarchiv* refers to a town or city archive.

Because they can be hard to find, city archives are an often untapped source of genealogical records. Their collections frequently include property and citizenship records as well as city histories and local family genealogies. In addition to the fact that they can be hard to locate, some may assume that only localized records are kept in city repositories. In Germany, there is no clear determination as to which records are kept in which type of archives. For example, in one German area probate records may be kept in state archives and in a neighboring area they may be in city archives.

WIth increasing frequency, city archives have developed websites and some have even begun hosting inventories of their holdings online. Researchers searching the Internet for the address of a city or town archive will find the ensuing list of archive names and terms helpful:
Aachen: Stadtarchiv, Fischmarkt 3, 52062 Aachen
Aalen: Stadtarchiv, Marktplatz 30, 73430 Aalen, Postfach 1740, 73407 Aalen
Abenberg: Stadtarchiv, Stillaplatz 1, 91183 Abenberg, Postfach 8, 91181 Abenberg
Abensberg: Stadtarchiv, Rathaus, 93326 Abensberg
Achern: Stadtarchiv, Rathausplatz 1, 77855 Achern
Achim: Stadtarchiv, Rathaus Achim, Am Westerfeld 15, 28832 Achim-Uesen
Ahaus: Stadtarchiv, Rathausplatz 1, 48683 Ahaus, Postfach 1462 48681 Ahaus
Ahlen: Stadtarchiv. See Kreis Warendorf
Aichach: Stadtarchiv, Am Plattenberg 20, 86551 Aichach, Postfach 1110, 86542 Aichach
Aichtal: Stadtarchiv, Waldenbucher Str. 30, 72631 Aichtal
Aindling: Marktarchiv, Waldweg 1°, 86447 Aindling
Aken: Stadtarchiv, Stadtverwaltung, 06385 Aken
Albstadt: Stadtarchiv, Bildungszentrum, Johannesstr. 5, 72458 Albstadt-Ebingen
Aldenhoven: Gemeindearchiv, 52457 Aldenhoven, Postfach 1363, 52447

Aldenhoven
Alfeld: Stadtarchiv, Museum der Stadt Alfeld, Am Kirchhof 4/5, 31061 Alfeld (Leine)
Alfter: Gemeindearchiv, Rathaus, 53347 Alfter
Alsfeld: Stadtarchiv, Beinhaus, Post: Stadtverwaltung, 36304 Alsfeld, Postfach 560, 36295 Alsfeld
Altdorf: Stadtarchiv, Oberer Markt 2, Postfach 24, 90518 Altdorf b. Nürnberg
Altena: Stadtarchiv, Rathaus, Lüdenscheider Str. 22, 58762 Altena
Altenau: See Clausthal-Zellerfeld
Altenbeken: Gemeindearchiv, Gemeindeverwaltung, 33184 Altenbeken
Altenberge: Gemeindearchiv, Kirchstr. 25, 48341 Altenberge
Altenburg: Stadtarchiv, Markt 1, 04600 Altenburg
Altenstadt: Gemeindearchiv, Rathaus, Frankfurter Str. 11, 63674 Altenstadt
Alzenau: Stadtarchiv, Postfach 1280, Hanauer Str. 1, 63755 Alzenau
Alzey: Archiv der Stadt, Ernst-Ludwig-Str. 42, 55232 Alzey
Amberg: Stadtarchiv, Zeughausstr. 1, Postfach 2155, 92224 Amberg (Oberpfalz)
Amerang: Gemeindearchiv, Rathaus, Wasserburger Str. 11, 83123 Amerang
Amorbach: Stadtarchiv, Stadtverwaltung, Kellereigasse 1, Postfach 1280, 63916 Amorbach
Andernach: Stadtmuseum und -archiv, Hochstr. 99, 56626 Andernach
Angermünde: Stadtarchiv, Berliner Str. 42, 16278 Angermünde
Annaberg-Buchholz: Archiv, Postfach 53, 09441 Annaberg-Buchholz
Annweiler am Trifels: Verbandsgemeindearchiv, Rathaus, Meßplatz 1, 76855 Annweiler am Trifels
Anröchte: Gemeindearchiv, Rathaus, Hauptstr. 72-74, 59609 Anröchte
Ansbach: Stadtarchiv, Karlsplatz 7/9, 91522 Ansbach
Arnsberg: Stadt- und Landständearchiv, Rathausplatz 1, 59759 Arnsberg, Postfach 2340, 59713

Arnsberg
Arnstadt: Stadtarchiv. See Ilm-Kreis
Arolsen: Stadtarchiv, Große Allee 26, 34454 Arolsen
Arzberg: Stadtarchiv, Stadtverwaltung, Friedrich-Ebert-Str. 6, 95659 Arzberg (Oberfranken), Postfach 1145, 95653 Arzberg (Oberfranken)
Aschaffenburg: Stadt- und Stiftsarchiv, Schönborner Hof, Wermbachstr. 15, 63739 Aschaffenburg
Ascheberg: Gemeindearchiv, Talstr. 8, 59387 Ascheberg, Postfach 2154, 59380 Ascheberg
Aschersleben: Stadtarchiv, Stadtverwalt-ung, Bahnhofstr. 1, 06449 Aschersleben
Asperg: Stadtarchiv, Schulstr. 12, 71674 Asperg, Postfach 1254, 71674 Asperg
Attendorn: Stadtarchiv, Rathaus, 57439 Attendorn, Postfach 420, 57428 Attendorn
Aub: Stadtarchiv, Rathaus, Marktplatz 1, 97239 Aub
Augsburg: Stadtarchiv, Fuggerstr. 12, 86150 Augsburg
Auma (Thüringen): Stadtverwaltung, Stadtarchiv, Marktberg 9, 07955 Auma (Thüringen)
Babenhausen: Stadtarchiv, Burgmannenhaus, Post: Stadtverwaltung, 64832 Babenhausen (Hessen), Postfach 1109, 64824 Babenhausen (Hessen)
Backnang: Stadtarchiv, Maubacher Str. 60-22, 71522 Backnang, Postfach 1569, 71505 Backnang
Bad Abbach: Stadtarchiv, Markt Bad Abbach, Kaiser-Karl-V.-Allee 12, 93077 Bad Abbach
Bad Bellingen: Stadtarchiv, 79415 Bad Bellingen
Bad Bentheim: Stadtarchiv, Stadtverwaltung, Schloßstr. 2 A, 48455 Bad Bentheim
Bad Bergzabern: Verbandsgemeindearchiv, Schloß, 76887 Bad Bergzabern
Bad Berka: Stadtarchiv, Zeughausplatz 11, 99438 Bad Berka, Post: Stadtverwaltung Bad Berka, Marktplatz 10,

Postfach 20, 99438 Bad Berka
Bad Berleburg: Stadtarchiv, Stadtverwaltung, Poststr. 42, 57319 Bad Berleburg
Bad Bevensen: Archiv der Samtgemeinde Bevensen sowie der Stadt Bad Bevensen, Hauptamt, Rathaus, Lindenstr. 1, 29549 Bad Bevensen
Bad Blankenburg: Stadtverwaltung Bad Blankenburg, Stadtarchiv, Markt 1, 07422 Bad Blankenburg, Dienstsitz: Bürgerhaus, Untere Markststr. 16, 07422 Bad Blankenburg
Bad Buchau: Stadtarchiv, Stadtverwaltung, 88422 Bad Buchau
Bad Camberg: Stadtarchiv, Stadtverwaltung, Am Amthof 15, 65520 Bad Camberg
Bad Driburg: Stadtarchiv, Stadtverwaltung, Rathausstr. 2, 33014 Bad Driburg
Bad Dürkheim: Stadtarchiv, Stadthaus, Mannheimer Str. 24, 67098 Bad Dürkheim
Bad Dürrheim: Stadtarchiv, Postfach 1465, 78068 Bad Dürrheim
Bad Ems: Stadtarchiv, Postfach 1153, Römerstr. 97, 56130 Bad Ems
Baden-Baden: Stadtarchiv, Küferstr. 3, 76530 Baden-Baden, Postfach 621, 76520 Baden-Baden
Bad Friedrichshall: Stadtarchiv, Stadtverwaltung, 74177 Bad Friedrichshall
Bad Hersfeld: Stadtarchiv, Am Treppchen 1, 36251 Bad Hersfeld
Bad Homburg: Stadtarchiv, Gotisches Haus, Tannenwaldweg 102, 61350 Bad Homburg
Bad Honnef: Stadtarchiv, Stadtverwaltung, 53604 Bad Honnef, Postfach 1740, 53587 Bad Honnef
Bad Kissingen: Stadtarchiv, Villa Bringfriede, Promenadestr. 6, 97688 Bad Kissingen
Bad König: Stadtarchiv, Magistrat der Stadt, Schloßplatz 3, 64732 Bad König
Bad Königshofen im Grabfeld: Stadtarchiv, Marktplatz 2, 97631 Bad Königshofen im Grabfeld

Bad Kreuznach: Stadtarchiv, Schloßparkmuseum, Dessauer Str. 49, 55545 Bad Kreuznach, Postfach 563, 55529 Bad Kreuznach
Bad Laasphe: Stadtarchiv, Stadtverwaltung, Mühlenstr. 20, 57334 Bad Laasphe
Bad Langensalza: Stadtverwaltung Bad Langensalza, Stadtarchiv, Markt 1, 99947 Bad Langensalza, Dienstsitz: Kleinspehnstr. 20/21, 99947 Bad Langensalza
Bad Lauterberg im Harz: Stadtarchiv, Rathaus, Ritscherstr. 13, 37431 Bad Lauterberg im Harz, Postfach 340, 37423 Bad Lauterberg im Harz
Bad Liebenwerda: Stadtarchiv Bad Liebenwerda, Markt 1, 04924 Bad Liebenwerda
Bad Lippspringe: Stadtarchiv, Stadtverwaltung, Friedrich-Wilhelm-Weber-Platz 1, 33175 Bad Lippspringe, Postfach 1480, 33169 Bad Lippspringe
Bad Mergentheim: Stadtarchiv, Hans-Heinrich-Ehrler-Platz 35, 97980 Bad Mergentheim
Bad Münder am Deister: Stadtarchiv, Rathaus, 31848 Bad Münder, Postfach 1140, 31841 Bad Münder
Bad Münstereifel: Stadtarchiv, Marktstr. 11, 53902 Bad Münstereifel, Postfach 1240, 53896 Bad Münstereifel
Bad Nauheim: Stadtarchiv, Rathaus, Friedrichstr. 3, 61231 Bad Nauheim, Postfach 1669, 61216 Bad Nauheim
Bad Neuenahr-Ahrweiler: Stadtarchiv, Hauptstr. 116, 53474 Bad Neuenahr-Ahrweiler, Postfach 101051, 53448 Bad Neuenahr-Ahrweiler
Bad Neustadt an der Saale: Stadtarchiv, Alte Pfarrgasse 3, 97616 Bad Neustadt an der Saale, Postfach 1640, 97615 Bad Neustadt an der Saale
Bad Oeynhausen: Stadtarchiv, Bahnhofstr. 43, 32545 Bad Oeynhausen, Postfach, 32543 Bad Oeynhausen
Bad Oldesloe: Stadtarchiv, Rathaus, Markt 5, 23843 Bad Oldesloe
Bad Pyrmont: Stadtarchiv, Bismarckstr. 14, 31812 Bad Pyrmont, Postfach 1630,

31798 Bad Pyrmont

Bad Reichenhall: Stadtarchiv, Stadtverwaltung, Rathausplatz 1 und 8, 83435 Bad Reichenhall, Postfach 1140, 83421 Bad Reichenhall

Bad Sachsa: Stadtarchiv, Bismarckstr. 1, 37441 Bad Sachsa, Postfach 1260, 37438 Bad Sachsa

Bad Säckingen: Stadtarchiv, Bürgermeisteramt, Rathausplatz 1, 79713 Bad Säckingen, Postfach 1143, 79702 Bad Säckingen

Bad Salzdetfurth: Stadtarchiv, Rathaus, Oberstr. 6, 31162 Bad Salzdetfurth

Bad Salzuflen: Stadtarchiv, Martin-Luther-Str. 2, 32105 Bad Salzuflen

Bad Salzungen: Stadtverwaltung Bad Salzungen, Stadtarchiv, Postfach 5, 36421 Bad Salzungen, Dienstsitz: Ratsstr. 2, 36433 Bad Salzungen

Bad Schandau: Stadtarchiv, Ernst-Thälmann-Str. 3, 01814 Bad Schandau

Bad Schussenried: Stadtarchiv, Stadtverwaltung, 88427 Bad Schussenried

Bad Schwalbach: Stadtarchiv, Stadtverwaltung, 65307 Bad Schwalbach

Bad Schwartau: Stadtarchiv, Schillerstr. 8, 23611 Bad Schwartau

Bad Segeberg: Stadtarchiv, Oldesloer Str. 20, 23795 Bad Segeberg

Bad Soden: Stadtarchiv, Magistrat der Stadt, 65812 Bad Soden am Taunus

Bad Sooden-Allendorf: Stadtarchiv, Stadtverwaltung, Rathaus, 37242 Bad Sooden-Allendorf

Bad Tennstedt: Verwaltungsmeinschaft Bad Tennstedt, Stadtarchiv, Markt 1, 99955 Bad Tennstedt

Bad Urach: Stadtarchiv, Elsachstr. 7, Städt, Kurverwaltung, 72574 Bad Urach (Württemberg)

Bad Vilbel: Stadtarchiv, Altes Rathaus, Am Marktplatz 5, 61118 Bad Vilbel

Bad Waldsee: Stadtarchiv, nächst St. Peter, Klosterhof 3, 88339 Bad Waldsee, Postfach 1420, 88331 Bad Waldsee

Bad Wildungen: Stadtarchiv, Stadtverwaltung, 34537 Bad Wildungen,

Postfach 1563, 34525 Bad Wildungen

Bad Wilsnack: Amts- und Stadtarchiv, Am Markt 1, 19334 Bad Wilsnack

Bad Wimpfen: Stadtarchiv, 74206 Bad Wimpfen, Postfach 120, 74200 Bad Wimpfen

Bad Windsheim: Stadtarchiv, Stadtverwaltung, Marktplatz 1, 91438 Bad Windsheim, Postfach 260, 91425 Bad Windsheim

Bad Wörishofen: Stadtarchiv, Rathaus, Bgm.-Ledermann-Str. 1, 86825 Bad Wörishofen, Postfach 1663, 86819 Bad Wörishofen

Baesweiler: Stadtarchiv, Mariastr. 2, 52499 Baesweiler, Postfach 1180, 52490 Baesweiler

Balingen: Stadtarchiv, Postfach 1840, 72336 Balingen

Ballenstedt: Stadtarchiv, Stadtverwaltung, Rathausplatz 12, 06493 Ballenstedt

Bamberg: Stadtarchiv, Untere Sandstr. 30a, 96049 Bamberg

Barnstorf: Samtgemeindearchiv, Am Markt 4, 49406 Barnstorf, Postfach 140, 49406 Barnstorf

Barntrup: Stadtarchiv, Stadtverwaltung, Mittelstr. 38, 32683 Barntrup, Postfach 1320, 32679 Barntrup

Barsinghausen: Stadtarchiv, Rathaus II am Bahnhof, 30890 Barsinghausen

Barth: Stadtarchiv, Teergang 2, 18356 Barth

Bassum: Stadtarchiv, Mittelstr. 4, 27211 Bassum

Baunatal: Stadtarchiv, Marktplatz 14, 34225 Baunatal

Bautzen: Stadtarchiv, Stadtverwaltung, Lessingstr. 7c, 02625 Bautzen, Postfach 1109, 02607 Bautzen

Bayreuth: Stadtarchiv, Maxstr. 64, Postfach 101052, 95410 Bayreuth

Bebra: Stadtarchiv, Hauptamt, Rathausmarkt 1, 36179 Bebra

Beckum: Stadtarchiv . See Kreis Warendorf

Bedburg: Stadtarchiv, Stadtverwaltung, 50181 Bedburg, Postfach 1253, 50173 Bedburg

Beelen: Gemeindearchiv. See Kreis Warendorf
Beerfelden: Stadtarchiv, Metzkeil 1, 64743 Beerfelden
Beeskow: Stadtarchiv, Liebknechstr. 13/14, 15848 Beeskow
Belgern: Stadtarchiv, Markt 3, 04874 Belgern
Bensheim: Archiv der Stadt Bensheim, An der Stadtmühle 3, 64625 Bensheim
Berchtesgaden: Archiv des Marktes, Rathausplatz 1, 83471 Berchtesgaden
Bergen: Stadtarchiv, Am Museum 2, 29303 Bergen, Postfach 1199, 29296 Bergen
Bergisch Gladbach: Stadtarchiv, Hauptstr. 310, 51465 Bergisch Gladbach, Postfach 200920, 51439 Bergisch Gladbach
Bergkamen: Stadtarchiv, Rathaus, 59192 Bergkamen
Bergneustadt: Stadtarchiv, Othestr. 2-4, 51702 Bergneustadt
Bernau: Stadtarchiv, Bürgermeisterstr. 1, 16321 Bernau
Bernburg: Stadtarchiv. See Landkreis Bernburg
Bersenbrück: Archiv der Samtgemeinde, Rathaus, Lindenstr. 2, 49593 Bersenbrück
Besigheim: Stadtarchiv, Marktplatz 12, 74354 Besigheim
Biberach: Stadtarchiv Biberach. See Landkreis Biberach
Biblis: Gemeindearchiv, Rathaus, Darmstädter Str. 25, 68647
Biebesheim: Gemeindearchiv, Bahnhofstr. 2, 64584 Biebesheim/Rhein, Postfach 1145, 64580 Biebesheim/Rhein
Bielefeld: Stadtarchiv und Landesgeschichtliche Bibliothek, Rohrteichstr. 19, 33602 Bielefeld, Postfach 100111, 33501 Bielefeld
Bietigheim-Bissingen: Stadtarchiv, Hauptstr. 61/63, 74321 Bietigheim-Bissingen, Postfach 1762, 74307 Bietigheim-Bissingen
Bingen am Rhein: Stadtarchiv, Stadtverwaltung, 55411 Bingen am Rhein,

Postfach 1751, 55387 Bingen am Rhein
Bischofswerda: Stadtarchiv, Rudolf-Breitscheid-Str. 7, 01877 Bischofswerda, Postfach 1173, 01871 Bischofswerda
Bischofswiesen: Gemeindearchiv, Rathaus, 83483 Bischofswiesen
Bitterfeld: Stadtarchiv, Markt 7, 06749 Bitterfeld
Blankenfelde: Amtsarchiv Blankenfelde-Mahlow, Karl-Marx-Str. 4, 15827 Blankenfelde
Blankenheim: Gemeindearchiv, Rathausplatz 16, 53945 Blankenheim
Blaubeuren: Stadtarchiv, Karlstr. 2, 89143 Blaubeuren
Blomberg: Stadtarchiv, 32825 Blomberg, Postfach 1452, 32820 Blomberg
Bocholt: Stadtarchiv, Münsterstr. 76, 46397 Bocholt
Bochum: Stadtarchiv, Kronenstr. 47, 44789 Bochum, Postfach 102269, 44777 Bochum
Bockenem: Stadtarchiv, Rathaus, 31167 Bockenem
Bodenwerder: Stadtarchiv, Stadtverwaltung, Münchhausenplatz 1, 37619 Bodenwerder
Böblingen: Stadtarchiv, Rathaus, 71032 Böblingen
Bönen: Gemeindearchiv, Bahnhofstr. 235, 59199 Bönen
Bomlitz: Gemeindearchiv, Schulstr. 4, 29699 Bomlitz
Bonn: Stadtarchiv und Stadthistorische Bibliothek, Stadthaus, Berliner Platz 2, 53103 Bonn
Borgentreich: Stadtarchiv, Am Rathaus 13, 34434 Borgentreich, Postfach 4, 34432 Borgentreich
Borgholzhausen: Stadtarchiv, Rathaus, Schulstr. 5, 33829 Borgholzhausen, Postfach 1261, 33826 Borgholzhausen
Borken: Stadtarchiv, Stadtverwaltung, Im Piepershagen 17, Postfach 1764, 46322 Borken
Borna: Stadtarchiv, Markt 1, 04552 Borna
Bornheim: Stadtarchiv, Rathausstr. 2, 53332 Bornheim

Bottrop: Stadtarchiv, Blumenstr. 12-14, Postfach 101554, 46215 Bottrop

Bovenden: Plesse-Archiv, Rathausplatz 1, 37120 Bovenden

Brackenheim: Stadtarchiv, Verwaltungs-stelle Hausen, Nordhausener Str. 4, 74336 Brackenheim-Hausen (Württemberg)

Brake (Unterweser): Stadtarchiv, Rathaus, Schrabberdeich 1, 26919 Brake (Unterweser), Postfach 1453, 26914 Brake (Unterweser)

Brakel: Stadtarchiv, Rathaus, Am Markt, 33034 Brakel

Brandenburg: Stadtarchiv, Altstädtischer Markt 8, 14770 Brandenburg

Brand-Erbisdorf: Stadtarchiv, Haasenweg, 09618 Brand-Erbisdorf, Postfach 17, 09614 Brand-Erbisdorf

Braunlage: Stadtarchiv, Stadtverwaltung, Herzog-Johann-Aolbrecht-Str. 2, 38700 Braunlage

Braunschweig: Stadtarchiv, 38100 Braunschweig, Löwenwall 18 B, Postfach 3309, 38023 Braunschweig

Breckerfeld: Stadtarchiv, Rathaus, Frankfurter Str. 38, 58339 Breckerfeld, Postfach 180, 58333 Breckerfeld

Breisach am Rhein: Stadtarchiv, Rathaus, Münsterplatz 1, 79206 Breisach am Rhein

Bremerhaven: Stadtarchiv, Stadthaus 5, Postfach 210360, 27524 Bremerhaven

Bremervörde: Stadtarchiv, Rathaus, Rathausmarkt 1, 27432 Bremervörde, Postfach 1465, 27424 Bremervörde

Bretten: Stadtarchiv, Untere Kirchgasse 9, 75015 Bretten

Brieselang: Amtsarchiv Brieselang, Vorholzstr. 57, 14656 Brieselang

Brilon: Stadtarchiv, Amtshaus, 59929 Brilon

Bruchhausen-Vilsen: Samtgemeindearchiv, Vilser Schulstr. 17, 27305 Bruchhausen-Vilsen

Bruchsal: Stadtarchiv, Am Alten Schloß 4, 76646 Bruchsal, Postfach 2320, 76613 Bruchsal

Brüggen: Gemeindearchiv, Klosterstr. 38, 41379 Brüggen, Postfach 1252, 41374 Brüggen

Brühl: Stadtarchiv, Rathaus, Franziskanerhof, Alte Feuerwache, 50321 Brühl

Buchen: Stadtarchiv, Wimpinaplatz 3, 74722 Buchen (Odenwald)

Buchholz in der Nordheide: Archiv der Stadt, Königsberger Str. 9, 21244 Buchholz in der Nordheide

Büchen: Amtsarchiv Büchen, Amtsplatz, 21514 Büchen

Bückeburg: Stadtarchiv, Schloß, 31675 Bückeburg, Postfach 1350, 31665 Bückeburg

Büdingen: Stadtarchiv, Zum Stadtgraben 7, Post: Stadtverwaltung, 63654 Büding-en, Postfach 1360, 63643 Büdingen

Bühl: Stadtgeschichtliches Institut, Hauptstr. 92, 77815 Bühl, Postfach 1420, 77804 Bühl

Bünde: Stadtarchiv, Saarlandstr. 5, 32257 Bünde

Büren: Stadtarchiv, Rathaus, Königstr. 16, 33142 Büren

Büttelborn: Gemeindearchiv, 64572 Büttelborn, Postfach 102, 64570 Büttelborn

Burg auf Fehmarn: Stadtarchiv, Rathaus, Am Markt 1, 23769 Burg auf Fehmarn, Postfach 1140, 23763 Burg auf Fehmarn

Burg bei Magdeburg: Stadtarchiv. See Landkreis Jerichower Land

Burgbernheim: Stadtarchiv, Rathaus, Rathausplatz 1, Postfach 47, 91593 Burgbernheim

Burgdorf: Stadtarchiv, Rathaus II, Vor dem Hann. Tor 1, 31303 Burgdorf

Burghausen: Stadtarchiv, Rathaus, 84489 Burghausen, Postfach 1240, 84480 Burghausen

Burgkunstadt: Stadtarchiv, Vogtei 5, 96224 Burgkunstadt, Postfach 1255, 96220 Burgkunstadt

Buttstädt: Stadtverwaltung Buttstädt, Stadtarchiv, Lohstr. 6a, 99628 Buttstädt (Thuringen)

Butzbach: Stadtarchiv Butzbach, Solms-Braunfelser-Hof (Museum), Färbgasse 16, Post: Marktplatz 1, 35510 Butzbach
Buxtehude: Stadtarchiv, Stavenort 5, 21614 Buxtehude, Postfach 1555, 21605 Buxtehude
Calw: Stadtarchiv, Im Zwinger 20, 75365 Calw
Camburg: Stadtverwaltung Camburg, Stadtarchiv, Rathausstr. 1, 07774 Camburg
Castrop-Rauxel: Stadtarchiv, Europaplatz 1, 44575 Castrop-Rauxel
Celle: Stadtarchiv, Westerceller Str. 4, 29227 Celle
Cham: Stadtarchiv, Spitalplatz 22, 93413 Cham
Chemnitz: Stadtarchiv, Aue 16, 09112 Chemnitz
Clausthal-Zellerfeld: Archiv der Samtgemeinde Oberharz mit den Mitgliedsgemeinden Altenau, Clausthal-Zellerfeld, Schulenberg im Oberharz und Wildemann, Hindenburgplatz 8, 38678 Clausthal-Zellerfeld
Coburg: Stadtarchiv, Rosengasse 1, 96450 Coburg, Postfach 3042, 96419 Coburg
Cochem: Stadtarchiv, Stadtverwaltung, Markt 1, 56812 Cochem, Postfach 1444, 56804 Cochem
Coesfeld: Stadtarchiv, Walkenbrückenstr. 25, 48653 Coesfeld, Postfach 1729, 48637 Coesfeld
Cossebaude: Gemeindearchiv, Gemeindeverwaltung, Dresdner Str., 01462 Cossebaude
Coswig: Stadtarchiv, Hauptstr. 18/20, 01640 Coswig
Cottbus: Stadtarchiv Cottbus, August-Bebel-Str. 85, 03046
Creglingen: Stadtarchiv, Rathaus, 97993 Creglingen, Postfach 20, 97991 Creglingen
Crimmitschau: Stadtarchiv, Leipziger Str. 76, 08451 Crimmitschau
Cuxhaven: Stadtarchiv, Altenwalder Chaussee 2, 27474 Cuxhaven
Dahlem: Gemeindearchiv, Rathaus,

Hauptstr. 23, 53949 Dahlem
Dahme (Mark): Amtsarchiv Dahme, Hauptstr. 48/49, 15936 Dahme (Mark)
Dannenberg/Elbe: Gemeindearchiv (Samtgemeinde), 29451 Dannenberg, Postfach 1260, 29446 Dannenberg/Elbe
Darmstadt: Stadtarchiv, Karolinenplatz 3, 64289 Darmstadt
Dassel: Stadtarchiv, Postfach, 37582 Dassel
Datteln: Stadtarchiv, Verwaltungsgebäude, Kolpingstr. 1, 45711 Datteln
Deggendorf: Stadtarchiv, Östlicher Stadtgraben 28, 94469 Deggendorf
Delitzsch: Stadtarchiv. See Landkreis Delitzsch
Delmenhorst: Stadtarchiv, Rathaus, 27747 Delmenhorst
Dessau (Anhalt): Stadtarchiv, Lange Gasse 22, 06844 Dessau (Anhalt)
Dieburg: Stadtarchiv, Stadtverwaltung, 64807 Dieburg, Postfach 1207, 64802 Dieburg
Diemelstadt-Rhoden: Stadtarchiv, Stadtverwaltung, 34474 Diemelstadt-Rhoden
Diepholz: Stadtarchiv, Rathausmarkt 1, 49356 Diepholz, Postfach 1620, 49346 Diepholz
Dießen am Ammersee: Gemeindearchiv, Marktplatz 1, 86911 Dießen am Ammersee
Dietenheim: Stadtarchiv, Königstr. 63, 89165 Dietenheim
Dietzenbach: Stadtarchiv, Stadtverwaltung, Offenbacher Str. 11, 63128 Dietzenbach, Postfach 1120, 63111 Dietzenbach
Diez: Stadtarchiv, Stadtverwaltung, Pfaffengasse 27, 65582 Diez (Lahn)
Dillenburg: Stadtarchiv, Stadtverwaltung, Postfach 429, 35664 Dillenburg
Dillingen: Stadtarchiv, Königstr. 38, 89407 Dillingen an der Donau, Postfach 1210, 89402 Dillingen an der Donau
Dingelstädt: Stadtverwaltung Dingelstädt, Stadtarchiv, Geschwister-Scholl-Str. 28, 37351 Dingelstädt
Dingolfing: Stadtarchiv, Rathaus, 84130

Dingolfing

Dinkelsbühl: Stadtarchiv, Rathaus, Segringer Str. 30, 91550 Dinkelsbühl

Dinslaken: Stadtarchiv, Rathaus, Platz d'Agen 1, 46535 Dinslaken, Postfach 100540, 46525 Dinslaken

Ditzingen: Stadtarchiv, Am Laien 4, 71254 Ditzingen, Postfach 1455, 71252 Ditzingen

Doberlug-Kirchhain: Stadtarchiv, Rathaus, Am Markt 8, 03251 Doberlug-Kirchhain

Döbeln: Stadtarchiv, Rathaus, Obermarkt 1, 04720 Döbeln

Dörentrup: Gemeindearchiv, Hauptstr. 2, 32694 Dörentrup, Postfach 1154, 32690 Dörentrup

Donaueschingen: Stadtarchiv, Rathaus, Rathausplatz 1, 78166 Donaueschingen

Donauwörth: Stadtarchiv, Rathaus, 86609 Donauwörth, Postfach 1453, 86604 Donauwörth

Donzdorf: Stadtarchiv - Heimatge-schichtliche Sammlungen, Stadtver-waltung, Hauptstr. 44, 73072 Donzdorf, Postfach 1363, 73069 Donzdorf, Dienstsitz: Hauptstr. 60, 73072 Donzdorf

Dorfen: Stadtarchiv, Justus-von-Liebig-Str. 5, 84405 Dorfen

Dormagen: Stadtarchiv, Gabrielstr. 6, 41542 Dormagen, Postfach 100120, 41538 Dormagen

Dornburg: Stadtverwaltung Dornburg, Stadtarchiv, Markt 21, 07778 Dornburg

Dornstetten: Stadtarchiv, 72280 Dornstetten

Dorsten: Stadtarchiv, Im Werth 6 (Bildungzentrum Maria-Lindenhof), 46282 Dorsten

Dortmund: Stadtarchiv, Friedensplatz 5, 44122 Dortmund, Postfach 105053

Dossenheim: Gemeindearchiv, Am Rathausplatz 1, 69221 Dossenheim, Postfach 1165, 69215 Dossenheim

Dransfeld: Archiv der Samtgemeinde und Stadt, Kirchplatz 1, 37125 Dransfeld

Dreieich: Stadtarchiv, Buchschlager Allee 8, 63303 Dreieich, Postfach 102020, 63266 Dreieich

Dresden: Stadtarchiv, Marienallee 3, 01099 Dresden, Postfach 120020, 01001 Dresden

Drolshagen: Stadtarchiv, Hagener Str. 9, 57489 Drolshagen

Duderstadt: Stadtarchiv, Christian-Blank-Str.1, 37115 Duderstadt, Postfach 1160, 37104 Duderstadt

Dülmen: Stadtarchiv, Stadtverwaltung, Markt 1-3, 48249 Dülmen, Postfach 1551, 48236 Dülmen

Düren: Stadtarchiv. See Kreis Düren

Düsseldorf: Stadtarchiv, Heinrich-Ehrhardt-Str. 61, 40468 Düsseldorf

Duisburg: Stadtarchiv, Karmelplatz 5, 47049 Duisburg

Eberbach (Baden): Stadtarchiv, Stadt-verwaltung, 69412 Eberbach (Baden), Postfach 1134, 69401 Eberbach (Baden)

Ebermannstadt: Stadtarchiv, Rathaus, 91320 Ebermannstadt, Postfach 43, 91316 Ebermannstadt

Ebersbach an der Fils: Stadtarchiv, Postfach 1129, 73055 Ebersbach an der Fils

Ebersberg: Stadtarchiv, Rathaus, Marienplatz 1, 85560 Ebersburg

Eberswalde: Stadtarchiv. See Landkreis Barnim

Eckernförde: Stadtarchiv, Gartenstr. 10, 24340 Eckernförde, Postfach 1420, 24334 Eckernförde

Edenkoben: Stadtarchiv, Verbands-gemeinde, 67480 Edenkoben (Landes-archiv Speyer serves as the depository)

Egestorf: Gemeindearchiv, Hinter den Höfen 9, 21272 Egestorf

Eggenfelden: Stadtarchiv, Rathausplatz 1, Postfach 1220, 84307 Eggenfelden

Ehingen: Stadtarchiv, Stadtverwaltung, Marktplatz 1, 89584 Ehingen (Donau)

Ehrenfriedersdorf: Stadtarchiv, Stadt-verwaltung, Markt 1, 09427 Ehren-friedersdorf

Eichstätt: Stadtarchiv, Marktplatz 11, 85072 Eichstätt, Postfach 1344, 85067 Eichstätt

Eilenburg: Stadtarchiv, Marktplatz 1, 04838 Eilenburg

Einbeck: Stadtarchiv, Steinweg 11, 37574 Einbeck, Postfach 1824, 37559 Einbeck
Eisenach: Stadtverwaltung Eisenach, Stadtarchiv, Am Markt 24, 99817 Eisenach
Eisenberg: Stadtverwaltung Eisenberg, Stadtarchiv, Postfach 22, 07601 Eisenberg, Dienstsitz: Markt 27, 07607 Eisenberg
Eisenhüttenstadt: Stadtarchiv, Am Trockendock 1a, 15890 Eisenhüttenstadt
Eisfeld: Museum Otto Ludwig, Museum für regionale Volkskunde, Stadtarchiv, Markt 2, Schloß, 98673 Eisfeld
Lutherstadt Eisleben: Stadtarchiv, Markt 1, 06295 Lutherstadt Eisleben
Eislingen: Stadtarchiv, Rathaus, 73054 Eislingen
Eitorf: Gemeindearchiv, Markt 1, 53783 Eitorf
Elbmarsch: Samtgemeindearchiv, Elbuferstr. 98, 21436 Marschacht
Ellingen: Stadtarchiv, Franziskanerkloster, Hausner Gasse 7, 91792 Ellingen
Ellwangen: Stadtarchiv, Stadtverwaltung, Spitalstr. 4, 73479 Ellwangen (Jagst)
Elsdorf: Gemeindearchiv, Gladbacher Str. 111, 50189 Elsdorf, Postfach 1155, 50182 Elsdorf
Elsterberg: Stadtarchiv, Markt 1, 07985 Elsterberg
Elsterwerda: Stadtarchiv, Hauptstr. 13, 04910 Elsterwerda
Elterlein: Stadtarchiv, Rathaus/Markt, 09481 Elterlein
Eltville am Rhein: Stadtarchiv, Stadtverwaltung, Matheus-Müller-Str. 3, 65343 Eltville am Rhein, Postfach 65334 Eltville am Rhein
Elze: Stadtarchiv, Rathaus, Hauptstr. 61, 31008 Elze, Postfach 1353, 31003 Elze
Emden: Stadtarchiv, Rathaus am Delft, Postfach 2254, 26721 Emden
Emmendingen: Stadtarchiv, Kirchstr. 7, 79314 Emmendingen (Baden)
Emmerich: Stadtarchiv, Stadtverwaltung, Martinikirchgang 2, 46446 Emmerich

Emsbüren: Gemeindearchiv, Markt 18, 48488 Emsbüren
Emsdetten: Stadtarchiv, Am Markt 1, 48282 Emsdetten, Postfach 1254, 48270 Emsdetten
Endingen: Stadtarchiv, Rathaus, 79346 Endingen
Engen: Stadtarchiv, Rathaus, 78234 Engen (Hegau)
Enger: Stadtarchiv, Kirchplatz 10 (Widukind-Museum), 32130 Enger
Ennepetal: Stadtarchiv, Lindenstr. 8, 58256 Ennepetal
Ennigerloh: Stadtarchiv. See Kreis Warendorf
Eppingen: Stadtarchiv, Bürgermeisteramt, Rathausstr. 14, 75031 Eppingen, Postfach 265, 75021 Eppingen
Eppstein: Stadtarchiv, Rathaus II, Rossertstr. 21, 65817 Eppstein (Taunus)
Erbach: Stadtarchiv, Stadtverwaltung, Neckarstr. 3, 64711 Erbach
Erding: Archiv der Stadt, Landshuter Str. 1, 85435 Erding
Erftstadt: Stadtarhiv, Rathaus, Holzdamm 10, 50374 Erftstadt
Erfurt: Stadt- und Verwaltungsarchiv, Gotthardstr. 21, 99084 Erfurt, Postfach 243, 99005 Erfurt
Erkelenz: Stadtarchiv, Johannismarkt 17, 41812 Erkelenz
Erkrath: Stadtarchiv, Bahnstr. 16, 40699 Erkrath
Erlangen: Stadtarchiv, Cedernstr. 1, 91054 Erlangen
Erwitte: Stadtarchiv, Stadtverwaltung, 59597 Erwitte, Postfach 1065, 59591 Erwitte
Eschborn: Stadtarchiv, Eschenplatz 1, 65760 Eschborn (Taunus), Postfach 5980, 65734 Eschborn (Taunus)
Eschede: Samtgemeindearchiv, Am Glockenkolk 1, 29346 Eschede
Eschershausen: Stadtarchiv, Postfach 1269, 37629 Eschershausen
Eschwege: Stadtarchiv, Stadtverwaltung, Postfach 1560, 37269 Eschwege

Espelkamp: Stadtarchiv, Rathaus, Wilhelm-Kern-Platz 1, 32339 Espelkamp
Essen: Stadtarchiv, Steeler Str. 29, 45121 Essen
Esslingen: Stadtarchiv, Marktplatz 20, 73728 Esslingen am Neckar, Postfach 269, 73726 Esslingen am Neckar
Esterland: Amtsarchiv Esterland, Hauptstr. 58, 03253 Schönborn
Ettlingen: Stadtarchiv, Schloß, 76261 Ettlingen, Postfach 0762, 76261 Ettlingen
Euskirchen: Stadtarchiv, Kölner Str. 75, 53879 Euskirchen, Postfach 1169, 53861 Euskirchen
Eutin: Stadtarchiv, Sparkasse Ostholstein, Am Rosengarten, 23701 Eutin, Postfach 328, 23693 Eutin
Everswinkel: See Kreis Warendorf
Extertal: Gemeindearchiv und Fotothek, Bösingfeld, 32699 Extertal
Falkenberg (Uebigau): Amtsarchiv Falkenberg (Uebigau), Markt 3, 04895 Falkenberg/Elster
Falkenberg-Höhe: Amtsarchiv Falkenberg-Höhe, Lindenstr. 2, 15848 Falkenberg (Mark)
Falkensee: Stadtarchiv, Falkenhagener Str. 45, 14612 Falkensee
Falkenstein (Vogtland): Stadtarchiv, Clara-Zetkin-Str. 1, 08223 Falkenstein (Vogtland)
Fallingbostel: Stadtarchiv, Stadtverwaltung, Vogteistr. 1, 29683 Fallingbostel
Fehrbellin: Amtsarchiv Fehrbellin, Johann-Sebastian-Bach-Str. 6, 16833 Fehrbellin
Fellbach: Stadtmuseum und Archiv, Hintere Str. 26, 70734
Feuchtwangen: Stadtarchiv, Rathaus, Hindenburgstr. 5/7, 91555 Feuchtwangen, Postfach 1257, 91552 Feuchtwangen
Filderstadt: Stadtarchiv, Lange Str. 83, 70794 Filderstadt-Sielmingen, Postfach 1180, 70772 Filderstadt
Finnentrop: Gemeindearchiv, 57413 Finnentrop, Postfach 220, 57402 Finnentrop
Finsterwalde: Stadtarchiv, Schloßstr. 7-8, 03238 Finsterwalde
Flensburg: Stadtarchiv, Rathaus, 24937 Flensburg, Postfach 2742, 24917 Flensburg
Flöha: Stadtarchiv, Augustusburger Str. 90, 09557 Flöha
Forchheim: Stadtarchiv, St.-Martin-Str. 8, 91301 Forchheim, Postfach 85, 91299 Forchheim
Forst (Lausitz): Stadtarchiv, Promenade 9, 03149 Forst (Lausitz)
Frankenberg (Sachsen): Stadtarchiv, Markt 15, 09669 Frankenberg (Sachsen)
Frankenthal: Stadtarchiv, Rathaus, 67227 Frankenthal (Pfalz)
Frankfurt am Main: Institut für Stadtgeschichte, Karmelitergasse 5, 60311 Frankfurt am Main
Frankfurt/Oder: Stadtarchiv, Collegien-str. 8/9, 15230 Frankfurt/Oder
Frauenau: Gemeindearchiv, Rathaus, Rathausplatz 4, 94258 Frauenau
Frechen: Stadtarchiv, Rathaus, 50226 Frechen, Postfach 1960, 50209 Frechen
Freiberg (Sachsen): Stadtarchiv, Obermarkt 24, 09596 Freiberg (Sachsen)
Freiburg im Breisgau: Stadtarchiv, Grünwälder Str. 15, 79098 Freiburg im Breisgau
Freilassing: Stadtarchiv, Stadtverwaltung, Münchener Str. 15, 83395 Freilassing, Postfach 1620, 83383 Freilassing
Freising: Stadtarchiv, Rathaus, Obere Hauptstr. 2, 85354 Freising
Freren: Stadtarchiv, Stadtverwaltung, Markt 1, 49832 Freren
Freudenberg: Stadtarchiv, Stadtverwaltung, Bahnhofstr. 18, 57258 Freudenberg
Freudenstadt: Stadtarchiv, Stadtverwalt-ung, Marktplatz 1, 72250 Freudenstadt
Friedberg (Bayern): Stadtarchiv, Pfarrstr. 6, 86313 Friedberg (Bayern), Postfach 1453, 86313 Friedberg (Bayern)
Friedberg (Hessen): Stadtarchiv im Bibliothekszentrum Klosterbau, Augustinergasse 8, 61169 Friedberg (Hessen), Postfach 100964, 61149 Friedberg

(Hessen)
Friedrichroda: Stadtverwaltung, Stadt-
und Kurbibliothek, Stadtarchiv,
Hauptstr. 45, 99894 Friedrichroda
Friedrichsdorf: Stadtverwaltung,
Hugenottenstr. 55, 61381 Friedrichsdorf,
Postfach 1340, 61364 Friedrichsdorf
Friedrichshafen: Stadtarchiv, Katharin-
enstr. 55, 88045 Friedrichshafen
Friedrichstadt: Stadtarchiv, Wester-
lilienstr. 7, 25840 Friedrichstadt
Fritzlar: Stadtarchiv, Rathaus, 34560
Fritzlar
Fröndenberg: Stadtarchiv, Rathaus,
Kirchplatz 2, 58730 Fröndenberg
Fürstenau: Stadtarchiv, Postfach 1160,
49578 Fürstenau
Fürstenfeldbruck: Stadtarchiv, Fürsten-
feld 3d, Post: Hauptstr. 31, 82256 Fürst-
enfeldbruck, Postfach 1645, 82245
Fürstenfeldbruck
Fürstenwalde: Stadtarchiv Fürsten-
walde, Eisenbahnstr. 18, 15517
Fürstenwalde (im Aufbau)
Fürth: Stadtarchiv, Schloßhof 12, 90768
Fürth
Füssen: Kloster- und Stadtarchiv, Lech-
halde 3, 87629 Füssen
Fulda: Stadtarchiv, Palais Buttlar,
Bonifatiusplatz 1-3, 36037 Fulda
Furth im Wald: Stadtarchiv, 93437 Furth
im Wald
Furtwangen: Stadtarchiv, Marktplatz 4,
78120 Furtwangen, Postfach 30, 78113
Furtwangen
Gaggenau: Stadtarchiv, Hauptstr. 71,
76571 Gaggenau, Postfach 1520, 76555
Gaggenau
Gaildorf: Stadtarchiv, Schloßstr. 20,
74405 Gaildorf, Postfach 150, 74402
Gaildorf
Gangelt: Gemeindearchiv, Burgstr. 10,
52538 Gangelt
Gangkofen: Archiv des Marktes,
Marktplatz 21, 84140 Gangkofen
Garbsen: Stadtarchiv, Lehmstr. 1, 30826
Garbsen
Gardelegen: Stadtarchiv, Rathausplatz
10, 39638 Gardelegen

Garmisch-Partenkirchen: Marktarchiv,
Rathausplatz 1, 82467 Garmisch-
Partenkirchen
Gartz/Oder: Amtsarchiv Gartz, Stettiner
Str. 15, 16307 Gartz/Oder
Gedern: Stadtarchiv, Stadtverwaltung,
63688 Gedern
Geesthacht: Stadtarchiv, Krügersches
Haus, Bergedorferstr. 28, 21502
Geesthacht
Gehrden: Stadtarchiv, Kirchstr. 1-3,
30989 Gehrden
Gehren: Stadtverwaltung Gehren,
Stadtarchiv, Obere Marktstr. 1, 98708
Gehren
Geilenkirchen: Stadtarchiv, Markt 9,
52511 Geilenkirchen
Geisa: Stadtverwaltung Geisa, Stadt-
archiv, Marktplatz 27, 36419 Geisa
Geislingen an der Steige: Stadtarchiv,
Altes Rathaus, Hauptstr. 19, 73312
Geislingen an der Steige, Postfach 1162,
73301 Geislingen an der Steige
Geithain: Stadtarchiv, Leipziger Str. 17
(Stadtbibliothek), 04643 Geithain
Geldern: Stadtarchiv, Kulturamt,
Issumer Tor 36, 47608 Geldern
Gellersen: Archiv der Samtgemeinde,
Dachtmisser Str. 1, 21391 Reppenstedt
Gelnhausen: Stadtarchiv, ehem.
Augustaschule, Am Obermarkt, Post:
Stadtverwaltung, 63571 Gelnhausen,
Postfach 1763, 63557 Gelnhausen
Gelsenkirchen: Institut für Stadtge-
schichte, Stadtarchiv, Bildungszentrum,
Ebertstr. 19, 45875 Gelsenkirchen,
Postfach 100101
Gemünden am Main: Stadtarchiv,
Stadtverwaltung, Scherenbergstr. 5,
97737 Gemünden am Main
Gengenbach: Stadtarchiv,
Bürgermeister-amt, 77723 Gengenbach,
Postfach 1165, 77717 Gengenbach
Genthin: Stadtarchiv, Lindenstr. 2, 39307
Genthin
Georgsmarienhütte: Stadtarchiv,
Museum Villa Stahmer, Carl-Stahmer-
Weg 13, 49124 Georgsmarienhütte
Gera: Stadtarchiv, Prof.-Simmel-Str. 1,

07548 Gera, Postfach 100, 07501 Gera
Gerlingen: Stadtarchiv, Urbanstr. 5/1, 70839 Gerlingen
Germersheim: Stadtarchiv, Stadtverwaltung, Kolpingplatz 3, 76726 Germersheim
Gernrode: Stadtarchiv, Stadtverwaltung, Marktstr. 20, 06507 Gernrode
Gernsbach: Stadtarchiv, Stadtverwaltung, 76593 Gernsbach, Postfach 1154, 76584 Gernsbach
Gernsheim: Stadtarchiv, Stadthaus, Stadthausplatz 1, 64579 Gernsheim/Rhein, Postfach 1262, 64574 Gernsheim
Gerolzhofen: Stadtarchiv, Rathaus, Brunnengasse 5, 97447 Gerolzhofen
Gescher: Stadtarchiv, Marktplatz 1, 48712 Gescher, Postfach 1361, 48706 Gescher
Geseke: Stadtarchiv Wichburgastr. 9, 59590 Geseke, Postfach 1442, 59585 Geseke
Gevelsberg: Stadtarchiv, Am Schultenhof 1, 58265 Gevelsberg, Postfach 2360 und 2380, 58265 Gevelsberg
Geyer: Stadtarchiv, Altmarkt 1, 09468 Geyer
Giengen an der Brenz: Stadtarchiv, Kirchplatz 2, 89537 Giengen an der Brenz
Giesen: Gemeindearchiv, Rathausstr. 27, 31180 Giesen
Gießen: Stadtarchiv, Behördenzentrum, Ostanlage 45, 35390 Gießen, Postfach 110820, 35353 Gießen
Gifhorn: Stadtarchiv, Schloßstr., 38518 Gifhorn
Gladbeck: Stadtarchiv, Willy-Brandt-Platz 2, 45956 Gladbeck
Glinde: Stadtarchiv, Rathaus, Markt 1, 21509 Glinde
Glückstadt: Stadtarchiv, Brockdorff-Palais, Am Fleth 43, 25348 Glückstadt
Goch: Stadtarchiv, Stadtverwaltung, Markt 2, 47574 Goch
Göppingen: Stadtarchiv, Alter Kasten, Schloßstr. 14, 73033 Göppingen, Postfach 1149, 73011 Göppingen
Görlitz: Stadtarchiv, Untermarkt 8, 02826 Görlitz

Göttingen: Stadtarchiv, Neues Rathaus, Hiroshimaplatz 4, 37083 Göttingen, Postfach 3831, 37028 Göttingen
Golßener Land: Amtsarchiv Golßener Land, Hauptstr. 41, 15938 Golßen
Goslar: Stadtarchiv, Zehntstr. 24, 38640 Goslar, Postfach 2569, 38615 Goslar
Grabow: Stadtarchiv, Am Markt 1, 19300 Grabow
Grafenau: Stadtarchiv, Rathausgasse 1, 94481 Grafenau
Grebenau: Stadtarchiv, Stadtverwaltung, Amthof 2, 36323 Grebenau
Greifswald: Stadtarchiv, Stadtverwaltung der Hansestadt Greifswald, Postfach 253, 17461 Greifswald
Greven: Stadtarchiv, Rathausstr. 6, 48268 Greven
Grevenbroich: Stadtarchiv, 41513 Grevenbroich
Grimma: Stadtarchiv, Markt 17, 04668 Grimma
Groitzsch: Stadtarchiv, Markt 1, 04539 Groitzsch
Gronau/Leine: Stadtarchiv, Blankestr. 16, 31028 Gronau/Leine
Groß-Bieberau: Stadtarchiv, Stadtverwaltung, Marktstr. 28, 64401 Groß-Bieberau
Großbottwar: Stadtarchiv, Im Schulzentrum Lindenstr., 71723 Großbottwar
Großbreitenbach: Stadtverwaltung Großbreitenbach, Stadtarchiv, Markt 11, 98701 Großbreitenbach
Großeutersdorf: Gemeindeverwaltung Großeutersdorf, Gemeindearchiv, Am Kirchberg, 07768 Großeutersdorf
Groß-Gerau: Stadtarchiv, Stadtverwaltung, Marktplatz, 64521 Groß-Gerau, Postfach 1561, 64505 Groß-Gerau
Groß Pankow: Amtsarchiv Groß Pankow, Steindamm 51, 16929 Groß Pankow
Groß Räschen: Amtsarchiv Groß Räschen, Ernst-Thälmann-Str. 47, 01983 Groß Räschen
Groß-Umstadt: Stadtarchiv, Unterdorf 41, 64823 Groß-Umstadt/Raibach, Der

Magistrat der Stadt, Markt 1, 64823 Groß-Umstadt
Grünberg: Stadtarchiv, Stadtverwaltung, Postfach 1265, 35301 Grünberg/Hessen
Guben: Stadtarchiv, Stadtverwaltung, Uferstr. 22-26, 03172 Guben
Güglingen: Stadtarchiv, Stadtverwaltung, 74361 Güglingen
Günzburg: Stadtarchiv, Schloßplatz 1, 89312 Günzburg
Güstrow: Stadtarchiv, Markt 1, 18273 Güstrow
Gütersloh: Stadtarchiv, Hohenzollernstr. 30a, 33330 Gütersloh
Gummersbach: Stadtarchiv, Rathausplatz 1, 51643 Gummersbach, Postfach 100852, 51608 Gummersbach
Gundelfingen an der Donau: Stadtarchiv, Postfach 28, 89421 Gundelfingen an der Donau
Gunzenhausen: Stadtarchiv, Rathaus, Marktplatz 23, 91710 Gunzenhausen
Haar: Gemeindearchiv, Bahnhofstr. 7, 85540 Haar b. München
Hachenburg: Stadtarchiv, Mittelstr. 2, 57627 Hachenburg, Postfach 1308, 57622 Hachenburg
Hagen (Westfalen): Stadtarchiv, Rathausstr. 12, Postfach 4249, 58042 Hagen (Westfalen)
Hainichen: Gemeindeverwaltung Hainichen, Gemeindearchiv, Dorfstr. 27, 07778 Hainichen
Halberstadt: Stadtarchiv, Domplatz 49, 38820 Halberstadt
Haldensleben: Stadtarchiv. See Ohre-Kreis
Halle/Saale: Stadtarchiv, Rathausstr. 1, 06108 Halle/Saale
Halle (Westfalen): Stadtarchiv, Kiskerstr. 2, 33790 Halle (Westfalen), Postfach 1563 und 1564, 33780 Halle (Westfalen)
Hallenberg: Stadtarchiv, Stadtverwaltung, Rathausplatz 1, 59969 Hallenberg, Postfach 1155, 59965 Hallenberg
Haltern: Stadtarchiv, Stadtbücherei, Lavesumer Str. 19, 45721 Haltern

Hameln: Stadtarchiv, Osterstr. 2 (Hochzeitshaus), 31785 Hameln
Hamm: Stadtarchiv, Altes Amtshaus Pelkum, Kamener Str. 177, 59077 Hamm, Postanschrift: Stadtverwaltung Hamm, Postfach 2449, 59061 Hamm
Hamminkeln: Gemeindearchiv, Rathaus, Brüner Str., 46499 Hamminkeln
Hanau: Stadtarchiv, Schloßplatz 2, 63450 Hanau
Hann. Münden: Stadtarchiv, Schloßplatz 5, 34346 Hann. Münden, Postfach 1528, 34335 Hann. Münden
Hannover: Stadtarchiv, Am Bokemahle 14-16, 30173 Hannover
Hanstedt: Gemeindearchiv, Gemeindeverwaltung, 21271 Hanstedt
Harburg: Stadtarchiv, Schloßstr. 1, 86655 Harburg
Haren/Ems: Stadtarchiv, Neuer Markt 1, 49733 Haren/Ems
Harpstedt: Gemeindearchiv (Samtgemeinde), Amtshof, 27243 Harpstedt
Harsefeld: Samtgemeindearchiv, Herrenstr. 25, 21698 Harsefeld
Harsewinkel: Stadtarchiv, Münsterstr. 14, 33428 Harsewinkel
Hartenstein: Stadtarchiv, Marktplatz 9, 08118 Hartenstein
Harzgerode: Stadtarchiv, Stadtverwaltung, Markt 1, 06493 Harzgerode
Haselünne: Stadtarchiv, Krummer Dreh 18/19, 49740 Haselünne
Haslach im Kinzigtal: Stadtarchiv, Rathaus, 77716 Haslach im Kinzigtal
Hattingen: Stadtarchiv, Stadtverwaltung, Im Welperfeld 23, 45527 Hattingen
Hatzfeld/Eder: Stadtarchiv, Stadtverwaltung, 35116 Hatzfeld/Eder
Hechingen: Bürgermeisteramt, Stadtarchiv, Postfach 222, 72375 Hechingen
Heide: Archiv der Stadt, Neue Anlage 5 (Bürger-Haus), 25746 Heide
Heideblick: Amtsarchiv Heideblick, Luckauer Str. 21, 15926 Langengrassau
Heidelberg: Stadtarchiv, Heiliggeiststr. 12, 69117 Heidelberg
Heidenheim an der Brenz: Stadtarchiv,

Rathaus, Grabenstr. 15, 89522 Heidenheim an der Brenz

Heilbronn: Stadtarchiv, Eichgasse 1 (Deutschhof), 74072 Heilbronn/Neckar

Heiligenhaus: Stadtarchiv, Hauptstr. 157 (Rathaus), 42579 Heiligenhaus, Postfach 100553, 42570 Heiligenhaus

Heiligenstadt: Stadtverwaltung Heilbad Heiligenstadt, Stadtarchiv, Postfach 337, 37303 Heilbad Heiligenstadt, Ägidienstr. 20, 37308 Heilbad Heiligenstadt, Dienstsitz: Kollegiengasse 10, 37308 Heilbad Heiligenstadt

Heimbach: Stadtarchiv, Hengebachstr. 14, 52396 Heimbach

Heldrungen: Stadtverwaltung Heldrungen, Stadtarchiv, Hauptstr. 49/50, 06577 Heldrungen

Helmstedt: Stadtarchiv, Rathaus, Markt 1, 38350 Helmstedt, Postfach 1640, 38336 Helmstedt

Hemer: Stadtarchiv, Hauptstr. 201, 58651 Hemer

Hennef: Stadtarchiv, Beethovenstr. 21, 53773 Hennef

Heppenheim: Stadtarchiv, Großer Markt 1, 64646 Heppenheim, Postfach 1808, 64636 Heppenheim

Herbolzheim: Stadtarchiv, Friedrichstr. 2 A, 79336 Herbolzheim

Herborn: Stadtarchiv, Rathaus, 35745 Herborn

Herdecke: Stadtarchiv, Kulturhaus, Goethestr. 14, 58313 Herdecke, Postfach, 58311 Herdecke

Herford: Kommunalarchiv, Archiv des Kreises und der Stadt, Elverdisser Str. 12, 32052 Herford

Hermsdorf: Stadtverwaltung Hermsdorf, Stadtarchiv, Eisenbergerstr. 56, 07629 Hermsdorf

Herne: Stadtarchiv, Eickeler Str. 7, Postfach 101820, 44651 Herne

Herrenberg: Stadtarchiv, Marienstr. 21, 71083 Herrenberg, Postfach 1209, 71071 Herrenberg

Hersbruck: Stadtarchiv, Rathaus, Postfach 540, 91214 Hersbruck

Herten: Stadtarchiv, Kurt-Schumacher-Str. 16-22, 45699 Herten

Herzberg am Harz: Stadtarchiv, Rathaus, 37412 Herzberg am Harz, Postfach 1340, 37403 Herzberg am Harz

Herzebrock-Clarholz: Gemeindearchiv, Clarholzer Str. 76, 33442 Herzebrock-Clarholz

Herzogenaurach: Stadtarchiv, Marktplatz 11, 91074 Herzogenaurach

Herzogenrath: Stadtarchiv, 52134 Herzogenrath, Postfach 1280, 52112 Herzogenrath

Hessisch Oldendorf: Stadtarchiv, Stadtverwaltung, Marktplatz 13, 31840 Hessisch Oldendorf, Postfach 128, 31833 Hessisch Oldendorf

Hettstedt: Stadtarchiv, Stadtverwaltung, Markt, 06333 Hettstedt

Heusenstamm: Stadtarchiv, Im Herrengarten 1, 63150 Heusenstamm

Hiddenhausen: Gemeindearchiv, Rathausstr. 1, 32120 Hiddenhausen

Hilchenbach: Stadtarchiv, Rathaus, Markt 13, 57271 Hilchenbach, Postfach 1360, 57261 Hilchenbach

Hildburghausen: Stadtarchiv. See Land-kreis Hildburghausen

Hilden: Stadtarchiv, Am Holterhöfchen 34, 40724 Hilden

Hildesheim: Stadtarchiv und Stadtbiblio-thek, Am Steine 7, 31134 Hildesheim

Hille: Marktarchiv, Am Rathaus 4, 32479 Hille (Hartum)

Hindelang: Gemeindearchiv, Eisenhammerweg 35, 87541 Hindelang

Hinterzarten: Stadtarchiv, Hauptamt, 79856 Hinterzarten

Hirschberg/Saale: Verwaltungsgemeinschaft Hirschberg/Saale, Stadt-archiv, Marktstr. 2, 07927 Hirschberg/Saale

Hirschhorn/Neckar: Städtisches Archiv, Rathaus, Neckarsteinacher Str. 8-10, 69434 Hirschhorn/Neckar, Postfach 1151, 69430 Hirschhorn/Neckar

Hitzacker: Archiv, Stadtverwaltung (Samtgemeinde), Am Markt 1, 29456 Hitzacker

Hochheim am Main: Stadtarchiv,

Stadtverwaltung, Kulturamt, Burgeffstr. 30, 65239 Hochheim am Main, Postfach 1140, 65233 Hochheim am Main

Hockenheim: Stadtarchiv, Stadtverwaltung, Rathausstr. 1, 68766 Hockenheim

Höchberg: Gemeindearchiv, Gemeindeverwaltung, 97204 Höchberg

Höchst im Odenwald: Gemeindearchiv, Montmelianer Platz 4, 64739 Höchst im Odenwald

Höchstadt an der Aisch: Stadtarchiv, Altes Kommunbrauhaus, 91315 Höchstadt an der Aisch

Höchstädt an der Donau: Stadtarchiv, Bahnhofstr. 10, 89420 Höchstädt an der Donau

Höxter: Stadtarchiv, Stadthaus am Petritor, 37671 Höxter

Hof an der Saale: Stadtarchiv, Unteres Tor 9, 95028 Hof an der Saale, Postfach 1665, 95015 Hof an der Saale

Hofgeismar: Stadtarchiv, Rathaus, Markt 1, 34369 Hofgeismar

Hofheim am Taunus: Stadtarchiv, Kulturamt, Chinonplatz 2, 65719 Hofheim am Taunus, Postfach 1340, 65703 Hofheim am Taunus

Hohe Elbegeest: Amtsarchiv. See Archivgemeinschaft Schwarzenbek

Hohenstein-Ernstthal: Stadtarchiv, Altmarkt 30, 09337 Hohenstein-Ernstthal

Hohenwart: Marktarchiv, 86557 Hohenwart

Holzminden: Stadtarchiv, Bahnhofstr. 31, 37603 Holzminden, Postfach 1404, 37594 Holzminden

Holzwickede: Gemeindearchiv, Rathaus, Postfach, 59439 Holzwickede

Homberg/Ohm: Stadtarchiv, Rathaus, 35315 Homberg/Ohm

Homburg/Saar: Stadtarchiv, Am Marktplatz, 66424 Homburg/Saar, Postfach 1653, 66407 Homburg/Saar

Hoppegarten: Amtsarchiv Hoppegarten, Lindenstr. 14, 15366 Dahlwitz-Hoppegarten

Horb am Neckar: Stadtarchiv, Oberamteigasse 2, 72160 Horb am Neckar

Horn-Bad Meinberg: Stadtarchiv, Stadtverwaltung, Rathausplatz 4, 32805 Horn-Bad Meinberg

Hornburg: Stadtarchiv, Heimatmuseum, 38315 Hornburg

Hoya: Stadtarchiv, Postfach 150, 27318 Hoya

Hoyerswerda: Stadtarchiv, Schloßplatz 1, 02977 Hoyerswerda

Hude: Gemeindearchiv, Parkstr. 53, 27794 Hude

Hückelhoven: Stadtarchiv, Parkhofstr. 76, 41836 Hückelhoven, Postfach 1360, 41825 Hückelhoven

Hückeswagen: Stadtarchiv, Stadtverwaltung, Postfach 166, 42499 Hückeswagen

Hüfingen: Stadtarchiv, Stadtverwaltung, 78183 Hüfingen

Hüllhorst: Gemeindearchiv, Löhner Str. 1, 32609 Hüllhorst

Hünxe: Gemeindearchiv, Dorstener Str. 24, 46569 Hünxe

Hürtgenwald-Kleinhau: Gemeindearchiv, August-Scholl-Str. 5, 52393 Hürtenwald-Kleinhau

Hürth: Stadtarchiv, Rathaus, Friedrich-Ebert-Str. 40, 50354 Hürth, Postanschrift: Stadt Hürth, 50351 Hürth

Hütten: Amtsarchiv Hütten, Schulberg 6, 24358 Ascheffel

Hungen: Stadtarchiv, Kaiserstr. 7, 35410 Hungen

Husum: Stadtarchiv. See Kreis Nordfriesland

Ibbenbüren: Stadtarchiv, Alte Münsterstr. 16, 49477 Iibbenbüren, Postfach 1565, 49465 Ibbenbüren

Ichenheim: Stadtarchiv, Ortsverwaltung, 77741 Neuried-Ichenheim

Idar-Oberstein: Stadtarchiv, Am Markt 2, 55743 Idar-Oberstein

Idstein: Stadtarchiv, Stadtverwaltung, 65510 Idstein, Postfach 1140, 65501 Idstein

Iffezheim: Gemeindearchiv, Bürgermeisteramt, Hauptstr. 54, 76473 Iffezheim

Ilmenau: Stadtverwaltung Ilmenau, Stadtarchiv, Am Markt 7, 98693 Ilmenau,

Dienstsitz: Naumannstr. 22, 98693 Ilmenau
Ilsede: Gemeindearchiv, Eichstr. 3, 31241 Ilsede
Immenstadt im Allgäu: Stadtarchiv, 87509 Immenstadt im Allgäu, Postfach 1461, 87504 Immenstadt im Allgäu
Ingelheim am Rhein: Stadtarchiv, Stadtverwaltung, Postfach 60, 55218 Ingelheim am Rhein
Ingolstadt: Stadtarchiv, Auf der Schanz 45, 85049 Ingolstadt, Postfach 210964, 85024 Ingolstadt
Iphofen: Stadtarchiv, Rathaus, 97346 Iphofen
Iserlohn: Stadtarchiv, An der Schlacht 14, 58644 Iserlohn
Isny (Allgäu): Stadtarchiv, Rathaus, 88316 Isny (Allgäu), Postfach 1162, 88305 Isny (Allgäu)
Isselburg: Stadtarchiv, Stadtverwaltung, Markt 14/16, 46419 Isselburg
Issum: Gemeindearchiv, Herrlichkeit 7-9, 47661 Issum
Itzehoe: Gemeinsames Archiv des Kreises Steinburg und der Stadt Itzehoe. See Kreis Steinburg
Jena: Stadtarchiv, Löbdergraben 18, 07743 Jena
Joachimsthal-Schorfheide: Amtsarchiv Joachimsthal-Schorfheide, 16247 Joachimsthal
Jöhstadt: Stadtarchiv, Markt 185, 09477 Jöhstadt
Jork: Gemeindearchiv, Am Gräfengericht 2, 21635 Jork
Jüchen: Gemeindearchiv, Postfach 1101, 41353 Jüchen
Jülich: Stadtarchiv, Kulturhaus, Kleine Rurstr. 20, 52428 Jülich, Postfach 1220, 52411 Jülich
Jüterbog: Stadtarchiv Jüterbog, Markt 1, 14913 Jüterbog
Kaarst: Stadtarchiv, Am Neumarkt 2, 41564 Kaarst
Kahl am Main: Gemeindearchiv, Aschaffenburger Str. 1, 63792 Kahl am Main
Kahla: Stadtverwaltung Kahla, Stadtarchiv, Markt 10, 07768 Kahla

Kaiserslautern: Stadtarchiv, Rathaus, Postfach 1320, 67653 Kaiserslautern
Kalkar: Stadtarchiv, Hanselaerstr. 5, 47546 Kalkar, Postfach 1165, 47538 Kalkar
Kalletal: Gemeindearchiv, Rintelner Str. 5, 32689 Kalletal
Kamen: Stadtarchiv, Rathausplatz 1, 59174 Kamen, Postfach 1580, 59172 Kamen
Kamenz: Stadtarchiv, Markt 1, 01917 Kamenz
Karben: Stadtarchiv, Bürgerzentrum, Rathausplatz 1, Post: Stadtverwaltung, 61184 Karben, Postfach 1107, 61174 Karben
Karlsruhe: Stadtarchiv, Markgrafenstr. 29, 76133 Karlsruhe, Post: Stadt Karlsruhe, Stadtbibliothek, Archiv, Sammlungen, Ständehausstr. 2, 76133 Karlsruhe bzw. 76124 Karlsruhe
Karlstadt: Stadtarchiv, Stadtverwaltung, Helfensteinstr. 2, 97753 Karlstadt
Kassel: Stadtarchiv, Marstallgebäude, Wildemannsgasse 1, 34117 Kassel
Kaufbeuren: Stadtarchiv, Hauberrisserstr. 8, 87600 Kaufbeuren, Postfach 1752, 87577 Kaufbeuren
Kehl: Stadtarchiv, Haupt- und Verkehrsamt, Großherzoz-Friedrich-Str. 19, 77694 Kehl
Kelheim: Stadtarchiv, Alleestr. 21, 93309 Kelheim
Kelkheim (Taunus): Stadtarchiv, Stadtverwaltung, Gagernring 6, 65779 Kelkheim (Taunus), Postfach 1560, 65765 Kelkheim
Kempen: Stadtarchiv. See Kreis Viersen
Kempten (Allgäu): Stadtarchiv, Rathaus-platz 3-5, 87435 Kempten (Allgäu)
Kenzingen: Stadtarchiv, Rathaus, Hauptstr. 15, 79341 Kenzingen, Postfach 1119, 79337 Kenzingen
Kerken: Gemeindearchiv, Dionysiusplatz 4, 47647 Kerken, Postfach 1164, 47639 Kerken
Kerpen: Stadtarchiv, Rathaus, Jahnplatz 1, 50171 Kerpen, Postfach 2109, 50151 Kerpen

Kevelaer: Stadtarchiv, Stadtverwaltung, Postfach 75, 47612 Kevelaer
Kiefersfelden: Gemeindearchiv, Rathausplatz 1, 83088 Kiefersfelden
Kiel: Stadtarchiv, Rathaus, Fleethörn, 24103 Kiel
Kierspe: Stadtarchiv, ehem. Amtshaus, Friedrich-Ebert-Str. 380, 58566 Kierspe
Kindelbrück: Verwaltungsgemeinschaft Kindelbrück, Stadtarchiv, Puschkinplatz 1, 99638 Kindelbrück
Kirchberg: Stadtarchiv, Neumarkt 2, 08107 Kirchberg
Kirchheim unter Teck: Stadtarchiv, Wollmarktstr. 48, 73230 Kirchheim unter Teck
Kirchhundem: Gemeindearchiv, Hundemstr. 35, 57399 Kirchhundem
Kirchlengern: Gemeindearchiv, Am Rathaus 2, 32278 Kirchlengern
Kirchseeon: Gemeindearchiv, Rathausstr. 1, 85614 Kirchseeon
Kirn: Stadtarchiv, Kirchstr. 3, 55606 Kirn, Postfach 93, 55602 Kirn
Kitzingen: Stadtarchiv, Landwehrstr. 23, 97318 Kitzingen
Kitzscher: Stadtarchiv, Ernst-Schneller-Str. 1, 04567 Kitzscher
Kleve: Stadtarchiv, Tiergartenstr. 41, 47533 Kleve, Postfach 1960, 47517 Kleve
Klingenthal: Stadtarchiv, Kirchstr. 14, 08248 Klingenthal
Koblenz: Stadtarchiv, Burgstr. 1, 56068 Koblenz, Postfach 2064, 56020 Koblenz
Köln: Historisches Archiv der Stadt, Severinstr. 222-228, 50676 Köln
Königslutter am Elm: Stadtarchiv, Rathaus, Postfach 26, 38154 Königslutter am Elm
Königstein im Taunus: Stadtarchiv, Stadtverwaltung, Postfach, 61462 Königstein im Taunus
Königswinter: Stadtarchiv, 53637 Königswinter
Königs Wusterhausen: Stadtarchiv, Karl-Marx-Str. 23, 15711 Königs Wusterhausen
Köthen: Stadtarchiv, Stadtverwaltung, Markt 1-3, 06366 Köthen

Konstanz: Stadtarchiv, Benediktinerplatz 5, 78467 Konstanz
Korbach: Stadtarchiv, Stadtverwaltung, Postfach 340, 34497 Korbach
Korntal-Münchingen: Stadtarchiv, Bürgermeisteramt, Rathausgasse 2, 70825 Korntal-Münchingen, Postfach 1405, 70810 Korntal-Münchingen
Kornwestheim: Stadtarchiv, Stadtverwaltung, Jakob-Sigle-Platz 1, Postfach 1840, 70806 Kornwestheim
Korschenbroich: Stadtarchiv, Arndtstr. 27, 41352 Korschenbroich
Kranenburg: Gemeindearchiv, Klever Str. 4, 47559 Kranenburg
Kranichfeld: Stadtverwaltung Kranichfeld, Stadtarchiv, Alexanderstr. 7, 99448 Kranichfeld
Krefeld: Stadtarchiv, Girmesgath 120, 47803 Krefeld, Postfach 2740, 47727 Krefeld
Kreuzau: Gemeindearchiv, Bahnhofstr. 7, 52372 Kreuzau
Kreuztal: Stadtarchiv, Stadtverwaltung, Siegener Str. 5, 57223 Kreuztal
Krölpa: Verwaltungsgemeinschaft Krölpa, Archiv, Pößneckerstr. 24, 07387 Krölpa
Kronach: Stadtarchiv, Rathaus, Marktplatz 5, 96317 Kronach, Postfach 1761, 96307 Kronach
Kronberg im Taunus: Stadtarchiv, Stadt-verwaltung, Katharinenstr. 7, 61476 Kronberg im Taunus, Postfach 1280, 61467 Kronberg im Taunus
Krumbach (Schwaben): Stadtarchiv, Nattenhauserstr. 5, 86381 Krumbach (Schwaben)
Kühbach: Marktarchiv, Markt Kühbach, Schönbacher Str. 1, 86556 Kühbach
Künzelsau: Stadtarchiv, Stadtverwaltung, Stuttgarter Str. 7, 74653 Künzelsau
Kürten: Gemeindearchiv, Marktfeld 1, 51515 Kürten
Kulmbach: Stadtarchiv, Pestalozzistr. 8, 95326 Kulmbach
Laatzen: Stadtarchiv, Amt für Kultur, Schulen und Sport, Marktplatz 13, 30880

Laatzen, Postfach 110545, 30860 Laatzen
Laer: Gemeindearchiv, Kulturamt der Gemeinde Laer, Mühlenhoek 1, 48366 Laer
Lage: Stadtarchiv, Clara-Ernst-Platz 5, 32791 Lage (Lippe)
Lahnstein: Stadtarchiv, Altes Rathaus, Hochstr. 34, 56112 Lahnstein, Postfach 2180, 56108 Lahnstein
Lahr: Stadtarchiv, Rathaus, Rathausplatz 4, 77933 Lahr (Schwarzwald)
Laichingen: Stadtarchiv, Bürgermeisteramt, 89150 Laichingen
Lampertheim: Stadtarchiv, Stadtverwaltung, Römerstr. 102, 68623 Lampertheim, Postfach 1120, 68601 Lampertheim
Landau in der Pfalz: Stadtarchiv und Museum, Marienring 8, 76829 Landau in der Pfalz
Landsberg am Lech: Stadtarchiv, Lechstr. 132 °, 86899 Landsberg am Lech
Landshut: Stadtarchiv, Stadtresidenz, Altstadt 79, 84026 Landshut
Landstuhl: Stadtarchiv, Verbandsgemeindeverwaltung, 66849 Landstuhl
Langen: Stadtarchiv, Kulturhaus, Altes Amtsgericht, Darmstädter Str. 27, 63225 Langen
Langenau: Stadtarchiv, Stadtverwaltung, Pfleghof, 89129 Langenau
Langenberg: Gemeindearchiv, Klutenbrinkstr. 5, 33449 Langenberg
Langenfeld (Rheinland): Stadtarchiv, Rathaus, Konrad-Adenauer-Platz, 40764 Langenfeld (Rheinland)
Langenhagen: Stadtarchiv, Niedersachsenstr. 3, 30853 Langenhagen
Langenzenn: Archiv der Stadt, Denkmalplatz 4, 90579 Langenzenn
Langerwehe: Gemeindearchiv, Postfach 1240, 52379 Langerwehe
Langewiesen (Thüringen): Stadtverwaltung Langewiesen, Stadtarchiv, Ratsstr. 2, 98704 Langewiesen
Laubach (Hessen): Stadtarchiv, Stadt-

verwaltung, Rathaus, Friedrichstr. 11, 35321 Laubach (Hessen), Postfach 1242, 35317 Laubach (Hessen)
Lauda-Königshofen: Stadtarchiv, Bürgermeisteramt, 97922 Lauda-Königshofen
Lauenburg: Stadtarchiv, Elbstr. 2, 21481 Lauenburg
Lauf an der Pegnitz: Stadtarchiv mit Städt, Sammlungen, Spitalstr. 5, 91205 Lauf an der Pegnitz
Laufen: Stadtarchiv, Rathausplatz 3, 83410 Laufen
Lauffen am Neckar: Stadtarchiv, Stadtverwaltung, Rathaus, 74348 Lauffen am Neckar
Lauingen: Archiv der Stadt, Rathaus, 89415 Lauingen
Laupheim: Stadtarchiv, Marktplatz 1, 88471 Laupheim
Lauscha: Stadtverwaltung Lauscha, Stadtarchiv, Postfach, 98734 Lauscha, Dienstsitz: Bahnhofstr. 12, 98724 Lauscha
Lauterbach (Hessen): Stadtarchiv, Obergasse 44, Schulanbau zum "Güldenen Esel", Post: Stadtverwaltung, Rathaus, 36341 Lauterbach (Hessen)
Leer (Ostfriesland): Stadtarchiv, Rathausstr. 1, 26789 Leer, Postfach 2060, 26770 Leer
Lehrte: Stadtarchiv, 31275 Lehrte
Leichlingen: Stadtarchiv, Stadtverwaltung, Am Büscherhof 1, 42799 Leichlingen, Postfach 1665, 42787 Leichlingen
Leinfelden-Echterdingen: Stadtarchiv, Schloßbergweg 17, 70771 Leinfelden-Echterdingen, Postfach 100351, 70747 Leinfelden-Echterdingen
Leipzig: Stadtarchiv, Torgauer Str. 74, 04318 Leipzig, Postfach 780, 04007 Leipzig
Leisnig: Stadtarchiv, Markt 1, 04703 Leisnig
Lemförde: Samtgemeindearchiv, Bahnhofstr. 10 A, 49488 Lemförde
Lemgo: Stadtarchiv, Rampendal 20a, 32655 Lemgo, Postfach 740, 32655 Lemgo
Lengenfeld: Stadtarchiv, Hauptstr. 1, 08485 Lengenfeld

Lengerich: Stadtarchiv, Rathausplatz 1, 49525 Lengerich, Postfach 1540, 49525 Lengerich
Lenggries: Gemeindearchiv, Rathausplatz 1, 83661 Lenggries
Lennestadt: Stadtarchiv, Kölner Str. 57, 57368 Lennestadt-Grevenbrück
Leonberg: Stadtarchiv, Altes Rathaus Eltingen, Carl-Schmincke-Str. 37, 71229 Leonberg, Postfach 1753, 71226 Leonberg
Letschin: Amtsarchiv Letschin, Bahnhofstr. 30a, 15324 Letschin
Leutkirch: Stadtarchiv, Stadtverwaltung, 88299 Leutkirch, Postfach 1260, 88292 Leutkirch
Leverkusen: Stadtarchiv, Landrat-Trimborn-Platz 1 und Stadtgeschichtliches Dokumentationszentrum, Haus-Vorster-Str. 6, 51379 Leverkusen (Opladen), Post: Postfach 101140, 51311 Leverkusen
Lich: Städtisches Archiv, Unterstadt 1, 35423 Lich
Lichtenau: Archiv des Marktfleckens Lichtenau, Gemeindeverwaltung, 91586 Lichtenau
Lichtenfels: Stadtarchiv, Rathaus, Markt-platz 5, 96215 Lichtenfels
Lichtenstein: Stadtarchiv, Poststr. 4, 09350 Lichtenstein
Liebenwalde: Amtsarchiv Liebenwalde, Am Markt 20, 16559 Liebenwalde
Lienen: Gemeindearchiv, Hauptstr. 14, 49536 Lienen
Limburg an der Lahn: Stadtarchiv, Schloß, 65549 Limburg an der Lahn
Lindau/Bodensee: Stadtarchiv, Altes Rathaus, Reichsplatz, 88131 Lindau/Bodensee
Linden: Stadtarchiv, Stadtverwaltung, Konrad-Adenauer-Str. 25, 35440 Linden, Postfach 1155, 35436 Linden
Lindlar: Gemeindearchiv, Borromäusstr. 1, 51789 Lindlar
Lingen/Ems: Stadtarchiv, Postfach 2060, 49803 Lingen/Ems
Linz am Rhein: Stadtarchiv, Klosterstr. (Servitessenkirche), 53545 Linz am Rhein,

Postfach 101, 53542 Linz am Rhein
Lippstadt: Archiv- und Museumsamt, Soeststr. 8, 59555 Lippstadt, Postfach 2540, 59535 Lippstadt
Lobenstein: Stadtverwaltung Moorbad Lobenstein, Stadtarchiv, Postfach 130, 07353 Lobenstein, Dienstsitz: Markt 1, 07356 Lobenstein
Löbau: Stadtarchiv, Altmarkt 1, 02708 Löbau, Postfach 180, 02701 Löbau
Löhne: Stadtarchiv, Stadtverwaltung, Oeynhausener Str. 41, 32584 Löhne
Lörrach: Stadtarchiv, Bürgermeisteramt, Rathaus, Luisenstr. 16, 79539 Lörrach, Postfach 1260, 79537 Lörrach
Lohmar: Stadtarchiv, Hauptstr. 83, 53797 Lohmar
Lohne: Stadtverwaltung, Vogtstr. 26, 49393 Lohne
Lommatzsch: Stadtarchiv, Rathaus, 01623 Lommatzsch
Lorch: Stadtarchiv, Stadtverwaltung, Hauptstr. 19, 73547 Lorch
Lorsch: Stadtarchiv, Kaiser-Wilhelm-Platz 1, 64653 Lorsch
Lucka: Stadtverwaltung Lucka, Stadtarchiv, Postfach 55, 04611 Lucka, Dienstsitz: Pegauer Str. 17, 04613 Lucka
Luckau: Stadtarchiv, Am Markt 34, 15926 Luckau
Luckenwalde: Stadtarchiv, Stadtverwalt--ung, Markt 10, 14943 Luckenwalde
Ludwigsburg: Stadtarchiv, Kaiserstr. 14, 71636 Ludwigsburg, Postfach 249, 71602 Ludwigsburg
Ludwigsfelde: Stadtarchiv, Potsdamer Str. 48, 14974 Ludwigsfelde
Ludwigshafen am Rhein: Stadtarchiv, Rottstr. 17, 67061 Ludwigshafen, Postfach 211225, 67012 Ludwigshafen
Lübbecke: Stadtarchiv, Am Markt (Altes Rathaus), 32312 Lübbecke, Postfach 1453, 32294 Lübbecke
Lübeck: Archiv der Hansestadt, Mühlen-damm 1-3, 23552 Lübeck
Lüchow: Stadtarchiv, Burgstr., 29439 Lüchow
Lüdenscheid: Stadtarchiv, Stadtverwalt-

ung, Rathausplatz 2, 58507 Lüdenscheid
Lüdinghausen: Stadtarchiv, Borg 2, 59348 Lüdinghausen, Postfach 1531, 59335 Lüdinghausen
Lügde: Stadtarchiv, Stadtverwaltung, 32676 Lügde, Postfach 1352 und 1353, 32670 Lügde
Lüneburg: Stadtarchiv, Rathaus, Postfach 2540, 21315 Lüneburg
Lünen: Stadtarchiv, Stadtverwaltung, Rathaus, 44530 Lünen
Magdeburg: Stadtarchiv, Bei der Hauptwache 4-6, 39104 Magdeburg, Post: Landeshauptstadt Magdeburg, Der Oberbürgermeister, Stadtarchiv, 39090 Magdeburg
Mainz: Stadtarchiv, Rheinallee 3 B, 55116 Mainz
Mannheim: Stadtarchiv, Collinicenter, 68161 Mannheim
Marbach am Neckar: Stadtarchiv, Marktstr. 25, 71672 Marbach am Neckar, Postfach 1115, 71666 Marbach am Neckar
Marburg: Stadtarchiv, Friedrichsplatz 15, 35037 Marburg, Post: Magistrat der Stadt Marburg, 35035 Marburg
Marienberg: Stadtarchiv, Markt 1, 09496 Marienberg
Marienmünster: Stadtarchiv, Schulstr. 1, 37696 Marienmünster (Vörden)
Markdorf: Stadtarchiv, Stadtverwaltung, Rathaus, 88677 Markdorf (Baden), Postfach 1240, 88670 Markdorf (Baden)
Markgröningen: Stadtarchiv, Finstere Gasse 3, 71706 Markgröningen, Postfach 1262, 71703 Markgröningen
Markneukirchen: Stadtarchiv, Am Rathaus 2, 08258 Markneukirchen
Marktoberdorf: Stadtarchiv, Rathaus, Jahnstr. 1, 87616 Marktoberdorf
Marktredwitz: Stadtarchiv, Neues Rathaus, Egerstr. 2, 95615 Marktredwitz, Postfach 609, 95606 Marktredwitz
Marl: Stadtarchiv, Rathaus, Creiler Platz 1, 45768 Marl
Marsberg: Stadtarchiv, Lillerstr. 8, 34431 Marsberg, Postfach 1341, 34419 Marsberg

Massenheim: Stadtarchiv. See Hochheim am Main
Maulbronn: Stadtarchiv, Rathaus, Klosterhof 31, 75433 Maulbronn, Postfach 47, 75429 Maulbronn
Mayen: Stadtarchiv, Genovevaburg, Eifeler Landschaftsmuseum, 56727 Mayen
Mechernich: Stadtarchiv, Postfach 1260, 53894 Mechernich-Kommern
Meckenheim (Rheinland): Stadtarchiv, Stadtverwaltung, 53340 Meckenheim (Rheinland), Postfach 1180, 53333 Meckenheim (Rheinland)
Meerbusch (Büderich): Stadtarchiv, Karl-Borromäus-Str. 2a, 40667 Meerbusch (Büderich), Postfach 1664, 40641 Meerbusch (Büderich)
Meersburg (Bodensee): Stadtarchiv, Kulturamt der Stadt Meersburg, Postfach 1140, 88701 Meersburg (Bodensee)
Meinerzhagen: Stadtarchiv, Altes Rathaus, Oststr. 5, 58540 Meinerzhagen
Meiningen: Stadtarchiv, Schloß Bibrabau, Schloßplatz 1, 98617 Meining-en
Meißen: Stadtarchiv, Kleinmarkt 5, 01662 Meißen
Meldorf: Stadtarchiv, Dithmarscher Landesmuseum, Bütjestr. 2-4, Landwirtschaftsmuseum, Jungfernstieg 4, 25704 Meldorf
Melle: Stadtarchiv (Stored in Niedersächsischen Staatsarchiv in Osnabrück)
Mellrichstadt: Stadtarchiv, Hauptstr. 4, 97638 Mellrichstadt
Memmingen: Stadtarchiv, Ulmer Str. 19, 87700 Memmingen, Postfach 1853, 87688 Memmingen
Menden (Sauerland): Archiv der Stadt, Altes Rathaus, Postfach 660, 58688 Menden (Sauerland)
Mengen: Stadtarchiv, Stadtverwaltung, 88512 Mengen
Meppen: Stadtarchiv, Markt 43, 49716 Meppen
Merseburg: Historisches Stadtarchiv, Stadtverwaltung, Wilhelm-Liebknecht-Str. 1, 06217 Merseburg

Merzenich: Gemeindearchiv, Valdersweg 1, 52399 Merzenich
Meschede: Stadtarchiv, Verwaltungsstelle Freienohl, Hauptstr. 38-40, 59872 Meschede
Meßkirch: Stadtarchiv, Rathaus, Conradin-Kreutzer-Str. 1, 88605 Meßkirch
Metelen: Stadtarchiv, Sendplatz 18, 48629 Metelen
Mettingen: Gemeindearchiv, Rathausplatz 1, 49497 Mettingen
Mettmann: Stadtarchiv, Neanderstr. 85, 40822 Mettmann
Metzingen: Stadtarchiv, Postfach 1363, 72544 Metzingen
Meuselwitz: Stadtverwaltung Meuselwitz, Stadtarchiv, Postfach 331, 04607 Meuselwitz, Dienstsitz: Rathausstr. 1, 04610 Meuselwitz
Meyenburg: Stadtarchiv, Freyensteiner Str. 42, 16945 Meyenburg
Michelstadt: Stadtarchiv, Löwenhof, Marktplatz, Post: Stadtverwaltung, Frank-furter Str. 3, 64720 Michelstadt
Michendorf: Amtsarchiv Michendorf, Potsdamer Str. 33-37, 14552 Michendorf
Miesbach: Stadtarchiv, Stadtverwaltung, Rathausplatz 1, 83714 Miesbach, Postfach 29, 83711 Miesbach
Milda: Gemeindeverwaltung Milda, Gemeindearchiv, Dorfstr. 60, 07751 Milda
Miltenberg: Stadtarchiv, Rathaus, 63897 Miltenberg, Postfach 1740, 63887 Miltenberg
Mindelheim: Stadtarchiv, Verwaltung Städttische Museen, Hermelestr. 4, 87719 Mindelheim
Minden: Kommunalarchiv Minden (Archiv der Stadt Minden und des Kreises Minden-Lübbecke), Tonhallenstr. 7, 32423 Minden, Postfach 3080, 32387 Minden
Mittenwald: Marktarchiv, Dammkarstr. 3, 82481 Mittenwald
Mittweida: Stadtarchiv, Rochlitzer Str. 1, 09642 Mittweida
Mölln: Stadtarchiv, Stadthaus, Wasserkrüger Weg 16, 23879 Mölln

Mönchengladbach: Stadtarchiv, Aachener Str. 2, 41050 Mönchengladbach
Mörfelden-Walldorf: Stadtarchiv, Westendstr. 8 und Flughafenstr. 37, 64546 Mörfelden-Walldorf
Moers: Stadtarchiv, Unterwallstr. 17, 47441 Moers
Monheim: Stadtarchiv, Tempelhofer Str. 13, 40789 Monheim
Monschau: Stadtarchiv, Laufenstr. 84, 52156 Monschau
Montabaur: Stadtarchiv, Josef-Kehrein-Schule, Gelbachstr., 56410 Montabaur
Moosburg an der Isar: Stadtarchiv, Stadtplatz 13, 85368 Moosburg an der Isar
Moringen: Stadtarchiv, Amtsfreiheit 8, 37186 Moringen
Morsbach/Sieg: Gemeindearchiv, Bahnhofstr. 2, 51597 Morsbach/Sieg
Mosbach (Baden): Stadtarchiv, Hauptstr. 29, 74821 Mosbach (Baden), Postfach 1162, 74819 Mosbach (Baden)
Much: Gemeindearchiv, Hauptstr. 57, 53804 Much
Mühlacker: Stadtarchiv, Stadtverwaltung, Postfach 1163, 75415 Mühlacker
Mühlberg: Stadtarchiv, Schloßplatz 1, 04931 Mühlberg
Mühldorf am Inn: Stadtarchiv, Rathaus, 84453 Mühldorf am Inn
Mühlhausen: Stadtverwaltung Mühlhausen, Stadtarchiv, Postfach 29 und 40, 99961 Mühlhausen, Dienstsitz: Ratsstr. 19, 99974 Mühlhausen
Mühlheim an der Donau: Stadtarchiv, Stadtverwaltung, 78570 Mühlheim an der Donau
Mühltroff: Stadtarchiv, Postfach, 07917 Mühltroff
Mülheim an der Ruhr: Stadtarchiv, Aktienstr. 85, 45473 Mülheim an der Ruhr, Postfach 101953, 45466 Mülheim an der Ruhr
Müllheim (Baden): Stadtarchiv, Rathaus, Bismarckstr. 3, 79379 Müllheim (Baden)
Münchberg (Oberfranken): Stadtarchiv, Kirchplatz 7, 95213 Münchberg

(Oberfranken), Postfach 467, 95213 Münchberg (Oberfranken)

Müncheberg: Amts- und Stadtarchiv Müncheberg, Rathausstr. 1, 15372 Müncheberg

München: Stadtarchiv, Winzererstr. 68, 80797 München

Münnerstadt: Stadtarchiv, Postfach 129, 97702 Münnerstadt

Münsingen: Stadtarchiv, Bachwiesenstr. 7, 72525 Münsingen, Postfach 1140, 72521 Münsingen

Münster: Stadtarchiv, Hörsterstr. 28, 48143 Münster

Münzenberg: Stadtarchiv, Hauptstr. 22, 35516 Münzenberg, Stadtteil Gambach

Munderkingen: Stadtarchiv, Stadtverwaltung, 89597 Munderkingen

Murnau: Archiv des Marktes, Untermarkt 13, 82418 Murnau am Staffelsee

Mylau: Stadtarchiv, 08499 Mylau

Nagold: Stadtarchiv, Badgasse 3, 72202 Nagold, Postfach 1444, 72194 Nagold

Nassau: Stadtarchiv, Rathaus, Postfach 1107, 56371 Nassau

Nauen: Stadtarchiv, Rathausplatz 1, 14641 Nauen

Naumburg: Stadtarchiv, Stadtverwaltung, Georgenberg 6, 06618 Naumburg

Neckargemünd: Stadtarchiv, Rathaus Villa Menzer, Dilsberger Str. 2, 69151 Neckargemünd

Neckarsteinach: Städt. Archiv, Hauptstr. 7, 69239 Neckarsteinach

Neckarsulm: Stadtarchiv, Binswanger Str. 3, 74172 Neckarsulm

Nennhausen: Amtsarchiv Nennhausen, Platz der Jugend, 14715 Nennhausen

Nettersheim: Gemeindearchiv, Krausstr. 2, 53947 Nettersheim

Netzschkau (Vogtland): Stadtarchiv, Markt 12/13, 08491 Netzschkaau (Vogtland)

Neubrandenburg: Stadtarchiv, Stadtver-waltung Neubrandenburg, Postfach 1814, 17008 Neubrandenburg; Dienstsitz: Friedrich-Engels-Ring 53, 17033 Neubrandenburg

Neuburg an der Donau: Stadtarchiv, Bahnhofstr. B 142, 86633 Neuburg an der Donau

Neuenrade: Stadtarchiv, Stadtverwaltung, Alte Burg 1, 58809 Neuenrade

Neu-Isenburg: Stadtarchiv, Rathaus, Hugenotten-Allee 53, 63263 Neu-Isenburg

Neukirchen-Vluyn: Stadtarchiv, Hans-Böckler-Str. 26, 47504 Neukirchen-Vluyn

Neumünster: Stadtarchiv, Grossflechen 68 und Parkstr. 17, 24534 Neumünster, Post: Stadtverwaltung, Postfach 2640, 24516 Neumünster

Neunburg vorm Wald: Stadtarchiv, 92431 Neunburg vorm Wald

Neunkirchen: Stadtarchiv, Rathaus, Postfach 1163, 66511 Neunkirchen

Neuötting: Stadtarchiv, Rathaus, 84524 Neuötting

Neuseddin: Verwaltungsgemeinschaftsarchiv Neuseddin, Kiefernweg 5, 14554 Neuseddin

Neuss: Stadtarchiv, Oberstr. 15, 41460 Neuss

Neustadt (Sachsen): Stadtarchiv, Markt 1, 01841 Neustadt (Sachsen)

Neustadt an der Aisch: Stadtarchiv, An der Bleiche 1, 91413 Neustadt an der Aisch, Postfach 1669, 91406 Neustadt an der Aisch

Neustadt an der Donau: Stadtarchiv, Stadtplatz 1, 93333 Neustadt an der Donau, Postfach 1452, 93330 Neustadt an der Donau

Neustadt an der Dosse: Amtsarchiv Neustadt, Bahnhofstr. 6, 16845 Neustadt an der Dosse

Neustadt in Holstein: Stadtarchiv, Stadtverwaltung, Am Markt 1, 23730 Neustadt in Holstein

Neustadt an der Orla: Stadtverwaltung, Stadtarchiv, Markt 1, 07801 Neustadt an der Orla

Neustadt an der Weinstraße: Stadtarchiv, Klemmhof, 67433 Neustadt an der Weinstraße, Postfach 100962, 67409 Neustadt an der Weinstraße

Neustrelitz: Stadtarchiv, Markt 1, 17235 Neustrelitz

Neu-Ulm: Stadtarchiv, Rathaus, Augsburger Str. 15, 89231 Neu-Ulm
Neuwied: Stadtarchiv, Landeshauptarchiv Koblenz - Außenstelle Rommersdorf -mit Stadtarchiv Neuwied, Abtei Rommersdorf, 56566 Neuwied
Neu Wulmstorf: Gemeindearchiv, Bahnhofstr. 39, 21629 Neu Wulmstorf, Postfach 1120, 21624 Wulmstorf
Nidda: Stadtarchiv, Stadtverwaltung, Rathaus, 63667 Nidda, Postfach 1250, 63659 Nidda
Nideggen: Stadtarchiv, Stadtverwaltung, Rathaus, Zülpicher Str. 1, 52385 Nid-eggen, Postfach 1161, 52383 Nideggen
Niederer Fläming: Amtsarchiv Niederer Fläming, Chausseestr. 12a, 14913 Hohenseefeld
Niedergörsdorf: Amtsarchiv Niedergörsdorf, Dorfstr. 14, 14913 Niedergörsdorf
Niederkassel: Stadtarchiv, Rathausstr. 19, 53859 Niederkassel
Niederzier: Gemeindearchiv, Postfach 1120, 52380 Niederzier
Nieheim: Stadtarchiv, Rathaus, 33039 Nieheim
Nienburg (Weser): Stadtarchiv, "Villa Holscher", Verdener Str. 24, 31582 Nienburg (Weser), Postfach 1780, 31567 Nienburg (Weser)
Nördlingen: Stadtarchiv, Hallgebäude, Weinmarkt 1, 86720 Nördlingen
Nörvenich: Gemeindearchiv, Bahnhofstr. 25, 52388 Nörvenich
Nordenham: Stadtarchiv, Enjebuhrer Str. 10, 26954 Nordenham-Abbehausen
Norderney: Stadtarchiv, 26548 Norderney
Nordhausen: Stadtarchiv, Markt 1, Postfach 132, 99732 Nordhausen
Nordhorn: Stadtarchiv, Bahnhofstr. 24, 48529 Nordhorn, Postfach 2429, 48522 Nordhorn
Northeim: Stadtarchiv, St. Blasien, Am Münster 30, 37154 Northeim
Nortorf: Stadtarchiv, Rathaus, Niedernstr. 6, 24589 Nortorf, Postfach 1162, 24585

Nortorf
Nossen: Stadtarchiv, Rathaus, Markt 31, 01683 Nossen
Nottuln: Gemeindearchiv, Stiftsplatz 7, 48301 Nottuln
Nürnberg: Stadtarchiv, Egidienplatz 23, 90403 Nürnberg, Post: 90317 Nürnberg
Nürtingen: Stadtarchiv, Hauptamt, 72622 Nürtingen, Postfach 1920, 72609 Nürtingen
Oberammergau: Gemeindearchiv, Schnitzlergasse 5, 82487 Oberammergau
Oberharz: See Clausthal-Zellerfeld
Oberhausen (Rheinland): Stadtarchiv (Schloß Oberhausen), Konrad-Adenauer-Allee 46, Postfach 101505, 46042 Oberhausen (Rheinland)
Oberkirch: Stadtarchiv, Kultur- und Verkehrsamt, Eisenbahnstr. 1, 77704 Oberkirch
Oberlungwitz: Stadtarchiv, Hofer Str. 203, 09353 Oberlungwitz
Obermoschel: Stadtarchiv, Rathaus, 67823 Obermoschel
Oberndorf am Neckar: Stadt- und Zeitungsarchiv, Stadtverwaltung, Klosterstr. 14, 78727 Oberndorf am Neckar, Postfach 1105, 78720 Oberndorf am Neckar
Obernkirchen: Stadtarchiv (Stored in Niedersächsischen Staatsarchiv Bückeburg)
Oberstdorf: Gemeindearchiv, Marktplatz 2, 87561 Oberstdorf, Postfach 1540, 87561 Oberstdorf
Oberursel (Taunus): Stadtarchiv, Schulstr. 32, 61440 Oberursel (Taunus)
Oberviechtach: Stadtarchiv, Haus der Bäuerin 1, 92526 Oberviechtach
Oberwiesenthal: Stadtarchiv, Stadtverwaltung, Markt 8, Postfach 44, 09482 Kurort Oberwiesenthal
Ochsenfurt: Stadtarchiv, Rathaus, 97199 Ochsenfurt, Postfach 1153, 97195 Ochsenfurt
Ochsenhausen: Stadtarchiv, Stadtverwaltung, 88416 Ochsenhausen
Ochtrup: Stadtarchiv, Prof. -Gärtner - Str. 4, 48607 Ochtrup
Odenthal: Gemeindearchiv, Altenberger-

Dom-Str. 31, 51519 Odenthal
Oederan: Stadtarchiv, Markt 5, 09569 Oederan
Öhringen: Stadtarchiv, Stadtverwaltung, Marktplatz 15, 74613 Öhringen, Postfach 1209, 74602 Öhringen
Oelde: Stadtarchiv. See Kreis Warendorf
Oelsnitz (Vogtland): Stadtarchiv, Markt 1, 08606 Oelsnitz (Vogtland)
Oer-Erkenschwick: Stadtarchiv, Christoph-Stöver-Str. 2 (Realschule), Oer-Erkenschwick
Oerlinghausen: Stadtarchiv, Hauptstr. 14 A, 33813 Oerlinghausen, Postfach 1344, 33806 Oerlinghausen
Oestrich-Winkel: Stadtarchiv, Stadtver-waltung, Hauptstr. 31, 65375 Oestrich-Winkel, Postfach 1108, 65370 Oestrich-Winkel
Offenbach: Stadtarchiv, Herrnstr. 61, 63065 Offenbach am Main
Offenburg: Stadtarchiv, Ritterstr. 10, 77652 Offenburg
Olbernhau: Stadtarchiv, Stadtverwaltung, Grünthaler Str. 28, 09526 Olbernhau
Oldenburg (Oldenburg): Stadtarchiv, Damm 41, Postfach 2427, 26105 Oldenburg
Olfen: Stadtarchiv, Kirchstr. 5, 59309 Olfen, Postfach 134, 59396 Olfen
Olpe/Biggesee: Stadtarchiv, "Altes Lyzeum", Franziskanerstr. 6/8, 57462 Olpe/Biggesee
Olsberg: Stadtarchiv, Stadtverwaltung, 59939 Olsberg, Postfach 1462, 59933 Olsberg
Ortenberg: Stadtarchiv, Kasinostr., Post: S t a d t v e r w a l t u n g / H a u p t a m t, Lauterbacher Str. 2, 63683 Ortenberg
Ortrand: Amts- und Stadtarchiv Ortrand, 01990 Ortrand
Oschatz: Stadtarchiv, 04758 Oschatz
Ostbevern: Gemeindearchiv. See Kreis Warendorf
Osterholz-Scharmbeck: Stadtarchiv, Rathausstr. 1, 27711 Osterholz-Scharmbeck
Osterode am Harz: Stadtarchiv, Altes Rathaus, Martin-Luther-Platz 2, 37520

Osterode am Harz, Postfach 1720, 37507 Osterode am Harz
Ostfildern: Stadtarchiv, Klosterhof Nellingen, 73760 Ostfildern, Postfach 1120, 73740 Ostfildern
Ottobeuren: Stadtarchiv, Rathaus, Marktplatz 6, 87724 Ottobeuren
Owen/Teck: Stadtarchiv, Bürgermeisteramt, Postfach 1151, 73277 Owen/Teck
Paderborn: Stadtarchiv, Marienplatz 2a, 33095 Paderborn
Parchim: Stadtarchiv, Putlitzer Str. 56, 19370 Parchim
Passau: Stadtarchiv, Rathausplatz 2, 94032 Passau, Postfach 2447, 94014 Passau
Pausa: Stadtarchiv, Newmarkt 1, 07952 Pausa
Peine: Stadtarchiv, Windmühlenwall 26, 31224 Peine, Postfach 1760, 31207 Peine
Peitz: Amtsarchiv Peitz, Markt 1, 03185 Peitz
Penig: Stadtarchiv, Markt 6, 09322 Penig
Perleberg: Stadtarchiv, Rathaus, Großer Markt, 19348 Perleberg
Petershagen: Stadtarchiv, Rathaus, Bahnhofstr. 63, 32469 Petershagen, Postfach 1120, 32458 Petershagen
Pfaffenhofen an der Ilm: Stadtarchiv, Hauptplatz 1, 85276 Pfaffenhofen an der Ilm
Pforzheim: Stadtarchiv, Brettener Str. 19, 75177 Pforzheim
Pfullendorf: Stadt- und Spitalarchiv, Bürgermeisteramt, 88630 Pfullendorf (Baden)
Pfullingen: Stadtarchiv, Bürgermeisteramt, 72793 Pfullingen
Pfungstadt: Stadtarchiv, Stadtverwaltung, Kirchstr. 12-14, Postfach 64319 Pfungstadt
Philippsburg: Stadtarchiv, Rote-Tor-Str. 10, 76661 Philippsburg
Pirmasens: Stadtarchiv, Stadtverwaltung, 66953 Pirmasens
Pirna: Stadtarchiv, Klosterhof 3, 01796 Pirna
Plauen (Vogtland): Stadtarchiv, Unterer Graben 1, 08523 Plauen (Vogtland)

Plettenberg: Stadtarchiv, Bahnhofstr. 103, 58840 Plettenberg
Plochingen: Stadtarchiv, Stadtverwaltung, Schulstr. 5, 73207 Plochingen
Plön: Archiv der Stadt, Schloßberg 4, 24306 Plön
Pößneck: Stadtarchiv, Rathaus, Markt 11, 07381 Pößneck, Postfach 126, 07373 Pößneck
Pöttmes: Marktarchiv, v.-Gumppenberg-Str. 19, 86554 Pöttmes
Pohlheim: Stadtarchiv, 35415 Pohlheim, Postfach 1154, 35411 Pohlheim
Porta Westfalica: Stadtarchiv, Kempstr. 1, 32457 Porta Westfalica, Postfach 1463, 32440 Porta Westfalica
Potsdam: Stadtarchiv, Freidrich-Ebert-Str. 79-81, 14469 Potsdam
Premnitz: Amtsarchiv Premnitz, Liebigstr. 43, 14727 Premnitz
Prenzlau: Stadtarchiv, Am Steintor 4, 17291 Prenzlau
Preußisch Oldendorf: Stadtarchiv, Rathausstr. 3, 32361 Preußisch Oldendorf, Postfach 1260, 32353 Preußisch Oldendorf
Prien am Chiemsee: Marktarchiv, Rathaus, Hauptverwaltung, Rathausplatz 1, 83209 Prien am Chiemsee
Prüm: Stadtarchiv, Rathaus, 54595 Prüm, Postfach 1060, 54591 Prüm
Püttlingen/Saar: Stadtarchiv, Postfach 101240, 66338 Püttlingen/Saar
Pulheim: Stadtarchiv, Rathaus, Alte Kölner Str. 26, 50259 Pulheim, Postfach 1345, 50241 Pulheim
Quakenbrück: Stadtarchiv, 49610 Quakenbrück (Stored in Niedersächsischen Staatsarchiv in Osnabrück)
Quedlinburg: Stadtarchiv, Stadtverwaltung, Markt 1, Postfach 97, 06472 Quedlinburg
Querfurt: Stadtarchiv, Stadtverwaltung, Markt 1, 06268 Querfurt
Radeberg: Stadtarchiv, Markt 19, 01454 Radeberg
Radebeul: Stadtarchiv, Gohliser Str. 1, 01445 Radebeul, Postfach 010121, 01435 Radebeul

Radevormwald: Stadtarchiv, 42477 Radevormwald
Radolfzell: Stadtarchiv, Löwengasse 12, 78315 Radolfzell am Bodensee
Rahden: Stadtarchiv, Lange Str. 9, 32369 Rahden
Rain: Stadtarchiv, Hauptstr. 60, 86641 Rain
Rastatt: Stadtarchiv, Herrenstr. 11, 76437 Rastatt
Rastenberg: Stadtarchiv, Markt 1, 99636 Rastenberg
Rathenow: Stadtarchiv, Jahnstr. 34, 14712 Rathenow
Ratingen: Stadtarchiv, Mülheimer Str. 47, 40878 Ratingen
Raunheim: Stadtarchiv, Rathaus, Schulstr. 2, 65479 Raunheim
Ravensburg: Stadtarchiv, Kuppelnaustr. 7, 88212 Ravensburg, Postfach 2180, 88191 Ravensburg
Recke: Gemeindearchiv, 49509 Recke, Postfach 1252, 49506 Recke
Recklinghausen: Stadt- und Vestisches Archiv, Hohenzollernstr. 12, 45659 Recklinghausen
Rees: Stadtarchiv, Sahlerstr. 8, 46459 Rees
Regen: Stadtarchiv, Stadtverwaltung, Rathaus, 94209 Regen
Regensburg: Stadtarchiv, Keplerstraße 1, 93047 Regensburg, Postfach 110643, 93019 Regensburg
Rehau (Oberfranken): Stadtarchiv, Stadtverwaltung, Martin-Luther-Str. 1, 95111 Rehau (Oberfranken), Postfach 1560, 95105 Rehau (Oberfranken)
Rehden: Samtgemeindearchiv, Schulstr. 18, 49452 Rehden
Rehna: Stadtarchiv, Mühlenstr. 1, 19217 Rehna
Reichenbach (Vogtland): Stadtarchiv, Markt 6, 08468 Reichenbach (Vogtland)
Reinbek: Stadtarchiv, Rathaus, Hamburger Str. 7, 21465 Reinbek
Reinheim: Stadtarchiv, Kirchstr. 24 (IM Hofgut), Stadtverwaltung, Cestasplatz 1, 64354 Reinheim
Remagen: Stadtarchiv, Rathaus, 53424

Remagen

Remda: Verwaltungsgemeinschaft Remda, Stadtarchiv, Rudolstädter Str. 8-10, Haus II, 07407 Remda

Remscheid: Stadtarchiv, Honsberger Str. 4, 42849 Remscheid

Remseck am Neckar: Stadtarchiv, Bürgermeisteramt, 71686 Remseck am Neckar, Postfach 1163, 71480 Remseck am Neckar

Renchen: Stadtarchiv, Stadtverwaltung, Hauptstr. 57, 77871 Renchen

Rendsburg: Archiv der Stadt, Am Gymnasium 4, 24768 Rendsburg

Rethem (Aller): Stadtverwaltung, Lange Str. 4, 27336 Rethem (Aller), Postfach 1240, 27335 Rethem (Aller)

Reutlingen: Stadtarchiv, Rathaus, Marktplatz 22, 72764 Reutlingen, Postfach 2543, 72715 Reutlingen

Rheda-Wiedenbrück: Stadtarchiv, Rathausplatz 13, 33378 Rheda-Wiedenbrück, Postfach 2309, 33375 Rheda-Wiedenbrück

Rhede: Hauptamt, Archiv, Rathausplatz 9, 46414 Rhede, Postfach 64, 46406 Rhede

Rheinbach: Stadtarchiv, Himmeroder Wall 6, 53359 Rheinbach, Postfach 1128, 53348 Rheinbach

Rheinberg: Stadtarchiv, Alte Kellnerei, Innenwall 104, 47495 Rheinberg, Postfach, 47493 Rheinberg

Rheine: Stadtarchiv, Marktstr. 12, 48431 Rheine, Postfach 2063, 48410 Rheine

Rheinfelden (Baden): Stadtarchiv, Kirchplatz 2, 79618 Rheinfelden (Baden), Postfach 1560, 79605 Rheinfelden (Baden)

Rheurdt: Gemeindearchiv, Rathausstr. 35, 47509 Rheurdt

Rhinow: Amtsarchiv Rhinow, Lilienthalstr. 3, 14728 Rhinow

Ribnitz-Damgarten: Stadtarchiv, Im Kloster 3, 18303 Ribnitz-Damgarten

Riedenburg: Stadtarchiv, Postfach 28, 93337 Riedenburg

Riedlingen: Stadtarchiv, Stadtverwaltung, 88499 Riedlingen

Rieneck: Stadtarchiv, Bürgerzentrum, Schulgasse 4, 97794 Rieneck

Rietberg: Stadtarchiv, Rügenstr. 1, 33397 Rietberg

Rinteln: Stadtarchiv, Marktplatz 7 (Bürgerhaus), 31737 Rinteln, Postfach 1460, 31724 Rinteln

Rodewisch: Stadtarchiv, Wernesgrüner Str. 32, 08228 Rodewisch

Rodgau: Stadtarchiv, Stadtteil Dudenhofen, Altes Rathauss, Georg-August-Zinn-Str.1 und Stadtteil Jügesheim, Neues Rathaus, Hintergasse 15, 63110 Rodgau

Roding: Stadtarchiv, Stadtverwaltung, Schulstr. 12, 93426 Roding

Rödermark: Stadtarchiv, Stadtverwaltung, 63322 Rödermark

Rödinghausen: Gemeindearchiv, Heerstr. 2, 32289 Rödinghausen

Römhild: Stadtverwaltung Römhild, Stadtarchiv, Griebelstr. 28, 98631 Römhild, Dienstsitz: Schloß "Glücks-burg", 98631 Römhild

Rommerskirchen: Gemeindearchiv, Nettesheimer Weg (Schulgebäude), 41569 Rommerskirchen, Postfach 101160, 41565 Rommerskirchen

Romrod: Stadtarchiv, Stadtverwaltung, 36329 Romrod

Rosendahl: Gemeindearchiv, Hauptstr. 30, 48720 Rosendahl, Postfach 1109, 48713 Rosendahl

Rosengarten: Ortsteilarchive Westheim, Rieden und Uttenhofen, Post: Gemeindeverwaltung, 74538 Rosengarten

Rosengarten: Gemeindearchiv, Bremer Str. 42, 21224 Rosengarten-Nenndorf, Postfach 240, 21222 Rosengarten-Nenndorf

Rosenheim (Oberbayern): Stadtarchiv, Max-Bram-Platz 2a, 83022 Rosenheim (Oberbayern)

Rostock: Archiv der Hansestadt Rostock, Hinter dem Rathaus 5, 18050 Rostock

Rot am See: Gemeindearchiv, Rathaus, Raiffeisenstr. 1, 74585 Rot am See

Rotenburg/Wümme: Stadtarchiv, Rathaus, Große Str. 1, 27356 Rotenburg/ Wümme

Roth (Mittelfranken): Stadtarchiv, Hauptstr. 1, 91154 Roth (Mittelfranken), Postfach 40, 91142 Roth (Mittelfranken)

Rothenburg ob der Tauber: Stadtarchiv, Büttelhaus, Milchmarkt 2, 91541 Rothenburg ob der Tauber

Rottenburg am Neckar: Stadt- und Spitalarchiv, Obere Gasse 12, 72108 Rottenburg am Neckar, Postfach 29, 72101 Rottenburg am Neckar

Rottweil: Stadtarchiv, Engelgasse 13, 78628 Rottweil, Postfach 1753, 78617 Rottweil

Rudolstadt: Stadtarchiv, Rathaus, Markt 7, 07407 Rudolstadt

Rüdesheim: Stadtarchiv, Stadtverwaltung, Rathaus, Markt 16, 65385 Rüdesheim am Rhein

Rümmingen: Gemeindearchiv, Rathaus, Lörracher Str. 9, 79595 Rümmingen

Rüsselsheim: Stadtarchiv, In der Festung, Hauptmann-Scheuermann-Weg 4, 65428 Rüsselsheim

Rüthen: Stadtarchiv, Stadtverwaltung, Hochstr. 14, 59602 Rüthen, Postfach 1026, 59598 Rüthen

Ruhpolding: Gemeinde Ruhpolding, Gemeindearchiv, Postfach 1180, 83318 Ruhpolding

Saalburg: Stadtverwaltung Saalburg, Stadtarchiv, Markt 1, 07929 Saalburg

Saalfeld: Stadtarchiv, Rathaus, Markt 1, 07318 Saalfeld

Saarbrücken: Stadtarchiv, Nauwieserstr. 3, 66111 Saarbrücken

Saarlouis: Stadtarchiv, Alte Brauereistr., Kaserne VI, 66740 Saarlouis

Sachsenheim (Württemberg): Stadtarchiv, Äußerer Schloßhof, 74343 Sachsenheim (Württemberg), Postfach 1260, 74338 Sachsenheim (Württemberg)

Salem: Gemeindearchiv, Bürgermeisteramt, 88682 Salem-Neufrach

Salzgitter: Stadtarchiv, Nord-Süd-Str. 155, 38206 Salzgitter

Salzhausen: Archiv der Samtgemeinde, 21376 Salzhausen

Salzwedel: Stadtarchiv, Stadtverwaltung, Mönchskirche 7, 29410 Salzwedel

Sangerhausen: Stadtarchiv, Stadtverwaltung, Markt 1, 06526 Sangerhausen

Sankt Augustin/Sieg: Stadtarchiv, Rathaus, Markt 1, 53757 Sankt Augustin/ Sieg

Sankt Goar: Stadtarchiv, Grundschule, Heerstr., Post: Stadtverwaltung, Heerst. 130, 56329 Sankt Goar

Sankt Ingbert/Saar: Stadtarchiv, Stadtverwaltung, Am Markt 12, 66386 Sankt Ingbert/Saar

Sankt Wendel (Saarland): Stadtarchiv, Mia-Münster-Haus (Mott), 66606 Sankt Wendel (Saarland)

Sarstedt: Stadtarchiv, Kirchplatz 2, 31157 Sarstedt, Post: Steinstr. 22, 31157 Sarstedt

Sassenberg: Stadtarchiv. See Kreis War-endorf

Saterland: Gemeindearchiv, Ramsloh, Hauptstr. 507, 26683 Saterland, Postfach 1164, 26677 Saterland

Saulgau: Stadtarchiv, Bürgermeisteramt, Postfach 1151, 88340 Saulgau

Sayda: Stadtarchiv, Schulgasse 7, 09619 Sayda

Schaafheim: Gemeindearchiv, Gemeindeverwaltung, Wilhelm-Leuschner-Str. 3, 64850 Schaafheim

Schauenburg: Gemeindearchiv, Raiffeisenstr. 5, 34270 Schauenburg

Scheibenberg: Stadtarchiv, Rudolf-Breitscheid-Str. 35, 09481 Scheibenberg

Schelklingen: Stadtarchiv, Stadtverwalt-ung, 89601 Schelklingen

Schieder-Schwalenberg: Stadtarchiv, Domäne 3, 32816 Schieder-Schwalenberg, Postfach 1265, 32807 Schieder-Schwalenberg

Schiltach: Stadtarchiv, Stadtverwaltung, Postfach 1144, 77757 Schiltach

Schleiden (Eifel): Historisches Archiv der Stadt, Blankenheimer Str. 2-4 (Behördenhaus), 53937 Schleiden (Eifel)

Schleiz: Stadtarchiv, Bahnhofstr. 1, 07907 Schleiz

Schleswig: Stadtarchiv, Plessenstr. 7, 24837 Schleswig

Schlettau: Stadtarchiv, Markt 1, 09487 Schlettau

Schliersee: Gemeindearchiv, Rathaus, 83727 Schliersee

Schlitz: Stadtarchiv, An der Kirche 4, 36110 Schlitz

Schloß-Holte/Stukenbrock: Gemeindearchiv, Rathausstr. 2, 33758 Schloß-Holte/Stukenbrock

Schlüchtern: Stadtarchiv, 36381 Schlüchtern

Schmalkalden: Stadtarchiv (See Landkreis Schmalkalden-Meiningen)

Schmallenberg: Stadtarchiv, Stadtverwaltung, 57392 Schmallenberg, Postfach 1140, 57376 Schmallenberg

Schneeberg: Stadtarchiv, Kirchgasse 3, 08289 Schneeberg

Schönau am Königsee: Gemeindearchiv, Rathaus, 83471 Schönau am Königsee

Schönebeck/Elbe: Stadtarchiv, Burghof 1, 39218 Schönebeck/Elbe

Schöneck (Vogtland): Stadtarchiv, Sonnenwirbel 3, 08261 Schöneck (Vogtland)

Schöningen: Stadtarchiv, Rathaus, 38364 Schöningen

Schöppingen: Gemeindearchiv, 48624 Schöppingen, Postfach 1107, 48620 Schöppingen

Schongau: Stadtarchiv und Stadtmuseum, Christophstr. 55-57, 86956 Schongau

Schopfheim: Stadtarchiv, Hauptstr. 29, 79650 Schopfheim, Postfach 1160, 79641 Schopfheim

Schorndorf (Württemberg): Stadtarchiv, Archivstr. 4, 73614 Schorndorf (Württemberg), Postfach 1560, 73605 Schorndorf (Württemberg)

Schotten (Hessen): Stadtarchiv, Stadtverwaltung, 63679 Schotten (Hessen)

Schramberg: Stadtarchiv, Im Schloß, 78713 Schramberg

Schriesheim: Stadtarchiv, Rathaus, 69198 Schriesheim

Schrobenhausen: Stadtarchiv, Lenbach-platz 18, 86529 Schrobenhausen, Postfach 1380, 86523 Schrobenhausen

Schüttorf: Stadtverwaltung, Rathaus, 48459 Schüttorf, Postfach 1420, 48459 Schüttorf

Schulenberg: (See Clausthal-Zellerfeld)

Schwabach (Mittelfranken): Stadtarchiv, Stadtverwaltung, 91126 Schwabach (Mittelfranken), Postfach 2120, 91114 Schwabach (Mittelfranken)

Schwabmünchen: Stadtarchiv, Fuggerstr. 50, 86830 Schwabmünchen, Postfach 1252, 86827 Schwabmünchen

Schwäbisch Gmünd: Stadtarchiv, Augustinerstr. 3, 73525 Schwäbisch Gmünd

Schwäbisch Hall: Stadtarchiv, Am Markt 5 und Nonnenhof 4, 74523 Schwäbisch Hall

Schwalbach am Taunus: Stadtarchiv, Stadtverwaltung, Marktplatz 1-2, 65824 Schwalbach am Taunus, Postfach 2710, 65820 Schwalbach am Taunus

Schwandorf (Bayern): Stadtarchiv, Stadtverwaltung, Kirchengasse 1, 92421 Schwandorf (Bayern), Postfach 1880, 92409 Schwandorf (Bayern)

Schwarzenbach an der Saale: Stadtarchiv, 95126 Schwarzenbach an der Saale

Schwarzenbek: Stadtarchiv, Rathaus, Ritter-Wulf-Platz 1, 21493 Shwarzenbek

Schwedt/Oder: Stadtverwaltung, Schwedt/Oder, Dezernat Kultur und Bildung, Kulturamt, Stadtarchiv, Bahnhofstr. 21, 16303 Schwedt/Oder, Postfach 66, 16284 Schwedt/Oder

Schweinfurt: Stadtarchiv , Friedrich-Rückert-Bau, Martin-Luther-Platz 20, 97421 Schweinfurt

Schwelm: Stadtarchiv, Haus Martfeld 1, 58332 Schwelm

Schwenningen: (See Villingen-Schwenningen)

Schwerin: Stadtarchiv, Platz der Jugend 12-14 und Johannes-Stelling-Str. 2, 19053 Schwerin

Schweringen: Gemeindearchiv, Dorfstr. 5, 27333 Schweringen

Schwerte: Stadtarchiv, Brückstr. 14, 58239 Schwerte

Schwetzingen: Stadtarchiv, Bürgermeist-eramt, Hebelstr. 1, 68723 Schwetzingen, Postfach 1920, 68721 Schwetzingen

Sebnitz: Stadtarchiv, Kirchstr. 5, 01855 Sebnitz, Postfach 182, 01851 Sebnitz

Seevetal: Gemeindearchiv, Am Schulteich 1, 21217 Seevetal

Selbitz (Oberfranken): Stadtarchiv, Rathaus, 95152 Selbitz (Oberfranken)

Selfkant: Gemeindearchiv, Gemeindedirektor, Hauptamt, 52538 Selfkant, Postfach 1315, 52539 Selfkant

Seligenstadt (Hessen): Stadtarchiv, Rathaus, Post: Stadtverwaltung, Postfach 63500 Seligenstadt (Hessen)

Selm: Stadtarchiv, Rathaus, 59379 Selm

Senden: Gemeindearchiv, Münsterstr. 30, Postfach 1251, 48303 Senden

Sendenhorst: Stadt- und Heimatarchiv, Stadtverwaltung, Rathaus, Kirchstr. 1, 48324 Sendenhorst

Siegburg: Stadtarchiv, Stadtverwaltung, Nogenter Platz 10, 53721 Siegburg, Postfach 53719 Siegburg

Siegen: Stadtarchiv, Oranienstr. 15, 57072 Siegen, Postfach 100352, 57003 Siegen

Simmern: Rhein-Hunsrück-Archiv, Schloß, 55469 Simmern

Simmerath: Gemeindearchiv, Rathaus, 52152 Simmerath

Sindelfingen: Stadtarchiv, Rathausplatz 1, 71063 Sindelfingen, Postfach 180, 71043 Sindelfingen

Singen (Hohentwiel): Stadtarchiv, August-Ruf-Str. 7, 78224 Singen (Hohentwiel), Postfach 760, 78207 Singen (Hohentwiel)

Sinsheim: Stadtarchiv, Wilhelmstr. 14-16, 74889 Sinsheim, Postfach 74877 Sinsheim

Sömmerda: Stadtarchiv, Marktplatz 2-4, 99610 Sömmerda

Soest: Stadtarchiv, Jakobistr. 13, 59494 Soest, Postfach 2252, 59491 Soest

Solingen: Stadtarchiv, Gasstr. 22b, 42657 Solingen

Soltau: Stadtarchiv, Altes Rathaus, 29614 Soltau, Postfach 1444, 29604 Soltau

Sondershausen: Stadtverwaltung Sondershausen, Stadtarchiv, Postfach 30, 99701 Sondershausen, Dienstsitz: Markt 7, 99706 Sondershausen

Sonneberg: Stadtarchiv, Stadtverwaltung, Bahnhofsplatz 1, 96515 Sonneberg, Postfach 169, 96504 Sonneberg

Sonnewalde: Stadtarchiv, Schloßstr. 21, 03249 Sonnewalde

Sonsbeck: Gemeindearchiv, Herrenstr. 2, 47665 Sonsbeck

Sonthofen: Stadtarchiv, Rathausplatz 1, 87527 Sonthofen

Spaichingen: Stadtarchiv, Stadtverwaltung, 78549 Spaichingen

Spenge: Stadtarchiv, Stadtverwaltung, Rathaus, Lange Str. 52-56, 32139 Spenge

Speyer: Stadtarchiv, Maximilianstr. 12, 67346 Speyer

Spiegelau: Gemeindearchiv, 94518 Spiegelau

Sprendlingen: Stadtarchiv, Stadtverwalt-ung, 6079 Sprendlingen

Springe: Stadtarchiv, Hauptamt, Auf dem Burghof 1, 31832 Springe

Sprockhövel: Stadtarchiv, 45549 Sprockhövel, Postfach 922040, 45541 Sprockhövel

Stade: Stadtarchiv, Johannisstr. 5, 21677 Stade

Stadthagen: Stadtarchiv, 31655 Stadthagen, Postfach 327, 31653 Stadthagen

Stadtlengsfeld: Stadtverwaltung Stadtlengsfeld, Stadtarchiv, Amtsstraße 8, 36457 Stadtlengsfeld

Stadtlohn: Stadtarchiv, Stadtverwaltung, Postfach 1465, 48695 Stadtlohn

Starnberg: Stadtarchiv, Stadtverwaltung, Vogelanger 2, 82319 Starnberg, Postfach 1680, 82306

Starnberg
Staßfurt: Stadtarchiv, Bernburger Str. 13, 39418 Staßfurt
Staufen (Breisgau): Stadtarchiv, Bürgermiesteramt, 79219 Staufen (Breisgau)
Steinach: Stadtverwaltung Steinach, Stadtarchiv, Postfach 81, 96520 Steinach, Dienstsitz: Marktplatz 4, 96523 Steinach
Steinbach: Stadtarchiv, 76487 Baden-Baden Steinbach
Steinfurt: Stadtarchiv An der Hohen Schule 13, 48565 Steinfurt, Postfach 2480, 48553 Steinfurt
Steinhagen: Gemeindearchiv, Am Pulverbach 25, 33803 Steinhagen
Steinheim (Westfalen): Stadtarchiv, Marktstr. 2, 32839 Steinheim (Westfalen)
Stelle: Gemeindearchiv, Unter den Linden 18, 21435 Stelle
Stendal: Stadtarchiv, Markt 1, 39576 Stendal
Sternberg: Stadtarchiv, Mühlenstr. 14, 19406 Sternberg
Stockach: Stadtarchiv, Rathaus, Adenauerstr. 4, 78333 Stockach
Stolberg (Rheinland): Stadtarchiv, Rathausstr. 11-13, 52222 Stolberg (Rheinland), Postfach 1820, 52205 Stolberg (Rheinland)
Straelen (Niederrhein): Stadtarchiv, Kuhstr. 21, 47638 Straelen (Niederrhein), Postfach 1353, 47630 Straelen (Niederrhein)
Stralsund: Stadtarchiv, Badenstr. 13, 18439 Stralsund
Straubing: Stadtarchiv, Rathaus, Theresienplatz 20, 94315 Straubing, Postfach 0352, 94303 Straubing
Strausberg: Stadtarchiv, Markt 10, 15344 Strausberg
Stuhr: Gemeindearchiv, 28816 Stuhr, Postfach 2130, 28808 Stuhr
Stuttgart: Stadtarchiv, Silberburgstr. 191, 70178 Stuttgart
Südlohn: Gemeindearchiv, Gemeindeverwaltung, Postfach 1030, 46349 Südlohn
Suhl: Stadtarchiv, Stadtverwaltung, Straße der Opfer des Faschismus 5, 98527

Suhl, Postfach 640, 98504 Suhl
Sulingen: Stadtarchiv, Lange Str. 67, 27232 Sulingen, Postfach 1240, 27223 Sulingen
Sulz am Neckar: Stadtarchiv, Stadtverwaltung, 72172 Sulz am Neckar, Postfach 1180, 72168 Sulz am Neckar
Sulzbach-Rosenberg: Stadtarchiv, Spitalgasse 21, 92237 Sulzbach-Rosenberg, Postfach 1254, 92230 Sulzbach-Rosenberg
Sundern: Stadtarchiv, Stadtverwaltung, 59846 Sundern, Postfach 1109, 59831 Sundern
Syke: Stadtarchiv, Nienburger Str. 5, 28857 Syke, Postfach 1365, 28847 Syke
Sylt: Sylter Archiv, Stadtarchiv, Alte Post, 25980 Westerland
Tangermünde: Stadtarchiv, Arneburger Str. 94, 39590 Tangermünde
Tann (Rhön): Stadtarchiv, Stadtverwaltung, 36142 Tann (Rhön)
Tanna: Stadtverwaltung Tanna, Stadtarchiv, Markt 1, 07922 Tanna
Tannroda/Ilm: Stadtverwaltung Tannroda, Stadtarchiv, Bahnhofstr. 18, 99448 Tannroda/Ilm
Taucha: Stadtarchiv, Schloßplatz 13, 04425 Taucha
Taunusstein: Stadtarchiv, Magistrat, Stadtteil Hahn, Erich-Kästner-Str. 5, 65232 Taunusstein, Postfach 1552, 65223 Taunusstein
Telgte: Stadtarchiv, Rathaus, Hauptamt, Baßfeld 4-6, 48291 Telgte, Postfach 220, 48284 Telgte
Teltow: Stadtarchiv, Potsdamer Str. 47, 14513 Teltow
Tettnang: Stadtarchiv, Bürgermeisteramt, 88069 Tettnang
Thale: Stadtarchiv, Stadtverwaltung, Rathausstr. 1, 06502 Thale
Themar: Stadtverwaltung Themar, Stadtarchiv Themar, Postfach 58, 98657 Themar, Dienstsitz: Markt 1, 98660 Themar
Tirschenreuth: Stadtarchiv, Maximilianplatz 35, 95643 Tirschenreuth
Titisee-Neustadt: Stadtarchiv, Stadtver-

waltung, Rathaus, 79822 Titisee-Neustadt

Tittmoning: Stadtarchiv, Postfach 1106, 84525 Tittmoning

Titz: Gemeindearchiv, Hauptamt, Landstr. 4, 52445 Titz

Tönning: Archiv der Stadt, Rathaus, 25832 Tönning

Toppenstedt: Gemeindearchiv, Lehmelweg 4, 21442 Toppenstedt

Torgau: Stadtarchiv, Markt 1, 04860 Torgau

Tostedt: Samtgemeindearchiv, Schützen-str. 24, 21255 Tostedt

Traunstein (Oberbayern): Stadtarchiv, Stadtplatz 39, 83278 Traunstein (Oberbayern), Post: Stadtarchiv, Stadt Traunstein, Große Kreisstadt, 83276 Traunstein (Oberbayern)

Trebbin: Amtsarchiv Trebbin, Markt 1-3, 14959 Trebbin

Treuchtlingen: Stadtarchiv, Rathaus, 91757 Treuchtlingen

Treuen: Stadtarchiv, Markt 7, 08233 Treuen, Postfach 10032, 08229 Treuen

Triebes: Verwaltungsgemeinschaft Triebes, Stadtarchiv, Schäferstr. 2, 07950 Triebes

Trier: Stadtarchiv, Weberbach 25, 54290 Trier

Triptis: Stadtverwaltung Triptis, Stadtarchiv, Postfach 8, 07817 Triptis, Dienstsitz: Markt 1, 07819 Triptis

Troisdorf: Archiv der Stadt Troisdorf, Am Schirmhof, 53827 Troisdorf-Sieglar

Trostberg: Stadtarchiv, Hauptstr. 24, 83308 Trostberg

Tübingen: Stadtarchiv, Am Markt 1, 72070 Tübingen, Postfach 2540, 72015 Tübingen

Tuttlingen: Stadtarchiv, Rathaus, Rathausstr. 1, 78532 Tuttlingen

Twistringen: Stadtarchiv, Rathaus, Lindenstr. 14, 27239 Twistringen, Postfach 1265, 27234 Twistringen

Überlingen: Stadtarchiv, Stadtverwaltung, Rathaus, 88662 Überlingen (Bodensee), Postfach 101863, 88648 Überlingen (Bodensee)

Uelzen: Stadtarchiv, An der Sankt Marienkirche 1, Postfach 2061, 29525 Uelzen

Ulm: Stadtarchiv, Schwörhaus, Weinhof 12, 89073 Ulm, Postfach 3940, 89070 Ulm

Ulrichstein: Stadtarchiv, Hauptstr. 9, 35327 Ulrichstein

Ummerstadt: Stadtarchiv. See Landkreis Hildburghausen

Unkel: Stadtarchiv, Graf-Blumenthal-Str. 13, 53572 Unkel

Unna: Stadtarchiv, Klosterstr. 12, 59423 Unna, Postfach 2113, 59411 Unna

Unterhaching: Gemeindearchiv, 82008 Unterhaching

Usingen: Stadtarchiv, Stadtverwaltung, Postfach, 61250 Usingen

Uslar: Stadtarchiv, Graftplatz 3, 37170 Uslar

Vaihingen an der Enz: Stadtarchiv, Spitalstr. 8, 71665 Vaihingen an der Enz

Varel: Stadtverwaltung, Rathaus, Windallee 4, 26316 Varel, Postfach 1669, 26306 Varel

Vechta: Stadtarchiv (Stored in Niedersächsischen Staatsarchiv in Oldenburg)

Velbert: Stadtarchiv, Zum Hardenberger Schloß 4, 42553 Velbert

Velen: Gemeindearchiv, Ramsdorfer Str. 19, 46342 Velen, Postfach 1260, 46335 Velen

Vellmar: Stadtarchiv, Stadtverwaltung, Rathausplatz 1, 34246 Vellmar

Ventorf: Gemeindearchiv (See Archivgemeinschaft Schwarzenbek)

Verden (Aller): Stadtarchiv, Ritterstr. 22, 27283 Verden (Aller)

Verl: Gemeindearchiv, Paderborner Str. 3/5, 33415 Verl

Versmold: Stadtarchiv, Schulstr. 14, 33775 Versmold, Postfach 1464, 33762 Versmold

Vettweiß: Gemeindearchiv, Gereonstr. 14, 52391 Vettweiß, Postfach 1124, 52389 Vettweiß

Vienenburg: Stadtverwaltung, 38690 Vienenburg

Viernheim: Stadtarchiv, Stadtverwaltung, 68519 Viernheim, Postfach 1640,

68506 Viernheim
Viersen: Stadtarchiv, Wilhelmstr. 12, 41747 Viersen
Villingen-Schwenningen: Stadtarchiv, Lantwattenstr. 4, 78050 Villingen-Schwenningen, Postfach 1260, 78002 Villingen-Schwenningen
Vilshofen: Stadtarchiv, Bürg 3, 94474 Vilshofen
Vlotho: Stadtarchiv, Lange Str. 60, 32602 Vlotho, Postfach 1705, 32591 Vlotho
Völklingen/Saar: Stadtarchiv, Neues Rathaus, Hindenburgplatz, 66333 Völklingen/Saar
Voerde (Niederrhein): Stadtarchiv, Rathausplatz 20, 46562 Voerde (Niederrhein)
Vohburg an der Donau: Stadtarchiv, Rathaus, Ulrich-Steinberger-Platz 12, 85088 Vohburg an der Donau
Volkach: Stadtarchiv in der Kartause Astheim, Verwaltungsgemeinschaft, 97332 Volkach
Vreden: Stadtarchiv, Burgstr. 14, 48686 Vreden, Postfach 1351, 48691 Vreden
Wachenheim an der Weinstraße: Stadtarchiv, Weinstr. 16, 67157 Wachenheim an der Weinstraße
Wachtberg: Gemeindearchiv, Rathausstr. 34, 53343 Wachtberg
Wachtendonk: Gemeindearchiv, Rathaus, Weinstr. 1, 47669 Wachtendonk
Wadersloh: Gemeindearchiv (See Kreis Warendorf)
Wächtersbach: Stadtarchiv, Stadtverwaltung, Postfach 1164, 63601 Wächtersbach
Waiblingen: Stadtarchiv, Kurze Str. 25, 71332 Waiblingen, Postfach 1751, 71328 Waiblingen
Waldbröl: Stadtarchiv, 51545 Waldbröl, Postfach 1620, 51536 Waldbröl
Waldfeucht: Gemeindearchiv, Lambertusstr. 13, 52525 Waldfeucht
Waldkirch: Stadtarchiv, Marktplatz 5, 79183 Waldkirch
Waldkraiburg: Stadtarchiv, Stadtplatz 26, 84478 Waldkraiburg, Postfach 1180, 84464 Waldkraiburg

Waldsassen: Stadtarchiv, Stadtverwaltung, Basilikaplatz 3, 95652 Waldsassen
Waldshut-Tiengen: Stadtarchiv, Stadtverwaltung, Kaiserstr. 28-32, 79761 Waldshut-Tiengen, Postfach 1941, 79746 Waldshut-Tiengen
Walsrode: Stadtarchiv, Rathaus, Lange Str. 22, 29664 Walsrode, Postfach 1440, 29654 Walsrode
Waltrop: Stadtverwaltung, Rathaus, Münsterstr. 1, Postfach 120, 45722 Waltrop
Wangen: Stadtarchiv, Rathaus, 88239 Wangen im Allgäu, Postfach 1154, 88227 Wangen im Allgäu
Warburg: Stadtarchiv, Sternstr. 35, 34414 Warburg
Waren: Stadtarchiv, Lange Str. 22, 17192 Waren
Warendorf: Stadtarchiv. See Kreis Warendorf
Warstein: Stadtarchiv, Rathaus, Dieplohstr. 1, 59581 Warstein
Wassenberg: Stadtarchiv, Roermonder Str. 25-27, 41849 Wassenberg, Postfach 1220, 41846 Wassenberg
Wasserburg am Inn: Stadtarchiv, Stadtverwaltung, 83512 Wasserburg am Inn, Postfach 1680, 83506 Wasserburg am Inn
Wasungen: Stadtverwaltung Wasungen, Stadtarchiv, Markt 7, 98634 Wasungen
Weeze: Gemeindearchiv, Cyriakusplatz 13/14, 47652 Weeze, Postfach 1265, 47649 Weeze
Wegberg: Stadtarchiv, Rathausplatz 25, 41844 Wegberg
Wehr: Stadtarchiv, Bürgermeisteramt, Hauptstr. 16, 79664 Wehr
Weida: Stadtverwaltung Weida, Stadtarchiv, Petersberg 2, 07570 Weida
Weiden in der Oberpfalz: Stadtarchiv, Kulturzentrum Hans Bauer, Pfarrplatz 4, 92637 Weiden in der Oberpfalz
Weikersheim: Stadtarchiv, Stadtverwalt-ung, Postfach 9, 97990 Weikersheim
Weil am Rhein: Stadtarchiv, Stadt-

verwaltung, Schillerstr. 1, 79576 Weil am Rhein

Weil der Stadt: Stadtarchiv, Stadtverwaltung, Postfach 1120, 71261 Weil der Stadt

Weilburg: Historisches Archiv der Stadt, Schloßplatz 1 , 35781 Weilburg, Postfach 1420, 35781 Weilburg

Weilerswist: Gemeindearchiv, Bonner Str. 29, 53919 Weilerswist

Weilheim an der Teck: Stadtarchiv, Marktplatz 6, 73235 Weilheim an der Teck, Postfach 1154, 73231 Weilheim an der Teck

Weilheim (Oberbayern): Stadtarchiv, Admiral-Hipper-Str. 20, 82362 Weilheim (Oberbayern), Postfach 1664, 82360 Weilheim (Oberbayern)

Weimar: Stadtarchiv, Postfach 14, 99421 Weimar, Dienstsitz: Markt 1, 99423 Weimar

Weingarten (Württemberg): Stadtarchiv, Schützenstr. 3/1, 88250 Weingarten (Württemberg)

Weinheim (Bergstraße): Stadtarchiv, Schulstr. 5/1, 69469 Weinheim (Bergstraße), Postfach 100961, 69449 Weinheim (Bergstraße)

Weinstadt: Stadtarchiv, Postfach 1327, 71373 Weinstadt

Weißenburg in Bayern: Stadtarchiv, Postfach 569, 91780 Weißenburg in Bayern

Weißenfels: Stadtarchiv, Nikolaistr. 13, 06667 Weißenfels

Weißensee: Stadtverwaltung Weißensee, Stadtarchiv, Marktplatz 26, 99631 Weißensee

Weismain: Stadtarchiv, Stadtverwaltung, Am Markt 19, 96260 Weismain, Postfach 27, 96258 Weismain

Welzow: Stadtarchiv Welzow, Rathaus, 16278 Welzow

Wemding: Stadtarchiv, Postfach 29, 86650 Wemding

Wentorf: Gemeindearchiv, Hauptstr. 2, 21465 Wentorf bei Hamburg

Werdau: Stadtarchiv, Markt 12, 08412 Werdau

Werder/Havel: Stadtarchiv, Eisenbahnstr. 13/14, 14542 Werder/Havel

Werdohl: Stadtarchiv, Stadtverwaltung, Goethestr. 51, 58791 Werdohl

Werl: Stadtarchiv, Rathaus, Hedwig-Dransfeld-Str. 23, 59457 Werl, Postfach 6040, 59455 Werl

Wermelskirchen: Stadtarchiv, Stadtver-waltung, 42929 Wermelskirchen, Postfach 1110, 42904 Wermelskirchen

Werne: Stadtarchiv, Kirchhof 9, 59368 Werne, Postfach 1552, 59358 Werne

Werneuchen: Amtsarchiv Werneuchen, Am Markt 5, 16356 Werneuchen

Wernigerode: Stadtarchiv, Burgstr. 49, 38855 Wernigerode

Wertheim: Stadtarchiv. See Staatsarchiv Wertheim (Archivverbund Main-Tauber)

Werther (Westfalen): Stadtarchiv, Kulturamt, Mühlenstr. 2, 33824 Werther (Westfalen)

Wesel: Stadtarchiv, Rathaus, Klever-Tor-Platz 1, 46483 Wesel

Wesseling: Stadtarchiv, 50379 Wesseling, Postfach 1564, 50389 Wesseling

Westerkappeln: Gemeindearchiv, Große Str. 13, 49492 Westerkappeln

Westerstede: Stadtarchiv, Albert-Post-Platz 19, 26653 Westerstede

Wetter (Ruhr): Stadtarchiv, Burgstr. 17, 58300 Wetter (Ruhr), Postfach 146, 58287 Wetter (Ruhr)

Wettringen: Gemeindearchiv, Kirchstr. 19, 48493 Wettringen

Wetzlar: Stadtarchiv, Rathaus, Hauser Gasse 17, 35578 Wetzlar, Postf. 2120, 35573 Wetzlar

Weyhe: Gemeindearchiv, Ortsteil Sudweyhe, Im Mühlengrunde 15 (Wassermühle), Post: Rathausplatz 1, 28844 Weyhe, Postfach 1160, 28838 Weyhe

Wiehe: Stadtverwaltung, Stadtarchiv, Postfach 6, 06571 Wiehe; Dienstsitz: Leopold-von-Ranke-Str. 33, 06571 Wiehe

Wiesbaden: Stadtarchiv, Im Rad 20, 65197 Wiesbaden, Postfach 3920, 65029 Wiesbaden

Wiesensteig: Stadtarchiv, Hauptstr. 25, 73349 Wiesensteig
Wiesloch: Stadtarchiv, 69168 Wiesloch, Postfach 1520, 69156 Wiesloch
Wietze: Gemeindearchiv, Steinförder Str. 4, 29321 Wietze
Wildemann: (See Clausthal-Zellerfeld)
Wildenfels: Stadtarchiv, Poststr. 26, 08134 Wildenfels
Wilhelmshaven: Stadtarchiv, Rathausplatz 10, 26382 Wilhelmshaven, Postfach 1180, 26359 Wilhelmshaven
Wilkau-Haßlau: Stadtarchiv, Dezernat Hauptverwaltung, Postfach 9, 08110 Wilkau-Haßlau
Willich: Stadtarchiv, Albert-Oetker-Str. 98-102, 47877 Willich
Wilster: Stadtarchiv, Klosterhof 28, 25554 Wilster
Windischeschenbach: Stadtarchiv, Rathaus, Hauptstr. 34, 92670 Windischeschenbach
Winnenden: Stadtarchiv, Marktstr. 47, 71364 Winnenden, Postfach 280, 71350 Winnenden
Winsen/Aller: Gemeindearchiv, Am Amtshof 8, 29308 Winsen/Aller
Winsen/Luhe: Stadtarchiv, Rathausstr. 1, 21423 Winsen/Luhe, Postfach 1240, 21412 Winsen/Luhe
Winterberg (Westfalen): Stadtarchiv, Stadtverwaltung, 59955 Winterberg (Westfalen), Postfach 1005, 59941 Winterberg (Westfalen)
Winterstein: Gemeindeverwaltung Winterstein, Gemeindearchiv, Liebensteiner Str. 14, 99891 Winterstein
Wipperfürth: Stadtarchiv, Marktplatz 1, 51688 Wipperfürth, Postfach 1460, 51678 Wipperfürth
Wismar: Stadtarchiv, Vor dem Fürstenhof 1, 23966 Wismar
Witten: Stadtarchiv, Stadt Witten, 58449 Witten
Wittenberg: Stadtarchiv der Lutherstadt, Schloß, 06886 Lutherstadt Wittenberg
Wittenberge: Stadtarchiv, August-Bebel-Str. 10, 19322 Wittenberge

Witzenhausen: Stadtarchiv, Stadtverwaltung, Rathaus, 37213 Witzenhausen
Wörth am Main: Stadtarchiv, Postfach 20, 63939 Wörth am Main
Wolfach: Stadtarchiv, Rathaus, Hauptstr. 41, 77709 Wolfach
Wolfratshausen: Stadtarchiv, Marienplatz 1, 82515 Wolfratshausen, Postfach 1460, 82504 Wolfratshausen
Wolfsburg: Stadtarchiv, Porschestr. 43c, 38440 Wolfsburg, Postfach 100944, 38409 Wolfsburg
Wolfstein: Stadtarchiv, Rathaus, Hauptstr. 2, 67752 Wolfstein
Wolgast: Stadtarchiv, Pestalozzistr. 42, 17438 Wolgast
Wolmirstedt: Stadtarchiv, August-Bebel-Str. 24, 39326 Wolmirstedt
Worms: Stadtarchiv, Raschi-Haus, Hintere Judengasse 6, 67547 Worms, Postfach 2052, 67510 Worms
Wriezen: Amtsarchiv Wriezen, Freienwalder Str. 50, 16269 Wriezen
Wülfrath: Stadtarchiv, Wilhelmstr. 189, 42489 Wülfrath
Würselen: Stadtarchiv, Stadtverwaltung, Morlaixplatz 1, 52146 Würselen, Postfach 1160, 52135 Würselen
Würzburg: Stadtarchiv, Neubaustr. 12, 97070 Würzburg
Wunsiedel: Stadtarchiv, Rathaus, 95632 Wunsiedel, Postfach 140, 95620 Wunsiedel
Wunstorf: Stadtarchiv, Stadtverwaltung, Südstr. 1, 31515 Wunstorf, Postfach 1280, 31502 Wunstorf
Wuppertal: Stadtarchiv, Friedrich-Engels-Allee 89-91, 42285 Wuppertal (Barmen)
Wyk auf Föhr: Föhrer Inselarchiv, c/o Stiftung Nordfriesland, Im Schloß, 25813 Husum
Xanten: Stadtarchiv, Rathaus, Karthaus 2, 46509 Xanten, Postfach 1164, 46500 Xanten
Zaberfeld: Gemeindearchiv, Schloßberg 5, 74373 Zaberfeld

Zeitz: Stadtarchiv. See Burgenlandkreis
Zella-Mehlis: Stadtverwaltung Zella-Mehlis, Stadtarchiv, Rathausstr. 1, 98544 Zella-Mehlis, Dienstsitz: Friedebergstr. 60, 98544 Zella-Mehlis
Zimmern: Gemeindeverwaltung Zimmern, Gemeindearchiv, Dorfstr. 33, 07778 Zimmern
Zirndorf (Mittelfranken): Stadtarchiv, Rathaus, Fürther Str. 8, 90513 Zirndorf (Mittelfranken), Postfach 1160, 90505 Zirndorf (Mittelfranken)
Zittau: Stadtarchiv, Neustadt 47, 02763 Zittau, Postfach 228, 02754 Zittau
Zossen: Amtsarchiv Zossen, Marktplatz 20/21, 15806 Zossen
Zschopau: Stadtarchiv, Altmarkt 2, 09405 Zschopau
Zülpich: Stadtarchiv, Stadtverwaltung, Markt 21, 53909 Zülpich, Postfach 1354, 53905 Zülpich
Zweibrücken: Stadtarchiv, Stadtverwalt-ung, Herzogstr. 1, Postfach 171, 66468 Zweibrücken
Zwickau: Stadtarchiv, Lessingstr. 1, 08058 Zwickau
Source: *Archive in der Bundesrepublik Deutschland, Österreich und der Schweiz*, Ardey-Verlag, Münster, 1995.

UNIVERSITY ARCHIVES

For addresses of German university archives, see pages 407 ff of this book:

Verein deutscher Archivare. *Archive in der Bundesrepublik Deutschland, Österreich und der Schweiz.* Münster: Ardey-Verlag, 1995.

In the years that have passed since the publication of the current edition of this work, the information included in the directory has been transferred to an electronic database (CD,) which is updated every two years. The CD-ROM now accompanies the printed volume.

LUTHERAN CHURCH ARCHIVES

**Lutheran Church:
central and state archives**
*(Evangelische Kirche:
Zentral- und Landsarchive)*
For updated contact information regarding central and state Lutheran archives in Germany visit: http://home.bawue.de/~hanacek/info/darchi18.htm.
Evangelisches Zentralarchiv in Berlin, Jebensstr. 3, 10623 Berlin [see next section]
Vereinigte Evangelisch-Lutherische Kirche Deutschlands, Archiv des Lutherischen Kirchenamts, Richard-Wagner-Str. 26, 30177 Hannover, Postfach 510409, 30634 Hannover
Evangelische Landeskirche Anhalts, Landeskirchenamt, Landeskirchliches Archiv, Friedrichstr. 22, 06844 Dessau
Evangelische Landeskirche in Baden, Evangelischer Oberkirchenrat, Landeskirchliches Archiv, Blumenstr. 1, 76133 Karlsruhe
Evangelisch-Lutherische Kirche in Bayern, Landeskirchliches Archiv, Veilhofstr. 28, 90489 Nürnberg
Evangelische Kirche in Berlin-Brandenburg: See Evangelisches Zentralarchiv in Berlin
Evangelisch-lutherische Landeskirche in Braunschweig, Landeskirchliches Archiv, Alter Zeughof 1, 38100 Braunschweig. Note: older records held in Nied-ersächsisches Staatsarchiv in Wolfen-büttel; see State Archives
Bremische Evangelische Kirche, Landeskirchliches Archiv, Franziuseck 2-4, 28199 Bremen, Postfach 106929, 28069 Bremen
Evangelisch-Lutherisches Landeskirch-enamt Sachsens, Palaisplatz 2 b, 01097 Dresden
Evangelisch-Lutherische Landeskirche Hannovers, Landeskirchliches Archiv,

Hildesheim Str. 165-167, 30173 Hannover; Postfach 5740, 30173 Hannover
Evangelische Kirche in Hessen und Nassau, Zentralarchiv, Ahastr. 5a, Post: Paulusplatz 1, 64285 Darmstadt
Evangelisch Lutherischer Kirchenkreis Kiel, Falckstr. 9, 24103 Kiel
Evangelische Kirche von Kurhessen-Waldeck, Landeskirchliches Archiv, Heinrich-Wimmer-Str. 4, 34131 Kassel-Wilhelmshöhe
Lippische Landeskirche, Archiv der Lippischen Landeskirche, Leopoldstr. 27, 32756 Detmold
Evangelisch-Lutherische Landeskirche Mecklenburgs, Landeskirchliches Arch-iv, Münzstr. 8, Postfach 011003, 19010 Schwerin
Nordelbische Evangelisch-Lutherische Kirche, Nordelbisches Kirchenamt, Dänische Str. 21-35, 24103 Kiel, Postfach 3449, 24033 Kiel
-Archiv der Nordelbischen Evangelisch-Lutherischen Kirche: Nordelbisches Kirchenarchiv Kiel, Dänische Str. 21-35, 24103 Kiel
-Archiv des Kirchenkreises Alt-Hamburg, Neue Burg 1, 20457 Hamburg
Evangelisch-reformierte Kirche in Nordwestdeutschland und Bayern, (Synode der evangelisch-reformierten Kirchen in Nordwestdeutschland und Bayern), Archiv des Synodalrates der Evangelisch-reformierten Kirche, Saarstr. 6, 26789 Leer, Postfach 1380, 26763 Leer
Evangelisch-Lutherische Kirche in Oldenburg, Archiv des Evangelisch-Lutherischen Oberkirchenrats, Philosoph-enweg 1, 26121 Oldenburg, Postfach 1709, 26007 Oldenburg
Evangelische Kirche der Pfalz, Zentralarchiv, Domplatz 6, 67346 Speyer, Postanschrift: 67343 Speyer
Pommersche Evangelische Kirche, Landeskirchliches Archiv, Postfach 187, 17461 Greifswald, Bahnhofstr. 35/36, 17489 Greifswald, Besucheradresse [visitors' address]: Karl-Marx-Platz 15

Evangelische Kirche im Rheinland, Archiv, Hans-Böckler-Str. 7, 40476 Düsseldorf, Postfach 320340, 40418 Düsseldorf
Evangelische Archivstelle Koblenz, Karmeliterstr. 1-3, 56068 Koblenz
Evangelische Kirche der Kirchenprovinz Sachsen, Evangelisches Konsis-torium, Am Dom 2, 39104 Magdeburg
Evangelisch-Lutherische Landeskirche Sachsens, Landeskirchenarchiv, Lukasstr. 6, 01069 Dresden
Evangelische Kirche der Schlesischen Oberlausitz, Konsistorium, Schlaurother Str. 11, 02827 Görlitz
Evangelisch-Lutherische Kirche in Thüringen, Landeskirchliches Archiv, Schloßberg 4 a, 99817 Eisenach
Evangelische Kirche von Westfalen, Landeskirchliches Archiv, Altstädter Kirchplatz 5, 33602 Bielefeld, Postfach 101051, 33510 Bielefeld
Evangelische Landeskirche in Württemberg, Landeskirchliches Archiv, Gänsheidestr. 4, 70184 Stsuttgart, Postfach 101342, 70012 Stuttgart

EVANGELISCHES ZENTRALARCHIV (EZA) BERLIN

Held in the *Evangelisches Zentralarchiv* (Evangelical Central Archive, or "EZA," at Bethaniendamm 29, 10997 Berlin, Tel. 01149 30 22504536, www.ezab.de) are most of the church records from Berlin, Berlin-Brandenburg, and a few books from the former German territories of Pommern, Westpreußen, Ostpreußen, Posen, eastern Brandenburg, and Schlesien.

Preparation for research at the EZA

The following publications are recommended for prior reading (available at the EZA):

♦ *Verzeichnis der Kirchenbücher Teil I. Die östlichen Kirchenprovinzen der evangelischen Kirche der altpreußen*

Union [Inventory of Parish Registers in the Protestant Central Archive in Berlin – eastern provinces], by Christa Stache, Berlin, 1992, and a supplement, Berlin 1998.

♦*Verzeichnis der Kirchenbücher TeilII, Alt-Berlin,* by Christa Stache, Berlin, 1987.

♦*Archivbericht - Beihefte.* This publication contains a register showing all the available Berlin church records on microfiche.

Registers published
no. 1 Berlin-Charlottenburg, 1708-1945
no. 2 Berlin-Schöneberg, 1760-1945
no. 3 Kreuzburg, 1694-1945
no. 4 Neukölln, 1639-1945
no. 5 Reinickendorf, 1690-1945
no. 6 Spandau, 1571-1945
no. 7 Steglitz, 1605-1945
no. 8 Tempelhof, 1606-1945
no. 9 Tiergarten-Friedrichswerder, 1835-1945
no. 10 Wedding, 1935-1945
no. 11 Wilmersdorf, 1714-1945
no. 12 Zehlendorf, 1642-1945
no. 13 Französische reformierte-Kirche, 1658-1945
no. 14 Berlin - Stadt I, 1583-1945
no. 15 Berlin III, 1712-1945
no. 16 Friedrichshain, 1723-1945
no. 17 Lichtenberg, 1667-1945
no. 18 Oberspree, 1642-1945
no. 19 Pankow, 1611-1945
no. 20 Berlin-Weissensee, 1595-1945
no. 21 Königs Wusterhausen, 1613-1945
no. 22 Teltow, 1578-1945

Nearly one hundred additional books in this series feature church records from towns near Berlin (all of them in the province of Brandenburg). They can be purchased from this archive at the cost of ˎ 3 plus postage.

A preliminary step
Because there were more than seventy Lutheran parishes in the city of Berlin by the year 1900, it is important to determine the ancestor's adress before searching for him in church rcords. To find an address, one may search in the city directories (*Adreßbücher)* that are available on microfilm at the Family History Library. The collection comprises the years 1799 to 1964 on 316 microfilmes, the first of which is 1633880. The original books are housed in the Stadtarchiv Berlin, at Breitestraße 36.

Using EZA facilities
The research center's reading room (*Lesesaal)* is at Bethaniendamm 29, 10997 Berlin. Visiting hours are Monday through Friday 9 am to 4 pm and Tuesdays also from 4:30 to 8 pm. No documents are retrieved after noon.

Reservations should be requested by email at reservierung@ezab.de, at least three months in advance.

Research costs
♦Use of the archives: ˎ 7,00 per day
♦Research performed by EZA staff: ˎ 12,00 per quarter hour; photocopies: ˎ 6,00 each.

Privacy law
It is vital to keep in mind that Germany's Privacy Law (*Datenschutz)* makes records unavailable from specific dates until the present. Records made within the last thirty years are restricted.

One may obtain records of direct ancestors by filling out an order form available from the EZA. Proof of one's relationship to the ancestor for whom one is searching is usually required.

EZA inventory
Note this book: *Das evangelische Zentralarchiv in Berlin und seine Bestände* [The Protestant Central Archive in Berlin and Its Inventory], by Christa Stache, Alektor-Verlag, Berlin 1992. FHL 943.155/B1 k23sc.

Sources:
♦"Research at the EZA in Berlin," by Sonia Nippgen-Holz, *Der Blumenbaum,* Vol. 16, No. 2, 1998.
♦www.ezab.de/e/edframe.html

CATHOLIC CHURCH ARCHIVES AT BISHOPRICS, DIOCESES AND CATHEDRALS (Katholische Kirche: Bistums-, Diözesan- und Domarchive)

For updated contact information regarding Catholic archivs in Germany visit: http://home.bawue.de/~hanacek/info/darchi17.htm.
Note: A central archive for information about Catholic records is,
Sekretariat der Deutschen Bischofskonferenz, Archiv, Kaiserstraße 163, 53113 Bonn.
Bistum Aachen, Diözesanarchiv, Kloster-platz 7, 52062 Aachen, Postfach 210, 52003 Aachen
-Domarchiv Aachen, Ritter-Chorus-Str. 7, 52062 Aachen
Bistum Augsburg, Archiv des Bistums Augsburg, Hafnerberg 2, 86152 Augsburg
Erzbistum Bamberg, Archiv des Erzbistums Bamberg, Domplatz 3, 96049 Bamberg, Postfach 120153, 96033 Bamberg
Erzbistum Berlin, Diözesanarchiv Berlin, Götzstr. 65, 12099 Berlin
Diözese Dresden-Meißen, Bischöfliches Ordinariat, Käthe-Kollwitz-Ufer 84, 01309 Dresden
Bistum Eichstätt, Diözesanarchiv, Luitpoldstr. 1, 85072 Eichstätt
Bistum Erfurt, Bistumsarchiv, Hermannsplatz 9, 99084 Erfurt, Postfach 296, 99006 Erfurt, Besucheradresse [visitors' address]: Domstr. 9, Eingang [entrance on] Stiftsgasse
Bistum Essen, Bistumsarchiv, Zwölfling 16, 45127 Essen, Postfach 100464, 45004 Essen
-Münsterarchiv, Zwölfling 16, 45127 Essen
Erzbistum Freiburg, Erzbischöfliches Archiv, Herrenstr. 35, 79098 Freiburg im Breisgau
Bistum Fulda, Bistumsarchiv, Bischöf-

liches Generalvikariat, Paulustor 5, 36037 Fulda, Postfach 147, 36001 Fulda
Bistum Görlitz, Ordinariatsarchiv, Carl-von-Ossietzky-Str. 41, 02826 Görlitz, Postfach 127, 02802 Gorlitz
Erzbistum Hamburg: See Osnabrück
Bistum Hildesheim, Bistumsarchiv, Pfaffenstieg 2, 31134 Hildesheim, Postfach 100263, 31102 Hildesheim
Erzbisbum Köln, Historisches Archiv, Gereonstr. 2-4, 50670 Köln
Bistum Limburg, Diözesanarchiv Limburg, Roßmarkt 4, 65549 Limburg (Lahn), Postfach 1355, 65533 Limburg (Lahn)
Bistum Magdeburg, Bischöfliches Zentralarchiv, Generalvikariat, Max-Josef-Metzger-Str. 1, 39104 Magdeburg
Bistum Mainz, Dom- u. Diözesanarchiv, Heringsbrunnengasse 4, 55116 Mainz, Postfach 1560, 55005 Mainz
Erzbistum München und Freising, Archiv, Karmeliterstr. 1 (Eingang [entrance on] Pacellistr.), 80333 München, Postfach 330360, 80063 München
Bistum Münster, Bistumsarchiv, Georgs-kommende 19, 48143 Münster
-Außenstelle Xanten des Bistumsarchivs Münster, Kapitel 21, 46509 Xanten
-Bischöflich Münstersches Offizialat Vechta, Offizialatsarchiv, Kolpingstr. 25, 49377 Vechta
Bistum Osnabrück, Bischöfliches Generalvikariat, Diözesanarchiv, Große Domsfreiheit 10, 49074 Osnabrück
Erzbistum Paderborn, Erzbistumsarchiv Paderborn, Domplatz 3, 33098 Paderborn
◆**Bistum Passau**, Archiv des Bistums Passau, Luragogasse 4, 94032 Passau
Bistum Regensburg, Bischöfliches Zentralarchiv Regensburg, St.-Peters-Weg 11-13, 93047 Regensburg, Postfach 110228, 93015 Regensburg
Bistum Rottenburg-Stuttgart, Diözesan-archiv Rottenburg, Eugen-Bolz-Platz 1, 72108 Rottenburg am Neckar, Postfach 9, 72101 Rottenburg am Neckar
Bischöfliches Amt Schwerin, Bistums-

archiv, Landower Str. 14-16, 19057
Schwerin
Bistum Speyer, Archiv des Bistums
Speyer, Kleine Pfaffengasse 16, 67346
Speyer, Postanschrift [postal address]:
67343 Speyer
Bistum Trier, Bistumsarchiv,
Jesuitenstr. 13b, 54290 Trier, Postfach
1340, 54203 Trier
Bistum Würzburg, Diözesanarchiv,
Bruderhof 1 a, Post: Domerschulstr. 2,
97070 Würzburg

OTHER ECCLESIASTICAL ORGANIZATIONS (Sonstigekirchliche Einrichtungen)

**Archiv des Synodalrates der Evan-
gelisch-reformierten Kirche,** Postfach
1380, 26763 Leer [headquarters of the
Evangelical Reformed church]
Deutscher Hugenotten-Verein e.V. [Ger-
man Huguenot Society], Archiv, Hafen-
platz 9 A, 34385 Bad Karlshafen
Das Rauhe Haus, Archiv, Beim Rauhen
Hause 21, 22111 Hamburg
**Zentralarchiv zur Erforschung der Ge-
schichte der Juden in Deutschland**
[Central Archive for research of the
history of Jews in Germany], Bienenstr.
5, 69117 Heidelberg
Johannes-Ronge-Archiv, Freireligiöse
Landesgemeinde der Pfalz, Wörthstr. 6
A, 67059 Ludwigshafen
**Russisch-orthodoxe Diözese des ortho-
doxen Bischofs von Berlin und Deutsch-
lands** [Russian Orthodox Diocese of the
Orthodox Bishops of Berlin and Ger-
many], KdöR, Schirmerweg 78, 81247
München
Source: *Archive in der Bundesrepublik
Deutschland, Österreich und der Schweiz,*
15. Ausgabe, Ardey-Verlag Münster, 1995.

ARCHIVES WITH HOLDINGS COVERING WIDER AREAS

Bundesarchiv
Potsdamer Straße 1
56075 Koblenz
(mailing address: Postfach 320
56003 Koblenz)
poststelle@hundesarchiv.de
www.bundesarchiv.de
   This is the federal archive of Germany.
The *Bundesarchiv* covers all records
that originated in offices or agencies of
the central government from 1815 to the
present., and holds as well records of
the Kingdom of Prussia and its predecessor, the Electorate of Brandenburg,
dating from the 13th century to 1945. It
also contains information on ethnic Germans in eastern Europe during the Hitler
era.

**Geheimes Staatsarchiv Preußischer
Kulturbesitz**
Archivstraße 12-14
14195 Berlin
Tel. 030/226 44 75 00
Fax 030/266 44 31 26
gsta.pk@gsta.spk-berlin.de
www.gsta.spk-berlin.de
   This is the Prussian State Privy Ar-
chives covering eastern Germany, in-
cluding military records for the Prussian
army before 1866, military church records,
and local and provinncial records from
the provinces of Prussia that became
part of Poland in 1919 (Posen, northern
Silesia) and 1945 (West Prussia, East
Prussia, Pomerania, and southern
Silesia).
For an inventory of this archive, see
*Übersicht über die Bestände des
Geheimen Staatsarchivs in Berlin-
Dahlem, Teil I Provincial und Lokal-
behörden* (Inventory of the Secret State
Archives of Berlin-Dahlem), by Hans
Branig, et al. FHL 943 A5gs.

Bundesarchiv Abteilung Militärarchiv
Wiesentalstraße 10
79115 Freiburg im Breisgau
Tel. 0761/47817-0
Fax 0761/47817-900
militaerarchiv@bundesarchiv.de
www.bundesarchiv.de/aufgaben_or
ganisation/abteilungen/ma/

This archive holds personnel records of the German army, navy, and air force for individuals serving in both World Wars; also hospital and medical records of all branches of the military for persons who became ill or injured during their service, and who were born before 1890. Medical records for persons born after 1890 are at the Krankenbuchlager Berlin, Wattstraße 11-13, 13355 Berlin. Personnel files and medical files are indexed.

Deutsche Zentralstelle für Genealogie
Sächsisches Archiv
Staatsarchiv Leipzig
Schongauerstraße 1
04329 Leipzig
Tel. 49 341/25 555 51
Fax 49 341/25 555 55
poststelle-1@sta.smi.sachsen.de
www.leipzig.de/de/buerger/bildung/
archive/staat/
[For information about this archive, see the following sections.]
Source: "The Bundesarchive of Germany," by Raymond S. Wright III, *Ancestry,* Vol. 15, No. 4, July/August 1997.

CENTRAL OFFICE FOR GENEALOGY, LEIPZIG
(Die deutsche Zentralstelle für Genealogie)

In the early twentieth century in Germany, a group of researchers pooled their research and created an organization, much of whose data was microfilmed following the reunification of Germany. This manuscript collection, filmed by the Church of Jesus Christ of Latter-day Saints, is available at the Family History Library in Salt Lake City and through Family History Centers. It is known as the *Ahnenlistenumlauf* (literally, "circulation of ancestor lists)," now commonly referred to as the ALU.

One of the several segments of the ALU is the 14-volume *Ahnenlistenkartei* (ancestor list cards) which is described elsewhere in this book. This body of information is the result of the decision of a group of German researchers in the 1970s to circulate their ancestor lists among contributors.

The ALA

Considerably older than the ALU is the *Ahnenlistenaustausch* (ancestor list exchange), begun in 1921 in Dresden, and known now as the ALA.

These data, which consist of a half million German pedigrees, are indexed in a collection called *Die Ahnenstammkartei des deutschen Volkes* (pedigree index of Germans), or "ASTAKA." The index contains 2.7 million cards. This body of information, whose emphasis lies with eastern Germany and its German neighbors to the east, is housed in *Die deutsche Zentralstelle für Genealogie* (German Central Office for Genealogy) in Leipzig, generally shortened to "DZfG."

Thus researchers of German family histories have two important collections available on Family History Library microfilm: ALU and ASTAKA.

Keys to the microfilms

An index to the German pedigrees, whose time periods range in time between 1650 and 1800, with exceptions at both ends, can be accessed by using this book:

♦ *An Introduction and Register to Die Ahnenstammkartei des deutschen Volkes of the Deutsche Zentralstelle für Genea-logie Leipzig 1922-1991,* compiled by Thomas Kent Edlund, The Family History Library, Salt Lake City,

1993. FHL 943 A33e 1995
* The pedigree films are accessed through the Family History Library under computer number 677728.

Using ASTAKA

The most complete explanation of the use of the ASTAKA may be found in "*Die Ahnenstammkartei des Deutschen Volkes* Pedigree Collection from Leipzig, Germany," by Laraine K. Ferguson and Larry O. Jensen, *German Genealogical Digest*, Winter 1993, pages 110-124.

The microfilms of ASTAKA are available through local Family History Centers of the Family History Library in Salt Lake City.

Online Tools for ASTAKA

A surname index to about 11,300 pedigree files is hosted online by The Federation of East European Family History Societies, also known as FEEFHS. Begin the search at www.feefhs.org/links/Germany/astaka/ask-idx.html. If you find your surname in the index, write down the microfilm number to the right. A copy of the original pedigree(s) can be found on this microfilm at the LDS Family History Library in Salt Lake City or through one of many local Family History Centers.

INDEX TO ZENTRALSTELLE HOLDINGS

The index to the holdings of *Die deutsche Zentralstelle für Genealogie* (German Central Office for Genealogy) consists of a four-volume work, *Bestands-verzeichnis der deutschen Zentralstelle für Genealogie,* by Martina Wermes, Renate Jude, Marion Bahr and Hans-Jürgen Voigt (Verlag Degener & Co., Neustadt/Aisch, 1991-94. Vol . I, 1991; Vol. II, 1991; Vol. III, 1994)

Teil (Part) I: *Die Kirchenbuchunterlagen der östlichen Provinzen Posen, Ost- und Westpreußen, Pommern und Schlesien.* [The Parish Registers of the Eastern Provinces of Posen, East and West Prussia, Pomerania and Silesia]
This volume lists parish registers for the German eastern provinces (1905 borders) excluding East Brandenburg. FHL 943.21/L2 K23w pt. 1 1994

Teil (Part) II: *Die archivalischen und Kirchen-buchunterlagen deutscher Siedlungsgebiete im Ausland: Bessarabien, Bukowina, Estland, Lettland und Litauen, Siebenbürgen, Sudetenland, Slowenien und Südtirol.* [The Parish Registers of the German Settlements in Other Areas: Bessarabia, Bukovina, Estonia, Latvia and Lithuania, Transylvania, the Sudetenland, Slovenia and South Tyrol] FHL 943.21/L2 K23wpt. 2
This volume lists records for the areas mentioned above, but for specifics see the book, Brandt, Edward R., *Germanic Genealogy: A Guide to Worldwide Sources and Migration Patterns.*

Teil (Part) III: *Die Kirchenbuchunterlagen der Länder und Provinzen des Deutschen Reiches (mit Ausnahme der östlichen Provinzen Preußens* [Church records of the territories and provinces of Germany (with the exception of the eastern provinces of Prussia)]. This volume covers Berlin, Schleswig-Holstein, Thuringia, Baden, Bavaria, Brandenburg (including the part now in Poland), Hamburg, Hanover, Hesse, Mecklenburg, the Rhine province, the Kingdom of Saxony, the Prussian Province of Saxony, Westphalia, Anhalt, Brunswick, Hesse-Nassau, Lippe, Oldenburg, the Saarland, Schaumburg-Lippe, and Württemberg. FHL 943.21L2 K23w pt. 3

Teil (Part) IV: *Ortsfamilienbücher mit Standort Leipzig in Deutscher Bücherei und Deutscher Zentralstelle für Genealogie.* [Family lineage books located in Leipzig in the German Library and the German Central Office for Genealogy]. Contains an inventory of (village) family books available at the locations stated in the title. FHL 943.21/L2 K23w pt. 4. The authors of this fourth volume,

Volkmar Weiss and Katja Münchow, have placed a list of these lineage books online at www.v-weiss.de/ofbmeur-a.html.
To purchase these books, contact, Verlag Degener & Co.
Postfach 1360
91403 Neustadt a.d. Aisch
Germany

HOW TO REACH
THE ZENTRALSTELLE

Deutsche Zentralstelle für Genealogie
Schongauerstraße 1
04329 Leipzig
Germany
Die deutsche Zentralstelle für Genealogie (the German Central Office for Genealogy) in Leipzig, located in the building of the Sächsisches Staatsarchiv (Saxony State Archives) Leipzig, is the home of the *Ahnenstammkartei,* or ASTAKA. The *Zentralstelle* holds also a good selection of *Ortssippenbücher* and *Matrikel* Registers.
    To reach this archive from central Leipzig, take the number 3, 6, or 8 trolley in the direction of Sommerfeld, which is the end of the line for all three lines. Ride the trolley to the end of the line.
    The *Sächsisches Staatsarchiv* is located in the suburb of Paunsdorf. From the end of the trolley line, go one long block on Leipzigerstraße to Schongauer-straße in the direction of Paunsdorf Center. The *Sächsisches Staatsarchiv* is on the corner, facing Schongauerstraße. The *Zenralstelle* is located on the second floor (the German "first floor" – in the elevator press the "1" button).

THE BERLIN
DOCUMENT CENTER

    The Berlin Document Center is the world's largest Nazi-records archive,
consisting of about 75 million pages of 30 million Nazi documents, filling racks 7.4 miles long. It is the most comprehensive collection of Nazi files for the years 1933-1945.
    These records were collected prior to 1945 by American, British, French and Soviet troops, from archives, libraries, and evacuation sites such as barns, caves, and salt and potash mines, and sent to document collection centers.
    Records which were biographic in nature were stored in building complexes in and around Berlin; thus the collection came to be known as the Berlin Document Center (BDC). Because this repository held biographic data of Germans and their participation agencies of the Nazis, the BDC was able to supply evidence to the Nürnburg Trials.
    For almost 50 years, the collection was in American custody, but on 1 July 1994 it was turned over to the *Bundesarchiv,* the Central Archives of Germany's federal government. It includes the almost complete membership files of the NSDAP (*Nationalsozialistische Deutsche Arbeit-erpartei*, or National Socialist German Workers'Party — the Nazi party), with data on its 10.7 million party members.
    Among the records are 600,000 applications for party membership, personal files on 260,000 members of the SA (*Sturmabteilung*, forerunner of the Nazi storm division in the early Nazi era), 329,000 files on the SS (*Schutzstaffel*, the Nazi's name for the "Blackshirts"), 185,000 files on the *Kulturkammer* (the Culture Commission, NSDAP's suborganization for writers, musicians, and other artists), 500,000 files on the *NS-Lehrerbund* (the NSDAP suborganization for teachers), 238,000 files on the RaSHA (*Rasse- und Siedlungshauptamt der SS,* the Race and Resettlement Department, responsible for review of marriage applications by members of the SS), 2.1 million files on the EW

(*Einwandererzentral-stelle Litzmannstadt*, ethnic Germans from Poland, Russia, Baltic States, etc., who were resettled in Germany), 72,000 files on the *Reichsärztekammer* (the medical directory of the NSDAP suborganization for physicians), as well as 50,000 files of the *Volksgerichtshof*, the Nazi's supreme court.

Following the United States' agreement to relinquish jurisdiction over the files to the Germans in July 1994, many scholars familiar with their content expressed the fear that the transfer could have disastrous consequences for historians and Nazi-hunters.

Upon receipt of the master copy of the files by the National Archive in Washington, to consist of 40,000 rolls of microfilm, work was begun on making available a users copy for researchers. These documents are indexed and housed in the National Archives Textual Reference Branch at Archives II in College Park, Maryland. Although The National Archives and Records Administration does not provide a search service for researchers, the staff will search the index for named persons and advise researchers about which rolls of film contain the files of the person of interest. The documents may then be viewed at the National Archives, or copies of the pertinent rolls of microfilm may be purchased.

Inquiries may be sent by email to berlin@bundesarchiv.de.

Reference

For an excellent discussion of the history and post-war management of these documents, see "Secrets of the Files," by Gerald Posner, *The New Yorker*, March 14, 1994, p. 39.

Sources:

♦Christel K. Converse, "The Challenge of the Berlin Document Center Library," *The Record* (National Archives and Records Adminstration), November 1998.

♦Raymond S. Wright III, "The Impact of Nazi Records on German Genealogical Research," *Ancestry*, Vol. 16, No. 6, Nov./Dec./1998.

INTERNATIONAL TRACING SERVICE

The ITS in Bad Arolsen serves victims of Nazi persecutions and their families by documenting the fate of inmates of concentration camps, foreign forced laborers in Germany and German civilians. The principal archive in Germany is located at Bad Arolsen in Lower Saxony. The website is www.its-arolsen.org.

THE 'GAUCK' FILES

In the 40 years before reunification of Germany, the *Staatssicherheit*, better known as the Stasi, or the East German secret police, had prepared and collected immense quantities of documents detailing the private lives of millions of East German citizens. The East Germany police state engaged 95,000 full-time Stasi agents, more than double the number of Gestapo agents in Nazi Germany, which had four times the population. From the 15 Stasi offices whose documents were turned over to the federal government came 35.6 million index cards and thousands of cassettes and diskettes of taped material.

Many of the records were shredded in the days just following the opening of the border. When the shredding machines broke down, Stasi members were ordered to tear up the records by hand. Thus 5,800 huge sacks of paper scraps were left waiting to be pieced together.

After the fall of the wall in November 1989, Joachim Gauck, a clergyman and a dissident from Rostock, was elected to the *Volkskammer* (the parliament of the German Democratic Republic) and became involved in the Stasi problem. He was given the charge of analyzing and releasing the 6 million files of the East German Stasi.

On 30 August 1989, a law was passed establishing an authority to regulate the use of the files, and Gauck was elected to head it. The new body, with head-quarters in Berlin, came to be known as the *Gauck-Behörde,* or the Gauck Authority. The official title created for the position was "The Federal Commissioner for Documentation of the State Security Service of the Former German Democratic Republic."

The mission assigned to Gauck and his 3,100 employees was to provide citizens with access to information filed about them and to protect citizens from misuse of their files.

Because the law under which Gauck served allowed only one reappointment, the chairmanship passed in 1999 to Marianna Birthler, former Minister for Educational Affairs in Brandenburg and member of the Green Party, through appointment by Chancellor Gerhard Schröder.

Examination of the files by private citizens began in January 1992. As of October 1995, almost 2.9 people had applied to look at their Stasi files. As of the end of 1999, about 15,000 people each month were applying to see their files, and more than 300,000 people were still waiting to see theirs.

Sources:
*"The Gauck Commission in Berlin," by Joachim Nowrocki, *Deutschland,* August 1995. pp. 138-140.
*"East Germany's Secret Files," interview by Pilar Wolfsteller, *German Life,* February/March 1996, pp. 12-15.
*Roger Cohen, "Germany's East Is Still Haunted by Big Brother. *New York Times,* Nov. 29, 1999
*_____, "For the Wall's Fall, East Germans Are Given Their Due." *New York Times,* Nov. 10, 1999

EWZ ANTRÄGE

In the period 1939 to 1945, a great number of ethnic Germans living outside Germany applied for naturalized German citizenship.

More than 400,000 of these applications are collected in the body of records known as the *EWZ (Einwanderungszentralstelle) Anträge* (applications).

Applications may contain background information about the applicant, as well as the applicant's parents, spouse, and children. Files may also contain naturalization forms (a naturalization application, declaration and final certificate) along with any correspondence related to the application process.

EWZ applications were originally part of the Berlin Document Center, but since 1992, they have been held at the *Bundesarchiv* (Federal Archive) in Berlin (Finckensteinallee 63, 12205 Berlin).

Microfilm copies of these records are now also stored by the National Archives and Records Administration (publication A3342). Contact james.kelling@arch2.nara.gov to find out which roll holds the surname you are seeking.

The collection is listed in the Family History Library under Einwandererkartei 1939-1945 of the EWZ.

INSTITUT FÜR PFÄLZISCHE GESCHICHTE UND VOLKSKUNDE

Institut für Pfälzische Geschichte und Volkskunde
Benzinoring 6
67657 Kaiserslautern
Germany
Tel. 0631 3647 303
Fax 0631 3647 324
info@institut.bv-pfalz.de
www.pfalzgeschichte.de

This respository for information regarding Palatine emigration (Institute of Palatine history and culture) maintains one million card files on more than 300,000 Palatine emigrants. Information is categorized by surname, town of residence before emigration, and persons who have submitted information. The archive is sometimes known as the Pfalz Emigration File.

The Institut's director, Dr. Roland Paul, encourages researchers to submit information about ancestors, including name, where settled, marriage, village in the Pfalz from whence the ancestor emigrated, and the date if known. Researchers may request a check of the Institute's files concerning their Palatine ancestors.

As 1995, the Institute held manuscripts or published volumes of extracts from churchbooks, which at that time included the following localities:

Abtweiler, Alsenborn, Banat, Bann, Barbelroth, Battweiler, Baumholder, Becherbach, Biedershausen, Bierbach, Billigheim, Blickweiler, Blieskastel, Bous, Breitenbach, Brücken, Busenberg, Contwig, Dellfeld, Desloch, Enkenbach, Ernsteweiler, Fehrbach, Fischbach, Frankenthal, Gerhardsbrunn, Glan-Münchweiler, Großbundenbach, Großeniedes-heim, Großsteinhausen, Gutenbrunnen, Hangard, Heidelberg, Hengstbach, Hermersberg, Herschberg, Heuchelheim, hinterweidenthal, Hochspeyer, Hochstadt, Homburg, Horbach, Hornbach, Hütsch-enhausen, Hundsbach, Jeckenbach, Jettenbach, Kaiserslautern, Kirchen-arnbach, Kirchenbollenbach, Kirchmohr, Klingen, Knopp, Kübelberg, Labach, Ladenburg, Lambsborn, Landstuhl, Leimen, Lemberg, Limbach, Mannheim, Martinshöhe, Meisenheim, Merzalben, Mimbach, Mittelbach, Mittelbrunn, Merzalben, Mimbach, Mittelbach, Mittelbrunn, Mittelreidenbach, Mörlheim, Mörs-bach, Neunkirchen/Saar,

Neunkirchen/Potzberg, Nünschweiler, Oberhausen, Offenbach am Glan, Otterberg, Pirmisens, Queidersbach, Ramstein, Reichenbach, Rheingönheim, Rieschweiler, Rodalben, Rumbach, Schaffhausen, Sembach, Sien, Stambach, Thaleischweiler, Trippstadt, Trulben, Ulmet, Waldfischbach, Wald-mohr, Wallhalben, Walsheim, Weben-heim, Weilerbach, Wiesbach, Winterbach, Wolfstein, Zeselberg, Zweibrücken, Zweybrücken

Main source: "Institut für Pfälzische Geschichte," by Jean Nepsund, *German American Genealogy* (Immigrant Genealogy Society), Spring 1998.

REICHSBAHN EMPLOYEE FILES

The *Deutsche Reichsbahn* (German Federal Railway) was formed from 11 provincial railways in 1920, with two provincial regions: Prussia and Bavaria.

This office keeps records of former employees of the *Reichsbahn:*
♦Reichsbahndirektion Berlin
Ruschestraße 59
10365 Berlin

The following German railway employee genealogy study group for the Hannover area may also have information:
♦Gruppe Familien- und Wappenkund im Bundesbahn - Sozialwerk
Ortsgruppe Hannover
Bahndirektion, Büro SF
30159 Hannover
Germany

WORKING IN A
A GERMAN ARCHIVE

The rules for using archival records are more or less the same at all German archives. The researcher acknowledges these rules by signing the application (*Benutzerantrag*) before using the archive.

Before you leave home . . . .

• Precisely define your research problem, determining with what kinds of records the problem may be solved and where the records may be found.

• Determine whether the archive you plan to visit holds the records you are seeking. If so, check to find out whether such records have been microfilmed for use in the Family History Library in Salt Lake City so that you can search them first in the United States.

After you arrive in Germany . . . .

• Telephone or email the archive before your planned visit to make certain that it will be open on the day you plan to visit. Also, check the hours that the archive is open.

• As you enter the archive, leave your coat and belongings in a locker in the room provided (*Garderobe*). Ask the way to the reading room (*Lesesaal, Benützersaal*) to complete the application form.

• Relate your problem to the archivist, who may either inform you that the records for solving the problem are not available at the archive or direct you to the appro-priate catalogs or to the catalog room.

• Write down on an order slip the numbers of the specific files you wish to examine, then submit the slip to the archivist. Usually an archive's files may be accessed only during specified hours of the day. In some archives, the number of records which may be requested per day is limited.

• After you receive the records you have requested, take them to your desk to examine them. When you are finished, return them to the archivist or to the place designated for this purpose.

• Because it is not the archivist's responsibility to read or translate entries on records you have requested, you should be sure that your language abilities are sufficient before ordering a record.

• Do not eat, drink, smoke, or talk loudly in the reading room.

• Do not take notes on paper laid on top of archive records.

• Reproductions of documents on paper or microfilm are usually provided upon request, but for your private use only. The copyright of archival records remains with the archive.

Without written permission, you may not forward a copy to anyone else or publish it.

If you publish a record from an archive, you must submit a free copy of the publication to the archive.

• Many archives will be able to refer you to a local or regional professional genealogist who is available for further research.

After you return home . . . .

Share your experiences by writing short articles for American genealogical magazines. Thus, other researchers will be forewarned against mistakes you may have made and may learn about sources they had not known about before.

Source: Friedrich R. Wollmershäuser, M.A., Accredited Genealogist, Herrengasse 8-10, 89610 Oberdischingen, Germany. © Friedrich R. Wollmershäuser, 1997.

See also: Minert, Roger P. and Shirley J. Riemer, *Researching in Germany: A Handbook for your Visit to the Homeland of Your Ancestors*, Sacramento: Lorelei Press, 2001.

RECOMMENDATIONS FOR ONSITE RESEARCH IN GERMANY

The following suggestions will be helpful to family history researchers with limited or no previous research experience in Europe:

1. Make an appointment (for the exact day and hours, if possible), with the director, pastor, etc. Have a record of this appointment in writing from the office; even appointments made over the tele-

phone can be forgotten. If at all possible, make the appointments in the host language, employing competent linguistic help if your language skills are not sufficient. Misunderstandings can be disastrous when you consider the time and money you will invest to make the visit.

2. Leave plenty of time to locate the archive. Except for the small-town church, it seems that the locals never know where the office or building is.

3. Do not expect the pastor or his secretary to assist, or even to be in the office for more than a few hours at a time. Smaller parish offices are often open less than eight hours per week.

4. Contrary to what you may have heard, most of the people you will deal with in this work do not speak English. Of those who do, most cannot deal with the technical terminology your research may entail.

5. Do not expect archive personnel to hurry.

6. Reading help is seldom available. As the years pass, we find that fewer pastors and their secretaries are able to read the old handwriting. Archive staff members usually can, but they often have no time to do so.

7. Good maps are not often available where you conduct your research (even in major archives), although listings of local towns are usually on hand. Bring along the best map you can get for the immediate vicinity and for your target town(s).

8. Bring enough cash to pay required fees, as well as unanticipated charges.

9. Photocopies of church book pages often cannot be made. Where this service is available, costs are usually about 25 to 50 cents per page. Making the copies or waiting for the copies to be made can consume valuable research time.

10. Lunchtime shut-downs are virtually universal. Bring your lunch along. It can take some time to locate a place to buy your lunch and eat it and still get back to the archive when they open up for the afternoon.

11. Never abuse the records of the facility. The mistakes you make could easily hurt the chances of the next United States visitor who wishes to see the same records.

12. When working in parish offices or when visiting private researchers, offer a donation or compensation for extraordinary services (20 is a suitable amount after a short visit). If your offer is rejected – as it often will be – do not be pushy or try to negotiate. Europeans usually mean what they say the first time.

13. Send thank-you notes soon after the visit. These notes can be in English; the message will get through. In situations where the visit has lasted more than a day and specific persons have rendered exceptional service, it is appropriate to purchase some flowers at a local shop and hurry back with them before the office closes. One might also sincerely volunteer to procure for the host certain items in the United States and send them later as a return favor.

Source: Minert, Roger P. and Shirley J. Riemer, *Researching in Germany: A Handbook for your Visit to the Homeland of Your Ancestors*, Sacramento: Lorelei Press, 2001.

GENEALOGY-RELATED ORGANIZATIONS IN GERMANY

The following societies related to genealogy and family history are listed alphabetically by locality.

When writing to an organization listed below, do not include the location before the colon (example: Berlin:). It has been added merely for the reader's convenience and should not be used as part of the mailing address. In correspondence, be sure to add "Germany" (not *Deutschland*) as the last line of each address.

The abbreviation *e.V.* stands for *einge-tragener Verein,* indicating a court-registered society that is incorporated.

Bad Karlshafen: German Huguenots Society
Deutscher Hugenotten-Verein e.V., Deutsches Hugenotten-Zentrum, Hafen-platz 9 a, 34385 Bad Karlshafen.

Beckedorf: Registry of Pedigrees for the *Deutsche Arbeitsgemeinschaft Genealogischer Verbände*
Ahnenlistenumlauf der DAGV, Rainer Bien,Hauptstr. 70,31699 Beckedorf.

Bensheim: Friedrich Wilhelm Euler Society for Genealogical Research
Friedrich-Wilhelm-Euler-Gesellschaft für personengeschichtliche Forschung e.V., (Ehem. Institut zur Erforschung historischer Führungsschichten e.V.),Ernst-Ludwig-Str. 21, 64625 Bensheim.

Berlin: Siemens Employees of Berlin Society for Family History
Arbeitsgemeinschaft für Familiengeschichte im Kulturkreis Siemens e.V. , Göbelstr. 143-145, 13629 Berlin.

Berlin: HEROLD, Society for Heraldry, Genealogy, and Related Studies
HEROLD, Verein für Heraldik, Genealogie und verwandte Wissenschaften, Archivstr. 12-14, 14195 Berlin (Dahlem).

Berlin: Sponsors and Supporters of the Central Office for Genealogy and Family History
Verein zur Förderung der Zentralstelle für Personen- und Familiengeschichte e.V. (Zentralstellenverein), Archivstr. 12-14, 14195 Berlin (Dahlem).

Berlin: Genealogy Society of Berlin
Interessengemeinschaft Genealogie Berlin, Heinrich-Heine-Str. 11, 10179 Berlin.

Bielefeld: Salzburger Society
Salzburger Verein e.V.,Memeler Str. 35 (Wohnstift Salzburg), 33605 Bielefeld.

Bolanden: Mennonite History Society
Mennonitischer Geschichtsverein e.V., Am Hollerbrunnen 7, 67295 Bolanden.

Bonn: Organization of Genealogy Societies
Bund der Familienverbände e.V.,Lorenz-von-Stein-Ring 20, 24340 Eckernförde.

Braunschweig: Academy for Genealogy, Heraldry, and Related Studies
Akademie für Genealogie, Heraldik und verwandte Wissenschaften e.V., Gutenbergstr. 12 B, 38118 Braunschweig.

Bremen: "The Mouse" Society for Genealogy
Die Maus, Gesellschaft für Familienforschung e.V., Am Staatsarchiv 1/ Fedelhöen (Staatsarchiv), 28203 Bremen.

Bretten: Baden Homeland Society for Historical and Cultural Studies
Landesverein Badische Heimat e.V., Heilbronner Str. 3, 75015 Bretten.

Brühl: German Association of Genealogy Societies (DAGV) [an umbrella organization of many German genealogical societies]
Deutsche Arbeitsgemeinschaft genealogischer Verbände e.V., Schloßstr. 12, 50321 Brühl.

Brühl: North Rhine-Westphalia Genealogical Archive, Rhineland Section
Nordrhein-Westfälisches Personenstands-archiv Rheinland, Schlossstr. 12, 50321 Brühl.

Chemnitz: Genealogical Society of Chemnitz
Fachgruppe Genealogie Chemnitz, c/o Armin Lippmann, Straße Usti nad Labem 23, 09119 Chemnitz.

Darmstadt: German-Baltic Genealogical Society
Deutsch-Baltische Genealogische Gesell-schaft e.V., Herdweg 79, 64285 Darmstadt.

Dortmund: Roland at Dortmund
Roland zu Dortmund e.V.,Postfach 103326, 44033 Dortmund.

Dresden: Genealogy Society of Dresden
Interessengemeinschaft Genealogie Dres-den, c/o Eberhard Stimmel, Friedrich-Wolf-Str. 3, 01465 Langebrück

Düren: Lineage Society of Wallmich-rath
Sippenverband Wallmichrath e.V., Rüt-ger-von-Scheven-Str. 63a,52349 Düren

Düsseldorf: Stoye Foundation
Stiftung Stoye, Jürgen Wagner, Rheinallee 159, 40545 Düsseldorf

Erfurt: Genealogical Society of Thuringia
Arbeitsgemeinschaft Genealogie Thüringen e.V.,Martin-Andersen-Nexö-Str. 62, 99096 Erfurt

Erlangen: Siemens Employees of Erlangen Genealogical Society
Genealogischer Kreis in der Kameradschaft Siemens Erlangen e.V., Postfach 3240, z.H. Th. Lonicer, Abt. VT 611, 91050 Erlangen

Friedrichsdorf: Central Office for Genealogy and Family History
Zentralstelle für Personen- und Familiengeschichte (Institut für Genealogie), Birk-enweg 13, 61381 Friedrichsdorf

Garbsen: Lower Saxony, Bremen, and Eastfalia Genealogy Society
Familienkundliche Kommission für Niedersachsen und Bremen sowie angrenzende ostfälische Gebiete e.V., Steinfeldstr. 34,
30826 Garbsen

Göttingen: Genealogy and Heraldry Society at Göttingen
Genealogisch-Heraldische Gesellschaft Göttingen, e.V., Postfach 2062, 37010 Göttingen

Hagen: Society for Genealogy in Hagen
Arbeitskreis für Familienforschung im Hagener Heimatbund e.V., Hochstr. 74, 58095 Hagen

Halle: Halle Researchers "Ekkehard"
Hallischer Familienforscher "Ekkehard" e.V., c/o Bernd Hofestädt, Otto-Hahn-Str.2
06122 Halle-Neustadt

Hamburg: Genealogy Society at Hamburg
Genealogische Gesellschaft, Sitz Hamburg, e.V. , Postfach 302042, 20307 Hamburg

Hamburg: Hamburg Society for Genealogy in East- and West Prussia
Verein für Familienforschung in Ost- und Westpreussen e.V., In der Krümm 10, 21147 Hamburg

Hannover: Lower Saxony Society for Genealogy
Niedersächsischer Landesverein für Fami-lienkunde e.V., Am Bokemahle 14-16 (Stadtarchiv), 39171 Hannover

Hannover: Heraldry Society of "Clover Leaf"
Heraldischer Verein zum Kleeblatt e.V., Erhardt Haacke, Berliner Str. 14E, 30457 Hannover

Heidelberg: Genealogical Association of English-Speaking Researchers in Europe
Genealogical Association of English-Speaking Researchers in Europe,c/o Alexander Fülling, Kaiserstraße 12, 51643 Gummersbach

Hemau: Society for Genealogy in the Upper Palatinate (Bavaria)
Gesellschaft für Familienforschung in der Oberpfalz e.V., Karl-Heinz Kriegelstein, Pustetstr. 13, 93155 Hemau

Herdecke: Society for Eastern Central European Studies
Gesellschaft für ostmitteleuropäische Landeskunde und Kultur e.V., Klaus-Dieter Kreplin,Zum Nordhang 5,58313 Herdecke

Herne: Society of East German Genealogical Researchers
Arbeitsgemeinschaft ostdeutscher Famil-ienforscher e.V.(AgoFF), Detlef Kühn,
Zum Block 1 a, 01561 Medessen

Hessian Family History Society
Hessische familiengeschichtliche Verein-igung e.V. (HFV), Karolinenplatz 3 (Staatsarchiv), 64289 Darmstadt

Ilmenau: Organization of Genealogical Societies
Bund der Familienverbände e.V., Kirchgasse 18, 98693 Ilmenau

Kaiserslautern: Institute for Palatine History and Culture

Institut für pfälzische Geschichte und Volkskunde, Benzinoring 6, 67657 Kaiserslautern

Kassel: Society for Family History Research in Kurhessen and Waldeck
Gesellschaft für Familienkunde in Kurhessen und Waldeck e.V., Postfach 101346, 34013 Kassel

Kassel: Society of Genealogical Organizations in Hessen
Arbeitsgemeinschaft der familienkundlichen Gesellschaften in Hessen,Gräfestr. 35, 34121 Kassel

Kiel: Schleswig-Holstein Society for Genealogy and Heraldry
Schleswig-Holsteinische Gesellschaft für Familienforschung und Wappenkunde e.V., Postfach 3809, 24037 Kiel

Kleve: Mosaik Genealogical Society for the Kleve District
Mosaik Familienkundliche Vereinigung für das Klever Land e.V., Mosaik-Archiv, Lindenallee 54, 47533 Kleve

Köln: Leps-Milke Foundation
Leps-Milke Stiftung, Gerhard Leps, Neusser Wall 12, 50670 Köln

Köln: West German Genealogical Society
Westdeutsche Gesellschaft für Familienkunde e.V., Sitz Köln , Unter Gottes Gnaden 34, 50859 Köln

Leipzig: Leipzig Genealogical Society
Leipziger Genealogische Gesellschaft e.V.
Marion Bähr, c/o Deutsche Zentralstelle für Genealogie,Postfach 274, 04002 Leipzig

Leipzig: German Central Office of Genealogy
Deutsche Zentralstelle für Genealogie, Sächsisches Staatsarchiv Leipzig, Abt. Deutsche Zentralstelle für Genealogie, Schongauer Str. 1, 04329 Leipzig

Lübeck: Society for Genealogy Lübeck
Arbeitskreis für Familienforschung Lübeck e.V.,Mühlentorplatz 2 (Mühlentorturm), 23552 Lübeck

Ludwigshafen: Society for Palatine and Rhineland Genealogy
Arbeitsgemeinschaft für Pfälzisch-Rheinische Familienkunde e.V.,Rottstr. 17, 67061 Ludwigshafen

Lünen: Society for the Promotion of Computer-Assisted Genealogical Research
Verein zur Förderung EDV-gestützter familienkundlicher Forschungen e.V., Schlorlemmerskamp 20, 44536 Lünen

Magdeburg: Magdeburg Genealogical Society
Arbeitsgemeinschaft Genealogie Magde-burg,Thiemstr. 7, 39104 Magdeburg

Marburg: German Nobility Archive
Deutsches Adelsarchiv, Schwanallee 21, 35037 Marburg

Markkleeberg: Society for Middle Germany Genealogy
Arbeitsgemeinschaft für mitteldeutsche Familienforschung e.V., Waldweg 5 , 04416 Markkleeberg

Mörfelden-Walldorf: Historical Society of Walldorf
Arbeitsgemeinschaft für Walldorfer Geschichte, Waldstr. 100, 64546 Mörfelden-Walldorf

München: Bavarian Genealogy Society
Bayerischer Landesverein für Familienkunde e.V., Ludwigstr. 14/I, 80539 München

München: Document Center for German Expatriates and Refugees from Eastern Europe (Silesia, East Prussia, Pomerania, etc.), Zentralstelle der Heimatsortskarteien, Lessingstr. 1, 80336 München

Münster: Westphalia Society for Genealogy and Family History
Westfälische Gesellschaft für Genealogie und Familienforschung, Postfach 6125, 48133 Münster

Neuenhaus: Historical and Cultural Society of Emsland Region, Genealogical Section
Arbeitskreis Familienforschung der „Emländischen Landschaft e.V." c/o Jan Ringena, Grafenstraße 11, 49828

Nürnberg: Society for Family History Research in Franconia
Gesellschaft für Familienforschung in Franken e.V., Archivstr. 17 (Staatsarchiv), 90408 Nürnberg

Oldenburg: Oldenburg Genealogical Society
Oldenburgische Gesellschaft für Familien-kunde, Lerigauweg 14, 26131 Oldenburg

Oldenburg: Research Center, Lower Saxons in the USA
Forschungsstelle Niedersächsische Aus-wanderer in den USA, Carl von Ossietzky Universität, Ammerländer Heerstraße 114-118, 26111 Oldenburg

Peine: Railway Employees' Society for Genealogy and Heraldry
Gruppe Familien- und Wappenkunde im Bundesbahn-Sozialwerk, Weissdornstr. 10, 31228 Peine

Plauen: Society for History and Culture of Vogtland Region Genealogical Section
Arbeitskreis Vogtländische Familien-forscher" im Verein für vogtländische Geschichte, Volks- und Landeskunde e.V., c/o Frau Andrea Hanisch, Alfred-Schlagk-Str. 12, 08523 Plauen

Püttlingen: Society for Saarland Genealogy
Arbeitsgemeinschaft für Saarländische Familienkunde e.V., Hebbelstr. 3, 66346 Püttlingen

Ratingen-Lintorf: Dusseldorf Society for Genealogy
Düsseldorfer Verein für Familienkunde e.V., Krummenweger Str. 26, 40885 Ratingen-Lintorf

Regensburg: Association of Sudeten German Genealogists
Vereinigung Sudetendeutscher Familien-forscher, Sudetendeutsches Genealo-gisches Archiv, Erikaweg 58, 93053 Regensburg

Sindelfingen: Society of Danube Swabian Genealogy
Arbeitskreis donauschwäbischer Fami-lienforscher, Goldmühlestr. 30, 71065 Sindelfingen

Söhlde: Hildesheim Genealogical Society
Familienkundlicher Verein Hildesheim, Nr 66, 31185 Söhlde

Sondershausen: Interest Group of the Middle Germany Family History Research:
Arbeitsgemeinschaft für mitteldeutsche Familienforschung e.V., Straße der Freundschaft 2, 99706 Sondershausen [Deals with the new eastern states, including Berlin]

Stuttgart: Society for Family History and Heraldry in Württemberg and Baden
Verein für Familien- und Wappenkunde in Württemberg und Baden e.V., Postfach 10 54 41, 70047 Stuttgart

Wiesbaden: Genealogical Society for Nassau and Frankfurt
Familienkundliche Gesellschaft für Nassau und Frankfurt e.V. (Hessisches Hauptstaatsarchiv), Mosbacher Str. 55 65187 Wiesbaden

Wilhelmshaven: Genealogical Society for East Frisia
Upstalsboom-Gesellschaft für historische Personenforschung und Bevölkerungs-geschichte in Ostfriesland e.V., Prof. Dr. Harro Buss, Flotowweg 4, 26386 Wilhelmshaven

Worms: Historical Society for the Siebenbürg Region (Romania) **Genealogical Section**
Arbeitskreis für Siebenbürgische Landes-kunde e.V., Abteilung Genealogie, Michäl Fleischer, Holderbaumstr. 9, 67549 Worms

Wuppertal: Society for Genealogy of the Bergisches Land Region
Bergischer Verein für Familienkunde e.V., Dr. Wolfram Lang, Zanellastr. 52, 42287 Wuppertal

Locality and topic index to the above-listed societies
Baden: see Bretten, Stuttgarg
Baltics: see Darmstadt
Bayern: see Hemau, München

Bensheim: see Bensheim
Bergische Land: see Wuppertal
Berlin: see Berlin
Braunschweig: see Braunschweig
Bremen: see Bremen, Garbsen
Chemnitz: see Chemnitz
Computers: see Lünen
DAGV: see Beckedorf, Brühl
Danube Swabians: see Sindelfingen
Dortmund: see Dortmund
Dresden: see Dresden
Düsseldorf: see Ratingen-Lintorf
Eastern Germany: see Herne, Sonders-
   hausen
Eastern-Central Europe: see Herdecke
Emsland: see Neuenhaus
English-speaking researchers: see
Heidel   berg
Franconia: see Nürnberg
Frankfurt: see Wiesbaden
Göttingen: see Göttingen
Hagen: see Hagen
Halle: see Halle
Hamburg: see Hamburg
Heraldry: see Berlin, Braunschweig,
   Göttingen, Hannover, Kiel, Marburg,
   Peine
Hessen: see Darmstadt, Kassel
Hildesheim: see Söhlde
Huguenots: see Bad Karlshofen
Kleve: see Kleve
Kurhessen: see Kassel
Leipzig: see Leipzig
Lübeck: see Lübeck
Magdeburg: see Magdeburg
Mennonites: see Bolanden
Middle Germany: see Markkleeberg
Mouse, The: see Bremen
Nassau: see Wiesbaden
Niedersachsen: see Garbsen, Hannover,
   Oldenburg
Nobility: see Marburg
Nordrhein-Westfalen: see Brühl
Oberpfalz (Bayern): see Hemau
Oldenburg: see Oldenburg
Ostfriesland: see Wilhelmshaven
Ostpreußen refugees: see München
Ostpreußen: see Hamburg
Palatine: see Ludwigshafen, Kaisers-

lautern
Pfalz: see Ludwigshafen, Kaiserslautern
Pommern refugees: see München
Railway employees: see Peine
Refugees: see München
Rheinland: see Ludwigshafen
Romania: see Worms
Saarland: see Püttlingen
Salzburger: see Bielefeld
Schlesien refugees: see München
Schleswig-Holstein: see Kiel
Siemens employees: see Berlin, Erlangen
Sudeten Germans: see Regensburg
Thüringen: see Erfurt
Transylvania (Siebenbürgen): see
Worms
Umbrella organizations: see Beckedorf,
   Berlin, Bonn, Brühl, Friedrichsdorf,
   Ilmenau, Leipzig
Vogtland: see Plauen
Waldeck: see Kassel
Wallmichrath: see Düren
Western Germany: see Köln
Westfalen: see Münster
Westpreußen: see Hamburg
Württemberg: see Stuttgart

HISTORICAL SOCIETIES IN GERMANY

Aachen: Aachener Geschichtsverein e.V.,
Fischmarkt 3 (Stadtarchiv),52062 Aachen
Bad Aibling: Historischer Verein für Bad
Aibling und Umgebung,
Wilhelm-Leibl-Platz 2 (Heimatmuseum
Bad Aibling), Geschäftsstelle: Frühling-
str. 34,83043 Bad Aibling.
Alsfeld: Geschichts-   und
Museumsverein   Rittergasse   3-5
(Regionalmuseum), 36304 Alsfeld.
Ansbach: Historischer Verein für
Mittelfranken e.V., Staatliche Bibliothek
(Schloßbibliothek), Reitbahn 5, 91522
Ansbach
Arolsen: Waldeckischer
Geschichtsverein e.V., Schloßstr. 24
(Schreibersches Haus), 34454 Arolsen.
Aschaffenburg: Geschichts- und Kunst-

verein Aschaffenburg e.V.,Wermbachstr. 15 (Schönborner Hof), 63739 Aschaffenburg.

Augsburg: Heimatverein für den Landkreis Augsburg, e.V., Prinzregentenplatz 4 (Landratsamt), 86150 Augsburg.

-Historischer Verein für Schwaben, Schaezlerstr. 25, 86152 Augsburg.

-Schwäbische Forschungsgemeinschaft bei der Kommission für bayerische Landesgeschichte bei der Bayerischen Akademie der Wissenschaften, Universitätsstr. 10 (Universität Augsburg), 86159 Augsburg.

Bamberg: Historischer Verein für die Pflege der Geschichte des ehemaligen Fürstbistums Bamberg, Postfach 1624, 96007 Bamberg.

Bayreuth: Historischer Verein für Oberfranke, Ludwigstr. 21 (Neues Schloß), 95444 Bayreuth.

Berchtesgaden: Verein für Heimatkunde des Berchtesgadener Landes e.V., 2. Vorsitzender: Hellmut Schöner, Salzburger Str. 18, 83471 Berchtesgaden.

Berlin: Historische Kommission zu Berlin, Kirchweg 33, 14129 Berlin.

-Historische Gesellschaft zu Berlin Habelschwerdter Allee 39-45, 14195 Berlin.

-Landesgeschichtliche Vereinigung für die Mark Brandenburg, Britzer Damm 23, 12169 Berlin.

-Verein für die Geschichte Berlins, Geschäftsstelle: Frau Ingeborg-Schröter Brauerstr. 31, 12209 Berlin

Biberach: Gesellschaft für Heimatpflege, Kunst- und Altertumsverein Biberach e.V., Gustav E. Gerster, Memminger Str. 36, 88400 Biberach.

Bielefeld: Historischer Verein für die Grafschaft Ravensberg e.V., Rohrteichstr. 19, 33602 Bielefeld

Bingen: Vereinigung der Heimatfreunde am Mittelrhein e.V.,Sitz Bingen, Geschäftsstelle: Rheinkai 21 (Städtisches Verkehrsamt), 55411 Bingen/Rh.

Bischofsheim: Heimat- und Geschichtsverein Bischofsheim,Geschäftsführer: Hans Leoff, Schillerstr. 25, 65474 Bischofsheim.

Böblingen: Heimatgeschichtsverein für Schönbuch und Gäu e.V,. Parkststr. 1,71005 Böblingen

Bonn: Bonner Heimat- und Geschichtsverein e.V, Berliner Platz 2 (Stadtarchiv), 53111 Bonn

-Verein für geschichtliche Landeskunde der Rheinlande, Am Hofgarten 22, 53113 Bonn

-Historischer Verein für den Niederrhein, insbesondere für das alte Erzbistum Köln, Geschäftsstelle: Prof. Dr. Giesbert Knopp, GrafZeppelin-Str. 36, 53757 Sankt Augustin

Braunschweig: Braunschweigischer Geschichtsverein e.V., Löwenwall 18 b (Stadtarchiv), 38100 Braunschweig.

-Harzverein für Geschichte und Altertumskunde, Burgplatz 1, 38100 Braunschweig.

Bremen: Historische Gesellschaft Bremen e.V., Am Staatsarchiv 1, 28203 Bremen

Bremerhaven: „Männer vom Morgenstern," Heimatbund an Elb- und Wesermündung, Geschäftsstelle: Bernd Behrens, Müggenburgweg 2, 27607 Langen.

Bückeburg: Schaumburg-Lippischer Heimatverein, Vorsitzende: Frau Dr. Roswitha Sommer, Lübingstr. 4, 31675 Bückeburg.

Büdingen: Büdinger Geschichtsverein, 1. Vorsitzender: Leitender Schulamtsdirektor Willi Luh, In der Langgewann 58, 63654 Büdingen.

Burghhausen: Heimatverein Burghausen /Salzach, Burg 40 (Josef Schneider), 84469 Burghausen.

Butzbach: Geschichtsverein für Butzbach und Umgebung, Brudergasse 8 (Winfried Schunk), 35510 Butzbach.

Coburg: Historische Gesellschaft Coburg e.V., Eupenstr. 108 (Oberstudiendirektor Har-

ald Bachmann), 96450 Coburg.
Darmstadt: Hessische Historische Kommission, Karolinenplatz 3 (Staatsarchiv), 64289 Darmstadt
-Historischer Verein für Hessen, Carolinenplatz 3 (Staatsarchiv), 64289 Darmstadt
-Hessische Kirchengeschichtliche Vereinigung, Ahastr. 5 a (Zentralarchiv der Evangelischen Kirche in Hessen und Nassau), 64285 Darmstadt.
Detmold: Naturwissenschaftlicher und Historischer Verein für das Land Lippe, Willi-Hofmann-Str. 2 (Staatsarchiv), 32756 Detmold
Dillingen: Fürstl. und Gräfl. Fuggersches Familien- und Stiftungsarchiv, Ziegelstr. 29, 89407 Dillingen/Donau
-Historischer Verein Dillingen/Donau Westendstr. 34 (OstudDir. Dieter M. Schienhammer), 89407 Dillingen.
Donauschingen: Verein für Geschichte und Naturgeschichte der Baar, Haldenstr. 3 (Fürst. Fürstenbergisches Archiv), 78166 Donaueschingen.
Dortmund: Gesellschaft für Westfälische Wirtschaftsgeschichte e.V., Märkische Str. 120, 44009 Dortmund
-Historischer Verein für Dortmund und die Grafschaft Mark e.V,. Geschäftsstelle: Stadtarchiv Dortmund, Friedensplatz 5, 44135 Dortmund
Düren: Dürener Geschichtsverein, Vorsitzender: Dr. Hans J. Domsta, Stadt- und Kreisarchiv Düren, Postfach 356, 52303 Düren
Düsseldorf: Düsseldorfer Geschichtsverein e.V., Mauerstr. 55 (Hauptstaatsarchiv), 40476 Düsseldorf.
Duisburg: Mercator-Gesellschaft, Karmelplatz 5 (Stadtarchiv), 47049 Duisburg
Eichstätt: Historischer Verein Eichstätt, Kobenzl-Schlößchen, 85072 Eichstätt
Erlangen: Heimat- und Geschichtsverein Erlangen e.V., Marktplatz 1, 91054 Erlangen
-Zentralinstitut für Fränkische Landes-

kunde und allgemeine Regionalforschung der Universität Erlangen-Nürnberg, Kochstr. 4, 91054 Erlangen.
Essen: Historisher Verein für Stadt und Stift Essen, Vorsitzender: Dr. G. Annen, Laubendakler Landstr. 1, 45239 Essen.
Esslingen: Geschichts- und Altertumsverein am Neckar e.V., Stadtmuseum Hafenmarkt 7, 73728 Esslingen.
Euskirchen: Verein der Geschichts- und Heimatfreunde Euskirchen e.V., Kreisverwaltungsarchiv, Jülicher Ring, Postfach 1145, 53861 Euskirchen.
Flensburg: Gesellschaft für Flensburger Stadtgeschichte e.V., Am Pferdewasser 1, 24937 Flensburg.
Frankfurt (Main): Frankfurter Historische Kommission, Karmelitergasse 5 (Stadtarchiv), 60311 Frankfurt/M.
-Frankfurter Verein für Geschichte und Landeskunde e.V., Karmelitergasse 5 (Stadtarchiv), 60311 Frankfurt/M.
-Verein für Geschichte und Altertumskunde e.V., Frankfurt/M.-Höchst, Museum im Höchster Schloß, Schloßplatz 16 ,65929 Frankfurt/M.-Höchst.
Freiburg: Breisgau-Geschichtsverein, Schau ins Land, Grünwälder Str. 15 , 79098 Freiburg i. Br.
Freising: Historischer Verein Freising e.V., Rathaus/Stadtarchiv, 85354 Freising.
Friedberg: Friedberger Geschichtsverein e.V., Augustinergasse 8, Bibliothek-zentrum Klosterbau, 61169 Friedberg i. Hessen.
Fürth: „Alt-Fürth," Verein für Geschichte und Heimatforschung e.V., Schloßhof 12, 90768 Fürth.
Fulda: Fuldaer Geschichtsverein, Stadt-schloß/Kulturamt, Postfach 1020, 36010 Fulda.
Geldern: Historischer Verein für Geldern und Umgebung e.V., Kapuzinerstr. 34 (Kreisarchiv), 47608 Geldern.
Gelsenkirchen-Buer: Verein für Orts- und Heimatkunde Gelsenkirchen-Buer,

Postfach 200417, 45839 Gelsenkirchen
Gießen: Oberhessischer
Geschichtsverein Gießen e.V., Ostanlage
45, 35390 Gießen
Göppingen: Geschichts- und Altertums-
verein Göppingen, Postfach 809
(Kreisarchiv), Orcher Str. 6, 73033
Göppingen
Göttingen: Geschichtsverein für
Götting-en und Umgebung e.V.,
Geismarlandstr. 4 (Neues Rathaus),
37083 Göttingen
-Historische Kommission für ost- und
westpreußische Landesforschung,
Eich-ener Str. 32,53902 Bad
Münstereifel-Houverath, (Prof. Dr. Udo
Arnold).
Goslar: Geschichts- und Heimatschutz-
verein Goslar, Cehntstr. 24 (Stadtarchiv),
Postfach 2569, 38615 Goslar.
Grafing: Arbeitsgemeinschaft für Heim-
atkunde e.V., Dobelweg 16 (Dr. Rolf
Klinger), 85567 Grafing b. München
Großostheim: Geschichtsverein Bach-
gau, Stettiner Str. 6, 63762 Großostheim
II
Günzburg: Historischer Verein Günzburg
e.V., Sophienstr. 3 , 89312 Günzburg.
Gunzenhausen: Verein für Heimatkunde
Gunzenhausen e.V., Sonnenstr. 8, 91710
Gunzenhausen.
Hamburg: Verein für Hamburgische
Geschichte, ABC-Str. 19 (Staatsarchiv),
20354 Hamburg.
Hanau: Hanauer Geschichtsverein,
Schloßplatz 3, 63450 Hanau.
Hannover: Gesellschaft für Niedersächs-
ische Kirchengeschichte, Rote Reihe 6
,30169 Hannover.
-Historischer Verein für Niedersachsen,
Am Archiv 1 (Hauptstaatsarchiv),
30169 Hannover
Heilbronn: Historischer Verein Heil-
bronn e.V., Eichgasse 1 (Stadtarchiv),
Postfach 2030, 74010 Heilbronn.
Heiligenhaus: Geschichtsverein Heilig-
enhause e.V., Rathaus 42579 Heiligen-
haus.
Herborn: Geschichtsverein Herborn e.

V. Schloßstr. 3 (Rechtsanwalt J.
Wienecke) 55758 Herborn
Hof: Nordoberfränkischer Verein für
Natur-, Geschichts- und Landeskunde
e.V., Unteres Tor 9 (Stadtarchiv), 95028
Hof/Saale.
Bad Homburg v.d. Höhe: Verein für
Geschichte und Landeskunde e.V., Bad
Homburg v.d. Höhe, Ernst-Moritz-Arndt
Str. 2 b, 61348 Bad Homburg v. d. Höhe.
Hünfeld: Hünfelder Kultur- und Mus-
eumsgesellschaft e.V., Geschäftsstelle
Kirchplatz 4 ,36088 Hünfeld
Ingelheim: Historischer Verein Ingel-
heim, Museum bei der Kaiserpfalz, Am
alten Rathaus, 55218 Ingelheim a. Rh.
Ingolstadt: Historischer Verei
,Ingolstadt Geschäftsstelle: Auf der
Schanz 4 (Stadtarchiv), 85049
Ingolstadt.
Kassel: Verein für hessische Geschichte
und Landeskunde e.V., Mönchebergstr.
19 (Gesamthochschule Kassel), 34125
Kassel
(Vorsitzender: Leitender Bibliotheks-
director Dr. H.-J. Kahlfuß).
Kempten: Heimatverein Kempten e.V. im
Heimatbund Allgäu e.V., (Anton J. Keil),
Amselweg 5, 87439 Kempton/Allgäu.
Kiel: Gesellschaft für Kieler Stadtge-
schichte, Rathaus/Stadtarchiv, 24103
Kiel.
Koblenz: Verein für Kunst und Ge-
schichte des Mittelrheins, Karmeliter-str.
1/3 (Landeshauptarchiv), 56068 Kob-
lenz.
Köln: Gesellschaft für Rheinische
Geschichtskunde, Severinstr. 222-228,
50676 Köln
-Kölnischer Geschichtsverein, Universi-
täts und Stadtbibliothek, Universitätsstr.
33, 50923 Köln
Königstein: Verein für Heimatkunde,
Königstein im Taunus, Hauptstr. 3, 61462
Königstein i. Ts.
Konstanz: Verein für Geschichte des
Bodensees und seiner Umgebung,
Deutsche Geschäftsstelle: Stadtarchiv
Konstanz, Benediktinerplatz 5 (Prof. Dr.

Mauerer), 78467 Konstanz
Koslar: Geschichtsverein Koslar e.V., Lebsgasse 15, 52428 Koslar
Bad Kreuznach: Verein für Heimatkunde für Stadt und Kreis Bad Kreuznach e.V., Geschäftsstellen: Dr. Horst Silbermann Dienheimer Berg 11, 55545 Sobernheim, und in der Bücherei im Hauses der Kreisverwaltung, Salinenstr. 47, 55543 Bad Kreuznach
Kronberg: Verein für Geschichte und Heimatkunde der Stadt Kronberg im Taunus e.V., Geschäftsstelle: Dr. Bruno Langhammer Kronberger Str. 7, 61462 Königstein.
Kulmbach: Freunde der Plassenburg e.V., E.-C.-Baumann-Str. 5, 95326 Kulmbach
Landsberg a. Lech: Historischer Verein für Stadt und Kreis Landsberg a. Lech, Klaus Münzer, Galgenweg 17, 86899 Landsberg a. Lech.
Landshut: Historischer Verein für Niederbayern, Altstadt 79, Residenz, 84028 Landshut.
Lauterbach: Lauterbacher Museum, Berliner Platz 1 (Hochhaus), 66333 Lauterbach.
Lichtenfels: Colloquium Historicum Wirsbergense, Heimat und Geschichtsfreunde am Obermain e.V., Vorsitzender: Dr. Emil Singer ,Neubaustr. 2, 96257 Redwitz.
Limburg/Lahn: Bischöfliches Ordinariat Limburg, Roßmarkt 4, 65549 Limburg a. d. L.
Lindau: Museumsverein Lindau,Dr. Karl Bachmann, Schweizerhofweg 18, 88131 Lindau.
Ludwigsburg: Historischer Verein Ludwigsburg für Stadt und Kreise e.V., Stadtarchiv, Kaiserstr. 14, 71636 Ludwigsburg.
Lübeck: Hansischer Geschichtsverein Mühlendamm 1-3 (Archiv der Hansestadt Lübeck), 23552 Lübeck.
-Verein für Lübeckische Geschichte und Altertumskunde, Mühlendamm 1-3 (Archiv der Hansestadt Lübeck) 23552 Lübeck.

Lüneburg: Museumsverein für das Fürstentum Lüneburg, Wandrahmstr. 10 (Museum), 21335 Lüneburg
Mainz: West- und Süddeutscher Verband für Altertumsforschung, Institut für Vorund Frühgeschichte Schillerstr. 11, 55166 Mainz.
Marburg: Hessisches Landesamt für geschlichtliche Landeskunde, Wilhelm-Roepke-Str. 6 c, 35039 Marburg/Lahn.
-Historische Kommission für Hessen Friedrichsplatz 15, 35037 Marburg/Lahn.
-Gesellschaft für Hessen, Friedrichsplatz 15, 35037 Marburg/Lahn
-Gesellschaft für pommersche Geschichte, Altertumskunde und Kunst e.V., Johann-Gottfried-Herder-Institut, Gisonenweg 5-7, 35307 Marburg/Lahn
Minden: Mindener Geschichtsverein, Tonhallenstr.7 (Kommunalarchiv Minden), 32423 Minden.
Monschau: Geschichtsverein des Monschauer Landes, Dr. E. Neuß M.A,. Görlitzer Str. 33, 48157 Münster.
München: Collegium Carolinum e.V. Forschungsstelle für böhmische Länder, Hochstr. 8/II, 81669 München
-Historische Kommission der Sudetenländer e.V., Hochstr. 8, 81669 München
-Historischer Verein von Oberbayern Winzererstr. 68, 80797 München
-Institut für baycrische Geschichte an der Universität München, Ludwigstr. 14, 80539 München
-Kommission für bayerische Landesgeschichte bei der Bayerischen Akademie der Wissenschaften, Marstallplatz 8, 80539 München
-Studiengruppe für Sächsische Geschichte und Kultur e. V., Geschäftsstelle: Grün-walder Str. 225 d, 81445 München
-Verband für Orts- und Flurnamenforschung in Bayern e.V., Leonrodstr. 57, 80636 München
Münster: Kopernikus-Vereinigung zur Pflege der Heimatkunde und Geschichte Westpreußens e.V., Sitz Münster/West-

falen, Geschäftsstelle: Norbert Str. 29,
48151 Münster.
-Historische Kommission für Westfalen,
Warendorfer Str. 24 , 48145 Münster
-Historischer Verein für Ermland, Erm-
landweg 22 (Ermlandhaus), 48159
Mün-ster
-Westfälisches Institut für Regional-
geschichte, Warendorfer Str. 14, 48745
Münster.
-Verein für Geschichte und Alter-
tumskunde Westfalens Abt. Münster
Geschäftsstelle: Warendorfer Str. 14,
48133 Münster
-Verein für Westfälische Kirchenge-
schichte ,
An der Apostelkirche 1-3,
48143 Münster
Neu-Ulm: Verein für Heimatgeschechte
Nagold e.V.,
Haiterbacher Str. 58,
72202 Nagold
-Historischer Verein Neu-Ulm,
Illerholzweg 18,
89231 Neu-Ulm.
-Verband zur Vorbereitung der Kreis-
beschreibung für die Stadt- und Land-
kreise Günzburg, Illertissen, Krumbach
und Neu-Ulm e.V., Geschäftsführender
Vorstand:Rechts-anwalt Horst Gaiser
Donaucenter, Marienstr. 1, 89231 Neu-
Ulm.
Nördlingen: Historischer Verein für
Nördlingen und das Ries, Stadtarchiv
Nördlingen, Rathaus, Marktplatz 1, 86720
Nördlingen.
Northeim: Heimat- und Museumsverein
für Northeim und Umgebung, Postfach
1323, 37154 Northeim.
Nürnberg: Abteilung für
Vorgeschichte der Naturhistorischen
Gesellschaft e.V.,
Gewerbemuseumsplatz 4 (Luitpold-
haus), 90403 Nürnberg
-Verein für die Geschichte der Stadt
Nürnberg , Egidienplatz 23 (Stadt-
archiv), 90403 Nürnberg
Oberursel: Verein für Geschichte und
Heimatkunde Oberursel (Taunus) e.V.,

Postfach 1146, 61401 Oberursel/Ts.
Offenburg: Historischer Verein für
Mittelbaden, Postfach 1569, 77605
Offenburg.
Osnabrück: Verein für Geschichte und
Landeskunde von Osnabrück, Schloßstr.
29 (Staatsarchiv), 49072 Osnabrück.
Osterrode: Heimat-   und
Geschichtsverein Osterrode am Harz
und Umgebung e.V. Martin-Luther-Platz
2, Altes Rathaus,
37520 Osterrode a. H.
Paderborn: Verein für Geschichte und
Altertumskunde Westfalens, Abt. Pader-
born, Leostr. 21, 33098 Paderborn
Pottenstein: Heimatverein Pottenstein.
Hauptstr. 19, 91278 Pottenstein
Ratzeburg: Heimatbund   und
Geschichts-verein   Herzogtum
Lauenburg   e.V.,   Domhof   12
(Kreismuseum), 23909 Ratzburg.
Recklinghausen: Verein für Orts und
Heimatkunde Recklinghausen, .Stadt-
archiv, Hohenzollernstr. 12, 45659
Recklinghausen
Regensburg: Fürst Thurn und Taxis
Zen-tralarchiv-Hofbibliothek,
Emeramsplatz,
93047 Regensburg
-Historischer Verein für Oberpfalz und
Regensburg, Dachauplatz 4, 93047
Regensburg
Rosenheim: Historischer Verein Rosen-
heim,Stadt und Landkreis, Geschäfts-
stelle: Kulturamt, Max-Bram-Platz 2 a,
83022 Rosenheim.
Rott: Heimatverein für Wasserburg am
Inn und Umgebung (Historischer Verein)
e.V., Arnikaweg 10, 83543 Rott am Inn.
Rottenburg: Sülchgauer
Altertumsverein,   Geschäftsführer:
Karlheinz Geppert M.A., Stadtarchiv,
Postfach 29, 72101 Rotten-burg a. N.
Saarbrücken: Historischer Verein für die
Saargegend e.V., Stadtarchiv, Postfach
439, 66104 Saarbrücken.
-Institut für Landeskunde im Saarland,
Universität, Bau 35 (Herr Güth), 66123
Saarbrücken.

-Kommission f. Saarländische Landesge-schichte u. Volksforschung, Scheidter Str. 114, 66130 Saarbrücken.
Schleswig: Gesellschaft für Schleswig-Holsteinische Geschichte, Frau Sylvia Günther, Harder Koppel 15, 24217 Schönberg/Holstein.
Schrobenhausen: Historischer Verein Schrobenhausen, Paarstr. 5, 86529 Schrobenhausen
Schwäbisch-Hall: Historischer Verein für Württembergisch Franken, Münzstr. 1, 74523 Schwäbisch-Hall.
Schweinfurt: Historischer Verein Schweinfurt e. V., Petersgasse 3, 97421 Schweinfurt.
Siegburg: Geschichts- und Altertums-verein und dem Rhein-Sieg-Kreis e.V., Rathaus, 53721 Siegburg
Sigmaringen: Hohenzollerischer Ge-schichtsverein,Karlstr. 3, 72488 Sigmar-ingen
-Landeskundliche Forschungsstelle Hohenzollern in der Kommission für geschichtliche Landeskunde in Baden-Württemberg, Karlstr. 3, 72488 Sigmar-ingen
Singen: Verein für Geschichte des Hegau e.V., August-Ruf-Str. 7 (Stadtarchiv), 78224 Singen (Hohentwiel)
Soest: Verein für Geschichte und Heim-atpflege Soest e.V., Jakobistr. 13 (Stadtarchiv und wissenschaftliche Stadt-bibliothek), 49494 Soest.
Spalt: Heimatverein Spalter Land e.V. Heinrich Heubusch, Lerchenbuck 28, 91174 Spalt.
Speyer: Historischer Verein der Pfalz e.V. Domplatz (Historisches Museum der Pfalz), 67324 Speyer.
-Pfälzische Gesellschaft zur Förderung der Wissenschaften, Große Pfaffengasse 7 (Historisches Museum der Pfalz), 67346 Speyer.
Stade: Niedersächsisches Staatsarchiv Stade, Am Sande 4 c, 21682 Stade.
-Stader Geschichts- und Heimatverein, Rathaus, Postfach 2025, 21660 Stade.
Straubing: Historischer Verein für

Straubing und Umgebung e.V., Fraun-hoferstr. 9, 94315 Straubing.
Stuttgart: Württembergischer Ge-schichts- und Altertumsverein e.V., Konrad-Adenauer-Str. 4 (Hauptstaats-archiv), 70173 Stuttgart
Tittmoning: Historischer Verein Tittmoning e.V., Poschacher Str. 2 a, 84529 Tittmoning.
Traunstein: Historischer Verein für den Chiemgau zu Traunstein e.V., Heimat-hausstr., Postfach 1829, 83268 Traunstein
Trier: Gesellschaft für nützliche For-schungen Trier, a) Ostalled 44, 54290 Trier
Ihre Sektion: Arbeitsgemeinschaft für Landesgeschichte und Volkskunde des Trierer Raumes, Weberbachstr. 25 (Stadtarchiv), 54290 Trier
Ulm: Verein für Kunst und Altertum in Ulm und Oberschwaben, Weinhof 12 (Stadtarchiv), 89073 Ulm.
Waldshut-Tiengen: Geschichtsverein Hochrhein e.V., Waldshut-Tiengen Vorsitzender: Fritz Schächtelin, Rathaus-str. 19, 79761 Waldshut-Tiengen.
Weiden: Heimatkundlicher Arbeitskreis im Oberpfälzer Waldverein, Geschäfts-stelle: Pfarrplatz 4 (Stadtarchiv), 92637 Weiden (Oberpfalz).
Weißenhorn: Heimat- und Museums-verein Weißenhorn und Umgebung, Wolf-gang Ott M. A., Kirchplatz 4, 89264 Weißenhorn (Schwaben)
Wertheim: Historischer Verein Wertheim e.V., Rathausgasse 10, 97877 Wertheim/ Main
Wetzlar: Wetzlarer Geschichtsverein e.V., Vorsitzende: Ingeburg Schäfer, Engelsgasse 8, 35578 Wetzlar.
Wiesbaden: Historische Kommission für Nassau, Mosbacher Str. 55 (Hessisches Hauptstaatsarchiv), 65187 Wiesbaden.
-Verein für Nassauische Altertumskunde und Geschichtsforschung e.V., Mos-bacher Str. 55 (Hessisches Hauptstaats-archiv), 65187 Wiesbaden.

Würzburg: Bischöfliches Ordinariat
Würzburger
Diözesangeschichtsverein,
Vorsitzender: Prof. Dr. Klaus Wittstadt,
Universität Würzburg, Sanderring 2,
97070 Würzburg.

Source: Wolfgang Ribbe and Eckart Henning, *Taschenbuch für Familiengeschichtsforschung.* Verlag Degener & Co., Neustadt an der Aisch, 1995.

Section 8: Life in Our German Ancestors' Times

◆

Names: Patterns, changes, and cultural history
Calendars, holidays, observances
Churches, religions
Education, universities
Measurements, monetary units
Military records, wars, nobility, heraldry

◆

A BRIEF HISTORY OF GERMAN NAMES

Germanic names

Originally, sons and daughters born into Germanic tribes had but one name, which consisted mostly of two words or syllables like,

Bernhart: *bêr* (bear) + *hart* (strong)
Kuonrad: *kuon* (bold) + *rad* (advise)

Other words or syllables like these were often used –

- *ger* (spear)
- *hari* (army)
- *brant* (sword)
- *wulf* (wolf)
- *run* (magic)

– showing that Germanic names usually revolved around bravery, glory, honor, battles, victory, prosperity – things and ideas held in high esteem.

Very early, abbreviations and short forms of these names – today called *Kosename* (nicknames) came into use, especially for children:

Bernhart >> Bernd

Kuonrad >> Kuno, Kurt
Audomar >> Otto
Hugibert >> Hugo

Many of these old Germanic names, especially their abbreviated forms, still exist and are widely used as given names (*Vorname*) today.

Christian names
(*Taufnamen*)

During the early days of Christianity in Germany, it was mostly adults who converted and were baptized. The church did not require them to change their Germanic names, but this happened nevertheless, following the example of the Roman Saulus, who became *Paulus*. In this way, biblical names and names of saints and martyrs of Hebrew, Greek and Latin origin came into use.

When the idea of baptizing infants (around the third century) gained ground, this ceremony usually coincided with the naming of the child. The name given to the child was therefore called the *Taufname* (Christian name).

Only after the Council of Trent, in the catechism of 1566, did the Roman Catholic Church require that a child must be given the name of a saint. Often (but not always), the name of the saint was chosen whose day of commemoration the calendar showed on the child's birthday. In case the dates differed, this created a tradition of celebrating the child's *Namenstag* (name day) in addition to (or instead of) his or her birthday. For example, a boy born on July 10 and named Nikolaus celebrates his *Namenstag* on December 6. This tradition is still alive today in predominantly Catholic regions like Bavaria and the Rhineland.

Maria and *Joseph* (*Josef*) thus became the most popular names – to such a degree that boys were named *Maria* (in addition to another first name – like the composer Carl-Maria von Weber) or girls *Josephine* or *Josefa*. Other popular Christian names were *Joachim* and *Anna* (names ascribed to the parents of Maria) and *Elisabeth*, the name ascribed to the mother of John, the Baptist (*Johannes der Täufer*). Next were the four evangelists *Matthäus, Markus, Lukas and Johannes* – followed by the apostles *Andreas, Bartholomäus, Jakobus, Thomas, Johannes, Matthäus, Matthias, Petrus, Philippus, Simon and Thaddäus* (*Judas* was omitted).

Archangels chosen as namesakes were *Gabriel, Michael,* and *Raphael*. The names of the 14 *Nothelfer* (saints as helpers in need) also were used: *Achatius, Ägidius, Barbar, Blasius, Christopherus, Cyriak, Dionysius, Erasmus, Eustachius, Georg, Katharina, Margarete, Pantalon,* and *Vitus*. Even popes' names became popular choices: *Alexander, Anastasius, Benedict, Eugen, Felix, Gregor, Klemens, Leo, Linus, Paul, Pius, Stephan*.

Some of these Latin names were germanized: *Antonius >>Anton*; *Augustus >> August*; *Aemilius >>Emil*.

Greek names were introduced and adopted in a similar way, including *Aga-* *tha, Andreas, Barbara, Christoph, Helene, Katharina, Peter, Petra, Sophie,* and *Theodor.*

The use of the names of saints and popes was, of course, restricted to Roman Catholic areas, as Protestants did not believe in these ideas. They used names from the Old and New Testaments as Christian names or (later, in the Pietist movement of the seventeenth and eighteenth centuries) invented new names like *Gottlieb* (loves God or loved by God), *Leberecht* (live a decent life), or *Fürchtegott* (fear God).

Family names
(last names)

With an increasing population and interaction between its members, soon one Christian name was no longer sufficient for distinguishing persons from one another. Thus, "important," aristocratic families started to add the name of their origin (region or location of a castle) to their Christian names (Rudolf von Habsburg), thus creating in Germany by the eleventh century the concept of the *Familien* name (family name). Since it was added to the Christian name – that is, it came after it – it is also called *Nachname* or *Zuname* (surname).

This same idea was employed by commoners (*Konrad von Würzburg, Walter von der Vogelweide*). Not until about 1600 was the prefix "von" definitely restricted to show an aristocratic lineage.

By the fourteenth/fifteenth century, the use of family names had spread to most of the population.

Either the name of the father (*Patronym*) was added (*Martin, Ernst, Paul*), or the region of origin (*Schwab* = Swabia, *Heß* = Hessia), the hometown (*Nürnberger, Darmstädter*), the profession (*Bäcker* = baker, *Bauer* = farmer, *Schmidt* = smith, *Schneider* = tailor) or bodily or intellectual characteristics (*Klein* = small, *Klug* = smart), etc.

Most of the Jewish population

adopted family names only after being forced to do so by local laws in the eighteenth and early nineteenth centuries. The prime categories for Jewish surnames are topographical descriptions (*Lilienthal* = valley of the lilies), animal names (Löw = lion), and city or regional origins (Offenbacher = from or involved with Offenbach).

The Humanist period (around the sixteenth/seventeenth centuries) with its revival of ancient Greek and Roman ideals led some families to use Latin versions (*Molitor* for *Müller*, *Pastorius* for *Schäfer*) or Greek versions (*Melanchthon* for *Schwarzerde*) of their German names.

In Germany, the general practice was for a woman to adopt her husband's surname upon marriage. A infrequent exception occured when a groom assumed his wife's surname if she were the heiress of the family property (in northwestern Germany).

Some confusion can arise from the fact that some names, like *Karl, Otto* or *Hein-rich* can be used both as first and last names, so documents should be checked carefully as to which name is the *Vorname* and which one is the *Nachname* or *Familienname*.

Hofnamen
(names of farms)

In rural areas, the owners of a farm sometimes are known to their neighbors by a totally different family name than the one shown in the birth or marriage register. This can happen when the original, often centuries-old, name of a farm is passed on despite changes in the owners' names. So a farm once owned by a family named *Pfleger* was known as *Pflegerhof* (Pfleger's farm). Today's owner may still be called Pfleger (now deriving his name from the farm), even though his official name is Maier.

This is called his *Hofname* (name of the farm).

When a groom assumed the suname of the bride and thus became the farm owner, the records sometimes show both surnames. The birth surname was given first, followed by the term *oder, alias, gennant* (called), *modo*, or *colon*. For example, Claus Richter *colon* Meinert was born Claus Richter, married Angela Meinert and died as Claus Meinert. All children born to this couple bore the surname Meinert.

Vornamen
(given names)

A *Vorname* is basically the same as the *Taufname* except that this word takes into account that, with the start of the Age of Enlightenment in Germany (around the seventeenth century), religious influences generally receded. Therefore, the naming of children was less likely to be connected with their baptism. The word *Vorname* states neutrally that this name is the one that stands before the family name.

Choice of first names was increasingly secularized and, in the nineteenth and early twentieth centuries, turned to names of kings, emperors, and other political leaders (*Friedrich, Wilhelm, Ludwig*). For obvious reasons, the popularity of *Adolf* dropped sharplely after 1945.

Although most Germans today have more than one "first" name, this additional name is rarely used or represented by a middle initial. While the conventional view on this may change, its use is often considered "showy" like a loud tie. When two "first" names are used, it is most often in hyphenated form, like *Franz-Xaver* or *Hans-Jochen*.

Official registration
of names

Since the fifteenth century (there are regional variations), parishes kept track of their members by entries and updates in the *Kirchenbücher* or *Pfarrbücher* (church registers). The pastor's most important duty was to keep complete records of batisms (*Taufregister*), marriages (*Trauregister*) and deaths *(Sterberegister)*. The names recorded therein became the official, legally binding names of the parishoners.

While these church records are still kept today for church purposes, since 1876 and the introduction of the law called the *Reichspersonenstandsgesetz,* the legally binding names are those officially regis-tered by the *Standesamt* (registry office).

The Rufname

Many children had more than one given name (aristocrats may have a dozen or so) as is evident from the birth records. Usually, the last of the given names was the one by which the parents wanted the child to be primarily known and called (*Rufname*). As further clarification, some recorders underlined the *Rufname* in the church books. This is not forever binding for the person involved, who later on in life may choose one of his other names as a *Rufname*.

Sources:
♦Rainer Thumshirn, Heimstetten, Germany.
♦Roger P. Minert, "Surname Changes in Northwestern Germany," *German Genealogical Digest*, 15:4 (Spring 2000), 6-17.

SOME ODDITIES IN NAMING PRACTICES

♦The surname of a woman was often represented by an *-in* ending —for example, *Schneiderin* as the female form of *Schneider*. The *-chen* ending on a given name signifies smallness, as in *Gretchen* (little Grete).
♦A name may have been recorded or transcribed in different languages in different time periods. For example, the German name *Johann (Hans)* might have been recorded as *Jean* in French, as

Joannes in Latin, or as *Jan* in Polish.
♦Variant spellings of names occurred according to similarities in pronunciation of certain letters of the alphabet, like these, for example,

♦v and f	♦j and y
♦b and p	♦k and g
♦b and v	♦ch and gh
♦f and ph	♦s and z
♦t and d	♦k and c
♦m and n	♦g and ch
♦z and tz	

♦In past times, how a name was spelled was unimportant. How it was pronounced was what counted. Many people could pronounce their own names, but they could not write or spell them.
♦Persons in a community with identical names were distinguished from one another by adding terms that separated them by age, like *alt-* (old), *älter* (older), *ältest* (oldest); *jung-* (young), *junger* (younger), *jungst* (youngest); *mitteln* (middle); and I, II, and III. These indicators usually pointed to differences in the ages of same-name persons, not blood rela-tionships. For example, three men named Karl Hartmann, might be recorded as *Karl Hartmann d. [der] jungste,* (Karl Hartmann the youngest), *Karl Hartmann d. mittlere* (the Karl Hartmann who is not the eldest or the youngest), and *Karl Hartmann d. älteste* (Karl Hartmann the eldest). Likewise, the identifiers I, II, and III separate men by age and do not infer family relationships.

Sources:
♦Arta F. Johnson, *How to Read German Church Records without Knowing Much German.* The Copy Shop, Columbus, OH, 1981.
♦Roger P. Minert, *Spelling Variations in German Names*, GRT Publications, Provo, UT 2000.

ABBREVIATED VERSIONS OF GERMAN GIVEN NAMES

The names in the left column below are abbreviated versions of the given names shown at the right, which persons may prefer to use in everyday life instead of their officially registered first names:

Male names

Achim	Joachim
Adi	Adolf
Alex	Alexander
Alf	Alfred
Alois	Aloysius
Andi, Andrä, Anderl	Andreas
Armin	Hermann
Arno	Arnold, Arnulf
Ben	Benedikt, Benjamin
Bernd	Bernhard
Bert, Berti	Albert, Herbert, Hubert, Norbert, Bertram, Engelbert
Chris,	Christian,
Christoph	Christopherus
Claus	Claudius, Nikolaus
Curd, Curt, Conny	Konrad
Didi, Dieter	Diethelm, Dietmar, Dietrich
Dolf	Adolf
Edi	Edgar, Eduard
Ferdi, Fertl	Ferdinand
Fips	Philipp
Fonse	Alfons
Fred	Alfred
Friedel, Frieder	Gottfried, Friedrich
Fritz, Fred	Friedrich
Georg	Jörg
Gerd, Gert	Gerhard(t), Gernot
Götz	Gottfried
Gus, Gustl, Gussi	Gustav, August
Hans, Hannes	Johannes
Harry	Harald, Heinrich
Hein, Heini, Heiner, Heinz,	
Heiko, Heino, Hinz	Heinrich
Herbert	Hubertus
Hias	Matthias
Ingo	Ingolf
Iwan	Johannes
Jan, Janosch	Johannes
Jackel	Jakob
Jochen, Jockel	Joachim
Jörg	Georg
Jos	Joseph
Juan	Johannes
Jupp	Joseph
Kirsten	Christian
Klaus	Nikolaus
Konny	Konrad
Lenz	Lorenz
Leo	Leonard(t), Leopold
Lois	Alois
Louis	Ludwig
Luggi	Ludwig, Lukas
Lutz	Ludwig
Manne, Manni, Männer	Manfred
Max	Maximilian
Matz, Matthes	Matthias
Mewes	Bartholomäus
Naz, Nazi	Ignaz
Niels	Nikolaus
Olli	Oliver
Pit	Peter
Poldi	Leopold, Luitpold
Rolf, Ralf	Rudolph
Roger	Rüdiger
Rudi	Rudolph
Schorsch	Georg
Sepp	Joseph
Sigi	Siegfried
Simmerl	Simon
Steffen	Stephan
Stoffel	Christoph
Theo, Teo	Theodor
Thies	Matthias
Thilo	Dieter
Tim	Timotheus
Tobi	Tobias
Tom	Thomas
Toni	Anton
Ulf	Wolfgang
Uli, Ulli	Ulrich
Veit	Valentin
Wasti, Wastl	Sebastian
Wiggerl	Ludwig
Willi, Willy, Wim	Wilhelm
Winni	Winfried
Wolf, Wulf	Wolfgang

Female names

Alex	Alexandra
Alice	Elisabeth
Andi	Andrea
Angela, Angi	Angelika
Anja, Änne, Anna, Antje	Annette
Annegret	Anna Margarete
Annemarie, Annamirl	Anna Maria
Babsi	Babette
Bärbel	Barbara
Bea	Beate
Bessie	Elisabeth
Beta	Elisabeth
Betty	Elisabeth, Bettina, Babette
Birgit	Brigitte
Burgi, Burgl	Walburga
Carola	Caroline
Christa, Christel	Christina
Claire	Clara, Klara
Conny	Cornelia, Constanze
Dorte, Dörte	Dorothea
Edda	Adelheid
Elfi	Elfriede
Elise	Elisabeth
Elke, Ellen, Elise, Else	Elisabeth
Erna	Ernestine
Emma	Emmerentia
Eva	Evelyn
Fanny, Franzi	Franziska
Finny, Fine	Josefine
Friedl	Friederike
Gabi	Gabriele
Geli	Angelika
Gerda, Gerdi	Gertrude
Gigi	Gisela, Brigitte
Gila	Gisela
Gina	Regina
Gitte, Gitti	Brigitte
Grete	Margarete
Gunda, Gundi	Gundula, Gunhild, Kunigunde
Gusti	Augustine, Gustava
Hanna	Johanna
Hedda	Hedwig
Heidi	Heidemarie
Hella	Helene, Helena
Helma	Wilhelmine
Henny	Henriette

Hetty	Henriette
Hilde	Hildegard, Brunhilde, Gernhilde, Mathilde
Inge	Ingeborg
Ika	Veronika
Ilona	Helene
Ilse	Elisabeth
Ina, Ines	Agnes
Irma, Irmi	Irmengard
Isa, Isabella	Elisabeth
Jean, Jenny	Johanna
Jella	Gabriele
Karin, Katrin, Käthe, Kati, Katja	Katharina
Karola	Karoline
Kerstin	Christine
Lena, Lene, Leni	Magdalena, Marlene, Helene
Lia, Lisa, Lise,	Elisabeth, Lieselotte
Lena	Madalena
Liesel, Lissi Lilo	Lieselotte
Lina	Helena
Lina, Line	Pauline
Lore	Eleanore, Hannelore
Lotte	Lieselotte
Magda	Magdalena
Margit, Margot, Margret	Margaretha
Marion	Maria
Marlene	Maria Helena
Marlis	Maria Elisabeth
Mascha, Mia	Maria
Minna	Wilhelmine
Mirjam	Maria
Nelli	Cornelia
Nora	Eleonore
Resi	Therese
Rika	Friederike
Rita	Roswitha
Rose	Rosemarie, Roswitha
Sandra	Alexandra
Sigi	Sigrid, Sieglinde
Silke	Gisela
Sissi, Sissy	Elisabeth
Stasi	Anastasia
Steffi	Stephanie
Susi	Susanne
Thea	Dorothea, Theolinde
Tina, Tine	Christina
Toni	Antonia

Traudl .... Gertraud, Waltraud,
                                   Edeltraud
Trina .... Catharina
Trude, Trudi .... Gertrude, Wiltrud
Ulla, Ursel, Uschi .... Ursula
Uli, Ulli .... Ulrike
Vera, Vroni .... Veronika, Verena
Wally .... Walburga, Waltraud
Wilma .... Wilhelmine
Zenzi .... Creszenzia

PATRONYMIC NAMES

The patronymic naming system incorporated the name of the father into
the name of the child. Generally, in
Scanda-navia, a male infant would be
named after the father's given name, followed by "son" or "sen." For females, it
would be followed by "datter" or "dotter."

For example Carl, the son of Peter
Hansen, would be named Carl Peterson,
not Carl Hansen.

The use of this system was prevalent
in Schleswig-Holstein and northwest
Hannover.

Laws were passed in various areas in
the eighteenth and nineteenth centuries
to establish permanent surnames: In 1771
such a law was passed in the Schleswig
area; in1811 in Ostfriesland; in Prussia
in 1816.[1] Compliance was only gradual.

[1] "The World of Germanic Names: Or, a
German by Any Other Name May Be Your
Ancestor," Larry O. Jensen, *German
Genealogical Digest,* Vol. IV, No. 1, 1988.

ABBREVIATIONS FOR TITLES OF PEOPLE

◆**Ang., Angst.** (*Angestellter*): employee
◆Genfldm. (*Generalfeldmarschall*): Gen-
eral of the Army
◆**Genltn.** (*Generalleutnant*): Major Gen-
eral
◆ **Genmaj.** (*Generalmajor*): Brigadier
General
◆**Genobst.** (*Generaloberst*): General
◆**Hptm.** (*Hauptmann*): Captain
◆**Hsfr.** (*Hausfrau*): Housewife
◆**Ing.** (*Ingenieur*): Engineer
◆**Kfm.** (*Kaufmann*): Businessman
◆**Ltn.** (*Leutnant*): Second Lieutenant
◆ **MdB** (*Mitglied des Bundestages*):
Member of the Federal Parliament
◆**MdL** (*Mitglied des Landtages*): Mem-
ber of Local Parliament
◆**Oberstltn.** (*Oberstleutnant*): Lieuten-
ant Colonel
◆**Obltn.** (*Oberleutnant*): First Lieuten-
ant
◆**Obst.** (*Oberst*): Colonel
◆**Pfr.** (*Pfarrer*): Pastor
◆**Präs.** (*Präsident*): President
◆**RA.** (*Rechtsanwalt*): Lawyer
◆**Reg. Rat.** (or **RR**) (*Regierungsrat*): Civil
Servant
◆**Sekr.** (*Sekretär*): Secretary
◆**Sen.** (*Senator*): Senator
◆**StuR.** (*Studienrat*): Teacher
◆**Vors.** (*Vorsitzender*): Chairman
◆**Wwe.** (*Witwe*): Widow

DIMINUTIVE ENDINGS FOR GERMAN NAMES

◆**-chen:** *Gretchen* from *Margarete*
◆**-lein:** *Hänslein* from *Johannes*
◆**-(e)l(e):** *Hänsel, Hansl, Hänsele* from
Johannes
◆**-li (Swiss):** *Margretli* from *Margarete*
◆**-i:** *Rudi* from *Rudolf*
◆**-y:** *Willy* from *Wilhelm*

NEXT PAGES: GERMAN , NON-GERMAN GIVEN NAMES

On the next pages are listed given names
of Germanic and foreign origin. During
the Third Reich, parents were urged to
choose names having Germanic roots.
Lists of such names were published to
help them choose "approved" names.

FEMALE GIVEN NAMES OF GERMANIC ORIGIN

Ada	Ellen	Hedda	Kunhild	Siegberta
Adda	Ellengard	Hedwig	Kunigard	Sieghild(e)
Adele	Elvira	Heide	Kunigund	Sieglinde
Adelgard	Emma	Heilburg	Leopolda	Siegrun
Adelgund	Engelberta	Heimtr(a)ud	Leopoldine	Sigberta
Adelheid	Engelgard	Helga	Liebgunde	Sigburg
Adeltraut	Erda	Helgard	Lina	Sighild
Adolfine	Erdmut(e)	Helma	Ludwiga	Siglind
Alberta	Erika	Helmtrud	Luitgard	Sigmut
Albertine	Ermgard	Henrike	Malwine	Sigrun
Almgard	Erna	Hergard	Mathild(e)	Sigtrub
Almtrud	Ernestine	Herma	Mechthild(e)	Solweig
Almut	Ferdinande	Hermine	Meinhild	Swanhild
Aloisia	Folkhild	Herta	Merlind	Theadelinde
Alrun	Frida	Hertr(a)ud	Miltrud	Thekla
Altrud	Friderun	Hildburg	Minna	Thusnelda
Alwine	Fridgarb	Hilde	Nortrud	Tilla
Amalie	Fridhild	Hildegard	Northild(e)	Traudlind(e)
Anselma	Fried(e)gard	Hildegund	Notburg(a)	Trude
Arngard	Frieda	Hildrun	Olga	U(da)lberta
Arnhild	Friedegund	Hiltr(a)ud	Orthild	Ulla
Arntrud	Friederike	Hulda	Ortlind	Ulrike
Berchthild	Frigga	Ida	Ortraud	Undine
Bernhild(e)	Froburg	Ilsa	Ortrud	Uta
Berta	Gesine	Ilse	Ortrun	Ute
Berthild(e)	Gelmut	Ingala	Osilde	Walburg
Bertraud	Genoveva	Inge	Oslinde	Walfriede
Bertrun	Gerburg	Ingeborg	Oswine	Walpurga
Borghild	Gerda	Ingeburg	Ottilie	Waltraud
Bothild	Gerharde	Ingeltrud	Radegund	Waltrud
Brita	Gerhild(e)	Ingrid	Reglind	Wanda
Brunhild(e)	Gerlind(e)	Irma	Reimunde	Werngard
Burghild	Gertraud	Irmburg	Reingard	Wernhild
Daglind	Gertrud	Irmela	Reinhild(e)	Wilburg
Dagmar	Gislinde	Irmfriede	Richarda	Wilfriede
Dietburg	Gisa	Irmgard	Roberta	Wilgard
Dietgard	Gisela	Irmhild	Rosa	Wilhelma
Dietlind	Giselheid	Irmlind	Rosamund(e)	Wilhelmine
Edelburg	Giseltr(a)ud	Irmlind(e)	Roswitha	Wilma
Edelgard	Gislind	Irmtr(a)ud	Rotraut	Wiltrud(t)
Edeltr(a)ud	Gotlind	Ishild(e)	Rotrud	Winfriede
Edith	Gudrun	Isolde	Rudolfine	Wolfhild
Ehrengard	Gudula	Karla	Runfrid	Wunhild
Eiltraut	Gunhild	Karoline	Runhild(e)	
Elfride	Gunthild(e)	Klothild(e)	Ruperta	
Elfriede	Hadburg	Kriemhild(e)	Selma	
Ella	Hadmut	Kunigunde	Senta	

MALE GIVEN NAMES OF GERMANIC ORIGIN

Adalbert	Dietger	Fritz	Helmbrecht	Lienhard
Adelbert	Diethard	Fromund	Helmund	Lothar
Adelhard	Diethelm	Frowein	Helmut	Ludolf
Adolf	Diether	Frowin	Helmuth	Ludwig
Alarich	Dietmar	Fürchtegott	Helwig	Luitpold
Albert	Dietrich	Gebhard	Helwin	Lutz
Albrecht	Dietwalt	Gerald	Henning	Manfred
Alfons	Eberhard	Gerd	Herbert	Markward
Alfred	Eckehard	Gerfried	Heribert	Markwart
Alois	Eckmar	Gerhard	Hermann	Markwin
Alwig	Edgar	Gerhold	Herwart	Marwig
Alwin	Edmund	Germut	Herwig	Meinhard
Anshelm	Eduard	Gernot	Hilbert	Meinhold
Armin	Edward	Gero	Hildebert	Meinrad
Arnhelm	Edwin	Gerolf	Hildebrand	Neidhard
Arno	Egbert	Gerwig	Hildemar	Neithard
Arnold	Eginhard	Gerwin	Hilmar	Norbert
Arnulf	Egon	Gilbert	Hinz	Norfried
Balduin	Eilert	Gisbert	Horstmar	Notker
Baldur	Eilhard	Giselher	(Horst)	Odilo
Baldwin	Einhard	Godecke	Hubert	Odo
Benno	Eisenhard	Gottfried	Hubert	Olaf
Bernd	Emmerich	Gotthard	Hugbert	Ortfrid
Bernhard	Erhard	Gotthelf	Hugo	Ortwig
Bernold	Erich	Gotthold	Humbert	Ortwin
Bernwart	Erkmar	Gottlieb	Ingbert	Oskar
Berther	Ernst	Gottwald	Ingo	Oswald
Berthold	Erwin	Götz	Ingolf	Oswin
Bertram	Ewalt	Guido	Ingomar	Otfrid
Bodmar	Falk	Gumprecht	Iwein	Otger
Bodo	Falko	Gundolf	Karl	Otmar
Bodwin	Ferdinand	Gunter	Karlmann	Otto
Bruno	Folker	Günter	Klodwig	Ottobert
Brunold	(Volker)	Guntram	Knut	Ottokar
Burckhard	Folkhard	Guntwig	Konrad	Ottomar
Burghard	Folkmar	Gustav	Kraft	Radbod
Dagabert	Folkrat	Hagen	Kunibert	Radulf
Dagbert	Frank	Harold	Kuno	Rainer
Dagmar	Franz	Harro	Kunold	Ralf
Dagobert	Fridbalt	Hartlieb	Kurt	Rambert
Dagomar	Fridbert	Hartmann	Lambrecht	Randolf
Dankmar	Fridhelm	Hartmut	Landhelm	Ratwin
Dankwart	Fridrich	Hartwig	Landolf	Reimar
Degenhard	Fridwalt	Hartwin	Lebrecht	Reimund
Detlef	Friedel	Heinrich	Leonhard	Reinalt
Diepold	Friedolin	Heinz	Leopold	Reiner
Dietbert	Friedrich	Helmar	Leuthold	Reinhard

Reinhold	Siegfried	Tejo	Volkwin	Willibalt
Reinulf	Siegmar	Theodebald	Waldemar	Willrich
Richard	Siegmund	Theoderich	Walter	Wilmar
Robert	Siegward	Tilmann	Walther	Winand
Roderich	Sigbert	Tilo	Warmund	Winfrid
Rodewalt	Sigfrid	Timm	Wernand	Winfried
Rodewin	Sighard	Traugott	Werner	Winild
Roger	Sigisbert	Tujoho	Widukind	Winrich
Roland	Sigismund	Udo	Wieland	Wiprecht
Rudolf	Sigmar	Ulbert	Wigand	Wittich
Rupert	Sigmund	Ulrich	Wigbert	Wolf
Ruprecht	Sigolf	Utz	Wighard	Wolfgang
Ruthard	Sigurd	Volker	Wilfrid	Wolfhard
Schwerthelm	Sigwart	Volkbert	Wilfried	Wolfram
Sebald	Sturmhard	Volkhard	Wilhelm	Wulf
Sebalt	Tassilo	Volkmar	Willi	
Siegbert	Tasso	Volkrad	Willibald	

FEMALE GIVEN NAMES OF FOREIGN ORIGIN

Agathe	Christel	Gabriele	Laura	Paula
Agnes	Christene	Grete(l)	Lene	Pauline
Alice	Crescentia	Hanna	Leonore	Renate
Alma	Dora	Helene	Liesbeth	Ruth
Angela	Dorothea	Henriette	Liese	Sophie
Angelika	Dörthe	Irene	Lieselotte	Stefanie
Anna	Elisabeth	Isabella	Lilli	Susanne
Anneliese	Elise	Johanna	Lore	Suse
Annemarie	Elsa	Josefa	Lotte	Therese
Auguste	Elsbeth	Josephine	Luise	Tine
Babette	Else	Jutta	Magdalene	Toni
Barbara	Emilie	Katharina	Margarete	Trine
Beate	Eugenie	Käthe	Marianne	Ursel
Bettina	Eva	Kathrein	Marie	Ursula
Brigitte	Fanni	Kathrine	Marie-Luise	Vareria
Cäcille	Florentine	Klara	Martha	Veronika
Charlotte	Franziska	Kreszenz	Meta	Viktoria

MALE GIVEN NAMES OF FOREIGN ORIGIN

Achim	Emil	Jochem	Leo	Philipp
Alexander	Felix	Jochen	Lorenz	Sebastian
Andrä	Florian	Johann(es)	Martin	Sepp
Andreas	Georg	Jörg	Matthias	Simon
Anton	Gregor	Josef	Max	Stefan
Artur	Hans	Julius	Merten	Theo
August	Ignatz	Jürgen	Michael	Theodor
Bartel	Immanuel	Karsten	Michel	Thomas
Benedikt	Jakob	Kaspar	Moritz	Veit
Christian	Joachim	Klaus	Paul	Viktor
Christoph	Jobst	Klemeno	Peter	Vinzenz

FURTHER READING
ON NAMING PRACTICES

◆Adolf Bach, *Deutsche Namenkunde*, 3 vols. (Heidelberg: Carl Winter, 1952-1956).
◆Hans Bahlow, *Dictionary of German Names*, trans. Edda Gentry. Friends of the Max Kade Institute for German-American Studies, Inc. Madison, Wisconsin, 1993.
◆George F. Jones, *German American Names*, 2nd Edition. Genealogical Publishing Co., Baltimore, 1995.
◆Werner König, *DTV-Atlas zur Deutschen Sprache* (München 1978).
◆Josef Karl Brechenmacher, *Deutsches Namenbuch*. Verlag von Adolf Bong & Comp., Stuttgart, 1928.
◆"The World of Germanic Names, or A German by Any Other Name May be Your Ancestor," by Larry O. Jensen, *German Genealogical Digest*. Part I, Vol. 4, No. 1, 1988; Part II, Vol. 4, No. 2, 1988.

Sources:
◆Larry O. Jensen, *A Genealogical Hand-book of German Research*, rev. ed. Logan, UT, 1995.
◆Albert Heintze, Die deutschen Familien-Namen, Verlag der Buchhand-lung des Waisenhauses, Halle/Saale, 1882.

NAME DAYS (NAMENSTAGE)
IN GERMAN-SPEAKING AREAS

Below is a selection of the best known and most popular "name days" (*Namens-tage*) in Germany and neighboring Grman-speaking areas. Regional variations in popularity may apply.

The "name day" is a tradition mostly in the Roman Catholic Church.

According to Roman Catholic tradition, the date shown is usually the death date (historically correct or as traditionally assumed).

It used to be customary for children to be named according to the day on which they were born.

Key

S = Patron saint for . . .
H = Helpers in case of . . . ; appealed to for or against . . .

January 6: Kaspar, Melchior, Bal-thasar [the Three Wise Men]
S: city of Cologne, travelers, pilgrims, game card producers
H: thunderstorm, epilepsy

January 14: Engelmar [hermit, martyr]
S: town of St. Englmar (Bavaria), farmers
H: good harvest, cattle diseases

January 20: Sebastian [martyr]
S: the dying, soldiers, wells, hardware dealers, potters, pewter makers, gardeners, tanners, stone masons, gunsmiths, brush makers, rifle marksmen
H: wounds, epidemics, cattle diseases

January 21: Agnes [martyr]
S: young women, the engaged, gardeners, chastity

January 22: Vinzenz [martyr]
S: vintners, sailors, roofers, lumberjacks
H: lost objects

January 28: Thomas von Aquin [monk]
S: Order of Dominican Monks, Catholic universities, students, book dealers, pencil makers, clergy
H: thunderstorms

February 1: Brigitta von Kildare [abbess]
S: city of Essen, pregnant women, children, cattle
H: disaster, persecution

February 3: Blasius [bishop, martyr]
S: physicians, wool traders, cobblers, tailors, weavers, bakers, construction workers, hat makers, musicians, domestic animals, horses
H: coughing, sore throats, diseases of the bladder, bleeding, toothaches, pestilence

February 4: Veronika [disciple]
S: priest's housekeepers, washer-women, weavers
H: gentle death, severe injuries, bleeding

February 5: Agatha [martyr]
S: Midwives, weavers, female shepherds, bell founders, miners, goldsmiths
H: fire, thunderstorm, earthquake, disaster, famine, infected wounds, diseases of the breast
February 6: Dorothea [martyr]
S: gardeners, miners, newlyweds, brides, pregnant women
H: birth labor, poverty, dying, false accusations
February 14: Valentin von Tern [bishop]
S: youth, travelers, beekeepers
H: good marriage, pestilence
February 24: Matthias [apostle]
S: dioceses of Trier, Goslar, Hanover, Hildesheim; construction workers; butch-ers; pastry makers; blacksmiths; tailors
H: coughing, infertility, start of school year for boys
February 25: Walburga [abbess]
S: diocese of Eichstätt, pregnant women, farmers, domestic animals
H: Coughing, dog bite, rabies, eye diseases, good harvest
March 17: Gertrud [nun]
S: hospitals, pilgrims, travelers, poor, widows, gardeners, crops
H: mice and rats
March 17: Patrick [bishop, missionary]
S: Ireland, barbers, blacksmiths, miners, coopers, cattle
H: vermin, cattle diseases, evil
March 19: Joseph von Nazareth [husband of Mary]
S: Catholic Church, Austria, Bavaria, Bohemia, Tyrol, Styria, Carinthia, dioceses of Osnabrück and Cologne, families, children, orphans, artisans, carpenters, engineers, travelers, teachers, undertakers, expatriates
H: eye diseases, temptation, desperation, homelessness
March 26: Kastulus [martyr]
S: herdsmen
H: lightning, flooding, horse theft

April 23: Adalbert [bishop, martyr]
S: Prussia, Bohemia
April 23: Georg [martyr]
S: diocese of Limburg, boy scouts, farmers, miners, saddlers, blacksmiths, coopers, artists, horses, cattle, hikers, hos-pitals, soldiers, prisoners, horsemen
H: war, temptation, bad weather, fever, pestilence
April 25: Markus [evangelist, martyr]
S: notaries, construction workers, basket makers, glaziers
H: favorable weather, good harvest, hail, lightning, sudden death
May 4: Florian [martyr]
S: Upper Austria, fire brigades, chimney sweeps, beer brewers, coopers, potters, blacksmiths, soap makers
H: fire, flooding, drought, infertility of fields, storm, burn injuries
May 12 Pankraz [martyr]
S: communicants, young plants, blossoms
H: headache, cramps, perjury, wrongful accusation
May 13: Servatius [bishop, martyr]
S: cities of Goslar, Limburg/Lahn, Quedlinburg; diocese of Worms; locksmiths; cabinetmakers
H: rheumatism, fever, sore feet, frost, mice and rats
May 16: Johannes von Nepomuk [vicar, martyr]
S: Bohemia, priests, bridges, sailors, rafters, millers, Hapsburg Dynasty
H: libel, confessional secrets, flooding, protection of property
June 2: Erasmus, also known as Elmo [bishop, martyr]
S: sailors (St. Elmo's fire), rope makers, weavers, domestic animals
H: cramps, colic, ulcers, childbirth, cattle diseases
June 3: Klothilde (Clothilde) [Queen of Franconia]
S: women, notaries, the lame
H: fever, sick children, sudden death, conversion of husband to Christianity
June 5: Bonifatius, also known as

Winfrid ("Apostle to Germany")
S: diocese of Fulda, Thüringen, tailors, file makers, beer brewers

June 13: Antonius von Padua [monk]
S: cities of Paderborn and Hildesheim, Franciscan monks, lovers, women, matrimony, children, the poor, travelers, bakers, miners
H: lost objects, childbirth, infertility, fever, cattle diseases, shipwreck, war, pestilence, emergencies of any kind

June 15: Veit, also known as Vitus [child martyr]
S: Lower Saxony; Bohemia; cities of Prague, Mönchengladbach, Ellwangen, Krems; youth; innkeepers; pharmacists; vintners; actors; beer brewers; miners; blacksmiths; domestic animals; dogs; poultry; springs; the mute; the deaf
H: rabies, epilepsy, hysterics, cramps, diseases of eyes and ears, bedwetting, lightning, thunderstorms, fire, infertility, good harvest

June 16: Benno von Meissen [bishop]
S: Bavaria, city of München, diocese of Dresden-Meissen, fishermen, weavers
H: pestilence, drought, thunderstorms

June 21: Alban von Mainz [priest, missionary, martyr]
S: city of Mainz, farmers
H: headache, sore throat, epilepsy, diseases of the urinal tract, thunderstorms

June 21: Aloisius von Gonzaga [monk]
S: youth, students
H: choosing a profession, pestilence, eye diseases

June 24: Johannes der Taufer (John the Baptist)
S: weavers, tailors, furriers, tanners, dyers, saddlers, vintners, innkeepers, coopers, chimney sweeps, blacksmiths, masons, carpenters, movie theater owners, farmers, herdsmen, architects, musicians, dancers, singers, vineyards, domestic animals, sheep, lambs
H: abstinence, epilepsy, headache, sore throat, dizziness, sick children, fear, hail

June 29: Paul (Paulus) [apostle, martyr]

S: the Pope, diocese of Osnabrück, butchers, carpenters, glaziers, watchmakers, locksmiths, potters, blacksmiths, construction workers, tile makers, bridge builders, weavers, net makers, fishermen, fish merchants, sailors, virgins, the repentant, stonemasons
H: snake bites, fever, rabies, sore feet, obsessions, theft, shipwreck

June 30: Otto von Bamberg [bishop]
S: dioceses of Bamberg and Berlin
H: fever, rabies

July 3: Thomas (apostle)
S: architects, construction workers, carpenters, masons, the clergy
H: backache, good marriage

July 4: Ulrich von Augsburg [bishop]
S: diocese and city of Augsburg, village of St. Ulrich in South Tyrol, vintners, fishermen, weavers, travelers, the dying
H: complications at childbirth, all kinds of illness, fever, rabies, mice and rats, flooding

July 11: Benedikt von Nursia [monk]
S: Europe, teachers, miners, coppersmiths, spelunkers, schoolchildren, the dying
H: fever, infections, poisoning, kidney stones, gallstones, witchcraft

July 13: Heinrich (German emperor)
S: diocese and city of Bamberg, diocese and city of Basel

July 13: Kunigunde (wife of Heinrich)
S: diocese of Bamberg, pregnant women, sick children

July 16: Irmgard (Irmengard) [abbess]
S: Lake Chiemsee district (Bavaria)
H: all kinds of needs

July 20: Margareta von Antiochien [martyr]
S: farmers, virgins, girls, midwives, wives, pregnant women
H: difficult childbirth, wounds, fertility

July 22: Maria Magdalena [present at Jesus' death]
S: women, penitents, students, prisoners, barbers, gardeners, vintners, coopers, wine merchants, glove makers, perfume makers

H: for children to learn to walk, eye infections, thunderstorms, pests
July 24: Christopher [martyr]
S: traffic, vehicle operators, rafters, coach-men, sailors, ferries, pilgrims, travelers, athletes, miners, carpenters, hatters, dyers, bookbinders, treasure hunters, gardeners, fruit dealers, fortifications, children
H: pestilence, sudden death, epidemics, fire, flooding, drought, thunderstorms, hail, eye diseases, toothaches, wounds
August 10: Lorenz (Laurentius) [martyr]
S: cities of Nürnberg, Wuppertal, and Kulm; librarians, archivists, cooks, beer brewers, innkeepers, washerwomen, pastrymakers, fire brigades, students
H: eye diseases, lumbago fever, skin diseases, fire, torments in purgatory, good grape harvest, pestilence
August 19: Sebald (Sebaldus) [missionary]
S: City of Nürnberg
H: cold weather
August 24: Bartholomäus [apostle]
S: cities of Frankfurt/Main, Pilsen, and Altenburg; miners; butchers; tailors; farmers; bookbinders; vintners; bakers
H: nervous diseases, skin diseases
August 25: Ludwig (king of France)
S: cities of München, Saarbrücken, Berlin, Saarlouis; science; pilgrims; bakers; barbers; painters; masons; merchants; jewelry makers; button makers; bailiffs
H: blindness, deafness, pestilence
September 1: Aegidius, also known as Egid, Till, Gilles [French hermit]
S: Carinthia, Styria, cities of Nürnberg, Osnabrück, Braunschweig, Graz; hungers; herdsmen; horse traders; the shipwrecked; beggars, lepers, breastfeeding mothers
H: infertility (human and livestock), mental diseases, drought, fire, storm, desolation, good confessions
September 8: Maria, mother of Jesus
S: All of Christianity, Bavaria, dioceses of Aachen and Speyer, innkeepers,

cooks, furriers, cloth makers, potters, sailors, gingerbread bakers, silk weavers, vinegar brewers
H: thunderstorms, lightning, in all kinds of distress and need
September 21: Matthäus [apostle]
S: bookkeepers, customs officials, tax collectors, bankers
H: alcoholism
September 22: Mauritius, also known as Moritz, Maurice [martyr]
S: soldiers, merchants, dyers, hat makers, glaziers, armorers, blade smiths, cloth makers, horses, vineyards
H: in wartime, gout, obsessions, diseases of the ears, horse diseases
September 24: Rupert von Salzburg [bishop]
S: city and diocese of Salzburg, salt miners, dogs
September 29: Michael [archangel]
S: the Catholic Church, all Germans, soldiers, pharmacists, tailors, glaziers, painters, cabinetmakers, merchants, scales makers, calibrators of scales, gilders, bankers, radio mechanics, cemeteries
H: painless death, lightning, thunderstorms
October 4: Franz von Assisi [monk]
S: Diocese of Basel, Franciscan monks, the poor, social workers, animals, environment, merchants, tailors, weavers
H: headache, pestilence
October 16: Hedwig von Andechs und Schlesien [duchess]
S: Silesia; cities of Berlin, Breslau, Trebnitz and Krakau; expatriates, engaged couples
October 21: Ursula [martyr]
S: city of Cologne, youth, female teachers, cloth merchants
H: good marriage, painless death, sick children
October 31: Wolfgang von Regensburg [bishop]
S: Bavaria, city and diocese of Regensburg, charcoal burners, herdsmen,

carpen-ters, sculptors, bargemen, lumber-jacks, innocent prisoners, cattle
H: gout, paralysis, eye diseases, bleeding, sore feet, stroke, dysentery, skin diseases, infertility, deformed child
November 3: Hubert (Hubertus) [bishop]
S: hunters, rifle marksmen, butchers, furriers, wood turners, opticians, metal-workers, mathematicians, hounds
H: dog bites (in French, *mal de St. Hubert*), snake bites, fear of water
November 11: Martin von Tours [bishop]
S: dioceses of Mainz and Rottenburg, province of Burgenland (Austria) and Schwyz (Switzerland), soldiers, cavalry, horsemen, farriers, armorers, weavers, tailors, tanners, glove makers, hat makers, hotel owners, millers, coopers, vintners, herdsmen, travelers, innkeepers, the poor, beggars, teetotalers, domestic animals, horses, geese
H: skin diseases, snakebite, good harvests
November 19: Elisabeth von Thüringen [countess]
S: Hessen, Thüringen, welfare organizations (Caritas), widows and orphans, beggars, innocently persecuted, the sick, the needy, bakers
November 22: Cäcilia [martyr]
S: sacred music, musicians, singers, builders of musical instruments, poets
November 25: Katharina von Alexandria [martyr]
S: girls, wives, teachers, students, libraries, orators, hospitals, attorneys
H: headaches, diseases of the tongue, discovery of drowned persons, good harvests
November 30: Andreas [apostle]
S: fishermen, fish merchants, butchers, miners, rope makers
H: gout, sore throat, cramps, swine fever, good marriage
December 3: Franz Xaver [missionary]
S: missionaries, sailors, Catholic news-papers
H: painless death, storms, pestilence
December 4: Barbara [martyr]
S: towers, miners, farmers, architects, construction workers, roofers, bell found-ers, masons, carpenters, undertakers, cooks, prisoners, girls, artillery, fortifications, fire brigades, the dying
H: painless death, fire, fever, thunder-storms, pestilence
December 6: Nikolaus von Myra [bishop]
S: province of Lothringen, altar boys, children, pilgrims, travelers, attorneys, merchants, judges, pharmacists, inn-keepers, bargemen, fishermen, sailors, rafters, millers, bakers, butchers, beer brewers, farmers, distillers, weavers, masons, quarry workers, coopers, candle makers, prisoners, fire brigades
H: good marriage, shipwreck, retrieval of stolen property, protection from thieves
December 24: Adam und Eva [first humans]
S: tailors, gardeners
December 26: Stephan [martyr]
S: horses, horsemen, coachmen, construc-tion workers, tailors, masons, carpenters, weavers, coopers
H: headaches, kidney stones, gallstones, stitches, obsessions, painless death
December 27: Johannes [apostle]
S: the clergy, civil servants, notaries, sculptors, painters, writers, book dealers, printers, bookbinders, paper makers, vintners, butchers
H: poisoning, burns, sore feet, epilepsy, hail, good harvests
December 29: David [king of Israel]
S: Musicians, singers, poets, miners
December 31: Silvester [pope]
S: domestic animals
H: good harvests of animal food, for a "happy new year"

OTHER NAME DAYS (NAMENSTAGE)

Achim .... Aug. 16	Andreas .... Nov. 30	Beata .... Sep. 6
Ada, Viktor .... Jul. 28	Andreas .... Nov. 10	Beate .... May 9
Adalbert .... Jun. 20	Angela .... Jan. 4	Beate .... Aug. 8
Adalbert .... Apr. 23	Angela .... Jun. 1	Beate .... Mar. 12
Adam .... Dec. 24	Angela .... Jan. 27	Beate .... Apr. 8
Adelheid .... Dec. 16	Angela .... Nov. 2	Beatrix .... Mar. 12
Adolf .... Jun. 17	Angelina .... Dec. 10	Beatrix .... Aug. 29
Adolf .... Jan. 3	Anke .... Jul. 26	Beatrix .... Jan. 17
Agatha .... Feb. 5	Anna .... Feb. 9	Benedikt .... Feb. 12
Agnes .... Jan. 21	Anna .... Jul. 26	Benedikt .... Jul. 11
Agnes .... Mar. 2	Anno .... May 23	Benedikt .... Oct. 8
Aja .... Apr. 18	Anonius .... Oct. 24	Benedikt .... Apr. 16
Alberich .... Nov. 14	Anselm .... Mar. 18	Benekikt .... Mar. 21
Alberich .... Oct. 17	Ansgar .... Feb. 3	Benjamin .... Mar. 31
Albert .... Apr. 8	Anton .... Jan. 17	Benno .... Aug. 3
Albert .... Aug. 7	Anton .... Jul. 5	Benno .... Jun. 16
Albert .... Sep. 5	Anton v. P. .... Jun. 13	Benno .... Jul. 28
Albert .... Nov. 15	Anton .... Feb. 12	Bernard .... Apr. 30
Albin .... Mar. 1	Antonia .... May 6	Bernadette .... Feb. 18
Alexander .... May 3	Antonius .... Jun. 13	Bernadette .... Apr. 16
Alexander .... Feb. 26	Antonius .... Jan. 17	Bernhard .... Aug. 20
Alexander .... Feb. 27	Apolonia .... Feb. 9	Bernhard .... Nov. 20
Alexandra .... Feb. 21	Ariane .... Aug. 2	Bernhard .... May 20
Alexandra .... Mar. 21	Armin .... Jun. 2	Bernhard .... Oct. 30
Alf .... Aug. 2	Arno .... Jan. 24	Bernulf .... Jul. 19
Alfons .... Aug. 1	Arnold .... May 1	Berta .... Jul. 4
Alfons R. .... Oct. 30	Arnold .... Jan. 15	Berta .... May 1
Alfons .... Aug. 1	Arnulf .... Sep. 19	Berta .... Mar. 24
Alfons .... Oct. 30	Arnulf .... Jan. 29	Berthilde .... Nov. 5
Alfred .... Oct. 28	Arthur .... Sep. 1	Bertold .... Jul. 27
Alfred .... Feb. 2	Arthur .... Nov. 1	Bertold .... Jul. 13
Alice .... Apr. 4	Asta .... Apr. 15	Bertold .... Sep. 19
Alice .... Feb. 5	Astrid .... Aug. 10	Bertram .... Jun. 30
Alice .... Jun. 12	Athanasius .... May 2	Bertram .... Jun. 6
Almud .... Mar. 12	Attila .... Oct. 5	Bertram .... May 10
Alois .... Jun. 21	Augustin .... Aug. 28	Bettina .... Jul. 8
Altmann .... Aug. 9	Augustin v. C. .. May 27	Bibiana .... Dec. 2
Alwin .... May 19	Augustin .... May 27	Birgit .... Jul. 23
Alwin .... Jan. 15	Augustinus ..... Aug. 28	Birgitta .... Jul. 23
Amadeus .... Mar. 30	Aurelia .... Oct. 13	Blandina .... Nov. 5
Amanda .... Mar. 19	Axel .... Mar. 21	Blanka .... Dec. 1
Ambrosius .... Dec. 7	Barbara .... Dec. 4	Blasius .... Feb. 3
Anastasia .... Dec. 25	Barbara .... Mar. 9	Bodo .... Feb. 2
Andrea .... Jul. 12	Bärbel .... Dec. 4	Bonifatius .... May 14
Andreas .... Feb. 4	Barnabas .... Jun. 11	Bonifaz .... Jun. 5
Andreas .... Sep. 20	Bartholomaüs .. Aug. 24	Boris .... May 2
Andreas .... Jun. 19	Basilius .... Jan. 2	Brigitta .... Feb. 1

Brunhilde .... Dec. 17
Bruno .... Oct. 6
Bruno .... Oct. 11
Bruno .... May 17
Bruno .... Dec. 10
Bruno .... Mar. 9
Burchard .... Apr. 7
Burkhard .... Oct. 14
Burkhard .... Jun. 14
Cäcilia .... Nov. 22
Camilla .... Sep. 16
Camillus .... Jul. 14
Carlo .... Dec. 15
Carmen .... Jul. 16
Carola .... Aug. 17
Carolina .... Apr. 6
Cäsar .... Apr. 1
Charlotte .... Jul. 17
Christa .... Jun. 4
Christian .... May 14
Christian .... Dec. 4
Christian .... Feb. 4
Christiana .... Dec. 15
Christiane .... Jul. 26
Christine .... Jul. 24
Christine .... Jun. 22
Christine .... Nov. 6
Christine .... Dec. 15
Christophorus .... Jul. 24
Claudia .... Mar. 20
Claudia .... May 18
Claudia .... Aug. 18
Claudia .... Sep. 10
Clementia .... Mar. 21
Constance .... Jun. 25
Corinna .... May 14
Cornelia .... Sep. 14
Corona .... May 16
Dagmar .... May 24
Dagobert .... Dec. 23
Damian .... Sep. 26
Daniel .... Dec. 11
Daniel .... Jul. 21
Daniel .... Jun. 27
Daniel(a) .... Jul. 21
Daria .... Oct. 25
David .... Jul. 15
Debor .... Sep. 21
Detlef .... Nov. 23

Detlef .... Apr. 28
Diana .... Jun. 9
Diana .... Jun. 10
Dieger .... Jan. 2
Diethard .... Sep. 10
Diethard .... Dec. 10
Diethilde .... Jun. 28
Dietmar .... Sep. 28
Dietmar .... Mar. 5
Dietmar .... May 17
Dietrich .... Oct. 29
Dietrich .... Dec. 16
Dietrich .... Jul. 1
Dietrich .... Sep. 27
Dolores .... Sep. 15
Dominikus .... Aug. 4
Donald .... Jul. 15
Donatus............ Aug. 7
Dorothea .... Feb. 6
Dorothea .... Jun. 25
Eberhard .... Jan. 9
Eberhard .... Apr. 17
Eckart .... Nov. 27
Eckart .... Jul. 1
Edeltraud .... Jun. 23
Edgar .... Sep. 10
Edgar .... Jul. 8
Edith .... Jan. 26
Edith .... Aug. 9
Edith .... Dec. 8
Edith .... Sep. 16
Edmund .... Oct. 20
Edmund .... Nov. 20
Eduard .... Jan. 5
Eduard .... Mar. 18
Eduard .... Oct. 13
Eduard .... Mar. 18
Edwin .... Oct. 4
Edwin .... Oct. 11
Egbert .... Nov. 25
Egbert .... Aug. 26
Egbert .... Apr. 24
Egmont .... Sep. 26
Egolf .... Sep. 3
Egon .... Jul. 15
Ekkehard .... Jun. 28
Eleanore .... May 27
Eleonore .... Feb. 21
Elfriede .... May 20

Elfriede .... Dec. 8
Elfriede .... Feb. 8
Elias .... Mar. 24
Elisabeth v. Th. Nov. 19
Elisabeth .... Apr. 3
Elke .... Feb. 5
Elmar .... Mar. 22
Elmar .... Aug. 28
Emanuel .... Oct. 1
Emil .... Dec. 6
Emil .... Mar. 10
Emil .... May 22
Emil .... Nov. 12
Emilia .... Jan. 5
Emilie .... Jan. 4
Emma .... Apr. 19
Emma .... Dec. 3
Emmerich .... Nov. 5
Engelbert .... Jul. 10
Engelbert .... Nov. 7
Engelbert .... Apr. 10
Engelbert .... Jun. 8
Ephräm .... Jun. 9
Erhard .... Jan. 8
Erich .... May 18
Erika .... Jul. 10
Erna .... Jan. 12
Ernst .... Nov. 7
Ernst .... Jun. 30
Ernst .... Jan. 12
Esther .... May 23
Eucharius .... Dec. 9
Eugen Jun.2
Eugen .... Dec. 20
Eugen .... Nov. 13
Eugen .... Jan. 23
Eugenie .... Sep. 26
Eva .... May 26
Eva .... Mar. 14
Eva .... Dec. 24
Ewald .... Oct. 3
Ewald .... Mar. 23
Fabian .... Jan. 20
Fabiola .... Dec. 27
Falko .... Feb. 20
Farah .... Dec. 7
Felicia .... Jun. 18
Felix .... Mar. 26
Felix .... Jul. 12

Felix .... Sep. 11	Gertrud .... Aug. 13	Heiko .... Feb. 5
Felix .... Feb. 14	Gertrud .... Nov. 17	Heinrich .... Jan. 23
Felix .... Nov. 20	Gertrud .... Mar. 17	Heinrich .... Jul. 13
Felix .... Jan. 14	Gervin .... Apr. 17	Helene .... Aug. 18
Ferdinand .... May 30	Gerwich .... Oct. 26	Helene .... Apr. 26
Fides .... Aug. 1	Gerwin .... Apr. 17	Helga .... Sep. 11
Flora .... Jul. 29	Gilbert .... Aug. 6	Helga .... Jun. 8
Flora .... Oct. 9	Gilbert .... Oct. 24	Helga .... May 7
Flora .... Nov. 24	Gisela .... May 7	Helmtrud .... May 30
Flora .... Jun. 11	Gislar .... Sep. 28	Helmut .... Mar. 29
Florence .... Oct. 10	Gordian .... May 12	Helmut .... Apr. 24
Florentina .... Jun. 20	Goswin .... Jul. 31	Hemma .... Jun. 27
Florian .... May 4	Gottfried .... Jan. 13	Herald .... Jun. 27
Folkard .... Nov. 30	Gottfried .... Nov. 8	Heribert .... May 25
Frank .... Oct. 6	Gottfried .... Feb. 16	Heribert .... Mar. 16
Franz .... Oct. 4	Gottfried .... Jul. 9	Heribert .... Apr. 27
Franz Xaver .... Dec. 3	Gotthelf .... Sep. 25	Heribert .... Aug. 29
Franz .... Apr. 2	Gottlieb .... Mar. 30	Heribert .... Aug. 30
Franz v. P. .... Apr. 2	Gottschalk .... Jun. 7	Hermann .... May 21
Franz v. S. .... Jan. 24	Gregor .... Jan. 2	Hermann .... Oct. 2
Franz v. A. .... Oct. 4	Gregor .... Aug. 26	Hermann .... Apr. 25
Franz .... Jan. 24	Gregor .... Nov. 17	Hermann .... May 21
Franz. B. .... Oct. 10	Gregor .... May 9	Hermelindis .... Oct. 29
Franziska .... Mar. 9	Gregor d. Gr. .... Sep. 3	Hermine .... Apr. 13
Franziska .... Dec. 14	Gudrun .... Jan. 8	Hermine .... Dec. 30
Fridolin .... Mar. 6	Guido .... Mar. 31	Herta .... Nov. 24
Frieda .... Oct. 19	Guido .... May 4	Hieronymus .... Feb. 8
Friedrich .... Nov. 29	Guido .... Sep. 12	Hilaria .... Aug. 12
Friedrich .... Jul. 18	Gundula .... May 6	Hilde .... Jan. 12
Gabriel .... Mar. 24	Gundula .... Mar. 3	Hildebald .... Oct. 2
Galesius .... Nov. 21	Gunnar .... Mar. 16	Hildebrand .... May 25
Gangolf .... May 11	Gunther .... Nov. 28	Hildegard .... Sep. 17
Gebhard .... Jun. 16	Günther .... Oct. 9	Hildegard .... Apr. 30
Gebhart .... Aug. 27	Günther .... Oct. 8	Hildegund .... Oct. 14
Genofeva .... Jan. 3	Gustav .... Aug. 8	Hildegund .... Apr. 20
Georg .... Apr. 23	Gustav .... Mar. 10	Hiltrud .... May 31
Gerald .... Mar. 13	Gutmar .... Oct. 11	Hiltrud .... Nov. 17
Gerald .... Dec. 5	Hadrian .... Sep. 8	Himana .... Oct. 21
Gerda .... Mar. 5	Hadwig .... Feb. 19	Holger .... Oct. 7
Gerda .... May 29	Hanno .... Mar. 27	Horst .... Oct. 12
Gerfried .... Sep. 12	Hanno .... Sep. 20	Hubert .... Nov. 3
Gerhard .... Apr. 23	Harald .... Nov. 1	Hugo .... Apr. 28
Gerhard .... Jan. 27	Hartmann .... Dec. 12	Hugo .... Apr. 1
Gerlinde .... Feb. 13	Hartwig .... Apr. 13	Hyppolyt .... Aug. 13
Gerlinde .... Dec. 3	Hartwig .... Jun. 14	Ida .... May 8
German .... May 28	Hedwig .... Oct. 16	Ida .... Nov. 26
Gernot .... Sep. 24	Hedwig .... Feb. 19	Ida .... Feb. 24
Gerold .... Apr. 19	Hedwig .... Apr. 14	Ida .... Apr. 13
Gerold .... Apr. 10	Hedwig .... Oct. 16	Ida .... Sep. 4

Ignatius .... Jul. 31
Ignaz .... Oct. 17
Ignaz v. L. .... Jul. 31
Ines .... Mar. 1
Ingbert .... Oct. 22
Ingeborg .... Jul. 30
Ingrid .... Sep. 2
Inis .... Mar. 2
Irene .... Sep. 18
Irene .... Apr. 3
Irene .... Apr. 1
Irene .... Feb. 21
Irene .... Jan. 22
Iris .... Sep. 4
Irmgard .... Mar. 20
Irmgard .... Feb. 19
Irmgard .... Feb. 24
Irmgard .... Sep. 14
Irmgard .... Dec. 30
Irmgard .... Sep. 4
Irmgard .... Jul. 17
Irmtrud .... May 29
Isabella .... Feb. 22
Isabella .... Jun. 8
Isabella .... Aug. 21
Isador .... Apr. 4
Isador .... May 10
Isolde .... Aug. 23
Isolde .... Apr. 6
Ivo .... Dec. 23
Jakob .... Oct. 6
Jakobus .... May 3
Jakobus .... Jul. 25
Jaqueline .... Jul. 23
Jaqueline .... Feb. 26
Jeanne .... May 30
Jeanne d'Arc .... May 29
Jenniver .... Jan. 3
Joachim .... Oct. 16
Joachim .... May 11
Johann Bosco ... Jan. 31
Johann B. .... Apr. 7
Johanna .... Dec. 12
Johanna .... Aug. 21
Johannes .... Jan. 31
Johannes .... Jan. 11
Johannes .... Sep. 13
Johannes .... Oct. 23
Johannes .... Jun. 12

Johannes .... Apr. 7
Johannes Ev. .... Dec. 27
Johannes v. G. .... Mar. 8
Johannes .... Jun. 24
  der Täufer
Johannes .... Dec. 14
Johannes .... Jun. 26
Jolanda .... Dec. 17
Jolande .... Nov. 29
Jonas .... Sep. 21
Jordan .... Feb. 20
Josef .... May 21
Josef .... Mar. 19
Joseph .... Mar. 19
Judas .... Oct. 28
Judith .... Sep. 7
Judith .... Mar. 25
Judith .... Mar. 13
Julia .... May 22
Julian .... Jan. 9
Julian .... Jan. 17
Julian .... Mar. 8
Juliana .... Feb. 16
Juliana .... Jun. 19
Julius .... Apr. 12
Justus .... Feb. 25
Jutta .... Aug. 17
Jutta .... Jan. 13
Jutta .... Feb. 13
Jutta .... Dec. 22.
Jutta .... Nov. 29
Jutta .... Mar. 25
Jutta .... May 5
Kajetan .... Aug. 7
Karin .... Nov. 7
Karin .... Apr. 30
Karl L. .... Jun. 3
Karl .... Mar. 2
Karl .... Jan. 28
Karl Borromäus .. Nov. 4
Karl .... Aug. 12
Karl .... Mar. 2
Karola .... Aug. 17
Kasimir .... Mar. 4
Kaspar .... Jan. 6
Kastor .... Feb. 13
Katharina .... Nov. 25
Katharina .... Mar. 23
Katharina .... Feb. 9

Katharina v. S .... Apr. 29
Katharina .... Nov. 24
Katharina .... Apr. 29
Kilian .... Jul. 8
Klara .... May 8
Klara .... Aug. 11
Klara .... Jun. 15
Klaus .... Sep. 25
Klemens .... Mar. 15
Klemens .... Nov. 23
Klemens .... Mar. 15
Kleopatra .... Apr. 9
Klothilde .... Jun. 3
Klothilde .... Jun. 4
Knut .... Jul. 10
Konrad Jun.1
Konrad .... Nov. 26
Konrad .... Apr. 9
Konrad .... Nov. 26
Konrad .... Mar. 14
Konrad .... Apr. 21
Konrad .... Dec. 19
Konstantia .... Feb. 18
Konstantin .... Apr. 12
Konstantin .... Feb. 17
Kordula .... Jun. 1
Kordula .... Oct. 22
Kunibert .... Nov. 12
Kunigunde .... Jul. 13
Kunigunde .... Mar. 3
Kuno .... May 19
Kuno .... Mar. 8
Kurt .... Feb. 14
Kurt .... Apr. 19
Kurt .... Nov. 26
Lambert .... Sep. 18
Larissa .... Mar. 26
Laura .... Oct. 19
Laurentius .... Jul. 21
Laurentius .... Aug. 10
Laurentz .... Sep. 5
Lea .... Mar. 22
Leander .... Feb. 27
Leo .... Jul. 3
Leo .... Jun. 12
Leo der Große .. Nov. 10
Leo .... Feb. 20
Leo .... Apr. 11
Leo .... Apr. 19

Priska .... Feb 18	Rosa .... Aug. 24	Sophie .... May 15
Radegund .... Aug. 12	Rosalie .... Aug. 23	Sophie .... May 24
Raimund .... Jan. 7	Rosalinde .... Oct. 7	Stanislaus .... Apr. 11
Raimund .... Aug. 31	Rose .... Aug. 29	Stanislaus .... Nov. 13
Rainer .... Jun. 17	Rosina .... Mar. 13	Stefan .... Aug. 2
Rainer .... Aug. 4	Roswitha .... Apr. 29	Stefan .... Dec. 26
Rainer ....Apr. 11	Rotraut .... Jun. 22	Stephan .... Dec. 26
Ralf ....Feb. 1	Rudger .... Dec. 27	Susanna........... Aug. 11
Ralph .... Sep. 7	Rüdiger .... Mar. 1	Susanne........... Aug. 11
Raphael .... Sep. 29	Rudolf .... Jul. 27	Susanne............. Jan. 18
Rasso .... Jun. 19	Rudolf............... Oct. 17	Sven................... Mar. 1
Rebekka .... Mar. 23	Rudolf .... Nov. 6	Sylvia .... Nov. 3
Regina .... Dec. 20	Rudolf.............. Apr. 17	Tamara .... Dec. 29
Regina ....Sep. 7	Rudolf .... Jun. 21	Tassilo .... Dec. 11
Regina .... Aug. 22	Rufus .... Nov. 21	Tasso .... Jan. 11
Regine .... May 10	Rupert .... Sep. 24	Thea.................... Jul. 25
Regine .... Jan. 18	Rupert .... Aug. 15	Thea .... Jan. 11
Reimund .... Jan 7	Rupert .... Mar. 4	Thea.....................Apr. 5
Reinbert .... May 16	Ruth .... Sep. 1	Thekla .... Sep. 23
Reiner ....Feb. 7	Rupert............... May 15	Thekla .... Oct. 15
Reiner .... Jan. 14	Sabine ....Feb. 1	Theo .... Aug. 16
Reinhard .... Mar. 7	Sabine .... Aug. 29	Theo .... Apr. 20
Reinhild .... May 30	Sabine .... Oct. 27	Theobald .... Jul. 1
Reinhild ....Feb. 13	Sandrina ....Apr. 2	Theobald .... Jan. 16
Renate .... May 22	Sebald............... Aug. 19	Theodor........... Dec. 28
Renate .... May 23	Sebastian .... Jan. 20	Theodor.............Feb. 11
René.....................Sep. 2	Sella .... Sep. 22	Theodor........... Aug. 16
Rheinhard .... Nov. 4	Senta ....Apr. 5	Theodor..............Feb. 7
Richard ....Feb. 7	Serena .... Jan. 30	Theodor............. Nov. 9
Richard .... Nov. 15	Servatius .... May 13	Theresia v. A. .... Oct. 15
Richard ....Apr. 3	Seuse .... Jan. 23	Theresia .... Mar. 11
Richard .... Jun. 9	Severin .... Oct. 25	Theresia................ Oct. 1
Rita .... May 22	Severin .... Jan. 8	Thikla .... Mar. 26
Robert .... May 13	Sibylle .... Oct. 9	Thomas .... Dec. 21
Robert .... Jun. 7	Sidonie .... Oct. 14	Thomas B. .... Dec. 29
Robert ....Sep. 17	Sidonie .... Nov. 14	Thomas .... Jan. 28
Roger .... Mar. 1	Siegfried ....Feb. 15	Thomas .... Jul. 3
Roland .... May 13	Sigismund .... May 2	Thomas .... Jun. 22
Roland .... Jul. 14	Sigrid .... Aug. 4	Thomas .... Jul. 3
Roland .... Sep. 15	Sigrid .... May 5	Thomas Becket Dec. 29
Roland .... Jan. 16	Sigrid .... Jan. 7	Timotheus .... Jan. 26
Roland .... Nov. 9	Sigurd .... Feb. 10	Titus .... Jan. 26
Roman .... Aug. 9	Silvana .... Feb. 10	Titus .... Jan. 25
Roman .... Nov. 18	Silvester............ Dec. 31	Tobias .... Mar. 3
Roman .... Oct. 1	Silvinus .... Feb. 17	Tobias .... Sep. 13
Roman ....Feb. 28	Simon .... Oct. 28	Torsten .... May 5
Romana .... Feb. 23	Sissy .... Nov. 22	Trudbert .... Apr. 26
Ronald .... Aug. 20	Sixtus .... Aug. 6	Uda .... Dec. 28
Rosa................. Aug. 23	Sola .... Dec. 5	Uda .... Oct. 3

Ulrich .... Mar. 11	Viktor .... Jul. 28	Wigbert .... Apr. 18
Ulrich .... Feb. 26	Viktoria .... Nov. 2	Wigmann .... Nov. 2
Ulrich .... Jan. 16	Vinzenz .... Jan. 22	Wilhelm .... Jan. 10
Ulrich .... Jul. 4	Vinzenz Ferr. .... Apr. 5	Wilhelm .... Jul. 5
Urban .... May 25	Vinzenz .... Sep. 27	Wilhelm .... Feb. 10
Urban .... Dec. 19	Viola .... May 3	Wilhelm .... Mar. 28
Ursula .... Jan. 20	Virgil .... Nov. 27	Wilhelm .... May 28
Ursula .... Oct. 21	Volker .... Mar. 7	Willibald .... Jul. 7
Ursus .... Sep. 30	Volkmar .... Jul. 18	Willibald .... Nov. 8
Uschi .... Oct. 21	Volkmar .... May 9	Willibald .... Jul. 7
Valentin .... Feb. 14	Walburga .... Feb. 25	Wilma .... Sep. 19
Valerian .... Apr. 14	Waldo .... Dec. 18	Wilpert .... May 23
Valerie .... Dec. 9	Walfried .... July. 7	Wiltrud .... May 21
Valerius .... Jan. 29	Walpurga .... Feb. 25	Winfried .... Jun. 5
Valerius .... Apr. 14	Walter .... May 17	Wolf .... Apr. 21
Veit .... Jun. 15	Walter .... Jan. 22	Wolf .... Mar. 8
Vera .... Aug. 29	Walter .... Oct. 15	Wolf .... Oct. 31
Vera .... Jan. 24	Walter ....Apr. 8	Wolf .... Jul. 19
Verena .... Jul. 22	Waltmann .... Apr. 15	Wolfgang .... Oct. 31
Verena .... Sep. 1	Waltraud .... Apr. 9	Wolfgang .... Mar. 23
Veronika .... Feb. 28	Waltrud .... Apr. 9	Wolfhard .... Oct. 27
Veronika .... Feb. 4	Wendelin .... Oct. 20	Wolfhelm .... Apr. 22
Veronika .... Jul. 9	Wenzel .... Sep. 28	Wolfram .... Jan. 25
Victoria .... Dec. 23	Werner .... Apr. 18	Wulf .... Oct. 31
Viktor .... Jan. 31	Werner .... Jun. 4	Wunibald .... Dec. 18
Viktor .... Sep. 30	Wigbert .... Aug. 13	Zita .... Apr. 27

MEASUREMENTS IN GERMAN-SPEAKING AREAS OF EUROPE AROUND 1800

Important: Before converting old measurements, make sure of the state and year in which they were used.

Key

m = meters; l. = liters; g = grams; q, QU = square

Acker

Schwarzburg-Sondershausen: 1 Acker = 1877.3m²
Sachsen-Altenburg: 1 Acker = 6443.1 m²
Meisenheim: 1 Acker = 2500 m²

Ar (a)
(plural Are)

Land measure

1 Ar = 100 square meters (119.5993 square yards, or .024711 acres)

Becher

Baden: 1 Becher = 0.15 l.
Lippe: 1 Becher = 2.768 l.
Österreich: 1 Becher = 0.48 l.

Dutzend

1 Dutzend = 1/12 Gros = 1/144 Maß = 12 Stück

Elle

Schleswig-Holstein: 1 Elle = 2 Fuß = 0.573 m
Weimar: 1 Elle = 0.564 m
Hamburg: Kurze [short] Elle = 0.573 m; Lange [long] Elle = 0.691 m
Braunschweig: 1 Elle = 2 Fuß = 0.571 m
Gera: 1 Elle = 0.579 m
Nürnberg: 1 Elle = 0.656 m

Fuder

A cart-load of hay, produce or wood; measure for wine equal to contents of cart-sized barrel (210-475 U.S. gallons or 800 - 1,800 liters, depending on the locality.

Fuß

Bayern: 1 Fuß = 0.292 m
Bremen: 1 Fuß (old) = 0.605 m; (new) = 0.289 m
Pommern: 1 Fuß = 0.292 m
Württemberg: 1 Fuß = 0.287 m

Gros

1 Gros = 12 Dutzend = 144 Stück

Hectar (ha)

1 ha = 4 Morgen = 2.47 acre = 0.067 Hufe
100 ha = 1 square kilometer = 0.39 square miles
1 ha = 100 Are (10,000 square meters), or about 2.5 acres

Hektoliter (hl)

100 liters, or 26.418 gallons for liquids, or 2.838 bushels as a dry measure [Guth]

Hufe

1 Hufe = 60 Morgen = 36.9 acres = 15 ha

Joch

Archaic measure, originally the area of land a team could plow in a day.
1 Joch = about 60 Are, or about 1.5 acres

Kanne

Dresden: 1 Kanne = 0.937 ltr.
Oldenburg: 1 Kanne = 1.368 ltr.

Lot

Frankfurt/Main,   Nassau, Hollenzollern: 1 Lot = 4 Quentchen = 15.625g
Kurhessen, Lippe: 1 Lot = 10 Quentchen = 16.667g

Malter

(singular and plural)

Antique German dry measure for grain; about 150 liters or 4.257 bushels; but sizes varied

Mandel

1 große (large) Mandel (or "Bauern") = 16 Stück (pieces)
1 kleine (small) Mandel = ˘ Schock = 15 Stück (pieces)

Maß

Generally: 1 Maß = 1 l.
Baden: 1 Maß = 10 Becher = 1.5 l.
Gotha: 1 Maß = 0.910 l.
Rheiinland: 1 Maß = 4 Achtel = 1.783 l.
Württemberg: 1 Maß = 1.831 l.

Meile

Generally: 1 Meile = 7420.4385 m
Baden: 1 Meile = 2 Wegstunden = 8888.89 m
Sachsen: 1 Meile = 16,000 Ellen = 9062.08 m
Hannover: 1 Meile = 1587.5 Ruten = 25400 Fuß = 7419.205 m

Morgen

(The Morgen was theoretically the amount of land that one man and an ox could plow in a morning. *Morgen* in German also means "morning.")
Aachen: 1 Morgen = 150 Qu-Ruten = 3053.26 qm
Danzig: 1 Morgen = 300 Qu-Ruten = 5555.46 qm
Koblenz: 1 Morgen = 160 Qu-Ruten = 3459.44 qm
Leipzig: 1 Morgen = 3273.2 qm
Preußen: 1 Morgen = 180 Qu-Ruten = 2553.224 qm
Sachsen: 1 Morgen = ° Acker = 150 Quadratruten = 2767.100 m^2)
Bayern: 1 Morgen = 4 Viertel = 400 Quadratruten = 3437 m^2; or 34.073 Are (about .85 acre)
Württemberg: 1 Morgen = 31.5 Are, or about .79 acre

Pfund (#)

Frankfurt/Main: 1 Pfund = 32 Lot =

500g (about 1.10 U.S. pounds)
Hamburg: 1 Old Pfund = 551.23 g;
middle 19th century = 484.848g
Österreich:
Wiener Pf. = 560g
Tiroler Pf = 564.26g
Apotheker Pf. = 420g
Schokoladen Pf = 490g
Zollpfund = 500g
Preußen:
1 Pfund = 32 Lot = 467.404g

Quentchen
Generally: 1 Quentchen (new) =
4 Gewichtspfennig = 4.385g
Hannover: 1 Quentchen = 3.654g
Preußen: 1 Quentchen = 4 Pfennig-
gewicht = 3.651g

Rute
Aachen: 1 Rute = 16 Fuß = 4.602 m
Bayern: 1 Alte (old) Rute = 15 Fuß =
4.378 m
Hamburg: 1 Rute = 16 Fuß = 4.585 m
Köln: 1 Rute = 16 Fuß = 4.602 m
Ulm: 1 Rute = 18 Fuß = 5.202 m

Schock
1 Schock = 4 Mandel = 5 Dutzend = 60
Stück (pieces)

Sheffel (Scheffel)
Bremen: 1 Sheffel = 79.201 l.
Dresden: 1 Sheffel = 106.298 l.
Hessen: 1 Sheffel = 8 Metzen = 80.368 l.
Potsdam before 1814: 1 Sheffel - 53.2 l.

Simmer/Simri
(plural *Simmeren*)
Dry measure
Palatinate: 1 Simmer = .25 Malter
Württemburg: 1 Simmer = .629 bushel

Zentner
1 Zentner = 100 German pounds, or about
110.23 U.S. pounds
Sources:
•Fritz Verdenhalven, *Alte Maße, Münzen und
Gewichte aus dem deutschen Sprachgebiet,*

Verlag Degener & Co. Neustadt/Aisc, 1968.
•*Helmut Kohnt and Berndt Knorr, Alte
Maße, Münzen und
Gewichte,*Bibliographisches Institut
Mannheim, Meyers Lexikon-Verlag. 1987.
•Helmut Guth, *Amish Mennonites in
Germany: Their Congregations, The Estates
Where They Lived, Their Families*. Masthof
Press, Morgan-town, PA, 1995.
•Eike Pies, *Löhne und Preise von
Dreizehnhundert bis 2000*. Wupperthal: E.
& U. Brockhaus, 2003.

GERMAN WEIGHTS AND MEASURES

Linear measure

1mm	**Millimeter** (millemeter) =1/1000 meter = 0.03937079 inches	
1 cm	**Zentimeter** (centimeter)=1/100 meter =0.9370 inches	
1 dm	**Dezimeter** (decimeter) =1/10 meter =3.9370 inches	
1 m	**Meter** (meter) =1.0936 yards =3.2809 feet =39.37079 inches	
1 km	**Kilometer** (kilometer) =1,000 meters =1,093.637 yards = 3,280.8692 feet =39,370.79 inches	

Square measure

1m	Quadratmeter (square meter) =1.19599 square yards = 10.7641 square feet = 1,550 square inches	
1 a	**Ar** (are) =100 square meters = 119.5993 square yards= 1,076.4103 square feet	
1 ha	**Hektar** (hectare) =100 acres = 10,000 square meters = 247.11	

acres =0.3861 square miles

1 km² **Quadratkilometer** (square kilometer) =1,000 cubic milli meters =0.061 cubic inches

Cubic measure

1 cm³ **Kubikzentimeter** (cubic centi-meter)

1 m³ **Kubikmeter** (cubic meter),

1 rm **Raummeter** (cubic meter),

1 fm **Festmeter** (cubic meter) =1,000 cubic decimeters =1.3079 cubic yards =35.3156 cubic feet

1 RT **Registertonne** (register ton) = 2.832m³ =100 cubic feet

1 l **Liter** (liter) =10 deciliters = 1.7607 pints (Br.) = 7.0431 gills (Br.) =0.2201 gallons (Br.) = 2.1134 pints (Am.) = 8.4534 gills (Am.) =1.0567 quarts (Am.) =0.2642 gallons (Am.)

1 hl **Hektoliter** (hectoliter =100 li ters = 22.009 (Br.) = 2.751 bush-els (Br.) = 26.418 gallons (Am.) =2.84 bushels (Am.)

Weights

1 mg **Milligram** (milligram) =1/1000 gram = 0.0154 grains

1 g **Gramm** (gram) =1/1000 kilo-gram = 15.4324 grains

1 Pfd **Pfund** pound (German) = ° ki logram =500 grams = 1.1023 pounds (avdp.) = 1.3396 pounds (troy)

1 kg **Kilogramm**, Kilo (kilogram) =1,000 grams =2.2046 pounds (advp.) = 2.6792 pounds (troy)

1 Ztr **Zentner** (centner) = 100 pounds (German) = 50 kilo grams = 110.23 pounds (advp)

1 dz **Doppelzentner** = 100 kilograms =1.9684 British hundred-weights = 2.2046 U.S. hundred-weights

1 t **Tonne** (ton) = 1,000 kilograms =0.984 British tons =1.1023 U.S. tons

KILOMETERS/MILES CONVERSIONS

The equivalents
1 kilometer = 0.621 miles
1 mile = 1.609 kilometers
To convert miles to kilometers
Divide the number of miles by 0.62.
For example, 24 miles divided by 0.62 equals 38.7 kilometers.
To convert kilometers to miles
Divide the number of kilometers by 1.6. For example, 204 kilometers divided by 1.6 equals 127.5 miles.

FAHRENHEIT/CELSIUS

Degrees Celsius/ Centigrade	Degrees Fahrenheit
-20	-4
-17.8	0
-15	5
-10	14
-5	23
0	32
1	33.8
2	35.6
3	37.4
4	39.2
5	41
6	42.8
7	44.6
8	46.4
9	48.2

10	50
15	59
20	68
25	77
30	88
35	95
40	104

quintillian	Trillion	18
sextillion	Sextillion	21
septillion	Quadrillion	24
octillion	Quadrilliarde	27

*Note: "1 million marks" is written as "eine Million Mark," but "2 million marks" is written "zwei *Millionen* Mark."

METRIC CONVERSIONS

When you know –
♦**millimeters,** multiply by 0.04 to find inches
♦**centimenters**, multiply by 0.39 to find inches
♦**meters**, multiply by 3.3 to find feet
♦**kilometers,** multiply by 0.62 to find miles
♦**hectares,** multiply by 2.47 to find acres
♦square kilomets, multiply by 0.39 to find square miles
♦**cubic meters,** multiply by 35.3 to find cubic feet
♦**liters,** multiply by 0.26 to find gallons
♦ **kilograms,** multiply by 2.2 to find pounds
♦**metric tons,** multiply by 0.98 to find long tons; by 1.1 to find short tons; by 2,204 to find pounds
♦**degrees Celsius (Centigrade)**, multiply by 1.8 and add 32 to find degrees Fahrenheit

MULTIPLES OF MILLIONS, AMERICAN TO GERMAN

Following is the terminology for expressing multiples of millions in American and German vocabularies respectively, clarified by indicating the number of zeroes following the "1" in the number "one million":

American	German	zeroes
million	Million*	6
billion	Milliarde	9
trillion	Billion	12
quadrillion	Billiarde	15

RENTENMARK, REICHSMARK, DEUTSCHE MARK, EURO

Rentenmark: Introduced November 20, 1923, the *Rentenmark* was issued as new currency in strictly limited quantities and was successful in stabilizing the monetary system following an inflationary period.
Reichsmark: Replacing the *Rentenmark* in 1924, the *Reichsmark* was convertible in gold or foreign currencies. The devaluation of the *Reichsmark* began with the world economic crisis when money circulation increased rapidly in Nazi Germany.
Deutsche Mark: Introduced by Allies in the western occupation zone on June 20, 1948, the *Deutsche Mark* brought about a stirring of the German economy, which was stabilized by vigorous anti-inflationary policies, leading to the "economic miracle" of the 1950s.
Euro: Supplanted the deutsche mark as of July 1, 2002.
Sources:
♦Wilfried Fest, ed., *Dictionary of Germany History 1806-1945*, St. Martin's Press, New York, 1978

NUMERALS ABOVE 100 IN GERMAN

In writing numbers, Germans use the period in places where Americans use the comma.

For example, the number written by Americans as 101,254 would be written by Germans as 101.254 (or sometimes it would be seen as 101 254).

Likewise, monetary amounts are written in the same manner. For example, forty-five Euro and twenty-five Cent is written as ¸ 45,25.

MONETARY HISTORY

The value of coins in circulation always was based on the weight and purity of the gold or silver they contained and therefore differed widely. Karl V was the first emperor to decree (in 1524) that a standard coin, the *Taler*, should be minted for universal use in his *Reich*.

The basis was the weight measure of the *Mark* (=° lb.) as defined in Cologne at 233,855 grams. Out of 1 Mark of 93.75 percent pure silver, 8 *Taler* could be minted.

However this was only parallel to a considerable variety of other coins also called *Taler* – but of different value.

To add to the confusion, the number of *Kreuzer, Groschen*, or *Pfennige* into which a *Taler* was divided, also could vary. The monetary systems reflected territorial variety.

It was not until the foundation of the *Deutsches Reich* in 1871 that a single currency was installed. It consisted of 1 *Mark* = 1/2790 kg of gold and was divided into 100 *Pfennige*. Equivalencies shown below, commonly used as standards for around 1800, don't really mean much unless they can be attributed to a particular territory. No such specific territorial area has been established for them.

1 *Taler* = 1° *Gulden* = 24 *Groschen* = 288 *Pfennige*
1 *Gulden* = 16 *Groschen* = 192 *Pfennige*
1 *Groschen* = 12 *Pfennige*

COINAGE REFERENCES

♦Craig, William D., *Germanic Coinages*

(Charlemagne through Wilhelm II), Author, Mountain View, Cal., 1954.
♦Engel, Franz, *Tabellen alter Münzen, Maße und Gewichte zum Gebrauch für Archivbenutzer*, Schaumburger Studien, Verlag C. Bösendahl, Rinteln, 1970.
♦Kahnt, Helmut & Bernd Knorr, *Alte Maße, Münzen und Gewichte*, Bibliographisches Institut/Meyers Lexikonverlag, Mannheim/Wien/Zürich, 1987.
♦Nicol, N. Douglas (comp.), *Standard Catalog of German Coins 1601 to Present*, 2nd ed., Krause Prublications, Iola, Wisc., 1998.
♦Verdenhalven, Fritz, *Alte Maße, Münzen und Gewichte aus dem deutschen Sprach-gebiet*, Verlag Degener & Co., Neustadt an der Aisch, 1968.

MONEY EQUIVALENCIES AROUND 1800

Thaler
The Thaler was in use from 1486 in Tirol until 1872 in Königreich Sachsen.

1 Thaler = 1° Gulden = 24 Groschen = 288 Pfennige (but note the caution stated in the item above)

Other Thaler equivalencies
1 Thaler = 24 Gute Groschen = 48 Sechser = 96 Dreier = 288 Pfennige
1 Thaler = 3 Mark = 9 Schillinge = 18 Flinderken = 72 Grote = 360 Schwaren

Note: In 1857 a monetary agreement attempted to unify the value of the Thaler by setting a weight of 18.518 grams and a composition of 90 percent silvered, but its value nevertheless fluctuated. In Austria it was worth 1° Austria gulden, 1∫ gulden in the southern German states, and 30 silver groschen if it was a Prussian coin. In 1871 when the Empire was formed by Prussia, the new unit of coinage became the mark.

Gulden and Groschen
1 Gulden = 16 Groschen = 192 Pfennige
1 Groschen = 12 Pfennige

Louis d'or

The louis d'or served as a trade coin which became the most important French gold coin of the seventeenth and eighteenth centuries. It was first struck in 1640 under Louis XIII and was valued at 10 livres. During the reign of Louis XV (ruled 1715-1774) the louis d'or was valued at 20, and later 24 livres.

The last of the coins were struck in 1793, followed by issuing of 24-livre pieces, which were the old louis d'or, whose official name had been changed. A few years later, France adopted a decimal system, without the louis d'or.

Sources:

- Helmut Kohnt and Berndt Knorr, *Alte Maße, Münzen und Gewichte.* Bibliographisches Institut Mannheim, Meyers Lexikonverlag, Mannheim/Wien, Zürich, 198.
- Richard G. Doty, *The Macmillan Encyclopedia Dictionary of Numismatics.* Macmillan Publishing Co., Inc., New York, 1982.

DOLLAR/EUROCONVERSIONS

To convert dollars to German currency:

Multiply dollars by the exchange rate. For example, to change $200 to Euro when the exchange rate is 0.67 (meaning that $1.00 = ˛0,67), $200 x 0,67 = ˛134,28.

To convert German currency to dollars:

Divide German currency by the exchange rate. For example, to change ˛88 to U.S. dollars when the exchange rate is 1.49 (˛1,00 = $1.49), ˛88 = $ 131.07.

END OF THE DEUTSCHE MARK

The deutschemark disappeared with the introduction of the Euro in 2002. First printed in the United States in 1948, and later in France and Britain as well, the deutschemark became one of the world's strongest and most successful currencies.

The East German mark, introduced later, never became a strong currency.

West Germany started printing its paper money in the 1960s. In 1999, Germany celebrated the 50th anniversary of its deutschemark (*Deutsche Mark*).

THE GUILDS (ZÜNFTE)

Background

Guilds (called *Gilden, Zünfte,* and *Innungen*) were associations of craftsmen or merchants, organized for self-protection and economic and social gain, which flourished between the 11th and 18th centuries in Europe. They became possible only after the rise of towns in the 10th and 11th centuries, enjoying their heydey from the 12th to the 15th centuries.

The guilds governed practices by which apprentices in the crafts gained experience in their respective trades. A decreee abolishing craft associations was enacted in Germany in 1859-60.

Stages of guild training

Apprentices *(Lehrlinge, Lehrjunge)* were young boys who lived with the family of a master (*Meister),* an established craftsman, who trained him for at least three years (usually five to nine years). Instead of wages, the apprentice received board and keep in addition to his training. To enroll a son as an apprentice, the family was required to pay a large sum of money to the master.

At the end of the apprenticeship, the *Lehrling* could take an examination *(Gesellenprüfung),* which, if he passed, earned him a journeyman's certificate *(Gesellenbrief),* and allowed him to go on to become a journeyman *(Geselle).* Traditionally the journeyman then set off on travels around the country *(Wanderschaft)* to work for master craftsmen and guilds in towns along his way. The journeyman's goal was to become accepted as a *Meister* so that he could in turn open a shop and train apprentices. Another examination (*Meisterprüfung*) was in many cases required before he could reach this stage.

Another step toward becoming a master was the construction of a *Meisterstück* (masterpiece) as a demonstration of the journeyman's technical competence in the given field and as a determiner of his admission into the guild.

Men who passed the master's test were recorded in a book of masters *(Meister-buch)*.

Some records associated with guilds

◆ The birth certificate (*Geburtsbrief)* or a statement of birth and origin (*Geburts- und Herkunftszeugnisse)* to prove "honorable birth and origin." (Illegitimatemate were not accepted into guilds.)

◆ Apprentice records were called *Ein- und Ausschreiben der Burschen* and *Lehr-briefe* (apprenticeship certificates).

◆ The traveling pass *(Wanderzettel)*, a record in which the journeyman's guild attested to his skills and verified his identity, and in which the various masters for whom he worked wrote to certify the quality of his performance.

◆ The journeyman was given a *Wander- buch* (journey book) as he set out on his travels. In it each employer would write down the nature of his work and the manner in which he performed it. Thus it became a record of his travels.

◆ The certificate of employment and conduct (*Kundschafts-Zettel*).

Availability of records

Guild records (*Zunftbücher*) may rarely be found in state and city archives, in modern guilds, and sometimes in the Family History Library Catalog. Few have been published or filmed. When available on film, they are found on the FLHC under "Occupations" (under Germany, or a German state, or a German town).

FHL-filmed guild records

A few guild records are available on microfilm through the Family History Library. Records for one or more guilds are available for:

◆ **Bavaria:** Augsburg, Nürnberg, München
◆ **Brandenburg:** Potsdam
◆ **Braunschweig**
◆ **Saxony:** Magdeburg
◆ **West Prussia:** Garnsee
◆ **Württemberg:** Göppingen
◆ **East Prussia:** Angerburg, Bartenstein, Bialla, Bischofstein, Braunsberg, Christburg, Darkehmen, Drengfurt, Frauenburg, Friedland, Gerdauen, Goldap, Gumbinn-en, Heiligenbeil, Insterburg, Johannisburg, Königsberg, Kreuzburg, Labiau, Lötzen, Lyck, Mehlsack, Memel, Mohrungen, Mühlhausen, Neidenburg, Ortelsburg, Osterode, Pillau, Preußisch Holland, Ras-tenburg, Rössel, Saalfeld, Schippenbeil, Seeburg, Soldau, Tapia, Tilsit, Wehlau, Zinten.

Guild archives (*Zunftarchive*) were formerly maintained in different cities in Germany, but guild records are now found in state and city archives, including,

◆ Staatsarchiv Amberg
◆ Stadtarchiv Augsburg
◆ Landesarchiv Berlin
◆ Staatsarchiv Bremen
◆ Staatsarchiv Hamburg
◆ Niedersächsisches Staatsarchiv Bückeburg
◆ Staatliches Archivlager Göttingen
◆ Staatsarchiv Oldenburg
◆ Staatsarchiv Wolfenbüttel
◆ Staatsarchiv Münster
◆ Landesarchiv Saarbrücken
◆ Landesarchiv Schleswig-Holstein
◆ Stadtarchiv Braunschweig

Further information

See "Guild Records in Germany," adapted from a lecture of Gerhard Jeske, *German Genealogical Digest*, Vol. 10, No. 4, Winter 1994.

Source of record and archive list: *German Genealogical Digest,* Winter 1994.

CHRONOLOGY OF GUILDS

1106: For the first time, guild regulations are put into writing (Fishermen in Worms)

1156: The guilds are mentioned as organizations in the Augsburg city code.

1356: Augsburg guilds are guaranteed in the laws of Augsburg. Since that time, guilds exist and are fully recognized in all towns. Between 20 and 50 masters belong to a guild. Augsburg develops into the world center of crafts. In 1466 there are 749 masters in the weavers guild alone.

1731: Cities forbid the guilds to hold meetings, to establish dues, and to create their own seals without the consent of the authorities.

18th century: Under pressure of the authorities and as a result of the French Revolution and several wars, the guilds disintegrate even further. By the end of the century in eastern Germany there are more masters than journeymen.

1810-1811: Trade regulations and business taxes destroy guilds' monopoly over certain trades, establishing the principle of freedom of trade (*Gewerbefreiheit*).

1848: Competition by industry, but also among the craftsmen themselves, puts the craftsmen in danger. As a result of the need for the maintenance of quality and per-formance, in this year occurs the first German trade congress in Frankfurt. There, 100 craftsmen from all over Germany draft trade regulations for mandatory guilds, as successors to guilds, which are adopted and given semi-official status.

1869: The North German Confederation proclaims free trade. Guild associations and laws are abolished.

1881: The government recognizes the guilds as corporations under public law and puts them in charge of the apprentice system.

1897: The reform movement of the craftsmen, out of which the last of the guilds developed, is acknowledged through the law protecting craftsmen.
Source: "Zunft: von den Anfängen bis zu den Innungen von heute" [Guilds: From Their Beginnings to the Craftsmen's Associations Today], *Das Große Illustrierte Wörterbuch der deutschen Sprache.* Verlag Das Beste, Stuttgart, Zürich, Wien, 1996.

GUILDS-RELATED VOCABULARY

Annahme der Meister: Acceptances of Masters
Ein- und Ausschreiben der Burschen: records of apprentices
Geburts und Herkunftszeugnis(se): statement(s) of birth and origin
Geburtsbrief(e): document(s)s of birth
Geselle(n): apprentice(s)
Gesellenbrief: journeyman's papers
Gesellenjahre: years between journeyman's and master's examinations
Gesellenprüfung: examination
Gewerbefreiheit: principle of freedom of trade
Gilde: guild
Gildebrief: guild's charter
Gildehaus: guild hall
Gildemitglied: member of a guild
Gilderbücher: guild records
Gilderichter: administrator of a guild
Handwerk: trade, craft
Handwerker: craftsman
Handwerksbursche: craft apprentice
Handwerksleute: craftsmen
Innung(en): guild(s)"
Innungsmeister: master of a local guild
Kundschaftszettel: certificate of employment and conduct
Lehrbriefe: Apprenticeship certificates
Lehrling(e): apprentice(s)
Lehrmeister: master of an apprentice
Meister: master craftsman

Meisterbuch: book of masters
Meisterprüfung: master craftsman's examination
Verzeichnis(se) der Berufsange-hörigen: list(s) of professional members
Wanderbuch: journey book
Wanderschaft: journey
Wandersmann: journeyman; traveler
Wanderzettel: passport attesting to craftsman's competence
Zunft/Zünfte: guild/s
Zunftbücher: guild records
Zunftmeister: guild master
Zunftwappen: coat of arms of a guild

OVERVIEW OF COIN VALUES IN GERMAN LANDS

♦**8th-13th centuries**
1 *Pfund* = 240 Pfennig;
1 *Mark* = 144 *Pfennig*
♦**Until 1557**
Mariengroschen = 6 to 8 *Pfennig*
Schreckenberger = 10 *Schilling*
1 *Mark* = 16 *Schilling* = 192 *Pfennig*
Gulden = 32 *Groschen*
Taler = 30 *Groschen*
12 *Heller* = 2° *Pfennig*
♦**Developments of the mid-16th century**
–**1551:** First *Augsburger Münzordnung, Taler* of 72 *Kreuzer*
–**1559:** Second *Augsburger Münzord-nung, Gulden* of 75 *Kreuzer*
–**1566:** *Taler* as basis for Imperial stan-dard (*Währungsmünze*), setting of weight and fineness (*Schrot und Korn*)
♦**1557 and after**
Fürstengroschen = 12 *Pfennig*
–**Groschen** = 16 *Pfennig* = 32 *Scherf* = 3 *Körtling* = 4 *Blaffert* = 9 *Witte* = 12 *Gosler* = 18 *Schwaar* = 36 *Lübesch* = 1/24 *Taler*
–**Taler** = 16 *lubische Doppelschillinge* = 21 *Schilling* = 24 *Neugroschen* = 30 *Stüber* = 36 *Mariengroschen* = 64 *Sechslinge* = 68 *Kreuzer* = 96 *Dreier* = 128 *Dreilinge*

–**Gulden** = 20/21 *Groschen* = 240 *Pfennig* = 36 *Groschen*
♦**ca. 1600-1650 (period of the Thirty Years' War)**
–*Taler* (*Reichstaler*) = 24 *Groschen* = 288 *Pfennig.*
A *Taler* also was equivalent to 16 *Doppelschillinge,* 4
, or 36 *Marien-groschen.*
–*Goldgulden* = 40 *Mariengroschen,* or 1 *Taler* + 4 *Mariengroschen*
♦***Kipper- und Wipperzeit*** (period of in-stability)
Taler in 1610 = 29 *Groschen*
Taler in 1617 = 49 *Groschen*
Taler in 1620 = 60 *Groschen*
Taler in early 1621 = 120 *Groschen*
Taler in late 1621 = 192 *Groschen*
Taler in 1622 = 24 *Groschen*
♦**18th century** after Convention between Austria and Bavaria of 1753 of Imperial standard of 10 Talers to be struck from fine mark of silver:
Species Taler = 1 1/3 *Reichstaler;*
Courant Taler = 1° *Reichstaler;*
Gulden = 16 *Groschen* = 2/3 *Taler;*
Batzen = 4 *Kreuzer;*
Groschen = 1/24 *Taler* = 3 *Kreuzer* = 12 *Pfennig;*
Mariengroschen = 1/36 *Taler;*
Mattier = 1/72 *Taler*
♦**19th century**
1837: *Münzverein Süddeutscher Staaten* (Munich Monetary Conven-tion)
1857: German-Austrian Monetary Con-vention, 30 *Talers* to be struck from mark of 500 grams
1871: German Empire, decimal system: 1 *Mark* = 100 *Pfennig;* 10 *Goldmark* = 3 1/3 *Vereinstaler* = 5 *Gulden,* 50 *Kreuzer* = 8 1/3 *Mark* of North German Standard
1876, 1 Jan.: New system legal in all parts of the German Empire
1878: Minor coinage of former states demonetized
Source: N. Douglas Nicol, comp., *Standard Catalog of German Coins 1601 to Present, 2nd ed.,*. Krause Publications, Iola, Wisc., 1998

COSTS OF LIVING IN JENA (PRUSSIA) IN 1804

	Taler	Groschen	Pfennige
1 *Scheffel Weizen* (wheat)	12	x	x
1 *Scheffel Hafer* (oats)	3	x	x
1 *Pfund Rindfleisch* (beef)	x	2	8-10
1 *Pfund Schweinefleisch* (pork)	x	2	0
1 *Rindszunge* (beef tongue)	x	10-12	x
1 *Bratwurst* (sausage)	x	1	x
1 *Kalbsleber* (calves liver)	x	3-4	x
1 *Pfund Blutwurst* (blood sausage)	x	4	x
1 *Pfund Speck* (bacon)	x	8	x
1 *Pfund Seife* (soap)	x	5	x
1 *Pfund gegossener Lichter* (candle)	x	7	6
° *Pfund* Butter	x	2	3-6
1 *Kanne Erbsen* (peas)	x	1	2
1 *Pfund Aal* (eel)	x	12-14	x
1 *Pfund Karpfen* (carp)	x	4	6
1 *Maß Graupen* (barley)	x	2	8
1 *Hase* (hare)	x	10-18	x
1 *Pfund Wildbret* (venison)	x	2	x
1 *Gans* (goose)	x	16	x
1 *Ente* (duck)	x	8	x
1 *Paar Tauben* (2 pigeons)	x	2	6
1 *Huhn* (chicken)	x	4	6
1 *alte Henne* (old hen)	x	6-7	x
1 *Maß Dorf- und Stadtbier* (local beer)	x	x	7
1 *Maß englisches Bier* (English beer)	x	2	10
1 *Mandel Eier* (eggs)	x	3	x
1 *Pfund Leinöl* (linseed oil)	x	9	x

IN JENA, IN 1804
A craftsman earned between 8 and 15 Talers per month.
1 Taler = 24 Groschen
1 Groschen = 12 Pfennige
1 Jenaer Scheffel = 160.12 Liter
1 Kanne = 0.89 Liter;
1 Elle = 0.56 Meter

Source: Stadtmuseum, Jena. "Lebensmittelpreise 1804," 1996 exhibit

NUMBERS OF GUILD-MEMBERS IN AUGSBURG IN 1474

Weber (weavers) 550

Zimmerleute (carpenters), also *Maurer* (masons), *Hafner* (potters), ... 200
　Kistler (box-makers), *Müller* (millers)

Krämer (peddlers), also *Nestler* (shoelace makers), *Säckler* (sack-makers), ... 163
　Gürtler (belt-makers) and others

Schmiede (smiths), including *Sattler* (saddle/harness-makers), ... 140
　Maler (painters), and *Goldschlager* (makers of gold leaf)

Metzger (butchers) 140

Brauer (brewers) 140

Schuster (cobblers) 124

Bäcker (bakers) 109

Kaufleute (merchants) 99

Schneider (tailors) 96

Salzfertiger (salt makers), also *Weinschenken* (wine tavern workers/waiters) 90

Kürschner (furriers) 86

Hucker (peddlers), also *Seiler* (rope merchants) 80

Loder (weavers of Loden cloth), also *Tucher* (clothmakers) 70

Fischer (fischermen), also *Floßleute* (raftsmen) 64

Lederer (leather makers) 42

Schäffler (coopers), also *Wagner* (wheel makers) and *Drechsler* (wood-turners) . 38

Bader (barbers, surgeons) 31

Total 2,239

Source: Schwabische Craft Museum, Augsburg, 1997 exhibit

NUMBERS OF CRAFTSMEN
EMPLOYED IN THE CITY OF JENA IN 1800

Schuster (cobblers) 55
Fleischhauer (butchers) 46
Bäcker (bakers) 33
Sattler, Gürtler, Riemer, Beutler (workers in leather belts, bags, saddles, ... 24
   and harnesses)
Tuchmacher, -färber und -scherer (cloth makers, dyers, and cutters 16
Schmiede — Huf-, Nagel-, und Kupferschmiede (blacksmiths, nailsmiths, ... 16
   coppersmiths) 16
Stumpfwirker (stocking makers) 15
Leineweber (linen weavers) 11
Tischler (cabinetmakers) 11
*Glaser (*glassmakers) 8
Seiler (rope makers) 8
Töpfer (potters) 8
Böttcher (coopers) 7
Buchbinder (bookbinders) 7
Müller (millers) 7
Schlosser (locksmiths) 7
Sporer (spur makers) 7
Seifensieder (soapmakers) 7
Hutmacher (hatmaker) 6
Wagner (coach-, wheelmaker) 6
Drechsler (wood turners) 4
Kürschner (furriers) 4
Nadler (needlemakers) 4
Zinngießer (tin founders) 4
Klempner (tinsmiths) 3
Goldarbeiter (gold workers) 3
Knopfmacher (button makers) 3
Mechaniker (fitters, mechanics) 3
Gerber (tanners) 3
Kammmacher (combmakers) 2
Korbmacher (basketmakers) 2
Posamentierer (lace/braid makers) 2
Bürstenmacher (brushmaker) 1
Papiermacher (papermaker) 1
Samtwirker (velvet worker) 1
Polierer (burnisher, polisher) 1
Schriftgießer (type founder) 1

Source: Stadtmuseum, Jena, 1996 exhibit.

THE ROMAN CALENDARS

The Romans used lunar calendars, starting the year in March. Therefore, the names of the months corresponded to March as the first month of the year. For example, September (the seventh month, from the word root *sept*, or seven), October (from the word root *oct*, or eight), November (from the word root *nov*, or nine) and December (from the word root *dec*, or ten).

Names of Roman months are *Januarius, Februarius, Martius, Aprilis, Majus, Junius, Julius (Quintilis), Augustus (Sex-tilis), September* (abbrev. 7ber), *October* (abbrev. 8ber), *November* (abbrev. 9ber), *December* (abbrev. 10ber or Xber).

Dates were reckoned from three points in the month: 1) the *Calende*, the first of the month; 2) the *Nones*, the fifth of the month except in March, May, July, and October, when it fell on the seventh; and 3) the *Ides*, the thirteenth of the month except in March, May, July, and October, when it fell on the fifteenth.

JULIAN, GREGORIAN, FRENCH REPUBLICAN CALENDARS

Old Style Julian calendar

Up to 1582, the Julian calendar (commonly referred to as the "Old Style," or "OS") was established by Julius Caesar in 46 BC, with 12 months, 365 days in the year for three years and a leap year of 366 days. It was based on one year equaling 365.25 days instead of the actual length of the year which is only 365.2422 days. By 1582, the calendar had lost 10 days — the vernal equinox had moved from 21 March to 10 March. The Julian calendar compensated for the loss by observing the leap year. New Years Day was observed on 25 March in me-dieval times in Christian nations under the Old Style Julian calendar.

New Style Gregorian calendar

In 1582, Pope Gregory XIII made a correction. He revised the calendar (commonly referred to as the "New Style," or "NS"), announcing that the day after 5 October 1582 would be 15 October 1582 and that century years not divisible evenly by 400 would no longer be counted as leap years. Instead of 25 March, New Years Day would change to 1 January. The New Style (NS) Gregorian calendar was adopted by Catholic areas in Germany in 1583-1585, but it was not accepted in Protestant areas until much later.

In Great Britain and America, the Gregorian calendar began on 1 January 1753.

French Republican Calendar

The French Republican Calendar was established during the French Revolution, based on the founding of the French Republic, and remained in effect only from 24 October 1793 to 31 December 1805.

Its days and months were unrelated to the Gregorian calendar. The French Republican calendar affected civil registration records in France and areas ruled by the French including modern Belgium, Luxembourg, and parts of Netherlands, Germany, Switzerland, and Italy.

The calendar was divided into 12 months, with 30 days each. The 5 or 6 extra days were added at the end of the year (celebrated as a festival), three 10-day weeks a month, and days divided into 10 hours. Each hour was divided into 100 minutes, and each minute was divided into 100 seconds.

The months were named *Vendémiaire, Brumaire, Frimaire, Nivôse, Pluviôse, Ventôse, Germinal, Floréal, Prairial, Messidor, Thermidor* (sometimes *Fervidor* was used instead), and *Fructidor*. (These months do not correspond to the standard months of

January through December.)

To calculate the standard date for a French Republican calendar date, see the *Research Outline: French Republican Calendar*, Family History Library, Salt Lake City, Utah. 1990.

See also John Dahl, *Conversion Tables, French Republican Calendar: An Aid for Family Research in France and Germany*, 2nd Edition. Deseret Books, Salt Lake City, 1972. FHL 944 A9d.

'30 DAYS HATH SEPTEMBER'....WHY?

The first Julian year began with the first of January of the 46th year before the birth of Christ. In the distribution of days in the months, Julius Caesar had changed the arrangement of days of the months, ordering that the first, third, fifth, seventh, ninth, and eleventh months (January, March, May, July, September, and November) should have each 31 days, and the other months 30, except February, which in common years should have only 29, but every fourth year 30 days. This order was interrupted to gratify the vanity of Augustus, by giving the month bearing his name as many days as July, which was named after the first Caesar. A day was accordingly taken from February and given to August; and in order that three months of 31 days might not come together, September and November were reduced to 30 days, and 31 given to October and December. For so frivolous a reason was the regulation of Caesar abandoned, and this arrangement introduced.

Source: *Encyclopedia Britannica,* 11th edition, 1910.

Library, Church of Jesus Christ of Latter-day Saints, 1991.

• Larry O. Jensen, *A Genealogical Handbook of German Research*, Pleasant Grove, Utah, 1983; Vol. 2.

♦George K. Schweitzer, *German Genealogy*

GREGORIAN CALENDAR: BEGINNING DATES

The Gregorian calendar was put in effect on the following dates in various areas of Europe and Asia:

Aachen .... 11 Jan. 1583
Appenzell .... Nov. 1724
Augsburg (diocese) .... 24 Feb. 1783
Augsburg (city) .... 16 Oct. 1583
Baden (margraviate) .... 27 Nov. 1583
Basel (diocese) .... 31 Oct. 1783
Basel (city) .... 12 Jan. 1701
Bayern/Bavaria (duchy) .... 16 Oct. 1582
Böhmen/Bohemia .... 17 Jan. 1584
Brabant .... 1 Jan. 1583
Breisgau .... 24 Oct. 1583
Brixen (South Tyrol) .... 16 Oct. 1583
Bulgarien/Bulgaria .... 1 Jan 1916
Cleve (duchy) .... 28 Nov. 1583
Dänemark/Denmark .... 1 Mar. 1700
Danzig 1582
Deutschland/Germany 1583-85
   (Catholic)
Deutschland/Germany .. 1 Mar. 1700-76
   (Protestant)
Dorpat .... 1617, after 1625 until
                                           World War I
Eichstätt .... 16 Oct. 1583
Elsaß/Alsace   1648 in the areas ceded
      through the Treaty of Westphalia;
      österreichisches Oberelsaß/Austrian
      Upper Alsace: 24 Dec. 1583
England .... 14 Sep. 1752
Estland/Estonia .... after World War I
Finnland/Finland 1753
Flandern/Flanders .... 1 Jan. 1583
Frankreich/France .... 20 Dec. 1582
                           (later in some parts)
Freiburg .... 22 Jan. 1584
Freising (diocese) .... 16 Oct. 1583
Friesland .... 12 Jan. 1701
Galizien/Galicia .... in World War I
   (Greek-Orthodox dioceses)
Graubünden 1812

Griechenland/Greece .... 1 Mar. 1923
Hennegau .... 1 Jan. 1583
Hildesheim (diocese) .... 26 Mar. 1631
Holland .... 1 Jan. 1583
Italien/Italy .... 15 Oct. 1582
                     (predominantly)
Jülich-Berg (duchy) .... 13 Nov. 1583
Jugoslawien/ .... after World War I
Yugoslavia   except for the Serbian-
                      Orthodox Church
Köln/Cologne .... 14 Nov. 1583
   (Archdiocese and city)
Kurland .... Partially from 1607
   until 28 Jan. 1796, then until World
   War I back to the Julian calendar
Lausitz .... 23 Jan. 1584
Lettland .... 18 Nov. 1918
Litauen/Lithuania .... Partially until
   13 Jan. 1800, then returning to the
   Julian Calendar until World War I
Lothringen/Lorraine .... 20 Dec. 1582
Lüttich .... 21 Feb. 1583
Luzern/Luzerne .... 22 Jan. 1584
Mainz (archdiocese) .... 22 Nov. 1583
Minden 1630
Mühlhausen .... 31 Oct. 1583
Münster (diocese) .... 28 Nov. 1583
Neuburg/Pfalz .... 24 Dec. 1615
Niederlande/Netherlands:
–Staatskanzlei/chancery . 25 Dec. 1583
–Antwerpen, Artois, ... 25 Dec. 1582
   Brabant, Flandern,   or 1 Jan. 1583
   Hennegau, Mecheln,
   Limburg, Luxemburg, Namur
–Bistum/Diocese Lüttich . 21 Feb. 1583
–Holland & Zeeland .... 25 Dec. 1582 or
                       1 Jan. 1583
–Groningen .... 11 Mar. 1583
   (until summer 1594, ultimately
   12 Dec. 1700/12 January 1701)
–Friesland .... 12 Jan. 1801
–Gelderland ...... 12 July or 12 Dec. 1700
–Overijssel .... 12 Dec. 1700
–Utrecht .... 1 Mar. 1700
Norwegen/Norway .... 1 Mar. 1700
Oberelsaß/UpperAlsace .... 24 Oct. 1583
(Austrian)
Osnabrück 1624
Österreich/Austria .... 29 Dec. 1583

(above the Enns)
Österreich .... 16 Oct. 1583
  (below the Enns)
Paderborn (diocese) .... 27 Jun 1585
Passau .... Feb. 1583
Polen/Poland 1583
(in Poland both calendars were used)
Portugal .... 15 Oct. 1582
Preußen/Prussia (duchy) ... 2 Sep. 1612
Regensburg .... 16 Oct. 1583
Rumänien/Romania .... after 1917
Rußland/Russia .... after 1917
Salzburg .... 16 Oct. 1583
Schaffhausen .... 12 Jan. 1701
Schlesien/Silesia ... 17 Jan.-23 Jan. 1584
Schweden/Sweden .... 1 Mar. 1753
  (with an interruption ca. 1600; in 1700
  the extra day in the calendar was
  omitted)
Schwyz/Switzerland .... 22 Jan. 1584
Siebenbürgen .... 25 Dec. 1590
Solothurn .... 22 Jan. 1584
Spanien/Spain .... 15 Oct. 1582
(and all Philipp II's lands)
St. Gallen 1724
Steiermark/Styria .... 25 Nov. 1503
Straßburg (diocese) .... 27 Nov. 1583
Straßburg (city) ...... 16 Feb.-1 Mar. 1682
Tirol/Tyrol .... 16 Oct. 1583
Trient .... 21 Feb. 1583
Trier .... 15 Oct. 1583
Türkei/Turkey 1926
Ungarn/Hungary .... 2 Feb. 1584;
           first by law 1 Nov. 1587
Unterwalden .... Jun. 1584
Uri .... 22 Jan. 1584
Westfalen/Westphalia .... 12 Jul. 1584
(duchy)
Würzburg (diocese) .... 15 Nov. 1583
Zug .... 22 Jan. 1584
Zürich .... 12 Jan. 1701

FEAST DAYS

Events marking the church calendar, rather than dates from the secular calendars, were in many cases used in recording births, marriages, and deaths in both Protestant and Catholic church records.

The church year was based on Christmas (December 25) and Easter (in March or April, date varies). Major feast days of the church calendar are listed below.

An asterisk (*) indicates that the observance date changes from year to year, based on solar-lunar cycles.

Advent (*Advents*)

◆ **Adventssonntag* (first Sunday in Advent, fourth Sunday before Christmas)
◆*Andreas* (St. Andrew), 30 November
◆ *Second Sunday in Advent, third Sunday before Christmas
◆ *Third Sunday in Advent, second Sunday before Christmas
◆*Thomas* (St. Thomas), 21 December
◆Fourth Sunday in Advent, first Sunday before Christmas
◆*Weihnachts* (Christmas), 25 December

Christmas (*Weihnachts*)

◆*Stephanus* (St. Stephen), 26 December
◆*First Sunday after Christmas
◆*Johannes* (St. John), 27 December
◆ *Unschuldige Kindlein* (Holy Innocents), 28 December
◆*Second Sunday after Christmas
◆*Beschneidung Christi* (Circumcision of Our Lord), 1 January

Epiphany (*Epiphanie/Erscheinung*)

◆*Epiphanie* (Epiphany), 6 January
◆ **Septuagesima* (Septuagesima Sunday), ninth Sunday before Easter
◆ **Sexagesima* (Sexagesima Sunday), eighth Sunday before Easter
◆ **Quinquasgesima* (Quinquagesima Sunday), seventh Sunday before Easter
◆*Pauli Bekehrung/Conversio* (Conversion of St. Paul), 25 January
◆*Praesentatio Domini Nostrum* (Presentation of Our Lord), 2 February
◆*Matthias* (St. Matthias), 24 February

Lent (*Fastenzeit*)

◆**Aschermitwoch* (Ash Wednesday), 46 days before Easter
◆**I Invocavit* (first Sunday in Lent), sixth Sunday before Easter
◆ **II Reminiscere* (second Sunday in Lent), fifth Sunday before Easter
◆**III Oculi* (third Sunday in Lent), fourth Sunday before Easter
◆**IV Laetare* (fourth Sunday in Lent), third Sunday before Easter
◆ **Passionssonntag* (fifth Sunday in Lent), second Sunday before Easter
◆**Palmsonntag* (sixth Sunday in Lent), first Sunday before Easter
◆**Karwoche* (Holy Week)
  Montag (Monday)
  Dienstag (Tuesday)
  Mittwoch (Wednesday)
  Gründonnerstag (Maundy Thursday)
  Karfreitag (Good Friday)
  Samstag (Easter Eve)

Easter (*Osternzeit*)

◆**Ostern* (Easter Sunday)
◆*Berkündigung Maria* (Annunciation), 25 March
◆**I Quasi Modo Geniti* (second Sunday of Easter), first Sunday after Easter
◆ **II Misericordia* (third Sunday of Easter), second Sunday after Easter
◆**III Jubilate* (fourth Sunday of Easter), third Sunday after Easter
◆**IV Cantate* (fifth Sunday of Easter), fourth Sunday after Easter
◆**V Rogate/Vocem Juncunditatis* (sixth Sunday of Easter), fifth Sunday after Easter
◆ **Himmelfahrt Christi* (Ascension Thursday), 40 days after Easter
◆**VI Exaudi* (7th Sunday of Easter), 6th Sunday after Easter
◆*Marcus* (St. Mark), 25 April
◆*Philippus und Jacobus* (St. Philip and St. James), 1 May

(continued on page 487)

◆ **Pfingsten* (Pentecost/Whitsunday), seventh Sunday or 50 days after Easter

Trinity (*Trinititatis*)

◆(*Trinity Sunday), eighth Sunday after Easter
◆ *Johannes der Täufer* (St. John the

(continued on page 506)

MONTHS OF THE YEAR IN FIVE LANGUAGES

ENGLISH	GERMAN	SWISS	FRENCH	LATIN
January	Januar/Hartung/ Eismonat	Januar/Jänner/ Jenner/Erster Monat	janvier	Januarius
February	Februar/Hornung/ Regenmonat	Februar/ Hornung	février	Februarius
March	März/Lenzing/ Lenzmond/ Windmonat	März/Lenz Frühlingsmonat	mars	Martius
April	April/Ostermond/ Ostermonat/ Wandelmonat	April/ Ostermonat	avril	Aprilis
May	Mai/Weidemonat/ Wonnemond/ Blütenmonat	Mai/ Wonnemonat	mai	Maius
June	Juni/Brachet/ Brachmonat/ Wiesenmonat	Juni/ Brachmonat	juin	Junius
July	Juli/Heuert/ Heumonat	Juli/ Heumonat	juillet	Julius
August	August/Ernting/ Erntemonat/ Hitzmonat	August/Augst/ Augstmonat/ Erntemonat	août	Augustus
September	September/ Fruchtmonat/ Scheiding/7ber	September/ Herbstmonat/ 7ber	septembre/ 7bre	September/ Septembris
October	Oktober/Gilbhard Weinmonat/8ber	Oktober/ Weinmonat/ 8ber	octobre/ 8bre	October/ Octobris
November	November/ Reifmonat/ Nebelmonat/9ber	November/ Wintermonat/ 9ber	novembre/ 9bre	November/ Novembris
December	Dezember/ Julmonat/ Schneemonat/ Christmonat/10bre	Dezember Christmonat/ Wolfmonat/ 10ber/Xber	décembre/ 10bre Xbre	December/ Decembris

DAYS OF THE WEEK IN FIVE LANGUAGES

ENGLISH	GERMAN	SWISS	FRENCH	LATIN
Sunday	Sonntag	Suntig	dimanche	dies dominica/dies Solis/feria prima
Monday	Montag	Mäntig	lundi	dies Lunae/feria secunda
Tuesday	Dienstag	Ziestig/ Zinstag	mardi	dies Martis/feria tertia
Wednesday	Mittwoch	Mittwuch	mercredi	dies Mercurii/feria quarta
Thursday	Donnerstag	Dunstig	jeudi	dies Jovis/feria quinta
Friday	Freitag/ Freytag/Frytig	Fritag/Frytig	venredi	dies Veneris/feria sexta
Saturday	Samstag/ Sonnabend	Samstag	samedi	dies Saturnia/feria septima/sabbatum

(concluded from page 504)

Baptist), 24 June
◆*Petrus und Paulus* (Sts. Peter and Paul), 29 June
◆*Heimsuchung Mariä* (Visitation), 2 July
w*Jacobus der Ältere* (St. James the Elder), 25 July
◆ *Umgestaltung/Verklärung* (Transfiguration of Our Lord), 6 August
◆*Himmelfahrt Maria* (Assumption of Mary), 15 August
◆*Bartholomäus* (St. Bartholomew), 24 August
◆ *Matthaeus* (St. Matthew), 21 September
w*Michael* (St. Michael and All Angels), 29 September
◆*Lucas* (St. Luke), 18 October
◆ *Simeon und Judas* (Sts. Simon and Jude), 28 October
◆*Reformations-Fest* (Reformation Day-Protestant), 31 October
◆*Allerseelen/Allerheiligen* (All Souls'/ All Saints' Day), 1 November

Sources: George K. Schweitzer, *German Genealogical Research*, 1995. *Encyclopedia Britannica,* 11th edition, 1910.

PERPETUAL CALENDAR

Use the perpetual calendar on the next two pages to determine the day of the week of a particular event since the Gregorian calendar was introduced in 1582. Pope Gregory XIII corrected errors in the Julian Calendar, starting on the day after October 4, which became 15 October.

The revised calendar is known as the New Style (NS) Gregorian calendar.

Personal Ancestral File (PAF), the software program (and some Internet programs) will also calculate day of the week and birth date from the death date.

Internet programs offer a "birth date calculator" to find the date of birth from age at death. The latter as frequently inscribed on grave stones.

1776-2000 CALENDARS

'76 ... 9	1814 ... 7	1852 ... 12	1890 ... 4	1928 ... 8	1966 ... 7
'77 ... 4	1815 ... 1	1853 ... 7	1891 ... 5	1929 ... 3	1967 ... 1
'78 ... 5	1816 ... 9	1854 ... 1	1892 ... 13	1930 ... 4	1968 ... 9
'79 ... 6	1817 ... 4	1855 ... 2	1893 ... 1	1931 ... 5	1969 ... 4
'80 ... 14	1818 ... 5	1856 ... 10	1894 ... 2	1932 ... 13	1970 ... 5
'81 ... 2	1819 ... 6	1857 ... 5	1895 ... 3	1933 ... 1	1971 ... 6
'82 ... 3	1820 ... 14	1858 ... 6	1896 ... 11	1934 ... 2	1972 ... 14
'83 ... 4	1821 ... 2	1859 ... 7	1897 ... 6	1935 ... 3	1973 ... 2
'84 ... 12	1822 ... 3	1860 ... 8	1898 ... 7	1936 ... 11	1974 ... 3
'85 ... 7	1823 ... 4	1861 ... 3	1899 ... 1	1937 ... 6	1975 ... 4
'86 ... 1	1824 ... 12	1862 ... 4	1900 ... 2	1938 ... 7	1976 ... 12
'87 ... 2	1825 ... 7	1863 ... 5	1901 ... 3	1939 ... 1	1977 ... 7
'88 ... 10	1826 ... 1	1864 ... 13	1902 ... 4	1940 ... 9	1978 ... 1
'89 ... 5	1827 ... 2	1865 ... 1	1903 ... 5	1941 ... 4	1979 ... 2
'90 ... 6	1828 ... 10	1866 ... 2	1904 ... 13	1942 ... 5	1980 ... 10
'91 ... 1	1829 ... 5	1867 ... 3	1905 ... 1	1943 ... 6	1981 ... 5
'92 ... 8	1830 ... 6	1868 ... 11	1906 ... 2	1944 ... 14	1982 ... 6
'93 ... 3	1831 ... 7	1869 ... 6	1907 ... 3	1945 ... 2	1983 ... 7
'94 ... 4	1832 ... 8	1870 ... 7	1908 ... 11	1946 ... 3	1984 ... 8
'95 ... 5	1833 ... 3	1871 ... 1	1909 ... 6	1947 ... 4	1985 ... 3
'96 ... 13	1834 ... 4	1872 ... 9	1910 ... 7	1948 ... 12	1986 ... 4
'97 ... 1	1835 ... 5	1873 ... 7	1911 ... 1	1949 ... 7	1987 ... 5
'98 ... 2	1836 ... 13	1874 ... 5	1912 ... 9	1950 ... 1	1988 ... 13
'99 ... 3	1837 ... 1	1875 ... 6	1913 ... 4	1951 ... 2	1989 ... 1
'00 ... 4	1838 ... 2	1876 ... 14	1914 ... 5	1952 ... 10	1990 ... 2
'01 ... 3	1839 ... 3	1877 ... 2	1915 ... 6	1953 ... 5	1991 ... 3
'02 ... 11	1840 ... 11	1878 ... 3	1916 ... 14	1954 ... 6	1992 ... 11
'03 ... 7	1841 ... 6	1879 ... 4	1917 ... 2	1955 ... 7	1993 ... 6
'04 ... 4	1842 ... 7	1880 ... 12	1918 ... 3	1956 ... 8	1994 ... 7
'05 ... 13	1843 ... 1	1881 ... 7	1919 ... 4	1957 ... 3	1995 ... 1
'06 ... 1	1844 ... 9	1882 ... 1	1920 ... 12	1958 ... 4	1996 ... 9
'07 ... 2	1845 ... 4	1883 ... 2	1921 ... 7	1959 ... 5	1997 ... 4
'08 ... 13	1846 ... 5	1884 ... 10	1922 ... 1	1960 ... 13	1998 ... 5
'09 ... 2	1847 ... 6	1885 ... 5	1923 ... 2	1961 ... 1	1999 ... 6
'10 ... 3	1848 ... 14	1886 ... 6	1924 ... 10	1962 ... 2	2000 ... 14
'11 ... 4	1849 ... 2	1887 ... 7	1925 ... 5	1963 ... 3	
'12 ... 11	1850 ... 3	1888 ... 8	1926 ... 6	1964 ... 11	
'13 ... 6	1851 ... 4	1889 ... 3	1927 ... 7	1965 ... 6	

Directions: The number opposite each year indicates the number of the calendar for that year, provided on these pages.

1

JANUARY · **FEBRUARY** · **MARCH** · **APRIL** · **MAY** · **JUNE** · **JULY** · **AUGUST** · **SEPTEMBER** · **OCTOBER** · **NOVEMBER** · **DECEMBER**

2

JANUARY · **FEBRUARY** · **MARCH** · **APRIL** · **MAY** · **JUNE** · **JULY** · **AUGUST** · **SEPTEMBER** · **OCTOBER** · **NOVEMBER** · **DECEMBER**

3

JANUARY · **FEBRUARY** · **MARCH** · **APRIL** · **MAY** · **JUNE** · **JULY** · **AUGUST** · **SEPTEMBER** · **OCTOBER** · **NOVEMBER** · **DECEMBER**

4

JANUARY · **FEBRUARY** · **MARCH** · **APRIL** · **MAY** · **JUNE** · **JULY** · **AUGUST** · **SEPTEMBER** · **OCTOBER** · **NOVEMBER** · **DECEMBER**

5

JANUARY · **FEBRUARY** · **MARCH** · **APRIL** · **MAY** · **JUNE** · **JULY** · **AUGUST** · **SEPTEMBER** · **OCTOBER** · **NOVEMBER** · **DECEMBER**

6

JANUARY · **FEBRUARY** · **MARCH** · **APRIL** · **MAY** · **JUNE** · **JULY** · **AUGUST** · **SEPTEMBER** · **OCTOBER** · **NOVEMBER** · **DECEMBER**

7

```
JANUARY               FEBRUARY              MARCH                 APRIL
S  M  T  W  T  F  S   S  M  T  W  T  F  S   S  M  T  W  T  F  S   S  M  T  W  T  F  S
               1               1  2  3  4  5         1  2  3  4  5                  1  2
2  3  4  5  6  7  8    6  7  8  9 10 11 12    6  7  8  9 10 11 12    3  4  5  6  7  8  9
9 10 11 12 13 14 15   13 14 15 16 17 18 19   13 14 15 16 17 18 19   10 11 12 13 14 15 16
16 17 18 19 20 21 22  20 21 22 23 24 25 26   20 21 22 23 24 25 26   17 18 19 20 21 22 23
23 24 25 26 27 28 29  27 28                  27 28 29 30 31         24 25 26 27 28 29 30
30 31

MAY                   JUNE                  JULY                  AUGUST
S  M  T  W  T  F  S   S  M  T  W  T  F  S   S  M  T  W  T  F  S   S  M  T  W  T  F  S
1  2  3  4  5  6  7            1  2  3  4                  1  2      1  2  3  4  5  6
8  9 10 11 12 13 14    5  6  7  8  9 10 11    3  4  5  6  7  8  9    7  8  9 10 11 12 13
15 16 17 18 19 20 21   12 13 14 15 16 17 18   10 11 12 13 14 15 16   14 15 16 17 18 19 20
22 23 24 25 26 27 28   19 20 21 22 23 24 25   17 18 19 20 21 22 23   21 22 23 24 25 26 27
29 30 31               26 27 28 29 30         24 25 26 27 28 29 30   28 29 30 31
                                              31

SEPTEMBER             OCTOBER               NOVEMBER              DECEMBER
S  M  T  W  T  F  S   S  M  T  W  T  F  S   S  M  T  W  T  F  S   S  M  T  W  T  F  S
         1  2  3                     1            1  2  3  4  5            1  2  3
4  5  6  7  8  9 10    2  3  4  5  6  7  8    6  7  8  9 10 11 12    4  5  6  7  8  9 10
11 12 13 14 15 16 17   9 10 11 12 13 14 15   13 14 15 16 17 18 19   11 12 13 14 15 16 17
18 19 20 21 22 23 24  16 17 18 19 20 21 22   20 21 22 23 24 25 26   18 19 20 21 22 23 24
25 26 27 28 29 30     23 24 25 26 27 28 29   27 28 29 30            25 26 27 28 29 30 31
                      30 31
```

8

```
JANUARY               FEBRUARY              MARCH                 APRIL
S  M  T  W  T  F  S   S  M  T  W  T  F  S   S  M  T  W  T  F  S   S  M  T  W  T  F  S
1  2  3  4  5  6  7            1  2  3  4               1  2  3   1  2  3  4  5  6  7
8  9 10 11 12 13 14    5  6  7  8  9 10 11    4  5  6  7  8  9 10    8  9 10 11 12 13 14
15 16 17 18 19 20 21   12 13 14 15 16 17 18   11 12 13 14 15 16 17   15 16 17 18 19 20 21
22 23 24 25 26 27 28   19 20 21 22 23 24 25   18 19 20 21 22 23 24   22 23 24 25 26 27 28
29 30 31               26 27 28 29            25 26 27 28 29 30 31   29 30

MAY                   JUNE                  JULY                  AUGUST
S  M  T  W  T  F  S   S  M  T  W  T  F  S   S  M  T  W  T  F  S   S  M  T  W  T  F  S
      1  2  3  4  5                  1  2   1  2  3  4  5  6  7            1  2  3  4
6  7  8  9 10 11 12    3  4  5  6  7  8  9    8  9 10 11 12 13 14    5  6  7  8  9 10 11
13 14 15 16 17 18 19   10 11 12 13 14 15 16   15 16 17 18 19 20 21   12 13 14 15 16 17 18
20 21 22 23 24 25 26   17 18 19 20 21 22 23   22 23 24 25 26 27 28   19 20 21 22 23 24 25
27 28 29 30 31         24 25 26 27 28 29 30   29 30 31               26 27 28 29 30 31

SEPTEMBER             OCTOBER               NOVEMBER              DECEMBER
S  M  T  W  T  F  S   S  M  T  W  T  F  S   S  M  T  W  T  F  S   S  M  T  W  T  F  S
                  1      1  2  3  4  5  6            1  2  3                     1
2  3  4  5  6  7  8    7  8  9 10 11 12 13    4  5  6  7  8  9 10    2  3  4  5  6  7  8
9 10 11 12 13 14 15   14 15 16 17 18 19 20   11 12 13 14 15 16 17    9 10 11 12 13 14 15
16 17 18 19 20 21 22  21 22 23 24 25 26 27   18 19 20 21 22 23 24   16 17 18 19 20 21 22
23 24 25 26 27 28 29  28 29 30 31            25 26 27 28 29 30      23 24 25 26 27 28 29
30                                                                  30 31
```

9

```
JANUARY               FEBRUARY              MARCH                 APRIL
S  M  T  W  T  F  S   S  M  T  W  T  F  S   S  M  T  W  T  F  S   S  M  T  W  T  F  S
            1  2  3   1  2  3  4  5  6  7   1  2  3  4  5  6  7            1  2  3  4
4  5  6  7  8  9 10    8  9 10 11 12 13 14    8  9 10 11 12 13 14    5  6  7  8  9 10 11
11 12 13 14 15 16 17  15 16 17 18 19 20 21   15 16 17 18 19 20 21   12 13 14 15 16 17 18
18 19 20 21 22 23 24  22 23 24 25 26 27 28   22 23 24 25 26 27 28   19 20 21 22 23 24 25
25 26 27 28 29 30 31                         29 30 31               26 27 28 29 30

MAY                   JUNE                  JULY                  AUGUST
S  M  T  W  T  F  S   S  M  T  W  T  F  S   S  M  T  W  T  F  S   S  M  T  W  T  F  S
                  1  2      1  2  3  4  5  6            1  2  3  4                     1
3  4  5  6  7  8  9    7  8  9 10 11 12 13    5  6  7  8  9 10 11    2  3  4  5  6  7  8
10 11 12 13 14 15 16   14 15 16 17 18 19 20   12 13 14 15 16 17 18    9 10 11 12 13 14 15
17 18 19 20 21 22 23   21 22 23 24 25 26 27   19 20 21 22 23 24 25   16 17 18 19 20 21 22
24 25 26 27 28 29 30   28 29 30               26 27 28 29 30 31      23 24 25 26 27 28 29
31                                                                   30 31

SEPTEMBER             OCTOBER               NOVEMBER              DECEMBER
S  M  T  W  T  F  S   S  M  T  W  T  F  S   S  M  T  W  T  F  S   S  M  T  W  T  F  S
         1  2  3  4               1  2  3   1  2  3  4  5  6  7            1  2  3  4  5
5  6  7  8  9 10 11    4  5  6  7  8  9 10    8  9 10 11 12 13 14    6  7  8  9 10 11 12
12 13 14 15 16 17 18  11 12 13 14 15 16 17   15 16 17 18 19 20 21   13 14 15 16 17 18 19
19 20 21 22 23 24 25  18 19 20 21 22 23 24   22 23 24 25 26 27 28   20 21 22 23 24 25 26
26 27 28 29 30        25 26 27 28 29 30 31   29 30                  27 28 29 30 31
```

10

```
JANUARY               FEBRUARY              MARCH                 APRIL
S  M  T  W  T  F  S   S  M  T  W  T  F  S   S  M  T  W  T  F  S   S  M  T  W  T  F  S
                  1  2      1  2  3  4  5  6         1  2  3  4  5                  1  2
3  4  5  6  7  8  9    7  8  9 10 11 12 13    6  7  8  9 10 11 12    3  4  5  6  7  8  9
10 11 12 13 14 15 16   14 15 16 17 18 19 20   13 14 15 16 17 18 19   10 11 12 13 14 15 16
17 18 19 20 21 22 23   21 22 23 24 25 26 27   20 21 22 23 24 25 26   17 18 19 20 21 22 23
24 25 26 27 28 29 30   28 29                  27 28 29 30 31         24 25 26 27 28 29 30
31

MAY                   JUNE                  JULY                  AUGUST
S  M  T  W  T  F  S   S  M  T  W  T  F  S   S  M  T  W  T  F  S   S  M  T  W  T  F  S
1  2  3  4  5  6  7            1  2  3  4                  1  2      1  2  3  4  5  6
8  9 10 11 12 13 14    5  6  7  8  9 10 11    3  4  5  6  7  8  9    7  8  9 10 11 12 13
15 16 17 18 19 20 21   12 13 14 15 16 17 18   10 11 12 13 14 15 16   14 15 16 17 18 19 20
22 23 24 25 26 27 28   19 20 21 22 23 24 25   17 18 19 20 21 22 23   21 22 23 24 25 26 27
29 30 31               26 27 28 29 30         24 25 26 27 28 29 30   28 29 30 31
                                              31

SEPTEMBER             OCTOBER               NOVEMBER              DECEMBER
S  M  T  W  T  F  S   S  M  T  W  T  F  S   S  M  T  W  T  F  S   S  M  T  W  T  F  S
         1  2  3                     1            1  2  3  4  5            1  2  3
4  5  6  7  8  9 10    2  3  4  5  6  7  8    6  7  8  9 10 11 12    4  5  6  7  8  9 10
11 12 13 14 15 16 17   9 10 11 12 13 14 15   13 14 15 16 17 18 19   11 12 13 14 15 16 17
18 19 20 21 22 23 24  16 17 18 19 20 21 22   20 21 22 23 24 25 26   18 19 20 21 22 23 24
25 26 27 28 29 30     23 24 25 26 27 28 29   27 28 29 30            25 26 27 28 29 30 31
                      30 31
```

11

```
JANUARY               FEBRUARY              MARCH                 APRIL
S  M  T  W  T  F  S   S  M  T  W  T  F  S   S  M  T  W  T  F  S   S  M  T  W  T  F  S
         1  2  3  4                     1   1  2  3  4  5  6  7            1  2  3  4
5  6  7  8  9 10 11    2  3  4  5  6  7  8    8  9 10 11 12 13 14    5  6  7  8  9 10 11
12 13 14 15 16 17 18   9 10 11 12 13 14 15   15 16 17 18 19 20 21   12 13 14 15 16 17 18
19 20 21 22 23 24 25  16 17 18 19 20 21 22   22 23 24 25 26 27 28   19 20 21 22 23 24 25
26 27 28 29 30 31     23 24 25 26 27 28 29   29 30 31               26 27 28 29 30

MAY                   JUNE                  JULY                  AUGUST
S  M  T  W  T  F  S   S  M  T  W  T  F  S   S  M  T  W  T  F  S   S  M  T  W  T  F  S
                  1  2      1  2  3  4  5  6         1  2  3  4                     1
3  4  5  6  7  8  9    7  8  9 10 11 12 13    5  6  7  8  9 10 11    2  3  4  5  6  7  8
10 11 12 13 14 15 16   14 15 16 17 18 19 20   12 13 14 15 16 17 18    9 10 11 12 13 14 15
17 18 19 20 21 22 23   21 22 23 24 25 26 27   19 20 21 22 23 24 25   16 17 18 19 20 21 22
24 25 26 27 28 29 30   28 29 30               26 27 28 29 30 31      23 24 25 26 27 28 29
31                                                                   30 31

SEPTEMBER             OCTOBER               NOVEMBER              DECEMBER
S  M  T  W  T  F  S   S  M  T  W  T  F  S   S  M  T  W  T  F  S   S  M  T  W  T  F  S
         1  2  3  4               1  2  3   1  2  3  4  5  6  7            1  2  3  4  5
5  6  7  8  9 10 11    4  5  6  7  8  9 10    8  9 10 11 12 13 14    6  7  8  9 10 11 12
12 13 14 15 16 17 18  11 12 13 14 15 16 17   15 16 17 18 19 20 21   13 14 15 16 17 18 19
19 20 21 22 23 24 25  18 19 20 21 22 23 24   22 23 24 25 26 27 28   20 21 22 23 24 25 26
26 27 28 29 30        25 26 27 28 29 30 31   29 30                  27 28 29 30 31
```

12

```
JANUARY               FEBRUARY              MARCH                 APRIL
S  M  T  W  T  F  S   S  M  T  W  T  F  S   S  M  T  W  T  F  S   S  M  T  W  T  F  S
               1            1  2  3  4  5            1  2  3  4                     1
2  3  4  5  6  7  8    6  7  8  9 10 11 12    5  6  7  8  9 10 11    2  3  4  5  6  7  8
9 10 11 12 13 14 15   13 14 15 16 17 18 19   12 13 14 15 16 17 18    9 10 11 12 13 14 15
16 17 18 19 20 21 22  20 21 22 23 24 25 26   19 20 21 22 23 24 25   16 17 18 19 20 21 22
23 24 25 26 27 28 29  27 28 29               26 27 28 29 30 31      23 24 25 26 27 28 29
30 31                                                               30

MAY                   JUNE                  JULY                  AUGUST
S  M  T  W  T  F  S   S  M  T  W  T  F  S   S  M  T  W  T  F  S   S  M  T  W  T  F  S
   1  2  3  4  5  6            1  2  3               1            1  2  3  4  5
7  8  9 10 11 12 13    4  5  6  7  8  9 10    2  3  4  5  6  7  8    6  7  8  9 10 11 12
14 15 16 17 18 19 20   11 12 13 14 15 16 17    9 10 11 12 13 14 15   13 14 15 16 17 18 19
21 22 23 24 25 26 27   18 19 20 21 22 23 24   16 17 18 19 20 21 22   20 21 22 23 24 25 26
28 29 30 31            25 26 27 28 29 30       23 24 25 26 27 28 29   27 28 29 30 31
                                              30 31

SEPTEMBER             OCTOBER               NOVEMBER              DECEMBER
S  M  T  W  T  F  S   S  M  T  W  T  F  S   S  M  T  W  T  F  S   S  M  T  W  T  F  S
                  1  2 1  2  3  4  5  6  7            1  2  3  4                  1  2
3  4  5  6  7  8  9    8  9 10 11 12 13 14    5  6  7  8  9 10 11    3  4  5  6  7  8  9
10 11 12 13 14 15 16  15 16 17 18 19 20 21   12 13 14 15 16 17 18   10 11 12 13 14 15 16
17 18 19 20 21 22 23  22 23 24 25 26 27 28   19 20 21 22 23 24 25   17 18 19 20 21 22 23
24 25 26 27 28 29 30  29 30 31               26 27 28 29 30         24 25 26 27 28 29 30
                                                                    31
```

13

```
JANUARY               FEBRUARY              MARCH                 APRIL
S  M  T  W  T  F  S   S  M  T  W  T  F  S   S  M  T  W  T  F  S   S  M  T  W  T  F  S
                  1  2    1  2  3  4  5  6      1  2  3  4  5  6               1  2  3
3  4  5  6  7  8  9    7  8  9 10 11 12 13    7  8  9 10 11 12 13    4  5  6  7  8  9 10
10 11 12 13 14 15 16  14 15 16 17 18 19 20   14 15 16 17 18 19 20   11 12 13 14 15 16 17
17 18 19 20 21 22 23  21 22 23 24 25 26 27   21 22 23 24 25 26 27   18 19 20 21 22 23 24
24 25 26 27 28 29 30  28                     28 29 30 31            25 26 27 28 29 30
31

MAY                   JUNE                  JULY                  AUGUST
S  M  T  W  T  F  S   S  M  T  W  T  F  S   S  M  T  W  T  F  S   S  M  T  W  T  F  S
                  1            1  2  3  4  5            1  2  3   1  2  3  4  5  6  7
2  3  4  5  6  7  8    6  7  8  9 10 11 12    4  5  6  7  8  9 10    8  9 10 11 12 13 14
9 10 11 12 13 14 15   13 14 15 16 17 18 19   11 12 13 14 15 16 17   15 16 17 18 19 20 21
16 17 18 19 20 21 22  20 21 22 23 24 25 26   18 19 20 21 22 23 24   22 23 24 25 26 27 28
23 24 25 26 27 28 29  27 28 29 30            25 26 27 28 29 30 31   29 30 31
30 31

SEPTEMBER             OCTOBER               NOVEMBER              DECEMBER
S  M  T  W  T  F  S   S  M  T  W  T  F  S   S  M  T  W  T  F  S   S  M  T  W  T  F  S
         1  2  3  4                  1  2      1  2  3  4  5  6            1  2  3  4
5  6  7  8  9 10 11    3  4  5  6  7  8  9    7  8  9 10 11 12 13    5  6  7  8  9 10 11
12 13 14 15 16 17 18  10 11 12 13 14 15 16   14 15 16 17 18 19 20   12 13 14 15 16 17 18
19 20 21 22 23 24 25  17 18 19 20 21 22 23   21 22 23 24 25 26 27   19 20 21 22 23 24 25
26 27 28 29 30        24 25 26 27 28 29 30   28 29 30              26 27 28 29 30 31
                      31
```

14

```
JANUARY               FEBRUARY              MARCH                 APRIL
S  M  T  W  T  F  S   S  M  T  W  T  F  S   S  M  T  W  T  F  S   S  M  T  W  T  F  S
1  2  3  4  5  6  7            1  2  3  4               1  2  3  4                     1
8  9 10 11 12 13 14    5  6  7  8  9 10 11    5  6  7  8  9 10 11    2  3  4  5  6  7  8
15 16 17 18 19 20 21   12 13 14 15 16 17 18   12 13 14 15 16 17 18    9 10 11 12 13 14 15
22 23 24 25 26 27 28   19 20 21 22 23 24 25   19 20 21 22 23 24 25   16 17 18 19 20 21 22
29 30 31               26 27 28               26 27 28 29 30 31      23 24 25 26 27 28 29
                                                                    30

MAY                   JUNE                  JULY                  AUGUST
S  M  T  W  T  F  S   S  M  T  W  T  F  S   S  M  T  W  T  F  S   S  M  T  W  T  F  S
   1  2  3  4  5  6            1  2  3               1            1  2  3  4  5
7  8  9 10 11 12 13    4  5  6  7  8  9 10    2  3  4  5  6  7  8    6  7  8  9 10 11 12
14 15 16 17 18 19 20   11 12 13 14 15 16 17    9 10 11 12 13 14 15   13 14 15 16 17 18 19
21 22 23 24 25 26 27   18 19 20 21 22 23 24   16 17 18 19 20 21 22   20 21 22 23 24 25 26
28 29 30 31            25 26 27 28 29 30       23 24 25 26 27 28 29   27 28 29 30 31
                                              30 31

SEPTEMBER             OCTOBER               NOVEMBER              DECEMBER
S  M  T  W  T  F  S   S  M  T  W  T  F  S   S  M  T  W  T  F  S   S  M  T  W  T  F  S
                  1  2 1  2  3  4  5  6  7            1  2  3  4                  1  2
3  4  5  6  7  8  9    8  9 10 11 12 13 14    5  6  7  8  9 10 11    3  4  5  6  7  8  9
10 11 12 13 14 15 16  15 16 17 18 19 20 21   12 13 14 15 16 17 18   10 11 12 13 14 15 16
17 18 19 20 21 22 23  22 23 24 25 26 27 28   19 20 21 22 23 24 25   17 18 19 20 21 22 23
24 25 26 27 28 29 30  29 30 31               26 27 28 29 30         24 25 26 27 28 29 30
                                                                    31
```

GREGORIAN CALENDAR KEY FOR 1583-1775

Find the year to be searched below for the years 1583-1775. The numbers beside each year are keyed to the 14 calendars on the previous two pages.

Note: The Gregorian Calendar began on October 15, 1582. From that date to 31 December 1582, use calendar 6.)

1583 7	1620 .. 11	1657 2
1584 8	1621 6	1658 3
1585 3	1622 7	1659 4
1586 4	1623 1	1660 .. 12
1587 5	1624 9	1661 7
1588 .. 13	1625 4	1662 1
1589 1	1626 5	1663 2
1590 2	1627 6	1664 .. 10
1591 3	1628 .. 14	1665 5
1592 .. 11	1629 2	1666 6
1593 6	1630 3	1667 7
1594 7	1631 4	1668 8
1695 1	1632 .. 12	1669 3
1596 9	1633 7	1670 4
1597 4	1634 1	1671 5
1598 5	1635 2	1672 .. 13
1599 6	1636 .. 10	1673 1
1600 .. 14	1637 5	1674 2
1601 2	1638 6	1675 3
1602 3	1639 7	1676 .. 11
1603 4	1640 8	1677 6
1604 .. 12	1641 3	1678 7
1605 7	1642 4	1679 1
1606 1	1643 5	1680 9
1607 2	1644 .. 13	1681 4
1608 .. 10	1645 1	1682 5
1609 5	1646 2	1683 6
1610 6	1647 3	1684 .. 14
1611 7	1648 .. 11	1685 2
1612 8	1649 6	1686 3
1613 3	1650 7	1687 4
1614 4	1651 1	1688 .. 12
1615 5	1652 9	1689 7
1616 .. 13	1653 4	1690 1
1617 1	1654 5	1691 2
1618 2	1655 6	1692 .. 10
1619 3	1656 .. 14	1693 ... 5

1694 6	1722 5	1750 5
1695 7	1723 6	1751 6
1696 8	1724 .. 14	1752 .. 14
1697 3	1725 2	1753 2
1698 4	1726 3	1754 3
1699 5	1727 4	1755 4
1700 6	1728 .. 12	1756 .. 12
1701 7	1729 7	1757 7
1702 1	1730 1	1758 1
1703 2	1731 2	1759 2
1704 .. 10	1732 .. 10	1760 .. 10
1705 5	1733 5	1761 5
1706 6	1734 6	1762 6
1707 7	1735 7	1763 7
1708 8	1736 8	1764 8
1709 3	1737 3	1765 3
1710 4	1738 4	1766 4
1711 5	1739 5	1767 5
1712 .. 13	1740 .. 13	1768 .. 13
1713 1	1741 1	1769 1
1714 2	1742 2	1770 2
1715 3	1743 3	1771 3
1716 .. 11	1744 .. 11	1772 .. 11
1717 6	1745 6	1773 6
1718 7	1746 7	1774 7
1719 1	1747 1	1775 1
1720 9	1748 9	
1721 4	1749 4	

THE MILLENNIAL GAP

The numbering of years from Jesus' birth has resulted in a gap that goes beyond the dispute about the third millennium start date, January 1, 2000 or January 1, 2001.

In 664, the Synod of Whitby accepted the recommendations of the monk Dionysius Exiguus, who created the system of counting years that we use today, starting from the year he (mistakenly) calculated Jesus was born. However, he was off by more than four years, as Herod, ruler of Judea when Jesus was born, died in 4 BC, and Jesus' own unrecorded birth must have occurred a year or two earlier. Therefore, Jesus' birth would have occurred around 5 or 6 BC. **Source:** *New York Times*, January 1, 1999.

HOLIDAYS AND OBSERVANCES IN GERMAN - SPEAKING AREAS

•**January 1:** *Neujahrstag, 1. Januar* (New Year); New Years Day is celebrated with fireworks and parties on New Year's Eve (*Silvester* or *Sylvester*); observed in Christendom since the sixth century; a legal holiday

•**January 6:** *Heilige drei Könige* (Holy Three Kings), *Epiphanias*; Epiphany; observed in Austria, Baden-Württemberg, and Bavaria in Germany, and in Catholic areas of Switzerland; since the ninth century A.D.

•**February 2:** *Maria Lichtmeß.* In the religious calendar this day commemorates the fortieth day after Jesus' birth when his mother Mary underwent ritual cleansing ceremonies in the temple. The English name is Candlemas. The day was also celebrated by farmhands, with feasting and merrymaking because it was the day when they were paid. Also it was believed to be the day when the weather for the next four (or six) weeks could be determined. One of the maxims/verses known by the peasants was, *Sonnt sich der Dachs in der Lichtmeßwoche/Geht er auf vier Wochen wieder zu Loche* (If the badger can bask in the sun during Candlemas week, /He'll go back into his hole for four more weeks.)

•**February 3:** *Maria Reinigung*; Purifica-tion

•**February/March:** *Aschermittwoch;* Ash Wednesday; first day of Lent (*Fasten*), 46 days before Easter

•**February/March:** *Fastnacht*; Shrove Tuesday; the day before Ash Wednesday

•**February/March:** *feister Sonntag*; fat Sunday; last Sunday before Lent

•**February/March:** *Rosenmontag;* 42 days before Easter; the climax of the *Karneval* celebrations, especially in the Rhineland

•**March 19:** *Josefstage*; Feast of St. Joseph

•**March 25:** *Verkündigung*; Annunciation

•**March/April:** *Palmsonntag*; Palm Sunday; Sunday before Easter

•**March/April:** *grüner Donnerstage*; Maundy Thursday; Thursday before Easter

•**March/April:** *Karfreitag, Stiller Freitag*; Good Friday; Friday before Easter, a legal holiday; observance of the crucifixion of Jesus; since the second century A.D.; the week before Easter is called "*Karwoche*"

•**March/April:** *Ostersonntag* (Easter Sunday); commemorates the resurrection of Jesus; Sunday after the first full moon after March 21 (always between March 22 and April 25); the basis for all movable Church feast days; established by the Council of Nicäa in 325 A.D; a legal holiday.

•**March/April:** *Ostermontag* (Easter Monday); Monday after Easter; a legal holiday

•**March/April:** *Quasimodogeniti*; Low Sunday; Sunday after Easter

•**May 1:** *Tag der Arbeit, Maifeiertag* (Labor Day, May Day); celebrated in most of Europe; a legal holiday; observed since 1890

•**May 11-15:** *Kalte Sophie* (Cold Sophie). The saints of the church calendar whose days are observed during this period are called *die Eisheiligen*, or the "Ice-Saints" (May 11, Mamertus; May 12, Pankraz; May 13, Servatius; May 14, Bonifatius; May 15, Sophie). The advice is not to plant anything sensitive to frost in the garden before *die Kalte Sophie* ("Cold Sophie") is over.

•**May/June:** *Christi Himmelfahrt* (Ascension Day); fortieth day after Easter, always on a Thursday; observed in Catho-lic regions; began in the fourth century A.D.; a legal holiday

•**May/June:** *Pfingstsonntag* (Whitsunday); also called Pentecost Sunday (*Pfingsten*) or Whitsun in English;

seventh Sunday after Easter; the season from Pentecost Sunday to Advent; observed since about 130 A.D; a legal holiday

•**May/June:** *Pfingstmontag* (Whit-monday); Monday after *Pfingsten*; *Pfingstsonntag* and *Pfingstmontag* fall between May 9 and June 13; a legal holiday.

•**May/June:** *Fronleichnam* (Corpus Christi Day); first Sunday after Pfingsten; a legal holiday only in the states of Baden Württemberg, Bavaria, Hessen, North Rhine-Westphalia, Rhineland-Palatinate; it is a holiday in communities in Saxony and Thuringia which have a majority of Catholic inhabitants; since 1254, pre-scribed by Urban IV.

•**June:** *Kindertag* (Day of the Child), celebrated on the first weekend in June since 1990 to promote more friendliness to children

•**June 24:** *Johannistage (Johannis des Täufers);* Feast of St. John the Baptist

•**June 27:** *Siebenschläfer-Tag:* ("Seven Sleepers Day"). A day known for its weather-forecasting qualities, June 27 was a saints' day commemorating seven young Christian men who were suppos-edly persecuted by the Romans for their faith. They fled into a cave, where they fell asleep while the cave was walled shut behind them. Almost 200 years later, the cave was opened, and the sleepers awoke, but died soon thereafter with halos around their heads, showing they had become saints. In the eighteenth century, the term *Siebenschläfer* came to be used as another name for a dor-mouse (*Haselmaus*) known for its long hibernation. Now the prediction is that if it rains on June 27, it will continue to rain for seven more weeks.

•**July 2:** *Heimsuchung Mariä;* Visitation of Maria. Legend has it that rain on this day predicts a long rainy spell.

•**August 1:** *Bundesfeier,* Swiss National Day; celebrates the founding of the Swiss Confederation, with fireworks, Alpine bonfires, lantern-lit nighttime parades, and political speeches

•**August 15:** *Mariä Himmelfahrt* (As-sumption of the Blessed Virgin); obser-vance of Mary's ascension into heaven; a legal holiday only Bavaria (in predom-inantly Catholic communities) and Saar-land; celebrated since Pope Pius XII announced the dogma of Mary's Assump-tion in 1950

•**September:** *Buß und Bettag* (Day of Repentance and Prayer); third Sunday in September; day of meditation in the Lutheran Church in Switzerland.

•**October 3:** *Tag der deutschen Einheit* (Day of German Unity); became a legal holiday in 1992; celebrates the official date of German reunification in 1990. It replaces the older June 17 holiday of the same name (marking the date of the East German workers' uprising in 1953). Although November 9 (the date of the opening of the Berlin Wall) might have seemed a more logical date for a "day of unity," it was unfortunately the anni-versary of the Kristallnacht ("night of glass") when Nazis systematically smashed storefronts of Jewish businesses.

•**October:** *Erntedankfest* (Harvest Thanksgiving); celebrated in many rural areas on the first Sunday in October (or the first Sunday after Michaelmas, which is September 29); not a legal holiday. In wine-growing areas, the *Winzer Fest* celebrates the the picking of the last grapes of the season.

•**October 26:** *Flag Day* in Austria, ob-serving the restoration of full sovereignty after World War II and declaration of neutrality on October 26, 1955.

•**October 31:** *Reformationstag*; Feast of the Reformation; only in states of Brandenburg, Mecklenburg-Vorpom-mern, Saxony, Saxony-Anhalt, and Thuringia

•**October:** *Königsfest Christi:* Feast of

Christ the King; first Sunday of October

•November 1: *Allerheiligen,* All Saints Day; observed in Austria and the Catholic regions of Germany and Switzerland (in Germany, a legal holiday only in Baden-Württemberg, Bavaria, North Rhine-Westphalia, Rhineland Palatinate, and Saarland); commemoration of all saints who are not honored with a saint's day of their own; since 835 A.D. In some rural districts, a woven straw decoration (*Heiligenstritzel*) is put outside the door as a reminder that the harvest has been gathered safely.

•November 2: *Allerseelen*; All Souls Day; Catholic memorial day observed by making supplication for the souls in purga-tory; also a day for decorating graves of relatives. At mid-day, the church bells ring for an hour to "free" the souls for a few hours until the bells are rung the next day. It was common to give bread to children and the poor on All Souls' Day; godparents gave their godchildren specially shaped pastries (*Seelenwecken, Seelenzelten,* or *Seelenzöpfe*). Children would go from house to house receiting All Souls' Day rhymes in return for the bread.

•November/December: *Buß und Bettag* (Day of Repentance and Prayer); Wednes-day before *Totensonntag* (Memorial Sun-day), observed as a day of meditation in the Lutheran Church in Germany; intro-duced in Prussia in 1816, then spread through Protestant areas; no longer a federal legal holiday since 1995 except in the state of Saxony

•November 11: *Martinstag* (St. Martin's Day); named after Bishop Martin of Tours, credited with giving half his cloak to a beggar. The day is celebrated with lantern marches and a meal of roast goose. St. Martin was said to have tried to hide in a flock of geese because he felt unworthy to be made bishop, but the geese began to cackle and gave him away. A more likely reason is that taxes were originally due at Martinmas, and,

since geese had been fattened at this time of year, they were often used to pay taxes in kind, just as eggs were given at Easter.

•November: *Volkstrauertag,* national (Protestant) day of mourning; Sunday before *Totensonntag* (two Sundays before the start of Advent); dedicated to victims of the National Socialist terror and the dead of the two World Wars. The Day of National Mourning was first established in 1922 in honor of the victims of World War I. Since 1952, it has been dedicated to the principles of atonement, understanding, and peace in the world.

•November: *Totensonntag,* or *Ewig-keitssonntag*; last Sunday before the first Advent; memorial day; Protestants visit graves of the dead and remember the dead in church services.

•November/December: Advent; starts on fourth Sunday before Christmas

•December 6: *Nikolaustag* (St. Nicholas Day); not a legal holiday; the day when Sankt Nikolaus (not Santa Claus) brings small gifts to children

•December 8: *Mariä Empfängnis, unbe-fleckte Empfängnis*; Day of Immaculate Conception; since the eighteenth century

•December 24: *Heiligabend, Weih-nachtsabend,* Christmas Eve; the most important day of the Christmas season; presents are exchanged

•December 25: *Weihnachtstag,* Christmas Day (commemoration of the birth of Jesus); celebrated on this day since 354 A.D.; a legal holiday in Germany

•December 26: *Weihnachtstag* (Second Christmas); a legal holiday in Germany

Sources:

◆Hyde Flippo, *The German Way.* Passport Books, Lincolnwood, Illinois, 1997.

◆German Research Association, *The German Connection.* Vol. 16, No. 1, January 1992.

◆Susan Steiner ed., *Federal Republic of Germany: Questions and Answers.* German Information Center, New York, 1996.

◆Rainer Thumshirn, "The Groundhog Knows," *Der Blumenbaum*, Vol. 11, No. 3, 1994.

OKTOBERFEST

Munich's Oktoberfest, a traditional celebration dominated by beer tents, music, and parades, is scheduled each year for 16 days, beginning on the third Saturday in September and running through the first Sunday in October.

The *Oktoberfest* tradition began in 1810 with a horserace on October 17 with a parade of military riders, music, and waving flags, on the occasion of the wedding feast of Bavarian King Maximilian Joseph's son, Prince Ludwig, and Princess Therese of Saxony-Hildburghausen.

The *Theresienwiese* (Therese's Meadow) where the *Oktoberfest* is held, is named after the bride. The citizens of Munich were invited to attend the festivities held in these fields in front of the city gates. The locals have since abbreviated the name simply to the "Wiesn."

The king, known as Max Josef, went so far as to invite Bavarian farmers, considered then as crude peasants, to join in the observance of the horse race in an attempt to revive patriotism, tradition, and the old ways. The decision to repeat the horse races in subsequent years gave rise to the tradition of the Oktoberfest.

Until the mid 1800s, the *Oktoberfest's* most popular attractions remained the horse race and the marksmen competitions. By the mid nineteenth century, the *Oktoberfest* became more of a country fair, where the beer tents were added.Today's *Oktoberfest* horse race is held ten miles from the beer tents, at the Reims track.

The opening parade, *Wies'n Einzug der Festwirte und Brauereien* (Meadow Appearance of Festival Hosts and Breweries), dates back to 1887. The main attraction is the horse-drawn beer wagons.

On the second day, Sunday, the *Oktoberfest Trachten und Schützen* (Oktoberfest Costume and Marksmen's) parade, which goes back to 1835, takes place, the largest *Oktoberfest* parade.

For more information about Munich's Oktoberfest, call the German National Tourist Office (see index).

Sources:
◆Dennis Burnside, "Oktoberfest Horses," *German Life*, October/November, 1996.
◆*Pazifische Rundschau*, September 1999.

KARNEVAL, FASCHING

The pre-Lenten celebrations noted for their high revelry (comparable to Mardi Gras in New Orleans), held mostly in Roman Catholic areas of Germany, are usually referred to in English as "*Karneval*," or "*Carneval*", but they carry different names in different areas.

For example, the festivities are known as *Karneval* in the Rhineland, North Rhine-Westphalia, and New Brandenburg; *Fassenacht* in Mainz; *Fasching* in Bavaria; *Fastnacht* or *Fasnet* in southwest Germany; *Fastloovend* in Cologne; and *Fasnacht* in Basel, Switzerland, where, incidentally, the celebration occurs *after* the onset of Lent (on the Monday following Ash Wednesday).

The differences are not merely in the titles of the events but in the manner in which they are celebrated, with each pre-Lenten celebration differing widely from one region to another.

The celebration is also known as *die närrische Zeit* (the foolish time). Those taking part in it are the *Narren* (the fools).

In Germany, *Carneval* officially begins on the 11th day of the 11th month, at 11:11 am, although it does not really get going until the New Year or sometime after Epiphany. The highpoint of

Fasching is *Rosenmontag* (the name derived from *rasender Montag,* or raving Monday), with parades and *Prunksitzungen* (gala meetings). On the stroke of midnight on *Faschingsdienstag* (Shrove Tuesday), all celebrations must end, as the clock ticks over into *Aschermittwoch* (Ash Wednesday), the first day of Lent.

Major locations famous for their *Karneval* spectaculars are Aachen, Cologne, Düsseldorf, Mainz, Munich, and Münster.

In Kitzingen (Bavaria), the *Deutsches Fastnachtmuseum,* at Hindenburgring Süd 3, displays dramatic costumes and masks used in *Fastnacht* celebrations.

Sources:

♦Jennifer M. Russ, *German Festivals and Customs,* Oswald Wolff, London, 1983.

♦*Cultural Life in the Federal Republic of Germany,* Inter Nationes, Bonn, 1993.

♦*German Life,* February/March, 1999.

♦ "Fools for Fasching," by Doris Faden, *German Life,* February/March 2000.

GERMAN - AMERICAN STEUBEN PARADE

The German-American Steuben Parade of New York takes place on the third Saturday of September. The name Steuben was selected to honor General Friedrich Wilhelm von Steuben's contributions to America.

One of the best known German immigrants, Baron von Steuben is credited with major contributions toward American victory in the Revolutionary War against the British.

(For information on the history and genealogy of Friedrich Wilhelm von Steuben, see "Baron von Steuben," *Der Blumenbaum* (Sacramento German Genealogy Society), Vol. 14, No. 3, 1997)

GERMAN - AMERICAN DAY

German-American Day was first instituted on October 6, 1983, the tricentennial of German emigration to America.

It was on October 6, 1683 that a group of Mennonites from Krefeld disembarked in Philadelphia from the *Concord* (the "German Mayflower"). This constituted the first group immigration of Germans to America.

The German-American Joint Action Committee (GAJAK) was formed with the main objective of promoting German-American events in Washington, D.C. and nationwide. It is made up of the German-American National Congress (DANK), the United German American Committee of the U.S.A., and the Steuben Society of America.

The designation "German" is used in a cultural, not in a political sense, thus including the German-speaking Swiss, Alsatians, Austrians, Germans from Eastern Europe, and German Jews.

Source: Ruth Reichmann, "A Celebration of German Heritage," *Indiana German Heritage Society Newsletter,* Vol. 14, No. 4, 1997.

CHRISTMAS IN GERMANY

Although the birthday of Jesus is dominent in most German Christmas traditions, they also incorporate many pre-Christian ideas of both Germanic and Roman origins.

Celebration of the longest and shortest day of the year is known from many ancient cults. What is December 25 in today's calendar was observed as the birthday of *Mithras,* a deity of sun and light of Indian and Persian origin, whose cult spread westward and encompassed most of the Mediterranean region. From there Roman legions brought it to

Germania.

There it coincided with the local Germanic celebration of winter solstice called *Julfest.* During these 12 to 20 days of festivities, the souls of the deceased were honored, as they were believed to haunt the earth for this period. Also, it was a time to pray and make offerings for the fertility of the fields in the year to come.

Early Christians first celebrated Jesus' birthday on January 6, but in 354 AD the date was moved up to December 25, to coincide with the heathen festivities for winter solstice, which the Romans had called *dies natalis invicti solis* (birthday of the undefeated sun). In early Germany, the festivities, now christianized, were called *ze wîhen nachten* (the holy nights) which became *Weihnachten* in modern German. The intermingling of these three sources can still be recognized in the traditions of the season.

Advent season

The first of the four Sundays of Advent marks the beginning of the Christmas season and the church year. Originally a time of fasting, it became the time when the faithful prepared for Christmas.

◆ The *Adventskranz* (Advent wreath): A relatively new tradition of Protestant origin, credited to Johann Heinrich Wichern. The founder of the *Innere Mission* (a Protestant charity organization) is said to have introduced the first one in 1860 during a church service in his native Hamburg. Today, mostly red candles and ribbons are used, replacing the original lilac ones which represented the liturgical color of the season. The wreath is made of fir twigs with four candles, the first of which is lighted on the first Sunday, two on the second, three on the third, until all four are burning together on the fourth Sunday of Advent.

◆ *Adventskranzweihe:* a service, where the church's wreath is consecrated.

◆ *Adventskalender:* A poster-calendar that helps children with the countdown toward Christmas. It is a poster, usually showing a Christmas-related scene, with 24 "windows," one to be opened every day, starting on December 1. When the "windows" are opened, they reveal child-pleasing pictures, candies, or little pouches numbered from 1 to 24 containing presents or a ladder with 24 rungs which a little figure climbs, one a day.

◆ *Adventsmarkt, Adventsbasar, Weihnachtsmarkt,* and *Christkindlsmarkt:* Christmas markets of which every town has at least one. The *Christkindlesmarkt* of Nürnberg, more than 300 years old, is particularly well known. Besides the usual Christmas tree decorations and statues for the nativity scenes, many of the following items are typically sold at these markets:

◆ *Lebkuchen:* Gingerbread from Nürnberg, world famous for centuries. The bakery of Haeberlein und Metzger, which still exists today, was founded in 1492. A purity law, similar to the one for brewing beer, existed for genuine *Lebkuchen*: Only honey, flour, and spices were to be used.

◆ *Zwetschgenmännlein (-weiblein)*: Little men (and women) made of dried plums (for limbs), dried figs (body) and a walnut (head) with pieces of wire as a "skeleton." The more elaborate ones even come with dresses.

◆ The *Räuchermännlein:* A carved, hollowed out wooden figure which can be separated in the middle to insert a glowing piece of incense. Rejoined, the smoke comes out of the mouth to create the impression of the figure smoking its pipe.

◆ *Rauschgoldengel*: A winged girlish figure wearing a long velvet gown, a crown and long blond curls, symbolizing the angel who brought to the shepherds the message of Christ's birth. Legend has it that the first such angel was made by a Nürnberg doll maker in memory of his daughter, killed in the Thirty Years War.

◆Kastanien or Maroni: The edible variety of the sweet or Spanish chestnut, which are roasted and sold by street vendors. They go very well with *Glühwein*, hot red wine to which spices and sugar are added.

◆Früchtebrot, or Kletzenbrot: A very sweet and rich fruitcake, consisting mostly of dried fruit in a shell of dough.

Christmas pageants, other traditions

◆ Adventssingen, or Krippenspiele: Christmas pageants. In eleventh-century Germany, the church began performing mystery plays depicting Bible stories as a means of educating a largely illiterate population. The plays would often start with the expulsion of Adam and Eve from the Garden of Eden, which was then linked to the coming of Christ, the savior. Others started with the Archangel Gabriel's annunciation. But all featured the popular elements: seeking a room at the inn, the shepherds' adoration, the assassination of the children in Bethlehem, the three wise men and – in the end – the flight to Egypt on the donkey.

Originally the actors were priests and monks, but more and more laymen took part, who even produced plays of their own, which then often included comic elements and all kinds of folklore.

Today, there are many such performances, ranging from amateur groups playing on an improvised stage in the village tavern or church to highly artistic and professional events at the largest concert halls. **◆ Anglöckeln, Klöpflgeher, Glöcklisinger, Kurrendesänger, and Bosseln:** Terms from various German regions describing groups of Christmas carolers who begin wandering from door to door on November 30, St. Andrews Day. After knocking on the door (*klopfen*) or ringing the door-

bell (*Glocke*) to call out the inhabitants, they sing for gifts. Some sources say this symbolizes the angel bringing the message of Christ's birth to Mary; other sources connect the "knocking" to secret signals used by the first Christians to gain entry at their places of assembly. Whatever the spiritual background, for a long time it was one of the few ways by which the poor could earn a meal during the winter season.

The duration of this tradition today varies widely and can last until Epiphany on January 6. Today it is mostly performed by children, who try to collect gifts for themselves or donations for some charity.

◆ Engelamt or Rorate: Daily special early morning masses in the Christmas season, where Christmas carols are sung and candles light the church. *Rorate* derives its name from a Latin song *Rorate coeli . . .* (thaw, oh heavens . . .). The service centered around the angel's annunciation. Every family who could afford it asked (and paid) for such an *Engelamt* to be celebrated. Tradition demands that every worshipper should bring his own candle and place it on the pew before him. Also, every family of the parish is expected to be represented by at least one member.

The *Quempassingen* is a variation in Pomerania, Saxony and Silesia, performed by groups of children located throughout the church who sing alternately. This name is derived from another song, *Quem pastores laudavere . . .* (He, whom the shepherds praised . . .).

◆Herbergssuche, or Frauentragen: A procession reminding people of the story of Mary and Joseph vainly seeking a room at the inn. In some local traditions, this is symbolized when a statue of Mary is carried through the village at night and each family hosts it for one night.

◆Krippe füllen: A tradition designed especially for children. A manger is placed in the living room on the First Sunday of

Advent. For every time they have been nice, have helped in the household, or have otherwise been considerate of others, children were allowed to place a straw into the manger. The more the straw accumulated by Christmas Eve, the more comfortable the Christchild would be.

♦*Weihnachtsbäckerei* (Christmas goodies): *Plätzchen, Stollen*

Plätzchen (cookies) come in literally hundreds of different varieties and shapes. Recipes often are passed on from generation to generation as are the cookie cutters and models to produce them.

Christstollen is the standard Christmas cake. It is made of a yeast dough with raisins, almonds, and candied lemon and orange peels, and dusted with powdered sugar. The best recipe is said to originate from Dresden.

Not only were these goodies baked and stocked in large quantities for guests and carolers, but the supply had to feed the family as well, as tradition (especially in northern Germany) forbade baking during the twelve days between Christmas and Epiphany.

Other Pre-Christian traditions

A wide variety of mythical figures do their haunting during the long nights of December. It is not always clear how and where they originated, as sometimes different and even conflicting characteristics are ascribed to the same figure. Mostly they reward good children and punish naughty and lazy ones. These are some of them:

♦The *Pelzmärtel*, found in Frankonia and Swabia, is a combination of St. Martin and St. Nicholas.

♦The *Berchtel* and *Schiache Perchten* are fantastic animal-shaped demons who haunt children in Bavaria and Austria.

♦The *Budelfrau* in Lower Austria is dressed all in white.

♦The *Busebrecht* of the Augsburg region is a woman dressed in ragged black clothes who dusts unsuspecting passers-by with flour.

♦*Hans Trapp* in the Upper Rhine Valley and the Alsace is the scary companion of the *Christkind*. He is named for Hans Dratt, a sixteenth-century Palatinate whose cruel rule made him a nightmare.

♦*St. Peter* and *Ruprecht* visit children in the Erzgebirge.

♦The *Erbsbär* (pea-bear) wears a costume decorated with dried pea plants. He is accompanied by an angel and a devil.

♦ St. Nicholas, called *Schimmelreiter,* appeared on a white horse in northern Germany.

♦The *Stutenfrau*, dressed all in white, brings cakes for the children of the Ucker-mark. Sometimes she is accompanied by three helpers also dressed in white and three others dressed in black. The latter performed wild dances while sweeping the floor with their brooms. If they managed to hit someone, this persons's good luck was swept away.

♦The *Rauhnächte* are a reminder of another belief carried over from heathen times (*rauch* = furry). During these nights the devil and other furry evil spirits and witches were thought to roam the earth. On the three major *Rauhnächte*, Christmas Eve, New Years Eve, and Epiphany (in today's calendar) those spirits are smoked out of houses, stables, barns, beehives, and fields with incense. During these twelve haunted nights, *Rübezahl* (in Silesia), *Frau Holle* (in Hessia) and *Frau Gode* (in Mecklenburg) might come to inspect the house. If they didn't find it clean and proper, they might destroy it. Also, all borrowed items had to be returned before the *Rauhnächte* began.

♦The twelve *Sperrnächte* or *Dunkelnächte* (barricaded or dark nights) refer to the same basic idea with a slight variation of dates as they occur from December 13-25 when in some regions it was customary to encircle with a rope the farm, or even an entire village with young men standing guard to prevent entry of evil spirits.

♦ *Julfriede* (Yuletime peace) also refers to the nights between December 24 and January 6, when in pre-Christian times all hostilities between individuals and tribes had to cease.

♦ *Losnächte* (*lozen* = old German for fortune-telling) are the nights of December 20, 24, and 31, when one might catch a glimpse of the future. For girls the most interesting question seems to have been when and to whom they would be married. These were some of the ways to find out:

– *Scheitlklauben* required one to pick up a handful of wooden kindlings and count them. An even number told you that you would get married next year.

– Girls throw a shoe over their shoulder; if its tip points toward the door, a bridegroom will enter through it next year.

– Girls also could go out into the orchard at midnight to shake a plum tree. If a dog barked, the direction from which the sound originated indicated the direction from which a bridegroom could be expected.

– During the *Thomasnacht* on December 20 (St. Thomas Night), girls kick their bedsteads and ask St. Thomas to show them their future sweetheart and husband in their dreams that night:

> *Bettstatt, i tritt di,*
> *Heiliger Thomas, i bitt di,*
> *Laß mir erscheinen*
> *Den Herzallerliebsten meinen!*

(Bedstead, I hit you, Saint Thomas, I beg you, let my dearest sweetheart appear to me.)

– *Vielliebchen* (Dearest Love) is a game for two utilizing hazelnuts or almonds which sometimes house two kernels instead of the regular single one. The two participants then each eat one of the twin kernels. The winner is determined the next day; it is the one who first remembers to greet the other saying "*Guten Morgen, Vielliebchen*" (Good morning,

dearest love!"). The winner then receives a small gift or is granted a wish by the loser.

Special Dates before Christmas

♦ **December 1**: The day Sodom and Gomorrha are said to have perished is an especially perilous day, requiring great caution. You have to finish all the chores you begin, and you must not make any mistake – otherwise this would be a bad omen for the next year.

♦ **December 4**: St. Barbara, the saint commemorated on this day, lived in Nikomedeia, the ancient Kingdom of Bithynia's capital, which at that time was one of the world's most prosperous cities. Barbara, the king's daughter, converted to Christianity against her father's will, who sentenced her to death. She was tortured and died as a martyr on December 4 of 237 AD (other sources say 306 or 317 AD). On her grave, flowers are said to have started blooming on every Christmas day.

In reverence to St. Barbara, branches are cut off a tree (mostly cherry, but also plum, apple, or pear) on December 4 and placed in a vase with water in a heated room. Usually blossoms appear on the *Barbarazweige* by Christmas.

♦ **December 6**: St. Nikolaus (St. Nicholas) commemorates Bishop Nicholas from Myra, the capital of the Kingdom of Lykia in the fourth century. Some sources say there was another Bishop Nicholas in southern Italy two centuries later. As both were benefactors to the poor and oppressed, probably events from the lives of both these holy men were merged into the figure of St. Nicholas. Among these deeds was the rescue of three poor girls from prostitution by giving them dowries so they could marry. He did this by throwing three balls of gold through the chimney of their father's house, where they fell into the girls' stockings which were hung to dry at the fireplace. (St Nicholas is often depicted holding these three golden balls.)

In another legend, St. Nicholas revived three scholastics who had been killed by a cannibal.

In the Middle Ages, starting in Bari, Italy, where the saint's relics were kept, out of these legends evolved St. Nicholas as the bringer of gifts to poor children and students. Originally only boys were the recipients – girls received their gifts from St. Lucia.

As the custom spread, its contents shifted and blurred somewhat, especially in Germany. There, in predominantly Catholic regions, the Bishop appears as a fatherly figure with a long white beard, dressed in a red or white robe, wearing a mitre and carrying both a bishop's staff and a big book containing records of the children's behavior. St. Nicholas is accompanied by a wild, furry bugbear or hobgoblin called *Krampus*, who takes over the job of scaring and punishing the not-so-good children. The switch they use originally was not a tool for punishment, but touching a person with it was meant as a blessing.

This tradition of St. Nicholas' visit is very much alive and occurs mostly on the eve of St. Nicholas Day. Families ask friends to masquerade and make an appearance or hire a Bishop and Krampus through the job exchange for students. The pair also shows up in elementary school and even the braver children often start wondering if they might not be "real" after all.

Krampuslauf or *Klausentreiben* is an event on the same night in Alpine regions, most notably around Salzburg, Berchtes-gaden, and Füssen, where the *Krampus* (sometimes also called Klaus) appear without the benevolent St. Nicholas. Groups of older boys and young men masquerade in black furs, and with terrifying face masks they roam the streets after dark, whipping anybody who doesn't manage to escape.

♦**December 8**: *Mariä Empfängnis* (the day of Mary's Immaculate Conception)

used to be a legal holiday in predominantly Catholic regions of Germany, but is no longer. (However, it is still a holiday in Austria.) In the evening special masses are celebrated. This was the day when baking bread, cookies, cakes, and fruitcakes for Christmas started.

♦**December 13**: St. Lucia's day honors a martyred saint from Syracuse, Sicily. Her name is derived from Latin *lux* (light), and paying reverence to her memory merged with a Germanic goddess of light. In Scan-dinavia, St. Lucia is a gentle girlish figure who brings gifts to children, formerly only to girls. However, in the Alpine regions of Bavaria and Austria, this figure became the *Luzelfrau*, a scary old woman who raged through villages in search of lazy and ill-behaved children, threatening to cut open their bellies and stuff them with straw, pebbles, or whatever dirt she swept from the ground. For this reason, streets, courtyards, barns, stables and houses were carefully cleaned on the eve of December 13, so that the *Luzelfrau* would not find any material for her evil intentions.

A less dramatic tradition is the planting of *Lucienweizen* and *Lucienlinsen* (wheat and lentils) in a plate of wet cotton. Kept moist and warm, they would sprout by Christmas and could be used as "fields" in the nativity scene.

♦**December 17: The** *Lazarustag* (day of Lazarus, the poor leper from the Gospel of St. Luke) reminds people not to forget to visit and bring presents to the sick and frail on Christmas. In many predominantly Catholic regions, at 3 pm, all church bells are tolled because Christmas is but one week away (*Christkindl-Einläuten*).

♦**December 21**: The day of *St. Thomas* also is the day of winter solstice, the year's longest night and shortest day. *St. Thomas* is commemorated on this day because he was the last one of the apostles to become convinced of Jesus' resurrection – he was the one who for the longest time remained in the "night of unbelief and doubt." These are some of the traditions practiced on this day:

+ *Thomasfaulpelz* or *Domesel* (lazybone or donkey of St. Thomas day) were names given to the last person to get out of bed and for the last student to appear in class on that particular morning in Westphalia.

+ The *Rittbergische Hochzeit* (Rittberg wedding), also in Westphalia, was an opulent meal served in the belief that if you ate well on St. Thomas day, you could expect to do so all of the next year.

+ The *Segensfrüchte* (blessed fruit) represent basically the same idea. In southern Germany, it is hoped that when a bowl of fruit, vegetables and nuts is placed on the table, a lack of them in the year to come will be prevented. Exchanging gifts of apples and nuts extended this wish to neighbors and friends.

+ *Blutiger Damerl* (Bavarian dialect for bloody Thomas) and *Schweinethomas* (St. Thomas' pig) may seem odd terms in connection with a saint. They refer to the tradition that demanded that on Bavarian farms, and also elsewhere, the whole family and the farmhands sat down to an opulent meal of roasted pork on Christmas day. The pig, especially raised and fattened for this occasion, was called the *Weihnachter* (Christmas pig). It was usually slaughtered on this day to have the meat and sausages ready by Christmas.

Trying to steal a farmer's *Weihnachter*, either alive or when it was butchered, worked about the same way as stealing the Maypole, in that only stealth and cunning were allowed, not bodily force. Very cautious owners even slept in the pig sty, so they could better guard their *Weihnachter*.

Christmas schedule and customs

Christmas in Germany consists of *Heiliger Abend* (Christmas Eve) and the *Erster und Zweiter Weihnachtsfeiertag* (first and second days of Christmas).

In the early afternoon of Christmas Eve, public life comes to a virtual standstill. Factories, offices, shops and most restaurants close, and buses, trains and airlines run on a very thinned-out schedule. Children are taken for a walk (or put in front of the TV) while the Christmas tree is decorated.

After darkness falls, the *Christkind* rings a bell as a sign that the candles on the tree are lit and the family should gather for the *Bescherung* (distribution of the gifts placed under the tree). Later, many families serve a traditional, rather modest dinner. Attending midnight mass is becoming increasingly popular again.

+ **December 25 and 26**: These are both legal holidays. The first day, generally, is more family-oriented and the main festive meal is served at noon. The second day is often used for visits.

– *Heiliger Abend* (Christmas Eve): Predominent in Christmas Eve observances are the Christmas tree and the gift-bringers.

The Christmas tree

– *Christbaum, Weihnachtsbaum* (Christmas tree): The decorated fir tree as the quintessential symbol of a German Christmas predates Christianity. Pagan cults practiced winter solstice rites using greenery, especially those plants that remained green throughout the winter which symbolized the triumphant return of spring. Christian *Krippenspiele* took over this idea. At center stage stood the play's only prop, an evergreen known as the Paradise Tree, hung with apples to represent the forbidden fruit.

In the fifteenth century, the church tried to ban the plays on the grounds that they had become too secular. As in other cases, the old customs proved impossible to suppress, and the Paradise Tree appeared in homes. First descriptions place it in the Alsace, Baden and the Rhineland-Palatinate.

Martin Luther, around 1520 or 1530

was the first German to gather his family around a candle-lit Christmas tree which became the Protestants' Christmas symbol – as opposed to the *Weihnachtskrippe* (nativity scene) in Catholic areas. (Even today, Christmas trees in Roman Catholic churches often remain without candles and other decorations.)

All the way into the nineteenth century in Bavaria, a decorated Christmas tree was considered proper for the upper class only. It made its entry into homes in general via the rich citizens of Nürnberg and the Royal Court of Munich. There, two Protestant queens were instrumental in its introduction, which gave many loyal Catholics reason to oppose this "Protestant stuff."

From Germany, the idea spread out over Europe and the world. The first American Christmas tree is said to have been put up in 1746 by German immigrants in Pennsylvania. It became more popular when Hessian mercenaries, who fought for the British in the War for Independence, spread their custom. At Aus-tria's Royal and Imperial Court in Vienna, the first Christmas tree was introduced by a German princess in 1816. A princess from Mecklenburg surprised her French husband with a Christmas tree in 1840. In England, Queen Victoria's German husband Albert helped spread the popularity of the new idea.

Christmas tree ornaments

Today, two basic categories of *Christbaumputz* (or *-schmuck* – Christmas tree ornaments) can be distinguished:

◆For a traditional, rural and folkloric tree, the ornaments are stars and angels made of straw, polished red apples, nuts and fir cones painted silver or golden, and an endless variety of wooden penny toys, cookies and gingerbread.

◆ For a more urban and up-scale tree, which became popular in the late nineteenth century, ornaments are *Christbaumkugeln* (glass balls) with paper-thin

walls lined with shiny silver, glass birds and other figures produced by the same technique as the balls, and *Lametta* (silver tinsel).

In both cases, wax candles in matching colors complete the setup. (Electric candles, while safer and easier to use, are frowned upon by purists.)

Sometimes (but only rarely) the forerunner of the Christmas tree can still be found in German homes. It is a triangular, pyramid-shaped contraption formed of four apples and sticks, decorated with can-dles and ribbons. In Bavaria, these are called *Paradeisl* (little paradise) and in the Erzgebirge *Weihnachtspyramide* (Christmas pyramid).

A *Gästebaum* (Christmas tree for guests) is sometimes placed near the front door, decorated with small packages which contain gifts. Guests are invited to choose a package of their choice.

Early in the twentieth century, a new tradition was started, when miniature Christmas trees were placed on graves and the can-dles lit on Christmas Eve.

Christbaumstehlen is a positively un-Christian tradition, in which Bavarian farmers steal their Christmas tree from somebody else's forest – even if they themselves own the largest forest around. It is just more fun.

Nativity scenes

Weihnachtskrippe (Nativity scene): *Krippe* literally means the feeding crib into which the holy infant was laid after birth. In a broader sense, it describes the nativity scene as a whole. The first of these was displayed in 1223 in St. Francis' church in Assisi, Italy. From there the idea spread throughout Italy and later over the Alps to Bavaria and Austria. As mentioned before, in these areas the nativity scene was a more important symbol for Christmas than the tree – both in churches and homes. Usually the scene was set up or unveiled in early December and the display rearranged as the story unfolded. The displays range from small modest stables to entire landscapes and towns and from miniature statues to almost life-sized ones. The scenery and the dress of the persons in it usually reflect local traditions.

The *Bayerisches Nationalmuseum* in Munich has a huge collection of nativity scenes with more than 8,000 statues from Italy, Austria, and Bavaria.

A Bavarian tradition connected with the *Krippe* is to put some straw into your bed on Christmas Eve to sleep on and be reminded how Christ spent his first night on earth.

Gift-bringers
♦ *Weihnachtsmann* and *Christkind*
These are the two mythical figures who supply that important part of Christmas: gifts.

The *Weihnachtsmann* (Christmas Man or Santa Claus) always prevailed in middle, northern and eastern Germany. He is the figure of St. Nicholas merged with older, demonic winter figures like *Knecht Ruprecht* and *Krampus,* who accompanied St. Nicholas. His general appearance with the hooded coat and the beard was created by Moritz von Schwind, who portrayed *Herr Winter*, a secular figure, in a print published in 1847 in Munich. As it was mostly children who were recipients of his attentions, in keeping with nineteenth century educational theories, the *Weihnachtsmann* not only brought gifts, but he also handed out punishments. His switch no longer was used to bless children, but to whip them.

Santa Claus, the American version of the *Weihnachtsmann*, is a similar, but less stern figure. It was created by political cartoonist Thomas Nast and first appeared in *Harper's Weekly* in 1863. Thomas Nast also created the Republican elephant and Uncle Sam.

Martin Luther substituted the *Heiliger Christ* (Holy Christ) for (until then) the sole and popular Catholic *St. Nikolaus as* the bringer of gifts. Out of

this figure grew the *Christkind* (Christmas child) that eventually took precedence over other bringers of gifts in western, southwestern and (only in this century) southern Germany. The *Christkind* is a mysterious figure who rarely makes any concrete appearances. If it does (as in the opening ceremony of Nürnberg's *Christkindlesmarkt*), it resembles a *Rauschgoldengel*. However, the *Christkind* is not identical with the newborn Jesus, as the name might suggest. The gifts the *Christkind* brings are deposited "secretly" beneath the Christmas tree, where they are "found" by the children.

Making children the main recipients of gifts also was Martin Luther's idea. He and other reformers wanted to cleanse Christmas from heathen practices, as well as Catholic ceremonies. Children were easier to re-educate; to win them over, the most attractive aspect of Christmas for them, the distribution of gifts, was moved up to Christmas Eve.

Christmas Eve mass
Christmette or Christnachtfeier (Christmas Eve Mass): A midnight mass concludes Christmas Eve. Usually this is the most festive and crowded service of the entire year, when the congregation, the choir, the organ, the orchestra with its brass instruments and all church bells join in the *Gloria in excelsis Deo.*

The world's most famous *Weihnachtslied* (Christmas carol), *Stille Nacht, Heilige Nacht* (Silent night, holy night) was created for such an occasion in 1818. In the small town of Oberndorf (near Salzburg), the organ had broken down. To avoid the unthinkable – a Christmas Eve mass without music – assistant priest Joseph Mohr took a poem he had written to his friend, teacher Franz Xaver Gruber, and asked him to set it to music so they could sing it together, to guitar accompaniment.

They never even began to realize that

their carol was to become the most universal of all songs, sung in almost every language.

And yet it was only by coincidence that it survived its premiere. A handwritten copy of the words and the musical notation found its way to the Zillertal in Tyrol, which had a strong musical tradition. It was the home of folk choirs that performed all over Europe and in this way spread "Silent Night" wherever they went.

Had it not been for the curiosity of the director of the Royal Court Choir of Berlin, where the song had become the favorite of King Friedrich Wilhelm IV of Prussia, who researched the origins of the carol, we might never have learned of Joseph Mohr, Franz Xaver Gruber, and the circumstances which brought about the creation of this song.

The success of this song, especially with Germany's middle class, is typical for the deeply sentimental, sweet and partially secularized idea of Christmas that is most often associated with Germany. It is the one that evolved during the *Biedermeier* period, the feeling of which "Silent Night" and these other songs reflect:
–1795: *Ihr Kinderlein kommet. . .* (Oh come, all ye children. . .)
–1816: *Oh du fröhliche, oh du selige . . .* (Oh you merry, oh you blessed Christmas time . . . .)
–1818: *Stille Nacht, Heilige Nacht* (Silent Night, Holy Night)
–1824: *Oh Tannenbaum . . .* (Oh Christmas tree)

Two days of Christmas
♦ *Weihnachtstag, Christtag, Erster Feier-tag:* The first day of Christmas comes as an anti-climax after the long build-up which culminates on Christmas Eve. It is mostly a day of church services, festive dining, admiring the Christmas tree and the presents – and rest.
♦ *Stephanitag, Zweiter Feiertag*: The second day of Christmas is the name day of St. Stephan, the first martyr. As he is the patron saint for horses and people working with horses, in Bavaria riders and horse-drawn carriages parade in his honor, coming to church to be blessed.

Just as on the second day of Easter and Pentecost, a young man was allowed to ask his prospective girlfriend to promenade in public with him. To find out the girl's answer to this proposal, the young man would come and ask her for a *Kletzenbrot* (fruitcake). If he was given one, the answer was "yes"; if it was refused, he had to try to find another girl.

Christmas meals
The *Mettenmahl* (Christmas Eve dinner) comes in two versions: before and after midnight mass.

As Christmas Eve is still within the fasting period, the meal in the early evening still was frugal. After midnight mass, a *Mettensuppe* was served at the festively decorated table. Sometimes an extra (empty) plate was added for the last member of the family to have passed away. The meal was prepared by an elderly grandmother or maid servant who was too weak for the walk to church. When a pig had been butchered, part of it was cooked for the soup which was served with ingredients like sausages or noodles. Soups were also made from dried fruit and served with deep-fried doughnuts. Fish soup also was popular. Another favorite (in Silesia) is *Heringssalat* (salad of herring), while *Bratwurst* or *Leberwurst* (liver sausage) with *Sauerkraut* and mashed potatoes was more popular in southern Germany. In northern Germany, people expressed their joy about the return to normal eating habits by calling Christmas Eve *Vullbuuksabend* (full belly evening).

Even today, in many families the tradition of a special Christmas Eve meal is observed, although mostly in a modified way.

For centuries, the most popular dish on Christmas day (for those who could afford it) was roasted pork – in remembrance of the wild boar served at ancient Germanic festivities – as the main part of the *Weihnachter* was served at noon. Second in popularity, and of more recent origin, is a roasted goose. Traditional side dishes for both are bread or potato dumplings and red cabbage. The carp appeared on German tables for Christmas since monks started to breed and raise them in ponds in medieval times. They are boiled either in a vinegar sauce (*Blaue Karpfen*: blue carp) or a sweet sauce of gingerbread, almonds, and raisins (*Böhmischer Karpfen* – Bohemian carp). A third variety is *Gebackener Karpfen* (deep fried).

More Christmas traditions

◆*Das Christkind anschießen* (to fire a salute for the Christchild) usually happens on Christmas Eve. Shortly before everybody goes to midnight mass, blanks are fired from all available handguns and special salute guns (*Böller*). For Catholic Bavarians, the Christ child was something like a royal prince and therefore deserved a royal salute. In the Berchtesgaden and Salzburg region, this tradition was (and still is) especially popular and is extended from a week before Christmas to New Years Eve, with the main event on Christmas Eve, when gunfire echoes from all elevations surrounding the villages and towns. More than a ton of gunpowder is said to be used up on such an evening. Children have been known to fill big keys with gunpowder and detonate them with blows of a big hammer. One farmer carried a loaded salute-gun in his rucksack when he attended mass – where it went off. In 1894, another farmer blew up his flour mill when he tried to grind his gunpowder more finely.

◆*Gastfreundschaft* (**Open House**) is a tradition that combines the memory of the yuletime peace, when everybody was made welcome in any house he entered, with that of the Holy Family that was turned away because there was "no room at the inn."

◆ **The** *Julklotz, Mettenbrocken,* **or** *Weih-nachtsscheit* (**Yule-log**) also originates with ancient Germanic winter rites of bonfires in honor of their gods. This big decorated log was gradually fed into the fire to keep it burning for twelve days. Later it decreased in size and had to burn only long enough for the family to return from midnight mass on Christmas Eve.

◆**Animals deserve special attention** at Christmas time, which is shown by feeding extra rations to cattle, horses, cats, and dogs. Birds are fed grain, seeds and nuts. Oxen and cows are believed to speak on Christmas Eve, a distinction awarded to them because they warmed the Christ child with their breath. However, nobody may listen to them.

◆**Even fields and trees** are included in the festivities. On Christmas Eve, or after Christmas, leftovers from meals and drinks are "fed" to them. Trees also were decorated, shaken or knocked upon or even hugged by girls to entice them to bear rich fruit.

◆**Fortune-telling** was a favorite pastime, as on some other days, on Christmas Eve before it was time for church. Some examples:

–Twelve nuts are lined up, one for each month of the year. (In some regions, four nuts are used, one for each season.) Cracked open, their contents, or lack of it, prophesied how fortunate the person would be in the respective month or season.

–Onions could predict the amount of rain in the year to come. They were cut in half and picked apart. Twelve such bowl-shaped pieces were named for the months, then salted. The amount of water which gathered in the halves overnight indicated the amount of rain that could be expected.

–Apples were used in many different ways. In Westphalia, when presented with an apple, one must eat it immediately, or soon run out of money. Cutting an apple in half without damaging the seeds means good luck. Girls had various ways to find out about their future husbands from the shape of peelings on Christmas Eve. Boys had it easier. All they had to do was sit in front of the house on Christmas morning and eat an apple. The first girl to come into sight would be their future bride.

Special days after Christmas

◆**December 27**: On this day the *Apostel und Evangelist Johannes* (St. John) is commemorated. Special powers are ascribed to Christ's favorite apostle, which are shown by his having drunk from a cup of poisoned wine without coming to harm. Therefore, wine is brought to church on this day to be blessed and used on special occasions during the year as *Johanniswein* (St. John's wine).

◆ **December 28**: The *Tag der unschuldigen Kinder* (day of innocent children) is the day when King Herod had all the young children executed, hoping to get rid of the rival "newborn king" – the Christ child. This merged with the Germanic belief that Frau Holle (a good-natured female spirit) haunted the skies together with the souls of all children to be born during the next year. A bowl of soup often was placed outside the door for them.

Since about 1300, in some regions children were given special attention and even allowed to "rule" the household for a day, doing and saying things to their parents which would get them into deep trouble on any other day.

◆ **December 26, 28**: These days are known as *Pfeffertage* or *Pfefferleinstage* (pepper days). In this context, this is not a reference to the oriental spice but to rough treatment. Beating someone with switches from an ash tree or a juniper bush (gently, one presumes) was a tradition in southern Germany and Austria which brought blessings and good luck.

Gratitude for being "peppered" was shown by a gift of *Pfefferkuchen* (gingerbread), a *Pfeffernuss* (cookie), or – for grownups – a glass of *Pfefferbranntwein* (brandy).

The new year

Silvester/Neujahr (New Year's Eve/ New Year's Day): These holidays are celebrated during the Christmas season, but they are actually not part of it,

The Three Kings, Epiphany (January 6): *Dreikönigstag, Heilige Drei Könige, Erscheinungsfest, Epiphanias* (Three Kings Day, Holy Three Kings, Day of Apparition, Epiphany):

January 6 is a double holiday. The first Christians celebrated it as the day of Christ's baptism and his apparition as God and King (*Epiphania Domini*). It also is the day when the three wise men or magicians (in German they mostly are called "Kings") from the Orient, guided by the comet, found the Christ child. Because of their long voyage, they became the patron saints for travelers.

If a guesthouse is named *Zur Krone* (the crown), *Zum Stern* (the star), *Zum Mohren* (the moor), or *Zu den Drei Königen* (the three kings) – as many all over Germany are – it is named for the three wise men.

Their relics were brought to Cologne in 1163, where the gigantic Gothic cathedral was built to house them.

From New Years Day to January 6, the *Sternsinger* (star-singers) roam the streets. They are similar to the *Klöckler*, only now the groups are dressed as the three wise men, one of them with a face blackened with shoe polish or soot, and a fourth person who carries the comet before them. Today, these groups often collect money for a local charity.

After having received their gifts, they chalk a blessing for the new year onto the top of the door frame. For example, for the year 2001 the blessing would read thus: 20 + C + M + B+ 01, the abbreviation of *Christus Mansionem Benedicet*

(Latin for "May Christ bless this house"). People, especially in rural areas, who did not know Latin, interpreted the letters C + M + B as the abbreviations of the Three Wise Men's biblical names of Caspar, Melchior and Balthasar.

A tradition peculiar to this day is eating the *Bohnenkuchen* (bean cake) which is baked in many different forms. A bean is hidden inside and the person who finds it in his slice is the *Bohnenkönig* (bean-king) for the day, who then selects his queen. The whole household has to act as a "Royal Court" at their command. In some regions, the "Royal Couple" is determined by a bean and a pea – or two beans, one black and one white.

According to the church calendar, the Christmas season ends with Epiphany day on January 6. (In fact, Epiphany day was New Years day until 1582 when Pope Gregory moved it up to January 1.) The Christmas tree is emptied; however, the tradition to burn it became hard to observe in modern homes without ovens or fireplaces.

In rural Bavaria, Christmas trees were often kept until February 2, *Mariä Lichtmeß* (Candlemas Day), commemorating the fortieth day after Jesus' birth, when his Mother Mary underwent ritual cleansing ceremonies at the temple. However, that was in the days before central heating which nowadays causes firs to lose their needles long before that date. But outdoor Christmas trees with electric lights are often left standing until February 2.

Source: Rainer Thumshirn, "Fröhliche Weihnachten! A Selection of German Christmas Traditions," *Der Blumenbaum,* Vol. 15, Number 2, 1997.

THE CHURCH IN MODERN GERMANY

In 1993, about 35 percent of the German population was Catholic (about 28.4 million church members). Some 36.5 percent of the population at that time (27.5 million) was affiliated with the established Protestant (Evangelical) Church. In addition, there were some 1.9 million Muslims in the country. The number of Jews has risen steadily due to an influx from eastern Europe and now lies at about 50,000, while the two large churches have seen a small but steady decline in membership and attendance in recent years.

The Protestant Church in Germany (*Evangelische Kirche in Deutschland*) is a federation of the Lutheran, Reformed (Calvinist) and United (Calvinist and Lutheran) churches. Its legislative body is the Synod.

The Roman Catholic Church in Germany is organized into 27 dioceses, five of which are in the former East Germany. The Catholic Church hierarchy is headed by the German Bishops Conference, the main governing body of the Church.

Although many Germans are members of a church, few attend regularly. The number of churchgoers has been on the decline in recent years. In 1993, 5.4 million Catholics – 19 percent of registered Catholics in the country – attended Sunday mass. That is down from the 25.3 percent recorded in 1984. Only 1.2 million, or four percent, of the Protestants in Germany regularly attended Sunday services in 1992.

Germany has no state religion. The Basic Law guarantees freedom of faith and freedom of religion or ideological creed. Historical development, however, has resulted in religious concentrations in certain areas. Northern Germany is primarily Protestant, while the population in the West and South is primarily Catholic.

These regional groupings, however, are gradually being leveled out through the increasing migration and mobility of families since World War II.

Church financing

Germans who are members of a church support it through their taxes, not directly as in the United States.

When taxpayers list their religious affiliation on their employment record, an amount between eight and nine percent of their income tax is collected by the tax authorities and given to the church to which the taxpayer belongs. Churches pay the administration cost.

Thus, churches in the Federal Republic have a guaranteed annual income from their members. They do not engage in the kinds of fund-raising activities familiar in the United States.

Religious instruction

Religion is a subject in public schools. Children attend classes according to their faith. Parents may decide which class their children attend, or whether they should attend any class at all. From the age of 14 on, a student can decide whether or not to continue religious instruction. There are also parochial schools in Germany, but they have become less important in the last few decades.

Religion in everyday life

Churches play an important role in the field of public welfare and social services, and foreign aid. They take part in the debate about peace and disarmament, foreign worker and labor market policy, abortion, and protection of the environment.

In the former German Democratic Republic, the churches played an important political role by sheltering dissidents and providing a free space for discussion. They were instrumental in supporting the grassroots movements that eventually paved the way for unification.

Church holidays are often national holidays, and the religious pageantry associated with these holidays has become a part of the public spectrum of customs and festivals.

In the former East Germany, some religious ceremonies were replaced by secular ones. For example, the *Jugendweihe*, a non-religious coming-of-age ceremony took the place of confirmation.

The *Jugendweihe* was discarded after unification, like many other eastern German customs, but is now making a comeback.

Despite the celebration of religious holidays, however, Germans are generally less involved in religious activities on a daily basis than are Americans, though this varies from region to region. German leisure-time activities generally do not center around the church.

Source: Courtesy of the German Information Center; excerpted from *Federal Republic of Germany: Questions and Answers*, ed. Susan Steiner, German Information Center, New York, 1996.

OFFICIALLY RECOGNIZED RELIGIONS

Following the Reformation, the Roman Catholic church was strongest in Bavaria; the Lutheran church in the northern states; and the Reformed church in the Palatinate. Catholic (*katholisch*) records have been kept since 1563, usually written in Latin. Lutheran and Reformed records date from 1550, written in German. Also written in German were the Evangelical records.

Through the the Peace of Westphalia (1648), the treaty that ended the Thirty Years War, it was stipulated that only three religious confessions would be tolerated in the German nations: Catholic, Lutheran, and Reformed.

Any sects outside these religions

were outlawed. Thus it was understandable why so many of the emigrants were of Pietist persuasions who sought freedom to practice their religion in America.

Up to the time of Napoleon, the Protestant churches — Lutheran and Reformed — were separate but legal entities. Then in 1806 in the Palatinate, in 1807 in other southern German states, and in 1817 in Prussia, they were decreed legally to be one "Protestant Evangelical Christian Church."

The term *evangelisch* originally connoted the church's scriptural theological basis, but later it became simply a generic term for "Protestant," to distinguish these faiths from that of the Catholic Church.

Thus, the records since that time show a person's religion to be either *katholisch* or *evangelisch*.

Other smaller religious groups included Huguenots (French Protestants), Anabaptists (Mennonites and others), Waldensians, Moravians, Amish, Quakers, Dunkers, Separatists, and Schwenkfelders.

Further reading

For an informative overview of religious groups in Germany, including a bibliography and addresses of organizations, see *Germanic Genealogy: A Guide to Worldwide Sources and Migration Patterns*, by Edward R. Brandt, Ph.D. et al, Germanic Genealogy Society, 1995, pp. 110-121.

Sources:
♦Ruth Bailey Allen, "Church Records Relating to the Pennsylvania Germans," Palatines to America: Publications Plus, 1992, No. 2.
♦Wolfgang Glaser, *Americans and Germans*. Verlag Moos&Partner. Munich, 1985.

THE PIETISTS

The Pietists participated in a seventeenth and eighteenth century Lutheran reform movement in which the focus was placed on individual conversion and "living faith."

The term Pietism stems from the *collegia pietatis* (informal devotional meetings) which became the basis for the movement through the efforts of Philipp Jakob Spener, a Frankfurt pastor. In small groups involving study and prayer, the participants emphasized faith in Christ, not just acceptance of correct theological concepts, as well as the importance of education.

The University of Halle became the intellectual center of Pietism, which influenced younger Halle-educated pastors in Protestant Germany who subsequently became pastors in colonial America.

The pietist reform movement, beginning in the late seventeenth century with its focus on individual conversion and a devout way of life, strengthened Lutheranism in Germany and spread to other countries.[1]

These pietistic sects were represented in good numbers in the early German settlements in the United States, largely as a result of the stipulation of the Peace of Westphalia in 1648 (ending the Thirty Years' War), that only the Catholic, Lutheran, and Reformed religions were to be permitted in Germany. Other sects or religions were forbidden. In order to continue practicing their religion, many were forced to emigrate.[2]

[1]"Pietism," Microsoft (R) Encarta. 1994 Microsoft Corporation, Funk & Wagnalls Corporation, 1994.
[2]La Vern Rippley, The German-Americans, University Press of America, Inc. 1984.

ANABAPTISTS

In the early 1520s, religious leaders who were to become known as Anabaptists spoke out against the church and social practices of the time, in Switzerland, Germany, and Austria. They stressed the need for personal faith and for independent judgment, at the same time rejecting the formal ritualistic practices of the established churches.

Originally named *Täufer* (baptizers), they took their name from their belief in adult baptism, or "believer's baptism." They were also called *Wiedertäufer* (rebaptizers) and *"Taufgesinnte"* (baptism-minded) because of their belief in adult baptism.[1]

The history of the Anabaptists in Europe is one of persecution resulting in migrations.

Anabaptist groups were found spread through Europe under a number of different names, one being that of the Mennonites.

[1]Hermann Guth, *Amish Mennonites in Germany: Their Congregations, the Estates Where They Lived, Their Families.* Masthof Press, Morgantown, Pa., 1995.

MENNONITES (ANABAPTISTS)

The Mennonites whose faith grew out of Huldreich Zwingli's Reformation, take their name from the religious leader Menno Simons.

The views that were later called Mennonite originated in Zürich where in 1523, a small community left the state church and shortly thereafter adopted the tenet of believers' baptism. Because of their belief in adult baptism, the term "Anabap-tists," meaning "rebaptizers," came into being. The Mennonites' original name was *Täufer* (baptizers) or *Taufgesinnte* (baptism-minded).

Anabaptists were most active during the Reformation and shortly afterward in Germany and the Netherlands. They were forced to flee following the fierce opposition and persecutions by both Catholic and Protestant authorities. Their congregations survived only in isolated parts of Switzerland and Frisia,

with a few in the Pala-tinate.

In the Netherlands, the Frisian priest Menno Simons preached believers' baptism and nonresistance, which led to years of persecution of his Anabaptist followers. Mennonites took their name from that of Menno Simons.

Groups of the same persuasion appeared in southern Germany and in Austria (led by Jakob Hutter and his Hutterites).

In the 1520s, in Switzerland, Mennonites broke with Zwingli over infant baptism.

In 1620, the Swiss Mennonites broke into two parties, the Uplanders, known as Amish (after Jakob Amen or Ammann, their leader), and the Lowlanders.

Mennonites were persecuted in Switzerland, Germany, Holland, and France.

In the 18th century, the Swiss Brethren fled to the Rhineland, the Netherlands, Pennsylvania, and eastern Europe. Many Dutch Mennonites emigrated to Pennsylvania, Prussia, and Poland.

Large numbers of German Mennonite colonies were formed in southern Russia following the invitation by Catherine II, where they were attracted by religious liberty and freedom from military service.

Of the many colonies which emigrated to America, the oldest, a group of 13 families from Krefeld (Crefeld), was settled in 1683 at Germantown, Pennsylvania, under the leadership of Francis Daniel Pastorius, whose colonists were warmly welcomed by William Penn.

Germantown was the first permanent German settlement in North America. The Krefelders were later joined by some of the Quaker Mennonites from Kriegsheim.

The date of the Krefelders' arrival in Philadelphia, 6 October 1683 is a date celebrated to this day as the beginning of German-American history. (In recent years, 6 October has been declared German-American Day.)

Following the Krefelders were Dutch

and Swiss Mennonites. Among them were the Amish Mennonites.

In the first half of the 19th century, Mennonites from Switzerland and southern Germany settled in Ohio, to the west, and into Missouri.

Following the Civil War, Mennonites emigrated to Kansas, Nebraska, and South Dakota. After World War I, Mennonite groups migrated to Canada, primarily Saskatchewan.

Sources:

♦ *Encyclopedia Britannica: Dictionary of Arts, Sciences, Literature and General Information,* University Press, New York, Eleventh Edition, 1910.

♦ *The American Immigration Collection: The German Element in the United States*, Albert Bernhardt Faust, Arno Press and New York Times, New York 1969. Vol. I.

♦ *Amish Mennonites in Germany,* Herman Guth, Masthof Press, Morgantown, PA. 1995. Original work: *Amische Mennoniten in Deutschland.*

RESOURCES FOR MENNONITE RESEARCH

Libraries and societies

♦ **Lancaster Mennonite Historical Society** (Landis Library), 2215 Millstream Road, Lancaster, PA 17602

♦**Hiebert Library, Fresno Pacific Library,** 1717 S. Chestnut, Fresno, CA 93702. Within this library is the Center for Mennonite Brethren Studies, also known as the Archives.

♦**Associated Mennonite Biblical Seminary Library,** 3003 Benham Avenue, Elkhart, IN 46517-1999. (219) 296-6253

♦ **Mennonite Historical Library,** c/o Goshen College, 1700 South Main Street, Goshen, IN 46526-4724

♦**Mennonite Library and Archives,**c/o Bethel College, 300 East 27th Street, North Newton, KS 67117-0531. (316) 284-5363.E-mail <library@bethelks.edu>

♦ **Center for Mennonite Brethren Studies:** See Hiebert Library, Fresno Pacific Library, above.

♦ **Center for Mennonite Brethren Studies,** Tabor College, 400 South Jefferson, Hillsboro, KS 67063

♦**Germantown Mennonite Historic Trust,** 6133 Germantown Avenue, Philadelphia, PA 19144 (Collections: Hymnals, prayerbooks printed in Germantown in the eighteenth and nineteenth centuries; mostly Mennonite and Brethren, some Lutheran; Germantown Mennonite history)

♦**Illinois Mennonite Historical and Genealogical Society,** State Route 16, P.O. Box 819, Metamora, IL 61548-1007. (309) 367-2551; gnafzig@ juno.com

♦**Menno Simons Historical Library and Archives,** Eastern Mennonite University, 1200 Park Road, Harrisonburg, VA 22802-2462. (540) 432-4000. info@emu.edu; www.emu.edu

♦**Mennonite Family History Library,** 10 West Main Street, P.O. Box 171, Elverson, PA 19520-0171. (610) 286-0258

♦ **Mennonite Historians of Eastern Pennsylvania Library and Archives,** 565 Yoder Road, Box 82, Harleysville, PA 19438-0082. (215) 256-3020. info@mhep.org; www.mhep.org. (Collections: Local Mennonites; local genealogy, history, biography and churches in Bucks, Montgomery, Berks, Lehigh and Philadelphia counties; general Mennonite and Anabap-tist history and theology; Pennsylvania German studies, peace and non-resistance, Mennonite missions; congregational histories; congregational and conference archival collections for the Eastern District and Franconia Conferences; manuscript collections from families, ministers, for-mer organizations and businesses relating to Mennonites in the region; local cemetery records)

♦**Mennonite Historical Association of**

the **Cumberland Valley**, 4850 Molly Pit-cher Highway South, Chambersburg, PA 17201. (717) 375-4544, (301) 733-2184. (Collections: General history of Men-nonite and related church groups; genealogy books; Mennonite journals; archival collection focusing on Mennonite and related church groups in the Cumberland Valley of Maryland and Penn-sylvania)

♦**Mifflin County Mennonite Historical Society**, Walnut Street, P.O. Box 5603, Belleville, PA 17004-5603 (717) 935-5574. (Collections: Books on genealogy, local and church history; old family Bibles; church and local periodicals; Amish-related materials; Mennonite and Anabaptist local history; deeds, letters, local newspapers, pictures and records of the local Mennonite congregations)

♦**Muddy Creek Farm Library**, 376 N. Muddy Creek Road, Denver, PA 17517-9125. (717) 484-4849. (Collection: Old Order Mennonites and some kindred groups; many Old Order Mennonite and Old Order Amish magazines and many Mennonite periodicals; Mennonite bio-graphies, county histories, fraktur, general church histories, congregational and conference histories; emphasis on collecting of all known Mennonite devotional books from the sixteenth century to the present)

♦**Pequea Bruderschaft Library**, 176 North Hollander Road, P.O. Box 25, Gordonville, PA 17529 (Collections: Old Order Amish and some Mennonite publi-cations, genealogies, church and secular histories; books used in Amish schools; diaries, account books and ledgers, ceme-tery records of Lancaster County from 1794 to 1985; Amish death records in Lancaster County from 1794 to the present; newspaper clippings on the Amish)

♦**Mennonite Historical Society of Iowa, Mennonite Historical Museum,** 411 Ninth Street, P.O. Box 576, Kalona, IA 52247-0576. (319) 656-3271, (319) 656-

3732

♦**Mennonite Library and Archives**, Bethel College, 300 East 27th, North Newton, KS 67117

♦ **Brethren in Christ Archives/His-torical Society,** Messiah College, Grantham, PA 17027-0531. (316) 284-5304, (316) 284-5360. mla@ bethelks.edu; www.bethelka.edu/services/mla. (Collection: Focus on Brethren in Christ; also Anabaptism, Pietism and Wesley-anism)

♦ **Home Messenger Library,** 1438-H West Main Street, Ephrata, PA 17522 (Collections: Old Order Mennonites; bio-graphies, historical, devotional and secular books; letters, diaries, records and out-of-print material)

♦**Juniata Mennonite Historical Society,** P.O. Box 81, Richfield, PA 17086. (717) 694-3543. (Collections: Herald Press publications, local church histories, local county and state histories and family Bibles; genealogies, published and unpublished; Juniata County news-papers; Juniata District church records, community papers and records; deeds; land title records for Juniata and Snyder Counties)

♦ **Mennonite Heritage Centre**, 600 Shaftesbury Blvd., Winnipeg, Manitoba, Canada, R3P OM4

♦**"GRANDMA" Project.** "GRANDMA" (Genealogical Registry and Database of Mennonite Ancestry) is a project of the California Mennonite Historical Society's Genealogy Project Committee, through which large Mennonite databases are distributed on CD-ROM. Contact California Mennonite Historical Society, 4824 E. Butler Street, Fresno, CA 93727. http://sunthree.fresno.edu/cmhs/home. htm.

Publications
♦*Mennonite Cyclopedic Dictionary*, ed. Daniel Kaufman. Scottdale, PA: Men-nonite Publishing House 1937; reprinted 1978 by The Bookmark, Knightstown, IN

♦ *Amish Mennonites in Germany,* Herman Guth, Masthof Press, Morgantown, PA. 1995. Originally published as *Amische Mennoniten in Deutschland.* FHL 943.F2gh 1995

♦*The Palatine Immigrant,* Vol. V, No. 2 (Autumn 1979). Issue deals completely with Mennonites

♦ *Historic Background and Annals of the Swiss and German Pioneer Settlers of Southeastern Pennsylvania, and of Their Remote Ancestors,* by H. Frank Esch-leman, 1917. Reprinted by The Genealogi-cal Publishing Co., Inc., Baltimore, 1969.

♦ Kraybill, Paul N., *Mennonite World Handbook: A Survey of Mennonite and Brethren in Christ Churches.* Mennonite World Conference, Lombard, Ill., 1978. FHL 289.7025 M527

♦"Swiss Mennonite Family Names, An Annotated Checklist," Leo Schelbert and Sandra Luebking. *Newsletter* of the Swiss American Historical Society, Vol. XIV No. 2, June 1978.

♦*Krefeld Immigrants and Their Descendants,* LINKS Genealogy Publications, 7677 Abaline Way, Sacramento, CA 95823-4224. Creator of bi-annual publications for the descendants of the Krefeld immigrants, their families, and neighbors of those who established Germantown, Pennsylvania, their migration, religion, and history.

Back issues of the publications are available.

Source: Library holdings information partially based on Ray K. Hacker, comp., *The Eastern Mennonite Associated Libraries and Archives Directory.* Masthof Press, Morgantown, Pa., 1996.

LANCASTER MENNONITE HISTORICAL SOCIETY

Lancaster Mennonite Historical Society
2215 Millstream Road
Lancaster, PA 17602-1499

Tel. (717) 393-8751
Fax: (717) 393-9745
lmhs@lmhs.org
www.lmhs.org

The library and archives of the Lancaster Mennonite Historical Society emphasize Pennsylvania Mennonite and Amish history, genealogy, and theology. The Society serves as the official repository of the Mennonite Church.

The collection includes historical and genealogical materials related to southeastern and south-central Pennsylvania and other areas to which Mennonites moved from Pennsylvania, especially concerning denominations with a Swiss and German background such as the Church of the Brethren, United Brethren, Brethren in Christ, River Brethren, Moravians, Lutherans, and German Reformed.

Materials available include approximately 230,000 individual name cards in the genealogical card file, including all obituaries indexed from a major Mennonite periodical (*Herald of Truth/Gospel Herald*) since 1864; major Mennonite, Brethren and Amish periodicals; about 1,900 published genealogies; census records and court-related documents for Lancaster County and surrounding counties; important works pertinent to Pennsylvania genealogical research; and collections of notes and other documents of significance to researchers.

Availability

The facility is open Tuesday through Saturday, 8:30 am - 4:30 pm, except holidays. A users fee for non-members is charged.

MENNO SIMONS HISTORICAL LIBRARY AND ARCHIVES

Eastern Mennonite University
Harrisonville, VA 22801-2462
Fax: (540) 432-4977
info@emu.edu

www.emu.edu

The Menno Simons Historical Library and Archives is located in the Hartzler Library on the campus of Eastern Mennonite University. The library's primary purpose is to "collect, preserve and make available for study and research the recorded history, doctrines, life, and arts of Anabaptist and Mennonite groups." Provided also are materials on Shenandoah Valley history, culture and genealogy.

Holdings

The collection. spanning the years from 1501 to the present, has special strengths in the Protestant Reformation, Dutch and German Anabaptist Mennonite history and thought, the life and ideas of Mennonites and related groups in North America, and materials on history of Swiss and German immigrants as well as genealogical information.

The collections include Pennsylvania German materials such as Ephrata and Saur imprints, extensive materials pertaining to the Amish and an outstanding collection of central Shenandoah Valley imprints. The library focuses on the collecting of materials from the East and Southeast, including small Mennonite groups in the Southeast. Genealogical collections are listed in a seven-page handout.

Availability

Archives hours are largely by appointment. Persons traveling from a distance should contact the library in advance.

MENNONITE HISTORICAL LIBRARY

Mennonite Historical Library
1700 South Main Street
Goshen College
Goshen, IN 46526-9989
Tel. (219) 535-7433
mhl@goshen.edu

www.goshen.edu/mhl

The Mennonite Historical Library, located on the third floor of the Harold and Wilma Good Library of Goshen College, owns a genealogical collection of more than 2,800 volumes, including genealogical aids. It is particularly strong in the genealogy of Amish and Mennonite families coming from Switzerland and South Germany. Many Dutch, West Prussian and Russian families are also represented.

Holdings

The broadest areas of the general collection are publications of Pennsylvania German records and German immigration in the 18th and 19th centuries.

The collection includes 41,000 volumes (books, pamphlets, bound periodicals) documenting Reformation and Anabaptist history and the various Mennonite and related groups throughout the world.

The library maintains an obituary index to the *Herald of Truth* (1864-1908) and its successor, the *Gospel Herald.* There is also a computerized index to about 120 Amish genealogies.

AMISH

In 1663 occurred the "Amish Division," a split among the "Swiss Brethren" Mennonites.

The division was instigated by a Mennonite preacher in the canton of Bern, Jacob Amman, who pushed for the doctrine of *Meidung* (avoidance, or shunning). Most Swiss Brethren of the Palatinate and of the Emmenthal were not willing to accede to Amman's demand.

When an Amish person is put "under the ban" of shunning, the result is total ostracism – business, social, religious, and domestic. He is totally isolated from his fellow church members. Even his wife and children are forbidden to sit at the same table with him.

The Amish set for themselves restrictions in styles of dress and implemented the practice of footwashing. They were known as *Häftler* ("hook-and eyers"), because of their use of hooks and eyes instead of buttons on their clothing, and *Bartmänner* ("beardsmen") because of their prefernce for full beards, without mustaches. Liberal Mennonites who had refused to accede to Amman's principles were called *Knöpfler* (button-wearers).

In 1712, King Louis XI banished all "Anabaptists" from France. Many Amish groups migrated into Germany. None of these congregations survives.

All but one of the following congregations were located in what is present-day Germany (each represents a chapter in the Hermann Guth book, *Amish Mennonites in Germany*:

1. The Congregation of the Upper Palatinate
2. The Congregation of the Lower Palatinate
3. The Hofstätten Congregation
4. The Darmstadt Congregation
5. The Durlach Congregation
6. The Hochburg Congregation
7. The Weilburg Congregation
8. The Zweibrücken Congregation
9. The Frönsburg (Froensbourg) Congregation, today in France
10. The Waldeck Congregation (with Wittgenstein and neighboring areas)

In North America, the Amish are formally referred to as Old Order Amish Mennonites.

Known as the Plain People, they began migrating to North America in 1728, traveling to Pennsylvania, then to Ohio, Illinois, and Iowa, and more recently to Wisconsin, Minnesota, and Canada.

Note: *The Guidebook to Amish Communities in North America and Business Directory*, by Ottie A. Garrett, Hitching Post Enterprises, 1996 contains a list of all known Amish communities, as well as some families and church districts. It is available through Masthof Bookstore, Morgantown, Pennsylvania.

Sources:

♦Hermann Guth, *Amish Mennonites in Germany*. Masthof Press, Morgantown, PA, 1995.

♦Fredric Klees, *The Pennsylvania Dutch.* The Macmillan Company, New York, 1950.

♦La Vern J. Rippley, *The German Americans.* University Press of America, Inc., Lanham, Md., 1984.

THE SCHWENKFELDERS

Kaspar Schwenkfeld von Ossig (1490-1561), a German nobleman from Silesia who led the Reformation there, and a theologian, was maligned by Catholic and Protestant groups and was unable to settle a theological dispute with the reformer Martin Luther.

At his death in 1561, he left behind a band of loyal followers known as Schwenkfeldians, who continued his mission by forming a sect in Silesia.

When, in 1720, a Commission of Jesuits set out to convert the sect by force, most members fled to Saxony, then to Holland, England, and North America. All Schwenkfelder immigrants came from either Silesia or Saxony, and many from Silesia moved to Saxony shortly before going to Pennsylvania.[1]

During the period 1731-1737, about 206 Schwenkfelders fled persecution and settled in eastern Pennsylvania — in Philadelphia as well as in Montgomery, Bucks, Lehigh, and Berks counties.

In 1782, the Society of Schwenkfelders was organized. In 1909, descendants of these immigrants incorporated themselves under the name of The Schwenkfelder Church.

Schwenkfelders practice adult baptism, dedication of children, and open communion. They serve in the armed forces when called. The churches teach the right, privilege and obligations of individual conscience.

Five congregations exist today in southeastern Pennsylvania: Palm (in Montgomery County, founded soon after arrival of the Schwenkfelder immigrants in Philadelphia in 1734), Norristown (organized as a mission in 1904), Lansdale (begun in 1916), Worcester (in Montgomery County, where members originally worshiped in private homes, later in meeting houses in Salfor, Towamencin, and Worcester, after which a church building was constructed in 1951), and Philadelphia (at 30th and Cumberland Streets, originating as a mission in 1895), with a total membership of about 3000.

Organizations

♦Schwenkfelder Church, One Seminary Street, Pennsburg, PA 18073

♦Schwenkfelder Historical Society Library, Carnegie Library Building, Pennsburg, PA 18073

♦The Society of the Descendants of the Schwenkfeldian Exiles, c/o Schwenkfelder Historical Society Library (see address above). This society seeks to maintain interest in the genealogical and cultural heritage of the Schwenkfelder exiles and refugees of the eighteenth century.

♦ Samuel K. Brecht, *A Genealogical Record of the Schwenkfelder Families,* Board of Publications of the Schwenkfelder Church, Pennsburg, Pa., Chicago, 1923. FHL 974.8 F2b

♦ *Selections from the Genealogical Record of the Schwenkfelder Families*, the Schwenkfelder Church, Pennsburg, PA: Rand McNally, Chicago, 1923. 1923.

♦ Howard Wiegner Kriebel, *The Schwenkfelders in Pennsylvania: A Historical Sketch. Pennsylvania German Society Proceedings, vol. 13,* 1904. Reprint. AMS Press, New York, 1971. FHL Film 924112 item 2

[1]Aaron Spencer Fogleman, *Hopeful Journeys: German Immigration, Settlement, and Political Culture in Colonial America,*

1717-1775. Uni-versity of Pennsylvania Press, Philadelphia, 1996.

HUGUENOTS

The Huguenot Confession originated in France. Followers of the faith were influenced by John Calvin who, in Geneva, Switzerland, trained hundreds of exiles from France to serve as missionaries in their own country.

Following the revocation of the Edict of Nantes in 1685 (whereby Huguenots were generally granted freedom of religion and other benefits), Huguenots by the thousands fled France for Holland, British Isles, Germany and America – including Massachusetts, New York, and South Carolina. Estimates of the number of Huguenots who fled France run from 400,000 to 1 million. About 30,000 fled to Germany, with large numbers settling in Brandenburg, Hessen-Kassel, and the Pfalz. Names of settlers in German lands were commonly germanicized from the French.

By 1802, the Napoleonic Code granted full religious equality to Huguenots.

Resources

♦ *Deutsches Geschlechterbücher* [German lineage book], C.A. Starke, Limburg/Lahn, 1889 - (ongoing)

♦ *Lexikon deutscher Hugenotten-Orte,* [Dictionary of place names of Huguenot settlements in Germany], Verlag des Deutschen Hugenotten-Vereins, c. 1994 FHL 943 F2gd, V. 22

♦"The Huguenots in Germanic Areas," *German Genealogical Digest*, Vol. 2, No. 4, 1986.

♦ *Genealogisches Handbücher des Adels* [German Handbooks of Nobles], C. A. Starke, 1972 - .

♦ *Hugenotten in der Pfalz*, FHL microfiche 6001626

♦ *Archiv für Sippenforschung*, Vol. 28, 1967 (special edition of this periodical on Huguenots) and the August 1975 issue.

* *Der deutsche Hugenott*, March and June 1966.

Organizations

* National Huguenot Society, 9033 Lyndale Avenue South, Suite 108, Bloomington, MN 55420-3535.
* The Huguenot Society of America, 122 East 58th Street, New York, NY 10022
* Huguenot Historical Society Library and Archives, 88 Huguenot Street, New Paltz, NY 12561. (914) 255-6738

HUGUENOT CHRONOLOGY

1536: John Calvin's leadership role in Geneva enables him to train hundreds of exiles from France, who return as missionary pastors.

1560: Aristocratic families in France begin to accept the Calvinist religion. Rival fac-tions emerge (Roman Catholic extremists and supporters of royalty), leading to ten wars.

1562-1563: First Huguenot war

1567-1568: Second Huguenot war

1568-1570: Third Huguenot war

1572-1573: Fourth Huguenot war

1574-1576: Fifth Huguenot war

1577 (April-September): Sixth Huguenot war

1579-1580: Seventh Huguenot war

1586-1598: Eighth Huguenot war

1598: King Henry IV promulgates the Edict of Nantes, reaffirming the position of the Catholic church as the official religion and granting freedom of religion to Huguenots in much of France.

1617: Louis XIII becomes king

1621-1622: Ninth Huguenot war

1624: Cardinal Richelieu becomes part of the king's council; he destroys the political power of the Huguenots.

1625-1629: Tenth Huguenot war

1685: King Louis XIV revokes the Edict of Nantes; thousands of Huguenots flee France for Holland, America, British Isles, and Germany. About 30,000 flee to Germany, traveling through Elsaß-Lothringen, Saar, Pfalz, North Baden, North Württemberg, Hessen, South Hannover, Anhalt, Brandenburg and the Vorpommern area.

1787: Edict of Toleration restores most of the civil rights of Protestants.

1802: Napoleonic Code grants full religious equality.

Source: "The Huguenots in Germanic Areas," *German Genealogical Digest*, Vol. 2, No. 4, 1986.

THE HARMONISTS

Georg Rapp of Iptingen, in Württemberg, led members of a nineteenth century sect who had left the Protestant church in order to worship in a more informal and pietistic manner.

These Separatists, as they came to be known, were called upon to submit a declaration of their position. The "Articles of Faith" of 1798 defined their beliefs concerning the church, baptism, communion, the church school, government and oaths, and military service — and constituted the formal beginning of the Separatist movement.

In 1803, Rapp and a few other Separatists sailed to Philadelphia and built a prosperous community called Harmony in Pennsylvania, near Pittsburgh.

They became a corporate body in 1805, from which time they were called either Harmonists or Rappites. In 1814, the group resettled south of Vincennes, Indiana, building the town of New Harmony. Here they thrived from 1814 to 1824 and experienced phenomenal economic success, at one point even lending money to the new State of Indiana. Frederick Rapp, the adopted son of Georg Rapp, became a representative to Indiana's constitutional convention in 1816.

Then in 1824, the Harmonists moved

again, back to Pennsylvania, purchasing land on the Ohio River near Pittsburgh and building the town of Economy (now called Ambridge, after the American Bridge Company). All the Harmonists had moved there by 1825.

Not long after, the religious faith of the Harmonists began to decline, especially among the young. In 1906, the society was dissolved.

Of genealogical interest is a document that discloses the membership of the Harmonists — a power of attorney given by the membership in Indiana to Frederick Rapp to sell their property. This document, dated 21 May 1824 and recorded 20 April 20 1825, is found in Deed Record Book D, pages 116-127, at the Posey County courthouse in Mount Vernon, Indiana.

Nearly 500 names, male and female, are listed. The document, with a complete list of names, was published in the *Indiana Magazine of History,* Vol. XLVII, pp. 313-319 (1951).

The definitive work on the Harmony Society is Karl J. R. Arndt's *George Rapp's Harmony Society, 1785-1847,* revised edition, Fairleigh Dickinson Press, Rutherford, New Jersey, 1972.
Source: Based primarily on "Württembergers to America: The Harmonists," by Keith Boger. *The German Connection,* Vol. 14, No. 4, October 1990.

THE AMANA COLONIES

The Amana community had its beginnings in eighteenth century Europe when a group of German, Swiss, and French pietists founded a religion based on a belief in divine revelation through *Werkzeuge,* or "inspired prophets." The denominational name became Community of True Inspiration.

In 1843, some 600 Inspirationists, beset by political and religious persecution, emigrated to the United States from German lands under the leadership of a pietist, Christian Metz and founded the Ebenezer Society community near Buffalo, New York.

Around 1855, they moved west to the Iowa River Valley. There they lived a communal life for 77 years in seven villages that they founded, the oldest of which was Amana. The Amana Society was incorporated in 1859.

References
♦ Shambaugh, Bertha Maud (Horack), *Amana That Was and Amana That Is.* State Historical Society of Iowa, Iowa City, 1932. Reprint. Benjamin Blom, New York, 1971
♦ Perkins, William Rufus, and Barthinius L. Wick, *History of the Amana Society or Community of True Inspiration.* Reprint. Radical Tradition in America, Westport, Conn., Hyperion Press, 1976.
Source: "Iowa's Enduring Amana Colonies," by Laura Longley Babb; *National Geographic,* Dec. 1975.

THE MORAVIAN CHURCH

The Moravian Church has its roots in the provinces of Bohemia and Moravia in the present-day Czech Republic. The church goes back to the time of John Hus, burned at the stake in 1415 as an early Protestant heretic, whom the Moravian church honored as a martyr.

After 1458 when the first association of the church organized in Bohemia, the church was referred to as *Jednota Bratrska* (The Union of Brethren) or *Unitas Fratrum* (Unity of the Brethren).

The *Unitas Fratrum,* or Moravians, should not be confused with the United Brethren in Christ, which did not form until around 1800.

The Moravians, however, adopted the name United Brethren in Christ in the midwest.

In 1740, by invitation of Count von Zinzendorf, a small group of the faithful took refuge on his estate in Saxony, where they built the town of Herrnhut. Under Zinzendorf's leadership, in 1741, members of the church arrived in Philadelphia and settled in Northampton and Lehigh counties, Pennsylvania, founding the town of Bethlehem — and later, Nazareth, Lititz, and Emaus, also in Pennsylvania.

The group failed at their attempts to form colonies in Georgia, in Hope, New Jersey, and in Salem, North Carolina.

Almost all Moravian emigrants left Europe from Herrnhut (Saxony), Wetteravia, the Netherlands, or London.[1]

The count named the group Moravians because they came from northern Moravia. (Although Moravia was attached to Bohemia from the eleventh century, it became an Austrian crownland after the Revolution of 1848. When Czechoslovakia was formed in 1918, Moravia became a part of that country.)

Moravian Church members, a German-speaking pietist sect, were the most successful missionaries among American Indians in American history.

They settled around Winston-Salem, North Carolina, in 1753.

Their numbers have been greatest in Pennsylvania, North Carolina, and Wisconsin, in that order.

The United Brethren has consolidated with the Methodist Episcopal Church to become the United Methodists. In the midwest, the Moravians adopted the name "United Brethren in Christ."

Archives, libraries, society

♦**Moravian Archives,** 41 West Locust Street, Bethlehem, PA 18018 ["Northern Province"].

♦**Moravian Archives**, 4 East Bank Street, Winston-Salem, NC 27101-5307. Tel. (910) 722-1742 ["Southern Province"]. Records in this repository of the Southern Province, Moravian Church go back to 1753. The Archives provides research for a fee.

♦**Salem College, Granly Library**, Salem Square, Winston-Salem, NC 27108

♦**Gnadenhutten Public Library**, 160 N. Walnut, Gnadenhutten, OH 44629

♦**Moravian College Library**, Main and Elizabeth, Bethlehem, PA 18018

♦ **Moravian Heritage Society**, 31910 Road 160, Visalia, CA 93292. Tel. (209) 798-1490. Fax (209) 798-1922. A Moravian surnames database may be accessed for $2 per surname. Other research ser-vices are available.

References

♦Hamilton, John Taylor, *A History of the Church Known as the Moravian Church, or the Unitas Fratrum, or the Unity of the Brethren, During the Eighteenth and Nineteenth Centuries.* 1900. Reprint, AMS Press, New York, 1971. FHL 284.6 H18a

♦Johnson Arta F. "Old Moravian Cemeteries." *Palatine Immigrant*, Vol. V, No. 1, Summer 1979.

♦Reichel, Levin T., *Index to the Moravians in North Carolina, an Authentic History.* 1857. Reprint, Genealogical Publishing, Baltimore, 1968. FHL 975.6 F22 mr

[1]Aaron Spencer Fogleman, *Hopeful Journeys: German Immigration, Settlement, and Political Culture in Colonial America, 1717-1775,* University of Pennsylvania Press, Philadelphia, 1996.

HUTTERIAN BRETHREN

Known as Hutterites, the Hutterian Brethren began in an Anabaptist community in Moravia (now the Czech Republic) during the Reformation. Their name is derived from their original leader Jakob Hutter of Austerlitz, burned as a heretic in 1536.

In the seventeenth and eighteenth centuries, the Hutterites lived for more than a century in a German-language enclave in Slavic Moravia. To escape

persecution, they settled in Russia and stayed there for about 100 years, until 1874.

When Russia mandated the use of Russian in the schools and required military service, they emigrated to settle in Dakota territory during the period between 1874 to 1879, and later in Canada in Manitoba and Alberta. An early colony settled near Yankton, South Dakota in 1884. There still remain more than 50 Hutterite colonies in South Dakota. The Hutterites retain the German language in school instruction and in the home.

Resources
♦ Horsch, John, *Hutterite Brethren: 1528-1931*. The Mennonite Historical Society, Goshen, IN., 1931.
♦Gross, Paul S., *The Hutterite Way; the Inside Story of the Life, Customs, Religion, and Traditions of the Hutterites*. Freeman Publishing, Saskatoon, Saskatchewan, 1965.

UNITED CHURCH OF CHRIST

This church resulted from a merger of the Evangelical and Reformed Church (mostly German in background) and the General Council of the Congregational Churches.

CHURCH OF THE BRETHREN, OR GERMAN BAPTIST BRETHREN (DUNKERS)

Dunkers (or Tunkers, after the German verb *tunken*, "to dip," based on their method of baptismal immersion) were members of a late seventeenth century pietist sect, which became the Church of the Brethren.

They have also been known as German Baptist Brethren or German Brethren.

The sect's members followed the teachings of Andrew Mack of Swartz-

enau, Germany.

Shortly after the new sect was organized in Germany in 1708, its members took refuge in Holland to escape persecution, but then emigrated to Pennsylvania between 1719 and 1729. The sect left none of its members behind in Germany.

The first German Baptists in America, who settled in Germantown, Pennsylvania, came from Krefeld in the Rhineland.

The first congregation in America was organized in 1723 by Peter Becker at Germantown. There, in 1743, Christopher Saur, a printer by trade and one of the sect's first pastors, printed the first Bible published in a European language in America.

The Dunkers moved westward and south from Pennsylvania, settling also in Maryland, Virginia, Ohio, Indiana, Illinois, Iowa, Missouri, Nebraska, Kansas, and North Dakota.

A few of them separated from the original teachings and went to Ephrata Cloister in Pennsylvania, with Conrad Beissel. This group believed in celibacy and gradually died out. Ephrata Cloister disbanded in 1830.

By the time of the American Revolution, the Dunkers were called Brethren.

In the 1880s, the church divided into the Old-Order and Progressive Brethren and eventually formed separate organizations. The Progressive Brethren divided again in 1939.

The parent church today is called the Church of the Brethren (Conservative Dunkers).

Branches of the Brethren which consider themselves as outgrowths of the original group are the Old German Baptist Brethren, organized in 1881; Brethren Church, 1883; Fellowship of Grace Brethren Churches, 1939; and the Dunkard Brethren, 1926.

References
♦Brumbaugh, Martin Grovek, *A History of the German Baptist Brethren in*

Europe and America. Bookmark, Knightstown, Ind., 1977

♦ Doll, Eugene Edgar, *The Ephrata Cloister: An Introduction.,* Ephrata Cloister Associates, Ephrata, Pa., 1958. FHL 974.8A1

♦ Falkenstein, George N., "The German Baptist Brethren or Dunkers," *Pennsylvania German Society Proceedings* and Addresses 10 (1900): 1-48. Pennsylvania German Society, Lancaster, Pa., 1900.

♦ Fitzkee, Donald R. , *Moving Toward the Mainstream: 20th Century Change Among the Brethren of Eastern Pennsylvania,* Good Books, 1995.

♦ "Migration of Early German Baptist Brethren Within the United States," by Lester H. Binnie. *The Palatine Immigrant,* Vol. V, No. 1, Summer 1979.

Archives

♦ Church of the Brethren Historical Library, 1421 Dundee Avenue, Elgin, IL 60120

♦ Church of the Brethren Library, 2710 Kingston Road, York, PA 17402

♦ Bethany Theological Seminary, Butterfield and Meyers Roads, Oak Brook, IL 60521

♦ Ashland Theological Seminary, Ashland, OH 44805

♦ Ephrata Cloister, Ephrata, PA 17522

♦ McPherson College, Miller Library, McPherson, KS 67460

♦ Messiah College, Murray Center, Grant-ham, PA 17027

♦ Juniata College, 18th and Moore, Huntington, PA 16652

Sources:

♦ *Encyclopedia Britannica: Dictionary of the Arts, Sciences, Literature and General Information,* University Press, New York, 11th ed., 1910.

♦ La Vern J. Rippley,*The German-Americans.* University Press of America, Inc., Lanham, MD, 1984.

♦ Microsoft (R) Encarta, 1994 Microsoft Corp., Funk & Wagnalls Corporation, 1994.

UNITED BRETHREN IN CHRIST

The Church of the United Brethren in Christ was founded in 1800 in Pennsylvania primarily through the efforts of a German-born clergyman, Philip William Otterbein, and a German Mennonite preacher, Martin Boehm. Services were initially conducted in German.

In 1946, the United Brethren in Christ united with the former Evangelical church to form the Evangelical United Brethren church, which joined with the Methodist church in 1968 to form the United Methodist Church.

Resource

The Center for Evangelical United Brethren Heritage, United Theological Seminary Library, 1810 Harvard Boulevard, Dayton, OH 45406. Tel. (513) 278-5817 contains denominational resources of the United Brethren in Christ Church, the Evangelical Church, and the Evangelical United Brethren Church.

Generally, the Center advises, it is more profitable to inquire into local church records to find family information. The Center can help to direct searches by locating a church or by attempting to trace the history of a local church.

REFORMED CHURCH IN THE UNITED STATES

Founders of the Reformed Church emigrated to America from the Rhine area and from the German cantons of Switzerland in the early 18th century. Other emigrants included French and Dutch families of the Reformed faith. The Dutch Reformed arrived before the German emigrants.

In 1793, the congregations adopted the name German Reformed Church. In 1869 the church was renamed the Reformed Church in the United States.

In 1934, it merged, except for a group of 34 churches, with the Evangelical Synod of North America. The resulting union became the Evangelical and Reformed Church. The latter became part of the United Church of Christ in 1957.

Beliefs of the German Reformed Church were based on the thinking of such men as John Calvin, Heinrich Bullinger, and Ulrich Zwingli.

The document that best expresses the doctrine of the German Reformed churches is the Heidelberg Catechism, written in 1563.

The German Reformed Church limited baptism to children of communicants.

References

◆Good, James Isaac, "The Founding of the German Reformed Church in America by the Dutch," *American Historical Association,* Annual Report, 1897.

◆Dubbs, Joseph Henry, "History of the Reformed Church, German, by Joseph Henry Dubbs." *The American Church History Series 8*, 1895.

sources:

◆"Reformed Church in the United States," Microsoft (R) Encarta. Microsoft Corporation 1994, Funk & Wagnalls Corporation 1994.

◆Humphrey, John T.,"Baptismal Records: Understanding Their Meaning & Use." *Der Kurier,* Mid-Atlantic Germanic Society, Vol. 4, No. 2, June 1996.

EVANGELICAL AND REFORMED HISTORICAL SOCIETY LIBRARY

The Evangelical and Reformed Historical Society
Philip Schaff Library
555 West James Street
Lancaster, PA 17603
Tel. (800) 393-0654, ext. 104
Fax (717) 290-8704
erhs@lancasterseminary.edu
www.erhs.info

The Philip Schaff Library, located at the Lancaster Theological Seminary, is the repository for the records of the former German Reformed Church, the Reformed Church in the United States, and the Evangelical and Reformed Church.

Since the merger in 1957 with the Congregational Christian Churches, the denomination has been known as the United Church of Christ.

Society holdings

In addition to denominational records, the Society holds records from some for-mer German Reformed congregations, especially in southeastern and central Pennsylvania areas.

There are no surname indexes to records. The researcher needs to know the name of a specific Reformed church in which an ancestor was once a member before a search can be made to determine whether records for that church are available.

Most of the local church records, which include baptisms, marriages, and burials, have been microfilmed by and are available through the Family History Library.

The Society's holdings do not include records from other German denominations or sects.

Availability

The facility is open Monday through Thursday. A per-day fee is charged for genealogical research.

The Society does not consider itself to be primarily a genealogical research organization. Researchers are encouraged to call in advance if they wish to use the Society's resources.

EXPULSION OF THE SALZBURG PROTESTANTS

In 1686, the Archbishop of Salzburg expelled 621 Protestants from his bishopric. All children under the age of 15 had to be left behind to be reared by Catholics.

Then 45 years later, Salzburg's Archbishop Leopold Anton Freiherr von Firmian, seeking to stop the rise of Protestantism, signed into law on November 11, 1731 the *Emigrationspatent* (emigration order) forcing all domestic servants and employed workers to renounce Protestantism or to leave Salzburg by November 30. This meant an immediate exodus in the middle of winter with nowhere specific to go. Farmers, artisans, and merchants were given an additional five months in which they could try to sell their property, being under order to leave by April 24, 1732. The majority of the more than 30,000 emigrants headed for East Prussia, and smaller groups settled in southern Germany and Holland.

One group headed for the British colonies in North America and settled near Savannah, Georgia. Altogether, more than 20,000 Protestants were evicted from their homeland. Estimates are that approximately a quarter of them perished on their flight to a new homeland.

A band of Lutheran Salzburgers settled in the United States on the Savannah River in Purysburg, Georgia, in 1731. Many of these settlers later moved to the nearby village of New Ebenezer, founded in 1736.

The Georgia Salzburger Society is publishing an updated, multi-volume genealogy of the Salzburgers, *Georgia Salzburg-ers and Allied Families.* Contact: Georgia Salzburger Society, 2980 Ebenezer Road, Rincon, GA 31406. (912) 754-7001

Source: "Exodus of the Salzburg Protestants to Georgia," by Rainer Thumshirn. *Der Blumenbaum,* Vol. 13, No. 3, 1996

LUTHERAN CHURCH HISTORY IN THE UNITED STATES

1623: First permanent settlement of European Lutherans arrives at Manhattan Island from Holland.

1748: Congregations in Pennsylvania, New Jersey, New York and Maryland organize the country's first Lutheran synod, "the ministerium of Pennsylvania," under Pastor Henry Melchior Mühlenberg.

1838: German immigrants, forerunners of the Lutheran Church-Missouri Synod, arrive in Missouri (also in Michigan).

1918: Groups of Germans, Norwegians, Danes, Icelanders, Finns and Slovaks start a cooperative group, the National Lutheran Council.

1930: Norwegian and other groups unite in "old" American Lutheran Church.

1960: American Lutheran Church, largely of Norwegian, Danish and German roots, is formed by "old" American Lutheran Church, Evangelical Lutheran Church, and United Evangelical Lutheran Church. Three years later, Lutheran Free Church joins.

1962: Lutheran Church in America is formed by four bodies, largely of Swedish, German, Finnish and Danish background: Augustana, United Lutherans, Suomi Synod, and American Evangelical Lutherans.

1966: Lutheran Church in America, American Lutheran Church, and Missouri Synod form the Lutheran Council in the USA, successor to the National Lutheran Council (formed in 1918).

1972: American Lutheran Church, Lutheran Church of America, and Missouri Synod form the Consultation on Lutheran Unity.

1975: Consultation on Lutheran Unity dissolved by mutual consent of the three denominations.

1976: "Moderates" who split from the Missouri Synod form the Association of Evangelical Lutheran Churches.

1982: Lutheran Church in America, American Lutheran Church, and Association of Evangelical Lutheran Churches begin work toward merger.

1988: The new Evangelical Lutheran Church in America begins functioning.

Source: Based on "A Brief History of Lutheran Union in America," *The German Connection*, Vol. 11, No. 1, January 1987, as reprinted from *Perspective* (date not given).

RECENT LUTHERAN CHURCH MERGERS IN THE UNITED STATES

As of the early 1980s these five Lutheran bodies were active:

LCA: Lutheran Church in America

LCMS: Lutheran Church - Missouri Synod

ALC: American Lutheran Church

WELS: Wisconsin Evangelical Lutheran Synod

AELC: Association of Evangelical Lutheran Churches

ELCA: Beginning in 1988, the Lutheran Church in America (LCA), The American Lutheran Church (ALC), and the Association of Evangelical Lutheran Churches (AELC) were consolidated to form the Evangelical Lutheran Church in America (ELCA).

Lutheran Church in America

The Lutheran Church in America (LCA), based in New York and Philadelphia, formed in 1962 from the union of four separate Lutheran bodies.

The LCA dated from the mid-1660s, when Dutch Lutherans formed congregations in the New York area.

American Lutheran Church

The American Lutheran Church (ALC), with headquarters in Minneapolis, formed in 1960 as the result of a merger of four separate Lutheran groups.

Association of Evangelical Luthean Churches

The Association of Evangelical Lutheran Churches (AELC), based in St. Louis, was established in 1976 as a result of separation from the Lutheran Church-Missouri Synod.

Evangelical Lutheran Church in America

The Evangelical Lutheran Church in America (ELCA), based in Chicago, is the largest of the United States-based Lutheran bodies.

Lutheran Church – Missouri Synod

This is the second largest Lutheran church in the United States. *Missouri* is part of the name because the denomination was founded in that state by German emigrants in 1847.

The church's headquarters is in St. Louis.

Wisconsin Evangelical Lutheran Synod

This synod was organized in 1850 in Milwaukee as the German Evangelical Lutheran Synod of Wisconsin.

It merged with two other synods – Minnesota and Michigan – in 1917, to become the Evangelical Lutheran Joint Synod of Wisconsin and Other States.

The present name was adopted in 1959.

Source: Frank Spencer Mead, *Handbook of Denominations in the United States.* Abingdon Press, Nashville, TN., new 9th ed., rev. by Samual S. Hill, 1990.

CONCORDIA HISTORICAL INSTITUTE

Concordia Historical Institute
Department of Archives and History
801 DeMun Avenue
St. Louis, MO 63105
Tel. (314) 721-5934

Concordia Historical Institute is the Department of Archives for The Lutheran Church – Missouri Synod.

Most of the resources in its collection are related to the pastors and congregations of the Missouri Synod, which was organized in 1847. The Institute does not have a computer listing of all Lutherans, as functioning parishes should still have their own records.

In order for the Institute to determine whether its holdings contain information that would interest a researcher, it needs as specific information as possible, including the name of a specific Lutheran congregation or minister who served the family, or some other such specific connection with the Lutheran Church.

Such information will enable the Institute to determine whether its holdings will be useful in researching a given request.

WELS HISTORICAL INSTITUTE

The WELS Historical Institute, Dept. of Archives
Rev. Martin O. Westerhaus, Archivist
11831 N. Seminary Drive 65W
Mequon, WI 53092
Tel. (414) 242-7200

WELS Historical Institute maintains archives of the Wisconsin Evangelical Lutheran Synod (WELS), which dates back to 1850 when the German Evangelical Lutheran Synod of Wisconsin and other states was organized in Milwaukee. Pastors and members of this church were recent immigrants from Germany. For some decades, services were conducted in the German language.

Although WELS has member congregations in all 50 states, the largest concentration of churches is in the upper Midwest, especially the states of Wisconsin, Minnesota, and Michigan.

The WELS Archives primarily gather and preserve records of the Wisconsin Synod itself as well as historical information about member congregations and biographical information about pastors and teachers of the Synod. The Institute does not have records of sacred acts of member congregations, which are kept by the congregations themselves.

Records of closed or merged congregations usually went to the congregation which most members of the closing congregation joined.

The Institute can usually provide names and addresses of congregations where ancestors might have been members, and information on pastors.

ABDEL ROSS WENTZ LIBRARY

Abdel Ross Wentz Library
Lutheran Theological Seminary
66 North West Confederate Avenue
Gettysburg, PA 17325-1795
Tel. (717) 334-6286
Fax (717) 334-3469

The A.R.Wentz library building at the Seminary serves as a repository for the archives of synods in central Pennsylvania and Maryland. Original parish registers stored there are not available for genealogical research.

All information contained in the records is available on microfilm through the Family History Library of the Church of Jesus Christ of Latter-day Saints.

Many records are also available through the Genealogical Society of Pennsylvania Library, 1305 Locust Street Philadelphia, PA 19107-5405. Tel. (215) 545-0391.

Typed transcripts of a limited number of parish registers from central Pennsylvania and Maryland are available at Adams County Historical Society Drawer A, Gettysburg, PA 17325. Tel (717) 334-4723.

A researcher is available, for a fee, for responses to written requests for service through the microfilms created by the Church of Jesus Christ of Latter-day Saints.

ELCA ARCHIVES

The Evangelical Lutheran Church in

America has a network of archival centers, most associated with its college or seminary archives/libraries.

ELCA rents and sells microfilms of congregational records.

The Archives staff will inform researchers as to whether a particular set of records has been filmed.

These films are not available through inter-library loan. Typically, the films contain records of baptisms, confirmations, marriages, and funerals. Some contain membership lists and official meeting minutes.

Write to the Archives office in Chicago (address below) for specific information about loans and purchases of films and its research fee schedule.

The archives in New York and Pennsylvania will be of particular interest to researchers of German colonial ancestors; those in the Midwest to those researching the 19th century immigration waves.

The following list represents regional/synodical collections only.

Churchwide archives
 Evangelical Lutheran Church in America Archives
8765 West Higgins Road
Chicago, IL 60631-4198
Tel. (800) 638-3522
Fax (773) 380-1465
(Archives location: 321 Bonnie Lane, Elk Grove Valley)
E-Mail: archives@ELCA.ORG
◆Alaska, Idaho, Montana, Oregon, Washington
ELCA Region 1 Archives
Archives and Special Collections
Mortvedt Library
Pacific Lutheran University
Tacoma, WA 98447
Tel. (206) 535-7586
◆Arizona, California, Colorado, Hawaii, New Mexico, Nevada, Utah, Wyoming
ELCA Region 2 Archives
Pacific Lutheran Theological Seminary

2770 Marin Avenue
Berkeley, CA 94708-1597
Tel. (510) 524-5264
◆Minnesota, North Dakota, South Dakota
ELCA Region 3 Archives
2481 Como Avenue West
Saint Paul, MN 55108-1445
Tel. (612) 641-3205
◆Arkansas, Oklahoma
Arkansas-Oklahoma Synod
4803 South Lewis Avenue
Tulsa, OK 74105-5199
Tel. (918) 747-8617
◆Kansas, Missouri
Bethany College
Wallerstedt Learning Center
421 North First Street
Lindsborg, KS 67456-1897
Tel. (913) 227-3311, Ext. 8299
PearsonJ@Bethany.BethanyLB.edu
◆Texas, Louisiana
The Rev. Arnold Moede
205 Coventry
Seguin, TX 78155
Tel. (210) 379-6450
◆Nebraska
Nebraska Synod
4980 S. 118th Street, Suite D
Omaha, NE 68137-2220
Tel. (402) 896-5311
◆llinois, Iowa, Wisconsin, Upper Michigan
ELCA Region 5 Archives
333 Wartburg Place
Dubuque, IA 52003-7797
Tel. (319) 589-0320
◆Indiana, Kentucky, Michigan, Ohio
ELCA Region 6 Archives
Trinity Lutheran Seminary
2199 East Main Street
Columbus, OH 43209
Tel. (614) 235-4136, Ext. 4002
reg6archives@trinity.capital. edu
◆New York, New Jersey, Eastern Pennsylvania, New England and the non-geographic Slovak-Zion Synod
–For all synods named above except Metropolitan New York:

Lutheran Archives Center
Northeast Region Archives ELCA
7301 Germantown Avenue
Philadelphia, PA 19119-1799
Tel. (215) 248-4616, ext. 34
Fax (215) 248-4577
lutthelib@ltsp.edu
–For Metropolitan New York Synod:
Gloria Dei Church
22 East 18th Sstreet
Huntington Station, NY 11746
Tel. (516) 271-2466
–For Western Pennsylvania, West
Virginia, Western Maryland
Tri-Synod Archives
Thiel College
College Avenue
Greenville, PA 16125
Tel. (412) 589-2131
–For Central Pennsylvania, Delaware-
Maryland , and Metropolitan Washing-
ton, DC
A.R. Wentz Library
Lutheran Theological Seminary
Gettysburg, PA 17325
Tel. (717) 334-6286, Ext. 407
♦ North Carolina:
ELCA North Carolina Synod
1988 Lutheran Synod Drive
Salisbury, NC 28144
Tel. (704) 633-4861
♦ South Carolina
ELCA South Carolina Synod
P.O. Box 43
Columbia, SC 29202-0043
Fax (803) 252-5558
♦Alabama, Florida-Bahamas, Georgia,
Mississippi, Tennessee, and the
Caribbean Synod:
Archives, Lutheran Theological
Southern Seminary
4201 North Main Street
Columbia, SC 29203
Tel (803) 786-5150, ext. 234
archives@ltss.edu
♦ Virginia
ELCA Virginia Synod
P.O. Drawer 70
Salem, VA 24153

Tel. (540) 389-5962
VASYNOD.parti@ecunet.com

LUTHERAN CHURCHES WITH GERMAN-SPEAKING CONGREGATIONS

**German Evangelical Lutheran Con-
ference in North America**
Deutsche Evangelisch-Lutherische Kon-
ferenz in Nordamerika
9715 Lake Avenue
Cleveland, OH 44102
Tel. (216) 631-5007
Fax (216) 961-1735
[Purpose: Promotion and development
of the work of German-speaking Lutheran
churches in North America]

GERMAN METHODISTS

The German Methodist movement developed from the work of William Nast,
who descended from a long line of Swa-
bian pastors of the Lutheran church in
Württemberg.
    Germans joined with the church
through the Methodists Episcopal
Church.
    The growth in numbers of German
Methodists grew especially fast after
the Civil War.
    In 1924, the Methodist church took
steps to phase out its German wing of
the church.
Source: LaVern J. Rippley, *The German-
Americans,* University Press of America,
Inc., Lanham, Md., 1984.
                    Resources
♦**Methodist Historical Society**, Old St.
George Church, 326 New Street, Phila-
delphia, PA 19106
♦**United Methodist Archives Center,**
General Commission on Archives and
History of the United Methodist Church,
Drew University Library, 36 Madison

Avenue, Madison, NJ 07940. (973) 408-3189

♦Nippert Collection of German Methodism (full title: "Bethesda Hospital and Deaconess Association/Rev. Louis and Ida E. Nippert Memorial Library and Museum of German Methodism in America and Germany Records").

The materials relate to the conferences, churches, schools, hospitals, deaconess institutions, orphanages, missions, and individuals in the German Methodist Church in the United States, Germany, Switzerland, and China.

Contact: Dr. Jonathan Dembo, Archivist, The Museum Center, Cincinnati Union Terminal, Cincinnati, OH 45203, Tel. (513) 287-7030.

♦Archives of Indiana United Methodism, Roy O. West Library, DePauw University, Greencastle, IN 46153

♦Garrett-Evangelical Theological Seminary, 2121 Sheridan Road, Evanston, IL 60201

♦ The Historical Center of the Free Methodist Church, Winona Lake, IN 46590

♦Methodist Historical Library, Perkins School of Theology, Southern Methodist University, Dallas, TX 75222

♦New England Methodist Historical Society Library, Boston University, School of Theology, 745 Commonwealth Avenue, Boston, MA 02215

♦Pacific School of Religion, Charles Holbrook Library, 1798 Scenic Avenue, Berkeley, CA 94709

Publications

♦General Commission on Archives and History of the United Methodist Church, *The Directory.* United Methodist Church, Madison, N.J., 1981.

♦ Harmon, Nolan B., ed. *The Encyclopedia of World Methodism.* World Methodist Council and Commission on Archives and History, United Methodist Publishing House, Nashville, 1974. 2 vols.

ROMAN CATHOLICS

(Check websites for updated information.)

After the Thirty Years War, only Catholic, Lutheran, and Reformed churches were recognized state churches.

Almost half the German-Americans in the 1880s were Roman Catholics. John Martin Henni, appointed bishop of Milwaukee in 1844, was a leader among the German-Americans by building a foundation for a German-American clergy in his Midwest archdiocese.[1]

Some Catholic records may be found in local and state historical societies and other secular libraries.

Organizations

♦American Catholic Historical Society of Philadelphia, P.O. Box 84, Philadelphia, PA 19105.

♦The National Conference of Catholic Bishops (NCCB)
3211 Fourth Street, NE
Washington, DC 20017-1194
Tel. (202) 541-3000
Fax: (202) 541-3322

♦United States Catholic Conference (USCC)
3211 Fourth Street, NE
Washington, DC 20017-1194
Tel. (202) 541-3000
Fax (202) 541-3322

♦American St. Boniface Society
P.O. Box D
Bronx, NY 10466-0604
Tel. (718) 994-0989
Fax (718) 994-6119
[Supports the Catholic church in the eastern German states]

♦Archives of the University of Notre Dame, South Bend, IN 46624. (Archdiocese of New Orleans Records (1576-1865)

♦Barry University, 11300 NE Second Avenue, Miami Shores, FL 33161

♦Boston College Library, Chestnut Hill,

MA 02167
◆**Catholic University of America**, 620
Michigan Avenue N.E., Washington, DC
20013
◆**College of the Holy Cross,** College
Street, Worcester, MA 01610
◆**Conception Abbey Library,** Conception, MO 64433
◆**Diocese of Fresno Library**, 1510 N.
Fresno, Fresno, CA 93703
◆**Kenrich Seminary,** 7800 Kenrick Road,
St. Louis, MO 63119
◆**LeMoyne College Library,** LeMoyne
Heights, Syracuse, NY 13214
◆**Loyola University Library**, 6525 N.
Sheridan, Chicago, IL 60626 (773) 508-2658
◆**Loyola University Library**, 6363 St.
Charles, New Orleans, LA 70118
◆**Providence College, Phillips Library,**
Providence, RI 02918
◆**St. Anselm College, Geisel Library,**
Manchester, NH 03102
◆**St. Mary's College**, St. Albert Hall,
Moraga, CA 94575
◆**St. Bonaventure University**, Library
Center, St. Bonaventure, NY 14778
◆**St. Francis Seminary Library**, 3257 S.
Lake Drive, Milwaukee, WI 53207
◆**St. Michaels College**, 56 College Parkway, Winooski, VT 05404
◆**St. Paul Seminary, Ireland Library**, St.
Paul, MN 55105
◆**St. Vincent College Library**, Latrobe,
PA 15650
◆**Seton Hall University,** McLaughlin
Library, South Orange, NJ 02079
◆**SS Cyril and Methodius Seminary,**
3605 Perrysville Highway, Pittsburgh, PA
15214
◆**Stamford Catholic Library,** 195 Glenbrook, Stamford, CT 06902
◆**Texas Catholic Historical Society,** 16th
& Congress, Austin, TX 78711
◆**Villanova University, Falvey Library**,
Villanova, PA 19085

Publication

The Official Catholic Directory. P.J.
Kennedy & Sons. Wilmette, Ill, annually.

[1]La Vern J. Rippley, *The German Americans.*
University Press of America, Inc., Lanham,
Md. 1984.

JEWS

Jews were living in Germany since
medieval times, but from about 1400 they
were not permitted to hold citizenship in
German towns and had to live on assigned streets in a ghetto. They were
forced to take official family names starting in 1808, before which time children
were named after their fathers or paternal grandfathers, or they held the name
of the house where they lived. After 1808,
many Jewish people took their names
from towns of their ancestors. Following the "emancipation" of the early nineteenth century, when Jews were given
the full rights of citizenship, there were
created special civil registers for Jews,
which were in effect until enactment of a
general civil registsration law in Germany, effective January 1, 1876.

The best records exist in
Württemberg, where 209 of the 213 communities there still exist, and records back
to 1750 or sometimes earlier are available, but in other areas of Germany, the
situation is much more difficult.

Source: Wolfgang Glaser, *Americans and
Germans: Deutsche und Amerikaner.* Verlag
Moos & Partner, München, 1986.

BEGINNINGS
OF JEWISH FAMILY NAMES

Laws by which Jews were mandated
to take family names took effect on the
following dates for given areas:

Austria	17 July and 11 November 1787
Galicia	7 May 1789
South and East Prussia	17 July 1797
Russia	9 December 1804
West Galicia	21 February 1805

Westphalia .... (Decree by Jérome Napoleon 31 March 1808, repeated 4 July 1811)
France (including the .... 20 July 1808 German area left of the Rhine)
Hesse .... 15 December 1808
Baden .... 13 January 1812
Lippe .... 16 December 1809 and 10 November 1840
Mecklenburg .... 22 February 1812
Prussia .... 11 March 1812
Bavaria .... 10 June 1813
Denmark .... 29 March 1814
Kurhessen .... 14 May 1816
Saxony-Anhalt .... 20 June 1811 and 4 November 1821
Saxony-Weimar-Eisenach 20 June 1823
Württemberg .... 25 April 1828
Saxony .... 16 November 1834
Oldenburg 1852
Breslau .... 30 April 1791
Frankfurt/Main .... 30 November 1807 and 1811
Posen .... 1 June 1833 and 22 December 1833

Source: Wolfgang Ribbe, Eckart Henning, *Taschenbuch für Familiengeschichtsforschung.* Verlag Degener & Co., Neustadt an der Aisch, 1995, p. 169.

EXAMPLES OF TYPES OF JEWISH RECORDS IN GERMAN

The examples of types of Jewish records listed below were kept by municipal offices and Christian churches, as well as by Jewish synagogues.

All these types are available through the Family History Library in Salt Lake City, Utah.

- ◆**Bürgerbücher:** Citizenship records, records of residents without citizenship
- ◆**Dissidentenregister:** Dissenter Registers, in which Jews were often included
- ◆**Gerichtsakten:** Court records registering and verifying birth, marriage and death. Verification Jews were baptized

- ◆**Judenregister:** Register of Jews
- ◆**Juden Taufen:** Baptismal records of Jews
- ◆**Jüdische Familienliste:** List of Jewish families
- ◆ **Kirchbücher (Lutheran):** Includes non-conformist and Jewish birth, marriage and death records
- ◆**Kirchenbücher (Catholic):** Includes Protestants and Jewish birth, marriage, and death records
- ◆**Matrikeln (Registers),** a general term which included —
- -**Aufnahme neuer Mitglieder:** Admission of new members
- -**Austritte:** Record of people leaving the Jewish faith
- -**Beschneidungsbuch:** Circumcision records
- -**Ehescheidungen:** Divorce records
- -**Eingebürgerung:** Naturalization record
- -**Familienbuch:** Family books
- -**Friedhofsregister:** Cemetery record
- -**Gottesdienst:** Services held in the synagogue
- -**Gräberliste:** List of graves
- -**Judenliste:** List of Jews
- -**Mitgliederlisten:** Membership list
- -**Namensannahme:** Register of Jewish name changes
- -**Personenstandsfälle:** Legal status records
- -**Seelenliste:** List of members
- -**Synagogenbuch:** Synagogue records (in Hebrew)
- -**Übertritte:** Record of people joining the Jewish faith
- -**Wittwen u. Waisenunterstützungsfond:** Widow and orphan fund
- ◆ **Passover charity collections and disbursements:** Written in either Hebrew or Yiddish
- ◆**Schutzverwanten Protokolle:** Tax on persons with limited citizenship rights
- ◆**Volkszählung:** Census record (1938-39, of non-Germanic minorities with emphasis on the Jews)
- ◆**Vormundschaftsprotokolle:** Guardian-

ship records
◆**Zivilstandsregister:** Civil registration (vital records: births, marriages deaths)
◆**Heiratsbelege:** Verification of marriage
Source: Larry O. Jensen, "Jewish Records," *German Genealogical Digest,* Vol. 9, No. 1, 1993.

TWO GROUPS OF JEWS IN GERMANY

Historically, the two distinct groups of Jews in Germany are these:

The Ashkenazim are descendants of Jews who settled in central Europe, especially along the Rhine River as early as Roman times. They lived in Cologne by 321 AD. The Ashkenazim Jews came to speak a special dialect of medieval German called *Jüdisch* (Yiddish). They centered mainly in southwestern Germany in the seventeenth through the nineteenth centuries. Also they moved eastward into Slavic countries, particularly Poland, where occupational restrictions were not severe.

The Sephardim, also called Maranos, were the Jews who fled Spain and Portugal in the late 15th century during the time of the Inquisition. About 120 families of Marano Jews settled in and near Hamburg in the early sixteenth century. Their language, Ladino, is based on medieval Spanish. Their cemetery was at Altona, then Danish territory, and they had synagogues at Altona, Hamburg, and Wandsbek.

Source: Clifford Neal Smith and Anna Piszczan-Czaja Smith. *Encyclopedia of German-American Genealogical Research.* R.R. Bowker Co., New York, 1976.

JEWISH ORGANIZATIONS

Organizations in the United States
◆**Jewish Genealogy Society, Inc.,** P.O.

Box 6398, New York, NY 10128-0004. Tel. (212) 330-8257; JGSNY@ aol.com; www.jgsny. org
◆**World Jewish Genealogy Organization,** P.O. Box 190420, Brooklyn, NY 11219-0009
◆**Jewish Genealogical Society of Cleveland,** 996 Eastlawn Drive, Highland Heights, OH 44143
◆**Jewish Genealogical Society of Illinois.**P.O. Box 515, Northbrook, IL 60065-0515
◆**Jewish Genealogical Society of Los Angeles.** P.O. Box 55443, Sherman Oaks, CA 91413-5544
◆ **Jewish Genealogical Society of Pittsburgh,** 2131 Fifth Avenue, Pittsburgh, PA 15219
◆**Jewish Genealogical Society of Rochester,** 265 Viennawood Drive, Rochester, NY 14618
◆**Jewish Historical Society,** 914 Royal Avenue, S.W., Calgary, Alberta, Canada T2T 0L5
◆ **Leo Baeck Institute,** 129 East 73rd Street, New York, NY 10021Tel. (212) 744-6400. Fax (212) 988-1305
[Researches and preserves the cultural heritage of the Jews in Germany and in German-speaking countries; houses a public reference center consisting of a library, an archive, and an art collection.]
◆**United States Holocaust Memorial Museum,** 100 Raoul Wallenberg Place, SW, Washington, DC 20024-2150. Tel. (202) 488- 0400; www. ushmm.org
[Includes the exhibition section, a library, an archive, and an educational section]
◆**Holocaust Memorial Center,** 6602 West Maple Road, West Bloomfield, MI 48322. Tel. (313) 661-0840. Fax (313) 661-4204.
[Includes an exhibit section and a library]
◆**Beit Hashoah-Museum of Tolerance,** 9786 West Pico Boulevard, Los Angeles, CA 90035-4792. Tel. (310) 553-9036. Fax (310) 277-5558. [Holocaust memorial of the Simon Wiesenthal Center; includes an archive, a theater, and an educational

section]

◆ **B'nai B'rith International,**1640 Rhode Island Avenue, NW, Washington, DC 20036.Tel. (202) 857-6600. Fax (202) 857-1099. [Founded in 1843 as a fraternal order of Jews who had emigrated mainly from Germany and Austria]

◆ **American Jewish Congress,** Stephen Wise Congress House,15 East 84th Street, New York, NY 10028.Tel. (212) 879-4500. Fax (212) 249-3672

◆ **Anti-Defamation League (ADL),** 823 United Nations Plaza,New York, NY 10017.Tel. (212) 490-2525. Fax (212) 867-0779

◆ **Union of Orthodox Jewish Congregations of America,** 333 Seventh Avenue, New York, NY 10001

◆ **Simon Wiesenthal Center,**
New York: 342 Madison Avenue, Suite 633, New York, NY 10173. Tel. (212) 370-0320. Fax (212) 883-0895
Los Angeles: 9760 West Pico Boulevard, Los Angeles, CA 90035. Tel. (310) 553-9036. Fax (310) 553-8007

Organizations in Germany and Austria

◆ **Genkstätte, Haus der Wannsee-Konferenz,** Großen Wannsee 56-58, 14109 Berlin. Tel. (030) 80 50 01-0, -26.

◆ **Stiftung Brandenburgische Gedenkstätten mit den Gedenkstätten Sachsenhausen und Ravensbrück,** JVA Brandenburg, Heinrich-Grüber-Platz, 16515 Oranienburg. Tel. (03301) 81 09 18 **Gedenkstätte Ravensbrück,**16798 Fürstenberg, Tel. (03 30 93) 20 25. [Foundation dedicated to documenting Nazi persecution in former concentration camps and to performing international youth and educational services]

◆ **Gedenkstätte Bergen-Belsen,** 29303 Lohheide, Tel. (05051) 60 11

◆ **Gedenkstätte Buchenwald,** 99427 Buchenwald, Tel. (03643) 43 10 41

◆ **KZ-Gedenkstätte Dachau,** Alte Römerstraße 75,85221 Dachau. Tel. (08131) 17 41-42

◆ **Gedenkstätte Plötzensee für die Opfer**

des Nationalsozialismus aus dem In- und Ausland, Hüttigpfad, 13627 Berlin. (030) 3 44 32 26

◆ **Stiftung Topographie des Terrors,** Budapester Str. 40, 10787 Berlin. Tel. (030) 25 45 09-15. Fax (030) 26 13 00-2. [Documents National-Socialist persecution to which an exhibit on the grounds of the former Gestapo headquarters in Berlin is dedicated]

◆ [Jewish archive in Vienna]: **Israelitische Kulturgemeinde,** Schottenring 25, A-1010 Wien, Austria

◆ **Zentralrat der Juden in Deutschland,** Rüngsdorfer Strasse 6, 53173 Bonn, Germany. Tel. (0228) 35 70 23/24. Fax (0228) 36 11 48 [consisting of 16 state associations including 65 Jewish congregations joined together under the Central Council of Jews in Germany]

◆ **Hochschule für jüdische Studien,** Friedrichstr. 9,69117 Heidelberg, Tel. (06221) 16 31 31, Fax (06221) 16 76 96 [University for Jewish Studies, with close partnership with the Hebraic University in Jerusalem]

Publications

◆ *Stammbaum* [German-Jewish journal], 1601 Cougar Court, Winter Springs, FL 32708-3855

◆ *Avotaynu: The International Review of Jewish Genealogy,* 155 N. Washington Avenue, Bergenfield, NJ 07621. Tel. (800) 286-9298

◆ Mokoloff, Gary, *How to Document Victims and Locate Survivors of the Holocaust.* Genealogy Unlimited, Orem UT.

◆ Segall, Aryeh, ed., *Guide to Jewish Archives*, World Council on Jewish Archives, Jerusalem, New York, 1981. FHL 026.025924 G941

◆ Goldstein, Irene Saunders, ed., *Jewish Genealogy Beginner's Guide.* Jewish Genealogy Society of Greater Washington, 2nd ed., Vienna, VA, 1991. FHL 929.1 J556j 1991

♦Arnstein, George, "Genealogical Resources for German Jewish Ancestry," Chap. XII of *Germanic Genealogy: A Guide to Worldwide Sources and Migration Patterns*, by Edward R.Brandt et al., Germanic Genealogy Society, St. Paul, Minn., 1994.

♦Gilbert, Martin, *Jewish History Atlas*, William Morrow and Co., New York, rev. ed. 1993. FHL 296 G374j 1977

♦Kurzweil, Arthur, *From Generation to Generation: How to Trace Your Jewish Genealogy and Personal History*. Harper Collins, New York, 2nd ed. 1994

♦ Rottenberg, Dan, *Finding Our Fathers: A Guidebook to Jewish Genealogy*, Random House, New York, 1977. FHL 929.1 R747f

♦Weiner, Miriam, *Bridging the Generations: Researching Your Jewish Roots*. Secaucus, NJ, 1987

♦ Zubatsky, David S., and Irwin M. Berent, *Jewish Genealogy: A Sourcebook of Family Histories and Genealogies*. Garland Publishing Co., New York, Rev. ed., 2 vols., 1984 FHL 929.1 Z81j.

♦ Beider, Alexander, *A Dictionary of Jewish Surnames from the Former Russian Empire*. Avotaynu, Teaneck, NJ, 1993. FHL 947.2 D46b

♦ Beider, Alexander, *A Dictionary of Jewish Surnames from the Kingdom of Poland*. Avotaynu, Teaneck, NJ, 1996. FHL 943.8 D46b

STAMMBAUM: JOURNAL OF GERMAN-JEWISH GENEALOGICAL RESEARCH

Stammbaum is an English-language journal which supports research and publication of reliable family histories and facilitates the exchange of information, techniques, sources, and archival material.

The scope of *Stammbaum*, while focusing on Germany, includes Austria, Switzerland, Alsace, Bohemia, and other areas with linguistic and historic relevance.

This journal is published twice yearly by the Leo Baeck Institute. Back issues are available. Contact: Stammbaum, Leo Baeck Institute, 129 E. 73rd Street, New York, NY 10021; frank@lbi. com.

SOME JEWISH ARCHIVES

American Jewish Archives
Hebrew Union College
Jewish Institute of Religion
3101 Clifton Avenue
Cincinnati, OH 45220
Gesamtarchiv der deutschen Juden
Joachimstaler Str. 13
10719 Berlin, Germany
International Tracing Service
35534 Arolsen, Germany
Bundesarchiv
Am Wöllershof 12
56068 Koblenz, Germany
Archiv des Institutum Judaicum
Delitzschianum
Wilmergasse 1-4
48143 Münster, Germany
Israelitische Kultusgemeide [Austria]
Schottenring 25
A-1010 Wien, Austria
Leo Baeck Institute
129 E. 73rd Street
New York, NY 10021
YIVO Institute for Jewish Research
1048 Fifth Avenue (at 86th Street)
New York, NY 10028
Central Archive for the History of the Jewish People
Sprimzak Building, Givat Ram Campus
Hebrew University
P.O. Box 1149
IL- Jerusalem, Israel
The Jewish National and University Library
Givat Ram Campus
Hebrew University
IL- Jerusalem, Israel

EARLY EDUCATION IN GERMANY

Compulsory schooling begins at the age of six, when children enter elementary school (*Grundschule*) and continues for nine years (in some *Länder* for ten). With the start of secondary school, they begin to follow more specialized courses of study. During the fifth and sixth years of school, known in most states as the "orientation stage" (*Orientierungsstufe*), they make the transition to either pre-university or vocational high school programs.

Until the age of 18, all young people who do not continue at attend a full-time school must attend a part-time vocational school (*Berufsschule*). Primary education lasts four years and is provided free of charge.

After the *Grundschule*, children's education continues at one of four types of secondary school.

There are three traditional types of high school in Germany and a newer fourth type that combines features of the other three.

1) The *Gymnasium* (academic high school), which, including the orientation stage, lasts nine years in the western states, through grade 13, and eight years in four of five of the eastern states, through grade 12. Students who successfully complete their studies at academic high schools receive a diploma known as the *Abitur*. The *Abitur* is the basic requirement for admission to a university.

In 1990, the officials of the Federal Republic and the German Democratic Republic negotiating the terms of German unification agreed to defer making a decision on a common length for Gymnasium study until 1996. The state ministers of education decided in 1994, however, to postpone "educational unification" until 2000, following a comprehen-

sive review of the country's school system.

2) The *Realschule* (commercial high school), which offers instruction in both academic and business-related subjects and lasts through the tenth grade. Graduates of *Realschulen* receive diplomas that normally entitle them to admission to business and technical colleges, or, depending on their grades, to the last three years of *Gymnasium*.

3) The *Hauptschule* (general high school), which is vocationally oriented. After completing the ninth or tenth grade, depending on the state, *Hauptschule* students receive the diploma necessary to enter formal three-year training programs for technical and clerical professions. During those three years, students in training programs attend a mandatory eight to twelve hours of classroom instruction a week at a *Berufsschule* (vocational school).

In recent years, comprehensive schools, *Gemsamtschulen*, that offer academic, commercial, and vocational programs have become increasingly common. There are also special schools for disabled students.

Sources:
♦ German Information Center, *Federal Republic of Germany: Questions and Answers*, ed. Susan Steiner, New York, 1996.
♦ The Europa World Year Book 1999 (Vo.1 1), Europa Publications Limited, London, 1999.

GERMAN UNIVERSITIES

All institutions of higher education are referred to in German as *Hochschulen*. The two most common types of *Hochschulen* are universities and more specialized institutions called *Fachhochschulen* that are polytechnics and geared toward specific professions. There are *Fachhochschulen* for fields like public administration, economics, ag-

(continued on page 555)

Schultüten: German children's introduction to school

Every year, German children starting school can be seen carrying those large cone-shaped parcels called *Schultüten*, filled with candy and small presents, such as pencils and rulers.

After the children arrive at school, wearing their new book bags and carrying their *Schultüten*, they are permitted to open their cones and see what presents are inside.

With the older students feeling a bit more sophisticated and mature than the green newcomers, they might refer to the newbies as "*I-Dötze*" or I-*Männchen*," a throw-back to the days when children started to learn to write with the easiest letter of the alphabet, *i*.

Just about every first-day child must have a photograph taken to commemorate this memorable day.

Some of the parents take the day off work to witness this important day in their children's lives.

During World War II, when it was almost impossible for parents to afford or find an attractive *Schultüte*, there was only one child at a certain school whose parents were able to provide a beautiful *Schultüte*. Thus that *Schultüte*, and that one only, was held, in turn, by every other child, as a parent photographed the child. Thus all the parents could save for posterity a photo of that special day – complete with a quite handsome *Schultüte*.

As proud as the day may be for parents, the celebration has at times caused problems for the younger siblings. Therefore, as long ago as 1927, a practice was begun whereby the younger siblings still in kindergarten would receive smaller but similar *Geschwistertüten* (literally, "sibling bags"), also filled with goodies.

The tradition of the *Schultüten* began in Saxony, Thuringia, Silesia, and Bohemia. In 1817 in Jena and 1820 in Dresden, children were given simple conical bags on the first day of school, containing pastries or candy. Some children were given the opportunity to choose bags from a *Zuckertütenbaum* (sugar-bag tree).

Still in print in Germany today is an illustrated children's book first published in 1928, *Der Zuckertütenbaum,* by Albert Sixtus and Richard Heinrich.

As extravagant as *Schultüten* may be today, they have often in the past been denied to children whose parents were not able to afford such luxuries. In such cases, the less fortunate child had his picture taken holding a not too elegant-looking "*Zuckertüte*."

First day of school, about 1890

riculture, engineering, social work, music, and the visual arts. *Fach-hochschulen* offer many of the same types of academic courses as universities.

Germany also has special teacher training colleges *(pädagogische Hochschulen)* and academies of art and music *(Kunst-und Musikhochschulen)*.

There were about 320 institutions of higher education *(Hochschulen)* in Germany in 1996, with the numbers increasing following the 1989 reunification

University faculties

The faculty of German universities commonly belong either to an academic department *(Fachbereich)* or to a school within the university *(Facultät)*. Disciplines in the humanities, natural sciences, and social sciences are often organized as *Fachbereiche*; fields like law, medicine, and theology as *Fakultäten*.
Source: *Federal Republic of Germany: Questions and Answers.* German Information Center. New York, 1996.

ACADEMIC DEGREES IN GERMANY

In Germany, an academic degree can be conferred only on graduates of a *Hochschule* which is run by the state or recognized by it.

There are basically three different kinds of *Hochschule*:

* *wissenschaftliche Hochschule* (a university with scientific orientation)
* *Kunsthochschule* (art academy)
* *Fachhochschule* (similar to a college, professional orientation, requiring lesser qualifications than a university)

The student who passes the final examinations and has successfully written a *Diplomarbeit* (a lesser kind of dissertation), is awarded a *Diplom* by the *Hoch-schule*. A *Diplom* awarded by a university has an annex of *"Univ."* or no annex at all. A *Diplom* awarded by a *Fachhochschule* is marked by an annex

of "FH."

For example, a degree in engineering from an *Universität* is *Dipl.-Ing. Univ.* or just *Dipl.-Ing.*; from a *Fach-hochschule* it is *Dipl.-Ing.(FH)*. The latter was written as *Ing. grad.* until the early 1980s.

Degrees awarded only by universities

The title most widely seen is *Doktor*, a degree that can be awarded only by universities. One earns it after obtaining the *Diplom* by staying at the university for postgraduate studies. For this, the candidate must find a professor *(Doktorvater)* to assign a research project, the result of which will be the dissertation *(Doktorarbeit)*. In addition, the candidate must pass an oral examination by the *Doktor-vater* and two other professors. All dissertations must be published for distribution to the other universities and major scientific libraries.

Contrary to popular belief in Germany, the doctorate thus earned does not become part of one's name. However, *Doktor* may be used with one's name, have it entered on one's ID card *(Personalausweis)* or passport, or even on one's driver's license or credit card.

The highest academic degree, which can be earned only after an outstanding doctorate, is the *Habilitation* (the qualification to teach at universities). For this, the candidate usually must publish the results of a major research project or other studies in a *Habilitationsschrift* and also prove one's pedagogic abilities. In many cases, this is the first and most important step toward becoming a professor at a university. Thus a physician, for example, would become a *Prof. Dr. med.* Upon choosing a non-university career, the physician would call himself or herself *Dr. med. Habil.* to show this qualification.

Universities may bestow honorary doctorates upon deserving persons, usually for special achievements in public life or for major donations to a university.

This is called a *doctorate honoris causa,* abbreviated as *Dr. h.c.* However, not all recipients of such an honorary degree always remember to use the *h.c.,* and thus they become indistinguishable from a *Dr.* by academic achievement, which is sometimes the intention.

Combinations of degrees

Since the *Diplom* is the prerequisite of a doctorate, usually only the *Dr.* is used, not the additional *Dipl.*; it's just *Dr. Ing.,* not *Dipl.-Ing.Dr. Ing.* However, if one has another *Diplom* in a different field, it often is added. For example, a physician may display a *"Dr. med. Dipl.-Biol."* sign on his or her door.

Doctorates in two or more different fields can also be earned, which could be represented as *Dr. med. Dr. Phil.,* for example. A professor might also get a honorary doctorate and choose to use *Prof. Dr. Dr. h.c.*

A person either very active in public life or very generous might have multiple honorary doctorates and show this by adding *Dr. h.c. mult.* to his name. Former Chancellor Helmut Kohl, for example, held 19 honorary doctorates.

Foreign academic degrees

Non-German academic degrees may be used in public only with express permission from German authorities. Such permission is granted only if academic qualifications similar to those in Germany are required for this academic degree.

For improper use: a misdemeanor

A person improperly using an academic degree in public can be jailed for up to one year or fined according to §132a of Germany's penal code (*Strafgesetz-buch*). An example of improper use would be to call oneself a *Doktor* without having legally acquired the degree or using an unapproved doctorate acquired at a foreign university.

The degree in everyday life

In business, the use of academic degrees, especially the *Dr.,* is thought to be of advantage where it is felt necessary to impress clients and customers with special abilities and trustworthiness of the employees they come in contact with.

Business consultants or banks are good examples. A lawyer without a doctorate usually is considered of somewhat inferior quality. But otherwise, the importance of a doctorate to promote a career is declining.

Applicants for jobs are screened for other qualifications considered more important, like foreign languages or experience with computers.

Forms of address

Relations between employees of German companies are mostly quite formal. It is not very often that people call each other by their first names. Much less do they drop the *Doktor* when addressing a colleague or a superior unless invited to do so.

Other academic degrees like the *Diplom* are not used when orally addressing another person. However, they are widely used in letterheads, company names, advertising, phone listings – and obituaries.

Even in private life, the degree of *Doktor* is widely used to address a person who holds one.

Two people may know one another for years and unless they are close friends who call one another by their first names, the holder of the *Doktor* degree would still in many cases be *Herr Doktor X* or *Frau Doktor Y.* It is also correct usage to omit the name and just say *"Herr Doktor"* or *"Frau Doktor."*

One particular use of *Frau Doktor* has gone out of fashion: Until about 30 or 40 years ago, good manners required the wife of a *Herr Doktor* (a lawyer or physician, for example) to be addressed as "*Frau Doktor*," even if she never attended a *Hochschule*.

Interestingly enough, in the rare cases where the wife held a doctorate and the husband did not, he was not called "*Herr Doktor*."

A genealogical tip

When researching a person who held an academic degree, especially a doctorate, it could be helpful to contact the university in question and locate the dissertation, which usually also contains a *curriculum vitae* of the student.

For example, a librarian at the law school (*Juristische Fakultät*) of Munich's Ludwig-Maximilians-Universität states that the library has all dissertations published since 1840 and "a lot" of those published before that. Unless files and archives were lost during World War II, the situation should be about the same at all German universities.

Source: Rainer Thumshirn, Heimstetten, Germany

GERMAN AND AMERICAN UNIVERSITY DEGREES

Three of the four types of academic degrees granted by German universities are roughly comparable to the Masters of Arts or Masters of Science degree offered by American universities.

A doctoral degree, awarded in both arts and sciences, as well as law, medicine and theology, is the equivalent of an American Ph.D. Candidates must pass a series of examinations and write a dissertation.

Until recent years there were no degrees comparable to the American Bachelor of Arts or Sciences, but changes are on the horizon, with Germany's universities and specialized colleges heeding the call to adapt themselves to the era of globalization.

By 1999, German institutions of higher learning had launched more than 300 programs for students interested in earning the Anglo-American-style BA or MA rather than the traditional German Diplom degree.

About a third of the 202 bachelor programs were in the humanities and another third in enginneering, while most of the masters programs were in technical disciplines.

At the same time, university officials were also campaigning for reforms to help draw into Germany more scholars and scientists from other countries – including the establishment of as many as a dozen Max Planck Research Schools, each especially designed to attract and support outstanding scholars from outside Germany.

Sources:

♦Susan Steiner, ed., *Federal Republic of Germany: Questions and Answers,* German Information Center, 1996

♦ *The Week in Germany,* German Information Center, New York, 19 November 1999

BOOKS WRITTEN IN GERMAN

German is the native language of more than 100 million people. About one in ten books published throughout the the world has been written in German.

As regards translations into foreign languages, German is third after English and French, and more works have been translated into German than into any other language.

Source: *Facts About Germany*, Press and Information Office, Federal Republic of Germany, Societäts Verlag, 1999

DOCTORATES AWARDED BY UNIVERSITIES
IN GERMAN-SPEAKING COUNTRIES

The codes in parentheses after each title represent the following countries in which the titles have been used:
D = Bundesrepublik Deutschland (the former West Germany)
DDR = Deutsche Demokratische Republik (the former East Germany)
A = Österreich (Austria)
CH = Schweiz (Switzerland)

D., ehrenhalber verliehener Doktorgrad der Ev. Theologie Doktor der .... Honorary doctor of Protestant Theology

Dr. agr. (agronomiae), Landbauwiss., Landwirtschaftswiss. (D, DDR) .... Agriculture

Dr. disc. pol. (disciplinarum politicarum), Sozialwiss. (D) .... Social sciences

Dr. eh. (ehrenhalber), Ehrendoktor (DDR) .... Honorary doctor

Dr. e.h. (ehrenhalber), Dr. E.h. (Ehren halber), Ehrendoktor der TH, TU ... Honorary doctor of a technical university

Dr. forest. (rerum forestalium), Forstwirtschaft (D, DDR) .... Forestry

Dr. h.c. (honoris causa), Ehrendoktor der Univ. .... Honorary doctor of a university

Dr.-Ing. (ingenieur), Ingenieurwiss. (D, DDR) .... Engineering

Dr. iur./jur. (iuris, juris), Rechtswiss. (D, DDR, A, CH) .... Law

Dr. kur. can. (iuris canonici), Kirchenrecht (D) .... Canon law

Dr. iur. utr., Dr.j.u. (iuris utriusque), weltl. und Kirchenrecht (D), CH) .... Law and canon law

Dr. med. (medicinae), Medizin (D, DDR, CH) .... Medicine

Dr. med. dent. (medicinae dentariae), Zahnmedizin (D, DDR, A, CH) .... Dentistry

Dr. med.univ. (medicinae universae), Heilkunde (A) .... Medicine

Dr. med. vet. (medicinae veterinariae), Tierheilkunde (D, DDR, A, CH) .... Veterinarian

Dr. mont. (rerum naturalium technicarum), Bodenkultur (A) .... Agriculture

Dr. oec (oeconomiae),Wirschaftswiss., Verwaltungswiss. (DDR, CH) .... Economics

Dr. oec. (oeconomiae publicae), Staatswiss., Volkswirtschaft (D,CH) .... Economics

Dr. oec. troph. (oecotrophologiae), Hauswirtschaft, Ernährungswiss. (D) .... Dietetics

Dr. paed. (paedagogiae), Erziehungswiss. (DDR) .... Educational science

Dr. pharm. (pharmaciae), Pharmazie (CH) .... Pharmaceutics

Dr. phil (philosophiae_, Philosophie, Doktorgrad der Philosoph... All doctorates awarded by an Fakultät (D, DDR, A, CH) arts faculty (i.e., languages, history, philosophy, etc.)

Dr. phil. fac. theol. (philosophiae facultatis theologicae), Philosophie der Theolog. Fakultät Theology

Dr. Phil. nat. (philosophiae naturalis), Naturwiss. (soweit innerhalb der All doctorates in science Philosoph Fakultät. (D, CH) subjects, if taught within an arts faculty

Dr. rer. agr. (rerum agrarium), Landbauwiss., Landwirtschaft und Bodenkultur (D, DDR) Agriculture

Dr. rer. comm. (rerum commercialium), Handelswiss. (DDR, A) .... Economics

Dr. rer. forest. (rerum forestalium), Forstwiss. (D, DDR) .... Forestry

Dr. rer. hort. (rerum hortensiarum), Gartenbauwiss. (D, DDR, A, CH) .... Horticulture

Dr. rer. mont. (rerum montanarum), Bergbauwiss. (D, DDR, CH) .... Mining

Dr. rer. nat. (rerum naturalium), Naturwiss. (D, DDR, A, CH) .... All doctorates awarded by science faculties

Dr. rer. oec. (rerum oeconomicarum), Wirtschaftswiss. (D, DDR, A) .... Economics

Dr. rer. oec. publ. (rerum oeconomicarum publicarum), Staatswiss., ... Economics and
Wirtschaftswiss. (D) .... political science

Dr. rer. pol. (rerum politicarum, Staatswiss., Wirtschafts- und .... Economics and
Sozialwiss., Volkswirtschaft (D, DDR, A, CH) .... political science

Dr. rer. publ (rerum publicarum), Verwaltungswiss. (CH) .... Civil service

Dr. rer. sec. (rerum securitatis), Sicherheitstechnik, -wiss. (D) .... Safety engineering

Dr. rer. silv. (rerum silvaticarum), Forstwiss. (DDR) .... Forestry

Dr. rer. soc. oec. (rerum socialium oeconomicarumque), Sozial- .... Economics and
und Wirtschaftswiss. (A) .... social science

Dr. rer. techn. (rerum technicarum), techn. Wiss. (DDR) .... Technics

Dr. sc. agr. (scientiarum agrariarum), Landbauwiss., Landwirtschaftswiss. (D, DDR).. Agriculture

Dr. sc. jur. (scientiae juris), Rechtswiss. (DDR) .... Law

Dr. sc. math., Dr. scient. math. (scientiae mathematicae), Mathematik (CH) .... Mathematics

Dr. sc. med. (scientiae medicinae), Medizin (DDR) .... Medicine

Dr. sc. nat. Dr. scient. nat. (scientiae naturalium), Naturwiss. .... All doctorates awarded
(DDR, CH)   by science faculties

Dr. sc. oec., Dr. scient. oec. (scientiae oeconomiae), Wirtschaftswiss. (DDR) .... Economics

Dr. sc. paed. (scientiae paedagogiae), Erziehungswiss. (DDR) .... Educational science

Dr. sc. phil. (scientiae philosophiae), Philosophie (DDR)All doctorates awarded by an arts faculty

Dr. sc. pol. (scientiarum politicarum), Staatswiss., Sozialwiss., ... Political science
Volkswirtschaft (D)   and economics

Dr. sc. silv. (scientiae silvaticae), Forstwiss. (DDR) .... Forestry

Dr. sc. techn., Dr. scient. techn. (scientiarum technicarum), techn. Wiss. (CH)Technical science

Dr. techn. (technicae), techn. Wiss. (A) .... Technical science

Dr. theol. (theologiae), Theologie (D, DDR, A, CH) .... Theology

Dr. troph. (trophologiae), Ernährungswiss. (D) .... Dietetics

Dr. vet. (veterinariae), Tierheilkunde (DDR) .... Veterinarian

DIPLOM DEGREES AWARDED BY GERMAN UNIVERSITIES

Diplom-Agrarbiologe (Dipl.-Agr.Biol.) .... Agricultural biologist
Diplom-Agraringenieur (Dipl.-Ing.agr.) .... Agricultural engineer
Diplom-Agrarökonom .... Agricultural economist
Diplom-Anglist .... English philologist
Diplom-Architekt (Dipl.-Arch.) .... Architect
Diplom-Betriebswirt (Dipl.-Betriebsw.) .... Business management
Diplom-Bibliothekar (Dipl.-Bibl.) .... Librarian
Diplom-Biochemiker (Dipl.-Biochem.) .... Biochemist
Diplom-Biologe (Dipl.-Biol.) .... Biologist
Diplom-Chemieingenieur (Dipl.-Chem.Ing.) .... Chemical engineer
Diplom-Chemiker (Dipl.-Chem.) .... Chemist
Diplom-Designer (Dipl.-Des.) .... Designer
Diplom-Dokumentar .... Documentarian
Diplom-Dolmetscher (Dipl.-Dolm.) .... Interpreter
Diplom-Ernährungswissenschaftler .... Dietitian
Diplom-Fachsprachenexperte .... Technical translator

Diplom-Forstwirt .... Forestry
Diplom-Geograph (Dipl.-Geogr.) .... Geographer
Diplom-Geologe (Dipl.-Geol.) .... Geologist
Diplom-Geophysiker (Dipl.-Geophys.) .... Geophysicist
Diplom-Handelslehrer (Dipl.-HdL.) .... Teacher at a commercial school
Diplom-Haushaltsökonom .... Housekeeping economist
Diplom-Informatiker (Dipl.-Inform.) .... Computer specialist
Diplom-Ingenieur (Dipl.-Ing.) .... Engineer
Diplom-Journalist (Dipl.-Journ.) .... Journalist
Diplom-Kaufmann (Dipl.-Kfm.), -Kauffrau .... Economics and business administration
Diplom-Laborchemiker (Dipl.-Lab.Chem.) .... Laboratory chemist
Diplom-Landschaftsplaner .... Landscape architect
Diplom-Landwirt (Dipl.-Landw.) .... Agriculture
Diplom-Lebensmittelchemiker .... Food chemist
Diplom-Lebensmittel-Ingenieur .... Food engineer
Diplom-Lebensmitteltechnologe .... Food technology
Diplom-Literaturübersetzer .... Translator of literature
Diplom-Mathematiker (Dipl.-Math.) .... Mathematician
Diplom-Meteorologe (Dipl.-Met.) .... Meteorologist
Diplom-Mineraloge (Dipl.-Min.) .... Mineralogist
Diplom-Oecotrophologe (Dipl.oec.troph.) .... Dietetics
Diplom-Ökonom (Dipl.oec.) .... Economist
Diplom-Ozeanograph .... Oceanographer
Diplom-Pädagoge (Dipl.-Päd) .... Teacher
Diplom-Pharmakologe .... Pharmacologist
Diplom-Physiker (Dipl.-Phys.) .... Physicist
Diplom-Physikingenieur (Dipl.-Phys.Ing.) .... Physics engineer
Diplom-Politologe (Dipl.-Pol.) .... Political scientist
Diplom-Psychologe (Dipl.Psych.) .... Psychologist
Diplom-Romanist .... Romance philologist
Diplom-Sozialökonom .... Sociologist
Diplom-Sozialwissenschaftler (Dipl.-Soz.Wiss.) .... Sociologist
Diplom-Soziologe (Dipl.-Soz.) .... Sociologist
Diplom-Sportlehrer (Dipl.SportL.) .... Teacher of sports
Diplom-Sprachenlehrer (Deutsch als Fremdsprache) .... Teacher of German
as a foreign language
Diplom-Statistiker (Dipl.-Stat.) .... Statistician
Diplom-Übersetzer (Dipl.-Übers.) .... Translator
Diplom-Theaterwissenschaftler .... Theater studies, dramaturgy
Diplom-Theologe (Dipl.-Theol.) .... Theologian
Diplom-Umweltwissenschaftler .... Environmentalist
Diplom-Verfahrenschemiker (Dipl.-Verf.Chem.) .... Chemist
Diplom-Volkswirt (Dipl.-Volksw.) .... Economist
Diplom-Wirtschaftsingenieur (Dipl.-Wirtsch.Ing.) .... Economist and engineer

DIPLOM DEGREES AWARDED BY GERMAN FACHHOCHSCHULEN

Diplom-Bauingenieur .... Civic engineer

Diplom-Betriebswirt (Dipl.-Betriebsw.) .... Managerial economics
Diplom-Bibliothekar (Dipl.-Bibl.) .... Librarian
Diplom-Chemieingenieur .... Chemical engineer
Diplom-Designer (Dipl.-Des.) .... Designer
Diplom-Dokumentar (Dipl.-Dok.) .... Documentarian
Diplom-Dolmetscher (Dipl.-Dolm.) .... Interpreter
Diplom-Elektroingenieur .... Electrical engineer
Diplom-Fachlehrer .... Teacher specializing in ...
Diplom-Finanzwirt (Dipl.-Finanzw.) .... Public finance
Diplom-Forstingenieur .... Forestry engineer
Diplom-Heilpädagoge (Dipl.-Heilpäd.) .... Therapeutic pedagogist
Diplom-Informatiker (Dipl.-Inform.) .... Computer specialist
Diplom-Ingenieur (dipl.-Ing.) .... Engineer
Diplom-Maschinenbauingenieur .... Mechanical engineer
Diplom-Mathematiker.. Mathematician
Diplom-Nautiker .... Navigation
Diplom-Oecotrophologe (Dipl.-oec.troph.) .... Dietetics
Diplom-Physikingenieur.. Physics engineer
Diplom-Rechtspfleger (Dipl.-Rpfl.) .... Judicial officer
Diplom-Sozialarbeiter (Dipl.-Soz.Arb.) .... Welfare worker
Diplom-Sozialpädagoge (Dipl.-Soz.Päd.)..Teacher of social studies
Diplom-Übersetzer (Dipl.Übers.) .... Translator
Diplom-Verwaltungsbetriebswirt ....Economist with the Civil Service
(Dipl.-Verwaltungsbetriebsw.)
Diplom-Verwaltungswirt (Dipl.-Verwaltungsw.) .... Civil servant
Diplom-Wirtschaftsinformatiker ....Computer specialist and economist

Source: **Brockhaus Encyclopaedia**; English translations by Rainer Thumshirn

SELECTED EUROPEAN UNIVERSITIES (HOCHSCHULEN) FOUNDED BEFORE 1920

Institutions in Germany are listed by their last-known German name. Names of those in other countries are listed by their names in English.
KEY:
f = founded
* = no longer extant

German universities

Aachen: Rheinisch-Westfälische Technische Hochschule Aachen (Rhenish-Westphalian Technical University of Aachen); f 1870 as Polytechnikum; 1880 became Technische Hochschule; 1948 present title; 1970 reorganized. Koper-

nikusstr. 16, 52074 Aachen; www. rwth-aachen.de
Altdorf: Universität Altdorf*; f 1578
Bamberg: Otto-Friedrich-Universität Bamberg; f 1648; www.uni-bamberg.de
Berlin: Hochschule für Schauspielkunst Berlin (College of Theatrical Arts Berlin); f 1905; 1981 present title
Berlin: Technische Universität Berlin; f 1799 as Bauakademie (building academy); 1879 became Technische Hochschule; 1916 Bergakademie, f 1770, incorporated; 1946 reopened as Technische Universi-tät; /www.tu-berlin.de
Berlin: Humboldt-Universität zu Berlin (Humboldt University, Berlin); f 1810 as Friedrich-Wilhelms Universität;1948 renamed with present name. 10099 Berlin;

www.hu-berlin.de

Berlin: Bergacademie (mining); f 1770.

Bonn: Rheinische Friedrich-Wilhelms-Universität Bonn (Rhenish Friedrich-Wilhelms-Universität Bonn); f 1777; 1786 raised to university rank; 1794 dissolved during French occupation; 1818 refounded. Regina-Pacis Weg 3, 53113 Bonn; www.uni-bonn.de

Braunschweig: Technical Universität Carolo-Wilhelmina zu Braunschweig (Carolo-Wilhelmina Technical University of Brunswick); f 1745 as Collegium Carolinum; 1877 became Technische Hochschule; 1968 Technische Universität

Breslau: Universität Breslau; refounded 1811

Chemnitz: Technische Universität Chemnitz; f 1836; became college of engineering 1953; Technische Hochschule 1963; 1986 renamed Technische Universi-tät. Straße der Nationen 62, 09111 Chemnitz; www.tu-chemnitz.de

Clausthal: Technische Universität Clausthal; f 1775; became Bergakademie Clausthal 1864; 1920 acquired university status; 1968 present title conferred. Adolph-Roemer-Str. 2A, 38678 Clausthal-Zellerfeld

Cottbus: Hochschule für Bauwesen Cottbus (College of Building Technology Engineering of Cottbus); f 1836 as Höhere Gewerbeschule; became Technische Hochschule 1877; acquired university status 1895

Darmstadt: Technische Hochschule Darmstadt (University of Darmstadt); f 1836 as Höhere Gewerbeschule; 1877 became Technische Hochschule; 1895 acquired university status. Karolinenplatz 5, 64289 Darmstadt; www.th-darmstadt.de

Dillinger: Universität Dillinger*; f 1554

Dresden: Technische Universität Dresden; f 1826; 1890 renamed Polytechnische Schule, Technische Hochschule; 1961 conferred university status

Düsseldorf: Heinrich-Heine-University Düsseldorf; f 1907 as academy for practical medicine; 1923 university status; www.rz.uni-duesseldorf.de

Erfurt: Universität Erfurt*; f 1382

Erlangen: Friedrich-Alexander-Universität Erlangen-Nürnberg; f 1743; 1961 the former Hochschule für Wirtschafts-und Sozialwissenschaften Nürnberg was incorporated, and "Nürnberg" was added to the name. Schloßplatz 4, 91054 Erlangen; www.uni-erlangen.de

Frankfurt a. M.: Johann-Wolfgang-Goethe-Universität Frankfurt a. M; f 1914; Goethe name adopted 1932

Frankfurt a. O.: Universität Frankfurt a. O.; f 1506; 1811 united with Universität Breslau

Freiberg: Bergakademie Freiberg (Freiberg Mining Academy); f 1765; 1905 university status

Freiberg im Breisgau: Albert-Ludwigs-Universität Freiberg im Breisgau; f 1457. Fahnenbergplatz, 79085 Freiberg/Breisgau; www.uni-freiberg.de

Gießen: Justus-Liebig-Universität Gießen (Justus Liebig University of Gießen); f 1607 as university; 1946 became Justus-Liebig-Hochschule (academy); Ludwig-straße 23, 35390 Gießen; www.uni-giessen.de

Göttingen: Georg-August-Universität Göttingen; f 1737. Gossterstraße 5-7, 37073 Göttingen; www.uni-goettingen.de

Greifswald: Ernst-Moritz-Arnt-Universität Greifswald; f 1456; 1648 came under control of Sweden; 1815 became a Prussian university. Domstsraße 11, 17487 Greifswald; www.uni-greifswald.de

Halle: Martin-Luther-Universität Halle-Wittenberg; University of Wittenburg f 1502 as Universität Wittenberg; University of Halle; f 1694; 1817 the two merged; 1933 name changed to Martin-Luther-Universität. Universitätsplatz, 06099 Halle/S.

Hamburg: Universität Hamburg; f 1919. Edmund-Siemers-Allee 1, 20146 Hamburg

Hannover: Tierarztliche Hochschule Hannover (Hannover School of Veterinary Medicine); f 1778; 1887 university status

Hannover: Universität Hannover; f 1831 as secondary vocational school; 1847 became Polytechnische Hochschule; 1879 Königliche Technische Hochschule; 1880 acquired university status. Welfengarten 1, 30167 Hannover www.uni-hannover.de

Heidelberg: Ruprecht-Karls-Universität Heidelberg; f 1386. Grabengasse 1, 69117 Heidelberg; www.rektorat.uni-heidelberg.de

Helmstedt: Universität Helmstedt*; f 1576

Herborn: Universität Herborn*; f 1654

Hohenheim: Universität Hohenheim; f 1818; 1904 became Hochschule; 1919 acquired university status. Schloß, 70599 Stuttgart (Hohenheim); www.uni-hohenheim.de

Ingolstadt: Universität Ingolstadt*; f 1472

Jena: Friedrich-Schiller-Universität Jena; f 1558 (as academy); 1558 became university. Fürstengraben 1, 07743 Jena

Karlsruhe: Pädagogische Hochschule Karlsruhe (College of Education Karlsruhe); f 1768 as Schul-Seminarium; 1962 became college. Bismarckstraße 10, 76133 Karlsruhe

Karlsruhe: Universität Fridericiana Karlsruhe (Technische Hochschule); f 1825 as Polytechnische Schule; 1865 acquired university status. Kaiserstraße 12, 76128 Karlsruhe

Kiel: Christian-Albrechts-Universität zu Kiel; f 1665; 1773 became *Landesuniversität* for Schleswig-Holstein; 1867 became a Prussian university; 1945 reestablished as Landesuniversität. Olsbausenstsraße 40, 24098 Kiel; www.uni-kiel.de/index.html

Köln: Universität zu Köln; f 1388; from 1798 closed under French occupation; 1919 reestablished as university.

Albertus-Magnus Platz, 50923 Köln

Königsberg: Universität Königsberg i. Pr.; f 1544

Landshut: Universität Landshut*; f 1800; 1826 moved to München

Leipzig: Universität Leipzig; f 1409; 1953 became Karl-Marx-Universität; 1991 acquired present title. Augustusplatz 9-11, 04109 Leipzig; www.uni-leipzig. de

Löwen: Universität Löwen; f 1426

Mainz: Johannes Gutenberg-Universität Mainz; f 1477; 1816 closed, but Catholic theology faculty continued as a seminary; 1946 reestablished. Saarstraße 21, 55099 Mainz

Mannheim: Universität Mannheim; f 1907 as Stadtische Handelshochschule; 1933 attached to University of Heidelberg; 1946 became Wirtschafts-hochschule; 1967 university title conferred. Schloß, 68131 Mannheim; www.uni-mannheim.de

Marburg: Philipps Universität Marburg a. d. Lahn; f 1527. Biegensstraße 10, 35037 Marburg/Lahn; www.uni-marburg.de

München: Technische Universität München; f 1827 as Polytechnische Zentral-schule; 1868 became Polytechnisch Schule; 1877 became Technische Hoch-schule; 1970 acquired university status. Arcisstraße 21, 80333 München; www.tu-muenchen.de

München: Ludwig-Maximilians-Universität München; f 1472 at Ingolstadt; 1800 transferred to Landshut; 1826 to München. Geschwister-Scholl-Platz 1, 80539 München; www.uni-muenchen. de

Münster: Westfalische Wilhelms Universität Münster; f 1780 as university; 1818 became academy of philosophy and theology; 1902 restored to university status; 1907 acquired present title. Schloßplatz 2, 48149 Münster

Osnabrück: Universität Osnabrück*; f 1630

Paderborn: Universität Paderborn*; f 1614

Rostock: Universität Rostock; f 1419; 15th century moved temporarily to Greifswald and Lübeck; 1946 reorganized and reopened. Universitätsplatz 1, 18051 Rostock; www.uni-rostock.de

Schwäbisch Gmünd: Pädagogische Hochschule Schwäbisch Gmünd (Univer-sity of Education of Schwäbisch Gmünd); f 1825 as University College. Oberbettringer Straße 200, 73525 Schwäbisch Gmünd

Stuttgart: Universität Stuttgart; f 1829 as grammar and vocational school; 1840 became Polytechnische Schule; 1890 became Technische Hochschule; 1967 present title conferred. Postfach 106037, Keplerstraße 7, 70174 Stuttgart; www.uni-stuttgart.de

Trier: Universität Trier; f 1473; closed in Napoleonic era; 1970 reestablished. Universitätsring 15, 54286 Trier; www.uni-trier.de

Tübingen: Eberhard-Karls-Universität Tübingen; f 1477. Wilhelmstraße 7, 72074 Tübingen; www.uni-tuebingen.de

Vechta: Hochschule Vechta; f 1830 as school for teacher training; became college after World War II; 1973 became branch of University of Osnabrück; 1955 present status. Driverstraße 22, 49377 Vechta; www.uni-vechta.de

Weimar: Hochschule für Architektur und Bauwesen Weimar: f 1860 as academy of fine arts; 1926 became college; 1954 acquired university status. Geschwister-Scholl-Straße 8, 99423 Weimar; www.uni-weimar.de

Wittenberg: Universität Wittenberg*; f 1502; 1817 united with Halle

Würzburg: Bayerische-Julius-Maximilians Universität Würzburg; f 1402; 1582 refounded. Sanderring 2, 97070 Würzburg

Switzerland

Basel: Universität Basel; f 1460

Berne: Universität Berne; f 1528 as school; 18th century became academy; 1834 became university

Fribourg: Université de Fribourg; f 1889 Université de Genève; f 1559 as Schola Genevensis by Calvin; 1873 established as university

Lausanne: École polytechnique federale de Lausanne; f 1853 as private school; 1890 part of Faculty of Science in University of Lausanne; 1946 autonomous institute

Lausanne: Université de Lausanne; f 1537 as Académie de Lausanne, a theological seminary; 1890 became university

Université de Neuchâtel; f 1838 as academy; 1909 became university

St. Gallen: Hochschule St. Gallen für Wirtschafts-Rechts- und Socialwissenschaften (University of St. Gallen for Business Administration, Economics, Law, and Social Sciences); f 1898

Zürich: Eidgenössische Technische Hochschule Zürich (Swiss Federal Institute of Technology); f 1855

Zürich: Universität Zürich; f 1523 as a school; 1838 became university

Austria

Graz: Hochschule für Musik und darstellende Kunst in Graz (College of Music and Dramatic Art Graz); f 1803 as provincial School of Music; 1815 conservatory; 1963 Akademie; 1970 university institution with title of Hochschule. Leonhardstraße 15, 8010 Graz ; www.mhsg.ac.at

Graz: Karl-Franzens-Universität Graz; f 1585/86; 1782 university status withdrawn; 1827 reestablished as Karl Franzens Universität. Universitätsplatz 3, 8010 Graz; www.kfunigraz.ad.at

Graz: Technische Universität Graz; f 1811; 1865/66 university rank. Rechbauerstsaße 12, 8010 Graz; www.tugraz.ac.at

Innsbrück: Leopold-Franzens-Universität Innsbruck; f 1669. Innrain 52, 6020 Innsbruck; www.uibk.ac.at

Leoben: Montanuniversität Leoben (University of Mining and Metallurgy Leoben); f 1840 as mining institute; 1904 university status; 1975 present title. Franz-Josef-Straße 18, 8700 Leoben;

www.unileoben.ac.at
Salzburg: Hochschule für Musik und darstellende Kunst 'Mozarteum' in Salzburg; f 1841; 1914 conservatory; 1921 state institution; 1953 Akademie; 1970 university institution with title of Hoch-schule. Mirrabelplatz 1, 5020 Salzburg; www.moz.ac.at.
Salzburg: Universität Salzburg; f 1617 as school; 1622 university; 1810 dissolved; 1962 reestablished. Kapitelgasse 4, 5020 Salzburg; www.sbg.ad.at.
Wien: Akademie der bildenden Künste in Wien (Academy of Fine Arts Vienna); f 1692. Schillerplatz 3, 1010 Wien
Wien: Hochschule für Musik und darstellende Kunst in Wien (College of Music and Dramatic Art Vienna); f 1812 as a Conservatory; 1920 became Academy; 1970 university with title of Hoch-schule. Lothringerstraße 18, 1030 Wien; www.moz.ad.at
Wien: Universität für Bodenkultur Wien (University of Agriculture Vienna); f 1872 as Hochschule; 1975 present title. Gregor Mendelstraße 33, 1180 Wien; www.boku.ad.at
Wien: Hochschule für angewandte Kunst in Wien (University of Applied Arts Vienna); f 1868 as school; 1948 academy; 1970 university institution with title of Hochschule
Wien: Technische Universität Wien; f 1815 as institute of technology; 1872 university rank. Karlsplatz 13, 1040 Wien; www.info.tuwien.ad.at
Wien: Universität Wien; f 1365. Dr. Karl Lueger-Ring 1, 1010 Wien; www.univie.ad.at
Wien: Wirtschaftuniversität Wien (Vienna University of Economic and Busi-ness Administration); f 1898 as academy for foreign trade; 1919 became Hoch-schule für Welthandel, with university rank. Augasse 2-6, 1090 Wien; www.wu-wien.ad.at
Wien: Veterinärmedizinische Universität Wien (Vienna University of Veterinary Medicine); f 1767 as school; 1908 university status; 1975 present title. Veterinaerplatz 1, 1210 Wien; www.vu-wien.ac.at

Czechoslovakia (Czech Republic)
Brno: Masaryk University Brno; f 1919; 1939 closed; 1945 reopened as Jana Evangelista Purkyn University; 1989 reverted to former name
Brno: Technical University of Brno; f 1849; closed during German occupation; 1945 reopened
Brno: University of Agriculture Brno; f 1919
Brno: University of Veterinary Sciences Brno; f 1918; 1969 became university
Olomouc: Palacky University Olomouc; f 1573; closed during German occupation; 1946 reopened
Ostrava: Technical University of Mines and Metallurgy Ostrava; f 1716 as School of Mining and Metallurgy at Jáchymov in Bohemia; 1763 became part of University of Prague; 1770 moved to Slovakia; 1849 to Stiaynica and Pribram, Bohemia; 1894 acquired university status; 1945 moved to present location, Ostrava
Prague: Charles University Prague; f 1348; 1882 divided into separate Czech and German universities, each bearing title Charles-Ferdinand; 1918 present title adopted; November 1939 closed during German occupation; 1945 reopened when the German university was abolished
Prague: Czech Technical University of Prague; f 1707 as Czech State Engineering School; 1803 became Polytechnic; 1864 acquired university status; 1939 closed during German occupation; 1945 reopened
Prague: University of Agriculture Prague; f 1906; 1939 closed during the German occupation; 1945 reopened; 1952 de-tached and reestablished as separate institution

Lithuania
Vilnius: Vilnius University; f 1579 as

Academica and Universitas Vilnensis; 1781 and 1803 reorganized as Imperial University of Vilnius; 1832 closed; 1919 reopened; 1943 closed during German occupation. 11 Sauletekeo Avenue, 2040 Vilnius

Luxembourg

Luxembourg: University Centre of Luxumbourg; f 1848. Centre Universitaire de Luxembourg 162A, avenue de la Faïencerie, 1511 Luxembourg

Netherlands

Amsterdam: Free University Amsterdam; f 1880. De Boelelaan 1105, 1081 HV Amsterdam; www.vu.nl

Amsterdam: University of Amsterdam; f 1632; 1876 became university

Delft: Delft University of Technology; f 1842 as "Royal Academy"; 1986 acquired present title. Postbus 5, 2600 AA Delft; www.tudelft.nl

Groningen: University of Groningen; f 1614. Postbus 72, 9700 AB Groningen; www.rug.nl

Leiden: Leiden University; f 1575. Rijkuniversiteit Leiden, Postbus 9500, 2300 RA Leiden; www. leidenuniv.nl

Utrecht: Utrecht University; f 1636. Postbus 80125, Heidelberglaan 8, 3508 TC Utrecht; www.ruu.nl

Wageningen: Wageningen Agriculture University; f 1876 as national agricultural college; 1918 acquired university status. P.O. Box 9101, Costerweg, 6700 HB Wageningen; www.wau.nl

Poland

Crakow: Crakow University of Technology; 1945 succeeded Polytechnic Institute (1835); 1878 suppressed; 1970 reorganized. ul. Warszawska 24, 31-155 Krakow; www.pk.edu.pl

Cracow: Jagiellonian University Cracow; f 1364; 1939 closed during the German occupation; after 1942 operated as an underground university

Cracow: The Stanislaw Staszic University of Mining and Metallurgy Cracow; f 1919 as Akademia Gornicza, Academy of Mining; 1949 name changed to

Akademia Gorniczo-Hutnicza; ul.Mickewcza 30, 30-059 Krakow; www.uci.agh.edu.pl

Gdansk: Technical University of Gdansk; f 1904 as Technische Hochschule Gdansk, Prussia. ul. Narutowicza 11/12, 80-952 Gdansk; www.pg.gda.pl

Lublin: Catholic University of Lublin; f 1918; 1939 closed during the German occupation; 1944 reopened. Aleje Ractawicki 14, 20-950 Lublin; www.eber.kul.lublin.pl

Poznan: Adam Mickiewicz University of Poznan; f 1919. ul. Wieniawskiego 1, 61-712 Poznan; www.amu.edu.pl

Poznan: Poznan University of Technology; f 1919 as college; 1939 closed; 1945 reopened; 1955 acquired full university status. ul. Marii Sklodowskiej-Curie 5, 61-542 Poznan 60-965; www.put.poznan.pl

Poznan: Agricultural University August Cieszkowski of Poznan, f 1870 as Agricultural School; 1919 became Faculty of Agriculture and Forestry, Adam Mickiewicz University Poznan; 1951 detached as college; 1972 took present title. ul. Wojska Polskiego 28, 60-637 Poznan

Warsaw: University of Warsaw f 1808 as school of law; 1816 became university; almost completely destroyed during World War II; 1945 reopened. ul. Krakowskie Przedmiescie 26/28, 00-325 Warszawa; www.uw.edu.pl

Warsaw: Warsaw University of Technology; f 1826 as polytechnic institute; 1830 closed; 1898-1915 operated with Russian as medium of instruction; 1915 reorganized as Technical University of Warsaw; 1939-1944 closed during the German occupation. plac Politechniki 1, 00-661 Warszawa; www.pw.edu. pl-iso/index-en.html

Wroclaw: University of Wroclaw; f 1702 as Generale Litterarum Gymnasium; 1811 became university after union with the University of Frankfurt/Oder; 1945 German university closed and Polish university opened. pl. Universytecki 1, 50-137 Wroclaw; www.adm.uni. wroc.pl

Slovak Republic

Bratislava: Comenius University Bratislava; f 1919 to replace former Hungarian University established 1914. Safarikovo nam, 6, 818 06 Bratislava; www.uniba.sk **Kovice:** Technical University of Kovice; f 1864 as Mining and Metallurgical School at Banskabystrica. Letna 9, 042 00 Kovice; http://ccsun.tuke.sk/tu/tuke-a.html **Zvolen:** University of Forestry and Wood Technology Zvolen; f 1807 at Banska Stiaynica as School of Forestry

Yugoslavia

Belgrade: University of Belgrade; f 1808 as a school; 1838 lyceum; 1863 became college; 1905 university status. Studentski trg broj 1, 11000 Beograd

Sources:

♦ *International Handbook of Universities.* 13th ed. International Association of Universities. The Macmillan Press Ltd., London. 1993.

♦ *International Handbook of Universities,* 15th ed., International Association of Universities. Groves Dictionaries, Inc., New York, 1998.

♦ *Meyers Lexikon*, Bibliographisches Institut, Leipzig, 1930.

ARCHIVES IN SELECTED GERMAN AND AUSTRIAN UNIVERSITIES

(Check websites for updated information.)

Achen: Rheinisch-Westfälische Technische Hochschule Aachen Historisches Institut, Abt. Hochschularchiv, Templergraben 57, 52062 Aachen; Post: Kopernikusstr. 16, 52074 Aachen

Augsburg: Universität Augsburg, Univer-sitätsarchiv, Alter Postweg 120, 86159 Augsburg

Bamberg: Otto-Friedrich-Universität Bamberg, Universitätsarchiv, Kapuziner-str. 16, 96047 Bamberg; Postanschrift: 96045 Bamberg

Bautzen: Sorbisches Kulturarchiv, Bahn-hofstsr. 6, 02625 Bautzen

Bayreuth: Universität Bayreuth, Universitätsarchiv, Dezernat HB/ID, Universi-tätsstr. 30, 95447 Bayreuth

Berlin: Freie Universität Berlin, Universi-tätsarchiv, Kaiserswerther Str. 16-18, 14195 Berlin

- Hochschule der Künste Berlin, Hochschularchiv, Postfach 126720, 10595 Berlin, Bundesalle 1-12, 10719 Berlin

- Humboldt-Universität zu Berlin, Universitätsarchiv, Unter den Linden 6, 10099 Berlin

- Technische Fachhochschule Berlin, His-torisches Archiv, Luxemburger Str. 10, Haus Grashof, Raum 802, 13353 Berlin

- Technische Universität Berlin, Univer-sitätsbibliothek/Hoschschularchiv, Straße des 17. June 135, 10623 Berlin

- HEROLD, Verein für Heraldik, Genealogie und verwandte Wissenschaften, Archiv, Archivstr. 12-14, 14195 Berlin

Bochum: Ruhr-Universität Bochum, Universitätsarchiv, Ruhr-Universität, 44780 Bochum (im Aufbau)

Bonn: Rheinische Friedrich-Wilhelms-Universität Bonn, Universitätsarchiv, Am Hof, 53113 Bonn

Braunschweig: Technische Universität Carolo-Wilhelmina Braunschweig, Uni-versitätsarchiv, Pockelsstr. 4, 38106 Braunschweig

Bremerhaven: Förderverein Deutsches Auswanderermuseum e.V., Archiv, Inselstr. 6, 27568 Bremerhaven

Chemnitz: Technische Universität Chemnitz-Zwickau, Universitätsarchiv, Reichenhainer Str. 41, 09126 Chemnitz; Postfach 964, 09009 Chemnitz

Clausthal: Technische Universität Claus-thal, Universitätsarchiv, Leibnizstr. 2, 38678 Clausthal-Zellerfeld

Darmstadt: Technische Hochschule Darmstadt, Dokumentation und Hoch-schularchiv, Karolinenplatz 3, 64289

Darmstadt
Dortmund: Universität Dortmund, Universitätsarchiv, August-Schmidt-Str. 4, 44227 Dortmund-Eichlinghofen; Postanschrift: 44221 Dortmund
Dresden: Technische Universität Dresden, Universitätsarchiv, Mommenstr. 13, 01069 Dresden
Duisberg: Gerhard-Mercator-Universität-Gesamthochschule Duisburg, Archiv, Lotharstr. 65, 47048 Duisburg
Eichstätt: Katholische Universität Eichstätt, Archiv, Ostenstr. 26, 85071 Eichstätt
Erfurt: Pädagogische Hochschule Erfurt/Mühlhausen, Hochschularchiv, Nord-häuser Str. 63, 99089 Erfurt; Postfach 307, 99006 Erfurt
Erlangen-Nürnberg: Friedrich-Alexander-Universität Erlangen-Nürnberg, Universitätsarchiv, Schuhstr. 1a, 91052 Erlangen
Flensburg: Fachhochschule Flensburg, Hochschularchiv, Kanzleistr. 91-93 Block B, 24943 Flensburg
Frankfurt am Main: Johann Wolfgang Goethe-Universität Frankfurt (Main), Universitätsarchiv, Senckenberganlage 31, 60325 Frankfurt
Freiberg: Technische Universität Bergakademie Freiberg, Universitätsarchiv, Akademiestr. 6, 09596 Freiberg
Freiberg im Breisgau: Albert-Ludwigs-Universität Freiburg, Universitätsarchiv, Werthmannplatz 2, 79098 Freiburg im Breisgau; Postfach 1629, 79016 Freiburg im Breisgau
Gießen: Justus-Liebig-Universität Gießen, Universitätsarchiv, c/o Universitätsbibliothek, Otto-Behaghel-Str. 8, 35394 Gießen
Göttingen: Georg-August-Universität Göttingen, Universitätsarchiv, Goßlerstr. 12a, 37073 Göttingen; Postfach 3744, 37027 Göttingen
Graz (Austria): Karl-Franzens-Universität Graz, Universitätsarchiv, Universitätsplatz 3, A-8010 Graz
Halle: Martin-Luther-Universität Halle-

Wittenberg, Universitätsarchiv, Weidenplan 12, 06108 Halle (Saale)
Hamburg: Universitätsarchiv Hamburg, Staatsarchiv der Freien und Hansestadt Hamburg, ABC-Str. 19 A, 20354 Hamburg
Hannover: Universität Hannover, Universitätsarchiv, Welfengarten 1 B, 30167 Hannover
Heidelberg: Ruprecht-Karls-Universität Heidelberg, Universitätsarchiv, Friedrich-Ebert-Platz 2, 69117 Heidelberg; Postfach 105760, 69047 Heidelberg
-Zentralarchiv zur Erforschung der Geschichte der Juden in Deutschland, Bienenstr. 5, 69117 Heidelberg
Hohenheim: Universität Hohenheim, Universitätsarchiv, Museum zur Geschichte Hohenheims, Speisemeistereiflügel, Schloß Hohenheim, Postfach, 70599 Stuttgart (Hohenheim)
Ilmenau: Technische Universität Ilmenau, Universitätsarchiv, Dezernat Akademische und Rechtsangelegenheiten, Max-Planck-Ring 14, 98693 Ilmenau; Postfach 327, 98684 Ilmenau
Innsbruck (Austria): Universität Innsbruck, Universitätsarchiv, Innrain 52, A-6020 Innsbruck
Jena: Friedrich-Schiller-Universität Jena, Thüringer Universitäts- und Landesbibliothek, Universitätsarchiv, Postfach, 07740 Jena
-Fachhochschule Jena, Hochschularchiv, Tatzendpromenade 1b, 07745 Jena; Postfach 100314, 07703 Jena
Karlsruhe: Universität Fridericiana Karlsruhe (Technische Hochschule), Universitätsarchiv, Kaiserstr. 12, 76131 Karlsruhe; Postfach 6980, 76128 Karlsruhe
Kiel: Universitätsarchiv Kiel, Landesarchiv Schleswig-Holstein, Prinzenpalais, 24837 Schleswig
Köln: Universität Köln, Universitätsarchiv, Universitätsstr. 33 [entrance on Kerpener Str.], 50931 Köln
Konstanz: Universität Konstanz, Univer-

sitätsarchiv, Universitätsstr. 10, 78464 Konstanz; Postfach 5560, D75, 78434 Konstanz
Leipzig: Universitätsarchiv Leipzig, Beethovenstr. 6, 04107 Leipzig
- Hochschule für Technik, Wirtschaft und Kultur Leipzig (FH), Hochschularchiv, Eichendorffstr. 2, 04277 Leipzig; Postfach 66, 04251 Leipzig
Lüneberg: Universität Lüneburg, Hochschularchiv, Wilschenbruchweg 84, 21335 Lüneberg
Magdeburg: Otto-von-Guericke-Universität, Universitätsarchiv, Universitätsplatz 2, 39106 Magdeburg; Postfach 4120, 39016 Magdeburg
Mainz: Johannes Gutenburg-Universität Mainz, Universitätsarchiv, Forum 2, 55128 Mainz; Postfach 3980, 55099 Mainz
Mannheim: Universität Mannheim, Universitätsarchiv, Schloß, Dezernat I, Postfach 103462, 68034 Mannheim
Marburg/Lahn: Philipps-Universität Marburg (Lahn), Universitätsarchiv, Hessisches Staatsarchiv Marburg, Friedrichsplatz 15, Postfach 540, 35037 Marburg
München: Ludwig-Maximilians-Universität München, Universitätsarchiv, Geschwister-Scholl-Platz 1, 80539 München
Münster: Westfälische Wilhelms-Universität Münster, Universitätsarchiv, Steinfurter Str. 107, 48149 Münster
Oldenburg: Carl von Ossietzky-Universität Oldenburg, Universitätsarchiv, Hermann-Helmers-Archiv, BIS, Postfach 2541, 26015 Oldenburg
Paderborn: Universität-Gesamthochschule Paderborn, Universitätsarchiv, Warburger Str. 100, 33098 Paderborn
Passau: Universität Passau, Universitäts-archiv, Dr.-Hans-Kapfinger-Str. 22, 94032 Passau
Potsdam: Universität Potsdam, Universitätsarchiv, UNI-Potsdam, Postfach 601553, 14415 Potsdam
Reutlingen: Fachhochschule für Technik und Wirtschaft Reutlingen, Hochschul-archiv, Alteburgstr. 150,

72762 Reut-lingen
Rostock: Universität Rostock, Universitätsarchiv, Universitätsplatz 1, 188051 Rostock
Saarbrücken: Universität des Saarlandes, Universitätsarchiv, Postfach 151150, 66041 Saarbrücken
Salzburg (Austria): Universität Salzburg, Universitätsarchiv, Residenzplatz 1, Postfach 505, A-5010 Salzburg
Stuttgart: Universität Stuttgart, Universitätsarchiv, Universitätsbibliothek, Post-fach 104941, 70043 Stuttgart
Tübingen: Eberhard-Karls-Universität Tübingen, Universitätsarchiv, Wilhelmstr. 32, 72074 Tübingen
Ulm: Universität Ulm, Universitätsarchiv, 89069 Ulm
Wien (Austria): Universität Wien, Universitätsarchiv, Postgasse 9 (Alte Universität), A1010 Wien
–Technische Universität Wien, Universitätsarchiv, Karlsplatz 13, A-1040 Wien
Würzburg: Bayerische Julius-Maximilians-Universität Würzburg, Universitätsarchiv, Sanderring 2, 97070 Würzburg
Zwickau: Hochschule für Technik und Wirtschaft Zwickau (FH), Hochschularchiv, Dr.-Friedrich-Ring 2a, 08056 Zwickau; Postfach 35, 08001 Zwickau

UNIVERSITIES, TECHNICAL SCHOOLS, AND LIBRARIES OF THE SECOND EMPIRE

Second Empire universities

The 21 universities of the Second German Empire are listed below, with their respective dates of founding (in parentheses). All had faculties of theology, law, medicine, and philosophy except Münster, which had no faculty of medicine.

Berlin (1809); Bonn* (1818); Breslau* (1811); Erlangen (1743); Freiburg**(1457); Giessen (1607); Göttingen

(1737); Griefswald (1456); Halle (1694); Heidelberg (1385); Jena (1558); Kiel (1665); Königsberg (1544); Leipzig (1409); Marburg (1527); München** (1826); Münster** (1902); Rostock (1418); Strassburg (1872); Tübingen* (1477); Würzburg** (1582)

* = both Protestant and Catholic faculties for school of theology

** = exclusively Catholic faculty for school of theology

All others: exclusively Protestant faculty for school of theology

Technical High Schools (Polytechnica)

Ten technical high schools, with departments of architecture, building, civil engineering, chemistry, metallurgy and, in some cases, anatomy, had the power to grant certain degrees. They were Berlin (Charlottenburg), München, Darmstadt, Karlsruhe, Hannover, Dresden, Stuttgart, Aix-la-Chapelle, Braunschweig, and Danzig.

Among other higher technical schools were three mining academies of Berlin, Clausthal, in the Harz, and Freiberg in Saxony.

For instruction in agriculture were agricultural schools attached to several universities — notably Berlin, Halle, Göttingen, Königsberg, Jena, Poppelsdorf near Bonn, München and Leipzig.

Noted academies of forestry were those of Tharandt (in Saxony), Eberswalde, Münden on the Weser, Hohenheim near Stuttgart, Braunschweig, Eisenach, Giessen, and Karlsruhe.

Five veterinary academies were located at Berlin, Hannover, München, Dresden, and Stuttgart.

For military science there were the academies of war *(Kriegsakademien)* in Berlin and München, a naval academy in Kiel, and various cadet and non-commissioned officers' schools.

Libraries

The best known libraries were in these locations (holdings represent early twentieth century counts):

Berlin (1,000,000 volumes, 30,000 manuscripts)

München (1,000,000 volumes, 40,000 manuscripts)

Heidelberg (563,000 volumes, 8,000 manuscripts)

Göttingen (503,000 volumes, 6,000 manuscripts)

Strassburg (760,000 volumes)

Dresden (500,000 volumes, 6,000 manuscripts)

Hamburg (municipal library 600,000 volumes, 5,000 manuscripts)

Stuttgart (400,000 volumes, 3,500 manuscripts)

Leipzig (university library 500,000 volumes, 5,000 manuscripts)

Würzburg (350,000 volumes)

Tübingen (340,000 volumes)

Rostock (318,000 volumes)

Breslau (university library 300,000 volumes, 7,000 manuscripts)

Freiburg-im-Breisgau (250,000 volumes)

Bonn (265,000 volumes)

Königsberg (230,000 voumes, 1,100 manuscripts)

There were also famous libraries at Gotha, Wolfenbüttel, and Celle.

Source: *Encyclopedia Britannica: Dictionary of Arts, Sciences, Literature and General Infor- mation,* University Press, NY, 1910, 11th ed. e.

UNIVERSITY ADMISSIONS

The basic entrance requirement is the *Abitur,* the diploma awarded to students who have passed a series of final examinations in grade 13 of an academic high school or its equivalent.

Some university-level programs, particularly in technical fields and specialized subjects like agriculture, are open to graduates of two-year vocational colleges (*Fachoberschulen*). It is possible for individuals who did not attend either an academic high school or a *Fachoberschule* to earn the *Abitur* at night school or in a general education institution called a *Kolleg*. Some vocational programs have also begun increasing the number of general education courses they offer, thereby opening the possibility for students in those programs to go on to study for the *Abitur*. These efforts to give individuals who did not attend Gymnasium the opportunity for university-level study are known as "Second Chance Education" (*Zweiter Bildungsweg*).

German universities once offered virtually open enrollment to all holders of an *Abitur*. But the number of young people choosing to pursue an *Abitur* has been growing steadily, which has put tremendous pressure on the university system.

Overcrowding is common in many German universities, and admission to some fields of study is now restricted. Young people hoping to study medicine, dentistry, and veterinary medicine must take special admissions exams. Students wanting to study other high-demand fields, including architecture, law, economics, psychology, and pharmacy, must apply to the Central Office for the Allocation of Study Places (*ZVS: Zentralstelle für die Vergabe von Studienplätzen*) in Dortmund (North Rhine-Westphalia), which ranks students on the basis of their grades on the *Abitur* exams and how long they have been on the waiting list to enter the desired program. The limitation on the number of students admitted to study certain fields is known as the *Numerus Claus-us*.

Source: *Federal Republic of Germany: Questions and Answers,* ed. Susan Steiner . German Information Center, New York, 1996.

GLOSSARY: THE GERMAN EDUCATION SYSTEM

Abendgymnasium: General secondary night school for employed adults providing university entrance qualification

Allgemeine Hochschulreife: General university entrance qualification, as a rule obtained by taking a final examination (*Abiturprüfung*) after 13 years of schooling, including upper secondary education, in general at a *Gymnasium*. The holder has the right to study at all institutions of higher education without restrictions with regard to subject areas.

Berufliches Gymnasium: Vocational school at the upper level of secondary education (grades 11, 12, 13) which leads to a general university entrance qualification. Career oriented-subject areas and focuses such as economics and engineer-ing are added to the subjects otherwise available at the general education *Gymnasium*.

Berufsaufbauschule: Vocational extension school giving access to the upper level technical types of education by providing a qualification equivalent to that of the *Realschule* leaving certificate.

Berufsfachschule: Vocational school at the upper level of secondary education that prepares students for jobs or provides them with vocational training promoting at the same time general education. Depending on the objective of training, the requirements for admission (*Hauptschule* or *Realschule* certificate) vary as well as the period of training (from 1 year to 3 years).

Berufsgrundbildungsjahr: Basic vocational training year as the first stage of vocational training either in a full-time school or in the cooperative form of part-time school and on-the-job training.

Berufsschule: Part-time vocational school at the upper level of secondary education providing general and career-oriented education for students in initial vocational training; special attention is paid to the requirements of training in the dual system (part-time school and on-the-job training).

Fachgymnasium: See *Berufliches Gymnasium.*

Fachhochschule: Institution of higher education offering academic training with a practical bias, particularly in engineer-ing, economics, social work, agriculture and design.

Fachhochschulreife: Qualification obtained, as a rule, by taking a final examination after 12 years of schooling, the last two years at a *Fachoberschule.* It provides access to studies at *Fachhochschulen* and the corresponding courses of study at *Gesamthochschulen.*

Fachoberschule: Technical secondary school (grades 11 and 12) specialized in various areas and providing access to *Fachhochschulen.*

Fachschule: Technical school providing advanced vocational training.

Gesamthochschule: Institution of higher education existing in two *Länder* combining functions of the universities, *Fachhochschulen* and, in some cases, colleges of art and music. It offers courses of study of various durations and leading to different degrees.

Gesamtschule: Comprehensive school existing in two forms: the cooperative comprehensive school combines the schools of the traditional tripartite system under one roof and harmonizes the curricula in order to facilitate student transfer between the different coexisting types; the integrated comprehensive school admits all pupils of a certain age without differentiating between the tradi-tional school types. A number of the integrated comprehensive schools also have the upper secondary level, usually the *Gymnasiale Oberstufe*

Gymnasiale Oberstufe: Upper level of the *Gymnasium* (grades 11, 12, 13); the final examination (*Abiturprüfung*)

provides a general university entrance qualification.

Gymnasium: General education secondary school (grades 5 to 13) providing general university entrance qualification. See also *Allgemeine Hochschulreife.*

Hauptschule: General education secondary school – lower level – providing full-time compulsory education and leading normally to vocational education and training.

Kolleg: Institute of general education preparing adults for higher education.

Kunsthochschule: College of arts

Mittlerer   Bildungsabschluss: Equivalent to the *Realschule* certificate; this qualification can also be obtained in vocational schools (*Berufsschule, Berufsaufbauschule, Berufsfachschule*) in combination with a vocational qualification.

Musikhochschule: College of music

Orientierungsstufe: Grades 5 and 6 may be organized as an orientational stage during which the decision on a particular school type is left open. In some *Länder* the orientation stage may be a separate organizational unit independent of the traditional school types which then start with grade 7.

Pädagogische Hochschule: Teacher training college which exists in only three *Länder* where teachers are trained for careers in primary and lower secondary as well as special education. In the other *Länder*, courses for the above-mentioned teaching careers are offered by universities, *Gesamthochschulen* and colleges of art and music.

Realschule: General education secondary school – lower level, normally grades 5 to 10 – going beyond the level of the *Hauptschule* and granting access to upper secondary education where a higher education entrance qualification or a vocational qualification may be obtained.

THE GERMAN EDUCATION SYSTEM

Universities and other institutions of higher learning	Further-education
	Specialized College
	Specialized School

13			Other vocational schools (e.g. Specialized High School)	
12	Compre-hensive School	High School (Gymnasium)		Vocational School (Berufsschule) (Part-time)
11				
10			Intermediate School (Realschule)	10th grade
9				Junior Secondary School (Hauptschule)
8				
7				
6		Orientation grades (Orientierungsstufe)		
5				

4	
3	Primary School (Grundschule)
2	
1	

School year

| Kindergarten |

- - - Short-course Secondary Graduation (Hauptschulabschluβ)

••••• Intermediate Graduation (Mittlerer Abschluβ)

▬▬ University Maturity (Hochschulreife)

Source: German Information Center

Sonderschule: Special schools for children with learning disabilities, schools for the blind and visually handicapped, schools for the deaf and hard of hearing, schools for children with speech handicaps, schools for the physically handicapped, schools for mentally handi-capped children, and schools for children with behavioral disturbances.

Technische Universität/Technische

Hochschule: Technical university.
Verwaltungsfachhochschule: Special type of *Fachhochschule* offering administrative studies which include periods of on-the-job training for future civil servants at the middle echelon level in federal, *Land* or local authorities.
Source: Secretariat of the Standing Conference of the Ministers of Education and Cultural Affairs of the *Länder,* in the Federal Republic of Germany, 1990.

VOCATIONAL EDUCATION

Germany's vocational education program is known as the "dual system." Students combine on-the-job training, often as apprentices, and classroom instruction. Apprentices and job trainees usually spend three or four days a week in the work place and one or two days attending classes in trade schools (*Berufsschulen*). Usually about 40 percent of their school work is in basic academic subjects such as languages, mathematics, and sciences, and about 60 percent in subjects directly related to their chosen professions.

The dual system is a collaboration between the state, private employers, and trade unions. It offers a means of assuring that nationwide training standards for every occupation are maintained. Large companies often run their own trade schools, which must be state accredited.

In 1994, young people could participate in training programs in 380 different occupations ranging from automobile repair to diamond cutting. About a third of the young men and half the young women participating in vocational programs pursue the ten most popular careers: retail sales, engine repair, industrial sales and purchasing, banking, clerical work, wholesale trade, electrical installation, hair dressing, assisting doctors, and industrial mechanics.

Source: *The Federal Republic of Germany: Questions and Answers,* ed. Susan Steiner. German Information Center, 1996.

UNIVERSITIES, ACADEMIES, AND COLLEGES TODAY

Aachen: Rheinisch-Westfälische, Tech-nische Hochschule Aachen, Templer-graben 55, 52056 Aachen

Augsburg: Universität Augsburg, Universitätsstr. 2, 86135 Augsburg

Bamberg: Otto-Friedrich-Universität Bamberg, Kapuzinerstr. 16, 96045 Bamberg

Bayreuth: Universität Bayreuth,Univer-sitätsstr. 30, 95440 Bayreuth

Berlin: Freie Universität Berlin Kaiserswerther Straße 16-18, 14195 Berlin

Berlin: Humboldt-Universität zu Berlin Unter den Linden 6, 10099 Berlin

Berlin: Technische Universität Berlin, Straße des 17. Juni 135, 10623 Berlin

Berlin: EAP Europäische Wirtschaftshochschule Berlin, Europa-Center, 10789 Berlin

Bielefeld: Universität Bielefeld, Universitätsstr. 25, Postfach 100131, 33510 Bielefeld

Bochum: Ruhr-Universität Bochum, Universitätsstr. 150, 44780 Bochum

Bonn: Rheinische Friedrich-Wilhelms-Universität Bonn, Regina-Pacis-Weg 3, Postfach 2220, 53012 Bonn

Braunschweig: Technische Universität Carolo-Wilhelmina zu Braunschweig, Pockelsstr. 14, Postfach 3329, 38023 Braunschweig

Bremen: Hochschule Bremen, Neustadts-wall 30, 28199 Bremen

Bremen: Universität Bremen, Bibliothek-str. 1, Postfach 330440, 28334 Bremen

Bremerhaven: Hochschule Bremerhaven, An der Karlstadt 8, 27568 Bremerhaven

Chemnitz: Technische Universität Chemnitz-Zwickau, Straße der Nationen 62, 09107 Chemnitz

Clausthal: Technische Universität Claus-thal, Adolph-Roemer-Straße 2a, 38678 Clausthal-Zellerfeld

Cottbus: Technische Universität Cottbus, Karl-Marx-Straße 17, Postfach 101344, 03013 Cottbus

Darmstadt: Technische Hochschule Darmstadt, Karolinenplatz 5, 64289

Darmstadt
Dortmund: Universität Dortmund, August-Schmidt-Straße 4, 44221 Dortmund
Dortmund: International School of Management ISM, Otto-Hahn-Straße 37, 44227 Dortmund
Dresden: Technische Universität Dresden, Mommsensstr. 13, 01062 Dresden
Duisburg: Gerhard-Mercator-Universität-Gesamthochschule - Duisburg, Lotharstr. 65, 47057 Duisburg
Düsseldorf: Heinrich-Heine-Universität Düsseldorf, Universitätsstr. 1, 40225 Düsseldorf
Düsseldorf: Robert-Schumann-Hochschule Düsseldorf, Fischerstr. 110, 40476 Düsseldorf
Erfurt: Universität Erfurt, Krämerbrücke 9-11, 99084 Erfurt
Erfurt: Pädagogische Hochschule Erfurt-Mühlhausen, Nordhäuser Straße 63, Postfach 307, 99006 Erfurt
Erlangen: Friedrich-Alexander-Universität Erlangen-Nürnberg,Schloßplatz 4, Postfach 3520, 91023 Erlangen
Essen: Folkwang-Hochschule Essen, Klemensborn 39, Postfach 4428, 45224 Essen
Essen: Universität-Gesamthochschule-Essen, Universitätsstr. 2, 45117 Essen
Flensburg: Bildungswissenschaftliche Hochschule Flensburg-Universität, Mürwiker Straße 77, 24943 Flensburg
Frankfurt/Main: Johann-Wolfgang-Goethe-Universität, Senckenberganlage 31, 60054 Frankfurt/Main
Frankfurt/Oder: Europa-Universität, Viadrina Frankfurt/Oder, Große Scharmstr. 59, Postfach 776, 15207 Frankfurt/Oder
Freiberg: Technische Universität Bergakademie Freiberg, Akademiestr. 6, 09596 Freiberg
Freiburg/Breisgau: Albert-Ludwigs-Universität Freiburg/Breisgau, Heinrich-von-Stephan-Straße 25,79100 Freiburg/Breisgau

Freiburg/Breisgau: Pädagogische Hochschule Freiburg/Breisgau,Kunzenweg 21, 79117 Freiburg/Breisgau
Gießen: Justus-Liebig-Universität Gießen,Ludwigstr. 12, Postfach 111440, 35359 Gießen
Göttingen: Georg-August-Universität Göttingen Goßlerstr. 5-7, Postfach 3744 37027 Göttingen
Greifswald: Ernest-Moritz-Arndt-Universität Greifswald, Domstr. 11, 17487 Greifswald
Hagen: Fernuniversität - Gesamthochschule - Hagen, Feithstr. 152, 58084 Hagen
Halle: Martin-Luther-Universität Halle-Wittenberg, Universitätsplatz 10, 06099 Halle/Saale
Hamburg: Hochschule für Wirtschaft und Politik, Von-Melle-Park 9, 20146 Hamburg
Hamburg: Technische Universität Hamburg-Harburg, Denikestr. 22, 21071 Hamburg
Hamburg: Universität Hamburg, Edmund-Siemers-Allee 1, 20146 Hamburg
Hamburg: Universität der Bundeswehr Hamburg, Holstenhofweg 85, 22043 Hamburg
Hannover: Medizinische Hochschule Hannover, Konstanty-Gulschow-Straße 8, 30623 Hannover
Hannover: Tierärztliche Hochschule Hannover, Bünteweg 2, 30559 Hannover
Hannover: Universität Hannover, Welfengarten 1, 30167 Hannover
Heidelberg: Hochschule für Jüdische Studien Heidelberg, Friedrichstr. 9, 69117 Heidelberg
Heidelberg: Ruprecht-Karls-Universität Heidelberg, Grabengasse 1, Postfach 105760, 69047 Heidelberg
Heidelberg: Pädagogische Hochschule Heidelberg, Keplerstraße 87, 69120 Heidelberg
Hildesheim: Universität Hildesheim, Marienburger Platz 22, Postfach 101363, 31113 Hildesheim

Ilmenau: Technische Universität Ilmenau, Max-Planck-Ring 14, Postfach 327, 98684 Ilmenau
Jena: Friedrich-Schiller-Universität Fürstengraben 1, 07740 Jena
Kaiserslautern: Universität Kaiserslautern, Erwiin-Schrödlinger-Straße, Postfach 3049, 67653 Kaiserslautern
Karlsruhe: Universität Fridericiana zu Karlsruhe - Technische Hochschule, Kaiserstr. 12, 76131 Karlsruhe
Karlsruhe: Pädagogische Hochschule Karlsruhe, Bismarckstr. 10, Postfach 4960, 76032 Karlsruhe
Kassel: Gesamthochschule Kassel - Universität, Mönchebergstr.19, 34109 Kassel
Kiel: Christian-Albrechts-Universität zu Kiel., Olshausenstr. 40, 24098 Kiel
Kiel: Muthesius-Hochschule,Lorenzendamm 6-8, 24103 Kiel
Köln: Deutsche Sporthochschule Köln, Carl-Diem-Weg 6, 50927 Köln
Köln: Universität Köln, Albertus-Magnus-Platz, 50923 Köln
Konstanz: Universität Konstanz,Universitätsstr. 10, 78464 Konstanz
Leipzig: Universität Leipzig, Augustusplatz 9-11, 04081 Leipzig
Leipzig: Ostdeutsche Hochschule für Berufstätige, Konradstr. 52, 04315 Leipzig
Ludwigsburg: Pädagogische Hochschule Ludwigsburg, Reuteallee 46, Postfach 220, 71602 Ludwigsburg
Lübeck: Medizinische Universität zu Lübeck, Ratzeburger Allee 160, 23538 Lübeck
Lüneburg: Universität Lüneburg,Wilschenbrucher Weg 84, 21332 Lüneburg
Mainz: Johannes-Gutenberg-Universität Mainz, Saarstr. 21, 55099 Mainz
Mainz: Universität Koblenz-Landau, Hegelstr. 59, Postfach 1864, 55008 Mainz
Magdeburg: Otto-von-Guericke Universität Magdeburg, Universitätsplatz 2, Postfach 4120, 39016 Magdeburg
Mannheim: Universität Mannheim,

Schloß, 68131 Mannheim
Marburg/Lahn: Philipps-Universität Marburg, Biegenstr. 10, 35032 Marburg/Lahn
München: Hochschule für Philosophie Kaulbachstr.33, 80539 München
München: Ludwig-Maximilians-Universität München Geschwister-Scholl-Platz 1, 80539 München
München: Technische Universität München, Arcisstr. 21, 80290 München
Münster: Westfälische Wilhelms-Universität Münster, Schloßplatz 2, 48149 Münster
Neuendettelsau: Augustana-Hochschule in Neuendettelsau, Waldstr. 11, Postfach 20, 91561 Neuendettelsau
Neubiberg: Universität der Bundeswehr München, Werner-Heisenberg-Weg 39, 85579 Neubiberg
Oestrich-Winkel: European Business School, Schloß Reichartshausen, 65375 Oestrich-Winkel
Oldenburg: Carl-von-Ossietzky-Universität Oldenburg, Ammerländer Heerstr. 114-118, 26111 Oldenburg
Osnabrück: Universität Osnabrück, Neuer Graben - Schloß, 49069 Osnabrück
Paderborn: Universität - Gesamthochschule - Paderborn, Warburger Straße 100, 33098 Paderborn
Passau: Universität Passau, Dr.-Hans-Kapfinger-Straße 22,94030 Passau
Potsdam: Universität Potsdam, Am Neuen Palais 10, Postfach 601553, 14415 Potsdam
Regensburg: Universisät Regensburg, Universitätsstr. 31, 93040 Regensburg
Rostock: Universität Rostock, Universitätsplatz 1, 18051 Rostock
Saarbrücken: Hochschule für Technik und Wirtschaft des Saarlandes (HTW), Goebenstr. 40, 66117 Saarbrücken
Saarbrücken: Universität des Saarlandes im Stadtwald, Postfach 151150, 66041 Saarbrücken

Schwäbisch-Gmünd: Pädagogische Hochschule Schwäbisch-Gmünd,Oberbettringer Straße 200, 73525 Schwäbish- Gmünd
Siegen: Universität - Gesamthochschule - Siegen, Herrengarten 3, 57068 Siegen
Speyer: Hochschule für Verwaltungswissenschaften Speyer, Freiherr-vom-Stein-Straße 2, 67324 Speyer
Stuttgart: Universität Stuttgart, Keplerstr. 7, 70174 Stuttgart
Stuttgart: Universität Hohenheim, Schloß 1, 70593 Stuttgart
Trier: Universität Trier, Universitätsring 15, 54286 Trier
Tübingen: Eberhard-Karis-Universität Tübingen, Wilhelmnstr. 7, 72074 Tübingen
Ulm/Donau: Universität Ulm, Albert-Einstein-Allee, 89069 Ulm/Donau
Vallendar: Wissenschaftliche Hochschule für Unternehmensführung - Otto-Beisheim-Hochschule, Burgplatz 2, 56179 Vallendar
Vechta: Hochschule Vechta, Driverstr. 22, 49377 Vechta
Weilheim-Bierbronnen: Gustav-Siewerth-Akademie, Oberbierbronnen 1, 79809 Weilheim-Bierbronnen
Weimar: Hochschule für Architektur und Bauwesen,Geschwister-Scholl-Straße 8, 99421 Weimar
Weingarten: Pädagogische Hochschule Weingarten, Kirchplatz 2, 88250 Weingarten
Witten: Private Universität Witten-Herdecke, Alfred-Herrhausen-Straße 50, 58448 Witten
Würzburg: Bayerische Julius-Maximilians-Universität Würzburg, Sanderring 2, 97070 Würzburg
Wuppertal: Bergische Universität - Gesamthochschule - Wuppertal, Gaußstr.20, 42097 Wuppertal

HERALDRY

Coats of arms, originally created for identification on fields of battle, are the currency of heraldry, which deals with the history and description of armorial bearings.

The following explanation of the use of arms, "Heraldry for United States Citizens,"[1] is provided as a public-service bulletin by the Board for Certification of Genealogists:[2]

"Heraldry in the United States has no legal standing unless it has been registered as a trade mark or copyrighted under United States law. Citizens of the United States may adopt and use any arms, devices, or badges of his or her own creation as long as they do not infringe on insignia covered by such a registration or copyright. However, if the citizen adopts arms, devices, or badges acknowledged by the Heraldic Offices of a foreign nation as belonging to the descendants of any of their nationals, the person using those arms, etc. may find himself guilty of violation of the laws of another country — thus subject to penalties.

"Arms do not belong to a 'family name.' They belong to individuals who are acknowledged as their owner, or who receive a grant from them (from a foreign government), or make them up for themselves. Under the laws of most countries other than ours, the rules are generally as follows:

"Unbroken male line descendants of any person who has a legally recognized right to bear heraldic arms may use their progenitor's arms, inheriting them in the same manner that they inherit anything else. If a male line descendant changes his name — as, for instance, from Smith to Jones — he still may bear his father's arms, even though he now uses a different surname. He does not bear different arms associated in someone's mind with another person of his new surname. This is clear evidence that there is no such thing as "arms of your family name."

"Daughters have the right to use their father's coat armour as long as they remain unmarried, or they may combine (by *impaling* or *escutcheon of pretense*) their father's arms with those of their husband's. If their spouses have no arms, they may continue for life to use their paternal arms, but this right is not inherited by their children and expires with their deaths. If an *armiger* (one who has the right to bear heraldic arms) has no sons but only daughters, then under British law the daughters are heraldic heiresses and their children may *quarter* the arms of their mother with those of their father. If their father has no arms, the right is lost — unless the arms are regranted to them as heirs of their maternal grandfather.

"Anyone whose uninterrupted male-line immigrant ancestor from England was entitled to use a coat of arms has the right under English law, to use this same coat of arms. If that ancestor had no such right, then neither does the descendant — unless he or she buys a grant of arms from the College of Arms. Thus, to establish the right under English (or German, French, Swiss, etc.) law to a coat-of-arms, it is necessary to prove one's uninterrupted male-line descent from someone who was legally entitled to use this coat of armor. No 'heraldry institute' or 'heraldic artist' can 'look up a surname' and provide the correct arms for a client without first proving the client's descent from the distant forebear, with legally acceptable proof at every generation. Any claim to 'research,' without proving the entire lineage, constitutes fraud.

"Several organizations in the United States seek to register and codify the use of arms. All these organizations operate on a voluntary basis. Excellent as their intentions may be, they have no

legal standing and are unable to enforce the registration or uniform use of coats of arms."

Footnotes

[1]*The Report*, Ohio Genealogical Society, Spring 1996.

[2]The Board for Certification of Genealogists, P.O. Box 5816, Falmouth, VA 22403-5816.

THE 'FAMILY COAT-OF-ARMS': NO SUCH THING

To reinforce a statement made in the previous section by the Board for Certification of Genealogists, "Arms do not belong to a family name," below is quoted a comment by a prominent writer on genealogy:

". . . there is no such thing [as a family coat-of-arms]. The right to bear arms was granted to an individual by the ruler of a country. The right belonged to one man and his descendants who were the first sons in a direct line. The [grant] from a ruler was usually because the recipient had done the ruler an [extraordinary service] . . . Since your ancestors and mine were probably peasants, they were not likely to have had the chance to do the ruler a favor, and so the great majority of us are not likely to have any right at all to a coat-of-arms."

Source: "Tonight Our Speaker Is . . . ," by Angus Baxter, *Heritage Quest*, May/June 1998, #75.

THE GERMAN WAPPENBÜCHER

The traditions in German-speaking parts of Europe are not the same as those in England. Helmut Nickel, who has written on topics of heraldry, states, "In some countries, such as Germany and Switzerland, that once were parts of the Holy Roman Empire, it was and still is the privilege of any free man to choose and adopt his family arms, as long as they do not infringe on the rights of others."[1]

Coats of arms for non-nobles

Myron R. Falck, who writes on German heraldry, states, "Of the many Siebmacher volumes that I looked at it is clear that numerous volumes are given to the presentation of *"Bürgerliche Wappen"*; that is, coats of arms for non-noble persons and families.

"A *Bürger* is described most simply as a citizen, but is also sometimes described as a free man or a burgher (a word not much in style anymore); in any case, a *Bürger* was a member of the community with rights to own property, hold office, and to participate in the governance of the community."[2]

J. Siebmacher's Wappenbuch

The best known work on German heraldry is the *Wappenbuch* (or *J. Siebmachers großes und allgemeines Wappen-buch...*) by Johann Siebmacher, a Nürnburg graphic artist who died in 1611. [*Wappen* means coat of arms; *Wappenbuch* means "heraldry book"; the plural is *Wappenbücher*.] This work was printed and reprinted until 1806, with revisions and additions in 18 volumes carrying titles that generally identify them as the "Old Siebmacher." The "New Siebmach-er" was published in a series of 101 volumes from 1854 to 1961.

In the Siebmacher *Wappenbücher*, the depicted coats of arms are presented in tables. Textual material, usually independent of the table but with references to the table, is also included for most of the depicted arms. These descriptions often include significant genealogical information; for example, the names of family members, locations of land holdings, castle names, as well as other information about families. In some of the volumes, a technical description of the coat of arms, sometimes known as the blazon, is included. The language used is German in contrast to the stylized French blazon found for British arms. It usually describes the shield and its divisions, the charges on the shield, the colors to be represented, as well as the wreath, the mantling, the helmet, and the crest. There are occasional entries for persons in the extended Holy Roman Empire and the Hapsburg Empire; a few Russian and Swedish arms from the Baltic area and some Hungarian arms are also entered.

Depictions of coats of arms

A coat of arms usually has a number of parts; it includes the most important element that may stand alone: the shield (*Schild* in German). A more complete coat of arms included the helmet (*Helm*) with a wreath or binding (*Wulst*) that, with six twists, binds the crest (*Kleinod*) to the helmet; and the mantling (*Decken*) that provides an elaborate and decorative fabric cover for the helmet, presumably for the protection of the neck and shoulders of the warrior. There are also numerous technical terms for the division of the shield, the images (charges) placed on it, and their locations, and for the stances of any animals that may be shown on the shield or crest.

Index to the Wappenbücher

The essential guide to the many volumes of the *Wappenbücher* is this index:

Jäger-Sunstenau, Hanns. *General-Index zu den Siebmacher'schen Wappen-büchern 1605-1961.* Graz, Austria: Akademische Druck und Verlagsanstalt, 1964. (FHL film 1181781 item 4).

Among other aids found in this one-volume work, an index for some 130,000 names, mostly German, is included, with a key to finding the coats of arms, as well as descriptive text as found in the Siebmacher *Wappenbücher*.

Using the index[4]

Care must be taken in going from the *Index* to the *Wappenbücher* because of the many republications.

The reverse of the title page may offer some help in deciding which section of the books to check. The filmed version of the *Index* [FHL film 1181781 item 4] explains at the very beginning of the roll a conversion needed to use the books on the Family History Library shelves. As one goes through the filmed *Wappenbücher,* it may be necessary to roll through several volumes to get to the table being searched.

Beginning on page 24 of the *General-Index* is a catalog of all the *Wappenbücher* with complete bibliographic information. There is a description of the contents of each volume. At the beginning of each listing, in parentheses right after the volume or edition number, is the abbreviation for the volume that is used in the alphabetical surname index; for example, *Bg5* refers to the fifth *bürgerliche* volume. All of the 14 *bürgerliche* volumes are listed beginning on page 24.

On page 39 begins a chronological list telling which volumes were published each year from 1605 to 1961. On page 43 is a list telling how the initial letters are grouped together: *b* includes *p; d* includes *dh, t,* and *th; f* includes *v; i* includes *j* and *y; k* includes *kh, c, ch, g,* and *gh; w* includes *v;* and *z* includes *zh, zs zsch, c, ch, cs,* and *cz.* (There are initial *v* listings under both *w* and *f.*) On page 46 are listed all the abbreviations.

This is an example of an entry:
FALK- . . . .

-. . . .
-(Baden) Bg5 75
This entry signifies that there is a Falk family from Baden with a coat of arms described on page 75 of the fifth burgher division. One then locates the Siebmacher volume containing this division.

Footnotes
[1]Helmut Nickel, "Heraldry," *Dictionary of the Middle Ages,* ed. Joseph Reese Strayer. New York, Charles Scribner's Sons, 1985, vol. 6, p. 172.
[2]Myron R. Falck, *Coats of Arms for the*

Name Falck and Variations of That Name as Found in the Siebmacher Wappenbücher. Myron R. Falck, 1996 .
[4]Helen Boyden, "Tips on Using the General-Index," *The German Connection,* German Research Association, Vol. 20, No. 2, 1996.
Source: The information in this section is based on and in large part excerpted, by permission of the author, from "German Coats of Arms," by Myron R. Falck, *The German Connection,* Vol. 20, No. 2 (1996).

RESOURCES FOR HERALDRY

♦Fox-Davies, Arthur Charles. *The Art of Heraldry: an Encyclopedaedia of Armory,* Arno, New York, 1904, reprint 1976.
♦Meyer, Mary Keysor and P. William Filby, eds. *Who's Who in Genealogy and Heraldry,* Savage, Md., 1990
♦ Neubecker, Ottfried. *Heraldry: Sources, Symbols, and Meaning.* McGraw Hill, New York, 1976.
♦Roland, Victor and Henri, *General Illustrated Armorial,* Sauvegarde historique, Lyon, 1953; 6 vols. FHL 940 D6ro; film 1045421 (vols. 1-5), and 1045422 item 1 (vol. 6)
♦*Der Schlüssel: Gesamtinhaltsverzeichnisse mit Ortsquellennachweisen für genealogische, heraldische und historische Zeitschriftenreihen,* Göttiger Genealogisch-Heraldischen Gesellschaft. FHL 943 D25sc
♦ Stephenson, Jean. *Heraldry for the American Genealogist.* National Genealogical Society, Washington, DC, 1959
♦Woodcock, Thomas, and John Martin Robinson. *The Oxford Guide to Heraldry.* Oxford University Press, Oxford, 1988.

THE GERMAN NOBILITY

The German system of nobility, as indeed the European system in general, is quite different from the English system with which most Americans are familiar. The English have a peerage system and not an extensive system of nobility, though their squires or landed gentry would tend to be the closest thing. In England, only the eldest son usually inherits the title and the rest are considered commoners, though they may bear "courtesy titles" if their father has more than one, or may be called "Lord" or "Lady" without actually being one.

The German nobility is divided into two major divisions, that of the lower (*niedriger Adel*) and the high (*hoher Adel*). It is further divided into the ancient nobility (*Uradel*) and the newer nobility (commonly known as *Briefadel*, or literally, nobility by letter-cachet, but also including other groups.) The *Uradel* may be of either the lower or high nobility, but the *Briefadel* is always of the lower.

In Germany, all legitimate children of a nobleman become nobles themselves, and most titles pass onto all the children with few exceptions. All the children of sovereigns did not, of course, become kings or electors, but did become princes or princesses. In the last decades of the German Empire, in imitation of the English system, a few families were ennobled with titles that passed on only to the eldest son, the remainder retaining either their father's former title (which he also still carried) or just untitled nobility.

The hereditary and legal privileges of the nobility as the first class of the realm ended in August of 1919 when the Constitution of the so-called Weimar Republic came into force. The laws that concerned the nobility for some one thousand years before 1919 stated that hereditary nobility could only be passed on through legitimate biological descent from a noble father but not through adoption and especially not through purchase. When non-nobles were adopted, the family name could be carried by the adoptee, but none of the noble designations of the family (such as a title or the "*von*".) If such an adoptee wished to become noble, he or she had to apply to their sovereign for such status in the same manner as any other subject. An exemption to this was and is still made by the "legitimatio per matrimonium subsequens", which allowed the legitimation of children born out of wedlock after the marriage of their noble parents. By this, the children became full hereditary nobles, though some social stigma still remained.

Since 1919, according to the German republican government, the nobility no longer exists as a legal entity. Nevertheless, the titles and noble designations of the nobility have not been abolished, as they have in Austria, and may still be carried. Legally, they are now merely parts of the family name and in theory convey no status. Following this rule, all children of, for example, a Count von Beust, whether male or female, would have the family name Count von Beust. Similarly you could find ladies named Elisabeth Duke of Saxony or Luise Prince of Prussia. A woman married to the Hereditary Grand Duke of Baden would, in law, also be named Hereditary Grand Duke of Baden, as would all their children. To avoid making all this seem too ridiculous, the German government ignores much of its own law and allows the wives and children of nobles to take the gender-specific titles appropriate to their sex.

Another example of society ignoring the 1919 law and following traditional practice is that in all German telephone books a person named, for instance, Baron von Richthofen would be listed under a "R" for Richthofen rather than a "v" for "von" or a "B" for "Baron". The U.S. telephone books are (unwittingly) more compliant with current German legal writ by listing all persons with a "von" under "v".

The 1919 law also causes difficulties in the case of children inheriting senior titles of their fathers. For example, in certain families, only the senior member is a count, and the rest are untitled nobles. For a child to use the inherited title of "count" upon his father's death would involve a court petition for a name change, which is not always granted when the judge or magistrate has an anti-noble bias.

Current law allows a person adopted by a noble to use the noble family name, and since the title is considered part of the name, that is also conveyed by adoption. It should be noted that the German nobility never acknowledges such persons to be noble, no matter what they call themselves.

Those persons who claim nobility through adoption or purchase, such as the notorious Claus von Bülow, the Nazi foreign minister von Ribbentrop, or Zsa-Zsa Gabor's husband who uses a Saxon princely title, are not recognized as part of the historical nobility and are no more members of that class than anyone else claiming a status to which they are not entitled. Most such persons are essentially deluding themselves while trying to fool others.

German nobles, especially the *Uradel*, have a particular class consciousness and consider themselves interrelated and cousins even if they don't know exactly how. Often, in the case of the ancient families, this is correct due to centuries of intermarriage. All members of the *Uradel* are considered by themselves to be of the same status, whether they are untitled, barons, counts, or whatever else they may be. The particular title of a person is far less important among the nobility than the age and standing of the family. This is particularly true as a number of old families have branches of various levels. For instance, the Counts, Barons, and un-titled von Bothmers are all part of the same family. The *Uradel* also tend to look down on the *Briefadel* as parvenus, even when the Briefadel may have been noble for centuries. I recall visiting a cousin on the Lüneburger Heath in Lower Saxony who had a brass plate on his front door stating "*Lieferanten und Briefadel zur Hintertür,*" meaning "Deliveries and Briefadel to the rear entrance". Though meant as a joke, there was still a bit of seriousness behind it.

The Noble Designation

The basic designation of the nobility is the predicate "*von*", which the vast majority of German nobles carry. There are a small number of noble houses, almost exclusively of the *Uradel*, which have never used the "*von*" or any other noble predicate, but are nevertheless of fully equal standing with those that do.

In northern and eastern Germany, there are a substantial number of families (such as the von Kranichfelds) that use the "*von*" as designations of the towns where they come from (as is the case with most older noble families) but have never been noble and make no pretense to be so.

A few noble houses use "*von und zu,*" meaning they are not only from the place mentioned but still retain it. Another *Uradel* house is named "*aus dem* Winckel" instead of "*von dem* Winckel" but having the same meaning. Other noble predicates sometimes seen are "*von dem,*" "*von der*", or "*vom.*" "*Van*" is not used by German nobles but is Dutch or Flemish and does not usually connote nobility in those countries.

As a way of differentiating themselves from non-nobles, the aristocracy of northern Germany in most cases uses the abbreviation "*v.*", instead of writing out the "*von,*" while still pronouncing the whole word. The southern Germans most often write out the "*von.*" It is always spelled with a small "v" unless it would be grammatically incorrect, such as in the beginning of a sentence.

Bibliography

Notwithstanding regional preferences, the "Bible" of the nobility, the *Genea-logisches Handbuch des Adels* (Genealogical Handbook of the Nobility), published by C. A. Starke in Limburg/Lahn, uses the "v." to designate nobles and spells out the "*von*" for non-noble families or individual non-nobles within aristocratic families. This handbook, colloquially known as the "Gotha" for its predecessor the *Almanach de Gotha* (in German, *Gothaisches Hofkalender*) attempts a comprehensive listing of all German noble houses currently or recently in existence and comes out in several volumes on a yearly basis, listing all living members of a family and all those deceased since the last edition. The handbook is divided into several series with the binding in different colors: Royal and Princely houses, Counts, Barons, Untitled nobles, and Family histories. Within these series, the families are, except since recently the Counts and Barons, divided into *Uradel* or *Briefadel*.

The advantage of having these books is obvious: there is a wealth of genealogical information, and as it lists addresses, many potential contacts can be found. It is also a way of being able to investigate people's claims to noble status, though this kind of checking is not considered "gentlemanly". The listings are thorough and are checked for accuracy, though they depend to a large degree on the individual's honesty in telling the truth about themselves.

Not every German noble family is included, as most often the family concerned must contribute financially to its inclusion, or the family may be too small, poor, or unwilling to warrant repeated updating. For instance, my own family, with some 70 members, appeared lastly in 1985 and will do so again in 1999, but that of my grandmother, von Bulmerincq,

has not appeared since 1939. The current series of books has been published since 1951, and is available at a number of larger libraries.

Divisions of the German Nobility

Uradel

This oldest level of the nobility is made up of those houses which by no later than 1400 were members of the knightly class, or patricians of a free Imperial city such as Frankfurt/Main. Most often these houses are counted as noble since "time immemorial" as at their first appearance in written records they were already noble. The families that make up this segment of the nobility usually descend from the knights or most important warriors of a sovereign that were the basis of his fighting force, or more rarely from a senior civil official of the time. The *Uradel* often had legal privileges over the newer nobility certifying their higher standing, such as in the Nobles Law of the Kingdom of Saxony of 1902. There are far fewer *Uradel* families still in existence than *Briefadel* due to the fact that families die out over the centuries and no *Uradel* has been created in almost 600 years.

Briefadel

This level of the nobility is made up of those houses which were ennobled since the beginning of the 15th Century through the end of the German or Austrian Empires in 1918. There were widely differing prerequisites for this level of the nobility, though most often military or civil service to the sovereign were the qualities most valued. The *Briefadel* includes houses ennobled or recognized as noble by the Emperor or one of the sovereigns of the high nobility. Also included are patricians of the free Imperial cities and non-German noble houses that immigrated over the centuries, such as the Counts von Polier from France or the Herren von Zerboni di Sposetti from Italy.

High Nobility

The High Nobility is made up of those families that had *Reichsstandschaft*, or had a seat in the Parliament of the Holy Roman Empire. These seats were reserved for sovereign houses. These families were also *Reichsunmittelbar*, or in a feudal sense, holding their lands directly from the Holy Roman Emperor, who for four centuries, until the end of the empire in 1806, came from the house of Habsburg. In essence, these families were rulers of their own countries, often in times of a weak emperor paying only lip service to their subservience to him. Their relationship to the emperor was then much like that of today's Commonwealth rulers to the British Queen. Even in times of a strong emperor, he was to them more like a chairman of the board rather than a ruler. Up to the early 19th century, there were some baronial and untitled families that held lands directly of the emperor, so essentially being their own rulers, but had no seat in the Parliament, thus being members of the lower nobility. Many families of the high nobility have house laws applicable to their members. Often these laws do not allow marriage outside their ranks, even to the lower nobility which would be considered a morganatic alliance. Even today, the children of a member of the high nobility who marries morganatically become members of the lower nobility.

Ranks of the High Nobility

Within this division of the nobility, the highest title is Emperor, or *Kaiser*, deriving from Caesar in Latin. Through most of German history, there was only one of these, the Holy Roman Emperor of the German Nation, lasting from the crowning of Charlemagne in the year 800 through the renunciation of the last emperor, Franz II, in 1806 under the influence of Napoleon, who by then had proclaimed himself Emperor of the French. Kaiser Franz had already declared himself Emperor of Austria, as Franz I, in

1804. In essence, the emperor just changed his title so as to more accurately reflect the political realities of the time.

A second German empire was established in 1871 after the victory of the German states over Napoleon III, when King Wilhelm I of Prussia was proclaimed German Emperor. He was never titled Emperor of Germany, as this nation was not a unitary state but a federation of monarchies and free city-states with quasi-republican governments. The title of German Emperor was always carried in conjunction with that of King of Prussia, and he was addressed as *Kaiserliche und Königliche Majestät* (Imperial and Royal Majesty). The Austrian Emperor, based to a large degree upon his position as King of Hungary, was addressed as Apostolic Majesty.

Both German and Austrian empires ceased to exist after World War I, and the imperial titles have not been carried since the last emperors died (Wilhelm II of Germany in 1941, Karl of Austria in 1922). The last empress, Zita of Austria, died in 1989. The children of the German emperor were *Prinzen von Preußen* (Princes of Prussia, not Germany) and royal highnesses, except the eldest, who was German *Kronprinz* (Crown Prince) and addressed as Imperial and Royal Highness. The current heir to the throne is titled the, rather than a, Prince of Prussia, and is the only one in Germany still addressed as Imperial and Royal Highness. The children of the Austrian emperor were titled Archdukes or Archduchesses of Austria rather than princes, and called Imperial and Royal Highnesses.

Next we come to *König* and *Königin*, or King and Queen, which was carried by the rulers of the larger German states (Bavaria, Hanover, Prussia, Saxony, Würt-temberg). They were addressed as Majesty, and their children, princes or princesses, as Royal Highnesses.

After these came the *Großherzog*, or Grand Duke, who were styled "royal highness," and were rulers of somewhat smaller states, such as the two Mecklenburgs or Luxemburg (which until 1918 was considered a German state). The heir to these thrones was known as an *Erbgroßherzog*, or hereditary grand duke, and the other children were princes or princesses. Additionally in the Saxon kingdom, grand duchy, and duchies, all the children of the ruler were also styled dukes or duchesses.

The next level is that of *Herzog*, or Duke, who was normally styled Highness.

Kurfürst, or Elector in English, ranked with a Duke. The electors were originally the greatest lords of the Holy Roman Empire, both temporal and spiritual, who elected the Emperor before the throne became hereditary. They later became sovereigns no different from the rest. The last ruling Elector, Hesse-Cassel, lost his throne to Prussia in 1866.

Landgraf (Landgrave), *Markgraf* (Margrave), and *Pfalzgraf* (Palsgrave or Count Palatine) ranked somewhat with a Duke and are usually considered higher than a *Fürst*. All sovereigns of this rank were eventually "promoted" to higher titles, but the titles were sometimes used instead of crown prince for their states, and are currently used for the Heads of the Houses of Baden, Hesse and Saxony. Depending on circumstances, they could be styled Royal Highness or simply Highness. In the Middle Ages, some sovereigns were *Burggraf*s, or Burgraves, but all these took higher titles early on and *Burggraf* became a title and sometimes function, like *Wildgraf*, of the lower nobility.

Next follows *Fürst* (for which there is no good translation in English, but which is confusingly called Prince). These are styled *Durchlaucht*, translated as Serene Highness. Children of dukes, kurfürsts, and fürsts were all princes or princesses.

In the third generation, their descendants sometimes become counts, except for the ruling line, which retains the princely title.

The last category of the high nobility still in existence is that of *Graf*, or Count. The last sovereigns of this rank ceased ruling after the Congress of Vienna in 1815. They are styled *Erlaucht*, or Illustrious Highness. Their children are all counts or countesses. A former, somewhat higher rank of *gefürsteter Graf*, or princely count, no longer exists.

Among all the higher nobility, the idea of *Ebenbürtigkeit* exists, meaning all of them, no matter what the title, are considered of equal birth and standing.

Ranks of the Lower Nobility

Very often, a certain level of income, wealth, or social standing was necessary for appointment to these ranks, so as to demonstrate the ability of the person ennobled to maintain himself at a proper level.

The highest rank of the non-sovereign nobility is *Herzog* or Duke, a title almost never given them and then only "ad personam", or much like an English life peer. An example is Otto von Bismarck as Duke of Lauenburg. He was styled Serene Highness.

The highest rank that normally was part of the lower nobility is *Fürst*. This title, like Duke, was given to them only in the last centuries of the monarchy. Their children were rarely princes, but more usually counts or barons, depending on what was the original title of the *Fürst*.

Next in rank is *Graf* or Count, which in modern times could be given primogeniture (inherited only by the eldest son), but was usually given to all the children of the new count. A very few houses also carry the title *Burggraf* which is approximately equivalent to Count.

Baron follows, which is almost always called *Freiherr* in Germany, but given as *Baron* to the Germans of the Baltic regions. For many years it was in dispute whether *Baron* was equivalent to *Freiherr* (which was deemed "better"), but this was settled in the last century in an affirmative manner. The wife of a *Freiherr* is a *Freifrau*, the daughter a *Freiherrin*. This last title is sometimes abbreviated *Freiin*. The wife of a Baron is a *Baronin*, the daughter a *Baronesse*. Another variant of this rank is called *Edler Herr*, or *Edle Herrin* for females, which is borne by only a few very old families (such as the Gans zu Putlitz).

The last level is that of the untitled nobility, which nevertheless includes some titled families. Normally, an untitled noble is addressed as *Herr*, in this context meaning Lord.

In former times, untitled nobles, especially those from the eastern regions, were addressed as *Junker*, a title still in usage in the Netherlands as *Jonkheer*. It is no longer normally used in Germany. In Bavaria and especially Austria, the hereditary title of *Ritter* (Knight) was given to families, but they were still considered part of the untitled nobility. Much the same applies to the title of *Edler*, which is mainly northern and central German. While the wife and daughters of an Edler were titled *Edle*, the wife of a *Ritter* was called a *Frau* (in this sense Lady) and not *Ritterin*.

Affiliations of the German Nobility

Though the formal power of the German nobility is gone, it still remains a considerable social force. After the debacle of World War II, the aristocracy gradually reformed in groups based on religious affiliation or province of origin. For well over 30 years, these groups have been affiliated as the "*Vereinigung der Deutschen Adelsverbände*" and published the monthly *Deutsches Adelsblatt* in the small town of Westerbrak (now part of Kirchbrak). The legalistic *Deutsches Adelsrechtsausschuß* was set up, composed of members from various noble and chivalric organizations, to determine in questionable cases who belongs to the nobility or if a person has a right to a noble title he claims. Only if there is a positive judgment by this organization can someone join one of the nobles' associations or have their family listed in the Gotha.

It has been estimated that there are some 40,000 nobles of all ranks in Germany today.

by Gilbert von Studnitz
© Gilbert von Studnitz 1992

THE GENEALOGICAL HANDBOOK OF THE NOBILITY AND ADELSLEXIKON

In 1951 in Limburg, C.A.Starke Verlag began publishing the *Genealogisches Handbuch des Adels* (Genealogical Handbook of the Nobility), which has, as of 1999, run to 114 volumes.

(See the "Bibliography" segment of the preceding section, "The German Nobility," for a further discussion of this series.)

The work is commonly referred to as "the Gotha," from its predecessor – *Gothaisches Hofkalender* (in German), and *Almanach de Gotha* (in French), which was an annual genealogical and political work, published in Gotha by Justus Perthes concerning the states of Europe and its ruling Houses.

Its purpose was to list all German noble houses currently or recently in existence, with each successive volume listing all living members of a family and those deceased since the previous edition. See FHL 943 D2ga.

Gradually, the same publisher produced annual series of genealogical handbooks conerning the other levels of the nobility – for the counts from around 1850, for the barons from around 1880, and a separate series for the *Uradel* and *Briefadel* from 1901. (These were called *Gothaisches Genealogisches Taschen-buch der Gräflichen/ Freiherrlichen/Adeligen* [respectivley] Häuser.

This enterprise ended with World War II, not to be pursued again until 1951, as mentioned above, with the publication of the *Genealogisches Handbuch des Adels,* considered the successor to "the Gotha," as it is colloquially referred to.

These handbooks provide a wealth of genealogical information – extremely thorough and frequently checked for accuracy. They include addresses of the nobles listed (at the time of the publication of each volume).

The bindings of the handbooks categorize each series. For example, red covers indicate information about higher nobility (including the entire higher nobility of Europe; green covers, the counts; dark red covers, the barons; the grey covers, the other nobility.

In 1994, an index (*Stammfolgen-Verzeichnisse 1994)* was published to cover the this publication as well as the "German Lineage Book" series (*Deutsches Geschlechterbuch).*

In 1972, C.A.Starke Verlag began publication of the *Adelslexikon* (lexicon of nobility), a series within the Gotha listing alphabetically the names of all German noble houses except for lineages that became extinct before 1800.

Sources:

♦Horst A. Reschke, "The Genealogical Handbook of the Nobility, *German Genealogical Digest,* Vol. 12, No. 4, Winter 1996.

♦Gilbert von Studnitz, "The German Nobility," *Der Blumenbaum,* Sacramento German Genealogy Society, Vol. 9, No. 4, 1992; as well as additional contributed information from this author.

• *German Festivals and Customs,* by Jennifer M. Russ. O. Wolff, London, c. 1982

EUROPEAN/GERMAN ORGANIZATION OF NOBILITY

The overall European organization of the nobility is CILANE, or *Commission d'Information et de Liaison des Associations Noble d'Europe.*

The German member of CILANE is VdDA, or *Vereinigung der deutschen Adelsverbände* (Union of German Aristocratic Associations), or VdDA. Its business office address is,

Vereinigun der deutschen Adelsverbände
Nonnenstrombergerstraße 34
53757 St. Augustin
Germany

As of 2000, the VdDA president is HSH Prince Alfred-Ernst zu Löwenstein-Wertheim-Freudenberg.

The next Noble's Congress of CILANE will be held in Berlin in September 2002. The previous Congress was held in September 1999.

DICTIONARY OF THE NOBILITY OF PRUSSIA

Neues preußisches Adels-Lexicon oder genealogische und diplomatische Nachrichten.... is a dictionary of the houses of nobility of Prussia, available in six volumes on five rolls of FHL microfilm.

The following FHL film numbers apply:

Vol. 1, A-D: 496856
Vol. 2, E-H: 496857
Vol. 3, I-O: 496858
Vol. 4, P-Z: 496859
Vol. 5 (Supp. 1 A-Z); and
Vol. 6 (Supp. 2) A-Z: 496860

USE OF 'VON'

The preposition *"von,"* meaning

"from" or "of," originated because no method existed to distinguish someone of the low nobility from a commoner.

In conjunction with a name, it was initially designed to fix the place of origin of the individual. Sometimes that aim was facilitated by writing "*von dem,*" or "*von der,*" both meaning "of the." In those instances it was not a sure-fire indication that the bearer of the name was of the nobility, but he or she might have been.

That place of origin generally denoted possession of land, villages, estates, castles and if so, it usually set a person apart as belonging to the nobility.

It has become an accepted practice to abbreviate the "von" as "v.," thereby signaling that the prefix connotes nobility. Still, there are noble German families, especially in Niedersachsen, the old state of Hannover, which have no distinguishing "von" as part of their name.
Source: "German Questions and Answers," by Horst A. Reschke, *Heritage Quest,* Sep./ Oct. 1999.

ABOLISHMENT OF NOBILITY

After the end of World War I, privileges of the nobility were abolished. German nobility, in effect, ceased to exist. Noble titles were relegated to becoming part of the name and new titles were no longer to be bestowed.

The privilege of being addressed in an especially deferential manner, such as "Highness" for a prince, was also abolished.

The new (in 1919) laws of the German Republic provided that the erstwhile noble title become a component of the surname of a common citizen. Thus "Count Ewald v. Hohensee" (a hypothetical example) would become "Ewald Count v. Hohensee." Yet the conventions pertaining to the nobility, including the protocol and decorum at social

gatherings, are still being observed.
Source: Horst A. Reschke, "German Questions and Answers," Heritage Quest, Sep./Oct. 1999 .

NOBILITY AND ROYALTY TERMINOLOGY

Adel	nobility, aristocracy
Adeliger	nobleman
Adelsstand	nobility
Baron	baron
Burggraf	burgrave
Edelknecht	squire
Edelmann	nobleman
Freiherr/Freiherrin	baron/baroness
or *Freifrau*	
Fürst/(-in)	prince/princess
Fürstentum	principality
Graf/Gräfin	count/countess
Grafschaft	county
Großherzog/-in	grand duke/grand duchess
Großherzogtum	duchy
Herr	master, lord, Lord
Herrengut	noble estate
Herrschaft	domain
Herzog/(-in)	duke/duchess
Herzogtum	duchy
Kaiser/(-in)	emperor/empress
Kanzler	chancellor
König/-in	king/queen
Königreich	kingdom
Krönprinz	crown prince
Kurfürst	elector
Kurfürstentum	electorate
Landgraf	landgrave, count
*Landgräfi*n	landgravine/landraviate, countess
Landgrafschaft	landgraviate, county
Landgut	country estate
Mark	march, borderland
Markgraf/	margrave/margravine
Markgräfin	marquis/marquise
Markgrafschaft	margraviate, marquisage
Pfalzgraf	earl, count palatine
Pfalzgraf	Count Palatinate/Palatine

Prinz/-essin .... prince/princess
Reich .... empire
Reichsfreiherr .... baron (prince
     of the Holy Roman Empire)
Ritter .... knight
Rittergut .... knight's estate
Ritterorden .... order of knighthood
Ritterschaft .... knighthood
Truchseß .... lord high steward

OTHER NOBILITY RESOURCES

Deutsches Adelsarchiv
Schwanallee 21
35037 Marburg/Lahn
Germany
[This organization deals with information on nobles from all Germanic countries]
Augustan Society
P.O. Box 75
Daggett, CA 92327-0075
Tel. (760) 254-9223
Fax (760) 254-1953
rcleve@msn.com
This is an "international genealogical, historical heraldic and chivalric society" which maintains a library and museum and publishes scholarly materials; keeps registration of coats of arms, orders of chivalry, knighthood and merit; and records family genealogies, lineages, and pedigrees.

    The society's publication is *The Augustan,* a quarterly journal of history, heraldry, genealogy, and chivalry.

SELECTED EUROPEAN WARS AND WORLD WARS SINCE 1500 INVOLVING GERMANIC PEOPLE AND THEIR NEIGHBORS

1524-25: Peasants Revolt — Lutheran peasants revolt in southern Germanic area and are suppressed (Austria, south-ern Germany).

1562-98:Wars of Religion — Civil wars between Catholics and Protestants (Huguenots) in France
1618 (May 22) - 1648 Oct. 24): Thirty Years War — Denmark, Sweden, France against the Hapsburg dynasty and the Holy Roman Empire, which is devastated by the war. Many German areas devasted.
1652-78: **Dutch Wars** — Trade wars, one between England and United Provinces (Netherlands) in 1652-1654, and the other being a general European war resulting from French expansionism, 1672-1678.
1689-97: War of the Grand Alliance — Expansionist aims of French king Louis XIV result in invasion of the Rhineland.
1700-21: Great Northern War — Russia gains Baltic territories.
1701-14:War of the Spanish Succession — Great Britain, Netherlands, Holy Roman Empire, Poland, and others wage war against Spain and France.
1733-38: .... **War of the Polish Succession** — Struggle for Polish throne; France on one side, Austria and Russia on the other
1740-48: War of Austrian Succession — France, Spain, Prussia and others against Great Britain and Austria; known in America as King George's War
1756-63: **Seven Years War** — France, Austria, Russia, Saxony, Sweden, and Spain against Great Britain and Prussia. Prussia, under Prussian king Frederick the Great, wins more territory and establishes Prussia as an important European power.
1789-1802: **French Revolution and Revolutionary Wars** — Austria and Prussia become allies against France.
1803-15: **Napoleonic Wars** — Between France and Great Britain, Russia, Austria, and Sweden. German troops serve throughout Europe. France tem-porarily occupies the

Rhineland.
1864: **Austro-Prusso-Danish War** — Schleswig, Holstein, and Lauenburg are ceded to Prussia and Austria.
1866: **Prusso-Austrian War (Seven Weeks War)** — Prussian chancellor Otto von Bismarck provokes war between Prussia and Austria, resulting in Prussia's exclusion of Austria from confederation of northern German states and leading to the establishment of the Austro-Hungarian Empire in 1867. Hannover, Electoral Hesse-Kassel, Nassau, Frankfurt am Main, and that part of Hesse-Darmstadt lying to the north of the Main River are annexed to Prussia. (**Note:** In 1867, Prussia absorbs the armies of all other states except Bavaria, Saxony, and Württemberg.)
1870-71: **Franco-German War** — France defeated. Armistice signed on January 29, 1871. The new German Reich included 25 states: four kingdoms, five grand duchies, 13 duchies and principalities, three free cities, and the Reichsland of Alsace-Lorraine.
1912-13: Balkan Wars — Two wars, becoming precursors to World War I
1914-18: World War I — Between Allies, including France, Great Britain, Russia, Italy, United States; and Central Powers, including Germany, Austria-Hungary, and Ottoman Empire. Alsace-Lorraine returned to France. (War ends 11 November 1918.)
1917-22: Russian Revolution and Civil War — Result in formal adoption of the name "Union of Soviet Socialist Republics"
1918-20: Baltic War of Liberation — Estonia, Latvia, and Lithuania successfully fight off invasions of Bolsheviks and Germans at end of World War I.
1919-20: Russo-Polish War — Poland gains some territory in Ukraine and Byelorussia.
1936-39: Spanish Civil War — Spanish nationalists defeat Loyalists, resulting in dictatorship of General Francisco Franco and contributing to outbreak of World War II.
1939-45: World War II — Allies, including United States, Great Britain, France, Russia and Russia, defeat Axis, including Germany, Italy, and later Japan, resulting in westward shift in Polish border and large gains in territory for USSR. Many German records are destroyed. (World War II began 1 September 1939 and ended 8 May 1945.)
1939-40 Russo-Finnish War Soviet Union fights for Finnish territory.
Sources:
♦Bruce Wetterau, *The New York Public Library Book of Chronologies.* Prentice Hall, New York 1990.
♦*The World Almanac and Book of Facts.* Pharos Books, New York, 1993.
♦David Brownstone and Irene Franck, *Timelines of War: A Chronology of Warfare from 100,000 BC to the Present.* Little, Brown and Company, Boston 1994.

GERMAN MILITARY RECORDS VOCABULARY

A.K. .... Armee Korps
A.O.K. ....*Armee Oberkommando* (army high command)
Abteilung .... draft
Abtlg. .... *Abteilung* (draft)
Aushebung .... conscription, draft, enlistment, recruitment
Ausgehuniform .... walking-out dress
Aushebungbezirk ... recruiting officer's district
Bataillon (Batl.) .... battalion
Batterie (Battr.) .... battery (artillery)
Beurlaubtenstand .... reserve status
Brigadegeneral .... brigadier general
Cantonment .... military quarters
Corporal .... corporal
Dragoner (Drag.) .... dragoon
Ehren .... medal decoration
Ehrenbuch .. book of honors bestowed
Ehrentoddeath given for one's country
Erkenntnis ..... verdict, award, sentence

Erkrankung .... illness, disease
Errichtet .... raised, established
Ersatzreserve .. military body of reserve
Ersatztruppe .... draft
Eskadron (Esk.) .... squadron
F.A.(*Feld Artillerie*) .... field artillery
Fähnrich .... flagbearer (military)
Feldmarschall .... general of the army
Feld .... field
Felddienst .... active service
Feldheer .... field force
Feldherr ... general, commander in chief
Feldjäger .... chasseur, courier
Feldlager .... camp
Feldlazarett .... field hospital
Feldprediger .... field chaplain
Feldschreiber .... military clerk
Feldsoldat ..... soldier on active service
Feldwebel .... sergeant major,
                                    sergeant first class
Feldzug .... campaign
Fourier .... quartermaster
Freilassungs-Schein .... release from
                                future military service
Freischein .... discharge from
                                        military duty
Freiwillinger .... volunteer
Füselier .... light infantryman
Fußsoldat .... foot soldier
Fußsoldaten mit Gewehr .. armed foot
                                                    soldier
Garnison .... garrison
Garnisonskirchenbuch .... garrison
                                            church book
Garnisonslazarett .... garrison
                                    military hospital
Gefecht .... battle, engagement
Gefechtbereitschaftreadiness for action
Gefechtsausbildung .... combat training
Gefreiter (Gefr.) . infantry lance-corporal
Geldstrafe .... monetary fine
Generalfeldmarschall .... general
                                            of the army
Generalleutnant (army) major general
Generalmajor .... major general
Generaloberst .... (army) general
Gestellung .... reporting for duty
Grenadier ...... grenadier, infantryman
Gruppe .... squad

Hauptgefreiter .... private first class
Hauptmann (Hpt.) .... captain
Heer .... army
Heeresdienst .... military service
Heeresmacht .... (military) forces
Heidentod .... death in battle
Husar .... hussar
I.B. .... *Infanterie Brigade*
I.D. .... *Infanterie Division*
Invalide(n) .... disabled soldier(s)
I.R. .... *Infanterie Regiment*
Jäger .... rifleman
Jägerbatallon .... rifle brigade
Kanonier .... gunner
Kapitän (navy) .... captain
K.S. .... *Kavallerie-Division*
Kompanie .... company (infantry)
Königlich [sächsische] Armee .. Royal
                                            [Saxon] Army
Korps .... corps
Krieg .... war
Kriegsdienst .... military service
Kriegsknecht .... mercenary
Kriegerdenkmal .... war memorial
Kriegsheer .... field army
Kriegsherr .... commander
Kriegslisten .... military records
Kriegsuntauglich .... unfit for
                                        active service
Kriegsversehrte .... disabled
                                    ex-serviceman
k.u.k. .... *kaiserliche und königlich*
                                (imperial and royal)
Landwehr .... militia
Leibregiment .... sovereign's
                                        own regiment
Leutnant (Ltn.) ...... second lieutenant
loskaufen .... to buy out of service
Major .... major
Mannschaftsstammrollen . troop rolls
Militäranwörter . soldier having served
                                    his time and claims
                                    civil employment
Militärarzt ...... military medical officer
Militäraushebungsrollen .... military
                                        levying rolls
Militärbezirk .... military district
Militärgericht .... military court
Militärgesetze .... military regulations

Militärkirchenbücher .. military parish records
Militärstrafe .... military punishment
Milizen .... militia
Musterungslisten .... muster rolls
Oberfeldwebel .... staff sergeant
Obergefreiter .... private first class
Oberleutnant (Oblt.) .. first lieutenant
Oberst (Obst.) .... colonel
Oberstleutnant .... (army) lieutenant colonel
Obrist .... *Oberst* (colonel)
Offizier (Offz.) .... officer
Offiziernachweise .... officer records
Offiziersstammrollen .... officer rolls
Panzer .... tank, armor plate
Pionier .... engineer
Quartiermeister .... quartermaster
Quartierzettel .... requisition for billets
Ranglisten .... tables of ranks, officer rolls
Regimentsgeschichten .... regimental histories
Regimentsquartiermeister ..... regiment quartermaster
Regimentsstab regimental headquarters
Reiter .... rider, cavalry soldier
Restantenlisten .... lists of arrears
Res. Div. ......:.............. reserve division
Res.K. .... *Reserve Korps*
Ritt. .... *Rittmeister,* (cavalry captain)
Rittmeister .... captain (of cavalry)
S. .... *Stab* (staff)
Schlacht .... battle
Schlachtfeld .... battlefield
Schuss .... shot
Schusswunde .... gunshot wound
Schütze .... rifleman
Sergt. .... sergeant
Soldat .... soldier
Stammrollen .... records of common soldiers and noncommissioned officers
Treffen .... battle
Truppenaushebung .... levy of troops
Ulanen .... lancers
Umkreis .... area, vicinity
Unteroffizier (Untffz.) .... corporal
Untoff .... Unteroffizier (corporal)

Verlust-Liste .... list of casualties
Verlustmeldungs .... casualty report
Vermögens .... property, wealth
verwundet .... wounded
Wachsoldat .... military guard
Wachtmeister .... sergeant major
Wehrdienstpflichtige .... draftee
Wehrmann .... soldier

Wehrmannscaft .... militia
Wehrpflicht .... obligation to serve in army
Wehrpflict (allgemeine) .... universal conscription
Zug .... platoon

GERMAN MILITARY RECORDS: AN OVERVIEW

Before 1871, when the Franco-Prussian War ended, there was no "German" army, but rather armies of the many states and principalities. In 1867, however, many of the non-Prussian troops in Germany were combined with the Prussian Army, which meant that after that year there was no longer an army consisting of solely Prussian soldiers. (The exceptions were Bavaria, Saxony, Württemberg, and Austria.)

Military records, dating from the 17th century, consist of military church records, records of common soldiers and noncommissioned officers, officers' rolls, and regimental histories.

The *Research Outline: Germany*, published by the Family History Library (an outline available at almost every Family History Center), provides this summary of the types of German military records:

"The earliest German military records, which began around 1485, usually list only the names of the soldiers. Records from the middle 1800s often give information about promotions, places served, pensions, conduct, and other details concerning the soldier's military career.

In addition, these records may include the soldier's age, birthplace, residence, occupation, and physical description as well as the names of family members. However, many German military records provide very few details about individuals other than those who served as officers."

Military records include the following:

• **Military church records** (*Militärkirchenbücher*), which give the same kind of information as church registers kept by clergymen not stationed in army camps. These records include garrison (*Garni-sons-*) records, parish registers, and regimental (*Regiments-*) church records. They date from 1672. Military church registers do not list deaths, which were recorded by the local churches in the garrison town.

• **Personnel files, or muster rolls** (*Stammrollen*) were kept for petty officers and soldiers who were non-commissioned. Before 1850, they include the soldier's name and place of origin, the period of his military service, and his height. After 1850, they list the name, place of origin, period of military service, height, and the town of birth.

• **Troop lists** (*Stammlisten*) vary in the information given. Some of the records are extensive, giving names of wives, the names and birthdates of children, and the place and date of marriage.

• **Officer rolls or rank lists** (*Ranglisten*) consist of information about officers only. Dating back to 1784, they include the officer's name, the title of his commission, and sometimes other data.

• **Regimental histories** (*Regimentsgeschichten*) usually list the names and dates of soldiers who were killed in action and who were decorated for bravery.

The excellent 12-page pamphlet, *German Military Records as Genealogical Sources,* by Horst A. Reschke, is essential as an orientation to military record searches.

This introduction to the topic, which discusses in general terms the German military records that are available, in which German states they can be found, and what time periods they cover, is available on microfiche (FHL fiche 6,001,596). It is no longer available for purchase.

Sources:

♦ *German Military Records as Genealogical Sources*, by Horst A. Reschke, 1990.

♦ *Research Outline: Germany,* Church of Jesus Christ of Latter-day Saints.

♦ "Searching German Military Sources," by Robert E. Ward, *Journal of German-American Studies: A Journal of History, Literature, Biography, and Genealogy*, Vol. XV, No. 1, March 1980.

GERMAN 'IMPERIAL' ARMIES

Research in German military records must always begin by first determining the army in question, i.e., Prussian, Saxon, Bavarian, etc. If family tradition reports military service in the 'imperial' (German = *Kaiserliche*) army, it never refers to the Prussian army, but, prior to 1804, would always indicate the Austrian army, and after 1804 would have reference to Napoleon's French army and all of its attached allied regiments. During the second half of the nineteenth century, the letters 'k.u.k.' (German = *kaiserlich und königlich,* i.e. "imperial and royal") always denoted Austro-Hungarian troops.

Source: Horst A. Reschke, *Military Record Sources in Germany* (FHL fiche 6001596).

FINDING A GERMAN ANCESTOR'S 'LOCAL DRAFT BOARD'

To find the location of the military

authority/office to which a male ancestor was obliged to report, see the gazetteer *Meyers Orts- und Verkehrslexikon des Deutschen Reichs* (see film and fiche numbers below) under the ancestor's native place name, to see whether the abbreviation: *BKdo* appears, followed by a place name. *BKdo* stands for *Bezirkskommando*, or district military authority.

Note this explanation by Horst A. Reschke: "Most native places were too small to have their own *Bezirkskommando*. Look in *Meyers* for the *Kreis*, or *Bezirksamt*, or *Domäneamt*, or *Amt*, or *Oberamt* – all terms for an administrative body akin to our American "county" – and find the *BKdo* which applies to it. (Such a variety of terminologies exist because the different German states did not have a uniform word for their "county seat," usually a city.) By finding the local *Bezirkskommando* (*BKdo*), one identifies the "local draft board" at which the ancestor was obliged to show up, register, and report for military duty."

The unit designations and garrisons of the German army are listed in the *Einteilung und Standorte der deutschen Wehrmacht.* beginning on page 53 of the Appendix of *Meyers Orts- und Verkehrslexikon,* at the end of fiche number 28 (see FHL fiche numbers above). The sixth column of this tabular listing, with the heading *Standort* (garrison), contains the name of the town in which each listed regiment was garrisoned. Here also can be found the armies of all the German states listed together, except for the Bavarian army, which appears in a separate list.

To find the location of non-Prussian military records (Prussian records were almost completely destroyed by fire in 1945), see the references noted in "Finding Military Records.".

(*Meyers Orts- und Verkehrslexikon des*

deutschen Reichs: FHL film 496,640 and 496,641; fiche 6,000,0001 [29 fiche]}
Source: "Beginning Your Military Research," by Horst A. Reschke, *The German Connection* , Vol. 20, No. 3, 1996.

PRUSSIAN ARMY MILITARY SERVICE: REFORM OF 1814

"In Prussia, under the army law of 1814, after a three-year period in the army, the individual draftee stayed for only two more years in the army reserve, which was designed to bring up the regular regiments to full strength in case of war. After these five years, the reservists changed over to the national guard, which was divided into two levies. The individual belonged to either for a period of seven years. The regiments of the first levy of the national guard, comprising men of the age of 25 to 32, were in wartime placed in the field army, where each brigade consisted of one regular and one national guard regiment, while the second levy, of men of 32 to 39, served as fortress garrisons and noncombat troops. . . .

"In the 1820s, the period of service in the regular army was lowered from three to two and half, and, in the 1830s to two years. Finally, close to one half of the first levy of the national guard was composed of 'recruits.'"
Source: Hajo Holborn, *A History of Modern Germany 1840-1945,* Princeton University Press, New Jersey, 1969; pp. 136, 137.

THE MALE'S MILITARY RESPONSIBILITIES DURING THE SECOND GERMAN EMPIRE

During the time of the Second German Empire (1871-1918), every male person had a military obligation extending from age 17 to age 45. That responsibility was divided into several categories, including,

* Active duty in the standing armed forces, at age 20, for three years
* Reserve duty in the standing army, for four years,
* The militia (*Landwehr*) of the first contingent, for five years, and of the second contingent for seven years, and
* Home guard duty, which extended from age 17 to age 45

Source: Horst A. Reschke

ARCHIVES FOR NON-PRUSSIAN MILITARY RECORDS

In 1945, during the battle of Berlin, the records for the Prussian army, housed in the *Heeresarchiv* at Potsdam, were almost entirely destroyed by fire. Only a few records which happened to be stored in locations less affected by bombing and combat survived.

Prior publication of some of the military source material in either book or magazine form preserved it for the genealogical researcher.

Inventory of non-Prussian military records can be found in various regional archives, as noted below. (The year shown indicates the end of the record-keeping period.) Documents generated after 1867 (or 1871, as indicated) were kept at the Prussian *Heersarchiv*, at Potsdam, where they suffered the common fate of oblivion by fire.

* **Anhalt** troops (until 1867): Landesarchiv Oranienbaum, Schloss, 06782 Oranienbaum, Germany
* **Austrian** army (complete until 1919): Österreichisches Staatsarchiv, Abteilung IV: Kriegsarchiv, Nottendorfer Gasse 3, A-1030 Wien, Austria
* **Baden** army (before 1871): Badisches Generallandesarchiv, Nördliche Hilda-Promenade 2, 76133 Karlsruhe, Germany; (after 1871): Hauptstaatsarchiv Stuttgart, Konrad-Adenauer Str. 4, 70173 Stuttgart, Germany

* **Bavarian** (Bayerische) army: (complete until 1919) Kriegsarchiv, Leonrodstr. 57, Postfach 221152, 80501 München, Germany
* **Bergische** (Rhineland) troops: (until 1815) Hauptstaatsarchiv, Mauerstr. 55, 40476 Düsseldorf, Germany
* **Braunschweig** army (before 1867): Niedersächsisches Staatsarchiv Wolfenbüttel, Forstweg 2, 38302
* **Hannover** army (before 1867): Niedersächsische Hauptstaatsarchiv, Am Archiv 1, 30169 Hannover, Germany
* **Hessen-Darmstadt** army (before 1871): Staatsarchiv Darmstadt, Karolinenplatz 3, 64289 Darmstadt, Germany
* **Hessen-Kassel** army (before 1867): Staatsarchiv Marburg, Friedrichsplatz 15, Postfach 540, 35037 Marburg, Germany
* **Lippe-Detmold** troops (before 1867): Personenstandsarchiv für Westfalen-Lippe, Willi-Hofmann-Str. 2, 32756 Detmold, Germany
* **Mecklenburg** army (before 1867): Landeshauptarchiv Schwerin, Graf-Schack-Allee 2, 19053 Schwerin, Germany
* **Nassau** army (before 1867): Hessisches Hauptstaatsarchiv Wiesbaden, Mosbacher Str. 55, 65187 Wiesbaden, Germany
* **Oldenburg** army (until 1867): Niedersächsisches Staatsarchiv Oldenburg, Damm 43, 26135 Oldenburg, Germany
* **Electoral Saxon and Royal Saxon** army (complete until 1919): Sächsisches Haupt-staatsarchiv, Archivstr. 14, 01097 Dres-den, Germany
* **Schaumburg-Lippe** army (before 1867): Niedersächsisches Staatsarchiv in Bückeburg, Schloss Westflügel, 31675 Bückeburg, Germany
* **Schleswig-Holstein** troops (before 1867):
—All military records of the State of Denmark: Rigsarkivet 3. Afdeling, Forsvarets Arkiver, Rigsdagsgarden 5, DK-1218

Copenhagen, Denmark
–Duchy of Schleswig-Holstein-Gottorf
to 1773 and Schleswig-Holstein 1848-
1851: Landesarchiv Schleswig-Holstein,
Prinz-enpalais, 24837 Schleswig, Germany
–Additional details may be found in:
Stolz, Gerd, "Genealogische Quellen für
das Militär in Schleswig-Holstein seit
dem 18. Jahrhundert" [Genealogical
Sources for the Military in Schleswig-
Holstein since the 18ᵗʰ Century]
*Familienkundliches   Jahrbuch
Schleswig-Holstein,* 1982. FHL 943.51
B5fj.
◆**Thuringian** units including Weimar,
Eisenach, Meiningen, Reuss, Gotha and
Altenburg (before 1867), in the various
archives of their respective states:
–Thüringisches Staatsarchiv Gotha,
Schloss Friedenstein, 99867 Gotha, Germany
–Thüringisches Staatsarchiv Greiz,
Oberes Schloss 7, 07973 Greiz, Germany
–Thüringisches Staatsarchiv Mein-
ingen, Schloss Bibrabau, 98617
Meiningen, Germany
–Thüringisches   Staatsarchiv
Rudolstadt, Schloss Hedecksburg, 07407
Rudolstadt, Germany
– Thüringisches Hauptstaatsarchiv
Weimar, Postfach 726, 99408 Weimar,
Germany
◆**Württemberg** army (before and after
1871): Hauptstaatsarchiv Stuttgart,
Konrad-Adenauer Str. 4, 70173 Stuttgart,
Germany
    Note: Dr. Th. J. Niemeyer, Director of
the Military Museum Rastatt, has stated
that because of the loss of the German
armed forces archives at Potsdam, there
is hardly a chance to find anything about
common soldiers and noncommissioned
officers. "Also all inquiries in which the
soldier's assignment to a given army
(Bad-ensian, Bavarian, Hessian, etc.) is
not known could not be answered by
the particular state archives which
house those armies' records."

    He did state, however, regarding the
badische Armee (the Badensian army),
"The museum has a number of records
of common soldiers and noncommissioned officers (*Stammrollen*), for the
years between 1812 and 1860. They contain the following information about the
regiments' troops: Surname, given name,
birth date, home residence, length and
occupation. The majority of these
records are at the Generallandesarchiv,
at Karlsruhe."
    This museum, Wehrgeschichtliches
Museum, Postfach 1633, 76406 Rastatt,
Germany, has more than 50,000 volumes
of titles on military history and might
possibly be a source for information on
the history of a particular regiment, rather
than information on a particular individual. The museum holds no detailed
archival material except for the Baden
army.
Source: Submitted by Horst A. Reschke
(from *The German Connection,* German
Research Association, Vol. 20, No. 3, 1996).

MILITARY REFERENCES, INCLUDING UNIFORMS

◆*Die altpreussische Armee 1714-1806
und ihre Militärkirchenbücher* [the old
Prussian army 1714-1806 and its military
church records], Alexander v. Lyncker,
(reprint of 1937 edition), Verlag Degener
& Co., Neustadt/Aisch, 1980. FHL 943
B4b v 23. Film 477,806 item 1
◆*Army Uniforms of World War I,* A.
Mollo/P. Turner, Blandford Press Ltd.,
Dorset, 1977.
◆ *Bibliographie der Geschichten
deutscher Regimenter* [bibliography of
the histories of German regiments], in
"Schrifttumsberichte zur Genealogie,"
eighth literature report, Dr. Fritz Runge,
Verlag Degener, Neustadt/Aisch, 1955.
◆*Dienstalters-Liste der Offiziere der
Königlich-Preussischen Armee und des
XIII (Königlich Württembergischen)*

Armeekorps [seniority list of the officers of the Royal Prussian Army and of the XIII (Royal Württemberg) Army Corps], Ernst Siegfried Mittler und Sohn, Berlin, 1917. FHL 943 M2d. Film 1,573,185 item 2

♦ *Einteilung und Standorte der deutschen Wehrmacht* [assignments and garrisons of the German armed forces], appendix V to *Meyers Orts- und Verkehrslexikon*, [9 pp.] compiled by E. Ütrecht, Leipzig, 1912.

♦ *Genealogische Quellen für das Militär in Schleswig-Holstein seit dem 18. Jahr-hundert* [genealogical sources of the military in Schleswig-Holstein, since the 18th century], Gerd Stolz, [8 pp.] in "Familienkundliches Jahrbuch Schleswig-Holstein," Kiel, 1982.

♦ *The German Connection*, Vol. 20, No. 3, third quarter 1996, contains eight essays pertaining to German military research. Published by the German Research Association, Inc., San Diego, 1996.

♦ "German Military Records: History and Genealogical Records," Part I, "The Wars of Unification," by Laraine K. Ferguson, *German Genealogical Digest*, Volume 11, No. 2, Summer 1995.

♦ *German Military Records as Genealogical Sources*, Horst A. Reschke, published by the author, Salt Lake City, 1990. FHL 943 M2r; fiche 6,001,596.

♦ *Heeres- und Truppengeschichte des Deutschen Reiches und seiner Länder, 1806 bis 1918* [army and troop history of the German empire and her states 1806 until 1918] a bibliography, Eike Mohr, Biblio Verlag, Osnabrück, 1989.

♦ *Histories of 251 Divisions of the German Army Which Participated in the War 1914-1918*, U.S. War Office, Reproduction of first edition of 1920, The London Stamp Exchange Ltd., London, 1989.

♦ *Kirchenbücher* [churchbooks], Eckart Henning and Christel Wegeleben, Verlag Degener, Neustadt/Aisch, 1991. Bibliog-

raphy of articles on military records appearing in German genealogical publications. FHL 943 D25gi v. 23

♦ *Literatur-Jahreskatalog 1997* [annual military literature catalog 1997] issued by Preussisches Bücherkabinett, Knesebeck-str. 88, 10623 Berlin, Germany; fax 011 40 30 3131180.

♦ *Militärgeschichte, Militärwissenschaft, Uniformkunde, Ordenskunde, Waffenkunde, Festungswesen* [military history, military science, uniform, medal, weapon & fortress expertise], catalog of publications, 182 pp., issued by Biblio-Zeller Verlag, Osnabrück, 1998 (address: Post-fach 1949, 49009 Osnabrück, Germany)

♦ *Military Uniforms 1686-1918*, Rene North, Bantam Books, Toronto, New York, London, 1970

♦ *Personengeschichtliche Quellen in den Militaria-Beständen des Niedersächsischen Hauptstaatsarchivs in Hannover* [sources pertaining to individual soldiers, as found in military documents of the Lower Saxony main state archive, Hannover], Jörg Walter, Vandenhoeck & Ruprecht, Göttingen, 1979. FHL 943.59 A3v No. 38. Film 1,917,267 item 9

♦ *Die Preussische Armee 1807-1867 und ihre sippenkundlichen Quellen* [the Prussian army 1807-1867 and its genealogial sources], Alexander v. Lyncker, reprint of 1939 edition, Verlag Degener & Co., Neustadt/Aisch, 1981. FHL Film 477,807 item 1

♦ *Preussisch-Deutsche Uniformen von 1640-1918* [Prussian-German uniforms from 1640 to 1918] Georg Ortenburg and Ingo Prömper, Orbis Verlag, 1991

♦ *Die preussischen Ranglisten und Stammrollen als Hilfsmittel für die genealogische Militariaforschung* [the Prussian officers' rolls and soldiers' records as tools for genealogical research of the military records] Alexander v. Lyncker, in "Familie, Sippe, Volk" magazine, 6 pp., 4th year, issue 6, Berlin, 20

June 1938
Searching German Military Sources,
Robert E.Ward, 6 pp., in "Ward's German-American Genealogical Workshop Bulletin," Cleveland, OH, 1982. FHL 973 F25wr

Stammregister und Chronik der Kur- und Königlich Sächsischen Armee [soldiers' rolls and history of the electoral and royal Saxon army] from 1670 to the beginnings of the 20th century, Heinrich August Verlohren, Verlag von Carl Beck, Leipzig, 1910. FHL 943 B4b v. 28

Uniformen der Alten Armee [uniforms of the old army], listing and explanation of the various army units, plus 312 color plates of the various German uniforms, Waldorf Astoria, München, ca. 1935

Uniforms of the World, Richard & Heinrich Knotel & Herbert Sieg, Exeter Books, New York, 1980

Verlust-Listen der Königlich Preussischen Armee und der Großherzoglich Badischen Division aus dem Feldzuge 1870-71 [list of casualties of the army of the Kingdom of Prussia in the 1870-71 campaign], Berlin, 1871.
Lists wounded and deaths in the Franco-Prussian war, arranged by regiment. Places of birth are usually included. A number of pages are missing from the FHL copy. FHL Film 1,340,524, pages 1-1285

Verzeichnis der Militärkirchenbücher in der Bundesrepublik Deutschland, [index of military Protestant church records in the Federal Republic of Germany (the former West Germany)] as of 30 Sept. 1990, Wolfgang Eger, Verlag Degener & Co., Neustadt/Aisch, 1993. FHL 943 K23 va, vol. 18

Verzeichnis der Militärkirchenbücher in der Bundesrepublik Deutschland, [index of the military church records in the Federal Republic of Germany] (new federal states and Roman Catholic Church), Wolfgang Eger, Verlag Degener & Co., Neustadt/Aisch, 1996. FHL 943 K23 va vo.. 23

Vocabulary of German Military Terms and Abbreviations, 219 pp., the War Office, London, 1943
Note: For further military sources, consult the Family History Library Catalog for listings under the topics "Military History" and "Military Records" in areas such as Germany; Germany, Prussia; Germany, [German state of interest]; or Austria.

Sources:
* Horst A. Reschke
* "German Military Records, Part I –the Wars of Unification," Laraine K. Ferguson, *German Genealogical Digest,* Vol. 11, No. 2.
* Family History Library Catalog

GERMANY'S 'IRON CROSS'

Germany's most famous military medal, the Iron Cross, was introduced by the Prussians in 1813 during the Napoleonic wars. Even after the German states unified under Bismarck in 1871, the Iron Cross survived. Hitler, a corporal in World War I when he received the award for bravery, gave out so many Iron Crosses during World War II that he had to invent even more exalted forms of awards as the war dragged on. The result was the Knight's Cross, which was worn around the neck and was personally awarded by *der Führer*. There were only 8,500 soldiers who received a Knight's Cross.

Frederick the Great, who led a campaign to build up the Prussian military, awarded what is believed to be the first medal for combat bravery, the *Pour le Merite*, nicknamed the "Blue Max" because of its color. (Frederick admired the French.) That medal was held in such respect that when a German officer arrived at a military base wearing it, the guards saluted the medal, not the officer.

Since World War II there has been a backlash against medals because of their association with the Nazis. The loss of so many Germans in World War II has led heroism in battle to be viewed as folly by many. Germany does have an award called the Federal Service Cross, but some feel that it has been devalued from having been given to second-rate actresses and others for dubious contributions.

Source: "Question of Medals Is Still Up in the Air For Luftwaffe Pilots," by Greg Steinmetz, *Wall Street Journal,* April 23, 1999.

MILITARY CHURCHBOOKS/ MILITARY PARISH RECORDS

"Military parish records . . . are only good, i.e., contain information, if a soldier either got married in a garrison church (*Garnisonkirche*) or, as a married soldier, had children who were baptized or confirmed and thus made it into the record books," states Horst A. Reschke, who writes frequently on German military matters. "If a soldier died or was killed while on active status, his death might be recorded. Regimental church records were kept by the regiment's chaplain and were regarded as his personal property."

Military churchbook index for the former West Germany

♦ Wolfgang Eger, *Verzeichnis der Militärkirchenbücher in der Bundesrepublik Deutschland (nach dem Stand vom 30. September 1990)* [index to the military churchbooks in the Federal Republic of Germany (according to their status as of September 30, 1990)], Vol. 18, Verlag Degener & Co., Neustadt/ Aisch, 1993. (A publication of the Work Group of the Protestant Church's archives and libraries) FHL 943 K23 va, vol. 18.

(Note: Three days after the September 30, 1990 date included in this book's title, on October 3, 1990, five additional

states, those of the former East Germany, were officially joined with the former West Germany; therefore, this volume deals with Protestant churchbooks of the former West Germany only. See volume 23, described below, for coverage of church-books of the former East Germany.)

In addition to the locations of more than 4,000 military Protestant churchbooks in the former West Germany, including Berlin (many of which are available on FHL microfilm), this index includes regimental church records (678 man central office for genealogy) in Leipzig.

Useful sections of this volume

Pages 418-430: "Register of Towns and Areas of Origin, and Persons Who Commissioned or Commanded Military Units" (nobles, generals, etc.). This section lists alphabetically the places including towns, cities, states, and provinces in which the military church books originated. The persons include the names of nobles, military commanders, and others after whom military units were named.

Pages 1-408: "Storage Locations of Military Churchbooks": Addresses for all these repositories are given in this "*Lagerorte*" (storage locations) section. (The postal codes given in these addresses may be updated by referring to *Das Postleitzahlenbuch.*

Pages iii - iv (*Inhaltsverzeichnis*): This section can be useful for locating military churchbooks in specific cities or provinces by checking these storage locations.

When the name of the military unit and the time of service are known, these sections of Volume 18 should be checked:

1) pages 314-314: Reference to these pages could be useful if the subject served in a Prussian infantry regiment numbered 1-52 or 54-60; on these pages, commanders of those regiments are given by sequential regiment numbers, with their dates of command.

2) Pages 431-445: The *"Register der militärischen Einheiten"* (register of military units) lists units alphabetically.

3) Pages 409-417: The *"Index der Regimentskirchenbücher"* (index of regimental churchbooks), now located at the *Deutsche Zentralstelle für Genealogie* (German central office for genealogy) in Leipzig, could be useful if the name of the military regiment and/or the name of its commander is known. (Many such records have been filmed and may be borrowed from the Family History Library. Check the *Findbuch der Regiments Kirchen-bücher 1714-1942* [inventory of military parish registers of the Prussian army] on FHL Film 492,737.

Military churchbook index for the former East Germany, and for Catholic church records

♦ Wolfgang Eger, *Verzeichnis der Militär-kirchenbücher in der Bundesrepublik Deutschland (neue Bundesländer – Römisch-Katholische Kirche)* [index of military churchbooks in the Federal Republic of Germany (new federal states – Roman Catholic Church)], Vol. 23, Verlag Degener & Co., Neustadt/Aisch, 1996. (A publication of the Work Group of the Protestant Church's Archives and Libraries) FHL 943 K23 va, vol. 23

This Volume 23 indexes about 1,200 military Protestant churchbooks of the former East Germany (and some in the former West Germany too). It also indexes Catholic military records in all of Germany.

The storage locations (*Lagerorte*) of the churchbooks are listed alphabetically by locality. Included are the following:

1) Index for storage locations for places included in Volume 18 (the above-mentioned volume containing military church-book listings for the former West Germany)

2) Index for storage locations for places included in this Volume 23 (containing military churchbook listings for the former East Germany)

3) A place- and person-index (*Orts- und Personenregister*), combined for both volumes 18 and 23: Page numbers given in boldface type in this index refer to Volume 23; those in normal type refer to Volume 18.

Source: "A Guide to Military Churchbooks," by Merriam M. Moore, *The German Connection* (German Research Association), Vol. 20, No. 3 (1996), page 59.

NAVY AND AIR FORCE CHURCHBOOKS

It is reported that the Central Churchbook Depository of the Army found no specific navy or air force churchbooks. In reference to such records, the following statement (in translation) appears in Wolfgang Eger's *Verzeichnis der Militärkirchenbücher in der Bundesrepublik Deutschland* (volume 18): "It is known that navy records before 1670 are found in the army churchbooks. After 1670 they are found in the navy sea-fortifications churchbooks *(Marine-Seefestungs-Kirchenbüchern)* in Pillau and in the sea garrisons' churchbooks; after about 1850, in the navy garrisons' church books.

The closed navy churchbooks were housed at navy bases (*Marinedienststellen*). The last navy churchbook archive is the *Dienststelle des Stationspfarrers der Marine-Station der Nordsee, Marinedekan Ronneberger* (office of the station pastor of the North Sea naval station, Naval Dean Ronneberger).

"The air force had no religious ministry of its own. Depending on their location, air force units were ministered to by the clergy of the army or navy; therefore air force entries are scattered among army and navy churchbooks."

Source: "A Guide to Military Churchbooks," by Merriam M. Moore, *The German Connection* (German Research Association), Vol. 20, No. 3 (1996).

GERMAN ARCHIVES FOR MILITARY RESEARCH

(Check websites for updated information.)

In order to make use of German archives and libraries for military research, it is necessary to know the name of the ancestor, the army in which he served, the regiment, and the company.

Some important archives

Note: The overwhelming majority of parish registers indexed in Wolfgang Eger's two volumes of indexes to military church-books in Germany, "Military Church-books/Parish Registers" are held among the first four of these archives:

♦ **Deutsche Zentralstelle für Genealogie**
Schongauer Strasse 1, 04329 Leipzig

♦ **Evangelisches Zentralarchiv in Berlin**
Jebenstrasse 3, 10623 Berlin
See Wolfgang Eger's *Verzeichnis der Militärkirchenbücher in der Bundesrepublik Deutschland* for the military parish register holdings for this archive (located in Charlottenburg). FHL 943 K23va Vol. 18.

♦ **Geheimes Staatsarchiv Preussischer Kulturbesitz**
Archivstrasse 12-14, 14195 Berlin
Military churchbook holdings for this archive are found in Wolfgang Eger's *Verzeichnis der Militärkirchenbücher in der Bundesrepublik Deutschland.* FHL 943 K23va Vol. 18.

♦ **Kirchliches Archiv des Katholischen Militärbischofs**
Kaiserstrasse 141, 53113 Bonn
(Post office address: Katholisches

Militär-bischofsamt, Adenauerallee 115, 53113 Bonn)

♦ **Bundesarchiv-Militärarchiv**
(Abteilung VI des Bundesarchivs)
Wiesenthalstrasse 10, 79115 Freiburg i. Br.
Prussian records 1867-1945. (The Freiburg archives are being combined with the military archive in Potsdam.)

♦ **Bundesarchiv-Militärisches Zwischenarchiv** Potsdam, Zeppelinstrasse 127/128, 14471 Potsdam

♦ **Militärgeschichtliches Forschungamt**
Grünwälderstrasse 10-145, 79098 Freiburg i. Br.
This library contains military history publications.

♦ **Krankenbuchlager Berlin**
Wattstrasse 11-13, 13355 Berlin
This is the agency that administers the military units' sick records from the World War I era.

Archives of states whose armies were not joined with the Prussian army

Below are archives of the four German states whose armies were not integrated into the Prussian army in 1867:

♦ **Sachsen:**
Staatsarchiv, Archivstrasse 14, 01097 Dresden

♦ **Bayern:**
Bayerisches Hauptstaatsarchiv, Abt. Kriegsarchiv, Schönfeldstrasse 5, 80539 München

♦ **Baden:**
Generallandesarchiv, Nördliche Hilda-promenade 2, 76133 Karlsruhe

♦ **Württemberg:**
Hauptstaatsarchiv, Konrad-Adenauer Strasse 4, 70173 Stuttgart

GERMAN EXPELLEES, 1944-1949

On October 16, 1944, a massive Soviet offensive set off a mass flight and evacuation of ethnic Germans from East Prussia, continuing into the spring of 1945, at which time Germans from central Poland followed. In May, Germans from Czechoslovakia took flight to the west. Germans fled from East Prussia, Eastern Brandenburg, Eastern Pomerania, Silesia, Czechoslovakia (primarily Bohemia and the Sudetenland), central Poland, Yugoslavia, Hungary, Romania, and the Baltic states.

The expulsion of 7.5 million people from today's Poland and the Russian part of East Prussia caused the deaths of an estimated 1.4 million people. The flight, brought on by the realignment of Poland's frontiers, to the benefit of the Soviet Union, continued through 1949.

The Bonn government estimated that as of 1950, 11,700,000 Germans had fled or were displaced, of whom 2,100,000 died en route.

As a result of this expulsion, many of the *Vertriebenen* (expellees) were lost from their families and former neighbors, inducing organizations in Germany to form organizations for the purpose of gaining and exchangiing information about individuals who have been reported missing.

In the following section are a few of the organizations involved in such activity.

Source: John Dornberg, "Germany's Expellees and Border Changes: An Endless Dilemma?" *German Life*, June/July 1995

SELECTED WAR-RELATED RESOURCES IN GERMANY

♦**German War Graves Commission:**
Volksbund Deutsche Kriegsgräberfürsorge e.V.
Bundesgeschäftsstelle
Werner-Hilpert Strasse 2
34112 Kassel
Germany

♦**Deutsche Dienststelle** (or WASt, abbreviation for "Wehrmachtsauskunftsstelle" [information center on members of the former German army]

The Deutsche Dienststelle (WASt) holdings deal with records on POWs (prisoners of war), MIAs (missing in action), and KIAs (killed in action). It also holds data on casualties, military hospitals, gravesites, medals and decorations, estates and inheritances, and death records.

Its records are available subject to provisions of Germany's privacy law (*Datenschutz*).
–Deutsche Dienststelle (WASt)
Eichborndamm 179, Tor 6
13403 Berlin
Mailing address:
Postfach 51 06 57
13400 Berlin
Tel. (030) 41904-0
Fax (030) 41904-100

♦**Internationaler Suchdienst Bad Arolsen** (international search service), deals with Germans and non-Germans who were held in concentration camps, forced labor camps, and otherwise imprisoned between 1933 and 1945.
–Internationaler Suchdienst
Große Alle 5-9
34454 Bad Arolsen
Tel. (05691) 60 37

♦**Deutsches Rotes Kreuz – Suchtdienst Hamburg** [German Red Cross, Hamburg search service], with many services including searching for family members separated during or after the war
–Deutsches Rotes Kreuz
Generalsekretariat
Suchdienst Hamburg
Amandastraße 74
20357 Hamburg
Tel. (040) 432 02-0
Fax: (040) 432 02-200
DRK-Suchdienst-Hamburg@drk-sdhh.de

♦**Deutsches Rotes Kreuz – Suchdienst**

München [German Red Cross, Munich], search services including reuniting missing people
–Deutsches Rotes Kreuz
Generalsekretariat
Suchdienst München
Chiemgaustraße 109
81549 München
Tel. (089) 680 773-0
Fax (089) 680 745 92
DRK-Suchdienst-Muenchen@t-online.de
♦Kirchlicher Suchdienst: Heimatortskarteien (HOK)[church-based organization gathering information for people missing since the expulsions following World War II]
–Zentralstelle der Heimatortskarteien
Lessingstraße 3
80336 München
Tel. (089) 544 97-0
Fax (089) 544 97-207
The following are addresses for branches concentrating in specific areas, which are indicated in parentheses:
– **Stuttgart:** Rosenbergstraße 50, 70176 Stuttgart (Germans from Hungary, Rumania, Yugoslavia, Slovakia, Ruthenia, Russia, Bessarabia, Bulgaria, Dobrudia)
–**Bamberg:** Postfach 16 48, 96007 Bamberg (Niederschlesien)
–**Passau:** Ostuzzistraße 4, 94032 Passau (Oberschlesien)
–**Augsburg:** Postfach 10 14 20, 86004 Augsburg (Mark Brandenburg)
–**Hannover:** Engelbosteler Damm 72, 30167 Hannover (Germans from Wartheland Poland)
–**Regensburg:** Postfach 11 01 55, 93014 Regensburg (Sudeten Germans)
– **Lübeck:** Vorwerker Straße 103, Block 33, 23554 Lübeck (Northeast Europe: East Prussia and Memel, Danzig-West Prussia, Pomerania, Estonia, Latvia, Lithuania)
♦**Bundesarchiv-Zentralnachweisstelle**
This archive has some military service records.
Abteigarten 6

52076 Aachen
♦**Verband der Kriegs- und Wehrdienstopfer, Behinderten und Rentner Deutschland** [Organization of the Victims of Wars and Military Services]
Wurzerstraße 4A
53175 Bonn
Tel. (40) 228 82093 0
♦ **Verband der Heimkehrer, Kriegsgefangenen und Vermisstsenangehörigen Deutschlands** [Organization of soldiers returning from the war, of POWs and family members of missing persons]
Konstantinstraße 17
53179 Bonn
Tel. (49) 228 95714 0

MILITARY ARCHIVES: AUSTRIA, FRANCE, DENMARK

♦**Austria**
Österreichisches Staatsarchiv
Abteilung IV: Kriegsarchiv
Stiftgasse 2
1010 Vienna
Austria
♦**France:**
Les Archives Militaires
Château de Vincennes
94304 Vincennes
France
♦**Denmark**
Haerens Archive
Slotsholmsgade 4
1216 Copenhagen K
Denmark

MILITARY CEMETERIES, WORLD WAR I AND II

–*Atlas deutscher Kriegsgräber: Frankreich, Belgien, Luxemburg, Niederlande,* (Atlas of German war graves: France, Belgium, Luxembourg, Netherlands), by Adolf Barth, and Willi Kammerer, *Volksbund Deutsche Kriegsgräber-fürsorge,* Kassel (1973?).

FHL 943 V3v
Illustrated atlas describing burial sites
of German soldiers from both world wars,
located in France, Belgium, Luxembourg,
and the Netherlands; includes some information about French, British, American and other military sites in these countries; includes an index)
–*Atlas deutscher Kriegsgräberstätten
des 1. und 2. Weltkrieges in der Bundesrepublik Deutschland* (Atlas of World
War I and World War II military cemeteries in Germany) by the German War
Graves Commission, *Volksbund
Deutsche   Kriegsgräberfürsorge,*
(1980?). FHL 943 V3a
Includes a brief history, numbers of
graves, index.
–*Schicksal in Zahlen* (History and description of German military cemeteries
worldwide. Includes excerpts from international treaties securing burial sites and
an alphabetical listing, together with enumeration of graves, and of German
miitary cemeteries in Germany and
abroad for those who fell in World War I
and World War II), by Volksbund
Deutsche   Kriegs-gräberfürsorge,
Kassel, 1985. FHL 943 V3b

GERMAN NAVY MEMORIAL

The "Monument of Honor of the German Navy" may be found at this address:
Marine-Ehrenmal
Strandstraße
24235 Laboe
Tel. (49) 4343 4270 0

THE MILITARY PASS

The "military pass" (*Militärpaß*) is
an official record of service that was issued to all German soldiers at the end of
their active duty, as they passed to reserve status (*Beurlaubtenstand*).

It included information dealing with
family members and addresses, the
soldier's ranks, the division he was assigned to, the battles in which he participated, his time in army hospitals, a
personal description, and finally, his discharge.
Source: Maryann Forster, "A Military
Pass," *The German Connection*, Vol. 20, No.
3, p. 59.

GERMAN PRISONERS OF WAR IN THE UNITED STATES DURING WORLD WAR II

More than three million prisoners
of war were held by the Allies during
World War II, of which about 425,000
were encamped in the continental
United States. Of these, between
360,000 and 372,000 prisoners (estimates vary) were Germans. In World
War I, Americans held a total of only
1,346 prisoners of war.[1]

Three general groups of German
prisoners were sent to the United
States: 1) Germans captured during the
fighting in North Africa in late 1942 and
in 1943 (by the end of 1943 there were
123,440 German POWs in the United
States), 2) about 50,000 Germans, most
of whom were captured in the fighting
in Italy, and 3) the 182,000 Germans
captured after the landing at
Normandy on June 6, 1944.[2]

It was decided in 1942 that all prisoners taken by the United States would
be shipped to the States, rather than
keeping them in Europe, to be transported in ships that were returning to
American shores practically empty after carrying troops and supplies overseas.

At first, prisoner-of-war encamp-
ments were established in old Civilian
Conservation Corps (CCC) camps or
in unused camps built in the Southwest for enemy aliens. In the first few

months, quarters were prepared to hold 76,218 more men, and structures for 144,000 more were begun in case they were needed. At first, tents were generally used to hold the prisoners until more substantial structures could be built.

At that time, the pertinent treaty in effect was the 1929 "Geneva Convention Relative to the Treatment of Prisoners of War," under which prisoners were to be treated humanely.

Under this convention, prisoners were to get the same housing, food, clothing, pay and work hours as provided to soldiers of the capturing nation. Only enlisted men (if they were healthy) could be put to work. Non-commissioned officers could be required only to supervise enlisted men, and officers could not be required to work.[3]

Americans honored the Geneva Convention almost to the letter, and often beyond its minimum requirements. Reasons for this strict attention to international law were, 1) prisoners were entitled to humanitarian treatment, 2) the United States felt a duty to live up to an agreement which it had signed, 3) living up to the agreement would not give the German government justification to treat American prisoners inhumanely, 4) the belief that well-treated prisoners would make better workers, and 5) German soldiers might well be encouraged to surrender, knowing they would be well treated by the Americans.[4]

Under the Geneva Convention, prisoners were not to be "reeducated" or denationalized. At the urging of Eleanor Roosevelt, however, the United States government did secretly undertake an extensive effort to inculcate democratic principles among German prisoners of war.

In 1944, the Prisoner of War Special Projects Division was created, whose personnel put together in a matter of weeks a program to reeducate 372,000 Germans. The project and its results form an intriguing undertaking that had distinguished, if controversial, effects.[5]

A sampling of some of the courses offered to the prisoners includes
- The Democratic Way of Life
- The Constitution of the United States
- Political Parties, Elections, and Parliamentary Procedures
- Education in the United States
- American Family Life
- The American Economic Scene
- American Military Government
- Democratic Traditions in Germany
- Why the Weimar Republic Failed; Democratic Traditions in Germany
- The World of Today and Germany
- New Democratic Trends in the World Today[6]

The interpreter shortage

The problem of interpreters was severe. It was not unusual for only a single translator to be available for up to 10,000 prisoners. The choices related to such a dilemma were not attractive: either use English-speaking German prisoners, (Nazis or anti-Nazis), or just forget about the prisoners and let them run themselves. Between these two choices it was decided that the better plan was to use the English-speaking Germans for communication, although the Nazi influence in the camps was a definite risk, which often backfired.[7]

Prisoner segregation

Only superficial separation of German personnel took place, with army personnel separated from air force, and officers from enlisted men. Nazis and anti-Nazis were housed together, causing serious problems later on. By 1945, only a total of 4,500 visibly loyal Nazis were interned at Alva, Oklahoma, and 3,300 of the most visibly dedicated anti-

Nazis were shipped to Fort Devens, Massachusetts, and Camp Campbell, Kentucky. There were numerous incidents in which rabid Nazis tried (and too often succeeded) to murder or harm anti-Nazi prisoners of war.[8]

Escape attempts

Fewer than 1 percent of the total number of German prisoners in the United States made attempts to escape. Working in favor of the War Department in this respect were three major factors: 1) the Germans formed a tightly obedient military unit, with each rank responsible to its immediate superior, 2) the prisoners were immediately attracted to a comprehensive recreational and educational program offered to them, and 3) there was simply no place to go (long train rides had impressed on prisoners the vastness of the American landscape).

Yet some prisoners tried to escape, and indeed, not only was it legal under the Geneva Convention of 1929, but it was the duty of captured soldiers to escape, charged by their oath of service to escape at every opportunity.

A copy of a "Memorandum Addressed to German Soldiers" provided to all German POWs as guaranteed by the Geneva Convention, reminded the soldiers that they were to keep physically strong, to become fully familiar with their rights, and to take every opportunity to escape.

The number of escapes was small: monthly about 3 escapees per 10,000 captives, a record better than that of the American penitentiary system. The great majority of escapees were returned to military control within 24 hours of their escape, when they were routinely interrogated, given a token punishment as required under the Geneva Convention, and returned to the prisoner community.

The War Department reported that 46 percent of the escapes occurred at base camps, 16 percent from branch camps, and 30 percent from work details.[9]

Of the total of 2,222 German prisoners of war who escaped, only 17 remained at large in late 1947; by 1951 only six were at large. Four were discovered or surrendered by 1959. The last escapee, Georg Gaertner, who escaped in September 1945, was never located [10]

A time of horrors

In 1945, the big news from Europe was that of the millions who had perished in the Nazi extermination camps. The War Department made mandatory the showing of films of the Nazi atrocities to German prisoners of war. The orders were the same for all camps: all prisoners were forced to attend, silence was to be maintained during the film, and no discussion afterwards was permitted.

Responses varied. Some were horrified, destroyed their German uniforms, and even took up collections for concentration camp survivors.Others credited the films as Hollywood fabrications, or as Russian propaganda. The most common response: "Why did they show that to us? We didn't do it."[11]

The reaction of the War Department, in May 1945, was to reduce the food allowances of the prisoners. At Camp Stark, New Hampshire, for example, the daily food ration was reduced from 5,500 to 1,800 calories; the canteen no longer sold beer, milk, cigarettes, or can-dy; and the lumber-cutting work quota was raised.[12]

In the midst of this new anxiety, the German prisoners at Camp Stark got word of another piece of news that put fear in their hearts: Some new guards were coming into the camp, American soldiers who had just returned to the United States after suffering as prisoners of war in Germany. These men, captured during the Battle of the Bulge, had been marched without food for four days from Belgium to Germany, and had endured a four-day rail journey locked in a box car with 60 men without food or water. Then they were marched to Bad Orb where for the next 100 days they existed on grass soup with a few potatoes. These men, the War Department declared, "who have experienced captivity and detention by the enemy, are considered to be eminently qualified for these duties."

The big surprise came when the American prisoners of war arrived and bore no animosity to the German prisoners. Rather, close friendships were formed between these two groups who shared the experience as prisoners of war. The Germans heard first-hand news of the situation in Germany from their new guards – and as bad as the news was, at least it was reliable. Also, the Americans empathized with the plight of the German prisoners of war. When rations were cut for the German prisoners, the American guards slipped food and cigarettes to the Germans in order to communicate their lack of support for the American policy.[13]

Dashed hopes

The end of the war raised great hopes for the Germans that they could return home. But in the end, the emptying out of the American prisoner of war camps triggered great disappointment and resentment in many Germans who had come to admire the United States. About half the German prisoners of war found that they were not going to go home after all, but that they were instead to be traded off primarily to France and Eng-land to help reconstruct those war-damaged countries. The anger stirred in the prisoners by this deal made by the Allies was remembered for years after.[14]

The majority of the prisoners shunted off to France, England, Netherlands, Scandinavia, Czechoslovakia, Yugoslavia, and Greece served in labor battalions for about four to six months, although many thousands were held much longer.[15]

Endnotes

[1] Allen V. Koop, *Stark Decency: German Prisoners of War in a New England Village* (New York: Hanover: University Press of New England, 1988), 24

[2] Helmut Hörner, *A German Odyssey: The Journal of a German Prisoner of War* (Golden, Colorado: Fulcrum Publishing, 1991) ix

[3] Hörner, *A German Odyssey: The Journal of a German Prisoner of War*, viii

[4] Hörner, *A German Odyssey: The Journal of a German Prisoner of War*, viii

[5] Judith M. Gansberg, *Stalag: U.S.A. The Remarkable Story of German POWs in America,* (New York: Thomas Y. Crowell Company, 1977)

[6] Hörner, *A German Odyssey: The Journal of a German Prisoner of War*, 360

[7] Arnold Krammer, *Nazi Prisoners of War in America* (New York: Stein and Day, 1979), 5

[8] Krammer, *Nazi Prisoners of War in America*, 169-174

[9] Krammer, *Nazi Prisoners of War in America*, 116-121

[10] Krammer, *Nazi Prisoners of War in America*, 136-139

[11] Koop, *Stark Decency: German Prisoners of War in a New England Village,* 99-100

[12] Koop, *Stark Decency: German Prisoners of War in a New England Village*, 99-101

[13] Koop, *Stark Decency: German Prisoners of War in a New England Village*, 103

[14] Koop, *Stark Decency: German Prisoners of War in a New England Village*, 111

[15] Krammer, *Nazi Prisoners of War in America*, 248

Source: Shirley J. Riemer, "German Prisoners of War in America," *Der Blumenbaum*, Vol. 14, No. 3 1997

MAJOR GERMAN PRISONER OF WAR INTERNMENT CAMPS IN THE UNITED STATES

- Camp Algoma, Idaho
- Camp Aliceville, Alabama
- Camp Alva, Oklahoma
- Camp Angel Island, California
- Camp Ashby, Virginia
- Camp Ashford, West Virginia
- Camp Atlanta, Nebraska
- Camp Atterbury, Indiana
- Camp Barkeley, Texas
- Camp Beale, California
- Camp Blanding, Florida
- Camp Bowie, Texas
- Camp Brady, Texas
- Camp Breckinridge, Kentucky
- Camp Butner, North Carolina
- Camp Campbell, Kentucky
- Camp Carson, Colorado
- Camp Chaffee, Arkansas
- Camp Claiborne, Louisiana
- Camp Clarinda, Iowa
- Camp Clark, Missouri
- Camp Clinton, Mississippi
- Camp Como, Mississippi
- Camp Concordia, Kansas
- Camp Cooke, California
- Camp Croft, South Carolina
- Camp Crossville, Tennessee
- Camp Crowder, Missouri
- Camp David, Maryland
- Camp Dermott, Arkansas
- Camp Douglas, Wyoming
- Camp Edwards, Massachusetts
- Camp Ellis, Illinois
- Camp Evelyn, Michigan
- Camp Fannin, Texas
- Camp Farragut, Idaho
- Camp Florence, Arizona
- Camp Forrest, Tennessee
- Camp Gordon Johnston, Florida
- Camp Grant, Illinois
- Camp Gruber, Oklahoma
- Camp Hale, Colorado
- Camp Hearne, Texas
- Camp Hood, Texas
- Camp Houlton, Maine
- Camp Howze, Texas
- Camp Hulen, Texas
- Camp Huntsville, Texas
- Camp Indianola, Nebraska
- Camp Jerome, Arkansas
- Camp Lee, Virginia
- Camp Livingston, Louisiana
- Camp Lordsburg, New Mexico
- Camp McAlester, Oklahoma
- Camp McCain, Mississippi
- Camp McCoy, Wisconsin
- Camp McLean, Texas
- Camp Mackall, North Carolina
- Camp Maxey, Texas
- Camp Mexia, Texas
- Camp Monticello, Arkansas
- Camp New Cumberland, Pennsylvania
- Camp Ogden, Utah
- Camp Opelika, Alabama
- Camp Papago Park, Arizona
- Camp Peary, Virginia
- Camp Perry, Ohio
- Camp Phillips, Kansas
- Camp Pickett, Virginia
- Camp Pima, Arizona
- Camp Polk, Louisiana
- Camp Popolopen, New York
- Camp Pryor, Oklahoma
- Camp Reynolds, Pennsylvania
- Camp Jos. T. Robinson, Arkansas
- Camp Roswell, New Mexico
- Camp Rucker, Alabama
- Camp Rupert, Idaho
- Camp Ruston, Louisiana
- Camp Scottsbluff, Nebraska
- Camp Shelby, Mississippi
- Camp Sibert, Alabama
- Camp Somerset, Maryland
- Camp Stewart, Georgia
- Camp Stockton, California
- Camp Sutton, North Carolina
- Camp Swift, Texas
- Camp Tonkawa, Oklahoma
- Camp Trinidad, Colorado
- Camp Van Dorn, Mississippi
- Camp Wallace, Texas
- Camp Wheeler, Georgia
- Camp White, Oregon

•Camp Wolters, Texas
•Fort Benjamin Harrison, Indiana
•Fort Benning, Georgia
•Fort Bliss, Texas
•Fort Bragg, North Carolina
•Fort Crockett, Texas
•Fort Curtis, Virginia
•Fort Custer, Michigan
•Fort Devens, Massachusetts
•Fort Dix, New Jersey
•Fort DuPont, Delaware,
•Fort Eustis, Virginia
•Fort Gordon, Georgia
•Fort Greely, Colorado
•Fort Jackson, South Carolina
•Fort Kearny, Rhode Island
•Fort Knox, Kentucky
•Fort Leavenworth, Kansas
•Fort Leonard Wood, Missouri
•Fort Lewis, Washington
•Fort McClellan, Alabama
•Fort Meade, Maryland
•Fort Niagara, New York
•Fort Oglethorpe, Georgia
•Fort Ord, California
•Fort Patrick Henry, Virginia
•Fort Reno, Oklahoma
•Fort Riley, Kansas
•Fort Robinson, Nebraska
•Fort D.W. Russell, Texas
•Fort Sam Houston, Texas
•Fort Sheridan, Illinois
•Fort Sill, Oklahoma
•Fort F.E. Warren, Wyoming
•Edgewood Arsenal, Maryland
•Eglin Army Air Field, Florida
•Glennan General Hospital, Oklahoma
•Halloran General Hospital, New York
•Hampton Roads Port of Embarkation, Virginia
•Indiantown Gap Military Reservation, Pennsylvania
•Holabird Signal Depot, Maryland
•McCloskey General Hospital, Texas
•Memphis General Depot, Tennessee
•New Orleans Port of Embarkation, Louisiana
•Olmsted Field, Pennsylvania
•Pine Bluff Arsenal, Arkansas

•Richmond ASF Depot, Virginia
•Tobyhanna Military Reservation, Pennsylvania
•Westover Field, Massachusetts

RESEARCHING GERMAN PRISONERS OF WAR IN THE UNITED STATES

After World War II, the United States sent relevant prisoner-of-war personnel files to Germany. The holder of such records is the *Wehrmachts-auskunftsstelle* ("information center on members of the former German army") abbreviated as "WASt," [Wehrmachts-auskunftsstelle].

WASt
Eichborndamm 179, Tor 6
13403 Berlin

National Archives records

Most of the records in the custody of the National Archives and Records Administration (NARA) as they relate to POW camps in the United States can be found in Record Group 389, Records of the Office of the Provost Marshal General.

Many POW camp records were destroyed after the war. While NARA usually has some material about the major camps in the United States, it has very little documentation about the small branch or satellite camps which existed. RG 389 files in NARA's custody which are camp specific include the following:

Inspection Reports: These include reports by the United States War Department, and by neutral observers such as the International Red Cross and the Swiss Legation. These files docu-ment camp facilities and activities, and may include blueprints and maps.

Special Projects Division Files: Include documents related to prisoner re-education and cultural activities.

Detention Rosters: Although not necessarily complete for each camp, the rosters contain name, service number, POW number, birth date, date of capture and possible SS affiliation.

Labor Report Forms: Forms covering a two-week period and list total POW man-hours available and how those hours were broken down into various activities. Sometimes the "remarks" sec-tion of these forms was used to record important administrative events.

Technical Service Division Files: Contain examples of administrative forms and some reports relating to the operation of the camps.

Construction Files: Documents relating to the construction of camps, although many of the enclosures and attachments described in cover sheets are not in these files.

Administrative Files: Containing infor-mation about the transfer of specific POWs in and out of the camps. Cor-respondence contains some lists of POWs.

In addition to the camp-specific files described above, RG 389 contains several correspondence files relating to Axis POWs interned in the United States.

Other record groups in NARA's cus-tody also contain related information. For example, Record Group 211, Records of the War Manpower Com-mission, contains several series of records relating to the use of POW la-bor in the United States during World War II.

Sources:
* National Archives II, Textual Reference Branch, 1996 .
* WASt information: Rainer Thumshirn, Heimstetten, Germany.

SUGGESTED READING ON GERMAN PRISONERS OF WAR

* Judith M. Gansberg, *Stalag U.S.A.: The Remarkable Story of German POWs in America.* Thomas Y. Crowell Co., New York, 1977
* Arnold Krammer, *Nazi Prisoners of War in America.* Stein and Day, New York, 1979
* Allen V. Koop, *Stark Decency: German Prisoners of War in a New England Village.* University Press of New England, Hanover, 1988
* Helmut Hörner, *A German Odyssey: The Journal of A German Prisoner of War.* Fulcrum Publishing, Golden, Col-orado, 1991
* Glenn Thompson, *Prisoners on the Plains: German POWs in America.* Gamut Publications, 1993
* R. Robin, *The Barbed-Wire College: Reeducating German POWs in the United States During World War II.* Princeton University Press, 1995

Section 9: Collections of information

•

Periodicals for German research
Emigration records
German libraries, museums, cultural institutions
Sister cities, German-related organizations
Telephones, folk costumes, cooking measurements
and vocabularies

◆

CITY DIRECTORIES

The city directory serves an especially useful function as a complement to the U.S. Federal Census.

For example, during the decade of the 1880s, the number of German immigrants almost doubled that of the previous decade. The immigrants of that decade would likely have been counted in the U.S. census of 1890, but unfortunately, that census was almost completely destroyed. And even those immigrants who arrived in the 1870s and were counted in the 1880 census would not be soundexed in that census unless they were members of families with at least one child age 10 or younger.

Working against inclusion of German immigrants in the United States census during the heavy immigration decades is the fact that so many immigrants were moving about – traveling to join relatives, looking for work, heading for the gold fields, and seeking land. In this sense, the censuses were often aiming at thousands of moving targets, and when they were found, it was only at ten-year intervals.

If, however, immigrants lived in a locality where city (or other) directories were published during the second half of the nineteenth century and into the twentieth century, they could possibly be recorded in these directories – not just every ten years, but consecutively through each year of residency.

The city directory is an excellent tracking tool for German immigrants from about 1850 forward because it may provide clues as to when a person arrived in a given locality and when he or she either died or moved on.

Although city directories were published much earlier, they were at first sporadic, and it was not until around the middle of the nineteenth century that they became somewhat standardized.

City directories (as well as directories for business and professional groups, members of specific industries, members of religious organizations, and social and military organizations) can offer significant clues in tracking immigrants from their ports of entry to their final destinations.

City directories generally list names of residents, their home addresses and occupations, names and addresses of businesses, and listings that include churches, cemeteries, schools, and other municipal and social institutions. Each volume of a city directory usually covers only one specific year, but occasionally two. City directories are now for the most part replaced by telephone directories.

The Library of Congress has the largest collection of city and county directories. Check first in local public and university libraries for city as well as professional organization directories.

Numerous United States city directories are made available through the LDS Family History Library (FHL) in Salt Lake City and its local branch archives. The FHL holdings include directories for about 250 cities and regions from the late 1700s to 1901. Pre-1860 city directories are on more than 6,000 microfiche. Directories for 1861 to 1901 are on 1,119 microfilms. To locate city directories in the Family History Library Catalog, search by "Place Name" and scroll down the alphabetized list of sources that appear for that location.

References
♦ Ethridge, James, ed. *Directory of Directories*. Detroit: Gale Research, 1980.
♦ Spear, Dorothea N. *Bibliography of American Directories Through 1860*. Worcester, MA: American Antiquarian Society, 1961.

MANUSCRIPT COLLECTIONS

Since 1959, the Library of Congress has requested from libraries and other repositories the descriptions of their manuscript collections, which have been catalogued in the *National Union Catalog of Manuscript Collections*. (NUCMC), Washington, DC. Library of Congress, 1959- (ongoing).

The Library of Congress operates the NUCMC as a free-of-charge cooperative cataloging program, which lists manuscripts found in the Library of Congress and in other North America libraries. Eligible repositories must be located in the United States and its territories, must regularly admit researchers, and must lack the capability of entering their own manuscript cataloging into either RLIN or OCLC systems.

NUCMC is available for searching on the Internet. The home page can be found at http://lcweb.loc.gov/coll/nucmc/.

This source can be valuable in identifying the ancestral home of German immigrant families.

The volumes are indexed. One might check the index using many topics, a few suggestions for which follow:
♦ a surname of interest
♦ Genealogy, then the surname of interest
♦ Germany
Germans in the United States, Prussia
♦ specific churches, such as the Reformed Church
♦ localities of interest
♦ Hessians or other specific interest groups
♦ Germans from Russia
♦ school records

The index provides the year the item was catalogued and the entry number for that year. Entries are arranged alphabetically in the catalog and include the title, a short description of the manuscript, location of the collection, brief description of the contents, name of the donor, and an indication as to whether a finding aid exists in the repository for the collection.

Further information
Library of Congress, Cooperative and

Instructional Programs Division, NUCMC Program, 101 Independence Avenue, SE, Stop 4231, Washington, DC 20540-4231. Tel. (202) 707-7954; Fax (202) 252-2082; nucmc@loc.gov.

Sources:
♦ "Locating the Ancestral Home: Manuscript Collections," *German Genealogical Digest*, Vol. II, No. 2, 1986.
♦ "NUCMC, free cataloging proram operated by Library of Congress," by Ruby Coleman, *Antique Week*, 8 June 1998.
♦ NUCMC Team, Library of Congress

GERMAN NEWSPAPERS IN THE UNITED STATES

The earliest German newspapers were published in Philadelphia. They included *Die Philadelphische Zeitung,* 1732; *Der Hoch-Deutsch Pensylvanische Geschicht-Schreiber,* 1739; *Die Zeitung,* 1748; and *Der Wochentliche Philadelphische Staatsbote,* 1762.

A German-language newspaper, the *Germantowner Zeitung,* holds the distinction of having first printed the news of American independence in its edition of July 3, 1776,[1] scooping all English language newspapers.

The major influence on the German press came with the immigration of the Forty-eighters (Germans who had been active in the brief revolution in Germany in 1848), who were heavily involved in literary, musical, gymnastic, and political affairs. Forty-eighters at one time controlled a majority of all German newspapers in the United States.

In 1840, there were about 40 German newspapers being published in the United States. That number had almost doubled in 1848. By 1852, there were 133 German-language newspapers in the United States, and by 1860 there were about 266. Between 1848 and the start of the Civil War, the United States experienced the golden age of German-lan-

guage newspapers.

In 1885, of all the foreign-language newspapers in the United States, German-language papers represented 79 percent. Their popularity crested in 1894, when more than 800 papers were in circulation.

World War I severely drained the energy of the German press. In 1917, Congress enacted a law whereby all war-related matters prepared for print were to be submitted to the local postmaster for censoring until the loyalty of the paper could be established. By 1920, there were found to be only 278 German-language publications, many of which were house organs for lodges, churches, and social organizations. By 1930, only 172 German-language publications remained; by 1950, only 60.[2]

[1] Laraine Ferguson, "Newspapers: Unique Sources for German Family and Local History," *German Genealogical Digest* 3, no. 3 (1987).
[2] La Vern J. Rippley, *The German-Americans* (Lanham, MD: University Press of America, 1984), 163-166.

GERMAN-AMERICAN NEWSPAPER RESOURCES

The largest collections of newspapers on microfilm can be found at state libraries and state archives. Small towns may have microfilmed their old newspapers as well. Microfilm versions of newspapers are available on interlibrary loan to more than 6,000 public libraries in the United States.

♦ Karl J. R. Arndt, and May E. Olson, comps., *German-American Newspapers and Periodicals, 1732-1955: History and Bibliography* 2nd rev. ed. 1961. Reprint. Johnson Report Corp., New York. Vol. 2. FHL film 824,091 item 1
♦ Karl J. R. Arndt and May E. Olson, *The German Language Press of the Americas 1732-1968: A History and*

Bibliography Die deutschsprachige Presse der Ameri-kas. Munich: Verlag Dokumentation, 1973-1976. (2 vols.). FHL 973 B33a
♦Clarence Saunders Brigham, *History and Bibliography of American Newspapers, 1690-1820.* 2 vols. American Antiquarian Society, Worcester, Mass., 1947. (Additions and corrections published in 1961.) FHL 973 A3bc
♦*Ethnic Press in the United States: Lists of Foreign Language Nationality and Ethnic Newspapers and Periodicals in the United States,* comp. by American Council for Nationalities Service, New York, 1974.
♦ Winifred Gregory, ed. *American Newspapers, 1821-1936: A Union List of Files Available in the United States and Canada.* Reprint, Kraus Reprint Corp., New York. 1967. FHL 970 B33a 1967; film 430,291; also 483,713 item 1
♦Betty M. Jarboe, *Obituaries: A Guide to Sources.* Boston, G.K. Hall & Co., 1982. FHL 973 V43; FHL film 430,291
♦ Anita Cheek Milner, *Newspaper Indexes: A Location and Subject Guide for Researchers.* Scarecrow Press, Metuchen, NJ, 1977. (U.S. newspapers only). FHL 973 B32m (3 vols.)
♦ United States, Library of Congress. *Chronological Index of Newspapers for the Period 1801-1967 in the Collections of the Library of Congress.* Comp. by Paul E. Swigart. Washington, DC, Library of Congress, 1956.
♦Julie Winklepeck, ed. *Gale Directory of Publications and Broadcast Media* formerly *(Ayer Directory of Publications).* Annual since 1869. Gale Research Inc., Detroit, Michigan.
♦ Grace D. Parch (ed.), *Directory of Newspaper Libraries in the U.S. and Canada.* New York: Special Libraries Association, c 1976. FHL 970 E4pa
♦Lubomyr R. Wynar and Anna T. Wynar, *Encyclopedic Directory of Ethnic Newspapers and Periodicals in the*

United States. Littleton, Colo.: Libraries Unlimi-ted, c 1976. FHL 973 E4w
♦ Lubomyr R. Wynar, *Guide to the American Ethnic Press: Slavic and East European Newspapers and Periodicals.* Kent, Ohio: Center for the Study of Ethnic Publications, 1986. FHL 973 B34w]
♦*Broadcast Media. . . . an Annual Guide to Newspapers, Magazines, Journals, and Related Publications* (formerly *Ayer Directory of Publications*). Published annually since 1869. IMS Press.
♦*Benn's Media Directory International.* Tonbridge, England: Benn's Business Information Services, annual. (Arranged by nation and city of the newspaper)
♦*Newspapers in Microform,* Library of Congress, Washington DC, 1973- (ongoing).This multi-volume publica-tion, found in virtually every library in the United States, is used by local inter-library loan librarians to locate and pro-cess inter-library loan requests.

LOCALITIES OF GERMAN-AMERICAN NEWSPAPERS

Localities where German newspapers and periodicals were once published, from *The German Language Press of the Americas* (see list above):

Alabama: Birmingham, Cullman, Mobile, Warrior
Arizona: St. Michaels
Arkansas: Fort Smith, Little Rock, St. Joe
California: Anaheim, Fresno, Glendale, Lodi, Los Angeles, Mokelumne Hill, Mountain View, Oakland, Petaluma, Sacramento, San Diego, San Francisco, San Jose, Santa Barbara, Santa Rosa, Stockton
Colorado: Denver, Greeley, Leadville, Pueblo
Connecticut: Bridgeport, Hartford, Meri-den, New Haven, Norwich, Rockville,

Southbury, Waterbury
District of Columbia: Washington
Delaware: Wilmington
Florida: Jacksonville, Miami, Pensacola, San Antonio
Georgia: Atlanta, Savannah
Idaho: Cottonwood
Illinois: Addison, Alton, Apple River, Arlington Heights, Aurora, Beardstown, Beecher, Belleville, Bloomington, Brookfield, Cairo, Carlinville, Carlyle, Carmi, Centralia, Champaign, Chester, Chicago, Danville, Decatur, Dundee, East St. Louis, Edwardsville, Effingham, Elgin, Evanston, Forest Park, Freeport, Galena, German Valley, Hawthorne, Highland, Hoyleton, Joliet, Kankakee, Kewanee, La Salle, Lensburg, Leonore, Lincoln, Litchfield, McHenry, Mascoutah, Mattoon, Mendota, Mundelein, Mt. Olive, Naperville, Nashville, Nauvoo, Nokomis, Okawville, Ottawa, Pekin, Peoria, Peru, Quincy, Ravenswood, Red Bud, Rock Island, Rockford, Springfield, Staunton, Sterling, Streator, Techny, Urbana, Vandalia, Warsaw, Waterloo, Wheaton, Woodstock
Indiana: Anderson, Batesville, Berne, Bowling Green, Brazil, Brookville, Collegeville, Crown Point, Elkhart, Evansville, Fort Wayne, Goshen, Hamburg, Hammone, Huntingburg, Indianapolis, Jeffersonville, Lafayette, La Port, Logansport, Michigan City, Mount Vernon, New Albany, Richmond, Rockport, St. Meinrad, Seymour, South Bend, Tell City, Terre Haute, Vincennes
Iowa: Ackley, Alton, Andrew, Boone, Breda, Burlington, Carroll , Cascade, Cedar Bluffs, Cedar Rapids, Charles City, Clinton, Council Bluffs, Davenport, Decatur, Denison, Des Moines, Dubuque, Dumont, Dysart, Earling, Elkader, Essex, Fort Dodge, Grundy Center, Guttenberg, Holstein, Ida Grove, Independence, Iowa City, Keokuk, Lansing, Le Mars, Lyons, Manning, Maquoketa, Marshalltown, Monticello, Muscatine, New Hampton, Newton,

Osage, Ottumwa, Postville, Reinbeck, Remson, Rock Rapids, Rockford, Schleswig, Sigourney, Sioux City , Spirit Lake, Sumner, Tama City, Toledo, Vinton, Walcott, Waterloo, Waverly, Wellsburg, Wheatland
Kansas: Alma, Atchison, Atwood, Burrton, Canada, Ellinwood, Emporia, Fort Scott, Great Bend, Halstead, Hays, Hillsboro, Hutchinson, Inman, Kansas City, Kingman, Kinsley, Lacrosse, Lawrence, Leavenworth, Lehigh, Lindsborg, Marion, Marysville, McPherson, Newton, Paola, Pittsburg, Russell, Topeka, Wichita, Winfield, Wyandotte
Kentucky: Berea, Covington, Louisville, Newport, Stanford
Louisiana: Lafayette, New Orleans
Maryland: Baltimore, Cumberland , Fredericktown, Hagerstown, New Windsor
Massachusetts: Boston, Clinton, Fitchburg, Greenfield, Holyoke, Lawrence, Lowell, Springfield, West Roxbury
Michigan: Adrian, Ann Arbor, Au Gres, Battle Creek, Bay City, Coldwater, Detroit, Grand Rapids, Jackson, Lansing, Manistee, Marquette, Menominee, Monroe, Muskegon, Pigeon, Port Huron, Saginaw, Sebewaing, Sturgis, West Bay City
Minnesota: Carver, Chaska, Duluth, Fairmont, Freeport, Glencoe, Jordan, Lake City, Little Falls, Mankato, Melrose, Minneapolis, Mountain Lake, New Ulm, Owatonna, Perham, Red Wing, Rochester, St. Cloud, St. Paul, Shakopee, Springfield, Stillwater, Wabasha, Waconia, Winona, Wykoff
Missouri: Boonville, California, Cape Girardeau, Centreton, Chamois, Clayton, Clyde, Concordia, Festus, Franklin, Fulton, Hannibal, Hermann, Higginsville, Jackson, Jefferson City, Joplin, Kansas City, Lexington, Marthasville, Moberly, O'Fallon, St. Charles, St. Joseph, St. Louis, Ste. Genevieve, Sedalia, Springfield, Starkenburg, Stewartsville,

Warrenton, Washington, Westphalia
Montana: Butte, Great Falls, Helena, Plevna
Nebraska: Arago, Auburn, Beatrice, Bellevue, Bloomfield, College View, Columbus, Crete, Deshler, Fairbury, Falls City, Fremont, Grand Island, Hartingon, Hastings, Jansen, Leigh, Lincoln, Meadow Grove, Nebraska City, Norfolk, Omaha, Schuyler, Seward, Steinauer, Sterling, Sutton, West Point, York
Nevada: Virginia City
New Hampshire: Manchester
New Jersey: Atlantic City, Bayonne, Bound Brook, Camden, Carlstadt, Egg Harbor, Elizabeth, Fairview, Hoboken, Irvington, Jersey City, Newark, New Brunswick, Orange, Passaic, Paterson, Riverside, Sea-Isle City, Town of Union, Trenton, Union, Union City
New York: Albany , Amsterdam, Auburn, Bardonia, Brooklyn, Buffalo, Camden, College Point, East New York, Elmhurst, Elmira, Erie, Forest Hills, Long Island, Haverstraw, Hicksville, Huntington, Ithaca, Jamaica, Kingston (Rondout), Lockport, Long Island City, Morrisania, Mount Vernon, Newburgh, Newtown, New York, Oswego, Poughkeepsie, Rochester, Schenectady, Sea Cliff, Staten Island, Syracuse, Tonawanda, Troy, Utica, Williamsburgh, Yonkers
North Carolina: Goldsboro
North Dakota: Arthur, Ashley, Berwick, Beulah, Bismarck, Dickinson, Fargo, Fessenden, Golden Valley, Harvey, Havelock, Hebron, Jamestown, Linton, McClusky, Mannhaven, Medina, Minot, New Salm, Richardton, Rugby, Stanton, Strassburg, Wahpeton, Wishek, Zap
Ohio: Akron, Baltic, Bellaire, Berea, Bluffton, Bowling Green, Bridgeport, Bucyrus, Canton, Carthagena, Celina, Chillicothe, Cincinnati, Cleveland, Columbiana, Columbus, Coshocton, Dayton, Defiance, Delphos, East Liverpool, Elyria, Findlay, Fremont, Germantown, Greenville, Hamilton,

Ironton, Kenton, Kingsville, Lancaster, Lima, Lorain, Mansfield, Marietta, Marion, Massillon, Millersburg, Minster, Morrow, Napoleon, New Bremen, New Philadelphia, Newark, Norwalk, Oak Harbor, Osnaburgh, Ottawa, Pauling, Perrysburg, Piqua, Pomeroy, Port Clinton, Portsmouth, Sandusky, Sidney, Springfield, Steubenville, Teutonia, Tiffin, Toledo, Upper Sandusky, Wapakoneta, Waterloo, Weinsberg, Woodsfield, Woodville, Wooster, Worthington, Xenia, Youngstown, Zanesville, Zoar
Oklahoma: Bessie, El Reno, Enid, Guthrie, Kingfisher, Medford, Okeene, Oklahoma City, Perry
Oregon: Astoria, Bend, Portland, St. Benedict, Salem
Pennsylvania: Aaronsburg, Abbottstown, Adamsburg, Allegheny (see Pittsburgh), Allentown, Altoona, Berlin, Bath, Berwick, Bethlehem, Boyertown, Carlisle, Cattawissa, Chambersburg, Chartiers, Chestnut-Hill, Columbia, Danville, Doylestown, Easton, Economy, Ephrata, Erie, Gap, Germantown, Gettysburg, Greensburg, Hamburg, Hanover, Harrisburg, Hazleton, Hellertown, Herman, Honesdale, Huntingdon, Jefferson, Jim Thorpe, Johnstown, Kutztown, Lancaster, Lansdale, Lebanon, Lewisburg, Mansfield, Marietta, Marklesburg, Mauchchunk, McKeesport, Meadville, Mercersburg, Meyerstown, Middleburg, Mifflintown, Milford Square, Millheim, Nanticoke, Nazareth, New Berlin, Norristown, Orwigsburg, Pennsburg, Perkasie, Philadelphia, Philipsburg, Pittsburgh, Pottstown, Pottsville, Quakertown, Reading, Schellsburg, Scottdale, Scranton, Selinsgrove, Sharpsburg, Shrewsbury, Skippack, Somerset, Souderton, South Bethlehem, Strassburg, Stroudsburg, Sumneytown, Sunbury, Telford, Thurlow, Vincent, Weissport, West Chester, Wilkes-Barre, Williamsport,

Womelsdorf, York, Zieglerville
Rhode Island: Providence
South Carolina: Charleston
South Dakota: Aberdeen, Eureka, Herreid, Java, Mitchell, Olivet, Orient, Parkston, Pierre, Redfield, Sioux Falls, Watertown, Yankton
Tennessee: Chatanooga, Columbia, Hohenwald, Memphis, Nashville, Robbins
Texas: Austin, Bastrop, Bellville, Boerne, Brenham, Castroville, Comfort, Cuero, Dallas, Denison, Fort Worth, Franklin, Fredericksburg, Gainsville, Galveston, Giddings, Gonsales, Hallettsville, Houston, Independence, La Grange, Lockart, Marlin, Meyersville, New Braunfels, Rosebud, San Antonio, Schulenberg, Seguin, Shiner, Taylor, Temple, Victoria, Waco, Windhorst
Utah: Logan, Salt Lake City
Virginia: Alexandria, Bridgewater, New Market, Norfolk, Richmond, Staunton, Winchester
Washington: Bellingham, Everett, Ritzville, Seattle, South Bend, Spokane, Tacoma, Walla Walla
West Virginia: Wheeling
Wisconsin: Antigo, Appleton, Arcadia, Ashland, Athens, Beaver Dam, Beloit, Burlington, Cedarburg, Chilton, Chippewa Falls, Clintonville, Cochrane, Columbus, Cumberland, Dorchester, Durand, Eagle, Eau Claire, Fond Du Lac, Fort Atkinson, Fountain City, Glidden, Grand Rapids, Green Bay, Hamburg, Horicon, Janesville, Jefferson, Juneau, Kaukauna, Kenosha, Kewaunee, Kiel, La Crosse, Lomira, Madison, Manitowoc, Marathon, Marinette, Marshfield, Mauston, Mayville, Medford, Menasha, Menomonie, Merrill, Merrimack, Milwaukee, Monroe, Neillsville, New Glarus, Oshkosh, Phillips, Platteville, Plymouth, Port Washington, Portage, Princeton, Racine, Reedsburg, Ripon, St. Francis, St. Nazianz, Sauk City, Schlessingerville (now Slinger), Shawano, Sheboygan, Spokane, Stevens Point,

Stockbridge, Superior, Theresa, Watertown, Wasau, Wauwatosa, West Bend, Weyauwega, Wittenberg
Wyoming: Laramie

GERMAN LANGUAGE NEWSPAPERS/PUBLICATIONS IN THE USA

◆ **Amerika Woche**, 4732 N. Lincoln Avenue, Chicago, IL 60625. Tel. (773) 275-5054; Fax (773) 275-0596; amwoche@mail.idt.net; Weekly. German language.
◆**Aufbau**, 2121 Broadway, New York, NY 10023. Tel. (212) 873-7400; Fax (212) 496-5736; aufbau2000@aol. com; Published every two weeks. German language.
◆**Buffalo Volksfreund/People's Friend,** 295 MainStreet, Ellicott Square Building, Suite 947, Buffalo, NY 14203. Tel. (716) 849-9606; Fax (716) 882-7300; Published six times per year. German and English language.
◆**California Staats-Zeitung**, 24763 Kay Avenue, Hayward, CA 94545. Tel. (510) 783-2072; Fax (510) 782-1840; Los Angeles office: 1201 N. Alvarado Street, P.O. Box 26308, Los Angeles, CA 90026-3126. Tel. (213) 413-5500; Fax (213) 413-5469; Weekly. German language.
◆**Deutschland Nachrichten,** weekly e-mailed German-language newsletter of the German Information Center, free to subscribers through GIC's website www.germany-info.org
◆**Eintracht,** 9456 N. Lawler Avenue, Skokie, IL 60077. Tel. (847) 677-9456; Fax (847) 677-9471; Weekly. German language.
◆**Das Fenster,** 1060 Gaines School Road, Suite C-3, Athens, GA 30605. Tel. (706) 548-4382; Fax (706) 548-8856; Monthly. Short articles, poetry, stories, timely topics. German language.
◆ **Florida Journal,** 6249 Presidential Court, Fort Myers, FL 33919. Tel. (941) 481-7511; Fax (941) 481-7753;

behr@floridajournal.com; Quarterly magazine. German language.

◆**Freie Zeitung,** 500 S. 31st Street, Kenilworth, NJ 07033. Tel. (908) 245-7995; Fax (908) 245-7997; Weekly. German language.

◆**The German-American Journal,** 4740 N. Western Avenue, Chicago, IL 60625-2013. Tel. (773) 275-1100; Fax (773) 275-4010; dankorg@mail.megsinet.net; www.dank.org; Monthly. German and English language.

◆**Der Hermann Sohn,** 1935 Via Lacqua, St. Lorenzo, CA 94580. Tel./Fax (510) 278-1252; Newspaper for members of the lodges of the fraternal organization, the *Hermann Söhne.* German language.

◆**Neue Presse,** 42263 50th Street W., P.O.Box 316, Quartz Hill, CA 93536. Tel. (661) 722-2668; Fax (661) 943-4880; neuepresse@qnet.com; Weekly. German language. *Neue Presse* has offices as well in Oakland, CA; San Diego, CA; Kenilworth, NJ; and St. Petersburg, FL. German language.

◆**New-Yorker Staats-Zeitung und Herold,** 160 W. 71st Street, Suite 2B, New York, NY 10023. Tel. (212) 875-0769; Fax (212) 875-0534; NYstaatsZ@aol.com; www.nysz.net; Weekly. German language with English supplement.

◆**Nordamerikanische Wochen-Post** 1301 W. Long Lake, Suite 105, Troy, MI 48098-7088. Tel (248) 641-9944; Fax (248) 641-9946; nwp@earthlink. net; http://home.earthlink.net/~nwp/; German language.

◆**Pazifische Rundschau,** 4131 11th Avenue NE PH1, Seattle, WA 98105-6397. "A German Language Newspaper for the Pacific Northwest." Tel. (206) 523-3535; Fax (206) 523-3494; pazif_rund@msn.com; Bi-weekly. German language (with English-language section, titled "Panorama.")

◆**Reisefieber,** 2430 Shadowlawn Drive, Suite 11, Naples, FL 34112. Tel. (914) 775-7100; Fax (914) 775-7044; reisefieber @naplesinfo.com; www.naplesinfo.

com; Monthly. Travel agency and travel information. German language.

◆**San Francisco-Neue Presse** (See *Neue Presse;* the *San Francisco-Neue Presse* office is incorporated with that of *Neue Presse* at the Quartz Hill, CA, address above.)

◆**Saxon News Volksblatt,** 5393 Pearl Road, Cleveland, OH 44129-1597. Newspaper of the fraternal membership society, Alliance of Transylvanian Saxons. German language.

◆**Washington Journal,** 23-03 45th Road, Suite 401, Long Island City, NY 11101. Tel. (718) 349-0500; Fax (718) 349-9355; wj@ultinet.net; Weekly. German language.

◆**The Week in Germany,** weekly English-language e-mail newsletter of the German Information Center on politics, the economy, sports and the arts in Germany, free to subscribers through GIC's website www.germany-info.org.

◆**Wochen-Post** (See Nordamerikanische Wochen-Post)

GERMAN TELEVISION IN THE UNITED STATES

◆**Deutsche Welle German TV,** 2800 Shirlington Road, Suite 901, Arlington, VA 22206. Tel. (703) 931-6644; Fax (703) 931-6662; news@dwelleusa.com; www.dwelle.de; Programs prepared in German and English.

SPECIAL-INTEREST AIDS AND GENEALOGY PERIODICALS

◆*Ancestry*, 440 South 400 West Suite D, Salt Lake City, UT 84101. Tel. (800) 531-1790; Fax. (800) 531-1798; www.ancestry com; Published six times annually. 32 pages. Illustrated, wide range of topics in articles written by established genealogists. Geared toward beginning and intermediate researchers.

◆*Der Blumenbaum*, quarterly journal of the Sacramento German Genealogy Society, P.O. Box 660061-0061, Sacramento, CA 95866-0061. Fax (916) 421-8032; www.SacGerGenSoc.org. $30 per year membership dues ($35 for a couple), includes subscription to the quarterly 48-page *Der Blumenbaum,* containing articles on a wide range of German genealogical, historical, and cultural topics. No advertising. Back issues $5.00 each.

◆**Der Buchwurm** [supplier of German books, music, movies, periodical subscriptions], P.O. Box 268, Templeton, CA 93465-0268. Tel (805) 238-2353; Fax (805) 238-9523; buchwurm@ tcsn.net

◆ *Deutschland* **[Magazine]** Publisher: Societäts-Verlag, in cooperation with the Press and Information Office of the German Federal Government. Frankfurter Societät, Postfach 100801, 60008 Frankfurt am Main, Germany. U.S. distribution by Aluta Company, International Press Service, 5108 Wally, El Paso, TX 79924. Available online. www.bundesregierung. de, redaktion. deutschland@rhein-main.net

◆ *Gemütlichkeit*, 288 Ridge Road, Ashland, OR 97520. Tel. (800) 521-6722 or (541) 488-8462; Fax (541)488-8468; gemut@mind.net. English language. Travel information.

◆*German-American Genealogy,* quarterly publication of the Immigrant Genealogical Society, P.O. Box 7369, Burbank, CA 91510-7369. Tel. (818) 363-0721; ural@juno.com; www. immigrant gensoc.org. Dues ($25 per year for individuals; $30 for families); includes a subscription to *German-American Genealogy* and a monthly newsletter. Society provides many research services for reasonable fees.

◆ **The German Connection,** quarterly journal of the German Research Association, Inc. P.O. Box 711600, San Diego, CA 92171-1600. http://feefhs.org/gra/frg-gra.html; Annual membership includes a subscription to *The German Connection.* Articles are clearly written and pertinent to interests of German genealogists.

◆*German Life,* Zeitgeist Publishing, Inc. 1068 National Highway, LaVale, MD 21502. Tel. (301) 729-6190; Fax (301) 729-1720; info@germanlife.com; www.ger manlife.com; Subscriptions go to German Life, P.O. Box 3000, Denville, NJ 07834-9723) Subscription price: $19.95 for 6 issues per year. Illustrated in beautiful color, wide range of topics of interest to germanophiles. First-rate presentation, style, and information. Archives may be searched on website.

◆ *Maibaum*, quarterly journal of the Deutschheim Verein, of Hermann, Missouri: Deutschheim, 109 W. 2nd Street, Hermann, MO 65041. Tel. (573) 486-2200; Fax (573) 486-224; deutschh@ktis.net; Offers accounts of German everyday life in early America, whimsical anecdotes, historical features – all recalling the ways and culture of our Germa immigrant ancestors. A free copy will be sent on request.

EMIGRATION RECORDS IN GERMAN NEWSPAPERS

Many American genealogical researchers write to Germany to obtain copies of their ancestors' "emigration record," without really knowing what such a file might contain.. It is often assumed that such a record includes biographical information on the emigrant, the port of embarkation and debarkation, the dates of departure and arrival, and the exact destination in the country of settlement.

Actually, most of these items were of little interest to the authorities in the German countries. The main objectives for emigration records were the following:
•To have a legally valid declaration of the abandonment of citizenship

•To make sure that passports were not issued to young men under conscription
•To have proof that the emigrants had sufficient travel funds, so his home country would not have to support him when he ran out of money on the trip
•To make sure the emigrant paid his debts before he left
•To make sure that under-age emigrants had sufficient protection by accompanying adults and were protected at their place of settlement
•To collect data for statistical purposes
Emigration records therefore contain only some data to identify the emigrant (such as name, age or birthdate, and occupation) and his family members, proof that the emigrant was clear of debts or a declaration of a warrant that he would be liable for such, indication of the property he exported, agreements by the guardians of children that they have no objection, similar agreements by military authorities, and sometimes a contract with an emigra-tion agent. Most emigration records do not, however, include all this information.

Where to look for records

Emigration records may be searched, obviously, through the records available at or near the emigrant's place of origin. But if the specific place of origin is not known, and if all sources in the country of destination (the United States, for example) have been exhausted without finding the exact location, then one should consult the emigration indexes of the state archive for the country of origin (Bavaria, Hesse, etc.).

If this search proves unsuccessful, one may try to find the place of origin by checking the main newspapers of the country of origin. This requires a good knowledge of the year – or even better, the months – of emigration, and it requires some trust in the lawfulness of the ancestor. Illegal emigrants are often mentioned too, but usually not close to

the time when they left; therefore, such entries can be located only with the help of overall indexes.

Local newspapers

Common types of newspaper announcements that contain or may contain names of emigrants include,
•Summons to a deserter from the armed forces to appear before court
•Summons to appear before court or lose citizenship after illegal emigration
•Search for fugitive persons who are suspected of having committed a crime
•Summons to missing or absent persons to appear before court or being declared legally deceased.
•Call for missing heirs

Official Newspapers

Besides local newspapers and papers with statewide circulation (in which announcements appeared concerning summons to missing persons, or notifications of emigrations of persons who may have had creditors, etc.), there were also official newspapers used for the same purpose. These had statewide circulation and generally served as enclosures in other media.

In Prussia, a "Public Advertiser" (*Öffentlicher Anzeiger*) was published as an enclosure to every issue of the "Official Newsletter of the Royal Government" (*Amtsblatt der Königlichen Regierung*) for each government seat (for example, *Amtsblatt der Königlichen Regierung Aachen,* or "Official Newsletter of the Royal Government in Aachen"). It contained warrants, names of missing heirs, names of absent divorcees, summons to missing persons, and summons to draft-dodgers. Similar entries were published in the *Öffentlicher Anzeiger*, an enclosure to a newspaper with the following names:
1819: *Allgemeine Preußische Staatszeitung*
1843: *Allgemeine Preußische Zeitung*

1848: *Preußischer Staatsanzeiger*
1849: *Kgl. Preußischer Staatsanzeiger*
1871: *Deutscher Reichsanzeiger und Königlichen Preußischer Staatsanzeiger*
1918: *Deutscher Reichsanzeiger und Preußischer Staatsanzeiger* (to 1945)

This *Reichsanzeiger*, as a nationwide official newspaper, was used as an instrument for notifications to and warrants for persons who were assumed to be somewhere in Prussia, or, from 1871 onward, somewhere in Germany or were being summoned by German authorities.

Some local papers

Listed below are a few local newspapers which carried emigration announcements:

Baden

c **1800-1871**: *Karlsruher Zeitung* (indexed by Friedrich R. Wollmershäuser)

c **1800-1868**: *Großherzoglich Badisches Anzeigeblatt für...* (from 1832 to 1856 four series, then on until 1868 by the title *Großherzoglich Badisches Allgemeines Anzeigeblatt*)
c **1800-1871**: local newspapers

Württemberg

c **1800-1850**: *Schwäbischer Merkur* and enclosure *Schwäbische Chronik*
c **1800-1870**: *Stuttgarter Anzeigen von allerhand Sachen (etc.)* and other titles, beginning 1850 by the name *Staatsanzeiger für Württemberg* (very incomplete to the late 1820s)
c **1820-1870**: local newspapers.

Hohenzollern

1809-1834: *Wochenblatt für das Fürsten-tum Hohenzollern-Sigmar-ngen.*
1829-1836: *Wochenblatt für das Fürsten-tum Hohenzollern-Hechingen*
1837-1844: *Verordnungs und Intelli-zenzblatt für das Fürstentum Hohen-*

zollern-Hechingen
1845-1850: *Verordnungs- und Anzeige-blatt für das Fürstentum Hechingen*
1855-1933: *Amtsblatt der Königlich Preußischen Regierung zu Sigmaringen* (and enclosure) *Öffentlicher Anzeiger*

Bayern (Bavaria)

Emigrations announced in local newspapers and gazettes

Braunschweig

1846-1871: *Braunschweigische Anzeigen*, and other papers. Emigration entries published by Fritz Gruhne, *Auswandererlisten des ehemaligen Herzogtums Braunschweig ohne Stadt Braunschweig und Landkreis Holzminden. Quellen und Forschungen zur braunschweigischen Geschichte 20. Braunschweig: Geschichtsverein 1971.*

Waldeck

1829-1872: *Fürstlich Waldeckisches Regierungsblatt.* Entries on emigrants published by Karl Thomas, *Die waldeck-ische Auswanderung zwischen 1829 und 1872.* 2 vols. (Köln and Eslohe: privately published by the author, 1983).

Kurhessen

1831-1866: *Wochenblatt für die Provinz Niederhessen.*

Nassau

1849-1868: *Nassauisches Intelligenz-blatt.* Names of emigrants published by Wolf-Heino Struck, *Die Auswanderung aus dem Herzogtum Nassau (1806-1866).* Geschichtliche Landeskunde 4 (Wiesbaden: Steiner 1966), 133-203.

Prussia

1819-1843: *Allgemeine Preußische Staatszeitung.*
1843-1848: *Preußische Staatszeitung.*
1848: *Preußischer Staatsanzeiger.*
1849-1871: *Königlicher Preußischer Staatsanzeiger.*

German Empire

1871-1918: *Deutscher Reichsanzeiger und Königlicher Preußischer Staatsanzeiger.* (These years were b abstracted by the Germanic Emigrants Register, P.O. Box 1720, 49347 Diepholz, Germany.)

Bibliography

◆ Martin Hankel, Rolf Taubert, *Die Deutsche Presse 1848-1850. Eine Bibliographie Deutsche Presseforschung,* Band 25. (München: K.G. Saur, 1986)

-The revolution of 1848-49 and the German press, with a listing of most German periodicals published then and their current locations.

◆ Winifred Gregory (ed.), *List of the Serial Publications of Foreign Governments, 1815-1931* (New York: H.W. Wilson, 1932, reprint Millwood, NY: Kraus, 1973).

- An impressive bibliography of official gazettes published all over the world. Entries on Germany are found on pp. 226 to 271; they cover Germany in general, the German Empire from 1871 onward, and the German states alphabetically, from Alsace Lorraine, Anhalt, Baden, etc. to Württemberg.

◆Gert Hagelweide (comp.), *Literatur zur deutschsprachigen Presse: eine BibliographieDortmunder Beiträge zur Zeitungsforschung,* Band 35. (München: K.G. Saur, 1985).

-An exhaustive bibliography of writings about the press in the German-speaking area in general, newspapers in individual states and towns, and the use and impact of newspapers. Catalogues of newspaper holdings in libraries and archives are listed on pp. 80 to 106.

◆ Oskar Michel (comp.), *Handbuch Deutscher Zeitungen 1917* (Berlin: Elsner, 1917).

-Includes all newspapers published at that date in the German Empire, with their names, publishers, years of foundation, and other details.

◆ Hartmut Walravens (ed.), *Internationale Zeitungsbestände in deutschen Bibliotheken: ein Verzeichnis von 19 000 Zeitungen, Amtsblättern und zeitungs-ähnlichen Periodika mit Besitznachweisen und geographischem Register* (International newspaper holdings in German libraries) (München: K.G. Saur, 1993).

-Includes the titles of 18,000 German newspapers and official gazettes with (not quite complete) references to current locations

◆ *Zeitschriften-Datenbank (ZBD)* 30th edition (Berlin: Deutsches Bibliotheksinstitut, 1994).

-419 microfiches and a manual in German and English. Includes 2,250,400 locations in Germany for 719,346 periodicals.

Source: Contributed by Friedrich R. Wollmershäuser, M.A: Accredited Genealogist, Herrengasse 8-10. 89610..Oberdischingen, Germany. © Friedrich R. Wollmershäuser, 1997.

LOCATING U.S. NEWSPAPERS (GALE DIRECTORY OF PUBLICATIONS)

The *Gale Directory of Publications and Broadcast Media,* available on the reference shelves of many public libraries, can help the researcher determine which current newspapers (and other publications) were being published during an ancestor's residency in a particular town or city in the United States. Only publications which are still in business are listed in this reference tool, however

Organized in three volumes, the *Gale Directory's* first two volumes list alphabetically all states of the United States subdivided into towns and cities; the third volume contains indexes, tables and maps.

Many of the periodicals listed are trade publications, which may be help ful if an ancestor is known to have been active in a particular business or trade.

Founding dates of newspapers and other publications which circulated in an ancestor's settlement area can be determined in this directory.

For example, the researcher may seek to learn which currently published newspapers were in business between the year an ancestor immigrated to Cincinnati in 1852 and 1898, the year he moved away. The answer is found by checking the directory first for the state, then the town or city where the immigrant settled, and by looking through the list of newspapers and magazines in that location to see if any of them were publishing between 1852 and 1898. Thus, one may learn not only which current publications were in existence during an ancestor's residency in an area, but which publications should be eliminated as possibilities.

The directory is updated periodically.

LEADING NEWSPAPERS IN GERMANY

The leading German national newspapers are the *Süddeutsche Zeitung* (published in Munich), *Frankfurter Allgemeine Zeitung* (published in Frankfurt am Main), *Die Welt* (published in Berlin) and the *Frankfurter Runschau* (Frankfurt). The leading tabloid is *Bild-Zeitung*, which is published in Hamburg.

Before reunification, the official state newspaper in the German Democratic Republic was *Neues Deutschland*. It still exists as an independent paper, but with a much-reduced readership.

The largest and most influential eastern German newspapers include *Berliner Zeitung, Leipziger Volkszeitung, Sächsische Zeitung* (published in Dresden), *Freie Presse* (Chemnitz, Saxony) and *Mitteldeutsche Zeitung* (Halle, Saxony-Anhalt).

Since reunification of Germany, nearly all the eastern newspapers have been bought up by western or foreign media concerns.

Source: German Information Center, *Federal Republic of Germany*, ed. Susan Steiner, New York, 1996.

PRINCIPAL NEWSPAPERS IN GERMANY

f. = founded in
Postfach= post office box (for use in correspondence)

Aachen
–Aachener Nachrichten: Dresdner Str. 3, 52068 Aachen. Postfach 110, 52002 Aachen. Fax (241) 5101399; f. 1872; circ. 67,000
–Aachener Zeitung: Dresdner Str. 3, 52068 Aachen. Postfach 500110. Fax (241) 5101396; f. 1946; circ. 105,000
Ansbach
–Fränkische Landeszeitung: Nürnberger Str. 9-17, 91522 Ansbach. Postfach 1362, 91504 Ansbach. Fax (981) 13961; circ. 50,000
Aschaffenburg
–Main-Echo: Weicherstr. 20, 63741 Aschaffenburg a. M. Postfach 548. Fax (6021) 396499; redaktions sekretariat@main-echo.de; circ. 93,000
Augsburg
–Augsburger Allgemeine: 86133 Augsburg; Curt-Frenzel-Str. 2, 86167 Augsburg. Fax (821) 704471; Mon. to Sat.; circ. 370,000
Baden-Baden
–Badisches Tagblatt: Stefanienstr. 1-3, 76530 Baden-Baden; Postfach 120, 76481 Baden Baden. Fax (7221) 215240; circ. 41,000
Bamberg
–Fränkischer Tag: Gutenbergstr. 1, 96050 Bamberg. Fax (951) 188113; circ. 75,800
Barchfeld

–Südthüringer Zeitung: Postfach 1225, 36456. Circ. 22,000

Bautzen
–Serbske Nowiny: Tuchmacher Str. 27, 02625 Bautzen. Sorbian language paper; circ. 1,500

Berlin
–Berliner Kurier am Abend/. . . am Morgen: Karl-Liebknecht-Str. 29, 10178 Berlin. Fax (30) 2442274; circ. 186,800
–Berliner Morgenpost: Axel-Springer-Str. 65, 10888 Berlin. Fax (30) 2516071; redaktion@berlinermorgenpost.de; www.berlinermorgenpost.de; f. 1945; circ. 181,773
–Berliner Zeitung: Karl-Liebknecht-Str. 29, 10178 Berlin. Fax (30) 23275533; www.berlinonline.de; f. 1945; circ. 208,018
–BZ (Berliner Zeitung): Kochstr. 50, 10969 Berlin. Fax (30) 2516071; www.bz-berlin.de; f. 1877; circ. 292,130
–Junge Welt: Mauerstr. 39-40, 10117 Berlin. Fax (30) 1302865; f. 1947; circ. 158,000
–Neues Deutschland: Alt-Strolan 1-2, 10245 Berlin. Fax (30) 29390600; f. 1946; circ. 74,200
–Der Tagesspiegel: Potsdamer Str. 87, 10785 Berlin; Postfach 304330, 10723 Berlin. Fax (30) 26009332; f. 1945; circ. 130,200
–Die Welt: Axel-Springer-Str. 65, 10888 Berlin. Fax (30) 25911929; www.welt.de; f. 1946; circ. 215,763

Bielefeld
–Neue Westfälische: Niedernstr. 21-27, 33602 Bielefeld; Postfach 100225, 33502 Bielefeld. Fax (521) 55348; f. 1967; circ. 219,850
–Westfalen-Blatt: Südbrackstr. 14-18, 33611 Bielefeld. Fax (521) 585370; f. 1946; circ. 147,000

Bonn
–Bonner Rundschau: Thomas-Mann-Str. 51-53, 53111 Bonn; Postfach 1248, 53002 Bonn. Fax (228) 721230; f. 1946; circ. 23,700
–General-Anzeiger: Justus-von-Liebig-Str. 15, 53100 Bonn. Fax (228) 6688170; f.

1725; circ. 90,000

Braunschweig
–Braunschweiger Zeitung: Hamburger Str. 277, 38114 Braunschweig; Postfach 3263, 38022 Braunschweig. Fax (531) 3900610; circ. 170,400

Bremen
–Bremer Nachrichten, Martinistr. 43, 28195 Bremen; Postfach 107801, 28078 Bremen. Fax (421) 3379233; f. 1743; circ. 44,000
–Weser-Kurier: Martinistr. 43, 28195 Bremen; Postfach 107801, 28078 Bremen. Fax (421) 3379233; f. 1945; circ. 185,000

Bremerhaven
–Nordsee-Zeitung: Hafenstr. 140, 27576 Bremerhaven. circ. 77,500

Chemnitz
–Freie Presse, Brückenstr. 15, 09111 Chemnitz; Postfach 261. Fax (371) 643042; f. 1963; circ. 461,900

Cologne: See Köln

Cottbus
–Lausitzer Rundschau: Str. Der Jugend 54, 03050 Cottbus. Fax (355) 481245; www.lr-online.de; circ. 190,000

Darmstadt
–Darmstädter Echo: Holzhofallee 25-31, 64295 Darmstadt; Postfach 100155, 64276 Darmstadt. Fax (6151) 387307; f. 1945. circ. 87,300

Dortmund
–Ruhr-Nachrichten: Pressehaus, Westen-hellweg 86-88, 44137 Dortmund. Postfach 105051. f. 1949; circ. 215,400
–Westfälische Rundschau, Brüderweg 9 44135 Dortmund; Postfach 105067, 44047 Dortmund. Fax (201) 8042841; circ 250,000

Dresden
–Dresdner Morgenpost, Ostra Allee Dresden 01067. Fax (51) 4951116; circ 126,700
–Dresdner Neueste Nachrichten Union: Hauptstr. 21, Dresden 01097. Fax (351) 8075212; circ. 40,400
–Sächsische Zeitung: Ostra-Allee 20 Haus der Presse, 01067 Dresden. Fax (351) 48642354; redaktion@sz-online.de

www.sz-online.de; f. 1946
Düsseldorf
–*Handelsblatt:* Kasernenstr. 67, 40213
Düsseldorf; Fax (211) 329954; 5 a week;
circ. 156,473
–*Rheinische Post:* Zülpicherstr. 10, 40196
Düsseldorf. Fax (211) 5047562; f. 1946;
circ. 349,200
–*Westdeutsche Zeitung:* Königsallee 27,
40212 Düsseldorf; Postfach 101132,
40002 Düsseldorf. Fax (211) 83822392;
circ. 176,800
Eisenach
–*Mitteldeutsche   Allgemeine:*
Eisenbahnstr. 2, 99817 Eisenach.; circ.
18,000
–Thüringer Tagespost: A.-Puschkin-Str.
107-109, 99817 Eisenach; circ. 80,000
Erfurt
–*Thüringer Allgemeine:* Gottstedter
Landstr. 6, 99092 Erfurt. Fax (361)
2275144; f. 1946; circ. 330,000
Essen
–*Neue Ruhr Zeitung:* Friedrichstr. 34-38,
45128 Essen; Fax (201) 8042621; circ.
215,000
–*Westdeutsche Allgemeine Zeitung:*
Friedrichstr. 34-38, 45128 Essen;
Postfach 104161; circ. 650,000
Frankfurt am Main
–*Frankfurter Allgemeine Zeitung:*
Hellerhofstr. 2-4, 60327 Frankfurt a.m. Fax
(69) 75911743; www.faz.de; f. 1949; circ.
400,200
–*Frankfurter Neue Presse*, Frankenallee
71-81, 60327 Frankfurt a.M.; Fax (69)
75014292; Postfach 100801, 60008 Frank-
furt a.M.; circ. 110,000
–*Frankfurter Rundschau*, Grosse
Eschenheimer Str. 16-18. Fax (69) 2199521;
circ. 189,000
Frankfurt an der Oder
–*Märkische Oderzeitung:* Kellenspring
6, 15230 Frankfurt a.d.Oder. Fax (335)
23214; circ. 150,633
Freiburg im Breisgau
–*Badische Zeitung:* Pressehaus,
Baslerstr. 88, 79115 Freiburg i. Br. Fax
(761) 496552; circ. 171,005

Gera
–*Ostthüringer Zeitung:* De-Smit-Str. 18,
07545 Gera. Fax (70) 51233; circ. 237,537
Göttingen
–*Göttinger Tageblatt:* Dransfelder Str.
1, 37079 Göttingen; Postfach 1953, 37009
Göttingen. Fax (551) 901229; f. 1889; circ.
50,200
Hagen
–*Westfalenpost:* Schürmannstr. 4, 58097
Hagen.   Fax   (2332)   9174263;
westfalenpost@cityweb.de; f. 1946; circ.
160,000
Halle
–*Hallesches Tageblatt:* Gr. Brauhausstr.
16-17, 06108 Halle. Fax (46) 28691; f. 1945;
circ. 37,400
–*Mitteldeutsche Zeitung:* Str. Der DSF
67, 06201 Merseburg. Fax (46) 845351; f.
1946; circ. 425,000

Hamburg
–*Bild:* Axel-Springer-Platz 1, 20355 Hamburg. Fax (40) 345811; www.bild.de; f.
1952; circ. 4,509,545
–*Hamburger Abendblatt:* Axel-
Springer-Platz 1, 20355 Hamburg; Fax
(40) 343180; www.abendblatt.de; circ.
311,279
–*Hamburger Morgenpost:* Griegstr. 75,
22763 Hamburg. Fax (40) 88303349;
i a m e d i e n @ w w w . m o p o . d e ;
www.mopo.de; circ. 154,700
Hannover
–*Hannoversche Allgemeine Zeitung:*
Bemeroder Str. 58, 30559 Hannover; Fax
(511) 513175; circ. 269,600

Heidelberg
–*Rhein-Neckar-Zeitung:* Hauptstr. 23,
69117 Heidelberg; Postfach 104560,
69035 Heidelberg. Fax (6221) 519217; f.
1945; circ. 104,600
Heilbronn
–*Heilbronner Stimme:* Allee 2, 74072
Heilbronn. Fax (7131) 615200; f. 1946;
102,500
Hof-Saale
–*Frankenpost:* Poststr. 9-11, 95028 Hof;

Postfach 1320. Fax (9281) 816283; fp-
redaktion@frankenpost.de; circ. 100,000

Ingolstadt
–*Donaukurier*: Stauffenbergstr. 2A,
85051 Ingolstadt. Fax (841) 9666255;
redaktion@donaukurier.de; f. 1872; circ.
84,700

Karlsruhe
–*Badische Neueste Nachrichten*:
Linken-heimer Landstr. 133, 76149
Karlsruhe; Postfach 311168l; circ. 165,500

Kassel
–*Hessische/Niedersächsische Allgemeine*: Frankfurter Str. 168, 34121 Kassel;
Postfach 101009. Fax (561) 2032406; f.
1959; circ. 189,200

Kempten
–*Allgäuer Zeitung*: Kotternerstr. 64,
87435 Kempten; Postfach 1129, 87401
Kempten; Fax (831) 206354; f. 1968; circ.
117,900

Kiel
–*Kieler Nachrichten*: Fleethörn 1-7,
24103 Kiel; Postfach 1111, 24100 Kiel.
Fax (431) 903935; circ. 115,200

Koblenz
–*Rhein-Zeitung*: August-Horch-Str. 28,
56070 Koblenz; Postfach 1540. Fax (261)
892476; circ. 246,100

Köln
–*Express*: Breite Str. 70, 50667 Köln;
Postfach 100410; f. 1964; circ. 370,000
–*Kölner Stadt-Anzeiger*: Breite Str. 70,
50667 Köln; Postfach 100410, 50450
Köln. Fax (221) 2242524; circ. 294,400
–*Kölnische Rundschau*: Stolkgasse 25-
45, 50667 Köln; Postfach 102145, 50461
Köln. Fax (221) 1632491; circ. 155,100

Konstanz
–*Südkurier*: Max-Stromeyer-Str. 178,
78467 Konstanz; Presse- und Druck-
zentrum, Postfach 102001, 78420
Konstanz. Fax (7531) 26785;
redaktion@suedkurier.de; www.skol.de;
f. 1945; circ. 148,990

Leipzig
–*Leipziger Volkszeitung*: Petersstein-
weg 3, 04107 Leipzig. Fax (41) 310592; f.
1894; circ. 320,700

Leutkirch
–*Schwäbische Zeitung*: Rudolf-Roth-Str.
18, 88299; Postfach 1145, 88291
Leutkirch. Fax (7561) 80134;
redaktion@schwäbische.de; f. 1945; circ.
196,000

Lübeck:
–*Lübecker Nachrichten*: Herrenholz 10-
12, 23556 Lübeck; Fax (451) 1441022; f.
1945; circ. 117,800

Ludwigshafen
–*Die Rheinpfalz*: Amtsstr. 5-11, 67059
Ludwigshafen/Rhein; Postfach 211147,
67011 Ludwigshafen. Fax (621) 5902546;
circ. 249,410

Magdeburg
–*Magdeburger Volksstimme*: Bahnhofstr. 17, 39104 Magdeburg. Fax (391)
388400; f. 1890; circ. 316,900

Mainz
–*Allgemeine Zeitung*: Grosse Bleiche 44-
50, 55116 Mainz; Postfach 3120, 55021
Mainz. Fax (6131) 144275; circ. 134,000

Mannheim
–*Mannheimer Morgen*: Postfach 102164,
68021 Mannheim. Fax (621) 3921376;
redaktion@mamo.de; www.mamo.de; f.
1946; circ. 97,600

München
–*Abendzeitung*: Sendlingerstr. 10, 80331
München; Fax (89) 2377499; f. 1948; circ.
213,200
–*Münchner Merkur*: Paul-Heyse-Str. 2-
4, Pressehaus, 80336 München. Fax (89)
5306651; www.merkur-online.de; circ.
203,200
–*Süddeutsche Zeitung*: Sendlingerstr. 8,
80331 München. Fax (89) 2183789; f.
1945; circ. 413,590
–*tz*: Paul-Heyse-Str. 2-4, 80336 München. Fax (89) 5306640; f. 1968; circ.
154,600

Münster
–*Münstersche Zeitung*: Neubrückenstr.
8-11, 48143 Münster; Postfach 5560,
48030 Münster. Fax (251) 5928450; mz-
redaktion@westline.de;
www.westline.de; f. 1871; circ. 46,860

—Westfälische Nachrichten: ZENO-Zeitungen, Soester Str. 13, 48155 Münster. Fax (251) 690705; circ. 125,900

Neubrandenburg
—Neubrandenburg Nordkurier: Flurstr. 2, 17034 Neubrandenburg. Fax (395) 4575694

Nürnberg
—Nürnberger Nachrichten, Marienstr. 9, 90402 Nürnberg. Fax (911) 2162326; f. 1945; circ. 344,000

Oberndorf-Neckar
—Schwarzwälder Bote: Postfach 1380, 78722 Oberndorf-Neckar. Fax (7423) 7873; circ. 104,300

Oelde
—Die Glocke: Engelbert-Holterdorf-Str. 4-6, 59302 Oelde. Fax (2522) 73216; circ. 65,500

Offenbach
—Offenbach-Post: Grosse Markstr. 36-44, 6050 Offenbach; Postfach 164. f. 1947; circ. 53,200

Oldenburg
—Norwest-Zeitung: Peterstr. 28-34, 26121 Oldenburg; Postfach 2527, 26015 Oldenburg. Fax (441) 99882029; www.nwz-online.de; circ. 130,000

Osnabrück
—Neue Osnabrücker Zeitung: Breiter Gang 10-14 (and Grosse Str. 17/19), 49074 Osnabrück; Postfach 4260, 49032 Osnabrück. Fax (541) 325696; f. 1967; circ. 179,700

Passau
—Passauer Neue Presse: Dr.-Hans-Kapfinger-Str. 30, 94032 Passau. Fax (851) 802256; f. 1946; circ. 162,900

Potsdam
—Märkische Allgemeine: Friedrich-Engels-Str. 24, 14473 Potsdam; Fax (331) 2840301; f. 1990; circ. 220,400

Regensburg
—Mittelbayerische Zeitung: Margareten-str. 4, 93047 Regensburg; Fax (941) 207307; www.donau.de; f. 1945; circ. 134,150

Rostock
—Ostsee-Zeitung: Richard-Wagner-Str., 18055 Rostock. Fax (81) 365244; f. 1952; circ. 214,300

Saarbrücken
—Saarbrücker Zeitung: Gutenbergstr. 11-23, 66117. Fax (681) 5022500; f. 1761; circ. 183,500

Schwerin
—Schweriner Volkszeitung: Gutenbergstr. 1. Fax (385) 3975140; f. 1946; circ. 144,800

Straubing
—Straubinger Tagblatt: Ludwigsplatz 30, 94315 Straubing. Fax (9421) 940206; service@iolowa.de; f. 1860; circ. 140,000

Stuttgart
—Stuttgarter Nachrichten: Plieninger Str. 150, 70567 Stuttgart; Postfach 104452, 70039 Stuttgart. Fax (711) 7205747; f. 1946; circ. 59,300

—Stuttgarter Zeitung: Plieninger Str. 150, 70567 Stuttgart; Postfach 106032, 70049 Stuttgart; Fax (711) 7205516; f. 1945; circ. 151,600

Suhl
—Freies Wort: Wilhelm-Pieck-Str. 6, 98527 Suhl. Fax (66) 21400; circ. 136,500

Trier
—Trierischer Volksfreund: Am Nikolaus-Koch-Platz 1-3, 54290 Trier; Postfach 3770, 54227. Fax (651) 7199990; circ. 100,000

Ulm
—Südwest Presse: Fraunstr. 77, 89073. Fax (731) 156308; circ. 107,800

Weiden
—Der Neue Tag: Weigelstr. 16, 92637 Weiden; Postfach 1340, 92603 Weiden. Fax (961) 44747; circ. 87,400

Weimar
—Thüringische Landeszeitung: Marienstr. 14, 99423 Weimar. Fax (3643) 206413; f. 1945; circ. 62,000

Wetzlar
—Wetzlarer Neue Zeitung: Elsa-Brandström-Str. 18, 35578 Wetzlar; Postfach 2940. Fax (6441) 71684; circ. 75,000

Wiesbaden
—Wiesbadener Kurier: Langgasse 21,

65183 Wiesbaden; Postfach 6029, 65050 Wiesbaden. Fax (611) 355377; circ. 86,700
Würzburg
–*Main-Post*: Berner Str. 2, 97084 Würzburg. Fax (931) 6001-242; www.mainpost.de; f. 1883; circ. 153,300

Sunday and weekly papers
Berlin
–*BZ am Sonntag*: Kochstr. 50, 10969 Berlin. Fax (30) 2516071; f. 1992; circ. 157,714
–*Wochenpost*: Ritterstr. 3, 10969 Berlin; weekly; circ. 102,900

Bonn
–*Rheinischer Merkur*: Godesberger Allee 91, 53175 Bonn. Fax (228) 884199; f. 1946; weekly; circ. 110,100
Frankfurt
–*Frankfurter Allgemeine Sonntagszeitung*: Hellerhofstr. 2-4, 60327 Frankfurt a.M.. Fax (69) 75911773; www.faz.de; Sunday; circ. 95,000
Hamburg
–*Bild am Sonntag*: Axel-Springer-Platz 1, 20350 Hamburg. Fax (40) 3435811; f. 1956; Sunday; circ. 2,542,426
–*Deutsches Allgemeines Sonntagsblatt*, Mittelweg 111, 20149 Hamburg; Fax (40) 41419111; f. 1948; Friday; circ. 97,592
–*Welt am Sonntag*: Axel-Springer-Platz 1, 20355 Hamburg. Fax (40) 34724912; www.welt.de; Sunday; circ. 401,766
München
–*Bayernkurier*: Nymphenburger Str. 64, 80636 München; weekly; circ. 156,300
Stuttgart
–*Sonntag aktuell*: Plienigerstr. 150, 70567 Stuttgart. Fax (711) 7205930; Sunday; circ. 869,500
Source: *The Europa World Year Book 1999*, Vol. 1, Europa Publications Limited, London, 1999.

SISTER CITIES INTERNATIONAL

Sister Cities International
1301 Pennsylvania Ave. NW, Ste. 850
Washington, DC 20004
Tel. (202) 347-8630
Fax (202) 3393-6524

The following are pairings of cities in the United States (in force in early 2000) with cities in Germany, Austria, Switzerland, Netherlands, and Poland, as organized through Sister Cities International:

Germany
Aachen	Arlington County, VA
Altenberg	Western Piedmont, NC
Ansbach	Bay City, MI
Apolda	Rapid City, SD
Augsburg	Dayton, OH
Bad Königshofen	Arlington, TX
Bad Schandau	Twentynine Palms, CA
Bad Zwischenahn	Centerville, OH
Berlin:	Los Angeles, CA
Berlin-Spandau (see Spandau)	
Bexbach	Goshen, IN
Billerbeck	Englewood, OH
Bingen am Rhein	Bingen-White Salmon, WA
Bissendorf	Huntingburg, IN
Braunfels	New Braunfels, TX
Braunschweig	Omaha, BE
Büdingen	Tinley Park, IL
Chemnitz	Akron, OH
Coburg	Garden City, NY
Crailsheim:	Worthington, MN
Cranzahl:	Running Springs, CA
Dorfen	Constantine, MI
Dortmund	Buffalo, NY
Dresden	Columbus, OH
Eberbach	Ephrata, PA
Eichstatt:	Lexington, VA
Eisenach	Waverly, IA
Erfurt	Shawnee, KS
Emmerich	Kirkland, WA
Erlangen	Greater Richmond Partnership, VA
Esslingen:	Sheboygan, WI

Eutin .... Lawrence, KS
Frankfurt-Oder .... Yuma, AZ
Freiburg im Breisgau ..... Fryburg, PA,
                             Madison, WI
Friedrichshafen: .... Peoria, IL
Friolzheim: .... Williamsville, NY
Fulda .... Wilmington, DE
Füssen .... Helen, GA
Garbsen .... Farmers Branch, TX
Garmisch-Partenkirchen ..... Aspen, CO
Gau-Algesheim .... Redford, MI
Gedern .... Columbia: IL
Gera .... Fort Wayne, IN
Gießen .... Waterloo, IA
Gotha .... Gastonia, NC
Gottelfingen: .... Botkins, OH
Greifswald ..Bryan-College Station, TX
Gross-Bieberau .... Millstadt, IL
Grünstadt ....Bonita Springs, FL
Guellesheim ....Lawton, OK
Gunzenhausen .... Frankenmuth, MI
Hamburg ....Chicago, IL
Hamm: .... Chattanooga, TN,
                           Santa Monica, CA
Hannover .... Kansas City, MO
Helmstedt .... Albuquerque, NM,
                             Oxford, MS
Herford .... Quincy, IL
Hof .... Ogden, UT
Holzerlinger ....Crystal Lake, IL
Ingelheim .... Ridgefield, CT
Kaiserslautern .... Davenport, IA
Kleve .... Fitchburg, MA
Koblenz .... Austin, TX
Königs Wusterhausen ... Germantown,
                                    TN
Krefeld .... Charlotte, NC
Kronach .... Greenville, MS
Kubelstein Stadt Scheßlitz ...... Victoria,
                                    KS
Kusel .... Marietta, OH
Landsberg am Lech ....Hudson, OH
Leinfelden-Echterdingen .... York, PA
Leipzig: .... Houston, TX
Leinfelden-Echterdingen: .... York, PA
Lengerich .... Wapakoneta, OH
Leonberg .... Seward, NE
Lichtenfels: .... Vandalia, OH
Lienen .... St. Mary's, OH

Linz am Rhein: .... Marietta, GA
Lübeck .... Spokane, WA
Lüdinghausen .... Deerfield, IL
Ludwigsburg .... St. Charles, MO
Ludwigshafen am Rhein Pasadena, CA
Lüneburg .... Thomasville, GA
Lutherstadt Wittenberg ...... Springfield,
                                    OH
Mainz: .... Louisville, KY
Malsch: .... Dinuba, CA
Mannheim .... Manheim, PA
Marbach am Neckar . Washington, MO
Marl ....Midland, MI
Markham .... Metrocrest, TX
Melsungen .... Elmira, NY
Memmingen .... Glendale, AZ
Meßstetten .... Toccoa, GA
Montabaur .... Fredricksburg, TX
Mörzheim .... Frederick, MD
Mühlacker .... Tolleson, AZ
München .... Cincinnati, OH
Münster .... Fresno, CA; Radcliff, KY
Neckargemünd .... Missoula, MT
Neu Ulm .... New Ulm, MN
Neusäß .... Redwood Falls, MN
Neustadt an der Waldnaab ... Hays, KS
Nienburg .... Las Cruces, NM
Nittenau .... Lake Zurich, IL
Nordhausen .... Custer, SD
Ofterdingen .... Dexter, MI
Osnabrück .... Evansville, IN
Paderborn .... Belleville, IL
Passau .... Hackensack, NJ
Pfaffenweiler .... Jasper, IN
Pinneberg .... Rockville, MD
Porta Westfalica: .... Waterloo, IL
Potsdam .... Sioux Falls, SD
Prum .... Fort Madison, IA
Quakenbruck .... Conway, AR
Radebeul .... Sierra Vista, AZ
Rastatt .... New Britain, CT
Ratingen .... Vermillion, SD
Regensburg .... Tempe, AZ
Rheinsberg .... Huber Heights, OH
Rödental .... Eaton, OH
Saarbrücken .... Pittsburgh, PA
Saarpfalz-Kreis, Saarland .... Henrico
                               County, VA
Schaumburg .... Schaumburg, IL

Schifferstadt .... Frederick, MD
Schorndorf .... Tuscaloosa, AL
Schwabisch-Gmund ...... Bethlehem, PA
Schwerin .... Milwaukee, WI
Schwieberdingen .... Belvidere, IL
Seevetal .... Decatur, IL
Soltau .... Coldwater, MI
Sonderhausen .... Rolla, MO
Spandau District, Berlin ... Boca Raton,
                                                      FL
Stuttgart .... St. Louis, MO
Sulzfeld .... El Cajon, CA
Taufkirchen .... West Chicago, IL
Tegernsee .... Ketchum, ID
Teterow .... Greater Tri-Cities TN/VA
Tirschenreuth .... Santa Fe Springs, CA
Trier .... Fort Worth, TX
Trossingen .... Beavertown, OR
Tübingen .... Ann Arbor, MI
Ul: .... New Ulm, MN
Waldsrode .... Hibbing, MN
Walldorf: .... Astoria, OR
Wasserburg .... Vincennes, IN
Weimar .... Weimar, TX
Wesel .... Hagerstown, MD
Wiernsheim .... New Harmony, IN
Wiesloch .... Sturgis, MI
Wilhelmshaven .... Norfolk, VA
Winterlingen: .... Shiner, TX
Wittenberg (see Lutherstadt Wittenberg)
Wittmund: .... Simsbury, CT
Wolfach .... Richfield, OH
Wolfenbüttel .... Kenosha, WI
Worms .... Mobile, AL
Würzburg .... Rochester, NY
Zittau .... Portsmouth, OH
Zweibrücken .... York County, VA

Austria

Abentenau .... Big Bear Lake, CA
Graz .... Montclair, NJ
Innsbruck .... New Orleans, LA
Kitzbuhl .... Sun Valley, ID
Lilienfeld .... Laconia, NH
Linz .... Kansas City, KS
St. Anton .... North Conway, NH
St. Johann .... Redford, MI
Salzburg .... Atlanta, GA
Solden .... Galesburg, MI
Stegersbach .... Northampton, PA

Steyr .... Kettering, OH

Switzerland

Bern .... New Bern, NC
Chur .... Olathe, KS
Crans Montana .... Zionsville, IN
Davos .... Aspen, CO
Liestal .... Sacramento, CA
Luzerne .... Chicago, IL
Saasfee .... Steamboat Springs, CO
St. Moritz .... Vail, CO
Sursee .... Highland, IL
Winterthur .... Ontario, CA

Netherlands

Delft .... Green Bay, WI
Dieren .... South Holland, Il
Enschede .... Palo Alto, CA
Grijpskerk .... La Grange,IN
Kapelle .... Zeeland, MI
Maastricht .... Englewood, NJ
Nijmegen .... Albany, NY
Rhenen .... Hillsdale, MI
Rotterdam .... Baltimore, MD
Soest .... Titusville, FL
Voorburg .... Temecula, CA

Poland

Bialystok .... Milwaukee County, WI
Bielsko-Biala .... Grand Rapids, MI
Czestochowa .... South Bend, IN
Gdansk .... Cleveland, OH
Gorzow Wielkopolski .... Hazleton, PA
Gulcz .... Stevens Point, WI
Gdynia .... Seattle, WA
Jelenia Gora .... Tyler, TX
Katowice .... Mobile, AL
Krakow .... Rochester, NY
Lomianki .... Columbia Heights,MN
Lomza .... Muscatine, IA
Lublin .... Erie, PA
Milanowek .... Winsted, CT
Moryn .... Bronson, MI
Naklo Nad Notecia .... Seymour, CT
Olsztyn .... Richmond, VA
Opole .... Roanoke County, VA
Plock .... Fort Wayne, IN
Poznan .... Bay City, MI, Toledo, OH
Pultusk .... New Britain, CT
Rzeszow .... Buffalo, NY
Slomniki .... Sparta, MI
Szczecin .... St. Louis, MO

VARIETIES OF GERMAN MUSEUMS

The number of Germans who visit museums in a year's time is huge; the 4,274 German museums which make their figures available counted a total of 92.7 million visitors in 1998, an increase of 2.1 million over the year before.

There are more than 3,000 museums in the Federal Republic: state, municipal, society, and private museums; museums of local history and culture; museums of church diocesan and cathedral treasures; and residential, castle, palace and open-air museums.

Below are listed just a few of the types of museums in Germany which present the culture, occupations, and living conditions of Germans in centuries past.

◆ The many *Freilichtmuseen* (open-air museums) in Germany demonstrate crafts and other everyday work of times past.

◆ Probably the most common museum type, however, is the *Heimatmuseum.* This "hometown" museum is sometimes given the title *Dorfstube,* or *Heimat-stube,* as well as various other similar terms, all indicating that the items on display are based strictly on the history and traditions of the residents of a particular small local area. The "hometown" museum, portrays the history of the clothing, tools, furniture, crafts, and other articles of everyday life in the village or town where the museum is situated.

◆ The *Stadtisches Museum* (city/town museum) exhibits artifacts portraying the history of the city or town.

◆ The *Kreismuseum* displays articles pertinent to its *Kreis,* which is the political unit similar to the American county.

◆ Frequently a *Schloßmuseum* (castle museum) is established within the walls of an old castle.

◆ The *Volkskundemuseum* (folkart museum) recounts the history of the dress styles, the furniture, the occupations, the crafts, and the traditions of a particular area. In every museum of this type, one will see articles displayed that are substantially different from those in any other part of Germany.

◆ The *Bauernmuseum* (farm museum) portrays farmlife in times past. This museum may often take the form of a *Freilichtmuseum,* even though the museum name may not contain that designation.

Germany is known for its often whimsical creation of museums with exceedingly specialized focuses – such as museums displaying one narrow topic only, such as clocks, wallpaper, puppetry, bread, typewriters, hats, hairdressing, and leather. There are dog museums, a chamber-pot museum, a potato museum, and a trumpet museum, to name just a very few.

The next section provides examples of some specialized German museums.

SELECTED MUSEUMS PORTRAYING GERMAN ETHNOLOGY

◆ **Berlin :** *Museum für Deutsche Volkskunde SMPK* (Museum of German Ethnology), devoted to the popular culture, urban and rural, of German-speaking central Europe, from the 16th century to the present

◆ **Böblingen (Baden-Württemberg):** *Deutsches Fleischermuseum* (German

Butchers' Museum), displaying the history of the butcher trade in Germany and the slaughtering and processing techniques used at different periods

♦ **Bochum (Northrhine-Westphalia):** *Deutsches Bergbau-Museum* (German Mining Museum), showing the past and present of mining in Germany, with demonstration mine galleries beneath the museum building

♦ **Cloppenburg (Lower Saxony):** *Museumsdorf* (Museum Village), the largest open-air museum in Germany

♦ **Detmold (Northrhine-Westphalia):** *Westfälisches Freilichtmuseum* Detmold, *Landesmuseum für Volkskunde, Krummes Haus* (Westphalia Open-Air Museum), with rural houses, farm buildings, and workshops from different parts of Westphalia

♦ **Dortmund (Northrhine-Westphalia):** *Deutsches Kochbuchmuseum,* literally, the German cookbook museum, which presents a cultural history of eating and drinking

♦ **Grossweil (Upper Bavaria):** *Freilichtmuseum des Bezirks Oberbayern* (Open-Air Museum of Upper Bavaria) contains a large collection of rural buildings, including farmhouses, granaries, barns, mills, flax-kilns, and a fisherman's hut

♦ **Hagen (Northrhine-Westphalia):** *Westfälisches Freilichtmuseum, Landesmuseum für Handwerk und Technik* (Westphalian Open-Air Museum of Technology), offering regular demonstrations of, for example, a scythe mill, a rope-walk, different forges, a printing shop, a paper mill, and a sawmill

♦ **Hamburg:** *Museumsdorf* (Museum Village), with a reconstruction of a Holstein village, including a village inn, smithy, drive-through barn, mill, and farmhouse

♦ **Hersbruck (Bavaria):** *Deutsches Hirtenmuseum* (German Shepherds' Museum), illustrating the life and duties of shepherds and cowboys from all over the world, but especially from Germany,

with the traditional life of rural Franconia

♦ **Iphofen (Bavaria):** *Fränkisches Bauern- und Handwerkermuseum* (Franconian Museum of Farming and Handicrafts), with 17 craftsmen's workshops, 12 galleries showing farm implements and 6 for vineyard cultivation and wine production

♦ **Kiel (Schleswig-Holstein):** *Schleswig-Holsteinisches Freilichtmuseum* (Schleswig-Holstein Open-Air Museum), includes rural houses, mills, barns and workshops, with regular demonstrations of basket-making, weaving and blacksmith's work

♦ **Marktrodach (Bavaria):** *Flössermuseum Unterrodach* (Unterrodach Raftsmen's Museum), illustrating the history and techniques of log-floating in the Frankenwald region

♦ **Molfsee (Schleswig-Holstein):** *Schleswig-Holsteinisches Freilichtmuseum* (Schleswig-Holstein Open-Air Museum), with 16th-19th century buildings and their furniture, domestic equipment, agricultural implements, windmills, farmhouses, and an apothecary's shop

♦ **Neu-Anspach (Hesse):** *Freilichtmuseum Hessenpark* (Hessenpark Open-Air Museum), a market place, surrounded by old buildings, contains restaurants, shops in which regional handicrafts are on sale, and exhibition rooms

♦ **Sobernheim (Rhineland-Palatinate):** *Rheinland Pfälzisches Freilichtmuseum* (Open-Air Museum of the Rhineland Palatinate), comprising rural buildings which include houses, farm buildings, and work-shops

♦ **Tann (Hesse):** *Freilichtmuseum 'Rhöner Museumsdorf'* (Rhön Museum Village), illustrating the way of life of a well-to-do rural family around 1800

♦ **Triberg (Baden-Württemberg):** *Schwarzwald-Museum* (Black Forest Museum), dealing mainly with traditional handicrafts of the Black

Forest

♦**Ulm (Baden-Württemberg):** *Deutsches Brotmuseum* (German Bread Museum), concerned with the history of bread-making, including a display of the history of hunger in the 19th and 20th centuries
Source: Kenneth Hudson and Ann Nichols, *The Cambridge Guide to the Museums of Europe.* Cambridge University Press, New York and Cambridge, 1991.

MUSEUMS AND SITES IN ROMAN GERMANY

After 400 years of existence, the Roman Empire left hundreds of thousands of ruins that lie in present-day Germany, mostly still unexplored. A few of these ruins and Roman artifacts can be seen in the following locations:

♦ *Via Romana*: The 50-mile-long "Roman Road" that runs from Nijmegen, Holland to Xanten, Germany, connecting eight towns, each of which has Roman ruins, excavations, and outdoor museums or archaeological theme parks
♦**Roman Route:** 175 miles of ancient Roman roads from Xanten to Detmold. (For information: Münsterland Touristik "*Grünen Band*," Hohe Schule 13, 48565 Steinfurt, Germany)
♦**Xanten:** The *Archaeologischer Park.* (For information: Xanten Tourist Office, Karthaus 2, 46509 Xanten, Germany)
♦ **Osnabrück-Kalkriese:** *Kultur-geschichtliches Museum* (Museum of Cultural History), Heger-Tor-Wall 28.
♦ **Cologne:** *Römisch-Germanisches Museum* (Roman-Germanic Museum), at Roncalliplatz 4. (Information: Tourist Office, Unter Fettenhennen 19, 50667 Köln.)
♦ **Trier:** *Rheinisches Landesmuseum,* Ostallee 44 (has the most comprehensive collection of Roman finds); also the Porta Nigra, Amphitheater, Imperial Baths and Basilika. (For information: Verkehrsamt-Touristik Information, An der Porta

Nigra, 54292 Trier)
♦ **Mainz:** *Antikes Schiffahrtsmuseum* (Antique Ships Museum), 2-B Neutor-strasse; also the *Römisch-Germanisches Zentralmuseum* in Kurfürstliches Schloss; and the *Mittelrheinisches Landesmuseum,* on Grosse Bleiche. (For information: Verkehrsverein Mainz, Bahnhofstrasse 15, 55116 Mainz)
♦**Saalburg:** The castellum, just outside Bad Homburg. (For information: Saalburgmuseum, Saalburg-Römerkastell, 61352 Bad Homburg)
♦ **Schwarzenacker:** *Römermuseum.* (Schwarzenacker is a suburb of Homburg/ Saarland.)
♦**Köngen:** *Römerpark*
♦ **Hechingen:** *Villa Rustica* and the *Römisches Freilichtmuseum* (Roman Open Air Museum) in the suburb of Steir
♦**Aalen:** The *Limes Museum*, St. Johann-Strasse 5
♦**Rottweil:** *Stadtmuseum,* Hauptstrasse 20
♦**Augsburg:** *Römisches Museum*, in the former Dominican St. Magdalene church at Dominikaner Strasse 15
♦ **Kempten:** *Archaeologischer Park*, Campodonum Weg 3
♦ **Regensburg:** *Museum der Stadt Regensburg*, Dachauplatz 2-4 (For information: Krauterermarkt 3, 93047 Regensburg
Source: "Living Roman Legacy," by John Dornberg. *German Life*, April/May 1995.

MUSEUM REFERENCES

♦*Museums of the World,* 6th revised and enlarged edition, K.G. Saur, München, 1997. [Arranged by subjects – for example, "Farms and Farming," "Railroads," "Printing," "Paper," Peasant Life and Traditions," and "Folklore." Within each subject area, the pertinent museums are listed by country – Germany, Switzerland, Ireland, South Africa, etc.]
♦**Deutscher Museumsbund e.V.**

In der Halde 1
14195 Berlin
Tel. 49/30/841095-17
Fax 49/30/841095-19

and Answers, ed. Susan Steiner. German Information Center, New York, 1996.
♦ *Facts about Germany,* Societäts Verlag, Press and Information Office of the Federal Government, Frankfurt am Main, 1999.

PUBLIC RESEARCH LIBRARIES IN GERMANY

The most important public research libraries are in Munich (*Bayerische Staatsbibliothek,* or Bavarian State Library), Berlin (*Preussischer Kulturbesitz,* or State Library of the Prussian Cultural Heritage Foundation), Frankfurt am Main (*Deutsche Bibliothek,* or The German Library), including the Federal Republic's bibliographical center, and Leipzig (*Die Deutsche Bücherei,* or the German Library). The German Library in Frankfurt am Main has at least one copy of all books published in the German language since 1945.

The state and university libraries likewise have large stocks. One library with an outstanding reputation is the well-preserved Herzog-August-Bibliothek in Wolfenbüttel, which has more than 660,000 volumes, including 12,000 priceless medieval manuscripts.

In the Federal Republic of Germany, there are about 13,500 public libraries, with more than 129 million volumes. Most of these libraries are maintained by local authorities and churches.

Many of these libraries feature public readings by authors, special events and exhibitions, and have thus become centers of cultural activity – in many smaller communities, the only such center. They also cater to the special interests of users by offering special sections for children and young people as well as music and art libraries. Many cities and communities operate bookmobiles serving suburban areas and villages.

Sources:
♦ *Federal Republic of Germany: Questions*

CREATION OF A NATIONAL LIBRARY

Great libraries of all sizes and specialties Germany has in abundance. What it lacked until recent years was a central national library like the Library of Congress or the British Library that serves as a copyright repository collection. The German Library (*Die deutsche Bücherei*) in Leipzig took on that role, but only beginning in 1913, some four and a half centuries after Gutenberg opened the age of print with the invention of moveable type.

Die deutsche Bibliothek in Frankfurt also functioned as a copyright collection, but only for books printed during the 20th century.

In August 1990, under terms of the Unification Treaty, the two libraries merged under the name *Die Deutsche Bibliothek,* which is the central archive of all German-language writings and the national bibliographical information center of the Federal Republic. Its stocks total about 13 million volumes.

In recognition of the lack of a national library for so many years, five major German libraries joined forces to build as complete a collection as possible of books printed in Germany since 1450. The "Collection of German Imprints 1450-1912" is to be a "virtual" one, with each of the five libraries having been assigned a period of time and asked to collect the books printed in Germany (or in the lands that became part of modern Germany) during that period as completely as possible. Researchers can find the location of books through a general catalog that is accessible on-line.

Responsibility for making acquisitions has been divided among the five libraries according to their existing strengths. The libraries and their assignments are,

♦ **Bavarian State Library, Munich:** First century and a half of printing
♦ **Herzog August Library, Wolfenbüttel (Lower Saxony):** Seventeenth century
♦ **University Library of Göttingen (Lower Saxony):** Eighteenth century
♦ **Frankfurt's Public and University Library:** 1801-1870
♦ **Prussian State Library, Berlin**: 1871-1912

Although the results of the libraries' collecting efforts have been impressive, many titles are still lacking. Of the estimated one million titles printed during the nineteenth century, for example, about one-third were destroyed and are lost forever.

Of the two-thirds remaining, experts estimate, the Frankfurt Public and University Library's comprehensive collection of early- and mid nineteenth-century works encompasses all but 100,000-150,000 titles. Coming up with those missing works could take another half century.

Source: *The Week in Germany,* German Information Center, New York, 20 October 1995.

STATUS OF THE MERGED NATIONAL LIBRARY

The two libraries – *Die Deutsche Bibliothek* in Frankfurt and *Die Deutsche Bücherei* in Leipzig, under the Unification Treaty of 1990 merged to become *Die Deutsche Bibliothek*. Each of the facilities has been assigned a different task related to its collecting of all materials published in and about Germany. (See the list in the column at the left.)

These two-libraries-in-one hold a collection as complete as possible of those German publications since 1913 which survived the wars. The merged *Deutsche Bibliothek* is funded solely through the German federal government.

A brief description of the major roles of the two parts of this library follows:

♦ **Deutsche Bücherei Leipzig**
Deutscher Platz 1
04103 Leipzig
This library holds a complete collection of books for the German-speaking world since 1913, as well as translations of works from German after 1941. It also includes holdings of the *Reichsbibliothek* (Imperial Library) after 1848, a *Hochschulschriften* (higher education literature) collection, a collection of translations of German works which appeared in other countries, as well as of foreign-language Germanica, a collection of exile literature, a collection of literary phonograph records and other recorded sources (*Tonträgersammlung*), and about a half million dissertations.

This library in Leipzig is to be responsible for all aspects of book preservation and for related text storage technologies. Also, it is to be the German research center for the history of the book and is responsible for maintaining the museum on the history of writing and the book. Presently its sections include the Center for Book Preservation and the German Museum of Books and Writings.

♦ **Deutsche Bibliothek Frankfurt a.M.**
Zeppelinallee 4 - 8
60325 Frankfurt am Main
As of 1994, the Frankfurt library held 4,750,000 volumes, in addition to 280,000 microforms and 62,000 current periodicals. Special collections include the German emigration of 1933 to 1945, Germanica, and manuscripts and books of German authors since 1945.

Decisions concerning collections

Decisions as of 1994 concerning collections have been made as follows:

◆Each library will continue to receive a copy of every current publication in Germany; therefore, each will be comprehensive for German publications from 1991 onward. It is likely, however, that the library in Leipzig will be more complete for the period from 1913 to 1949 than the library in Frankfurt.

◆The German Exile Archive 1933-1945 will continue to be in two parts. Because the library in Frankfurt has a significantly larger collection, it might be assumed that it will become the leader in this field.

◆The library in Leipzig will continue to focus on collecting all works related to Germany (including translations of German works) wherever published.

◆The *Reichsbibliothek* (Imperial Library) of 1848 (about 4,600 volumes), a library that was the predecessor of a national library, will continue to be stored in Leipzig, separated from the general collection, but accessible to users.

◆ The collection "Sozialistica," with strong holdings for the period from 1830 until 1912, will continue to be held in Leipzig.

◆The library in Leipzig will collect published works about music. The German Music Archive in Berlin, founded in 1970 as a special section of the Frankfurt *Deutsche Bibliothek*, will continue to have responsibility for printed music and sound recordings.

Source: *Archives and Libraries in a New Germany,* by Erwin K. Welsch and Jürgen Danyel, with Thomas Kilton. Council for European Studies, New York, 1994.

BOOKS/LIBRARIES TRADES: ADDRESSES IN GERMANY

◆German Publishers & Booksellers Association:
Börsenverein des Deutschen Buch-handels e.V., Grosser Hirschgraben 17-21, 60311 Frankfurt am Main. 101513.1345@compuserve.de; www. buchhandel.de

◆German Library Association:
Deutscher Bibliotheksverband e.V., Alt-Moabit 101 A,10559 Berlin. www.bdbibe. de/db;dbv@dbi-berlin.de

BOOK PUBLISHING IN GERMANY

There are more than 2,000 publishers in Germany. Although 100 of them have an annual turnover of more than DM 25 million, none of them dominates the market. Many small companies also contribute to the variety of literature available to the public. After World War II, book clubs attracted a wider readership. Today about 6.6 million readers belong to a book club.

The Frankfurt Book Fair is the outstanding event of the year for the international book trade. The second major book fair is held every spring in Leipzig. It especially serves as an intermediary with the countries of Eastern Europe.

In terms of book production, Germany ranks third in the world behind the United Kingdom and China. Several cities are major publishing centers: Munich, Berlin, Frankfurt am Main, Stuttgart, Cologne, and Hamburg.

Source: *Facts about Germany,* Societäts Verlag, Press and Information Office of the Federal Government, Frankfurt am Main, 1999.

GERMAN PUBLISHERS

◆Ardrey-Verlag GmbH,
Bohlweg 22, 48147 München.
Tel. (0251) 41320; Fax (0251) 413220
◆ Aschendorffsche Verlagsbuch-handlung, Soester Str. 13, 48155 Münster.
Tel. (0251) 6900; Fax (0251) 690105

◆**Verlag C. H. Beck,** Wilhelmstr. 9, 80801 München. Tel. (089) 381890; Fax (089) 38189402 ; bestellung@beck.de

◆**C. Bertelsmann GmbH,** Neumarkter Str. 18, 81673 München 80. Postfach 800360, 81603 München 80.

◆ **Bettendorf'sche Verlagsanstalt GmbH,** Knorrstr. 66, 80807 München. Tel (089) 356384-0; Fax (089) 356384-20

◆**Böhlau Verlag GmbH & Co.**, Theodor-Heuss-Strasse 76, 51149 Köln. Tel. (02203) 307021. Fax (410) 625-9004

◆**Verlag E. u. U. Brockhaus,** Am Wolfshahn 31, 42117 Wuppertal. Tel. 01149 202 44 74 74; mail@verlag-brockhaus.de; www.verlag-brockhaus. de.

◆ **Degener & Co. Manfred Dreiss Verlag,** Nürnberger Str. 27, 91413 Neustadt a d Aisch

◆**Institut für pfälzische Geschichte und Volkskunde,** Benzinoring 6, 67657 Kaiserslautern. Tel. (0631) 3647302; Fax (0631) 63597

◆**Landbuch-Verlagsgesellschaft,** Kabelkamp 6, 30179 Hannover. Postfach 160 30001 Hannover. Tel. (0511) 6780635; Fax (0511) 6780680; info@ landbuch.de

◆**Langenscheidt Group,** Neusser Str. 3, 80807 München. Postfach 401120. 80807 München 40. Tel. (089) 36096-0; Fax (089) 36096222

◆**Gerhard Rautenberg Druckerei und Verlag GmbH & Co. KG,** Blinke 8, 26787 Leer. Postfach 1909, 26767 Leer. Tel. (0491) 929704 Fax (0491) 929706

◆**C.A. Starke Verlag,** Frankfurter Str.51-53, Postfach 1310, 65549 Limburg/Lahn. Tel. (06431) 96150; Fax (06431) 961515

◆ **Verlag Walter de Gruyter & Co.**, Genthiner Weg 13, Berlin 19785. Tel. (030) 2600; Fax (030) 26005251

Source: *International Literary Market Place*, R.R. Bowker, 1999.

AMERICAN UNIVERSITIES IN GERMANY

◆**Stanford Univeristy (Berlin):** Pacelli-

Allee 18-20,14195 Berlin. Tel. (030) 8 31 30 88; Fax (030) 8 31 30 - 79

◆ **University of Southern California (USC), Germany:** Hohenstaufenstr., 180801 München. Tel. (089) 34 59 54; Fax (089) 33 60 04

◆**University of Maryland (Mannheim),** Grenadierstr. 4, Gebäude 485, 68167 Mannheim. Tel. (0621) 337 40; Fax (0621) 337 4103

◆**University of Maryland (Heidelberg):** Im Bosseldorn 30, 69126 Heidelberg. Tel. (06221) 3 78 - 0; Fax (06221) 3 78 - 300

◆ **University of Maryland University College:** Postfach 20 23, 73510 Schwäbisch Gmünd. Tel. (07171) 18070; Fax (07171) 37525, or 37776

◆ **Schiller International University (Heidelberg),** Admissions Office and Central Administration, Bergstraße 106, 69121 Heidelberg. Tel. (06221) 4 91 59; Fax (06221) 40 27 03

AMERICAN AND INTERNATIONAL SCHOOLS IN GERMANY

◆ **John-F.-Kennedy-Schule,** Teltower Damm 87-93, 14167 Berlin. Tel. (030) 8 07 - 27 10; Fax (030) 8 07 - 33 77

◆**International School of Düsseldorf e.V.,** Leuchtenberger Kirchweg 2 40489 Düsseldorf. Tel. (0211) 94 066; Fax (0211) 4 08 07 74

◆**The Frankfurt International School,** An der Waldlust 15, 61440 Oberursel. Tel. (06171) 2 02 - 0; Fax (06171) 2 02 - 3 84

◆ **Hamburg International School,** Internationale Schule Hamburg, Holmbrook 20, 20605 Hamburg. Tel. (040) 8 83 00 10; Fax (040) 8 81 14 05

◆ **Europäische Schule Karlsruhe,** Albert- Schweitzer-Straße 1, 76139 Karlsruhe-Waldstadt. Tel. (0721) 68 00 90; Fax (0721) 68 72 33

◆**Europäische Schule München,** Elise-Aulinger-Straße 21, 81739 München. Tel. (089) 6 37 84 18

◆**Munich International School,** Percha-

Schloß Buchhof, 82319 Starnberg. Tel
(08151) 366 - 0; Fax:(08151) 366 119

ACADEMIC AND CULTURAL
ORGANIZATIONS IN GERMANY

◆ **Atlantik-Brücke e.V.,** Adenauerallee
131, 53113 Bonn. Postfach 11 47, 53001
Bonn. Tel. (0228) 2 14 1 60 or -2 60; Fax
(0228) 2 14 - 6 59
◆ **The German Marshall Fund of the
United States,** Berlin Office, Friedrichstr.
113a, 10117 Berlin. Tel. (030) 2 83 48 33; 2
83 48 43; Fax (030) 2 83 48 53
◆ **Inter Nationes,** Kennedyallee 91-103,
53175 Bonn. Tel. 49-228-880-0; Fax 49-
228-880-457; info@inter-nationes.de
◆ **Deutscher Akademischer Austausch-
dienst (DAAD),** Kennedyalee 50, 53175
Bonn. Tel. 49 (0)2 28/8 82-0.
◆ **Städte-Brücke e.V.,** Deutsch-
Amerikanischer Rundfunk - und
Fernseh- Arbeitskreis, Postfach 76 04 44,
22054 Hamburg. Tel. (040) 20 46 47; Fax
(040) 2.00 26 55. (Organizes exchanges
between Germans and Americans;
focuses on arranging meetings between
Germans and Americans with the same
surname.)
◆ **Verband der Deutsch-Amerikanisch-
en Clubs e.V.,** Kniebisstraße 16, 68163
Mannheim. Tel./Fax (0621) 81 78 89

U.S. EMBASSY OFFICES
IN GERMANY

◆ **Berlin office** – Außenstelle Berlin,
Clayallee 170, 14195 Berlin. Tel. (030)
8305-0; Fax (030) 8305-1215;
ACSBerlin@state.gov; Consular
jurisdiction: Berlin, Brandenburg,
Bremen, Hamburg, Mecklenberg,
Western Pomerania, Lower Saxony,
Saxony, Saxony-Anhalt, Schleswig-
Holstein, Thuringia
◆ **Düsseldorf – Consulate General of hte
United States of America,** Willi-Becker-

Allee 10, 40227 Düsseldorf. Tel. (0211)
788-8927; Fax (0211) 788-8938
◆ **Frankfurt – Consulate General of the
United States of America,** General-
konsulat der Vereinigten Staaten von
Amerika, Gießener Str. 30, 60435 Frankfurt
am Main. Tel. 069) 7535-0; Fax (069) 7535-
2277; http://frankfurt.usconsulate.gov/
frankfurt/contact.htm.; Consular jurisdic
tion: States of Hesse, Rhineland-
Palatinate, Saarland; Lower Franconia
County of the state of Bavaria; Baden-
Württemberg
◆ **Leipzig – Consulate General of the
United States of America,** Wilhelm-
Seyfferth-Straße 4, 04107 Leipzig. Tel.
(0341)   213-840;   http://
leipzig.usconsulate.gov
◆ **München – Consulate General of the
United States of America,** Königstraße
5, 80539 München. Tel. (089) 2888-0; Fax
(089)   280-9998;   ConsMunich@
state.gov; Consular jurisdiction: State of
Bavaria (except Lower Franconia
County).
◆ **Hamburg – Consulate General of the
United States of America,** Generalkonsu-
lat der Vereinigten Staaten von Amerika,
Alsterufer 27/28, 20354 Hamburg. Tel.
(040) 411 71-100; Fax (040) 41 32 79 33;
http://hamburg.usconsulate.gov

GERMAN 'CHAMBER OF
COMMERCE' ORGANIZATIONS

◆ **Federation of German Industries,**
Bundesverband   der   Deutschen
Industrie, Gustav-Heinemann-Ufer 84-88,
50968 Köln. www.bdi-online.de;
presse@bdi-online.de
◆ **Association of German Chambers of
Industry and Commerce,** Deutscher
Industrie- und Handelstag, Adenauer-
allee   148,   53113   Bonn.
www.diht.dediht@bonn.diht.ihk.de

SISTER-CITY PARTNERSHIPS IN GERMANY

◆**Deutscher Städtetag (DST),** Linden-allee 13 - 17, 50968 Köln. Tel. (0221) 37 71 - 0; Fax (0221) 37 71 - 1 27 or -8. (Issues information on sister-city partnerships)
◆**Institut für europäische Partner-schaft en und internationale Zusam-menarbeit e.V. (IPZ),** Mirecourtstr. 7, 53225 Bonn. Tel. (0228) 46 72 83; Fax (0228) 47 72 86. (Promotes sister-city partnerships)

AMERICA HOUSES (Amerika-Häuser)

◆**Amerika-Haus Berlin,** Hardenbergstr. 22-24, 10623 Berlin. Tel. (030) 31 00 01 13/14; Fax (030) 31 00 01 27, E-mail <covbera@usia.gov>
◆**Amerika-Haus Frankfurt,** Staufenstr. 1, 60232 Frankfurt (Main). Tel. (069) 97 14 48 28; Fax (069) 17 49 62; bibifran@usia.gov
◆**Amerika-Haus Hamburg,** Tesdorpfstr. 1, 20148 Hamburg. Tel. (040) 45 01 04 23; Fax (040) 44 80 96 98; csghamb@usia.gov
◆**Amerika-Haus Köln,** Apostelnkloster 13-15, 50672 Köln. Tel. (0221) 209 01 47; Fax (0221) 209 01 57; ahlcolo@usia.gov
◆ **Amerika-Haus Leipzig,** Wilhelm-Seyfferth-Straße 4, 04107 Leipzig. Tel. (0341) 2 13 84 25; Fax (0341) 2 13 84 43; ustleip@usia.gov
◆**Amerika-Haus München,** Karolinen-platz 3, 80333 München. Tel. (089) 55 25 37 21; Fax: (089) 55 35 78; mapmuni@usia.gov

GERMAN-AMERICAN INSTITUTES IN GERMANY

◆**Carl-Schurz Haus,** Kaiser- Joseph-Straße 266, 79098 Freiburg. Tel. (0761) 3 16 45; Fax (0761) 3 98 27
◆ **Deutsch-Amerikanisches Institut,** Sofienstr. 12, 69115 Heidelberg. Tel. (06221) 2 47 71; Fax (06221) 1 49 25
◆**Kennedy-Haus,** Holtenauerstr. 9, 24103 Kiel. Tel. (0431 55 48 66
◆ **Deutsch-Amerikanisches Institut,** Gleissbühlstr. 13, 90402 Nürnberg. Tel. (0911) 20 33 27; Fax: (0911) 20 87 67
◆ **Deutsch-Amerikanisches Institut,** Haidplatz 8, 93047 Regensburg. Tel. (0941) 5 24 76; Fax (0941) 5 21 98

TOURISM HEADQUARTERS IN GERMANY

Deutsche Zentrale für Tourismus DZT, Beethovensstraße 69, 60325 Frankfurt am Main. Tel. 49 (0)69.9 74 64-0; Fax 49 (0)30/75 19 03; www.germany-tourism. de

GERMAN COOKING MEASUREMENTS AND VOCABULARY

German cooking measurements
◆ *Eßlöffel (Eßl.):* tablespoon
◆ *Teelöffel (Teel.):* teaspoon
◆ *Tasse(n):* cup(s)
◆*Messerspitze (Messp.):* point of a knife
◆*kg:* kilogram
◆*g:* gram
◆*l:* liter

Equivalencies
◆ 1 kg (kilogram) = 1000 g (grams). One kilogram (*Kilo*) is 2.204 pounds
◆ ° kg (kilogram) = 500 g (grams) = 1 *Pfund* (pound).
One-half kilogram is about one Ameri-can pound.
◆ 1 l (liter) water = 1 kg (kilogram) = 2 *Pfund* (pounds).
One liter is 1.06 American quarts

◆ 1/10 liter water = 6-7 *Eßlöffel* (tablespoons)
◆ 1 cup (*Tasse*) flour = 100 g (grams)
◆ 1 cup (*Tasse*) sugar = 200 g (grams)

Cooking vocabulary

abgießen: .... to pour off, drain, strain
abgegoss- (adj.): ...... drained, strained
abkochen: .... to boil
abschmecken: .. to taste for seasoning
allseitig: .... all around
anbraten: .... sauté
anordnen: .... to arrange
anrichten: .... to serve (a dish)
anrühren: .... to mix, stir
auffüllen: .... to fill up
aufkochen: to warm up, bring to a boil
Auflauf: .... soufflé
ausgefüllt- (adj.): .... filled
Backofen: .... oven
beifügen: .... add
Beilagen: .... accompanying foods,
            garnishing, side dishes
belegt- (adj.): ... covered (as in *belegtes
            Brot*: (open) sandwich)
bereiten: .... prepare
bestäuben: .... to dust, sprinkle
bestreichen: ..... to spread (over), cover
bestreuen: .... to dust (with),
            sprinkle (with)
beträufeln: .... to sprinkle
beziehen: .... to cover
bisfest: .... firm, not overdone
Blatt: .... leaf (as, a leaf of gelatin,
            a leaf of cabbage)
braten: .... to roast, bake
Butterflöckchen belegen: ... to dot with
            butter
dämpfen: .... to steam
Deckel: .... lid to a pan or dish
Dose: .... can (containing food)
dünsten: .... to simmer, braise, stew
durchschneiden: .... to cut through
            (*der Länge nach durchschneiden*:
            to cut lengthwise)
einfüllen: .... to pour in, put in
einkochen: .... to boil down
einrühren: .... to stir in, mix in
Eintopf: .... a stew

Eis: .... ice cream
fein schneiden: .... to cut finely
feuerfeste Schüssel: .... fireproof dish
Flasche: .... bottle
gar dünsten: .... to steam until done
garnieren: .... to garnish
gebunden- (adj.): tied, bound together
gedünstet- (adj.) .... steamed
gefüllt- (adj.): .... stuffed
gehackt- (adj.): .... minced (ground)
gehäuft- (adj.): .... rounded measure
            (as in, "1 rounded teaspoon")
gekocht- (adj.): .... cooked
gelegentlich wenden: .... turn from
            time to time
Gericht: .... a dish (a prepared food)
gerieben- (adj.): .... grated
gerührt- (adj.): .... stirred (in)
geschält- (adj.): .... peeled
gestrichen: .... leveled off measure
            (as in, "a level teaspoon")
hacken: .... to chop, mince
Halbstunde: .... a half hour
hartgekochte Eier: ... hard-cooked eggs
heiß machen: .... to heat
Kartoffelbrei: .... mashed potatoes
Kartoffelsalat: .... potato salad
Klops: .... meat ball
Klößen: .... dumplings
klump(e)rig- (adj.): .... lumpy
knapp (adj.): .... scant
Knödel: .... dumpling
kochen ..... (darf nicht kochen!): do not
            allow to boil
kochendes Wasser: .... boiling water
kreuzweise: .... crosswise
Kuchen: .... cake, pastry
Kuchenblech: .... cake tin
Kühlschrank: .... refrigerator
legen: .... to lay
Marmelade: .... jelly, jam
Menge: .... quantity, amount
mittelgroß- (adj.): .... middle-size
nacheinander: .... one after the other
Oberhitze: .... high heat
Pfanne: .... pan, bowl
Pfannkuchen: .... pancakes
Prise: .... pinch (eine Prise Zucker =
            a pinch of sugar)

Reibekuchen: .... potato pancakes
reichen: .... to serve (a prepared dish)
roh- (adj.): .... raw
rühren: .... to stir
Salzkartoffeln: .... salted potatoes
Schale: .... skins of vegetables
(*mit Schale*: with skins)
schälen: .... to peel
Schaumgebäck: .... meringue
Scheibe(n): .... slice(s)
schlagen: .... to beat
schmoren: .... to stew
Schüssel: .... dish, bowl
Schwarzbrot: .... black bread
sieden: .... to simmer
Spaten: .... slices
Spätzle: .... small dumplings
Spiegeleier: .... fried eggs
Streifen: .... strips
Stück: .... piece
Suppe: .... s o u p
Teigwaren: .... baked goods
Topf: .... saucepan
Torte: .... flat cake, tart
Torteform: .... baking tin
Tunke: .... gravy
überbacken: .... to brown
übergießen: .... to pour over, baste
Unterhitze: .... low heat
unterziehen: .... to fold in carefully
verdampft: .... to boil down, reduce
verlesen: .... to select
vermengen: .... to mix together
vermischen: .... to mix, blend
verteilen: .... to spread out
verzieren: .... to decorate, garnish
verziert- (adj.): .... garnished, decorated
Viertelstunde: .... a quarter hour
wälzen: .... to roll, rotate
Wasser (*unter fließendem Wasser
wasch-en*): to wash under running water
zerlassen: .... to melt (in the pan)
zerteilen: .... to divide, separate
ziehen lassen: .... to let set (for a
certain length of time)
zugeben: .... to add
zum kochen bringen: . to bring to a boil
Zutaten: .... ingredients

Source: Erna Zietzschmann, *Das große Kochbuch*, C. Bertelsmann Verlag Gütersloh, 1952.

COOKING INGREDIENTS, PREPARED FOODS

Ananas: .... pineapple
Anis: .... anise
Äpfel: .... apples
Apfelmus: .... apple sauce
Apfelsinen: .... oranges
Aprikosen: .... apricots
Aubergine: .... eggplant
Auflauf: .... soufflé, casserole
Backpulver: .... baking powder
Bananen: .... bananas
Barsch: .... perch
Basilikum: .... basil
Beeren: .... berries
Berliner: .... yeast donut, no hole, filled
Bienenstich: ..... rich custard filled cake
Bierwurst: .... a fresh sausage
Birnen: .... pears
Blätterteig: .... puff pastry
Blau: .... refers to poached fish
Blaukraut: .... red cabbage
Blumenkohl: .... cauliflower
Blutwurst: .... blood sausage
Bockwurst: .... a kind of sausage
Bohnen: .... beans
Braten: .... a roast (meat)
Bratkartoffeln: .... fried potatoes
Bratwurst: .... a kind of sausage
Brombeeren: .... blackberries
Brösel: .... bread crumbs
Brot: .... bread
Brötchen: .... a roll
Brühe: .... broth
Brunnenkresse: .... watercress
Buchweizen: .... buckwheat
Butterkäse: .... a mild cheese
Champignon: .... mushroom
Crevetten: .... shrimp or prawns
Dampfnudeln: . puffy sweet dumplings
Dill: .... dill
Dorsch: .... cod
Dotter: .... egg yolk

Eidotter: .... egg yolk
eingelegt: .... pickled
Eier: .... eggs
Eis: .... ice cream
Eisbein: .... pickled pork knuckles
Eischeibe: .... an egg slice
Eiweiß: .... egg white
Ente: .... duck
Erbsen: .... peas
Erdbeeren: .... strawberries
Erdnüsse .... peanuts
Essig: .... vinegar
Estragon: .... tarragon
Fasan: .... pheasant
Fenchel: .... fennel
Fett: .... fat
Fische: .... fish
Fleisch: .... meat
Forelle: .... trout
Frikadelle: .... a type of hamburger
Früchte: .... fruit
Gans: .... goose
Gebäck: .... pastries, cookies
gefüllt: .... filled, stuffed
gekocht .... cooked, boiled
Gemüse: .... vegetables
Gerstengraupen: .... pearl barley
Gerstenmehl: .... barley flour
Getränke: .... drinks
Gewürze: .... herbs, condiments
Grieß: .... semolina
Gurken: .... cucumbers, pickles
Hackfleisch: .... ground meat
Haferflocken: .... rolled oats
Hafergrütze: .... groats
Hammelfleisch: .... mutton
Hase: .... hare
Haxen: .... knuckles, hocks
Hefe: .... yeast
Heidelbeeren: .... blueberries
Hering: .... herring
Himbeeren: .... raspberries
Hirn: .... brains
Hirsch: .... deer
Honig: .... honey
Huhn: .... fowl
Hühnerbrust: .... chicken breast
Hummer: .... lobster
Ingwer: .... ginger

Innereien: .... innards
Johannisbeeren: .... currants
Kabeljau .... cod
Kaffee: .... coffee
Kaiserschmarrn: .... shredded pancakes
      fried with rum-soaked raisins
Kalb: .... veal
Kakao: .... cocoa
Kalbfleisch: .... veal
Kalbshaxe: .... leg of veal
Kaninchen: .... rabbit
Kapern: .... capers
Kardamom: .... cardamon
Karotten: .... carrots
Karpfen: .... carp
Kartoffelbrei: .... mashed potatoes
Kartoffeln: .... potatoes
Kartoffelpuffer: . fried potato pancakes
Käse: .... cheese
Kasseler: .... pickled smoked pork
Kastanien: .... chestnuts
Kehkse: .... cookies
Kerbel: .... chervil
Kirschen: .... cherries
Klopse: .... meatballs
Klösse: .... dumplings
Knoblauch: .... garlic
Knochensuppe: .... soup made
                              with bones
Knödel: .... dumpling
Kohl: .... cabbage
Konfitüre: .... jam, preserves
Kopfsalat: .... head lettuce
Kotelett: .... cutlet, chop
Krabbe: .... crab, schrimp
Kraftbrühe: .... consommé
Kräuter: .... herbs
Krebse: .... crustaceans
Kümmel: .... caraway, cumin
Kürbis: .... pumpkin
Lachs: .... salmon
Lammfleisch: .... lamb
Lauch: .... leek
Leberknödel: .... liver dumplings
Leberwurst: .... liverwurst
Lebkuchen: .... gingerbread
Liebstöckel: .... lovage
Linsen: .... lentils
Lorbeerblatt: .... bay leaves

Lungen: .... lungs
Mais: .... corn
Majoran: .... marjoram
Makkaroni, Nudeln: .... pasta
Mandarinen: .... tangerines
Mandeln: .... almonds
mariniert: .... marinated
Maronen: .... chestnuts
Matjesheriing: .... fillets of salt-cured
herring
Meeresfrüchte: .... seafood
Meerrettich: .... horseradish
Mehl: .... flour
Melonen: .... melons
Milch: .... milk
Mirabellen: .... yellow plums
Mohn: .... poppy seed
Möhren: .... carrots
Müllerin Art: .... dredged in flour
and pan-fried
Muscheln: .... mussels
Muskat/Muskatnuss: ... mace, nutmeg
Nelken: .... cloves
Nelkenpfeffer: .... allspice
Nieren: .... kidneys
Nudeln: .... pasta, noodles
Nüsse: .... nuts
Obst: .... fruit
Ochsenfleisch: .... ox meat
Pampelmuse: .... grapefruit
Pellkartoffeln: .... potatoes cooked
in their skins
Petersilie: .... parsley
Pfeffer: .... pepper
Pfefferkuchen: .... gingerbread
Pfirsiche: .... peache
Pflaumen: .... plums
Pilzen: .... mushrooms
Pökelfleish: .... salted or cured meat
Pommes frites: .... french fries
Presskopf: .... head cheese
Preiselbeeren: .... cranberries
Pumpernickel: ... dark, dense, rye bread
Puter: .... turkey
Quark: .... fresh curd cheese
Ragout: .... ragout, stew
Rahm: .... cream
Rebhuhn: .... partridge
Reh: .... game (deer, rabbit, etc.)

Reibekuchen: .... potato pancakes
(in Rhineland)
Reis: .... rice
Rettiche: .... radishes
Rhabarber: .... rhubarb
Rinderzunge: .... beef tongue
Rindfleisch: .... beef
Rippchen: .... rib cut of meat
Roggenmehl: .... rye flour
Rollmops: stuffed pickled herring rolls
Rosenkohl: .... Brussels sprouts
Rosinen: .... raisins
Rosmarin: .... rosemary
Rostkartoffeln: .... pan-fried potatoes
Rote Beete: .... beets
Rotkohl: .... red cabbage
Rotwild: .... deer, venison
Rüben: .... turnips
Rührei: .... scrambled eggs
Saft: .... juice
Sago: .... tapioca
Sahne: .... cream
Salat: .... head of lettuce, also a salad
Salatblättern: .... lettuce leaves
Salbei: .... sage
Salm: .... salmon
Salz: .... salt
Sauerampfer: .... sorrel
Sauerbraten: .... marinated pot roast
Saure Milch: .... sour milk
Saurer Rahm: .... sour cream
Schalentiere: .... shellfish (in general)
Schinken: .... ham
Schlagsahne: .... whipped cream
Schnecken: .... snails
Schnittlauch: .... chives
Schnitzel: .... cutlet of veal
Schokolade: .... chocolate
Scholle: .... plaice
Schweinefleisch: .... pork
Schwenkbraten: ...... grilled pork steaks
Sellerie: .... celeriac
Semmelknödel: .... bread dumplings
Semmelmehl: .... white or wheat flour
Senf: .... mustard
Spanferkel: .... roast suckling pig
Spargel: .... asparagus
Spätzle: .... tiny egg noodles
Speck: .... bacon

Spinat: .... spinach
Stachelbeeren: .... gooseberries
Stangensellerie: .... celery
Stärkemehle: .. starch flour (cornstarch)
Suppe: .... soup
Taube: .... pigeon
Teigwaren: .... baked goods
Thunfisch: .... tuna fish
Thymian: .... thyme
Tomaten: .... tomatoes
Trauben: .... grapes
Truthahn: .... turkey
Vanillezucker: .... vanilla flavored sugar
Wacholder: .... juniper
Wallnüsse: .... walnuts
weiße Rüben: .... turnips
Weißwein: .... white wine
Weizen: .... wheat
Weizenmehl: .... wheat flour
Wild: .... game, deer
Wildgeflügel: .... game birds
Wildschwein: .... wild boar
Wurst: .... sausage
Wurstsalat: .... salad that includes
              strips of cold sausage
Zimt: .... cinnamon
Zitrone: .... lemon
Zitronensaft: .... lemon juice
Zucker: .... sugar
Zunge: .... tongue
Zwetsch(g)en: .... plums
Zwiebel: .... onion

TRACHTEN: TRADITIONAL FOLK COSTUMES

The folk costumes, or *Trachten*, symbolized typically by the *Dirndl* and *Leder-hosen* so consistently seen at festive events in Germany, are a relatively modern development.

Centuries ago these "costumes" were everyday work clothes. The *Dirndl* was sewn by the women of the family, and the men's sturdy leather pants were constructed by the saddler – to last a lifetime!

The Germans of past centuries, like those living today, had their "Sunday best" folk costumes for church and festivals, but their everyday wear was just a more simple and practical version. Today, the costumes are reserved mostly for special occasions.

The popularity of *Trachten* today is relatively new. By the end of the 19th century, *Trachten* were nearly out of fashion. It was only in 1880 that the first *Trachten* club was organized in Germany, in an attempt to keep the old culture from dying out. Gradually, wearing *Trachten* became chic.

Today there are more than 800 *Trachtenvereine* (folk costume societies) in Bavaria alone. These organizations not only present their own regional versions of style in traditional dress, but in addition, they present and preserve the distinctive traditional music, songs, dances and customs of their ancestors. It is now not unusual to see people in their *Trachten* performing rather everyday activities, particularly in Bavaria.

On the second day of Munich's *Oktoberfest*, the dressed-up members of a number of Bavarian and Austrian *Trachten* clubs parade through the city, in the event that is known as the *Trachten und Schützenzug*.

The Bavarian style of *Trachten*, based on that in the Miesbach region, became popular at the end of the 19th century. The clothing is constructed from completely natural fabrics, and it actually does last a lifetime. The famous German *Loden* fabric is 100 percent wool – woven, shrunken and mechanically treated to become nearly as waterproof as modern chemically treated fabrics.

The story of one's locale is told both by the style of one's *Tracht* and its accessories. The colors of the clothing items, the jewelry, the hair styles, and the hats worn by the women, as well as the suspenders and jackets of the men – all quietly reveal the locale from which the wearers come.

The clothing, accessories, and jewelry aspects of the *Trachten* are relatively uniform in nomenclature, if not in colors and styles. The woman donning her *Tracht* will need at least a half hour before she can appear appropriately dressed. Her costume will include fresh flowers arranged over the bodice, at her chest. The male may not need as much time to present himself, yet the pertinent customs and accessories are also precise.

Following are the parts of the *Trachten* worn by women and by men:

The woman's *Tracht*

* **Rock:** The skirt, the length of which may be measured by the rule of thumb for the Miesbacher Dirndl – *Ein Maßkrug vom Boden,* or the height of a one-liter beer mug from the floor up, measured without shoes on. The skirt's pleats are not pressed. It is made of a solid color wool or silk, with blue, red, green, and black being the predominant colors.
* **Janker:** A long sleeved blouse of the same color and fabric as the skirt
* **Schmiesel** or **Vorhemd:** This white linen dickey with lace across the front is the base for the outfit, as it is what shows when the Janker is worn.
* **Leibl:** If the *Schmiesel* and *Janker* are not worn, the *Leibl,* a white linen blouse with short puffy or flat sleeves takes their place.
* **Kropkette:** The choker, made of silver with a gold clasp can indicate the wealth of the family. It is often set with garnets and seed pearls.
* **Mieder:** A black, corset-like bodice with hidden hooks or a complicated *Schnur-lochleiste* to help create the desire "hourglass" figure. It is worn on top of the *Janker* and under the skirt. It is ornately decorated with chains, charms, and flowers.
* **Geschnür:** A beaded silver chain used to cinch the *Mieder,* at least 2° meters

long and laced around silver hooks and decorated with coins, medals and amulets
* **Miederleibe:** Fresh flowers, worn in the spring, drawing attention to the cleavage area of the dress.
* **Schürze:** The apron was originally worn to protect the skirt, but it developed into a decorative addition. Sometimes the aprons are made of silk that matches the *Schal.* In some regions, single women tie their apron strings on the left, and married women on the right.
* **Schal,** or **Schultertuch:** The shawl, whether in pastel or bright colors, is usually made of patterned silk. It is worn over the shoulders and tucked into the *Mieder.* The color of the shawl matches the apron (*Schürze*). It is usually white linen or pastel silk when worn with wool; it is made of silk if the *Tracht* is silk.
* **Strümpfe:** Stockings – for church they are black; for other occasions, white
* **Schuhe:** Shoes. Women's *Trachten* shoes are always black.
* **Hut:** The hat. In Miesbach, the *Schnurhut,* a hat with the crown wrapped in silver or gold cording with two tassels, which hang over the hat rim in back. In some areas a *Riegelhaube,* a type of crown-like hat is worn at the back of the head. Silver is reserved for single women, gold for married, and black or dark blue for widows. With a white linen apron and shawl, a woman might wear a green velour shallow *Miesbacher* hat, usually with a *Gamsbart* (see men's clothing terms). The hat may be worn tilted slightly tilted toward the front. No pins are allowed to be worn on the *Trachtenhut.*
* **Trachtenschmuck:** Jewelry – predominantly silver, with gold accents. Garnets are the the usual stone. The most popular necklace, the *Halskette,* in Bavaria has at least five rows of chains, with a front clasp, that fits tightly around the neck.
* **Unterwäsche** or **Unterrock**: The slip is made the same width and nearly the same

length as the skirt. It is proper to wear a "modesty slip" which is cut straighter and does not go up when turning while dancing. Instead of the "modesty slip," bloom-ers, loosely fitted and knee high, may be worn. Sometimes as many as seven starched petticoats are worn underneath the skirt to emphasize its bell-like shape.

The man's *Tracht*

♦*Hemd*: The shirt, usually white cotton or linen, always with long sleeves, buttoned at the wrist. Men may be seen with the sleeves rolled up, especially when dancing.

♦*Trachtenjoppe:* The jacket, worn at all times except when the men are dancing. In light gray or charcoal or loden green (for hunters). Some jackets are embroidered on the front or have appliques on the lapels and cuffs. These decorations, as well as the buttons and pleats, reveal the wearer's home region or rank in his club.

♦ *Weste:* The vest, worn only in some areas, is usually green wool with narrow red piping.

♦*Lederhosen:* The leather pants can be short to the knee or shorter. *Bundhosen* (knickers) may also be worn. Black is the most popular color, but the *Lederhosen* all eventually wear to a beautiful brown color. Hand-stitched embroidery may be seen on the flap and legs, in gold, green or off-white. A knife may be carried in the knife pocket. Usually the knife handle is made of stag horn with silver caps.

♦*Schlips, Binder,* or *Krawatte:* The tie, most commonly knitted or crocheted. In some areas men wear silk scarves, with a broach at the neck.

♦*Gürtel:* The belt, like the other accessories, are usually handed down from generation to generation. The belt can be decoratively stitched, with the favorite design made with peacock quilt stitching. In Bavaria, vests and belts are not worn together.

♦ *Hosenträger:* Suspenders, with a cross-piece that can be embroidered.

♦*Hut:* The hat is usually green, made from a velour material, decorated with a feather or chamois tail, or *Gamsbart* (see below). Only for a special occasion do men wear a flower or greenery on their hats. Only honor and club pins are worn on these hats; all other pins are worn on an alpine-style hat (*Wanderhut*), usually gray in color.

♦*Gamsbart:* A tuft for the hat made of hair of the chamois, a small goat-like animal, indicating originally that the wearer was a hunter, with the tuft of hair worn like a hunting trophy. These tufts, the longer the better, should be dark at the base and light at the tips to produce a halo-like effect.

♦*Charivari:* Originally used as a watch-chain when a man was wearing a pocket watch. The chain is decorated with lucky charms, including the *Dachspfote* (badger's paw) for luck in love, *Berg-kristall* (rock crystal) for good fortune, and *Koralle* (coral) for potency. *Charivari* can be worn on *Lederhosen* or vests.

♦*Socken:* Either white or gray, with green trim. Long knee-high socks are for the *Bundhosen* (knickers). Very short socks and separate calf-warmers (*Waden-strümpfe*, or *Loferl*) are for the short *Leder-hosen*. Each region has a different design on the socks. The calf-warmers show off the muscular calves of the strong man.

♦*Schuhe:* Shoes, usually black, with different regions having different styles, like buckles, flaps, or laces.

♦*Haferlschuh:* Black leather shoe with lacing on the side and square-formed toe. Some areas wear *Altenstiefel* – leather boots with pleats at the ankles indicating a man's wealth and his standing in society.

Sources:

♦Teresa Fisher, "High on the Hill Is a Lonely Goatherd," *Munich Found*, October 1994.

♦Elsa Meinig and Brigitte Hoppe, "Men's Trachten," *Pazifische Rundschau*, July 1999.

♦Elsa Meinig and Brigitte Hoppe, "Women's Trachten," *Pazifische Rundschau*, August 1999..

SPECIAL GREETINGS, THANKS, IN GERMAN

Christmas and New Years

♦*Frohe Weihnachten und viel Glück im neuen Jahr!* Merry Christmas and a prosperous new year

♦*Frohe Weihnachten und alles Gute im Neuen Jahr!* Merry Christmas and many blessings in the New Year

♦ *Fröliche Weihnachten und ein gesundes Neues Jahr!* Merry Christmas and good health in the New Year

♦ *Wir wünschen Ihnen [or Dir] ein fröhliches gutes Weihnachtsfest und ein glückliches gesundes neues Jahr 2001* [using the formal "you"] We wish you a very merry Christmas holiday and a prosperous New Year 2001

♦*Ich hoffe, daß Ihr alle ein glückliches Weihnachts- und Neujahrsfest verbringen werdet* [Using the informal "you"] I hope you will all have a very happy Christmas and New Year

♦*Ich hoffe, daß Sie alle ein glückliches Weihnachts- und Neujahrsfest verbringen werden* [using the formal "you"] I hope you will all have a very happy Christmas and New Year

♦*Ein gesegnetes Weihnachtsfest*

New Years

♦*Guten Rutsch ins neue Jahr!* [Have a] good slide into the new year

♦*Ich wünsche Ihnen Glück zum neuen Jahre* [using the formal "you"] I wish you a happy new year

♦Viel Glück in neuen Jahr

Birthday

♦*Herzliche Glückwunsche zum Geburtstag* Hearty best wishes on your birthday

♦*Die besten Wünsche zum Geburtstag* Best wishes on your birthday

♦ *Alles Gute zum Geburtstag!* Many happy returns of the day!

Congratulations

♦*Herzlichen Glückwünsch* Hearty congratulations

Thanks

♦ *Vielen herzlichen Dank* Thank you very much

FORMAL SALUTATIONS FOR LETTER-WRITING

Note: The formal salutation in German is followed by a comma; in English by a colon.

Sehr geehrter Herr Koch, Dear Mr. Koch:

Sehr geehrte Frau Koch, Dear Mrs. Koch:

Sehr geehrte Damen und Herren, Dear Madam, dear Sir:

Sehr geehrter Herr Doktor, Dear Dr. (Hess):

Sehr geehrter Herr Dr. Koch, Dear Dr. Hess:

Sehr geehrte Frau Doktor, Dear Doctor (Hess):

Sehr geehrte Frau Dr. Hess, Dear Dr. Hess:

Sehr geehrter Herr Professor, Dear Professor (Hamm):

Sehr geehrter Herr Professor Hamm, Dear Professor Hamm:

Sehr geehrter Herr Bürgermeister, Dear Mayor (Holz):

INFORMAL SALUTATIONS

Note: The informal salutation in both German and English is followed by a comma.
Lieber Heinz, Dear Heinz,
Liebe Maria, Dear Maria,
Lieber Heinz, liebe Maria, Dear Heinz and Maria,
Mein lieber Heinz, My dear Heinz,
Meine liebe Maria, My dear Maria,

CLOSINGS OF LETTERS

Note: Closings in German are not followed by commas as they are in English.

Formal closings
Mit freundlichen Grüßen Sincerely (literally, "With friendly greetings,")
Mit freundlichen Gruß Sincerely (literally, "With a friendly greeting,")
Mit vorzüglicher Hochachtung Very respectfully yours, (literally, "With the most excellent and highest regard,")
Hochachtungsvoll Respectfully yours, (literally, "With high respect,")

Informal closings
Mit besten Grüßen . Best regards,
Mit herzlichem Gruß Love, (literally, "With a hearty greeting,")
Mit herzlichen Grüßen Love, (literally, "With hearty greetings,")
Grüße und Küsse Love, (literally, "Greetings and kisses,")
Alle guten Wünsche! Best wishes,
Mach's gut Take care,

FORMS OF ADDRESS

Note: *Professor* and *Doktor*, academic titles considered part of the name, are written before the name. Diplomas and vocational and occupational job titles are used in the written address, but not in the salutation. *Herr* and *Frau* are not abbreviated in forms of address.
Examples:
Address: Herrn Professor Dr. Eduard Hoffmann
Salutation: Sehr geehrter Herr Professor, *(or)* Sehr geehrter Herr Professor Weimer,

Address: Herrn Rechtsanwalt Dr. Josef Keller
Salutation: Sehr geehrter Herr Dr. Keller

Address: Herrn Dipl. Ing. Helmut Metzger,
Salutation: Sehr geehrter Herr Metzger,

Address: Frau Direktor Silke Molter
Salutation: Sehr geehrte Frau Molter,

Address: Herrn Bürgermeister Wolf,
Salutation: Sehr geehrter Herr Wolf,
Source of salutations, closings, and forms of address: *Ultimate German Advanced,* by Birgit Nielsen, Living Language, Random House, New York, 1995.

BOOKING A ROOM IN GERMAN

Whereas most hotels in Germany have had websites for several years, an increasing number of less expensive lodgings (Hotel Garni, Pension, Gasthof, etc.) are establishing websites.

Reservations can be made via email and in some cases, the potential guest uses drop-down menus to select arrival and departure dates as well as room sizes.

When using a computer translation program to produce the text for an email message, make your message very concise and avoid colloquialisms.

It should be mentioned that many German hotels (even small hotels) offer non-smoking rooms (*"nichtraucher Zimmer"*).

Note: The following letter may be sent to a German place of lodging to request the reservation of a room. The asterisks refer to variations in the number of nights requested, the date, and the number of people to occupy the room. See "Text variations" below.

Sehr geehrte Herren,
würden Sie mir bitte für zwei Nächte*
vom 5.-7. September** ein Einzel-
zimmer*** mit Bad oder Dusche
reservieren?
Mit freundlichen Grüßen
[name of sender]

Text variations
* Instead of *"zwei Nächte"* ("two nights") one may use *eine Nacht* (one night); *drei Nächte* (three nights); *vier Nächte* (four nights); etc.
**Instead of *"ein Einzelzimmer,"* (a single room), one may state *"ein Doppelzimmer"* (double room)
***Instead of *"5.-7. September"* (from the fifth to the seventh of September), write the appropriate date similarly; for example, *10.-14. April;* or *30. Januar-2. Februar.* (Note that each number is followed by a period). Four months of the year are spelled in German the same as their English counterparts. Those spelled differently are *Januar, Februar, März, Mai, Juni, Juli, Oktober,* and *Dezember.*

English translation
Dear Sirs,
Please reserve a single room with bath or shower for me for the nights of September 5 and 7.
Sincerely,

POSTAL EXPRESSIONS

Absender .... Sender; From:
per Adresse, bei .... c/o (=care of)
Bitte nicht knicken! .... Do not fold
(or bend)

Dringend! .... Urgent
*Drücksache (Infopost)*printed paper(s)
Eilbrief/Eilpaket . express letter/parcel
Eilzustellung .... express delivery
Einschreiben .. registered letter/parcel
Einschreiben gegen Rückschein regis-
tered letter with
confirmation of delivery
Internationaler Antwortschein... Inter-
national Reply Coupon
(Per) Luftpost .... by airmail
Luftpostleichbrief .... aerogramme
Muster ohne Wert .... sample of
no commercial value
Nachgebühr .... excess to pay
Nachnahme .... COD
oben! .... This Way Up!
Persönlich .... private, personal
Postfach .... post office box
Postlagernd .... general delivery
Vorsicht, zerbrechlich! ..... handle with
care
Vertraulich .... confidential
Wertbrief .... registered letter
Source: *Langenscheidts großes*
Schulwörterbuch: deutsch-englisch,
Langenscheidt, Berlin, 1996.

VACATION DAYS IN GERMANY

Federal law in Germany requires a legal minimum for vacation time of 18 work days for adults, and 25-30 days for young adults up to the age of 18 years. However, due to collective bargaining agreements, 70 percent of all employees enjoy at least six weeks of paid vacation, and most of the others get between five and six weeks.

As for school children, in all the federal states they have six weeks of summer vacation, two or three weeks at Easter and at Christmastime, and a one-week vacation in the fall. Additional days off from school vary from state to state. The major summer vacations are scheduled by the various states each year according to a staggered timetable. This is done to alleviate traffic congestion on the high-ways, because German families tend to travel when summer vacations begin.

Source: German Information Center, Federal Republic of German: *Questions and Answers,* ed. Susan Steiner (New York, 1996).

VIDEO SYSTEMS: GERMANY VS. UNITED STATES

Video equipment systems in Germany and the United States are for the most part different. Germany uses the PAL system, which is not compatible with the NTSC system prevalent in the United States. There are, however, some films in Germany which are specially made with NTSC equipment for the United States market and can be run on American VCRs.

It is common to have video cassettes recorded on the PAL system converted electronically to NTSC for use on American systems.

SPEED LIMITS IN GERMANY

Speed limits in Germany exist on state and local highways (100 km/h or 62 mph), and in towns and cities (50 km/h or 31 mph). The Autobahns have a recommended maximum speed of 130 km/h or 81 mph, but normally no mandatory speed limit. It is important to take note of the changing speed limit signs posted at various points along the Autobahn

The legal age for driving is 18 for driving cars and trucks, 16 for mopeds and motorscooters.

TELEPHONE CARDS IN GERMANY

Very few public telephones in Germany accept coins any longer. Almost all are operated by the *Telekom Telefonkarte,* a card sold in German post offices for 10 .

The *Telefonkarte* can be used in Germany only, not in any other country. To make calls to points outside Germany with a *Telefonkarte*, look for a booth displaying the word "International."

Frequent visitors to Germany carry a mobile phone ("Handy') which is geared specifically to international calling capabilities.

Appendix

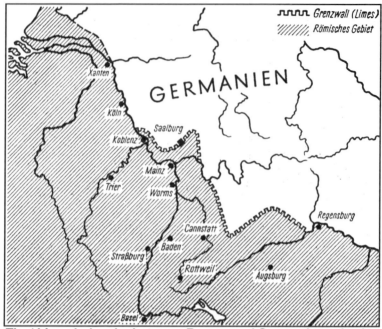

The ' Limes' – border between Roman and Germanic territories

Waterways of the German Empire
(The Oder-Neisse boundary, shown as the vertical dotted line, was drawn after World War II as the boundary between Germany and Poland.)

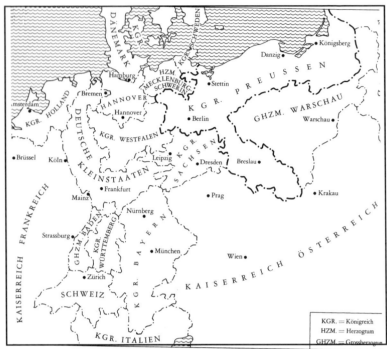

German lands under Napoleon (1807)

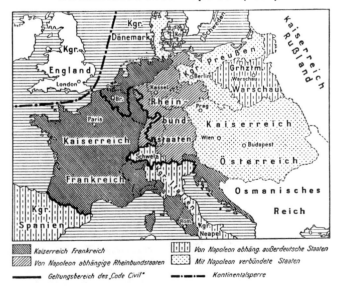

Napoleon's "Grand Empire" (1812)

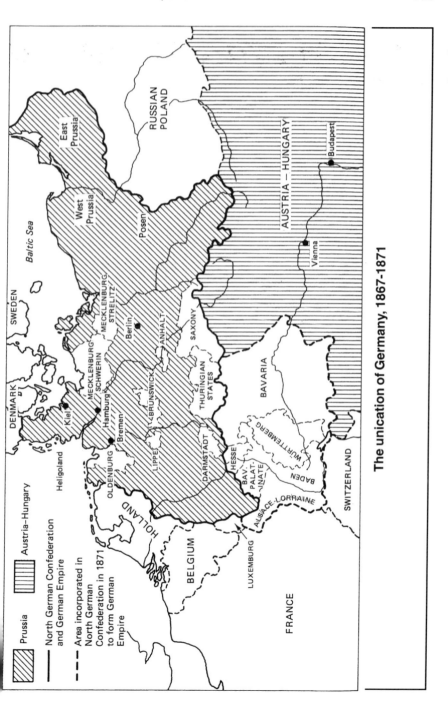

The unication of Germany, 1867-1871

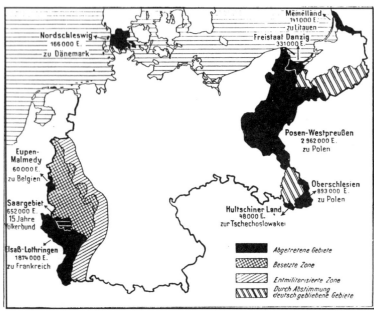

**Geographic losses mandated by the Treaty of Versailles
after World War I (1919)**

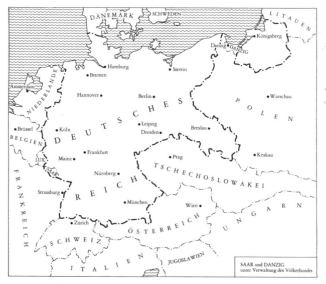

Germany's Weimar Republic (about 1925)

THE SECOND
GERMAN EMPIRE
1871-1918

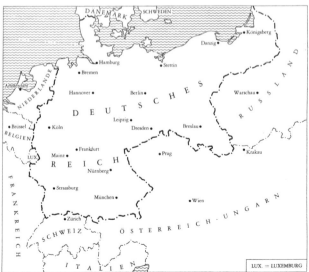

The Second Empire with adjacent countries, 1871

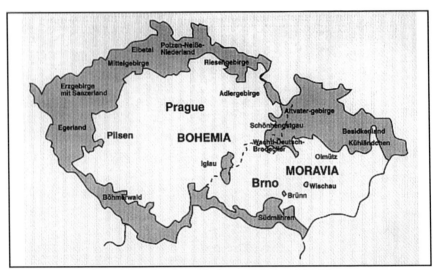

The Czech portion of Czechoslovakia from 1938 to 1945. The gray area was known as the Sudetenland – the portion inhabited predominately by ethnic Germans (an area occupied by the German army in September 1938).

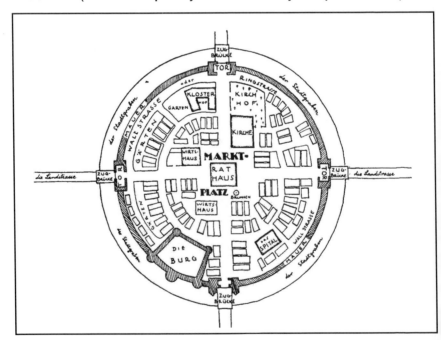

Typical layout of a German town in the Middle Ages

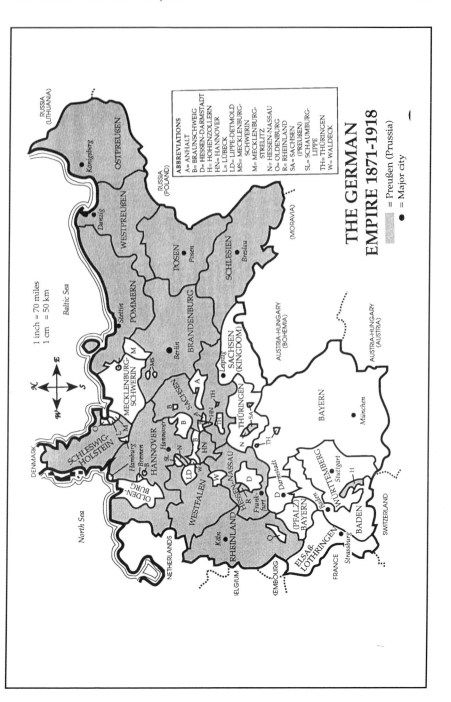

THE GERMAN
EMPIRE 1871-1918

= Preußen (Prussia)
● = Major city

ABBREVIATIONS
A= ANHALT
B= BRAUNSCHWEIG
D= HESSEN-DARMSTADT
H= HOHENZOLLERN
HN= HANNOVER
L= LÜBECK
LD= LIPPE-DETMOLD
MS= MECKLENBURG-
SCHWERIN
M= MECKLENBURG-
STRELITZ
N= HESSEN-NASSAU
O= OLDENBURG
R= RHEINLAND
(PREUßEN)
SL= SCHAUMBURG-
LIPPE
SA= SACHSEN
TH= THÜRINGEN
W= WALDECK

1 inch = 70 miles
1 cm = 50 km

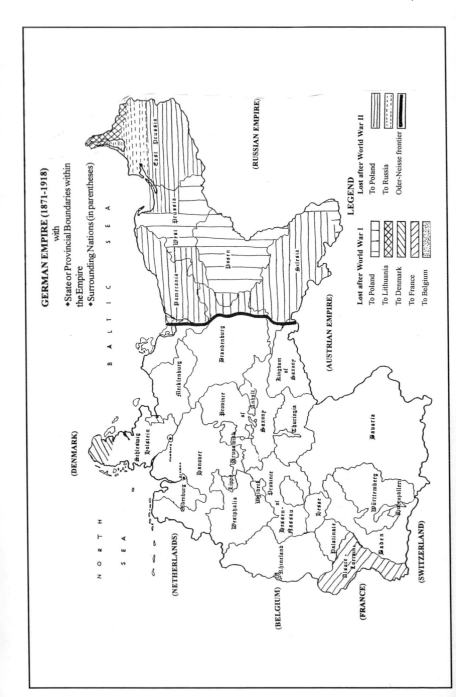

GERMAN EMPIRE (1871-1918)
with
♦State or Provincial Boundaries within
the Empire
♦Surrounding Nations (in parentheses)

LEGEND

Lost after World War I

To Poland
To Lithuania
To Denmark
To France
To Belgium

Lost after World War II

To Poland
To Russia
Oder-Neisse frontier

**The Second German Empire as compared
with the state of Texas**

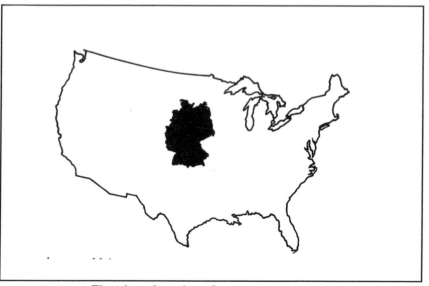

**The size of modern Germany compared
with the continental United States**

Germany from 1949 to 1989, when it was divided between the Federal Republic of West Germany, and the German Democratic Republic (East Germany)

German emigrants bid their country farewell.

Castle Garden served as the processing center
for immigration from 1855 to 1890.

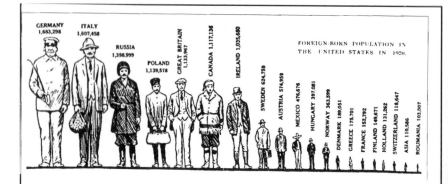

Overview of German Immigration

• More persons immigrated to the United States from Germany than from any other country in the world.

• Between 1820 and 1996 the largest ethnic groups were, in order, Germany (7 million), Mexico (5.5 million), Italy (5.3 million); Great Britain (5.1 million), and Ireland (5.1 million).

• Little immigration occurred between 1776 and 1819 (because of the War of Independence, 1775-1783; and The War of 1812-14).

• About 5,000 Hessian prisoners of war stayed in America after the War of Independence.

• Many German speakers emigrated from Austria-Hungary and Russia but were not counted as Germans.

• German immigrants, choosing the best farmland, settled mainly in Maryland, Pennsylvania, Ohio, Indiana, Michigan, Wisconsin, Illinois, Minnesota, Iowa, Missouri, North Dakota, South Dakota, Nebraska, and Kansas.

• In 1900, about 40% of the farmlands of the U.S.A. were owned by German Americans.

• Many U.S. cities had a high percentage of Germans. In 1900, American cities had the following percentage of German immigrants and their children compared to total populations: Milwaukee (70%), Davenport (62%), Hoboken (58%), Cincinnati (54%), St. Louis (45%), Buffalo (43%) and Detroit (41%).

• Baltimore, the terminal of immigration ships from Bremerhaven, in 1900 counted 28% of its population as first- and second-generation Germans. Among whites that year, 42 percent first- and second-generation Germans inhabited Baltimore.

Other large American cities with a high percentage of first- and second-generation Germans in 1900 were New York (32%), Chicago (35%), and Cleveland (38%).

Source: Edward A. Fleckenstein, "The Distinguished German Ethnic Population of America – (XVI)" in *Der Volksfreund/ People's Friend* (Buffalo) May/June 1998; as reported in "Germans: The largest immigrant group in the United States," by Gary Carl Grassl, *The German-American Heritage Society of Greater Washington, D.C. Newsletter*, Vol. XVII, No. 4, July 2000.

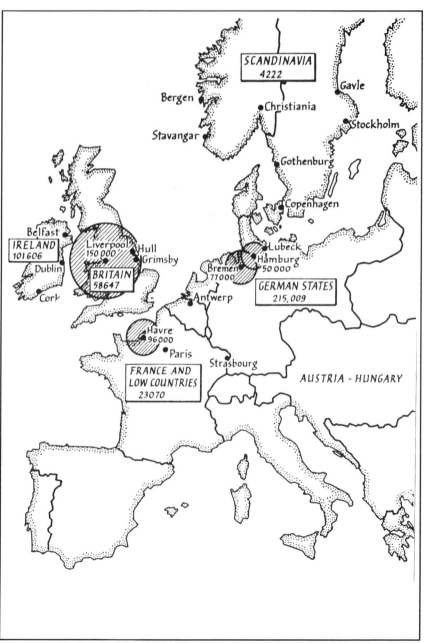

**Emigration to the U.S., 1854 : Ports of embarkation,
Including the route through the port of Liverpool**

Translation of labels relating to steamship decks, compartments, and facilities, as illustrated on the next page

Kommando-Brücke: bridge
First deck: *Sonnendeck:* sundeck; *Grillroom:* bar; *Passag.-Kammer I Cl :* first-class cabin; *Sonnendeck:* sundeck
Second deck: *Promenadendeck:* promenade deck; *Rauchsalon I Cl.:* first-class smoking salon; *Gesellschaftssalon:* first-class lounge; *Promenaden-deck:* promenade deck
Third deck: *Gang:* walkway; *Post Bureau:* post office; *Gang:* walkway; *Luxus-Cabine:* luxury cabin.
Fourth deck: *Speise-Salon I Classe:* first-class dining room.
Fifth deck: *Passag. II Cl. Küche f. Zwischendeck:* second-class kitchen for "tween-decks" (steerage) passengers; *Speise- u. Schlafraum f. Zwischen-decker:* dining and sleeping room for steerage passengers; *Barbier:* barber services
Sixth deck: *Schlachterei:* butchery; *Gang:* walkway; *Fleisch.:* meat storage; *Proviant-Raum.* dry goods storage; *Obst.:* fruit storage; *Gang:* walkway; *Gepäck:* luggage
Seventh deck: *Kohlen:* coal; *Ladung:* cargo
Hold: *Heiz Raum:* boiler room

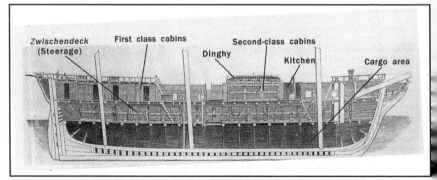

Cutaway of an emigrant ship in the first half of the 19th century

**Cross-section of a passenger steamship in1895
(See on the previous page the translations of deck
and compartment designations.)**

**Zwischendeck (steerage) quarters
in an emigrant passenger ship**

**400 years in the development
of sailing ships**

Front: "Santa Maria," a 1492 caravel (*Karavelle*)
Middle: "Spindrift," English clipper ship
(*englisher Klipper*) 1867
Behind: The "Preussen," five-masted full-rigged
ship (*Fünfmastvollschiff*), 1902-1910

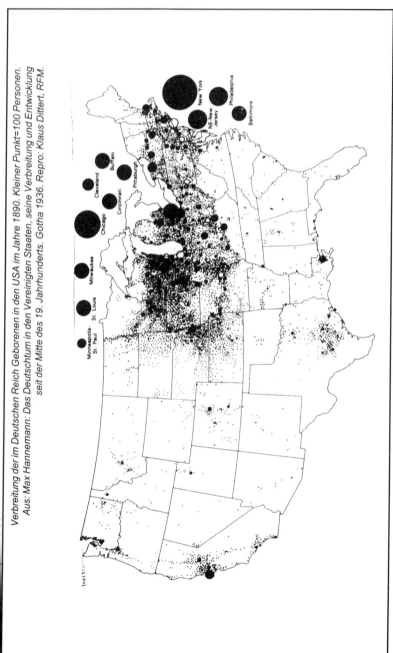

Verbreitung der im Deutschen Reich Geborenen in den USA im Jahre 1890. Kleiner Punkt=100 Personen. Aus: Max Hannemann: Das Deutschtum in den Vereinigten Staaten, seine Verbreitung und Entwicklung seit der Mitte des 19. Jahrhunderts. Gotha 1936. Repro: Klaus Dittert, RFM.

Map showing distribution of German-born population in the United States in 1890. Each dot represents 100 people.

Immigrants' migration routes by 1920

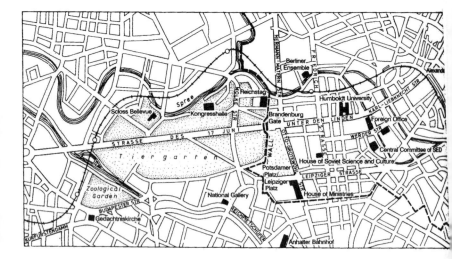

The Berlin Wall, in central Berlin

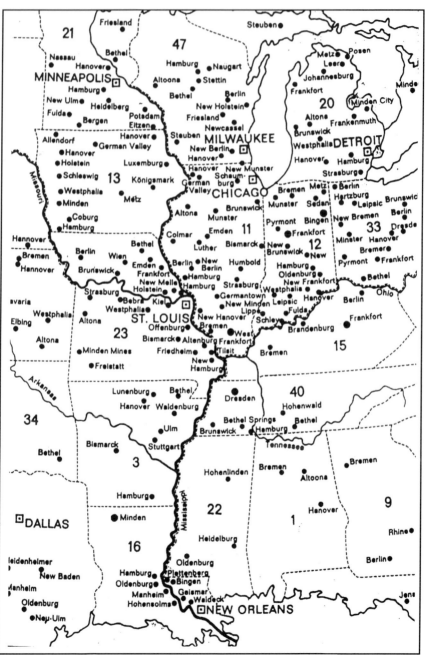

German place-names in the American Midwest

**Shop of a master shoemaker
(Schumacher,meister or Schustermeister)**

A typical Jahrmarkt (annual market) in the Schwarzwald

Der Vierseithof in Kleinlosnitz (Lkr. Hof)

Layout of a Bauernhof (independent farm with home, animal stalls, and out-buildings)

A Christening/Baptism Procession
Here the Hebamme (midwife) leads the procession of parents
and godparents to the church where the infant is to be christened/baptized.

Kirmes (annual church celebration) in a German town

From the third century, it became customary after the dedication of a church to celebrate the *Kirchweih* (church consecration) – always on a Sunday between the summer solstice, June 24, and St. Martin's Day, November 11. These festivals are usually held in the fall, after the grain harvest and the pasture season have ended, and the demand of work in the fields is no longer an obstacle to engaging in often wild and frenzied activity.

This *Kirchweih* was called "*Kirmes*," which derived from the Middle High German word, *Kirmesse*, referring to the *Messe* (mass) that served to give the new church its stature as holy ground.

That event is what begins the annual celebration – whether it be called a *Kirchweih*, a *Kirmes*, a *Jahrmarkt,* or a *Volksfest*, among other names.

The nature of the *Kirchweih* celebrations changed over the decades and centuries, with harvest festivals (*Erntedankfeste*) and shooting festivals (*Schützenfeste*), among others, becoming the themes, with very little, if any emphasis on the *Kirchweih* celebration.

Villages in a given area take care to schedule their festivals so that they don't conflict with those of their neighbors, so that any villager can hop-scotch from one festival to the next without missing a day of fun.

Depending on the local dialect, *Kirchweih* is known as "Kirwe," "Kilbe," "Kirta" (for "church day"), "Kirwe," "Kärwe," "Kirbe," and "Kerb" – among other names.

At the Standesamt (civil registry office), a marriage is taking place as the registrar has the bride, groom, and witnesses sign the record book. The marriage is then official. A Church wedding may then take place, but it is optional.

During World War II in Germany, children enjoyed Kartoffelferien ("potato vacation), when they were released from school)to pick potatoes during the labor shortage. Many children enjoyed the experience!

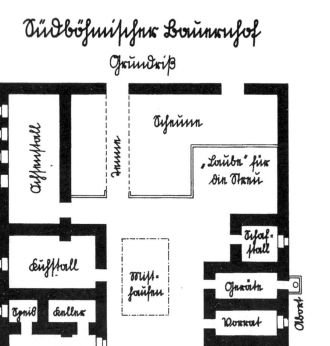

Use this floor plan of a southern Bohemian farmhouse to practice reading Sütterlin script. The Sütterlin alphabet below may be helpful. Answers appear on the next page.

Transliterations and translations of terms,
from the floor plan on the previous page

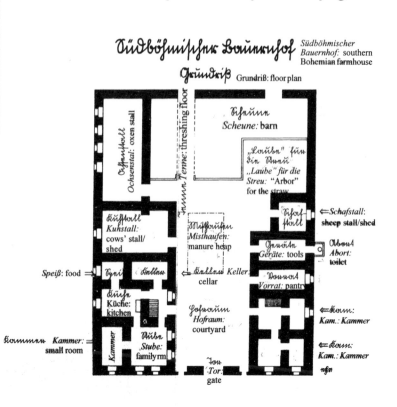

Südböhmischer Bauernhof: southern Bohemian farmhouse

Grundriß: floor plan

Scheune: barn

Ochsenstall: oxen stall

Tenne: threshing floor

"*Laube*" für die Streu: "Arbor" for the straw

⇐*Schafstall*: sheep stall/shed

Kuhstall: cows' stall/shed

Misthaufen: manure heap

Geräte: tools

Abort: toilet

Speiß: food ⇒

⇐ Keller: cellar

Vorrat: pantry

⇐*Kam.: Kammer*

Küche: kitchen

Hofraum: courtyard

Kammer: small room ⇐

Stube: family rm

⇐*Kam.: Kammer*

Tor: gate

Index

A

C

The German Research Companion
makes a great gift

– as a holiday or birthday gift

– as a contribution to a genealogy society or library

– as a gift to a relative interested in researching your common German roots

Use the order form below or order the book through your PayPal account.

- -

ORDER FORM

(Photocopy this page and send your order to the address below.)

Copies of *The German Research Companion,* Third Revised Edition, may be ordered by personal check:

Please ship _____ copy/copies of *The German Research Companion,* Third Revised Edition, each at $28.00 plus $5.00 (shipping/handling), to me at the address below.

I enclose my check in the amount of _____, payable to "Lorelei Press."

NAME_____

ADDRESS_____

_____

E-mail address _____

Mail this order form with your check to:

Lorelei Press
P.O. Box 1845
Provo, UT 84603-1845

You may also purchase the book using PayPal at www.LoreleiPress.com